Cost Management

A Strategic Emphasis

Edward J. Blocher
University of North Carolina at Chapel Hill
Kenan-Flagler School of Business

Kung H. Chen
University of Nebraska
School of Accountancy

Thomas W. Lin
University of Southern California
Levanthal School of Accounting

Irwin
McGraw-Hill

Boston   Burr Ridge, IL   Dubuque, IA   Madison, WI   New York   San Francisco   St. Louis
Bangkok   Bogotá   Caracas   Lisbon   London   Madrid
Mexico City   Milan   New Delhi   Seoul   Singapore   Sydney   Taipei   Toronto

Irwin/McGraw-Hill

A Division of The McGraw·Hill Companies

COST MANAGEMENT: A STRATEGIC EMPHASIS

This book is printed on acid-free paper.

international   2 3 4 5 6 7 8 9 0   VNH/VNH   9 3 2 1 0 9
domestic   2 3 4 5 6 7 8 9 0   VNH/VNH   9 3 2 1 0 9

ISBN 0-07-005916-0

Vice president and editorial director: *Michael W. Junior*
Publisher: *Jeffrey J. Shelstad*
Associate editor: *Rebecca M. Page*
Developmental editor: *Marc Chernoff*
Senior marketing manager: *Rhonda Seelinger*
Marketing coordinator: *Melissa Caughlin*
Project manager: *Margaret Rathke*
Senior production supervisor: *Melonie Salvati*
Senior designer: *Laurie J. Entringer*
Cover and interior design: *ZGraphics*
Supplement coordinator: *Kimberly D. Stack*
Compositor: *GTS Graphics, Inc.*
Typeface: *10.5/12 Goudy*
Printer: *Von Hoffmann Press, Inc.*

Material from the Certificate in Management Accounting
Examinations, Copyright (1977–1996) by the Institute of
Management Accountants is adapted with permission.

Library of Congress Cataloging-in-Publication Data

Blocher, Edward.
    Cost Management: a strategic emphasis/Edward Blocher, Kung H.
Chen, Thomas W. Lin.
      p.   cm.
    Includes indexes.
    ISBN 0-07-005916-0
    1. Cost accounting. 2. Managerial accounting. I. Chen, Kung H.
II. Lin, W. Thomas. III. Title.
HF5686.C8B559 1999
658.15'52–dc21   98-8633

www.mhhe.com

To our wives: Sandy, Mary, and Angela

And children: Joseph and David
Robert and Melissa
Bill and Margaret

Blocher

Edward J. Blocher is Professor of Accounting at the Kenan-Flagler School of Business at the University of North Carolina. He received his bachelor's degree in economics from Rice University, his MBA degree from Tulane University, and his PhD in accounting from the University of Texas at Austin. He has been on the faculty of Northwestern University, and at the University of North Carolina since 1976.

Professor Blocher is an active member of the American Accounting Association, where he presents workshops on cost management and founded the section on Artificial Intelligence and Expert Systems. He is also active in the American Institute of CPAs, where he currently serves on a task force.

While he is involved in a number of accounting organizations, Professor Blocher has been the most continuously active in the Institute of Management Accountants. He is a Certified Management Accountant (CMA), has taught review courses for the CMA exam, and has served on the Institute's national education committee. He remains active in the Raleigh-Durham chapter of the Institute, where he has served in many positions and is currently director of manuscripts.

Professor Blocher is the author of a book on analytical procedures (Prentice Hall) and a research monograph on management fraud (Institute of Management Accountants), as well as coauthor on monographs of the American Accounting Association and the American Institute of CPAs. He is also author or coauthor of several articles appearing in various journals, including *The Accounting Review, Management Accounting, Journal of Accountancy, Accounting and Business Research, Accounting, Organizations and Society,* and *Auditing: A Journal of Practice and Theory.*

Putting research and teaching into practice is important to Professor Blocher, who has worked closely with other firms and organizations to assist in developing products, publications, and teaching materials. He was the principal designer of an accounting analysis system for Prentice Hall Professional Software, and has worked with Blue Cross and Blue Shield of North Carolina, the American Institute of CPAs, KPMG Peat Marwick, Grant Thornton, and the Chancellor's Office at the University of North Carolina at Chapel Hill, among others.

Chen

Kung H. Chen is the Steinhardt Foundation Professor of Accounting and the Director of Graduate Programs in the School of Accountancy at the University of Nebraska–Lincoln. A graduate of National Taiwan University, he has his MBA degree from West Virginia University and a PhD from the University of Texas–Austin.

Professor Chen has published his research in various journals, including *The Accounting Review, Encyclopedia of Accounting, Internal Auditor, Journal of Business Finance & Accounting, Behavioral Research in Accounting, Journal of Accounting Literature, Advances in Accounting, Financial Management,* and *International Journal of Accounting,* and has presented research papers to audiences in several countries including the United States of America, New Zealand, Japan, Taiwan, Korea, and China.

Thomas W. Lin is the Accounting Circle Professor of Accounting at the Leventhal School of Accounting at the University of Southern California. He received his BA in business administration from National Taiwan University, MBA from National Chengchi University in Taiwan, MS in accounting and information systems from UCLA, and a PhD in accounting from the Ohio State University. He has experience as a management accountant, a systems analyst, and an assistant to the president of a multinational plastics firm, and as a computer auditor in an international accounting firm.

Lin

Professor Lin has published 3 books and over 50 papers in various journals, including *The Accounting Review, Journal of Management Accounting Research, Journal of Accountancy, Journal of Business Finance and Accounting, Advances in Accounting, Journal of Information Systems, IS Audit & Control Journal,* and *Auditing: A Journal of Practice and Theory.* He has presented seminars on new developments in cost management in North America and Asia.

Professor Lin has worked with many companies, including Times Mirror, Carnation, Western Refuse and Hauling, City of Chino, Formosa Plastics, Intex Plastics, Zee Toys, FCB Taiwan California Bank, and General Bank. He is active in the American Accounting Association and the Institute of Management Accountants. A Certified Management Accountant (CMA), he was awarded a Certificate of Distinguished Performance by the Institute of Certified Management Accountants.

Over the past 10 years, we have seen a dramatic shift in the way educators and practitioners view the field of cost accounting. This changing view is the result of an increasingly competitive environment due to the introduction of new manufacturing and information technologies, the focus on the customer, and the growth of worldwide markets. Accounting information plays a vital role in determining the most appropriate strategic direction for the organization. In particular, cost information is a critical type of information needed for effective management. For this reason, the role of the cost accountant has expanded. Once viewed as technical experts in accounting methods and procedures, accountants are now participants on multifunctional management teams. Procedural cost accounting methods are important, but equally important is knowing how and when to apply them for more effective decision making. Employers, today, are looking for accounting professionals who understand the business environment and can interpret important cost information in ways that contribute to the firm's success.

Our new text, *Cost Management: A Strategic Emphasis*, addresses these changing needs. Our goal in writing this book is **to better prepare students to understand the critical role cost management information plays in the overall success of an organization.** In order to do this, we have presented cost and management accounting in an entirely new way—first, by organizing the topics according to the functions of management, and second, by presenting the topics in conjunction with the basic concepts of strategy. Throughout the text, you will discover a running theme: **How does the topic we are discussing help the firm more effectively compete in its industry?** This organization helps students gain an understanding of how learning cost accounting techniques can better serve the company as a whole.

WHY THE STRATEGIC EMPHASIS?

In taking a strategic emphasis, *Cost Management* looks to the long-term competitive success of the firm. Management reports that focus only on short-term financial results will not suffice. Each successful firm maintains a competitive advantage based on a unique strategy. The strategy sets out the critical success factors the firm must achieve. These success factors include financial measures such as profit and nonfinancial measures such as new product development, product quality, and customer satisfaction. Only by succeeding at these critical success factors will the firm maintain its strategic competitive advantage. The role of cost management is to identify, measure, collect, analyze, and report information on these critical factors reliably and in a timely manner. Cost management information provides the critical information the manager needs to develop and implement successful strategies.

For more than a decade, educators and cost management practitioners have called for a strategic emphasis in cost management and accounting education. In addition, the Accounting Education Change Commission, the American Institute of Certified Public Accountants (AICPA), the American Accounting Association, as well as many of the large accounting firms have called for change in accounting education—change to reflect the broader responsibilities of the practicing accountant. The expectation is very clear now that the accountant must be knowledgeable about business and be able to effectively work as part of a management team for the success of the firm or organization.

An example of the forces behind these changes is a survey of 800 management accountants commissioned by the Institute of Management Accountants (IMA) and completed in 1996. The *Practice Analysis of Management Accounting* revealed the changing expectations top managers have for management accountants. Instead of financial reporting specialists only, managers now expect management accountants to develop and interpret information that will help the firm succeed. For example, a respondent from ITT automotive indicated that management accountants need to be far more knowledgeable about the operations of the business.

Another indicator of the importance of strategy is the regular series of columns on "Strategic Cost Management" (since January 1998) in the IMA's magazine, *Management Accounting*, edited by Robin Cooper and Regine Slagmulder. The series is prompted in part by Robin Cooper's two-part article on the changes in management accounting, "Look Out, Management Accountants," in the May and June 1996 issues of *Management Accounting*. Cooper stresses the need for a broader, more active role in the management process for the management accountant. The IMA has taken other steps. It has inaugurated a certificate program, the Certificate in Financial Management, that provides an opportunity for recognition of broader skills by management accountants who achieve the certificate.

The AICPA has taken similar steps. It has initiated a new program, called the "Center for Excellence in Financial Management," to redefine and enhance the role of management accountants. The program envisions the skills and competencies for the management accountant to include a strategic business orientation, facilitating of business and human performance, and creative and dynamic leadership.

Michael Porter in *Competitive Advantage* (New York: The Free Press, 1985) prepared the way for a strategic emphasis in cost management by developing a simple and useful framework for identifying a firm's competitive strategy. Porter's concepts of cost leadership and differentiation have had a strong influence on management education. These concepts provide the foundation on which the strategic approach to cost management is based because they explain what a firm does to succeed. Thus, there are two steps in strategic cost management: first, to identify (using Porter's framework) what managers must do to make the firm succeed, and second, to develop cost management methods and practices to facilitate management's efforts.

In accounting, the importance of the strategic emphasis was first demonstrated to us by John Shank and Vijay Govindarajan in *Strategic Cost Analysis* (Homewood, IL: Richard D. Irwin, 1989). Several leading authors have continued to develop the strategic theme, including, in particular, Robert S. Kaplan and David Norton in *The Balanced Scorecard* (Harvard Business School Press, 1996).

GOALS OF COST MANAGEMENT: A STRATEGIC EMPHASIS

This evolution in the field of cost accounting has created a need for contemporary teaching materials that **help students make the connection between learning basic accounting methods and serving the overall needs of the company.** Our specific goals in writing this book are to help students:

1. Understand how a firm or organization chooses its competitive strategy, including the identification and measurement of critical success factors.

2. Learn how cost management methods and practices are used to help the firm succeed.

3. Understand and apply appropriate cost management methods in each of the four management functions:
   a. strategic management;
   b. planning and decision making;
   c. preparation of financial reports; and
   d. management and operational control.

4. See the effect of the contemporary business environment on cost management methods and practices, including: the global business environment, new manufacturing and information technologies, the increasing focus on the customer, new management organizational forms, and other social, ethical, political, and cultural considerations.

5. Understand the role of cost management in the firm's use of contemporary management techniques such as: total quality management, benchmarking,

continuous improvement, activity-based management, reengineering, the theory of constraints, mass customization, target costing, life-cycle costing, and the balanced scorecard.

ORGANIZATION AND CONTENT DIFFERENCES

Along with the important traditional methods and procedures, the text includes relevant discussions of strategy. This unique strategic emphasis is integrated in the text in three ways:

1. **Strategic framework.** The book is organized to emphasize the role of cost management information in each of the management functions. In this way, each cost management method is clearly linked not only to the firm's overall strategy, but also to the management function that uses the method. Each part of the book develops the role of cost management information in each of the four management functions:
   - Strategic Management—Parts I and II
   - Planning and Decision Making—Part III
   - Product Costing and Financial Reporting—Part IV
   - Operational Control and Management Control—Parts V and VI, respectively

2. **Early coverage of basic strategic concepts.** The introductory chapters develop important strategic concepts that are then used throughout the book. These chapters explain how firms compete, and the nature of the key measures that managers must use to gain and maintain a competitive advantage.

3. **Running theme: How does this topic contribute to the success of the firm?** A key feature of the book is that the strategic theme is used to integrate the individual chapters into a coherent whole—one wherein each of the parts contributes to the overall strategic emphasis. For example, most chapters start with an explanation of the strategic role of the chapter topic in cost management.

The following chart demonstrates how these three differentiating aspects of the book are applied to three different types of chapters: (1) a chapter covering a traditional topic that is usually presented in a procedural manner, (2) a chapter covering a contemporary topic that involves a significant advancement upon a traditional cost management method, and (3) a chapter covering strategic topics—contemporary management methods used to enhance the firm's competitiveness.

Key Differences in Each Chapter

Chapter 1: Cost Management: An Overview

This chapter introduces the central theme of the book, the strategic role of cost management. The chapter describes the contemporary business environment and explains how it has affected the role of cost management. The strategic role of cost management is then linked to the development of 10 new management techniques, including total quality management, target costing, and the balanced scorecard.

Chapter 2: Strategic Analysis and Strategic Cost Management

This chapter explains how firms develop strategies to succeed. The concepts of strategy and how a firm develops a competitive strategy are presented using Michael Porter's framework: cost leadership, differentiation, and focus. Coverage includes an introduction to the concept of critical success factors, the strategic role of the balanced scorecard, and an explanation of value chain analysis.

Chapter 3: Cost Drivers and Basic Cost Concepts

This topic can often seem like a glossary of somewhat related concepts. In contrast, in this book the basic cost terms and concepts are presented as they relate to the

	Strategic Framework: Organization by Management Function	Strategic Concepts: Covered Early in the Book	Strategic Theme: Integrated Throughout the Book
		Traditional Topic	
Job Costing (Chapter 12)	Cost management systems such as job order costing have an important role in the management function — preparing financial reports for both internal and external use. This management function is covered in Part IV of the book, with Chapter 12 as the introductory chapter.	The coverage of strategy in Chapter 2 provides a good foundation in which to explain why job order costing can add value and competitiveness for a company. The chapter explains the business purpose of job costing, linking it to the firm's strategy, as developed in Chapter 2.	The job order costing chapter begins with an explanation of the different costing systems, including job order costing, with the objective of showing the business purpose of the different systems.
		Contemporary Topic	
Activity-Based Costing and Management (Chapter 4)	Activity-based costing is covered early in the book, in Part II, Contemporary Cost Management Concepts, because the activity approach to cost management is a critical feature of many management methods and practices. For example, early coverage of activity-based costing means we can more effectively integrate activity-based costing into the later chapters on cost estimation, cost-volume-profit, and decision making.	The early coverage of strategy allows us to explain the importance of contemporary topics such as activity-based costing in the context of the firm's critical success factors. For example, activity-based costing is most important for firms that compete on price/low cost, and have somewhat complex sales/production processes.	Activity-based costing is a critical cost management method for firms that compete on cost leadership and have complex manufacturing environments. The chapter begins with an explanation of the contemporary manufacturing environment, and explains how activity-based costing is used to improve management decision making.
		Strategic Topics	
Target Costing, Theory of Constraints, and Life-Cycle Costing (Chapter 5)	Target costing, life-cycle costing, and the theory of constraints are three contemporary management techniques that are used to enhance the competitiveness of the firm. The topics deal directly with the first management function of strategic management and are covered in Part II, Contemporary Cost Management Concepts.	Since strategic management, including the topics of Chapter 5, is the most important of the management functions, we cover it at the beginning of the book in Parts I and II.	Each of the topics in Chapter 5 is presented from the perspective of how the method can help the firm become more successful, that is, how it can best achieve its strategy.

four management functions, to emphasize the use of the terms in actual cost management methods and practices. This organization emphasizes the role of cost management in each of the four management functions, and thus provides greater motivation for learning the terms as it is clear from the start how they will be used later in the book.

Chapter 4: Activity-Based Costing and Management

Activity-based costing is presented thoroughly in this chapter, including value-added and non-value-added activities; activity-based management; applications in manufacturing, marketing, and administration; and applications in service firms and not-for-profit organizations. The topic is motivated by reference to the contemporary manufacturing environment (JIT, robotics, and FMS) and the limitations of volume-based costing.

Chapter 5: Target Costing, Theory of Constraints, and Life-Cycle Costing

Several new cost management topics are explained in this chapter—target costing, the theory of constraints, life-cycle costing, and sales life-cycle analysis. An organizing theme is used: the life cycle of the product from both a cost and a sales perspective. From the cost perspective, the cost life-cycle of the product begins with the upstream activities of research, development, and testing; then manufacturing; and finally the downstream activities of delivery, support, and service. Target costing is developed for the upstream activities, while the theory of constraints is developed for the manufacturing phase, and life-cycle costing looks at the entire cost life cycle. In addition, sales life-cycle analysis is explained as a method for managing the product's costs from the time the product is introduced, to the growth in its market, to finally its removal from the market.

Chapter 6: Total Quality Management

The entire chapter is devoted to total quality management. The types of quality conformance, the different costs of quality, and the means to detect defects are covered extensively. A special feature of the chapter is an extensive section on cost of quality reports, including the cost of quality matrix.

Chapter 7: Cost Estimation

This chapter integrates the strategic theme in both the text of the chapter and the problem material. The emphasis is on the role of cost estimation and on the choice of estimation method. The presentation of each method explains the expected reliability and accuracy of the method as a basis for understanding its proper use in management accounting practice. Special emphasis is given to regression analysis; it is the most reliable and accurate of the estimation methods.

Chapter 8: Cost-Volume-Profit Analysis

This chapter begins with the strategic role of cost-volume-profit analysis, then covers four different methods: the equation and the ratio method, each developed for breakeven in units or dollars. The strategic theme is emphasized in an extensive section on sensitivity analysis, which includes a discussion of operation leverage and its use in analyzing a firm's strategy. A unique section develops a cost-volume-profit analysis when using activity-based costing.

Chapter 9: Strategy and the Master Budget

A unique aspect of this chapter is the full development of the budgeting process, including the formulation of the budget committee through to the review and approval of the final budget, and the ethical and behavioral issues that arise in the budget process.

Chapter 10: Decision Making with a Strategic Emphasis

This chapter goes beyond the typical focus on the determination of relevant costs. It includes a discussion of the importance of taking a strategic approach in using relevant cost analysis. Several examples are used. There is a particular emphasis on managerial incentives in decision making and the strategic role of profitability analysis, both with single and with multiple products and limited resources.

Chapter 11: Capital Budgeting

The strategic focus is an integral part of this chapter. The coverage is complete and thorough, including all the current methods, the tax effects, and the techniques for project evaluation and review. A unique aspect of the chapter is the careful treatment of the determination of cash flows in using each of the capital budgeting methods.

Chapter 12: Job Costing

Rather than simply presenting the procedural aspects of this method, the discussion has been expanded to include an explanation of why a firm would choose to use the job costing method. It addresses how the design of the cost system and choice of a system such as job order costing fit the strategic objectives of the firm. The different costing methods are explained, and there is a discussion of when and why each is used.

Chapter 13: Process Costing

Continuing the discussion of cost systems in Chapter 12, this chapter explains the business context in which the process costing method is used. The procedural aspects of the method are then carefully developed. Several actual examples are used to demonstrate how the method fits different operating conditions.

Chapter 14: Cost Allocation: Service Departments and Joint Product Costs

The chapter looks at the traditional issues of cost allocation among production and service departments and where joint production processes are involved. The coverage is objective-based; it begins with strategic, implementation, and ethical issues involved in cost allocation. The development of the procedural aspects is comprehensive. Examples show the complete cost allocation cycle—the allocation of costs to department, the reallocation of costs for service departments to production departments, and the allocation to products.

Chapter 15: The Flexible Budget and Standard Costing: Direct Materials and Direct Labor and Chapter 16: Standard Costing: Factory Overhead

These two chapters begin with an introduction to the use of standard costing within the management function, operational control. Particular emphasis is placed on the strategic role of standard costing—which firms use it and why. Also, a unique aspect of the chapter is the careful development of how cost standards are determined in practice, taking into account new manufacturing environments and using benchmarking and activity analysis.

Chapter 17: Managing Productivity and Marketing Effectiveness

The critical success factors for most firms include both the productivity of operations and the effectiveness of sales and marketing. The presentation of productivity is a natural follow-up to the standard costing material presented in Chapters 15 and 16. A unique aspect of the presentation is its unified approach—the different forms of analysis are presented in a way that clearly demonstrates how they are interrelated and can be integrated. Similarly, a special feature of the sales and marketing analysis is the unified approach. All the variances are shown in an integrated manner.

Chapter 18: Management Control and Strategic Performance Measurement

The emphasis is on strategic business units (SBUs) and how managers of these units are motivated, evaluated, and rewarded to contribute most effectively to the success of the firm. We look at two types of strategic business units in this chapter: one evaluated on cost only and the other based on the profitability of the SBU. Unique aspects of this chapter include the use of the balanced scorecard, the role of outsourcing for cost SBUs, the development of the principal-agent model, the explanation of the role of the sales life cycle in management control, and a special section on determining which type of SBU a firm should use, based on its competitive strategy.

Chapter 19: Strategic Investment Units and Transfer Pricing

Return on investment for investment centers is a topic that is often criticized for its failure to provide a strategic motivation and evaluation of managers. We have addressed this by presenting both the limitations and contributions of return on investment for a strategic business unit, and also new ways in which strategic business units are evaluated, including economic value added and the balanced scorecard. The second topic of the chapter, transfer pricing, is treated in a very up-to-date manner, including international taxation, an increasingly important issue for multinational companies.

Chapter 20: Management Compensation and the Evaluation of the Firm

Two of the emerging issues in cost management are covered in this chapter. Executive compensation is an important part of the strategy for most firms because of the increasing competition for top executives. Our coverage presents the strategic objectives, as well as many of the operational issues of implementing compensation plans, including the different types of bonus plans, tax issues, and financial reporting issues. Also, the valuation of the firm is increasingly important, both as a means to evaluate the firm's management and as a basis for investors to assess the value of the company. Several of the common valuation methods are covered.

IMPORTANT PEDAGOGICAL DIFFERENCES

way in the search for sustainable competitive advantage. This is what we refer to as "strategic cost analysis."[2]

BusinessWeek

Who Made Your Car?

Large auto parts manufacturers such as Textron, Inc., and Johnson Controls are being forced by Detroit automakers to assume new responsibilities, including the design of some of the parts they manufacture and the supervision of some of the smaller suppliers. Chrysler Corporation, for example, requires Textron, Inc., to coordinate the work of other suppliers of parts for its minivans. In addition, Magna International, a Canadian parts manufacturer, is scheduled to produce the entire interior for a new Ford sport-utility vehicle to be introduced in the 2000 model year. Other parts manufacturers supply entire seat systems, floor systems, rear compartment systems, and other major auto parts systems for the automakers. By outsourcing the parts, the automakers expect to have cost savings of as much as 50 percent over in-house manufacturing.

Why does outsourcing parts manufacturing save automakers so much in costs? *Find out on page 44 of this chapter.*

---

[1] Peter F. Drucker, *Managing the Future*, New York, Penguin, 1994, p. 305.
[2] John K. Shank and Vijay Govindarajan, *Strategic Cost Analysis*, Burr Ridge, Ill., Irwin, 1989, p. xi.

(BUSINESS WEEK) CHAPTER OPENING VIGNETTES.
Drawn from recent issues of *Business Week*, these chapter opening vignettes add relevance and increase student interest. Each chapter begins with a synopsis of an article that demonstrates how an actual company has been faced with cost management issues and challenges. An intriguing question leads the student into the chapter, providing a context in which to think about the material.

Later, after going through the related topics in the chapter, the answer to the question is presented, so students can see how concepts have been applied in a real company situation.

reducing ... viding ... or serv

BusinessWeek

Why Is Outsourcing "In" for Automakers?
(Continues from page 27)

A: In three words, value-chain analysis.
To understand the cost-saving role of the parts manufacturers, automakers use value-chain analysis. Automakers look at their upstream costs of design and engineering and find that the specialized design teams of parts manufacturers are sometimes more cost efficient. One example is the seat systems for Chrysler cars. "At one time we had 250 engineers here, just designing seat covers," says Thomas T. Stallkamp, Chrysler's executive vice president for procurement and supply. "Now, the suppliers are the experts." In effect, what Chrysler has done is to examine its cost competitiveness at each step in the value chain, and has found that in seat systems, it is better to outsource.

The trend is for the parts manufacturers to sell *entire* parts systems. For example, Lear Corporation can now supply almost entire passenger compartments for the automakers, according to Lear Chairman Kenneth L. Way. The same trend appears to be true for other systems—brakes, fuel systems, and exterior trim, among others—with one analyst pointing out that a total interior supplier could save $600 of the $900 it costs Ford and Chrysler for these systems. Essentially, a value-chain analysis for automakers shows that increasing reliance on outsourcing in manufacturing is providing an important way to reduce costs.

For further reading, see the following source: "Get Big or Get Out: How Detroit Is Driving Consolidation in the Auto-Parts Biz," *Business Week*, September 2, 1996, pp. 60–62.

STRATEGIC MATERIAL HIGHLIGHTED.
The strategic icon highlights the important discussions of strategy within each chapter. Refer to the detailed Table of Contents for the locations of these passages.

... of top managers

ronment will also be included in cost management. The environmental factors are as critical as the financial factors in assessing the potential for the firm's long-term success.

THE STRATEGIC FOCUS OF COST MANAGEMENT

The lowest form of thinking is the bare recognition of the object. The highest is the comprehensive intuition of the man who sees all things as part of the system.

PLATO

As the Greek philosopher observed, the successful individual, like the successful firm, is the one that thinks strategically. The competitive firm incorporates the emerging and anticipated changes in the contemporary environment of business into its business planning and practices. The competitive firm is customer-driven, uses advanced manufacturing technologies where appropriate, anticipates the effect of changes in regulatory requirements and customer tastes, and recognizes the complex social, political, and cultural environment of the firm. Guided by strategic thinking, the management accountant focuses on the factors that make the company successful, rather than only calculating costs and other financial measures. We are reminded of the story of the Scottish farmer who had prize sheep to take to market. When asked why his sheep were always superior to those of his neighbors, the

11

Problem Material. The end-of-chapter material was designed to promote better understanding of the strategic role of the cost management methods and practices presented in that chapter. We have taken great care in developing unique problems and cases that effectively demonstrate the strategic issues presented in the chapter. Types of problem material include: **Self-study problems** (with answers provided at the end of the chapter), **Questions** to test comprehension of key concepts, and **Problems** for more comprehensive practice of important concepts and procedures. A variety of problems are included that deal with emerging strategic, international, service, and ethics issues. These problems are marked appropriately for easy identification.

 Strategy   *International*   *Service*  *Ethics*

SUPPORT MATERIALS

Web Resources. This book is supported by a dynamic Web site located at http://www.mhhe.com/business/accounting/blocher. The site contains information about the book, the authors, and additional on-line resources designed for both students and instructors. Be sure to check out the unique interactive spreadsheets, created by Leslie Turner (Northern Kentucky University). These are downloadable spreadsheet applications for use with selected end-of-chapter problems. We invite you and your students to visit the site often to stay current or to give us feedback.

Cases & Readings in Strategic Cost Management. Automatically shrink-wrapped with each copy of the book, this supplement contains a host of value-added resources. It includes an extensive set of longer cases pertaining to a variety of important topics. These case scenarios put students into situations that allow them to think strategically and to apply concepts that they have learned in the course. Key readings have been chosen to give students more background into the evolution of strategic cost management topics.

Cost Management, The *Business Week* Edition. (ISBN# 007-561947-4) The price of this version of the text includes a 10-week subscription to *Business Week*, the best-selling business magazine in the world. This unique real-world offering gives students and instructors the opportunity to keep up with current events and bolster in-class discussions.

Especially for Students

Study Guide. Prepared by Roger Doost (Clemson University), this booklet reviews the highlights of each chapter and includes a variety of self-study questions for student review. Every chapter includes short-answer questions organized by learning objective, multiple-choice questions, and thorough exercises. Suggested answers to all questions and exercises are included.

Ready Notes. This booklet of Ready Show screen printouts enables students to take notes during Ready Show presentations. This supplement changes the nature of note-taking. Rather than spending time copying material that is already in the book, students can focus on what is being discussed in the classroom.

Instructor Support

Instructor's Manual. Written by the lead author, Ed Blocher, this helpful guide includes lecture outlines, teaching tips, and ideas for additional class discussion. Suggested teaching notes are also provided to accompany the *Cases & Readings in Strategic Cost Management* booklet.

Solutions Manual. This is prepared by the authors. This booklet contains fully worked solutions to questions and problems from the text. All solutions have been carefully reviewed for accuracy by outside sources. The solutions manual is available in electronic format as well.

Solutions Transparencies. Solutions to all problems are available on transparencies for classroom presentations.

Check Figures. This is prepared by the authors. This list of answers is available to allow students to check their work. Order the handouts in packs of 30 or simply download the list from the Web site and distribute as needed.

Test Bank. Prepared by Greg Lowry (Troy State University) and Leo Ruggle (Professor Emeritus—Mankato State University), this test bank is designed to help instructors create exams consistent with the text's strategic emphasis. Each chapter includes true/false, multiple-choice questions, brief essays, and extended problems requiring strategic thinking.

Computest (available for both Windows and Macintosh systems). The Computest is a computerized version of the manual test bank for more efficient use.

Ready Shows. Prepared by Douglas Cloud (Pepperdine University), Ready Shows use PowerPoint software to illustrate chapter concepts.

ACKNOWLEDGMENTS

In writing this book, we were fortunate to have received extensive feedback from a number of accounting educators. We want to thank our colleagues for their careful and complete review of our work. The comments that we received were invaluable in helping us to shape the manuscript. We believe that this collaborative development process helped us to create a text that will truly meet the needs of today's students and instructors. We are sincerely grateful to the following individuals for their participation in the process:

Progyan Basu, Howard University; Bruce Bradford, Fairfield University; Gregory P. Cermignano, Widener University; Peter Clarke, University College Dublin; G. R. Cluskey Jr., Bradley University; Roger K. Doost, Clemson University; Lila H. Greco, Orange County Community College; Susan Hamlen, SUNY at Buffalo; Dick Houser, Northern Arizona University; Mohamed E. A. Hussein, University of Connecticut; Michele E. Johnson, University of Sioux Falls; David Keys, Northern Illinois University; Zafar U. Khan, Eastern Michigan University; Leslie Kren, University of Wisconsin–Milwaukee; Gregory K. Lowry, Troy State University; David Marcinko, SUNY–Albany; Fred Nordhauser, University of Texas at San Antonio; Marilyn Okleshen, Mankato State University; David Pariser, West Virginia University; Diane D. Pattison, University of San Diego; Shirley Polejewski, University of St. Thomas; Anthony H. Presutti Jr., Miami University; Leo A. Ruggle, Mankato State University; Ali Sedaghat, Loyola College in Maryland; Douglas Sharp, Wichita State University; Kenneth P. Sinclair, Lehigh University; James C. Stallman, University of Missouri–Columbia; Sandra Weber, Truman State University; Stacey Whitecotton, Arizona State University; and Martin G. H. Wu, New York University

Finally, we are most appreciative of the outstanding assistance and support provided by the professionals of Irwin/McGraw-Hill: Jeff Shelstad, our publisher, for his guidance; Becky Page, our associate editor, for her creativity; our developmental editor, Marc Chernoff, for his invaluable suggestions; Rhonda Seelinger, our marketing manager, for her significant promotional efforts; Maggie Rathke, our project manager, for her attention to detail; Laurie Entringer, for the outstanding presentation of the text; and Kimberly Stack, our supplements coordinator, for her timeliness and accuracy in delivering the support material. A special thanks goes to Gina Huck, for her work on the *Business Week* chapter opening vignettes.

Ed Blocher
Kung Chen
Tom Lin

CONTENTS

*Entries highlighted in blue and bolded refer to important discussions of strategy and strategic cost management topics.

Contents

CHAPTER 6   **Total Quality Management**   162

PART III   **Management Planning and Decision Making**   199

CHAPTER 7   **Cost Estimation**   200

CHAPTER 8   **Cost-Volume-Profit Analysis**   248

Contents

CHAPTER 13

Process Costing   490

CHAPTER 14

Cost Allocation: Service Departments and Joint Product Costs   542

Contents

 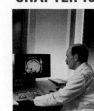

Contents

Part I

Introduction to Cost Management

1

Cost Management

An Overview

1

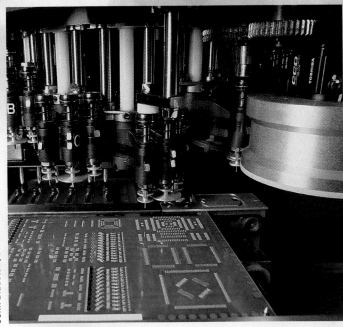

After studying this chapter you should be able to ...

1 Explain the use of cost management in each of the four functions of management and in different types of organizations, with emphasis on the strategic management function

2 Explain the concepts of cost object and cost driver

3 Explain how the contemporary business environment has influenced cost management

4 Explain the contemporary management techniques and how they have influenced cost management

5 Describe the professional environment of the management accountant, including professional organizations, professional certifications, and professional ethics

6 Understand the principles and rules of professional ethics and explain how to apply them

John Blaustein/Gamma Liaison.

> The most successful man in life is the man who has the best information.
>
> BENJAMIN DISRAELI, A NINETEENTH-CENTURY
> PRIME MINISTER OF ENGLAND

This book is about developing, understanding, and using cost management information. As Disraeli knew in the nineteenth century, having the best information is the key to success. In today's business environment, the development and use of information—especially cost management information—is a critical factor in the effective management of a firm or organization. As the business environment has changed, the role of cost management information has expanded to serve all management functions.

THE USES OF COST MANAGEMENT

Cost management information is a broad concept. It is the information the manager needs to effectively manage the firm or not-for-profit organization—both *financial information* about costs and revenues, and relevant *nonfinancial information* about productivity, quality, and other key success factors for the firm.[1]

Financial information alone can be misleading, because it tends to have a short-term focus. For competitive success, a firm needs to focus primarily on longer-term factors, such as product and manufacturing advances, product quality, and customer loyalty. For example, an emphasis on financial information alone could lead managers to stress cost reduction (cost is a financial measure), while ignoring or even lowering quality standards (a nonfinancial measure). This decision could be a critical mistake, leading to the loss of customers and market share in the long term. Internationally known business consultants, such as W. Edwards Deming, Peter Drucker, and others, point out the importance of looking at nonfinancial and longer-term measures of operating performance if a firm is going to compete successfully. A central theme of this book, then, is that cost management information includes all the information—both financial and nonfinancial and both short-term and long-term—that managers need to lead their firms to competitive success.

Those who develop cost management information are most often referred to as management accountants, though they are also called cost analysts or cost

◀ **LEARNING OBJECTIVE 1**
Explain the use of cost management in each of the four functions of management and in different types of organizations, with emphasis on the strategic management function.

Cost management information is the information the manager needs to effectively manage the firm or not-for-profit organization.

BusinessWeek

? How Does Dell Do It?

The growth in the price of Dell Computer's common stock outperformed that of IBM, Cisco Systems, Hewlett-Packard, Compaq, Intel, and Microsoft through 1996 and early 1997. The computer manufacturer's return on invested capital was almost twice the nearest competitor in the first quarter of 1997. And that's not all. All of this was accomplished in a very price-sensitive industry, where price wars and cost cutting are constant, and customer expectations are ever increasing. Competition forces computer makers to increase the features of their products while decreasing the cost and/or price. For a computer manufacturer and direct marketer such as Dell, a large portion of total costs is made up of selling costs and the costs of components used in the assembly of the computers.

Q: How can Dell reduce costs and at the same time add value to the product? *Find out on page 15 of this chapter.*

---

[1] Cost is often defined as the use of a resource that has a financial consequence. In this text we use the broader concept of cost management information as defined above—to include nonfinancial information as well as financial information.

accountants. The responsibility for cost management typically falls within the role of the controller, who reports to the chief financial officer (CFO) of the firm. The controller has a number of other duties, including financial reporting, maintaining financial systems, and other reporting functions (to industry organizations, governmental units, etc.), as illustrated in Exhibit 1–1. The CFO has the overall responsibility for the financial function, while the treasurer manages investor and creditor relationships, and the chief information officer (CIO) manages the firm's use of information technology, including computer systems and communications.

In contrast to the management accounting function, the financial reporting function involves preparation of financial statements for external users such as investors and government regulators. Financial accounting requires compliance with external reporting requirements, whereas cost management information is developed for use within the firm, to facilitate management. The main focus of cost management information therefore must be *usefulness* and *timeliness*, whereas the focus of financial reports must be *accuracy* (in compliance with the reporting requirements). However, strict adherence to accuracy will often compromise the usefulness and timeliness of the information. The function of the financial systems department is to develop and maintain the financial reporting system and related systems such as payroll, financial security systems, and tax preparation. The challenge for the controller is to reconcile these different and potentially conflicting roles.[2]

The Four Functions of Management

The management accountant develops cost management information for the CFO and other managers to use in managing the firm, to make the firm more competitive and successful. Cost management information is provided for each of the four major management functions: (1) strategic management, (2) planning and decision making, (3) management and operational control, and (4) preparation of financial statements. The most important function is **strategic management,** which is the

Strategic management is the development of a sustainable competitive position.

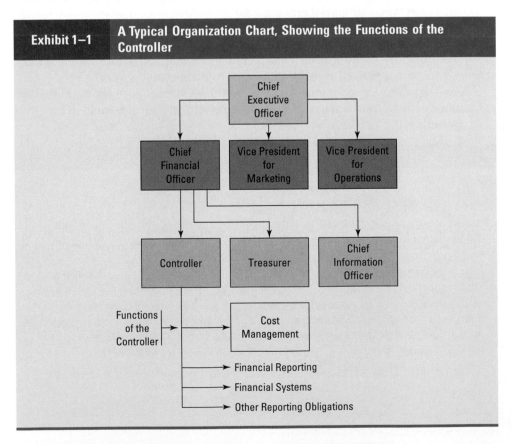

Exhibit 1–1	A Typical Organization Chart, Showing the Functions of the Controller

[2] A history of cost management is provided by Robert S. Kaplan, "The Evolution of Management Accounting," *The Accounting Review,* July 1984, pp. 390–418.

Cost Management Information Is Needed for Each of the Four Management Functions

1. **Strategic Management.** Cost management information is needed to make sound strategic decisions regarding choice of products, manufacturing methods, marketing techniques and channels, and other long-term issues.

2. **Planning and Decision Making.** Cost management information is needed to support recurring decisions regarding replacing equipment, managing cash flow, budgeting raw materials purchases, scheduling production, and pricing.

3. **Management and Operational Control.** Cost management information is needed to provide a fair and effective basis for identifying inefficient operations, and to reward and support the most effective managers.

4. **Preparation of Financial Statements.** Cost management information is needed to provide accurate accounting for inventory and other assets, in compliance with reporting requirements, for the preparation of financial reports and for use in the three other management functions.

development of a sustainable competitive position in which the firm's competitive advantage provides continued success. A **strategy** is a set of goals and specific action plans which, if achieved, will provide the desired competitive advantage. Strategic management involves the identification and implementation of these goals and action plans. Next, management is responsible for **planning and decision making,** which involves budgeting and profit planning, cash flow management, and other decisions related to the operations of the firm, such as when to lease or buy a facility, when to repair or replace a piece of equipment, when to change a marketing plan, and when to begin the development of a new product.

The third area of responsibility, control, consists of two functions, operational control and management control, involving managers at both the top and mid-management levels. **Operational control** takes place when mid-level managers (e.g., plant managers, product managers, regional managers) monitor the activities of operating-level managers and employees (e.g., production supervisors and various department heads). In contrast, **management control** is the evaluation of mid-level managers by upper-level managers (the controller or the CFO).

In the fourth function, **preparation of financial statements,** management complies with the reporting requirements of the industry, of relevant professional groups (such as the Financial Accounting Standards Board), and of relevant federal government authorities (for example, the Internal Revenue Service and the Securities and Exchange Commission).[3] The financial statement information also serves the other three management functions, because this information is often an important part of planning and decision making, control, and strategic management.

Strategic Management and Strategic Cost Management

Effective strategic management is critical to the success of the firm or organization, and it is thus a pervasive theme of this book. The growing pressures of global competition, technological innovation, and changes in business processes have made cost management much more critical and dynamic than ever before. Managers must think *competitively*, and to do so requires a strategy. They need to think about the long term and to think integratively.

Long-term thinking involves anticipating changes; products and production processes are designed to accommodate expected changes in customer demands. Flexibility is important. The ability to make fast changes is critical, as illustrated by the new management concepts of speed to market and agile manufacturing. Product life cycles, the time from the introduction of a new product to its removal from the market, are expected to get shorter and shorter. Success in the short term is no longer a measure of ultimate success; it is long-term success firms seek, and that goal requires strategic, long-term thinking.

A **strategy** is a set of goals and specific action plans that, if achieved, will provide the desired competitive advantage.

Planning and decision making involves budgeting and profit planning, cash flow management, and other decisions related to operations.

Operational control takes place when mid-level managers monitor the activities of operating-level managers and employees.

Management control is the evaluation of mid-level managers by upper-level managers.

Preparation of financial statements. In preparing financial statements, management complies with the financial reporting requirements of the industry and of regulatory agencies.

---

[3] The professional groups are identified and explained at the end of this chapter.

The strategic emphasis also requires integrative thinking, that is, the ability to identify and solve problems from a cross-functional view. The business functions are often identified as marketing, production, finance, and accounting/controllership. Instead of viewing a problem as a production problem, or a marketing problem, or a finance and accounting problem, the integrative approach combines skills from all the functions simultaneously, using cross-functional teams. The integrative approach is necessary in a dynamic and competitive environment. The firm's attention is focused on satisfying the customers' needs, and all the firm's resources, *from all the functions*, are directed to that goal.

Because strategic issues are growing in their importance to management, cost management has moved from a traditional role of product costing and operational control to a broader, strategic focus—to strategic cost management. **Strategic cost management** is the development of cost management information to facilitate the principal management function, strategic management.

Strategic cost management is the development of cost management information to facilitate the principal management function, strategic management.

Types of Organizations

Cost management information is useful in a wide range of organizations—business firms, governmental units, and not-for-profit organizations. Business firms are usually categorized by industry, the main categories being merchandising, manufacturing, and service. Merchandising firms purchase goods for resale. Merchandisers that sell to other merchandisers are called wholesalers, while those selling directly to consumers are called retailers. Examples of merchandising firms are the large retailers, such as Sears, Wal-Mart, and Radio Shack.

Manufacturing firms use raw materials, labor, and manufacturing facilities and equipment to produce products. These products are sold to merchandising firms or to other manufacturers as raw materials for additional products. Examples of manufacturers are General Motors, IBM, and Sony.

Service firms provide a service to customers that offers convenience, freedom, safety, or comfort. Common services include transportation, health care, financial services (banking, insurance, accounting), personal services (physical training, hair styling), and legal services. In the United States, service industries are growing at a much faster rate than manufacturing or merchandising, in part because of the increased demand for leisure and convenience and the increased complexity of society.

Governmental and not-for-profit organizations provide services, much like the firms in service industries. However, the services provided by these organizations are such that there is often no direct relationship between the amount paid and the services provided. Instead, both the nature of the services to be provided and the customers to receive the services are determined by government or philanthropic organizations. The resources are provided by governmental units and/or charities. The services provided by these organizations are often called public goods to indicate that there is no typical market for the services. There are a number of unique characteristics of public goods, such as the impracticality of limiting consumption to a single customer (clean water and police and fire protection are provided for *all* residents).

Most firms and organizations use cost management information. For example, the typical manufacturing firm requires cost management information because of the critical need to manage production costs. Similarly, large retail firms such as Wal-Mart use cost management information to manage stocking, distribution, and customer service. Firms in the service industries, such as those providing financial services or other professional services, use cost management information to identify the most profitable services and to manage the costs of providing those services.

Cost management information is used in a wide variety of ways. Whether the firm's business is not-for-profit or profit, that firm must know the cost of new products or services, the cost of making improvements in existing products or services, and the cost of finding a new way of producing the products or providing the services. Cost management information is used to determine prices, to change product or service offerings to improve profitability, to update manufacturing facilities in a timely fashion, and to determine new marketing methods or distribution channels. For example, manufacturers such as Hewlett-Packard study the cost implications of design options for each new product. The design study includes analysis of projected manufacturing costs as well as those costs incurred after the product is completed, which include service and warranty costs. Service and warranty costs are often called downstream costs because they occur after manufacturing. By analyzing both manufacturing and downstream costs, Hewlett-Packard is able to discover whether product enhancements might cause manufacturing and downstream costs to be out of line with expected increases in customer value and revenue for that feature.

Users of cost management information are both large and small firms, in all types of industries. A firm's degree of reliance on cost management depends on the nature of its competitive strategy. Many firms compete on the basis of being the low-cost provider of the industry's goods or services, and for these firms, cost management is critical. Other firms, such as cosmetics, fashion, and pharmaceutical firms, compete on the basis of product differentiation, in which the unique or innovative features of the product make the firm successful. For these firms, the critical management concern is maintaining product differentiation through product development and marketing. The role of cost management is to support the differentiation strategy through cost management of research and development and marketing expenses, as well as manufacturing expenditures. Historically, some governmental units and not-for-profit agencies have tended to focus on their responsibility to spend in approved ways, rather than to spend in efficient and effective ways. Increasingly, however, these types of organizations are using cost management for efficient and effective use of their financial resources.

For not-for-profit organizations especially, it is important to be able to predict the effect of an anticipated budget cut or increase on planned service levels. Cost management information usually serves as a starting point in assessing the effect of changing funding levels on activities and services. For example, Durham Service Corps, a nonprofit provider of educational services, had its funding cut by approximately 30 percent in a recent period. Through a study of its cost structure, the agency was able to project a cutback in service of approximately 50 percent, based on the fact that a significant proportion of its costs (for facilities and administration) were not directly involved in providing the educational services and could not be reduced. Therefore, the cuts had to come from costs for classroom teachers. Thus the analysis of the organization's cost structure explains why a 30 percent change in the budget had a greater effect on direct services.

COST OBJECTS AND COST DRIVERS

The focus of the management accountant's attention varies with the nature of the firm or organization and its cost objects. A **cost object** is any item or activity for which management desires to accumulate costs. The five main types of cost objects are:

1. Product, or a related group of products.
2. Service.
3. Customer.
4. Department (e.g., engineering, human resources).
5. Project, such as a research project, marketing promotion, or community service effort.

For business firms, the cost object is usually the product or service provided by the firm. Sometimes an individual customer or a related group of customers is selected as the cost object, to allow for further analysis of the cost of providing products and services to these customers. Generally, the cost object is the focus of profitability analysis—which products and which customers are most profitable? For not-for-profit organizations, the cost object is the service provided.

A **cost object** is any item or activity for which costs are accumulated for management purposes.

◀ **LEARNING OBJECTIVE 2**
Explain the concepts of cost object and cost driver.

For any organization or firm, a cost object can also be a department within the firm or organization, or a project, such as a research-and-development venture or a community service effort. In these cases, the management accountant is concerned mainly with the management of costs incurred to provide the service of the organization, department, or project and/or with maintaining an accurate accounting of costs incurred.

A **cost driver** is any factor that has the effect of changing the level of total cost for a cost object.

The total amount of cost for a cost object is influenced by cost drivers. A **cost driver** is any factor that has the effect of changing the level of total cost for a cost object. For example, the cost of electricity in a plant (the cost object) is influenced by the number of machine hours; thus the number of machine hours is a cost driver for the cost of electricity. Other common cost drivers are the number of products manufactured, the number of machine setups, the number of design changes made for the product, and the number of marketing promotions and distribution channels. The identification and analysis of cost drivers is a critical step in the strategic analysis of the firm and in cost management for the firm. It provides a basis for accurately determining the cost of a cost object and for controlling costs for that cost object.

THE CONTEMPORARY BUSINESS ENVIRONMENT

LEARNING OBJECTIVE 3 ▶
Explain how the contemporary business environment has influenced cost management.

Many changes in the business environment in recent years have caused significant modifications in cost management practices. The primary changes are (1) an increase in global competition, (2) advances in manufacturing and information technologies, (3) a greater focus on the customer, (4) new forms of management organization, and (5) changes in the social, political, and cultural environment of business.

The Global Business Environment

A key development that drives the extensive changes in the contemporary business environment is the growth of international markets and trade. Businesses and not-for-profit organizations, as well as consumers and regulators, are all significantly

---

Manufacturing and Information Technology Drives Globalization

Senior executives from 150 of the Fortune 1000 companies report that the use of information technology is considered the major driver of globalization, allowing these firms to respond quickly to changing conditions around the world.

Over 80 percent of the executives viewed information technology as a strategic investment. The responding firms reported using information technology to track financial and operating events in the firm (74 percent), to improve service quality (41 percent), to improve profits (30 percent), and to improve product quality (24 percent).

Source: Based on information in the *Deloitte & Touche Review,* November 25, 1996, p. 3.

Responding to an Environment of Continuous Change

According to a recent survey of American business leaders, sponsored by Deloitte & Touche LLP, change has become an integral part of corporate culture. On average, senior executives are investing about 8 percent of corporate revenues in major changes (including reorganizations, acquisitions, mergers, and sell-offs), and they expect to earn 30 percent return on their investments. Some key findings:

- A full 91 percent of the business leaders surveyed report that change within their own companies has increased in the past two years, and half characterize their companies as being in a constant state of change and expect it to continue in the near term.

- Cost leadership (cited by 37 percent) is the major goal for change programs, followed by flexibility and agility (24 percent), quality improvement (23 percent), innovation (22 percent), and growth (21 percent).

- The key external factors driving change within companies are (1) intensified competition, (2) the changing regulatory environment, and (3) heightened customer requirements.

Source: Based on information in the *Deloitte & Touche Review,* April 17, 1995, p. 2.

affected by the rapid growth of economic interdependence and increased competition from other countries. The North American Free Trade Agreement (NAFTA), the World Trade Organization (WTO), the European Union (EU), and the growing number of alliances between large multinational firms make it clear that the opportunities for growth and profitability lie in global markets. Most consumers benefit as low-cost, high-quality goods are traded worldwide. Managers and business owners know the importance of pursuing sales and production activities in foreign countries, and investors benefit from the increased opportunities for investment in foreign firms.

The increasing competitiveness of the global business environment means that firms increasingly need cost management information in order to be competitive. Firms need financial and nonfinancial information about doing business and competing effectively in other countries.

Manufacturing and Information Technologies

To remain competitive in the face of the increased global competition, firms around the world are adopting new manufacturing and information technologies. These include just-in-time inventory methods to reduce the cost and waste of maintaining large levels of raw materials and unfinished product. Also, many U.S. firms and firms in other countries are adopting the methods applied in Japanese manufacturing, methods that have produced significant cost and quality improvements through the use of quality teams and statistical quality control. Other manufacturing changes include flexible manufacturing techniques, developed to reduce setup times and allow fast turnaround of customer orders. A key competitive edge in what is called speed to market is the ability to deliver the product or service faster than the competition.

Another main area of manufacturing process change is the gradual *increase in facilities costs relative to the costs of materials and labor* in the product. That is, the cost of maintaining the capacity to produce with plant and equipment has increased relative to the materials and labor used in producing the product. Firms that once viewed facilities costs as uncontrollable and focused their attention on managing labor and materials costs have now redirected their attention to controlling facilities costs.

In addition to changes in the makeup of production costs, there have been some significant changes in the makeup of the so-called life-cycle costs of developing, manufacturing, and selling and servicing a product. The upstream costs of design and of developing vendor relationships have become extremely important, because of the increased awareness that design decisions significantly affect all the costs incurred later in manufacturing, selling, and service. A design that is simple and reliable to service and to manufacture can provide significant savings over other designs throughout the life cycle of the product, even though the design effort may have been more costly. Similarly, the downstream costs of marketing, selling, distributing, and servicing the product are an important part of the total life cycle cost of the product. Cost management techniques must therefore be relevant for upstream and downstream costs, as well as for the manufacturing costs of the product.

Upstream and Downstream Costs Increasing Faster Than Production Costs

In a recent *Fortune* magazine analysis of the auto industry, Kurt Brown, an economic forecaster, noted that upstream (incurred before manufacturing) and downstream (incurred after manufacturing) costs are a growing part of the total cost of designing (upstream), producing, and selling and servicing (downstream) the product.

Now it takes about 20 worker-hours to assemble a Ford Taurus. Because labor costs about $42 an hour, the total direct labor expense is about $840—5 percent of the sticker price of the car. In contrast, Martin Anderson, the retailing expert of MIT's International Motor Vehicle Program, reports that the cost of marketing and distributing the car is about 30 percent of the sticker price.

The implication is that cost management must be relevant for upstream and downstream costs as well as production costs.

Source: Based on information from "The New Golden Age of Autos," *Fortune*, April 4, 1994, pp. 50–66.

Focus on the Customer

A key change in the environment of business is increased *consumer expectations* for product functionality and quality. The result has been shorter product life cycles, as firms seek to add new features and new products as quickly as possible, thereby increasing the overall intensity of competition.

In manufacturing and marketing in past years, a business typically succeeded by focusing on only a relatively small number of products with limited features and by organizing production into long, low-cost, and high-volume production runs, aided by assembly-line automation. The new business process focuses instead on customer satisfaction. Producing value for the customer changes the orientation of managers from low-cost production of large quantities to *quality, service, timeliness of delivery, and the ability to respond to the customer's desire for specific features.* The critical success factors today are all customer-oriented. Cost management practices are also changing; cost management reports now include specific measures of customer preferences and customer satisfaction.

Management Organization

Management organization has changed in response to the changes in marketing and manufacturing. Because of the focus on customer satisfaction and value, the emphasis has shifted from financial and profit-based measures of performance to customer-related, nonfinancial performance measures such as quality, time to delivery, and service. Similarly, the hierarchical command-and-control type of organization is being replaced by a more flexible organizational form that encourages teamwork and coordination among business functions. In response to these changes, cost management practices will also change to include reports that are useful to cross-functional teams of managers; the reports will reflect the multifunctional roles of these teams and include a variety of operating and financial information: product quality, unit cost, customer satisfaction, and production bottlenecks, for example.

The changes in manufacturing, marketing, and management organization in the environment of business are summarized in Exhibit 1–2.

Social, Political, and Cultural Considerations

In addition to changes in the business environment, significant changes have taken place in the social, political, and cultural environment that affect business. These changes include a more ethnically and racially diverse workforce, a renewed sense of ethical responsibility among managers and employees, and increased deregulation of business by the federal government.

The consequences of the new environment are to enhance the firm's need to be flexible and adaptable, and to place greater responsibility in the hands of a more highly skilled workforce. Additionally, the changes tend to focus the firm on factors *outside* the production of its product or service, that is, on the ultimate consumer and the global society in which the consumer lives. Although cost management will continue to include financial performance measures as an important evaluation of a firm's current success and long-term potential, the additional measures of the firm's effect on the environment and its response to changes in the envi-

---

Customer Service–Driven Firms to Dominate Manufacturing in the Twenty-First Century

According to a survey of midsized manufacturers, what customers increasingly will demand in the coming years is the best product at the best price, whenever and wherever they need it. Quality and a good price are taken for granted. What will differentiate firms is their customer service—speed of delivery, ability to accommodate special orders, and other services such as vendor-managed inventory. Manufacturers are responding by using information technology to improve the speed and flexibility of their operations and by using a variety of contemporary management techniques [discussed later in this chapter] to achieve dramatic improvements in customer service.

Source: Based on information in Grant Thornton, *Manufacturing Issues,* Summer 1995, pp. 1–7; and the *Deloitte & Touche Review,* January 6, 1997, p. 3.

Exhibit 1–2	Comparison of Prior and Contemporary Business Environments	
	Prior Business Environment	**Contemporary Business Environment**
	Manufacturing	
Basis of competition	Economies of scale, standardization	Quality, functionality, customer satisfaction
Manufacturing process	High volume, long production runs, significant levels of in-process and finished inventory	Low volume, short production runs, focus on reducing inventory levels and other non-value-added activities and costs
Manufacturing technology	Assembly-line automation, isolated technology applications	Robotics, flexible manufacturing systems, integrated technology applications connected by networks
Required labor skills	Machine-paced, low-level skills	Individually and team-paced, high-level skills
Emphasis on quality	Acceptance of a normal or usual amount of waste	Goal of zero defects
	Marketing	
Products	Relatively few variations, long product life cycles	Large number of variations, short product life cycles
Markets	Largely domestic	Global
	Management Organization	
Type of information recorded and reported	Almost exclusively financial data	Financial and operating data, the firm's strategic success factors
Management organizational structure	Hierarchical, command and control	Network-based organization forms, teamwork focus—employee has more responsibility and control, coaching rather than command and control
Management focus	Emphasis on the short term, short-term performance measures and compensation, concern for sustaining the current stock price, short tenure and high mobility of top managers	Emphasis on the long term, focus on critical success factors, commitment to the long-term success of the firm, including adding shareholder value

ronment will also be included in cost management. The environmental factors are as critical as the financial factors in assessing the potential for the firm's long-term success.

THE STRATEGIC FOCUS OF COST MANAGEMENT

> The lowest form of thinking is the bare recognition of the object. The highest is the comprehensive intuition of the man who sees all things as part of the system.
>
> PLATO

As the Greek philosopher observed, the successful individual, like the successful firm, is the one that thinks strategically. The competitive firm incorporates the emerging and anticipated changes in the contemporary environment of business into its business planning and practices. The competitive firm is customer-driven, uses advanced manufacturing technologies where appropriate, anticipates the effect of changes in regulatory requirements and customer tastes, and recognizes the complex social, political, and cultural environment of the firm. Guided by strategic thinking, the management accountant focuses on the factors that make the company successful, rather than only calculating costs and other financial measures. We are reminded of the story of the Scottish farmer who had prize sheep to take to market. When asked why his sheep were always superior to those of his neighbors, the farmer responded, "While they're weighing their sheep, I'm fattening mine."[4] Similarly, cost management focuses not on measurement per se, but on the *identification of those measures that are critical* to the success of the firm. Robert Kaplan's classification of the life cycle of the development of cost management systems describes this shift in focus:[5]

> **Stage 1:** In the first stage, cost management systems are basic transaction reporting systems.
>
> **Stage 2:** As they develop into the second stage, cost management systems focus on external financial reporting. The objective is reliable financial reports; accordingly, the usefulness for cost management is limited.
>
> **Stage 3:** In the third stage of development, cost management systems track key operating data and develop more accurate and relevant cost information for decision making; cost management information is developed.
>
> **Stage 4:** In the final stage, strategically relevant cost management information is an integral part of the system.

The first two stages of cost system development focus on the management accountant's measurement and reporting role, while the third stage shifts to operational control. In the fourth stage, the ultimate goal, the management accountant is viewed as an integral part of management, not as a reporter but as a full business partner, with the skills of identifying, summarizing, and reporting the critical factors that are necessary for the firm's success. **Critical success factors (CSFs)** are measures of those aspects of the firm's performance that are essential to its competitive advantage, and therefore to its success. Many of these critical success factors will be financial, but many will also be nonfinancial operating information. The unique factors for any given firm will depend on the nature of the competition facing the firm. Two such factors are product quality and customer service, which along with others, are illustrated in Exhibit 1–3.

Critical success factors (CSFs) are measures of those aspects of the firm's performance that are essential to its competitive advantage, and therefore to its success.

CONTEMPORARY MANAGEMENT TECHNIQUES

LEARNING OBJECTIVE 4 ▶
Explain the contemporary management techniques and how they have influenced cost management.

Managers commonly use the following tools to implement the firm's broad strategy and to facilitate the achievement of success on critical success factors—benchmarking, total quality management, continuous improvement (*kaizen*), activity-based costing, reengineering, the theory of constraints, mass customization, target costing, life-cycle costing, and the balanced scorecard. These techniques are introduced here, and most are covered more fully in later chapters.

Benchmarking

Benchmarking is a process by which a firm identifies its critical success factors, studies the best practices of other firms (or other units within a firm) for these critical success factors, and then implements improvements in the firm's processes to match or beat the performance of those competitors. Benchmarking was first implemented by Xerox Corporation in the late 1970s.[6] Today many firms use benchmarking, and some of these firms are recognized as leaders, and therefore benchmarks, in selected areas (see Exhibit 1–3).

Benchmarking is a process by which a firm identifies its critical success factors, studies the best practices of other firms (or other units within a firm) for these critical success factors, and then implements improvements in the firm's processes to match or beat the performance of those competitors.

Benchmarking efforts are facilitated today by cooperative networks of noncompeting firms that exchange benchmarking information. For example, the Institute of Management Accountants (IMA) has a Continuous Improvement Center to help organizations benchmark and thereby improve their financial processes. The IMA

---

[4] Sheep farmer story adapted from IEEE, *Spectrum,* January 1992, p. 25.

[5] Robert S. Kaplan, "The Four-Stage Model of Cost System Design," *Management Accounting,* February 1990, pp. 22–26.

[6] R. C. Camp, *Benchmarking: The Search for Industry Best Practices that Lead to Superior Performance* (Milwaukee, Wis.: American Society for Quality Control Press, 1989); and Alexandra Biesada, "Strategic Benchmarking," *Financial World,* September 29, 1992, pp. 30–58.

Exhibit 1–3	Benchmarking: Leading Firms in Selected Critical Success Factors				
Flexible Manufacturing	**Labor Relations and Employee Retraining**	**Data Processing**	**Customer Service**	**Product Development**	**Quality**
Allen-Bradley	Corning	PepsiCo/Frito-Lay	L.L. Bean	3M	Xerox
Motorola	Ford Motor Company	American Express	Federal Express	Motorola	Ford
	Federal Express	MCI	Xerox	NCR	IBM
	General Electric		AT&T	Hewlett-Packard	Motorola
	Milliken				Westinghouse

Source: Based on information in "Beg, Borrow, and Benchmark," *Business Week,* November 30, 1992, pp. 74–75.

program includes access to a benchmark database, assistance in assessing CSFs, programs to assist firms in implementing improvement opportunities, and a recognition program that honors firms that achieve outstanding levels of continuous improvement. The Houston International Benchmarking Clearinghouse also assists firms in strategic benchmarking.

Total Quality Management

Total quality management (TQM) is a technique in which management develops policies and practices to ensure that the firm's products and services exceed customers' expectations. This approach includes increased product functionality, reliability, durability, and serviceability. It is important to realize that quality in the context of TQM is a very *broad* concept, reaching much further than the conventional concept of quality as a measure of reliability only. Cost management is used to analyze the cost consequences of different design choices for TQM and to measure and report the many aspects of quality, including, for example, production breakdowns and production defects, wasted labor or raw materials, the number of service calls and the nature of the complaints, warranty costs, and product recalls.

TQM efforts can build brand loyalty and help the company improve product quality and competitiveness more quickly. For example, Hewlett-Packard has a policy of taking back products returned by customers to retailers—something many computer manufacturers do only reluctantly. This policy builds retailer and customer loyalty, and it provides Hewlett-Packard with early warning of product problems.[7]

> **Total quality management (TQM)** is a technique in which management develops policies and practices to ensure that the firm's products and services exceed customers' expectations.

Continuous Improvement

> Whether you think you can or whether you think you can't—you're right.
>
> HENRY FORD

Henry Ford realized that the right attitude is important to success. That belief is what continuous improvement is all about. **Continuous improvement** (the Japanese word is *kaizen*) is a management technique in which managers and workers commit to a program of continuous improvement in quality and other critical success factors. Its origin is attributed to Japanese manufacturers, with their tireless pursuit of quality. Continuous improvement is very often associated with benchmarking and total quality management, as firms seek to identify other firms as models to learn how to improve their critical success factors.

> **Continuous improvement** (the Japanese word is *kaizen*) is a management technique in which managers and workers commit to a program of continuous improvement in quality and other critical success factors.

Activity-Based Costing and Management

Many firms have found they can improve planning, product costing, operational control, and management control by using **activity analysis** to develop a detailed description of the specific activities performed in the operations of the firm. The activity analysis provides the basis for activity-based costing and activity-based

> **Activity analysis** is used to develop a detailed description of the specific activities performed in the operations of the firm.

---

[7] "The Printer King Invades Home PCs," *Business Week,* August 21, 1995, pp. 74–75.

Activity-based costing (ABC) is used to improve the accuracy of cost analysis by improving the tracing of costs to cost objects.

Activity-based management (ABM) uses activity analysis to improve operational control and management control.

management. **Activity-based costing (ABC)** is used to improve the accuracy of cost analysis by improving the tracing of costs to cost objects. ABC is used for many different cost objects, including individual products, and related groups of products, and individual customers. **Activity-based management (ABM)** uses activity analysis to improve operational control and management control. Although ABC and ABM have been in practice for some time, only in recent years have they become widely used. These techniques are especially useful when operations are complex, with a large number of products and manufacturing processes or steps in providing the service to customers. When operations are complex, the identification of and cost tracing for activities can provide a good understanding of cost drivers and cost behavior that is difficult to obtain without detailed activity analysis. ABC and ABM are key strategic tools for firms with complex operations.

Reengineering

Reengineering is a process for creating competitive advantage in which a firm reorganizes its operating and management functions, often with the result that jobs are modified, combined, or eliminated.

Reengineering is a process for creating competitive advantage in which a firm reorganizes its operating and management functions, often with the result that jobs are modified, combined, or eliminated. It has been defined as the "fundamental rethinking and radical redesign of business processes to achieve dramatic improvements in critical, contemporary measures of performance, such as cost, quality, service, and speed."[8] Under the pressure of global competition, many firms look to reengineering as a way to reduce the cost of management and operations, and as a basis for careful reanalysis of the firm's strategic competitive advantage. Cost management supports the reengineering effort by providing the relevant information.

The Theory of Constraints

The **theory of constraints (TOC)** is a strategic technique to help firms effectively improve the rate at which raw materials are converted to finished product.

The **theory of constraints (TOC)** is a strategic technique to help firms effectively improve a very important critical success factor—cycle time, the rate at which raw materials are converted to finished product.[9] The key concept in TOC is *throughput,* the rate at which the firm generates cash through sales, which is equal to sales *less* the materials required in product sold. Throughput is improved directly by increasing the speed at which product is moved through the plant and sold. TOC helps identify and eliminate bottlenecks in the production process, that is, places where partially completed products tend to accumulate as they wait to be processed.

In the competitive global marketplace common to most industries, the ability to be faster than the competitors is often a critical success factor. Many managers argue that the focus on speed in the TOC approach is crucial. They consider speed in product development, in product delivery, and in manufacturing to be paramount, as global competitors find ever higher customer expectations for rapid product development and prompt delivery. Many mail-order firms, including sellers of computer products, clothing, and other consumer goods, are finding that promise of prompt

The Importance of Time

By connecting its computers to those of its largest customers (such as Wal-Mart and J.C. Penney) VF Corporation, the Wyomissing, Pennsylvania, clothing supplier, is able to resupply these customers as quickly as overnight. Moreover, VF is able to help its retail customers lower their inventory levels by focusing only on those articles that are in high demand. Ultimately, VF plans to use this technology to assist its customers in forecasting demand and appropriate stocking levels. CEO Lawrence Pugh credits the approach for VF's strong growth and profits in a competitive market.

Source: "Just Get It to the Stores on Time," *Business Week,* March 6, 1995, pp. 66–67.

---

[8] The definition is provided by Michael Hammer and James Champy, *Re-Engineering the Corporation* (New York: Harper Press, 1993). Another useful reference is the book by Roy Harmon and Leroy D. Peterson, *Re-Inventing the Factory* (New York: Free Press, 1990).

[9] Two of the best sources for descriptions of the theory of constraints are the following books: E. Goldratt and J. Cox, *The Goal* (New York: Free Press, 1986); and E. Goldratt, *The Theory of Constraints* (New York: North River Press, 1990).

delivery is sometimes the only way to make a sale, since competition has forced all competing firms to provide excellent quality products and services.

In many industries, speed of product development and the ability to meet a rapidly growing market demand for a product are critical to the firm's profitability. For example, in the computer software industry, it is often the firm that reaches the market first with a high-quality system that captures the market. This was true of Netscape's Navigator and Intuit's Quicken. An example of what can happen when speed is not paramount comes from IBM Corporation. In the early 1990s IBM developed popular new computers, the Thinkpad notebook computer and the Aptiva desktop, but initially lacked the manufacturing and distribution resources to meet the demand. The rising demand was then met by Compaq and other manufacturers, which were better prepared.

Bottlenecks can appear in areas other than manufacturing, such as purchasing and distribution. Firms are adopting global strategies for sourcing materials and distributing product. Such strategies involve global dispersion of plant operations and increasing reliance on transportation, especially air transport. In North Carolina, a global-transpark facility is under development to provide North Carolina manufacturers and others who locate near this facility with the ability to source materials, assemble products, and distribute products worldwide in 48 hours. Efforts are under way to develop freighters that will cut the time of transatlantic voyages in half.[10] With these innovations, firms located nearby will continue to set a new, higher standard for global competition.

Mass Customization

Increasingly, many manufacturing and service firms find that customers expect products and services to be developed for each customer's unique needs. For example, a particular bicycle customer might expect the product to be designed to fit his or her height, weight, and usage requirements. Or a computer manufacturer such as Dell or Gateway will assemble a computer based on the customer's exact specifications.

BusinessWeek

How Does Dell Outperform Its Competitors?
(continues from page 3)

A: Think quick! ... Dell's secret is speed.

- Speed in **order taking:** Orders are confirmed to customers in five minutes.
- Speed in **manufacturing:** An order received by 9 AM Monday is shipped by 9 PM Tuesday.
- Speed in **collections:** Within 24 hours, phone and Web orders are collected in cash; in contrast, rival manufacturers that sell through dealers wait from a month or more to collect on sales
- Speed in **resupply:** Circuit boards are restocked at the Austin, Texas, plant from suppliers in Mexico within 15 hours of an order.

Speed is how Dell has managed to make a low-margin, mail-order business profitable. According to Michael Dell, "Speed is everything in this business. We're setting the pace for the industry." Speed reduces costs, adds value for the customer, and makes the firm more profitable. Speed in order taking reduces costs of processing the order. Speed in manufacturing reduces manufacturing and handling costs, and provides a valued service for customers. Speed in collections reduces costs of holding receivables, and speed in resupply reduces the costs of holding inventory.

For further reading, see the following sources: "Whirlwind on the Web," *Business Week,* April 7, 1997, pp. 132–36; "There's Something Wrong Out There," *Business Week,* December 29, 1997, pp. 38–40.

---

[10] "Warp Speed on the High Seas," *Business Week,* September 18, 1995, pp. 155–56.

Mass customization is a management technique in which marketing and production processes are designed to handle the increased variety that results from delivering customized products and services to customers.

Many firms have found that they can compete successfully with a strategy that targets customers' unique needs. In **mass customization,** marketing and production processes are designed to handle the increased variety that results from this type of business.[11] This redesign involves a larger number of smaller production runs in manufacturing, and specially designed marketing and service functions. The greater variety and complexity of production under mass customization will increase a portion of production costs, though the costs of marketing and servicing the product might be reduced. Mass customization can be an effective way for a firm to compete in an industry where the price and quality expectations of many consumers are met by existing manufacturers, and a firm must distinguish itself by providing a fast, customized service. The growth of mass customization is, in effect, another indication of the increased attention given to satisfying the customer.

Target Costing

Target costing determines the desired cost for a product on the basis of a given competitive price, such that the product will earn a desired profit.

Target costing is a tool that has arisen directly from the intensely competitive markets in many industries.[12] **Target costing** determines the desired cost for a product on the basis of a given competitive price, such that the product will earn a desired profit. Cost is thus determined by price. The firm using target costing must often adopt strict cost-reduction measures or redesign the product or manufacturing process in order to meet the market price and remain profitable.

$$\text{Target cost} = \text{Market-determined price} - \text{Desired profit}$$

Target costing forces the firm to become more competitive, and like benchmarking, it is a common strategic form of analysis in intensely competitive industries, where even small price differences will attract consumers to the lower-priced product. The computer software industry is a good example of the application of target costing. Competing software producers will often sell at a market-determined price level (sometimes a price set by the industry leader), and try to differentiate their product in terms of the quality and quantity of new features in each upgrade or new version of the software. The automobile industry follows a similar pattern.

Life-Cycle Costing

Life-cycle costing is a management technique used to identify and monitor the costs of a product throughout its life cycle.

Life-cycle costing is a management technique used to identify and monitor the costs of a product throughout its life cycle. The life cycle consists of all the steps from product design and purchase of raw materials to delivery and service of the finished product. The steps include (1) research and development; (2) product design, including prototyping, target costing, and testing; (3) manufacturing, inspecting, packaging, and warehousing; (4) marketing, promotion, and distribution; and (5) sales and service. Cost management has traditionally focused only on costs incurred at the third step, manufacturing. Thinking strategically, management accountants now manage the full life cycle of costs for the product, including upstream and downstream costs as well as manufacturing costs. This expanded focus means that careful attention is paid especially to product design, since design decisions lock in most subsequent life-cycle costs.

The Balanced Scorecard

Strategic information using critical success factors provides a road map for the firm to use to chart its competitive course, and serves as a benchmark for competitive success. Financial measures such as profitability reflect only a partial, and frequently only a short-term, measure of the firm's progress. Without strategic information, the firm is likely to stray from its competitive course, to make strategically wrong prod-

---

[11] Find out more about mass customization in articles by James H. Gilmore, "Reengineering for Mass Customization," *Journal of Cost Management,* Fall 1993, pp. 22–29; and Joseph P. Pine II, Bart Victor, and Andrew C. Boynton, "Making Mass Customization Work," *Harvard Business Review,* September–October 1993, pp. 108–19.

[12] A useful reference for target costing is the book by Y. Monden and M. Sakurai (eds.), *Japanese Management Accounting: A World Class Approach to Profit Management* (Cambridge, Mass.: Productivity Press, 1993).

uct decisions—for example, choosing the wrong products or the wrong marketing and distribution methods.

To emphasize the importance of using strategic information, *both financial and nonfinancial*, accounting reports of a firm's performance are now often based on critical success factors in four different dimensions. One dimension is financial; the other three dimensions are nonfinancial:

1. **Financial performance.** Measures of profitability and market value, among others, as indicators of how well the firm satisfies its owners and shareholders.

2. **Customer satisfaction.** Satisfaction measures of quality, service, and low cost, among others, as indicators of how well the firm satisfies its customers.

3. **Internal business processes.** Measures of the efficiency and effectiveness with which the firm produces the product or service.

4. **Innovation and learning.** Measures of the firm's ability to develop and utilize human resources to meet the firm's strategic goals now and into the future.

An accounting report based on the four dimensions is called a **balanced scorecard.** The concept of balance captures the intent of broad coverage, financial and nonfinancial, of all the factors that contribute to the success of the firm in achieving its strategic goals. The balanced scorecard provides a basis for a more complete analysis than is possible with financial data alone. The use of the balanced scorecard is thus a critical ingredient of the overall approach that firms take to become and remain competitive.

The **balanced scorecard** is an accounting report that includes the firm's critical success factors in four areas: (1) financial performance, (2) customer satisfaction, (3) internal business processes, and (4) innovation and learning.

THE PROFESSIONAL ENVIRONMENT OF COST MANAGEMENT

The man who is cocksure he has arrived is ready for the return journey. So are business concerns. When they become satisfied that there is nothing more for them to learn, and that they can dispense with any and every aid to success, they are headed for trouble.

B. C. FORBES

Mr. Forbes, the founder and publisher of *Forbes* magazine, noted the importance of continuous learning in business. His words apply equally well to the management accountant. Management accountants must continuously improve their technical and other skills as well as maintain a constant high level of professionalism, integrity, and objectivity about their work. Many professional organizations, such as the Institute of Management Accountants (IMA) and the American Institute of CPAs (AICPA), encourage their members to earn relevant professional certifications, participate in professional development programs, and continually reflect on the professional ethics they bring to their work.

◄ **LEARNING OBJECTIVE 5**
Describe the professional environment of the management accountant, including professional organizations, professional certifications, and professional ethics.

Professional Organizations

The professional environment of the management accountant is influenced by two types of organizations—one that sets guidelines and regulations regarding management accounting practices, and one that promotes the professionalism and competence of management accountants.

The first group of organizations includes a number of federal agencies, such as the Internal Revenue Service, which sets product costing guidelines for tax purposes, and the Federal Trade Commission (FTC), which, in order to foster competitive practices and protect trade, restricts pricing practices and requires that prices in most circumstances be justified on the basis of cost. The FTC also requires line-of-business reporting. In addition, the Securities and Exchange Commission (SEC) provides guidance, rules, and regulations regarding financial reporting; in this way it directs the manner in which the management accountant develops product costs.

> ### Where to Look for Information on Professional Organizations
>
> American Institute of CPAs (AICPA):   http://www.aicpa.org/
> Federal Trade Commission (FTC):   http://www.ftc.gov/
> Financial Executives Institute (FEI):   http://www.fei.org
> Institute of Internal Auditors (IIA):   http://www.rutgers.edu/Accounting/raw/iia
> Institute of Management Accountants (IMA):   http://www.mythbreakers.com/ima/
> Internal Revenue Service (IRS):   http://www.irs.ustreas.gov/prod/coverhtml
> Securities and Exchange Commission (SEC):   http://www.sec.gov/
> Society of Management Accountants (SMAC, Canada):   http://www.cma-Canada.org/
> American Accounting Association Management Accounting Section (MAS):
> http://aaa-mas.byu.edu/

In the private sector, the Financial Accounting Standards Board (FASB), an independent organization, and the AICPA supply additional guidance regarding financial reporting practices. The AICPA also provides educational opportunities in the form of newsletters, magazines, professional development seminars, and technical meetings for management accountants.

The Cost Accounting Standards Board (CASB) was established by Congress in 1970 (Public Law 91–379) and operates under the Office of Federal Procurement Policy "to make, promulgate, amend and rescind cost accounting standards and interpretations thereof designed to achieve uniformity and consistency in the cost accounting standards governing measurement, assignment, and allocation of cost to contracts with the United States federal government." The objective of the CASB is to achieve uniformity and consistency in the cost accounting standards used by government suppliers, in order to reduce the incidence of fraud and abuse. There are 20 cost accounting standards that cover a broad range of issues in cost accounting.

Another group of organizations supports the growth and professionalism of management accounting practice. The Institute of Management Accountants (IMA) is the principal organization devoted primarily to management accountants in the United States. The IMA has magazines, newsletters, research reports, management accounting practice reports, professional development seminars, and monthly technical meetings that serve the broad purpose of providing continuing education opportunities for management accountants. In Canada, the Society of Management Accountants (SMA) performs a similar role. Similar organizations are present in most other countries around the world.

In areas related to the management accounting function, the Financial Executives Institute (FEI) provides services much like those provided by the IMA for financial managers, including controllers and treasurers. Because of the nature of its membership, the FEI tends to focus on management and operational control issues, with less emphasis placed on the product costing, planning, and decision-making functions.

Since one of the management control responsibilities of the management accountant is to develop effective systems to detect and prevent errors and fraud in the accounting records, it is common for the management accountant to have strong ties to the control-oriented organizations such as the Institute of Internal Auditors (IIA). In addition, for those with a significant amount of experience in management accounting, particularly experience with federal government contractors, the Institute of Cost Analysis provides a useful set of services much like those provided by the IMA, FEI, and IIA.

Professional Certifications

The role of professional certification programs is to provide a distinct measure of experience, training, and performance capability for the management accountant. The certification is one way in which the management accountant shows professional achievement and stature. Three types of certification are relevant for management accountants. The first is the Certified Management Accountant (CMA) designation administered by the Institute of Management Accountants, which is achieved by passing a qualifying exam and satisfying certain background and experience requirements. The exam covers four areas of knowledge relevant to the practice of management accounting: (1) economics, finance, and management; (2) financial accounting and reporting; (3) management analysis and reporting; and (4) decision analysis and information systems. The material required for part (3) of the exam is covered throughout this book; sections of parts (1), (2), and (4) are also covered.

The second relevant certification is the Certified Financial Manager (CFM) program of the IMA. This program is intended for the broader responsibilities of the financial manager, such as those of the chief financial officer. The exam includes topics related to corporate financial management, in addition to the topics covered on the CMA exam.

The third certification is the Certified Public Accountant (CPA) designation. Like the CMA and CFM, the CPA is earned by passing a qualifying exam, which is prepared and graded by the AICPA, and by satisfying certain background, education, and experience requirements. Unlike the CMA, which is an international designation, the CPA certificate is awarded and monitored by each state in the United States, and each state has its own set of criteria. While the CPA is critical for those accountants who practice auditing, the CMA is widely viewed as the most relevant for those dealing with cost management issues.[13] Many countries have certificates that are equivalent to the CPA.

Professional Ethics

Ethics is an important aspect of the management accountant's work and profession. Professional ethics can be summed up as the commitment of the management accountant to provide a useful service for management. This commitment means that the management accountant has the competence, integrity, confidentiality, and objectivity to serve management effectively.

◄ **LEARNING OBJECTIVE 6**
Understand the principles and rules of professional ethics and explain how to apply them.

The IMA Code of Ethics

The ethical behavior of the management accountant is guided by the code of ethics of the Institute of Management Accountants (IMA). The IMA code of ethics specifics *minimum* standards of behavior that are intended to guide the management accountant and to inspire an overall very high level of professionalism. By complying with these standards, management accountants enhance their profession and facilitate the development of a trusting relationship in which managers and others can confidently rely on their work.

The IMA code of ethics contains four main sections: (1) competence, (2) confidentiality, (3) integrity, and (4) objectivity (Exhibit 1–4). The standard of competence requires the management accountant to develop and maintain the skills necessary for her or his area of practice, and to continually reassess the adequacy of those skills as the firm grows and becomes more complex. The standard of confidentiality requires adherence to the firm's policies regarding communication of data, to protect the firm's trade secrets and other confidential information. Integrity refers to behaving in a professional manner (e.g., refraining from activities that would discredit the firm or profession, such as unfair hiring practices) and to avoiding conflicts of interest (e.g., not accepting a gift from a supplier or customer). Finally, objectivity refers to the need to maintain impartial judgment (e.g., not developing analyses to support a decision that the management accountant knows is not correct).

How to Apply the Code of Ethics

Handling situations in which an ethical issue arises can be very challenging and frustrating. Using the following step-by-step approach can be helpful.

---

[13] A fourth type of certification, the title of Certified Cost Analyst (CCA), is sponsored by the Institute of Cost Analysis. As for the others, there is a qualifying exam; in addition, eight years of experience in cost analysis is required. The orientation of this exam and certification is accounting for federal contractors, especially defense contractors.

First, the management accountant must consider the ethical principles or standards that might apply in the situation—competence, integrity, confidentiality, and objectivity. Also important is keeping in mind the broad objective of the code of ethics, which is to maintain management's confidence in the profession. The management accountant must consider how the resolution of the situation would affect a manager's trust and reliance on her- or himself and on other management accountants.

Exhibit 1–4   Institute of Management Accounts Code of Ethics

Competence

- Maintain an appropriate level of professional competence by ongoing development of knowledge and skills.
- Perform professional duties in accordance with relevant laws, regulations, and technical standards.
- Prepare complete and clear reports and recommendations after appropriate analyses of relevant and reliable information.

Confidentiality

- Refrain from disclosing confidential information acquired in the course of the work except when authorized, unless legally obligated to do so.
- Inform subordinates as appropriate regarding the confidentiality of information acquired in the course of the work and monitor one's activities to assure the maintenance of that confidentiality.
- Refrain from using or appearing to use confidential information acquired in the course of the work for unethical or illegal advantage either personally or through third parties.

Integrity

- Avoid actual or apparent conflicts of interest and advise all appropriate parties of any potential conflict.
- Refrain from engaging in any activity that would prejudice one's ability to carry out his or her duties ethically.
- Refuse any gift, favor, or hospitality that would influence or would appear to influence one's actions.
- Refrain from either actively or passively subverting the attainment of the organization's legitimate and ethical objectives.
- Recognize and communicate professional limitations or other constraints that would preclude responsible judgment or successful performance of an activity.
- Communicate unfavorable as well as favorable information and professional judgments or opinions.
- Refrain from engaging in or supporting any activity that would discredit the profession.

Objectivity

- Communicate information fairly and objectively.
- Disclose fully all relevant information that could reasonably be expected to influence an intended user's understanding of the reports, comments, and recommendations presented.

Source: Statement on Management Accounting No. 1C, "Standards of Ethical Conduct for Management Accountants," Institute of Management Accountants, Montvale, N.J., June 1, 1983, pp. 1–2.

A Value-Based Approach to Global Competition Is Good Strategy

At least some firms have found that an ethical, value-based approach can be effective in competing in the global marketplace. For example, British Petroleum, Co. (BP), takes a strong interest in the social and economic welfare of the cities and towns where it does business. This includes job training programs and support of small businesses in South Africa, the use of computer technology in Vietnam to help control flooding, and the financing of replanting of a forest in Turkey. In Colombia, BP recycles its waste material into bricks for local homebuilding, and in Zambia it supplies materials and equipment for medical doctors. Have these efforts hurt BP's bottom line—global earnings? To the contrary, BP's CEO John Browne says, "These efforts have nothing to do with charity, and everything to do with our long-term self-interest." BP's earnings in the last six years appear to prove the point—profits have increased more than four times, and shareholders' return has been in excess of 30 percent annually.

Source: "Globalism Doesn't Have to Be Cruel," *Business Week,* February 9, 1998, p. 26.

Second, the management accountant should discuss the situation with a superior. If the superior is part of the situation, then the management accountant should seek out the person or persons *within the firm* who have the equivalent or higher level of responsibility, such as a manager in the firm's human resources department or a member of the audit committee. In keeping with the standard of confidentiality, the accountant does not communicate such problems outside the firm, except as indicated in the fourth step below.

Third, if the ethical conflict cannot be resolved, and if the matter is significant, then the management accountant may have to resign from the firm and communicate the reasons to the appropriate management level.

Fourth, the management accountant must, if resigning, consider his or her responsibility to communicate the matter outside the firm, to regulatory authorities or to the firm's external auditor.

SUMMARY

The central theme of this book is that cost management information includes all the information managers need to manage effectively, to lead their firms to competitive success. Cost management information includes both financial and non-financial information critical to the success of the firm. The specific role of cost management in the firm will differ depending on the firm's competitive strategy, the type of industry and organization (manufacturing firm, service firm, merchandising firm, non-for-profit organization, or governmental organization), and the management function to which cost management is applied (the functions are strategic management, planning and decision making, management and operational control, and preparation of financial statements).

Of particular importance is how changes in business, especially the increase in global competition and the changes in management techniques, have created the need for a new, strategic approach to management and to cost management. Cost management can assist the firm in using the new management techniques: benchmarking, total quality management, continuous improvement, activity-based costing and management, reengineering, the theory of constraints, mass customization, target costing, life-cycle costing, and the balanced scorecard.

A variety of professional organizations support management accounting, including the Institute of Management Accountants (IMA), the American Institute of Certified Public Accountants (AICPA), and the Financial Executives Institute (FEI), among others. Several relevant certification programs recognize competence and experience in management accounting; they include the Certified Management Accountant (CMA) and the Certified Financial Manager (CFM) programs of the IMA, and the Certified Public Accountant (CPA) program of the AICPA.

The management accountant is responsible to the firm and to the public to maintain a high standard of performance, as set forth in the IMA code of professional ethics. The professional ethics standards of the management accountant include competence, integrity, objectivity, and confidentiality.

KEY TERMS

SELF-STUDY PROBLEM

(For solution, please turn to the end of the chapter.)

An Ethical Problem

An example of an ethical situation involving potential manipulation of accounting earnings occurred in Bausch & Lomb's (B&L) contact lens unit. Apparently, B&L used inappropriate accounting methods to inflate year-end sales. The story, as reported by *Business Week* (December 19, 1994, pp. 108–110), is as follows:

September 1993: Independent contact lens distributors say B&L asks them to buy 4 to 6 months' worth of inventory. B&L says buildup supports a new marketing program, but distributors say uneven results leave them with 4 to 12 months' inventory in early December.

December 13, 1993: B&L calls a meeting and tells distributors to take additional inventories ranging from one to two years' worth or face cutoff. B&L says the buildup is needed for programs aimed at getting high-volume accounts to buy from distributors rather than from the company.

December 24, 1993: Insisting lenses be ordered by December 24, B&L rushes out shipments. That tactic adds sales of $25 million, but distributors say B&L gave verbal assurances that the distributors would pay for lenses only when sold. B&L says small payments were set through June, when balances were due.

June 15, 1994: With the new promotions lagging, less than 10 percent of the inventory is sold—or paid for. When the final payments fall due, most distributors refuse to pay. Meanwhile, B&L continues to sell directly to some high-volume accounts at prices below what the distributors paid.

October 1994: With the majority of the inventory unsold, B&L takes most back. Distributors pay sharply discounted prices for the rest. B&L's third-quarter revenues drop 10 percent, to $449 million, and earnings plummet 86 percent, to $7.7 million, as a result of inventory reduction efforts and price cuts.

Required What are the ethical issues in this case?

QUESTIONS

1–1 Give four examples of firms you think would be significant users of cost management information and explain why.

1–2 Give three examples of firms you think would *not* be significant users of cost management information and explain why.

1–3 What is meant by the term *cost management*? Who in the typical firm or organization is responsible for cost management?

1–4 Name three professional cost management organizations and explain their roles and objectives.

1–5 What type of professional certification is most relevant for the management accountant and why?

1–6 List the four functions of management. Explain what type of cost management information is appropriate for each.

1–7 Which is the most important function of management, and why?

1–8 Identify the different types of business firms and other organizations that use cost management information, and explain how the information is used.

1–9 Name a firm or organization you know of that you are reasonably sure uses strategic cost management and explain why it does so.

1–10 What is a cost object? Do all organizations have the same cost objects?

1–11 Identify different types of cost objects and give at least one example for each type.

1–12 What are some of the factors in the contemporary business environment that are causing changes in business firms and other organizations, and how are the changes affecting the way those firms and organizations use cost management information?

1–13 Contrast past and present business environments with regard to the following aspects—basis of competition, manufacturing processes and manufacturing technology, required labor skills, emphasis on quality, number of products, number of markets, types of cost management information needed, management organizational structure, and management focus.

1–14 Name the ten contemporary management techniques and describe each briefly.

PROBLEMS

1–15 **AN EXERCISE IN LOGIC.** It is important for the management accountant to be able to think clearly and logically. The following is an exercise in logical thinking. Imagine there are four cards on a table in front of you, showing the numerals 2, 4, 3, and 7.

Required If you are asked to verify the truth of the rule stating that if a 2 is printed on one side, then a 7 is printed on the other, for these four cards, which ones would you have to turn over? If you turn any over unnecessarily, you lose.

1–16 **THE THEORY OF CONSTRAINTS, MANUFACTURING VS. RETAIL** Manufacturing firms such as Saturn, Caterpillar, and Apple utilize the concept of the theory of constraints and emphasize speed of throughput in their manufacturing operations.

Required Discuss whether the concept of throughput in the theory of constraints is appropriate for retail and service industries. Take as a specific example the Wal-Mart chain of retail stores. How would you, or could you, apply this management technique to Wal-Mart?

1–17 **CONTEMPORARY MANAGEMENT TECHNIQUES** Tim Johnson is a news reporter and feature writer for *The Wall Street Review*, an important daily newspaper for financial managers. Tim's assignment is to develop a feature article on target costing, including interviews with chief financial officers and operating managers. Tim has a generous travel budget, and funds for research into company history, operations, and market analysis for the firms he selects for the article.

Required

1. Tim has asked you to recommend industries and firms that would be good candidates for the article. What would be your advice? Explain your recommendations.

2. Assume Tim's assignment is a feature article on life-cycle costing. Answer as you did for requirement 1.

3. Assume Tim's assignment is a feature article on the theory of constraints. Answer as you did for requirement 1.

1–18 PROFESSIONAL ORGANIZATIONS AND CERTIFICATION Ian Walsh has just been hired as a management accountant for a large manufacturing firm near his hometown of Canton, Ohio. The firm manufactures a wide variety of plastic products for the automobile industry, the packaging industry, and other customers. At least initially, Ian's principal assignments have been to develop product costs for new product lines. His cost accounting professor has suggested to Ian that he begin to consider professional organizations and professional certifications that will help him in his career.

Required Which organizations and certifications would you suggest for Ian, and why?

1–19 BALANCED SCORECARD Johnson Industrial Controls, Inc. (JIC), is a large manufacturer of specialized instruments used in automated manufacturing plants. JIC has grown steadily over the past several years on the strength of technological innovation in its key product lines. The firm now employs 3,500 production employees and 450 staff and management personnel in six large plants located across the United States. In the past few years, the growth of sales and profits has declined sharply, because of the entrance into the market of new competitors. As part of a recent strategic planning effort, JIC identified its key competitive strengths and weaknesses. JIC management believe that the critical strengths are in the quality of the product, and that the weakness in recent years has been in customer service, particularly in meeting scheduled deliveries. The failure to meet promised delivery dates can be quite costly to JIC's customers, because it is likely to delay the construction or upgrading of the customers' plants and therefore delay the customers' production and sales.

JIC's management believes that the adoption of the balanced scorecard for internal reporting might help the firm become more competitive.

Required

1. Explain how the balanced scorecard might help a firm like JIC.
2. Develop a brief balanced scorecard for JIC. Give some examples of the items which might be included in each of the four parts of the scorecard: (1) customer satisfaction, (2) financial performance, (3) manufacturing and business processes, and (4) human resources.

Service

1–20 ACTIVITY ANALYSIS IN A BANK Mesa Financial is a small bank located in west Texas. As a small bank, Mesa has a rather limited range of services: mortgage loans, installment loans (mostly auto loans), commercial loans, checking and savings accounts, and certificates of deposit. Mesa's management has learned that activity analysis could be used to study the efficiency of the bank's operations.

Required

1. Explain how activity analysis might help a bank like Mesa.
2. Give six to eight examples of activities you would expect to identify in Mesa's operations.

International

Strategy

1–21 STRATEGY, INTERNATIONAL In the mid-1980s, Toyota and General Motors formed a strategic alliance to jointly manufacture certain engine parts in an old General Motors plant in Fremont, California. For Toyota, the expected benefit was to gain the experience working with U.S. suppliers, trade groups, and employee groups. Such experience would be useful when Toyota later built its own manufacturing plants in the United States. For General Motors, the expected benefit was to obtain firsthand experience with the Japanese carmaker's manufacturing and management techniques, as a basis for potential improvements in General Motors's own management methods.

Required

1. Identify and explain the critical success factors for both Toyota and General Motors that provided the motivation for the strategic alliance at Fremont.

2. What are some of the risks for Toyota and for General Motors in this alliance?

1–22 **ETHICS, PRODUCT QUALITY** HighTech, Inc., is a manufacturer of computer chips and components. HighTech has just come out with a new version of its memory chip, which is far faster than the previous version. Because of high product demand for the new chip, the testing process has been thorough but hurried. As chief of operations for the firm, you discover after the chip has been on the market for a few months and is selling very well that there is a minor fault in the chip that will cause hard-to-discover failures in certain, very unusual circumstances.

 *Ethics*

Required Now that you know of the chip's faults, what should you disclose and to whom should you disclose it?

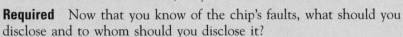

SOLUTION TO SELF-STUDY PROBLEM

An Ethical Problem

As reported above, B&L has apparently made several direct efforts to improperly inflate earnings through forced sales to distributors. The ethical principles involved are integrity and objectivity, both of which have been violated in this case.

Strategic Analysis and Strategic Cost Management

2

After studying this chapter, you should be able to . . .

Explain competitive strategy and show how strategy is influenced by the contemporary business environment **1**

Identify the three principal types of competitive strategy **2**

Demonstrate how a firm identifies its own competitive strategy, including determining its critical success factors, and how it designs a strategic cost information system **3**

Explain how the balanced scorecard is used to help a firm achieve its strategic goals **4**

Explain value-chain analysis and show how it is used to better understand a firm's competitive advantage **5**

Understand the implications of strategic analysis for cost management **6**

Joe Caputo/Gamma Liaison.

When I first took over as general manager, I asked the cost accountant for some cost information. What I received was several computer output reports containing unanalyzed raw data. There was no question about the accuracy of the numbers, but what surprised me was how unfamiliar this individual was with the manufacturing process for making the products. He had difficulty in associating the figures contained in the reports with the factory operations behind the figures.

A MANAGER, QUOTED IN COST ACCOUNTING DESK REFERENCE
BY DUDICK, BEST, AND KRAUS (1986, P. 258)

The stereotype of the cost or management accountant is very well known, and sometimes it is even harsher than the manager's assessment cited above. The good news is that this perception is changing. It is now widely recognized that the management accountant's role has shifted away from having a focus only on financial reporting to include a more significant role in the strategic management of the company. The change is due in part to increased global competitiveness and the wide-ranging changes in management techniques and business processes, described in Chapter 1. Cost management has a key role in helping a firm find and maintain a competitive position. As Peter Drucker points out:

> Bean counters do not enjoy a good press these days. They are blamed for all the ills that afflict U.S. manufacturing. But the bean counters will have the last laugh. In the factory of 1999, manufacturing accounting will play as big a role as it ever did and probably even a bigger one. But the beans will be counted differently. The new manufacturing accounting, which might more accurately be called "manufacturing economics," differs radically from traditional cost accounting in its basic concepts. Its aim is to integrate manufacturing with business strategy.[1]

And as Shank and Govindarajan note:

> A sophisticated understanding of the firm's cost structure can go a long way in the search for sustainable competitive advantage. This is what we refer to as "strategic cost analysis."[2]

BusinessWeek

 ### Who Made Your Car?

Large auto parts manufacturers such as Textron, Inc., and Johnson Controls are being forced by Detroit automakers to assume new responsibilities, including the design of some of the parts they manufacture and the supervision of some of the smaller suppliers. Chrysler Corporation, for example, requires Textron, Inc., to coordinate the work of other suppliers of parts for its minivans. In addition, Magna International, a Canadian parts manufacturer, is scheduled to produce the entire interior for a new Ford sport-utility vehicle to be introduced in the 2000 model year. Other parts manufacturers supply entire seat systems, floor systems, rear compartment systems, and other major auto parts systems for the automakers. By outsourcing the parts, the automakers expect to have cost savings of as much as 50 percent over in-house manufacturing.

Why does outsourcing parts manufacturing save automakers so much in costs? *Find out on page 44 of this chapter.*

---

[1] Peter F. Drucker, *Managing the Future* (New York: Penguin, 1994), p. 305.

[2] John K. Shank and Vijay Govindarajan, *Strategic Cost Analysis* (Burr Ridge, Ill.: Irwin, 1989), p. xi.

LEARNING OBJECTIVE 1 ▶
Explain competitive
strategy and show how
strategy is influenced by
the contemporary
business environment.

A **strategy** is a set of
policies, procedures, and
approaches to business to
produce long-term
success.

Understanding how cost management can facilitate the development of a success-ful business strategy requires a knowledge of the principles and practices of strate-gic management—the process of developing a competitive strategy.

HOW A FIRM SUCCEEDS: THE COMPETITIVE STRATEGY

A firm succeeds by finding a sustainable, long-term **strategy,** that is, a set of poli-cies, procedures, and approaches to business to produce long-term success. Finding a strategy begins with determining the purpose and long-range direction, and there-fore the mission, of the company. Exhibit 2–1 lists the mission statements of sev-eral companies. The mission is developed into specific performance objectives, which are then implemented by specific corporate strategies, that is, specific actions to achieve the objectives that will fulfill the mission. See the Sara Lee corporate strategy in Exhibit 2–2. Note how Sara Lee's broad mission statement is explained in terms of more specific objectives, which are in turn operationalized through spe-cific corporate strategies.

Firms have responded to the changes in business in many ways, including reengi-neering operational processes, downsizing the workforce, outsourcing service func-tions, and developing smaller, more efficient, and more socially responsible organi-zational policies and structures. They have attempted to become more adaptable as the pace of change increases.

Exhibit 2–1	**Mission Statements of Selected Companies**

Ford Motor Company

To be a low-cost producer of the highest-quality products and services that provide the best customer value.

General Electric

To become the most competitive enterprise in the world by being number one or number two in market share in every business the company is in.

Quaker Oats Company

To achieve return on equity at 20 percent or above, attain "real" earnings growth averaging 5 percent or better over time, be a leading marketer of strong consumer brands, and improve the profitability of low-return businesses or divest them.

Eastman Kodak

To be the world's best in chemical and electronic imaging.

Federal Express

To continue the expansion of Federal Express's global network linking key markets around the world by merging dissimilar networks, providing service to additional countries, increasing the number of flight destinations, expanding our fleet of aircraft, operating new hubs, and adding U.S. gateways for the distribution of packages and freight.

IBM

To be the most successful information-technology company in the world.

Xerox

To be The Document Company

General Motors

To be the world leader in transportation products and related services. We will earn our customers' enthusiasm through continuous improvement driven by the integrity, teamwork, and innovation of GM people.

Sarah Lee

To be the leading brand-name food and consumer packaged goods company with major market share positions in key consumer markets worldwide.

Firms also are beginning to make use of cost management to support their strategic goals. Cost management has shifted away from a focus on the stewardship role—product costing and financial reporting. The new focus is on a management-facilitating role—the development of cost and other information to support the management of the firm and the achievement of its strategic goals. Before the changes in business processes, a focus on detailed methods for product costing and control at the departmental level was appropriate for the high-volume, standardized, infrequently changing manufacturing processes of that time. Now, a firm's cost accounting system must be more dynamic to deal with the more rapidly changing environment and the increasing diversity of products and manufacturing processes. The cost management system must be able to assist management in this dynamic environment by facilitating strategic management; the contemporary business environment will focus on critical success factors, including both financial and nonfinancial factors (Exhibit 2–3).

Strategic Measures of Success

The strategic cost management system develops strategic information, including both financial and nonfinancial information. In the past, firms tended to focus primarily on financial performance measures, such as growth in sales and earnings, cash flow, and stock price. In contrast, firms in the contemporary business environment use strategic management to focus primarily on strategic measures of success, many of which are nonfinancial measures of operations, such as market share, product quality, customer satisfaction, and growth opportunities (see Exhibit 2–4). The financial measures show the impact of the firm's policies and procedures on the firm's *current financial position*, and therefore its *current* return to the shareholders. In contrast, the nonfinancial factors show the firm's *current and potential competitive*

Exhibit 2–2	Sara Lee Corporate Strategy

Entrepreneurial Management

We shall reinforce and seek to institutionalize the entrepreneurial character and culture of Sara Lee Corporation management while maintaining essential financial and strategic control and a high degree of professionalism.

Consumer Value

We shall market products and brands that have real and demonstrable value for our consumers.

Global Expansion

We shall accelerate growth by extending major brands and selected product positions worldwide, investing in the global expansion of strong U.S. and European businesses, and making strategic acquisitions to gain competitive leadership in key markets.

Improved Returns

We shall seek to increase our return on invested assets.

Source: Sara Lee Corporation 1993 Annual Report.

Exhibit 2–3	Cost Management Focus in Prior and Contemporary Business Environments

	Prior Business Environment	Contemporary Business Environment
Cost management focus	Financial reporting and cost analysis; common emphasis on standardization and standard costs; the accountant as functional expert and financial scorekeeper	View of cost management as a tool for the development and implementation of business strategy; the accountant as business partner

Exhibit 2–4	**Financial and Nonfinancial Measures of Success** **Critical Success Factors**

Financial Measures of Success

Sales growth
Earnings growth
Dividend growth
Bond and credit ratings
Cash flow
Increase in stock price

Nonfinancial Measures of Success

Customer Measures
Market share and growth in market share
Customer service
On-time delivery
Customer satisfaction
Brand recognition
Positions in favorable markets

Internal Business Processes
High product quality
Manufacturing innovation
High manufacturing productivity
Cycle time
Yield and reduction in waste

Innovation and Learning (Human Resources)
Competence and integrity of managers
Morale and firmwide culture
Education and training
Innovation in new products and
manufacturing methods

Exhibit 2–5	**Consequences of Lack of Strategic Information**

Decision making based on guesses and intuition only
Lack of clarity about direction and goals
Lack of a clear and favorable perception of the firm by customers and suppliers
Incorrect investment decisions; choosing products, markets, or manufacturing processes inconsistent
  with strategic goals
Inability to effectively benchmark competitors, resulting in lack of knowledge about more effective
  competitive strategies
Failure to identify most profitable products, customers, and markets

position, as measured from three additional perspectives: (a) the customer, (b) internal business processes, and (c) innovation and learning (i.e., human resources). Strategic financial and nonfinancial measures of success are also commonly called critical success factors (CSFs).

Without strategic information, the firm is likely to stray from its competitive course, to make strategically wrong manufacturing and marketing decisions—to choose the wrong products or the wrong customers. Some of the consequences of a lack of strategic information are shown in Exhibit 2–5.

DEVELOPING A COMPETITIVE STRATEGY: STRATEGIC POSITIONING

LEARNING OBJECTIVE 2 ▶
Identify the three principal
types of competitive
strategy.

The concept of competitive strategy developed by Michael Porter identifies three main types of competitive strategies—cost leadership, differentiation, and focus. A firm conducts a three-step strategic competitive analysis to identify its competitive strategy.[3]

---

[3] This section is adapted from Michael Porter, *Competitive Advantage* (New York: Free Press, 1985), chap. 1. The Porter concept of competitive strategy is widely used. Other common views of competitive strategy are the Boston Consulting Group's use of the market growth/market share matrix [B. D. Henderson, *Henderson on Corporate Strategy* (Cambridge, Mass.: Abt Books, 1979)] and the concept of the confrontation strategy based on quality, price, and functionality [Robin Cooper, *When Lean Enterprises Collide* (Boston: Harvard Business School Press, 1995)].

A Framework for Strategic Competitive Analysis

In developing a sustainable competitive position, each firm will purposefully or as a result of market forces arrive at one of the three competitive strategies—cost leadership, differentiation, or focus.

Cost Leadership

Cost leadership is a strategy in which a firm outperforms competitors by producing products or services at the lowest cost. The cost leader makes sustainable profits at lower prices, thereby limiting the growth of competition in the industry through its success at price wars and undermining the profitability of competitors, which must meet the firm's low price. The cost leader normally has a relatively large market share and tends to avoid niche or segment markets, using the price advantage to attract a large portion of the broad market. While most firms make strong efforts to reduce costs, the cost leader may focus almost exclusively on cost reduction, thereby ensuring a significant cost and price advantage in the market.

Cost advantages usually arise from productivity in the manufacturing process, in distribution, or in overall administration. For example, technological innovation in the manufacturing process and labor savings from overseas production are common routes to competitive productivity. Firms known to be successful at cost leadership are typically very large manufacturers and retailers, such as Wal-Mart, Texas Instruments, DuPont, and Compaq.

A potential weakness of the cost leadership strategy is the tendency to cut costs in a way that undermines demand for the product or service, for example, by deleting key features. The cost leader remains competitive only as long as the consumer sees that the product or service is (at least nearly) equivalent to competing products that cost somewhat more.

> **Cost leadership** is a competitive strategy in which a firm succeeds by producing products or services at the lowest cost in the industry.

Differentiation

The **differentiation** strategy is implemented by creating a perception among consumers that the product or service is unique in some important way, usually by being of higher quality. This perception allows the firm to charge higher prices and outperform the competition in profits without reducing costs significantly. There are differentiated firms in most industries, including automobiles, consumer electronics, and industrial equipment. The appeal of differentiation is especially strong for product lines for which the perception of quality and image is important, as in cosmetics, jewelry, and automobiles. Tiffany, Bentley, Caterpillar, Rolex, Maytag, and Kitchen Aid are good examples of firms that stress differentiation.

A weakness of the differentiation strategy is the firm's tendency to undermine its strength by attempting to lower costs or by ignoring the necessity of having a continual and aggressive marketing plan to reinforce the perceived difference. If the consumer begins to believe that the perceived difference is not significant, then lower-cost rival products will appear more attractive.

> **Differentiation** is a competitive strategy in which a firm succeeds by developing and maintaining a unique value for the product, as perceived by consumers.

Focus

The third strategy, **focus,** is implemented by a firm's targeted, careful attention to a specific segment of a market—as defined, for example, by type of customer, segment of the product line, or geographic area. This strategy is used to choose market niches where competition is the weakest, or where the firm has a strong competitive advantage because of technology or other form of differentiation. The focused firm succeeds by avoiding direct competition. It has either strong differentiation or low cost advantage (or both) for its market segment. For example, many small CPA firms succeed by focusing on the tax and personal financial service needs of their smaller clients, in contrast to the attest services offered by the larger firms to their larger clients.

An important disadvantage of the focused strategy is that the niche may suddenly disappear because of technological change in the industry or change in consumer tastes. A company that specializes only in gourmet coffees, for example, would have a difficult time recovering if consumer tastes shifted to other beverages.

> **Focus** is a competitive strategy in which a firm succeeds by targeting its attention to a specific segment of a market.

Other Strategic Issues

A firm succeeds, then, by adopting and effectively implementing one of the strategies explained above (and summarized in Exhibit 2–6). Recognize that while one strategy is generally dominant, a firm is most likely to employ two or more of the strategies at the same time, for example, by combining low cost and product differentiation. However, a firm following two or more strategies is likely to succeed only if it achieves significantly on one of them. A firm that does not achieve on at least one strategy is not likely to be successful. This situation is what Michael Porter calls "getting stuck in the middle." A firm that is stuck in the middle is not able to sustain a competitive advantage. This often happens when a successfully differentiated firm attempts to diversify outside its area of expertise, the area where it can compete effectively. Focus firms have failed by moving outside their area of focus. For example, People Express airline lost its successful geographic niche when it began to expand to a national market, where it could not compete successfully.

Another common way for a company to get stuck in the middle arises from the normal progression of a firm from one type of strategy to another as it grows. Often, a firm will begin small and succeed through effective differentiation or focus. Then, as the firm grows and its product or service matures in the marketplace, the firm will begin to focus on cost leadership as the principal way to succeed. A firm must be careful to identify these stages in its growth and appropriately adapt its corporate strategies to them.

Critical Success Factors and SWOT Analysis

LEARNING OBJECTIVE 3 ▶
Demonstrate how a firm identifies its own competitive strategy, including determining its critical success factors, and how it designs a strategic cost information system.

SWOT analysis is a systematic procedure for identifying a firm's critical success factors—its internal *strengths* and *weaknesses*, and its external *opportunities* and *threats*.

Skills or competencies that the firm employs especially well are called **core competencies**.

Identifying a sustainable competitive strategy for a given firm can be described as a three-step process. (Step 1 is discussed in this section; steps 2 and 3, in the following two sections.)

Step 1: Obtain a strategic analysis of the firm using SWOT analysis. What are its strengths and weaknesses, opportunities and threats? Determine the firm's overall strategy (cost, differentiation, focus) and its critical success factors.

SWOT analysis is a systematic procedure for identifying a firm's critical success factors—its *internal* strengths and weaknesses, and its *external* opportunities and threats. Strengths are skills and resources that the firm has more abundantly than other firms. Skills or competencies that the firm employs especially well are called **core competencies**. The concept of core competencies is important because it points to areas of significant competitive advantage for the firm; core competencies can be used as the building blocks of the firm's overall strategy. In contrast, weaknesses represent a lack of important skills or competencies, relative to the presence of those resources in competing firms.

Exhibit 2–6	Distinctive Aspects of the Three Competitive Strategies		
Aspect	**Cost Leadership**	**Differentiation**	**Focus**
Strategic target	Broad cross-section of the market	Broad cross-section of the market	Narrow market segment
Basis of competitive advantage	Lowest cost in the industry	Unique product or service	Uniqueness or low cost in a specific market segment
Product line	Limited selection	Wide variety, differentiating features	Targeted to selected market segment
Production emphasis	Lowest possible cost with high quality and essential product features	Innovation in differentiating products	Appropriateness for selected market segment
Marketing emphasis	Low price	Premium price and innovative, differentiating features	Firm's unique ability to serve the selected market segment

Source: Based on information from A. A. Thompson and A. J. Strickland, *Strategic Management* (Burr Ridge, Ill.: Irwin, 1993), p. 104.

Strengths and weaknesses are most easily identified by looking inside the firm at its specific resources:

- **Product lines.** Are the firm's products innovative? Are the product offerings too wide or too narrow? Are there important and distinctive technological advances?
- **Management.** What is the level of experience and competence?
- **Research and development.** Is the firm ahead or behind competitors? What is the outlook for important new products and services?
- **Manufacturing.** How competitive, flexible, productive, and technologically advanced are the current manufacturing processes? What plans are there for improvements in facilities and processes?
- **Marketing.** How effective is the overall marketing approach, including promotion, selling, and advertising?
- **Strategy.** How clearly defined, communicated, and effectively implemented is corporate strategy?

Opportunities and threats are identified by looking outside the firm. Opportunities are important favorable situations in the firm's environment. Demographic trends, changes in regulatory matters, and technological changes in the industry might provide significant advantages or disadvantages for the firm. For example, the gradual aging of the U.S. population represents an advantage for those firms that specialize in products and services for the elderly. In contrast, threats are major unfavorable situations in the firm's environment. These might include the entrance of new competitors or competing products, unfavorable changes in government regulations, and technological change that is unfavorable to the firm.

Opportunities and threats can be identified most easily by analyzing the industry and the firm's competitors:

- **Barriers to entry.** Do certain factors, such as capital requirements, economies of scale, product differentiation, and access to selected distribution channels, protect the firm from newcomers? Do other factors, including the cost of buyer switching, government regulations and policies that favor the firm, and educational and licensing restrictions, restrict competition? To what degree is the firm protected from competition from new entrants to the industry?
- **Intensity of rivalry among competitors.** Intense rivalry can be the result of high entry barriers, specialized assets (and therefore limited flexibility for a firm in the industry), rapid product innovation, slow growth in total market demand, or significant overcapacity in the industry. How intense is the overall industry rivalry facing the firm?
- **Pressure from substitute products.** Will the presence of readily substitutable products increase the level of intensity of competition for the firm?
- **Bargaining power of customers.** The greater the bargaining power of the firm's customers, the greater the level of competition facing the firm. Bargaining power of customers will likely be higher if there are relatively low switching costs and if the products are not differentiated.
- **Bargaining power of suppliers.** The greater the bargaining power of a firm's suppliers, the greater the overall level of competition facing the firm. The bargaining power of suppliers will be higher when the group of suppliers to the firm is dominated by a few large firms, and when these suppliers have other good outlets for their products.

SWOT analysis guides the strategic analysis by focusing attention on the strengths, weaknesses, opportunities, and threats critical to the company's success. By carefully identifying the critical success factors in this way, executives and managers can discover differences in viewpoints. For example, what some managers might view as a strength, others might view as a weakness. SWOT analysis therefore also serves as a means for obtaining greater understanding, and perhaps also consensus, among managers regarding the factors that are crucial to the firm's

SWOT Analysis at NEC Corporation

NEC Corporation, a Japanese manufacturer of electronic products, based its marketing strategy for personal computers on its success in semiconductor and VCR sales in the United States. NEC felt that its technology and quality leadership in semiconductors and VCRs would give it a competitive advantage in breaking into the personal computer (PC) market in the United States.

However, while spending over $150 million over the last 10 years to break into the U.S. market, NEC sold only about 260,000 PCs in the United States in 1991—a small fraction of the millions of PCs sold by the leading manufacturers. NEC did not take into account the weaknesses and threats in their strategy:

1. NEC assumed it could sell proprietary Japanese computers when most buyers in the United States wanted machines compatible with the IBM PC. It was unlikely NEC would be able to establish a successful product that was not compatible with the IBM PC.

2. Although NEC was first with a notebook computer (Ultralite), Compaq came out with a laptop that included a floppy drive rather than NEC's semiconductor memory cards. The floppy drive was much more attractive to the average consumer.

3. NEC's marketing was not as effective as that of Compaq, Apple, IBM, and others. NEC appeared to assume that quality and technological achievement would be recognized without effective marketing.

NEC relied on the quality and technology strengths that it had used in semiconductors and VCRs as applicable in the U.S. PC market. Their threats and weaknesses in competing with IBM, Apple, Compaq, and others were underestimated.

Source: Based on information from "The Invasion that Failed," *Forbes,* January 20, 1992, p. 102.

success. In addition, a careful consideration of its CSFs will lead to identification of the appropriate overall strategy for the firm—cost leadership, differentiation, or focus. The ultimate objective of the SWOT analysis, then, is to identify the overall strategy and the CSFs of the firm, and to begin to develop a consensus among executives and managers regarding them.[4]

Cost, Quality, and Time

Many firms find that a consideration of critical success factors yields a renewed focus on the three key factors: cost, quality, and speed of product development and product delivery. Increasingly, firms find that they must compete effectively on each of these three factors.[5] Consumer expectations are very high for quality, cost, and speed. Retail businesses such as Wal-Mart and Home Depot succeed by providing high-quality goods at low prices in desired quantities. Suppliers to these firms expect

Success Through Focus on Time: Toyota Motor Company

When a fire in the manufacturing plant of a supplier destroyed the main source of brake parts for Toyota in February 1997, experts were expecting Toyota's own manufacturing plants would be down for several days or weeks, waiting for a new source for the critical parts. In contrast, because Toyota has developed a close-knit family of suppliers over the years, it was able to use this large support system of 36 suppliers (including a sewing machine company that had never made car parts) to replace the lost manufacturing capacity within five days, a remarkably fast recovery. Toyota clearly showed that it could avoid the risk of reliance on suppliers, as in this case, by building a loyal network of a closely knit family of suppliers that would come to Toyota's aid in a crisis. All the members of the "family" knew how important it was to recover Toyota production as quickly as possible.

Source: Based on information in "Toyota's Fast Rebound after Fire at Supplier Shows Why It Is Tough," *The Wall Street Journal,* May 8, 1997, p. 1.

---

4 The Bank of Scotland has developed a SWOT-based system called COMPASS, which evaluates the strategic position of potential loan customers (Alan Sangster, "COMPASS—The Future of Bank Lending," *Expert Systems with Applications* 8, no. 3 1995).

5 This point is made in Robin Cooper's concept of the confrontation strategy based on quality, price, and functionality [Robin Cooper, *When Lean Enterprises Collide* (Boston: Harvard Business School Press, 1995)].

to meet very high standards of quality (including inspections by the retailer at the manufacturer's plant) and to meet increasingly demanding delivery terms, in many cases delivering product directly to the retail location, bypassing any warehousing operation. Cost, time, and quality are discussed in greater detail in Part Two.

Measures for Critical Success Factors

The second step in the process of identifying a sustainable competitive strategy follows the identification of the firm's CSFs.

Step 2: Develop relevant and reliable measures for the critical success factors identified in the first step.

Developing measures for the CSFs involves a careful study of the business processes of the firm. Product development, manufacturing, marketing, management, and financial functions are looked at to determine in which specific ways these functions contribute to the success of the firm. The objective at this step is to determine those specific measures that will allow the firm to monitor its progress toward achieving its strategic goals. Exhibit 2–7 lists sample CSFs and ways in which they might be measured.

Exhibit 2–7	**Measuring Critical Success Factors**
Critical Success Factor	**How to Measure the CSF**
Financial Factors:	
• Profitability	Earnings from operations, earnings trend
• Liquidity	Cash flow adequacy, trend in cash flow, interest coverage, asset turnover, inventory turnover, receivables turnover
• Sales	Level of sales in critical product groups, sales trend, percent of sales from new products, sales forecast accuracy
• Market value	Share price
Customer Factors	
• Customer satisfaction	Customer returns and complaints, customer survey
• Dealer and distributor	Coverage and strength of dealer and distributor channel relationships
• Marketing and selling	Trends in sales performance, training, market research activities
• Timeliness of delivery	On-time delivery performance, time from order to customer receipt
• Quality	Customer complaints, warranty expense, service speed and effectiveness
Internal Business Processes	
• Quality	Number of defects, numbers of returns, customer survey, amount of scrap, amount of rework, field service reports, warranty claims, vendor quality defects
• Productivity	Cycle time (from raw materials to finished product); labor efficiency; machine efficiency; amount of waste, rework, and scrap
• Flexibility	Setup time, cycle time, scheduling effectiveness
• Equipment readiness	Downtime, operator experience, machine capacity, maintenance activities
• Safety	Number of accidents, effects of accidents
Learning and Innovation	
• Product innovation	Number of design changes, number of new patents or copyrights, skills of research-and-development staff
• Timeliness of new product	Number of days over or under the announced ship date
• Skill development	Training hours, skill performance improvement
• Employee morale	Employee turnover, number of complaints, employee survey
• Competence	Rate of turnover, training, experience, adaptability, financial and operating performance measures
Other Factors	
• Governmental	Number of violations, and community service activities

Information Systems for Critical Success Factors

The final step in identifying competitive advantage follows the development of measures for the firm's CSFs.

Step 3: Develop a strategic cost information system for supporting the firm's overall strategy and for reporting critical success factors to appropriate managers.

Strategy and Customer Service at Leading Firms

A substantial number of firms (including Whirlpool Corporation, PepsiCo, AT&T, Conrail, and Otis Elevator) have found that a given critical success factor may contribute to the success of the firm in many different ways. For example, while prompt and effective customer service has become a critical success factor for most firms, a number of firms are also finding that data derived from customer service activities can help the firm elsewhere:

1. Effective use of data from field service of the firm's products

can lead to the identification of manufacturing processes or parts that require redesign or replacement; the result can be a significantly improved product.

2. The field service data is a valuable source of information regarding the quality of the firm's vendors; the rate of defect in specific parts from specific vendors can be tracked for later use in negotiations with the vendor regarding quality.

3. The field service information also provides a means to identify customer preferences in a very clear and timely way; the result can be new products and improved products that are more likely to win quick customer acceptance.

Source: Based on information from "The Gold Mine of Data in Customer Service," *Business Week,* March 21, 1994, pp. 113–114.

Exhibit 2–8	**Effects of Competitive Strategy on Required Skills, Reporting Systems, and Cost Management Systems**		
Strategy	**Required Skills and Resources**	**Organization and Reporting Requirements**	**Strategic Cost Management System**
Cost leadership	Substantial capital investment and access to capital	Tight cost control	Part Five: Cost Accounting and Operational Control
	Process engineering skills	Frequent, detailed control reports	
	Intense supervision of labor	Structured organization and policies	
	Products designed for ease of manufacture	Incentives based on meeting strict, quantitative targets	
Differentiation	Strong marketing abilities	Strong coordination among functions— research, product development, manufacturing, and marketing	Part Six: Management Control
	Product engineering		
	Corporate reputation for quality or technological leadership		
	Long tradition in the industry or unique skills drawn from other businesses		
Focus	Skills and resources of cost leadership and differentiation directed at the particular strategic target	Policies of cost leadership and differentiation directed at the particular strategic target	Parts Five and Six: Operational and Management Control

Source: Based on information from Michael E. Porter, *Competitive Advantage* (New York: Free Press, 1985), p. 40.

The third and final step is to develop a strategic cost accounting system to facilitate the achievement of the CSFs and the broad strategy. A starting point in determining the focus of the strategic information system is to consider the identification of the competitive strategy. Cost management can play an important role here. For example, if the firm's broad strategy is cost leadership, then the cost system should record and report concise quantitative information that will assist in cost control. The techniques require careful monitoring of the manufacturing and service operations where the costs are incurred. These techniques are explained in Part Five.

On the other hand, if the firm's objective is to succeed through product differentiation, then the techniques require a focus on coordination and performance evaluation at the management level where decisions related to product design and enhancement are made. These techniques are explained in Part Six. Finally, if the firm has a focus strategy, which requires attention to elements of both the cost leadership and differentiation strategies, then the most appropriate strategic information system will incorporate elements of both operational control and management control. The impact of a firm's competitive strategy on management is summarized in Exhibit 2–8.

Once the CSFs have been identified and measured, the final step is the development of a strategic information system to measure and report them. This is often done in the form of a balanced scorecard (see the following section). Most often, timeliness of reports will be crucial; many firms achieve timely reporting by using on-line computer systems networked throughout the firm—from manufacturing operations areas to marketing and financial management offices.

In addition to timeliness, the reporting procedure should consider the nature of the organizational structure of the firm. If the focus of the organizational structure is on relatively autonomous teams, then the accounting reports should focus on team performance for relevant CSFs. Alternatively, in the hierarchical organization, the accounting reports should flow upward, aggregating the information as they do so.

Exhibit 2–9 illustrates that a corporate-level CSF such as quality (as measured in part by warranty return rate) can be linked to CSFs at each level in the hierarchy

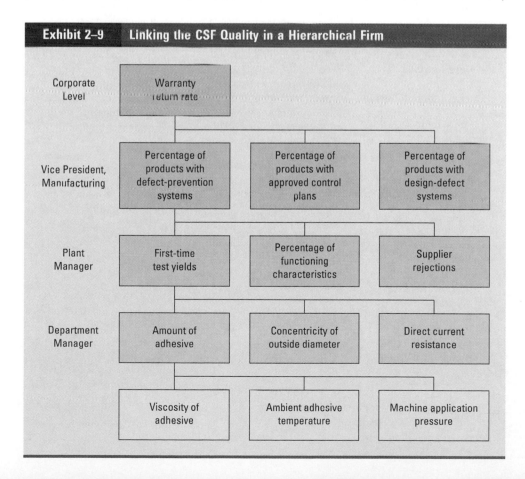

Exhibit 2–9   Linking the CSF Quality in a Hierarchical Firm

Corporate Level
- Warranty return rate

Vice President, Manufacturing
- Percentage of products with defect-prevention systems
- Percentage of products with approved control plans
- Percentage of products with design-defect systems

Plant Manager
- First-time test yields
- Percentage of functioning characteristics
- Supplier rejections

Department Manager
- Amount of adhesive
- Concentricity of outside diameter
- Direct current resistance

- Viscosity of adhesive
- Ambient adhesive temperature
- Machine application pressure

of manufacturing management.[6] Whereas, at the corporate level, the CEO and board of directors are concerned with the warranty return rate, the vice president of manufacturing deals with specific CSFs, each of which can be linked to the reduction of the warranty return rate—for example, the percentage of products with defect-prevention systems. Similarly, the plant managers will have CSFs that can be linked to the CSFs of the manufacturing vice president. In the same manner, department managers and operations on the shop floor can be linked upwardly to the overall corporate CSF of reducing warranty returns.

A final consideration is that the development and reporting of CSFs must be linked to the financial objectives of the firm. For example, if quality is a corporate goal, making the warranty return rate a relevant quality-related CSF, then the strategic information system should develop relevant information about the costs and benefits of reducing the warranty return rate. One question to be asked could be, What will be the net impact of the warranty return rate on short- and long-term earnings? The strategic management of the firm requires managers to attend to CSFs and monitor their progress in achieving strategic goals by watching short- and long-term profitability goals, using the strategic information system.

THE BALANCED SCORECARD

LEARNING OBJECTIVE 4 ▶
Explain how the balanced scorecard is used to help a firm achieve its strategic goals.

The balanced scorecard is the accounting report developed from the strategic information system described above. It is used for linking CSFs to strategy and for monitoring the firm's achievement toward its strategic goals. The balanced scorecard serves as an action plan, a basis for implementing the strategy expressed by the CSFs. Because of its broad, strategic role, the balanced scorecard includes *all* the firm's critical success factors, which, as noted earlier, are typically shown in four areas: (1) financial performance, (2) customer satisfaction, (3) internal business processes, and (4) innovation and learning (examples of these CSFs are shown in

The Balanced Scorecard at Three Leading Firms

Caterpillar, Inc.: Using Nonfinancial Measures to Focus on Long-Term Issues
Caterpillar's Wheel Loaders and Excavators Division (WLED) was concerned about the possible excessive focus on short-term profits by managers as the firm moved to a greater focus on profits in each of the divisions. Since all employees at WLED are compensated on the basis of division profits, they would have a short-term focus and would not properly attend to the CSFs, which were important for long-term success. WLED used a team of staff-level employees to identify nonfinancial critical success factors for the division. Additional teams identified the action plans needed to achieve these CSFs. The plan is used to make sure that employees understand that attending to CSFs is an important way to contribute to current as well as long-term earnings.

Bank of Montreal: Linking CSFs to Long-Term Profits
The primary objective of the bank's performance evaluation system is to maximize long-term return on investment to shareholders. Management's view was that this was best done by focusing on key financial and nonfinancial measures. The objective was fourfold: (1) to communicate to those in-

side and outside the bank the CSFs that contribute to long-term return on investment, (2) to focus bank managers' attention on the critical success factors, (3) to serve as a basis for management action, through the regular monitoring of achievement on the CSFs, and (4) to provide a basis for rewarding managers.

Dow Chemical: Focus on Learning and Innovation
Dow Chemical became concerned about the management of its patents some years ago. The response was to create a director of intellectual assets, who works with Dow's researchers and others to analyze the competition and technology gaps in the market to better plan the firm's research programs and to develop patents that are more competitively useful.

Source: Based on information in J. A. Hendricks, D. G. Defreitas, and D. K. Walker, "Changing Performance Measures at Caterpillar," *Management Accounting*, December 1996, pp. 18–24; A. A. Atkinson, J. H. Waterhouse, and R. B. Wells, "Strategic Performance Measurement: Theory and Practice," paper presented at the Conference on Strategic Cost Management, The University of Alberta, Canada, May 1996; and "Your Company's Most Valuable Asset: Intellectual Capital," *Fortune*, October 3, 1994, pp. 68–74.

---

[6]   M. E. Beischel and K. R. Smith, "Linking the Shop Floor to the Top Floor," *Management Accounting*, October 1991, p. 27.

Exhibit 2–7).[7] Each group of CSFs in the balanced scorecard summarizes the firm's overall performance for that strategic objective (see Exhibit 2–10). The four areas represent the key strategic areas for most firms. Some firms, however, may elect to use fewer groups if appropriate. Other firms may use additional groups to reflect the importance of additional strategic concerns, such as the environmental impact of the firm's operations, or the broad economic and social effects of the firm's operations on the community in which it operates.[8]

The balanced scorecard is comprehensive, since it includes all the CSFs that contribute to competitive success. For this reason, it can help focus managers properly on

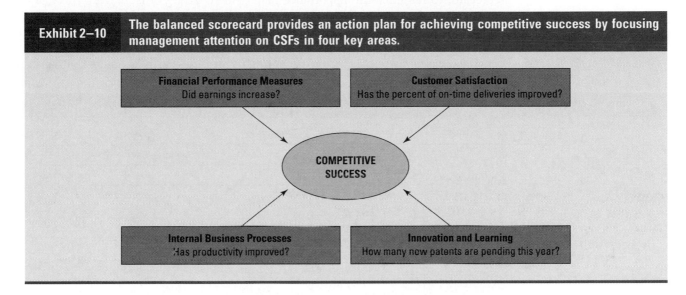

| **Exhibit 2–10** | **The balanced scorecard provides an action plan for achieving competitive success by focusing management attention on CSFs in four key areas.** |

Financial Performance Measures
Did earnings increase?

Customer Satisfaction
Has the percent of on-time deliveries improved?

COMPETITIVE SUCCESS

Internal Business Processes
Has productivity improved?

Innovation and Learning
How many new patents are pending this year?

The Balanced Scorecard at Champion International Corporation

The Champion International paper mill in Hamilton, Ohio, uses the balanced scorecard approach to provide monthly financial and nonfinancial indicators of the mill's performance. The key nonfinancial measures are developed and used in monthly production meetings with production supervisors. "For the first time, because of the balanced scorecard, line managers understand the numbers presented . . . Now that accountants are not bogged down in trying to explain GAAP absorption and variance from plan, they can concentrate on conveying the results of actions that are controllable by the mill."

Customer Focus	**Units of Measure**
Quoted lead times	Days
Complaints	Number
Customer Satisfaction Index	Score out of 100

Process Improvement	
First-pass yield	Percent
Finish yield	Percent
Litho	Percent
Cover	Percent
Colorcast	Percent
Fiber usage	Output/ton
Machine 2 yield	Percent
Machine 9 yield	Percent

Source: Kim Constantinides and John K. Shank, "Matching Accounting to Strategy: One Mill's Experience," *Management Accounting*, September 1994, pp. 32–36.

---

[7] The balanced scorecard is explained in Robert S. Kaplan and David P. Norton, "The Balanced Scorecard—Measures That Drive Performance," *Harvard Business Review*, January–February 1992, pp. 71–79; John Hoffecker and Charles Goldenberg, "Using the Balanced Scorecard to Develop Companywide Performance Measures," *Journal of Cost Management*, Fall 1994, pp. 5–17; Robert S. Kaplan and David P. Norton, "Using the Balanced Scorecard as a Strategic Management System," *Harvard Business Review*, January–February 1996, pp. 75–85; and Robert S. Kaplan and David P. Norton, "Why Does Business Need a Balanced Scorecard?" *Journal of Cost Management*, May/June 1997, pp. 5–10.

[8] In Europe, particularly in France, managers have used a performance measurement approach, the *tableau de bord*, which is very much like the balanced scorecard. The *tableau de bord* identifies drivers of competitive success in four areas: logistics, manufacturing, personnel, and administration.

the firm's CSFs and alleviate the myopic attention to profits that is often found in accounting reports based on financial results only. It is also forward-looking, since many of the nonfinancial CSFs, such as quality and customer service measures, when achieved, provide benefits well into the future.

Making the Balanced Scorecard Most Effective

First, for the balanced scorecard to be most effective, it should be developed at the detail level, so that employees can see how their actions contribute to the success of the firm. Moreover, employee compensation should be based on the balanced scorecard, to reinforce the importance management places on achieving the CSFs.

Second, the scorecard should have both leading and lagging indicators. Leading indicators are those that point to future competitive success, such as patents pending in research development, or improvements in operations or customer service. In contrast, lagging indicators are primarily output measures, such as productivity mea-

Exhibit 2–11	Operating Data and Scorecard Results for Conner Valve Company			

Panel A: Operating Data

		Operating Data		
		April	**May**	**June**
Vendor	Number of defects	6	2	3
	Number of shipments received	456	488	473
	Number of on-time deliveries	433	448	413
Materials handling	Number of routing errors	4	8	12
	Number of routings	1,228	1,654	1,997
Production	Number of units completed and shipped	332,786	377,619	356,118
	Number of units in process (incomplete)	23,998	11,542	44,928
	Downtime (hours)	21	18	11
	Machine run time (hours)	310	303	345
	Reworked units	12	3	13
	Scrapped units	4	18	98
	Quality defects	33	12	21
Distribution	Number of working days	21	21	22
	Number of shipments	1,025	998	1,335
	Number of shipping errors of all types	18	45	31
	Number of on-time deliveries	1,001	903	1,300
	Total pounds shipped	478,556	511,827	499,816

Panel B: Scorecard Results

		Scorecard Results		
Purchasing		**April**	**May**	**June**
Vendor quality	Number of defects/number of shipments received	1.32%	0.41%	0.63%
Vendor delivery	Number of on-time deliveries/number of shipments received	94.96%	91.80%	87.32%
Materials Control/Materials Handling				
Routing efficiency	Number of routing errors/number of routings	0.33%	0.48%	0.60%
Inventory level	Units in process/units shipped	7.21%	3.06%	12.62%
Manufacturing				
Downtime	Hours downtime/hours of machine run time	6.77%	6.04%	3.22%
Machine efficiency	Units shipped/machine run time	1,073.50	1,246.27	1,032.23
Rework	Number of units reworked	12	3	13
Scrap	Number of units scrapped	4	18	98
Quality	Number of defects	33	12	21
Distribution/Shipping				
Shipping accuracy	Number of errors/Number of shipments	1.76%	4.51%	2.32%
Shipping efficiency	Average shipments/day	48.81	47.52	60.68
	Average pounds shipped/day	22,788	24,373	22,719
Delivery timeliness	Number on-time deliveries/number of shipments	97.66%	90.48%	97.38%

sures, unit cost, and profits. Financial measures tend to be lagging indicators, while nonfinancial measures can be of either type. Much like economists who use these two types of indicators, the management accountant develops a comprehensive scorecard that helps management predict future and assess past performance.

An Illustration of the Balanced Scorecard

The Connor Valve Company (CVC), a large manufacturer of industrial valves, provides an example of how the balanced scorecard can be used. CVC is planning to develop the scorecard initially for internal business processes only, and in that context will focus only on those processes directly related to manufacturing: purchasing, materials handling, manufacturing, and shipping. The other three areas of the scorecard—financial performance, customer satisfaction, and innovation and learning—are to be developed later. CVC developed the relevant data for the most recent quarter, as shown in Exhibit 2–11. Panel A shows the key operating data; panel B shows the critical success factors and how they are measured. The data and the scorecard results are shown for the months of April, May, and June.

The scorecard results have important information for CVC. Looking first at the results for purchasing and materials handling, note in particular the rapid decline in vendor delivery performance over the three months. There should be an investigation into why this has happened. How will the decline affect operations in the coming months? Next, looking at manufacturing, note the unusually large number of units scrapped in June. And finally, for shipping, note the overall good performance in terms of shipping errors and on-time deliveries, especially for April and June. CVC's scorecard provides a basis for management planning and action on achieving the critical success factors, and thereby making progress toward competitive success.

VALUE-CHAIN ANALYSIS

Value-chain analysis is a strategic analysis tool used to better understand the firm's competitive advantage, to identify where value to customers can be increased or costs reduced, and to better understand the firm's linkages with suppliers, customers, and other firms in the industry.[9] The value chain identifies and links the various strategic activities of the firm. The nature of the value chain depends on the nature of the industry, and differs among manufacturers, service firms, and not-for-profit organizations. The value chain of a manufacturing industry is illustrated in Exhibit 2–12. The objective of the value-chain analysis is to identify stages of the value chain where the firm can increase value to the customer or reduce cost. The reduction in cost or increase in value makes the firm more competitive. The increase in

> **Value-chain analysis** is a strategic analysis tool used to identify where value to customers can be increased or costs reduced, and to better understand the firm's linkages with suppliers, customers, and other firms in the industry.

> ◄ **LEARNING OBJECTIVE 5**
> Explain value-chain analysis and show how it is used to better understand a firm's competitive advantage.

> ### Application of Value-Chain Analysis: Improved Supplier Relationships at Mercedes-Benz in Alabama
>
> To speed up manufacturing and reduce costs, the Mercedes-Benz plant in Vance, Alabama, is reducing the number of suppliers to 100 from the approximately 1,000 that are required for the E-Class sedan. In addition, suppliers will have more flexibility in the design of parts, allowing them to adapt previously designed parts, thus saving design and testing costs for the supplier and for Mercedes. Also, in order to develop longer-term relationships with suppliers, Mercedes is offering multiyear contracts (usually with an annual 5 percent price reduction) rather than requiring suppliers to bid for new contracts each year.
>
> **Source:** Based on information from "Mercedes' Maverick in Alabama," *Business Week*, September 11, 1995, p. 65.

---

[9] The concepts in this section are adapted in part from John K. Shank and Vijay Govindarajan, *Strategic Cost Analysis* (Burr Ridge, Ill.: Irwin, 1989); and *Strategic Cost Management* (New York: Free Press, 1993).

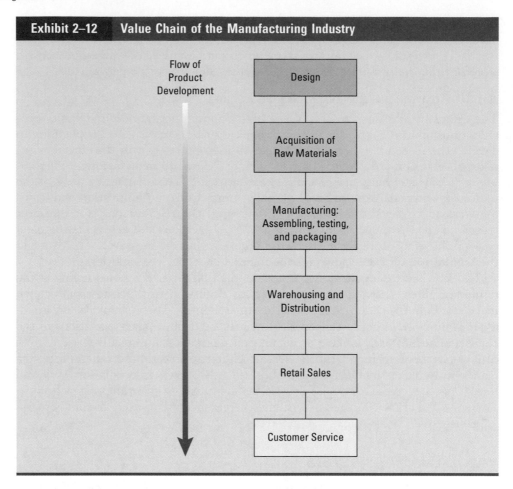

Exhibit 2–12 Value Chain of the Manufacturing Industry

value or reduced cost can be achieved by seeking better terms with suppliers, by simplifying the distribution of product, by outsourcing (i.e., having the component or service provided by another firm, rather than providing it internally), and by identifying areas where the firm is not competitive, among other means.

The value-chain analysis focuses on the total value chain of the product, from the design of the product, to the manufacture of the product, to service after the sale. The underlying concept of the analysis is that each individual firm occupies a selected part or parts of this entire value chain.

The determination of which part or parts of the value chain to occupy is a strategic analysis, based on consideration of comparative advantage for the individual firm, that is, where the firm can best provide value to the ultimate consumer at the lowest possible cost. For example, some firms in the computer-manufacturing industry focus on the manufacture of chips (Texas Instruments), while others manufacture primarily processors (Intel), or hard drives (Seagate and Western Digital), or monitors (Sony). Some manufacturers combine purchased and manufactured components to manufacture the complete computer (IBM, Compaq), while others depend primarily on purchased components (Dell, Gateway). In the sport-shoe industry, Reebok manufactures its shoes and sells them to large retailers, while Nike concentrates on design, sales, and promotion, contracting out all the manufacturing to others. In effect, each firm establishes itself in one or more parts of the value chain, on the basis of a strategic analysis of its competitive advantage.

Value-chain analysis has three steps:

Step 1: Identify the value-chain activities.

The firm identifies the specific **value activities** that firms in the industry must perform in the process of design, manufacturing, and customer service. Some firms may be involved in a single activity or a subset of the total activities. For example,

Value activities are activities that firms in the industry must perform in the process of taking raw material and converting it to final product, including customer service.

some firms may only manufacture, while others distribute and sell the product. See the value chain for the computer-manufacturing industry in Exhibit 2–13.

The development of a value chain will differ depending on the type of industry. For example, in a service industry, the focus will be on operations and on advertising and promotion rather than on raw materials and manufacturing (an example of a service industry value chain is shown in self-study problem 1 at the end of the chapter). Also, the activities should be determined at a relatively detailed level of operations, that is, at the level of a business unit or process just large enough to be managed as a separate business activity (in effect, the output of the process has a market value). For example, while the completion of a chip or computer board is likely to be an activity (the output has a market), it is unlikely that the operation of testing or packaging the chip or board would be an activity in a value-chain analysis.

Step 2: Identify the cost driver(s) at each value activity.

As noted in Chapter 1, a cost driver is any factor that changes the level of total cost.[10] The objective in this step therefore is to identify activities where the firm has a current or potential cost advantage. For instance, an insurance agency might find that an important cost driver is the cost of maintaining records on customers' accounts. This strategic cost driver information can lead the agency to look for ways to reduce or outsource these costs, possibly by hiring an outside computer-service firm to handle the data processing tasks, so as to reduce overall costs and maintain or improve competitiveness.

Step 3: Develop a sustainable competitive advantage by reducing cost or adding value.

Exhibit 2–13	Value Chain for the Computer-Manufacturing Industry*	
Step in the Value Chain	**Activities**	**Expected Output of Activities**
Step 1: Design	Research and development	Completed product design
Step 2: Acquiring raw materials	Mining, development, and refining	Silicon, plastic, various metals
Step 3: Assembling materials into components**	Converting raw materials into components and parts used in the manufacture of the computer	Desired components and parts
Stage 1	Conversion, assembly, finishing, testing, and grading	Chips, processors, other basic components
Stage 2		Boards, higher-level components
Step 4: Computer manufacturing	Final assembly, packaging, and shipping the final product	Completed computers
Step 5: Wholesaling, warehousing, and distribution	Moving products to retail locations and warehouses, as needed	Rail, truck, and air shipments
Step 6: Retail sales	Retail sale	Cash receipts
Step 7: Customer service	Processing returns, inquiries, and repairs	Serviced and restocked computers

* Although this example shows two stages of component manufacturing under step 3, there may be one, two, or several stages depending on the nature of the industry.

** This step requires two stages—one for the chips and processors and other basic components, and another for the boards and other components that are made up of chips and other basic components.

---

[10] The difference between a value activity and a cost driver activity is that the value activity is a higher level of aggregation; in effect, one or more cost drivers are likely to be involved in any one value activity.

In this step, the firm determines the nature of its current and potential competitive advantage by studying the value activities and cost drivers identified above. In doing so, the firm must take into account the following:

1. Identify competitive advantage (cost leadership or differentiation). The analysis of value activities can help management better understand the firm's strategic competitive advantage and the firm's proper positioning in the overall industry value chain. For example, in the computer industry, certain firms (e.g., Hewlett-Packard) focus primarily on innovative design, while others (e.g., Texas Instruments and Compaq) focus on low-cost manufacturing.

2. Identify opportunities for added value. The analysis of value activities can help identify activities in which the firm can add significant value for the customer. For example, it is more common now for food-processing plants and packaging plants to be located near their largest customers to provide faster and cheaper delivery. Similarly, large retailers such as Wal-Mart use computer-based technology to coordinate with suppliers to efficiently and quickly restock each of the stores. In banking, ATMs (automated teller machines) were introduced to provide improved customer service and to reduce processing costs. Now banks are developing on-line computer technologies to further enhance customer service and to provide an opportunity to further reduce processing costs.

3. Identify opportunities for reduced cost. A study of its value activities and cost drivers can help a firm determine those parts of the value chain for which it is *not* competitive. For example, Intel Corporation once manufactured computer chips and certain computer boards, such as modems, but for a variety of reasons, it abandoned those portions of the industry value chain and now focuses primarily on processors. Similarly, some firms might reconfigure their value activities in order to reduce cost. For example, Iowa Beef Processors moved its processing plants to be near the feedlots in the southwest and midwest states, thereby saving transportation costs and reducing the loss in weight that the animals usually suffered during transportation.

In summary, value-chain analysis supports the firm's strategic competitive advantage by facilitating the discovery of opportunities for adding value for the customers and/or by reducing the cost of providing the product or service.

BusinessWeek

 Why Is Outsourcing "In" for Automakers?

(Continues from page 27)

A: In three words, value-chain analysis.

To understand the cost-saving role of the parts manufacturers, automakers use value-chain analysis. Automakers look at their upstream costs of design and engineering and find that the specialized design teams of parts manufacturers are sometimes more cost efficient. One example is the seat systems for Chrysler cars. "At one time we had 250 engineers here, just designing seat covers," says Thomas T. Stallkamp, Chrysler's executive vice president for procurement and supply. "Now, the suppliers are the experts." In effect, what Chrysler has done is to examine its cost competitiveness at each step in the value chain, and has found that in seat systems, it is better to outsource.

The trend is for the parts manufacturers to sell *entire* parts systems. For example, Lear Corporation can now supply almost entire passenger compartments for the automakers, according to Lear Chairman Kenneth L. Way. The same trend appears to be true for other systems—brakes, fuel systems, and exterior trim, among others—with one analyst pointing out that a total-interior supplier could save $600 of the $900 it costs Ford and Chrysler for these systems. Essentially, a value-chain analysis for automakers shows that increasing reliance on outsourcing in manufacturing is providing an important way to reduce costs.

For further reading, see the following source: "Get Big or Get Out: How Detroit Is Driving Consolidation in the Auto-Parts Biz," *Business Week,* September 2, 1996, pp. 60–62.

Value Chain Analysis in Computer Manufacturing

The computer industry offers excellent opportunities to experience value-chain analysis in action. The Computer Intelligence Company (CIC), a disguised representation of an actual company, manufactures computers for small businesses in the Raleigh–Durham, North Carolina, area. CIC has an excellent reputation for service and reliability, and a growing list of customers. The manufacturing process consists primarily of assembling components purchased from various electronics firms, plus a small amount of metalworking and finishing. The manufacturing operations cost $250 per unit. The purchased parts cost CIC $500, of which $300 is for parts that CIC could manufacture in its existing facility for $190 in materials for each unit, plus an investment in labor and equipment that would cost $55,000 per month. CIC is considering whether to make or to continue to buy these parts.

CIC is considering contracting out to another Durham firm, JBM Enterprises, the marketing, distribution, and service for its units. This would save CIC $175,000 in monthly materials and labor costs. The cost of the contract would be $130 per machine sold, for the average of 600 units sold per month. CIC uses value-chain analysis to study the effect of these options on its strategy and costs. The analysis is summarized in Exhibit 2–14.

The value chain analysis in Exhibit 2–14 shows that CIC can save $108,000 per month ($355,000 − $247,000) by choosing option 2; thus, from a cost advantage, option 2 is preferred. However, CIC also needs to consider its strategic competitive position. If its customers rely on CIC primarily for its service and reliability, then contracting out the marketing, distribution, and service functions is unwise; CIC should retain control over these critical success factors. Moreover, by moving to a strategy of making rather than buying the components, CIC is moving in the direction of

Exhibit 2–14	Value-Chain Analysis for CIC Manufacturing Company	
Value Activity	**Option 1: Current Operations**	**Option 2: Manufacture Components and Contract Out Marketing, Distribution, and Service**
Acquisition of raw materials	CIC is not involved at this step in the value chain.	CIC is not involved at this step in the value chain.
Manufacture of computer chips and other parts	CIC is not involved at this step in the value chain; the cost of these parts is $200 to CIC.	CIC is not involved at this step in the value chain; the cost of these parts is $200 to CIC.
Manufacture of components, some of which CIC can make	CIC purchases $300 of parts for each unit.	CIC manufactures these parts for $190 per unit, plus monthly costs of $55,000.
Assembly	CIC's costs are $250.	CIC's costs are $250.
Marketing, distribution, and service	CIC's costs are $175,000 per month.	CIC contracts out services to JBM Enterprises for $130 per unit sold.
	Summary of Costs that Differ between Options	
	1. Unit costs for purchased components: $300 2. Monthly costs for marketing, distribution, and service: $175,000	1. Unit costs for manufacture of components ($190) plus cost of JBM contract ($130): $320 2. Monthly costs for labor and equipment: $55,000
	Total relevant costs for this option (assuming 600 units sold per month): $300 × 600 + $175,000 = $355,000 per month	Total relevant costs for this option (assuming 600 units sold per month): $320 × 600 + $55,000 = $247,000 per month

Note: Items in color are those activities of the value chain in which CIC operates.

competing on cost leadership with other computer manufacturers. It is unlikely that CIC can succeed at cost leadership because of its relatively small size and the presence of effective competitors already in this part of the value chain (IBM, Compaq, Dell, and Gateway, to name a few). Thus, option 2 pulls CIC away from its proven competitive advantage of emphasis on customer service. From a strategic view, option 1 is preferred, even though the costs are higher.[11] The value-chain analysis provides a useful framework for studying the options facing CIC—where it can reduce costs and where it can compete most effectively on the value chain.

STRATEGIC COST MANAGEMENT IN NOT-FOR-PROFIT ORGANIZATIONS

For not-for-profit or governmental organizations, strategic cost management is likely to serve a somewhat different role. Governmental and not-for-profit organizations must satisfy funding authorities, political leaders, and the general public as to their effectiveness and efficiency. The balanced scorecard can be used to monitor and evaluate the organization's performance on the key internal processes (e.g., efficiency measures such as pounds of trash removed), customer satisfaction measures (where the customers are the public and political leaders), key financial measures (e.g., credit rating, fund balance), and human resources measures.

Additionally, value-chain analysis can be used for determining at what points costs can be reduced or value added in the organization's value chain. In contrast to the acquisition of raw materials or the process of advertising and promotion, the first step in the value chain for a not-for-profit or governmental organization will likely be a statement of the broad social mission of the organization, including the specific public needs served. The second step is the development of resources for the organization, including both personnel and facilities. The third and fourth steps are the operations of the organization and the delivery of the service to the public, respectively.

IMPLICATIONS OF STRATEGIC ANALYSIS FOR COST MANAGEMENT

LEARNING OBJECTIVE 6
Understand the implications of strategic analysis for cost management.

As a result of changes in the environment of business, the role of cost management has been transformed. The introduction of new manufacturing and information technologies, the focus on the customer, the growth of worldwide markets, and other changes require that firms develop strategic information systems to effectively maintain their competitive advantage in the industry. This means that cost management must provide appropriate types of information that have not been provided under traditional cost accounting systems.

First, there is a need for information that addresses the strategic objectives of the firm. Reports that focus only on operational issues, such as those often summarized in financial reports, will not suffice. The critical success factors to which the firm must attend are diverse, and many of them relate to long-term issues such as new-product development, quality, customer relations, and other CSFs. Only by succeeding at these CSFs will the firm maintain its competitive advantage. The role of cost management then must be to identify, collect, measure, and report information on the CSFs reliably and in a timely manner. Many of the CSFs will be nonfinancial measures, such as delivery speed, cycle time, and customer satisfaction. The cost manager is thus involved in the development of both financial and nonfinancial information. This information is reported in the balanced scorecard.

Second, the efforts to sustain a competitive advantage require long-term plans. SWOT analysis and value-chain analysis are used to identify the firm's strategic posi-

---

[11] The options facing CIC can also be viewed as two separate outsourcing decisions, one for the manufacture of components and the other for marketing, distribution, and service. Both favor outsourcing. The manufacturing decision favors outsourcing for a savings of $11,000 ($300 × 600 − $190 × 600 − $55,000), and the marketing, distribution, and service decision favors outsourcing for a savings of $97,000 ($175,000 − $130 × 600).

tion in the industry. Success in the short term is no longer a measure of ultimate success, since long-term success requires strategic, long-term planning and action.

Third, the strategic approach requires integrative thinking, that is, the ability to identify and solve problems from a cross-functional view. Instead of viewing a problem as a marketing problem, or a production problem, or a problem in finance and accounting, the integrative approach utilizes skills from many functions simultaneously, very often in a team setting. The integrative approach is necessary because the firm's attention is focused on satisfying the customers' needs, and all the firm's resources, from all the different functions, are directed to this goal.

Spurred by the growing importance of strategic issues in management, cost management has adopted a strategic focus. The role of cost management has become that of a strategic partner, no longer simply a function of record keeping and reporting.

SUMMARY

The use of cost management facilitates the strategic management of a firm. The management accountant has moved from a procedural, stewardship role to become more of a strategic facilitator, to have a business partnership role in the firm. Michael Porter's work in strategic management explains the fundamentals of how firms compete. It is this grounding in the competitive environment of the firm that determines the cost management role. That is, it is necessary to know how a firm competes and to identify its critical success factors to know how the cost management system for the firm should be designed.

The three main types of competitive strategy are cost leadership, differentiation, and focus. Cost leadership is a strategy that relies on lowest-cost production and distribution, while differentiation relies on outstanding quality or product features. The focus strategy relies on differentiation or cost leadership for a particular product or market. Critical success factors are the specific, measurable aspects of the firm's products and operations, such as speed of service, safety of the workplace, and customer satisfaction, which, when achieved, lead to successful competition.

Three important strategic management techniques are SWOT analysis, the balanced scorecard, and value-chain analysis. SWOT analysis is a technique for identifying a firm's strategy and critical success factors, based on an identification of the firm's strengths, weaknesses, opportunities, and threats in the business environment. The balanced scorecard is a cost management report that summarizes the critical success factors for the attention of management. Value-chain analysis is a technique for determining the strategic competitive advantage of the firm, and for assisting the management accountant in identifying opportunities for reducing cost and/or adding value to the firm's products and services.

KEY TERMS

Core competencies 32	Strategy 28
Cost leadership 31	SWOT analysis 32
Differentiation 31	Value activities 42
Focus 31	Value-chain analysis 41

SELF-STUDY PROBLEMS

(For solutions, please turn to the end of the chapter.)

1. Value-Chain Analysis

Jack Smith, a consultant for the Greensboro Bulls AA baseball team, has been asked to complete a value-chain analysis of the franchise with a particular focus on comparison with a nearby competing team, the Durham Buffaloes. Jack has been able to collect selected cost data, as shown below, for each of the six steps in the value chain. Single-ticket prices range from $4.50 to $8, and average paying attendance is approximately 2,200 for Greensboro and 5,000 for Durham.

Average Cost per Person at Scheduled Games

Greensboro Bulls	Steps in the Value Chain	Durham Buffaloes
$ .45	Advertising and general promotion expenses	$ .50
.28	Ticket sales: local sporting goods stores and at the ballpark	.25
.65	Ballpark operations	.80
.23	Management compensation	.18
.95	Players' salaries	1.05
.20	Game-day operations: security, special entertainment, and game-day promotions	.65
$2.76	Total cost	$3.43

Required Develop an analysis of the value chain to help Jack better understand the nature of the competition between the Bulls and the Buffaloes, and to identify opportunities for adding value and/or cost reduction at each step.

2. Competitive Strategy, Ethics

Ethics

Frank Sills, the CEO and founder of Enviro-Wear, is facing the first big challenge of his young company. Frank began the company on the principle of environmental consciousness in the manufacture of sports and recreation wear. His idea was to develop clothing that would appeal to active people who were concerned about quality, waste in manufacturing and packaging, and the environmental impact of the manufacture of the goods they purchased. Starting with a small shop in Zebulon, North Carolina, Frank was able to develop his small business through strategic alliances with mail-order merchandisers and through effective public relations about his environmentally concerned processes. A special advantage for the young firm was Frank's knowledge of accounting and his prior experience as a CPA in a national public accounting firm and as a controller of a small manufacturing firm.

Enviro-Wear had reached $25,000,000 in sales in its sixth year when a disastrous set of events put the firm and its prospects in a tailspin. One of the key sales managers, while telling jokes about the poor quality of the firm's clothing, was overheard by a news reporter, and the story spread quickly. At the same time, rumors (largely unfounded) spread that the firm was not really as environmentally conscious in its manufacturing and packaging as it claimed. The result was an immediate falloff in sales, and some retailers were returning the goods.

Frank intends to fire the manager and deny publicly any association with the manager's comments, as well as to defend the firm's environmental record.

Required

1. On the basis of Porter's analysis of strategic competitive advantage, what type of competitive strategy has Enviro-Wear followed? What type of strategy should it follow in the future?
2. What are the ethical issues involved in the case, and how would you resolve them?

QUESTIONS

2–1 Identify and explain the three types of competitive strategy.

2–2 Identify three or four well-known firms that succeed through cost leadership.

2–3 Identify three or four well-known firms that succeed through product differentiation.

2–4 Identify two or three firms that succeed through product or market focus.

2–5 Explain the process of identifying a sustainable competitive advantage for a firm.

2–6 What is the meaning of "getting stuck in the middle" in the context of competitive strategy, and how does the situation arise?

2–7 What is SWOT analysis? What is it used for?

2–8 What is the role of the cost manager regarding nonfinancial performance measures such as delivery speed and customer satisfaction?

2–9 Explain the difference between short-term and long-term performance measures, and give two or three examples of each.

2–10 What is a critical success factor, and what is its role in strategic management and in cost management?

2–11 Identify four or five potential critical success factors for a manufacturer of industrial chemicals, and explain why you consider those factors critical for the firm to be successful.

2–12 Identify four or five potential critical success factors for a large savings and loan institution.

2–13 Identify four or five potential critical success factors for a small chain of retail jewelry stores.

2–14 Identify four or five potential critical success factors for a large retail discount store that features a broad range of consumer merchandise.

2–15 Identify four or five potential critical success factors for a small auto-repair shop.

2–16 What is a balanced scorecard? What is the primary objective when using a balanced scorecard?

2–17 Contrast using the balanced scorecard with using only financial measures of success.

2–18 What are the implications of strategic analysis for cost management?

2–19 Explain what is meant by value-chain analysis.

2–20 Are strategic analysis and value-chain analysis applicable for service and not-for-profit organizations?

Strategy

Each of the following problems incorporates one or more key strategic issues that must be resolved as part of the answer.

PROBLEMS

2–21 **SPECIAL ORDER, STRATEGY** Joel Deaine, CEO of Deaine Enterprises, Inc. (DEI), is considering a special offer to manufacture a new line of women's clothing for a large department store chain. DEI has specialized in designer women's clothing sold in small, upscale retail clothing stores throughout the country. In order to protect the very elite brand image, Deaine has not sold clothing to the large department stores. The current offer, however, may be too good to turn down. The department store is willing to commit to a large order, which would be very profitable to Deaine, and the order would be automatically renewed for two more years, presumably to continue after that point.

Required Analyze the choice Joel faces, based on a competitive analysis.

2–22 **STRATEGY, COMPETITIVE ADVANTAGE** In the mid-1970s a large retailer of auto parts, Best Parts, Inc. (BPI), was looking for ways to invest an accumulation of excess cash. BPI's success was built on a carefully developed inventory control system that guaranteed a customer would be able to purchase a desired part 99 percent of the time on demand, and the remaining 1 percent of the time within one business day. The speed and quality of service set BPI apart from other parts dealers, and the business continued to grow.

On the advice of close friends and consultants, the owner and CEO of BPI decided to invest a significant portion of the excess cash in a small chain of gift and craft stores. The stores would be placed in shopping malls.

Required   Determine the competitive advantage (cost leadership, or differentiation) of BPI in the auto-parts business. Assess how this competitive advantage would or would not facilitate success in the new venture.

2-23   STRATEGY, CONTEMPORARY MANAGEMENT TECHNIQUES (REVIEW OF CHAPTER 1)   One of the large auto manufacturers in the 1970s developed a sport version of its family sedan. The new version was equipped with a small V-8 engine and other performance improvements. The car was called the Pirouette, because of its graceful appearance and performance. Unfortunately, there was a difficulty in servicing the vehicle. The engine was too large for the space available, and it had to be moved slightly on the engine mounts in order for one of the spark plugs to be changed.

Required   Comment on the strategic competitive advantage of the Pirouette. What type of management technique was likely used in its design? What type of design approach should have been used?

2-24   STRATEGIC ANALYSIS   Jim Hargreave's lifelong hobby has been racing small sailboats. Jim has been successful both at the sport and in the design of new pieces of equipment to be used on small sailboats to make them easier to sail and more effective in racing. Jim is now thinking about starting a mail-order business in his garage to sell products he favors, as well as some he has designed himself. He plans to contract out most of the manufacturing for the parts and equipment to machine shops and other small manufacturers in his area.

Required   Develop a strategic analysis for Jim's new business plan. What should be his competitive position; that is, how should he choose to compete in the existing market for sailboat supplies and equipment? How is he likely to use cost management information in building his business?

2-25 THE BALANCED SCORECARD   Refer to the description of the Connor Valve Company in the chapter, and the operating data and scorecard results for the firm in Exhibit 2–11.

Required

1. Study the scorecard results in panel B of Exhibit 2–11. Using the operating data in panel A of Exhibit 2–11, develop your own scorecard, to replace what is now in panel B. Explain why your scorecard is an improvement over the one in the exhibit.

2. Connor's balanced scorecard in Exhibit 2–11 focuses only on the internal manufacturing processes of the firm. A complete balanced scorecard would also include three other perspectives. What are the three additional perspectives? Develop examples of the types of operating data, financial data, and CSFs that would be used for each of these additional perspectives.

Service

2-26 STRATEGIC ANALYSIS   Consider the following cases, each of which is a consulting client:

1. Performance Bicycles, a mail-order company that supplies bicycles, parts, and bicycling equipment and clothing.

2. The Oxford Omni, a downtown hotel that serves primarily convention and business travelers.

3. The Orange County Public Health Clinic, which is supported by tax revenues of Orange County and public donations.

4. The Harley-Davidson motorcycle company.

5. The Merck pharmaceutical company.

6. St. Sebastian's College, a small, private liberal arts college.

Required   For each client, determine the competitive strategy and the related critical success factors for the organization or firm.

2–27 **STRATEGIC ANALYSIS, THE COMPUTER INDUSTRY**   Compaq Corporation and Hewlett-Packard (HP) are two significant competitors in the computer industry, though they have somewhat different product lines and quite different approaches to competition. Both have a reputation for the highest-quality product and for innovation. However, some important differences exist in the ways they compete. Compaq sustains competitive advantage by developing products with competitive functionality and quality, while maintaining low cost. These products compete directly with those of other manufacturers in basic functionality. In contrast, HP puts the greatest focus on innovation—the products are unique and the features are innovative. These differences lead to differences in manufacturing and marketing practices. Compaq emphasizes low-cost manufacturing, high volume, and relatively few plant locations, while HP has a larger number of small plants and a focus on product development and innovation rather than cost. In research and development, Compaq looks for ways to improve value and lower cost for standard products, while HP spends its R&D dollar on developing new and innovative products. While the product life cycle in both firms is relatively short, that of HP is somewhat shorter. Because HP tends to lead in product development, when competitors catch up, it moves on to new and advanced products.

International

Required

1. Identify and describe the competitive strategies of HP and Compaq using Porter's framework.

2. Using Exhibit 2–13, which shows the value chain for the computer-manufacturing industry, identify where HP and Compaq fit in the industry. Which steps of the value chain are most important to HP? To Compaq?

3. How would your answer in requirement 2 differ if you were to assume that HP and Compaq operated exclusively in one country, the United States? What does your answer say about the importance of global issues in competitive analysis?

2–28 **STRATEGIC ANALYSIS, THE CAMERA INDUSTRY**   Olympus, Nikon, Canon, and other firms in the market for low-cost cameras have experienced significant changes in recent years. The rate of introduction of new products has increased significantly. Entirely new products, such as the digital camera, are coming down in cost, so they are likely to be a factor in the low-cost segment of the market in the coming years. Additionally, product life cycles have fallen from several years to several months. The new products in this market are introduced at the same price as the products they replace, but the new products have some significant advance in functionality—such as integrated flash, zoom lens, and "red eye" reduction. Thus, there are price points at which the customer expects to purchase a camera of a given functionality. In effect, the camera manufacturers compete to supply distinctive and therefore competitive functionality at the same cost as that of the previous models.

Strategy

The manufacturing process for Olympus, one of the key firms in the industry, is representative of the others. Olympus makes extensive use of suppliers for components of the camera. The quality of the parts is assured by working closely with the suppliers, not only in a supplier's manufacturing process, but also in the supplier's design of the parts. Each supplier is, in effect, part of a team that includes the other suppliers and Olympus's own design and manufacturing operations.

Required

1. How does this type of competition differ from the Porter framework of cost leadership, differentiation, and focus?

2. Develop a value chain for Olympus camera company. What are the opportunities for cost reduction and/or value enhancement for Olympus?

Strategy

2–29 STRATEGIC ANALYSIS, THE BALANCED SCORECARD, AND VALUE-CHAIN ANALYSIS; THE PACKAGING INDUSTRY Dana Packaging Company is a large producer of paper and coated-paper containers, with sales worldwide. The market for Dana's products has become very competitive in recent years, because of the entrance of two large European competitors. In response, Dana has decided to enter new markets where the competition is less severe. The new markets are principally the high end of the packaging business—products that require greater technological sophistication and better materials. These more advanced products are used by the food and consumer products companies that are the customers of Dana, to enhance the appeal of their high-end products. In particular, more sturdy, more colorful and attractive, and better-sealing packaging has some appeal in the gourmet food business, especially in coffees, baked goods, and some dairy products. As a consequence of the shift, Dana has had to reorient its factory to produce the smaller batches of product that are associated with this new line of business. This change has required additional training for plant personnel and some upgrading of factory equipment to reduce setup time.

The manufacturing process for Dana starts with pulp paper, which is produced in Dana's own mills around the world. Some of the pulp material is purchased from recycling operators, when price and availability are favorable. The pulp paper is then converted into paperboard, which is produced at Dana's own plants or purchased at times from outside vendors. In most cases, the paperboard plants are located near the pulp mills. At this point in the manufacturing process, the paperboard might be coated with a plastic material, a special embossing, or some other feature. This process is done at separate plants owned by Dana. On occasion, but infrequently, the coating and embossing process is outsourced to other manufacturers, when Dana's plants are very busy. The final step in the process is the filling of the containers with the food product or consumer product. This step is done exclusively in plants owned by Dana. Dana has tried to maintain a very good reputation for the quality of the filling process, stressing safety, cleanliness, and low cost to its customers.

Required

1. Develop a value chain for Dana Company. What are the opportunities for cost reduction and/or value enhancement for Dana?

2. Evaluate Dana's new strategic competitive position.

3. Dana's management is considering a balanced scorecard for the firm. For each of the four areas within the balanced scorecard, list two or three examples of measurable critical success factors that should be included.

Service

2–30 VALUE-CHAIN ANALYSIS

Required Develop a value chain for the airline industry. Show the analysis in appropriate graphical form. Identify areas wherein any given airline might find a cost advantage by modifying the value chain in some way. Similarly, identify areas of the value chain where the airline might be able to develop additional value for the airline customer. For example, consider in what ways the ticketing operation might be reconfigured for either cost or value-added advantage.

2–31 VALUE-CHAIN ANALYSIS, IDENTIFYING FIRMS

Required For the airline value chain developed in problem 2–30, identify two or three firms currently or previously operating in the industry and locate them on the value chain. Do they operate at each step in the value chain? To the best of your knowledge, how do they differ in terms of cost and service at each of the steps in the chain?

2–32 VALUE-CHAIN ANALYSIS, COST MANAGEMENT REPORTS

Required For the airline value chain discussed in problems 2–30 and 2–31 above, determine the proper role of cost management for a firm in this industry. What types of information should the management accountant report to airline management?

2–33 VALUE-CHAIN ANALYSIS Sheldon Radio manufactures yacht radios, navigational equipment, and depth-sounding and related equipment from a small plant near Raleigh–Durham, North Carolina. One of Sheldon's most popular products, making up 40 percent of its revenues and 35 percent of its profits, is a marine radio, model VF4500, which is installed on many of the new large boats produced in the United States. Average production and sales are 500 units per month. Sheldon has achieved its success in the market through excellent customer service and product reliability. The manufacturing process consists primarily of assembly of components purchased from various electronics firms, plus a small amount of metalworking and finishing. The manufacturing operations cost $110 per unit. The purchased parts cost Sheldon $250, of which $130 is for parts that Sheldon could manufacture in its existing facility for $80 in materials for each unit, plus an investment in labor and equipment that would cost $35,000 per month.

Sheldon is considering outsourcing to another Raleigh firm, Brashear Enterprises, the marketing, distribution, and servicing for its units. This would save Sheldon $125,000 in monthly materials and labor costs. The cost of the contract would be $105 per radio.

Required

1. Prepare a value-chain analysis for Sheldon to assist in the decision whether to purchase or manufacture the parts, and whether to contract out the marketing, distribution, and servicing of the units.

2. Should Sheldon (a) continue to purchase the parts or manufacture them, and (b) continue to provide the marketing, distribution, and service, or outsource this activity to Brashear? Explain your answer.

SOLUTIONS TO SELF-STUDY PROBLEMS

1. Value-Chain Analysis

The cost figures Jack has assembled suggest that the two teams' operations are generally quite similar, as one would expect in AA baseball. However, an important difference is the amount the Durham team spends on game-day operations—more than three times that of the Greensboro Bulls. That difference has, in part, built a loyal set of fans in Durham, where gate receipts average more than twice that of Greensboro ($28,500 versus $12,350). It appears that the Buffaloes have found an effective way to compete—by drawing attendance to special game-day events and promotions.

To begin to compete more effectively and profitably, Greensboro might consider additional value-added services, such as game-day activities similar to those offered in Durham. While Greensboro's costs per person are somewhat lower than Durham's, the cost savings are not enough to offset the loss in revenues.

On the cost side, the comparison with Durham shows little immediate promise for cost reduction; Greensboro spends on the average less than Durham in every

53

category except management compensation. Perhaps this is a further indication that instead of reducing costs, Greensboro should spend *more* on fan development. The next step in Jack's analysis might be to survey Greensboro fans to determine the level of satisfaction and to identify desired services that are not currently provided.

2. Competitive Strategy, Ethics

1. Enviro-Wear's strategy to this point is best described as the differentiation strategy, wherein Frank has been able to succeed by differentiating his products as environmentally sound. This approach has appealed to a sufficient number of customers of sportswear, and Enviro-Wear has grown accordingly. However, given the unfortunate jokes made by the sales manager and the rumors, the differentiation strategy is unlikely to continue to work; the offense of the jokes and the disclosure of some discrepancies in the manufacturing methods will undermine the appeal of environmentally sound manufacturing. Frank will have to work quickly to maintain differentiation, perhaps through a quick response that effectively shows the firm's commitment to quality and environmental issues. If that fails, Frank should quickly decide what change in strategy will be necessary for his firm to survive and continue to succeed. Frank should consider a new strategy, perhaps based on cost leadership or competitive focus. The cost leadership strategy would bring Frank into competition with different types of firms, and the question for Frank would be whether his firm could successfully compete in that type of market.

2. There are a number of ethical issues in the case, which are especially important to Frank as a CPA with previous experience in public accounting practice, where ethics are very important. Frank should try to identify and understand the different options and the ethical aspects of the consequences of those options. For example, should Frank deny all charges against the company? Should he undertake an investigation to determine what his other sales managers think (do they have the same view as the offensive sales manager)? Do the manufacturing processes of the firm really live up to the claimed quality and environmental standards? The relevant ethical issue requires communicating unfavorable as well as favorable information and disclosing fully all relevant information that could reasonably be expected to influence a consumer's understanding of the situation. To disguise or mislead consumers and others would be in conflict with the professional standards Frank is very familiar with.

Also at issue is whether it is appropriate to fire the offensive sales manager. Most would probably agree that the firing is appropriate, since the sales manager has publicly put himself at odds with the strategic goals of the firm. However, others might want to consider the consequences of the firing and its fairness to the employee.

3

Cost Drivers and Basic Cost Concepts

After studying this chapter, you should be able to . . .

1 Explain the cost driver concepts at the activity, volume, structural, and executional levels

2 Explain the cost concepts used in product and service costing

3 Demonstrate how costs flow through the accounts

4 Prepare an income statement for both a manufacturing firm and a merchandising firm

5 Explain the cost concepts related to the use of cost information in planning and decision making

6 Explain the cost concepts related to the use of cost information for management and operational control

© Tony Freeman/Photo Edit.

> When asked the difference between a fixed and a variable cost, one
> worker replied, "A fixed cost? If it's broke, I fix it and it costs me."
> R. SUSKIND, *WALL STREET JOURNAL*, FEBRUARY 26, 1992, P. B1

As suggested in the story above, a number of cost management concepts are not
well understood. For example, the definition of *fixed cost* is based not on the need
for repair jobs, but on the behavior of total cost in response to changes in output
levels. This chapter explains the cost concepts that relate to each of the four management functions: (1) strategic management, (2) planning and decision making,
(3) product and service costing for preparing financial statements, and (4) management and operational control.[1]

◀ **LEARNING OBJECTIVE 1**
Explain the cost driver
concepts at the activity,
volume, structural, and
executional levels.

COST DRIVER CONCEPTS FOR STRATEGIC MANAGEMENT

A critical first step for achieving a competitive advantage is to identify the key cost
drivers in the firm or organization. A cost driver is any factor that has the effect of
changing the level of total cost. For a firm that competes on the basis of cost leadership, the management of the key cost drivers is essential. For example, to achieve
its low-cost leadership in manufacturing electronic products, Texas Instruments
watches carefully the design and manufacturing factors that drive the costs in its
products. Design improvements are made when necessary, and the manufacturing
plants are designed and automated for the highest efficiency of use of materials,
labor, and equipment. For firms that are not cost leaders, the management of cost
drivers may not be as critical, but attention to the key cost drivers contributes
directly to the success of the firm. For example, an important cost driver for retailers is loss and damage to merchandise. So most retailers have careful procedures for
handling, displaying, and storing merchandise.

Cost Drivers, Cost Pools, and Cost Objects

A **cost** is incurred when a resource is used for some purpose. For example, a company producing kitchen appliances has costs of materials (such as sheet metal and
bolts for the enclosure), costs of manufacturing labor, and other costs. Sometimes
costs are collected into meaningful groups called **cost pools.** There are many

A **cost** is incurred when a
resource is used for some
purpose.

Costs are sometimes
collected into meaningful
groups, called **cost pools**.

BusinessWeek

Does More Mean Less for Procter & Gamble?

Procter & Gamble Co. (P & G), one of the world's largest manufacturers of consumer
products, finds that in manufacturing and marketing, life has become quite complex. On
today's store shelf, there are now 31 varieties of Head & Shoulders shampoo, and 52
versions of Crest (one for every week in the year!). In addition, there are a variety of trade
promotions, including discounts, rebates, and coupons, and large product turnover, with
new products being added and others deleted each year. The practice of identifying and
moving quickly to satisfy consumer wants has led to a proliferation of products and
marketing practices.

Q: How does this complex environment affect costs and
profitability, and what is Procter & Gamble doing about it?

Find out on page 67 of this chapter.

---

[1]   Useful information on cost terms is also available in the IMA's Statement on Management Accounting
No. 2, "Management Accounting Terminology," Institute of Management Accountants, Montvale, N.J.,
June 1, 1983.

different ways to group the individual costs, and therefore many different ways to define a cost pool, including by type of cost (labor costs in one pool, material costs in another), by source (department 1, department 2, and so on), or by responsibility (manager 1, manager 2, and so on). For example, an assembly department or a product engineering department might be treated as a cost pool.

A cost object is any product, service, or organizational unit to which costs are assigned for some management purpose. Products and services are generally cost objects, while manufacturing departments are considered either cost pools or cost objects, depending on whether management's main focus is on the costs for the products or for the manufacturing departments. The concept of cost objects is a broad concept. It includes not only products, services, and departments, but also groups of products, services, and departments; customers; suppliers; telephone service providers; and so on. Any item to which costs can be traced and that has a key role in management strategy can be considered a cost object.

Cost Assignment and Cost Allocation: Direct and Indirect Costs

Cost assignment is the process of assigning costs to cost pools, or from cost pools to cost objects. A **direct cost** can be conveniently and economically traced directly to a cost pool or a cost object. For example, the cost of materials required for a particular product is a direct cost because it can be traced directly to the product. Also, an airline's cost of preparing and processing a traveler's airline ticket is a direct cost of the service provided that customer.

In contrast, with an **indirect cost,** there is no convenient or economical trace from the cost or cost pool to the cost pool or cost object. That is, the indirect cost is caused by two or more cost pools or objects and cannot be conveniently or economically traced directly to any one. The cost of supervising manufacturing employees and the cost of handling materials are good examples of costs that generally cannot be traced to individual products, and are therefore indirect costs for the products. Similarly, the cost of fueling an aircraft is an indirect cost when the cost object is the individual airline customer, since the aircraft's use of fuel cannot be traced directly to that customer. In contrast, if the cost object for the airline is the flight, then the cost of fuel is a direct cost that can be traced directly to the aircraft's use of fuel for that flight.

Since indirect costs cannot be traced to the cost pool or cost object, the assignment for indirect costs is done by using cost drivers. For example, if the cost driver for materials handling cost is the number of parts, then the total cost of materials handling can be assigned to each product on the basis of its total number of parts relative to the total number of parts in all other products. The result is that costs are assigned to the cost pool or cost object that caused the cost in a manner that is fairly representative of the way the cost is incurred. For example, a product with a large number of parts should bear a larger portion of the cost of materials handling than a product with fewer parts. Similarly, a department with a large number of employees should bear a large portion of the cost of supervision provided for all departments.

The assignment of indirect costs to cost pools and cost objects is called **cost allocation,** a form of cost assignment in which direct tracing is not possible, so cost drivers are used instead. The cost drivers used to allocate costs are often called **allocation bases.** The relationships between costs, cost pools, cost objects, and cost drivers are illustrated in Exhibit 3–1 and Exhibit 3–2, for the case of appliance manufacturing. This simplified example includes two cost objects (dishwasher, washing machine), two cost pools (assembly department, packing department), and five cost elements (electric motor, materials handling, supervision, packing material, and final inspection of the product). The electric motor is traced to the assembly department, and from there, directly to the two products. Similarly, the packing material is traced directly to the packing department, and from there, directly to the two products. In contrast, since there is no cost pool for it, the cost of final inspection is traced directly to each of the two prod-

---

Sidebar notes:

Cost assignment is the process of assigning costs to cost pools, or from cost pools to cost objects.

A **direct cost** can be conveniently and economically traced directly to a cost pool or a cost object.

An **indirect cost** has *no* convenient or economical trace from the cost or cost pool to the cost pool or cost object.

The assignment of indirect costs to cost pools and cost objects is called **cost allocation.**

The cost drivers used to allocate costs are often called **allocation bases.**

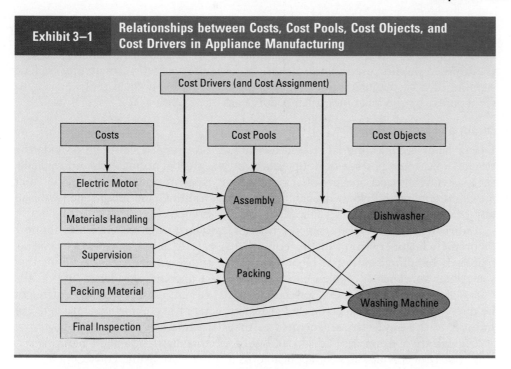

Exhibit 3–1 Relationships between Costs, Cost Pools, Cost Objects, and Cost Drivers in Appliance Manufacturing

Exhibit 3–2 Selected Examples of Costs, Cost Pools, Cost Objects, and Cost Drivers in Appliance Manufacturing

Cost	Cost Driver	Cost Pool	Cost Driver	Cost Object
Direct Costs				
Electric motor	Direct trace	Assembly department	Direct trace	Dishwasher and washing machine
Packing material	Direct trace	Packing department	Direct trace	Dishwasher and washing machine
Final inspection	Direct trace	Not applicable	Not applicable	Dishwasher and washing machine
Indirect Costs				
Supervision	Allocation base: number of employees in the department	Assembly and packing departments	Allocation base: direct labor-hours for each product	Dishwasher and washing machine
Materials handling	Allocation base: number of parts in the product	Assembly and packing departments	Allocation base: number of parts in the product	Dishwasher and washing machine

ucts. The two indirect costs, supervision and materials handling, are allocated to the two cost pools (assembly and packing departments) and are then allocated from the cost pools to the products (the allocation bases are shown in Exhibit 3–2).

Direct and Indirect Materials

Direct materials include the cost of materials in the product or other cost object (less purchase discounts but including freight and related charges) and usually a reasonable allowance for scrap and defective units (e.g., if a part is stamped from strip

Direct materials include the cost of the materials in the product and a reasonable allowance for scrap and defective units.

steel, the material lost in the stamping is ordinarily included as part of the direct materials of the product).[2]

On the other hand, the cost of materials used in manufacturing that are not in the finished product are **indirect materials.** Examples of indirect materials include supplies used by manufacturing employees, such as rags and small tools, or materials required by the machines, such as lubricant.[3]

The cost of materials used in manufacturing that are not physically part of the finished product are **indirect materials.**

Direct and Indirect Labor

Direct labor includes the labor used to manufacture the product or to provide the service, plus some portion of nonproductive time that is normal and unavoidable, such as coffee breaks and personal time. Other types of nonproductive labor that are discretionary and planned, such as downtime, training, and setup time, will usually be included not as direct labor, but as indirect labor.[4]

Direct labor includes the labor used to manufacture the product or to provide the service.

Indirect labor provides a support role for manufacturing. Examples of indirect labor include supervision, quality control, inspection, purchasing and receiving, materials handling, janitorial labor, downtime, training, and cleanup. Note that sometimes an element of labor can be both direct and indirect depending on the cost object; for example, labor for the maintenance and repair of equipment might be direct to a given manufacturing department where the equipment is located, but indirect to the products manufactured in that department.

Indirect labor includes supervision, quality control, inspection, purchasing and receiving, and other manufacturing support costs.

Though these examples of direct and indirect costs are from a manufacturing setting, the concepts are equally applicable to a service company. For example, in a restaurant where the cost object is each meal served, the food and food preparation costs are direct costs, while the costs of purchasing, handling, and storing food items are indirect costs. Similarly, in professional services firms such as law firms or accounting firms, the professional labor and materials costs for providing client service are direct costs, while the cost of research materials, the cost of nonprofessional support staff, and the cost of training professional staff are indirect costs.

Other Indirect Costs

In addition to labor and materials, other types of indirect costs are necessary for manufacturing the product or providing the service. They include the facilities costs, the equipment used in manufacturing the product or providing the service, and any other support equipment, such as that used for materials handling.

All the indirect costs—indirect materials, indirect labor, and other indirect costs—are commonly combined into a single cost pool called **overhead.** In a manufacturing firm, it is called **factory overhead.**

All the indirect costs are commonly combined into a single cost pool called **overhead** or, in a manufacturing firm, **factory overhead.**

The three types of costs—direct materials, direct labor, and overhead—are sometimes combined for simplicity and convenience. Direct materials and direct labor are sometimes considered together and called **prime costs.** Similarly, direct labor and overhead are often combined into a single amount, which is called **conversion cost.** For many firms that have highly automated operations, the labor component of total manufacturing costs is relatively low, and these firms often choose to place their strategic focus on materials and facilities/overhead costs by combining labor costs with overhead.

Direct materials and direct labor are sometimes considered together and called **prime costs.**

Direct labor and overhead are often combined into a single amount, which is called **conversion cost.**

Types of Cost Drivers

Most firms, especially those following the cost leadership strategy, use cost management to maintain or improve their competitive position. Cost management requires

---

[2] For additional information about the nature of direct materials cost, see Statement on Management Accounting No. 4E, "Practices and Techniques: Definition and Measurement of Direct Material Cost," Institute of Management Accountants, Montvale, N.J., June 3, 1986.

[3] For cost-benefit reasons, those direct materials that are a very small part of materials cost, such as glue and nails, are sometimes not traced to each product but included instead in indirect materials.

[4] For additional information about the nature of direct labor cost, see Statement on Management Accounting No. 4C, "Practices and Techniques: Definition and Measurement of Direct Labor Cost," Institute of Management Accounts, Montvale, N.J., June 13, 1985.

Military Downsizing and Direct vs. Indirect Costs

The determination of whether a cost is direct or indirect can be critical in some situations, as for example, in the case of a contractor supplying a product for the U.S. government when, because of budget problems or other reasons, the contract is canceled. The costs that are direct costs for the contract are reimbursable, but what about the indirect costs? Indirect costs can be a problem when contracts are terminated because established cost assignment procedures are no longer appropriate.

To understand the problem, consider this typical case. A contractor enters into a multiyear, fixed-price development contract with the military. The job calls for a significant investment in test equipment that is to be used only for the military contract. However, equipment cost is not treated as direct because governmental cost standards require depreciation costs of all similar assets to be treated consistently, either as direct or indirect costs, and thus the inspection equipment must be treated as an indirect cost. Since the equipment is an indirect cost, the cost will not be fully recovered until the project is completed, and if the contract is terminated early, only a portion of the cost of the inspection equipment can be recovered.

In recognition of this problem, and of the large number of contract appeals it has caused, the various federal boards of contract appeals have ruled in favor of treating certain indirect costs as direct costs in situations such as these:

1. In an appeal filed by Fiesta Leasing & Sales, Inc., the board allowed depreciation on buses purchased for a bus leasing contract when the Defense Department terminated the contract. The board allowed depreciation costs because the costs were incurred for the contract and because these costs could not be discontinued after the contract was terminated.

2. In an appeal brought by Essex Electric Engineers, Inc., the Department of Transportation (DOT) Contract Appeals Board allowed recovery of the full cost of equipment remaining at a plant when the contract was terminated for the convenience of the DOT. The reason for the ruling is that the equipment purchased by Essex for the DOT contract was far beyond its needs for its other business.

Source: Based on information from Margaret M. Worthington, "As Military Downsizes, Contract Termination Becomes a Challenge," *Journal of Accountancy,* March 1992, pp. 88–90.

a good understanding of how the total cost of a cost object changes as the cost drivers change. There are four ways to describe how costs change, that is, four types of cost drivers—activity-based, volume-based, structural, and executional cost drivers. Activity-based cost drivers are developed at a detailed level of operations and are associated with a given manufacturing activity (or activity in providing a service), such as machine setup, product inspection, materials handling, or packaging. In contrast, volume-based cost drivers are developed at an aggregate level, such as an output level—the number of units of product produced or the number of direct labor-hours used in manufacturing. An important difference between volume-based and activity-based cost drivers is that volume-based cost drivers are often developed at a very aggregated level, such as total output or total labor-hours, while activity-based measures are generally developed at a detailed level of analysis—at the activity level, sometimes involving an individual machine or work unit. Structural and executional cost drivers involve strategic and operational decisions that affect the relationship between the cost drivers and total cost.

Activity-Based Cost Drivers

Activity-based cost drivers are identified by using activity analysis, a detailed description of the specific activities performed in the operations of the firm. The description includes each of the steps in the manufacture of the product or in providing the service. And, for each activity, a cost driver is developed to explain how the costs incurred for that activity change. For example, the activities and cost drivers for a hospital are illustrated in Exhibit 3–3. Note how the analysis lists each activity in the treatment of the patient from start (schedule the patient) to finish (bill insurance). The total cost to the hospital is affected by the cost driver for each of the activities.

The detailed description of the firm's activities helps the firm achieve its strategic objectives by helping the firm develop more accurate costs for its products and/or services. Also, the activity analysis helps improve operational and management control in the firm, since performance at the detailed level can be monitored and evaluated, for example, by (1) identifying which activities are contributing value to the

Exhibit 3–3	Activities and Cost Drivers in a Hospital

	Activity	Cost Driver
1	Schedule patient.	Number of patients scheduled
2	Verify insurance.	Number of verifications
3	Admit patient.	Number of admissions
4	Prepare patient's room.	Number of preparations
5	Review doctor's report.	Number of reviews
6	Feed patient.	Number of meals
7	Order tests.	Number of orders (*not* number of tests)
8	Move to/from laboratory.	Number of moves
9	Administer lab tests.	Number of tests
10	Order pharmaceuticals.	Number of orders (*not* number of pharmaceuticals)
11	Complete patient report.	Number of reports
12	Check patient's vital signs.	Number of checks
13	Prepare patient for operation.	Number of preparations
14	Move to/from operating room.	Number of moves
15	Perform operation.	Number of operating room procedures employed; measures of complexity of the operation
16	Collect charges.	Number of charges to the patient
17	Discharge patient.	Number of discharges
18	Bill insurance.	Number of billings

Source: Based on information from James A. Brimson and John Altos, *Activity-Based Management for Service Industries, Government Entities and Nonprofit Organizations* (New York: Wiley, 1994), pp. 328–329.

Exhibit 3–4	Total Cost and the Effect of Capacity Limits

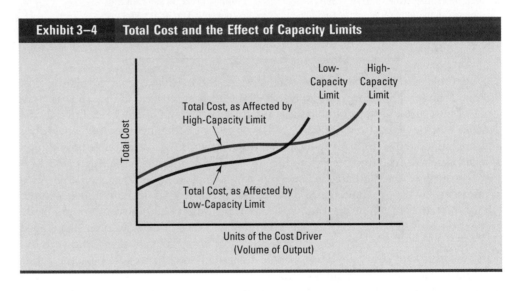

customer and which are not, and (2) focusing attention on those activities that are most costly or differ the most from expectations. These two benefits are achieved by activity-based costing and activity-based management, which are explained in the following chapter.

Volume-Based Cost Drivers

Many types of costs are volume-based, such as direct materials and direct labor. Total cost for a volume-based cost has a nonlinear relationship with the volume-based cost driver, the number of units of output for the product or service. As illustrated in Exhibit 3–4, at low values for the cost driver, costs increase at a decreasing rate, due in part to factors such as more efficient use of resources and higher productivity through learning. The pattern of increasing costs at a decreasing rate is often referred to as increasing marginal productivity, which means that the inputs are used more productively or more efficiently as manufacturing increases.

At higher levels of the cost driver, costs begin to increase at an increasing rate, due in part to inefficiency associated with operating nearer the limit of capacity—the less efficient resources are now being used, overtime may be required, and so on. This cost behavior in the higher levels of the cost driver is said to satisfy the

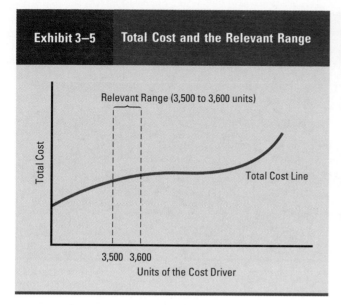

Exhibit 3–5   Total Cost and the Relevant Range

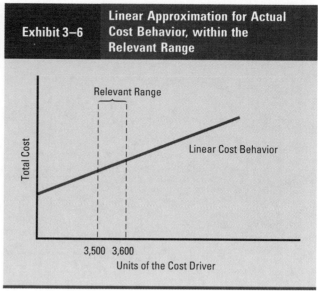

Exhibit 3–6   Linear Approximation for Actual Cost Behavior, within the Relevant Range

law of diminishing marginal productivity. When a company faces these increasing costs, it will very often add capacity, and an entirely different cost curve will arise. The new cost curve based on higher capacity will have unit costs increasing at a higher level of the cost driver.

The nonlinear cost relationships depicted in Exhibit 3–4 present some difficulties in estimating costs and in calculating total costs, since linear, algebraic relationships cannot be used. Fortunately, we are often interested in only a relatively small range of activity for the cost driver. For example, we might know in a certain instance that the *volume-based* cost driver will fall somewhere between 3,500 units and 3,600 units of product output. And we observe that within this range the total cost curve is approximately linear. The range of the cost driver in which the actual value of the cost driver is expected to fall, and for which the relationship is assumed to be approximately linear, is called the **relevant range.**

This simplification process is illustrated in Exhibit 3–5 and Exhibit 3–6. Exhibit 3–5 shows the curved actual total cost line and the relevant range of 3,500 to 3,600 units; Exhibit 3–6 shows the linear approximation of actual total cost—within the relevant range the behavior of total cost approximates that shown in Exhibit 3–5.

Fixed and Variable Costs

Total cost is made up of a portion that is variable cost and a portion that is fixed cost. **Variable cost** is the change in total cost associated with each change in the quantity of the cost driver. In contrast, **fixed cost** is that portion of the total cost that does not change with a change in the quantity of the cost driver, within the relevant range. *Total* fixed costs and *unit* variable cost are expected to remain approximately constant within the relevant range. Fixed cost is illustrated as the horizontal line at $3,000 in Exhibit 3–7. Variable cost is $1 per unit, total cost is the upward-sloping line, and total variable cost is the difference between total cost and fixed cost. Total cost of $6,500 at 3,500 units is made up of fixed cost ($3,000) plus total variable cost (3,500 × $1 = $3,500); similarly, total cost at 3,600 units is $6,600 ($3,000 fixed cost plus 3,600 × $1 = $3,600 variable cost).

Common examples of variable costs are direct materials and direct labor. Fixed costs include many of the indirect costs, especially facility costs (depreciation or rent, insurance, taxes on the plant building, and so on), production supervisors' salaries, and other manufacturing support costs that do not change with the number of units produced. However, some of the indirect costs are variable, since they change with the number of units produced. An example is lubricant for machines. The term **mixed cost** is used to refer to total cost when total cost includes both variable and fixed components, as illustrated above.

The determination of whether a cost is variable depends on the nature of the cost object. In manufacturing firms, the cost object is typically the product. In

The range of the cost driver in which the actual value of the cost driver is expected to fall, and for which the relationship is assumed to be approximately linear, is called the **relevant range.**

Variable cost is the change in total cost associated with each change in the quantity of the cost driver.

Fixed cost is that portion of the total cost that does not change with a change in the quantity of the cost driver, within the relevant range.

Mixed cost is the term used to refer to total cost when total cost includes both variable and fixed cost components.

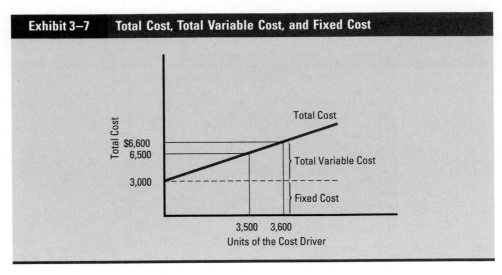

Exhibit 3–7   Total Cost, Total Variable Cost, and Fixed Cost

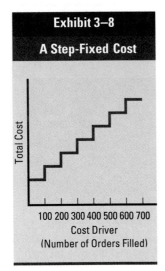

Exhibit 3–8

A Step-Fixed Cost

A cost is said to be **step-fixed** when it varies with the cost driver, but in discrete steps.

service firms, however, the cost object is often hard to define, because the service may have a number of qualitative as well as quantitative dimensions. Consider education, and in particular, a single course offering. How is the cost object defined? Is it the student who receives course credit? Is it each class meeting? Or is it the section offered? Also, is the focus on the university's costs, or the student's costs, or on both? Each of the above definitions for the cost object could be useful, but there will be significant differences in what is considered variable and fixed cost. The choice of cost object will determine how to properly classify the cost of the textbook, the costs for maintaining the classroom, and the instructor's salary.

It is important to understand that the distinction between variable and fixed cost is *not* affected by the passage of time. While it is true that many fixed costs do change over time (for example, the cost of rent might increase from year to year), that does not mean these costs are variable. Strictly interpreted, a variable cost is a total cost that changes *only as a function of changes in the level of a cost driver.*[5]

Step-Fixed Costs

A cost is said to be **step-fixed** when it varies with the cost driver, but does so in discrete steps (Exhibit 3–8). Step-fixed costs are characteristic of certain clerical tasks, such as order filling and claims processing. For example, if a warehouse clerk can fill 100 orders in a day, then 10 clerks will be needed to process approximately 1,000 orders; as demand exceeds 1,000 orders, an eleventh clerk must be added. The steps correspond to specific levels of the cost driver for which an additional clerk is required, so, in effect, each step corresponds to 1 additional clerk. The steps will be relatively narrow if clerks are added for relatively small increases in the cost driver; for large increases, steps will be wider.

The management accountant's determination of whether a cost should be treated as a variable, fixed, or step-fixed cost is based on a consideration of how the choice will affect the use of the information.

Unit cost (or average cost) is the total of manufacturing costs (materials, labor, and overhead) divided by units of output.

Unit Cost and Marginal Cost

Unit cost (or **average cost**) is the total of manufacturing costs (materials, labor, and overhead) divided by units of output. It is a useful concept in setting prices and in evaluating

Illustration of Per-Unit and Total Fixed Cost and Variable Cost

	Units of Output	
	10,000	20,000
Fixed Cost		
Per unit	$ 10	$ 5
Total	$100,000	$100,000
Variable Cost		
Per unit	$ 8	$ 8
Total	$80,000	$160,000

---

5   While fixed costs do not vary over time, they become differential over time, as explained later in this chapter.

Survey of Practice: Cost Classification in U.S. Firms

A survey of 350 U.S. manufacturing firms provides the following results regarding how these firms treat selected indirect cost categories (the data show the percentage of the firms treating each type of indirect cost as a variable, step-fixed, or fixed cost).

Activity	Variable	Step-Fixed	Fixed	Other
Setup labor	49	20	12	19
Material handling labor	40	29	15	16
Quality control labor	28	30	25	17
Repairs and maintenance	23	36	24	17
Tooling	24	27	25	24
Energy	21	36	23	20
Supervision	3	22	58	17
Engineering	5	18	61	16
Data processing	2	12	69	17
Building occupancy	1	5	77	17
Taxes and insurance	1	9	74	16
Depreciation—machinery and equipment	1	6	78	15
Work-in-process inventory carrying cost	19	25	24	32

Source: Il-Woon Kim and Ja Song, "Accounting Practices in Three Countries," *Management Accounting,* August 1990, p. 28.

product profitability, but it can be subject to some misleading interpretations. To properly interpret unit cost, we must distinguish *unit variable* costs, which do not change as output changes, from *unit fixed* costs, which do change as output changes. For example, if total fixed costs are $100,000 and the output level is 20,000 units, then average fixed cost is $5; if the output is 10,000 units, then average fixed cost is $10. In contrast, if the per-unit variable cost is $8 at the 10,000 unit level, it will also be $8 at the 20,000 unit level. Because fixed cost does not change with the output level, average fixed cost and average total cost cannot be interpreted without knowing the output level. For example, a driver's cost per mile will likely be lower for a person who keeps a car for 200,000 miles than for a person who keeps a car for only 40,000 miles, because the fixed costs are spread over a greater number of miles. These relationships are illustrated graphically in Exhibit 3–9. The management accountant is careful in using the terms *average cost* and *unit cost* because of the potential for misleading interpretations.

The term **marginal cost** is used to describe the additional cost incurred as the cost driver increases by one unit. Under the assumption of linear cost within the relevant range, the concept of marginal cost is equivalent to the concept of unit variable cost.

Marginal cost is the additional cost incurred as the cost driver increases by one unit.

Structural and Executional Cost Drivers

Structural and executional cost drivers are used to facilitate strategic and operational decision making.[6] **Structural cost drivers** are strategic in nature because they involve plans and decisions that have long-term effects. Issues such as the following are considered:

1. **Scale.** How much should be invested? How large should the firm become? Larger firms have lower overall costs as a result of economies of scale. For example,

Structural cost drivers are strategic in nature and involve plans and decisions that have a long-term effect with regard to issues such as scale, experience, technology, and complexity.

---

[6] See John K. Shank and Vijay Govindarajan, *Strategic Cost Analysis* (New York: Free Press, 1993), pp. 20–22. Also see D. Riley, "Competitive Cost Based Investment Strategies for Industrial Companies," *Manufacturing Issues* (New York: Booz, Allen, Hamilton, 1987).

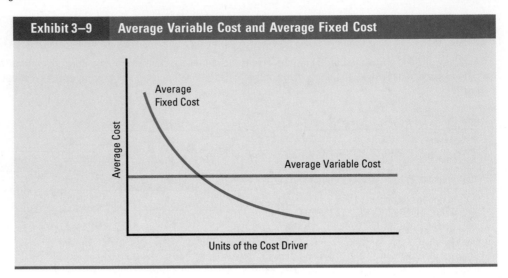

Exhibit 3–9   Average Variable Cost and Average Fixed Cost

a retail firm such as Wal-Mart must determine how many new stores it should open in a given year to achieve its strategic objectives and compete effectively as a retailer.

   2. **Experience.** How much prior experience does the firm have in its current and planned products and services? The more experience, the lower the development, manufacturing, and distribution costs are likely to be. For example, a manufacturer such as Hewlett-Packard uses existing manufacturing methods as much as possible for new products in order to reduce the time and cost necessary for workers to become proficient at manufacturing the new product. Additionally, health care management firms such as Columbia/HCA use their knowledge of experience-related cost drivers to reduce the time and cost necessary to improve the profitability of newly acquired hospitals.

   3. **Technology.** What process technologies are used in the manufacturing and distribution of the product or service? New technologies can reduce these costs significantly. For example, manufacturers such as Procter & Gamble use computer technology to monitor the quantities of its products its customers (typically, large retailers) have on hand so that it can promptly restock these products as needed.

   4. **Complexity.** How many different products does the firm have? Firms with many products have higher costs of scheduling and managing the production process, as well as the upstream costs of product development and the downstream costs of distribution and service. These firms often use activity-based costing to better identify the accurate costs and therefore the profitability of its different products, suppliers, and customers.

   Strategic analyses using structural cost drivers help the firm improve its competitive position. These analyses include value-chain analysis and activity-based management. Value-chain analysis can help the firm assess the long-term consequences of its current or planned commitment to a structural cost driver. For example, the growth in size and capability of parts manufactures for automakers should cause the automakers to reassess whether the manufacture of certain parts should be outsourced.

   Executional cost drivers are factors the firm can manage in short-term, operational decision making to reduce costs. These include:

   1. **Workforce involvement.** Are the employees dedicated to continual improvement and quality? If the workforce has this commitment, costs will be lower. Firms with strong employee relationships, such as Federal Express, can reduce operating costs significantly.

   2. **Design of the production process.** Can the layout of equipment and processes and the scheduling of production be improved? Speeding up the flow of

Executional cost drivers are factors the firm can manage in the short term to reduce costs, such as workforce involvement, design of the production process, and supplier relationships.

66

BusinessWeek

What's Procter & Gamble's equation for success?
(Continues from page 56)

A: P & G's answer is simple ... simplify!

Like other large consumer products manufacturers, P&G has developed a huge assortment of products of different varieties (size, color, features, etc.), each subject to a variety of marketing promotions (coupons, discounts, rebates, etc.). One shopper in a P&G survey explained in frustration, "There's this vast array of products. A lot of times I end up getting what's on sale." P&G's president, Durk Jager, observed: "It's mind-boggling how difficult we've made it for them (shoppers) over the years."

As importantly, the complexity and variety of the products and marketing methods have been costly for P&G, which is engaged in a program of simplification. Between 1991 and 1996, it cut its total number of items for sale from approximately 3,300 to just over 2,000. Also, packaging is now standardized, and the number of trade promotions reduced. Additionally, marginally profitable brands were identified and deleted, and there are fewer new product launches. These moves to reduce complexity have saved the company millions in advertising, reduced processing costs, and lowered manufacturing costs. Earnings have increased, and the 8.6 percent profit on sales is the highest in 45 years. In addition, consumers have responded positively, with the result being an increase in sales from a 2 percent annual sales increase in 1991 to an almost 6 percent increase in 1996. The message from P&G: simplify and improve your profits.

For further reading, see the following source: "Make it Simple," *Business Week,* September 9, 1996, pp. 96–104.

product through the firm can reduce costs. Innovators in manufacturing technology, such as Motorola and Allen-Bradley, can reduce manufacturing costs significantly.

3. **Supplier relationships.** Can the cost, quality, or delivery of materials and purchased parts be improved? Improvements here can reduce overall costs. Wal-Mart and Toyota, among other firms, are able to maintain a low-cost advantage in part by agreements with suppliers that have explicit requirements for quality, timeliness of delivery, and other features of the supplied products or parts.

Plant managers study executional cost drivers to find ways to reduce costs. Such studies are done as a part of operational control, which is covered in Part Five.

COST CONCEPTS FOR PRODUCT AND SERVICE COSTING

Accurate information about the cost of products and services is important in each of the management functions—strategic management, planning and decision making, management and operational control, and financial statement preparation. The cost accounting systems to provide this information are explained in this section.

◄ **LEARNING OBJECTIVE 2**
Explain the cost concepts used in product and service costing.

Cost Accounting for Products and Services

Cost accounting systems differ significantly between the firms that manufacture products and the merchandising firms that resell those products. Merchandising firms include both retailers, which sell the final product to the consumer, and wholesalers, which distribute the product to retailers. Service firms often have little or no inventory, so their costing systems are relatively simple.

Product Costs and Period Costs

Product inventory for both manufacturing and merchandising firms is treated as an asset on the firm's balance sheet. As long as the inventory has market value, it is considered an asset until the product is sold; then the cost of the product is transferred

When inventory is sold, the cost of the product is transferred to the income statement as **cost of goods sold**.

Product costs for a manufacturing firm include *only* the costs necessary to complete the product—direct materials, direct labor, and factory overhead.

All nonproduct expenditures for managing the firm and selling the product are called **period costs**.

LEARNING OBJECTIVE 3 ▶
Demonstrate how costs flow through the accounts.

Materials inventory is the store of materials used in the manufacturing process or in providing the service.

Work-in-process inventory accounts for all costs put into manufacture of products that are started but not complete at the financial statement date.

Finished goods inventory is the cost of goods that are ready for sale.

to the income statement as **cost of goods sold,** an expense. This is the life cycle of product cost, from design and manufacture (or purchase and stocking, in the merchandising firm) to sales and service, that is, from asset on the balance sheet to expense on the income statement.

Product costs for a manufacturing firm include *only* the costs necessary to complete the product:

1. Direct materials—the materials used in the manufacture of the product, which become a physical part of the final product.
2. Direct labor—the labor used in the manufacture of the product.
3. Factory overhead—the indirect costs for materials, labor, and facilities used to support the manufacturing process.

Product costs for a merchandising firm include the purchase cost of the product plus the transportation costs paid by the retailer or wholesaler to get the product to the location from which it will be sold or distributed.

All other expenditures for managing the firm and selling the product are expensed as they are incurred, and for that reason they are called **period costs.** These costs are expensed because there is no expectation that they will produce future value; in contrast, the sale of inventory will produce future cash flow. Period costs include primarily the general, selling, and administrative costs that are necessary for the management of the company, but which are *not* involved directly or indirectly in the manufacturing process (or in the purchase of the products for resale). Advertising costs, data processing costs, and executive and staff salaries are good examples of period costs. In a manufacturing or a merchandising firm, period costs are also sometimes referred to as operating expenses or selling and administrative expenses. In a service firm, all these costs will often be referred to as operating expenses.

Manufacturing, Merchandising, and Service Costing

The cost flows in both manufacturing and retail firms are illustrated in Exhibits 3–10a and 3–10b, 3–11, 3–12a, and 3–12b. The left-hand side of Exhibit 3–10a presents a graphic representation of the flows of costs for a manufacturing firm: from the initial cost elements (materials, labor, and overhead) to the work-in-process account, through to finished goods inventory and cost of goods sold. The first step of the manufacturing process is to purchase materials to be used in manufacturing. The second step involves adding the three cost elements—materials used, labor, and overhead—to work in process. As the products are completed, these three factors of production are added to the work-in-process account. In the third step, as production is completed, the production costs that have been accumulating in the work-in-process account are transferred to finished goods, and from there to cost of goods sold when the products are sold.

In the merchandising firm, shown on the right-hand side of Exhibit 3–10a, the process is somewhat simpler. Merchandise is purchased and placed in the inventory account. When sold, it is transferred to the cost of goods sold account. The merchandising and manufacturing firms in Exhibit 3–10a are shown side by side to emphasize the difference: Inventory is purchased in the merchandising firm, while inventory is manufactured using materials, labor, and overhead in the manufacturing firm. Cost flows in a service firm are shown separately, in Exhibit 3–10b, to emphasize how they differ: Service firms have little or no inventory.

In a service firm, there are few or no finished goods and little or no merchandise inventory for sale, so there is usually only a small amount of materials used in providing the service. Materials, labor, and operating costs are traced to the services that are provided, as illustrated in Exhibit 3–10b.

In manufacturing, there are three inventory accounts: (1) **materials inventory,** the store of materials used in the manufacturing process; (2) **work-in-process inventory,** which accounts for all costs put into manufacture of products that are started but not complete at the financial statement date; and (3) **finished goods inventory,**

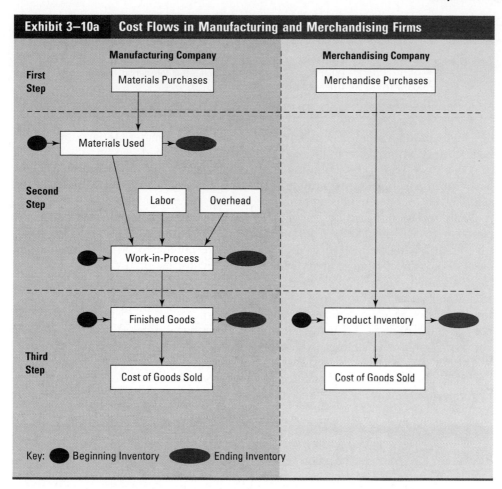

Exhibit 3–10a Cost Flows in Manufacturing and Merchandising Firms

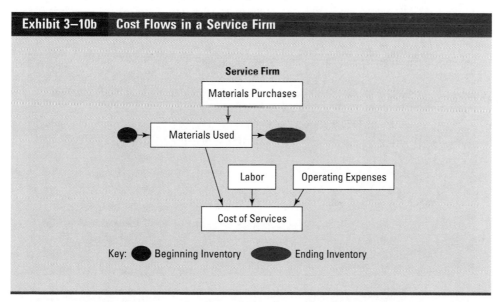

Exhibit 3–10b Cost Flows in a Service Firm

the cost of goods that are ready for sale. Each of these accounts has its own beginning and ending balances.

An inventory formula relates the inventory accounts, as follows:

Beginning inventory + Cost added = Cost transferred out + Ending Inventory

The terms *cost added* and *cost transferred out* have different meanings depending on which inventory account is considered:

Inventory Account	Cost Added	Cost Transferred Out
Materials	Purchases of materials	Cost of materials used in production
Work-in-process	1. Cost of materials used 2. Labor cost 3. Overhead cost	Cost of goods manufactured, for products completed this period
Finished goods inventory	Costs of goods manufactured	Cost of goods sold

LEARNING OBJECTIVE 4 ▶

Prepare an income statement for both a manufacturing firm and a merchandising firm.

The inventory formula is a useful concept to show how materials, labor, and overhead costs flow into work in process, then into finished goods, and finally into cost of goods sold. Exhibit 3–11 illustrates the effects of the cost flows on the accounts where, in the manufacturing firm, materials are converted into finished product and sold, and in the merchandising firm, merchandise inventory is sold.

The illustration in Exhibit 3–11 shows a manufacturing company that begins the period with $10 in materials, $10 in work in process, and $20 in finished goods inventory. During the period, $70 of materials are purchased, $75 of materials are used, $80 of direct labor is used, and $100 is spent for factory overhead. Also during the period, $215 of goods are completed and transferred from work in process to finished goods inventory, and $210 of goods are sold. These events leave ending inventories of $5 in materials, $50 in work in process, and $25 in finished goods. For the merchandising company, merchandise purchases of $250 and sales of $230 are shown, and merchandise inventory increases from $40 to $60.

Exhibit 3–12a shows how the accounting relationships are then finally represented in the income statements for the two types of firms. Note that the manufacturing firm requires a two-part calculation for cost of goods sold—the first part

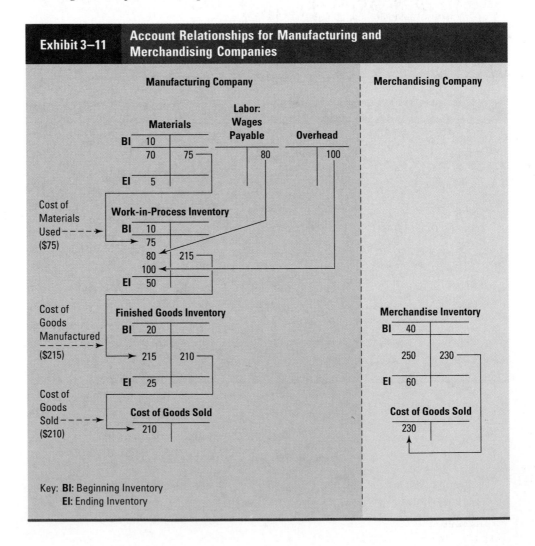

Exhibit 3–11 — **Account Relationships for Manufacturing and Merchandising Companies**

Exhibit 3–12a   Income Statements for Manufacturing and Merchandising Firms

MANUFACTURING, INC. **Income Statement** **For the Year Ended December 31, 19X5**			**MERCHANDISING, INC.** **Income Statement** **For the Year Ended December 31, 19X5**		
Cost of Goods Manufactured Statement			**(No need for a Cost of Goods Manufactured Statement)**		
Current Manufacturing Cost This Period:					
Materials Used					
Beginning Inventory	$10				
Add: Purchases	70				
Less: Ending Inventory	(5)				
Materials Used		$ 75			
Direct Labor Used		80			
Factory Overhead		100			
Total Manufacturing Cost		$255			
Account for Change in Work-in-Process					
Add: Beginning Work-in-Process		10			
Less: Ending Work-in-Process		(50)			
Cost of Goods Manufactured		$215			

MANUFACTURING, INC. **Income Statement** **For the Period Ended December 31, 19X5**			**MERCHANDISING, INC.** **Income Statement** **For the Period Ended December 31, 19X5**		
Sales		$300	Sales		$300
Less: Cost of Goods Sold			Less: Cost of Goods Sold		
Beginning Finished Goods Inventory	20		Beginning Finished Goods Inventory	40	
Add: Cost of Goods Manufactured	215		Add: Purchases	250	
Less: Ending Finished Goods Inventory	(25)	210	Less: Ending Finished Goods Inventory	60	230
Gross Margin		90	Gross Margin		70
Selling and Administrative Expenses		30	Operating Expenses		40
Net Income		60	Net Income		30

Exhibit 3–12b   Income Statement for a Service Firm

SERVICE, INC. **Income Statement** **For the Year Ended December 31, 19X5**		
Revenues		$300
Operating Expenses		
Materials	$ 60	
Labor	40	
Other Operating Expenses	100	200
Operating Income		$100

combines the flows affecting the work-in-process account to determine the amount of **cost of goods manufactured,** the cost of goods that were finished and transferred out of work in process this period. The second part combines the flows for the finished goods account to determine the amount of cost of goods sold. Exhibit 3–12b shows the income statement for a service firm with $300 in sales, $60 in materials costs, $40 in labor costs, and $100 in other operating expenses, for an operating income of $100.

Cost of goods manufactured is the cost of goods that were finished and transferred out of work-in-process this period.

COST CONCEPTS FOR PLANNING AND DECISION MAKING

To facilitate management decision making and planning, the management accountant provides relevant, timely, and accurate information, at a reasonable

◄ **LEARNING OBJECTIVE 5**
Explain the cost concepts related to the use of cost information in planning and decision making.

cost. Relevance is the most critical of the decision-making concepts; timeliness, accuracy, and cost are unimportant if the information is irrelevant.

Relevant Cost

The concept of relevant cost arises in situations in which the decision maker must choose between two or more options. To determine which option is best, the decision maker will determine which option has the highest benefit, usually in dollars. Thus, the decision maker will need information on relevant costs. A **relevant cost** has two properties: (a) it *differs for each decision option*, and (b) it will be *incurred in the future*.

A **relevant cost** has two properties: (a) it *differs for each decision option,* and (b) it will be *incurred in the future.*

If a cost is the same for each option, including it in the decision can only waste time and increase the possibility for simple error. Also, costs that have already been incurred or committed are irrelevant because there is no longer any discretion about them.

The two qualities of relevant cost information provide a useful basis for introducing three additional concepts—differential cost, opportunity cost, and sunk cost. All three are important for effective decision making.

Differential Cost

A **differential cost** is a cost that differs for each decision option and is therefore relevant.

A **differential cost** is a cost that differs for each decision option and is therefore relevant for the decision maker's choice, if it is an expected *future* cost. A differential cost will arise either as the direct cost of selecting an option (the purchase cost of a new machine is the direct effect of replacing an old machine), or as the indirect cost associated with the choice among options (replacing a machine creates a difference in certain costs, such as maintenance or electric power).

Differential costs must be carefully distinguished from variable costs. Some differential costs are fixed and others are variable. Recall that variable costs are those that change as the cost driver changes. Variable costs in a given decision context may or may not be differential. For example, if the variable cost of electricity per unit of product for the new machine will not differ from the cost of electricity per unit of product for the old machine, then this variable cost is not differential and is irrelevant. Also, though fixed costs do not change with the cost driver, certain fixed costs can be differential. For example, the fixed cost of the new machine would be a differential fixed cost.

In using differential costs, the management accountant must also choose either costs based on *cash flows*, or costs based on *accounting net income*. Cash flow measures and accounting income are ordinarily different because some noncash revenues and expenses (for example, depreciation) are used to arrive at accounting income. In some cases the decision maker may be interested primarily in the effect of a decision on cash flows (for example, for cash management purposes, or for evaluating the firm's ability to generate cash flows). In other cases the principal focus will be on accounting net income. Thus, the treatment of the differential cost for the new equipment will depend on whether the decision maker is interested in cash flow or accounting income. (The remainder of the book will use the cash flow concept of differential costs to focus on the firm's ability to generate cash flows.)

Differential costs are affected by the *time period* used in the analysis. For longer periods, a greater portion of the costs involved in a given decision will become differential. Alternatively, for very short periods, fewer costs will be differential. This difference is due to the *nature of fixed costs,* which cannot be changed in the short run but which can become differential in the long term. For example, a manufacturer may be under a lease contract to pay rent on warehouse space for the next 48 months, after which time the lease is renewed on a month-to-month basis. For the next 48 months the cost is nondifferential; thereafter, however, it becomes differential because it can be canceled at the end of any month in which the manufacturer is ready to give up the warehouse space.

The concept of differential cost is often misapplied. Consider this newspaper account of the organizational changes at Greyhound Corporation:

> Greyhound Corp.'s famed running dog is limping, but Chairman John W. Teets says the company's bus lines can return to the fast lane by franchising routes for the first time in its 71-year history . . . Sample routes on the block: Clarksdale to Jackson, Miss. . . . and San Francisco to Calistoga, Calif. . . . The routes were only marginal *because of corporate overhead* and terminal upkeep, says assistant general counsel Robert W. Wilmoth. (emphasis added)[7]

The statement above is misleading in that corporate overhead is unlikely to be a differential cost within the context of the sale of a few routes. That is, Greyhound's total corporate overhead costs are unlikely to change whether or not it drops a few bus routes. Whether Greyhound included corporate overhead in this analysis or whether overhead might have changed to some degree is unclear from this article, but it is unlikely that a principal reason for selling the routes was the largely undifferential corporate costs. In cases such as this, the concept of differential cost is an important tool for determining which costs are relevant in decision making.

Opportunity Cost

Opportunity cost is the benefit lost when choosing one option precludes receiving the benefits from an alternative option. If the management accountant ranks the monetary outcomes of the alternative options, then it is possible to calculate the opportunity cost of the option chosen by determining the maximum alternative benefit that would have been obtained if the effort, action, or capacity had been applied to some alternative use. For example, if a person chooses to leave a job (earning, say, $20,000 per year) and return to school for an advanced degree, then the opportunity cost of returning to school is $20,000 per year.

> **Opportunity cost** is the benefit lost when choosing one option precludes receiving the benefits from an alternative option.

The concept of opportunity cost is used to measure the potential economic impact of alternatives of a decision; the measurement is made on the basis of factors that may not be easily quantified. For example, it might be that the benefit of returning to school for the advanced degree is the expected higher earnings in future years, an amount that at the time of the decision may not be easily quantified.

Sunk Cost

Sunk costs are costs that have been incurred or committed in the past, and are therefore irrelevant because the decision maker no longer has discretion over them and they will not affect future *discretionary* cash flows. For example, if a company purchased a new machine without warranty and it failed the next day, the purchase price would be *irrelevant* for the present decision to replace the machine or repair it. Only future cash flows are relevant, and the purchase price of the recently acquired machine will have no effect on future cash flows.[8] The relationships among the cost concepts for planning and decision making are illustrated in Exhibit 3–13.

> **Sunk costs** are costs that have been incurred or committed in the past, and are therefore irrelevant.

An important additional issue must be considered when sunk costs are present in the decision situation. It is commonly observed that decision makers improperly seek to include sunk costs as relevant to the analysis. There is apparently an inherent bias to do so. Studies by psychologists Kahneman and Tversky found that decision makers are more willing to invest money to "recover" sunk costs than to invest the money to earn the same net return. Similarly, a study by Whyte finds that decision makers tend to escalate commitments even though those commitments are sunk. The practical implication of these findings is that cost analysts and cost system designers must be particularly careful to develop information for

---

[7] "Greyhound Will Leave Some Driving to Others," *USA Today*, March 14, 1985.

[8] An important exception to the concept that sunk costs do not affect future cash flows is the use of depreciation as a tax shield; that is, the depreciation arising from the sunk assets generates positive cash flow in the form of reduced tax costs, since depreciation is tax deductible. A complete analysis will take the tax effect into account.

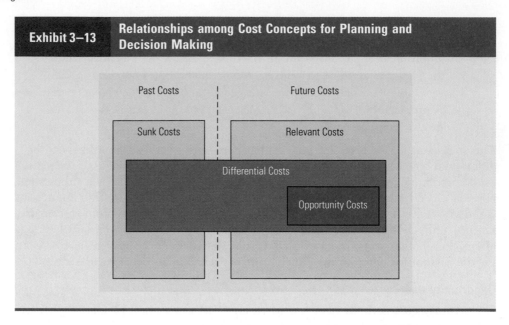

Exhibit 3–13 | **Relationships among Cost Concepts for Planning and Decision Making**

decision makers which can effectively deal with the bias.[9] An important part of an informative cost report, then, is to separate sunk costs from expected future costs.

Attributes of Cost Information for Decision Making

Accuracy

The experienced decision maker will *not* use accounting information without giving consideration to the potential for inaccuracy. Inaccurate data can mislead, resulting in potentially costly mistakes. A primary means for ensuring accurate data for decision making is to design and monitor an effective system of internal accounting controls. The system of **internal accounting controls** is a set of policies and procedures that restrict and guide activities in the processing of financial data, with the objective of preventing or detecting errors and fraudulent acts.

The accuracy of the accounting data and the design of the system of internal accounting controls are the responsibility of the controller, who is assisted by external and internal auditors. The external auditor will periodically provide an evaluation of the control environment and recommendations for improved effectiveness, while the internal auditor provides an ongoing monitoring role.

> The system of **internal accounting controls** is a set of policies and procedures that restrict and guide activities in the processing of financial data, with the objective of preventing or detecting errors and fraudulent acts.

Timeliness

Cost management information must be available to the decision maker in a timely manner, to facilitate effective decision making. The cost of delay can be significant in many decisions, such as in filling rush orders that may be lost if the necessary information is not timely. Also, the cost of identifying quality deficiencies *early* in a manufacturing process may be far less than the cost of materials and labor wasted until the deficiency is detected later in the process.

Cost and Value of Cost Information

Thinking of cost management information as having a certain cost and value emphasizes that the management accountant is an information specialist, very much like other financial professionals, such as tax advisors, financial planners, and consultants. The management accountant provides an information service that has both a preparation cost and a value to the user. The preparation costs for cost manage-

---

9 Daniel Kahneman and Amos Tversky, "Prospect Theory: An Analysis of Decisions Under Risk," *Econometrica*, March 1979, pp. 263–91; and Glen Whyte, "Escalating Commitment to a Course of Action: A Reinterpretation," *Academy of Management Review*, 1986, pp. 311–21.

ment information should be controlled, just as for any other service provided within the firm. These preparation costs will likely be influenced by the desired accuracy, timeliness, and level of aggregation; where greater accuracy, timeliness, and detail are desired, the preparation costs will be higher.

COST CONCEPTS FOR MANAGEMENT AND OPERATIONAL CONTROL

A crucial role for cost management information is to provide a basis for controlling, motivating, and rewarding managers' and employees' efforts and effectiveness. Key cost concepts applicable for this management function include controllability and risk preferences.

Controllability

A cost is said to be **controllable** if the manager or employee has discretion in choosing to incur the cost or can significantly influence the amount of the cost within a given, usually short, period of time. For example, rent expense and insurance on the plant facility would ordinarily *not* be controllable by the shop supervisor, nor would the division manager ordinarily have discretion over the amount of corporate-level administrative costs. In contrast, employees will typically have control over the labor and materials used in their work area. Also, costs such as advertising and maintenance will ordinarily be within the scope of the product or division manager's control.

There are two views of the importance of controllability in the context of employee and manager motivation. One view holds that the manager or employee should be responsible only for the management of controllable costs. This view is consistent with the argument that to hold managers responsible for changes in costs beyond their control is unfair and unmotivating. The second view is that many "uncontrollable costs," such as corporate-level administrative costs, are in fact controllable by all managers *taken as a whole*; thus to include these costs on the managers' costs reports sends a clear message that the firm benefits when managers manage these costs properly.

As in many instances where cost accounting concepts apply, the proper application of this concept is *context-specific*. It is important to know the specific needs of the firm. For example, if maintenance costs are perceived to be too high, then those costs should be treated as controllable by the appropriate production managers, to help set a firmwide goal of reducing the overall expenditures on maintenance. Conversely, if the productivity of the equipment is declining because of a lack of preventive maintenance, then maintenance should be treated as *not* controllable by the individual managers and therefore as a free resource, to motivate increased use of maintenance. Regardless of which view is taken, it is clear that the management accountant should carefully consider the anticipated effects on the manager's motivation before deciding to include uncontrollable costs in accounting reports.

The Effect of Risk Preferences on Motivation and Decision Making

A manager's risk preferences are important in management and operational control because they can have unexpected and undesirable effects on the manager's behavior. Assume a manager is facing a decision in which each option has a different outcome, and some outcomes are more certain to happen than others. **Risk preferences** describe the way individuals differentially view decision options, because they place a weight on *certain* outcomes that differs from the weight they place on *uncertain* outcomes. The risk associated with uncertain outcomes may be undesirable (or desirable) to the decision maker, irrespective of the value of the outcome itself. It is necessary to separate the value of the outcome from the positive or negative weight associated with the risk due to uncertainty. For example, it is common for people to dislike risk, and thus to prefer a certain $50 over a 50-50 chance at $100. People who prefer risk, on the other hand, would choose to have the chance at winning the $100.

Many managers are risk-averse; that is, they seek to avoid options with high risk, and would choose an option with lower expected value if it had less risk. Other managers are risk-prone. They seek out risky projects that promise some chance of a high benefit, even though there is a significant risk of a low benefit. These differences in risk preferences can have significant effects on motivation under different supervision and reward techniques. For example, the risk-averse manager is most likely to be highly motivated by supervision and rewards that reduce risk, while the reverse may be true for the risk-prone manager.

Moreover, risk preferences can interfere with proper decision making. For example, a risk-averse manager may choose not to take a risky action that top management would take (for example, to install a costly new machine that would probably reduce operating costs) because of the personal consequences to the manager of a potential unfavorable outcome. For proper motivation and decision making, management and operational control systems should be designed to reduce the negative effects of risk preferences. These systems are explained in Chapters 18–20.

SUMMARY

The management accountant must understand several important concepts to be an effective information professional. Those concepts are related to the four management functions: strategic management, product and service costing for preparing financial statements, planning and decision making, and management and operational control.

In strategic management, the most important concepts relate to the four types of cost drivers: activity-based, volume-based, structural, and executional. Activity-based cost drivers are at a detail level of operations—equipment setup, materials handling, clerical, or other tasks. In contrast, volume-based cost drivers are at an aggregate level, usually the number of units produced. The most important volume-based concepts are variable costs, which change with a change in the level of the cost driver, and fixed costs, which do not. Direct costs are defined as costs that can be traced directly to a cost object, in contrast to indirect costs, which cannot. Also, structural cost drivers involve plans and decisions having long-term effects, while executional cost drivers are those with short-term decision frames.

The important concepts in product costing are product costs, which are the direct materials, direct labor, and indirect manufacturing costs (called overhead) that are required for the product and production process. Nonproduct costs (also called period costs) are the selling, administrative, and other costs that are not involved in manufacturing. The inventory formula is used to determine the cost of materials used in production, the cost of materials manufactured (transferred from work in process into finished goods), and the cost of goods sold for a given period.

The important concept in planning and decision making is relevant cost. When considering options, the management accountant considers relevant costs—the costs that differ for each option and that will occur in the future. All past costs (also called sunk costs) are irrelevant because they will not change irrespective of the option chosen.

The two key concepts in management and operational control are controllability and risk preferences. It is important to distinguish controllable costs from other costs, because managers should be evaluated only on the basis of controllable costs; it can be very unmotivating to be evaluated, even in part, on the basis of costs one cannot control. Also, it is important for the management accountant to recognize in the development of cost management systems that managers tend to be relatively risk-averse, which can cause the manager to make decisions that are not consistent with top management's objectives.

KEY TERMS

Allocation bases 58

Average cost 64

Controllable cost 75

Conversion cost 60

Cost 57

Cost allocation 58

Cost assignment 58

Cost of goods manufactured 71

Cost of goods sold 68

Cost pools 57

Differential cost 72

Direct cost 58

Direct labor 60

Direct materials 59

Executional cost drivers 66

Factory overhead 60

Finished goods inventory 68

Fixed cost 63

Indirect cost 58

Indirect labor 60

Indirect materials 60

Internal accounting controls 74

Marginal cost 65

Materials inventory 68

Mixed cost 63

Opportunity cost 73

Overhead 60

Period costs 68

Prime costs 60

Product costs 68

Relevant cost 72

Relevant range 63

Risk preferences 75

Step-fixed cost 64

Structural cost drivers 65

Sunk costs 73

Unit cost 64

Variable cost 63

Work-in-process inventory 68

SELF-STUDY PROBLEM

(For solution, please turn to the end of the chapter.)

The following data pertain to Spartan Products Company:

Sales Revenue	$1,000,000
Direct Materials Inventory, Jan. 1, 19X2	20,000
Direct Labor—Wages	350,000
Depreciation Expense—Plant and Equipment	80,000
Indirect Labor—Wages	5,000
Heat, Light, and Power—Plant	12,000
Supervisor's Salary—Plant	40,000
Finished Goods Inventory, Jan. 1, 19X2	35,000
Work-in-Process Inventory, Dec. 31, 19X2	25,000
Supplies—Administrative Office	6,000
Property Taxes—Plant	13,000
Finished Goods Inventory, Dec. 31, 19X2	40,000
Direct Materials Inventory, Dec. 31, 19X2	30,000
Sales Representatives' Salaries	190,000
Work-in-Process Inventory, Jan. 1, 19X2	35,000
Direct Materials Purchases	100,000
Supplies—Plant	4,000
Depreciation, Administrative Office	30,000

Required Prepare a statement of cost of goods manufactured and an income statement for Spartan Products Company.

QUESTIONS

3–1 Relevant cost information is needed to accomplish what particular management function?

3–2 Distinguish between direct and indirect costs and give a few examples of each.

3–3 Are all direct costs variable? Explain.

3–4 Are all fixed costs indirect? Explain.

3–5 Define *cost driver*.

3–6 What is the difference between variable and fixed costs?

3–7 Explain step-fixed costs and give an example.

3–8 Define *relevant range* and explain its use.

3–9 What is a conversion cost? What are prime costs?

3–10 Why might the term *average cost* be misleading?

3–11 How do total variable costs, total fixed costs, average variable costs, and average fixed costs react to changes in the cost driver?

3–12 What is meant by marginal cost?

3–13 Distinguish between product costs and period costs.

3–14 Explain the difference between costs based on cash flows and costs based on accrual accounting.

3–15 What are the three types of inventory in a manufacturing firm?

3–16 Cost management information should be relevant, timely, and accurate. Which of these attributes is most important? Why?

3–17 What is a relevant cost?

3–18 Define *differential cost*, *opportunity cost*, and *sunk cost*.

3–19 Should managers be responsible for the costs they cannot control directly? Why or why not?

3–20 What problem can arise if the firm and its employees have different risk preferences? What can be done about this problem?

PROBLEMS

3–21 **CLASSIFICATION OF COSTS** The following costs were taken from the accounting records of the Ajax Company:

1. State income taxes
2. Insurance on the manufacturing facilities
3. Merchandise purchased for resale
4. Wages for employees in the assembly department
5. Wages for employees who deliver the product
6. Interest on notes payable
7. Materials used in production process
8. Rent for the sales outlet in Sacramento
9. Electricity for manufacturing equipment
10. Depreciation expense on delivery trucks
11. Wages for the sales staff
12. Factory supervisors' salaries
13. Salary of the company president
14. Advertising expense

Required Classify each item as either a product cost or a period cost.

3–22 **CLASSIFICATION OF COSTS** Following is a list of costs from the Oakland Company, a manufacturer of furniture:

1. Wood used in chairs
2. Salaries of inspectors
3. Lubricant used in machinery
4. Factory rent
5. Wages of assembly workers
6. Workers' compensation insurance
7. Sandpaper
8. Fabric used for upholstery

9. Property taxes
10. Depreciation on machinery

Required   Classify each cost as direct or indirect with respect to the firm's product.

3–23 **CLASSIFICATION OF COSTS**   The following costs are incurred by the Oakland Company, a manufacturer of furniture:

1. Wood and fabric used in furniture
2. Depreciation on machinery
3. Property taxes on the factory
4. Labor costs to manufacture the furniture
5. Electricity cost to operate the machinery
6. Factory rent
7. Production supervisor's salary
8. Sandpaper and other supplies
9. Fire insurance on factory
10. Commissions paid to salespersons

Required   Classify each cost as either variable or fixed.

3–24 **VARIABLE COSTS, CHANGE IN BUDGET**   The Community Help Center provides clothing and canned food to needy people in the community. Of the Help Center's costs, 40 percent are fixed and 60 percent are variable. Because of rising unemployment in the community, monetary contributions are down by 20 percent this year. The center's budget was $100,000 last year.

Service

Strategy

Required   What will be the percentage change in the amount of services the Help Center can provide this year?

3–25 **AVERAGE AND TOTAL COSTS**   The Business Students Association wants to have a Christmas dance for its members. The cost of renting a nightclub is $250, and the cost of refreshments will be $1 per person.

Required

1. What is the total cost if 100 people attend? What is the average cost?

2. What is the total cost if 200 people attend? What is the average cost?

3. Explain why average total cost differs with changes in total attendance.

3–26 **COST CLASSIFICATION**   The Fran McPhair Dance Studios is a chain of 45 wholly owned dance studios that offer private lessons in ballroom dancing. The studios are located in various cities throughout the southern and southeastern states. McPhair offers a set of 12 private lessons; while the student may pay for the lessons one at a time, each student is required to enroll for at least a 12-lesson plan. There are also 20-, 40-, and 100-lesson plans, which offer savings. Each dance instructor is paid a small salary plus a commission based on the number of dance lessons provided.

Service

Strategy

Required

1. McPhair's owner is interested in a strategic analysis of the business. Overall profitability has declined slightly in the most recent year, while other studios in the area seem to be doing well. The owner wants to understand why. What would be the proper choice of a cost object to begin this analysis? Explain your choice.

2. Using the cost object you chose in requirement 1 for each cost element listed below, determine its cost classification (in some cases, two or more classifications will apply).

Cost Elements

1. Salary for each dancing instructor.
2. Manager's salary.
3. Music tapes used in instruction.
4. Utilities for the studio.
5. Part-time receptionist at the studio.
6. Planning and development materials sent from the home office.
7. Free lessons given by each studio as a promotion.
8. McPhair places regional TV and radio advertisements several times a year.

Cost Classifications

a. Direct
b. Indirect
c. Variable
d. Fixed
e. Controllable by studio manager
f. Uncontrollable by studio manager

3-27 COST CLASSIFICATION A portion of the costs incurred by business organizations is designated direct labor cost. As used in practice, the term *direct labor cost* has a wide variety of meanings. Unless the meaning intended in a given context is clear, misunderstanding and confusion are likely to ensue. If a user does not understand the elements included in direct labor cost, erroneous interpretations of the numbers might occur and could result in poor management decisions.

The Institute of Management Accountants has issued Statement on Management Accounting No. 4C, "Practices and Techniques: Definition and Measurement of Direct Labor Cost," to assist management accountants in dealing with problems that may arise in interpreting and understanding direct labor costs. Along with providing a conceptual definition of direct labor cost, this Statement describes how direct labor costs should be measured. Measurement of direct labor costs has two aspects: (1) the quantity of labor effort that is to be included, that is, the types of hours or other units of time that are to be counted; and (2) the unit price by which each of these quantities is multiplied to arrive at a monetary cost.

Required

1. Distinguish between direct labor and indirect labor.
2. Explain why some nonproductive labor (e.g., coffee breaks, personal time) is treated as direct labor while other nonproductive labor (e.g., downtime, training) is treated as indirect labor.
3. Presented below are labor cost elements that a company has classified as (a) direct labor, (b) factory overhead, or (c) either direct labor or factory overhead depending upon the situation.
   a. Direct labor. Included in the company's direct labor are cost production efficiency bonuses and certain benefits for direct labor workers, such as FICA (employer's portion), group life insurance, vacation pay, and workers' compensation insurance.
   b. Factory overhead. The company's calculation of manufacturing overhead includes the cost of the following: wage continuation plans, the company-sponsored cafeteria, the human resources department, and recreational facilities.
   c. Direct labor or factory overhead. The costs that the company includes in this category are maintenance expense, overtime premiums, and shift premiums.

   Explain the reasoning used by the company in classifying the cost elements in each of the three categories.

   (CMA adapted)

3-28 BASIC COST TERMS Following are descriptions of costs for a small-town cafe (column A) and cost type (column B):

A	B
1. Cost of part-time workers (seasonal fluctuations in breakfast and lunch trade)	a. Variable cost
	b. Step-fixed cost
2. Rent of the cafe building	c. Fixed cost
3. Cost of full-time workers (seasonal fluctuations in breakfast and lunch trade)	
4. Cost of utilities (includes telephone, gas, electric, and trash)	
5. Cost of a leased gas-powered grill	
6. Cost of eggs, sausage, flour, and sugar	

Required Match each cost in column A to a cost type in column B.

3–29 **OPPORTUNITY COST AND RELEVANT COSTS** Emilio earns $34,000 annually as a marketing specialist in Saltillo, Mexico. He has applied for admission to the University of Mexico M.B.A. program. If accepted, he will resign and move to Mexico City. The relevant data are as follows:

Emilio's annual salary	$34,000
Annual tuition and fees	6,000
Annual book and supply expense	700
Monthly living expenses in Saltillo	800
Monthly living expenses in Mexico City	1,200
Monthly auto expenses (auto required in both cities)	350
Cost of two business suits purchased just prior to resigning	600
Moving expenses	400

Required Calculate Emilio's opportunity cost of earning an M.B.A. degree if it will take 12 months to complete the program.

3–30 **COST CLASSIFICATION** Lester-Sung, Inc., is a large general construction firm in the commercial building industry. Following is a list of costs incurred by this company:

1. Cost of a laborer for 8 hours at $6 an hour.
2. Cost of a forklift purchased 3 years ago that is now in storage. Since the company is now subcontracting the masonry, the forklift is no longer needed.
3. Cost of 1,000 board feet of 2×4 lumber.
4. The company has the opportunity to bid on a very profitable project that will start in 3 months. If taken, the new project will require the delay or cancelation of other projects.
5. CEO's salary.
6. Cost of insurance for the carpenters.

Required Classify each cost above using the following categories:

a. Selling and administrative cost
b. Direct material
c. Direct labor
d. Overhead cost
e. Opportunity cost
f. Sunk cost

3–31 **COST CLASSIFICATION, PROFIT ANALYSIS** Specialty Automobiles is an upscale, high-priced, specialty carmaker based in Los Angeles, California. The management accountant for Specialty Automobiles has compiled information for various levels of automobile output:

Automobile Output

	2,500 Cars	5,000 Cars	7,500 Cars
Variable production costs	$19,000,000	$_____	$_____
Fixed production costs	_____	30,125,000	_____
Variable selling costs	2,875,000	_____	_____
Fixed selling costs	10,500,000	10,500,000	_____
Total costs	_____	_____	_____
Selling price per auto	40,000	33,500	29,500
Unit cost	25,000	_____	_____
Profit per auto	_____	_____	_____

Required

1. Using your knowledge of unit costs and the relationships between fixed and variable costs, fill in the blanks with the correct figures.

2. Which of the three levels of output gives the highest profit per auto?

3–32 COST CLASSIFICATION The XYZ company sells computer accessories using sales representatives. The sales department incurs the following types of costs during each fiscal quarter:

1. Sample product mailed out to prospective customers
2. Phone charges by sales representatives for calling on customers
3. Repair of faulty products under warranty
4. Travel expenses on business trips
5. Copying expenses
6. Salaries paid to sales representatives
7. Computer time charged to the sales department

Required   Determine whether the listed costs are controllable or uncontrollable by the sales manager and general manager. Use the following classifications:

a. Controllable by sales manager
b. Uncontrollable by sales manager
c. Controllable by general manager
d. Uncontrollable by general manager

Service

3–33 DIFFERENTIAL COSTS A nonprofit health organization is studying two methods of increasing the measles immunization level of schoolchildren in the area. The first method would involve hiring an educator at $25,000 a year. The educator's expenses, including materials, would be $40,000.

A second method being considered would be to strictly enforce an existing law requiring all schoolchildren to be immunized as they enroll for kindergarten. A staff would be hired to review all necessary paperwork, to send home notices if a child is not in compliance, and to do whatever follow-up work is necessary. Two clerical workers at a total cost of $35,000, including benefits, would be needed to accomplish the task. It would take $15,000 in supplies and other materials to support the new staff in their jobs.

Required   The health organization must choose between the methods.

1. What are the relevant costs in the decision?

2. What other information might be important?

International

3–34 PRODUCT COSTS AND PERIOD COSTS Galletas Americanas is a cookie company in Guadalajara, Mexico, that produces and sells American-style cookies with very high quality and service. The owner would like to identify the various costs incurred during each year in order to plan and control the costs in the business. Galletas Americanas's costs are the following (in thousands of pesos):

Utilities for the bakery	$ 1,600
Paper used in packaging product	70
Salaries and wages in the bakery	15,000
Cookie ingredients	27,000
Bakery labor and fringe benefits	1,000
Administrative costs	800
Bakery equipment maintenance	600
Depreciation of bakery plant and equipment	1,500
Uniforms	300
Insurance for the bakery	600
Rent for administration offices	13,200
Advertising	1,500
Boxes, bags, and cups used in the bakery	700
Manager's salary	10,000
Overtime premiums	2,000
Idle time	400

Required

1. What is the total amount of product costs and period costs?

2. Assume that Galletas is planning to expand its business into the United States and Canada, targeting initially the United States. This expansion will not require additional baking facilities, but labor and materials costs will increase. Additionally, advertising costs and packaging costs will increase substantially. Also, United States authorities will require certain documentation and inspections that will be an added cost for Galletas.

   a. Which of the additional costs are product costs?

   b. Which costs are relevant for the decision whether or not to expand into the United States?

3-35 COST CLASSIFICATION Advanced Technical Services, Ltd., has many products and services in the medical field. The Clinical Division of the company does research and testing of consumer products on human participants in controlled clinical studies. The division has the following costs:

Service

1. Director's salary
2. Part-time help
3. Payment on purchase of medical equipment
4. Allocation of companywide advertising
5. Patches used on participants' arms during the study
6. Stipends paid to participants

Required Determine whether each cost is best classified as a fixed, variable, or step-fixed cost.

3-36 COST OF GOOD MANUFACTURED The following information pertains to the Piper Company:

Prime costs	$150,000
Conversion costs	170,000
Direct materials used	65,000
Beginning work in process	75,000
Ending work in process	62,000

Required Determine the cost of goods manufactured.

3-37 COST RELATIONSHIPS The following inventory data relate to the Sunshine Company:

	Beginning	Ending
Finished goods inventory	$100,000	$ 95,000
Work-in-process inventory	65,000	80,000
Direct materials	90,000	100,000

Costs incurred during the period are as follows:

Total manufacturing costs	$689,000
Factory overhead	153,000
Direct materials Ïused	120,000

Required Calculate direct materials purchased, direct labor costs, and cost of goods sold.

3-38 COST OF GOODS MANUFACTURED AND SOLD The Designer Company produces women's clothing. During 19X5, the company incurred the following costs:

Factory rent	$100,000
Direct labor	260,000
Utilities—Factory	25,000
Purchases of direct materials	400,000
Indirect materials	70,000
Indirect labor	55,000

Inventories for the year were as follows:

	January 1	December 31
Direct materials	$ 70,000	$ 50,000
Work-in-process	90,000	100,000
Finished goods	115,000	95,000

Required

1. Prepare a statement of cost of goods manufactured.
2. Calculate cost of goods sold.

3–39 **COST OF GOODS MANUFACTURED** The following data pertain to the Wheeler Company:

	End of 19X1	End of 19X2
Direct materials inventory	$40,000	$47,000
Work-in-process inventory	37,000	35,000
Finished goods inventory	18,000	20,000
Purchases of direct materials		70,000
Direct labor		30,000
Indirect labor		10,000
Factory insurance		12,000
Depreciation—Factory and equipment		13,000
Repairs and maintenance—Factory and equipment		5,000
Marketing expenses		49,000
General and administrative expenses		30,000

Sales in 19X2 were $400,000.

Required Prepare a schedule of cost of goods manufactured and an income statement for the Wheeler Company.

3–40 **COST OF GOODS MANUFACTURED AND INCOME STATEMENT** The following data (in millions) pertain to the Underwood Company:

	January 1, 19X1	December 31, 19X1
Direct materials inventory	$ 20	$10
Work-in-process inventory	12	7
Finished goods inventory	30	18
Factory utilities	$ 10	
Sales	400	
Direct labor	45	
Property taxes on factory	2	
Miscellaneous factory overhead	12	
Depreciation—Factory and equipment	12	
Direct materials purchased	90	
Factory supplies used	5	
Indirect labor	22	
Marketing and administrative expenses	85	

Required Prepare a schedule of cost of goods manufactured and an income statement for the Underwood Company.

3–41 **COST OF GOODS MANUFACTURED AND SOLD** The following information pertains to the Shell Company:

Direct labor	$200,000
Direct materials	180,000
Factory overhead	150,000
Ending work-in-process	40,000
Beginning finished goods inventory	190,000
Ending finished goods inventory	220,000
Cost of goods sold	480,000

Required

1. Calculate the cost of goods manufactured.
2. Calculate beginning work in process.

3–42 **COST OF GOODS MANUFACTURED, CALCULATING UNKNOWNS** The following information was taken from the accounting records of the Ross

Manufacturing Company. Unfortunately, some of the data were destroyed by a computer malfunction.

	Case A 19X1	Case B 19X2
Sales	40,000	?
Finished goods inventory, Jan. 1, 19X5	5,000	5,000
Finished goods inventory, Dec. 31, 19X5	6,000	?
Cost of goods sold	?	10,000
Gross margin	15,000	3,000
Selling and administrative expenses	?	2,000
Net income	10,000	1,000
Work-in-process, Jan. 1, 19X5	?	4,000
Direct material used	6,000	5,000
Direct labor	7,000	4,000
Factory overhead	10,000	?
Total manufacturing costs	?	15,000
Work-in-process, Dec. 31, 19X5	4,000	?
Cost of goods manufactured	?	13,000

Required Calculate the unknowns indicated by question marks.

SOLUTION TO SELF-STUDY PROBLEM

The Spartan Products Company

SPARTAN PRODUCTS COMPANY
Statement of Cost of Goods Manufactured
For the Year Ended December 31, 19X2

Direct Materials		
Direct Materials Inventory, Jan. 1, 19X2	$ 20,000	
Purchases of Direct Materials	100,000	
Total Direct Materials Available	120,000	
Direct Materials Inventory, Dec. 31, 19X2	30,000	
Direct Materials Used		$ 90,000
Direct Labor		350,000
Factory Overhead		
Heat, Light, and Power—Plant	12,000	
Supplies—Plant	4,000	
Property Taxes—Plant	13,000	
Depreciation Expense—Plant and Equipment	80,000	
Indirect Labor	5,000	
Supervisor's Salary—Plant	40,000	
Total Factory Overhead		154,000
Total Manufacturing Costs Incurred during the Year		594,000
Add: Beginning Work-in-Process, Jan. 1, 19X2		35,000
Total Manufacturing Costs to Account for		629,000
Less: Ending Work-in-Process, Dec. 31, 19X2		25,000
Cost of Goods Manufactured		$604,000

SPARTAN PRODUCTS COMPANY
Income Statement
For the Year Ended December 31, 19X2

Sales Revenue		$1,000,000
Cost of Goods Sold		
Finished Goods Inventory, Jan. 1, 19X2	$ 35,000	
Cost of Goods Manufactured	604,000	
Total Goods Available for Sale	639,000	
Finished Goods Inventory, Dec. 31, 19X2	40,000	
Cost of Goods Sold		599,000
Gross Margin		401,000
Selling and Administrative Expenses		
Sales Representatives' Salaries	190,000	
Supplies—Administrative Office	6,000	
Depreciation Expense—Administrative Office	30,000	
Total Selling and Administrative Expenses		226,000
Net Income		$175,000

Part II Contemporary Cost Management Concepts

Activity-Based Costing and Management

4

After studying this chapter, you should be able to . . .

© Paul Conklin/Photo Edit.

88

A new method of cost accounting developed in the past 10 years—called "activity-based" accounting   records all costs. And it relates them, as traditional cost accounting cannot, to value added. Within the next 10 years it should be in general use. And then we will have operational control in manufacturing.

PETER F. DRUCKER, *THE WALL STREET JOURNAL*,
APRIL 13, 1993, P. A14.

Since the early 1980s, many U.S. companies, such as IBM, Hewlett-Packard, Allen-Bradley, Westinghouse, General Motors, General Electric, Eastman Kodak, and Lockheed, have adopted advanced manufacturing technologies to meet global competition. The modernization of U.S. factories increased quality and lowered costs. Along with these changes, cost management practices as well as manufacturing processes have been changed and improved.

While describing various techniques used in the contemporary manufacturing environment, this chapter identifies the major problems cost accounting has in providing accurate and relevant cost information. It also explains activity-based costing (ABC)—its definition, description, benefits, and limitations. Lastly, this chapter describes activity-based management (ABM) and ABC/ABM applications in manufacturing, marketing, administrative, service, and not-for-profit organizations.

ABC helps firms reduce distortions caused by the traditional costing system and obtains more accurate product costs. It provides a clear view of how a firm's diverse products, services, and activities contribute in the long run to the bottom line.

ABM focuses on managing activities to promote business efficiency and effectiveness, and to increase not only the value received by customers but also the firm's profits.

ABC/ABM systems have been developed and implemented at many companies, such as General Motors, Data Technologies, Hewlett-Packard, Advanced Micro Devices, Avery International, Cal Electronic Circuits, General Electric, Siemens Electric Motor Works, John Deere Component Works, Merck, Tektronix, Texas Instruments, Alexandria Hospital, Union Pacific Railroad, Amtrak, Data Services, AT&T, Fireman's Fund, American Express, and Naval Supply System Command.

ABC and ABM are closely tied to strategic cost management. Managers receive more meaningful information to answer strategic questions such as these:

BusinessWeek

What's the Lowdown on Overhead?

During the 1980s, Corporate America fought to reduce labor costs by eliminating positions and laying off millions of hourly workers. In the 1990s the major challenge shifted to reducing high overhead costs. A 1990 survey conducted by Boston University found that overhead equaled 26 percent of sales for U.S. manufacturers versus 21 percent for Western Europe's and 18 percent for Japan's. General Motors, Du Pont, and other manufacturers reorganized with great fanfare in the 1980s, but today they find they are still fighting overhead in today's corporate environment. Weyerhaeuser Co. found itself in the same position, and like other companies, discovered a way to help manage its overhead.

Q: What's Weyerhaeuser's strategy in keeping overhead costs down? *Find out on page 104 of this chapter.*

- What are the potential impacts on pricing and product-line decisions if a firm switches from the traditional costing system to an activity-based costing system?
- What are potential cost savings if a firm uses ABM to identify and eliminate non-value-added activities to achieve its low-cost strategy?
- How can ABC/ABM help a firm achieve its competitive strategy of high performance and short lead time in delivering its products?
- How can ABC/ABM help a firm analyze its major customer profitability, and develop a customer-focused strategy?

THE CONTEMPORARY MANUFACTURING ENVIRONMENT

LEARNING OBJECTIVE 1 ▶
Describe the key features of contemporary manufacturing techniques.

Over the past decade an increasing number of national and international companies have made changes in their manufacturing plants. In attempts to reduce costs, increase productivity, improve product quality, and increase flexibility in response to customer needs, these companies have taken some or all of the following innovative approaches: (1) adopting just-in-time (JIT) manufacturing systems using kanban and work cells tools; (2) using various automation techniques such as robots, computer-aided design (CAD), and computer-aided manufacturing (CAM); and (3) applying integration approaches such as flexible manufacturing systems (FMS) and computer-integrated manufacturing (CIM) to improve manufacturing productivity.

The Just-in-Time System

A **just-in-time (JIT) system** is a comprehensive production and inventory system in which materials and parts are purchased or produced as needed and just in time to be used at each stage of the production process.

A **just-in-time (JIT) system** is a comprehensive production and inventory management system in which materials and parts are purchased or produced as needed and just in time to be used at each stage of the production process. JIT is a philosophy that can be applied to all aspects of business, including purchasing, production, and delivery. The goals of JIT are to produce and deliver products just in time to be sold profitably, and to purchase materials and parts just in time to be placed into manufacturing processes. JIT focuses on eliminating waste, reducing inventories, developing a strong supplier relationship, increasing employee involvement, and developing customer-focused programs. The degree of coordination needed to implement effective JIT manufacturing systems highlights existing problems such as bottlenecks, inventory shrinkage, and unreliable suppliers. JIT helps organizations to become more efficient and better managed, as well as to earn more profits than their competitors.

Because the JIT environment allows only small inventory buffers, each organizational unit must maintain close communication with other units, customers, and outside vendors. This constant exchange of information causes any inefficiencies to be located quickly. Problems concealed earlier in inventory, such as inadequate product or process quality or obsolescence, become evident when JIT is implemented.

Many companies have used JIT successfully to cut inventories, improve production efficiency, and raise product quality. For example, Oregon Cutting Systems (OCS), a $250 million company headquartered in Portland, manufactures steel products for cutting saws, timber harvesting equipment, and sporting equipment. OCS developed its own version of JIT, called a zero inventory production system,

JIT Helps Harley-Davidson

Harley-Davidson used JIT to save more than $22 million within one year, due to the reduction of work-in-process inventory. Under the JIT, only enough parts to satisfy one day's production are manufactured and shipped to the job site with high quality. It reduces working capital requirements for warehousing surplus parts and permits much better quality control.

Source: William T. Turk, "Management Accounting Revitalized: The Harley-Davidson Experience," *Journal of Cost Management*, Winter 1990, pp. 28–39.

that has three major components: (1) JIT manufacturing to improve supplier relationship, smooth the production line, and reduce setup time and inventory; (2) continual improvement to upgrade quality and reduce waste; and (3) employee development and empowerment to promote their personal commitments to the company.

OCS started implementing JIT in the early 1980s; within five years it managed to reduce defects by 80 percent and cut scrap and rework by 50 percent. Other results also were remarkable. For example, at one Canadian plant, setup times were reduced from 390 minutes to 1 minute 40 seconds, space requirements were reduced by 40 percent, lead times were cut from 21 days to 3 days, and inventory was reduced by 50 percent.[1]

JIT is not just for manufacturers. It can be applied to service and retailing firms, such as banks, insurance companies, hospitals, department stores, and accounting firms. In nonmanufacturing applications, JIT focuses management's attention on non-value-added processes and just-in-time delivery and service.

Kanban

In Japanese, **kanban** means "card." Workers use a set of control cards to signal the need for materials and products to move from one operation to the next in an assembly line. Kanban is used with JIT to greatly reduce lead times, decrease inventory, and improve productivity by linking all production operations in a smooth, uninterrupted flow.[2]

Kanban is essentially a communication system; it can be a card, a label, a box or bin, a series of in-trays, or simply a number of squares painted or taped on the factory floor or work surface. Its purpose is to inform the previous step in the process to make a part. The kanban card typically contains information identifying the part, its descriptive name, how many of each part should accompany the card, the delivery location, the reorder point on the shelf stack, and the turnaround time negotiated between the internal customer and producer or the plant and an external subcontractor.[3]

Under a kanban system, the previous process or step cannot send in-process parts or components to the subsequent step unless requested by means of a kanban card from the downstream process. The subsequent step controls the amount produced. Thus, no overproduction occurs, priority in production becomes obvious, and control of inventory becomes easier.

Work Cells

Work cells are small groups of related manufacturing processes organized in clusters to assemble parts of finished products. Major characteristics of work cells are (1) related manufacturing processes organized in clusters, (2) operations moved together, (3) all production activities from the raw materials stage to finished goods

> **Kanban** is a set of control cards that are used to signal the need for materials and products to move from one operation to the next in an assembly line.

> **Work cells** are small groups of related manufacturing processes organized in clusters to assemble parts of finished products.

Dell Computer Uses JIT to Minimize Its Inventories

Dell Computer Corporation uses JIT to minimize the need for computer inventories. The firm builds computers to customers' specifications after the orders are received. This makes its inventories much lower. Dell keeps 35 days of inventory on hand compared to 110 days for Compaq Computer Corporation.

Source: "The Computer Is in the Mail (Really)," *Business Week*, January 23, 1995, pp. 76–77.

---

[1] Jack C. Bailes and Ilene K. Kleinsorge, "Cutting Waste with JIT," *Management Accounting*, May 1992, pp. 28–32.

[2] Bruce R. Neumann and Pauline R. Jaouen, "Kanban, ZIPS, and Cost Accounting: A Case Study," *Journal of Accountancy*, August 1986, pp. 132–41.

[3] Richard B. Kitney, "Production Systems with Pull," *CMA Magazine*, July–August 1994, pp. 22–24.

stage in the same cell, and (4) visual control is easy; when problems occur as a result of a line slowdown or stoppage, feedback is immediate.

Automation

Automation means the replacement of human effort with machines. The goal of automation is to increase efficiency and effectiveness. Factory automation has become a necessity for many industries. The most popular forms are robots, computer-aided design, and computer-aided manufacturing tools.

Robots

A **robot** is a computer-programmed and controlled machine that performs repetitive activities.

More companies are using robots than ever before. A **robot** is a computer-programmed and controlled machine that performs repetitive activities. By using robots, companies have increased their capacity, decreased the time to manufacture a part (by using more efficient routings), and consequently reduced past-due orders. They are achieving major cost savings with automation by decreasing direct labor costs and tooling costs.

Computer-Aided Design and Manufacturing

Computer-aided design (CAD) is the use of computers in product development, analysis, and design modification to improve the quality and performance of the product.

Computer-aided manufacturing (CAM) is the use of computers to plan, implement, and control production.

Computer-aided design (CAD) is the use of computers in product development, analysis, and design modification to improve the quality and performance of the product. **Computer-aided manufacturing (CAM)** is the use of computers to plan, implement, and control production. General Motors, Ford, and Chrysler use CAM to produce cars. The CAM system dispatches production orders to electronic machine tools, robots, and other automated work stations.

In the factories of the future, more companies will introduce CAD and CAM to respond to changing consumer tastes more quickly. These innovations allow companies to significantly reduce the time necessary to bring their products from the design process to the distribution stage.

Integration

A **flexible manufacturing system (FMS)** is a computerized network of automated equipment that produces one or more groups of parts or variations of a product in a flexible manner.

Computer-integrated manufacturing (CIM) is a totally integrated manufacturing system that integrates all functions of the offices and factories within a company via a computer-based information network, to allow hour-by-hour manufacturing management.

Automation requires a relatively large investment in computers, computer programming, machines, and equipment. Many firms add automation equipment gradually, one process at a time. To improve efficiency and effectiveness continuously, firms must integrate people and equipment into the smoothly operating teams that have become a vital part of manufacturing strategy. Flexible manufacturing systems (FMS) and computer-integrated manufacturing (CIM) are two integration approaches.

A **flexible manufacturing systems (FMS)** is a computerized network of automated equipment that produces one or more groups of parts or variations of a product in a flexible manner. It uses robots and computer-controlled materials-handling systems to link several stand-alone numerically controlled machines in switching from one production run to another.

Computer-integrated manufacturing (CIM) is a totally integrated manufacturing system that integrates all functions of the offices and factories within a company via a computer-based information network, to allow hour-by-hour manufacturing management.

The major characteristics of modern manufacturing companies that are adopting FMS and CIM are high-quality products and services, low inventories, high degrees of automation, fast throughput, greater flexibility, and advanced information technology. These innovations shift the focus away from large production volumes necessary to absorb fixed overhead to a new emphasis on marketing efforts, engineering, and product design. Every world-class manufacturing company needs a world-class cost management system to produce high-quality accounting information for more effective management decisions.

Managers use financial information to judge the impact of their decisions on company profits. Accurate and relevant cost information is an important key for an enterprise to survive, grow, and make profits in this highly competitive environment. Therefore, having a suitable cost system helps a company evaluate both the profitability of products and the effects of the resource allocation decisions on profit. Also, it can be used in budgets for planning and control.

LIMITATIONS OF TRADITIONAL COSTING SYSTEMS

The traditional, volume-based costing systems are useful when direct labor and materials are the predominant factors of production, when technology is stable, and when there is a limited range of products. Traditional costing systems measure the resources consumed in proportion to the number of individual products produced. However, accompanying the revolution taking place in the business world, many organizational resources, such as setup or materials-handling costs for activities and transactions, are unrelated to the physical volume of units produced. Consequently, traditional costing systems do a poor job of attributing the expenses of these support resources to the production and sale of individual products. The expenses typically are allocated to products using unit- or volume-based measures, such as direct labor-hours, direct materials costs, direct labor costs, machine-hours, or units produced. The product costs generated by such allocations are distorted because products do not consume most support resources in proportion to their production volumes.

◄ **LEARNING OBJECTIVE 2**
Explain why traditional costing systems tend to distort product costs.

Traditional costing systems no longer reflect how specific activities in an automated plant cause variations in major cost categories. Product costs typically have been monitored under three components: direct materials, direct labor, and factory overhead. Traditional costing systems were developed when the labor component dominated total manufacturing costs—products requiring the highest labor input were driving most of the production costs. Hence, the focus of these systems was on measuring and controlling direct labor costs.

Factory overhead, defined as the sum of all production costs that cannot be identified directly with any product line (the sum of all indirect costs), was traditionally not a major cost element. It included expenses such as factory maintenance, utilities, insurance, and supervisory salaries. In the contemporary manufacturing environment, most of the expenditures associated with factory automation now are included in the factory overhead account: new equipment depreciation and insurance, salaries for technicians and product engineers, and research and development. As a result, the percentage of total manufacturing costs related to direct labor has consistently decreased, with a corresponding increase in fixed overhead costs.

The major limitation of traditional costing systems is the use of volume-based plantwide or departmental rates. These rates produce inaccurate product costs when a large share of factory overhead costs is not volume-based, and when firms produce a diverse mix of products with different volumes, sizes, and complexities.

Volume-Based Plantwide and Departmental Rates

The traditional costing system uses either a single plantwide overhead rate or several departmental overhead rates based on output volume to allocate factory overhead cost to products or services. A plantwide rate assumes that, in proportion to the overhead allocation base (e.g., direct labor-hours) used, all products or services benefit from the overhead costs incurred. The departmental rates method uses a separate volume-based predetermined overhead rate (e.g., one uses direct labor-hours while the other uses machine-hours) for each department. Therefore, product costs are more likely to reflect different usages in departments than with the plantwide rate. Still, department rates do not consider the varying costs of different processes or activities within a department.

In traditional costing systems, overhead often is allocated to products using volume-based direct labor-hours or dollars. Firms usually adopt a plantwide overhead rate, as a result of dividing total budgeted overhead costs by total budgeted direct labor costs. Only a decade ago, overhead rates of 150 percent of direct labor costs were fairly typical. Now it is common to see overhead rates of 600 percent or even 1,000 percent in highly automated plants. As products move through a plant, they

Old Costing System Distorted Product Costs at Hewlett-Packard

The old product costing system at Hewlett-Packard (HP) used the volume-based labor cost as the cost driver for all nonmaterial costs, regardless of the actual cost drivers. On average, labor costs were only 2 percent of total costs, so it was unlikely that they were the major cause of most other costs. The result of using labor cost was significant cost distortion—products with higher labor costs were overcosted whereas products with lower labor costs were undercosted. Managers did not have confidence in the product cost predictions using this old labor-based system.

Therefore, HP decided to switch to an activity-based costing system. It measured cost behavior as part of its companywide implementation of activity-based costing. HP used detailed engineering analysis to revise its accounting system at many of its manufacturing sites.

Source: Mike Mertz and Aelene Hardy, "ABC Puts Accountants on Design Team at HP," *Management Accounting,* September 1993, pp. 22–27.

are charged overhead costs based on the plantwide rate times the cost of direct labor required by each product.

Such overhead cost allocations in a factory using automation can cause serious distortions. To allocate overhead based on direct labor cost, we have to assume that products with higher direct labor contents are responsible for greater overhead costs, so they need to be charged higher overhead allocations. In automated environments, however, overhead allocations based on direct labor systematically overstate the costs of products with high direct labor content and understate the costs of other products that utilize more automated processes. Also, because fixed manufacturing costs are associated with groups of products, allocation of factory overhead to any individual product becomes more difficult.

Volume, Size, and Diversity Complexity

The distortions from unit- or volume-based product cost systems are most severe in firms producing a diverse mix of products. Products that differ in volume, size, and complexity consume support resources in significantly different amounts. As product diversity increases, the quantities of resources required for handling transaction and support activities rise, thereby increasing the distortion of reported product costs from traditional cost systems.

Cooper demonstrates how traditional costing systems overcost large-size, high-volume products and undercost small-size, low-volume products when product diversity exists within the same operation.[4]

Traditional costing systems using unit- or volume-based measures or cost drivers can cause distorted inventory measurement (even if they are perfectly within financial accounting standards). This distortion, in turn, may cause undesirable strategic effects, such as wrong product-line decisions, unrealistic pricing, and ineffective resource allocations.

ACTIVITY-BASED COSTING

To evaluate the profitability of different product lines, it is necessary to do a proper tracing of factory overhead costs to the end products, given the greater relative importance of factory overhead. However, because factory overhead costs are related only indirectly to end products, management accountants have had to devise some reasonable basis of applying such costs to individual products. Activity-based costing is the result of the improvement efforts by management accountants.

Activities, Resources, Cost Objects, and Cost Drivers

Before discussing the definition of the activity-based costing, we should define these terms: *activity, resource, cost object, cost pool, cost element,* and *cost driver.*

---

[4] Robin Cooper, "The Rise of Activity-Based Costing—Part One: What Is an Activity-Based Cost System?" *Journal of Cost Management,* Summer 1988, pp. 45–54.

An *activity* is work performed within an organization.[5] Activities are actions, movements, or work sequences. An activity also is defined as an aggregation of actions performed within an organization that is useful for purposes of activity-based costing. For example, moving inventory is a warehousing activity.

A *resource* is an economic element that is applied or used in the performance of activities. Salaries and materials, for example, are resources used to perform activities.

A *cost object* is any end item for which the cost measurement is desired. Examples of cost objects include any customer, product, service, contract, project, or other work unit for which a separate cost measurement is desired.

A **cost element** is an amount paid for a resource consumed by an activity and included in a *cost pool*. For example, a machinery cost pool may include power cost, engineering cost, and depreciation cost elements.

A *cost driver* is any factor that causes a change in the cost of an activity. It is also a measurable factor used to assign costs to activities and from activities to other activities, products, or services.[6] The two kinds of cost drivers are resource drivers and activity drivers.

A **resource driver** is a measure of the quantity of resources consumed by an activity. It is the cost driver used to assign a resource cost consumed by an activity to a particular cost pool. An example of a resource driver is the percentage of total square feet occupied by an activity.

An **activity driver** is a measure of frequency and intensity of demands placed on activities by cost objects. An activity driver is used to assign cost pool costs to cost objects. An example is the number of different parts in a finished product used to measure the consumption of materials-handling activities by each product.

> A **resource** is an economic element that is applied or used in the performance of activities.
>
> **Cost element** is an amount paid for a resource consumed by an activity and included in a cost pool.
>
> A **resource driver** is a measure of the quantity of resources consumed by an activity.
>
> An **activity driver** is a measure of frequency and intensity of demands placed on activities by cost objects.

What Is Activity-Based Costing?

Activity-based costing (ABC) is a costing approach that assigns costs to products or services based on their consumption of the resources caused by activities. The premise of this costing approach is that a firm's products or services are performed

> ◄ **LEARNING OBJECTIVE 3**
> Describe an activity-based costing system and its benefits, limitations, and two-stage allocation procedures.

Cost Drivers at Cal Electronic Circuits, Inc.

Cal Electronic Circuits, Inc., uses 10 cost drivers for the production of printed circuit boards (PCB):

1. Number of setups.
2. Number of holes drilled in PCB.
3. Number of layers in PCB.
4. Number of drill sizes required.
5. Number of images per panel in PCB.
6. PCB length and width.
7. Number of parts per panel.
8. Number of engineering hours.
9. Lot size.
10. Volume of chemical waste.

Source: John Lee, "Activity Based Costing at Cal Electronic Circuits," *Management Accounting,* October 1990, pp. 36–38.

---

[5]   Norm Raffish and Peter B. B. Turney, "Glossary of Activity-Based Management," *Journal of Cost Management,* Fall 1991, pp. 53–63. Other definitions from this glossary also are used in this chapter.

[6]   Institute of Management Accountants, "Statement No. 4T: Implementing Activity-Based Costing," 1993, p. 34. Cost drivers reflect the consumption of costs by activities and the consumption of activities by other activities, products, or services.

by activities and that the required activities use resources incurring costs. Resources are assigned to activities, then activities are assigned to cost objects based on their use. ABC recognizes the causal relationships of cost drivers to activities.

With ABC, factory overhead costs are assigned to cost objects such as products or services by identifying the resources, the activities, and their costs and quantities needed to produce output. A cost driver is used to calculate the resource cost of a unit of activity. Then each resource cost is assigned to the product or service by multiplying the cost of each activity by the quantities of each activity consumed in a given period.

Activity-based costing is a system that maintains and processes financial and operating data on a firm's resources based on activities, cost objects, cost drivers, and activity performance measures. It also assigns costs to activities and cost objects.

Two-Stage Allocation Procedures

A **two-stage allocation** assigns a firm's resource costs, namely factory overhead costs, to cost pools and then to cost objects based on how cost objects use those resources. In traditional costing systems, factory overhead costs are assigned to plant or departmental cost pools or cost centers, and then to production outputs (see Exhibit 4–1). This traditional two-stage assignment procedure, however, distorts reported product or service costs considerably. Especially in the second stage, the traditional costing system assigns factory overhead costs from plant or departmental cost pools to outputs using volume-based or unit-level cost drivers, such as direct labor- and machine-hours, direct materials costs, direct labor costs, and output units. Because many factory overhead resources are not used in proportion to the number of output units produced, the traditional systems may provide highly inaccurate measures of the costs of support activities used by individual products or services.

Activity-based costing systems differ from traditional costing systems by modeling the usage of a firm's resources on activities performed by these resources, and then linking the cost of these activities to cost objects such as products or services (see Exhibit 4–2). In particular, activity-based costing systems measure more accurately the cost of activities that are not proportional to the volume of outputs produced.

Under activity-based costing systems, the first-stage allocation is a resource cost assignment process by which factory overhead costs are assigned to activity cost pools or groups of activities called activity centers by using appropriate resource drivers.

A **two-stage allocation** assigns a firm's resource costs, namely factory overhead costs, to cost pools and then to cost objects.

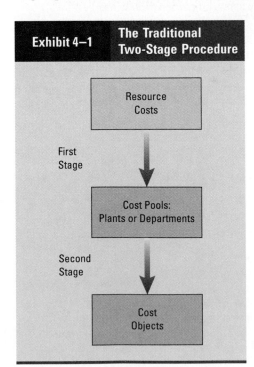

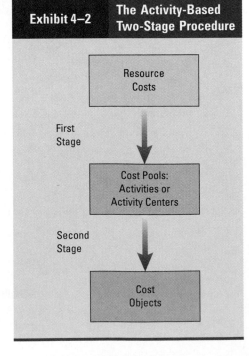

The second-stage allocation is an activity cost assignment process by which the costs of activities are assigned to cost objects using appropriate activity drivers. An activity driver measures how much of an activity is used by a cost object.

Activity-based costing systems differ from traditional costing systems in two ways: First, cost pools are defined as activities or activity centers rather than production plant or department cost centers. Second, the cost drivers used to assign activity costs to cost objects are activity drivers based on cause–effect relationships. The traditional approach uses a single volume-based driver that often bears little or no relationship to either the resource cost or the cost object.

These modifications to the two-stage procedure allow activity-based costing systems to report more accurate costs than a traditional costing system because they identify clearly the costs of the different activities being performed in the firm. They also assign the costs of those activities to output cost objects using measures that represent the types of demands individual output products or services make on those activities.

When Is an Activity-Based Costing System Needed?

Activity-based costing systems provide better costing and can help firms manage efficiently as well as understand their competitive advantages, strengths, and weaknesses. In the past, activity-based costing systems were implemented only when (1) the cost of measuring the activities and their costs was reduced, perhaps because of computerized scheduling systems on the production floor; (2) stronger competition increased the cost of errors caused by erroneous pricing; and (3) product diversity was high in volume, size, or complexity.[7] All firms should use the ABC system when the benefits of such a system exceed the costs of implementing it.

Steps in Designing an Activity-Based Costing System

The three major steps in designing an activity-based costing system are to (1) identify resource costs and activities, (2) assign resource costs to activities, and (3) assign activity costs to cost objects.

Step One: Identify Resource Costs and Activities

The first step in designing an ABC system is to identify resource costs and conduct an activity analysis. Resource costs are incurred to perform various activities. Most resource costs are in the subaccounts of the general ledger, such as materials, supplies, purchasing, materials handling, warehousing, office space, furniture and fixtures, buildings, equipment, utilities, salaries and benefits, engineering, and accounting.

An *activity analysis* is the identification and description of the work done (activities) in an organization. Activity analysis includes gathering data from existing documents and records, and using survey questionnaires, observation, and ongoing interviews of key personnel. ABC project team members typically ask each key employee or manager questions such as these:

- What work or activities do you do?
- How much time do you spend performing the activities?
- What resources are required to perform the activities?
- Which operational data best reflect the performance of the activities?
- What value does the activity have for the organization?

The team also collects activity data by observing and listing the work performed.

Manufacturing processes have four categories of activities:

1. A **unit-level activity** is performed for each unit of production. Unit-level activities are performed every time a unit of production volume is performed. Examples of

A **unit-level activity** is performed for each unit of production.

---

[7]   Robin Cooper, "The Rise of Activity-Based Costing—Part Two: When Do I Need an Activity-Based Cost System?" *The Journal of Cost Management*, Fall 1988, pp. 41–48.

A **batch-level activity** is performed for each batch of products rather than for each unit of production.

A **product-sustaining activity** is performed to support the production of a different product.

A **facility-sustaining activity** is performed to support the production of products in general.

unit-level (volume-based or unit-based) activities include using direct materials, using direct labor-hours, inserting a component, inspecting every item, and running machines.

2. A **batch-level activity** is performed for each batch or group of products rather than for each unit of production. Batch-level activities are performed every time a batch of product is produced. Examples of batch-level activities are machine setup, purchase ordering, production scheduling, inspection of every batch, and materials handling.

3. A **product-sustaining activity** is performed to support the production of a different product. Examples of product-sustaining activities include product design, parts administration, issuance of engineering change orders, and expediting.

4. A **facility-sustaining activity** is performed to support the production of products in general.[8] Examples of facility-sustaining activities include security, safety, maintenance, plant management, plant depreciation, and payment of property taxes.

Step Two: Assign Resource Costs to Activities

Activities drive the cost of resources used. Resource drivers are used to assign resource costs to activities. An important criterion for choosing a good resource driver is the cause–effect relationship. Typical resource drivers include (1) meters for utilities; (2) the number of employees for payroll-related activities; (3) the number of setups for a machine setup activity; (4) the number of moves for a materials-handling activity; (5) machine-hours for a machine running activity; and (6) square feet for a janitorial cleaning activity.

Although the company's general ledger is a good starting point to find information about the cost of resources used to perform activities, most general ledger systems report the costs of different resources, such as indirect labor, electricity, equipment, and supplies, but do not report the cost of activities performed. New accounting systems are needed to obtain this information.

The cost of the resources can be assigned to activities by direct tracing or estimation. Direct tracing requires measuring the actual usage of resources by activities. For example, power used to operate a machine can be traced directly to that machine's operation by observing meter usage.

If direct measurement is not available, department managers or supervisors are asked to estimate the percentage of time (or effort) spent by employees on each of the identified activities.

For example, at the New River Valley Works of AT&T, multiple resource cost drivers are used to allocate different costs of resources to activity center cost pools (different shops). Factory overhead at the New River Valley plant is allocated as shown in Exhibit 4–3.[9]

Activities and Cost Drivers at Siemens Electric Motor Works

Cost Driver	Activity Level
1. Direct labor-hours	Unit
2. Machine-hours	Unit
3. Direct materials dollars	Unit
4. Value added	Unit
5. Number of product orders	Batch
6. Number of special components	Batch

Source: Robin Cooper, "Cost Classification in Unit-Based and Activity-Based Manufacturing Cost Systems," *Journal of Cost Management,* Fall 1990, pp. 4–14.

---

[8] Robin Cooper, "Cost Classification in Unit-Based and Activity-Based Manufacturing Cost Systems," *Journal of Cost Management,* Fall 1990, pp. 4–14.

[9] F. B. Green, Felix Amenkhienan, and George Johnson, "Performance Measures and JIT," *Management Accounting,* February 1991, pp. 50–53.

Sample Resource Drivers at Hughes Aircraft

For years, Hughes Aircraft had allocated service department costs to operating departments using the number of employees as the primary resource driver because of its simplicity. In 1991, the company adopted activity-based costing to improve its costing system. For example, Hughes Aircraft uses the following service departments and resource drivers:

Service Department (Resources)	Allocation Bases (Resource Drivers)
1. Human resources	Number of employees
	Number of new hires
	Training hours
2. Security	Square footage
3. Data processing	Lines printed
	CPU minutes
	Storage units

Source: Jack Haedicke and David Feil, "Hughes Aircraft Sets the Standard for ABC," *Management Accounting,* February 1991, pp. 29–33.

Exhibit 4–3   Resource Cost Drivers at AT&T New River Valley Plant

Resources	Resource Cost Drivers
Personnel	Number of workers in shop
Storeroom	Number of "picks" used by shop
Engineers	Time worked in or for shop
Materials management	Time worked in or for shop
Accounting	Time worked in or for shop
Research and development	New codes developed for production
Quality	Time worked in or for shop
Utilities	Square-footage

Source: F. B. Green, Felix Amenkhienan, and George Johnson, "Performance Measures and JIT," *Management Accounting,* February 1991, p. 53.

Step Three: Assign Activity Costs to Cost Objects

Once the cost activities are known, it is necessary to measure the cost per unit of activity with which these activities are carried out. This is done by measuring the cost per unit of output produced by the activity. Appropriate comparisons over time and with other organizations can be used then to determine the efficiency (productivity) of these activities.

Outputs are the cost objects for which activities are performed. Typical outputs for a cost system can include products, services, customers, projects, or business units. For example, in an insurance company, the outputs could be the individual products or services offered to customers, the customers themselves, the insurance agents, or the divisions that are receiving benefits from corporate resources.

Activity drivers are used to assign activity costs to the cost objects. Typical activity drivers are the number of purchase orders, number of receiving reports, number of inspection reports or hours, number of parts stored, number of payments, direct labor-hours, machine-hours, number of setups, and manufacturing cycle time.

For example, John Deere Component Works started its ABC system in 1985 with eight activities (cost pools) and activity (cost) drivers as shown in Exhibit 4–4:[10]

---

[10] Robin Cooper and Robert S. Kaplan, *The Design of Cost Management Systems* (Englewood Cliffs, N.J.: Prentice Hall, 1991), pp. 291–310.

Exhibit 4–4	Activity Drivers at John Deere Component Works	
Activity	**Level**	**Driver**
Materials purchasing	Unit	Material cost
Direct labor support	Unit	Direct labor cost
Machine operation	Unit	Machine-hours
Setup	Batch	Setup hours
Production order	Batch	Number of orders
Materials handling	Batch	Number of loads
Part administration	Product	Number of parts
General and administrative	Facility	Amount of value-added

Source: Robin Cooper and Robert S. Kaplan, *The Design of Cost Management Systems: Solution Manual and Teaching Notes* (Englewood Cliffs, N.J.: Prentice Hall, 1991), p. 310.

Cost Driver Selection Process at Hewlett-Packard's Surface Mount Center

At HP's Surface Mount Center in Boise, the ABC system has been fully operational since early 1993. This facility manufactures about 50 different electronic circuit boards for internal HP customers. The center's accounting, production, and engineering staffs jointly conducted an intense analysis of the production process and cost behavior patterns to select cost drivers. This combination of regression analysis of accounts and engineering analysis helped the management to choose cost drivers.

Source: C. Mike Merz and A. Hardy, "ABC Puts Accountants on Design Team at HP," *Management Accounting,* September 1993, pp. 22–27.

Activity drivers should explain why an activity's costs go up or down. Once the cost of each activity and what drives it are known, activity drivers can be used to determine which products are consuming activities. Cost is allocated in proportion to the cost drivers used by each product or product line.

Benefits and Limitations

Benefits

Activity-based costing helps reduce distortions caused by traditional cost allocations. It provides a clear view of how the mix of a firm's diverse products, services, and activities contributes to the bottom line in the long run.

Major benefits of the activity-based costing are:

1. ABC provides more accurate and informative product costs, which lead to more accurate product profitability measurements and to better-informed strategic decisions about pricing, product line, customer market, and capital expenditure.

2. ABC provides more accurate measurements of activity-driving costs, which helps managers improve product and process value by making better product design decisions, controlling costs better, and fostering various value-enhancement projects.

3. ABC provides managers with easier access to relevant costs for making business decisions.

Limitations

Although activity-based costing provides better tracing of costs to individual products, it does have limitations that managers should be aware of before using it to calculate product costs:

1. **Allocations.** Even if activity data are available, some costs probably require allocations to departments and products based on arbitrary volume measures because

> ### Activity-Based Costing Helps Original Bradford Soap Works
>
> The Original Bradford Soap Works, a New England–based manufacturer of 5,000 private-label soap products, faced a crisis in the mid-1980s when the firm increased the variety of its products and the volume of all product types, and new customers demanded unique service requirements. The firm decided to implement an activity-based costing system to track the job costs of products based on activities consumed to produce the products.
>
> The ABC system provided Bradford managers with useful information for making pricing and product-mix decisions, and for cost and profit control purposes. In addition, ABC continues to help Bradford employees identify opportunities for improvement on the plant floor, reinforcing the total quality process.
>
> **Source:** Frances Gammell and C. L. NcNair, "Jumping the Growth Threshold through Activity-Based Cost Management," *Management Accounting,* September 1994, pp. 37–46.

finding a specific activity that causes the incidence of the costs may not be practical. Examples are some of the facility-sustaining costs, such as cleaning the factory and managing the production process.

2.   Omission of costs. Another limitation of ABC is that some costs identified with specific products are omitted from the analysis. Activities that cause such costs may include marketing, advertising, research and development, product engineering, and warranty claims. The additional costs simply would be traced to individual products and added to the manufacturing costs to determine the total product cost. Traditionally, marketing and administrative costs have not been included in product costs because of GAAP financial reporting requirements that they be included in period costs.

3.   Expense and time consumed. An ABC system is very expensive to develop and implement. It is also very time-consuming. Like most innovative management or accounting systems, it usually takes more than a year to develop and implement ABC successfully.

Comparison of Traditional and Activity-Based Costing Systems

An activity-based costing system traces costs to products through activities. Factory overhead costs are assigned to homogeneous cost pools or activity centers rather than to departments. Activity center costs are assigned to products or services. The process has three steps: First, costs traced to the same or similar resource drivers are assigned to the same cost pool or activity center. Second, an overhead rate is calculated for each activity center based on a selected activity driver. Finally, the overhead costs are assigned to each product by multiplying the specific overhead rate by the quantity of the activity driver consumed in that product. The major differences between the traditional costing and the activity-based costing system lie in the second and third steps.

The following example contrasts steps 2 and 3 of the traditional costing system, using direct labor-hours as the cost driver, with the activity-based costing system, using both volume-based and non-volume-based cost drivers.

Northern High-Tech, Inc., has successfully produced and sold two quality printers. Assume the company has the following financial and cost data for the two products:

◀ **LEARNING OBJECTIVE 4**
Compute product costs under a traditional costing system and an activity-based costing system.

	Deluxe	Regular
Production volume	5,000	15,000
Selling price	$400.00	$200.00
Unit direct material and labor costs	$200.00	$80.00
Direct labor-hours	25,000	75,000

The company's management accountant has identified the following activities, budgeted cost pools, and activity drivers:

Activity	Budgeted Cost Pool	Activity Driver
Engineering	$ 125,000	Engineering hours
Setups	300,000	Number of setups
Machine running	1,500,000	Machine-hours
Packing	75,000	Number of packing orders
Total	$2,000,000	

These are the actual activity units or transactions for both products:

	Activity Consumption		
Activity Driver	Deluxe	Regular	Total
Engineering hours	5,000	7,500	12,500
Number of setups	200	100	300
Machine-hours	50,000	100,000	150,000
Number of packing orders	5,000	10,000	15,000

Traditional Costing Analysis   In the traditional costing approach, the factory overhead (OH) is allocated on the basis of direct labor-hours (DLH):

Total direct labor-hours: 25,000 + 75,000 = 100,000 DLH

Overhead rate per DLH: $2,000,000/100,000 = $20 per DLH

OH assigned to Deluxe: $20 × 25,000 = $500,000

Deluxe OH cost per unit: $500,000/5,000 = $100

OH assigned to Regular: $20 × 75,000 = $1,500,00

Regular OH cost per unit: $1,500,000/15,000 = $100

Exhibit 4–5 presents a product profitability analysis under the traditional costing system.

Activity-Based Costing Analysis   In the activity-based costing approach, the cost driver rate for each activity cost driver—that is, the activity rate—is calculated as follows:

(1) Activity Driver	(2) Cost	(3) Activity Consumption	(4) = (2)/(3) Activity Rate
Engineering hours	$125,000	12,500	$10
Number of setups	300,000	300	1,000
Machine-hours	1,500,000	150,000	10
Number of packing orders	75,000	15,000	5

Factory overhead costs are assigned to both products, as shown by these calculations:

Deluxe Printer

(1) Activity Driver	(2) Activity Rate	(3) Number of Activities	(4)=(2)×(3) Total OH	(5) Unit OH
Engineering hours	$10	5,000	$50,000	$10
Number of setups	1,000	200	200,000	40
Machine-hours	10	50,000	500,000	100
Number of packing orders	5	5,000	25,000	5

Regular Printer

(1) Activity Driver	(2) Activity Rate	(3) Number of Activities	(4)=(2)×(3) Total OH	(5) Unit OH
Engineering hours	$10	7,500	$75,000	$5.00
Number of setups	1,000	100	100,000	6.67
Machine-hours	10	100,000	1,000,000	66.67
Number of packing orders	5	10,000	50,000	3.33

Exhibit 4–5	Product Profitability Analysis under the Traditional Costing System	
	Deluxe	**Regular**
Unit selling price	$400	$200
Unit product cost		
Direct material and labor	$200	$80
Factory overhead	100	100
Cost per unit	$300	$180
Product margin	$100	$20

Exhibit 4–6	Product Profitability Analysis under the ABC Costing System				
		Deluxe		*Regular*	
Unit selling price		$400			$200.00
Unit product cost					
Direct material and labor		$200		$80.00	
Factory overhead					
Engineering	$ 10			$ 5.00	
Setups	40			6.67	
Machine running	100			66.67	
Packing	5	155		3.33	81.67
Cost per unit			355		161.67
Product margin			$ 45		$ 38.33

Exhibit 4–7	Comparison of Alternative Costing Approaches		
	Allocation Method		
	(1) **Traditional**	**(2)** **ABC**	**(1) – (2)** **Difference**
Deluxe			
Total overhead	$500,000	$775,000	$(275,000)
Unit OH cost	100	155	(55)
Unit margin	100	45	55
Regular			
Total overhead	$1,500,000	$1,225,000	$275,000
Unit OH cost	100	81.67	18.33
Unit margin	20	38.33	(18.33)

Exhibit 4–6 presents a product profitability analysis under the activity-based costing system.

Exhibit 4–7 presents a comparison of product costs and profit margins under the two costing systems.

Remember, one major limitation of the traditional costing system is that it generally undercosts complex low-volume products and overcosts high-volume products. The activity-based costing system presents a more accurate measurement pattern of overhead consumption. The preceding comparison shows that the traditional product costing system may significantly undercost the Deluxe printer (a low-volume product) and overcost the Regular printer (a high-volume product), compared with the actual overhead consumption. Consequently, traditional product costing can cause distorted inventory measurement, incorrect product-line decisions, unrealistic pricing, ineffective resource allocations, misplaced strategic focus, misidentified critical success factors, and lost competitive advantage.

BusinessWeek

How Is Weyerhaeuser Bringing Down Its Overhead?

(Continued from page 89)

A: It boils down to activity-based costing.

After years of staff buildup, white-collar layoffs may be an unavoidable first step, but eliminating positions just isn't enough. Many companies have found that it's just as important to get a handle on overhead costs—thus, like Weyerhaeuser, they've turned to activity-based costing to track costs. This technique assigns costs to each task performed by employees—even mail opening and telephone answering—making it easier to identify waste.

The idea, says Kenneth J. Stancato, vice president and controller at Weyerhaeuser Co., is to analyze work processes and eliminate as many "redundancies and non-value-added activities" as possible. At Weyerhaeuser, overhead barely ticked down, to 9.65 percent of revenues in 1991 from 9.7 percent in 1989, because sagging lumber and paper prices depressed revenues. Now, the company is vowing to keep overhead flat as prices recover and revenues rise. It's a drama that will be played out at hundreds of companies throughout the coming years.

For further reading, see the source: "Can Corporate America Get Out from Under Its Overhead?" *Business Week,* May 18, 1992.

ACTIVITY-BASED MANAGEMENT

What Is Activity-Based Management?

LEARNING OBJECTIVE 5 ▶
Describe an activity-based management system and value-added and non-value-added activities.

After implementing activity-based costing, firms often take on activity-based management. Broadly speaking, under activity-based management both the value received by customers and the firm's profits from providing this value increase.[11]

Activity-based management (ABM) is the management of activities to improve the value received by the customer and to increase the profit achieved by providing this value.[12] ABM draws on ABC as its major source of information.

Major advantages of the ABM approach include:

1. ABM measures the effectiveness of the key business processes and activities and identifies how they can be improved to reduce costs and to increase value to customers.

2. ABM improves management focus by allocating resources to key value-added activities, key customers, key products, and continuous-improvement methods to maintain the firm's competitive advantage.

Cost driver analysis is the examination, quantification, and explanation of the effects of cost drivers.

A **cause-and-effect diagram** maps out a list of causes that affect an activity, process, stated problem, or a desired outcome.

Pareto analysis is a management tool that shows 20 percent of a set of important cost drivers are responsible for 80 percent of the total cost incurred.

Activity-based management uses cost driver analysis, activity analysis, and performance measurement. **Cost driver analysis** is the examination, quantification, and explanation of the effects of cost drivers. The purpose of cost driver analysis is to search for the root causes of activity costs. Tools used in cost driver analysis include benchmarking, cause-and-effect diagrams, and Pareto analysis.

Benchmarking is the search for the best practices within and across industries to improve a firm's performance of a task, activity, or process. A **cause-and-effect diagram** maps out a list of causes that affect an activity, process, stated problem, or a desired outcome. Because the shape of the diagram is similar to a fishbone, it is called a fishbone diagram. **Pareto analysis** is a management tool that shows 20 percent of a set of important cost drivers are responsible for 80 percent of the total cost incurred. These tools are discussed in more detail in Chapter 6.

Recall that an *activity analysis* identifies and describes the activities in an organization. Through interviews, questionnaires, observation, and a review of documentation, an activity analysis collects information.

---

[11]   Peter B. B. Turney, "Activity-Based Management," *Management Accounting,* January 1992, pp. 20–25.

[12]   Norm Raffish and Peter B. B. Turney, "Glossary of Activity-Based Management," *Journal of Cost Management,* Fall 1991, p. 57.

Activity-Based Management at Stockham Valve and Fittings

Stockham Valve and Fittings implemented activity-based management and was able to:

1. Produce parts at the lowest cost.
2. Design parts to minimize manufacturing costs.
3. Modify equipment to reduce costs.
4. Increase prices of products priced below ABC cost, and drop unprofitable products.

Source: Peter B. B. Turney, "Activity-Based Management," *Management Accounting,* January 1992, pp. 20–25.

The Role of ABC/ABM Tools

Critical Questions	ABC/ABM Tools
1. What do we do?	1. Activity analysis, cause-and-effect diagram, Pareto analysis
2. How much does it cost?	2. Activity-based costing
3. How well do we do it?	3. Performance measurement
4. How can we do it better?	4. Benchmarking, just-in-time, process redesign, eliminating non-value-added activities

General Motors Supplies Eliminated Non-Value-Added Activities

General Motors Corporation uses ABC/ABM to force its parts suppliers to cut their costs and prices by eliminating these non-value-added activities: (1) overproducing, (2) overstocking, (3) moving, (4) processing in too many steps, (5) waiting, (6) reworking, (7) idling equipment, (8) idling space, and (9) making a product with features not required by customers.

Source: Joe Cyr, "Waste Removal—Now," *CMA Magazine,* June 1993, p. 23.

Performance measurement identifies indicators of the work performed and the results achieved in an activity, process, or organizational unit. Performance measures should include both financial and nonfinancial measures. Examples of financial performance measures are the cost per unit of output, return on sales, and the gross cost of every department's value-added and non-value-added activities. Nonfinancial performance measures evaluate customers, manufacturing processes, and human resources. Examples of nonfinancial performance measures are the number of customer complaints, customer satisfaction survey results, defective parts or outputs, output units, cycle time, frequency of on-time delivery, number of employees' suggestions, and employee morale survey results. Recall that Chapter 2 discussed the balanced scorecard performance measurement concept, which includes financial performance, customer satisfaction, internal business processes, and innovation and learning.

Performance measurement identifies indicators of the work performed and the results achieved in an activity, process, or organizational unit.

Value-Added and Non-Value-Added Activities

Activity-based management focuses on identifying activities that can be eliminated and making sure that needed activities are carried out efficiently. To improve operations, management must search out unnecessary or inefficient activities, determine the cost drivers for the activities, and change the level of those cost drivers. A major task of the activity analysis is to identify value-added and non-value-added activities.

A **value-added activity** is an activity that contributes to customer value and satisfaction or satisfies an organizational need. Examples include designing products, processing by direct labor, adding direct materials, machining, and delivering products.

A **value-added activity** is an activity that contributes to customer value and satisfaction or satisfies an organizational need.

Summary of Value-Added and Non-Value-Added Activities

Activity	Value-Added	Non-Value-Added
Designing product	X	
Setting up		X
Waiting		X
Moving		X
Processing	X	
Reworking		X
Repairing		X
Storing		X
Inspecting		X
Delivering product	X	

Daton Technologies Identifies Value-Added and Non-Value-Added Activities

Daton Technologies uses five questions to classify activities as value-added or non-value-added:

1. Is the activity of value to an external customer?
2. Is the activity required to meet corporate rules?
3. Is the activity required for sound business practices?
4. Is the activity of value to an internal customer?
5. Is the activity a waste?

The company classifies answers to the first two questions under value-added activities and to the last three questions under non-value-added activities. Examples of value-added activities in Daton Technologies are extrusion runs, shipping, designing parts, and making tools. Examples of non-value-added activities are setup, inspection, regrind, and process returns.

Source: Neal R. Pemberton, Logan Arumugam, and Nabil Hassan, "ABM at Daton Technologies: From Obstacles to Opportunities," *Management Accounting,* March 1996, pp. 20–27.

Exhibit 4–8	A Television News Broadcasting Firm's Value-Added and Non-Value-Added Activities

A *value-added activity* is one that, if eliminated, would affect the accuracy and effectiveness of the newscast and decrease total viewers as well as ratings for that time slot.
1. **Activities that augment accuracy**
   - Verification of story sources and acquired information.
2. **Activities that augment effectiveness**
   - Efficient electronic journalism to ensure effective taped segments.
   - Newscast story order planned so that viewers can follow from one story to the next.
   - Field crew time used to access the best footage possible.
   - Meaningful news story writing.
   - Contents of the newscast planned so that viewers get the best possible package of stories.

A *non-value-added activity* is one that, if eliminated, would not affect the accuracy and effectiveness of the newscast. Therefore, the activity contributes nothing to the quest for viewer retention and improved ratings.
1. **Activities that generate excess**
   - Developing stories from beginning to end but not using them in a newscast.
   - Assigning more than one person to develop each process of the same news story.
2. **Activities that augment delay (downtime)**
   - Newscast not completed on time because some step in the process was inefficient.
   - Too many employees on a particular shift with not enough work to go around.

A **non-value-added activity** does not contribute to customer value or to the organization's needs. Examples include setting up, moving, waiting, repairing, inspecting, and storing.

Exhibit 4–8 presents an example of a television news broadcasting firm's value-added and non-value-added activities.

A non-value-added activity does not contribute to customer value or to the organization's needs.

MANUFACTURING INDUSTRY APPLICATIONS

Activity-based costing initially was developed for manufacturing industry applications. Many manufacturing companies, such as Hewlett-Packard and Advanced Micro Devices, have implemented activity-based costing and management systems successfully.

◄ **LEARNING OBJECTIVE 6**
Explain how activity-based costing systems are used in manufacturing industry.

ABC at Hewlett-Packard

The Roseville Network Division (RND) of Hewlett-Packard (HP) was one of the first divisions to use activity-based costing. Because RND's products were increasing in number and decreasing in length of product life, the design of new products and their production processes was especially important to the division's success. The old costing system, however, did not provide information managers could use to compare the production costs of different designs.

RND's new costing system focused on the costs of each production process—the different activities of the division. The ABC system started with only two cost drivers—direct labor-hours and number of insertions; now it has nine cost drivers, as shown in Exhibit 4–9.

Engineering managers at RND were pleased with the activity-based costing system that greatly influenced the design of new products. For example, once it became clear that manual insertion was three times as expensive as automatic insertion, designs were modified to include more automatic insertion. The system clearly had the desired effect of influencing the behavior of product designers.[13]

Advanced Micro Devices

Advanced Micro Devices (AMD), a major semiconductor manufacturer, performed its first activity-based costing project in a test and assembly facility in Penang, Malaysia. The new ABC system at Penang identified significant product cost distortions (high-volume, simple products were overcosted by 20 to 30 percent, and low-volume, complex products were undercosted by 600 to 700 percent). ABC provided AMD management with a more accurate basis for setting transfer prices between manufacturing and the divisions.

Exhibit 4–9	Cost Drivers at HP's Roseville Network Division
Cost Driver	**Activity Level**
1. Number of axial insertions	Unit
2. Number of radical insertions	Unit
3. Number of DIP insertions	Unit
4. Number of manual insertions	Unit
5. Number of test hours	Unit
6. Number of solder joints	Unit
7. Number of boards	Product
8. Number of parts	Product
9. Number of slots	Product

Source: Robin Cooper and Peter B. B. Turney, "Internally Forced Activity-Based Cost Systems," in *Measures for Manufacturing Excellence*, ed. R. S. Kaplan (Boston: Harvard Business School Press, 1990), p. 17.

[13] Robin Cooper and Peter B. B. Turney, "Internally Forced Activity-Based Cost Systems," in *Measures for Manufacturing Excellence*, ed. R. S. Kaplan (Boston: Harvard Business School Press, 1990).

Exhibit 4–10	Cost Drivers for Marketing Activities
Marketing Activity Cost Pool	**Cost Driver**
Advertising	Sales units or dollars
	Number of sales calls
Selling	Sales dollars
	Number of orders obtained
Order filling, shipping, warehousing	Weight of shipped product
	Number, weight, or size of units ordered
	Units of shipped product
General office (e.g., credit and collection)	Number of customer orders
	Number of invoice lines

Source: Ronald J. Lewis, "Activity-Based Costing for Marketing," *Management Accounting,* November 1991, pp. 34–35.

Some of the key non-volume-based cost drivers included (1) number of line items (for production scheduling and setup activities); (2) number of quality problems that were encountered (for some process-sustaining activities); and (3) number of times a product fell below a certain point for yield and quality improvement activities.

The high total of expenses driven by these non-volume-based costs underscored the inaccuracies in the old system that allocated all expenses to products using labor- and machine-hours.

The success of the project was described by the director of finance, who stated, "ABC provided AMD with a cost system solution which will enable and support AMD's strategy of managing profitable growth."[14]

MARKETING AND ADMINISTRATIVE APPLICATIONS

LEARNING OBJECTIVE 7 ▶
Describe how activity-based costing systems are used in marketing and administrative activities.

Activity-based costing also can be applied to marketing and administrative activities, such as selling, advertising, order filling, shipping, warehousing, billing, and payroll accounting. After taking a look at marketing activities and related cost drivers, we present AT&T's application of ABC to billing activities.

Marketing activities include advertising, selling, order filling, shipping, warehousing, and credit and collection by the general office. To apply ABC to marketing activities, management accountants trace marketing costs to activity cost pools; then they trace them to product lines and territories to measure profitability. Exhibit 4–10 presents example cost drivers for marketing activities.[15]

AT&T turned to ABC after its breakup into smaller, more focused business units. The breakup and price deregulation made understanding and managing costs, rather than simply allocating them, critical for AT&T. As a result, AT&T managers implemented an activity-based costing system to help them understand the activities driving their business.

The business billing center was selected for the ABC pilot project. The business billing center activities included monitoring billing records; editing checks; validating data; correcting errors; and printing, sorting, and dispatching invoices to business customers. A cross-functional team prepared a flowchart of the business operations that identified the relationships between resources and activities, between activities and processes, and between process outputs and services provided to each customer.

The cost of services provided to different customers was determined by identifying activity and cost driver consumption characteristics. The firm selected sev-

---

14 Robin Cooper, Robert Kaplan, Lawrence Maisel, Eileen Morrissey, and Ronald Oehm, *Implementing Activity-Based Cost Management: Moving from Analysis to Action—Implementing Experiences at Eight Companies* (Montvale, N.J.: Institute of Management Accountants, 1992).

15 Ronald J. Lewis, "Activity-Based Costing for Marketing," *Management Accounting,* November 1991, pp. 33–36.

eral cost drivers, including the number of customers tested, change requests, service orders, customer locations, bill resolution groups, printer hours, and pages printed.

AT&T managers found the pilot ABC model useful in helping the firm manage costs and improve its internal operating processes, supplier relationships, and customer satisfaction.[16]

SERVICE AND NOT-FOR-PROFIT APPLICATIONS

ABC has been applied mainly to manufacturing companies; it also can be useful for service and not-for-profit organizations. ABC has been developed and implemented at Alexandria Hospital; Union Pacific Railroad; Amtrak Auto-Ferry Service; Data Services, Inc.;[17] AT&T;[18] Fireman's Fund;[19] American Express;[20] and the Naval Supply System Command.[21]

◀ **LEARNING OBJECTIVE 8**
Demonstrate how activity-based costing systems are used in service and not-for-profit organizations.

Service and most not-for-profit organizations have many distinct characteristics that distinguish them from manufacturing companies. Outputs often are harder to define, service request activity is less predictable, and overhead and indirect costs are difficult to relate to product or service outputs.

Suppose that the accounting firm of Achuck, Buniel & Hinckley performs two audits this week. The traditional direct labor-based costing system uniformly assigns the cost of activities to the cost object, an audit. One cost driver, professional labor-hours, is used to allocate overhead. Both audits have required a total of 100 professional labor-hours. The firm pays $25 per hour to each of its audit staff members.

In the first audit, the audit team spent much time in researching material, faxing, and making phone calls to complete the engagement, whereas the second audit did not require as many of these activities. So, if professional labor-hours is the only method of overhead allocation, the audit that is resource-intensive would be undercosted and the audit that is less resource-intensive would be overcosted.

Total labor dollars for the week (DL)	$5,000
Total overhead costs for the week (OH)	$8,000
Overhead allocation rate = OH/DL	160% per DL

Traditional Costing System

Under the traditional costing system, total overhead cost is allocated to each audit by multiplying total labor costs by the overhead allocation rate.

	(1) DL Hours	(2) DL Rate	(3)=(1)×(2) DL Cost	(4) OH Rate	(3)×(4) Applied OH
Audit 1	100	$25/hour	$2,500	160%	$4,000
Audit 2	100	$25/hour	$2,500	160%	$4,000

As you can see, under the traditional costing system, both audits have the same overhead cost of $4,000, but audit 1 is more resource-intensive and audit 2 is less

16 Terrence Hobdy, Jeff Thomson, and Paul Sharman, "Activity-Based Management at AT&T," *Management Accounting*, April 1994, pp. 35–39.

17 William Rotch, "Activity-Based Costing in Service Industries," *Journal of Cost Management*, Summer 1990, pp. 4–14.

18 Hobdy, Thomson, and Sharman, "Activity-Based Management at AT&T."

19 Michael Crane and John Meyer, "Focusing on True Costs in a Service Organization," *Management Accounting*, February 1993, pp. 41–45.

20 David A. Carlson and S. Mark Young, "Activity-Based Total Quality Management at American Express," *Journal of Cost Management*, Spring 1993, pp. 48–58.

21 David J. Harr, "How Activity Accounting Works in Government," *Management Accounting*, September 1990, pp. 36–40.

Distorted Medicare Reimbursements with Inappropriate Cost Drivers

Hospitals must annually complete a Medicare Cost Report to be eligible for government reimbursement for services rendered to Medicare patients. This cost information is used in determining values of Medicare reimbursement parameters. This same cost information often is used as the basis for determining the charges for privately insured patients. For inpatient care costs, Medicare reporting requires that all operating costs pertaining to patient care are allocated to patients based only on the number of patient-days. Thus Medicare cost reporting does not explicitly take into account the possibility of multiple cost drivers.

In a recent study, Hwang and Kirby noted that patient care costs can be attributed to at least two cost drivers: (1) the number of days a patient spends in the hospital and (2) the number of inpatients admitted. Patient-day costs include costs such as meals, laundry, and basic nursing care, while admission costs include costs related to taking patients' history upon admission, preparing patients for surgery, intensively tending them immediately following surgery, preparing rooms for new patients, and handling medical coding and billing. Patient-days are a unit-level cost driver, and admissions are a batch-level cost driver.

Using publicly available data, Hwang and Kirby compared the results of current Medicare reimbursement procedures, which use a single volume-based, unit-level cost driver (patient-days), with the results that would be obtained if Medicare reimbursements were based on two cost drivers: a unit-level cost driver (patient-days) and a batch-level cost driver (number of admissions). Their study results suggest that Medicare is potentially overcharged for hospital patient care by between $66 million and $1.98 billion per year! The main reason is that Medicare patients tend to be older and have a much longer average length of hospitalization than private insurance patients. Because Medicare reimbursements only consider patient-days, Medicare is charged for a disproportionately large share of admitted patients.

Source: Yuchang Huang and Alison L. Kirby, "Distorted Medicare Reimbursements: The Effect of Cost Accounting Choices," *Journal of Management Accounting Research,* Fall 1994, pp. 128–43.

---

resource-intensive. Therefore, under the traditional costing system, audit 1 is undercosted and audit 2 is overcosted. To determine costing more accurately, the ABC system should be used.

Activity-Based Costing System

An activity-based costing system focuses on activities as the fundamental cost objects. This example has one cost pool and one cost driver per activity.

Activities	OH Costs	Cost Drivers	Indirect Cost Application Rate	Total Activities
Direct labor		Number of hours	$25 an hour	200
Copying/faxing	$ 900	Number of copies/faxes	$0.10 a copy/fax	9,000
Long-distance calls	1,600	Number of calls made	$10 a call	160
Research/information services	4,500	Number of calls	$50 a call	90
Data processing	1,000	Number of pages	$10 a page	100
Total	$8,000			

Audit 1 is more resource-intensive. This means more photocopies, long-distance calls, information service calls, and data processing were done to complete the audit.

Activity	Amount	Rate		Applied OH
Copying/faxing	5,000 copies	$0.10 a copy	=	$ 500
Long distance calls	100 calls	$10 a call	=	1,000
Research/information services	80 calls	$50 a call	=	4,000
Data processing	70 pages	$10 a page	=	700
			Total =	**$6,200**

In contrast, audit 2 is less resource-intensive. The breakdown of activities is

Activity	Amount	Rate		Applied OH
Copying/faxing	4,000 copies	$0.10 a copy	=	$ 400
Long distance calls	60 calls	$10 a call	=	600
Research/information services	10 calls	$50 a call	=	500
Data processing	30 pages	$10 a page	=	300
		Total	=	**$1,800**

Under the ABC system, the engagements clearly are costed more accurately than under the traditional costing system.

ACTIVITY-BASED COSTING AND STRATEGIC COST MANAGEMENT

◀ **LEARNING OBJECTIVE 9**
Relate activity-based costing to strategic cost management.

Activity-based costing is closely tied to strategic cost management. ABC assigns costs to products or customers according to the resources they consume. It shows how activities consume resources and how products or customers trigger activities. ABC describes a firm as a series of activities designed to satisfy customer needs. It provides information for managers to manage activities to improve competitiveness and to achieve strategic goals.

Activities are determined by strategic choices. Successful firms put their resources into those activities that lead to the greatest strategic benefit. ABC/ABM helps managers understand the relation between the firm's strategy and the activities and resources needed to put the strategy into place.

Cost leadership is a business strategy for achieving competitive advantage. ABC/ABM is critical to this strategy because it identifies key activities, drivers, and ways to improve processes to reduce cost. Providing superior customer value is another business strategy for achieving competitive advantage. ABC/ABM can help managers identify value-enhancement opportunities. ABC/ABM also can help managers develop a customer strategy, support a technological leadership strategy, or establish a pricing strategy by identifying and analyzing key activities, processes, cost drivers, and improvement methods.

Specifically ABC/ABM provides answers to these strategic cost management questions:

- How do the cost structures and profits of a firm measure up to its competition?
- What are the potential impacts on pricing, product design, process design, manufacturing technology, and product-line decisions when a firm switches from the traditional costing system to an activity-based costing system?
- What are the cost impacts on different products when a firm adopts a new strategy; for example, to change from mass production of standardized products to the production of small lots of customized products?
- What behavior changes occur for the product designers when a firm selects a cost driver to encourage the use of common components instead of many specialized components?
- Could the production process of a particular product be changed to allow a firm to reduce the unit cost of this product?
- Has a firm adopted the most profitable distribution system in its product market?
- How would changes in activities and components affect the suppliers and customers in the value chain?
- What impact will changes in a firm's processes have on the bottom line?
- What are the potential cost savings if a firm uses ABM to identify and eliminate non-value-added activities to achieve its low-cost strategy?
- How can ABC/ABM help a firm achieve its competitive strategy of high performance and short lead time in delivery of its products?

BEHAVIORAL AND IMPLEMENTATION ISSUES

LEARNING OBJECTIVE 10 ▶
Identify key factors for a
successful ABC/ABM
implementation.

Behavioral and organizational factors play an important role in implementing ABC/ABM. For a successful ABC/ABM implementation, management accountants need to cooperate with engineers, manufacturing, and operating managers to form a design team. Activities and cost drivers need to be identified; both financial and nonfinancial performance indicators are required. The basic information necessary to implement these cost system changes usually is not available because most companies do not collect it.

To obtain the information necessary for new cost management and measurement systems, the people directly involved in operating activities need to be interviewed. Each operating and support department should be carefully studied to analyze its multiple activities. This process will allow the identification of cost pools where homogeneous cost drivers are responsible for each cost category. For example, a quality control department may have three cost pools: inspection of incoming materials (cost driver: number of purchase orders), inspection of work in process (cost driver: number of setups), and inspection of finished goods (cost driver: cost of goods sold).

Understanding the production process and identifying cost drivers require a significant amount of persistent effort. In some cases, companies may decide that their particular manufacturing environment does not require such sophisticated cost and performance measurement systems. The effort to redesign cost systems is rewarded when there is high product diversity, various cost drivers, multiple channels of distribution, and a wide range of batch sizes.

Six ways to avoid failure in implementing ABC/ABM are

Implementing Strategy	Justification
1. Involve management and employees in the creation of an ABC system	Involving management and employees allows them to become familiar with ABC/ABM. They may then be more willing to implement the system because they feel included and share in ownership of the new system.
2. Maintain a parallel system	Maintaining a parallel system allows individuals to adapt gradually to the ABC/ABM system. Abruptly changing cost systems can confuse and frustrate management and employees.
3. Use ABC/ABM on a job that will succeed	ABC/ABM should be used on a simple job in which the probability for its success is high. This implementation will show how and why it works. Successfully completing one job enables individuals to see the benefits of ABC/ABM more clearly.
4. Keep the initial ABC/ABM design simple	Keeping the initial ABC/ABM design simple avoids overwhelming users and holds costs down. Simple design also reduces implementation time.
5. Create desired incentives	Change often is met with resistance. By offering desired incentives, the firm reassures employees that they are properly evaluated in accordance with their performance.
6. Educate management	Seminars educating management about ABC/ABM enable them to understand the concept and appreciate the benefits. Management becomes aware of the activities that drive the business.

A survey of 143 companies conducted by Shields and McEwen in September–November 1993 showed that 75 percent had received a financial benefit from ABC.[22] The chief reason for unsuccessful implementations of ABC was that many companies overemphasized the architectural and software design of ABC systems and failed to pay adequate attention to behavioral and organizational issues.

Using the results of their survey, Shields and McEwen developed seven factors for a successful ABC implementation: (1) top management support; (2) linkage to competitive strategy, stressing quality and JIT/speed; (3) linkage to performance evaluation and compensation; (4) training; (5) nonaccounting ownership (the belief

---

[22] Michael D. Shields and Michael A. McEwen, "Implementing Activity-Based Costing Systems Successfully," *Journal of Cost Management*, Winter 1996, pp. 15–22.

by nonaccountants that the ABC system is of practical use to people throughout the company, not just to the accounting department); (6) adequate resources; and (7) consensus and clarity of the objectives of ABC.

SUMMARY

Over the past decade an increasing number of national and international companies have made changes in their manufacturing plants. In attempts to reduce costs, increase productivity, improve product quality, and increase flexibility in response to customer needs, these companies have taken some or all of these innovative approaches: (1) adopted just-in-time manufacturing systems with kanban and work cells tools; (2) used various automation techniques, such as robots, computer-aided design, and computer-aided manufacturing; and (3) applied integration approaches such as flexible manufacturing systems and computer-integrated manufacturing to improve manufacturing productivity.

One major limitation of traditional costing systems is the use of a single plantwide factory overhead rate, such as direct labor-hours, or volume-based departmental rates, such as machine-hours and direct materials cost to firms with diverse products, processes, and volume. These rates produce inaccurate product costs when more factory overhead costs, such as setup and materials handling costs, are not volume-based, and when firms produce a diverse mix of products with different volumes, sizes, and complexities.

Activity-based costing (ABC) assigns costs to products or services based on their consumption of the activities. This system is based on the premise that a firm's products or services are performed by activities and that the required activities incur costs. After resources are assigned to activities, activities are assigned to cost objects according to their use. ABC recognizes the causal relationships of cost drivers to activities.

ABC systems use a two-stage procedure to assign costs to products. The first-stage allocation is a resource cost assignment process by which factory overhead costs are assigned to activity cost pools or groups of activities called activity centers by using appropriate cost drivers. The second-stage allocation is an activity cost assignment process by which the costs of activities are assigned to products or services using appropriate cost drivers.

Activity-based costing helps to reduce distortions caused by the traditional costing system and obtains more accurate product costs. It provides a clear view of how a firm's diverse products, services, and activities contribute to the bottom line in the long run. Developing and implementing an ABC system is expensive and time-consuming. Management accountants should get involved as team players to help their firms develop and implement successful ABC systems.

Activity-based management (ABM) focuses on improving business efficiency and effectiveness, and increasing not only the value received by customers but also the firm's profits.

ABC and ABM have been applied successfully in manufacturing, marketing, and administrative organizations as well as service and not-for-profit groups.

Activity-based costing is closely tied to strategic cost management. Managers can have more meaningful information to answer the question, What are the potential impacts on pricing, product design, process design, manufacturing technology, and product line decisions if a firm switches from the traditional costing system to an activity-based costing system?

Behavioral and organizational factors play important roles in implementing ABC/ABM. To be successful, management accountants need to cooperate with engineers, manufacturing, and operating managers to form a design team. Activities and cost drivers need to be identified; both financial and nonfinancial performance indicators are required.

KEY TERMS

SELF-STUDY PROBLEM

(For the solution, please turn to the end of the chapter.)

Traditional Cost vs. ABC

Carter Company uses a traditional two-stage cost allocation system. In the first stage, all factory overhead costs are assigned to two production departments, A and B, based on machine-hours. In the second stage, direct labor-hours are used to allocate overhead to individual products, Deluxe and Regular.

During 19X8 the company has a total factory overhead cost of $1,000,000. Machine-hours in production departments A and B were 4,000 and 16,000 hours, respectively. Direct labor-hours in production departments A and B were 20,000 and 10,000, respectively.

The following information relates to products Deluxe and Regular for the month of January 19X8:

	Deluxe	Regular
Units produced and sold	200	800
Unit cost of direct materials	$100	$50
Hourly direct labor wage rate	$25	$20
Direct labor-hours in department A per unit	2	2
Direct labor-hours in department B per unit	1	1

Carter Company is considering implementing an activity-based costing system. Its management accountant has collected this information for activity cost analysis:

Activity	Driver	OH Rate	Driver Consumption Deluxe	Driver Consumption Regular
1. Material movement	Number of production runs	$20	150	300
2. Machine setups	Number of setups	800	25	50
3. Inspections	Number of units	30	200	800
4. Shipment	Number of shipments	20	50	100

Required

1. Calculate the unit costs for each of the two products under the existing traditional costing system.

2. Calculate the unit costs for each of the two products if the proposed ABC system is adopted.

QUESTIONS

4–1 Define the following terms: *just-in-time*, *kanban*, *work cells*, *robots*, *computer-aided design*, *computer-aided manufacturing*, *flexible manufacturing systems*, and *computer-integrated manufacturing*.

4–2 Explain how a traditional costing system using either a plantwide overhead rate or volume-based departmental rates can produce distorted product costs.

4–3 What is meant by product diversity?

4–4 What is activity-based costing, and how can it improve the costing system of an organization?

4–5 What is the first-stage procedure in tracing costs to products when using an activity-based costing system?

4–6 What is the second-stage procedure in tracing costs to products when using an activity-based costing system?

4–7 When does a company need an activity-based costing system?

4–8 What four general levels of activities can be identified in a company?

4–9 Give three examples of unit-level activities.

4–10 Give three examples of batch-level activities.

4–11 Give three examples of product-sustaining activities.

4–12 Give three examples of facility-sustaining activities.

4–13 Why do product costing systems using a single, volume-based cost driver tend to overcost high-volume products? What undesirable strategic effects can such product cost distortion have?

4–14 What is activity-based management?

4–15 Give three examples of value-added activities.

4–16 Give three examples of non-value-added activities.

4–17 How can activity-based costing and management be used in service organizations?

PROBLEMS

4–18 ACTIVITY LEVELS

Required Classify the following costs as unit-level, batch-level, product-sustaining, or facility-sustaining activity costs:

1. Direct materials
2. Direct labor wages
3. Purchase order clerk labor wages
4. Materials-handling labor wages
5. Parts administrators' salaries
6. Setup labor wages
7. Equipment maintenance
8. Plant building insurance
9. Plant building rent expense
10. Plant building depreciation

4–19 ACTIVITY LEVELS

Required Classify the following costs as unit-level, batch-level, product-sustaining, or facility-sustaining activity costs:

1. Direct materials and parts
2. Setup wages
3. Computer programming, FMS
4. Property taxes
5. Engineering design
6. Natural gas, heating
7. Plant custodial wages
8. Electricity, light
9. Inspection
10. Machine depreciation

Service

4–20 ACTIVITY LEVELS

Required   Au's is a small hamburger shop at a nearby university. Classify Au's costs as unit-level, batch-level, product-sustaining, or facility-sustaining activity costs:

1.	Bread	6.	Advertising
2.	Cook's wages	7.	Cheese
3.	Store rent	8.	Utilities
4.	Beef	9.	Server's wages
5.	Catsup	10.	Napkins and bags

4–21 COST DRIVERS

Required   Identify a cost driver for each of the following activities:

1.	Engineering	6.	Payroll accounting
2.	Custodial service	7.	Product testing
3.	Machine maintenance	8.	Warehouse expense
4.	Plant building depreciation	9.	General and administration
5.	Production orders	10.	Production supervision

4–22 COST DRIVERS

Required   Identify a cost driver for each of the following activities:

1.	Product design	6.	Direct labor related overhead
2.	Production scheduling	7.	Machine setups
3.	Materials ordering	8.	Plant administration
4.	Parts administration	9.	Quality control
5.	Materials receipts	10.	Utilities

4–23 COST DRIVERS

Required   Identify a cost driver for each of the following activities:

1.	Accounts payable	6.	Receiving and component stores
2.	Accounts receivable		
3.	Inventory control	7.	Incoming inspection
4.	Material planning and control	8.	Quality control
		9.	Vendor evaluations
5.	Purchasing	10.	Vendor certification

Service

4–24 COST DRIVERS

Required   Identify a cost driver for each of these activities for the U.S. Postal Service:

1. Selling to major customers
2. Responding to customer concerns
3. Maintaining express mail program
4. Accepting bulk mail
5. Distributing mail
6. Administering rules to customers

Identify a cost driver for each of the activities for an electric utility company:

1. Installing electricity to homes
2. Installing electricity to commercial firms
3. Installing new electric lines for community
4. Call-backs/not working
5. Repairing electricity in homes
6. Repairing common electric lines

4-25 VALUE-ADDED AND NON-VALUE-ADDED ACTIVITIES

Service

Required Classify each hospital radiology activity as a value-added or non-value-added activity:

1. Receive patients
2. Load film and X-ray
3. Develop X-ray
4. Counsel patients
5. Wait on patients
6. Equipment repairs

Classify each hospital nursing activity as a value-added or non-value-added activity:

1. Record medical records
2. Attend to patients
3. Coordinate lab/ radiology/pharmacy
4. Coordinate housekeeping
5. Idle
6. Training

4-26 COST DRIVERS

Required Supertech Corporation is a computer manufacturing company that applies the just-in-time system to its production flow. The following costs are budgeted for December:

Direct materials and parts	$400,000
Engineering design	60,000
Depreciation, building	50,000
Depreciation, machine	40,000
Electrical power	30,000
Insurance	20,000
Property taxes	15,000
Machine maintenance—labor	10,000
Machine maintenance—materials	9,000
Natural gas (for heating)	8,000
Packaging	7,000
Inspection of finished goods	6,000
Setup wages	5,000
Receiving	4,000
Inspection of direct materials	3,000
Purchasing	2,000
Custodial labor	1,000

Required Separate these costs into cost pools and identify the cost driver for each cost pool.

4-27 DISTORTION OF PRODUCT COSTS

Strategy

Junghans Computer Company has two product lines, computer A and computer B. Overall, the company profit has been declining in the last six months. According to the controller, computer A costs $500 and is a high-volume product with sales over 1,000. Competitors produce a similar computer with an average market price of $380 that has cut into Junghans' sales volume for computer A. On the other hand, the company makes a large profit margin from sales of computer B because it costs only $400 to produce and the selling price is $750. The marketing vice president suggests shifting the sales mix in favor of computer B. Unfortunately, computer B is more complicated to make and few are produced.

Required Do you think that Junghans Computer Company's marketing strategy should focus its sales on the computer A? Or is it better to focus on the computer B as suggested by the marketing vice president? Provide analysis for your answer.

Strategy

4–28 ACTIVITY-BASED COSTING, VALUE CHAIN ACTIVITIES   The Hoover Company uses activity-based costing and provides this information:

Manufacturing Activity Area	Cost Driver Used as Application Base	Conversion Cost per Unit of Base
1. Materials handling	Number of parts	$ 0.45
2. Machinery	Machine-hours	51.00
3. Assembly	Number of parts	2.85
4. Inspection	Number of finished units	30.00

Assume that 75 units of a component for packaging machines have been manufactured. Each unit required 105 parts and 3 machine-hours. Direct materials cost $600 per finished unit. All other manufacturing costs are classified into one category, conversion costs.

Required

1. Compute the total manufacturing costs and the unit costs of the 75 units.

2. Suppose upstream activities for the company's internal value chain, such as research and development and product design, are analyzed and applied to this component at $180 per unit. Moreover, similar analyses are conducted of downstream activities, such as distribution, marketing, and customer service. The downstream costs applied to this component are $1,050 per unit. Compute the full product cost per unit, including upstream, manufacturing, and downstream activities. What are strategic implications of this new cost result?

3. Explain to the Hoover Company the usefulness of calculating the total value chain cost, and breaking it down by different value-creating activities.

4–29 ACTIVITY-BASED COSTING   Nixon Company has the following data:

OH Cost Pool	Budgeted OH Cost	Budgeted Level for Cost Driver	Cost Driver	OH Rate
Direct materials	120,000	3,000 pounds	Weight of raw material	40
Machine setup	9,750	325 repetitions	Number of repetitions	30
Machine repair time	1,045	5 units	Units of time*	209
Inspections	8,100	135 inspects	Number of inspections	60
Requirements for Job 747				
Raw materials		100 pounds		
Machine setup		25 repetitions		
Machine repair time		0.5 hours		
Inspections		10 inspections		

*One unit equals 15-minute intervals.

Required   Compute the total overhead that should be assigned to job 747.

4–30 ACTIVITY-BASED COSTING   Shieh Company has identified the following overhead cost pools and cost drivers:

Cost Pools	Activity Costs	Cost Drivers
Machine setup	$180,000	1,500 setup hours
Materials handling	50,000	12,500 pounds of materials
Electric power	20,000	20,000 kilowatt-hours

The following cost information pertains to the production of products X and Y:

	X	Y
Number of units produced	4,000	20,000
Direct materials cost ($)	$20,000	$25,000
Direct labor cost ($)	$12,000	$20,000
Number of setup hours	100	120
Pounds of materials used	500	1,500
Kilowatt-hours	1,000	2,000

Required Use the activity-based costing approach to calculate the unit cost for each of the two products.

4–31 TRADITIONAL COSTING Madison, Inc., manufactures box radios in three different styles:

Elite box radio, annual sales 8,000 units

Standard box radio, annual sales 12,000 units

Junior box radio, annual sales 10,000 units

Madison uses a traditional volume-based costing system in applying factory overhead using direct-labor dollars. The cost of each product is

	Elite	Standard	Junior
Direct materials	$ 29.25	$19.50	$ 9.75
Direct labor:			
1.0 × $13.50 =	13.50		
0.8 × $13.50 =		10.80	
0.6 × $13.50 =			8.10
Factory overhead	75.38	45.90	34.43
Total	$100.13	$76.20	$52.28

Predetermined overhead rate = 425%

Direct labor budget per annual sales:

Elite radio	8,000 × $13.50	=	$108,000
Standard radio	12,000 × $10.80	=	129,600
Junior radio	10,000 × $8.10	=	81,000
Total			$318,600

Factory overhead:

Engineering and design	$ 400,799		
Quality control	238,312		
Machinery	557,869	Predetermined rate	
Miscellaneous overhead	157,070	$\dfrac{\$1,354,050}{\$318,600} = 4.25$	
Total	$1,354,050		

Madison's retail price for radios is usually marked up at 175 percent of its full cost.

	Elite	Standard	Junior
Product cost	$100.13	$ 76.20	$ 52.28
Target price	175.23	133.35	91.49
Actual price	150.95	133.35	110.50

Madison has noticed that it is able to charge more for Junior box radios with no effect on sales. Unfortunately, Madison has had to lower its price on the Elite radio to obtain purchase orders.

Required

1. According to this information, what is Madison's most profitable product?

2. What is its least profitable product?

4–32 ACTIVITY-BASED COSTING (Continuation of 4–31) Madison's controller has been researching activity-based costing and has decided to switch to it. A special study determined Madison's three radio models are responsible for these proportions of each cost driver:

Strategy

	Elite	Standard	Junior
Engineering and design	25%	50%	25%
Quality control	20	30	50
Machinery	35	10	55
Miscellaneous overhead	25	59	16

Required

1. Use the data in Problems 4–31 and 4–32 to develop unit product costs for each of the three products using activity-based costing.

2. Compare and explain unit cost differences between the traditional costing and activity-based costing.

3. Calculate the activity-based costing target prices for three products using Madison's pricing formula. Compare and explain differences between new target prices with actual selling prices and target prices based on traditional costing.

4. What are the implications for Madison's pricing strategy?

4–33 TRADITIONAL COSTING VS. ABC   The Robertson Company manufactures laser printers. It uses these overhead cost drivers:

OH Cost Pool	Cost Driver	OH Cost	Budgeted Level for Cost Driver	Budgeted OH Rate
Quality control	Number inspections	$ 50,000	1,000	$ 50
Machine repetitions	Number repetitions	100,000	1,000	100
Accounts receivable	Number invoices	650	25	26
Other OH cost	Direct labor-hours	30,000	3,000	10

Robertson has an order for 500 laser printers; production requirements for this order are

Number of inspections	25
Number of repetitions	200
Number of invoices processed	250
Direct labor-hours	300

Required

1. What is the total overhead assigned to the 500 units using an activity-based costing method?

2. What is the cost per laser printer?

3. If Robertson expressed its overhead rate in direct labor-hours, how much overhead would be applied to the entire order for laser printers?

4. Would you recommend ABC or the direct labor-based method to this company? Why?

Service

4–34 TRADITIONAL COSTING VS. ABC   Budgeted cost and operating data are given for the Get Well Soon Hospital:

The hospital has a hospitalwide overhead rate based on direct labor-hours. The intensive care unit (ICU) applies overhead using machine-hours.

Budgeted information:	
Hospital total overhead	$5,360,000
Hospital total direct labor-hours	80,000
Machine-hours for ICU	30,000

Cost Driver Information for ICU:

Cost Pool	Budget Cost	Budget Level for Cost Driver	OH Rate	Cost Drivers
Beds	$2,100,000	700	$3,000	Number of beds
Equipment	175,000	3,500	50	Number of monitors
Personnel	180,000	2,000	90	Number of staff

For the month of March, Get Well's intensive care unit recorded the following data:

3,600 direct labor-hours
5,800 machine-hours
60 beds were occupied
330 monitors were used
170 staff worked

Required

1. Calculate Get Well's ICU overhead costs for the month of March using:
   a. The hospitalwide rate
   b. The ICU department-wide rate
   c. The cost drivers for the ICU department
2. Explain the differences and determine which overhead rate is more appropriate.

4–35 TRADITIONAL COSTING VS. ABC   The controller for California Cooking Oil Company has established overhead cost pools and cost drivers.

Overhead Cost Pool	Budgeted Overhead	Cost Driver	Estimated Cost Driver Level
Machine setups	$100,000	Number of setups	100 setups
Material handling	80,000	Number of barrels	8,000 barrels
Quality control	200,000	Number of inspections	1,000 inspections
Other overhead cost	100,000	Machine-hours	10,000 machine-hours
Total	$480,000		

An order of 500 barrels of cooking oil has used:

Machine setups	6 setups
Materials handling	500 barrels
Quality inspections	20 times
Machine-hours	1,000 hours

Required

1. If California uses a single-cost driver system based on machine-hours, how much is the total overhead applied to an order of 500 barrels?
2. How much is the overhead assigned for each barrel of cooking oil under the single-cost driver system?
3. If California uses a multiple-cost driver system based on total overhead cost, will the total overhead applied for 500 barrels be different than requirement 1? If yes, compute the total overhead cost under a multiple-cost driver system.
4. How big is the difference in the overhead cost per barrel under the single-cost driver system and a multiple-cost driver system?

4–36 TRADITIONAL COSTING VS. ABC   Elteha Chemical Company produces three products:

Strategy

Product A with annual sales of 1,000 units

Product B with annual sales of 3,000 units

Product C with annual sales of 500 units

The company allocates the overhead costs based on direct labor dollars, and the total unit costs for each product are computed as follows:

	Product A	Product B	Product C
Direct materials	$ 50.00	$ 60.00	$ 65.00
Direct labor	20.00	20.00	10.00
Factory overhead*	116.00	116.00	58.00
Total	$186.00	$196.00	$133.00

*Factory overhead budget:

Machine setups	$ 8,000
Materials handling	100,000
Hazardous material control	250,000
Quality control	75,000
Other overhead costs	60,000
Total	$493,000

Direct labor dollars budgeted:

Product A	1,000 × $20.00	=	$20,000
Product B	3,000 × $20.00	=	60,000
Product C	500 × $10.00	=	5,000
Total			$85,000

Predetermined overhead rate = $493,000 / $85,000
= 5.80

The target and actual selling prices are

	Product A	Product B	Product C
Product cost	$186.00	$196.00	$133.00
Target price (150%)	279.00	294.00	199.50
Actual price	280.00	250.00	300.00

Required

1. Is product B the least profitable and product C the most profitable?
2. The controller, who conducted research about product costing, comes up with the following proportion of each cost driver that each product absorbed:

Overhead	Cost Driver	Product A	Product B	Product C
Machine setup	Number of setups	20%	50%	30%
Materials handling	Weight of direct materials	40	25	35
Hazardous control	Number of inspections	25	45	30
Quality control	Number of inspections	30	35	35
Other overhead	Direct labor-hours	20	70	10

   Given these percentages, what is the new product cost for the three products based on the activity-based costing system?
3. What is the new target price for each product based on 150 percent of the new costs? Compare with the actual selling price and comment on the result. Assuming that you are a manager of the Elteha Chemical Company, describe what actions you would take based on the information provided by the activity-based unit costs.

4–37 VALUE-ADDED AND NON-VALUE-ADDED ACTIVITIES

Required   Classify each of the following warehouse activities as a value-added or non-value-added activity.

1. Receive goods
2. Inspect goods
3. Move goods to warehouse
4. Move goods to stores
5. Expedite goods
6. Manage employees

Classify each of the following engineering activities as a value-added or non-value-added activity.

1. Develop the bill of materials
2. Maintain the bill of materials
3. Develop routing
4. Maintain routing
5. Capacity studies
6. Tooling design
7. Training
8. Management and administration

4–38 VALUE-ADDED AND NON-VALUE-ADDED ACTIVITIES

Required   Classify each of the following vendor invoice paying activities as a value-added or non-value-added activity.

1. Receive a purchase order
2. Receive a warehouse receiving receipt
3. Receive a vendor invoice
4. Match the invoice with the purchase order and the receiving receipt
5. Enter data
6. Determine errors
7. Expedite payment
8. Make payment: computer
9. Make payment: manual
10. Document file

4–39 VALUE-ADDED AND NON-VALUE-ADDED ACTIVITIES

Required   Classify each of the Best Keyboard Company's ordering activities as a value-added or non-value-added activity.

1. Receive call or call companies
2. Fill in sales form
3. Enter data into computer
4. Print order form
5. Deliver to supervisor
6. Supervisor approval
7. Deliver to vice president
8. Vice president final approval
9. Deliver to accounting
10. Accounting department entry
11. Deliver to warehouse
12. Box and load order
13. Call UPS for shipping or delivery

4–40 ETHICS, COST SYSTEM SELECTION   Aero Dynamics is a manufacturer of airplane parts and engines for a variety of military and civilian aircraft. The company is the sole provider of the rocket engines for the U.S. government with a selling price equal to the full cost plus a 5 percent markup.

Ethics

The current cost system at Aero Dynamics is a traditional direct labor-hour-based overhead allocation system. Recently, the company has conducted a pilot study using the activity-based costing system. The study shows that the new ABC system, while more accurate and timely, will result in lower costs being assigned to the rocket engines and higher costs being assigned to the company's other products. Apparently, the current (less accurate) direct labor-based costing system overcosts the rocket engines and undercosts the other products. On hearing of this, top management has decided to scrap the plans for adopting the new activity-based costing system, because the rocket engine business with the government is a significant part of Aero Dynamics's business, and the reduced cost would reduce the price and thus the profit for this part of Aero Dynamics's business.

Required   As the management accountant participating in this ABC pilot study project, how do you see your responsibility when you hear of the decision of top management to cancel the plans for the new activity-based costing system? Can you ignore your professional ethics code in this case? What would you do?

International

4–41 LIBRARY RESEARCH, INTERNATIONAL ABC

Required Go to your library or use a business periodicals database to select one article describing an application of the activity-based costing system to a company or companies outside of the United States. Your written report should include:

1. Title, source, and the abstract of the article.
2. Description of the application situation, cost drivers used, as well as benefits and problems encountered in applying the ABC system.

4–42 TEAM PROJECT ASSIGNMENT, ACTIVITY ANALYSIS

Required This is a group assignment. Each group is to select a real world organization and conduct an activity analysis of one of its processes such as sales and collection, purchase and payment, college admissions, student enrollment, warehousing, or bank deposits. Your written report should include:

1. Organization name, background information, persons contacted or interviewed.
2. Descriptions of activities and cost drivers in this process.
3. Process inputs, outputs, and performance measures.
4. Value- and non-value-added activities.
5. Suggested improvements.

4–43 JUST-IN-TIME SYSTEM

Required Fontana Machinery Company has lost its market share in recent years. In a recent executive meeting, the company president asked the controller to recommend a cost reduction and productivity improvement tool. The controller suggested to adopt a just-in-time inventory management system.

1. Describe the just-in-time (JIT) system.
2. What are roles of kanban and work cells in a JIT system?
3. The use of JIT is likely to impact the amount of working capital required by Fontana Machinery Company. Give two examples that the adoption of the JIT system will reduce the company's working capital.

Strategy

4–44 TRADITIONAL COSTING VS. ABC
The current manufacturing costing system of Auer Corporation has two direct cost categories (direct materials and direct labor). Indirect manufacturing costs are applied to products using a single indirect cost pool. The indirect manufacturing cost application base is direct labor-hours; the indirect cost rate is $120 per direct labor-hour.

Auer Corporation is switching from a labor-paced to a machine-paced manufacturing approach at its aircraft components plant. Recently, the plant manager set up five activity areas, each with its own supervisor and budget responsibility. Pertinent data follow:

Activity Area	Cost Driver Used as Indirect Cost Application Base	Cost per Unit of Application Base
Materials handling	Number of parts	$ .70
Lathe work	Number of turns	.35
Milling	Number of machine-hours	15.00
Grinding	Number of parts	.60
Shipping	Number of orders shipped	$2,180.00

Information technology has advanced to the point where all the necessary data for budgeting in these five activity areas are automatically collected.

The two job orders processed under the new system at the aircraft components plant in the most recent period had the following characteristics:

	Job Order 101	Job Order 102
Direct materials cost per job	$45,300	$5,700
Direct labor cost per job	$16,800	$1,400
Number of direct labor-hours per job	420	35
Number of parts per job	1,500	600
Number of turns per job	80,000	15,000
Number of machine-hours per job	750	70
Number of job orders shipped	1	1
Number of units in each job order	450	20

Required

1. Compute the per unit manufacturing cost of each job under the existing manufacturing costing system; that is, indirect costs are collected in a single cost pool with direct labor-hours as the application base.

2. Assume that Auer Corporation adopts an activity-based costing system. Indirect costs are applied to products using separate indirect cost pools for each of the five activity areas (materials handling, lathe work, milling, grinding, and shipping). The application base and rate for each activity area are described in the problem. Compute the per unit manufacturing cost of each job under the ABC approach.

3. Compare the per unit cost figures for Job Orders 101 and 102 computed in requirements 1 and 2. Why do they differ? Why might these differences be strategically important to Auer Corporation? How does ABC add to Auer's competitive advantage?

4–45 TRADITIONAL COSTING VS. ABC Gorden Company produces a variety of electronic equipment. One of its plants produces two dot-matrix printers: the superior and the regular. At the beginning of the year 19X8, the following data were prepared for this plant:

 *Strategy*

	Superior	Regular
Quantity	50,000	400,000
Selling price	$475.00	$300.00
Unit prime cost	$180.00	$110.00
Unit overhead cost	$ 20.00	$130.00

Overhead is applied using direct labor-hours.

Upon examining the data, the manager of marketing was particularly impressed with the per unit profitability of the superior printer and suggested that more emphasis be placed on producing and selling this product. The plant supervisor objected to this strategy, arguing that the cost of the superior printer was understated. He argued that overhead costs could be assigned more accurately by using multiple cost drivers that reflected each product's consumption. To convince top management that multiple rates could produce a significant difference in product costs, he obtained the following projected information from the controller for the preceding production output:

Overhead Activity	Cost Driver	Pool Rate*	Activity Consumption	
			Superior	Regular
Setups	Number of setups	$2,800	200	100
Machine costs	Machine-hours	100	100,000	400,000
Engineering	Engineering-hours	40	45,000	120,000
Packing	Packing orders	20	50,000	200,000

*Cost per unit of cost driver

Required

1. Using the projected data based on traditional costing, calculate gross profit percentage, gross per unit, and total gross profit for each product.

2. Using the pool rates, calculate the overhead cost per unit for each product. Using this new unit cost, calculate gross profit percentage, gross profit per unit, and total gross profit for each product.

3. In view of the outcome in requirement 2, evaluate the suggestion of the manager of marketing to switch the emphasis to the superior model.

4. How does ABC add to Gordon's competitive advantage?

4–46 TRADITIONAL COSTING VS. ABC Hairless Company manufactures a variety of electric shavers used by men and women for hair removal. The company's plant is partially automated; however, some manual labor is employed. The company uses the activity-based cost system. This cost driver information is used in the product-costing system:

OH Cost Pool	Budgeted OH Cost	Budgeted Level for Cost Driver	Cost Driver	OH Rate
Machine depreciation/maintenance	$ 27,000	140,400	Machine hours	$ 5.20
Factory depreciation/utilities/insurance	30,000	117,000	Machine hours	3.90
Product design	42,000	504,000	Hours in design	12.00
Material purchasing/storage	147,000	980,000	Raw materials	15% cost

Two current product orders have these requirements:

	15,000 Men's Shavers	20,000 Women's Shavers
Direct labor-hours	24	12
Raw material cost	29,400	25,725
Hours in design	15	37.5
Machine-hours	50	40

Required

1. What is the total overhead that should be assigned to each product order?

2. What is the overhead cost per shaver?

3. Compute the predetermined overhead rate if the direct labor budget allows for 1,015 hours of direct labor.

4. Compute the total overhead cost assigned to each production order using the predetermined rate.

5. What is the overhead cost per shaver using the predetermined rate?

Strategy

4–47 TRADITIONAL COSTING VS. ABC Alaire Corporation manufactures several different printed circuit boards; however, two of the boards account for the majority of the company's sales. The first of these boards, a television (TV) circuit board, has been a standard in the industry for several years. The market for this board is competitive and price sensitive. Alaire plans to sell 65,000 of the TV boards in 19X8 at $150 per unit. The second high-volume product, a personal computer (PC) circuit board, is a recent addition to Alaire's product line. Because the PC board incorporates the latest technology, it can be sold at a premium price. The 19X8 plans include the sale of 40,000 PC boards at $300 per unit.

Alaire's management group is meeting to discuss strategies for 19X8, and the current topic of conversation is how to spend the sales and promotion dollars for next year. The sales manager believes the market share for the TV board could be expanded by concentrating Alaire's promotional efforts in this area. In response to this suggestion, the production manager said, "Why don't you go after a bigger market for the PC board? The cost sheets that I get show the contribution from the PC board is more than double the contribution from the TV board. I know we get a premium price for the PC board; selling it should help overall profitability."

Alaire's current costing system shows these data for TV and PC boards:

	TV Board	PC Board
Direct materials	$80	$140
Direct labor	1.5 hours	4 hours
Machine time	.5 hour	1.5 hours

Variable factory overhead is applied on the basis of direct labor-hours. For 19X8, variable factory overhead is budgeted at $1,120,000, and direct labor-hours are estimated at 280,000. The hourly rates for machine time and direct labor are $10 and $14 respectively. Alaire applies a materials-handling charge at 10 percent of direct materials cost; this materials-handling charge is not included in variable factory overhead. Total 19X8 expenditures for direct materials are budgeted at $10,600,000.

Budgeted Overhead Costs		Cost Driver	Annual Activity for Cost Driver
Materials-related overhead:			
Procurement	$ 400,000	Number of parts	4,000,000
Production scheduling	220,000	Number of boards	110,000
Packaging and shipping	440,000	Number of boards	110,000
	$1,060,000		
Variable overhead:			
Machine setup	$ 446,000	Number of setups	278,750
Hazardous waste disposal	48,000	Pounds of waste	16,000
Quality control	560,000	Number of inspections	160,000
General supplies	66,000	Number of boards	110,000
	$1,120,000		
Manufacturing:			
Machine insertion	$1,200,000	Number of parts	3,000,000
Manual insertion	4,000,000	Number of parts	1,000,000
Wave soldering	132,000	Number of boards	110,000
	$5,332,000		

Required per Unit	TV Board	PC Board
Parts	25	55
Machine insertions	24	35
Manual insertions	1	20
Machine setups	2	3
Hazardous waste	.02 lb.	.35 lb.
Inspections	1	2

Ed Welch, Alaire's controller, believes that before the management group proceeds with the discussion about allocating sales and promotional dollars to individual products, it might be worthwhile to look at these products on the basis of the activities involved in their production. As Welch explained to the group, "Activity-based costing integrates the cost of all activities, known as cost drivers, into individual product costs rather than including these costs in overhead pools." Welch prepared the preceding schedule to help the management group understand this concept.

"Using this information," Welch explained, "we can calculate an activity-based cost for each TV board and each PC board and then compare it to the standard cost we have been using. The only cost that remains the same for both cost methods is the cost of direct materials. The cost drivers will replace the direct labor, machine time, and overhead costs in the old standard cost figures."

Required

1. Identify at least four general advantages associated with activity-based costing.

2. On the basis of Alaire's current volume-based costing system and its cost data (direct materials, direct labor, materials handling charge, variable overhead, and machine time overhead) given in the problem, calculate the total contribution margin expected in 19X8 for Alaire Corporation's (a) TV board and (b) PC board.

3. On the basis of activity-based costs, calculate the total contribution expected in 19X8 for Alaire Corporation's (a) TV board and (b) PC board.

4. Alaire's management group is meeting to discuss strategies for 19X8; they are especially interested in deciding how to spend the sales and promotion dollars. The sales manager is in favor of spending more on TV boards while the production manager is in favor of promoting the PC boards. Explain how the comparison of the results of the two costing methods may affect the sales, pricing, and promotion decisions made by Alaire Corporation's management group.

(**CMA** adapted)

Strategy

4–48 TRADITIONAL COSTING VS. ABC   Coffee Bean, Inc. (CBI), is a distributor and processor of a variety of different brands of coffee. The company buys coffee beans from around the world and roasts, blends, and packages them for resale. CBI currently has 15 different coffees that it offers to gourmet shops in one-pound bags. The major cost is direct materials; however, there is a substantial amount of factory overhead in the predominantly automated roasting and packing process. The company uses relatively little direct labor.

Some of the coffees are very popular and sell in large volumes, while a few of the newer brands have very low volumes. CBI prices its coffee at full product cost, including allocated overhead, plus a markup of 30 percent. If prices for certain coffees are significantly higher than the market, the prices are lowered. The company competes primarily on the quality of its products, but customers are price conscious as well.

Data for the 19X8 budget include factory overhead of $3,000,000, which has been allocated in its current costing system on the basis of each product's direct labor cost. The budgeted direct labor cost for 19X8 totals $600,000. Budgeted purchases and use of direct materials (mostly coffee beans) will total $6,000,000.

The budgeted direct costs for one-pound bags of two of the company's products are as follows:

	Mona Loa	Malaysian
Direct materials	$4.20	$3.20
Direct labor	.30	.30

CBI's controller believes the current traditional product costing system may be providing misleading cost information. She has developed this analysis of the 19X8 budgeted factory overhead costs:

Activity	Cost Driver	Budgeted Activity	Budgeted Cost
Purchasing	Purchase order	1,158	$ 579,000
Material handling	Setups	1,800	720,000
Quality control	Batches	720	144,000
Roasting	Roasting-hours	96,100	961,000
Blending	Blending-hours	33,600	336,000
Packaging	Packaging-hours	26,000	260,000
Total factory overhead cost			$3,000,000

Data regarding the 19X8 production of Mona Loa and Malaysian coffee follow. There will be no beginning or ending direct materials inventory for either of these coffees.

	Mona Loa	Malaysian
Budgeted sales	100,000 pounds	2,000 pounds
Batch size	10,000 pounds	500 pounds
Setups	3 per batch	3 per batch
Purchase order size	25,000 pounds	500 pounds
Roasting time	1 hour per 100 pounds	1 hour per 100 pounds
Blending time	.5 hour per 100 pounds	.5 hour per 100 pounds
Packaging time	.1 hour per 100 pounds	.1 hour per 100 pounds

Required

1. Using Coffee Bean, Inc.'s current traditional product costing system:
   a. Determine the company's predetermined overhead rate using direct labor cost as the single cost driver.
   b. Determine the full product costs and selling prices of one pound of Mona Loa coffee and one pound of Malaysian coffee.

2. Develop a new product cost, using an activity-based costing approach, for one pound of Mona Loa coffee and one pound of Malaysian coffee. Allocate all overhead costs to the 100,000 pounds of Mona Loa and the 2,000 pounds of Malaysian. Compare the results with those in requirement 1.

3. What are the implications of the activity-based costing system with respect to CBI's pricing and product mix strategies? How does ABC add to CBI's competitive advantage?

(CMA adapted)

SOLUTION TO SELF-STUDY PROBLEM

Traditional Costing vs. ABC

1. Traditional costing system

Stage 1 Allocation:

Total overhead allocated to Department A

$$\$1,000,000 \times (4,000/20,000) = \$200,000$$

Total overhead allocated to Department B

$$\$1,000,000 \times (16,000/20,000) = \$800,000$$

Stage 2 Allocation:

	(Per Unit Cost)	
	Deluxe	Regular
Overhead allocated to:		
Department A		
($200,000/20,000) × 2 =	$ 20	
($200,000/20,000) × 2 =		$ 20
Department B		
($800,000/10,000) × 1 =	$ 80	
($800,000/10,000) × 1 =		$ 80
Total	$100	$100

Product cost per unit:

	Deluxe	Regular
Direct materials	$100	$ 50
Direct labor		
$25 × (2 + 1) =	75	
$20 × (2 + 1) =		60
Factory overhead	100	100
Unit cost	$275	$210

2. ABC system

	Deluxe	Regular
Overhead allocated to:		
Material movement		
$20 × 150 =	$ 3,000	
$20 × 300 =		$ 6,000
Machine setups		
$800 × 25 =	20,000	
$800 × 5 =		40,000
Inspections		
$30 × 200 =	6,000	
$30 × 800 =		24,000
Shipment		
$20 × 50 =	1,000	
$20 × 100 =		2,000
Total	$30,000	$72,000
Unit overhead cost	$150	$90

Product cost per unit:

	Deluxe	Regular
Direct materials	$100	$ 50
Direct labor	75	60
Factory overhead	150	90
Unit cost	$325	$200

Note that the traditional costing system overcosts the high-volume Regular product and undercosts the low-volume Deluxe product.

Target Costing, Theory of Constraints, and Life-Cycle Costing

5

After studying this chapter, you should be able to ...

Explain how to use target costing to facilitate strategic management **1**

Apply the theory of constraints to strategic management **2**

Describe how life-cycle costing facilitates strategic management **3**

Outline the objectives and techniques of cost management over the sales life cycle **4**

Reuters

Time is the measure of business, as money is of wares.

FRANCIS BACON, SEVENTEENTH-CENTURY
ENGLISH WRITER, PHILOSOPHER, AND STATESMAN

This chapter focuses on the time dimension of cost management, as described by Francis Bacon. We consider both the effect of the timeliness of operations on total costs, and the way in which costs change over the life cycle of the product. Product life cycle is considered in each of two aspects—the cost life cycle and the sales life cycle. The **cost life cycle** is the sequence of activities within the firm that begins with research and development, followed by design, manufacturing (or providing the service), marketing/distribution, and customer service. It is the life cycle of the product or service from the viewpoint of costs incurred. The cost life cycle is illustrated in Exhibit 5–1.[1]

The **sales life cycle** is the sequence of phases in the product's or service's life in the market—from the introduction of the product or service to growth in sales and finally maturity, decline, and withdrawal from the market. Sales are at first small, then peak in the maturity phase and decline thereafter, as illustrated in Exhibit 5–2.

Important strategic cost management issues arise in each activity of the cost life cycle. The methods helpful in analyzing the cost life cycle are target costing, the theory of constraints, and life-cycle costing. Target costing is used for managing costs primarily in the design activity. The theory of constraints is a method for

> The **cost life cycle** is the sequence of activities within the firm that begins with research and development, followed by design, manufacturing, marketing/distribution, and customer service.
>
> The **sales life cycle** is the sequence of phases in the product's or service's life in the market—from the introduction of the product or service to growth in sales and finally maturity, decline, and withdrawal from the market.

BusinessWeek

Can Intel Keep Profits Up as Computer Prices Fall?

Intel Corp. makes the chips that run 90 percent of the personal computers now sold worldwide. In the past, Intel's strategy has been to maintain or increase this dominance by being the first to develop and deliver in large quantities upgraded versions of these chips. What this means is that it has essentially ignored the very low end of the computer market. The company once referred to personal computers (PCs) sold for under $1,000 as "segment zero" of the computer market—a dumping ground for obsolete computers, closeouts, and desperation sales. However, now that PCs sold for under $1,000 make up 25 percent or more of the market, with a rapidly rising share, Intel has decided that these computers are now priority one.

The problem is how to adapt a strategy of developing high-level chips to a new market that will not pay top dollar for a newer, better chip [not to mention, where the competition is very strong from rival chip makers Cyrix Corp. and Advanced Micro Devices, Inc. (AMD)]. The challenge for Intel in going forward with this new strategy is that the profit margins on its most advanced chips are 80 percent or more, while Cyrix and AMD have margins closer to 20–40 percent.

Q: How will Intel maintain its profitability while reaching into the low-end market? *Find out on page 139 of this chapter.*

---

[1]   The cost life cycle also is called a value chain by many writers, to emphasize that each activity must add value for the ultimate consumer [Michael Porter, *Competitive Advantage* (New York: Free Press, 1985)]. Note that this concept of the value chain differs from that introduced in Chapter 2. Chapter 2 describes the industry-level value chain, while the cost life-cycle concept in this chapter describes the firm-level value chain. We use the broader concept of the industry-level value chain in Chapter 2 to facilitate the strategic focus in that chapter. For a discussion of the two types of value chains, see Joseph G. San Miguel, "Value Chain Analysis for Assessing Competitive Advantage," *Management Accounting Guideline Number 41*, The Society of Management Accountants of Canada; and Mike Partridge and Lew Perren, "Assessing and Enhancing Strategic Capability: A Value-Driven Approach," *Management Accounting* (UK), June 1994, pp. 28–29.

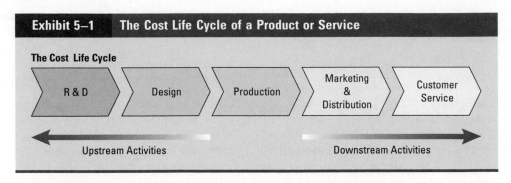

Exhibit 5–1   The Cost Life Cycle of a Product or Service

The Cost Life Cycle

R & D → Design → Production → Marketing & Distribution → Customer Service

← Upstream Activities   Downstream Activities →

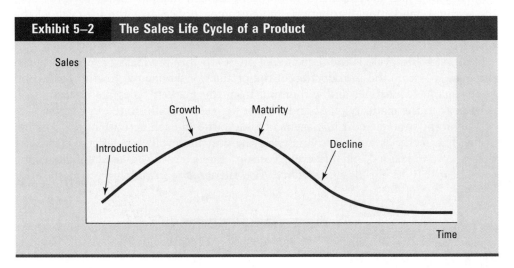

Exhibit 5–2   The Sales Life Cycle of a Product

Sales

Introduction   Growth   Maturity   Decline

Time

managing manufacturing costs. And life-cycle costing is used throughout the cost life cycle to minimize overall cost. Two of the methods, target costing and the theory of constraints, are particularly applicable for manufacturing firms because they deal primarily with product design and manufacture. However, each method also can be applied for service firms, to improve the efficiency and speed of the processes involved in providing the service. Each method is explained in Part One of this chapter. Part Two looks at the sales life cycle and explains the differences in critical success factors, pricing policy, and cost management systems at each of the phases of the sales life cycle.

PART ONE: COST MANAGEMENT OVER THE COST LIFE CYCLE

TARGET COSTING

Our policy is to reduce the price, extend the operations, and improve the article. You will notice that the reduction of price comes first. . . . We first reduce the price to the point where we believe more sales will result . . . the new price forces the costs down . . . the point is the fact that although one may calculate what a cost is, and of course all of our costs are carefully calculated, no one knows what a cost ought to be. One of the ways of discovering is to name a price so low as to force everybody in the place to the highest point of efficiency. The low price makes everybody dig for profits.

HENRY FORD, MY LIFE AND MY WORK, 1923

Henry Ford's thinking would fit well in the corporate boardrooms of today, where global competition and competitive pricing in many industries have forced firms to look for ways to reduce costs year after year, at the same time producing products with greater levels of quality and functionality. Ford is describing a technique called target costing, in which the firm determines the desired cost for the product or service, given a competitive market price, so the firm can earn a desired profit:

◀ LEARNING OBJECTIVE 1
Explain how to use target costing to facilitate strategic management.

Target cost = Competitive price − Desired profit

The firm has two options for reducing costs to a target cost level:

1. By integrating new manufacturing technology, using advanced cost management techniques such as activity-based costing, and seeking higher productivity through improved organization and labor relations, firms can reduce costs. This approach is implemented using standard costing or *kaizen* costing, which is explained in a later section entitled "Target Costing and Kaizen Costing."

2. By redesigning the product or service, a company can reduce cost to a target cost level. This method is the more common of the two, because it recognizes that design decisions account for much of the total product life cycle costs (see Exhibit 5–3).[2] By careful attention to design, significant reductions in total cost are possible. This approach to target costing is associated primarily with Japanese manufacturers; Toyota is credited with developing the method in the mid-1960s.[3]

Target Costing: Honda's Civic Lesson

Because of the appreciating yen and increased global competition, Honda faced some hard choices in the redesign of its 1996 Civic, choices that were helped in part by target costing at the design stage.

Honda was looking for ways to improve the Civic and still reduce the cost of manufacture. Honda reduced costs in ways that customers won't notice, trying to avoid the critics who say that some Japanese automakers have gone so far in reducing the cost of the auto

that they are removing desirable features. To reduce costs on the 1996 Civic, Honda:

- Replaced the rear disk brakes with cheaper drums.
- Switched to a simpler antilock system.
- Integrated the dashboard clock into the radio display.
- Replaced the trunk hinge with a simpler design.
- Used fewer threads in rear seat

materials and replaced vinyl and interior trim with cheaper fabrics.

- Redesigned bumpers, the dashboard, and other parts; they now have fewer pieces, cutting manufacturing costs.
- Installed air-conditioning at the factory rather than at the dealership, to save installation costs.

Source: Based on information in "Honda's Civic Lesson," *Business Week*, September 18, 1995.

Target Costing at Ford Motor Company

Ford Motor Company knew that the real opportunities for cutting costs were in the design phase, according to Jim Harbor, an industry analyst. Ford's engineers and factory workers were asked how to trim costs from the manufacture of the 1997 Taurus model. Some of the suggestions and the per car savings are

- A new, integrated bracket for the air conditioner ($4).
- Recycled instead of new plastic in splash shields (45 cents).

- Elimination of a plastic part from the wiring harness behind the instrument panel (10 cents).
- Redesigned door hinge pins ($2).
- Plastic moldings for the moon roof instead of metal moldings ($7.85).
- Antilock circuits are no longer installed in cars without the system ($1).

Source: Based on information in "How Ford Cut Costs on the 1997 Taurus, Little by Little," *The Wall Street Journal*, July 18, 1996.

---

[2] The Westinghouse Corporate Services Council estimates that 85 percent of a product's life-cycle cost is determined in the design phase (Karlos A. Artto, "Life Cycle Cost Concepts and Methodologies," *Journal of Cost Management*, Fall 1994, pp. 28–32).

[3] Takao Tanaka, "Target Costing at Toyota," *Journal of Cost Management*, Spring 1993, pp. 4–11.

Target Costing at Toyota

Toyota's design approach was based on the realities of global competition and the trade difficulties associated with the increasing value of the yen against the dollar. Design engineers looked for ways to cut costs that had the least impact. Several hundred dollars are saved by reducing the number of speeds on both manual and auto-matic transmissions. Because the loss of a high-speed gear increases noise, the engineers also designed a lighter rear axle to reduce noise. Also to reduce cost, Toyota designed a new integrated grill and an integrated headlight/running light assembly. Changes also were made inside the car. For example, the seats in the new Paseo model were covered with a less expensive nylon cover instead of the velour fabric in other Toyota cars.

Source: Based on information in "The Japanese Formula: Nylon Seat Covers and a Falling Yen," *The Wall Street Journal,* July 18, 1996, and "More Camry for Less Cash," *Business Week,* November 11, 1996, p. 186.

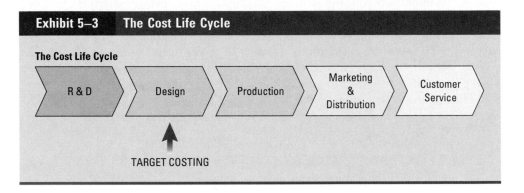

Exhibit 5–3   The Cost Life Cycle

The Cost Life Cycle

R & D → Design → Production → Marketing & Distribution → Customer Service

↑

TARGET COSTING

Many firms employ both methods—operational control to achieve productivity gains and target costing to determine low-cost design. Some managers argue that, unlike the kaizen concept of continual improvement, target costing provides a more distinct goal, a specific cost level. Because the goal is more definite, it appears more achievable and therefore more motivating.

Many auto manufacturers, software developers, and other consumer product manufacturers also must, in the design process, determine the number and types of features to include in periodic updates of a product, using cost and market considerations. Target costing, based on analysis of functionality/cost tradeoffs, is an appropriate management tool for these firms. With its positioning in the early, upstream phases of the cost life cycle, target costing can clearly help a firm reduce total costs.[4]

Japanese industry and a growing number of firms worldwide are using target costing. The Cadillac division at General Motors Corporation; Toyota; Mercedes-Benz; Compaq Computer Inc.; Intel, Inc.; and many others are using target costing. Many firms find it difficult to compete successfully on cost leadership or differentiation alone; they must compete on both price and functionality.[5] Target costing is a very useful way to manage the needed trade-off between increased functionality and higher costs.

There are five steps in implementing a target costing approach:

1. Determine the market price.
2. Determine the desired profit.
3. Calculate the target cost at market price less desired profit.
4. Use value engineering to identify ways to reduce product cost.
5. Use kaizen costing and operational control to further reduce costs.

---

[4]   B. S. Blanchard, *Design and Manage to Life-Cycle Cost* (Portland, OR: M/A Press, 1978).

[5]   Robin Cooper, *When Lean Enterprises Collide* (Boston: Harvard Business School Press, 1995).

Target Costing at Mercedes-Benz

In a move that surprised automakers and consumers alike, Helmut Werner, CEO of Mercedes, announced the firm would make lower-priced vehicles. The move is necessary because of declining sales and profits at Mercedes. Consumers were saying that the firm's

autos were overpriced for the value received. One aspect of the new strategy was that engineers, who have dominated the culture at Mercedes, must design cars from a market price perspective rather than the usual cost-plus pricing approach of earlier times.

Prices are being set by the market, and engineers and manufacturing units have to meet that target price.

Source: Based on information in "Mercedes Is Downsizing—And That Includes the Sticker," *Business Week*, February 8, 1993, p. 38.

The first three steps require no additional explanation. The following sections explain the fourth and fifth steps: the role of value engineering, operational control, and kaizen costing.

Value Engineering

Value engineering is used in target costing to reduce product cost by analyzing the trade-offs between (1) different types and levels of product functionality and (2) total product cost. An important first step in value engineering is a consumer analysis performed during the design stage of the new or revised product. The consumer analysis identifies critical consumer preferences that define the desired functionality for the new product.

The type of value engineering used depends on the functionality of the product. For one group of products—including automobiles, computer software, and many consumer electronic products such as cameras and audio and video equipment—functionality can be added or deleted relatively easily. These are products that have frequent new models or updates, and customer preferences change frequently. The manufacturer in effect chooses the particular bundle of features to be included with each new model of the product. For automobiles, this means new performance and new safety features; whereas for computer software, it might mean the ability to perform certain new tasks or analyses.

In contrast, for another group of products best represented by specialized equipment and industrial products such as construction equipment, heavy trucks, and specialized medical equipment, the functionality of the product must be designed into the product rather than added on. In contrast to the first group, customer preferences here are rather stable.

Target costing is more useful for products in the first group because there are a larger number of features about which the firm has some discretion. A common type of value engineering employed in these firms is **functional analysis,** in which the performance and cost of each major function or feature of the product is examined. The objective of the analysis is to determine a desired balance of performance and cost. An overall desired level of achievement of performance for each function is obtained while keeping the cost of all functions below the target cost.

Benchmarking often is used at this step to determine which features give the firm a competitive advantage. In a release of new software, for example, each desired feature of the new updated version is reviewed against the cost and time required for its development. The objective is an overall bundle of features for the software that achieves the desired balance of meeting customer preferences while keeping costs below targeted levels. In another example, auto manufacturers must decide which performance and safety features should be added to the new model. This decision is based on consumer analysis and a functional analysis of the feature's contribution to consumer preferences compared to its cost. For instance, improved safety air bags could be added, but due to target cost constraints an improved sound system may be delayed until a later model year.

Design analysis is the common form of value engineering for products in group two, industrial and specialized products. The design team prepares several possible

Value engineering is used in target costing to reduce product cost by analyzing the trade-offs between (1) different types and levels of product functionality and (2) total product cost.

Functional analysis is a common type of value engineering in which the performance and cost of each major function or feature of the product is examined.

Design analysis is a common form of value engineering in which the design team prepares several possible designs of the product, each having similar features that have different levels of performance and different costs.

designs of the product, each having similar features that have different levels of performance and different costs. Benchmarking and value chain analysis help guide the design team in preparing designs that are both low cost and competitive. The design team works with cost management personnel to select the one design that best meets customer preferences while not exceeding the target cost.

A useful comparison of different target costing and cost reduction strategies in three Japanese firms, based on the field research of Robin Cooper, is illustrated in Exhibit 5–4.[6] Note that the different market demands for functionality result in different cost reduction approaches. Where customers' expectations for functionality are increasing, as in Nissan and Olympus, there is more significant use of target costing. In contrast, at Komatsu the emphasis is on productivity analysis.

Other cost reduction approaches include cost tables and group technology. **Cost tables** are computer-based databases that include comprehensive information about the firm's cost drivers. Cost drivers include, for example, the size of the product, the materials used in its manufacture, and the number of features. Firms that manufacture different sized parts from the same design (pipe fittings, tools, and so on) use cost tables to show the difference in cost for parts of different sizes and different types of materials.

Group technology is a method of identifying similarities in the parts of products a firm manufactures, so the same parts can be used in two or more products, thereby reducing costs. Large manufacturers of diverse product lines, such as in the automobile industry, use group technology in this way. A point of concern in the use of group technology is that, while manufacturing costs are reduced, service and warranty costs might be increased if a failed part is spread over many different models, with the result that a product recall will affect many more customers. Of course, the combination of group technology and total quality management can result in lower costs in both manufacturing and service/warranty.

Cost tables are computer-based databases that include comprehensive information about the firm's cost drivers.

Group technology is a method of identifying similarities in the parts of products a firm manufactures, so the same part can be used in two or more products, thereby reducing costs.

Target Costing and Kaizen Costing

The fifth step in target costing is to use kaizen costing and operational control to further reduce costs. Kaizen costing occurs at the manufacturing stage, so that the effects of value engineering and improved design are already in place; the role for cost reduction at this phase is to develop new manufacturing methods (such as flexible manufacturing systems) and to use new management techniques such as operational control (Chapters 15, 16, and 17), total quality management (Chapter 6), and the theory of constraints (next section) to further reduce costs. Kaizen means "continual improvement," that is, the ongoing search for new ways to reduce costs in the manufacturing process of a product with a given design and functionality.

---

[6]   Ibid.

Exhibit 5–4	Target Costing in Three Japanese Firms		
Firm/Industry	**Functionality**	**Cost Reduction Approach**	**Strategy**
Nissan/Auto	Rapidly increasing; easy to add or delete functionality	**Value engineering;** then increase price or reduce functionality	Prices are set by desired customers' expectations about functionality; after functionality is set, target cost is used to find savings, especially from suppliers
Komatsu/Construction equipment	Static; must be designed in	**Design analysis** to determine alternative designs; **Functional analysis** to develop cost/functionality trade-offs; **Productivity analysis** to reduce the remaining costs	Primary focus is on cost control rather than redesign or functionality analysis
Olympus/Cameras	Increasing rapidly; is designed in	Greater focus on redesign and functionality; the concept of distinctive functionality for the **price point**, plus supportive functionality	Heavy focus on managing functionality, like Nissan, but more so; importance of price points

Target Costing in Health Product Manufacturing

Health Products International, Inc. (HPI), is conducting a value engineering project by making a target costing analysis of a major product, a hearing aid. HPI sells a reliable second-generation hearing aid for $750 (cost of $650) and has obtained 30 percent of this market worldwide at a profit of $100 per aid. However, in recent years a competitor has introduced a new third-generation hearing aid that incorporates a computer chip that improves performance considerably while increasing the price to $1,200. Through a consumer analysis, HPI has determined that cost-conscious consumers will stay with HPI, and HPI will maintain its market share as long as the price does not exceed $600. HPI must meet the new lower price and would like to maintain its current rate of profit ($100 per unit), by redesigning the hearing aid and/or the manufacturing process.

BusinessWeek

How Will Intel Reach the Low-Price Target Market?

(continues from page 133)

A: Through target costing!

Intel's strategy for meeting the growth of the under $1,000 computer market uses target costing. Specifically, Intel focused its attention on the costs of specific parts; in this case, cache memory. Intel plans to ship a simplified version of the Pentium II that excludes the cache memory previously included with it. (For the curious, cache memory speeds processing by making frequently used data more readily accessible to the processor.) A consulting firm, Micro Design Resources, Inc., estimates the removal of cache memory will save $15 of Intel's $103 manufacturing cost for each Pentium II. By targeting cache memory, Intel can now meet the new price expectations of the low-price computer market.

In related moves, Intel is developing ways to reduce costs on other computer parts such as chip sets which, like cache memory, work with the Pentium II processor. The new chip sets will be simpler and cost less. In total, Intel expects to save computer manufacturers about $50 per computer through the redesigned parts. Together with the reduced manufacturing costs for the Pentium II, Intel will be able to compete more effectively with Cyrix Corp. and Advanced Micro Devices, Inc. (AMD), for processors and chips in the low-price sector of the computer market.

For further reading, see the following source: "Intel: Can Andy Grove Keep Profits Up in an Era of Cheap PCs?" *Business Week,* December 22, 1997, and "How the Competition Got Ahead of Intel in Making Cheap Chips," *The Wall Street Journal,* February 12, 1998, p. 1.

The target cost for the new aid is $600 − $100 = $500, a reduction in cost of $150 from the current model. Because the product has no add-on features, HPI decides to use design analysis, with the following changes and related savings per unit:

Alternative A: Reduce research and development expenditures ($50), replace the microphone unit with one of nearly equivalent sensitivity ($30), replace toggle power switch with a cheaper and almost as reliable slide switch ($30), replace the current inspection procedure with an integrated quality review process at each assembly station ($40). Total savings: $150.

Alternative B: Replace the amplifier unit with one having slightly less power, not expected to be a noticeable difference for most users ($50), replace the microphone unit with one of nearly equivalent sensitivity ($30), replace toggle power switch with a cheaper and almost as reliable slide switch ($30), replace the current inspection procedure with an integrated quality review process at each assembly station ($40). Total savings: $150.

Alternative C: Increase research and development activity to develop the new third-generation computer chip type of hearing aid (increase of $40). Replace the amplifier unit with one of slightly less power, not expected to be a noticeable difference for most users ($50), replace the microphone unit with one of nearly equivalent sensitivity ($30), replace toggle power switch with a cheaper and almost as reliable slide switch ($30), replace the current inspection procedure with an integrated quality review process at each assembly station ($40), renegotiate contract with supplier of plastic casing ($20), replace plastic earpiece material with material of slightly lower quality, but well within the user's expectations for 6 to 10 years of use ($20). Net savings: $150.

After a review of its options, HFI chose alternative C, primarily because it included an increase in research and development expenditures that would enable the firm at some future time to compete in the market for the new type of hearing aid. Manufacturing and marketing managers agreed that the design changes proposed in all the options would not alter significantly the market appeal of the current product. Also, key managers thought that this alternative was strategically important because the new technology, while only a fraction of the market now, would be dominant in the next 10 to 15 years as prices came down on the new units and user awareness of the benefits of the computer chip became more well known.

THE THEORY OF CONSTRAINTS

LEARNING OBJECTIVE 2 ▸
Apply the theory of constraints to facilitate strategic management.

Throughput is defined as sales less direct materials costs, including purchased components and materials handling costs

In contrast to target costing, which focuses on the early phases of the cost life cycle, the theory of constraints focuses on manufacturing activity. The theory of constraints (TOC) was developed by Goldratt and Cox to help managers improve the overall profitability of the firm.[7] This theory focuses the manager's attention on the constraints, or bottlenecks, that slow the production process. The main idea is that a firm succeeds by maximizing the overall rate of manufacturing output, which is called the throughput of the firm. **Throughput** is defined as sales less direct materials costs, including purchased components and materials handling costs.

TOC directs managers' attention to the speed with which the product's raw materials and purchased components are processed into final products and delivered to the customer (see Exhibit 5–5). TOC emphasizes the improvement of throughput by removing or reducing the bottlenecks in the production process that slow the rate of output. Manufacturing and distribution processes that do not affect throughput are nonbinding constraints that receive less attention than bottlenecks or binding constraints.

---

[7]   E. Goldratt and J. Cox, *The Goal* (New York: Free Press, 1986); and E. Goldratt, *The Theory of Constraints* (New York: North River Press, 1990).

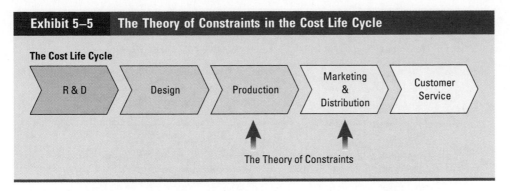

Exhibit 5–5   The Theory of Constraints in the Cost Life Cycle

Using the Theory of Constraints in Pharmaceutical and Health Product Manufacturing

To illustrate, suppose a small pharmaceutical firm, Skincare Products, Inc. (SPI), manufactures a variety of topical skin creams including insect repellents and sun screen. The firm mixes the active and inert ingredients of each cream in a large vat. The mixing process is a binding constraint because the packaging and labeling operations must wait until the mixing is done and raw materials must wait until the vat is empty. The objective of a TOC analysis is to identify and remove the binding constraints, to facilitate the speedy and efficient throughput of raw materials. The search for improved throughput means finding ways to reduce process time, to better coordinate production scheduling, to reduce setup time, and to reduce the size of production batches. By focusing attention on throughput, the TOC approach provides a clear and well-defined goal for managers. Moreover, the TOC approach is strategically important to firms in dynamic markets because it leads to a more responsive and flexible manufacturing environment. Fast throughput enables firms to be better prepared for quick product changeovers and changes in customer preferences.

Steps in Theory of Constraints Analysis

There are five steps in TOC analysis:

1. Identify the binding constraint(s).
2. Determine the most efficient utilization for each binding constraint.
3. Manage the flows through the binding constraint.
4. Add capacity to the binding constraint.
5. Redesign the manufacturing process for flexibility and fast throughput.

Step 1: Identify the Binding Constraint(s).

In the first step the management accountant works with manufacturing managers and engineers to identify binding constraints by developing a network diagram of the flow of production. A **network diagram** is a flowchart of the work done that shows the sequence of processes and the amount of time required for each. The purpose of the network diagram is to help the management accountant look for signs of a bottleneck. A bottleneck often is indicated by a process with relatively large amounts of inventory accumulating, or where there are long lead times. **Task analysis,** which describes the activity of each process in detail, also could be used to identify binding constraints.

The network diagram in Exhibit 5–6 illustrates the production flow for Skincare Products, Inc., which involves six manufacturing processes:

Process 1: Receive and inspect raw materials.

Process 2: Mix raw materials.

Process 3: Second inspection.

Process 4: Filling and packaging.

A **network diagram** is a flowchart of the work done that shows the sequence of processes and the amount of time required for each.

Task analysis describes the activity of each process in detail, to help identify binding constraints.

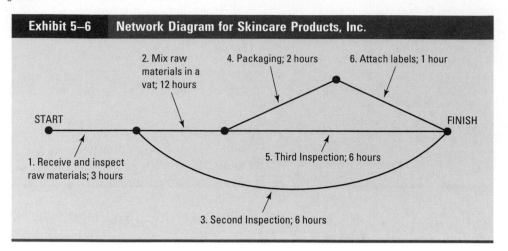

Exhibit 5–6 Network Diagram for Skincare Products, Inc.

Process 5: Third inspection.

Process 6: Attach labels.

Note the production flow and time required for each of the six processes in Exhibit 5–6. Because of Food and Drug Administration (FDA) requirements, SPI inspects the product at three points: (1) the raw materials received by SPI, (2) the mix of raw materials during the mixing process, and (3) the final product after packaging. The first and second inspections check the materials for correct chemical content and potency, while the third inspection focuses on correct weight or item count. Through a visual analysis of the network, we see that the critical processes, *the binding constraints*, are

1. Process 1: Receive and inspect raw materials; required time, 3 hours
2. Process 2: Mix raw materials in vat; 12 hours
3. Process 5: Third inspection of packaged product; 6 hours

The total time for the entire manufacturing process cannot be less than the total time of these three processes added together (3 + 12 + 6 = 21 hours), since these processes must follow in sequence and they cannot overlap. The remaining processes—3, 4, and 6—are not binding. They can be delayed one or more hours without delaying the entire production process, and the amount of the delay can be determined as follows. Process 3 requires 6 hours and must be completed while processes 2 and 5 are being done, but because processes 2 and 5 require 12 + 6 = 18 hours and process 3 requires only 6 hours, there are 12 hours (18 − 6) of slack for finishing process 3.[8]

Step 2: Determine the Most Efficient Utilization for Each Binding Constraint.

In this step, the management accountant determines how to most efficiently utilize the firm's resources. The approach differs somewhat depending on whether there is one product, or two or more (as SPI has). If there is one product, the management accountant looks for ways to maximize the flow of production through the constraint. Exhibit 5–7 explains how this might be done. For two or more products, however, the determination of which product or which product mix to produce becomes important, as does maximizing the flow through the constraint. Different products are likely to require different times on the binding constraint. Thus, managers must determine the *most profitable mix of the products*. Determining the most profitable product mix involves careful analysis of the profitability of each product as well as the time required for each product on the binding constraint.[9]

---

[8] Similarly, since processes 4 (2 hours) and 6 (1 hour) together require only 3 hours, and they must be done during process 5 (6 hours), there are in effect 3 hours of slack on processes 4 and 6 combined (6 hours for process 5 less 3 hours, the total time for processes 4 and 6).

[9] For determining the most profitable product mix using constraint analysis techniques, refer to the section in Chapter 10, "Multiple Products and Limited Resources."

Exhibit 5–7	Maximizing Flow through the Binding Constraints

To maximize the flow through a binding constraint:
1. Simplify the bottleneck operation:
   - Simplify the product design.
   - Simplify the manufacturing process.
2. Look for quality defects in raw materials that might be slowing things down.
3. Reduce setup time.
4. Reduce other delays due to unscheduled and non-value-added activities, such as inspections or machine breakdowns.
5. Simplify the binding constraint by removing all activities from the constraint that do not reduce the function of the operation.

Exhibit 5–8	The Drum-Buffer-Rope System for Production Flow Management

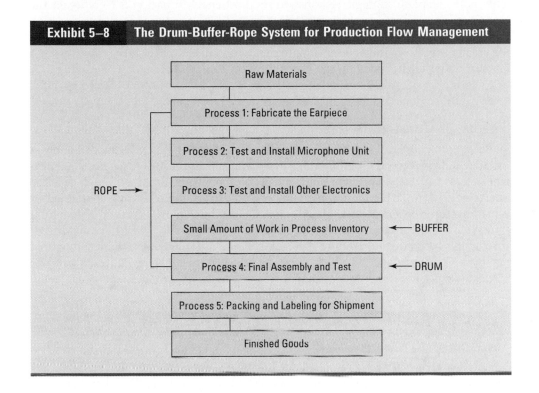

Step 3: Manage the Flows Through the Binding Constraint.

In step 3, the objective is to manage the flow of production in and out of the binding constraint to smooth the flow of production throughout the plant. The orderly scheduling of production prevents the buildup of materials or work-in-process inventory at various processes. An important tool for managing product flow in this context is the **drum-buffer-rope (DBR) system,** which is a system for balancing the flow of production through a binding constraint, illustrated in Exhibit 5–8 for Health Products International, Inc. HPI uses the DBR system in manufacturing its hearing aids; its five manufacturing processes are

Process 1: Fabricate the earpiece to fit the customer's ear.

Process 2: Test and install the microphone unit.

Process 3: Test and install remaining electronics.

Process 4: Final assembly and final test.

Process 5: Packing and labeling for shipment.

The binding constraint is process 4 because it requires a high level of a limited expertise.

This is how the DBR system works for HPI: In the DBR system, all production flows are synchronized to the drummer or the binding constraint, process 4. The rope

> The **drum-buffer-rope system** is a system for balancing the flow of production through a binding constraint, thereby reducing the amount of inventory at the constraint and improving overall productivity.

is the sequence of processes prior to and including the binding constraint. The objective is to *balance the flow of production* through the rope by careful timing and scheduling of activity on processes 1 through 3. The buffer is a minimum amount of work-in-process input for process 4 that is maintained to ensure that process 4 is kept busy.

Step 4: Add Capacity to the Binding Constraint.

As a longer-term measure to relieve the bottleneck and improve throughput, management should consider adding capacity to the binding constraints, by adding new or improved machines and/or additional labor.

Step 5: Redesign the Manufacturing Process for Flexibility and Fast Throughput.

The most complete strategic response to the bottleneck situation is to redesign the manufacturing process, including the introduction of new manufacturing technology, deletion of some hard-to-manufacture products, and redesign of some products for greater ease-to-manufacture. Simply removing one or more minor features on a given product might speed up the production process significantly. The use of value engineering as described earlier might help at this point. The five steps of TOC analysis are summarized in Exhibit 5–9.

Theory of Constraints Reports

When a firm focuses on improving throughput, eliminating bottlenecks, and improving speed of delivery, the performance evaluation measures also focus on these critical success factors. A common approach is to report throughput as well as selected operating data in a theory of constraints report. An example of this report used by a manufacturer of automotive glass is shown in Exhibit 5–10. Note in the exhibit that window styles H and B are the most profitable because they have far higher throughput based on the binding constraint, hours of furnace time. The throughput per hour is $3,667 and $2,370 for styles H and B, respectively; in contrast, the throughput per hour for styles C and A is less than $1,000. TOC reports are useful

---

Exhibit 5–9	**Summary of the Five Steps of TOC Analysis**

Step 1: Identify the Binding Constraint(s)

Use a network diagram. The binding constraint is a resource that limits production to less than market demand.

Step 2: Determine the Most Efficient Utilization of the Binding Constraint

Product mix decision: based on capacity available at the binding constraint; find the most profitable product mix.

Maximize flow through the constraint (see Exhibit 5–7)
- Reduce setups.
- Reduce lot sizes.
- Focus on throughput rather than efficiency.

Step 3: Manage the Flows through the Binding Constraint

Use the Drum-Buffer-Rope system: maintain a small amount of work in process (buffer) and insert materials only when needed (drum) by the constraint, given lead times (rope).

All resources are coordinated to keep the constraint busy without a buildup of work in process.

Step 4: Increase Capacity on the Constrained Resource

Invest in additional capacity if it will increase throughput greater than the cost of the investment.

Do not invest to increase capacity until steps 2 and 3 are complete. Instead, maximize the productivity of the process through the constraint with existing capacity.

Step 5: Redesign the Manufacturing Process for Flexibility and Fast Throughput

Consider a redesign of the product or production process, to achieve faster throughput.

Exhibit 5–10	The TOC Report for an Auto Glass Manufacturer

Theory of Constraints Report: Throughput for Four Auto Window Styles

	March 19X2			
	Style C	**Style A**	**Style H**	**Style B**
Window size	0.77	.073	7.05	4.95
Sales volume	High	Moderate	High	Moderate
Units in unfilled orders	1,113	234	882	23
Average lead time (days)	16	23	8	11
Market price	$2.82	$6.68	$38.12	$24.46
Direct production costs				
Materials	0.68	0.64	5.75	4.02
Scrap allowance	0.06	0.05	0.42	0.34
Material handling	0.12	0.12	1.88	1.61
Subtotal	.86	.81	8.05	5.97
Throughput value (TV)	$1.96	$5.87	$30.07	$18.49
Furnace hours/unit (FH)	.0062	.0061	.0082	.0078
Throughput per hour (TV/FH)	$316	$962	$3,667	$2,370

Source: Adapted from R. J. Campbell, "Pricing Strategy in the Automotive Glass Industry," *Management Accounting*, July 1989, pp. 26–34.

for identifying the most profitable product and for monitoring success in achieving the critical success factors.

ABC and the Theory of Constraints

Activity-based costing (ABC) is employed commonly by firms using such cost management methods as target costing and the theory of constraints. ABC is used to assess the profitability of products, just as TOC in the previous illustration. The difference is that TOC takes a short-term approach to profitability analysis, while ABC costing develops a long-term analysis. The TOC analysis has a short-term focus because of its emphasis only on materials-related costs, while ABC includes all product costs.

On the other hand, unlike TOC, ABC does not explicitly include the resource constraints and capacities of production activities. Thus, ABC cannot be used to determine the short-term best product mix, as for the auto window manufacturer in Exhibit 5–10. ABC and TOC are thus *complementary* methods; ABC provides a comprehensive analysis of cost drivers and accurate unit costs, as a basis for strategic decisions about long-term pricing and product mix. In contrast, TOC provides a useful method for improving the short-term profitability of the manufacturing plant through short-term product mix adjustments and through attention to production bottlenecks. The differences between ABC and TOC are outlined in Exhibit 5–11.[10]

LIFE-CYCLE COSTING

Typically, product or service costs are measured and reported for relatively short periods, such as a month or a year. Life-cycle costing provides a long-term perspective, because it considers the entire cost life cycle of the product or service (see Exhibit 5–12). It therefore provides a more complete perspective of product costs and product or service profitability. For example, a product that is designed

◀ **LEARNING OBJECTIVE 3**
Describe how life-cycle costing facilitates strategic management.

---

[10]   For a comparison of TOC and ABC, see Jay S. Holmen, "ABC vs. TOC: It's a Matter of Time," *Management Accounting*, January 1995, pp. 37–40; Robert Kee, "Integrating Activity-Based Costing with the Theory of Constraints to Enhance Production-Related Decision Making," *Accounting Horizons*, December 1995, pp. 48–61; and John B. MacArthur, "TOC and ABC: Friends or Foes?" *Journal of Cost Management*, Summer 1993, pp. 50–56.

Exhibit 5–11	Comparison of the TOC and ABC Costing Methods	
	TOC	**ABC**
Main objective	**Short-term focus;** throughput analysis based on materials and materials-related costs	**Long-term focus;** analysis of all product costs, including materials, labor, and overhead
Resource constraints and capacities	Included explicitly; a principal focus of TOC	Not included explicitly
Cost drivers	No direct utilization of cost drivers	Develop an understanding of cost drivers at the unit, batch, product, and facility levels
Major use	Optimization of production flow and short-term product mix	Strategic pricing and profit planning

Exhibit 5–12   Life-Cycle Costing

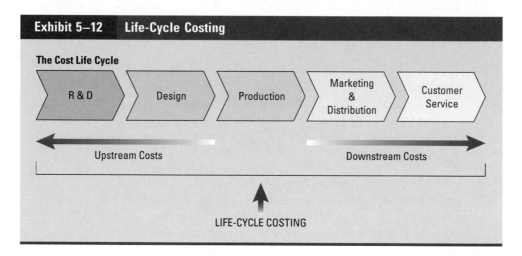

The Cost Life Cycle

R & D → Design → Production → Marketing & Distribution → Customer Service

Upstream Costs   Downstream Costs

LIFE-CYCLE COSTING

quickly and carelessly, with little investment in design costs, may have significantly higher marketing and service costs later in the life cycle. Managers are interested in the total cost, over the entire life cycle, and not manufacturing costs only. Total cost over the product's life cycle often is broken down into three components—upstream costs, manufacturing costs, and downstream costs:

Upstream costs
Research and development
Design: prototyping, testing, concurrent engineering, and quality development

Manufacturing costs
Purchasing
Direct manufacturing costs
Indirect manufacturing costs

Downstream costs
Marketing and distribution—packaging, shipping, samples, promotion, advertising
Service and warranty—recalls, service, product liability, customer support

While cost management methods have tended to focus only on manufacturing costs, upstream and downstream costs can account for a significant portion of total life-cycle costs, especially in certain industries:

Industries with high upstream and downstream costs
Pharmaceuticals
Auto manufacturing

Industries with high upstream costs
    Computer software
    Specialized industrial and medical equipment

Industries with high downstream costs
    Retail
    Perfumes, cosmetics, and toiletries

Upstream and downstream costs are managed in a number of ways, including by improving relationships with suppliers and distributors; the most crucial way is the design of the product and the manufacturing process. Also, value chain analysis, as explained in Chapter 2, can provide a useful means to identify upstream and downstream linkages for a manufacturing or service firm.

The Importance of Design

As managers consider upstream and downstream costs, decision making at the design stage is critical. Although the costs incurred at the design stage may account for only a very small percentage of the total costs over the entire product life cycle, design stage decisions commit a firm to a given production, marketing, and service plan. Therefore, they lock in most of the remaining life-cycle costs.

The critical success factors at the design stage include:

Reduced time-to-market—In a competitive environment where the speed of product development and the speed of delivery are critical, efforts to reduce time-to-market are the first priority.

Reduced expected service costs—By careful, simple design and the use of modular, interchangeable components, the expected service costs can be greatly reduced.

Improved ease-of-manufacture—To reduce production costs and speed production, the design must be easy to manufacture.

Process planning and design—The plan for the manufacturing process should be flexible, allowing for fast setups and product changeovers, using agile manufacturing concepts, computer-integrated manufacturing, computer-assisted design, and concurrent engineering.

The four common design methods are basic engineering, prototyping, templating, and concurrent engineering. See Exhibit 5-13. **Basic engineering** is the method in which product designers work independently from marketing and manufacturing to develop a design from specific plans and specifications. An advantage of this approach is that it can be quick and less costly than the others. The disadvantage is that because basic engineering is independent from marketing and production, the product might be inappropriate for the market (hard to sell and/or service), or it might be difficult and costly to manufacture. This method has high downstream costs as a result.

Basic engineering is the method in which product designers work independently from marketing and manufacturing to develop a design from specific plans and specifications.

Exhibit 5–13	Characteristics of the Four Design Methods		
Design Method	**Design Speed**	**Design Cost**	**Effect on Downstream Costs**
Basic engineering	Fast	Depends on desired complexity and functionality; should be relatively low	Can be very high; as marketing and production are not integral to the design process
Prototyping	Slow	Significant; materials, labor, and time	Potentially a significant reduction in downstream costs
Templating	Fast	Modest	Unknown; can have costly unexpected results if the scaling does not work in the market or in production
Concurrent engineering	Continuous	Significant; design is an integral, ongoing process	The best method for reducing downstream costs

Prototyping is a method in which functional models of the product are developed and tested by engineers and trial customers.

Templating is a design method in which an existing product is scaled up or down to fit the specifications of the desired new product.

Concurrent engineering, or simultaneous engineering, is an important new approach in which product design is integrated with manufacturing and marketing throughout the product's life cycle.

Prototyping is a method in which functional models of the product are developed and tested by engineers and trial customers. A good example of prototyping is the process of beta testing software products, in which customers of the software vendor provide a trial run of a new software system. The direct cost of prototyping can be high, for significant materials and labor are needed to prepare the prototype products. On the other hand, there is a great potential to reduce downstream costs, since the feedback from the engineers and trial customers is used to improve the product and/or the production process.

Templating is a design method in which an existing product is scaled up or down to fit the specifications of the desired new product. An example is the "Big Mac," "Biggie," "Double," or "Whopper" hamburger sandwiches that are derived from more simple sandwiches. Templating is a fast and low-cost design method; the impact on downstream costs depends on how well the scaling works—whether the production costs and market reaction are as expected.

Concurrent engineering, or simultaneous engineering, is an approach in which product design is integrated with manufacturing and marketing throughout the product's life cycle.

The Hidden Costs That Drive Up the Price of Your Car: The Importance of Downstream Costs

The Big Three automakers spend billions each year to repair customers' vehicles. The cost of warranties has risen dramatically, even though quality also has improved. This is due in part to the extended coverage offered under many auto warranties. The coverage has increased from one to two to three years on certain components of the automobile. Moreover, auto analyst David Bradley of J. P. Morgan Securities observes that most consumers purchase an extended coverage service contract with their new car, thus further increasing the automaker's liability for defects. The cost of repairs under warranty or service contract are conservatively estimated at $800 per vehicle, which works out to $1.8 billion per year for Chrysler, $3.1 billion for Ford, and $4 billion for GM.

Source: Based on information in "The Hidden Costs That Drive Up the Price of Your Car," *Fortune,* September 4, 1995, p. 28.

Upstream Life-Cycle Costing at German Automakers

To compensate in part for high labor costs in Germany, automakers are working hard to reduce upstream costs. For example, the German automakers are speeding up product development and are using virtual prototyping instead of the more costly physical prototyping methods. Also, Volkswagen and Mercedes are using ever-closer partnerships with suppliers to reduce design and materials acquisition costs.

Source: Based on information from "VW's Factory of the Future," *Business Week,* October 7, 1995, pp. 52–56; "Hot Wheels," *Business Week,* September 15, 1997, pp. 56–57.

Downstream Life-Cycle Costing at Haggar

Haggar Clothing Company, a large manufacturer of menswear, is reducing downstream costs for itself and its customers by automating customer records and stock replenishment programs for its large retail customers. The systems allow Haggar to focus on popular products and to provide enhanced customer service. For example, the clothing is shipped ready for display—on hangers, and with the customer's price tags attached. Automated equipment at the customer's warehouses helps to sort Haggar's products for each customer, so that the correct shipment is prepared for each of the customer's stores.

Source: Based on information from Grant Thornton LLP, "Haggar Wears a Coat of Many Colors to Meet Customer Needs," *Manufacturing & Distribution Issues,* Winter 1997, pp. 9–10.

Concurrent Engineering

An important new development in the design of products is concurrent engineering. It is replacing the basic engineering approach in which product designers work in isolation on specialized components and tasks of the overall design project. In contrast, concurrent engineering relies on an integrated approach, in which the engineering/design process takes place *throughout the cost life cycle* using cross-functional teams. Information is solicited and used at each of the phases of the value chain to improve the product design. For example, customer feedback in the service phase is used directly in the design of the product. Software developers and other manufacturers are increasingly using product design in a very flexible manner; improvements are incorporated in the product continuously. Some experts argue that this approach has saved firms as much as 20 percent of total product cost.[11]

Life-Cycle Costing in a Software Firm

As an example of applying life-cycle costing, consider software developer Analytical Decisions, Inc. (ADI), that provides specialized software for banks and other financial institutions. ADI software is used in analyzing loan loss reserves and planning loan portfolios. ADI has two products, ADI–1 for large banks and ADI–2 for smaller banks and savings and loans. Each product is updated every year, with an occasional special update during the year. Each update improves the functionality of the product in some significant way.

Initially, ADI analyzed profitability by using the accounting software widely used in the industry, which provided the report shown in Exhibit 5–14.

This analysis shows both products to be quite profitable, even in the presence of heavy R&D and selling costs; ADI–1 shows a somewhat higher gross margin (72%; $3,260,000/$4,500,000) than for ADI–2 (60%; $1,495,000/$2,500,000). However,

Exhibit 5–14	Product Line Income Statement for Analytical Decisions, Inc.		
	ADI–1	**ADI–2**	**Total**
Sales	$4,500,000	$2,500,000	$7,000,000
Cost of sales	1,240,000	1,005,000	2,245,000
Gross margin	3,260,000	1,495,000	4,755,000
Research and development			2,150,000
Selling and service			1,850,000
Income before tax			$ 755,000

Reducing Service Costs at Merisel, Inc.

In 1994 Merisel, a large distributor of computers located near Palo Alto, California, purchased a large computer retailer, Computerland, and found that other retailers (customers of Merisel) now required larger discounts because Merisel had become a competitor (through Computerland) as well as a supplier.

To keep this business, Merisel began to offer substantial discounts. This led quickly to the need to reduce costs, and Merisel looked at the life cycle of their cost structure to do this. The firm found that a considerable amount of its costs were tied up in distribution and other support costs, such as repairs and returns. In particular, its warehousing and distribution costs in the Palo Alto area were quite high. Thus, the firm began to look for a new location for its support center, where facility and labor costs would be somewhat lower.

---

[11] Terrance R. Ozan, "Innovation," *Business Week*, 1992 Bonus Issue.

Exhibit 5–15	Life-Cycle Costing for Analytical Decisions, Inc.		
	ADI–1	**ADI–2**	**Total**
Sales	$4,500,000	$2,500,000	$7,000,000
Cost of sales	1,240,000	1,005,000	2,245,000
Gross margin	3,260,000	1,495,000	4,755,000
Less:			
Research and development	1,550,000	600,000	2,150,000
Selling and service	1,450,000	400,000	1,850,000
Net income before tax	$ 260,000	$ 495,000	$ 755,000

the analysis is incomplete, since most of ADI's costs (R&D and selling) are not included in the product comparison. Because ADI's systems designers and programmers work in project teams, it is relatively simple to determine how the R&D costs should be assigned to the two products. Similarly, because ADI's sales and customer service efforts are logged by product, these costs also can be traced, as shown in Exhibit 5–15.

It is clear from the life-cycle cost analysis that ADI–2 is the more profitable of the two products, because the bulk of the R&D and selling costs are incurred by ADI–1. Moreover, the revised analysis provides a basis for ADI management to seek out possible cost reductions. For example, the ratio of research and development, selling and service costs to sales dollars is much higher for ADI–1 (67%; $3,000,000/$4,500,000) than for ADI–2 (40%; $1,000,000/$2,500,000). Management should investigate whether this is due to the nature of the different customers, or whether some quality problems in ADI–1 account for these higher costs. The manager can use this breakdown of costs throughout the product's life cycle to identify opportunities for cost savings.

PART TWO: COST MANAGEMENT OVER THE SALES LIFE CYCLE

Strategic pricing and the development of an appropriate cost management system depend on the position of the product or service in the phases of the sales life cycle. As the sales life cycles become shorter (only months in some industries such as consumer electronics), the analysis of the sales life cycle becomes increasingly important.[12] In contrast to the cost life cycle just described, the sales life cycle refers to the phase of the product's or service's sales in the market—from introduction of the product or service to decline and withdrawal from the market. (Exhibit 5–2 illustrates the phases of the sales life cycle.)

Phase 1: Product Introduction In the first phase there is little competition, and sales rise slowly as customers become aware of the new product or service. Costs are relatively high because of high R&D expenditures and capital costs for setting up production facilities and marketing efforts. Prices are relatively high because of product differentiation and the high costs at this phase. Product variety is limited.

Phase 2: Growth Sales begin to grow rapidly and product variety increases. The product continues to enjoy the benefits of differentiation. There is increasing competition and prices begin to soften.

Phase 3: Maturity Sales continue to increase but at a decreasing rate. There is a reduction in the number of competitors and of product variety. Prices

---

[12] Manash R. Ray, "Cost Management for Product Development," *Journal of Cost Management*, Spring 1995, pp. 52–64.

soften further, and differentiation is no longer important. Competition is based on cost, given competitive quality and functionality.

Phase 4: Decline Sales begin to decline, as do the number of competitors. Prices stabilize. Emphasis on differentiation returns. Survivors are able to differentiate their product, control costs, and deliver quality and excellent service. Control of costs and an effective distribution network are key to continued survival.

In the first phase, the focus of management is on design, differentiation, and marketing. The focus shifts to new product development and pricing strategy as competition develops in the second phase. In the third and fourth phases, management's attention turns to cost control, quality, and service as the market continues to become more competitive. Thus, the firm's strategy for the product or service changes over the sales life cycle, from differentiation in the early phases to cost leadership in the final phases.

Similarly, the strategic pricing approach changes over the life cycle of the product or service. In the first phase, pricing is set relatively high to recover development costs and to take advantage of product differentiation and the new demand for the product. In the second phase, pricing is likely to stay relatively high as the firm attempts to build profitability in the growing market. Alternatively, to maintain or increase market share at this time, relatively low prices (penetration pricing) might be used. In the latter phases, pricing becomes more competitive, and target costing and life-cycle costing methods are used, as the firm becomes more of a price taker rather than a price setter and makes efforts to reduce upstream (for product enhancements) and downstream costs.

Together with the change in strategy and pricing, there is a change in the cost management system. At the introduction and into the growth phases, the primary need is for value chain analysis, to guide the design of products in a cost-efficient manner. Master budgets (see Chapter 9) also are used in these early phases to manage cash flows; there are large developmental costs at a time when sales revenues are still relatively small. As the strategy shifts to cost leadership in the latter phases, the goal of the cost management system is to provide the detailed budgets and activity-based costing tools for accurate cost information.

The Sales Life Cycle in Computer Manufacturing

Exhibit 5–16 summarizes the relationship between life cycle phases, critical success factors, and desired pricing for a manufacturer of computer processors. The firm makes three processors: the Z300, Y300, and X300. The Z300 is a very fast processor, while the Y300 and X300 are somewhat slower. The Z300 has been introduced recently, the Y300 has a growing market, while the X300 is in a mature market, near the end of its product sales life cycle. The critical success factors of the Z300 focus on product differentiation, while those of the Y300 focus on production

---

Life-Cycle Costing vs. Sales Life-Cycle Analysis at Olympus Camera and Nissan

Some firms, such as Olympus Camera, use life-cycle costing to plan expected cost reductions. That is, the product might not be profitable initially, but with an expectation that upstream and downstream costs as well as manufacturing costs will be reduced later, Olympus expects the product to eventually become profitable. For example, the cost reductions in manufacturing can come about as a result of learning (see Chapter 7) or kaizen costing.

Other firms, such as Nissan, use sales life-cycle analysis to plan prices and costs so that the product is profitable over the entire sales life cycle. As the sales life cycle of products becomes shorter, as it has in many industries including automobiles and cameras, the use of life-cycle analysis becomes more important and useful.

Exhibit 5–16	Critical Success Factors and Pricing at Different Sales Life-Cycle Phases for Three Different Computer Processors		
Computer Processor (speed)	**Sales Life-Cycle Phases**	**Critical Success Factors**	**Strategic Pricing**
Z300 (very fast)	Introduction	Differentiation, quality	Price is set relatively high because of demand and differentiation, and to recover development costs
Y300 (fast)	Growth	Adequate capacity and financing, effective distribution channels	Prices still set relatively high because of product differentiation and demand
X300 (relatively slow)	Maturity and decline	Effective cost control and quality control, service	Use of target costing; prices set by a mature, competitive market

capacity, financing, and distribution. Those of the X300 focus on cost leadership and quality. Also, pricing strategy differs among the three products, with prices set relatively high for the Z300 and Y300. Because of increased competition, the X300 is in a price-taker market, and the firm uses target costing.

SUMMARY

The strategic cost management concepts introduced in the preceding chapters are extended here. First, we discussed three cost management methods used to analyze the product or service's cost life cycle: target costing, the theory of constraints, and life-cycle costing. Target costing is a tool for analyzing the cost structure to help management identify the proper design features and manufacturing methods to allow the firm to meet a competitive price. The five steps in target costing are (1) determine the market price, (2) determine the desired profit, (3) calculate the target cost (market price less desired profit), (4) use value engineering to identify ways to reduce product cost, and (5) use kaizen costing and operational control to further reduce costs.

The theory of constraints (TOC) is a tool that assists managers in identifying bottlenecks and scheduling production to maximize throughput and profits. There are five steps to TOC analysis: (1) identify the binding and nonbinding constraints, (2) determine the most efficient utilization for each binding constraint, (3) manage the flows through the binding constraint, (4) add capacity to the binding constraint, and (5) redesign the manufacturing process for flexibility and fast throughput.

Life-cycle costing assists managers in minimizing total cost over the product's or service's entire life cycle. Life-cycle costing brings a focus to the upstream activities (research and development, engineering) and downstream activities (marketing, distribution, service), as well as the manufacturing and operating costs that cost systems focus on. Especially important is a careful consideration of the effects of design choices on downstream costs. The analysis of design is done in four ways: (1) basic engineering in which engineering is done separately from marketing and production; (2) prototyping in which a working model of the product is developed for testing; (3) templating in which a new product is developed from the design of a similar existing product; and (4) concurrent engineering, an ongoing effort in which marketing, manufacturing, and design are integrated to continually improve a product's design.

The second part of the chapter considers strategic pricing and cost management issues as the product or service moves through the different phases of its sales life cycle. In the product introduction phase, value chain analysis and the master budget are important. In the growth phase, managers are more likely to need advanced costing methods such as activity-based costing and capital budgeting to deal with the increased complexity and growth of the manufacturing process. In the final two phases of the sales life cycle, maturity and decline, cost management focuses on operational and management control—the flexible budget and activity-based management.

KEY TERMS

SELF-STUDY PROBLEM

(For the solution, please turn to the end of the chapter.)

Best Brand Lighting, Inc.

Best Brand Lighting, Inc. (BBL), manufactures lighting fixtures. The two major markets for BBL products are the major retailers including Home Depot, Wal-Mart, and Kmart, and specialty lighting stores. The former sell primarily to homeowners, and the latter primarily to electrical contractors.

While standard sizes and models typically are sold to the large retailers, BBL's products with more specialized features and sizes are sold only to the specialty stores. Thus, the design and manufacturing costs of the products going to the specialty stores are slightly higher. The products in both markets have similar sales life cycles of about two years.

Because of the difference in consumers, BBL has a larger marketing cost for the products sold to the large retailers—advertising in major media to attract homeowners. In contrast, the marketing for the specialty shops consists mainly of catalogs and advertisements in trade publications resulting in a lower overall marketing cost. Also, the sales policies are somewhat different for the two markets. Sales to specialty stores are priced higher but include significant discounts and attractive return policies. In contrast, sales to the major retailers have restrictive return policies and little, if any, discount.

BBL management is interested in an in-depth analysis of the profitability of its two markets. As a first step, it has asked for the average costs and other data for all BBL products:

	Major Retailers	Specialty Stores
Design costs	$ .80	$ 1.10
Manufacturing costs	5.20	5.90
Marketing costs	.95	.10
Returns	.05	.95
Discounts	.10	.95
Average price	10.55	12.50
Total market ($000) in BBL's sales region	188,000	32,000
Current unit sales	56,000	14,000

Required   Using the methods of strategic cost management, develop an analysis of BBL's two market segments. What questions would you want to ask management and which fact-finding studies would be appropriate to support this analysis?

QUESTIONS

5–1   Explain the two methods for reducing total product costs to achieve a desired target cost. Which is most common in the consumer electronics industries? In the specialized equipment manufacturing industries?

5–2   What is meant by the sales life cycle? What are the phases of the sales life cycle? How does it differ from the cost life cycle?

5-3 Do pricing strategies change over the different phases of the sales life cycle? Explain how.

5-4 Do cost management practices change over the product's sales life cycle? Explain how.

5-5 What is target costing, and what types of firms use it?

5-6 What is life-cycle costing, and why is it used?

5-7 Name the five steps of the theory of constraints and explain the purpose of each. Which is the most important step and why?

5-8 What is meant by a binding constraint in the theory of constraint analysis? A nonbinding constraint?

5-9 What is the role of the network diagram in the theory of constraints analysis?

5-10 What are the different methods of product engineering used in product design and life-cycle costing?

5-11 What is meant by the concept of value engineering? How is it used in target costing?

5-12 What is the main difference between activity-based costing and the theory of constraints? When is it appropriate to use each one?

5-13 For what types of firms is the theory of constraints analysis most appropriate and why?

5-14 For what types of firms is target costing most appropriate and why?

5-15 For what types of firms is life-cycle costing most appropriate and why?

5-16 Explain the difference in intended application between sales life-cycle analysis and life-cycle costing.

PROBLEMS

5-17 **TARGET COSTING** DuoDrive manufactures a wide variety of parts for recreational boating, including a gear and driveshaft component for high-powered outboard boat engines. The component is purchased by OEM (original equipment manufacturers) such as Mercury and Honda, for use in large, more powerful outboards. The units sell for $510, and sales volume averages 25,000 units per year. Recently, DuoDrive's major competitor reduced the price of its equivalent part to $450. The market is very competitive, and DuoDrive realizes it must meet the new price or lose significant market share. The controller has assembled these cost and usage data for the most recent year for DuoDrive's production of 25,000 units:

	Standard Cost	Actual Quantity	Actual Cost
Materials	$5,125,000		$ 5,500,000
Direct labor	1,750,000		1,670,000
Indirect labor	2,500,000		2,359,000
Inspection (hours and cost)	—	2,000	350,000
Materials handling (number of purchases and cost)	—	56,000	245,000
Machine setups (number and cost)	—	3,500	980,000
Returns and rework (number of times and cost)	—	500	65,000
Total			$11,169,000

Required

1. Calculate the target cost for maintaining current market share and profitability.

2. Can the target cost be achieved? How?

5–18 STRATEGIC COSTING Optic Care Inc. (OCI) manufactures specialized equipment for polishing optical lenses. There are two models—one principally used for fine eyewear (L–25) and another for lenses used in binoculars, cameras, and similar equipment (BL–10).

Strategy

The manufacturing cost of each unit is calculated by activity-based costing, using these manufacturing cost pools:

Cost Pools	Allocation Base	Costing Rate
1. Materials handling	Number of parts	$1.85 per part
2. Manufacturing supervision	Hours of machine time	$11.40 per hour
3. Assembly	Number of parts	$2.55 per part
4. Machine setup	Each setup	$43.50 per setup
5. Inspection and testing	Logged hours	$35 per hour
6. Packaging	Logged hours	$15 per hour

OCI currently sells the BL–10 model for $1,050 and the L–25 model for $725. Manufacturing costs and activity usage for the two products are:

	BL–10	L–25
Direct materials	126.50	58.19
Number of parts	121	88
Machine hours	6.1	3.2
Inspection time	1.3	0.6
Packing time	0.7	0.4
Setups	2	1

Required

1. Calculate the product cost and product margin for each product.

2. A new competitor has entered the market for lens polishing equipment with a superior product at significantly lower prices—$750 for the BL–10 model and $550 for the L–25 model. To try to compete, OCI has made some radical improvements in the design and manufacturing of its two products. While the costing rates have stayed the same, the materials costs and activity usage rates have been decreased significantly:

	BL–10	L–25
Direct materials	111.50	48.30
Number of parts	96	77
Machine hours	5.7	2.9
Inspection time	1.0	0.5
Packing time	0.7	0.4
Setups	1	1

Calculate the total product costs with the new activity usage data. Can OCI make a profit with the new costs, assuming that OCI must meet the price set by the new competitor?

3. What cost management method might be useful to OCI at this time, and why?

5–19 TARGET COSTING IN A SERVICE FIRM ALERT Alarm Systems installs home security systems. Two of Alert's systems, the ICU 100 and the ICU 900, have these characteristics:

Service

Design Specifications	ICU 100	ICU 900
Video cameras	1	3
Video monitors	1	1
Motion detectors	5	8
Floodlights	3	7
Alarms	1	2
Wiring	700 ft.	1,100 ft.
Installation	16 hrs.	26 hrs.

Cost Data for Both Systems:

Video cameras	$150/ea.
Video monitors	$75/ea.
Motion detectors	$15/ea.
Floodlights	$8/ea.
Alarms	$15/ea.
Wiring	$0.10/ft.
Installation	$20/hr.

The ICU 100 sells for $810 installed, and the ICU 900 sells for $1,520 installed.

Required

1. What are the current profit margins on both systems?

2. ALERT's management believes it must drop the price on the ICU 100 to $750 and the ICU 900 to $1,390 to remain competitive in the market. Recalculate profit margins for both products at these price levels.

3. Describe two ways that ALERT could cut its costs to get the profit margins back to their original levels.

Strategy

5–20 TARGET COSTING, STRATEGY Benchmark Industries manufactures large workbenches for industrial use. Wayne Garrett, the vice president for marketing at Benchmark, has concluded from his market analysis that sales are dwindling for Benchmark's standard table because of aggressive pricing by competitors. Benchmark's table sells for $875 whereas the competition's comparable table is selling in the $800 range. Garrett has determined that dropping the price to $800 is necessary to regain the firm's annual market share of 10,000 tables. Cost data based on sales of 10,000 tables are:

	Budgeted Amount	Actual Amount	Actual Cost
Direct materials	400,000 sq. ft.	425,000 sq. ft.	$2,700,000
Direct labor	85,000 hrs.	100,000 hrs.	1,000,000
Machine setups	30,000 hrs.	30,000 hrs.	300,000
Mechanical assembly	320,000 hrs.	320,000 hrs.	4,000,000

Required

1. Calculate the current cost and profit per unit.

2. How much of the current cost per unit is attributable to non-value-added activities?

3. Calculate the new target cost per unit for a sales price of $800 if the profit per unit is maintained.

4. What strategy do you suggest for Benchmark to attain the target cost calculated in requirement 3?

5–21 TARGET COST; WAREHOUSING Yapley Ceramic, a wholesaler, has determined that its operations have three primary activities: purchasing, warehousing, and distributing. The firm reports the following pertinent operating data for the year just completed:

Activity	Cost Driver	Quantity of Cost Driver	Cost per Unit of Cost Driver
Purchasing	Number of purchasing orders	1,000	$100 per order
Warehousing	Number of moves	8,000	20 per move
Distributing	Number of shipments	500	80 per order

Yapley buys 100,000 units at an average cost of $5 per unit and sells them at an average unit price of $10. The firm also has a fixed operating cost of $100,000 for the year.

Yapley's customers are demanding a 5 percent discount for the coming year. Yapley expects to sell the same quantity if the demand for price reduction can be met. Yapley's suppliers, however, are willing to give only a 4 percent discount.

Required Yapley has estimated that the number of purchasing orders can be reduced to 800 and a $5 decrease in the cost of each shipment can be achieved with minor changes in its operations. Any further cost saving has to come from reengineering the warehousing processes. What is the maximum cost (i.e., target cost) for warehousing if the firm desires to earn the same amount of profit next year?

5–22 TARGET COSTING; INTERNATIONAL Harpers, Ltd., is a British manufacturer of casual shoes for men and women. It has sustained strong growth in the British market in recent years due to its close attention to fashion trends. Also, Harpers' shoes have a good reputation for quality and comfort. To expand the business, Harpers is considering introducing its shoes to the United States market, where comparable shoes sell for an average of $90 wholesale, more than $16 above what Harpers gets in Britain (average price, 46 pounds). Management has engaged a marketing consultant to obtain information about what features U.S. citizens desire in shoes. Those in the British market desire different features. Harpers also has obtained information on the approximate cost of adding these features:

International

Strategy

Features Desired in the United States	Cost to Add (in U.S. $)	Importance Rating (5 is most important)
Colorfast material	$4.50	3
Lighter weight	6.75	5
Extra-soft insole	3.00	4
Longer-wearing sole	3.00	2

The current average manufacturing cost of Harpers' shoes is 35 pounds (approximately $56 U.S.), which gives it an average profit of 11¼ pounds ($18 U.S.) per pair of shoes sold. Harpers would like to maintain this profit margin; however, the firm recognizes the U.S. market requires different features and shipping and advertising costs would increase approximately $10 U.S. per pair of shoes.

Required

1. What is the target manufacturing cost for shoes to be sold in the United States?

2. Which features, if any, should Harpers add for shoes to be sold in the United States?

3. Critically evaluate Harpers' decision to begin selling shoes in the United States.

5–23 THEORY OF CONSTRAINTS: IDENTIFYING THE CONSTRAINT Coble Inc. manufactures a part, X23, used in automobiles. Three processes are involved in the production of X23: drilling, inserting, and packaging. Each process is performed at a separate workstation and has these performance characteristics:

- The drilling function can drill 30,000 parts per hour.

- The inserting function can insert 3,000 parts per 5 minutes.

- The packaging function can package 10,000 parts per half hour.

Required How many units of X23 can be manufactured in a week, and which process is the binding constraint?

5–24 THEORY OF CONSTRAINTS: THE PRODUCT MIX DECISION Bell Company produces and sells three products (A,B,C). These data relate to the three products.

	A	B	C
Demand in units	120	110	100
Selling price per unit	$100	$120	$105
Raw material costs/unit	$50	$60	$60
Labor time in minutes/unit	12	17	7

157

Required

1. Calculate the contribution per labor minute for each product.

2. Determine the best product mix. Assume there are five employees; given time for breaks, training, and regular meetings, there are a total of 2,200 minutes available per day.

5–25 DETERMINING THE IMPACT OF EVALUATING LOCAL CONSTRAINTS Jim Gordon is a manufacturing manager at Perkins, Inc., with direct responsibility for the assembly department. Gordon's department is the second of four manufacturing operations:

Receiving → Assembly → Heat Treatment → Shipping

He has just finished a class in the theory of constraints and is now doing his best to reduce the time and increase the flow through his department. He is the only manager trying to do this at Perkins.

Required Explain the likely outcome of Jim's actions and how you would have attempted to improve the throughput at Perkins, Inc.

Ethics

5–26 LIFE-CYCLE COSTING Jim Waters, the COO of BioDerm, has asked his cost management team for a product line profitability analysis for his firm's two products, Xderm and Yderm. The two skin care products require a large amount of research and development and advertising. After receiving the following statement from BioDerm's auditor, Waters concludes that Xderm is the more profitable product, and that perhaps cost-cutting measures should be applied to Yderm.

	Xderm	Yderm	Total
Sales	$3,000,000	$2,000,000	$5,000,000
Cost of goods sold	(1,900,000)	(1,600,000)	(3,500,000)
Gross profit	$1,100,000	$ 400,000	$1,500,000
Research and development			(900,000)
Selling expenses			(100,000)
Profit before taxes			$ 500,000

Required

1. Explain why Waters may be wrong in his assessment of the relative performances of the two products.

2. Suppose that 80 percent of the R&D and selling expenses are traceable to Xderm. Prepare life-cycle income statements for each product and calculate the return on sales. What does this tell you about the importance of accurate life-cycle costing?

3. Consider again your answers in 1. and 2. above, with the following additional information. R&D and selling expenses are substantially higher for Xderm because it is a new product. Waters has strongly supported development of the new product, including the high selling and R&D expenses. He has assured senior managers that the investment in Xderm would pay off in improved profits for the firm. What are the ethical issues, if any, facing Waters as he reports to top management on the profitability of the firm's two products?

5–27 LIFE-CYCLE COSTING Starcom Communications Technologies, Inc., has introduced a new phone so small that it can be carried in a wallet. Starcom invested $400,000 in research and development for the technology, and another $800,000 to design and test the prototypes. Starcom predicts a four-year life cycle for this model and gathered this cost data for the wallet phone:

	Monthly Fixed Costs	Variable Costs
Manufacturing costs	$25,000	$20
Marketing costs	20,000	5
Customer service costs	3,000	8
Distribution costs	5,000	15

Sales predictions:
For price of $150—average annual sales of 20,000 units.
For price of $180—average annual sales of 15,000 units.
For price of $225—average annual sales of 12,000 units.

If the price of a wallet phone is $225, Starcom will have to increase the research and development costs by $100,000 and the prototyping costs by $400,000 to improve the model for the higher price. Fixed customer service costs also would increase by $500 per month and variable distribution costs would increase by $5 per unit to improve the customer service and distribution at the $225 level. At the lowest price level of $150, fixed marketing costs would be reduced by $5,000 per month because the low price would be the principal selling feature.

Required

1. Determine the life-cycle costs for each pricing decision.
2. What price will produce the most profit for Starcom for the wallet phone's life cycle?

5–28 **LIFE-CYCLE COSTING** Matt Simpson owns and operates Quality Craft Rentals. Quality Craft offers canoe rentals and shuttle service on the Nantahala River. Customers can rent canoes at one station and enter the river there. They can exit at one of two designated locations to catch a shuttle that returns them to their vehicles. Following are the costs involved in providing this service each year:

	Fixed Costs	Variable Costs
Canoe maintenance	$ 2,300	$2.50
Licenses and permits	3,000	0
Vehicle leases	5,400	0
Station lease	6,920	0
Advertising	6,000	0.50
Operating costs	21,000	0.50

Quality Craft Rentals began business three years ago with a $21,000 expenditure for a fleet of 30 canoes. These are expected to last seven more years, at which time a new fleet will be purchased.

Required Simpson is happy with the steady rentals that average 6,400 per year. For this number of rentals, what price should Simpson charge per rental for the business to make a 20 percent life-cycle return on investment?

5–29 **LIFE-CYCLE COSTING** The following revenue and cost data are for Turner Manufacturing's two radial saws. The TM 200 is for the commercial market and the TM 800 is for industrial customers. Both products are expected to have three-year life cycles.

	TM200		
	Year 1	Year 2	Year 3
Revenue	$ 500,000	$2,000,000	$2,500,000
Costs:			
Research and development	1,000,000	-0-	-0-
Prototypes	300,000	50,000	-0-
Marketing	60,000	320,000	475,000
Distribution	80,000	120,000	130,000
Manufacturing	20,000	800,000	1,000,000
Customer service	-0-	60,000	85,000
Income	$ (960,000)	$ 650,000	$ 810,000

159

	TM800		
	Year 1	**Year 2**	**Year 3**
Revenue	$ 900,000	$1,800,000	$2,000,000
Costs:			
Research and development	1,150,000	-0-	-0-
Prototypes	550,000	30,000	10,000
Marketing	124,000	200,000	260,000
Distribution	170,000	300,000	410,000
Manufacturing	85,000	600,000	700,000
Customer service	-0-	20,000	10,000
Income	$(1,179,000)	$ 650,000	$ 610,000

Required

1. How would a product life-cycle income statement differ from this calendar-year income statement?

2. Prepare a three-year life-cycle income statement for both products. Which product appears to be more profitable?

3. Prepare a schedule showing each cost category as a percentage of total annual costs. Pay particular attention to the research and development and customer service categories. What do you think this indicates about the profitability of each product over the three-year life cycle?

5–30 SALES LIFE-CYCLE ANALYSIS   The management accountant at the Huang Manufacturing Company has collected these data in preparation for a sales life-cycle analysis on one of its products, a leaf blower:

Item	This Year	Change over Last Year	Average Annual Change over the Last Four Years
Annual sales	$2,000,000	1.5%	19.6%
Unit sales price	$400	2.0	6.9
Unit profit	$180	(0.8)	2.5

Required   Determine what stage of the sales life cycle the leaf blower is in.

5–31 MATCHING MARKET CHARACTERISTICS WITH SALES LIFE-CYCLE STAGES

Activities and Market Characteristics	Sales Life-Cycle Stage
Decline in sales	_____
Advertising	_____
Boost in production	_____
Stabilized profits	_____
Competitors' entrance into market	_____
Market research	_____
Market saturation	_____
Start production	_____
Product testing	_____
Termination of product	_____
Large increase in sales	_____

Required   Insert the appropriate life-cycle stage in the space provided after each activity.

SOLUTION TO SELF-STUDY PROBLEM

Best Brand Lighting, Inc.

A thorough analysis will require a good deal more inquiry of management and fact-finding than is available from the limited information provided earlier, but a few useful observations can be made.

1. Encourage BBL to consider increasing the effort put into design to reduce manufacturing costs, and also to possibly reduce the relatively high rate of product returns in the speciality segment. The cost of design appears low relative to manufacturing and downstream costs, especially in the specialty segment. Inquire about which types of design approaches are being used. Urge BBL to adopt concurrent engineering-based methods, especially because of the relatively short market life cycles in the industry.

2. Consider a further analysis of pricing. Because of BBL's strong acceptance in the specialty segment, and because the differentiation strategy is likely to be important in that segment, an increase in price might yield higher profits with little or no loss in market share.

Cost leadership appears to be the appropriate strategy in the major retail segment; inquire what methods the company may be using to reduce overall product costs in this segment.

Also, investigate further the relatively high rate of customer returns of product. Is this due to design problems or problems in sales management?

3. Consider a further analysis of marketing expenses. Would an increase in marketing effort in the major retailer segment improve sales in this segment?

4. Consider the need to perform a detailed analysis by product category within each market segment. A detailed analysis might uncover important information about opportunities to reduce cost and add value within the products' value chain.

5. Because of the relatively short sales life cycles, consider whether target costing might be used effectively at BBL. How intense is the level of competition in the industry, and to what extent are trade-offs made between functionality and price in the development and introduction of each new product? If the level of competition is very intense, and trade-offs between functionality and price are key strategic decisions, target costing should be a useful management tool.

6. Investigate the costing system. Is the costing system activity-based? How accurate are the cost figures developed by the cost system?

Total Quality Management

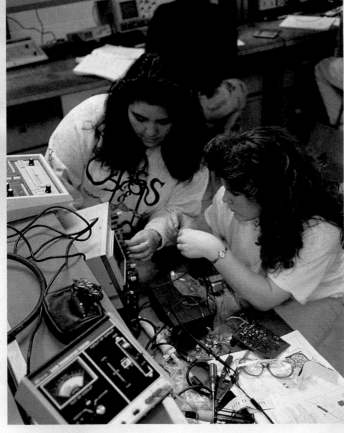

Dennis MacDonald/Photo Edit

After studying this chapter, you should be able to . . .

1. Define quality and total quality management, and devise guidelines for implementing total quality management

2. Distinguish between the two types of conformance and explain their effects on workers' behavior

3. Identify four major categories of quality costs

4. Prepare and interpret cost of quality reports

5. Describe methods commonly used to identify significant quality problems and their causes

6. Identify distinct characteristics of total quality management in service organizations

7. Explain the relationships between total quality management and productivity

8. Describe the role of management accountants in total quality management and challenges they face

> Nothing concentrates a man's mind so wonderfully as the prospect of being hanged in the morning.
>
> SAMUEL JOHNSON

Samuel Johnson's eighteenth-century remark describes the feelings of many U.S. business executives in the late 1970s and the early 1980s. In the glory days of the 1950s and 1960s, *Made in the U.S.A.* stood for the best that was available. As those decades became memories, however, many U.S. firms saw their fortunes take a turn for the worse. Against their will, U.S. manufacturers exchanged places with producers from foreign countries including West Germany and Japan. Once a term of mockery, *Made in Japan* became a term synonymous with quality. U.S. executives, especially those working for firms employing the traditional management techniques that had paid off so well a scant 20 years earlier, found themselves searching frantically for answers and desperately seeking to keep figurative nooses from tightening around their necks.

The world had changed. Global competition gave consumers abundant choices and they became more cost- and value-conscious, demanding high-quality products and services.

U.S. auto manufacturers realized in the late 1970s that Japanese auto manufacturers were somehow able to sell automobiles that performed better, had far fewer defects, and cost less than those made in the United States and still earn high returns. Likewise, when Hewlett-Packard tested the quality of more than 300,000 new computer chips in the early 1980s, HP found those made by Japanese manufacturers had zero defects per thousand. Those made by U.S. manufacturers had 11 to 19 defects per thousand. After 1,000 hours of use, the failure rate of U.S. chips was 27 times higher than those of the Japanese chips.[1]

It was no surprise, given these examples and others like them, that many U.S. firms experienced decreasing sales and diminishing market shares in both domestic and foreign markets. Operating profits in firms that failed to pay attention to quality eroded substantially and threatened the continuation of the firms' operations.

The 1980s became a decade of remarkable changes for many U.S. firms. Consumers have witnessed major efforts by U.S. manufacturers to improve quality. The *Challenger* disaster in 1986 also drove home the importance of achieving perfect

BusinessWeek

Do "the 3Rs + TQM = Success" for Today's Educational System?

The business world has known about Total Quality Management (TQM) for years, and witnessed its successful implementation by Japanese companies. This popular business technique, designed to create and instill quality in companies' products and services, is now transcending the border from the business world into the educational arena.

At Brooklyn's George Westinghouse Vocational & Technical High School, for example, students are participating in an educational experiment learning and using TQM. With help from corporate sponsors such as Ricoh, IBM and Xerox, students use TQM principles in their electronics classes (finishing repairs before deadlines and with few mistakes) and receive feedback from the companies on their work. The school administration also uses TQM in their efforts to improve attendance and parental involvement.

Q: How is education adopting TQM and using this business principle in educational reform? *Find out on page 185 of this chapter.*

---

[1] James R. Evans and William M. Lindsay, *The Management and Control of Quality*, 3rd ed. (New York: West Publishing Co., 1996), p. 7.

quality. Many firms in the United States have engaged in relentless efforts in the last two decades to improve the quality of their products and services.

In 1987, the U.S. government created the Malcolm Baldrige National Quality Award to recognize U.S. companies in manufacturing, small business, service, education, and health care that excel in quality achievement and quality management. The fierce competition among U.S. firms to win the award is evidence of the importance these firms place on being recognized for their high-quality operations. Simply applying for the award requires substantial investments in both time and money and the odds of winning are slim; no more than two awards are given in each category each year. Since the first award in 1988, winning firms have included Federal Express, Motorola, Inc., Ritz-Carlton Hotel Company, and Texas Instruments, Inc.

ISO 9000 is a set of guidelines for quality management and quality standards developed by the International Organization for Standardization in Geneva, Switzerland.

Many firms worldwide also have sought ISO 9000 certification. **ISO 9000** is a set of guidelines for quality management and quality standards developed by the International Organization for Standardization in Geneva, Switzerland. More than 90 countries have adopted it. ISO 9000 certification has become a seal of quality since the revised standards became effective in 1987.

To be ISO 9000 certified, a firm has to prove that it is following ISO 9000 operating procedures; these include inspecting production processes, maintaining equipment, training workers, testing products, and dealing with customer complaints. An independent test company audits the firm's operations and makes recommendations for certification.

Recognizing the high cost of failing to meet quality standards and the benefit from being recognized as having high-quality products or services also has prompted firms to improve the quality of their products and services.

The cost of quality can be substantial. On average, the cost of quality is 20 to 25 percent of sales for many U.S. firms.[2] Wolf, a consultant, estimates that 40 percent of the cost of doing business in the service sector can be attributed to poor quality.[3] On the other hand, firms with quality products or services gain sales and earn high profits. Attaining high quality and continuous improvement in the quality of products and services has become a way of life for most, if not all, organizations. Pursuing quality has become a global revolution affecting every facet of business. Quality reduces costs, increases customer satisfaction, and induces and maintains long-term success and profitability.

This chapter explains total quality management, defines quality and measurement of quality costs, illustrates the preparation of quality reports, examines approaches to detecting causes of deviations in quality, and explores decisions to investigate quality defects.

How Have U.S. Firms Done so Far?

In a survey of American business, *The Economist* reports that American firms have made tremendous progress in quality improvement. In 1994, AT&T became the first American company to win Japan's prestigious Deming Prize for quality control. Many other American firms have introduced vigorous quality-raising initiatives and have discovered their own versions of the Japanese *kaizen,* or continuous quality improvement.

Motorola's Six Sigma program that aims to reduce manufacturing defects to 3.4 per million has become part of quality lore. Some management consultants believe that for American firms quality is now old hat. They preach that it is time to take quality for granted and move on to the next new idea.

Source: Based on "American Business Survey," *The Economist,* September 16, 1995, p. 5.

---

[2] Michael R. Ostrega, "Return on Investment through Cost of Quality," *Journal of Cost Management,* Summer 1991, pp. 37–77.

[3] Ted Wolf, "Becoming a 'Total Quality' Controller," *The Small Business Controller,* Spring 1992, pp. 24–27.

QUALITY AND STRATEGIC COST MANAGEMENT

In the last two decades, the CEOs of many firms have come to realize that a strategy driven by quality improvements can lead to significant market advantages, improved profitability, and long-term prosperity. The line between planning for quality improvements and planning a standard business strategy has become increasingly blurred. Whether a firm competes through a strategy of low-cost or product differentiation, quality issues permeate every aspect of its operations. A firm choosing to compete through low prices is not choosing to produce low-quality products. Its low-priced products must meet customers' expectations. Similarly, a differentiation strategy fails whenever a firm fails to build quality into the products. The guiding principles underlying most quality-improvement programs are to satisfy customers' needs and to meet or exceed customers' expectations. This is also the goal of a strategic plan to gain competitive advantage.

Quality is significant for other reasons, too. Quality costs often are substantial portions of sales revenues. In many organizations, few other factors have as much effect on costs and the bottom line. It is not surprising, therefore, that the current trend is to integrate planning for quality improvements with business strategic planning, recognizing that quality drives the success of the organization.

PIMS Associates, Inc., examined more than 1,200 companies to determine the impact of product quality on corporate performance and found that:

- Product quality and profitability are closely related.
- Businesses that offer premium-quality products and services are more likely to have large market shares.
- Quality relates positively to a higher return on investment.[4]

Exhibit 6–1 shows that a firm with improved quality has several strategic competitive advantages and enjoys higher profitability and a higher return on investment. Customers perceive quality products as having higher values. Perceived high values allow the firm to command higher prices or to take a larger market share. Higher prices and greater market shares increase revenues. Improved quality decreases return rates, manufacturing costs, and throughput time. A lower return rate eases warranty cost and repair expenses. A faster throughput time enables the

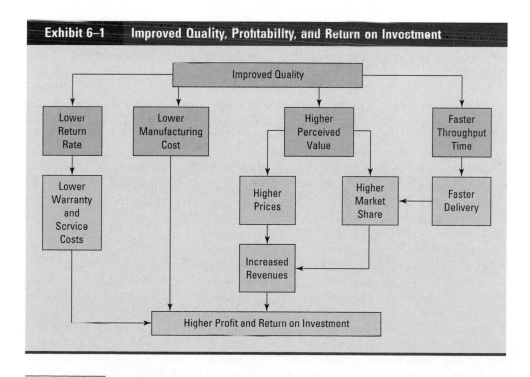

Exhibit 6–1   Improved Quality, Profitability, and Return on Investment

---

[4] Evans and Lindsay, *The Management and Control of Quality*, pp. 18–19.

firm to make fast deliveries. Prompt delivery makes happy customers, creates new demand, and increases the market share of the firm. Higher revenues and lower costs boost net income and increase the firm's return on investment. Focus on quality elevates the firm's opportunity and decreases competitive threats.

Cost, quality, and time are among the critical factors in all successful strategies. Having quality products allows firms that compete on differentiation to be effective in sustaining their strategy. A firm with low costs and quality products provides its customers with products equal to or better in quality at lower prices. Only with quality products can the firm truly be a cost leader.

TOTAL QUALITY MANAGEMENT

LEARNING OBJECTIVE 1
Define quality and total quality management, and devise guidelines for implementing total quality management.

To survive and be successful in today's global competitive environment, firms must manufacture quality products and provide quality services. Quality products and services also enhance any competitive advantages a firm may have.

What Is Quality?

There are many definitions of quality, and people often view quality differently because of differences in their roles in the production-marketing-consumption chain and in their expectations for the products or services. In simpler times, many CEOs perceived quality as a characteristic revealed by "I know it when I see it." Such an approach to quality provides no clear guideline for meeting quality and makes quality management very difficult.

The ultimate test of a quality product or service is whether the product or service meets or exceeds customers' expectations. The requirements to meet or exceed customers' expectations then serve as specifications for operations throughout the organization. Each individual, department, or subdivision throughout an organization needs to strive for conformity to specifications that meet and improve upon customer satisfaction.

Not all customers have the same expectations for a product or service. All 3/8-inch drill bits can drill 3/8-inch holes. Nevertheless, a firm can manufacture a 3/8-inch drill bit that costs $3 apiece for home use and an industrial strength drill bit that costs $15. The specifications and quality expectation for the less expensive drill bit will not be the same as those for the more expensive one. The industrial strength drill bit is designed for heavy continuous use and can be used for, say, 100 hours before it needs to be replaced. A drill bit for home use, on the other hand, is not designed for continuous use for long hours and has a shorter expected life of, say, 10 hours.

A **quality** product or service meets or exceeds customers' expectations at a competitive price they are willing to pay.

Both can be quality products if both meet their respective specifications and customers' expectations. A product is a **quality** product if it conforms with a design that meets or exceeds the expectations of customers at a competitive price they are willing to pay.

Expectations for services also differ. A tourist will not expect the same services from a Motel 6 as from a Ritz-Carlton Hotel, though both provide rooms for tourists. A mechanic performs quality service by changing a car's oil as specified: draining old oil, installing a new oil filter, lubricating the chassis, and adding clean new oil. The service is a quality service even if the mechanic used a regular oil, not a new synthesized oil that would improve engine performance, if the customer asked for a regular, not a deluxe, oil change. The mechanic has failed to deliver a quality service, however, if the new oil filter falls off the next morning due to improper installation or if the refill is four or six quarts of oil instead of the five quarts specified by the manufacturer. Conformity to the specifications determines the quality service of the job.

Procter & Gamble uses a concise and well-received definition of total quality management (TQM): "Total quality (management) is the unyielding and continually improving effort by everyone in an organization to understand, meet, and exceed the expectations of customers."[5] Procter & Gamble's description of total quality management points out that the core principles of TQM are processes that:

---

[5] Ibid., p. 17.

- Focus on satisfying the customer.
- Strive for continuous improvement.
- Involve the entire work force.

In Exhibit 6–2 we describe the critical factors for total quality management.

Focus on the Customer

TQM starts with identifying the firm's customers and their requirements. At some stage, everyone in a process or organization is a customer or supplier to someone else, either inside or outside the organization. The TQM process begins by identifying the requirements and expectations of external customers. These requirements and expectations are the bases for specifying requirements for each in a succession of internal customer/suppliers, and for the external suppliers to the firm.

A manufacturing firm translates the identified expectations and requirements of external customers into supplier specifications for each successive internal customer/supplier, including design requirements, part characteristics, manufacturing operations, production and external vendor requirements, and selling requirements.

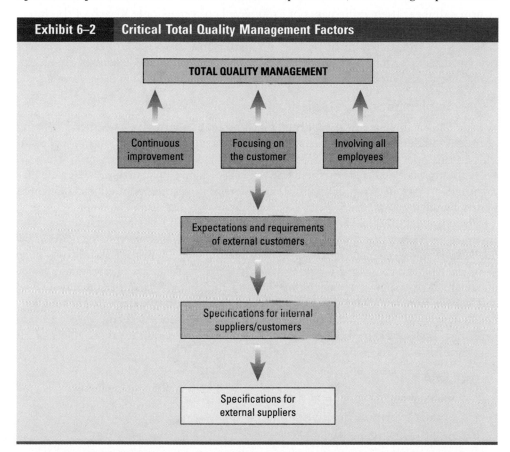

Exhibit 6–2   Critical Total Quality Management Factors

TOTAL QUALITY MANAGEMENT

Continuous improvement

Focusing on the customer

Involving all employees

Expectations and requirements of external customers

Specifications for internal suppliers/customers

Specifications for external suppliers

Quality Principles in the Coca-Cola Company

The continuous dominance of Coca-Cola as the number one brand in the global soft-drink market is no accident. Coca-Cola believes that

- Quality is the result of focused hard work and diligence; it is not an accident.

- Quality is a way of life; a job worth doing is worth doing right the first time.

- Excellence is the goal and nothing less is acceptable.

- Quality is not a destination; it's a way of life and continuous effort. There is no finish.

Source: Based on "Coca-Cola: A Taste for Quality," The Coca-Cola Company. As cited in James R. Evans and William M. Lindsay, *The Management and Control of Quality* (New York: West Publishing, 1996), p. 12.

A firm can serve its ultimate, external customer better if the firm meets fully all the requirements of each internal customer.[6] Ford used this approach to develop and manufacture Taurus, and in 1993, the Taurus overtook the Honda Accord as the top-selling car in America.

Continuous Improvement (Kaizen)

The Coca-Cola Company believes that quality is not a destination; it is a way of life. Coca-Cola Company states: "We know we will never arrive; there is no finish."

Taguchi and Wu believe that continuous quality improvement and cost reduction (kaizen) are necessary to remain competitive in today's global marketplace.[7] "With competitors forever trying to outperform us and customers exhibiting ever-changing expectations, a firm can never reach the ideal quality standard." The processes described in Exhibit 6–2 never end; firms need to continuously update specifications for both internal customers/suppliers and external suppliers to better serve external customers.

Full Involvement of the Entire Work Force

A firm can meet the requirements of its external customers only if each of the internal customers/suppliers in the process satisfies the requirements of the downstream customer. A breakdown in the process, no matter how insignificant, leads to a defective product or service and an unsatisfied customer. Full involvement of the entire workforce in the process is necessary to achieve total quality.

TQM Implementation Guidelines

A firm cannot implement a successful TQM program overnight. Superficial copying of quality circles, teamwork, kaizen, and other techniques popular among successful TQM firms does not make a TQM firm. It took Japanese companies more than 20 years to approach and surpass the quality levels of many U.S. firms. It will take any organization serious about achieving TQM several years of concerted and dedicated efforts by all its members to become a world-class quality firm.

The implementation of TQM is not an easy task and is time consuming. The Institute of Management Accountants (IMA) believes that a typical organization takes three to five years to move from traditional management to TQM. Most likely, the firm will not see many tangible benefits in the early years of implementation, although some specific projects along the way can quickly yield high returns.

Drawing from the experiences of winners of the Malcolm Baldrige award for effectively managing quality, IMA has devised an 11-phase process lasting three years to carry out TQM.[8] Throughout the process, the full and genuine involvement of all employees is essential for successful TQM.

Year One

- Create quality council and staff.
- Conduct executive quality training programs.
- Conduct quality audits.
- Prepare gap analysis.
- Develop strategic quality improvement plans.

Year Two

- Conduct employee communication and training programs.
- Establish quality teams.
- Create a measurement system and set goals.

---

[6]   Ibid., p. 5.

[7]   G. Taguchi and Y. Wu, *Introduction to Off-Line Quality Control* (Nagoya, Japan: Central Japan Quality Control Association, 1980).

[8]   Statement on Management Accounting No. 4-R: Managing Quality Improvements. (Montvale, NJ: Institute of Management Accountants, 1993), pp. 10–11.

Year Three

- Revise compensation/appraisal/recognition systems.
- Launch external initiatives with suppliers.
- Review and revise.

Create Quality Council and Staff

Most companies have found that successful implementation of TQM requires unwavering and active leadership from the CEO and senior managers. TQM is an undertaking that needs cooperation and the best efforts of all units of the organization. Without management support, a quality improvement program is likely to fail. As Shilliff and Motiska point out, "Every member of the (quality) team is important, but the most important member is the chief executive officer or top management. Without top management's wholehearted support, guidance, and direction, the quality program is doomed to mediocrity or eventual failure."[9]

However, the CEO or top management alone cannot bring forth all the desired benefits from TQM. Only with support from all managers in the top echelon can TQM attain the most desirable results. The necessary leadership often takes the form of an executive-level quality council. The quality council should include the top management team with the CEO chairing the council. The primary function of the council is to develop a quality mission and vision statements, companywide goals, and a long-term strategy.

Conduct Executive Quality Training Programs

To ensure senior management's unwavering and continuous support of TQM, the firm needs to conduct executive quality training programs. The primary function of the program is to (1) raise senior management's awareness of the need for a systematic focus on and continuous support of quality improvement, (2) create a common knowledge base on total quality, and (3) establish reasonable expectations and goals. Conducting executive quality training programs also helps avoid misunderstandings and miscommunication as the change effort progresses.[10]

Conduct Quality Audits

A quality audit assesses the firm's quality practices and analyzes the quality performance of the best practices, including those of other companies. Conducting a quality audit enables the firm to identify the company's strengths and weaknesses, develops a long-term strategic quality improvement plan, and identifies which quality improvement opportunities will yield the greatest return to the company in both the short and long term.

Prepare Gap Analysis

A gap analysis is a type of benchmarking that determines the gap in practices between the best-in-class and a specific firm. Following a quality audit that identifies the strengths and weaknesses of the firm's quality programs, a gap analysis identifies target areas for quality improvements and provides a common objective database for the firm to develop its strategic quality improvement.

Develop Strategic Quality Improvement Plans

The gap analysis results and the goal for quality improvement serve as bases for developing both short-term (one year) and long-range (three to five years) strategic plans for setting priorities in quality improvements. The initial plan should be limited and specific, and have the potential of yielding high, measurable quality benefits.

---

9 Karl A. Shilliff and Paul J. Motiska, *The Team Approach to Quality* (Milwaukee: ASQC Quality Press, 1992), p. xi.

10 Ibid., p. 11.

Conduct Employee Communication and Training Programs

Employee training programs serve as a communication tool to convey management's commitment to total quality and provide employees with necessary skills to achieve total quality; they play critical roles in successful quality improvement programs. In 1996, GE launched a $200 million quality improvement program to slash its defects to four per million. GE began by training 200 "master black belts" who became full-time quality teachers.[11]

Establish Quality Teams

A cross-functional quality team includes members from a variety of employee and management teams and functional units. The cross-functional quality team oversees the continuous improvement efforts and quality task forces throughout the organization and coordinates work to optimize the quality efforts, ensure adequate resources, and resolve issues.

Team members from throughout the organization should include individuals who can identify specific quality requirements and quality costs. Typical team members are product managers, engineers, production workers, customer service representatives, and management accountants.

Once established, quality teams become the main forces behind quality incentives, implementation and monitoring of quality programs, and continuous improvement. One major function of a quality team is to involve all employees in quality programs.

Create a Measurement System and Set Goals

A crucial factor for the success of TQM is having measures that truly reflect the needs and expectations of customers, both internal and external. A good measurement system that helps TQM often entails developing a new accounting system, because a traditional accounting system often divides and spreads important quality data among myriad accounts. A good measurement system for TQM also should enable all employees to know at all times the progress being made toward total quality and the additional improvements needed.

As an integral part of the firm's financial performance evaluation system, a traditional accounting system can be an impediment to quality improvement. All employees of the organization must understand that the measurements generated by a TQM system are tools for improvement, not punishment. A separate measurement system also facilitates total quality management by reducing concerns on the effect that expenditures for quality improvement have on short-term operating results.

Revise Compensation/Appraisal/Recognition Systems

Reward and recognition are the best means of reinforcing the emphasis on TQM. Moreover, a proper reward and recognition structure based on quality measures can be a very powerful stimulus to promote TQM in a company (see Chapter 20). Efforts and progress will most likely be short-lived if the firm makes no change to its compensation/appraisal/recognition system.

Launch External Initiatives with Suppliers

A supplier is as much a part of the company's operations as a division of the company. Suppliers that fail to deliver goods as specified can doom a firm's efforts to deliver only quality products or services. TQM efforts should include the entire business system that extends from raw materials to the final customer. Among the practices successful TQM firms use to ensure having quality suppliers are

---

[11] *The Wall Street Journal*, April 25, 1996, p. A4.

- Reducing the supplier base. A reduced supplier base reduces variations in quality, increases supplier commitment, and improves the efficient use of the firm's resources.

- Selecting suppliers based not only on price and their capability and willingness to improve quality, cost, delivery, and flexibility but also on their dedication to continuous improvement.

- Forming long-term relationships with suppliers as working partners.

- Specifying precise supplier expectations and ensuring suppliers' consistent delivery.[12]

Review and Revise

All employees, led by the quality council and quality team, should review quality progress and reassess quality improvement efforts at least annually. Again, as stated by many firms, including Coca Cola, there is no finish line in quality improvement.

TYPES OF CONFORMANCE

Quality is conformance with the specifications for the product or service that meet or exceed customer requirements and expectations. Conformance, however, may differ among individuals or firms, as it did at Sony, as we describe in the next section.

Goalpost Conformance

Goalpost conformance is conformance to a quality specification expressed as a specified range around the target. The target is the ideal value that the process is designed to attain.

For example, the target for a production process to manufacture .5-inch sheet metal is .5-inch thickness for all sheet metal manufactured. Recognizing that meeting the target every time in manufacturing is difficult, a firm often specifies a tolerance range. A firm that specifies a tolerance of ±.05 inch meets the quality standard if the thickness of its products is between .55 inch and .45 inch.

A goalpost conformance is a **zero-defects conformance.** Management expects the production process to have all output within the specified range of variations, thus achieving zero-defect conformance. Exhibit 6–3 depicts the goalpost conformance specifications for the sheet metal.

Absolute Quality Conformance

Absolute quality conformance or the robust quality approach requires all products or services to exactly meet the target value with no variation. The requirement for an absolute conformance requires all sheet metal to have a thickness of .5 inch,

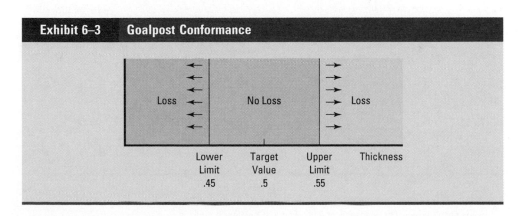

Exhibit 6–3   Goalpost Conformance

Loss — No Loss — Loss

| Lower Limit .45 | Target Value .5 | Upper Limit .55 | Thickness |

[12] Ibid., p. 17.

not .5 inch ± .05 inch or even .5 inch ± .0005 inch. Exhibit 6–4 depicts the robust quality conformance approach.

Goalpost or Absolute Conformance?

Goalpost conformance assumes that the firm incurs no quality or failure cost or loss if quality measures fall within the specified limits. The firm incurs quality costs or losses only when the measure is outside the limits. Alternatively, absolute conformance views quality costs or losses as a continuously increasing function starting from the target value. Quality costs, hidden or out-of-pocket, occur any time the quality measure deviates from its target value.

Which of these two approaches, goalpost or absolute conformance, is better? Perhaps we can find an answer in the experience Sony had in two of its plants that manufacture color televisions.[13]

The two Sony plants manufacture the same television sets and follow the same specification for color density. On examining the operating data of a period, Sony found that all the units produced at the San Diego plant fell within the specifications (zero-defect), while some of those manufactured at the Japanese plant did not. The quality of the Japanese units, however, was more uniform around the target value, while the quality of the San Diego units was uniformly distributed between the lower and upper limits of the specification, the goalpost, as depicted in Exhibit 6–5.

The average quality cost (loss) per unit of the San Diego plant was $0.89 higher than that of the Japanese plant. One reason for the higher quality cost for units produced at the San Diego plant is the need for more frequent field service. Customers are more likely to complain when the density is farther away from the target value. For a firm having long-term profitability and customer satisfaction as its goals, absolute conformance is the better approach.

Taguchi Quality Loss Function

Genichi Taguchi and Y. Wu proposed the absolute quality conformance approach as an *off-line* quality control.[14] Before engaging in manufacturing or servicing, this approach pays more attention to such activities as the design and the manufacturing or operation processes to facilitate manufacturing the product or providing the service. Taguchi believes that these dimensions need to be perfected before manufacturing the product.

Taguchi and Wu recognize that any variation from the exact specifications entails a cost or loss to the firm, as shown in Exhibit 6–4. The cost or loss can be depicted by a quadratic function.

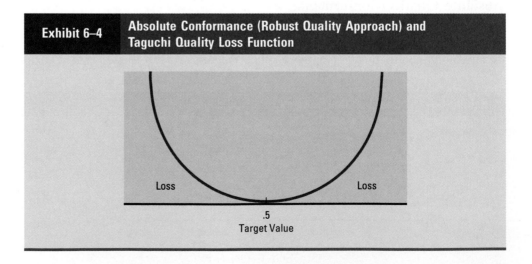

| Exhibit 6–4 | Absolute Conformance (Robust Quality Approach) and Taguchi Quality Loss Function |

---

[13] Evans and Lindsay, *The Management and Control of Quality*, p. 244.

[14] Taguchi and Wu, *Introduction to Off-Line Quality Control*. See also Evans and Lindsay, *The Management and Control of Quality*, pp. 243–48; and Thomas L. Albright and Harold P. Roth, "The Measurement of Quality Costs: An Alternative Paradigm," *Accounting Horizon*, June 1992, pp. 15–27.

| Exhibit 6–5 | Color Density of Sony TV Sets Manufactured in the San Diego Plant and a Japanese Plant |

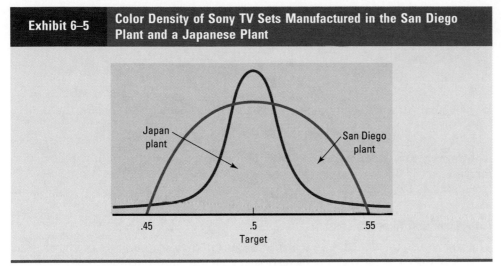

Source: James R. Evans and William M. Lindsay, *The Management and Control of Quality,* 3rd ed. (New York: West Publishing Co., 1996), p. 245.

The **Taguchi quality loss function** depicts the relationship between the total loss to a firm due to quality defects and the extent of quality defects. Overall, the loss grows larger as the variation increases (as a quadratic function)—the total loss increases as the magnitude of a quality characteristic of the product or service moves farther away from the target value. A quadratic function means that when the deviation from the target value doubles, the loss quadruples. For instance, if a deviation of 0.1 from the target value has a loss of $4, then a $16 loss occurs when the deviation doubles or is 0.2 from the target value.

Deviations from the quality standard increase manufacturing, service, and other hidden quality costs. Examples of the costs due to poor quality or failure to meet the absolute conformance standard are rework, warranty repair or replacement, additional production costs, and loss on disposal. The hidden quality losses include customer dissatisfaction, loss of future business, loss of market share, additional engineering costs, additional management costs, and additional inventory. The exact nature of the loss function for different quality characteristics may differ.

> **Taguchi quality loss function** depicts the relationship between the total loss to a firm due to quality defects and the extent of quality defects.

Quality Loss Function

Taguchi believes that a quadratic function provides a good approximation of losses. Losses increase at twice the rate of deviations from the target value. A general expression of the loss function, $L(x)$, for a quality characteristic of a product or service with the observed value of x is

$$L(x) = k(x - T)^2$$

where: x = an observed value of the quality characteristic
T = the target value of the quality characteristic
k = the cost coefficient

k is a constant that is estimated based on the total production and service costs and hidden costs due to deviation of the quality characteristic from the target value. The value of k for a quality characteristic can be determined using this relationship:

$$k = \frac{\text{Total quality cost}}{(\text{Tolerance allowed})^2}$$

Say, for example, a firm has determined that no customer will accept sheet metal deviating more than .05 inch from the target value in thickness, that the target thickness is .5 inch, and that the cost to the firm is $5,000 for each rejection by a customer. The $5,000 cost to the firm includes repair or replacement, processing, service costs, and other costs due to customer dissatisfaction. Then

$$k = \frac{\$5,000}{.05^2}$$

$$k = \$2,000,000$$

If the actual thickness of a unit is .47, then the estimated total loss for the unit is:

$$L(.47) = \$2,000,000(.47 - .5)^2 = \$1,800$$

If, however, the thickness is .46, then the estimated total loss from the deviation increases to $3,200.

$$L(.46) = \$2,000,000(.46 - .5)^2 = \$3,200$$

Total Loss and Average Loss

The losses just calculated represent the losses for each of the units produced. The total loss due to a quality characteristic for all the units manufactured during a period is the sum of the losses for each unit that varied from the standard.

Alternatively, one can determine the total loss due to variations in the quality characteristic by multiplying the average loss per unit and the total number of units manufactured. The average loss per unit is the expected loss due to variations in the quality characteristic. Exhibit 6–6 shows the results of operations in two plants identified as plant A and plant B.

The output from plant A spreads equally over the range from .46 to .54 with no unit falling outside the tolerance limits. The output from plant B concentrates near the specified target value, but not all units lie within the tolerance limits.

Albright and Roth show that the expected, or average, loss per unit can be determined using variance and the square of the mean deviation from the target value as follows:[15]

$$EL(x) = k(\sigma^2 + D^2)$$

where:

$EL(x)$ = expected or average loss for quality characteristic x
σ^2 = variance of the variation about the target value
D = the deviation of the mean value of the quality characteristic from the target, or $D = \bar{x} - $ Target value

The variance is .0008 for plant A and .000412 for plant B. The value of D is 0 for both plants. Thus,

Exhibit 6–6	Total Quality Loss					
x Measured Thickness	*L (x)* Quality Loss	Plant A Probability	Weighted Loss	Plant B Probability	Weighted Loss
.43	$9,800	0	$ 0	.02	$196
.46	3,200	.20	640	.03	96
.48	800	.20	160	.15	120
.50	0	.20	0	.60	0
.52	800	.20	160	.15	120
.54	3,200	.20	640	.03	96
.57	9,800	0	0	.02	196
Expected loss			$1,600		$824

[15] Ibid., p. 23.

Plant A: $EL(x) = \$2,000,000(.0008 + 0) = \$1,600$

Plant B: $EL(x) = \$2,000,000(.000412 + 0) = \$824$

Notice the similarity in the quality characteristic between plant A and those observed in the Sony plant in San Diego—all units are within the specified tolerance limits and spread somewhat evenly between the specified tolerance limits. The quality characteristic of plant B is similar to those observed in the Sony plant in Japan—not all units lie within the tolerance limit, but most units cluster around the target value. Some units, however, fall outside the tolerance limits. Plant B, like the Sony plant in Japan, incurs a smaller average cost per unit. Even though all units of plant A are within the tolerance limits while some units of plant B are outside of the limits, plant B has a much lower expected loss than that of plant A. The firm can expect a lower cost in plant B than in plant A.

Using Quality Loss Function for Tolerance Determination

Another use of the Taguchi quality loss function is to set tolerances for an operation. Assume that in the sheet metal example the cost to the firm is only $300 if the firm repairs the product that failed before shipping. The firm can determine the tolerances as follows:

$$\$300 = \$2,000,000(\text{tolerance})^2$$

Solve the equation,

$$\text{Tolerance} = .0122$$

Because it is less expensive to rework or repair before shipment, the specification should be set at $0.5 \pm .0122$.

COSTS OF QUALITY

Costs of quality are costs associated with the prevention, identification, repair, and rectification of poor quality, and with opportunity costs from lost production time and sales as a result of poor quality. Traditionally, quality costs had been limited to the costs of inspections and testing of finished units. Other costs of poor quality were included as overheads and not identified as quality costs.

Firms have discovered that in addition to manufacturing costs, quality costs include costs associated with supporting functions such as product design, purchasing, public relations, and customer services. Joseph Juran classifies costs of quality into four categories: prevention, appraisal, internal failure, and external failure. A main criterion in Juran's classification of quality costs is the time when quality costs are incurred. Exhibit 6–7 illustrates the components of quality costs.

Costs of quality are costs associated with the prevention, identification, repair, and rectification of poor quality, and with opportunity costs from lost production time and sales as a result of poor quality.

◄ **LEARNING OBJECTIVE 3** Identify four major categories of quality costs

Prevention Costs

Prevention costs are expenditures incurred to keep quality defects from occurring. Prevention costs include:

- **Quality training costs** Expenditures for internal and external training programs include salaries and wages for time spent in training, instruction

Prevention costs are costs incurred to keep quality defects from occurring.

Quality Is Free

Quality is not only free, it helps firms make a profit. Every penny a company doesn't spend on doing things wrong, over, or instead of, becomes a penny right on its bottom line. In these days of "who knows what is going to happen to our business tomorrow," there aren't many ways left to increase profits. If managers concentrate on making quality products or services, they can probably increase the firm's profit by an amount equal to 5 to 10 percent of sales. That is a lot of money for free.

Source: Philip Crosby, *Quality Is Free* (New York: McGraw-Hill, 1979).

Exhibit 6–7	Components of Quality Costs

Prevention Cost

Training cost
  Instructor fees
  Training equipment
  Tuition for external training
  Training wages and salaries
Planning and execution
  Salaries
  Cost of preventive equipment
  Cost of meetings
Promotion cost
  Awards
  Printing costs

Internal Failure Cost

Scrap
Rework
Loss due to downgrades
Reinspection costs
Loss due to work interruptions

Appraisal Cost

Raw materials inspection
Work-in-process inspection
Finished goods inspection
Test equipment
  Acquisition
  Salaries and wages
  Maintenance

External Failure Cost

Sales returns and allowance due to quality
  deficiency
Warranty cost
Contribution margin of cancelled sales orders
  due to quality deficiency
Contribution margin of lost sales orders due to
  perceived unsatisfactory quality

costs, clerical staff expenses and miscellaneous supplies, and costs expended to prepare handbooks and instructional manuals.

- **Quality planning costs**   Wages and overhead for quality planning and quality circles, new procedure designs, new equipment designs to enhance quality, reliability studies, and supplier evaluations.

- **Equipment maintenance costs**   Costs incurred to install, calibrate, maintain, repair, and inspect production instruments, processes, and systems.

- **Supplier assurance costs**   Costs incurred to select, evaluate, and train suppliers to conform with the requirements of TQM.

- **Information systems costs**   Costs expended for developing data requirements, and measurement, auditing, and reporting of quality.

Typically, as prevention costs increase, other costs of quality decrease. By far, the best way a firm can spend its cost-of-quality money is to invest in preventive actions. Usually, prevention costs are voluntary or discretionary costs and are the most cost-effective way to improve quality.

Appraisal Costs

Appraisal costs are incurred in the measurement and analysis of data to ascertain if products and services conform to specifications.

Appraisal (detection) costs are incurred in the measurement and analysis of data to find out if products and services conform to specifications. These costs are incurred after production but before sales. Firms incur appraisal costs to identify defective items and to ensure that all units meet or exceed customer requirements. Incurring these costs does not reduce the errors or keep defects from happening again; it only detects defective units before they are delivered to customers. Appraisal costs include:

- **Test and inspection costs**   Costs incurred to test and inspect incoming materials, work in process, and finished goods or services.

- **Test equipment and instruments**   Expenditures incurred to acquire, operate, or maintain facilities, software, machinery, and instruments for testing or appraising of quality in products, services, or processes.

- **Quality audits**   Salaries and wages of all personnel involved in appraising products and services quality and other expenditures incurred during quality appraising.

- **Laboratory acceptance testing.**

- **Field evaluation and testing.**

- **Information costs**   Costs to prepare and verify quality reports.

Internal Failure Costs

Internal failure costs are incurred as a result of poor quality found through appraisal prior to delivery to customers. These costs are not value-added and are never necessary. Some internal failure costs:

- **Costs of corrective action**   Costs for time spent to find the cause of failure and to correct the problem.

- **Rework and scrap costs**   Materials, labor, and overhead costs for scrap, rework, and reinspection.

- **Process costs**   Costs expended to redesign the product or processes, unplanned machine downtime for adjustment, and lost production due to process interruption for repair or rework.

- **Expediting costs**   Costs incurred to expedite manufacturing operations due to time spent for repair or rework.

- **Reinspect and retest costs**   Salaries, wages, and expenses incurred during reinspection or retesting of reworked or repaired items.

External Failure Costs

External failure costs are costs incurred to rectify quality defects after unacceptable products or services reach the customer, and profits lost from missed opportunities as a result of the unacceptable products or services delivered. These costs include:

- **Costs to handle customer complaints and returns**   Salaries and administrative overhead for a customer service department, repair of returned products, allowance or discount granted for poor quality, and freight charges.

- **Product recall and product liability costs**   Administrative costs to handle product recalls, repairs, or replacements; legal costs; and settlements resulting from legal actions.

- **Lost sales due to unsatisfactory products and customer ill will**   Lost contribution margins on canceled orders, lost sales, and decreased market shares.

Conformance and Nonconformance Costs

Quality expert Philip Crosby believes there are no quality problems, only product design, materials, labor, and manufacturing problems that lead to poor quality. Crosby proposes that quality costs have two components—the price of conformance and the price of nonconformance.[16] Prevention and appraisal costs are **costs of conformance** because they are incurred to ensure that products or services meet customers' expectations. Internal failure costs and external failure costs are **costs of nonconformance.** They are costs incurred and opportunity costs because of rejection of products or services. The cost of quality is the sum of conformance and nonconformance costs.

Prevention costs are usually the lowest and the easiest among the four costs of quality for management to control. Internal and external failure costs are among the most expensive costs of quality, especially external failure costs. In a typical scenario, the cost of prevention may be $0.10 per unit, the cost of testing and replacing poor quality parts or components during production may be $5, the cost of reworking or reassembling may be $50, and the cost of field repair and other external costs may be $5,000.

External failure costs can be rather substantial. For instance, in early 1996 Ford announced a recall to fix a poorly designed ignition system. Had the firm detected the problem earlier, the cost might have been less than $10,000. Ford estimated the cost of recall and repair would be more than $10 million, assuming no legal or liability costs and no loss in sales due to the quality problem.

---

16 Philip B. Crosby, *Quality without Tears* (New York: McGraw-Hill, 1984), p. 86.

Better prevention of poor quality clearly reduces all other costs of quality. With fewer problems in quality, less appraisal is needed because the products are made right the first time. Fewer defective units also reduce internal and external failure costs as repairs, rework, and recalls decrease. By spending more on prevention, companies spend less due to internal or external failures. The savings alone can be substantial. Meanwhile the firm enjoys higher perceived values of its products, increased sales and market share, and improved earnings and returns on investments.

Theoretically, a firm with a completely successful prevention effort incurs neither appraisal costs nor internal or external failure costs. It is easier to *design* and *build* quality in rather than to *inspect* or *repair* quality in. Appraisal costs decrease as quality improves.[17] Nonconformance costs, however, decrease at a much faster rate than prevention costs increase.

REPORTING QUALITY COSTS

LEARNING OBJECTIVE 4 ▶
Prepare cost of quality reports.

Reporting quality costs includes data definitions, identification of data sources, data collection, and preparation and distribution of quality cost reports.

Data Definition, Sources, and Collection

The first step in generating a quality cost report is to define quality cost categories and identify quality costs within each category. The preceding discussion described common quality cost categories; however, definitions of cost categories can vary among firms. Firms need to clearly state operational definitions of all quality costs and every member of the team needs to have a clear understanding of the firm's quality cost categories. One important step in identifying quality costs is to ask users and suppliers to identify specific costs incurred because of poor quality.

Ideally each quality cost should have its own account so that quality cost information is readily observable and not buried in several accounts. These quality cost accounts then become the source of quality cost information.

Cost of Quality Report

A report on cost of quality will be useful only if its recipients understand, accept, and can use the content of the report. Reports can be prepared in many ways. Each firm should select and design a reporting system (1) that can be integrated into its information system, and (2) that promotes TQM. Among considerations in establishing a quality cost report system are proper stratifications of quality cost reports by product line, department, plant, or division, and the time periods of the reports.

A cost of quality matrix, as illustrated in Exhibit 6–8, is a convenient and useful tool in reporting quality costs. With columns for functions or departments and

---

Analyzing Quality Costs in Formosa Plastics Group

Formosa Plastics Group developed an analytical program to evaluate its quality costs. In its corporate manual, the firm specifies these quality costs based on the ratio of:

- Total quality cost to sales revenue and cost of goods sold.
- External failure cost to sales revenue.
- Total failure cost to sales revenue.

- Voluntary cost (prevention and appraisal costs) to sales revenue.
- Total quality cost to direct labor hours.
- Total quality cost to plant assets.

Source: Based on Thomas P. Edmonds, Bor-Yi Tsay, and Wen-Wei Lin, "Analyzing Quality Costs," *Management Accounting*, November 1989, p. 29.

---

[17] One reason is that once suppliers are tested, screened, and monitored, a firm would spend much less time verifying compliance than it would otherwise.

Exhibit 6–8	Cost of Quality Matrix						
	Design Engineering	Purchasing	Production	Finance	Accounting	Other	Totals
Prevention Costs Quality planning Training Other							
Appraisal Costs Test and Inspect Instruments Other							
Internal Failure Costs Scrap Rework Other							
External Failure Costs Returns Recalls Other							
Totals							

Source: Based on James R. Evans and William M. Lindsay, *The Management and Control of Quality,* 3rd ed. (New York: West Publishing Co., 1996), p. 303.

rows for categories of quality costs, a cost of quality matrix enables each department to identify and recognize the effects of its actions on the cost of quality and to pinpoint areas of high-quality costs. The matrix can contain dollar amounts (actual or estimate) or relative percentages of the amounts in a base period. The base period can be the amount in the first year of implementing the TQM program, preselected benchmark amounts, or other appropriate amounts that management decides to use for monitoring progress.

An Illustration of a Cost of Quality Report

Exhibit 6–9 illustrates a cost of quality report.[18] Bally Company is a small midwestern manufacturing company with annual sales of approximately $50 million. The firm operates in a highly competitive environment and has been experiencing increasing cost and quality pressures from new and existing competitors. The report shows that the external failure costs for such items as warranty claims, customer dissatisfaction, and market-share loss accounted for 75 percent of the total cost of quality in year 0.

To be competitive and to regain market shares, Bally began a corporatewide three-year TQM process. The firm started with substantial increases in prevention and appraisal expenditures. The investment started to pay off in year 2. The internal failure, external failure, and total quality costs have all decreased.

Exhibit 6–9 compares the current year's quality costs to those of a base year. Alternative bases for comparisons can be the budgeted amounts, flexible budget costs, or long-range goals. A cost of quality report also should include output measures whenever possible.

PROBLEM FINDING

To achieve total quality management, firms need to identify and understand truly significant quality problems when they occur. Many helpful tools to identify significant quality problems are available, including control charts, histograms, Pareto

◄ **LEARNING OBJECTIVE 5**
Describe methods commonly used to identify significant quality problems and their causes.

---

[18] Adapted from IMA Statement No. 4R.

Exhibit 6–9	Cost of Quality Report		
	Year 2	**Year 0**	**Percent Change**
Prevention costs			
Training	$ 90,000	$ 20,000	350%
Quality planning	86,000	20,000	330
Other quality improvement	60,000	40,000	50
Supplier evaluation	40,000	30,000	33
Total	$ 276,000	$ 110,000	151
Appraisal costs			
Testing	120,000	100,000	20
Quality performance measurement	100,000	80,000	25
Supplier monitoring	60,000	10,000	500
Customer surveys	30,000	10,000	200
Total	$ 310,000	$ 200,000	55
Internal failure costs			
Rework and reject	55,000	150,000	(63)
Reinspection and testing	35,000	30,000	(16)
Equipment failure	30,000	50,000	(40)
Downtime	20,000	50,000	(60)
Total	$ 140,000	$ 280,000	(50)
External failure costs			
Product liability insurance	70,000	250,000	(72)
Warranty repairs	100,000	120,000	(17)
Customer losses (estimated)	600,000	1,400,000	(57)
Total	$ 770,000	$1,770,000	(56)
Total quality costs	$1,496,000	$2,360,000	(37)

diagrams, brainstorming, and cause-and-effect diagrams. These tools are most effective if management accountants take a proactive role throughout the process.

Control Charts

A **control chart** is a graph
that depicts successive
observations of an operation taken at constant intervals.

A **control chart** is a graph that depicts successive observations of an operation taken at constant intervals. The operation can be a machine, workstation, individual worker, work cell, part, or process that affects quality. Intervals can be time periods, batches, production runs, or other demarcations of the operation.

A typical control chart has a horizontal axis representing time intervals, batch numbers, or production runs, and a vertical axis denoting a measure of conformance to the quality specification. The vertical measure also has a specified allowable range of variations. Exhibit 6–10 contains control charts for the manufacturing of 1/8-inch drill bits in three workstations.

Say a firm has determined that all drill bits must be within .0005 inch of the specified diameter. All units from workstation A are within the specified range (±.0005″) and the firm needs to conduct no further investigation. Three units from workstation B are outside the specified range and suggest out-of-control occurrences. Management should investigate the cause of the aberration to prevent further failure of the quality standard. Although all units manufactured by workstation C are within the specified range acceptable to the firm, management may want to launch an investigation because the trend suggests that in the future the operation will most likely turn out drill bits outside the specified range if the trend continues.

Control charts are useful in establishing a state of statistical quality control, monitoring processes, and identifying causes of quality variations. A process is in statistical control if no sample observation is outside the established limits, all the observations are randomly distributed with no apparent patterns or runs, and an approximately equal number of observations are above and below the center line with most of the points nearing the center line. A process may be out of control if the observations show trends, cycles, clusters, or sudden shifts hugging the center

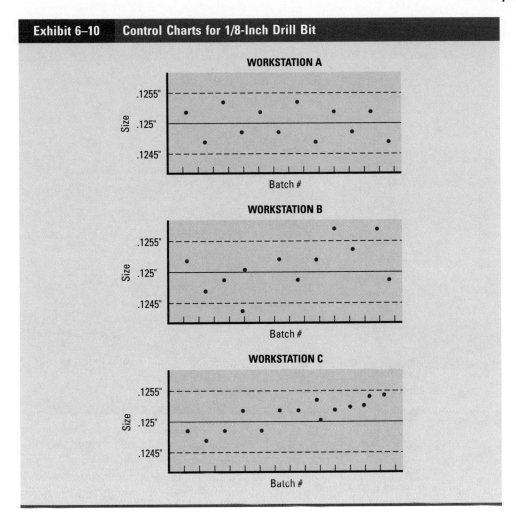

Exhibit 6–10   Control Charts for 1/8-Inch Drill Bit

line or the control limits. Many sophisticated statistical techniques are available to help determine whether a process is in or out of control.[19]

Histogram

A **histogram** is a graphical representation of the frequency of events in a given set of data. Patterns or variations that are often difficult to see in a set of numbers become clear in a histogram. Exhibit 6–11 contains a histogram of factors that contribute to the quality problems identified by a firm that makes chocolate mousse.

The firm has experienced uneven quality in one line of chocolate mousse. The firm identifies six factors: substandard chocolate, improper liqueur mixture, uneven egg size, uneven blending speed, variant blending time, and improper refrigeration after production. They identified 210 batches as having poor quality. The histogram in Exhibit 6–11 suggests that variations in egg size may be the largest contributor to the quality problem, followed by uneven speed in blending ingredients.

A **histogram** is a graphical representation of the frequency of events in a given set of data.

Pareto Diagram

A **Pareto diagram** is a histogram of factors contributing to the quality problem, ordered from the most to the least frequent. Joseph Juran observed in the 1950s that a few causes usually account for most of the quality problems, thus the name Pareto.[20] In Exhibit 6–12 we present a Pareto diagram of the chocolate mousse quality problem.

A **Pareto diagram** is a histogram of the frequency of factors contributing to the quality problem, ordered from the most to the least frequent.

---

[19] Evans and Lindsay, *The Management and Control of Quality*, pp. 697–98.

[20] Vilfredo Pareto, a nineteenth-century Italian economist, observed that 80 percent of the wealth in Milan was owned by 20 percent of its residents.

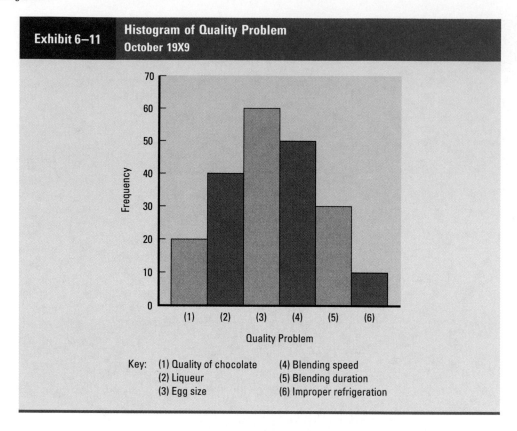

| Exhibit 6–11 | Histogram of Quality Problem October 19X9 |

Key: (1) Quality of chocolate (4) Blending speed
(2) Liqueur (5) Blending duration
(3) Egg size (6) Improper refrigeration

A Pareto diagram not only ranks the relative size of quality problems but also provides a useful visual aid. Often we also draw a cumulative curve as shown in Exhibit 6–12. Using a Pareto diagram, management can separate the few major causes of quality problems from the many trivial ones and identify areas for improvement. Then management can focus its efforts on achieving the greatest amount of quality improvement. For example, the cumulative line in Exhibit 6–12 shows that improper egg size and erratic blending speed account for 110 quality problems in the manufacturing of chocolate mousse. Pareto diagrams are especially useful in making an initial analysis of quality problems identified by a control chart as being outside the specified range.

Brainstorming

The ancient Greeks used brainstorming, which was revived by Alex Osborn in the 1940s, as a way to elicit ideas from a group of people in a short time.[21] Brainstorming can identify problems, find causes of a problem, and develop a solution to a quality problem.

A relaxed yet structured group session with members from a variety of backgrounds is conducive to effective brainstorming. Some basic rules for productive brainstorming are

1. No criticism of anyone's ideas by word or by gesture.
2. Once an idea has been put forth, there should be no further discussion of that idea during the session, except for clarification.
3. No idea is dumb or silly.
4. Each team member can introduce only one idea at a time.
5. Until most of the members have presented an idea, no member can introduce more than one idea.
6. No single individual should dominate the session.
7. No accusations of blame should occur during the session.[22]

---

[21] A. F. Osborn, *Applied Imagination* (New York: Scribner's, 1963).

[22] Howard Gitlow, Alan Oppenheim, and Rosa Oppenheim, *Quality Management* (Burr Ridge, Ill.: Irwin, 1995), p. 309.

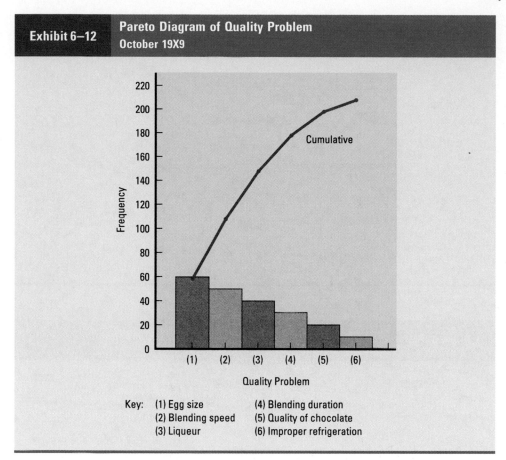

Exhibit 6–12 Pareto Diagram of Quality Problem
October 19X9

Cumulative

Frequency

Quality Problem

Key: (1) Egg size   (4) Blending duration
     (2) Blending speed (5) Quality of chocolate
     (3) Liqueur   (6) Improper refrigeration

Cause-and-Effect Diagram

The cause-and-effect, or Ishikawa, diagram organizes a chain of causes and effects to sort out root causes and identify relationships between causes or variables. Karou Ishikawa discovered the number of factors that could influence a process or lead to a problem overwhelmed most plant personnel. To cope with myriad factors, in 1943 he developed cause-and-effect diagrams as an organizing aid.[23] Because of its shape, a fishbone diagram is another name for this diagram.

A cause-and-effect or fishbone diagram consists of a spine, ribs, and bones. At the right end of the horizontal spine is the quality problem at hand. The spine itself connects causes to the effect—the quality problem. Each branch or rib pointing into the spine describes a main cause of the problem. Bones pointing to each rib are contributing factors to the cause. Look at Exhibit 6–13 to see the general structure of a cause-and-effect diagram.

Typical main causes for quality problems in manufacturing operations are

- Machines
- Materials
- Methods
- Manpower

Some users refer to the four main categories as 4M. In Exhibit 6–14 you can see a cause-and-effect diagram for the quality problems in the manufacturing of chocolate mousse.

The two basic types of cause-and-effect diagrams are dispersion analysis and process classification. A dispersion analysis identifies and classifies causes for a specific quality problem (as previously illustrated for the chocolate mousse problem). A process classification diagram identifies key factors that may have contributed to the poor quality at each step of the process or flow. A process analysis is used when

[23] Karou Ishikawa, *Guides to Quality Control*, 2nd ed. (Tokyo: Asian Productivity Organization, 1986).

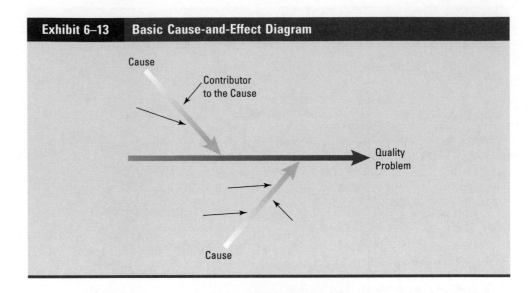

Exhibit 6–13   Basic Cause-and-Effect Diagram

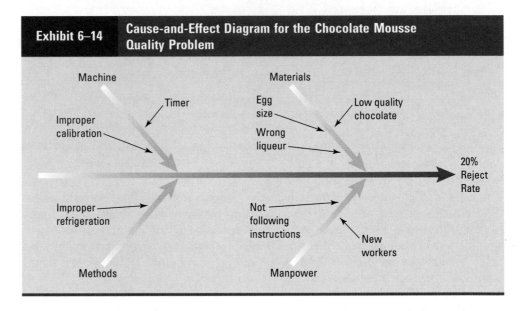

Exhibit 6–14   Cause-and-Effect Diagram for the Chocolate Mousse Quality Problem

a series of events, steps, or processes creates a problem and it is not clear which one is the major cause of the problem.

TOTAL QUALITY MANAGEMENT IN SERVICE ORGANIZATIONS

LEARNING OBJECTIVE 6 ▶
Identify distinct characteristics of total quality management in service organizations.

When forming an opinion about a company, nothing seems to stir people's passion more than dealing with its employees. The quality of service provided by a firm's frontline personnel—whether a receptionist or a service engineer—can have a huge impact on its image. We cannot overstate the importance of quality in service organizations.

Service organizations include firms rendering services to generate revenues and firms providing services to help sales of products. The cost of providing quality services is usually only a fraction of the total cost. Nevertheless, a customer unhappy with the quality of service most likely will not come back. Reichheld and Sasser report that companies can increase their profits by almost 100 percent if they retain just 5 percent more of their customers.[24]

---

[24] Frederick F. Reichheld and W. Earl Sasser, Jr., "Zero Defections: Quality Comes to Services," *Harvard Business Review* 68, no. 5 (September–October 1990), pp. 105–12.

BusinessWeek

How Will Education Mean Business with TQM?
(Continued from page 163)

A: It starts with the ABCs of TQM . . .

Although there are differences between business and education, educators are applying TQM principles to their environment—and with initial success. Westinghouse isn't alone in its use of TQM for reform. According to the American Society for Quality Control, the number of U.S. public school districts using TQM grew from 87 to 127 over a year's time. The schools adopt a variety of TQM principles to create improvements specific to their particular needs. For example, in keeping with TQM's emphasis on gathering data to identify and help solve problems, Westinghouse teachers and administrators monitor attendance and test scores to pinpoint problems. They then use the information to brainstorm with students to resolve truancy and classroom failures. Other TQM principles at work at Westinghouse include: using scatter diagrams to illustrate the relationship between two variables (e.g., how skipping homework leads to poor test grades); benchmarking (using a survey approach developed by Xerox to trace low PTA turnout to scheduling conflicts); and cause-and-effect (using prompter students to make wake-up calls to classmates, thus decreasing tardiness). All in all, TQM means business in education and its reform effort.

For further reading, see the following source: "Total Quality Management: Now, It's a Class Act," Business Week, October 31, 1994.

Although TQM for service organizations is similar to TQM for manufacturing, several differences exist. Service firms pursuing quality let customers determine their needs and requirements, then set performance standards consistent with this information. The needs and requirements can be difficult to define, however, because each customer is different.

Services are intangible outputs: a good service exists mostly in a customer's mind. We can, on the other hand, examine good products and identify and design into production the characteristics that make the product good.

The goals for service outputs are different from those of manufacturing outputs. While the goal in manufacturing is uniformity, the goal of services is customization. Medical doctors tailor their services to the need of each individual patient. Barbers provide quality service if they cut hair the way their customers want. Customization renders it difficult to set specifications.

A manufacturing firm can recall a product of poor quality to repair or replace it. A service firm that rendered poor quality service often can offer only apologies or reparations. An automaker, for example, can recall cars to replace a defective brake system. Rarely can a surgeon recall the patient to undo an operation wrongly executed.

The cost of failures can be astronomical for a service organization. Quality costs for service organizations also include prevention, appraisal, as well as internal failure and external failure costs. Differences in output characteristics between service and manufacturing organizations, however, make it necessary for service organizations to ensure that only qualified personnel can render services, that all personnel receive continuous education and training, and that quality is built into every step of the services provided to clients and customers.

TOTAL QUALITY AND PRODUCTIVITY

A common misconception is that improvements in quality decrease productivity. The reasoning behind this misconception is that quality improvement requires additional input efforts. Because productivity measures the relationship between output and input resources, an effort that requires additional input resources with no increase in output decreases productivity. Managers may believe that materials, labor

◀ **LEARNING OBJECTIVE 7**
Explain the relationships between total quality management and productivity.

hours, and other resources spent on rework, repair, or other activities to improve quality consume additional resources with no increase in output.

Studies have shown, however, that improvements in quality lead to *increases* in productivity.[25] The belief that quality improvement and productivity have an inverse relationship may have grown out of the misperception that all units, once manufactured, are good outputs, whatever the quality or required subsequent spending to rectify poor-quality products. A firm's accounting system may not include resources expended on rework or repair in the manufacturing cost of the unit. Rather, repair or rework costs are treated as manufacturing overheads to be shared by all products and units. The term *hidden factory* sometimes refers to the use of facilities and resources for repairs, rework, retests, and other remedial work for poor-quality products. They are hidden because these accounts often are included as part of the total manufacturing overhead shared by all.

Furthermore, many actions or decisions taken to achieve total quality management improve productivity. A simple and easy-to-make product design decreases defects and, at the same time, increases productivity. A decision to streamline the manufacturing process to reduce the chance for error also can increase productivity because it eliminates unnecessary operations.

In their study, Leonard and Sasser found many examples of quality improvement leading to increased productivity:

- Installation of a new clean room to reduce contaminants on printed circuit boards increased output by almost 35 percent.

- Elimination of rework stations at one manufacturing factory for televisions forced workers to find and solve their own quality problems. As a result, the firm experienced an increase in production rates per direct labor-hour. The firm also saved money on rework and rework stations.

- Efforts to do it right the first time and every time by a firm increase not only its manufacturing productivity but also the firm's sales productivity. Sales personnel no longer have to spend time processing returned defective products.[26]

THE CHALLENGE OF TOTAL QUALITY MANAGEMENT TO MANAGEMENT ACCOUNTANTS

LEARNING OBJECTIVE 8 ▶
Describe the role of management accountants in total quality management and the challenges they face.

The role of management accountants in total quality management includes gathering all relevant quality information, participating actively in all phases of the quality program, and reviewing and disseminating quality cost reports. A quality management system developed without active involvement of management accountants may fail to realize its potential. Too often a firm includes quality costs in diverse and scattered accounts for products, marketing, engineering, and services. The impact of these costs and benefits disappears as the firm allocates account balances. As a result, the firm pays scant attention to quality costs and quality results on financial performance.

With their training and expertise in analyzing, measuring, and reporting information, management accountants can help design and conduct comprehensive quality information gathering, measurement, and reporting systems. Management accountants can improve total quality management further by integrating the quality cost information into the existing management reporting and measurement systems. This integration facilitates constant and continuous attention to improving quality by making measurement, reporting, and evaluation of quality a regular, routine activity, rather than a special effort that will be dropped when the fad is over.

---

[25] Frank S. Leonard and W. Earl Sasser, "The Incline of Quality," *Harvard Business Review* 60, no. 5 (September–October 1982), pp. 163–71; and Y. K. Shetty, "Corporate Response to Productivity Challenges," *National Productivity Review*, Winter 1984–85, pp. 7–14.

[26] Leonard and Sasser, "*The Incline of Quality*," pp. 163–71.

A management accountant should be completely involved in all quality improvement activities of the enterprise. The IMA described these activities of an involved management accountant:

- Ensure full representation of management accountants on the main quality control committees and quality improvement teams.
- Make the company fully aware of the competitive benchmarks, competitive gaps, customers' retention rate, and cost of quality.
- Participate actively in identifying areas of greatest quality improvement opportunities and needs.
- Develop quality measures to monitor and assess ongoing progress toward quality goals.
- Be involved closely in vendor rating decisions.
- Review and evaluate quality control effectiveness and the value of training courses for quality control personnel and human resources staff.
- Gather and continually review scrap and recovery costs.[27]

To meet the challenges of total quality management, management accountants need to have a clear understanding of TQM methodology. They must be able to design, create, or modify information systems that measure and monitor quality and evaluate progress toward total quality as expected of each organizational unit and of the total enterprise. Some of the tasks are

- Determine which accounts contain significant data for TQM.
- Reorganize and restructure the existing accounting system to provide accurate and complete quality cost data.
- Revise the chart of accounts to reflect each quality cost category.

A traditional accounting system often fails to associate costs with activities. As a result, quality teams do not have the necessary information readily available to focus on quality problems. A management accountant needs to relate quality costs to activities so that quality teams can focus their efforts appropriately to ensure the success of the TQM effort. One approach is to apply techniques from activity-based costing to TQM so that cost drivers for quality costs are identified clearly (see Chapter 4).

Content of cost of quality reports can vary widely depending on the organization and its operating characteristics. Management accountants need to ensure that the measurement and reporting process meets the following criteria:

- Meets the need of the internal customers.
- Includes all relevant cost-of-quality measures including both financial and nonfinancial measures.
- Adjusts measures to reflect quality and business challenges.
- Adapts measures as the need changes.
- Is simple and easy to use, execute, and monitor.
- Provides fast and timely feedback to users and managers.
- Fosters improvement rather than just monitoring.
- Motivates and challenges team members to strive for the highest quality gains.[28]

SUMMARY

In today's global competition, with short product life cycles and rapidly changing technologies and consumer tastes, firms can sustain long-term survival and profitability only by manufacturing quality products and rendering quality services.

---

[27] IMA Statement No. 4R, p. 9.

[28] Ibid., p. 31.

Providing quality is the best strategy for firms to maintain long-term profitability. Businesses offering quality products and services usually have large market shares; studies show that quality is positively and significantly related to a higher return on investment.

A quality product or service meets or exceeds a customer's expectations at a price the customer is willing to pay. To achieve quality products or services, many firms adopt total quality management. Total quality management requires continuous efforts by everyone in an organization to understand, meet, and exceed the expectations of both internal and external customers.

Approaches to conform to quality specifications include goalpost or zero-defect conformance, which meets the quality standard within the specified range of the target, and absolute or robust quality conformance, which meets the specification exactly at the target value.

Four common categories for quality costs are prevention, appraisal, internal failure, and external failure. Prevention and appraisal costs are costs of conformance; and internal and external failure costs are costs of nonconformance.

Cost of quality reports should enable each department to identify and recognize the effects of its actions on the cost of quality and to pinpoint areas of high-quality costs. In generating a quality cost report, accountants define quality cost categories and identify all quality costs within each category. Ideally each quality cost should have its own account so that quality cost information is not buried in, or aggregated with, other accounts.

Tools that identify quality problems and find solutions to those problems include control charts, histograms, Pareto diagrams, brainstorming, and cause-and-effect (fishbone or Ishikawa) diagrams. A control chart is a graph that depicts successive observations of an operation taken at constant intervals; it is used often in identifying or discovering quality problems. Both histograms and Pareto diagrams depict graphically the frequency of quality problems or observations. A Pareto diagram orders quality problems from the largest to the smallest. Brainstorming is a useful way to elicit ideas in identifying quality problems, finding causes of a quality problem, or developing solutions to a quality problem. The cause-and-effect (fishbone or Ishikawa) diagram represents graphically a chain of causes and effects that lead to a quality problem. It is a useful way to sort out root causes and to identify relationships between causes or factors and the quality problem.

Organizations with quality services conform their performance standards with the needs and requirements of their customers. Although quality costs for a service organization or function include prevention, appraisal, internal failure, and external failure costs, service organizations pay the most attention to training and building quality into every step of service rendered because poor quality service usually cannot be recalled or replaced.

Improved quality increases productivity. Evidence has shown that the common misconception of inverse relationships between quality improvement and productivity is a result of including all units, regardless of quality, as good output.

Management accountants, with training and expertise in analyzing, measuring, and reporting information, can help design and conduct comprehensive quality information gathering, measurement, and reporting.

KEY WORDS

SELF-STUDY PROBLEMS

(For solution, please turn to the end of the chapter.)

1.   Taguchi Quality Loss Function

Marlon Audio Company manufactures cassette tapes. The desired speed of its model SF2000 is 2 inches per second. Any deviation from this value distorts pitch and tempo resulting in poor sound quality. The firm sets the quality specification to $2 \pm .25$ because an average customer is likely to complain and return the tape if the speed is off by .25 inch per second. The cost per return is $36. The repair cost before the tape is shipped, however, is only $3 per tape.

Required:

1. Compute $L(x)$ if x is 2.12 inches.
2. Estimate the tolerance for the firm to minimize its cost.

2.   Cost of Quality Report

Coolquietude Electric Instruments manufacturers fans for mini and micro computers. As a first step to focus on quality improvements, the firm has compiled the following operating data for the year just completed (in thousands):

Line inspection	$ 55
Training	120
Returns	100
Warranty repairs	68
Preventive equipment maintenance	20
Recalls	157
Design engineering	67
Scrap	30
Downtime	40
Product-testing equiment	88
Product liability insurance	20
Supplier evaluation	15
Reworks	35
Inspection and testing of incoming materials	25
Litigation costs to defend allegation of defective products	240

Required   Prepare a cost of quality report and classify the costs as prevention, appraisal, internal failure, and external failure.

QUESTIONS

6–1   Define quality.

6–2   Why do you think the cost of poor quality reached such an epidemic level before U.S. companies were motivated to do something about the problem?

6–3   What is TQM? At what point can a firm consider its effort to achieve total quality management complete?

6–4   What are the Malcolm Baldrige Award and an ISO 9000 certificate? Why do many firms in the United States seek them?

6–5   What are the core principles of total quality management?

6–6   Why is continuous quality improvement essential to achieve TQM and critical to an organization's success and competitive position?

6–7   Describe the processes for an effective implementation of TQM.

6–8   What are the purposes of conducting a quality audit?

6–9   What is gap analysis?

6–10   Why is it often necessary to revise a firm's compensation and appraisal systems when implementing TQM?

6–11 Describe goalpost conformance.

6–12 Discuss the difference between goalpost conformance and absolute quality conformance.

6–13 Taguchi argues that being within specification limits is not enough to be competitive in today's global economy. Do you agree? Why?

6–14 What is the likely cost to a firm when its product or service does not conform to customers' expectations for features or performance?

6–15 Name three types of costs associated with each of the following cost categories:
a. Prevention
b. Appraisal
c. Internal failure
d. External failure

6–16 Which of the following cost categories tend to increase during the early years of TQM? Which of them tend to decrease over the years due to successful total quality management? Why?
a. Prevention
b. Appraisal
c. Internal failure
d. External failure

6–17 What is cost of conformance? Nonconformance?

6–18 Many organizations found that investments in prevention and appraisal usually resulted in major cost savings in other areas. Explain this phenomenon.

6–19 What functions does COQ reporting play in a quality improvement program?

6–20 Name and briefly describe three methods that companies use to identify quality problems.

6–21 What is an Ishikawa diagram? What is its primary purpose?

6–22 What are the main causes of quality problems in a typical cause-and-effect diagram for manufacturing operations?

6–23 What is a Pareto chart? What is its function?

6–24 What are similarities and distinct characteristics in TQM between manufacturing and service firms?

6–25 What are the relationships between quality and productivity? Do efforts at productivity improvement help or hurt quality? Do quality improvement efforts help or hurt productivity? Why?

6–26 What roles do management accountants play in TQM?

6–27 How can management accountants meet the challenges of TQM?

PROBLEMS

6–28 **PARETO DIAGRAM** The following causes of absenteeism for a fellow student are for the year just completed:

Cause of Absenteeism	Occurrences
Personal illness	12
A child's illness	26
A car broke down	8
Personal emergency	32
Overslept	9
Unexpected visitor	11

Required Construct a Pareto diagram.

6-29 QUALITY COST CLASSIFICATION

Required Classify these following items into types of cost of quality:

a. Warranty repairs
b. Scrap
c. Allowance granted due to blemish
d. Contribution margins of lost sales
e. Tuition for quality courses
f. Raw materials inspections
g. Work-in-process inspection
h. Shipping cost for replacements
i. Recalls
j. Attorney's fee for unsuccessful defense of complaints about quality
k. Inspection of reworks
l. Overtime caused by reworking
m. Machine maintenance
n. Tuning of testing equipment

6-30 COST OF QUALITY REPORT

The Buster Company manufactures custom-designed milling machines and incurred the following cost of quality in 20X8 and 20X9:

	20X9	20X8
Rework	$200,000	$250,000
Quality manual	40,000	50,000
Product design	300,000	270,000
Testing	80,000	60,000
Retesting	50,000	90,000
Product recalls	360,000	500,000
Field service	230,000	350,000
Disposal of defective units	90,000	85,000

The total sales in each of the two years were $6,000,000. The firm's cost of goods sold is typically one-third of the net sales.

Required

1. Prepare a cost-of-quality report that classifies the firm's costs under the proper cost-of-quality category.

2. Calculate the ratio of each cost-of-quality category to sales in each of the two years. Comment on the trends in cost of quality between 20X8 and 20X9.

3. Give three examples of nonfinancial measures that Buster Company might want to monitor as part of a total quality management effort.

6-31 HISTOGRAM GRAPH

The Genova Company classifies its costs of quality into four categories. The costs of quality as a percentage of cost of goods sold for the last three years are

	20X3	20X2	20X1
Prevention costs	2.00%	4.00%	1.00%
Appraisal costs	1.50	2.50	3.00
Internal failure costs	14.00	23.00	27.00
External failure costs	12.00	18.00	31.00

Required

1. Prepare a histogram that shows the costs-of-quality trends as a percentage of costs of goods sold.

2. Comment on the trends in cost of quality over the three-year period from 20X1 to 20X3.

3. What can the firm expect of its cost of quality as percentages of its cost of goods sold in 20X4?

6–32 **QUALITY COST CLASSIFICATION**   A partial list of Josephson Manufacturing Company's activities during the past year includes:
a. Materials for repairs of goods under warranty.
b. Inspection of goods repaired under warranty.
c. Customer returns.
d. Canceled sales orders due to unsatisfactory products previously delivered to its customers.
e. Maintenance costs for testing equipment.
f. Inspecting finished goods.
g. Time spent to determine courses needed for quality training.
h. Debugging software before production.
i. Technical help to resolve a customer's production problems that may have been caused by bugs in the software shipped with the firm's equipment.
j. Supervision of testing personnel.

Required

1. Classify each of these costs into one of the following categories: prevention cost, appraisal cost, internal failure cost, external failure cost, or not a quality cost.

2. Identify conformance and nonconformance costs in the list of activities.

6–33 **QUALITY COST REPORT**   Scrabbling Enterprises is a pioneer in designing and producing scrabbling devices. SE's products were brilliantly designed but the manufacturing process was neglected by management; as a consequence, quality problems have been chronic. When customers complained about defective units, SE would simply send out a repairperson or replace the defective unit with a new one. Recently, several competitors came out with similar products that lack similar quality problems, causing SE's sales to decline. The firm's market share has declined from 60 to 40 percent in 20X5.

To rescue the situation, SE embarked on an intensive campaign to strengthen its quality control at the beginning of 20X6. These efforts met with some success—the downward slide in sales was reversed, and the firm's market share grew from 40 percent in 20X5 to 45 percent in 20X6. To help monitor the company's progress, costs relating to quality and quality control were compiled for the previous year (20X5) and for the first full year of the quality campaign (20X6). The costs, which do not include the lost sales due to a reputation for poor quality, appear in thousands:

	20X6	20X5
Product recalls	$ 600	$3,500
Systems development	980	120
Inspection	2,770	1,700
Net cost of scrap	3,300	800
Supplies used in testing	40	30
Warranty repairs	2,800	3,300
Rework labor	2,600	1,400
Statistical process control	270	—
Customer returns of defective goods	200	3,200
Cost of testing equipment	390	270
Quality engineering	1,650	1,080
Downtime due to quality problems	1,100	5,600

Required

1. Prepare a quality cost report for both 20X5 and 20X6. Carry percentage computations to two decimal places.

2. Prepare a histogram showing the distribution of the various quality costs by category.

3. Write an analysis to accompany the reports you have prepared in requirements 1 and 2 on the effectiveness of the changes the firm made in the last year.

4. Suppose the firm has just learned that its major competitor has reduced its price by 20 percent. SE can afford to lower its price only if it can cut costs. A sales manager suggests that the firm can reduce quality engineering and inspection work until the market stabilizes. The manager also points out that reduced inspections will decrease the net cost of scrap and losses of downtime due to quality problem. Do you agree?

6–34 **QUALITY COST REPORT**   Carrie Lee, the president of Lee Enterprises, was concerned about the result of her company's new quality control efforts. "Maybe the emphasis we've placed on upgrading our quality control system will pay off in the long run, but it doesn't seem to be helping us much right now. I thought improved quality would give a real boost to sales, but sales have remained flat at about $10,000,000 for the last two years."

Ethics

Lee Enterprises has seen its market share decline in recent years due to increased foreign competition. An intensive effort to strengthen the quality control system was initiated a year ago (on January 1, 20X6) in the hope that better quality would strengthen the company's competitive position and also reduce warranty and servicing costs. These costs (in thousands) relate to quality and quality control over the last two years:

	20X6	20X5
Warranty repairs	$140	$420
Rework labor	200	140
Supplies used in testing	6	4
Depreciation of testing equipment	34	22
Warranty replacements	18	60
Field servicing	120	180
Inspection	120	76
Systems development	106	64
Disposal of defective products	76	54
Net cost of scrap	124	86
Product recalls	82	340
Product testing	160	98
Statistical process control	74	
Quality engineering	80	56

Required

1. Prepare a quality cost report that contains data for both 20X5 and 20X6. Carry percentage computations to two decimal places.

2. Prepare a histogram showing the distribution of the various quality costs by category.

3. Prepare a written evaluation to accompany the reports you have prepared in requirements 1 and 2. This evaluation should discuss the distribution of quality costs in the company, changes in this distribution that you detect have taken place over the last year, and any other information you believe would be useful to management.

4. A member of the management team believes that workers will be more conscientious in their works if they are held responsible for mistakes. He suggests that workers should do reworking on their own time and that workers also should pay for disposals of defective units and the cost of scraps. The proposal estimates that the firm can save another $400,000 in quality costs and the workers are less likely to make as many errors. Should the firm implement the proposal?

(CMA Adapted)

Service

International

6–35 RELEVANT COSTS AND QUALITY IMPROVEMENT Lightening Bulk Company is a moving company specializing in transporting large items worldwide. The firm has an 85 percent on-time delivery rate. Twelve percent of the items are misplaced and the remaining 3 percent are lost in shipping. On average, the firm incurs an additional $60 per item to track down and deliver misplaced items. Lost items cost the firm about $300 per item. Last year the firm shipped 5,000 items with an average freight bill of $200 per item shipped.

The firm's manager is considering investing in a new scheduling and tracking system costing $150,000 per year. The new system is expected to reduce misplaced items to 1 percent and lost items to .5 percent. Furthermore, the firm expects the total sales to increase by 10 percent with the improved service. The average contribution margin is 40 percent.

Required

1. Should the firm install the new tracking system?
2. What other factors does the firm's manager need to consider in making the decision?
3. Upon further investigation the manager discovered that 80 percent of the misplaced or lost items either originated in or were delivered to the same country. What is the maximum amount the firm should spend to reduce the problems in that country by 90 percent?

Strategy

6–36 QUALITY IMPROVEMENT, RELEVANT COST ANALYSIS The Worrix Corporation manufactures and sells 3,000 premium quality multimedia projectors at $12,000 per unit each year. At the current production level, the firm's manufacturing costs include variable costs of $2,500 per unit and annual fixed costs of $6,000,000. Additional selling, administrative, and other expenses, not including 15 percent sales commissions, are $10,000,000 per year.

The new model, introduced a year ago, has experienced a flickering problem. On average the firm has to rework 40 percent of the completed units. The firm still has to repair under warranty 15 percent of the units shipped. The additional work required for rework and repair makes it necessary for the firm to add additional capacity with annual fixed costs of $1,800,000. The variable costs per unit are $2,000 for rework and $2,500, including transportation cost, for repair.

The chief engineer, Patti Mehandra, has proposed a modified manufacturing process that will almost entirely eliminate the flickering problem. The new process will require $12,000,000 for new equipment and installation, and $3,000,000 for training. Mehandra believes that current appraisal costs of $600,000 per year and $50 per unit can be eliminated within one year after the installation of the new process. The firm currently inspects all the units before shipment. Furthermore, warranty repair cost will be only $1,000 for no more than 5 percent of the units shipped.

Worrix believes that none of the fixed costs of rework or repair can be saved and that a new model will be introduced in three years. The new technology will most likely render the current equipment obsolete.

The accountant estimates that repairs cost the firm 20 percent of its business.

Required

1. What are the additional costs of choosing the new process?
2. What are the benefits of choosing the new process?
3. Should Worrix use the new process?
4. What factors should be considered before making the final decision?
5. A member of the board is very concerned about the substantial amount of additional funds needed for the new process. Because the

current model will be replaced in about three years, the board member suggests that the firm should take no action and the problem will go away in three years. Do you agree?

6–37 TAGUCHI LOSS FUNCTION Duramold specializes in manufacturing molded plastic panels to be fitted on car doors. The blueprint specification for the thickness of a high-demand model calls for 0.1875 ±.0025 inch. It costs $150 to scrap a part that doesn't meet the specifications. The thickness measure for the unit just completed is .1893 inch.

Required Use the Taguchi loss function to determine

1. The value of k.
2. The amount of loss for the unit.

6–38 TAGUCHI LOSS FUNCTION Use the data from problem 6–37 for Duramold. Duramold can eliminate the uneven thickness by adding a production worker at the critical production point for $6 per unit.

Required At what tolerance should the panel be manufactured?

6–39 TAGUCHI LOSS FUNCTION An electronic component has an output voltage specification of 125 ±5 millivolts. The loss to the firm for a component that does not meet the specification is $200. The output voltage for a sample unit is 122 millivolts.

Required Use the Taguchi loss function to determine

1. The value of k.
2. The amount of loss.

6–40 TAGUCHI LOSS FUNCTION Use the data for problem 6–39. The firm can adjust the output voltage in the factory by changing a resistor at a cost of $12.

Required At what voltage should the electronic component be manufactured?

6–41 COST OF QUALITY CATEGORY The management of Brooks Company thinks that its total costs of quality can be reduced by increasing expenditures in certain key costs of quality categories. The following costs of quality have been identified by management:

Cost of Quality	Costs
Rework	$ 6,000
Recalls	15,000
Reengineering efforts	9,000
Repair	12,000
Replacements	12,000
Retesting	5,000
Supervision	18,000
Scrap	9,000
Training	15,000
Testing of incoming materials	7,000
Inspection of work in process	18,000
Downtime	10,000
Product liability insurance	9,000
Quality audits	5,000
Continuous improvement	1,000
Warranty repairs	15,000

Required

1. Classify these costs into the four cost of quality categories.
2. Determine the total dollars being spent on each of the categories.
3. Based on the company's expenditures by cost of quality categories, on which cost category should the company concentrate its efforts to decrease its overall costs of quality?

6–42 **PREPARING A COST OF QUALITY REPORT** The Tarheel Company incurred these costs of quality:

	20X7	20X8
Calibration	$ 75,000	$100,000
Product design	150,000	175,000
Product liability	125,000	75,000
Product recalls	400,000	200,000
Retesting	250,000	200,000
Rework	325,000	100,000
Testing	50,000	150,000
Training	75,000	100,000
Warranty repairs	150,000	75,000

Required Prepare a cost of quality report that classifies each of the costs under the proper cost of quality category. Indicate whether the costs are increasing or decreasing and by how much.

6–43 **COST OF QUALITY PROGRAM, NONFINANCIAL INFORMATION**

International Tractor (IT) manufactures tractor parts. A major customer has just warned IT that if it did not improve its quality it would lose that firm's business. Duane Smith, the controller for IT, must develop a cost of quality program. He seeks your advice on classifying each of the following items as (i) a prevention cost, (ii) an appraisal cost, (iii) an internal failure cost, or (iv) an external failure cost:

a. Cost of tractor parts returned to International Tractor

b. Costs of having to rework defective parts detected by the engineering quality assurance team

c. Cost of inspecting the products on the production line by the IT quality inspectors

d. Labor cost of product designer at IT whose job is to design products that will not break under extreme pressure

e. Payment for employees who visit customers with complaints

Required

1. Classify the five individual items into one of the four categories.

2. Give two examples of nonfinancial performance measures that IT can use to monitor its total quality control effort.

3. Recommend an effective TQM implementation procedure to meet the customer's demand.

SOLUTION TO SELF-STUDY PROBLEMS

1. **Taguchi Quality Loss Function**

    1. $36 = k (0.25)^2$
       $k = 576
       $L(x = 2.12) = 576(2.12 - 2)^2 = $40,000$
    2. $3 = $576(\text{tolerance})^2$
       Tolerance $= 0.0722$
       Therefore, the specification should be set at 2 inches ± 0.0722 inch.

2. Cost of Quality Report

Coolquietude Electric Instruments
Cost of Quality Report
For the Year 20X1

Prevention costs:	
Training	$ 120
Design engineering	67
Preventive equipment maintenance	20
Supplier evaluation	15
Total prevention costs	$ 222
Appraisal costs:	
Line inspection	$ 55
Product-testing equipment	88
Inspection and testing of incoming materials	25
Total appraisal costs	$ 168
Internal failure costs:	
Scrap	$ 30
Downtime	40
Reworks	35
Total internal failure costs	$ 105
External failure costs:	
Returns	$ 100
Warranty repairs	68
Recalls	157
Product liability insurance	20
Litigation costs	240
Total external failure costs	$ 585
Total cost of quality	$1,080

Part III

Management Planning and Decision Making

Cost Estimation

After studying this chapter you should be able to . . .

Understand the strategic role of cost estimation **1**

Apply the six steps of cost estimation **2**

Use each of the cost estimation methods: account classification, visual fit, high-low method, work measurement, and regression analysis **3**

Explain the data requirements and implementation problems of the cost estimation methods **4**

Use learning curves in cost estimation when learning is present **5**

Use statistical measures to evaluate a regression analysis **6**

Lincoln Potter/Gamma Liaison

It's hard to make predictions—especially about the future.

ALLAN LAMPORT

Cost estimation is one of the most critical aspects of the strategic management function:

> The strategic cost literature points management accountants in the direction of active participation in early strategic decision making. Their contributions at early stages are likely to be in the form of (1) predicting costs of alternative activities, processes, or organizational forms—both of the firm and its competitors, (2) predicting financial and operational impacts of alternative strategic choices, and (3) predicting costs (dollars and time) of alternative implementation strategies. If management accountants do not fill this role, others will.[1]

As Jalinski and Selto indicate, a critical starting point for strategic cost management is accurate cost estimates. The strategic approach is forward looking, and thus cost estimation is an essential element of it. **Cost estimation** is the development of a well-defined relationship between a cost object and its cost drivers for the purpose of predicting the cost. It can be as simple as reading a graph, as formal as solving an algebraic equation, or as complex as building a statistical model.

THE STRATEGIC ROLE OF COST ESTIMATION

Cost estimation facilitates strategic management in two important ways. First, cost estimation helps predict future costs using previously identified activity-based, volume-based, structural, or executional cost drivers. Second, cost estimation helps identify the key cost drivers for a cost object. This latter use is particularly important in activity-based costing that commonly uses a number of detailed cost drivers. Cost estimation identifies which of these cost drivers are most useful in predicting cost.

Using Cost Estimation to Predict Future Costs

Strategic management requires accurate cost estimates for many applications, including:

1. To facilitate strategic positioning analysis. Cost estimates are particularly important for firms competing on the basis of cost leadership. Cost estimates guide

Cost estimation is the development of a well-defined relationship between a cost object and its cost drivers for the purpose of predicting the cost.

◀ **LEARNING OBJECTIVE 1**
Understand the strategic role of cost estimation.

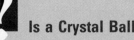

Is a Crystal Ball More Effective?

Chrysler Corp., Texas Instruments, Inc., and other firms use cost estimation methods to predict cost and revenue data. For example, among other applications, Chrysler uses these methods to estimate the cost of materials for its products, while Texas Instruments employs the methods to project the revenues in its various product lines. However, both firms face, as do many others, important limitations in using the estimation methods effectively.

Q: What limitations do today's corporations face in predicting costs and revenues? *Find out on page 217 of this chapter.*

---

[1] Dale W. Jalinski and Frank H. Selto, "Integration of Accounting and Strategy: A Longitudinal Field Study," working paper, University of Colorado at Boulder, July 1995.

201

management in determining which contemporary management techniques, such as target costing or total quality management, the firm should employ to succeed in its chosen strategy.

2. To facilitate value chain analysis. Cost estimates help the firm identify potential opportunities for cost reduction through reconfiguring the value chain. For example, cost estimates are useful in determining if overall costs and value to the product can be improved by manufacturing one of its components in-house, or by purchasing the component from a supplier.

3. To facilitate target costing and life cycle costing. Cost estimates are an integral part of target costing and life-cycle costing. Management uses cost estimates of different product designs as part of the process of selecting the particular design that provides the best trade-off of value to the customer versus manufacturing and other costs. Similarly, cost estimates are used in the process of determining the minimum expected life-cycle cost for a product or service.

Cost Estimation for Different Types of Cost Drivers

The cost estimation methods explained in this chapter can be used for any of the four cost drivers: activity-based, volume-based, structural, or executional. The relationships between costs and activity-based or volume-based cost drivers often are best fit by linear cost estimation methods because these relationships are at least approximately linear within the relevant range of the firm's operations. These linear methods are explained in a later section, "Cost Estimation Methods."

Structural cost drivers involve plans and decisions that have a long-term and therefore a strategic impact on the firm. Such decisions include manufacturing experience, scale of product, product or production technology, and product or production complexity. Technology and complexity issues often lead management to use activity-based costing and linear estimation methods. In contrast, experience and scale often require nonlinear methods. As a cost driver, experience represents the reduction in unit cost due to learning. The effect on total cost of experience is nonlinear: that is, costs decrease with increased manufacturing experience. The experience effect is explained in the first appendix to the chapter. Similarly, the relationship between the structural cost driver, scale, and total cost is nonlinear. *Scale* is the term used to describe the manufacture of similar products that differ in size—for example, pipe valves of different capacity. A common effect of scale is that total manufacturing cost increases more rapidly than the increase in the size of the product. For example, the manufacture of a 22-inch industrial valve requires more than twice the cost of an 11-inch valve. The relationship between manufacturing cost and valve size can be predicted by a mathematical estimation model called the power law that is used in industrial engineering.[2]

Using Cost Estimation to Identify Cost Drivers

Often the most practical way to identify cost drivers is to rely on the judgment of product designers, engineers, and manufacturing personnel. Those who know the product and production processes the best have the most useful information on cost drivers. Cost estimation sometimes can play a discovery role, and at other times a collaborative role to validate and confirm the judgments of the designers and engineers. For example, Hewlett-Packard uses cost estimation to confirm the usefulness of cost drivers selected by teams of engineers and production personnel.[3]

THE SIX STEPS OF COST ESTIMATION

LEARNING OBJECTIVE 2 ▶
Apply the six steps of cost estimation.

The six steps of cost estimation are (1) define the cost object for which the related costs are to be estimated, (2) determine the cost drivers, (3) collect consistent and

---

[2]   Based on information in Phillip F. Ostwald, *Cost Estimating for Engineering and Management* (Inglewood Cliffs, N.J.: Prentice Hall, 1974).

[3]   Based on information from Mike Merz and Arlene Hardy, "ABC Puts Accountants on Design Team at HP," *Management Accounting*, September 1993, pp. 22–27.

accurate data on the cost object and the cost drivers, (4) graph the data, (5) select and employ an appropriate estimation method, and (6) evaluate the accuracy of the cost estimate.

Step 1: Define the Cost Object to Be Estimated

Although it might seem elementary, defining the particular cost to be estimated requires care. Management accountants must answer these questions: What is the cost object? What is the level of aggregation? Also, they should consider *who* has incurred the cost, so that the cost estimate is relevant for the intended use. For example, for a city manager who is estimating the cost to the city of a certain public health program, the cost of materials and services provided by the state government (at no charge to the city) is irrelevant.

Step 2: Determine the Cost Drivers

Cost drivers are the causal factors used in the estimation of the cost. Some examples of estimated costs and their related cost drivers are

Cost to Be Estimated	*Cost Driver*
Fuel expense for auto	Miles driven
Heating expense for a building	Temperature to be maintained in the building
Maintenance cost in a manufacturing plant	Machine-hours, labor-hours
Product design cost	Number of design elements, design changes

Identifying cost drivers is the most important step in developing the cost estimate. There may be a number of relevant drivers, and some may not be immediately obvious. Fuel expense for a large delivery truck, for example, might be primarily a function of miles traveled, but it is also affected by the average weight delivered, the number of hours of operation, and the nature of the delivery area.

Step 3: Collect Consistent and Accurate Data

Once the cost drivers have been selected, the management accountant collects data on the cost object and cost drivers. The data must be consistent and accurate. Consistency means that each period of data is calculated on the same accounting basis and all transactions are properly recorded in the period in which they occurred.

The accuracy of the data depends on the nature of the source. Sometimes data developed within the firm are very reliable, due to management policies and procedures to ensure accuracy. Accuracy also varies among external sources of data, including governmental sources, trade and industry publications, universities, and other sources. The choice of cost drivers requires trade-offs between the causality of the drivers and the accuracy of the data.

Step 4: Graph the Data

The objective of graphing data is to identify unusual patterns. Any shift or nonlinearity in the data must be given special attention in developing the estimate. For example, a week's downtime due to installing new equipment would cause unusual production data for that week; such data should be excluded when developing a cost estimate. Any unusual occurrences can be detected easily by studying a graph.

Step 5: Select and Employ the Estimation Method

The five estimation methods presented in the next section of the chapter differ in their ability to provide superior accuracy in cost estimation relative to the cost of the expertise and resources required. The management accountant chooses the method with the best precision/cost trade-off for the estimation objectives. The five methods are (1) account classification, (2) visual fit, (3) high-low method, (4) work measurement, and (5) regression analysis.

Step 6: Assess the Accuracy of the Cost Estimate

A critical final step in cost estimation is to consider the potential for error when the estimate is prepared. This involves considering the completeness and appropriateness of cost drivers selected in step 2, the consistency and accuracy of data selected in step 3, the study of the graphs in step 4, and the precision of the method selected in step 5.

An Illustration of the Six Steps of Cost Estimation

Suppose Mary Koenig is the dean of a business school that graduates about 3,500 students each year. The university has a separate graduation ceremony for the business majors. As a part of the business school budget process, Dean Koenig must estimate the funds necessary for the graduation ceremony.

The first step in developing the cost estimate is to define the cost to be estimated. Dean Koenig defines total cost as those costs incurred by the school of business in the graduation ceremony. These include the costs of a speaker, rented folding chairs (the ceremony will be outside on a grassy area next to the business building), and light food and beverages.

The second step is to identify the cost drivers. In this case the principal cost driver is the expected number of graduates and guests because that factor affects the number of chairs and the amount of food required. The costs of rented chairs and refreshments are variable because they vary with the number of attendees. The cost of the speaker is not affected by the number attending; it is a fixed cost. The total cost of the graduation is the sum of the fixed and variable costs.

The dean must select the cost drivers carefully. Dean Koenig would know, for example, that the total number of graduates is irrelevant to the estimation. The relevant cost driver is the number of graduates *expected to attend* the ceremony because a significant number of graduates do not attend. Expected attendance requires further investigation, perhaps determining the number or percentage of business graduates actually attending the ceremony last year.

Moreover, there are often two or more cost drivers. Rainy weather might reduce the number attending and therefore reduce the expected cost of chairs, food, and beverages. Koenig should obtain a weather forecast; if she is using data from the prior year in her estimation, she must find out whether it rained during last year's graduation.

In the third step, the dean collects the data on the number of graduates who attended the ceremony in prior years; or if this is not available, it is approximated from the number of graduates in prior years. Then in the fourth step, the dean graphs these data to see whether there is a significant trend or shift in the data.

The fifth step is the choice of an estimation method. Five methods are explained later in this chapter. An illustration of estimating total costs based on the simplest method, the account classification method, follows. Suppose the costs are

- $5,000.00 for the speaker
- $.50 for each rental chair
- $1.50 for food and beverages for each person.

Further suppose that on average each graduate is expected to bring two guests. Koenig assumes the number graduating is similar to the prior year and that approximately 50 percent of the graduates will attend. Thus she develops the following cost estimate:

$$\text{Cost} = \text{Fixed cost} + \text{Cost driver quantity} \times \text{Unit variable cost}$$

$$\text{Cost} = \begin{bmatrix} \text{Cost of} \\ \text{speaker} \end{bmatrix} + \begin{bmatrix} \text{Expected number} & & \text{Number of} \\ \text{of attending} & \times & \text{graduates and guests} \\ \text{graduates} & & \text{per graduate} \end{bmatrix} \times \begin{bmatrix} \text{Total unit} \\ \text{variable} \\ \text{cost} \end{bmatrix}$$

$$\text{Cost} = \$5,000 + [(3,500 \times .5) \times (2 + 1)] \times [\$.50 + \$1.50]$$

$$= \$15,500$$

The final step is to assess the accuracy of the cost estimate. To do this, the dean reviews what she has done so far—identified the cost driver (the number attending), the per-unit variable cost, the fixed cost, and an estimate for total cost. The dean knows that the estimate would be improved if she knew the actual number of graduates this year, rather than using the average number of graduates in prior years. Although she has chosen one useful cost driver, other important cost drivers may improve the estimate. The goal is to achieve the most accurate estimate possible given cost/benefit considerations.

COST ESTIMATION METHODS

The five estimation methods are (1) account classification, (2) visual fit, (3) the high-low method, (4) work measurement, and (5) regression analysis. The methods are listed from least to most accurate. However, the cost and effort expended in employing the methods are inverse to this sequence; the account classification method is the easiest and least costly, while the regression analysis method is both the most accurate and most costly, requiring greater time, data collection, and expertise (see Exhibit 7–1). In choosing the best estimation method, management accountants must consider the level of accuracy desired and any limitations on cost, time, and effort.

◄ **LEARNING OBJECTIVE 3**
Use each of the cost estimation methods: account classification, visual-fit, high-low method, work measurement, and regression analysis.

The Account Classification Method

The **account classification method** requires classifying each cost account in the financial records as either a fixed or variable cost. Using this classification, accountants determine the total costs by summing the estimated unit variable cost and the total fixed cost. Dean Koenig used this method to estimate the costs of the graduation ceremony in the previous example. The advantages of the account classification method are its simplicity and ease of use. On the other hand, its limitation is that the estimates are likely inaccurate because of not only the subjectivity of the method but also some costs are a mix of both variable and fixed costs.

The **account classification method** requires the classification of each cost account in the financial records as either a fixed or variable cost.

The Visual Fit Method

The **visual fit method** calls for the management accountant to view the cost data from prior periods, in either tabular or graphical form, and use the graph or table to estimate the cost on the basis of visual judgment. This method is also very simple and easy to use; it requires no special estimation expertise.

For example, consider the case of Ben Garcia, the management accountant of a large manufacturing plant who is preparing a budget for plant expenditures for the coming year, 19X8. He is estimating various plant costs and giving special attention to maintenance costs that have fluctuated somewhat over the last seven years.

The **visual fit method** calls for the management accountant to view the cost data from prior periods, in either tabular or graphical form, and estimate the cost on the basis of visual judgment.

Ben Garcia's Data on Maintenance Costs

	19X1	19X2	19X3	19X4	19X5	19X6	19X7
Maintenance Cost ($)	22,843	22,510	22,706	23,030	22,413	22,935	23,175

Garcia graphs the data as shown in Exhibit 7–2. Based on a quick view of the data, he estimates approximately $23,200 of maintenance cost in 19X8. The visual

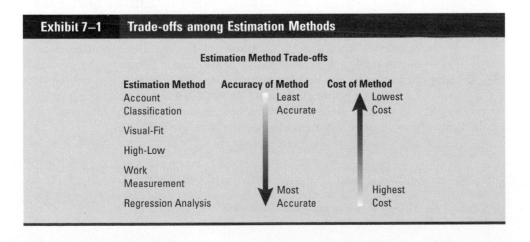

Exhibit 7–1   Trade-offs among Estimation Methods

Estimation Method Trade-offs

Estimation Method	Accuracy of Method	Cost of Method
Account Classification	Least Accurate	Lowest Cost
Visual-Fit		
High-Low		
Work Measurement		
Regression Analysis	Most Accurate	Highest Cost

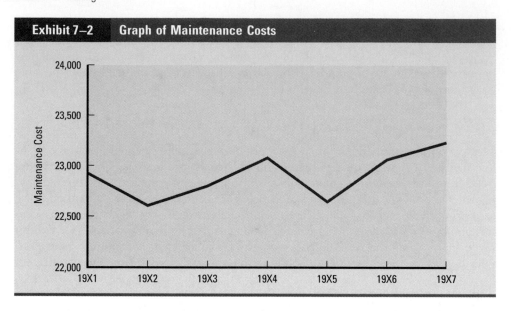

Exhibit 7–2   **Graph of Maintenance Costs**

fit method allows Garcia to obtain a relatively quick estimation. However, this approach has significant potential for error because of two inherent limitations:

1. The scale of a graph may affect the viewer's ability to estimate costs accurately. A relatively small scale tends to dampen perceptions of trend, whereas a relatively large scale tends to enhance perceptions of trend. Either can distort a cost estimate.

2. Studies have shown that users of both tabular and graphical reports make significant perception errors. One of the common findings is that, when a series of data has a significant upward trend, the unaided user tends to underestimate the amount of trend, while for a short series of data with little or no trend, the user tends to overestimate the amount of trend present. Other perception errors are explained in the accounting and psychology research.[4]

The High-Low Method

The **high-low method** improves on the accuracy of the account classification and visual fit methods by using algebra to determine a unique estimation line between representative low and high points in the data.

Management accountants can improve on the limited accuracy of the visual fit method with the **high-low method** that uses algebra to determine a *unique* estimation line between representative high and low points in the data. We continue with the maintenance cost example. Ben Garcia chooses the total hours of operation in the plant as a relevant cost driver for maintenance. Then he prepares a high-low estimate to predict the level of maintenance cost as a function of the expected operating hours in 19X8.

	19X1	**19X2**	**19X3**	**19X4**	**19X5**	**19X6**	**19X7**
Total Operating Hours	3,451	3,325	3,383	3,614	3,423	3,410	3,500
Maintenance Costs ($)	22,843	22,510	22,706	23,030	22,413	22,935	23,175

Garcia enters the data into a graph, as shown in Exhibit 7–3, and then selects two points from the data, one representative of the lower points in the data and the other representative of the higher points in the data. Often, these can be simply the lowest and highest points in the data. However, if either the highest or lowest point is a great distance from the other points around it, a biased estimation can result. Both points must be representative of the data around them.

---

[4] Representative papers in this research include those by William F. Wright, "Superior Loan Collectibility Judgments Given Graphical Displays," *Auditing: A Journal of Practice and Theory*, Fall 1995, pp. 144–54; Stanley F. Biggs and John J. Wild, "An Investigation of Auditor Judgment in Analytical Review," *The Accounting Review*, October 1985; and Edward R. Tufte, *The Visual Display of Quantitative Information* (Cheshire, CT: Graphics Press, 1983).

Exhibit 7–3   Ben Garcia's Data on Maintenance Cost and Hours

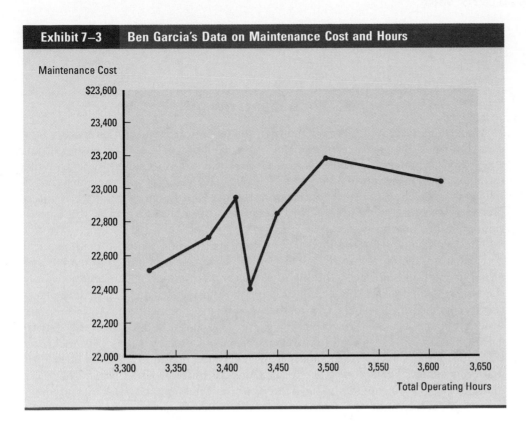

Maintenance Cost

Total Operating Hours

The high-low estimate is represented as:

$$Y = a + b \times H$$

where: $Y =$ the value of the estimated maintenance cost
  $H =$ the cost driver, the number of hours of operation for the plant
  $a =$ a fixed quantity that represents the value of Y when $H =$ zero
  $b =$ the slope of the line. In the plant maintenance example, it is the unit variable cost for maintenance

To obtain the high and low points, Ben draws a freehand line through the data to help in selecting the high and low points (try this yourself on Exhibit 7–3). He then chooses a high and a low point reasonably close to the freehand line. Suppose Ben has chosen the points for 19X2 and 19X7. Then, he calculates the value for b:

$$b = \text{Variable cost per hour}$$

$$= \frac{\text{Difference between \textbf{costs} for high and low points}}{\text{Difference for the value of the \textbf{cost driver} for the high and low points}}$$

$$b = \frac{\$23,175 - \$22,510}{3,500 - 3,325} = \$3.80 \text{ per hour}$$

Next, the value for a (the fixed quantity) can be calculated using either 19X2 or 19X7 data:
Using 19X7 data:

$$a = Y - (b \times H) = \$23,175 - \$3.80 \times 3,500 = \$9,875$$

Using 19X2 data gives the same value for a because fixed cost is the same at both levels of operating hours; only total variable costs differ between the two levels:
Using 19X2 data:

$$a = Y - (b \times H) = \$22,510 - \$3.80 \times 3,325 = \$9,875$$

So, the estimation equation using the high-low method is

$$Y = \$9,875 + \$3.80 \times H$$

This equation can be used to estimate maintenance cost for 19X8. Suppose 3,600 operating hours are expected in 19X8. Then, maintenance costs are estimated as follows:

$$\text{Maintenance cost in 19X8} = \$\ 9,875 + \$3.80 \times 3,600$$

$$= \$23,555$$

Management accountants find the high-low equation useful for estimating *total costs*, but not for approximating the amount of fixed costs alone. The reason is that the estimate applies only to the *relevant range* of the cost driver used to develop the estimate, the range from 3,325 to 3,614 hours. The value of a, a measure that is relevant at zero hours only, is too far from the relevant range to be properly interpreted as a fixed cost. Its role is to serve only as the constant part of the estimation equation, used to *predict total cost.*

The key advantage of the high-low method is providing a precise mathematical cost equation, in contrast to the subjectivity in using the account-classification and visual-fit methods. However, the high-low method is limited; it can represent only the best possible line for the two selected points, and the selection of the two points requires judgment. The next two methods, work measurement and regression, are generally more accurate than the previous three methods, because they use statistical estimation, which provides greater mathematical precision. Also, by including estimation error directly in the analysis, they provide useful measures of their estimation accuracy. The accuracy of the account classification, visual fit, and high-low methods can be evaluated only subjectively, while regression and work measurement have objective, quantitative measures of their estimation accuracy.

Work Measurement

Work measurement is a cost estimation method that makes a detailed study of some production or service activity to measure the time or input required per unit of output. For example, work measurement is applied to manufacturing operations to determine the labor and/or materials needed in the manufacture of the part or subassembly completed in that operation. In the nonmanufacturing context, the method is used to measure the time required to complete certain clerical tasks, such as processing receipts or processing bills for payment.

While a variety of work measurement methods are used in practice, the most common is work sampling. **Work sampling** is a statistical method that makes a series of measurements about the activity under study. These measurements are analyzed statistically to obtain estimates of the time and/or materials required for the activity.

As an example, suppose Kupper Insurance Company provides insurance coverage for automobile drivers. The cost of processing claims has increased significantly in recent years, and the firm is studying that cost. A careful statistical analysis is completed over a three-week period, including several different employees and several types of claims. The mean processing time is found to be 18 minutes, while the range is such that 95 percent of the claims required between 14 and 22 minutes. On the basis of this study, Kupper is able to estimate processing costs more accurately, and to evaluate the processing clerks more effectively and more fairly. For example, if a given claims processing clerk requires on average 24 minutes per claim, that clerk likely needs training or supervision because this time is outside the 95 percent likelihood range. Kupper considers the work measurement to be an ongoing activity, and continues to sample the processing times throughout the year, and to make adjustments to estimated times when needed.

Regression Analysis

Regression analysis is a statistical method for obtaining the unique cost estimating equation that best fits a set of data points. The regression line or equation obtained by regression analysis fits the data to *minimize the sum of the squares* of the estimation errors. Each error is the distance measured from the regression line to one of

Work measurement is a cost estimation method that makes a detailed study of some production or service activity to measure the time or input required per unit of output.

Work sampling is a statistical method that makes a series of measurements about the activity under study.

Regression analysis is a statistical method for obtaining the unique cost estimating equation that best fits a set of data points.

the data points. Errors are squared to magnify the largest differences, and therefore to highlight the importance of large errors in fitting the regression line. Because the regression analysis systematically minimizes the estimation errors in this way, it is called **least squares regression** and is widely viewed as one of the most effective methods for estimating costs.

There are two types of variables in a regression analysis. The **dependent variable** is the cost to be estimated.[5] The **independent** variable is the cost driver used to estimate the amount of the dependent variable. When there is one cost driver, the analysis is called a simple regression analysis. When there are two or more cost drivers, it is called multiple regression.

The regression equation has both an intercept and a slope term, much like the high-low method. In addition, the amount of the estimation error is considered explicitly in the regression estimate, which is

$$Y = a + bX + e$$

where: $Y =$ the amount of the *dependent variable*, the cost to be estimated

$a =$ a *fixed quantity*, also called the *intercept* or constant term, which represents the amount of Y when $X = 0$

$X =$ the value for the *independent variable*, the cost driver for the cost to be estimated; there may be one or more cost drivers

$b =$ the *unit variable cost*, also called the *coefficient* of the independent variable, that is, the increase in Y (cost) for each unit increase in X (cost driver)

$e =$ the regression *error*, which is the distance between the regression line and the data point

To illustrate the method, Exhibit 7–4A and the accompanying table show three months of data on supplies expense and production levels. (To simplify the presentation, only three data points are used; applications of regression usually involve 12 or more data points.) The management accountant's task is to estimate supplies expense for month 4, in which the production level is expected to be 125 units.

Month	Supplies Expense *(Y)*	Production Level *(X)*
1	$250	50 units
2	310	100
3	325	150
4	?	125

The regression for the data is determined by a statistical procedure that finds the unique line through the three data points that minimizes the sum of the squared error distances. Note that unique line in Exhibit 7–4B; the regression line is[6]

$$Y = \$220 + \$.75\ X$$

And the estimated value for supplies expense in month 4 is

$$Y = \$220 + \$.75 \times 125 = \$313.75$$

Regression analysis gives a management accountant an objective, statistically precise method for estimating supplies expense. Its principal advantage is that there is a unique estimate that produces the least estimation error for the data. On the other hand, since the errors are squared to find the best fitting line, the regression analysis can be influenced strongly by unusual data points called **outliers,** with the result

Least squares regression, which minimizes the sum of the squares of the estimation errors, is widely viewed as one of the most effective methods for estimating costs.

The **dependent variable** is the cost to be estimated.

The **independent variable** is the cost driver used to estimate the value of the dependent variable.

Outliers are unusual data points that strongly influence a regression analysis.

---

[5]   Although the dependent variable is a cost object in most of the cases we consider, the dependent variable also could be a revenue or some other type of financial or operating data.

[6]   The derivation of the intercept ($220) and coefficient ($.75) for this regression line is beyond the scope of this text, but it can be found in textbooks on basic probability and statistics such as that by Sheldon Ross, *Introductory Statistics* (New York: McGraw Hill, 1996). Also, there is a technical reference on regression analysis in Appendix B at the end of this chapter.

Exhibit 7–4A	Supplies Expense Data for Regression Application

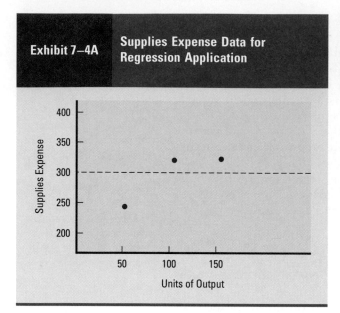

Exhibit 7–4B	The Regression Line for Supplies Expense, with Units of Output as the Cost Driver (i.e., independent variable)

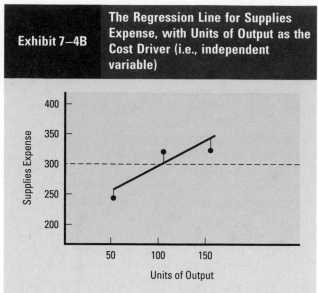

that the estimation line is not representative of most of the data. Such a situation is illustrated in Exhibit 7–5. To prevent this type of distortion, management accountants often prepare a graph of the data prior to using regression and determine whether any outliers are present. Each outlier is reviewed to determine whether it is due to a data-recording error, normal operating conditions, or a unique and unrecurring event. The accountant then decides whether to correct or remove the outlier, guided by the objective of developing the regression that is most representative of the data, one that provides the most accurate predictions.

Choosing the Dependent Variable

Development of a regression analysis begins with the choice of the cost object, the dependent variable. The dependent variable might be at a very aggregate level, such as total maintenance costs for the entire firm, or at a detail level, such as maintenance costs for each plant or department. The choice of aggregation level depends on the objectives for the cost estimation, data availability and reliability, and cost/benefit considerations. When a key objective is accuracy, a detailed level of analysis often is preferred. The detailed cost estimates can be aggregated if desired. For example, suppose the manager is estimating maintenance expense for a firm with several plant locations. Each plant most likely has unique cost drivers for maintenance, so the manager will get a more accurate overall estimate of maintenance expense by obtaining separate regression cost estimates for each plant and then aggregating the results.

Choosing the Independent Variables

To identify the proper independent variables, management accountants consider all the financial data, operating data, and other economic data that might be relevant for estimating the dependent variable. The goal is to choose a subset that (1) appears to be the most relevant, and (2) does not duplicate other independent variables. Exhibit 7–6 shows some dependent variables and the independent variables that might be appropriate for the selected dependent variables in the study of a chain of retail stores.

In developing a regression, it is not necessary to include a large number of independent variables. Often, one independent variable is sufficient, though commonly two to five variables are used. Generally, not more than five variables are used, because many candidates for independent variables will "tell the same story," that is, have the same basic relationship with the dependent variable.

A **dummy variable** is used to represent the presence or absence of a condition.

Most often the data in a regression analysis are numerical amounts in dollars or units. Another type of variable, called a **dummy variable,** represents the presence or absence of a condition. For example, dummy variables can be used to indicate

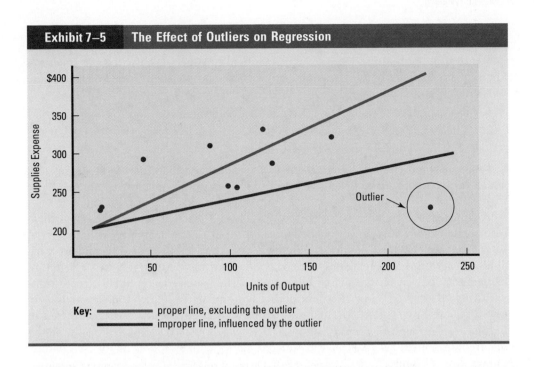

Exhibit 7–5   The Effect of Outliers on Regression

Key: ————— proper line, excluding the outlier
————— improper line, influenced by the outlier

Exhibit 7–6   Independent Variables for Selected Dependent Variables
Types of Independent Variables: Financial, Operating, Economic, and Other

Selected Dependent Variables	Financial Data	Operating Data	Economic Indicators	Other
1. Overhead expense	1. Materials cost 2. Labor cost	1. Machine-hours 2. Labor-hours		1. Activity or cost center
2. Inventory level	1. Sales	1. Size of store 2. Store type	1. Price level index 2. Index of local economic conditions	1. Dummy variable for difference in management policy
3. Labor expense	1. Total expenses 2. Sales or cost of goods	1. Hours worked 2. Dummy variable for changes in labor mix 3. Production level		1. Trend variable 2. Dummy variable for significant work stoppage or pay rate change
4. Utilities expense	1. Sales or cost of good manufactured	1. Average daily temperature 2. Dummy variable for plant additions 3. Production level		1. Dummy variable for significant change in utility rate 2. Trend variable
5. General expenses— office salaries and supplies, telephone, printing and duplicating, and repairs	1. Sales 2. Total expenses 3. Net fixed assets	1. Store type 2. Store size 3. Number of employees	1. Index of local price level	1. Age of store 2. Dummy variable for differences in office management-automation

seasonality. If the management accountant is estimating costs of production, and if production is always high in March, then a dummy variable with a value of one for March and zero for the other months could be used.

Evaluating a Regression Analysis

In addition to a cost estimate, regression analysis also provides several statistical measures of its precision and reliability. Precision refers to the accuracy of the estimates from the regression, and reliability indicates whether the regression reflects actual relationships among the variables. These measures can aid management accountants in assessing the usefulness of the regression.

Regression analysis produces several statistical measures. The three key measures are explained briefly here. These and other statistical measures are explained more fully in Appendix B.

R-squared is a number between zero and 1, and often it is described as a measure of the explanatory power of the regression; that is, the degree to which changes in the dependent variable can be predicted by changes in the independent variable(s).

The **t-value** is a measure of the reliability of each of the independent variables; that is, the degree to which an independent variable has a valid, stable, long-term relationship with the dependent variable.

Multicollinearity means that two or more independent variables are highly correlated with each other.

Correlation means that a given variable tends to change predictably in the same (or opposite) direction for a given change in the other, correlated variable.

1. R-squared, also called the coefficient of determination.
2. The t-statistic, or t-value.
3. SE, the standard error of the estimate.

R-squared and the t-value are used to measure the reliability of the regression, while the standard error is a useful measure of the precision, or accuracy, of the regression.

R-squared is a number between zero and 1, and often it is described as a measure of the explanatory power of the regression; that is, the degree to which changes in the dependent variable can be predicted by changes in the independent variables. A more reliable regression, then, is one that has a relatively high degree of explanatory power, an R-squared close to 1. When viewed graphically, regressions with high R-squared show the data points lying near the regression line, while in low R-squared regressions, the data points are scattered about, as demonstrated in Exhibit 7–7A (high R-squared) and 7–7B (low R-squared). Most regression analyses involving financial data have R-squared values above .5, and many have values in the .8 to .9 range.[7]

The **t-value** is a measure of the reliability of each of the independent variables. Reliability is the degree to which an independent variable has a valid, stable, long-term relationship with the dependent variable. A relatively small t-value (generally, the t-value should be greater than 2) is an indication of little or no relationship between the independent and dependent variables. A variable with a low t-value should be removed from the regression to simplify the model and because it can lead to less accurate cost estimates.

When there are two or more independent variables, the presence of a low t-value for one or more of these variables is a possible signal of what is called **multicollinearity,** which means that two or more independent variables are highly correlated with each other. As suggested by the name, independent variables are supposed to be independent of each other, and not correlated. **Correlation** among

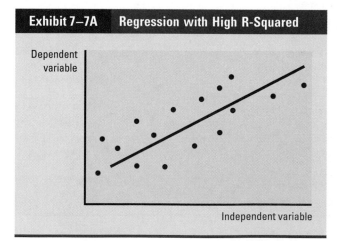

Exhibit 7–7A **Regression with High R-Squared**

Dependent variable

Independent variable

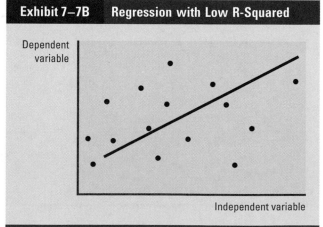

Exhibit 7–7B **Regression with Low R-Squared**

Dependent variable

Independent variable

[7] The square root of R-squared, or simply R, is called the **correlation coefficient** and is interpreted in the same manner as R-squared. The correlation coefficient is a number between −1 and +1, and a value near zero is interpreted as a lack of relationship between the independent and dependent variable. When R is positive, the relationship is direct; that is, when one variable increases, so does the other. When R is negative, the relationship is inverse; that is, when one variable increases, the other decreases.

variables means that a given variable tends to change predictably in the same (or opposite) direction for a given change in the other variable. For example, the number of machine-hours used in manufacturing is correlated with the number of labor-hours because both are affected by the same factor, the number of units produced. Moreover, because there tends to be a common trend affecting many types of financial data, it is common for accounting and operating data to be highly correlated.

The effect of multicollinearity is that the regression is less reliable and the estimates less accurate. Thus, when a management accountant has reason to believe that two or more of the variables in the equation are correlated and the t-values are relatively low, then additional regressions that remove one or more of these independent variables should be considered.

The **standard error of the estimate (SE)** is a measure of the accuracy of the regression's estimates. It is a range around the regression estimate in which we can be reasonably sure that the unknown actual value will fall. For example, if the regression estimate is $4,500, and the SE is $500, then there is reasonable confidence that the unknown actual value lies in the range $4,500 +/− $500, that is, between $4,000 and $5,000.[8]

Because it is used to measure a confidence range, the SE must be interpreted by its relationship to the average size of the dependent variable. If the SE is small relative to the dependent variable, then the precision of the regression can be assessed as relatively good. How small the SE value has to be for a favorable precision evaluation is a matter of judgment, but a threshold of approximately 5 to 10 percent of the average of the dependent variable can be used. The confidence ranges for two regressions are illustrated in Exhibit 7–8A (good precision) and 7–8B (relatively poor precision).

Note also from Exhibits 7–8A and 7–8B that the SE value increases as points on the regression line move farther in either direction from the mean of the independent variable. This is consistent with the concept of the relevant range. The estimate is most accurate near the mean of the independent variable and less accurate the farther it is from the mean.

> The **standard error of the estimate (SE)** is a measure of the accuracy of the regression's estimates.

Using Regression to Estimate Maintenance Costs

We continue the case developed earlier, Ben Garcia's estimation of maintenance costs. Following the six steps outlined in the first section of the chapter, Garcia has

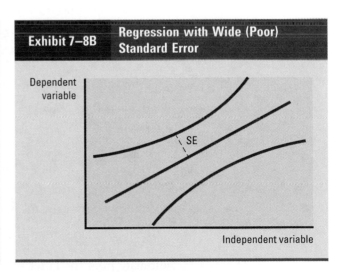

Exhibit 7–8A	Regression with Narrow (Good) Standard Error

Exhibit 7–8B	Regression with Wide (Poor) Standard Error

---

8   The standard error of the estimate provides a quantitative measure of the confidence one has with the accuracy of the estimate. See Appendix B for a more detailed explanation. An excellent discussion of the standard error and other regression measures, including a spreadsheet illustration, is provided in Adel M. Novin, "Applying Overhead: How to Find the Right Bases and Rates," *Management Accounting*, March 1992, pp. 40–43.

defined the cost object and the relevant cost driver as maintenance cost and operating hours, respectively. He also has collected and graphed the data (Exhibit 7–3). The next step is to solve the regression using regression software such as the EXCEL spreadsheet program, with the following findings (Y represents maintenance cost and H represents operating hours):

$$Y = \$15,843 + \$2.02 \times H$$

Garcia expects there will be approximately 3,600 operating hours in 19X8, so the amount of maintenance cost for 19X8 is estimated to be:

$$Y = \$15,843 + \$2.02 \times 3,600 = \$23,115$$

The statistical measures are

R-squared = .461

t-value = 2.07

Standard error of the estimate = $221.71

Ratio of SE to the mean of the dependent variable = .98%

Garcia notes that R-squared is less than .5, the t-value is greater than 2, and the SE is approximately 1 percent of the mean of the dependent variable. The SE and t-values are very good. However, since the R-squared is low (R-squared should be closer to .8 or .9), Garcia asks his accounting assistant, Kim Jan, to review the regression.

Jan looks at the regression and the related graphs and comments immediately that in 19X5 there was a significant drop in maintenance cost, and a modest drop in operating hours as well. Garcia observes that the drop in 19X5 was probably due to the unusually poor economic conditions that year; thus output was reduced and operating hours and maintenance fell accordingly. Recalling that dummy variables can be used to correct for isolated variations and seasonal or other patterns, Jan suggests that Garcia run the regression again with a dummy variable having a value of 1 in 19X5 and a value of zero otherwise (the symbol D represents this variable). The new regression is as follows:

$$Y = \$16,467 + \$1.856 \times H - \$408.638 \times D$$

With the revised regression, the estimate of maintenance costs for 19X8 is as follows (assuming no unusual unfavorable event in 19X8, and thus $D = 0$):

$$Y = \$16,467 + \$1.856 \times 3,600 - \$408.638 \times 0$$
$$= \$23,149$$

And the statistical measures are:

R-squared = .772

t-values:

  Hours: 2.60

  Dummy Variable: −2.33

Standard error of the estimate (SE) = $ 161.27

Ratio of SE to the mean of the dependent variable = .71%

Garcia observes that the inclusion of the dummy variable improves R-squared, the t-values, and the SE of the regression. For this reason, he should rely on the estimate from the latter regression.

Using Spreadsheet Software for Regression Analysis

Suppose WinDoor Inc. is developing a regression cost equation for the indirect costs in its plant. WinDoor manufactures windows and doors used in home construction; both products are made in standard and custom sizes. Occasionally, a very large order substantially increases the direct and indirect costs in a given month. The indirect costs are made up primarily of supplies, quality control and testing, overtime, and other indirect labor. Regression is to be used in budgeting indirect costs for the coming year, primarily for cash management purposes. The management accountant, Charlotte Williams, knows from prior years that both labor-hours and machine-hours in the plant are good independent variables for estimating indirect costs. She gathers the data in Exhibit 7–9 for the most recent 31 months.

Williams develops the regression for these data using a spreadsheet program, EXCEL. To use EXCEL, she selects **Regression** from the Tools/Data Analysis menu, then selects the X and Y ranges for the independent and dependent variables, and obtains the regression results in Exhibit 7–10 (where L represents labor-hours and M represents machine-hours):

$$Y = \$10,635 + \$67.944 \times L + \$33.166 \times M$$

And the statistical measures are:

R-squared = .85

t-values:

Labor-hours: 4.98

Machine-hours: 2.22

Standard error of the estimate (SE) = \$28,194

Ratio of SE to mean of the dependent variable = 10%

The regression satisfies our statistical criteria—R-squared is relatively high at .85, and the t-values and SE are good. Thus, WinDoor can use the regression for estimates with a reasonable degree of confidence.

Exhibit 7–9	Indirect Costs, Labor- and Machine-Hours for WinDoor Inc.		
Date	**Total Indirect Costs**	**Labor-Hours**	**Machine-Hours**
June 19X0	$274,500	2,694	2,009
July	320,000	3,569	3,057
August	323,200	3,258	3,523
September	219,900	2,458	1,856
October	232,100	1,995	2,168
November	342,300	3,433	3,056
December	427,800	4,318	3,848
January 19X1	231,000	2,129	1,999
February	257,300	2,843	2,290
March	248,700	2,466	1,894
April	248,400	2,787	2,134
May	338,400	3,194	3,145
June	294,500	2,642	1,874
July	275,800	3,125	2,865
August	339,400	3,334	2,435
September	225,400	1,888	1,893
October	276,300	2.767	2,232
November	324,500	3,226	3,078
December	457,600	4,593	3,811
January 19X2	210,300	2,041	2,195
February	205,600	2,673	2,045
March	487,400	4,215	3,445
April	278,400	2,345	2,453
May	234,500	1,872	1,720
June	291,200	2,876	2,216
July	209,300	2,446	1,934
August	287,300	3,334	1,783
September	256,300	2,434	1,977
October	238,400	2,452	2,090
November	247,600	2,329	2,189
December	236,400	2,755	2,093

Exhibit 7–10	EXCEL Regression Results for WinDoor Data					
SUMMARY OUTPUT						
Regression Statistics						
Multiple R	0.9222					
R Square	0.8504					
Adjusted R Square	0.8397					
Standard Error	28193.9143					
Observations	31					
ANOVA						
	df	*SS*	*MS*	*F*	*Sig. F*	
Regression	2	1.2653E+11	63263803112	79.587442	2.810226E-12	
Residual	28	2.2257E+10	794896805.4			
Total	30	1.4878E+11				
	Coeff.	*Std Err*	*t Stat*	*P-value*	*Lower 95%*	*Upper 95%*
Intercept	10635.777	22340.289	0.476	0.638	-35126.282	56397.84
Labor Hours	67.944	13.635	4.983	0.000	40.014	95.874
Machine Hours	33.166	14.942	2.220	0.035	2.560	63.773

DATA REQUIREMENTS AND IMPLEMENTATION PROBLEMS

LEARNING OBJECTIVE 4 ▶
Explain the data requirements and implementation problems of the cost estimation methods.

To develop a cost estimate using regression, or any of the other estimation methods, management accountants must consider those aspects of data collection that can significantly affect precision and reliability. Three main issues are (1) data accuracy, (2) the choice of the time period, and (3) nonlinearity.

Data Accuracy

All the methods previously explained rely on the accuracy of the data used in the estimation. Whether it be financial data, operating data, or economic indicators (examples shown in Exhibit 7–6), management must carefully consider the source of the data and its reliability. If the source is inside the firm (usually financial and operating data), management can develop reporting requirements to ensure the accuracy of the data. For external economic data, the firm determines the reliability of data by considering the source. For example, trade and industry associations commonly provide industry and economic data for association members; by reputation, some providers are more reliable than others. Also, economic data are available from the U.S. government, local and state governments, as well as research firms and universities; again some have better reputations for accuracy than do others. Management accountants must judge how much to rely on the data used in the estimation method.

Selecting the Time Period

1. **Mismatched time periods.** The data for each of the variables must be from the same time period. Mixing biweekly and monthly data would be a problem, as would using data for sales based on the calendar month and data for wages expense based on four consecutive weekly periods. Difficulties also arise when supplies are purchased in one period and used in the next.

These problems are most likely to appear where (1) a cash basis is used for accounting rather than an accrual basis, (2) significant lags in the recording of transactions make the data available to the management accountant incomplete and inaccurate, or (3) the data contain errors because transactions of one accounting period are recorded in another. Management accountants may have to reconstruct data so time periods are consistent.

2.   Length of time period. The period can vary from daily or weekly to annual. If the period is too short, there is a greater chance of mismatch as just described because of recording lags or recording errors. If the period is too long, important relationships in the data might be averaged out, and the regression will therefore not show much explanatory power. Moreover, a longer period reduces the number of data points needed to improve the standard error and the statistical reliability of the regression. Management accountants must spend some time considering which time period best satisfies the competing objectives for a reliable and precise regression.

Nonlinearity Problems

Other problems arise because of nonlinearity due to certain time-series patterns to the data. These patterns are trend, seasonality, shift, outliers, and fixed costs.

1.   Trend and/or seasonality. A common characteristic of accounting data is a significant trend due to changing prices and/or seasonality that can affect the precision and reliability of the estimate. When trend or seasonality is present, a management accountant can use a variety of techniques to deseasonalize or to detrend a variable. The most common techniques include:

- Use of a price change index to adjust the values of each variable to some common time period.
- Use of a decomposition technique that extracts the seasonal, cyclical, and trend components of the data series.[9]

BusinessWeek

Does Effective Cost Estimation Require Magic?
(Continues from page 201)

A: Not if you've got accurate data to start with . . .
Chrysler Corporation uses cost estimation methods to project the cost of materials to be used in manufacturing its products. The consumer price index (CPI) is a significant predictor variable in the Chrysler method. Unfortunately, the consumer price index is systematically in error, sometimes by as much as 100%. One reason is that the official U.S. government statistics on prices fail to take into account important changes in consumer buying patterns, improvements in the quality of products, and improvements in the functionality of products. For example, a product may cost a little more than a few years ago, but its quality and functionality make it a bargain relative to the prior year's product; the relevant price may have really dropped significantly. Also, consumers may have moved on to other products. Thus, Chrysler's ability to accurately predict its materials costs is limited by the inaccuracy of the CPI, which is an important input in the estimation method.

Similarly, Texas Instruments, Inc. (TI), relies upon industrial production statistics from the U.S. government in projecting revenues in its different product lines. These statistics are biased because they rely upon electricity consumption to measure industrial production, an approach termed "prehistoric" by TI's chief economist, Vladi Catto. Other distortions arise due to confusing and inconsistent means used to measure imports and exports, and biases in measuring capacity utilization and productivity in U.S. factories. Firms like TI and Chrysler find it difficult to develop accurate estimates of costs and revenues when key economic indicators are unreliable.

For further reading, see the following source: "The Real Truth about the Economy," *Business Week,* November 7, 1994, pp. 110–118.

---

[9]   An explanation of the decomposition of time series is beyond the scope of this introductory material. Decomposition is presented in basic texts on probability and statistics, such as *Introductory Statistics* by Sheldon Ross (New York: McGraw-Hill, 1996).

| Exhibit 7–11 | Adjusting for Trend and Seasonality Using First Differences or a Price Index | | |

| | | Price Index Adjustment | |
| | | Hypothetical Price Index for Supplies Expense | Supplies Expense Adjusted for Price Index |
Supplies Expense	First Differences		
$250	—	1.00	$250/1.00 = $250
310	$60	1.08	310/1.08 = 287
325	15	1.12	325/1.12 = 290

A **trend variable** is a variable that takes on values of 1, 2, 3, . . . for each period in sequence.

First differences for each variable are the difference between each value and the succeeding value in the time series.

- Addition of a trend variable. A **trend variable** takes on values of 1, 2, 3, . . . for each period in sequence.
- Replacement of the original values of each of the variables with the first differences. **First differences** for each variable are the difference between each value and the succeeding value in the time series.

You can see the index approach and the first differences approach in Exhibit 7–11, using the supplies expense data from Exhibit 7–2. Note that when either of these approaches is used, the data must be retransformed (transformed back into the original scale or units) in preparing the cost estimate.

Trend is present in virtually all financial time series data used in management accounting because of inflation and growth in the economy. Thus, it is a pervasive issue in the proper development of an estimate.

2. Outliers. As mentioned earlier, when an error in the data or an unusual or nonrecurring business condition affects operations for a given period, the result may be a data point that is far from the others, an outlier. Because outliers can significantly decrease the precision and reliability of the estimate, they should be corrected or adjusted (using, for example, a dummy variable) if it is clear that they are unusual or nonrecurring.

3. Data Shift. In contrast to the outlier, if the unusual business condition is long lasting, such as the introduction of new production technology or other permanent change, there is a distinct shift in the average direction of the data, and this shift should be included in the estimate. One way to handle this is the use of a dummy variable to indicate the periods before and after the shift.

SUMMARY

In the current dynamic environment of business, it is important that managers have accurate and timely estimates of product and service costs. This chapter presents five estimation methods. The first three are the account classification, visual fit, and high-low methods; although relatively simple to employ, these methods have relatively limited accuracy. The account classification method uses the accountant's classification of ledger cost accounts as either variable or fixed costs to develop the estimation equation as fixed cost plus average per unit variable cost. The visual fit method requires the accountant to graph the data and to visually draw in the estimation equation. The high-low method is superior to the other two because it develops a unique estimation equation using algebra and the representative low and high points in the data.

Two statistical methods also are presented—work measurement and regression analysis. Work measurement is a study of a work activity to measure the time or input required per unit of output. Regression analysis is a statistical method that obtains a unique best-fitting line for the data. The chapter's focus is on the proper interpretation of the three key measures of the precision and reliability of the regression: R-squared, the t-value, and the standard error of the estimate.

APPENDIX A

Learning Curve Analysis

One prominent example of nonlinear cost behavior is costs influenced by learning. When an activity has a certain labor component, and repetition of the same activity or operation makes the labor more proficient, the task is completed more quickly with the same or higher level of quality. Learning can occur in a wide variety of ways, from the individual level as new employees gain experience, to the aggregate level where a group of employees experiences improvement in productivity. We consider the latter instance in this appendix.

Costs are affected by learning in a wide variety of contexts, especially in large-scale production settings, such as the manufacture of airplanes and ships. In each of these cases, it is possible to model the expected improvement in productivity and to use this information in the estimation of future costs. A **learning curve analysis** is a systematic method for estimating costs when learning is present.

One of the first well-documented applications of learning curves was in the World War II aircraft industry.[10] Studies showed that the total time to manufacture two airplanes declined by approximately 20 percent of the total time without learning. In other words, the average *per-unit* time to build the first two units was 80 percent of the time for the first unit. For example, if the time to build the first unit is 20 hours, then the *average* time to build the first two units would be 16 hours (20 × .8), or a total of 32 hours (16 × 2) for two units. Without learning it would take 40 hours (20 × 2). The **learning rate** is the percentage by which average time (or total time) falls from previous levels, as output doubles. In this example the rate is 80 percent. The unit cost behavior of the learning curve is illustrated in Exhibit 7–12.

Additional evidence of the practical importance of learning curves is the common reference to start-up costs in corporate annual reports and the financial press. It is commonly accepted in business that new products and production processes have a period of low productivity followed by increasing productivity. Thereafter, the rate of improvement in productivity tends to decline over time until it reaches some equilibrium level, where the rate remains relatively stable until there is another change in the product line or production process.[11]

Learning Curves in Software Development

SofTech, Inc., is a software vendor for financial analysts. SofTech's development staff recently changed from its present development language, T-Base, to a new language, Z-Base, that permits faster development and provides certain object-oriented programming benefits. Now SofTech is figuring the learning time needed to get its programmers up-to-speed in the new language. These estimates are important because programming costs have increased 10 percent to $65 per hour in the past year and are expected to rise as quickly in the coming years. For purposes of this analysis, SofTech uses the convention of 500 lines of programming code as a unit of output. It estimates that the learning rate for Z-Base will be 80 percent and the initial time for coding 500 lines of good code in Z-Base will be 100 hours. The time

◄ **LEARNING OBJECTIVE 5**
Use learning curves in cost estimation when learning is present.

A **learning curve analysis** is a systematic method for estimating costs when learning is present.

The **learning rate** is the percentage by which average time (or total time) falls from previous levels, as output doubles.

---

[10] Frank J. Andress, "The Learning Curve as a Production Tool," *Harvard Business Review*, January–February 1954; and Harold Asher, "Cost Quality Relationships in the Airframe Industry," Report R–291 (Santa Monica, CA: The RAND Corporation, July 1956).

[11] As in the World War II airplane production example, the common learning rate is approximately 80 percent. There are two conventional models used in learning curve analysis. One measures learning on the basis of average unit cost; the other is based on marginal cost. Both models are conceptually and mathematically similar, though the average cost model tends to lead to lower unit costs. The average cost model is the most common, and for clarity and simplicity it is the only model we present here. For a full explanation and comparison of the two models, see J. Chen and R. Manes, "Distinguishing the Two Forms of the Constant Percentage Learning Curve Model," *Contemporary Accounting Research*, Spring 1985, pp. 242–52.

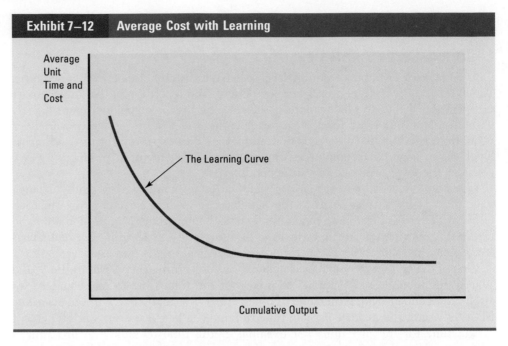

Exhibit 7–12   Average Cost with Learning

Average Unit Time and Cost

The Learning Curve

Cumulative Output

Exhibit 7–13   Softech, Inc.'s Learning Curve for Z-Base

Cumulative Output	Average Time	Total Time
1 unit (= 500 lines)	100 hours	100 hours
2 units (= 1,000 lines)	100 × .8 = 80 hours	80 × 2 = 160 hours
4 units (= 2,000 lines)	80 × .8 = 64 hours	64 × 4 = 256 hours
8 units (= 4,000 lines)	64 × .8 = 51.2 hours	51.2 × 8 = 409.6 hours

and related cost required for developing the first 4,000-line application in Z-Base can be determined by using the learning curve; see Exhibit 7–13.

Learning rates are obtained through the review and analysis of historical data. The methods vary from the simple high-low method to regression analysis based on fitting a nonlinear relationship to the historical data.[12]

Note that the learning curve has a more general application than we present here. For example, the learning rate can be derived and applied for any set increment in output, not only the output-doubling assumption shown here. However, since the 80 percent with output-doubling approach is commonly used, it is the model presented here.

Note also that a learning rate of *1.0 is equivalent to no learning. A learning rate of .5 is best interpreted as the maximum learning rate* because the total time for actual production is equal to the time for a single unit. Thus, the learning rate is always a number greater than .5 and less than 1.0. Actual case studies reveal the learning rate most often falls near .8.

---

[12] For example, to estimate the parameters of the model, *a* and *b*, using the high-low method, select two appropriate points and determine the learning equation for each point. Then substitute *a* for *b* and take the log of both sides of the new equation. Then solve for *b*. To determine the learning rate necessary to achieve a given level of output within a certain time limitation, use the methods described in Patrick B. McKenzie, "An Alternative Learning Curve Formula," *Issues in Accounting Education*, Fall 1987, pp. 383–88; and C. Carl Pegels, "Start Up or Learning Curves—Some New Approaches," *Decision Sciences*, October 1976, pp. 705–13.

Learning Helps Quality at Chrysler

The learning effect can help a firm improve quality as well as productivity. For example, at Chrysler, higher levels of quality were achieved for the second year of production on the new car, the Prowler. Reporters for the magazine, *Car and Driver,* indicated that the new Prowler seemed more solid. When asked about this, Plymouth officials reported that the difference was not due to design changes but to the increasing expertise of the assembly line workers.

Source: Based on information in "The Prowler Gets More Growl," *Car and Driver,* April 1998, p. 25.

What Decisions Are Influenced by Learning?

Because the productivity of labor is a vital aspect of any production process, learning curve analysis can be an important way to improve the quality of a wide range of decisions.[13] For example, when product prices are based in part on costs, learning curves would be used when a new product is introduced to determine a life-cycle plan for product pricing. Moreover, learning curves would be helpful in these areas:

1. **The make or buy decision (Chapter 10).** When the cost to make a part is affected by learning, the analysis can be used to more accurately reflect the total cost over time of the make option.

2. **Preparation of bids for production contracts; life-cycle costing (Chapter 5).** Here learning curves play an important role in ensuring that the contract cost estimates are accurate over the life of the contract.

3. **Cost-volume-profit analysis (Chapter 8).** The determination of a breakeven point might be significantly influenced by the presence of learning.[14] Failing to consider learning causes overstatement of the actual number of units required for breakeven.

4. **Development of standard product costs (Chapters 15 and 16).** When learning is present, standard costs will change over time, and the appropriate labor costs must be adjusted on a timely basis.[15]

5. **Capital budgeting (Chapter 11).** Learning curves capture cost behavior more accurately over the life of the capital investment, by including the expected improvements in labor productivity due to learning.

6. **Budgeting production levels and labor needs (Chapter 9).** Another useful application of learning curves is the development of the annual or quarterly production plan and related labor requirement budget. When the activity or operation is affected by learning, the production and labor budgets need to be adjusted accordingly.

7. **Management control (Chapters 18 and 19).** The use of learning curves is important in properly evaluating managers when costs are affected by learning. The evaluation should recognize the pattern of relatively higher costs at the early phase of the product life cycle.

Limitations of Learning Curve Analysis

Although learning curve analysis can significantly enhance the ability to predict costs when learning is present, three inherent limitations and problems are associated with the use of this method.

---

[13] A useful summary of applications of learning curves is presented by Eugene A. Imhoff Jr., "The Learning Curve and Its Applications," *Management Accounting*, February 1978, pp. 44–46.

[14] Edward V. McIntyre, "Cost-Volume-Profit Analysis Adjusted for Learning," *Management Science*, October 1977, pp. 149–60.

[15] Jackson F. Gillespie, "An Application of Learning Curves to Standard Costing," *Management Accounting*, September 1981, pp. 63–65.

The first and key limitation of using learning curves is that the approach is most appropriate for repetitive tasks, for which repeated trials improve performance, or learning. When the production process is designed to maximize flexibility and very fast set-up times for manufacturing machinery, using robotics and computer controls as many manufacturers do now, the manufacturing setting requires relatively little repetitive labor. When there is little repetitive labor, there is relatively little opportunity for learning. Learning curves are most applicable in labor-intensive contexts, where long production runs and repetition of tasks present the opportunity for continued learning.

A second limitation is that the learning rate is assumed to be constant (average labor time decreases at a fixed rate as output doubles). In actual applications the decline in labor time may not be constant. For example, the learning rate may be 80 percent for the first 20,000 units, 90 percent for the next 35,000 units, and 95 percent thereafter. Such differences indicate the recurring need to update projections based on the observed progression of learning.

Third, a carefully estimated learning curve might be unreliable because the observed change in productivity in the data used to fit the model was actually associated with factors other than learning. For example, the increase in productivity might have been due to a change in labor mix, a change in product mix, or some combination of other related factors. In such cases the learning model is unreliable and produces inaccurate estimates of labor time and cost.

APPENDIX B

Regression Analysis

LEARNING OBJECTIVE 6 ▶
Use statistical measures to evaluate a regression analysis.

This appendix uses an example to explain how a regression estimate and the related statistical measures are developed. Then, we interpret the statistical measures to assess the precision and reliability of the regression.

Simple Linear Regression

Simple linear regression is based on a single independent variable, in contrast to multiple regression, which includes two or more independent variables. Many of the statistical issues are the same for both types, though lack of independence among the independent variables (multicollinearity) is a concern in multiple regression analysis only.

The Regression Estimate

To illustrate the manner in which a regression estimate is obtained we use the data in Exhibit 7–4. Recall that regression analysis finds the unique line through the data that minimizes the sum of the squares of the errors, where the error is measured as the difference between the values predicted by the regression and the actual values for the dependent variable. In this example, the dependent variable, supplies expense (Y), is estimated with a single independent variable, production level (X). The regression for the three data points is

$$Y = a + b \times X = \$220 + \$.75 \times X$$

The intercept term, labeled a, and the coefficient of the independent variable, labeled b, are obtained from a set of calculations performed by spreadsheet programs and are described in basic textbooks on probability and statistics.[16] The calculations themselves are beyond the scope of this text. Our focus is on the derivation and interpretation of the statistical measures that tell management accountants something about the reliability and precision of the regression.

---

[16]   See, for example, Sheldon Ross, *Introductory Statistics* (New York: McGraw-Hill, 1996).

Statistical Measures

The statistical measures of the reliability and precision of the regression are derived from an analysis of the variance of the dependent variable. Variance is a measure of the degree to which the values of the dependent variable vary about its mean. The term *analysis of variance* is used because the regression analysis is based on a separation of the total variance of the dependent variable into error and explained components. The underlying concept is that in predicting individual values for the dependent variable, the regression is *explaining changes in the dependent variable* associated with changes in the independent variable. What is not explained is called the residual, or *error variance*. Thus, the regression's ability to correctly predict changes in the dependent variable is a key measure of its reliability, and is measured by the proportion of explained to error variances. How the variance measures are obtained is shown in Exhibit 7–14, based on the data in Exhibit 7–4.

The first two columns of Exhibit 7–14 show the data for the independent (X) and dependent (Y) variables. Column (3) shows the mean of the dependent variable (YM), and column (4) the regression prediction (YE) for each of the points. The last three columns indicate the three variance measures. Column (5) shows the total variance, or variance of the dependent variable, measured as the difference between each data point and the mean of the dependent variable ($Y - YM$). Column (6) shows the variance explained by the regression ($YE - YM$), and column (7) shows the error variance, ($Y - YE$). The measures in these last three columns are squared and summed to arrive at the desired values for *total* variance, explained variance, and error variance, respectively. The sum of the error and explained variance terms equals total variance. These terms are illustrated in Exhibit 7–15 and the values calculated in Exhibit 7–16.

Exhibit 7–14	Variance Components for Regression Analysis					
1	2	3	4	5	6	7
Dependent Variable Y	Independent Variable X	Mean of Y (YM)	Regression Prediction for Y (YE)	Total Variance of Y $(T) = (Y - YM)$	Regression Variance $(M) = (YE - YM)$	Error Variance $(E) = (Y - YE)$
250	50	295	257.5	(45)	(37.5)	(7.5)
310	100	295	295	15	0	15
325	150	295	332.5	30	37.5	(7.5)

Exhibit 7–15	Variance Components for Regression Analysis

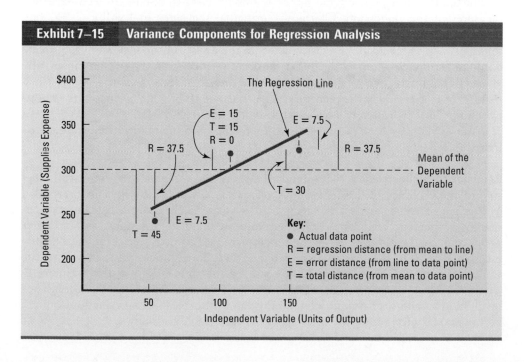

223

Exhibit 7–16	Analysis of Variance Table for Regression Analysis		
Source of Variance	Variance of Each Component of the Regression (Also called sum of squares)	Degrees of Freedom	Mean Squared Variance
Explained (Regression)	$37.5^2 + 0^2 + 37.5^2 = 2{,}812.5$	1	2,812.5
Error	$7.5^2 + 15^2 + 7.5^2 = 337.5$	1	337.5
Total	$(45)^2 + (15)^2 + (30)^2 = 3{,}150$	2	1,575

Exhibit 7–17	Six Key Statistical Measures

Precision

1. Precision of the regression (measured by the standard error of the estimate)

Reliability (and how measured)

2. Goodness of fit (R-squared)
3. Statistical reliability (F-statistic)
4. Statistical reliability for each independent variable (t-value)
5. Reliability of precision (Rank-order correlation)
6. Nonindependence of errors (Durbin-Watson statistic)

The **analysis of variance table** separates the total variance of the dependent variable into both error and explained variance components.

The **degrees of freedom** for each component of variance represent the number of independent choices that can be made for that component.

Mean squared variance is the ratio of the amount of variance of a component to the number of degrees of freedom for that component.

The three variance terms are the basic elements of the statistical analysis of the regression. This is best illustrated in the analysis of variance table in Exhibit 7–16. The **analysis of variance table** separates the total variance of the dependent variable into both error and explained components. The first two columns of the table show the type and amount of variance for each of the three variance terms. The third column shows the **degrees of freedom** for each component, which represents the number of independent choices that can be made for that component. Thus, the number of degrees of freedom for the explained variance component is always equal to the number of independent variables, and the total degrees of freedom is always equal to the number of data points less 1. The error degrees of freedom equal the total less the explained degrees of freedom.

The fourth column, **mean squared variance,** is the ratio of the amount of the variance of a component (in the second column) to the number of degrees of freedom (in the third column).

The analysis of variance table serves as a useful basis to discuss the key statistical measures of the regression. Of the six principal measures in Exhibit 7–17, one measure refers to the precision of the regression and five measures refer to the reliability of the regression. Precision refers to the ability of the regression to provide accurate estimates—how close the regression's estimates are to the unknown true value. Reliability refers to the confidence the user can have that the regression is valid; that is, how likely the regression is to continue to provide accurate predictions over time, and for different levels of the independent variables.

After explaining each of the statistical measures, we summarize the explanations in Exhibit 7–20.

Precision of the Regression   The standard error of the estimate (SE) is a useful measure of the accuracy of the regression's estimates. The standard error is interpreted as a range of values around the regression estimate such that we can be approximately 67 percent confident the actual value will lie in this range (see Exhibits 7–8A and 7–8B). As the size of the range increases, so does our confidence in the estimate. For example, doubling the range to two SE distances on each side of the estimate gives approximately a 95 percent confidence range for the estimation. There is an inverse relationship, and therefore a trade-off, between the confidence level and the width of the interval. The value of the SE for a given regression can be obtained directly from the analysis of variance table as follows:

$$SE = \sqrt{\text{Mean Square Error}}$$
$$= \sqrt{337.5} = 18.37$$

The precision and accuracy of the regression improve as the variance for error is reduced and as the number of data points is increased, as illustrated in the above formula for SE.

The standard error of the estimate also can be used to develop confidence intervals for the accuracy of the prediction, as illustrated in Exhibits 7–8A and B. A **confidence interval** is a range around the regression line within which the management accountant can be confident the actual value of the predicted cost will fall. A 67 percent confidence interval is determined by taking the regression line and identifying a range that is one standard error distance on either side of the regression line, while a 95 percent confidence interval would be determined from two standard error distances. Confidence intervals are a useful and precise way for a management accountant to describe the degree of accuracy obtained from the regression.

> A **confidence interval** is a range around the regression line within which the management accountant can be confident the actual value of the predicted cost will fall.

Goodness of Fit (R-squared)   R-squared (also called the coefficient of determination) is a direct measure of the explanatory power of the regression. It measures the percent of variance in the dependent variable that can be explained by the independent variable. R-squared is calculated in Exhibit 7–16:

$$R^2 = \frac{\sum \text{ of squares (explained)}}{\sum \text{ of squares (total)}}$$
$$= \frac{2,812.5}{3,150} = .892$$

The explanatory power of the regression improves as the explained sum of squares increases relative to the total sum of squares. A value close to 1 would reflect a well-fit regression with strong explanatory power.

Statistical Reliability   The **F-statistic** is a useful measure of the statistical reliability of the regression. Statistical reliability asks the question, Does the relationship between the variables in the regression actually exist, or is the correlation between the variables an accident of the data at hand? If only a small number of data points are used, it is possible to have a relatively high R-squared (if the regression is a good fit to the data points), but there is relatively little confidence that an actual stable relationship exists.

> The **F-statistic** is a useful measure of the statistical reliability of the regression.

The larger the F, the less the risk that the regression is statistically unreliable. While the determination of an acceptable F-value depends on the number of data points, the required F-value decreases as the number of data points increases. Most regression software programs will show the F-value and the related risk score, which should be less than approximately 5 percent. The F-statistic can be obtained from the analysis of variance table as follows:

$$F = \frac{\text{mean square (explained)}}{\text{mean square (errors)}}$$
$$= \frac{2,812.5}{337.5} = 8.333$$

The R-squared value and the F-statistic usually tell the same story; that is, they are both favorable or unfavorable. However, if the regression was done with a very large number of data points (a few hundred or more), then it is possible to have a good score for the F-statistic and a poor fit, based on the R-squared value. The number of data points in such a case is so large that the mean square error is very small (and therefore F is large) even though the sum of squares for error is large, and therefore R-squared is poor. In this case, management accountants should interpret the regression as having statistical reliability (it is not by chance), but having perhaps little practical reliability (goodness of fit). That is, the management accountant can be relatively confident that there is a poor regression. The reverse would be true for very small samples. The implication is that R-squared and the F-statistic must be interpreted carefully when the sample size is either very small or very large.

Statistical Reliability for Each of the Independent Variables (t-value) The t-value is a measure of the reliability of each independent variable, and as such it has an interpretation very much like that of the F-statistic. The t-value is equal to the ratio of the coefficient of the independent variable to the standard error of the coefficient for that independent variable. The standard error of the coefficient is not the same as the standard error of the estimate, but it is interpreted in the same way. However, the SE cannot be obtained directly from the analysis of variance table. For the data in Exhibit 7–14, the value of the standard error for the coefficient is .2598.[17] The t-value is thus:

$$t = .75/.2598 = 2.8868$$

A t-value larger than 2 would indicate that the independent variable is reliable at a risk level of approximately 5 percent and is therefore a reliable independent variable to include in the regression.

Reliability of Precision (NonConstant Variance) For certain sets of data, the standard error of the estimate varies over the range of the independent variable. The variance of the errors is not constant over the range of the independent variable. This is the case, for example, when the relationship between the independent and dependent variables becomes less stable over time. This type of behavior is illustrated in Exhibit 7–18.

If this is so, the SE value provided by the regression will not be uniformly accurate. To detect nonconstant variance, we calculate the rank-order correlation

> **Nonconstant variance** is the condition when the variance of the errors is not constant over the range of the independent variable.

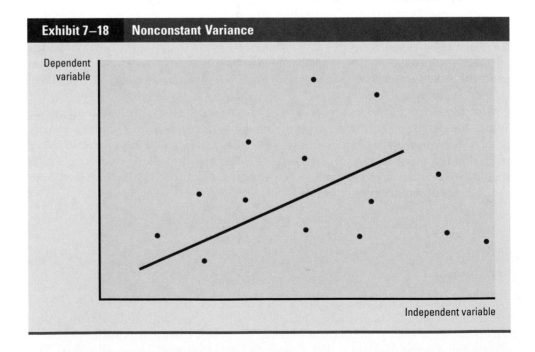

Exhibit 7–18   Nonconstant Variance

Dependent variable

Independent variable

---

[17] The standard error of the coefficient is calculated as:

$$\text{Standard error} = SE/(\text{Std. deviation of the indep. var.})$$

$$= \frac{18.37}{\sqrt{(50 - 100)^2 + (100 - 100)^2 + (150 - 100)^2}} = .2598$$

between the position of the data and the size of the error. The **rank-order correlation** is a statistic that measures the degree to which two sets of numbers tend to have the same order, or rank. A relatively high rank-order correlation would be evidence of nonconstant variance. For the data in Exhibit 7–14, the Spearman rank correlation coefficient is .125, a relatively small correlation that indicates little evidence of nonconstant variance. The calculation of rank-order correlation is beyond the scope of this introductory chapter, but found in many statistics texts.

To fix the problem of nonconstant variance, the management accountant should transform the dependent variable with the log or square root, and see whether this improves the behavior of the errors. If the condition is not fixed, the management accountant should be very cautious in interpreting the SE value.

Nonindependent Errors (Durbin-Watson Statistic) A key assumption of regression is that the relationship between the independent and dependent variables is linear. If the data are nonlinear because of seasonality, or a cyclical pattern, for example, the errors are systematically related to each other; that is, not independent. This assumption is violated frequently because financial data often are affected by trend, seasonality, and cyclical influences. Also, the relationship between the variables might be inherently nonlinear, as when learning is present or when there is a multiplicative rather than an additive relationship (such as predicting payroll costs from hours worked and wage rates). Then the regression is unreliable and subject to greater than expected estimation errors. One type of nonlinearity (nonindependence of errors) is illustrated in Exhibit 7–19.

A common way to detect nonlinearity is to use the **Durbin-Watson (DW) statistic.** The DW statistic is calculated from the amount and change of the errors over the range of the independent variable. The DW value falls between zero and 4; when there are 20 or more data points, a value of DW between approximately 1 and 3 would indicate little chance of a nonlinearity as described earlier, while values less than 1 or greater than 3 should indicate the need to study the data and to choose appropriate fixes if necessary.

The problem of nonindependent errors usually can be fixed by deseasonalizing the data, using a dummy variable for seasonality, or using an index to remove trend. Alternatively, what may be required is to convert a multiplicative relationship to an equivalent additive (that is, linear) relationship by taking the logarithm of the independent and dependent variables. The statistical measures,

The **rank-order correlation** is a statistic that measures the degree to which two sets of numbers tend to have the same order or rank.

The **Durbin-Watson (DW) statistic** is a measure of the extent of nonlinearity in the regression.

Exhibit 7–19 Nonindependence of Errors

227

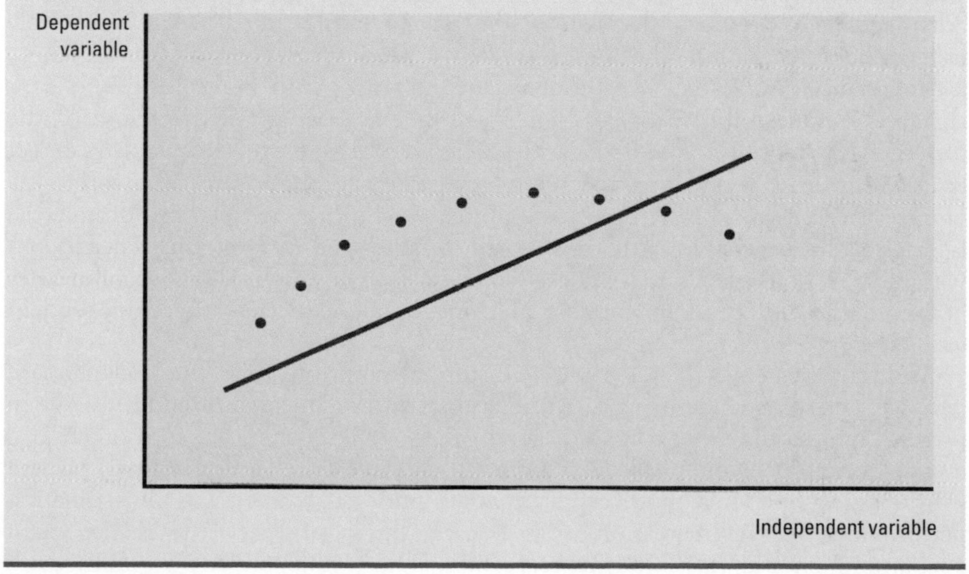

Exhibit 7–20	Summary of Statistical Measures			
Measure Is Concerned with	**Statistical Measure**	**What Is an OK Value?***	**What Is the Right Fix, If Not OK?**	**Consequence If Not Fixed**
Reliability— Goodness of fit	R-squared	Should be approximately .75 or better	* Add or delete independent variables * If DW is poor, may need transforms (lag, log, first differences, . . .) * Correct measurement errors in the data, for example, cutoff errors, or reporting lags (see "Data Requirements and Problems")	* Inaccurate estimates
Statistical reliability for the regression	F-statistic	Depends on sample size	* Increase sample size * Other changes as suggested for reliability—goodness of fit	* Inaccurate estimates
Statistical reliability for the independent variables	t-value	Should be greater than 2	* Delete or transform the independent variable	* Inaccurate estimates
Precision of the regression	Standard error of the estimate (SE)	Should be small relative to the dependent variable—10% or less	* Same considerations as for "reliability—goodness of fit" above	* Inaccurate estimates
Reliability of precision (non-constant variance)	Rank-order correlation	Should be small, less than 30%	* Square root or log transform the dependent variable * Add a dummy variable	*SE is unreliable
Reliability— Potential nonlinearity (nonindependence of errors)	Durbon-Watson statistic (DW)	Between 2 and 3	*For certain time series* * Deseasonalize * Detrend * Use dummy variable for shift *For nonlinear relationship* * Log transform * Some other nonlinear transform	* Inaccurate estimates * SE is unreliable

* The values shown here are useful for a wide range of regressions. The exact values for a specific regression depend on a number of factors including the sample size and the number of independent variables.

their indicators, and how to fix the underlying conditions, are summarized in Exhibit 7–20.

Multiple Linear Regression

Although the previous discussion illustrated simple linear regression (one independent variable), the same concerns are applicable for two or more independent variables. One additional concern arises with multiple independent variables—multicollinearity. Multicollinearity exists when two or more of the independent variables are significantly correlated. There are two ways to detect multicollinearity. A direct approach is to review the correlation values given in the output of the regression. An indirect approach, when the correlation information is not readily accessible, is to review the t-values for each of the independent variables. A nonsignificant t-value is an indication of potential multicollinearity between that independent variable and one or more of the other independent variables.

Multicollinearity violates the regression assumption that the independent variables are independent, that the relationships are linear and additive. When present, multicollinearity can show good values of R-squared, but it also can lead a management accountant to overestimate the degree of reliability actually present in the regression. Thus, multicollinearity does not so much degrade the estimation performance of the regression as it distorts the confidence the management accountant should have in the regression. Thus, independent variables with relatively low t-values should be reviewed for possible exclusion from the regression; these variables tend to add little to the precision or reliability of the regression.

KEY TERMS

SELF-STUDY PROBLEMS

(For solutions, please turn to the end of the chapter.)

1. Using the High-Low Method

Hector's Delivery Service uses four small vans and six pickup trucks to deliver small packages in the metropolitan area of Charlotte, North Carolina. Hector spends a lot of money on the gas, oil, and regular maintenance of his vehicles, which is done at a variety of service stations and repair shops. To budget his vehicle expenses for the coming year, he gathers data on his expenses and number of deliveries for each month of the current year.

	Total Vehicle Expenses	Total Deliveries
January	$145,329	5,882
February	133,245	5,567
March	123,245	5,166
April	164,295	6,621
May	163,937	6,433
June	176,229	6,681
July	180,553	7,182
August	177,293	6,577
September	155,389	5,942
October	150,832	5,622
November	152,993	5,599
December	201,783	7,433

Required Use the high-low estimation method to determine the relationship between the number of deliveries and the cost of maintaining the vehicles.

2. Using Regression Analysis

George Harder is the plant manager of one of the processing plants of the Imperial Foods Company. Harder is concerned about the increase in plant overhead costs in the recent months. He has collected data on overhead costs for the past 24 months and has decided to use regression to study the factors influencing these costs.

He also has collected data on materials cost, direct labor-hours, and machine-hours, as potential independent variables to be used in predicting overhead.

Harder runs two regression analyses on these data, with the following results:

	Regression 1 (Labor-Hours Only)	Regression 2 (Labor-Hours and Machine-Hours)
R-squared	.65	.58
Standard error	$12,554	$13,793
Standard error as a percent of the dependent variable	12%	14%
t-values:		
Materials cost	2.0	−1.6
Labor-hours	4.5	3.8
Machine-hours		1.4

Required Which of the two regressions is better and why?

3. Using Both High-Low and Regression

The John Meeks Company is a medium-size manufacturing company with plants in three small mid-Atlantic towns. The company makes plastic parts for automobiles and trucks, primarily door panels, exterior trim, and related items. The parts have an average cost of $5 to $20. Meeks has a steady demand for its products from both domestic and foreign automakers and has experienced growth in sales averaging between 10 and 20 percent over the last 8 to 10 years.

Currently, management is reviewing the incidence of scrap and waste in the manufacturing process at one of its plants. Scrap and waste is defined for Meeks as any defective unit that is rejected for lack of functionality or another aspect of quality. The plants have a number of different inspection points, and failure or rejection can occur at any of the inspection points. The number of defective units is listed in the table; management estimates that the cost of this waste in labor and materials is approximately $10 per unit.

There appears to be an unfavorable trend with regard to defects, and management has asked you to investigate, and to estimate the defective units in the coming months. A first step in your investigation is to identify the cost drivers of defective parts, to understand what causes them, and to provide a basis on which to estimate future defects. For this purpose you have obtained these recent data on the units produced, the units shipped, and the cost of sales, since these numbers are easily available and relatively reliable on a monthly basis:

	Units Produced (000s)	Cost of Sales (000s)	Units Shipped (000s)	Defective Units
Jan 19X5	55	689	50	856
Feb	58	737	53	1,335
Mar	69	886	64	1,610
Apr	61	768	56	1,405
May	65	828	60	1,511
Jun	69	878	64	1,600
Jul	75	962	70	1,570
Aug	81	1052	76	1,910
Sep	70	1104	80	2,011
Oct	79	1224	89	2,230
Nov	82	1261	92	2,300
Dec	70	1020	74	1,849
Jan 19X6	67	850	62	1,549
Feb	72	916	67	1,669
Mar	85	1107	80	2,012
Apr	75	968	70	1,756
May	81	1037	76	1,889
Jun	85	1103	80	1,650

Jul	92	1208	87	2,187
Aug	100	1310	95	2,387
Sep	91	1380	101	2,514
Oct	101	1536	111	2,787
Nov	105	1580	115	2,310
Dec	88	1270	92	2,311

Required Use the high-low method and regression analysis to estimate the defective units in the coming months and to determine which method provides the best fit for this purpose.

QUESTIONS

7–1   Define cost estimation and explain its purpose in each of the management functions.

7–2   Explain the assumptions used in cost estimation.

7–3   List the five methods of cost estimation. Explain the advantages and disadvantages of each.

7–4   Explain the implementation problems in cost estimation.

7–5   What are the six steps in cost estimation? Which one is the most important? Why?

7–6   Contrast how regression analysis and the high-low method are used to estimate costs.

7–7   How would cost estimation be used in activity-based costing?

7–8   Explain how to choose the dependent and independent variables in regression analysis.

7–9   What are nonlinear cost relationships? Give two examples.

7–10 List four advantages of regression analysis.

7–11 Explain what dummy variables are and how they are used in regression analysis.

7–12 How do we know when high correlation exists? Is high correlation the same as cause and effect?

7–13 What does the coefficient of determination (R-squared) measure?

7–14 Cost Classification

Required Match each of the costs described below to the appropriate cost behavior pattern shown in the graphs (a) through (l).

1. The cost of lumber used in the manufacture of wooden kitchen tables.

2. The cost of order-fillers in a warehouse. When demand increases, the number of order-fillers is increased, and when demand falls off, the number of order-fillers is decreased.

3. The salary of the quality control inspector in the plant, who inspects each batch of products.

4. The cost of water and sewer service to the manufacturing plant. The local municipality charges a fixed rate per gallon for usage up to 10,000 gallons, and a higher charge per gallon for usage above that point.

5. The cost of an Internet connection, which is $23.00 per month.

6. The cost of an Internet connection which is $10.00 per month plus $2 per hour of usage above 10 hours' usage.

7. The cost for making copies of a given document at a printing shop that reduces the per-copy charge for customers who make more than 100 copies of the document.

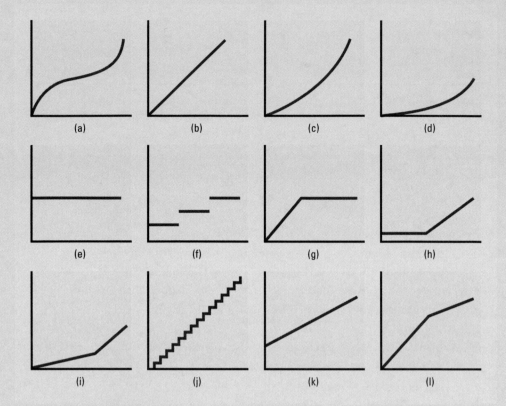

8. The total cost of manufacturing a new camera, over the entire life cycle of the camera.

9. To discourage excess usage and to level the demand, especially in peak load times, the local electric utility increases the per-kilowatt-hour charge for each additional 5,000 kilowatt-hours' usage.

10. The rental charge for a clothing store in the SunnyVale Mall is a fixed charge of $1,000 per month plus 2 percent of gross sales receipts.

11. The cost of repair for a machine used in manufacturing.

12. The rental charge for a shoe store in the SunnyVale Mall is 6 percent of gross sales receipts, up to a maximum of $3,000 per month.

PROBLEMS

7–15 COST ESTIMATION; HIGH-LOW METHOD Elias Manufacturing Inc. produces floor mats for automobiles. The owner, Joseph Elias, has asked you to assist him in estimating his maintenance costs. Together, you and Elias determine that the single best cost driver for maintenance costs is machine-hours. These data are from the previous fiscal year for maintenance expense and machine-hours:

Month	Maintenance Expense	Machine-Hours
1	$2,600	1,690
2	2,760	1,770
3	2,910	1,850
4	3,020	1,870
5	3,100	1,900
6	3,070	1,880
7	3,010	1,860

8	2,850	1,840
9	2,620	1,700
10	2,400	1,600
11	2,230	1,300
12	2,450	1,590

Required What is the cost equation for maintenance cost using the high-low method?

7–16 COST ESTIMATION WITH DIFFERENT METHODS Home Decorations Company recently obtained a short-term bank loan from First City Federal Bank. The bank requires that certain credit information and pro forma financial statements be maintained through the life of the loan. To prepare the pro forma statements, Home Decorations must forecast demand for its main product, a high-quality upholstery and drapery fabric. The sales manager's forecast for yards of fabric sold follows with actual sales data over the past six months:

Month	Yards of Fabric Sold	Manager's Forecast
January	2,450	2,400
February	2,680	2,500
March	2,300	2,400
April	2,470	2,600
May	2,550	2,700
June	2,690	2,700

Required Suppose that the bank is not completely satisfied with the accuracy of the manager's forecasts and has asked that you prepare forecasts for each month, July through September. Which estimation methods should you use? Explain your choice.

7–17 COST ESTIMATION; AVERAGE COST Maribeth's Cafe bakes croissants sold to local restaurants and grocery stores in the Raleigh, North Carolina, area. When 500 croissants are baked, the average cost is $0.55; and when 600 croissants are baked, the average cost is $0.50.

Required If the cost function for croissants is linear, what will be the average cost when 560 are baked?

7–18 COST RELATIONSHIPS CompuCo hired Daffner & Associates to design a new computer-aided manufacturing facility. The new facility is designed to produce 250 computers per month. The variable costs for each computer are $450 and the fixed costs total $62,250 per month.

Required What is the average cost per unit if the facility normally expects to operate at 90 percent of capacity?

7–19 COST RELATIONSHIPS The following costs are for Optical View Inc., a contact lens manufacturer.

Output	Fixed Costs	Variable Costs	Total Costs
250	$4,750	$ 7,500	$12,250
300	4,750	9,000	13,750
350	4,750	10,500	15,250
400	4,750	12,000	16,750

Required

1. Graph total cost, total variable costs, and total fixed costs.
2. Graph the per-unit total cost, per-unit variable cost, and per-unit fixed cost.
3. Discuss the behavior of fixed, variable, and total cost.

7–20 COST ESTIMATION USING GRAPHS; SERVICE Lawson Advertising Agency is trying to persuade Kansas City Sailboards Company to spend more money on advertising. The agency's argument is that there is a positive

Service

233

linear relationship between advertising and sales in the sailboard industry. Sue Lawson presents these data taken from the accounts of Sailboards Galore Company in Omaha, a store similar in size and market share to Kansas City Sailboards:

Advertising Expense	Annual Sales
$2,500	$ 95,000
3,000	110,000
3,500	124,000
4,000	138,000
4,500	143,000
5,000	147,000
5,500	150,000

Required

1. Graph annual sales and advertising expense.
2. Do the data prove Sue's point?

7–21 COST ESTIMATION; ACCOUNT CLASSIFICATION   Brown's Compact Disk Store expanded the size of its store in Westfield, New Jersey, two months ago. The owner, Montgomery Brown, has asked you to analyze the cost structure in his store, as a basis for assessing the profitability of his business. He provides you with account data for the most recent month, which he explains is representative of what these costs are in most months of the year; there is not much seasonality in his business. Last month 890 compact disks were sold.

Account	Amount
Salespersons' wages	$1,780
Compact disk purchases	6,675
Rent	1,025
Depreciation	40
Shopping bags	18
Insurance	75
Advertising	65
Utilities	125
Brown's salary	1,850

Assume that salespersons' wages are based on commissions only. Also, assume that Brown purchases promptly on a day-to-day basis to replace inventory so that the level of inventory remains constant.

Required

1. Develop the cost equation for Brown's store, using the account classification method, assuming that the cost object is the individual compact disk.
2. Brown plans to increase sales by 25 percent next month by reducing the price of his compact disks. Assuming a 25 percent increase in sales units, what is the lowest price Brown can sell his disks for if he wants to meet all costs plus make $1 profit per disk?
3. What would the profit per disk be if sales actually increased by only 15 percent and the disks were sold at the price calculated in requirement 2?

7–22 COST ESTIMATION; HIGH-LOW METHOD   The Bob Schmitz Company specializes in the purchase, renovation, and resale of older homes. Schmitz employs several carpenters and painters to do the work for him. It is essential for him to have accurate cost estimates so he can determine total renovation costs before he purchases a piece of property. If estimated renovation costs plus the purchase price of a house are greater than its estimated resale value, then the house would not be a worthwhile investment.

Schmitz has been using the home's interior square feet for his exterior paint cost estimations. Recently he decided to include the number of openings as a cost driver. Openings are the total number of doors and windows in a house. Their cost is significant because they require time-consuming preparatory work and careful brushwork. The rest of the house usually is painted either by rollers or spray guns, which are relatively efficient ways of applying paint to a large area. Schmitz has been keeping careful records of these expenses on his last 12 jobs:

House	Square Feet	Openings	Cost
1	2,600	13	$3,300
2	3,010	15	3,750
3	2,800	12 ·	3,100
4	2,850	12	3,150
5	4,050	19	4,700
6	2,700	13	3,250
7	2,375	11	2,800
8	2,450	11	2,800
9	2,600	10	2,875
10	3,700	16	4,100
11	2,650	13	3,200
12	3,550	16	3,950

Required

1. Using the high-low cost estimation technique, determine the cost of painting a 3,200-square-foot house with 14 openings. Also, determine the cost for a 2,400-square-foot house with 8 openings.

2. Plot the cost data against square feet and also against openings. Which variable is a better cost driver? Why?

7-23 COST ESTIMATION; MACHINE REPLACEMENT; ETHICS SpectroGlass Company manufactures glass for office buildings in Arizona and Southern California. As a result of age and wear, a critical machine in the production process has begun to produce quality defects. SpectroGlass is considering replacing the old machine with a new machine, of either brand A or brand B. The manufacturer of each machine has provided SpectroGlass with data on the cost of operation of the machine at various levels of output:

Ethics

Output (square yards)	Machine A Estimated Total Costs	Machine B Estimated Total Costs
4,000	$ 54,600	$ 70,000
7,000	78,800	100,000
9,000	90,300	115,000
14,000	114,900	137,000
16,000	132,400	146,000
24,000	210,000	192,000

Required

1. If SpectroGlass's output is expected to be 22,000 square yards, which machine should SpectroGlass purchase? At 15,000 square yards?

2. You are a cost analyst at Spectroglass, assigned to complete requirement 1. A production supervisor comes to you to say that the nature of the defect is really very hard to detect, and that most of the customers will not notice it anyway. So why replace the machine? He suggests that you should modify your calculations to justify keeping the present machine, to keep things the way they are and save the company some money. What do you say?

3. Assume Machine A is manufactured in Germany and Machine B is manufactured in Canada. As a United States–based firm, what considerations are important to SpectroGlass, in addition to those already mentioned in your answer to requirement 1?

7–24 to 7–28 REGRESSION ANALYSIS Problems 7–24 through 7–28 are based on Armer Company, which is accumulating data to be used in preparing its annual profit plan for the coming year. The cost behavior pattern of the maintenance costs must be determined. The accounting staff has suggested that linear regression be employed to derive an equation for maintenance hours and costs. Data regarding the maintenance hours and costs for the last year and the results of the regression analysis follow:

	Hours of Activity	Maintenance Costs
January	480	$ 4,200
February	320	3,000
March	400	3,600
April	300	2,820
May	500	4,350
June	310	2,960
July	320	3,030
August	520	4,470
September	490	4,260
October	470	4,050
November	350	3,300
December	340	3,160
Sum	4,800	$43,200
Average	400	3,600

Average cost per hour (43,200/4,800) = $9.00

a (intercept)	684.65
b coefficient	7.2884
Standard error of the estimate	34.469
R-squared	.99724
t-value for *b*	60.105

Required (7–24) If Armer Company uses the high-low method of analysis, the equation for the relationship between hours of activity and maintenance cost would be:

a. y = 400 + 9.0x

b. y = 570 + 7.5x

c. y = 3,600 + 400x

d. y = 570 + 9.0x

e. None of the above

(CMA Adapted)

Required (7–25) Based on the data derived from the regression analysis, 420 maintenance hours in a month would mean the maintenance costs would be budgeted at

a. $3,780

b. $3,461

c. $3,797

d. $3,746

e. None of the above

(CMA Adapted)

Required (7–26) The coefficient of determination for Armer's regression equation for the maintenance activities is

a. 34.469/49.515

b. .99724

c. square root of .99724

d. $(.99724)^2$

e. None of the above

(CMA Adapted)

Required (7–27)   The percent of the total variance that can be explained by the regression equation is

a. 99.724%

b. 69.613%

c. 80.982%

d. 99.862%

e. None of the above

(CMA Adapted)

Required (7–28)   At 400 hours of activity, Armer management can be approximately two-thirds confident that the maintenance costs will be in the range of

a. $3,550.50–$3,649.53

b. $3,551.37–$3,648.51

c. $3,586.18–$3,613.93

d. $3,565.54–$3,634.47

e. None of the above

(CMA Adapted)

7–29   **COST ESTIMATION; REGRESSION ANALYSIS**   A local realty company has purchased a regression program to help estimate the sale prices of homes. The realtors have run three different regressions using as the independent variables (1) square feet, (2) the number of bedrooms, and (3) both square feet and the number of bedrooms. The data and the results from their regression analyses are

Service

House	Square Feet	Bedrooms	Selling Price
1	2,300	3	$ 76,000
2	3,700	4	150,000
3	2,700	3	114,000
4	2,500	3	86,000
5	4,000	5	176,000
6	2,600	3	89,000
7	2,300	2	80,000
8	1,800	2	84,000
9	3,500	5	140,000
10	3,300	4	146,000
11	2,900	3	110,000
12	3,000	4	112,000
		mean =	$113,583

Regression using square feet only

Intercept: −24,425.67
Coefficient of the independent variable: 47.86 ($t = 9.23$)
R-squared: .8949
Standard error of the estimate: $11,117.31
F-statistic: 85.21 (p<.01)
Durbin-Watson statistic: 2.63

Regression using bedrooms only

Intercept: 17,160.31
Coefficient of the independent variable: 28,221.38 ($t = 5.32$)
R-squared: .7389
Standard error of the estimate: $17,528.19
F-statistic: 28.30 (p<.01)
Durbin-Watson statistic: 2.64

Regression using both square feet and bedrooms:

Intercept: −25,246.42	
Coefficients:	
Square feet: 49.65	t-values: 3.66
Bedrooms: −1262.48	−.14
R-squared: .8952	
Standard error of the estimate: $11,705.28	
F-statistic: 38.44 (p<.01)	
Durbin-Watson statistic: 2.61	

Required

1. Evaluate each of the three regressions on the basis of:
   a. precision of the regression
   b. goodness of fit
   c. statistical reliability
   d. potential nonlinearity
2. Does multicollinearity exist between square feet and the number of bedrooms?
3. Which is the best regression? Why?
4. What other potentially relevant cost drivers might you consider?

7–30 COST ESTIMATION; HIGH-LOW METHOD, REGRESSION ANALYSIS   Clothes for U is a large merchandiser of clothes for budget-minded families. Recently management has become concerned about the amount of inventory carrying costs and transportation costs between warehouses and retail outlets. As a starting point in further analyses, Gregory Gonzales, the controller, wants to test different forecasting methods and then use the best one to forecast quarterly expenses for 19X2. The relevant data for the previous three years:

Quarter	Warehouse and Transportation Expense ($000)
1 19X9	$12,500
2	11,300
3	11,600
4	13,700
1 19X0	12,900
2	12,100
3	11,700
4	14,000
1 19X1	13,300
2	12,300
3	12,100
4	14,600

The results of a simple regression analysis using all 12 data points yielded an intercept of $11,854.55 and a coefficient for the independent variable of $126.22 (R-squared = .19, t = 1.5, SE = 974).

Required

1. Calculate the quarterly forecasts for 19X2 using the high-low method and regression analysis. Recommend to Gonzales which method to use.
2. How does your analysis in requirement 1 change if Clothes for U is involved in global sourcing of products for its stores?

7–31 LEARNING CURVES   The Air Force Museum Foundation has commissioned the purchase of 16 "Four F Sixes," a pre–World War II aircraft. These will be built completely from scratch to the exact specifications used for the originals. As further authentication, the aircraft will be made using the technology and manufacturing processes available at the time the originals were built. Each of the 16 will be flown to Air Force and aviation museums throughout the country for exhibition.

Aviation enthusiasts also can visit the production facility to see exactly how such aircraft were built in 1938.

Soren Industries would like to bid on the aircraft contract and asked for and received certain cost information about the Four F Sixes from the Air Force. The information includes some of the old cost data from the builders of the original aircraft. The available information is for the total accumulated time as the first, eighth, and thirty-second aircraft, respectively, were completed.

Output	Total Hours
1	250
8	1,458
32	4,724

Required

1. If Soren Industries expects that the time spent per unit will be the same as it was in 1938, how many hours will it take to build the 16 aircraft for the Air Force Museum Foundation?

2. What is the role of learning curves in Soren Industries' business for contracts such as this?

7–32 **LEARNING CURVES** Moss Point Manufacturing recently completed and sold an order of 50 units that had the following costs:

Direct materials	$ 1,500
Direct labor (1,000 hours @ $8.50/hr)	8,500
Variable overhead (1,000 hrs. @ $4.00/hr)	4,000
Fixed overhead*	1,400
	$15,400

*10% of total variable costs

The company has been requested to prepare a bid for 150 units of the same product.

Required If an 80 percent learning curve is applicable, estimate Moss Point's total cost on this order.

(CMA Adapted)

7–33 **COST ESTIMATION; REGRESSION ANALYSIS** Plantworld is a large nursery and retail store specializing in house and garden plants and supplies. Jean Raouth, the assistant manager, is in the process of budgeting monthly supplies expense for 19X5. Raouth assumes that in some way supplies expense will be related to sales, either in units or in dollars. She has collected these data for sales and supplies expenses for June 19X2 through December 19X4, and she has estimated sales for 19X5:

Date	Supplies Expense	Sales Units	Sales Dollars
Jun 19X2	$2,745	354	$2,009
Jul	3,200	436	2,190
Aug	3,232	525	1,878
Sep	2,199	145	1,856
Oct	2,321	199	2,168
Nov	3,432	543	1,899
Dec	4,278	1,189	2,463
Jan 19X3	2,310	212	1,999
Feb	2,573	284	2,190
Mar	2,487	246	1,894
Apr	2,484	278	2,134
May	3,384	498	2,100
Jun	2,945	224	1,874

(continued on next page)

(continued from previous page)

Date	Supplies Expense	Sales Units	Sales Dollars
Jul	2,758	312	2,265
Aug	3,394	485	2,435
Sep	2,254	188	1,893
Oct	2,763	276	2,232
Nov	3,245	489	2,004
Dec	4,576	1,045	2,109
Jan 19X4	2,103	104	2,195
Feb	2,056	167	2,045
Mar	4,874	1,298	2,301
Apr	2,784	398	1,893
May	2,345	187	2,345
Jun	2,912	334	2,094
Jul	2,093	264	1,934
Aug	2,873	333	1,783
Sep	2,563	143	1,977
Oct	2,384	245	1,857
Nov	2,476	232	2,189
Dec	2,364	322	2,093
Jan 19X5 (estimated)		435	1,567
Feb		234	1,923
Mar		123	1,894
Apr		446	1,276
May		1,200	1,576
Jun		1,789	2,593
Jul		475	2,453
Aug		584	2,736
Sep		1,103	1,598
Oct		220	1,576
Nov		876	2,398
Dec		834	1,783

Required

1. Develop the regression Raouth should use based on these data and using the regression procedure in EXCEL or equivalent regression software. Evaluate the reliability and precision of the regression you have chosen.

2. What are the predicted monthly figures for supplies expense for 19X5?

7-34 LEARNING CURVES   Andrews & Henderson Inc. is a manufacturer of mining equipment in Colorado. Eric Andrews, the founder of the corporation, has just won a new contract from Shakley Inc. to build seven new tunneling machines for a price of $500,000 each. The machines are to be delivered in the next seven months. The costs associated with the production of the first machine follow. Andrews estimates that an 85 percent cumulative average learning rate exists for these types of projects. Following is the cost information for the first tunneling machine:

Direct materials:	$150,000
Direct labor (8,500 hours @ $50/hr)	425,000
Variable overhead (8,500 hours @ $10/hr)	85,000

Required

1. Prepare an estimate of the total hours for producing the second through eighth machines.

2. Determine the expected profit from this project.

7-35 LEARNING CURVES   Ben and David work for a landscaping company in Twin Cities, Oklahoma. Their principal job is to lay railroad ties to line the sidewalks around apartment complexes and to install flower boxes. The first time Ben and David undertook one of these projects, it took 17 hours. Their goal by the end of the summer was to be able to finish an apartment complex in 8 hours, one working day. They performed eight of these jobs and had an 80 percent learning curve. Assume all apartment complexes are approximately the same size.

Required Did they reach their goal? If not, what would the learning rate have to have been for them to have accomplished their goal?

7–36 LEARNING CURVES Emotional Headdress (EH) is a Des Moines, Iowa, manufacturer of avant garde hats and headwear. On March 11, 19X7, the company purchased a new machine to aid in the production of various established product lines. Production efficiency on the new machine increases with the experience of the workforce. It has been shown that as cumulative output on the new machine increases, average labor time per unit decreases up to the production of at least 3,200 units. As EH's cumulative output doubles from a base of 100 units produced, the average labor time per unit declines by 15 percent. EH's production varies little from month to month and averages 800 hats per month.

Emotional Headdress has developed a new style of men's hat called the Morrisey to be produced on the new machine. One hundred Morrisey hats can be produced in a total of 25 labor-hours. All other direct costs to produce each Morrisey hat are $16.25, excluding direct labor cost. EH's direct labor cost per hour is $15. Fixed costs are $8,000 per month, and EH has the capacity to produce 3,200 hats per month.

Required

1. Emotional Headdress wishes to set the selling price for a Morrisey hat at 125 percent of the hat production cost. At the production level of 100 units, what is the selling price?

2. The company has received an order for 1,600 Morrisey hats from Smiths, Inc. Smiths is offering $20 for each hat. Should the company accept Smiths' order and produce the 1,600 hats? Explain.

7–37 COST ESTIMATION; HIGH-LOW METHOD Antelope Park Amoco (APA) in Antelope Park, Alaska, has noticed that utility bills are substantially higher the colder the average monthly temperature is. The only thing in the shop that uses natural gas is the furnace. Because of prevailing low temperatures, the furnace is used every month of the year (though less in the summer months and very little in August). Everything else in the shop runs on electricity, and electricity use is fairly constant throughout the year.

For a year APA has been keeping track of the average daily temperature and the cost of its monthly utility bills for natural gas and electricity.

	Average Temperature	Utility Cost
January	31°F	$760
February	41	629
March	43	543
April	44	410
May	46	275
June	50	233
July	53	220
August	60	210
September	50	305
October	40	530
November	30	750
December	20	870

Required Use the high-low method to estimate utility cost for the upcoming months of January and February. The forecast for January is a near record average temperature of 10°F, while temperatures in February are expected to average 40°F.

International

7–38 REGRESSION ANALYSIS The Pilot Shop is a catalog business that provides a wide variety of aviation products to pilots throughout the world. Maynard Shephard, the recently hired assistant controller, has been asked to develop a cost function to forecast shipping costs. The previous assistant controller had forecast shipping department costs each year by plotting cost data against direct labor-hours for the most recent 12 months and visually fitting a straight line through the points. The results have not been satisfactory.

After discussions with the shipping department personnel, Shephard decided that shipping costs may be more closely related to the number of orders filled. Shephard based his conclusion on the fact that 10 months ago the shipping department added some automated equipment. Furthermore, Shephard believes that using linear regression analysis will improve the forecasts of shipping costs. Cost data for the shipping department have been accumulated for the last 25 weeks. Shephard ran two regression analyses of the data, one using direct labor-hours and one using the number of cartons shipped. The information from the two linear regressions is

	Regression 1	Regression 2
Equation	$SC = 804.3 + 15.68DL$	$SC = 642.9 + 3.92NR$
Coefficient of determination	.365	.729
Standard error of the estimate	2.652	1.884
t-value	1.89	3.46

where: SC = total shipping department costs
DL = total direct labor-hours
NR = number of cartons shipped

Required

1. Identify which cost function (regression 1 or regression 2) the Pilot Shop should adapt for forecasting total shipping department cost and explain why.

2. If the Pilot Shop projects 600 orders will be filled the coming week, calculate the total shipping department cost using the regression you selected in requirement 1.

3. Explain 2 or 3 important limitations of the regression you selected in requirement 1, and identify 1 or 2 ways the limitations can be addressed. Specifically include in your discussion the effect, if any, of the global nature of the Pilot Shop's business.

(CMA Adapted)

7–39 REGRESSION ANALYSIS The Danzer Company manufactures a line of lawn care products distributed primarily through landscaping companies and is in the process of developing its marketing strategy for the upcoming fiscal year. As in the past, the marketing strategy focuses on quality and customer service. Danzer employs linear regression to forecast sales by region. The marketing department has prepared the following regression models for the midwestern, the southern, and the eastern regions using actual sales data from the past 10 years. In general terms, the midwest region is characterized by rapid growth in recent years, while the eastern region is characterized by slow to little growth based on long-term relationships with nurseries, arboretums, and research units at local universities where new ideas are tested.

S_t = Forecasted sales for the region in time period t.

S_{t-1} = Actual sales for the region in time period $t-1$.

Howard Todesco, president of Danzer Company, and Frank Mulrooney, vice president of marketing, are wondering whether the results of the regression analysis can be relied on to develop the company's marketing strategy. The results of the analysis indicate that they should recommend to the board of directors that Danzer drop the eastern region; however, they have read recently that the economy of the eastern states in general, and the market for lawn care products specifically, is entering a period of rejuvenation.

	Midwestern Region	Southern Region	Eastern Region
Equation	$S_t = \$400 + 1.12S_{t-1}$	$S_t = \$445 + 1.06\ S_{t-1}$	$S_t = \$510 + 0.985\ S_{t-1}$
Coefficient of determination	.9025	.8649	.9216
Standard error of the estimate	$495,000	$480,000	$500,000
Calculated t-statistic for the regression coefficient	3.64	3.88	3.70

Required

1. Evaluate the three regressions in terms of precision and reliability.
2. Identify the basic assumptions underlying regression analysis.
3. If actual sales for the eastern region are $2,200,000 in the current year, calculate the sales forecast for the coming year.
4. Discuss the strategic issues that are important to whether or not the board of directors of Danzer Company should accept a recommendation to drop the eastern region.

(CMA Adapted)

SOLUTIONS TO SELF-STUDY PROBLEMS

1. Using the High-Low Method

Begin by graphing the data to determine whether there are any unusual patterns or outliers, as shown in Exhibit 7–21:

The graph shows no unusual patterns or outliers, so the high-low estimate can be determined directly from the low point (March) and the high point (December) as follows:

To determine the slope of the line (unit variable cost):

$$(\$201,783 - \$123,245)/(7,433 - 5,166) = \$34.644 \text{ per delivery}$$

To determine the intercept:

$$\$201,783 - 7,433 \times \$34.644 = -\$55,726$$
$$\$123,245 - 5,166 \times \$34.644 = -\$55,726$$

And the estimation equation is

$$\text{Vehicle costs} = -\$55,726 + \$34.644 \times \text{number of deliveries/month}$$

Note that the intercept is a negative number, which simply means the relevant range of 5,166 to 7,433 deliveries is so far from the zero point (where the intercept is) that the intercept cannot be properly interpreted as fixed cost. The estimation equation therefore is useful only within the relevant range of approximately 5,000 to 7,500 deliveries, and should not be used to estimate costs outside that range.

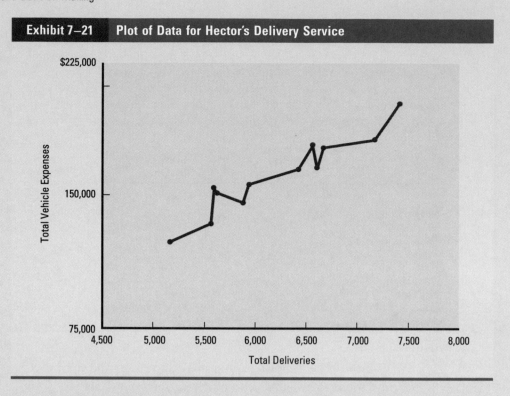

Exhibit 7–21 **Plot of Data for Hector's Delivery Service**

2. Using Regression Analysis

All the relevant criteria favor the first regression, based on higher R-squared and t-values, and lower standard error. Moreover, the sign on the materials cost variable in regression two is negative, which is hard to explain. This variable should have a direct relationship with overhead, and thus the sign of the variable should be positive. The reason for the improvement of regression 1 over regression 2 might be that machine-hours are highly correlated with either materials costs, labor-hours, or both, thus causing multicollinearity. By excluding machine-hours as an independent variable, Harder reduced or removed the multicollinearity, and the regression improved as a result. Harder should therefore use regression 1.

3. Using Both High-Low and Regression

Begin by graphing the data for the number of defective units, as shown in Exhibit 7–22. The objective is to identify any unusual patterns that must be considered in the development of an estimate.

Exhibit 7–22 shows that the number of defective units varies considerably from month to month, and that there has been a steady increase over the past two years. Knowing that the production level also has been increasing (as measured either by cost of sales, units produced, or units shipped), we now want to determine whether there has been a change in the relationship between defects and production level (Exhibit 7–23). We begin with units produced as the independent variable, since it should have the most direct relationship with defects; the other independent variables can be tried later. The second graph (Exhibit 7–23) makes clear there is a relationship between units produced and the number of defects.

The next step is to quantify this relationship with the high-low method and regression analysis. We begin with the high-low analysis. For Exhibit 7–23, we identify February 19X5 and December 19X6 as representative low and high periods respectively. We calculate the high-low estimate as follows (these two points are not the absolute lowest and highest points, but they are the best points to produce a line that is representative of the data):

| Exhibit 7–22 | Defective Units from January 19X5 to December 19X6 |

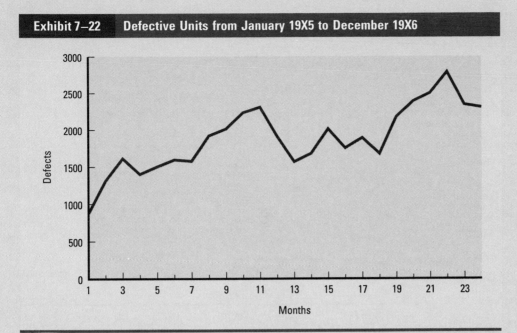

| Exhibit 7–23 | Defective Units vs. Production Level from January 19X5 to December 19X6 |

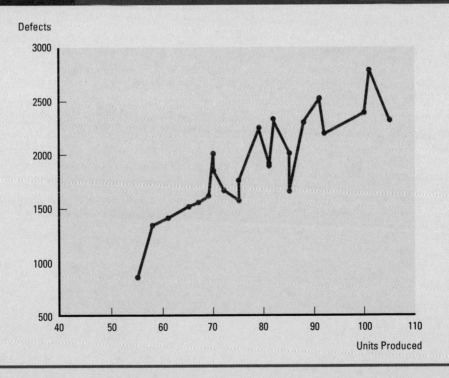

$$\text{slope} = (2,311 - 1,335)/(88 - 58) = 32.533$$

And:

$$\text{Intercept} = 2,311 - 32.533 \times 88 = 1,335 - 32.533 \times 58 = -552$$

Thus, the estimation equation is

$$\text{Number of defects} = -522 + 32.533 \times \text{production level}$$

The high-low estimate is subject to the limitations of subjectivity in the choice of high and low points and because of the fact that it uses only those two points of

Exhibit 7–24	Regressions for the Number of Defects

Intercept	Coefficient of Independent Variable	t-value for Independent Variable	R-squared	Standard Error of the Estimate
Regression 1				
103.20			.883	161
	−38.974 (units shipped)	−.44		
	−2.849 (units produced)	−.38		
	4.702 (cost of sales)	.72		
Regression 2				
92.24			.881	158
	−2.230 (units produced)	−.309		
	1.837 (cost of sales)	4.54		
Regression 3				
43.95			.881	155
	1.720 (cost of sales)	12.77		

the data to develop the estimate. So regression is done to provide a more precise estimate. Thus, the next step is to obtain a regression analysis from the previous data and to assess the precision and reliability of the regression estimate. The regression can be completed with a spreadsheet program or any of a number of available software systems. The results for three regression analyses are presented in Exhibit 7–24. The dependent variable in each case is the number of defective units.

Regression 1 has the following independent variables: cost of sales, units shipped, and units produced. While R-squared and SE are OK, we observe that all three t-values are less than two, indicating unreliable independent variables. Because a priori we expect correlation among these variables, and because of the low t-values, we suspect multicollinearity among these variables. To reduce the effect of multi-collinearity, we try regression 2, which removes the variable units shipped, since that variable is likely to be least associated with defective units and has among the lowest of the t-values. R-squared for regression 2 is essentially the same as for regression 1, while SE improves very slightly, and the t-value for cost of sales is now OK. The results of regression 3, with the cost of sales variable only, shows that SE and the t-value improve again, while R-squared is unchanged. Because it has the best SE and t-values, and a very good R-squared, the third regression is the best choice.

Cost-Volume-Profit Analysis

8

After studying this chapter you should be able to . . .

Explain cost-volume-profit (CVP) analysis, the CVP model, and the strategic role of CVP analysis **1**

Apply CVP analysis for breakeven planning **2**

Apply CVP analysis for revenue planning and cost planning **3**

Apply CVP analysis for activity-based costing **4**

Employ sensitivity analysis to more effectively use CVP analysis when there is uncertainty about actual sales **5**

Adapt CVP analysis for multiple products **6**

Apply CVP analysis in service firms and not-for-profit organizations **7**

Identify the assumptions and limitations of CVP analysis, and explain how they affect the proper interpretation of the results **8**

Gary A. Conner/Photo Edit

Annual income twenty pounds, annual expenditure nineteen six, result happiness. Annual income twenty pounds, annual expenditure twenty pounds ought six, result misery.

CHARLES DICKENS, *DAVID COPPERFIELD*

As noted in *David Copperfield*, there is an important relationship between income and expenditures. Similar relationships exist in the business environment between revenues, costs, and output. Management must understand how unit costs, unit selling price, and number of units sold are related. An important context in which these relationships play a key role is pricing of products and service. For example, a firm might reduce the price of a product or service to increase profits by increasing sales. However, profits will increase only if sales volume rises enough to compensate for the reduced price. Only a careful analysis based on an understanding of the relationships between costs, anticipated volume changes, and prices can determine the best pricing decision.

Cost-volume-profit (CVP) analysis is a method for analyzing how operating decisions and marketing decisions affect net income, based on an understanding of the relationship between variable costs, fixed costs, unit selling price, and the output level. CVP analysis has many applications:

- Setting prices for products and services.
- Introducing a new product or service.
- Replacing a piece of equipment.
- Deciding whether a given product or service should be made within the firm or purchased outside the firm.
- Performing strategic what-if analyses.

◀ **LEARNING OBJECTIVE 1**
Explain cost-volume-profit (CVP) analysis, the CVP model, and the strategic role of CVP analysis.

Cost-volume-profit (CVP) analysis is a method for analyzing how various operating decisions and marketing decisions will affect net income.

THE COST-VOLUME-PROFIT (CVP) MODEL

CVP analysis is based on an explicit model of the relationships between the three factors—costs, revenues, and profits—and how they change in a predictable way as the volume of activity changes. The CVP model is

$$\text{Profit} = \text{Revenues} - \text{Total costs}$$

BusinessWeek

How Does American Airlines Continue to Pass with Flying Colors?

American Airlines (AA) is a dominant player in the worldwide airline industry. It has been a powerful competitor, setting prices and competitive standards for the industry. In addition, it has been a key innovator, introducing frequent flyer programs, integrated reservations systems, and super-saver fares. CEO Robert L. Crandall is the controversial drive behind all this. Crandall sees the industry as a low-cost leadership type of industry. He models his strategy at AA after the successful bargain-fare airline, Southwest Air. He says, "The market is telling all the traditional airlines that they must compete in a low-cost, low-price world . . . This business is intensely, vigorously, bitterly, savagely competitive."

How does Crandall manage AA so that it can sustain the price wars in the industry? While many of its competitors are losing millions, and others such as Trans World Airlines and Continental have faced bankruptcy, AA continues to prosper.

Q: How does American Airlines continue to fly high amongst its competitors? *Find out on page 261 of this chapter.*

or equivalently, since total costs include both fixed and variable cost elements:

$$\text{Revenues} = \text{Fixed costs} + \text{Variable costs} + \text{Profit}$$

Now, replacing revenues with the number of units sold times price, and replacing variable cost with unit variable cost times the number of units sold, the CVP model is

$$\text{Units sold} \times \text{Price} = \text{Fixed cost}$$
$$+ \text{Units sold} \times \text{Unit variable cost}$$
$$+ \text{Profit}$$

For easier use, the model is commonly shown in a symbolic form,

where: Q = units sold
v = unit variable cost
f = total fixed cost
p = unit selling price
N = operating profit (profits *exclusive* of unusual or nonrecurring items and income taxes)

The CVP Model in Symbolic Form
$$p \times Q = f + v \times Q + N$$

The Contribution Margin, Ratio, and Income Statement

Effective use of the CVP model requires an understanding of three additional concepts: the contribution margin, the contribution margin ratio, and the contribution income statement. The contribution margin is both a unit and a total concept. The **unit contribution margin** is the difference between unit sales price and unit variable cost:

$$p - v = \text{Unit contribution margin}$$

The unit contribution margin measures the increase in profit for a unit increase in sales. If sales are expected to increase by 100 units, then profits should increase by 100 times the contribution margin. The **total contribution margin** is the unit contribution margin multiplied by the number of units sold.

For example, suppose Household Furnishings, Inc. (HFI), a manufacturer of home furnishings, is interested in developing a new product, a wooden TV table, that would be priced at $75 and would have variable costs of $35 per unit. The investment would require new fixed costs of $5,000 per month. HFI wants to achieve an increase in operating profit of at least $48,000 per year. The data for HFI are summarized in Exhibit 8–1.

The unit contribution margin for each table would be $40 ($75 − $35). Using the unit contribution margin, we see that if HFI expects to sell 3,000 tables per year, it can expect to increase total contribution margin by $120,000 ($40 × 3,000) and operating profit by $60,000 ($120,000 less $60,000 fixed cost), which is $12,000 greater than the desired operating profit of $48,000.

Another important concept is the **contribution margin ratio,** which is the ratio of the unit contribution margin to unit sales price $(p − v)/p$. The contribution mar-

Sidebar notes:

The **unit contribution margin** is the difference between unit sales price and unit variable cost, and is a measure of the increase in profit for a unit increase in sales.

The **total contribution margin** is the unit contribution margin multiplied by the number of units sold.

The **contribution margin ratio** is the ratio of the unit contribution margin to unit sales price $(p − v)/p$.

Exhibit 8–1	**Data for Household Furnishings, Inc. (HFI): TV Table**		
	Per Unit	**Monthly**	**Annual**
Fixed cost		$ 5,000	$ 60,000
Desired operating profit		4,000	48,000
Revenue	$75		
Variable cost	35		
Planned production		250 units	3,000 units
Planned sales		250 units	3,000 units

Exhibit 8–2	Contribution Income Statement for Household Furnishings, Inc.		
	19X1	**19X2**	**Change**
Sales	$180,000	$195,000	$15,000
Variable costs	84,000	91,000	7,000
Contribution margin	96,000	104,000	$ 8,000
Fixed costs	60,000	60,000	-0-
Profit	$ 36,000	$ 44,000	$ 8,000

gin ratio for HFI's proposed TV table is .533 = ($75 − $35)/$75. This ratio shows the net profit contribution per sales dollar. More profitable products have higher contribution margin ratios. Also, the ratio tells the amount of increase (or decrease) in profits caused by a given increase (or decrease) in sales dollars. What would be the effect on profits of an increase of $15,000 in sales? We can quickly calculate that profits will increase by $8,000 ($15,000 × .5333).

A useful way to show the information developed in cost-volume-profit analysis is to use the contribution income statement. The **contribution income statement** separates variable costs and fixed costs, in contrast to the conventional income statement shown in Chapter 3. Both income statements arrive at net income, but the contribution statement obtains the total contribution margin by subtracting all variable costs (both product and nonproduct) from sales; fixed costs are then deducted from the contribution margin. Exhibit 8–2 shows the contribution income statement for HFI, which shows total contribution margin and net income for 19X1 and 19X2. Note that the sales increase of $15,000 in 19X2 caused profits to increase by $8,000 in 19X2, as predicted by the contribution margin ratio. The contribution income statement is more useful than the conventional income statement for cost-volume-profit analysis because of the separation of fixed and variable costs; variable costs change directly with volume while fixed costs do not.

> The **contribution income statement** focuses on variable costs and fixed costs, in contrast to the conventional income statement in Chapter 3, which focuses on product costs and nonproduct costs.

THE STRATEGIC ROLE OF CVP ANALYSIS

CVP analysis has an important role in the strategic management of the firm. It is important in using both life-cycle costing and target costing. In life-cycle costing, CVP analysis is used in the early stages of the product's cost life cycle to determine whether the product is likely to achieve the desired profitability. Similarly, CVP analysis can assist in target costing at these early stages by showing the effect on profit of alternative product designs at expected sales levels.

In addition, CVP analysis can be used at later phases of the life cycle, during manufacturing planning, to determine the most cost-effective manufacturing process. Such manufacturing decisions include when to replace a machine, what type of machine to buy, when to automate a process, and when to outsource (or to bring inside the firm) a manufacturing operation. Also, CVP analysis is used in the final stages of the cost life cycle to help determine the best marketing and distribution systems. For example, CVP analysis can be used to determine whether it would be more cost effective to have salespeople on a salary basis or on a commission basis. Similarly, it can help to assess the desirability of a discount program or promotional plan. Some of the strategic questions answered by CVP analysis are outlined in Exhibit 8–3.

CVP analysis also has a role in strategic positioning. A firm that has chosen to compete on cost leadership needs CVP analysis primarily at the manufacturing stage of the cost life cycle. The role of CVP analysis here is to identify for planned activity levels the most cost-effective manufacturing methods, including automation, outsourcing, and total quality management. In contrast, a firm following the differentiation strategy needs CVP analysis in the early phases of the cost life cycle to assess the profitability of new products and the desirability of new features for existing products.

Exhibit 8–3	Strategic What-if Questions Answered by CVP Analysis

1. What is the expected level of profit at a given sales volume?
2. What additional amount of sales is needed to achieve a desired level of profit?
3. What will be the effect on profits of a given increase in sales?
4. What is the required funding level for a governmental agency, given desired service levels?
5. Is the forecast for sales consistent with forecasted profits?
6. What additional profit would be obtained from a given percentage reduction in unit variable costs?
7. What increase in sales is needed to make up a given decrease in price, to maintain the present profit level?
8. What sales level is needed to cover all costs in a sales region or product line?
9. What is the required amount of increase in sales to meet the additional fixed charges from a proposed plant expansion?
10. What additional sales are needed to improve profits by a desired amount?

CVP ANALYSIS FOR BREAKEVEN PLANNING

LEARNING OBJECTIVE 2 ▶
Apply CVP analysis for breakeven planning.

The **breakeven point** is the point at which revenues equal total cost and profit is zero.

The starting point in many business plans is to determine the **breakeven point,** the point at which revenues equal total costs and profit is zero. This point can be determined by using CVP analysis. The CVP model is solved by inserting known values for v, p, and f, setting N equal to zero, and then solving for Q. We can solve for Q in two ways: the equation method and the contribution margin method. Each method can determine the breakeven point in units sold, or sales dollars.

The Equation Method: For Breakeven in Units

The equation method uses the CVP model directly. For example, the equation for the analysis of HFI's sale of TV tables is

$$\$75 \times Q = \$5,000 + \$35 \times Q$$

Solving for Q, we determine the breakeven point is $Q = 125$ TV tables per month (1,500 units per year).

$$(\$75 - \$35) \times Q = \$5,000$$

$$Q = \$5,000/(\$75 - \$35)$$

$$Q = \$5,000/\$40 = 125 \text{ units per month}$$

The contribution to profit per TV table is measured directly by the unit contribution margin, $p - v$, which is $40 per table. So, since at sales of 125 units the profit is zero, at 126 units the profit is $40 (one unit past breakeven at $40), at 127 units the profit is $2 \times \$40 = \$80$, and so on. Using the unit contribution margin gives us a quick way to determine the change in profit for a change in sales units. At the 128-unit level profit would be

Sales: 128 units at $75/unit		$9,600
Less:		
Variable costs: 128 at $35/unit	$4,480	
Fixed costs	5,000	
Total costs		9,480
Total profit		$ 120

Or, using the unit contribution margin:

Three units in excess of breakeven × contribution margin

$$= 3 \times \$40 = \$120$$

The Equation Method: For Breakeven in Dollars

Sometimes units sold, unit variable cost, and unit sales price are not known, or it is impractical to determine them. Suppose a firm has many products and is interested in finding the overall breakeven level for all products taken together. Then we cannot find the breakeven in units, but it is possible to find the breakeven in sales dollars. We use the equation method in a revised form, where Y is the breakeven point in sales *dollars*:

$$Y = (v/p) \times Y + f + N$$

Using algebra, one can see this model is equivalent to the model used earlier for breakeven in units, except that Q is replaced by Y/p (i.e., sales in dollars $= Y = Q \times p$). Continuing with the HFI data in Exhibit 8–1, assume that we do not know that price is $75 and that unit variable cost is $35, instead, we know only total variable cost ($210,000) and total sales ($450,000). We can obtain the ratio, $v/p = .4667$ ($210,000/$450,000), and solve for monthly breakeven:

$$Y = .4667 \times Y + \$5,000$$

$$Y = \$9,375 \text{ per month}$$

To see that the dollar result agrees with the result for units, determine the total sales value for the breakeven level of 125 units, 125 units $\times$ $75 = $9,375, which agrees with the breakeven in dollars.

The Contribution Margin Method: For Breakeven in Units

A convenient method for calculating the breakeven point is to use the equation in its equivalent algebraic form (derived by solving the model for Q):

$$Q = \text{Fixed costs/Unit contribution margin}$$

$$= f/(p - v)$$

The contribution margin method (so-called because the contribution margin is the denominator of the ratio) produces the same result as the equation method:

$$Q = (\$5,000)/(\$75 - \$35) = 125 \text{ units per month}$$

Some people find it easier to use the equation method and others prefer to use the contribution margin method. We suggest you use the method with which you are most comfortable. Both methods produce the same results.

The CVP Graph and the Profit-Volume Graph

Breakeven analysis is illustrated graphically in Exhibit 8–4 that shows the CVP graph at the top and the profit-volume graph beneath. The **CVP graph** illustrates how the levels of revenues and total costs change over different levels of output. Note in the CVP graph that at output levels lower than 125 units, the revenue line falls below the cost line, resulting in losses. In contrast, there are profits for all points above the 125-unit level.

The **profit-volume graph** at the lower portion of the exhibit illustrates how the level of profits changes over different levels of output. At 125 units, profits are zero, and positive profits appear for output levels greater than 125. The slope of the profit-volume line is the unit contribution margin; therefore, the profit-volume graph can be used to read directly how total contribution margin, and therefore profits, will change as the output level changes.

The **CVP graph** illustrates how the levels of revenues and total costs change over different levels of output.

The **profit-volume graph** illustrates how the level of profits changes over different levels of output.

The Contribution Margin Method: For Breakeven in Dollars

It is also possible to find the breakeven point in dollars using the contribution margin method. Some managers are primarily interested in breakeven in dollars, or for a firm with many products it may not be practical to obtain a breakeven point in units. Instead of using the contribution margin for each product, the manager uses a single contribution margin ratio assumed to be the same for all products. (This is a reasonable assumption if all the products have approximately the same markup percentage.)

To use the contribution margin ratio method we multiply unit sales price by both sides of the CVP model used in the contribution margin method:

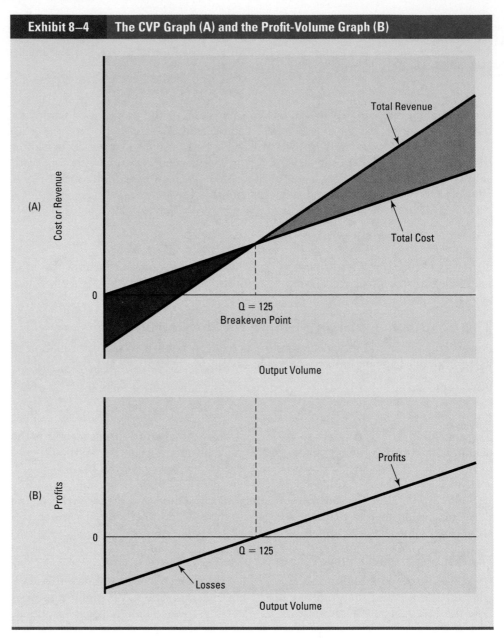

Exhibit 8–4   The CVP Graph (A) and the Profit-Volume Graph (B)

$$p \times Q = \frac{f \times p}{p - v}$$

or, alternatively:

$$p \times Q = \frac{f}{(p - v)/p}$$

The denominator in this equation is the contribution margin ratio. To continue with the HFI example, we compute the breakeven point in dollars as follows. The numerator is

$$f = \$5,000$$

And the denominator is

$$(p - v)/p = (\$75 - \$35)/\$75 = .5333$$

Thus the breakeven in dollars is computed as:

$$\$5,000/.5333 = \$9,375 \text{ per month}$$

Because the contribution margin method gives the same results as the equation method, it can be used interchangeably.

Summary of Breakeven Methods

The Equation Methods

1. Breakeven in units (Q = sales in units)

$$p \times Q = v \times Q + f + N$$

2. Breakeven in dollars (Y = sales in dollars)

$$Y = (v/p) \times Y + f + N$$

The Contribution Margin Methods

3. Breakeven in units =

$$\frac{(f + N)}{(p - v)}$$

4. Breakeven in dollars =

$$\frac{(f + N)}{(p - v)/p}$$

CVP ANALYSIS FOR REVENUE AND COST PLANNING

CVP analysis can be used to determine the level of sales needed to achieve a desired level of profit. The two possible objectives are revenue planning and cost planning.

◄ **LEARNING OBJECTIVE 3**
Apply CVP analysis for revenue planning and cost planning.

Revenue Planning

In revenue planning, CVP analysis assists managers in determining the revenue required to achieve a desired profit level. For example, if HFI's management wants to know the sales volume necessary to achieve $48,000 in annual profits, we would substitute $60,000 for fixed costs and $48,000 for desired profit; the solution in units is

$$Q = \frac{f + N}{p - v} = \frac{\$60,000 + \$48,000}{\$75 - \$35} = 2,700 \text{ units per year}$$

The solution in sales dollars is

$$p \times Q = \$75 \times 2,700 = \$202,500 \text{ per year}$$

Cost Planning

For cost planning decisions, the value of Q and the desired profit are known, and the manager wants to find the value of the required variable cost or fixed cost. Here are two examples.

Target Costing: Trade-offs between Different Costs

To facilitate target costing, CVP analysis is used to determine the most cost-effective trade-off between different types of costs. To continue with the HFI example, assume that sales will be 2,700 units per year. Management is now considering a new piece of production machinery that will reduce variable costs but also increase fixed costs by $2,250 per month. How much will unit variable costs have to fall to maintain the current level of profit, assuming sales volume and all other factors remain the same?

$Q = 2,700$ units

$p = \$75$

v = an unknown (it previously was $35)

$f = \$5,000 + \$2,250 = \$7,250$ per month ($87,000 per year)

$N = \$48,000$

Now, instead of solving for Q (Q is given as 2,700 units), we solve for v, as follows:

$$Q = \frac{f + N}{p - v}$$

$$p - v = \frac{(f + N)}{Q}$$

$$v = p - \frac{(f + N)}{Q}$$

$$v = \$75 - (\$87,000 + \$48,000)/2,700 = \$25$$

In effect, for profits to remain unchanged with the increase in fixed costs, unit variable costs would have to fall from \$35 to \$25.

Sales Commissions and Salaries

Another cost planning use of CVP analysis is to determine the most cost-effective means to manage downstream costs such as selling costs. To illustrate, management of HFI is reviewing sales salaries and commissions and finds that \$1,000 of the monthly \$5,000 fixed costs is sales salaries, and that \$7.50 of the \$35 of unit variable cost is a 10 percent sales commission. Suppose the salespeople are asking for a \$450 increase in salary. Management responds that the salaries can be raised only if the commission rate is decreased. How much would management have to reduce the commission rate to keep profits the same, assuming sales volume and all other factors remain unchanged?

With the proposed changes in variable and fixed costs to accommodate the new salary and commission plan, fixed costs increase by \$450 per month and variable costs decrease as a result of the decrease in the commission rate, r:

$$v = \text{commission rate} \times \text{sales price} + \text{other unit variable costs}$$

$$v = r \times \$75 + \$27.50$$

And: f = current monthly fixed costs + increase in monthly salary

$$f = \$5,000 + 450 = \$5,450 \text{ per month, or } \$65,400 \text{ per year}$$

Now we use the CVP model to solve for v:

$$Q = \frac{f + N}{p - v}$$

$$v = p - \frac{f + N}{Q}$$

and substituting for v and f:

$$r \times \$75 + \$27.50 = \$75 - (\$65,400 + \$48,000)/2,700$$

$$r = .0733$$

In this situation, the manager would have to reduce the commission rate from 10 to 7.33 percent to keep profits the same and pay an additional monthly salary of \$450 to the salespeople.

Including Income Taxes in CVP Analysis

The manager's decisions about costs and prices usually must include income taxes because taxes affect the amount of profit for a given level of sales. In the HFI example, if we assume the average tax rate is 20 percent, then to achieve the desired annual *after-tax* profit of \$48,000, HFI must generate before-tax profits of at least

$60,000 [$48,000/(1 − .2)]. Thus, when taxes are taken into account, the CVP model is as follows, where the average tax rate is t:

$$Q = \frac{f + \dfrac{N}{(1 - t)}}{(p - v)}$$

or:

$$Q = \frac{\$60,000 + \$48,000/(1 - .2)}{\$75 - \$35} = 3,000 \text{ units per year}$$

This amount is an increase of 300 units over the 2,700 units required for the before-tax profit level, as calculated earlier. The amount of the required sales to achieve a desired profit level thus increases as a result of taxes.

CVP ANALYSIS FOR ACTIVITY-BASED COSTING

The conventional approach to CVP analysis is to use a volume-based measure; that is, a measure based on units of product manufactured and sold. The preceding discussion has assumed a volume-based approach. An alternative approach is to use activity-based costing. In activity-based costing, cost drivers are identified for detailed-level indirect cost activities, such as machine setup, materials handling, inspection, and engineering. In contrast, the volume-based approach combines the costs of these activities and treats them as fixed costs, since they do not vary with output volume.

◀ **LEARNING OBJECTIVE 4**
Apply CVP analysis for activity-based costing.

Activity-based costing provides a more accurate determination of costs because the indirect costs are separately identified and traced to products, rather than being combined into a pool of fixed costs as in the volume-based approach. Returning to the HFI example, we show how CVP analysis can be adapted when activity-based costing is used.

The conventional, volume-based CVP analysis would provide:

$$Q = (\$60,000 + 48,000)/(\$75 - \$35) = 2,700 \text{ units}$$

What would the activity-based CVP analysis look like? Suppose the cost accounting staff has been able to trace approximately $10,000 of last year's fixed costs to batch-level activities such as machine setup and inspection. This estimate was made when the firm was operating at 100 batches per year. These costs can be traced directly to each batch, though not to each unit of output. Also, the staff has learned that this year's production of 3,000 units is to be produced in batches of 30 units, so there will be 100 batches produced again this year. If the manufacturing facility is sufficiently large, then we can assume batch-level costs increase in proportion to an increase in the number of batches produced during the year; that is, $100 per batch ($10,000/100). The activity-based CVP model is thus developed in the following way.

First, we define new terms for fixed cost: $f = f^{VB} + f^{AB}$,

where:

f^{VB} = the volume-based fixed costs, the portion of fixed costs that *do not* vary with the activity cost driver, $50,000 ($60,000 − $10,000)

f^{AB} = the portion of fixed costs that varies with the activity cost driver, $10,000; we assume that $10,000 is necessary for 3,000 units of output, requiring 100 production batches of 30 units each

Second, we define the following terms:

v^{AB} = the cost per batch for the activity-based cost driver, $10,000/100 = $100 per batch

b = the number of units in a batch, 30 units (3,000/100)
v^{AB}/b = the cost per unit of product for batch-related costs, when the batch is size b; v^{AB}/b = \$3.33 (\$100/30)

Third, the CVP model for activity-based costing is

$$Q = \frac{f^{VB} + N}{p - v - (v^{AB}/b)}$$

Fourth, substituting data from the HFI example,

$$Q = \frac{\$50,000 + \$48,000}{\$75 - \$35 - \$100/30} = 2,673 \text{ units}$$

The solution for the activity-based model (2,673 units) is slightly lower than for the conventional model (2,700 units), because a portion of the fixed costs in the conventional analysis is treated as variable costs in the activity-based model.[1]

To illustrate the effect of batch size on the solution, suppose production is scheduled in smaller batches of 20 units, and assume that batch costs continue to be \$100 each. How many units must be sold now to earn \$48,000? The answer is determined from the preceding equation for activity-based CVP analysis:

Batches of 20 units each

$$Q = (\$50,000 + \$48,000)/(\$75 - \$35 - \$100/20)$$

$$= 2,800 \text{ units}$$

or

$$= 140 \text{ batches } (2,800/20) \text{ of 20 units each}$$

We also can determine the solution for batches of 100:

Batches of 100 units each

$$Q = (\$50,000 + \$48,000)/(\$75 - \$35 - \$100/100)$$

$$= 2,513 \text{ units}$$

or

$$= 26 \text{ batches } (2,513/100, \text{ rounded})$$

Notice that the number of units to achieve the desired profit falls dramatically when we go from a 20-unit batch to a 100-unit batch, due to the decrease in batch-level costs. Fewer, larger batches means less batch-related cost and, therefore, a lower breakeven point. CVP analysis based on activity-based costing can provide a more precise analysis of the relationships among volume, costs, and profits by taking batch-level costs into account.[2]

LEARNING OBJECTIVE 5 ▸
Employ sensitivity analysis to more effectively use CVP analysis when there is uncertainty about actual sales.

The **margin of safety** measures the potential effect of the risk that sales will fall short of planned levels.

SENSITIVITY ANALYSIS OF CVP RESULTS

It is often important to answer the question, How much does it really matter if we fall short of the breakeven point? To examine the sensitivity of profits to changes in sales, we can use either of two measures: the margin of safety or operating leverage.

Margin of Safety

The **margin of safety** measures the potential effect of the risk that sales will fall short of planned levels.

---

[1]   While the increase in variable costs for the activity-based model has the effect of *increasing* the breakeven point, the effect of the decreased fixed costs is stronger because of the assumption that expected production levels are higher than the breakeven point.

[2]   There is a discussion of CVP analysis for activity-based costing in Lawrence M. Metzger, "The Power to Compete: The New Math of Precision Management," *The National Public Accountant*, May 1993, pp. 14–32.

Margin of safety = Planned sales − Breakeven sales

Returning to the HFI example, assume the planned sales of TV tables is 3,000 units per year; since the breakeven quantity is 1,500 units, the margin of safety would be

Margin of safety in units = 3,000 − 1,500 = 1,500 units

or

Margin of safety in sales dollars = 1,500 × \$75 = \$112,500

The margin of safety also can be used as a ratio, a percentage of sales:

Margin of safety ratio = Margin of safety/Planned sales

= 1,500/3,000 = 50 percent

The **margin of safety ratio** is a useful measure for comparing the risk of two alternative products, or for assessing the riskiness in any given product. The product with a relatively low margin of safety ratio is the riskier of the two products and therefore usually requires more of management's attention.

<aside>The **margin of safety ratio** is a useful measure for comparing the risk of two alternative products, or for assessing the riskiness in any given product.</aside>

Operating Leverage

Changes in the contemporary manufacturing environment include improved production techniques through automation, work-flow enhancements, and other techniques. As these changes take place, the nature of CVP analysis also changes. For example, in a fully automated production environment, labor costs are less important, and variable costs consist primarily of materials costs. In some settings, such as the manufacture of certain electrical parts and components, the materials cost is also relatively low, so that fixed costs are very high relative to total cost. In this context CVP analysis can play a crucial strategic role, because profits are more sensitive to the number of units manufactured and sold. In other manufacturing operations, with low fixed costs and relatively high variable costs, profits are less sensitive to changes in sales, and CVP is relatively less important.

Consider two firms: One has relatively low fixed costs and relatively high unit variable costs (a labor-intensive firm). The second has relatively high fixed costs and relatively low variable costs (a fully automated firm). Sample data for two such firms are shown in Exhibit 8–5.

These two situations are compared in Exhibit 8–6A (relatively high fixed costs) and Exhibit 8–6B (relatively low fixed costs). Note that the breakeven point is the same in each case, 50,000 units. However, if we examine the profit at 25,000 units above breakeven, or the loss at 25,000 units below breakeven, a strong contrast emerges. For the firm with relatively high fixed costs (Exhibit 8–6A), the loss at 25,000 units is relatively large, a \$250,000 loss, while the profit at 75,000 units is also relatively large, \$250,000. In contrast, when fixed costs are low (Exhibit 8–6B), the loss at 25,000 units is only \$75,000 and the profit at 75,000 units is only \$75,000.

It is apparent that a firm with high fixed costs is more risky because profits are very strongly affected by the level of activity. High profits are earned beyond breakeven, but high losses result from falling below breakeven. In this context, CVP analysis is

Exhibit 8–5	Contrasting Data for Fully Automated and Labor-Intensive Firms	
	Fully Automated: **High Fixed Cost**	**Labor-Intensive:** **Low Fixed Cost**
Fixed cost/year	\$500,000	\$150,000
Variable cost/unit	2	9
Price	12	12
Contribution margin	10	3

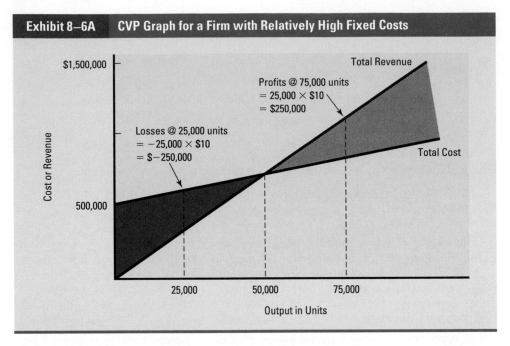

Exhibit 8–6A   CVP Graph for a Firm with Relatively High Fixed Costs

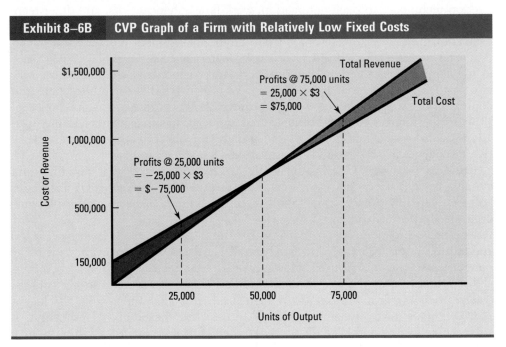

Exhibit 8–6B   CVP Graph of a Firm with Relatively Low Fixed Costs

particularly important in planning the use of new manufacturing technologies that have the potential to change the relationship between fixed and variable costs.

The potential effect of the risk that sales will fall short of planned levels, as influenced by the relative proportion of fixed to variable manufacturing costs, can be measured by operating leverage. **Operating leverage** is the ratio of the contribution margin to profit. For the HFI data (Exhibit 8–2), the operating leverage for 19X1 is as follows:

Operating leverage is the ratio of the contribution margin to profit.

$$\text{Operating leverage} = \text{Contribution margin/Profit}$$

$$= \$96,000/\$36,000 = 2.667$$

Operating leverage of 2.667 means that since HFI's sales increased 8.33 percent ($15,000/$180,000) from 19X1 to 19X2, profits should increase by 22.22 percent (2.667 × 8.33%). A quick calculation demonstrates that profit has increased by 22.22 percent ($8,000/$36,000).

A higher value for operating leverage indicates a higher risk in the sense that a given change in sales will have a relatively greater impact on profits. When sales volume is strong, it is desirable to have a high level of leverage, but when sales begin to fall, a lower level of leverage is preferable. Each firm chooses the level of operating leverage that is consistent with its competitive strategy. For example, a firm with a dominant position in its market might choose a high level of leverage to exploit its advantage. In contrast, a weaker firm might choose the less risky low-leverage strategy.

Operating Leverage at Chrysler Corporation

Chrysler management announced a planned new luxury car would not be built. The economics were just not there. But when asked about the number of cars needed to break even on the planned new car (Codename LX), management acknowledged a relatively small number, about 30,000 vehicles. The reason for the low breakeven is that Chrysler adds manufacturing capacity only in response to proven demand. Chrysler president Robert Lutz explained that in comparison to Ford, Chrysler has similar labor and materials cost. The big difference is in the per-unit fixed costs, where Lutz thinks Chrysler is $1,000 to $1,500 lower than Ford.

Source: Based on information from "The Car Chrysler Didn't Build," *Forbes,* August 12, 1996, pp. 89–90.

Operating Leverage at Conner and Seagate

In examining the two manufacturers of computer disk drives, Seagate and Conner, *Business Week* explains how the two firms differ on operating leverage. Conner buys rather than builds most of its components, and therefore has lower fixed costs. But when demand jumps, it can run short of parts. Seagate, however, makes many of its components. Thus, its fixed costs are relatively high, but it can increase production quickly when demand is strong. However, when demand is low, Seagate's high fixed costs cannot be avoided.

Seagate is the more highly leveraged of the manufacturers, and it benefits when demand is strong and suffers if demand falls.

Source: Based on information in "Quantum Has One Tough Hurdle to Leap," *Business Week,* May 8, 1991, p. 86, and "The Man in the Disk Driver's Seat," *Business Week,* March 18, 1996, pp. 71–73.

BusinessWeek

 What's American Airlines' Strategy for Continued Success?

(Continued from page 249)

A: It's a strategy grounded in Strategic Fundamentals.

There are a number of strategies CEO Robert Crandall has devised to compete in his low-cost leadership industry. The major strategy is strict cost control. For example, Crandall devised a two-tier salary structure in which new employees at American receive substantially lower salaries than the senior employees do. Thus, as the firm grows and adds employees, the average labor cost of the firm decreases. Crandall was also the first to effectively reduce costs of on-board meal service.

Secondly, Crandall watches operating leverage and is careful not to become over-committed. He prides himself on the low debt of the airline, and has cut orders for new airplanes when necessary to maintain low leverage. Elizabeth Bailey, an expert in the industry, observes, "Those (airlines) in trouble are in trouble by and large because they leveraged themselves in the 1980s. American didn't leverage itself in that crazy way." By keeping its leverage and fixed costs low, and by reducing operating costs (labor and meals), American is in a better position to meet the price wars in the industry.

For further reading, see the following sources "The Airline Mess," *Business Week,* July 6, 1992; "Stuck!" *Business Week,* November 15, 1993; and "Bob Crandall: An American Gladiator," *Business Week,* April 27, 1998, p. 44.

> ### The Role of Operating Leverage in Strategy at Unisys
>
> The CEO of Unisys, a large computer mainframe manufacturer, recognizes the effect of different cost structures on competitive strategy. Contrasting the computer manufacturing industry and the steel industry, he notes that while the steel industry has high fixed costs, the mainframe manufacturing industry does not. Therefore, he observes, it is more important for the computer manufacturer to control costs, while for the steel manufacturer it is more important to increase revenues.
>
> **Source:** Based on information from *Financial World,* October 12, 1993, p. 37.

> ### Operating Leverage in the Computer Industry: Microprocessors and Software
>
> In many industries, growth in demand for the product or service often leads to price inflation. In contrast, high-tech industries such as those that manufacture microprocessors or semiconductors and those that develop software, find that rising demand can actually drive prices down. The reason is that it requires a very large investment to be competitive in the semiconductor industry or in mainstream software products. The fixed costs of the investment, and the capacity to produce the chips or the programs, are very high while the variable costs of producing the chips or programs are relatively low. As the investment rises, the variable costs fall, and thus the trend to concentration in the industry and the ever-falling prices.
>
> **Source:** Based on information from "Cover Story: The Computer Industry," *Business Week,* March 31, 1997, p. 64.

CVP ANALYSIS WITH MULTIPLE PRODUCTS

LEARNING OBJECTIVE 6 ▶
Adapt CVP analysis for multiple products.

One of the simplifying assumptions made in the chapter to this point was to develop the CVP model for only a single product. How does the analysis change if we must deal with two or more products? What if the two or more products share the same fixed costs? Can we still calculate a breakeven value for each product? This section adapts the CVP model so that questions like these can be readily answered.

Our adaptation of the CVP model requires one key assumption, that the sales of the product will *continue at the same sales mix*. That is, the sales of each product will remain at the same proportion of total sales. The mix can be determined in either sales units or sales dollars; the important point is that it must remain constant.

Assuming that there is a constant sales mix allows us to treat the two or more products as one combined product mix, by computing a weighted-average contribution margin. The weighted-average contribution margin is used to determine the total sales necessary for attaining the desired operating result.

To illustrate, we use the example of Windbreakers, Inc., which is in the business of selling light-weight sport/recreational jackets. Windbreakers has three products, "Calm" (to wear in a light breeze), and "Windy" and "Gale" for wear in sterner weather. Relevant information for these products is in Exhibit 8–7. The total fixed costs for the period are expected to be $171,500.

Exhibit 8–7	Sales and Cost Data for Windbreakers, Inc.			
	Calm	**Windy**	**Gale**	**Total**
Last period's sales (units)	750,000	600,000	150,000	1,500,000
Percent of unit sales	50	40	10	100%
Price	$30	$32	$40	
Unit variable cost	25	27	36	
Contribution margin	$ 5	$ 5	$ 4	
Fixed costs				$171,500

From this information we can calculate the weighted-average contribution margin as follows, using the percent of sales units relative to total sales units for each product.

$$.5(\$5) + .4(\$5) + .1(\$4) = \$4.90$$

$$= \text{Weighted-average contribution margin}$$

The breakeven point for all three products can be calculated:

$$Q = f/(p - v) = \$171,500/\$4.90 = 35,000 \text{ jackets}$$

This means that for the Windbreakers business to breakeven, 35,000 units of all three products must be sold in the same proportion as last year's sales mix. The sales for each product are

For Calm:	.5(35,000) =	17,500 jackets
For Windy:	.4(35,000) =	14,000 jackets
For Gale:	.1(35,000) =	3,500 jackets
Total		35,000 jackets

The sale of 35,000 jackets in the correct sales mix would produce exactly the breakeven revenue of $171,500:

$$\$5(17,500) + \$5(14,000) + \$4(3,500) = \$171,500$$

The solution relies on the assumed constant sales mix for the products involved. If the sales mix does change, the analysis will be different. As new sales mix, price, or cost information becomes available, the breakeven analysis should be recomputed.

Graphical Analysis: Multiple Breakeven Points

When only two products are involved, a graphical approach can add to the manager's understanding of the cost-volume relationships for these products. The analysis is based on the fact that the breakeven point for the firm can be any one of many possible combinations of sales mixes for the two products. Fortunately, all possible combinations of sales mixes for breakeven are easy to identify graphically, once we know the breakeven points of each product. Using the previous example, suppose *only Windy and Gale are produced*, with these individual breakeven points:

Windy: $171,500/5 = 34,300 units

Gale: $171,500/4 = 42,875 units

All possible combinations of breakeven points lie on (and only on) the line joining the individual breakeven points for the two products, as illustrated in Exhibit 8–8. This is so because of the linear nature of the CVP relationship for each of these products. Any point on the line in Exhibit 8–8 can be determined from the equation for that line, which is

$$\text{Gale} = \frac{42,875}{34,300} \times (34,300 - \text{Windy})$$

Or:

$$\text{Units of Gale} = 42,875 - 1.25 \times (\text{Units of Windy})$$

For example, the breakeven quantity for units of Gale, if Windy is sold at the level of 19,000 units, would be

$$\text{Units of Gale} = 42,875 - 1.25 \times 19,000 = 19,125 \text{ units}$$

The total contribution margin of this product mix would be

$$19,000 \times \$5 + 19,125 \times \$4 = \$171,500$$

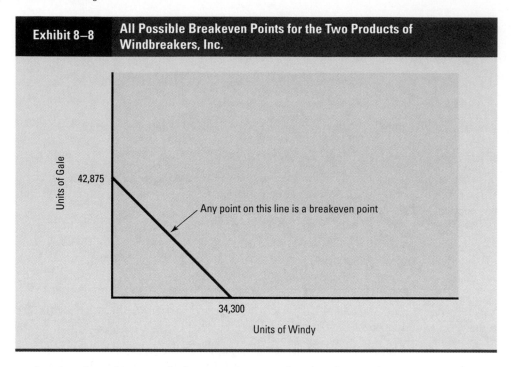

| Exhibit 8–8 | All Possible Breakeven Points for the Two Products of Windbreakers, Inc. |

Graphical analysis can help managers see that breakeven for two products can be achieved by many possible combinations of product mixes, specifically, all those product mix combinations that fall on the line segment in Exhibit 8–8.

CVP ANALYSIS FOR NOT-FOR-PROFIT ORGANIZATIONS AND SERVICE FIRMS

LEARNING OBJECTIVE 7 ▶
Apply CVP analysis in not-for-profit organizations and service firms.

CVP analysis also can be used in not-for-profit organizations. To illustrate, consider a small mental health agency experiencing financial difficulty. Orange County Mental Health Center's financial support comes from the county, whose revenues are underbudget because of a recession in the local economy. As a result, the county commissioners have set an across-the-board budget cut of about 5 percent for the new fiscal year. The center's funding was $735,000 last year and is projected to be approximately $700,000 next year. The center's director figures that variable costs (including medications, handout publications, and some administrative costs) amount to approximately $10 per visit for the almost 300 patients who regularly see counselors at the center. All other costs are fixed, including salaries for the counselors, record-keeping costs, and facilities costs. How will the budget cuts affect the level of services provided by the center?

To answer this question, we have to determine precisely the activity of the center with the associated fixed and variable costs. Though we could define activity in a variety of ways, we choose the number of patient visits as a logical measure of the center's activity. The director estimates there were 13,000 to 14,000 patient visits last year. With this information we can develop the cost equation illustrated in Exhibit 8–9. We have assumed that there were 13,500 visits last year and that unit variable costs are constant at $10 per visit in the range of 10,000 to 14,000 visits per year; total variable costs were therefore $135,000 ($10 × 13,500) last year. To determine total fixed costs for last year:

$$\text{Funding} = \text{Total cost}$$

$$= \text{Total fixed costs} + \text{Total variable costs}$$

$$\$735,000 = \text{Total fixed costs} + \$135,000$$

$$\text{Total fixed costs} = \$600,000$$

Now the director can analyze the effect of the budget change on the center's service levels. At the $700,000 budget level expected for next year, the activity would

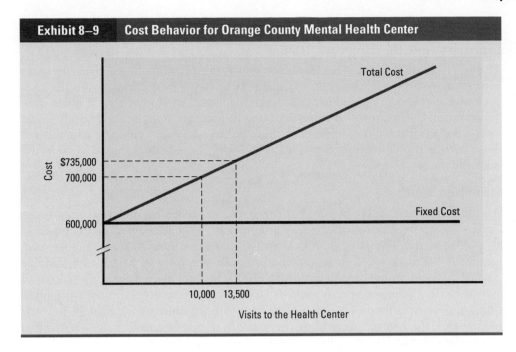

Exhibit 8–9   Cost Behavior for Orange County Mental Health Center

be approximately 10,000 visits. Total cost of $700,000 less fixed cost of $600,000 leaves variable costs of $100,000; thus, $100,000/$10 = 10,000 visits. The director can now see that the approximate 5 percent cut in the budget is expected to result in an approximate 26 percent drop in patient contact [(13,500 − 10,000)/13,500].

While the county commissioners might have expected that the center's activity would be reduced by approximately 5 percent with the budget cut, the actual contraction in services is much more severe (26 percent). Why? Because fixed costs are expected to remain constant into the new budget year, and expected savings from reducing activity levels will be less than the effect on the activity itself. The county commissioners should realize that the mental health center's costs are predominantly fixed costs, and therefore budget cuts might have more of an effect on services than expected.

As demonstrated earlier, CVP analysis also can be used in service firms; for example, in the airline industry or the medical care industry. Airline firms use CVP to identify profitable new routes and to manage variable costs to meet reduced revenues in times of fare wars in the industry. Similarly, firms that specialize in home health care, nursing homes, or outpatient care use CVP analysis to identify profitable new services and to help analyze the costs of delivering existing services.

BEHAVIORAL ISSUES IN USING CVP ANALYSIS

Occasionally a behavioral issue arises when using CVP analysis. As our example of the county mental health clinic illustrates, an understanding of cost-volume behavior may be necessary to appropriately and fairly decide issues regarding the use of public funds.

Behavioral issues arise because of the uncertainty in the factors of the CVP model—price, expected sales level, variable costs, and fixed costs. As we saw in Chapter 3, the presence of uncertainty means that risk-averse decision makers may be biased in their efforts to avoid unfavorable consequences. For example, a CVP analysis might show that a new product should be introduced because its breakeven point produces a reasonably high margin of safety; the firm would therefore wish to introduce the product. However, if there is significant uncertainty about the expected sales of the product, and if the choice is made by a risk-averse manager whose compensation and reputation are likely to be adversely affected by the potential for poor sales, the manager might choose not to introduce the product, against the firm's wishes. When uncertainty is significant in a CVP analysis, management must be aware of the bias resulting from risk aversion.

ASSUMPTIONS AND LIMITATIONS OF CVP ANALYSIS

Linearity and the Relevant Range

The CVP model assumes that revenues and total costs are linear over the relevant range of activity. Although actual cost behavior is not linear, we use the concept of the relevant range introduced in Chapter 3, so that within a given limited range of output, total costs are expected to increase at an approximately linear rate. The caution for the manager is therefore to remember that the calculations done within the context of a given CVP model should not be used outside the relevant range.

Step-Fixed Costs

As illustrated in Exhibit 8–10, the cost behavior under examination may be so "lumpy" (step-fixed costs) that an approximation via a relevant range is unworkable. Although CVP analysis can be done, it becomes somewhat more cumbersome. Exhibit 8–10 illustrates a situation wherein there is a price of $18, a unit variable cost of $10, an initial fixed cost of $100,000, and an incremental fixed cost of another $100,000 when output exceeds 10,000 units. The expenditure of the additional fixed cost will provide capacity for up to 30,000 units. A CVP analysis would require that the manager determine the breakeven point for each range (below and above the point at 10,000 units). For these data, we find that there is no breakeven below the 10,000 unit level of output, but the breakeven point can be obtained for the upper range as follows:

$$Q = f/(p - v) = \$200,000/(\$18 - \$10) = 25,000 \text{ units}$$

Thus, losses will be incurred up until the 25,000-unit level, and the additional investment in capacity will be necessary to achieve this production and sales level. Of potential concern to the manager is the relatively narrow range of profitability, between 25,000 and 30,000 units. Therefore, additional analysis might be advisable to better determine the extent of demand for the product and the cost of extending capacity beyond 30,000 units.

Identifying Fixed and Variable Cost for CVP Analysis

In the CVP analysis, it is not always easy to identify the dollar figures used for fixed costs and unit variable cost. Let's take a close look at how fixed and variable costs are determined for purposes of the CVP analysis.

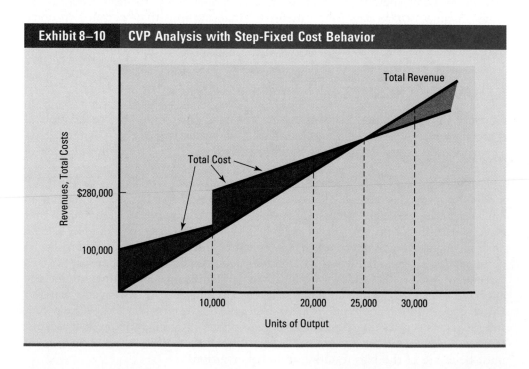

Exhibit 8–10   CVP Analysis with Step-Fixed Cost Behavior

Fixed Costs to Include

Suppose management wants to calculate the breakeven point for a new product for Household Furnishings, Inc. The new product is a computer table designed for easy assembly and intended for the low-price end of the market. Would the cost of the president's salary be a relevant fixed cost for this calculation? The answer is no. Because the president's salary does not change whether or not HFI introduces the computer table, it is a fixed cost for the corporation, but it is irrelevant for the analysis of the short-term profitability of the new product.

In a short-term analysis, relevant fixed costs are those expected to change with the introduction of the new product. These include costs of any new production facilities, salaries of new production personnel, and similar costs.

If a new product would not require any new fixed costs because there is existing capacity, facilities, and personnel to handle the added production, what would be the breakeven point? For a *short-term analysis*, the breakeven point would be zero, since there are no new fixed costs to be covered by the new product. That is, each product sold, beginning with the first, contributes to profit in the excess of price over variable cost. In contrast, for a *long-term analysis* of breakeven, all current and expected future fixed costs associated with the production, distribution, and sale of the product would be relevant.

Allocated Fixed Costs

Firms that have two or more products often allocate fixed costs to these products when the fixed costs are incurred jointly by the product lines. Do these allocated fixed costs belong in a CVP analysis? Following the previous thinking, for a short-term analysis the answer is no. For example, if we are calculating the breakeven point for a new product, we would not include any allocated fixed costs unless the new product is expected to increase these joint costs. Only the increase in fixed costs should be included.

The Period in Which the Cost Was Incurred

The fixed costs in a CVP analysis can include the expected cash outflows for fixed costs in the period for which breakeven is expected; alternatively, they can include the fixed costs as determined by accrual accounting. The cash flow fixed costs would include all cash outflows for insurance, taxes, and salaries, but would exclude the noncash items such as depreciation, amortization of patents, and other noncash expenses. The advantage of the cash flow approach is its focus on the cash needs of the company.

An accrual accounting approach to determine the amount of fixed costs would include all the costs normally expensed in the income statement, including depreciation, amortization, and accrued expenses. The advantage of this approach is that it ties the CVP analysis into the income statement. In choosing between these two approaches, a manager considers the relative benefits of information most relevant for cash flows or for accrual net profit.[3]

Unit Variable Costs

In measuring unit variable cost, the management accountant must be careful to include all relevant variable costs, not only production costs but also selling and distribution costs. Thus, commissions expense would be properly included as a unit variable cost. Also, any transportation or warehousing costs, if they change with level of output, would be relevant.

---

[3] Some useful references for cash flow and accrual breakeven analysis are Bipin Ajikkya, Rowland Atiase, and Linda Bamber, "Absorption versus Direct Costing: Income Reconciliation and Cost-Volume-Profit Analysis," *Issues in Accounting Education*, Fall 1986, pp. 268–81; David Solomons, "Breakeven Analysis under Absorption Costing," *The Accounting Review*, July 1968, pp. 447–52; Donald E. Ricketts and Charles R. Purdy, "The Effect of Cost-Volume-Profit Structure on Full and Direct Costing Net Income: A Generalizable Approach," *The Accounting Review*, July 1974, pp. 603–7; and Henry Wichmann, Jr., and Harold M. Nix, "Cost-Volume-Profit Analysis for Small Retailers and Service Businesses," *Cost and Management*, May–June 1984, pp. 31–35.

SUMMARY

This chapter develops CVP analysis, a linear model of the relationships between costs, revenues, and output levels. The analysis is used for breakeven planning, revenue planning, and cost planning.

Breakeven planning determines the output level at which profits are zero. Breakeven analysis is used in planning and budgeting to assess the desirability of current and potential products and services. CVP analysis also is used in revenue planning to determine the sales needed to achieve a desired profit level by adding desired profit to the breakeven equation of total sales equal total costs. In cost planning, CVP analysis is used to find the required reduction in costs to meet desired profits, or to find the required change in fixed cost for a given change in variable cost (or vice versa).

Revenue and cost planning are enhanced by two additional concepts—activity-based costing and sensitivity analysis. Activity-based costing breaks fixed costs into batch- and unit-related costs, so CVP analyses can be done at either (or both) the batch or unit level. Sensitivity analysis is useful because profits of firms with relatively high fixed costs are more sensitive to changes in the level of sales. The sensitivity, or risk, of changes in sales levels is measured by the margin of safety and operating leverage.

When there are two or more products, the use of CVP analysis requires the assumption of a constant sales mix between the products, and the weighted-average contribution margin is used to calculate the breakeven point.

KEY TERMS

Breakeven point   252

Contribution income statement   251

Contribution margin ratio   250

Cost-volume-profit (CVP) analysis   249

CVP graph   253

Margin of safety   258

Margin of safety ratio   259

Operating leverage   260

Profit-volume graph   253

Total contribution margin   250

Unit contribution margin   250

SELF-STUDY PROBLEM

(For solution, please turn to the end of the chapter.)

The following data refer to a single product, the TECHWHIZ, made by the Markdata Computer Company:

Sales price = $5,595

Materials cost (including purchased components) = $899

Direct labor cost = $233

Facilities cost (a highly automated plant; this is mainly rent, insurance, taxes, and depreciation) = $2,352,000 per year

Required

1. What is the unit contribution margin?
2. What is the breakeven point in units and dollars?
3. What is the desired level of sales if the company plans to increase fixed costs by 5 percent (to improve product quality and appearance) and achieve a desired before-tax profit of $200,000?
4. If the company's income tax rate is 22 percent, what unit sales are necessary to achieve an after-tax profit of $150,000?

QUESTIONS

8-1 What is the underlying relationship in CVP analysis?

8-2 When might it be better to find the breakeven point in sales dollars rather than in units?

8-3 What is the contribution margin ratio and how is it used?

8-4 What are the basic assumptions of CVP analysis?

8-5 Why might the percentage budget cut for a not-for-profit agency not equal the resultant change in the activity level?

8-6 If a new product does not require any new fixed costs because the company utilizes the existing capacity of facilities and personnel, what would be the breakeven point?

8-7 CVP analysis can be conducted by recognizing costs under either the cash or accrual basis. What are the advantages of each method?

8-8 Why does the issue of taxes not affect the calculation of the breakeven point?

8-9 Why is CVP analysis important in planning the use of new manufacturing technologies?

8-10 What type of risk does sensitivity analysis deal with?

8-11 Why does the management accountant use sensitivity analysis?

8-12 What is the margin of safety, and what is it used for?

8-13 What is operating leverage, and what is it used for?

8-14 How are allocated fixed costs treated in CVP analysis?

8-15 Desired before-tax net income is equal to the desired after-tax net income divided by _____?

8-16 How is CVP analysis used to calculate the breakeven point for multiple products?

8-17 Explain the four methods for calculating the breakeven point.

PROBLEMS

8-18 **CVP ANALYSIS; STRATEGY** Frank's Western Wear is a retailer of western hats in Dallas, Texas. Although Frank's carries numerous styles of western hats, each hat has approximately the same price and invoice (purchase) cost, as shown in the table. Sales personnel receive large commissions to encourage them to be more aggressive in their sales efforts. Currently the economy of Dallas is really humming, and sales growth at Frank's has been great. However, the business is very competitive, and Frank has relied on his knowledgeable and courteous staff to attract and retain customers, who otherwise might go to other western wear stores. Also, because of the rapid growth in sales, Frank is finding it more difficult to manage certain aspects of the business, such as restocking of inventory and hiring and training new salespeople.

Strategy

Sales price	$30.00
Per unit variable expenses	
Invoice cost	15.50
Sales commissions	4.50
Total per unit variable costs	$20.00
Total annual fixed expenses	
Advertising	$ 20,000
Rent	25,000
Salaries	105,000
Total fixed expenses	$150,000

Required

1. Calculate the annual breakeven point in unit sales and dollar sales.
2. If 20,000 hats are sold, what is Frank's net income or loss?
3. Frank is considering eliminating sales commissions completely and increasing salaries by $82,000 annually. What would be the new breakeven point in units? What would be the net income or loss if 20,000 hats are sold with the new salary plan?
4. Identify and discuss the strategic issues in the above decision about eliminating sales commissions (see requirement 3). How do these strategic concerns affect Frank's decision?

8–19 **MAKE OR BUY; TWO MACHINES**   The IZ & Z Company manufactures electronic equipment. Currently, the company purchases the special switches used in each of its products from an outside supplier. The supplier charges IZ & Z $2 per switch. IZ & Z's CEO is considering purchasing either machine A or machine B, so the company can manufacture its own switches. The projected data are

	Machine A	Machine B
Annual fixed cost	$145,000	$180,000
Variable cost per switch	.55	.40

Required

1. For each machine, give the minimum number of switches that must be made annually for total costs to equal outside purchase cost.
2. What is the most profitable alternative for producing 200,000 switches per year?
3. What volume level would produce the same total costs regardless of the machine purchased?

8–20 **MARGIN OF SAFETY**   The InfoTech Corporation expects to sell 20,000 phone switches. Fixed costs are $10,125,000, unit price is $3,225, and unit variable cost is $1,200.

Required

1. Calculate InfoTech's margin of safety and margin of safety ratio.
2. Explain the meaning of margin of safety.
3. Is a large margin of safety more or less risky? Why?

8–21 **OPERATING LEVERAGE**   These sales and cost data (000s) are for two companies in the transportation industry:

	Company A		Company B	
	Amount	Percent of sales	Amount	Percent of sales
Sales	$100,000	100%	$100,000	100%
Variable costs	60,000	60	30,000	30
Contribution margin	$ 40,000	40%	$ 70,000	70%
Fixed costs	30,000		60,000	
Net income	$ 10,000		$ 10,000	

Required

1. Calculate the operating leverage for each company. If sales increase, which company benefits more? How do you know?
2. Assume sales rise 10 percent in the next year. Calculate the percentage increase in profit for each company. Are the results what you expected?

8–22 CHANGE IN FIXED COSTS   The Riley Company manufactures high-level computer monitors. Following is a summary of its basic cost and revenue data:

	Per Unit	Percent of Sales
Sales price	$400	100%
Variable costs	240	60
Unit contribution margin	$ 160	40%

Assume the Riley Company is currently selling 500 computer monitors per month totaling $200,000. The sales manager believes that a $15,000 increase in the advertising budget would increase monthly sales by $50,000.

Required   Should the advertising budget be increased? Explain your answer.

8–23 CHANGE IN PRICE, FIXED COSTS   Refer to the data about the Riley Company in problem 8–22. Assume again that the Riley Company is currently selling 500 computer monitors per month. To increase sales, the manager wants to cut the selling price by $40 per unit and increase the advertising budget by $15,000. Management believes that unit sales will increase by 50 percent if these two steps are followed. Fixed costs are $50,000 per month.

Required

1. Should the Riley Company follow this new strategy?

2. Prepare a comparative income statement to prove your results.

8–24 MULTIPLE PRODUCTS CVP   The Brown Company can produce two types of lamps, the Brighter and Elegance. The data on the two lamps are

	Brighter	Elegance
Sales volume in units	500	600
Unit sales price	$200.00	$250.00
Unit variable cost	120.00	120.00
Unit contribution margin	$ 80.00	$130.00

It takes 1 machine-hour to produce Brighter and 2 hours to produce Elegance. Total fixed costs for the manufacture of both products is $132,000. Demand is high enough for either product to keep the plant operating at full capacity.

Required

1. What is the breakeven point in sales costs for the Brown Company, assuming that the sales mix remains constant in sales dollars?

2. Which of the two products do you think is more profitable? Why?

8–25 BUDGET CUTS   The Student Health Services Pharmacy provides certain medications to students free of charge. Currently, 40 percent of the pharmacy's costs are fixed; the other 60 percent are variable. The pharmacy's budget was $200,000 last year. The university recently cut the budget by 20 percent for this year.

Service

Required   What will be the percentage decrease in the amount of services the pharmacy can provide this year?

8–26 EFFECTS OF TECHNOLOGY ON CVP   Firms A and B both produce and sell computer cables. The sales price is $5 per cable. Data for both firms at 100 units are

	Firm A	Firm B
Sales	$500	$500
Variable costs	100	300
Total contribution margin	$400	$200
Fixed costs	300	100
Operating income	$100	$100

Required

1. Prepare graphs showing total revenue and total costs for each firm (from 0 to 100 units).

2. Which firm's profit or loss is more sensitive to changes in production?

8–27 THE ROLE OF INCOME TAXES   The Triad Company had fixed costs of $200,000 and variable costs of 80 percent of total sales revenue in 19X5. The company earned net income after taxes of $70,000 in 19X5. The income tax rate was 30 percent.

Required   Determine (1) before-tax operating income, (2) total contribution margin, (3) total sales, and (4) breakeven point in dollar sales.

8–28 CVP ANALYSIS WITH TAXES   The Jeffrey Company produces and sells socks. Variable costs are $3 per pair, and fixed costs for the year total $75,000. The selling price is $5 per pair.

Required   Calculate the following:

1. The breakeven point in units.

2. The breakeven point in sales dollars.

3. The units required to make a before-tax profit of $10,000.

4. The sales in dollars required to make a before-tax profit of $8,000.

5. The sales units and sales dollars required to make an after-tax profit of $12,000 given a tax rate of 40 percent.

8–29 BREAKEVEN ANALYSIS FOR MULTIPLE PRODUCTS   TexFab manufactures two products, GT450 and GT600, that have the following sales and cost information:

	Product GT450		Product GT600		Total	
	Amount	Percent	Amount	Percent	Amount	Percent
Sales	$25,000	100%	$75,000	100%	$100,000	100%
Variable costs	20,000	80	37,500	50	57,500	57.5
Contribution margin	$ 5,000	20%	$37,500	50%	$ 42,500	42.5%
Fixed costs					20,000	
Net income					$ 22,500	

Required

1. What is the breakeven point if sales remain at the same sales mix, at $100,000 per month?

2. If the TexFab Company sells $50,000 of product GT450 and $50,000 of product GT600, what is the breakeven point in sales dollars? Prepare an income statement for this scenario.

3. Why do the breakeven point and net income change?

8–30 MULTIPLE PRODUCT CVP ANALYSIS   The Neptune Company recently acquired the technology needed to produce small, standard, and super marine bilge pumps. Budgeted fixed costs for the manufacture of all three products total $425,000. The *budgeted* sales by product and in total for the coming year are

	Small		Standard		Super	
	Amount	Percent	Amount	Percent	Amount	Percent
Sales	$175,000	100%	$400,000	100%	$250,000	100%
Variable costs	120,000	69	100,000	25	125,000	50
Contribution	$ 55,000	31%	$300,000	75%	$125,000	50%

Actual sales for the year were not as planned; sales by product were

Small	$400,000
Standard	225,000
Super	200,000
	$825,000

Required

1. Prepare a contribution income statement for the year based on actual sales data.

2. Compute the breakeven sales for the year based on budgeted and actual sales, assuming the sales mix remains constant in sales dollars.

3. The president knows that total actual sales were $825,000 for the year, the same as budgeted. Because she had seen the budgeted income statement, she was expecting a nice profit from producing the bilge pumps. Explain to the president what happened.

8–31 **CVP ANALYSIS; TAXES** The Sunshine Company produces and sells dolls. It projects the following revenue and costs for production and sales:

Sales price per unit	$ 10.00
Variable production costs per unit	1.50
Fixed production costs (total)	170,000
Variable selling costs per unit	2.50
Fixed selling costs (total)	145,000

Required

1. Determine the breakeven point in units and dollars.

2. What will Sunshine's pretax profit be at 60,000 units?

3. Sunshine is subject to a tax rate of 30 percent. If the president wants to make an after-tax profit equal to $25,000, how many units must be produced and sold?

4. What must sales be (in units) to produce a before-tax profit equal to 20 percent of sales? Include a short income computation to prove your answer.

5. Sunshine Company is considering an alternate strategy to reduce fixed production costs by $70,000. However, this would cause variable production costs to increase to $2.50 per unit. What is the number of units at which the company is indifferent between the original production strategy and the new strategy?

8–32 **CVP ANALYSIS; TAXES** Fashions, Inc., is a retail store that sells sweaters and jackets. In the past, it has bought all its sweaters from a supplier for $20 per unit. However, Fashions has the opportunity to acquire a small manufacturing facility where it could produce its own sweaters. The projected data for producing its own sweaters are

Sales price	$30
Variable costs	15
Fixed costs	$150,000

Required

1. If Fashions acquired the manufacturing facility, how many sweaters would it have to produce and sell to break even?

2. To earn an after-tax profit of $125,000, how many sweaters would Fashions have to sell if it buys the sweaters from the supplier? If it produces its own sweaters? Fashion's tax rate is 30 percent.

3. At sales of how many units is Fashions indifferent between the two alternatives (ignore income-tax effects)? Show a computation of operating income to prove your answer.

8–33 CVP ANALYSIS; TAXES   The Elmire Company produces and sells watches. It projects the following revenue and costs for next year:

Sales price per unit	$60
Variable production cost per unit	30
Fixed production costs (total)	$200,000
Variable selling costs per unit	5
Fixed selling costs (total)	150,000

Required

1. Determine the breakeven point in units and dollars.

2. How many units does the company need to sell to earn a pretax profit of $150,000?

3. What will Elmire's pretax profit be at 40,000 units?

4. Elmire is subject to a tax rate of 40 percent. If the CEO wants an after-tax profit of $150,000, how many units must be sold?

5. Elmire Company is considering an alternate strategy to reduce fixed production costs by $50,000. However, this would cause variable production costs to increase to $35 per unit. What is the number of units at which the company is indifferent between the original production strategy and the new strategy?

6. Prepare a CVP graph based on the original data.

Strategy

8–34 CVP ANALYSIS   Peter Farrow is considering opening a franchised record store in a new shopping mall that has just been completed. Based on historical data from other franchise stores and a careful market study, he is confident that the store can achieve monthly sales of $180,000. Variable costs (excluding rent) will be approximately 70 percent of sales. Rent payable to the mall owners will be 7 percent of sales or $11,000, whichever is higher. Initial cost of the franchise is $25,000, paid for in one lump sum. Monthly fixed costs, totaling $33,000, consist of:

Installment loan for leasehold improvements	$ 800
Salaried employees (4 at $2,750)	11,000
Owner's salary	15,000
Franchise fee	4,000
Insurance, property taxes, etc.	2,200
Total fixed costs	$33,000

Farrow is aware that a department store with a large discount record department also is considering moving into the mall directly opposite his own location. Farrow knows that while his merchandise is carefully selected and his customer service is highly rated, the new store will take some of his business. If the department store moves in, he expects his own sales to decline by at least 10 but not more than 18 percent. A decline of even 10 percent would require him to reduce the cost of salaried employees to $10,000 by replacing one full-time employee with part-time help. Farrow considers a 15 percent minimum return on his initial investment in the franchise as the minimal return necessary to justify opening the store.

Required

1. Determine the sales volume per month necessary to achieve the desired return, assuming the competing department store does *not* rent space in the mall.

2. Determine the breakeven sales volume assuming the competing department store does move into the mall and sales are reduced by (a) 10 percent and (b) 18 percent.

3. Should Farrow open the store? What additional analysis should he undertake?

4. Assume a sales volume decrease of 18 percent. How far below $32,000 would Farrow have to reduce fixed costs to break even? Is it likely that he would be able to do this?

(Adapted, R. Shockley)

8-35 CVP ANALYSIS IN A PROFESSIONAL SERVICE FIRM A local CPA firm, Bidwell and Hope, has been asked to bid on a contract to perform audits for three counties in its home state. Should the firm be awarded the contract, it will be necessary to hire two new staff members at salaries of $30,000 each to handle the additional workload. (Existing staff are fully scheduled.) The managing partner is convinced that obtaining the contract will lead to additional new profit-oriented clients from the respective counties. Expected new work (excluding counties) is 800 hours at an average billing rate of $38.50. Other current relevant information on the firm's annual revenues and costs:

Service

Firm volume in hours (normal)	30,750
Expected hours of county work	900
Fixed costs	$470,000
Variable costs	$3.90/hr

Required

1. If the managing partner's expectations are correct, what is the lowest bid the firm can submit and still expect to increase annual net income?

2. If the contract is obtained at a price of $40,000, what is the minimum number of hours of new business in addition to the county work that must be obtained for the firm to break even on total new business?

(Adapted, R. Shockley)

8-36 CVP ANALYSIS; TAXES Soft Sport Company produces software for personal computers. The main product of the company is a golf training program called Swing! The total variable cost of the product is $23. Fixed manufacturing expenses are $6,000 per month, and the price of the product is $300. In the coming year the company plans to spend $100,000 for advertising and $50,000 for research and development. Because this proprietorship is managed from a personal residence, there are no other fixed costs. The federal and state tax rate for the proprietor is 40 percent. The company expects 700 units of sales for the next year.

Required

1. Determine the breakeven point for the coming year in number of units.

2. Determine the contribution margin ratio.

3. Determine the number of units required for the coming year to cover a 100 percent increase in advertising expenses and a $12,000 after-tax profit per month.

8–37 CVP ANALYSIS Headlines Publishing Company (HPC) specializes in international business news publications. HPC's principal product is *HPC-Monthly*, which is mailed to subscribers the first week of each month. A weekly version, called *HPC-Weekly*, is also available to subscribers over the World Wide Web at a higher cost. Sixty percent of HPC's subscribers are nondomestic customers. While there was a fast growth in subscribers in its first few years of operation, sales have begun to slow in recent years, as new competitors have entered the market. HPC has the following cost structure and sales revenue for its subscriptions operations on a yearly basis. All costs and all subscription fees are in U.S. dollars.

Fixed Cost		
$306,000 per month		

Variable Costs		
Mailing	$ .60	per issue
Commission	3.00	per subscription
Administrative	1.50	per subscription

Sales Mix Information	
HPC-Weekly	20 percent
HPC-Monthly	80 percent

Selling Price	
HPC-Weekly	$47.00 per subscription
HPC-Monthly	$19.00 per subscription

Required Use the data to determine:

1. Contribution margin for weekly and monthly subscriptions.
2. Contribution margin ratio for weekly and monthly subscriptions.
3. HPC's breakeven point in sales units and sales dollars.
4. HPC's breakeven point to reach a target before-tax profit of $75,000.
5. What are the critical success factors for HPC? For the domestic subscribers? For international subscribers? How can CVP analysis be used to make HPC more competitive?

8–38 CVP ANALYSIS Maria Ramirez operates a feedlot on a farm near Gretna, Nebraska. She buys steers that weigh about 700 pounds, feeds them, and sells them when they reach approximately 1,200 pounds. Her annual fixed expenses are for land (rent), silo, tractor, feedwagon, chopper, silage wagons, and a barn with a fence. Her monthly fixed costs are

Monthly Fixed Costs	
Land (100 acres at $20 each)	$2,000
Silo	1,000
Tractor	500
Feedwagon	200
Chopper	200
Silage wagons	200
Barn and fence	500
Total variable costs	$4,600

Variable costs to purchase and feed each 700-pound steer:

Purchase price	$700
Corn or sorghum	30
Silage	60
Medicine implants	10
Miscellaneous	64
Total variable costs	$864

All steers are sold on a per-pound basis.

Required

1. What is the breakeven selling price per pound if 200 steers are bought and sold per month?

2. What is the breakeven quantity of steers if Maria can contract a price of $76 per hundredweight (pounds)?

3. What is the selling price per pound needed for 200 steers figuring a $20,000 before-tax profit?

8–39 CVP ANALYSIS   A nonprofit Cardiac Diagnostic Screening Center (CDSC) is contemplating purchasing a blood gases analysis machine at a cost of $750,000. Useful life expectancy for this machine is 10 years. The screening center currently services 5,000 patients per year, 30 percent of whom need blood gases analysis data as part of their diagnostic tests. At present the blood samples are sent out to a private laboratory that charges $85 per sample. In-house variable expenses are estimated at $40 per sample if the blood gases analysis machine is purchased.

Service

Required

1. Determine the indifference point between purchasing the blood gases analysis machine or using the private laboratory.

2. Determine how many additional patients would be needed to cover all fixed and variable charges of the analysis machine if the $85 charge were used by the screening center.

3. Determine the amount the private laboratory charge must be so that CDSC would be indifferent between purchasing the analysis machine or using the private laboratory, assuming the current service level of 5,000 patients per year.

8–40 CVP ANALYSIS; OPERATING LEVERAGE   A potential franchisee of Subway Sandwich Shop Inc. is in the process of developing a business plan to present to potential investors. Following are various projected cost data for the operation:

Lease of store space	$500/month
Equipment lease	$500/month
License	$250/year
Advertising	2.5 percent of gross sales revenue
Royalty	8 percent of gross sales revenue
Salaries	$2,000/month
Utilities	$400/month
Insurance	$1,500 per year

The orders average $4, with a food cost of $2.

Required

1. What is the contribution of each sale toward covering fixed expenses?

2. What is the projected monthly breakeven point in units?

3. The potential franchisee has a target before-tax net profit of $2,000 per month. What level of sales (in units and in dollars) must be achieved?

4. What is the operating leverage of this sandwich shop at the target profit of $2,000?

5. What would be the impact on net income if sales dollars are increased by 5 percent?

8–41 MULTIPLE PRODUCT CVP ANALYSIS   Reader's Corner is a small book store that rents space in a neighborhood shopping mall for $19,200 a year. Utilities add another $7,800 yearly. The total staff salaries and benefits projected for next year equal $56,000. Also, Reader's Corner spends $900 on advertising and $2,400 on professional services. Other overhead expenses total $11,500.

Ms. Davis, the company's owner, would like to make a $40,000 profit after taxes next year. Her tax rate will be 33 percent. The book store sells hardbound books, paperback books, and magazines. The average cost of each category of items and Reader's markup on cost is: hardbacks, $12.00 and 50 percent; paperbacks, $2.40 and 60 percent; magazines, $1.90 and 60 percent.

In past years 70 percent of the store's sales revenue came from hardback books, 20 percent from paperbacks, and the remaining 10 percent from magazines.

Required

1. What is the contribution margin of each sales item?
2. What are the projected fixed costs of the company next year?
3. What is the breakeven point for Reader's Corner?
4. What sales level will the company need to reach the target after-tax profit?

Ethics

8–42   CVP ANALYSIS; COMMISSIONS; ETHICS   Marston Corporation manufactures pharmaceutical products sold through a network of sales agents in the United States and Canada. The agents are currently paid an 18 percent commission on sales; that percentage was used when Marston prepared the following budgeted income statement for the fiscal year ending June 30, 19X1.

MARSTON CORPORATION
Budgeted Income Statement
For the Year Ending June 30, 19X1
($000 omitted)

Sales		$26,000
Cost of goods sold		
Variable	$11,700	
Fixed	2,870	14,570
Gross profit		11,430
Selling and administrative costs		
Commissions	$ 4,680	
Fixed advertising cost	750	
Fixed administrative cost	1,850	7,280
Operating income		4,150
Fixed interest cost		650
Income before income taxes		3,500
Income taxes (40 percent)		1,400
Net income		$ 2,100

Since the completion of the income statement, Marston has learned that its agents are requiring an increase in their commission rate to 23 percent for the upcoming year. As a result, Marston's president has decided to investigate the possibility of hiring its own sales staff in place of the network of sales agents and has asked Tom Markowitz, Marston's controller, to gather information on the costs associated with this change.

Markowitz estimates that Marston will have to hire eight salespeople to cover the current market area, and the annual payroll cost of each of these employees will average $80,000, including fringe benefits expense. Travel and entertainment expense is expected to total $600,000 for the year, and the annual cost of hiring a sales manager and sales secretary will be $150,000. In addition to their salaries, the eight salespeople will each earn commissions at the rate of 10 percent on the first $2 million in sales and 15 percent on all sales over $2 million. For planning purposes, Markowitz expects that all eight salespeople will exceed the $2 million mark and that sales will be at the level previously projected. The president believes that Marston also should increase its advertising budget by $500,000.

Required

1. Determine Marston Corporation's breakeven point in sales dollars for the fiscal year ending June 30, 19X1, if the company hires its own sales force and increases its advertising costs.

2. If Marston Corporation continues to sell through its network of sales agents and pays the higher commission rate, determine the estimated volume in sales dollars for the fiscal year ending June 30, 19X1, that would be required to generate the same net income as projected in the budgeted income statement.

3. Describe the general assumptions underlying breakeven analysis that limit its usefulness.

4. What is the indifference point in sales for the firm to either accept the agents' demand or adopt the proposed change? Which plan is better for the firm?

5. Assume total sales for year ending June 30, 19X2, will remain approximately the same as for the year ending June 30, 19X1. Would you, as the head of the sales agents' union, demand an increase in commission rate?

6. What are the ethical issues, if any, Markowitz should consider before adopting the new program?

(CMA Adapted)

8–43 **CVP ANALYSIS** FastQ Company, a specialist in printing, has established 500 convenience copying centers throughout the country. To upgrade its services, the company is considering purchasing three new models of laser copying machines that produce high-quality copies. These high-quality copies would be added to the growing list of products offered in the FastQ shops. The selling price to the customer for each laser copy would be the same, no matter which machine is installed in the shop.

The three models of laser copying machines under consideration are 1024S, a small-volume model; 1024M, a medium-volume model; and 1024G, a large-volume model. The annual rental costs and the operating costs vary with the size of the machine. The machine capacities and costs are

	Copier Model		
	1024S	**1024M**	**1024G**
Annual capacity (copies)	100,000	350,000	800,000
Costs			
Annual machine rental	$ 8,000	$11,000	$20,000
Actual product costs	.02	.02	.02
Variable overhead costs	.12	.07	.03

Required

1. Determine the volume level in copies where FastQ Company would be indifferent between acquiring either the small-volume laser copier (1024S) or the medium-volume laser copier (1024M).

2. The management of FastQ Company can estimate the number of copies to be sold at each establishment. Present an analysis that would enable FastQ Company to select the most profitable machine without having to make a separate cost calculation for each establishment.

(CMA Adapted)

8–44 CVP ANALYSIS; DIFFERENT PRODUCTION PLANS The PTO Division of the Galva Manufacturing Company produces power take-off units for the farm equipment business. The PTO Division, headquartered in Peoria, has a newly renovated, automated plant in Peoria and an older, less-automated plant in Moline. Both plants produce the same power take-off units for farm tractors that are sold to most domestic and foreign tractor manufacturers.

The PTO Division expects to produce and sell 192,000 power take-off units during the coming year. The division production manager has the following data available regarding the unit costs, unit prices, and production capacities for the two plants.

- All fixed costs are based on a normal year of 240 working days. When the number of working days exceeds 240, variable manufacturing costs increase by $3 per unit in Peoria and $8 per unit in Moline. Capacity for each plant is 300 working days.

- Galva Manufacturing charges each of its plants a per-unit fee for administrative services such as payroll, general accounting, and purchasing, because management considers these services to be a function of the work performed at the plants. For each of the plants at Peoria and Moline, the fee is $6.50 and represents the variable portion of general and administrative expense.

Wishing to maximize the higher unit profit at Moline, PTO's production manager has decided to manufacture 96,000 units at each plant. This production plan results in Moline's operating at capacity and Peoria's operating at its normal volume. Galva's corporate controller is not happy with this plan because she does not believe it represents optimal usage of PTO's plants.

	Peoria	Moline
Selling price	$150.00	$150.00
Variable manufacturing cost	72.00	88.00
Fixed manufacturing cost	30.00	15.00
Commission (5 percent)	7.50	7.50
General and administrative expense	25.50	21.00
Total unit cost	131.50	131.50
Unit profit	$ 15.00	$ 18.50
Production rate per day	400 units	320 units

Required

1. Determine the annual breakeven units for each of PTO's plants.

2. Determine the operating income that would result from the division production manager's plan to produce 96,000 units at each plant.

3. Determine the optimal production plan to produce the 192,000 units at PTO's plants in Peoria and Moline, and determine the resulting operating income for the PTO Division. Be sure to support the plan with appropriate calculations.

(CMA Adapted)

8–45 CVP ANALYSIS Puppy Inc., maker of quality dog houses, has experienced a steady growth in sales over the past five years. Since his business has grown, the president of Puppy Inc. believes he needs an aggressive advertising campaign next year to maintain the company's growth. To prepare for the growth, the chief accountant has prepared and presented the president with the following data for the current year:

Variable costs per dog house	
Direct labor	$20.00
Direct materials	10.25
Variable overhead	4.50
Total variable costs	$34.75
Fixed costs	
Manufacturing	$ 28,000
Selling	35,000
Administrative	60,000
Total fixed costs	$123,000
Selling price per dog house	$60.00
Expected sales (30,000 units)	$1,800,000
Tax rate: 40%	

Required

1. If costs and sales prices remain the same, what is the projected net income for the coming year?
2. What is the breakeven point in units for the coming year?
3. The president has set the sales target at a level of 32,000 dog houses. He foresees an additional selling expense of $12,000 for advertising and expects all other costs to remain constant. What will be the net income if the additional $12,000 is spent on advertising?
4. What will be the new breakeven point if an additional $12,000 is spent on advertising?
5. If the additional $12,000 is spent for advertising the next year, what is the required sales level in units to equal the current year's net income?

SOLUTION TO SELF-STUDY PROBLEM

Breakeven Analysis

1. Unit contribution margin — $5,595 — $899 — $233 — $4,463
2. Breakeven:

    In units: $Q = (f + N)/(p - v)$

    $Q = \$2,352,000/\$4,463 = 527$ units

    In dollars: $pQ = \$5,595 \times 527 = \$2,948,565$

    Or

    $$p \times Q = \frac{(f + N)}{(p - v)/p} = \frac{\$2,352,000}{.797676} = \$2,948,565$$

3. New level of fixed costs = $2,352,000(1 + .05) = 2,469,600$

    Breakeven:

    $Q = (f + N)/(p - v)$

    $Q = (\$2,469,600 + \$200,000)/(\$4,463)$

    $= 599$ units

4. Incorporate a tax rate of 22 percent and desired profit of $150,000:

    $Q = [\$2,352,000 + (\$150,000)/(1 - .22)]/\$4,463 = 571$ units

281

Strategy and the Master Budget

9

After studying this chapter you should be able to . . .

1. Describe the role of a budget in planning, communicating, motivating, controlling, and evaluating performance

2. Discuss the importance of strategy and its role in budgeting and identify factors common to successful budgets

3. Outline the budgeting process

4. Prepare a master budget and explain the relationships among components of a master budget

5. Identify unique budgeting characteristics of service and not-for-profit organizations, and of organizations operating in international settings

6. Apply zero-base, activity-based, and kaizen budgeting

7. Discuss the roles of ethics and behavioral concerns in budgeting

AP/Wide World Photos

> You get what you expect to get. Seldom, if ever, do you get more.
>
> HAROLD S. GENEEN

The point made by Harold Geneen—the builder of ITT and its legendary CEO for nearly two decades—is that firms and organizations get, at most, what they plan to achieve. A well-managed firm implements the planned operations to attain the planned results. The growth of ITT from a relatively unknown company in the late 1950s to an international conglomerate can be attributed to careful planning.

Planning is a process of charting the future course to attain desired goals. Good planning helps managers attain goals, recognize opportunities, and minimize the negative effects of unavoidable events. Successful organizations usually are the result of good planning. Conversely, failure to plan often results in compromising goals and can lead to financial disaster. The budget is one aspect of planning used by many organizations—for-profit, not-for-profit, large or small, service or manufacturing.

THE ROLE OF A BUDGET

A **budget** is a quantitative plan of operations for an organization; it identifies the resources and commitments required to fulfill the organization's goals for the budgeted period. A budget includes both financial and nonfinancial aspects of the planned operations. The budget for a period serves as a guideline for operation for the budgeted period and a projection of the operating results. The process of preparing a budget is called **budgeting.**

Budgets and the budgeting process are intertwined with all aspects of management. In addition to being a plan of operations, a budget plays an important role in allocating resources, coordinating operations including identifying bottlenecks and communicating and authorizing actions, motivating and guiding implementation, providing guidelines for controlling operations and managing cash flows, and furnishing criteria for evaluating performance.

In preparing a budget, the management of a firm needs to be forward-looking in assessing future situations in light of the firm's strategic goals. Budget preparations allow management time to work out any problems the company may face in the coming periods. This extra time enables firms to minimize the adverse effects anticipated problems may have on operations. Because all divisions are not likely to think alike and have the same plan for their operations, completion of a budget for all units of an organization also mandates coordinating operations among all budgeted units and synchronizing the operating activities of various departments. The use of budgets thus helps firms to run smoother operations and achieve better results.

◄ **LEARNING OBJECTIVE 1**
Describe the role of a budget in planning, communicating, motivating, controlling, and evaluating performance.

A **budget** is a quantitative plan of operations for an organization; it identifies the resources and commitments required to fulfill the organization's goals for the budgeted period.

Budgeting is the process of preparing a budget.

BusinessWeek

Did Twentieth Century Fox Go Overboard on Titanic?

The long-anticipated launch of the biggest disaster movie in years, *Titanic,* arrived in 1998. Long before *Titanic* hit the theatres, the industry was speculating whether revenues would cover the huge amount of dollars sunk into the creation of this epic movie. In the end, *Titanic* achieved blockbuster status quickly after its release. So the question is why do moviemaking budgets often get out of hand? Doesn't the movie industry worry about budgets and profitability like other corporations and industries?

Q: What can moviemakers do to keep budgets from becoming a disaster? *Find out on page 299 of this chapter.*

Why Paramount Pictures Prepares Budgets

- To determine if they are going to make a loss or a profit (negative or positive cash flow).
- To compute the impact of certain decisions they plan to take or of market changes on an existing budget.
- To validate business decisions already taken.
- To set targets/management objectives.
- To determine tax rates, cash borrowing needs, and so on.

Source: Based on a presentation by Stephen P. Taylor, senior vice president, finance, Paramount Pictures, at the University of Southern California, November 14, 1991.

The budget also can help managers identify current and potential bottlenecks in operations. Critical resources can be mustered then to ease any bottlenecks and prevent them from becoming obstacles to attaining budgetary goals.

A budget is a formal expression of plans for future actions. In many organizations, budgets are the only formal expression of future plans. Thus, budgets also serve as communication devices. Through budgets, top management makes the plan and goal for the budgeted period known to the entire organization. Moreover, each division knows what it needs to do to satisfy its obligations to other divisions. The manufacturing division knows, for example, that it needs to complete the production of a given quantity before a given date if the marketing division budget calls for delivery of that quantity to a customer on that date. Budgets prescribe what performance the organization expects of all divisions and all employees for the period.

A budget also is a motivating device. With clearly delineated expected results for the budget period, workers know what is expected of them; this in turn sustains morale and keeps people working to attain the budgeted goals. The budget of an organization that employs participative budgeting involving all or most personnel in formulating all or part of it often can be an effective motivating device. Employees of such an organization identify the budget as their own, which motivates them to attain budget goals. There are other motivational aspects of budgets as well.

During the course of operations, budgets serve as frames of reference. They become guidelines for operations, criteria for monitoring and controlling activities, and authorizations for actions. The success of an organization requires that all subunits of the organization carry out their operations as planned. Budgets spell out the expected operations of each unit and subdivision of an organization enabling all units and subdivisions to coordinate activities. The authorization function of budgets is especially important for government and not-for-profit organizations because budgeted amounts often serve both as approvals of activities and as ceilings for expenditures.

At the end of an operating period, a firm's budget also serves as a basis for evaluating its performance. The budget represents the specific results expected of divisions and employees of the firm for the period against which actual operating results can be measured.

STRATEGY, THE LONG-TERM PLAN, AND THE MASTER BUDGET

The Importance of Strategy in Budgeting

LEARNING OBJECTIVE 2
Discuss the importance of strategy and its role in budgeting and identify factors common to successful budgets.

The strategy of a firm is the path the firm chooses for attaining its long-term goals and missions. It is the starting point in preparing the firm's plans and budgets. American Express Company considers itself a personal financial services company. Corporate financial services such as investment banking do not fit into the firm's strategic course and have been removed from its operations. B. F. Goodrich Company determined in the early 1980s that for competitive reasons it would not stay in the automobile tire business and focused its strategy on other rubber products. Finally, Varity Corporation, a leading maker of diesel engines and automotive parts, decided not to be in the farm-equipment business, even though its farm-equipment manufacturing subsidiary, Massey-Ferguson, accounted for nearly 90 percent of its total revenue. Again, for competitive reasons, the firm made the strategic decision to leave the farm-equipment business.

The process of determining a firm's strategy begins with assessing external factors that affect operations and evaluating internal strengths and weaknesses. External factors typically include competition and political, economic, social, regulatory, environmental, and technological factors. A careful examination of such factors can help the organization to identify opportunities, limitations, and threats. An organization's internal evaluation includes inspection of such operating characteristics as financial strength, organizational culture, managerial expertise, functional structure, and current operations. Matching the strength of the organization with identified opportunities enables an organization to form its strategy. Exhibit 9–1 shows the development of a firm's product strategy.[1]

The importance of strategy in planning and budgeting cannot be overemphasized. Without a good strategy, an organization may not be able to take full advantage of its opportunities and its strengths. Repeatedly missed opportunities may cause an organization to stagnate. In the worst cases, having an inappropriate strategy or no strategy eventually leads to the demise of organizations.

In the late 1960s and early 1970s U.S. auto manufacturers decided not to develop compact and subcompact automobiles; thus, they did not plan and budget necessary resources for developing and manufacturing such vehicles. This strategy later proved to be a costly mistake. The automakers suffered for almost 20 years because of this strategic decision. They did not begin to recover until the early 1990s.

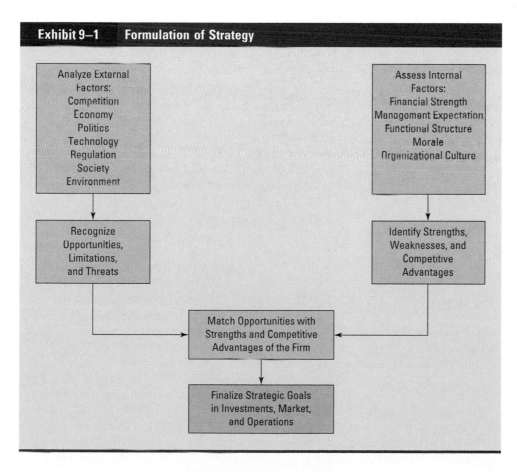

Exhibit 9–1   Formulation of Strategy

---

[1] Adapted from Robert N. Anthony and Vijay Govindarajan, *Management Control System*, 8th ed. (Burr Ridge, IL: Irwin, 1995), p. 265.

The success stories of many business firms are stories of the value of good strategy. Wal-Mart stores took advantage of its experience in operating stores in medium-size towns and expanded nationally into these markets, becoming first in the nation among retail stores.

Strategic Goals and Long-Term Objectives

A strategy is implemented through long-range planning, the capital budget, and the master budget. Strategy provides the framework within which a long-range plan is developed. The **long-range plan** of the organization identifies which actions are required during the typical 5- to 10-year period covered by the plan to attain the firm's strategic goal. For instance, B. F. Goodrich accomplished its strategic goal of not staying in the automobile tire business by gradually phasing out its automobile tire–manufacturing operations. Varity chose to liquidate Massey-Ferguson through downsizing and diversification. To divest its investment banking business, American Express Company decided in January 1994 to infuse more than $1 billion into its investment banking arm, Lehman Brothers Inc. The capital infusion lifted the credit rating of the subsidiary, and American Express was able to complete the sale of Lehman Brothers Inc. in May 1994. These actions required long-range planning and coordination for the organizations to attain the goals set forth in their strategies.

Long-range planning often entails capital budgeting. **Capital budgeting** is a process for evaluating and choosing between an organization's proposed long-range major projects such as purchase of new equipment, construction of a new factory, and addition of new products. A capital budget is a plan for major expenditures that have long-term effects on the organization. Capital budgets are prepared for the purpose of bringing an organization's capabilities in line with the needs of its long-range plan and long-term sales forecast. The capacity that an organization has is a result of capital investments made in prior budgeting periods. Also, the resources required and activities planned for the current period's capital budgeting need to be included in the budget.

Short-Term Objectives and the Master Budget

Long-term objectives and plans, operating results of the past periods, and expected future operating and environmental factors including economic, industry, and marketing conditions give rise to short-term objectives. These, in turn, serve as the basis for preparing the master budget for a period.

A **master budget** is a plan of operations for a business unit during a budgeted period. It sets specific goals for all major operations of the organization and provides a detailed plan for acquisitions and commitments of financial resources. The plan of operations is based on the goals of the strategic and long-range plans, expected future events, and the recent actual operating results of the organization. Exhibit 9–2 illustrates the relationship between strategic goals, objectives, budgets, operations, and controls.

Because a master budget commits limited resources to attain the goals set for the organization, such commitments must be made with a clear idea of where the organization is heading. The master budget must be consistent, therefore, with the goals prescribed in the strategic and long-range plans of the organization.

A master budget differs from a long-range plan in at least two respects: A master budget is a short-run operating plan that typically covers a period of one year; a long-range plan extends over a longer period, such as three to five years.[2] In addition, the focal point of a master budget is a responsibility center; a long-range plan is most likely structured along strategic business units, programs, activities, or product lines.

The operating results of recent years—including the year about to end—impose limitations on the courses of action available to the organization in preparing a master budget while the expected future events shape the set of actions from which a

Long-range plan is a plan that identifies which actions are required during the 5- to 10-year period covered by the plan to attain the firm's strategic goal.

Capital budgeting is a process for evaluating an organization's proposed long-range major projects.

A **master budget** is a plan of operations for a business unit during a budgeted period.

---

[2] It is not unusual for businesses with two distinct seasons to have two operating budgets within a year. For example, many sports teams have two operating budgets each year.

| Exhibit 9–2 | The Relationship between Strategic Goals, Long-Run Objectives, Budgets, and Operations |

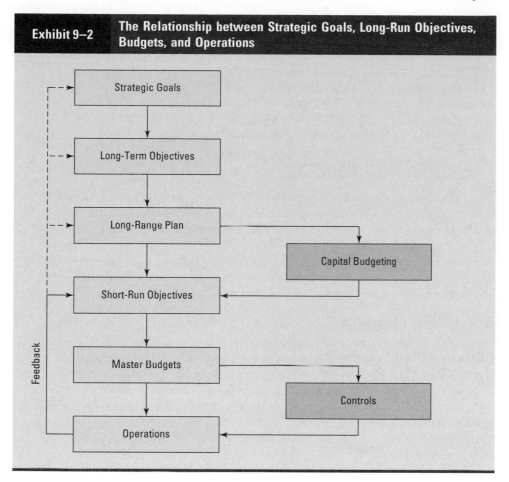

firm can choose to attain its goals. Both the operating results of recent years and the expected future events also can affect a firm's strategic goals and long-range plans.

A master budget also is a comprehensive financial summarization of the budgets and plans for operating activities of the organization and its subunits for the next year. It comprises operating budgets and financial budgets. **Operating budgets** are plans that identify needed resources and how these resources will be acquired for all day-to-day activities such as sales and services, production, purchasing, marketing, and research and development. Examples of operating budgets include production budgets, purchase budgets, personnel budgets, and sales promotion budgets. **Financial budgets** are plans that identify sources of funds from the budgeted operation and uses for these funds during a period to carry out the budget activities. Financial budgets usually include budgets for cash inflows and outflows, operating incomes, and financial position. Thus, a master budget includes all the planned activities and results of both operating and financing decisions for activities that will occur during the next operating period.

Operating budgets are plans that identify resources needed in operating activities and the acquisition of these resources.

Financial budgets identify sources and uses of funds for the budgeted operations to achieve the expected operating results for the period.

Common Factors of Successful Budgets

No single characteristic can define successful budgets. There are, however, many factors common to successful budgets. Most important among them is that a successful budget is accepted and supported by the key managers.

A successful budget often becomes a personalized budget of the people who have the responsibility for carrying it out. They feel it is *their* budget, not a detached, impersonal institutional budget. They own the budget and are the ones who bring the budgeted goal to fruition.

A budget is more likely to be successful if employees perceive it as a planning and coordinating tool to help them to do a better job, not as a pressure device to squeeze the last drop of their energy out of them. Nor is a budget likely to be an asset when viewed as a tool to be used by management in placing blame.

A successful budget is a motivating device that helps people work toward the goal and the improvement of the organization; it is never used as an excuse for not doing things strategically important to the organization. The expression *not in the budget* never crops up in an organization with a successful budget.

Finally, a successful budget contains technically correct and reasonably accurate numbers. A budget will not be accepted and thus will not do the job intended if it is not technically correct. A budget with inaccurate numbers will lose the confidence of the people affected by it and be rendered useless.

THE BUDGETING PROCESS

LEARNING OBJECTIVE 3 ▶
Outline the budgeting process.

The budgeting process can range from the informal simple process a small firm uses that may take only days to complete to the elaborate lengthy procedure a large firm or the federal government employs that requires several months or even more than a year to complete.

Budgeting processes usually include formation of a budget committee; determination of the budget period; specification of budget guidelines; preparation of the initial budget proposal; budget negotiation, review, and approval; and budget revision.

The Budget Committee

Most organizations have a budget committee that oversees all budget matters; it is composed of members of senior management. A typical budget committee includes the chief executive officer or one or more vice presidents, heads of strategic business units, and the chief financial officer. The size of the committee depends on such factors as the size of the organization, number of people involved in budget matters, extent of organization units' participation in budgetary processes, and management style of the chief executive officer. In some organizations the chief executive officer makes all the decisions and there is no budget committee.

The budget committee is the highest authority in an organization for all matters related to the budget. The committee sets or approves the overall budget goals for the organization and its major business units, directs and coordinates budget preparation, resolves conflicts and differences that may arise during budget preparation, approves the final budget, monitors operations as the year unfolds, and reviews the operating results at the end of the period. The budget committee also approves major revisions of the budget during the period.

The Budget Period

Budgets usually are prepared for a one-year period and coincide with the organization's fiscal year. Many companies also have quarterly or monthly budgets. Synchronizing budget periods with the fiscal period of the organization facilitates comparisons of actual operating results with the budgeted amounts.

Some companies use a continuous (or rolling) budget. A **continuous budget** is a budgeting system that has in effect a budget for a set number of months, quarters, or years at all times. Thus, as a month or quarter ends, the original budget is updated based on the newly available information, and the budget for a new month or quarter is added.

Johnson & Johnson uses a continuous budget and prepares two annual budgets each year, one for each of the next two years. Each year, the second-year budget is revised and updated based on the information that has become available since the last budget preparation period. This second-year budget then becomes the master budget for the coming period and a new second-year budget is prepared. In addition, Johnson & Johnson has 5- and 10-year budgets.

In practice, firms seldom have a budget for only one year. The budgets for the years beyond the coming year, however, usually contain only the essential operating data. Advantages of such a system include a longer strategic perspective for managers, one that allows them more time to make operating decisions, and the opportunity to assess the accuracy of forecasts.

A popular continuous budgeting system is to have 4 quarterly or 12 monthly bud-

*A **continuous budget** is a budgeting system that has in effect a budget for a set number of months, quarters, or years at all times.*

A popular continuous budgeting system is to have 4 quarterly or 12 monthly budgets in effect at all times. A survey showed that 15 percent of firms maintained 4 quarterly budgets; another 5 percent had 12 monthly budgets.[3] Firms using continuous budgets claim that the system makes it mandatory for managers to adopt a perspective that looks at operations beyond the immediate future at all times, not just once a year as the budget is prepared. Firms using continuous budgets also are more likely to have up-to-date budgets because the preparation of a budget for a new quarter or month often leads to revision of the existing budget.

Similar to a continuous budget, a **continuously updated budget** incorporates new information as the year unfolds. Unlike a continuous budget, however, a continuously updated budget does not maintain budgets for a constant period such as 4 quarterly or 12 monthly budgets. The objective of a continuously updated budget is that it takes advantage of newly available information to revise the operating guidelines for the year as set forth in the master budget.

> A **continuously updated budget** incorporates new information as the year unfolds.

Budget Guidelines

One of the responsibilities of the budget committee is to provide initial budget guidelines that set the tone for the budget and govern budget preparation. All responsibility centers (or budget units) follow the initial budget guidelines in preparing their budgets.

The starting point in developing budget guidelines is the firm's strategy. In developing the initial budget guidelines, the budget committee also needs to consider developments that have occurred since the adoption of the strategic plan; the general outlook of the economy and the market; the goal of the organization for the budgeting period; specific corporate policies such as mandates for downsizing, reengineering, and special promotions; and the operating results of the year to date.

The Initial Budget Proposal

Based on the initial budget guidelines, each responsibility center prepares its initial budget proposal.

A number of internal factors are considered by a budget unit in preparing an initial budget proposal:

- Changes in availability of equipment or facilities.
- Adoption of new manufacturing processes.
- Changes in product design or product mix.
- Introduction of new products.
- Changes in expectations or operating processes of other budget units that the budget unit relies on for its input materials or other operating factors.
- Changes in other operating factors or in the expectations or operating processes in those other budget units that rely on the budget unit to supply them components.

External factors to consider in forming an initial budget proposal include:

- Changes in the labor market.
- Availability of raw materials or components and their prices.
- Industry's outlook for the near term.
- Competitors' actions.

Budget Negotiation

The superior of budget units examines the initial budget proposal to see whether the proposal is within the budget guidelines. The superior also checks to see if the budget goals can be reasonably attained and are in line with the goals of the budget units at the next level up, and the budgeted operations are consistent with the

---

[3] William P. Cress and James B. Pettijohn, "A Survey of Budget-Related Planning and Control Policies and Procedures," *Journal of Accounting Education* 3, no. 2 (Fall 1985), pp. 61–78)

budgeted activities of other budget units, including units directly and indirectly affected. Each budget unit negotiates with its superior any changes in the budget proposals.

Negotiations occur at all levels of the organization. They are perhaps the core of the budgeting process and take up the bulk of budget preparation time. For a firm with a December 31 fiscal year-end, for example, it is not unusual for the budget process to start in May, and for the negotiation process to continue until September or October before the final budget is approved near the end of the calendar year.

Review and Approval

As budget units approve their budgets, the budgets go through the successive levels of the organization until they reach the final level, when the combined unit budgets become the budget of the organization. The budget committee reviews and gives final approval to the budget. The budget committee examines the budget for consistency with the budget guidelines, attainment of the desired short-term goals, and fulfillment of the strategic plan. The chief executive officer then approves the entire budget and submits the budget to the board of directors.

Revision

Procedures for budget revision vary from one organization to another. Once a budget has been approved, some organizations allow budget revision only under special circumstances; others, such as firms adopting continuously updated budgets, build into their budgeting system quarterly or monthly revisions.

For organizations that allow budget revisions only under special circumstances, approval to modify a budget can be difficult to obtain. Not all events, however, unfold as predicted in a budget. Strictly implementing a budget as prescribed even when the actual events differ significantly from those expected certainly is not a desirable behavior. In such cases, managers should be encouraged not to rely on the budget as the final guideline in operations.

Systematic, periodic revision of the approved budget or the use of a continuous budget can be an advantage in dynamic operations because the updated budget provides better operating guidelines. Regular budget revision, however, may encourage responsibility centers not to prepare their budgets with due diligence. Organizations with systematic budget revisions need to ensure that revisions are allowed only if circumstances have changed significantly.

THE MASTER BUDGET

LEARNING OBJECTIVE 4 ▶
Prepare a master budget and explain the interrelationships among components of a master budget.

The master budget is the operating budget for the period and consists of many interrelated budgets. Exhibit 9–3 delineates the relationships among components of a master budget.

Strategic Planning and Budgeting

The master budget is the document an organization relies on as it carries out its strategic goals and long-range plan for the coming operating period. An organization forms its budget guidelines for the coming period based on its strategic goals and long-range plan. The master budget for the period is then prepared following the budget guidelines; this is the organization's operating budget.

Budgeting for Sales

A firm attains its desired goals through sales. Almost all activities of a firm emanate from efforts to attain sales goals and sales growth. The importance of having the best sales budget for a firm cannot be overemphasized.

Sales Forecast

A sales forecast estimates future sales of the firm's products and is the starting point in preparing sales budgets for the period. An accurate sales forecast enhances the usefulness of the budget as a planning and control tool.

Exhibit 9–3	The Master Budget

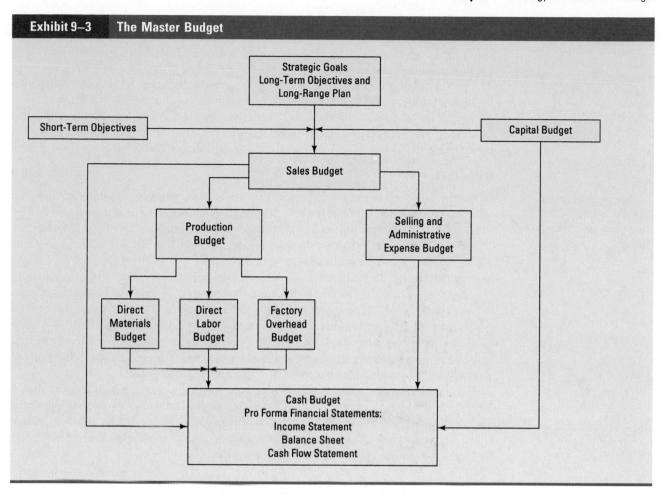

casts, as a standard procedure many firms generate several independent sales forecasts. A firm may, for example, have sales forecasts prepared by its market research unit, the manager of its business unit, and the sales department of its budget unit. The volume of sales in the sales budget, then, would be the one that all parties agree is the most likely prediction.

Among the factors that should be considered in sales forecasting:

- Current sales levels and trends of sales in the past few years.
- General economic and industry conditions.
- Competitors' actions and operating plans.
- Pricing policies.
- Credit policies.
- Advertising and promotional activities.
- Unfilled back-orders.

Many sales forecasting tools are available.[4] Among them are trend analysis and econometric models. A *trend analysis* can range from a simple visual plotting of past data on a graph to a sophisticated time-series model. An advantage of trend analysis is that all the data needed can be obtained easily from the firm's records because a trend analysis uses only past data. History, however, never repeats itself exactly. Forecast adjustments for future events that may cause results to deviate from the historical trend are needed.

Econometric models such as regression or time-series analyses incorporate past sales data and other factors that affect sales. A firm may use an econometric model that includes, for example, national and regional economic indicators, unemployment

---

[4]   Chapter 4 discusses in more detail quantitative techniques useful in sales forecasting.

includes, for example, national and regional economic indicators, unemployment rates, consumer-confidence indexes, and age-group distributions. The advantages of using econometric models in forecasting include objectivity, verifiability, and explicit measures of reliability.

The use of econometric models has become more common in recent years partly because of wider availability of powerful, inexpensive computers. No model, however, can replace human judgment, no matter how complete or sophisticated the model. A combination of experienced judgment and analyses often leads to a better forecast than does relying on only one technique or the other.

Sales Budget

A **sales budget** shows expected sales in units at their expected selling prices.

A **sales budget** shows expected sales in units at their expected selling prices. The usual starting point in preparing the sales budget for a period is the forecasted sales level, production capacity, and long-term and short-term objectives of the firm.[5]

A sales budget is the cornerstone of budget preparation because a firm can complete the plan for other activities only after the firm knows the expected sales level. A manufacturing firm cannot complete its production schedule without knowing the number of units to be produced, and the number of units to be produced can be ascertained only after the firm knows the number of units budgeted to be sold for the period. Once the units to be produced have been determined, then the units of materials to be purchased, the number of employees needed for the operation, and the required factory overheads can be determined. Expected selling and administrative expenses also are determined by the desired sales level.

Exhibit 9–4 illustrates the sales budget for Kerry Industrial Company for 20X0. Kerry has a March 31 fiscal period. After examining its sales forecast for the coming year, operating results of the year to date, strategic goals and the long-range plans for the firm and the product, and budget guidelines, Kerry has set the sales levels shown and a selling price of $30 per unit.

Budgeting at Borg-Warner Automotive

The Muncie, Indiana, plant of Borg-Warner Automotive drives its budget with cost targets by product line and department. The initial step in its budgeting processes is developing sales estimates for the coming year. Current costs then provide baselines. From there the firm incorporates basic assumptions, such as inflation, planned product and process changes, and special program costs, to arrive at a base budget. Before completing the budgeting processes, operating managers work with accounting to fine-tune assumptions and incorporate other goals and objectives.

Source: Based on George F. Hanks, Michael A. Freid, and Jack Huber, "Shifting Gears at Borg-Warner Automotive," *Management Accounting,* February 1994, p. 28.

Exhibit 9–4   Sales Budget

KERRY INDUSTRIAL COMPANY
Sales Budget
For the First Quarter Ended June 30, 20X0

	April	May	June	Quarter
Sales in units	20,000	25,000	35,000	80,000
Selling price per unit	× 30	× 30	× 30	× 30
Total sales	$600,000	$750,000	$1,050,000	$2,400,000

---

[5] Determination of sales levels and preparation of the sales budget for the budget period may not occur at the same time in some firms. When the sales budget includes marketing plans to attain sales, the sales budget and the firm's marketing plan have to be done at the same time.

Production Budget

The production budget follows the sales budget. A **production budget** is a plan for acquiring and combining the resources needed to carry out the manufacturing operations that allow the firm to satisfy its sales goals and have the desired amount of inventory at the end of the budget period. The total number of units to be produced depends on the budgeted sales, the desired amount of finished goods ending inventory, and the units of finished goods beginning inventory. This equation describes the determination of budgeted units of production:

$$\begin{array}{ccccccc} \text{Budgeted} & & \text{Budgeted} & & \text{Desired ending} & & \text{Beginning} \\ \text{production} & = & \text{sales} & + & \text{inventory} & - & \text{inventory} \\ \text{(in units)} & & \text{(in units)} & & \text{(in units)} & & \text{(in units)} \end{array}$$

Selecting the desired ending inventory for a period requires balancing opposing goals. On one hand, a firm does not want to lose sales because of insufficient inventory. On the other hand, having an inventory of excess finished goods is costly. Thus, the organization must determine how quickly it can increase production if demand warrants and then set its desired production and inventory levels accordingly. For a firm using a just-in-time system, for example, the desired ending as well as the beginning inventory will be zero or a small amount.

Other factors that may affect a production budget include company policies regarding stabilizing production versus flexible production schedules that minimize finished inventories, conditions of production equipment, availability of production resources such as materials and laborers, and experience with production yields and quality.

To illustrate, Kerry expects to have 5,000 units on hand on April 1 and desires to have 30 percent of the following month's (May) predicted sales (25,000 units) on hand at the end of the period. Kerry therefore has a production budget to manufacture 22,500 units in April as calculated here.

1. Determine the desired ending inventory level (April 30)

    30 percent of the next month's sales $= 30\% \times 25,000$ units

    $= 7,500$ units

2. Calculate the budgeted production units in April

    Budgeted sales in April + Desired ending inventory − Beginning inventory

    $= 20,000$ units $+ 7,500$ units $- 5,000$ units

    $= 22,500$ units

Exhibit 9–5 shows the production budget of the Kerry Industrial Company for the first quarter of 20X0. This budget is based on the sales budget in Exhibit 9–4 and the expected sales in July of 40,000 units.

> A **production budget** is a plan for acquiring and combining the resources needed to carry out the manufacturing operations that allow the firm to satisfy its sales goals and have the desired amount of inventory at the end of the budget period.

Exhibit 9–5   Production Budget

KERRY INDUSTRIAL COMPANY
Production Budget
For the First Quarter Ended June 30, 20X0

	April	May	June	Quarter
Budgeted sales in units	20,000	25,000	35,000	80,000
Add: Desired ending inventory of finished units	7,500	10,500	12,000	12,000
Total units needed	27,500	35,500	47,000	92,000
Less: Beginning inventory of finished units	5,000	7,500	10,500	5,000
Budgeted production	$22,500	$28,000	$36,500	$87,000

Exhibit 9–6	Direct Materials Usage Budget

KERRY INDUSTRIAL COMPANY
Direct Materials Usage Budget
For the First Quarter Ended June 30, 20X0

	April	May	June	Quarter	
Budgeted production	22,500	28,000	36,500	87,000	
Pounds of aluminum alloy for one unit of product	× 3	× 3	× 3	× 3	
Total pounds of aluminum alloy needed in production	67,500	84,000	109,500	261,000	A
Pounds of aluminum alloy from beginning inventory	7,000	8,400	10,950	7,000	B
Cost per pound	$ 2.40	$ 2.45	$ 2.50	$ 2.40	C
Total cost of aluminum alloy beginning inventory	$16,800	$20,580	$27,375	$16,800	D = B × C
Total cost of aluminum alloy purchases	168,805	216,375	284,310	669,490	E = Ex. 9–7
Total cost of aluminum alloy available	$185,605	$236,955	$311,685	$686,290	F = D + E
Desired ending inventory of aluminum alloy in units	8,400	10,950	10,800	10,800	G = Ex. 9–7
Cost per unit	$ 2.45	$ 2.50	$ 2.60	$ 2.60	H = Ex. 9–7
Aluminum alloy ending inventory	$ 20,580	$ 27,375	$ 28,080	$ 28,080	I = G × H
Total cost of aluminum alloy used in production	$165,025	$209,580	$283,605	$658,210	J = F − I

* Ex. = Exhibit

Most of the quarterly amounts are simply the sums of the appropriate monthly figures. For example, the budgeted sales for the quarter, 80,000 units, is the sum of the budgeted sales in April (20,000 units), May (25,000 units), and June (35,000 units). The desired ending finished inventory of the quarter, however, is the desired ending inventory of *June*, the end of the quarter, not the sum of the desired ending amount in each of the three months. Also, the beginning inventory of the quarter is the beginning inventory of *April*, the first month of the quarter. These two amounts refer to specific times in the quarter, not the amount for the entire period.

The production budget is reviewed by the production manager to ascertain that the firm can attain the budgeted level of production with the facilities available, keeping in mind the other activities scheduled for the same period. If the production level exceeds the maximum capacity available, management can either revise the budgeted sales level or find alternatives to satisfy the demand. If the available capacity exceeds the budgeted production level, management may want to find alternative uses for the idle capacity or schedule other activities such as preventive maintenance and trial runs of new production processes. This ability to coordinate sales needs and production activities is another benefit of having a budget that allows firms to identify mismatches between capacity and output.

The sales budget for the quarter shows that Kerry Industrial Company expects to have increasing sales. When sales vary over periods, management can either change the production level as needed—as Kerry Industrial Company did in the previous budget—or maintain a stable production level. With a total of 87,000 units to be produced during the quarter, Kerry may set the production level at 29,000 units per month.

Maintaining a constant production level enables the firm to keep a constant employment level. The trend, however, is away from maintaining a constant production level. New manufacturing technology and adoption of just-in-time operations in recent years have forced an increasing number of firms to adjust production activity to changes in sales volume, not to keep it steady.

Direct Materials Usage and Purchases

The production budget is the basis for the direct materials usage budget. A **direct materials usage budget** shows the direct materials required for production and their budgeted cost. The direct materials usage budget thus serves as the starting point for preparing a direct materials purchase budget. Firms prepare direct materials purchase budgets to ensure having sufficient direct materials available to meet production needs and the desired direct materials ending inventory.

The direct materials purchase budget also provides the budgeted cost for purchases of direct materials; this enables the firm to determine the total amount of funds needed for the purchase. A materials purchase budget depends on company policies regarding production activities, such as just-in-time purchases versus stocking critical materials, and the firm's experience with materials quality and the dependability of suppliers.

Kerry Industrial Company uses three pounds of an aluminum alloy for each unit produced. At the beginning of April, Kerry has 7,000 pounds of the aluminum alloy on hand at a cost of $2.40 per pound. The aluminum alloy price is expected to be $2.45 per pound in April, $2.50 per pound in May, and $2.60 per pound in June. The firm uses the FIFO inventory valuation method and desires to have on hand 10 percent of the direct materials needed for the next month's production at the end of each period. Exhibit 9–6 shows Kerry's direct materials usage budget for the first quarter of 20X0.

The last items in Exhibit 9–6 are the total direct materials to be used in manufacturing during the period. The quantity, or total aluminum alloy needed in production, also serves as a starting point for determining total purchases for the period.

> A **direct materials usage budget** shows the direct materials required for production and their budgeted cost.

Total direct materials needed in production	+	Desired direct materials ending inventory	=	Total direct materials needed for the period

Total direct materials needed for the period	−	Direct materials beginning inventory	=	Direct materials purchases

Exhibit 9–7 shows the first quarter of the 20X0 direct materials purchases budget for Kerry Industrial Company. Kerry expects to manufacture 36,000 units in July. The desired direct materials ending inventory in June, therefore, is 10,800 pounds of aluminum alloy (10 percent of the production need for the next period, which is 3 pounds per unit × 36,000 = 108,000 pounds).

Exhibit 9–7	Direct Materials Purchase Budget

KERRY INDUSTRIAL COMPANY
Direct Materials Purchase Budget
For the First Quarter Ended June 30, 20X0

	April	May	June	Quarter
Total direct materials needed in production (from Exhibit 9–6)	67,500	84,000	109,500	261,000
Add: Desired direct materials ending inventory	8,400	10,950	10,800	10,800
Total direct materials needed	75,900	94,950	120,300	271,800
Less: Direct materials beginning inventory	7,000	8,400	10,950	7,000
Total direct materials purchases	68,900	86,550	109,350	264,800
Purchase price per pound	$ 2.45	$ 2.50	$ 2.60	
Total cost for direct materials purchases	$168,805	$216,375	$284,310	$669,490

The total direct materials needed for each period is the sum of the total direct materials needed in production and the desired ending direct materials inventory. The total direct materials to be purchased in each of the periods is the difference between the total direct materials needed for the period and the direct materials beginning inventory.

Direct Labor Budget

The production budget also serves as a starting point for preparing the direct labor budget. A firm's labor force must include sufficient skilled workers required for the production of the finished goods scheduled for the period. The direct labor budget enables the personnel department to plan for direct labor and avoid emergency hiring or labor shortages, and to reduce the need to lay off workers. Erratic labor employment decreases employees' sense of loyalty, increases their insecurity, and leads to inefficiency.

Many firms have policies of stable employment or labor contracts that prevent them from hiring and laying off workers in direct proportion to their production needs. A direct labor budget enables the firm to identify circumstances when it can either reschedule the production or plan temporary reassignments of workers to perform other tasks. Manufacturing cells common to many of the firms that adopt new manufacturing technologies can use the direct labor budget to plan for maintenance, minor repair, installation, testing, learning to use new equipment, or other activities.

A direct labor budget usually is prepared for each type of labor needed in production. Kerry Industrial Company has two skill levels for its workers, skilled and semiskilled. The production process uses 0.5 hour of semiskilled labor and 0.2 hour of skilled labor. The hourly wages are $8.00 and $12.00 for semiskilled and skilled laborers, respectively. Exhibit 9–8 illustrates the direct labor budget for the first quarter of 20X0.

Factory Overhead Budget

The factory overhead budget includes all production costs other than direct materials and direct labor. Unlike direct materials and direct labor, which tend to vary

Exhibit 9–8	Direct Labor Budget

KERRY INDUSTRIAL COMPANY
Direct Labor Budget
For the First Quarter Ended June 30, 20X0

		April	May	June	Quarter
Semiskilled					
1.	Budgeted production	22,500	28,000	36,500	87,000
2.	Semiskilled direct labor-hours per unit	× .5	× .5	× .5	× .5
3.	Total semiskilled direct labor-hours needed	11,250	14,000	18,250	43,500
4.	Hourly wage rate of semiskilled labor	$ 8.00	$ 8.00	$ 8.00	$ 8.00
5.	Total wages for semiskilled labor	$ 90,000	$112,000	$146,000	$348,000
Skilled					
6.	Budgeted production	22,500	28,000	36,500	87,000
7.	Skilled direct labor-hours per unit	× .2	× .2	× .2	× .2
8.	Total skilled direct labor-hours needed	4,500	5,600	7,300	17,400
9.	Hourly wage for skilled labor	$ 12.00	$ 12.00	$ 12.00	$ 12.00
10.	Total wages for skilled labor	$ 54,000	$ 67,200	$ 87,600	$208,800
Total					
11.	Total direct manufacturing labor-hour (3) + (8)	15,750	19,600	25,550	60,900
12.	Total cost for direct manufacturing labor (5) + (10)	$144,000	$179,200	$233,600	$556,800

in direct proportion with the number of units manufactured, manufacturing overhead costs also include costs that do not vary in direct proportion with the units manufactured, but with the way the production is carried out. Examples include costs that vary with the batch size and number of setups in production. Manufacturing overhead also includes costs that are fixed, such as salaries of production supervisors and factory depreciation expenses.

Budgeting for factory overhead costs requires forecasting the units to be produced, determining the way in which production is to be carried out, and incorporating external factors that affect factory overhead. Many firms divide the factory overhead budget into variable and fixed overhead items. All factory overhead costs other than those that vary in direct proportion with the units manufactured are treated as fixed costs. Such practices are justified on the ground that nonvariable factory overhead costs usually remain the same within a given range of production activities. Exhibit 9–9 shows the factory overhead costs budget of Kerry Industrial Company for the first quarter of 20X0.

Cost of Goods Manufactured and Sold

The cost of goods manufactured and sold budget reports the total and per unit budgeted production cost in each period. Exhibits 9–5 through 9–9 provide the data needed to complete this budget. Exhibit 9–10 shows the cost of goods manufactured and sold budget for the first quarter of 20X0 prepared by Kerry Industrial Company. It is assumed the company's finished goods inventory on April 1 has a unit cost of $18.

Two of the items in this budget appear in other budgets for the same period. The income statement budget uses the cost of goods sold to determine the gross margin of the period, while the balance sheet includes the finished goods ending inventory in the total assets.

Merchandise Purchase Budget

A merchandising firm does not have a production budget. Instead, the production budget for a manufacturing firm, as illustrated in Exhibit 9–5, is replaced by a merchandise purchase budget.

The **merchandise purchase budget** of a firm shows the amount of merchandise it needs to purchase during the period. The basic format of a merchandise purchase

A **merchandise purchase budget** of a firm shows the amount of merchandise it needs to purchase during the period.

Exhibit 9–9	Factory Overhead Budget

KERRY INDUSTRIAL COMPANY
Factory Overhead Budget
For the First Quarter Ended June 30, 20X0

	April	May	June	Quarter
Total direct labor-hours	15,750	19,600	25,550	60,900
Variable factory overhead:				
Supplies	$ 1,890	$ 2,352	$ 3,066	$ 7,308
Indirect labor	15,750	19,600	25,550	60,900
Fringe benefits	47,250	58,800	76,650	182,700
Power	3,150	3,920	5,110	12,180
Maintenance	1,260	1,568	2,044	4,872
Total variable factory overhead	$ 69,300	$ 86,240	$112,420	$267,960
Fixed factory overhead:				
Depreciation	$ 30,000	$ 30,000	$ 40,000	$100,000
Factory insurance	2,500	2,500	2,500	7,500
Property taxes	900	900	900	2,700
Supervision	8,900	8,900	8,900	26,700
Power	1,250	1,250	1,250	3,750
Maintenance	750	750	750	2,250
Total fixed factory overhead	$ 44,300	$ 44,300	$ 54,300	$142,900
Total factory overhead	$113,600	$130,540	$166,720	$410,860

Exhibit 9–10	Cost of Goods Manufactured and Sold Budget

KERRY INDUSTRIAL COMPANY
Cost of Goods Manufactured and Sold Budget
For the First Quarter Ended June 30, 20X0

	April	May	June	Quarter
Direct materials	$165,025	$209,580	$283,605	$ 658,210
Direct labor	144,000	179,200	233,600	556,800
Factory overhead	113,600	130,540	166,720	410,860
Total cost of goods manufactured	$422,625	$519,320	$683,925	$1,625,870
Finished goods beginning inventory	90,000	140,875	194,745	90,000
Total cost of goods available for sale	$512,625	$660,195	$878,670	$1,715,870
Finished goods ending inventory	140,875	194,745	224,852	224,852
Cost of goods sold	$371,750	$465,450	$653,818	$1,491,018
Factory cost per unit	$18.7833	$18.5471	$18.7377	$18.6882

Exhibit 9–11	Selling and Administrative Expense Budget

KERRY INDUSTRIAL COMPANY
Selling and Administrative Expense Budget
For the First Quarter Ended June 30, 20X0

	April	May	June	Quarter
Selling expenses				
Variable selling expense				
Sales commissions	$ 30,000	$37,500	$52,500	$120,000
Delivery expenses	2,000	2,500	3,500	8,000
Bad debts expenses	9,000	11,250	15,750	36,000
Total variable selling expense	$41,000	$51,250	$71,750	$164,000
Fixed selling expense				
Sales salary	$ 8,000	$ 8,000	$ 8,000	$ 24,000
Advertising	50,000	50,000	50,000	150,000
Delivery expenses	6,000	6,000	6,000	18,000
Depreciation	20,000	20,000	20,000	60,000
Total fixed selling expense	$84,000	$84,000	$84,000	$252,000
Total selling expense	$125,000	$135,250	$155,750	$416,000
Administrative expenses (all fixed)				
Administrative salaries	$25,000	$25,000	$25,000	$75,000
Accounting and data processing	12,000	12,000	12,000	36,000
Depreciation	7,000	7,000	7,000	21,000
Other administrative expenses	6,000	6,000	6,000	18,000
Total administrative expense	$ 50,000	$ 50,000	$ 50,000	$150,000
Total selling and administrative expense	$175,000	$185,250	$205,750	$566,000

budget is the same as the production budget. Instead of budgeted production as shown in Exhibit 9–5, however, the last items in a merchandise purchase budget are *budgeted purchases*.

Selling and General Administrative Expense Budget

The selling and general administrative expense budget contains all nonmanufacturing expenses expected in the budget period. Exhibit 9–11 shows the selling and administrative expense budget for Kerry Industrial Company for the first quarter of 20X0. The selling and administrative expense budget is important as a guideline for operations. However, because many of the items included in it are discretionary expenditures and their impacts are mostly long term, using this budget to evaluate performance must be done carefully.

For example, a manager may cut expenditures for customer services from, say, $200,000 to $50,000 to improve earnings and to show that he has good control of expenses. The incentive for the manager is a reward in the form of a bonus or promotion because the likely short-term result from the reduction is improved profits. The reduction in customer services probably will not have any immediate effect on sales. It will, however, most likely have negative consequences for the firm in the future. Hence, firms have to be wary of taking a short-run perspective when preparing a selling and administrative expense budget.

Cash Budget

Having an adequate amount of cash on hand at all times is crucial to a business for survival and for capturing opportunities. A **cash budget** brings together the anticipated effects of all budgeted activities on cash. It also delineates cash receipts and disbursements during the period. By preparing a cash budget, management ensures having sufficient cash on hand to carry out its planned activities, arrange additional financing in advance to avoid the high costs of emergency borrowing, and plan investments to earn the highest possible return from any excess cash on hand. For smaller firms and those with seasonal business, the cash budget is especially critical to ensure smooth operations and avoid crises. The critical importance of having adequate cash to meet all operation needs leads many firms to consider cash budgets among their most important master budgets.

> A **cash budget** brings together the anticipated effects of all budgeted activities on cash.

A cash budget pulls together data from almost all parts of the budget. In preparing a cash budget, a firm needs to review all its budgets to identify all revenues, expenses, and other transactions that have effects on cash. Any items that affect cash flows are included in the cash budget.

A cash budget generally includes three major sections:

1. Cash available
2. Cash disbursements
3. Financing

The cash available section details the sources of cash available for operations. In general, the two sources are the cash balance at the beginning of the budget period and cash collections during that period.

BusinessWeek

How Can Moviemakers Keep Their Heads (Budgets) above Water?

(Continues from page 283)

A: The right accounting systems can keep them afloat . . .

According to Bill Mechanic, chairman at Twentieth Century Fox, they learned a lot regarding budget management from the making of *Titanic*. "We learned some lessons making Titanic . . . We have tightened up our budget controls, made sure we had more representatives on the set. Making movies for a budget is about planning and execution, and we have learned a great deal about that." Mechanic noted that having more accounting systems in place to keep track of where and why money is spent helps achieve effective cost control. As he put it, "You start to treat this like a real business . . . we all knew the budget [for *Titanic*] was a bit soft. It would have helped some if we had known ahead of time what we were really in for."

For further reading, see the following source: "Online Original: Q & A with Bill Mechanic of Twentieth Century Fox," *Business Week*, January 12, 1998.

Cash collections include cash sales and cash collections of accounts and notes receivable. Factors that may affect cash sales and cash collections of accounts include sales levels of the firm, the credit policy of the company, and the collection experience of the firm.

There are times when a firm engages in nonroutine transactions that generate cash. Examples are selling operating assets such as equipment or a building, or non-operating assets such as land purchased for the site of a factory that the firm no longer intends to build. All proceeds from such sales should be included in the cash available section.

The cash disbursements section lists all payments including payments for purchases of direct materials and supplies, wages and salaries, operating expenses, interest expenses, and taxes. The difference between cash available and cash disbursements is the ending cash balance.

A firm needs to borrow additional funds if its cash balance falls below the desired minimum balance set by the management. On the other hand, when the firm expects to have a significant amount of excess cash on hand, it must determine how the excess is to be invested. Return, liquidity, and risk must be weighed for alternative investments. Both the borrowing and the planned investments are included in the financing section.

Exhibit 9–12 shows the cash budget of the Kerry Industrial Company for the first quarter of 20X0. In addition to reviewing Exhibits 9–4 through 9–11 to identify items that have effects on cash, management must gather additional information about the operating characteristics and policies of the firm to complete the cash budget. Examples of such items and policies include:

1. The firm has a policy of maintaining a minimum cash balance of $50,000. It expects to have $75,000 cash on hand on April 1.

2. The firm expects 70 percent of its sales to be cash sales. The other sales are made to customers with open accounts with the firm. Also, the firm estimates that 40 percent of the cash customers use credit cards for their purchases. The bank charges a 3 percent service fee to process credit card charges.

3. The firm sends statements to its customers on the first of each month with terms of 2/10, n/eom.[6] Eighty percent of the accounts are paid within the month. Three-fifths of these payments are received by the firm within the discount period. Fifteen percent of the accounts send in their checks the following month. The firm has a 5 percent bad debt rate on its accounts receivable.

4. The typical term for the firm's purchases of direct materials is n/30. The firm pays 60 percent of its purchases in the month of the purchase and the remainder in the following month.

5. All expenses and wages are paid as incurred.

6. Total sales were $400,000 in February and $450,000 in March.

7. The firm purchased a total of $155,000 direct materials in March.

8. Equipment purchased in January for $200,000 will be delivered in May, terms COD.

9. The firm has a revolving 30-day account at 1 percent per month with the First National Bank for all temporary financing needs. The account has to be drawn in increments of $50,000 with repayment occurring no sooner than 30 days.

Budget Income Statement

The budget income statement shows the profit a firm can expect from its budgeted operations. Management assesses actions to take when the budgeted income for the

---

[6] Customers who pay within 10 days receive a 2 percent discount on the total amount due. The payment is due on or before the end of the month.

Exhibit 9–12   Cash Budget

KERRY INDUSTRIAL COMPANY
Cash Budget
For the First Quarter Ended June 30, 20X0

	April	May	June	Quarter
Cash available				
Cash balance, beginning	$ 75,000	$ 84,781	$ 91,916	$ 75,000
Cash collections				
Cash from cash sales*	$252,000	$315,000	$ 441,000	$1,008,000
Credit card sales*	162,960	203,700	285,180	651,840
Collections of accounts:				
Within cash discount period†	63,504	84,672	105,840	254,016
After the cash discount:				
From prior month's sales‡	43,200	57,600	72,000	172,800
From sales two months earlier§	18,000	20,250	27,000	65,250
Total cash collections	$539,664	$681,222	$ 931,020	$2,151,906
Total cash available	$614,664	$766,003	$1,022,936	$2,226,906
Cash disbursement				
Purchases of direct materials				
Current month purchases‖	$101,283	$129,825	$ 170,586	$ 401,694
Last month's purchases#	62,000	67,522	86,550	216,072
Total payment for direct materials purchases	$163,283	$197,347	$ 257,136	$ 617,766
Direct labor wages	$144,000	$179,200	$ 233,600	$ 556,800
Factory overheads	$ 83,600	$100,540	$ 126,720	$ 310,860
Operating expenses				
Sales commissions	$ 30,000	$ 37,500	$ 52,500	$ 120,000
Sales salary	8,000	8,000	8,000	24,000
Administrative salaries	25,000	25,000	25,000	75,000
Delivery expenses	8,000	8,500	9,500	26,000
Advertising	50,000	50,000	50,000	150,000
Accounting and data processing	12,000	12,000	12,000	36,000
Other administrative expenses	6,000	6,000	6,000	18,000
Total payment for operating expenses	$139,000	$147,000	$ 163,000	$ 449,000
Equipment purchase		$200,000		$ 200,000
Total cash disbursement	$529,883	$824,087	$ 780,456	$2,134,426
Cash balance before financing	$ 84,781	$ (58,084)	$ 242,480	$ 92,480
Financing				
First National Bank		$150,000		$ 150,000
Payment to First National Bank				
Principal			(150,000)	(150,000)
Interest			(1,500)	(1,500)
Total financing		$150,000	$ (151,500)	$ (1,500)
Cash balance	$ 84,781	$ 91,916	$ 90,980	$ 90,980

* *April*
Total cash sales in April: $600,000 × .7 = $420,000
Cash paying customers are $420,000 × .6 = $252,000
Collections from credit card sales are
$420,000 × .4 × .97 = $162,960

May
Total cash sales in May: $750,000 × .7 = $525,000
Cash paying customers are $525,000 × .6 = $315,000
Collections from credit card sales are
$525,000 × .4 × .97 = $203,700

June
Total cash sales in June: $1,050,000 × .7 = $735,000
Cash paying customers are $735,000 × .6 = $441,000
Collections from credit card sales are
$735,000 × .4 × .97 = $285,180

† For April from sales in March:
$450,000 × .3 × .8 × .6 × .98 = $63,504

For May from sales in April:
$600,000 × .3 × .8 × .6 × .98 = $84,672
For June from sales in May
$750,000 × .3 × .8 × .6 × .98 = $105,840

‡ For April from sales in March: $450,000 × .3 × .8 × .4 = $43,200
For May from sales in April: $600,000 × .3 × .8 × .4 = $57,600
For June from sales in May: $750,000 × .3 × .8 × .4 = $72,000

§ For April from sales in February: $400,000 × .3 × .15 = $18,000
For May from sales in March: $450,000 × .3 × .15 = $20,250
For June from sales in April: $600,000 × .3 × .15 = $27,000

‖ For April for purchases in April: $168,805 × .6 = $101,283
For May for purchases in May: $216,375 × .6 = $129,825
For June for purchases in June: $284,310 × .6 = $170,586

For April for purchases in March: $155,000 × .4 = $62,000
For May for purchases in April: $168,805 × .4 = $67,522
For June for purchases in May: $216,375 × .4 = $86,550

period falls short of the goal. In such cases, the budget is revised. Once the budget income statement has been approved, it becomes the benchmark against which the performance of the period is to be evaluated. Exhibits 9–4, 9–10, and 9–11 provide information needed to prepare the budget income statement for the period in Exhibit 9–13.

Budget Balance Sheet

A budget balance sheet completes the budget preparation cycle. The starting point in preparing the budget balance sheet is the expected balance sheet at the end of

Exhibit 9–13	Budget Income Statement

KERRY INDUSTRIAL COMPANY
Budget Income Statement
For the First Quarter Ended June 30, 20X0

	Reference	April	May	June	Quarter
Sales	Ex. 9–4	$600,000	$750,000	$1,050,000	$2,400,000
Cost of goods sold	Ex. 9–10	371,750	465,450	653,818	1,491,018
Gross margin		$228,250	$284,550	$ 396,182	$ 908,982
Selling and administrative expenses	Ex. 9–11	175,000	185,250	205,750	566,000
Net operating income		$ 53,250	$ 99,300	$ 190,432	$ 342,982
Less: Interest expense	Ex. 9–12			1,500	1,500
Income before taxes		$ 53,250	$ 99,300	$ 188,932	$ 341,482
Less: Income taxes (30%)		15,975	29,790	56,680	102,445
Net income		$ 37,275	$ 69,510	$ 132,252	$ 239,037

Exhibit 9–14	Budget Balance Sheet

KERRY INDUSTRIAL COMPANY
Budget Balance Sheet
March 31, 20X0

Assets

Current assets:			
Cash		$ 75,000	
Accounts receivable		153,000	
Raw materials inventory		16,800	
Finished goods inventory		90,000	
Office supplies		3,500	
Total current assets			$338,300
Plant, property, and equipment:			
Land		$ 40,000	
Buildings and equipment	$764,000		
Less: Accumulated depreciation	168,000	596,000	
Total plant, property, and equipment			636,000
Total assets			$974,300

Liabilities and Stockholders' Equity

Current liabilities:			
Accounts payable		$ 62,000	
Sales tax payable		4,500	
Total liabilities			$ 66,500
Stockholders' equity:			
Common stock		$303,300	
Retained earnings		604,500	
Total stockholders' equity			907,800
Total liabilities and stockholders' equity			$974,300

Exhibit 9–15	Budget Balance Sheet

KERRY INDUSTRIAL COMPANY
Budget Balance Sheet
June 30, 20X0

Assets

Current assets:		
Cash (Exhibit 9–12)	$ 90,980	
Accounts receivable[1]	333,000	
Raw materials inventory (Exhibit 9–6)	28,080	
Finished goods inventory (Exhibit 9–10)	224,852	
Office supplies	38,906	
Total current assets		$ 715,818
Plant, property, and equipment:		
Land (Exhibit 9–14)	$ 40,000	
Buildings and equipment	$964,000	
Less: Accumulated depreciation	349,000	615,000
Total plant, property, and equipment		655,000
Total assets		$1,370,818

Liabilities and Stockholders' Equity

Current liabilities:		
Accounts payable (Exhibits 9–7 and 9–12)	$113,724	
Sales tax payable	7,812	
Income tax payable (Exhibit 9–13)	102,445	
Total liabilities		$ 223,981
Stockholders' equity:		
Common stock (Exhibit 9–14)	$303,300	
Retained earnings (Exhibits 9–13 and 9–14)	843,537	
Total stockholders' equity		1,146,837
Total liabilities and stockholders' equity		$1,370,818

[1]	Total credit sales in June	$1,050,000 × 0.3 =	$315,000	
	Allowance for bad debts	$315,000 × 0.05 =	15,750	$299,250
	Total credit sales in May	$750,000 × 0.3 =	$225,000	
	Allowance for bad debts	$225,000 × 0.05 =	11,250	
	Total accounts receivable from May		$213,750	
	Collections in June	$225,000 × 0.8 =	180,000	33,750
	Accounts receivable, June 30, 20X0			$333,000

the current operating period, which is the beginning of the budget period. Exhibit 9–14 presents the budget balance sheet as of March 31, 20X0, the end of Kerry Industrial Company's current operating period.

In preparing the budget balance sheet, the firm incorporates expected changes during the budget period into the expected balance sheet at the end of the current period (see Exhibit 9–14). Exhibit 9–15 shows the budget balance sheet at the end of the budget period.

For example, the amount of cash in Exhibit 9–14 is taken from the ending cash balance on the cash budget of the period (Exhibit 9–12). The ending balance of Raw Materials is from Exhibit 9–6. And the gross amount of Building and Equipment is the sum of the beginning balance in the Building and Equipment account (Exhibit 9–14) and the purchase of new equipment during the budget period (Exhibit 9–12).

ADDITIONAL CONSIDERATIONS IN BUDGETING

Several other issues are of concern in budgeting. For example, service firms and not-for-profit organizations have different considerations than those of the manufacturing and merchandising firms discussed earlier. Moreover, firms operating in an international setting need to pay attention to particular environments in which they operate. In addition, many firms have benefited from budgeting approaches such as zero-based budgeting, activity-based budgeting, and kaizen budgeting. This section examines special concerns in budgeting for service firms and not-for-profit organizations as well as several budgeting approaches.

Budgeting in Service Industries

LEARNING OBJECTIVE 5 ▶
Identify unique budgeting characteristics of service and not-for-profit organizations, and of organizations operating in international settings.

The budgeting procedures are the same for both service and manufacturing or merchandising firms. A service firm carefully plans how to secure the resources required to render its services and fulfill its budgeted goals, just as a manufacturing firm plans its manufacturing activities and acquires materials, labor, and other resources for its budgeted sales. The primary difference between budgets for service firms and manufacturing or merchandising firms' budgets is the absence of production or merchandise purchase budgets and their ancillary budgets. Also the focal point of a service organization's budgeting is personnel planning. A service firm must ensure that it has personnel with the right skills to perform services required for the budgeted service revenue.

As an example, AccuTax, Inc., provides tax services to small firms and individuals. The firm expects to have these total revenues:

Revenues from business firms		$1,200,000
Revenues for individual tax returns:		
Simple tax forms	$300,000	
Complicated tax forms	500,000	800,000
Total revenues		$2,000,000

The firm charges $100 per hour for services rendered to business firms, $50 per hour for services rendered to individuals with complicated tax matters, and $30 per hour for services rendered to individuals with simple tax returns. The firm therefore needs to budget for the staff:

Staff hours to serve business firms	$1,200,000 ÷ $100 =	12,000 hours
Staff hours to serve individual taxpayers:		
with complicated tax forms	$500,000 ÷ $50 =	10,000 hours
with simple tax forms	$300,000 ÷ $30 =	10,000 hours
Total service hours budgeted		32,000 hours

Suppose, however, that most of the AccuTax, Inc., staff have the skills necessary to provide services to business firms. The higher wage rate for these highly skilled staff, when paid for completing individual returns that draw considerably less in revenue, causes the firm's earnings to drop. The budget projections, if followed, would have led to hiring a staff mix better suited for the expected work.

Many firms in service industries have people as their principal assets. A service organization with a good budgeting system can avoid short-run fluctuations in staff levels and achieve higher productivity from personnel than a firm without a budget system.

Budgeting in Not-for-Profit Organizations

Not-for-profit organizations such as governments, state universities or colleges, secondary and primary schools, charity organizations, museums, and foundations have different objectives from for-profit organizations. There is no single bottom-line amount, such as operating income, that is widely recognized as the ultimate criterion in budgeting.

The objective of a not-for-profit organization is to provide services efficiently and effectively as mandated in its charter, yet within the amount of expenditure allowed. With no clear standard by which to measure performance in delivering services, and with a clear mandate not to exceed budgeted expenditures, master budgets of not-for-profit organizations often become the means to plan and document *authorization for expenditures*. In effect, the budget for a not-for-profit organization is often the document that shows the limitations of expenditures of the organization during the budgeted period.

The starting point of budget preparation for a not-for-profit organization is estimating the total revenues for the budget period. Because not-for-profit organizations often do not have the option of increasing revenues by increasing marketing activities, they must decide how best to allocate limited resources to competing activities and to subunits. The budget must show that the organization can at least break even at the estimated amount of revenue.[7] Once approved, the budget shows how a not-for-profit organization plans to perform its activities. Seldom is revision made during the budget period and operations of the organization usually follow the budget.

Budgeting in International Settings

A multinational company (MNC) faces several unique budgeting issues. These arise because of cultural and language differences, dissimilar political and legal environments, fluctuating monetary exchange rates, and discrepancies in the inflation rates of different countries, among other causes. An operating procedure acceptable in one country may be against the law in another country. Also, fluctuating currency exchange rates and different inflation rates must be incorporated into the budget, because changes in these rates affect the budgeted purchasing power of the MNC.

Subsidiaries or subdivisions of a multinational firm often have their own budgets. They still have to follow the budget procedure of the firm and coordinate with other divisions of the firm because all budgets have to be approved by the MNC's budget committee. All international subsidiaries of ITT, for example, must negotiate their budgets with the regional headquarters. A subsidiary in Belgium negotiates its budget with the European headquarters in Geneva, Switzerland; and then the budgets have to be approved by corporate headquarters in New York City.

Zero-Base Budgeting

Zero-base budgeting is a budgeting process that requires managers to prepare budgets from ground zero. A typical budgeting process is an incremental process and starts with the budget for the current period. The process assumes that most, if not all, the current activities and functions will continue into the next budget period. The primary focus in a typical budgeting process is changes to the current operating budget.

In contrast, a zero-base budgeting process allows no activities or functions to be included in the budget unless managers can justify the need for having them. Zero-base budgeting requires managers or budgeting teams to perform in-depth reviews and analyses of all budget items. Such a budgeting process encourages managers to be aware of activities or functions that have outlived their usefulness or have been a waste of resources. A tight, efficient budget often results from zero-base budgeting.

Zero-base budgeting has drawn considerable attention since the 1970s. Although its popularity has faded since its heyday, many organizations still use zero-base budgeting, especially government and not-for-profit organizations.

A good budgeting process should follow the fundamental concept of zero-base budgeting; namely, regular, periodic review of all activities and functions. The amount of work and time needed to complete zero-base budgeting, however, makes it impossible for an organization to review and examine all its activities from the zero-budget level every year. Many organizations schedule zero-base budgeting periodically or perform zero-base budgeting for different divisions each year. For example, the highway department of a state government could adopt rotating five-year zero-base budgeting. All divisions of the department would be subject to in-depth review of their activities every fifth year, with the process applying to different divisions each year.

◄ **LEARNING OBJECTIVE 6**
Apply zero-base, activity-based, and kaizen budgeting.

Zero-base budgeting is a budgeting process that requires managers to prepare budgets from ground zero.

---

[7] The budget for the federal government of the United States is an exception.

Activity-Based Budgeting

Activity-based budgeting (ABB) is a budgeting process that focuses on costs of activities or cost drivers necessary for operations. ABB segregates costs into homogeneous cost pools based on cost drivers that result from activity-based costing.[8] Thus, activity-based budgeting begins with partitioning all budget costs into separate homogeneous cost pools such as unit, batch, product, and facility. Criteria for inclusion in a cost pool is that costs in that pool vary in similar proportions when the level of activity changes. A firm that uses activity-based costing already would have partitioned its costs into such cost pools. A review of the accuracy of the cost pools for the budget period, however, needs to be conducted before employing the same cost pools in budgeting, especially when a firm has experienced inexplicable variances.

Exhibit 9–16 contrasts traditional budgeting with ABB. An ABB budget is a budget of the costs of performing various activities, in contrast to the traditional budget that presents budgeted costs for each of the functional areas or spending categories. While traditional budgeting focuses on the cost elements such as materials, labor, and manufacturing overhead, ABB directs attention to the expected costs of performing various activities.

An ABB facilitates continuous improvement. The process in preparing an ABB highlights opportunities for cost reduction and elimination of wasteful activities. ABB reduces workloads required to the minimum level necessary to achieve organizational objectives. In contrast, history often is the underlying theme in a traditional budget. Resources for an activity are provided for in a traditional budget unless the organization has experienced difficulties.

A traditional budget confines its activities within the organization and seldom reaches beyond the loading docks of the firm. Such a firm treats the activities of its suppliers or customers as given conditions to the budget. In contrast, a successful ABB requires coordinating closely with suppliers and meeting the needs of customers.

As a control tool, a traditional budget focuses on minimizing variances and maximizing responsibility units' performances. The primary objective for control in an ABB is to coordinate and synchronize activities of the entire firm to serve customers.

Kaizen (Continuous Improvement) Budgeting

Chapter 1 noted that continuous improvement (kaizen) has become a common practice for firms operating in today's globally competitive environment. **Kaizen budgeting** is a budgeting approach that explicitly demands continuous improvement

Exhibit 9–16	Traditional vs. Activity-Based Budgeting	
	Traditional Budgeting	**Activity-Based Budgeting**
Budgeting unit	Expressed as the cost of functional areas or spending categories	Expressed as the cost of performing activities
Focus on	Required input resources	Output or work to be done
Orientation	History	Continuous improvement
Roles of suppliers and customers	Does not formally consider suppliers and customers in budgeting	Coordinates with suppliers and considers the needs of customers in budgeting
Control objective	Controls maximize managers' performances	Control processes synchronize activities companywide
Budget base	Based on cost behavioral patterns: variable and fixed costs	Based on utilized and unutilized capacity

[8]   Chapter 4 discusses activity-based costing in detail.

and incorporates all the expected improvements in the resultant budget. In a kaizen budgeting process budgets are based on the desired future operating processes rather than the continuation of the current practices as is often the case in traditional budgeting. A kaizen budget reflects all the resultant changes from the continuous improvement.

Kaizen budgeting begins with analyzing current practices to find improvements and determine expected changes needed to attain the desired improvements. Budgets are prepared based on improved practices or procedures. As a result, budgeted costs often are lower than those in the preceding period and the firm expects to be able to manufacture products or render services at a lower cost. Kaizen budgeting mandates, for example, a 10 percent decrease in a product's manufacturing cost. The manufacturing cost for a product that required labor costs of $500 previously has a budgeted manufacturing labor cost of $450 in a kaizen budget.

Kaizen budgeting is not limited to internal improvements. Many firms expect and demand continuous improvements of their suppliers and explicitly incorporate consequent effects on costs and delivery schedules of parts and components in budgeted production cost and manufacturing schedules.

Citizen Watch demands its suppliers decrease their costs a minimum of 3 percent per year. This 3 percent decrease in cost is included in the budget. Suppliers keep any cost saving in excess of 3 percent.[9]

A kaizen budget is not the same as the budget cuts we often see firms or governments make when facing a budget crunch because of diminishing profits, decreasing sales, or declining tax revenues. A budget cut often is a reluctant passive response to a mandate that is accomplished by reductions in productive activities or services. In contrast, kaizen budgeting promotes active engagement in reforming or altering practices. A decrease in cost in a kaizen budget is a result of doing the same activity more efficiently and with higher quality; it is not a result of arbitrarily eliminating activities or components.

ETHICAL, BEHAVIORAL, AND IMPLEMENTATION ISSUES IN BUDGETING

A budget can be successful only if the person responsible for its implementation makes it happen. To encourage persons responsible for budget preparation and implementation to attain the goals of the organization efficiently and effectively, firms need to consider the many ethical and behavioral aspects of budgeting.

◀ **LEARNING OBJECTIVE 7**
Discuss the roles of ethics and behavioral concerns in budgeting.

Ethics in Budgeting

Ethical issues permeate all aspects of budgeting. A significant portion of information used in budgeting is provided by people whose performance is evaluated against the budget. Employees breach the code of ethics if they deliberately furnish data for budgeting purposes that would lead to lower performance expectations.

A budget also is the result of negotiations. Too often people follow this motto: It is better to promise too little and deliver more than to promise too much and deliver less. This might involve negotiating a goal of 12 percent growth in earnings and achieving 14 percent rather than negotiating a goal of 16 percent and delivering 15 percent. The 15 percent actual performance is certainly better for a firm than 14 percent. Yet when facing a choice between offering a budget with the likelihood of 12 percent growth and one with 16 percent growth, managers usually choose the 12 percent budget because it represents a lower risk to their careers.

Including budget slack, or padding the budget, is the practice of knowingly including a higher amount of expenditure in the budget than managers truly feel is needed. Managers often justify such practices as insurance against uncertain future events. After all, no one knows exactly how the future will unfold. Padded

---

[9] Robin Cooper, *Citizen Watch Company, Ltd.*, Harvard Business School case 9–194–033. ©1993 by the President and Fellows of Harvard College.

budgets, however, waste resources and may lead employees to make half-hearted efforts to meet or exceed the budget. In any event, budget padding is not an honest action.

Spending the budget is another serious ethical issue in budgeting. Managers may believe that if they do not use up all the budgeted amounts, future budgets will be reduced. To avoid cuts in their budgets, managers may resort to wasteful spending to exhaust the remaining budgeted amount before the end of the period. As a result, precious resources are wasted on activities that yield little or no benefit to the firm. Or unnecessary assets are acquired to use up remaining funds. Furthermore, time is wasted on unproductive efforts in trying to use up the budget.

Goal Congruence

Goal congruence is consistency between the goals of the firm and the goals of its employees.

Goal congruence is consistency between the goals of the firm and the goals of its employees. A perfect goal congruence is the ideal for which many firms strive. Realistically, perfect goal congruence almost never exists because resources for satisfying short-term goals of individuals are often in conflict with those of the firm. For example, employees desire to earn a high salary with minimum effort, whereas a firm seeks to pay employees the lowest possible compensation while receiving maximum efforts from them.

Still, a firm needs its goals to be as consistent as possible with the goals of its employees. A budget devoid of considerations for goal congruence is most likely to be a failure. A budget that aligns the goals of the firm with those of its employees has a much better chance of leading to successful operations. One approach that encourages goal congruence is avoiding authoritative budgeting and using participative budgeting as much as possible. As employees identify a budget as their own in participative budgeting, the goals of the firm and those of its employees become the same.

Difficulty of the Budget Target

An easily attainable budget target may fail to bring out the employees' best efforts. A budget target that is very difficult to achieve, on the other hand, can discourage managers from even trying to attain it. Exhibit 9–17 depicts general relationships between the level of employees' efforts and level of difficulty of budget targets. Ideally, budget targets should be challenging, yet attainable. But what is a challenging and attainable budget target?

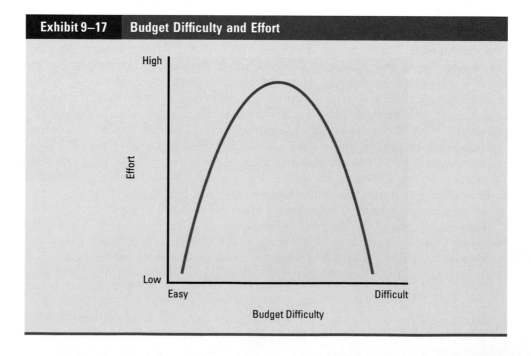

Exhibit 9–17	Budget Difficulty and Effort

In determining the difficulty level of a budget target, managers must consider the multiple functions a budget is expected to serve. A budget allows a manager to convert the organizational goals into budget goals for operating divisions. Budgeting, however, is a planning, coordinating, motivating, controlling, and evaluating tool. For planning and coordinating purposes, budget goals should be set at the level most likely to be attained by most managers. Good planning identifies those events most likely to occur. A budget including activities managers cannot perform as budgeted because of the difficulty of the budget target is no plan at all. The possibility of coordinating activities has been undermined. Firms should expect to achieve goals only if most managers can accomplish the activities and goals as budgeted.

For motivational purposes, a budget target easily attained by most managers may fail to spur these managers to put forth their best efforts. The optimal budget target should be set at a level attainable by, say, fewer than half the managers. On the other hand, a budget that allows fewer than half the operations to unfold as planned certainly is not a good plan. Nor is it a very good guideline for coordinating activities.

Research by Merchant and Manzoni suggests that a highly achievable target, a target achievable by most managers 80 to 90 percent of the time, serves quite well in the vast majority of organizations, especially when accompanied by extra rewards for performance exceeding the target.[10] According to Merchant (1990), the advantages of using a highly achievable budget target include:

1. Increasing managers' commitment to achieving the budget target.
2. Maintaining managers' confidence in the budget.
3. Decreasing organizational control cost.
4. Reducing the risk of managers engaging in harmful earnings management practices or violating corporate ethical standards. Twenty-nine percent of workers responding to a survey felt pressure to violate the ethical standards of their firms because of overly aggressive business goals.[11]
5. Allowing effective and efficient managers greater operating flexibility.
6. Improving predictability of earnings or operating results.
7. Enhancing usefulness of a budget as a planning and coordinating tool.

One risk in using highly achievable budgets is that some managers may not be challenged enough to put forth their maximum performances, especially managers who are not highly motivated. Merchant, however, points out that this problem may not be significant because most profit center managers already are highly motivated. Most have risen through the ranks because they are good performers with strong internal drives for competition and self-satisfaction. More likely than not, profit center managers will continue at the same pace even after they have attained the budget targets. And to ensure that managers do not slack off once they have achieved the budget target, some firms provide bonuses for performance exceeding the budget target.

Authoritative or Participative Budgeting

Budgeting processes are either top down or bottom up. In a top-down budgeting process top management prepares budgets for the entire organization, including those for lower-level operations. This process often is referred to as authoritative budgeting. A participative budgeting process, on the other hand, is a bottom-up approach that involves the people affected by the budget, including lower-level employees, in preparing the budget.

---

[10] Kenneth A. Merchant, "How Challenging Should Profit Budget Targets Be?" *Management Accounting*, November 1990, pp. 46–48; Kenneth A. Merchant, *Rewarding Results: Motivating Profit Center Managers* (Cambridge, MA: Harvard Business School Press, 1989); and Kenneth A. Merchant and J. Manzoni, "The Achievability of Budget Targets in Profit Centers: A Field Study, *The Accounting Review* 64, no. 3 (July 1989), pp. 539–58.

[11] *The Wall Street Journal*, March 10, 1995, p. A2.

Authoritative budgeting provides better decision-making control than participative budgeting. Top management sets the overall goals for the budget period and prepares a budget for operations to attain the goals. An authoritative budget, however, often lacks commitment on the part of the lower-level managers and workers responsible for the implementation of the budget. Furthermore, an authoritative budget does not communicate; it issues or dictates orders. People are likely to be resentful of orders. They are more willing to devote extra effort to attain goals they perceive as their own than they are to achieve goals they are ordered to attain.

A participative budget is a good communication device. The process of preparing a participative budget often gives top management a better grasp of the problems their people face and enables employees to gain a better understanding of the quandaries top management deals with. A participative budget is more likely to gain the employees' commitment to fulfill the budgetary goals.

Unless properly controlled, however, a participative budget may lead to easy budget targets or targets not in compliance with the organization's strategy or budget targets. An effective budgeting process therefore usually combines both top-down and bottom-up budgeting approaches. Divisions prepare their initial budgets based on the budget guidelines issued by the firm's budget committee. Senior managers review and make suggestions to the proposed budget before sending it back to the divisions for revisions. The final budget usually results from more participation, not enforced negotiations.

Top Management Involvement

To what extent should top management be involved in budgeting and how? The answer is complex. For a budget to be effective, top management needs to be involved and show strong interest in budget results. Too much involvement, however, may make the budget an authoritative budget and alienate lower managers. The right answer is a good balance of top management involvement with lower-level managers.

Top management ensures that budget guidelines are being followed through the budget review and approval process. Active involvement by top management in reviewing and approving the proposed budget is an effective way to discourage lower-level managers from playing budget games.[12] The active involvement of top management in budgeting also motivates lower managers to believe in the budget, be candid in budget preparation, and be dedicated to attaining the budget goals because they know the boss cares about the budget.

Role of the Budget Department or Controller

The budget department, and in some organizations the controller, stays active throughout the entire budget preparation process from examining the accuracy of data in the budget to analyzing the budget for consistency and conformity with the budget guidelines and the budget goals of the organization. The budget department provides the technicians who put the budget together.

Unfortunately, many of the tasks the budget department has to perform are perceived as negative. At times, the budget department may have to point out slack, excessive inventory, inefficient operations, and other potential problems in budgets. These certainly are not easy tasks. Yet they also are necessary if a firm is to have an efficient and effective budget for its operations.

Staff members in the budget department need to be good communicators. They also have to earn a reputation for being fair and impartial and for having personal integrity. A person who possesses such characteristics can go a long way as an effective facilitator and coordinator of budgeting.

---

[12]   Hofstede examines several budget games that people play. Among them are submitting budgets with easy targets and adding slack to a budget. For details see G. H. Hofstede, *The Game of Budget Control* (New York: Barnes & Noble, 1968).

SUMMARY

A budget for an organization is a quantitative plan that identifies the resources and commitments required to fulfill the organization's goal for the budget period. Budget preparation allows management to plan ahead, to communicate the plan and goals for the budget period to all divisions, and to motivate employees by having them involved in setting up plans. A budget also serves as the blueprint for operations, a guideline for controlling operations, and a basis for performance evaluation.

Strategy helps a firm to be more focused in its operations and to take advantage of its strengths and opportunities. A firm carries out its strategy through long-range plans and master budgets. Strategy provides the framework within which the long-range plan is developed. Both strategy and the long-range plan serve as starting points in preparing the annual master budget. A successful budget is accepted and supported by the key management people. It becomes a personalized budget for the people responsible for carrying out the budget; they perceive it as a tool to help them to do a better job, not as a pressure device. A successful budget also is a motivating device and has to be technically accurate.

Budgeting processes include formation of a budget committee; determination of the budget period; specification of budget guidelines; preparation of the initial budget proposal; budget negotiation, review, and approval; and budget revision. The budget committee usually consists of key members of senior management and its job is to oversee all budget matters. The committee issues budget guidelines based on plans that rely on the firm's strategy, external and internal factors, and experience gained from the implementation of the current budget. Based on the budget guidelines, managers of responsibility centers prepare initial budgets, then discuss and negotiate budget proposals with their superiors. The budget committee or the chief executive officer gives final approval of the budget.

The master budgets include sales, production, direct materials, direct labor, factory overhead, selling, and administration expense budgets, and the budgeted cash statement, income statement, and balance sheet.

A service firm prepares a budget following set procedures just as a manufacturing or merchandising firm does. A major difference between budgets for service firms and those for manufacturing or merchandising firms is the absence of a production budget or merchandise purchase budget and their ancillary budgets. The budgeting procedures and all other budget items are the same for both service and manufacturing or merchandising firms. A service firm needs to carefully plan its activities for securing the required resources, frequently focusing on manpower, to render the planned services to fulfill the budgeted sales.

A budget for a not-for-profit organization often becomes an authorization for its operating activities. A multinational company needs to consider carefully in its budget such issues as cultural and language differences, dissimilar political and legal environments, fluctuating monetary exchange rates, and discrepancies in inflation rates of different countries.

Zero-base budgeting requires managers to justify the need for their divisions or for engaging in any of the activities to be included in the budget. Activity-based budgeting focuses on costs of activities or cost drivers to carry out operations. The final budget thus reflects the budget costs of performing various activities. Kaizen budgeting prepares budgets on the basis of operations that are improvements over the current practices.

Ethical issues in budgeting include not revealing all information to avoid accepting a higher budget goal, inclusion of budget slack, and spending the budget. Behavioral issues in budgeting encompass the difficulty level of budget targets, drawbacks and advantages of authoritative and participative budgeting processes, the extent of involvement of the top management in budgeting, and the role of the budget department or controller in budgeting.

SELF-STUDY PROBLEMS

(For solutions, please turn to the end of the chapter)

1. MASTER BUDGET

The management of the Hansell Company wants to prepare budgets for one of its products, DuraFlex, for July 20X0. The firm sells the product for $40 per unit and has the following expected sales units for these months in 20X0:

April	May	June	July	August	September
5,000	5,400	5,500	6,000	7,000	8,000

The production process requires 4 pounds of Dura–1000 and 2 pounds of Flex-plas. The firm's policy is to maintain a minimum of 100 units of DuraFlex on hand at all times. The units on hand at the end of a period, however, should not fall below 10 percent of the expected sales for the following month. All materials inventories are to be maintained at 5 percent of the production needs for the next month, but not to exceed 1,000 pounds. The firm expects all inventories at the end of June to be within the guidelines. The purchase department expects the materials to cost $1.25 per pound and $5.00 per pound of Dura–1000 and Flexplas, respectively.

The production process requires direct labor at two skill levels. Workers at the K102 level earn $50 per hour and can process one batch of DuraFlex per hour. Each batch consists of 100 units. The manufacturing of DuraFlex also requires one-tenth of an hour of K175 workers' time for each unit manufactured. K175 workers earn $20 per hour.

Manufactured overhead is allocated at the rate of $200 per batch and $30 per direct labor-hour.

Required On the basis of the preceding data and projections, prepare the following budgets for July 20X0:

1. Sales budget (in dollars).
2. Production budget (in units).
3. Production budget for August (in units).
4. Direct materials purchase budget (in pounds).
5. Direct materials purchase budget (in dollars).
6. Direct manufacturing labor budget (in dollars).

2. CASH BUDGET AND BUDGET INCOME STATEMENT

Hansell Company expects its trial balance on June 30 to be as follows:

HANSELL COMPANY
Budget Trial Balance
June 30, 120X0

	Debit	Credit
Cash	$ 10,000	
Accounts receivable	80,000	
Allowance for bad debts		$ 3,500
Inventory	25,000	
Plants, property, and equipment	650,000	
Accumulated depreciation		320,000
Accounts payable		95,000
Wages and salaries payable		24,000
Note payable		200,000
Stockholders' equity		122,500
Total	$765,000	$765,000

Typically, 20 percent of sales are cash sales and 80 percent of sales are credit sales. Sales terms are 2/10, n/30. Hansell bills customers on the first day of each month. Experience has shown that 60 percent of the billings will be collected within the discount period, 25 percent by the end of the month after sales, 10 percent by the end of the second month after the sale, and 5 percent will be uncollectible. The firm writes off uncollectible accounts after 12 months.

The term of purchases for materials is 2/15, n/60. The firm makes all payments within the discount period. Experience has shown that 80 percent of the purchases are paid in the month of the purchase and the remainder are paid in the month immediately following. The firm budgeted in June 20X0 purchases of $25,000 for Dura–1000 and $22,000 for Flexplas.

Sixty percent of the factory overhead is variable. The firm has a monthly fixed factory overhead of $50,000, of which $20,000 is depreciation expenses. The firm pays all its manufacturing labor and factory overhead when incurred.

Total budgeted marketing, distribution, customer service, and administrative costs for 20X0 are $600,000. Of this amount, $270,000 is considered fixed and includes depreciation expenses of $150,000. The remainder varies with sales. The budgeted total sales for 20X0 are $2 million. All marketing and administrative costs are paid as incurred.

The management desires to maintain a minimum cash balance of $40,000. The firm has an agreement with a local bank to borrow in multiples of $1,000 up to $100,000 at an interest rate of 12 percent for short-term needs.

Required

1. Prepare the cash budget for July 20X0.
2. Prepare the budget income statement for July 20X0.

QUESTIONS

9–1 What is a budget?

9–2 What roles do budgets play in operations?

9–3 Explain the difference between strategic plans and a master budget.

9–4 What are the relationships between master and capital budgets?

9–5 What are master budgets, operating budgets, and financial budgets?

9–6 List some common characteristics of successful budgets.

9–7 What are the primary roles of a budget committee?

9–8 What is the difference between a sales forecast and a sales budget? What is the role of sales forecasting in budgeting?

9–9 The sales budget is the cornerstone of a budget. Do you agree?

9–10 When sales volume is seasonal in nature, certain items in the budget must be coordinated. What are the three most significant items to coordinate in budgeting seasonal sales volume? **(CMA Adapted)**

9–11 After a firm completes its sales budget for the budget period, what additional factors does the firm need to consider to complete the materials purchase budget?

9–12 What are the two most appropriate factors for budgeting factory overhead? **(CMA Adapted)**

9–13 What is a pro forma financial statement? What pro forma financial statements are prepared as part of the master budget?

9–14 Contrast budgeting considerations for service organizations with budgeting considerations for manufacturing companies.

9–15 What are the major differences in preparation and uses of budgets between a business firm and a not-for-profit organization?

9–16 What is zero-base budgeting?

9–17 Is kaizen budgeting the Japanese term for activity-based budgeting?

9–18 What is slack in a budget? Why is it not unusual to find slack in budgets?

9–19 What is a highly achievable budget? Why do firms prefer such a budget?

9–20 What is the role of top management in participative budgeting?

9–21 Kallert Manufacturing currently uses the company's budget only as a planning tool. Management has decided that it would be beneficial to also use budgets for control purposes. What must the management accountant do for the firm's budgeting and accounting systems to implement this change successfully? **(CMA Adapted)**

PROBLEMS

9–22 **BUDGETARY SLACK AND ZERO-BASED BUDGETING** Bob Bingham is the controller of Atlantis Laboratories, a manufacturer and distributor of generic prescription pharmaceuticals. He is currently in the process of preparing the annual budget and reviewing the current business plan. The business unit managers of Atlantis prepare and assemble the detailed operating budgets, with technical assistance from the corporate accounting staff. The final budgets are then presented by the business unit managers to the corporate executive committee for approval. The corporate accounting staff reviews the budget for adherence to corporate accounting policies, but no detailed review for reasonableness of the line items within the budget is conducted.

Bingham is aware that the upcoming year for Atlantis may be a difficult one due to the expiration of a major patent and the loss of a licensing agreement for another product line. He also knows that during the budgeting process, budgetary slack is created in varying degrees throughout the organization. Bingham believes this slack has a negative effect on the overall business objectives of Atlantis Laboratories and should be eliminated where possible.

Required

1. Define budgetary slack.
2. Explain the advantages and disadvantages of budgetary slack from the point of view of (a) the business unit manager who must achieve the budget and (b) corporate management.
3. Bob Bingham is considering implementing zero-based budgeting at Atlantis Laboratories.
    a. Define zero-base budgeting.
    b. Describe how zero-based budgeting could be advantageous to Atlantis Laboratories in controlling budgetary slack.
    c. Discuss the disadvantages Atlantis Laboratories might encounter in using zero-based budgeting.

(CMA Adapted)

9–23 DETERMINING QUANTITY OF RAW MATERIALS TO PURCHASE   Willard Company is budgeting sales of 100,000 units of its model GS30 small generator for the month of September. Production of one unit of GS30 requires two pounds of aluminum and three pounds of alloy. The beginning inventory and the desired ending inventory are

	Beginning Inventory	Desired Ending Inventory
GS30	20,000	10,000
Aluminum	25,000	18,000
Alloy	22,000	24,000

Required   How many pounds of aluminum and alloy is Willard Company planning to purchase during September?

9–24 PRODUCTION BUDGET   Merhendra Company's sales budget shows these projections for the year 20X4:

Quarter	Units
First	60,000
Second	80,000
Third	45,000
Fourth	55,000
	240,000

Inventory on December 31, 20X3, was budgeted at 18,000 units. The quantity of finished goods inventory at the end of each quarter is to equal 30 percent of the next quarter's budgeted sales of units.

Required   Determine the units to be produced in the production budget for the first two quarters of 20X4.

9–25 PRODUCTION AND MATERIALS PURCHASE BUDGETS   The DeVaris Corporation's budget calls for the following sales for next year:

Quarter 1	45,000 units
Quarter 2	38,000 units
Quarter 3	34,000 units
Quarter 4	48,000 units

Each unit of the product requires three pounds of direct material. The company's policy is to begin each quarter with an inventory of the product equal to 10 percent of that quarter's sales requirements and an inventory of direct materials equal to 20 percent of that quarter's direct materials requirements for productions.

Required   What would be the budgeted production of the product and the budgeted purchases of direct materials for the second quarter?

9–26 CASH BUDGET   Carla Inc. has the following budget data for 20X1:

Cash balance, beginning	$ 20,000
Collections from customers	150,000
Expenses:	
Direct materials purchases	25,000
Operating expenses	50,000
Payroll	75,000
Income taxes	6,000
Machinery purchases	30,000
Minimum cash balance desired	20,000

Operating expenses include $20,000 depreciation for buildings and equipment and cash expenditures of $30,000.

Required   Compute the cash financing needs or excess cash available to invest.

9–27 PRODUCTION BUDGET The Shocker Company's sales budget shows quarterly sales for the next year:

Quarter 1	10,000 units
Quarter 2	8,000 units
Quarter 3	12,000 units
Quarter 4	14,000 units

Company policy is to have a finished goods inventory at the end of each quarter equal to 20 percent of the next quarter's sales.

Required What would be budgeted production for the second quarter of the next year?

(CMA Adapted)

9–28 ESTIMATE CASH COLLECTIONS Ishikawa Corporation is preparing its cash budget for the month of May. The following information is available concerning its accounts receivable:

Estimated credit sales for May	$200,000
Actual credit sales for April	150,000
Estimated collections in May	
For credit sales in May	25%
For credit sales in April	70%
For credit sales prior to April	$16,000
Estimated write-offs in May for uncollectible accounts	8,000
Estimated provision for bad debts in May due to credit sales that month	7,000

Required What are the estimated cash receipts from accounts receivable collections in May?

(CPA Adapted)

9–29 CASH BUDGET Information pertaining to Noskey Corporation's sales revenue includes:

	November 20X2 (Actual)	December 20X2 (Budget)	January 20X3 (Budget)
Cash sales	$ 80,000	$100,000	$ 60,000
Credit sales	240,000	360,000	180,000
Total sales	$320,000	$460,000	$240,000

Management estimates that 5 percent of credit sales are uncollectible. Of the credit sales that are collectible, 60 percent are collected in the month of sale and the remainder in the month following the sale. Purchases of inventory each month are 70 percent of the next month's projected total sales. At the end of each quarter the firm assesses its inventory and adjusts the inventory to meet the requirement. All purchases of inventory are on account; 25 percent are paid in the month of purchase, and the remainders are paid in the month following the purchase. The purchase costs are approximately 60 percent of the selling prices.

Required Determine for Noskey

1. Budgeted cash collections in December 20X2 from November 20X2 credit sales.
2. Budgeted total cash receipts in January 20X3.
3. Budgeted total cash payments in December 20X2 for inventory purchases.

(CPA Adapted)

9–30 PRODUCTION AND MATERIALS BUDGETS Paradise Company budgets on an annual basis. The planned beginning and ending inventory levels (in units) for the fiscal year of July 1, 20X2, through June 30, 20X3, are:

	July 1, 20X2	June 30, 20X3
Raw material*	40,000	50,000
Work in process	10,000	20,000
Finished goods	80,000	50,000

* Two units of raw material are needed to produce each unit of finished products. All materials are added at the beginning of production.

Required

1. What is the number of units Paradise Company would have to manufacture if it plans to sell 480,000 units during the 20X2–3 fiscal year?

2. How many units of raw material need to be purchased if 500,000 finished units are to be manufactured during the 20X2–3 fiscal year by Paradise Company?

(CMA Adapted)

9–31 **CASH COLLECTION** Esplanade Company has the following historical pattern on its credit sales:

70 percent collected in the month of sale

15 percent collected in the first month after sale

10 percent collected in the second month after sale

4 percent collected in the third month after sale

1 percent uncollectible

These sales on open account (credit sales) have been budgeted for the last six months of 20X2:

July	$ 60,000
August	70,000
September	80,000
October	90,000
November	100,000
December	85,000

Required

1. Determine the estimated total cash collections from accounts receivable during October 20X2.

2. Compute the estimated total cash collections during the fourth quarter from credit sales of the fourth quarter.

(CMA Adapted)

9–32 **COLLECTION OF ACCOUNTS RECEIVABLE** The Doreen Company is preparing its cash budget for the month of May. The following information is available concerning its accounts receivable:

Actual credit sales for March	$120,000
Actual credit sales for April	$150,000
Estimated credit sales for May	$200,000
Estimated collections in the month of sale	25%
Estimated collections in the first month after the month of sale	60%
Estimated collections in the second month after the month of sale	10%
Estimated provision for bad debts in the month of sale	5%

The firm writes off all uncollectible accounts at the end of the second month after the month of sale.

Required Determine for Doreen Company for the month of May:

1. The estimated cash receipts from accounts receivable collections.

2. The gross balance of accounts receivable at the end of the month.

3. The net amounts of accounts receivable at the end of the month.

9–33 **SPREADSHEET APPLICATION** Alice Williams, the manager of the Financial Analysis Department, has been asked to forecast the cash position for the third quarter for the Linden Corporation. Williams will use the following pro forma income statement that was prepared by Jerry Miller, a former financial analyst who recently left the company. Miller prepared the pro forma income statement by using a common spreadsheet package on a microcomputer.

Pertinent information about the company's financial transactions:

- All sales are on account, and the accounts receivable have historically been paid, and are forecasted to be paid, 30 days after the sale.

- All other revenues are presumed to be paid as they occur.

- Cost of goods sold relate to raw materials that are purchased on account. Accounts payable are settled in 30 days. All other cash expenses are paid as incurred.

- Accrued taxes are equal to the tax liability and are paid 45 days after the end of the quarter. The second quarter's total tax liability was $95,000.

- Linden is purchasing a $25,000 microcomputer network to be delivered, installed, and paid in September. Depreciation on this equipment will be straight-line, over five years, with no salvage value at the end of five years. The depreciation expense for this equipment is not currently reflected in the projected expenses.

- In July, Linden will be receiving $500,000 from a public stock offering of 100,000 shares sold in June.

- On June 10, 20X0, the board of directors declared dividends of $75,000 to be distributed on August 15, to the shareholders of record as of June 30.

- The ending cash balance at June 30, 20X0, is projected to be $250,000.

- For forecasting purposes, Linden Corporation assumes that all cash flows and transactions consistently occur at the end of each month.

1	(A)	(B)	(C)	(D)	(E)
2					
3			**LINDEN CORPORATION**		
4			**20X0 Partial Pro Forma Income Statement**		
5			**(in thousands)**		
6		June	July	August	September
7	Revenues				
8	Sales	$230	$250	$260	$290
9	Other revenues	20	10	30	20
10	Total revenue	250	260	290	310
11	Expenses				
12	Cost of goods sold	80	90	120	110
13	Salaries	50	50	50	50
14	Depreciation	40	40	40	40
15	Other	0	10	10	20
16	Total expenses	170	190	220	220
17	Income before taxes	80	70	70	90
18	Taxes (40 percent)	32	28	28	36
19	Net income	$ 48	$ 42	$ 42	$ 54

Williams is preparing a projected internal cash flow report by referencing the amounts given in the pro forma income statement prepared by Miller and the previous financial transactions. Before Miller left Linden, he gave Williams a brief lesson on forecasting the cash flows by using the spreadsheet package and referencing income statement values. Although Miller had not developed any specific directions on using this spreadsheet model, he believed that Williams was proficient enough to prepare the cash flow projection. It should be noted that the pro forma income statement is correct. In reviewing the first draft of the following cash flow report, Williams observed six errors that are indicated by numbers 1 through 6.

Required

1. The six errors identified on Linden Corporation's third quarter 20X0 projected cash flow report displayed below were caused by either incorrect reasoning or spreadsheet logic. Describe the six errors and explain how to specifically correct each error by providing the correct spreadsheet formula using these notations:

    Spreadsheet Formula Notations

BB56	For cell references, column first and row second
= or @	To start formula
+	For addition
−	For subtraction
*	For multiplication
=SUM() or @SUM	For a summation formula
CF	Name for the Cash Flow Report file
IS	Name for the Income Statement file

    Use the following format for your answer:

Description of Error	Corrected Spreadsheet Formula
1.	
2.	
3.	
4.	
5.	
6.	

2. List at least three problems inherent in the use of spreadsheet models developed by users who are not trained in the procedural controls of systems design and development.

	(AA)	(BB)	(CC)	(DD)	
51					
52			**LINDEN CORPORATION**		
53			**Third Quarter 20X0 Projected Cash Flow Report**		
54			**(in thousands)**		
55		July	August	September	
56	Beginning cash balance	$250	$735	$735	#1
57	Cash receipts				
58	Sales receipts	250	260	290	#2
59	Other revenue	10	30	20	
60	Equity	500	0	0	
61	Total cash receipts	760	290	310	
62					
63	Cash disbursements				
64	Purchases and expenses	180	190	230	#3
65	Tax payments	95	0	0	#4
66	Dividends	0	75	0	
67	Other (capital purchases)	0	0	25	
68	Total cash disbursements	275	265	230	#5
69	Net cash contribution	485	25	80	
70	Ending cash balance	$735	$760	$1,045	#6

(CMA Adapted)

9–34 CASH BUDGET Riley Instruments, a rapidly expanding electronic parts distributor, is in the process of formulating plans for 20X4. Samantha

Carlson, the firm's director of marketing, has completed her 20X4 forecast and is confident that sales estimates will be met or exceeded. The following sales figures show the growth expected and provide the planning basis for the other corporate departments:

Forecasted Month	Forecasted Sales	Forecasted Month	Forecasted Sales
January	$1,800,000	July	$3,000,000
February	2,000,000	August	3,000,000
March	1,800,000	September	3,200,000
April	2,200,000	October	3,200,000
May	2,500,000	November	3,000,000
June	2,800,000	December	3,400,000

Bill Stockton, assistant controller, has been given the responsibility of formulating the cash flow projection, a critical element during a period of rapid expansion. The following information can be used in preparing the cash analysis.

- Riley has experienced an excellent record in accounts receivable collection and expects this trend to continue. Sixty percent of billings are collected in the month after the sale and 40 percent in the second month after the sale. Uncollectible accounts are nominal and will not be considered in the analysis.

- The purchase of electronic parts is Riley's largest expenditure; the cost of these items is equal to 50 percent of sales. Sixty percent of the parts are received by Riley one month prior to sale and 40 percent are received during the month of sale.

- Historically, 80 percent of accounts payable have been cleared by Riley one month after receipt of purchased parts and the remaining 20 percent have been cleared two months after receipt of purchased parts.

- Hourly wages, including fringe benefits, are a factor of sales volume and are equal to 20 percent of the current month's sales. These wages are paid in the month incurred.

- General and administrative expenses are projected to be $2,640,000 for 20X4. The composition of these expenses follows. All of these expenses are incurred uniformly throughout the year except the property taxes. The property taxes are paid in four equal installments in the last month of each quarter.

Salaries	$ 480,000
Promotion	660,000
Property taxes	240,000
Insurance	360,000
Utilities	300,000
Depreciation	600,000
	$2,640,000

- Income tax payments are made by Riley in the first month of each quarter based on the income for the prior quarter. Riley is subject to an effective income tax rate of 40 percent. Riley's net income after taxes for the first quarter of 20X4 is projected to be $612,000.

- Riley has a corporate policy of maintaining an end-of-month cash balance of $100,000. Cash is invested or borrowed monthly, as necessary, to maintain this balance.

- Riley uses a calendar year reporting period.

Required

1. Prepare a pro forma schedule of cash receipts and disbursements for Riley Instruments by month for the second quarter of 20X4. Be sure

that all receipts, disbursements, and borrowing/investing are presented on a monthly basis. Ignore the interest expense and/or income associated with borrowing/investing.

2. Discuss why cash budgeting is particularly important for a rapidly expanding company such as Riley Instruments.

(CMA Adapted)

9–35 **BUDGET REVISION** Molid Company was founded by Mark Dalid three years ago. The company produces a modulation-demodulation unit (modem) developed by Dalid and several of the firm's major stockholders for use with minicomputers and microcomputers. The modem can transit three times faster than other compatible products. Business has expanded rapidly since the company's inception.

Strategy

Bob Wells, the company's general accountant, prepared a budget for the fiscal year ending August 31, 20X2. The budget was based on the prior year's sales and production activity because Dalid believed that the sales growth experienced during the prior year would not continue at the same pace. The pro forma statements of income and cost of goods sold that were prepared as part of the budget process follow:

Statement of Income (in thousands)

Net sales		$31,248
Cost of goods sold		20,765
Gross profit		$10,483
Operating expenses		
Marketing	$3,200	
General and administrative	2,200	5,400
Income from operations before income taxes		$ 5,083

Statement of Cost of Goods Sold (in thousands)

Direct materials		
Materials inventory, 9/1/20X1	$ 1,360	
Materials purchases	14,476	
Materials available for use	15,836	
Materials inventory, 8/31/20X2	1,628	
Direct materials consumed		$14,208
Direct labor		1,134
Factory overhead		
Indirect materials	$ 1,421	
General factory overhead	3,240	4,661
Cost of goods manufactured		$20,003
Finished goods inventory, 9/1/20X1		1,169
Cost of goods available for sale		$21,172
Finished goods inventory, 8/31/20X2		407
Cost of goods sold		$20,765

On December 10, 20X1, Dalid and Wells met to discuss the first quarter operating results (i.e., results for the period September 1–November 30, 20X1). Wells believed that several changes should be made to the original budget assumptions that had been used to prepare the pro forma statements. Wells prepared the following notes that summarized the changes that did not become known until the first quarter results had been compiled. The following data were submitted to Dalid:

1. The estimated production in units for the fiscal year should be revised upward from 162,000 units to 170,000 units with the balance of production being scheduled in equal segments over the last nine months of the fiscal year. Actual first-quarter production was 35,000 units.

2. The planned ending inventory for finished goods of 3,300 units at the end of the fiscal year remains unchanged. The finished goods inventory of 9,300 units as of September 1, 20X1, had dropped to 9,000 units by November 31, 20X1. The finished goods inventory at the end of the fiscal year will be valued at the average manufacturing cost for the year.

3. The direct labor rate will increase 8 percent as of June 1, 20X2, as a consequence of a new labor agreement that was signed during the first quarter. When the original pro forma statements were prepared, the expected effective date for this new labor agreement had been September 1, 20X2.

4. Direct materials sufficient to produce 16,000 units were on hand at the beginning of the fiscal year. The plans for direct materials inventory to contain 18,500 units of production at the end of the fiscal year remain unchanged. Direct materials inventory is valued on a first-in, first-out basis. Direct materials equivalent to 37,500 units of output were purchased for $3,300,000 during the first quarter of the fiscal year.

   Molid's suppliers have informed the company that direct materials prices will increase 5 percent on March 1, 20X2. Direct materials needed for the rest of the fiscal year will be purchased evenly through the last nine months.

5. On the basis of historical data, indirect materials cost is projected at 10 percent of the cost of direct materials consumed.

6. One-half of general factory overhead and all of marketing and general and administrative expenses are considered fixed.

   After an extended discussion, Dalid asked for new pro forma statements for the fiscal year ending August 31, 20X2.

Required

1. Based on the revised data presented by Bob Wells, calculate Molid Company's sales for the year ending August 31, 20X2, in (a) number of units to be sold and (b) dollar volume of net sales.

2. Prepare the pro forma statement of cost of goods sold for the year ending August 31, 20X2, that Mark Dalid has requested.

3. Wells suggests that the firm should adopt a JIT strategy to better serve customers and to reduce obsolescence costs. He points out that the firm needs to incorporate new manufacturing technologies to maintain its competitive advantage. Dalid is reluctant to make changes. He does not want to upset the proven successful business. He knows that any changes cost money and he does not want to commit fresh capital just to change the way of doing business. Bob argues that no additional capital will be needed to fund the changes. He points out that a JIT system maintains no finished goods inventory and no more than the materials needed for the production of 100 units of the finished products needs to be maintained.
   a. What will be the saving, if any, for the firm to change to a JIT system?
   b. Should the firm follow Wells' suggestion?
   c. What other factors need to be considered in making the decision?

(CMA Adapted)

Strategy

9–36 VARIABLE COSTING PRO FORMA FINANCIAL STATEMENTS   Jacqueline Stern is a successful investor whose specialty is revitalizing failed businesses. Her goal is to maximize her profits within the limits of careful use of external financing, which usually means limiting growth rates and forgoing some potential profit. Stern believes this is the key to her success and that unlimited growth can easily lead to fatal financing problems. Stern is once again set to test her approach.

Five years ago, Robert West perfected a technique for joining the edges of laminated plastic parts so that the edges of subsurface layers were not visible. Since subsurface layers are a different color than the surface layer, West's edges greatly improved the appearance of the finished product. West then designed equipment that permitted large volume production of the edges. West's product was unique, and sales and production levels grew rapidly. Rapid growth, however, soon exceeded West's management ability and his ability to obtain financing. A few months ago, West's firm closed, leaving a regional bank holding the plant, equipment, and some inventory.

Stern believes the product has sales and profit potential and has offered the bank $400,000 in cash plus assumption of the loan for the plant, equipment, and inventory. The bank was only too happy to accept Stern's offer.

Stern has established Edge Company and contributed to it the acquired assets and $450,000 in cash. Edge Company's statement of financial position at the start of business is presented below.

THE EDGE COMPANY INC.
Statement of Financial Position
as of January 1, 20X3
(in thousands)

Assets

Cash	$ 450
Accounts receivable	0
Inventory	100
Plant and equipment	2,000
Total assets	$2,550

Liabilities and Equities

Accounts payable	$ 0
Current portion of long-term debt	90
Long-term debt	1,610
Common stock (no par value)	850
Retained earnings	0
Total liabilities and equities	$2,550

To implement her goal of making conservative use of external financing, Stern has established these financial objectives:

- Paying no dividends, thus keeping all cash generated within the company.

- Issuing no additional capital stock.

- Incurring no new long-term debt while servicing current interest and $90,000 of principal annually on the existing bank loan.

- Keeping the cash balance at no less than $50,000.

- Taking advantage of supplier credit but not allowing accounts payable to exceed $100,000.

The bank's loan officer had commented that West was unable to control costs and working capital, and Stern agreed. She plans to hold variable costs at 75 percent of sales. Even though the existing plant and equipment have a capacity of $12,000,000 in annual sales, Stern's plan is to budget a lump sum of $500,000 per year for fixed costs, including both depreciation and interest. Depreciation of plant and equipment is $100,000 per year.

In making her plans, Stern has used 20 percent as the average income tax rate applicable to Edge Company. Because some of the firms she acquires have been in income tax trouble, Stern makes a point of keeping tax payments current and aims to finish each year with no tax liability on the books.

Customers for products of this kind are notoriously slow payers;

however, Stern is confident that accounts receivable can be kept at 15 percent of annual sales. She also believes that inventories can be maintained at 20 percent of annual variable costs.

Some of West's former salespeople have been rehired, and they believe that Edge Company's first-year sales could easily reach $5,000,000. But Stern believes that managing growth is the most important part of the plan, and she plans to limit first-year sales to $2,100,000.

Required

1. Determine whether Jacqueline Stern's financial objectives can be achieved by preparing a pro forma income statement in a variable (direct) costing format for the Edge Company for the year ending December 31, 20X3, and a pro forma statement of financial position for the Edge Company as of December 31, 20X3. Assume that her projections occur and sales are limited to $2,100,000.

2. Without regard to your answer in requirement 1, assume that the following results from the company's first fiscal year ending December 31, 20X3, occurred, and that Stern's financial objectives were met.
   - Sales: $2,000,000
   - Net income: $0
   - Cash balance at December 31, 20X3: $60,000
   - Accounts payable at December 31, 20X3: $100,000
   - Net working capital at December 31, 20X3: $470,000

   Compute the maximum amount by which Edge Company could increase dollar sales in its second year (ending December 31, 20X4) and still achieve Stern's financial objectives.

3. Do you agree with Stern's strategy of limiting sales growth?

(CMA Adapted)

9-37 **MASTER BUDGET**   SecCo manufactures and sells security systems. The company started by installing photoelectric security systems in existing offices and has since expanded into the private home market. SecCo has a basic security system that has been developed into three standard products, each of which can be upgraded to meet the specific needs of customers. SecCo's manufacturing operation is moderate in size as the bulk of the component manufacturing is completed by independent contractors. The security systems are approximately 85 percent complete when received from contractors and require only final assembly in SecCo's plant. Each product passes through at least one of three assembly operations.

SecCo operates in a community that is flourishing. There is evidence that a great deal of new commercial construction will take place in the near future, and SecCo's management has decided to pursue this new market. To be competitive, SecCo will have to expand its operations.

In view of the expected increase in business, Sandra Becker, SecCo's controller, believes that SecCo should implement a master budget system. Becker has decided to make a formal presentation to SecCo's president explaining the benefits of a master budget system and outlining the budget schedules and reports that would be required.

Required

1. Explain what benefits can be derived from implementing a master budget system.

2. If Sandra Becker is going to develop a master budget system for SecCo:
   a. Identify, in order, the schedules and/or statements that will have to be prepared.
   b. Identify the subsequent schedules and/or statements that would be derived from the schedules and statements identified in requirement 2a.

(CMA Adapted)

9–38 **COMPREHENSIVE PROFIT PLAN** The Palms Manufacturing Company makes two basic products known as Cee and Dee. Data assembled by the managers follow:

	Cee	Dee
Requirements for finished unit		
Raw material 1	10 pounds	8 pounds
Raw material 2	none	4 pounds
Raw material 3	2 units	1 unit
Direct labor	5 hours	8 hours
Product information		
Sales price	$150	$220
Sales unit	12,000	9,000
Estimated beginning inventory	400	150
Desired ending inventory	300	200

	Raw Materials		
	1	2	3
Cost	$2.00	$2.50	$0.50
Estimated beginning inventory	3,000	1,500	1,000
Desired ending inventory	4,000	1,000	1,500

The direct labor wage rate is $10 per hour. Overhead is applied on the basis of direct labor-hours. The tax rate is 40 percent. The beginning inventory of finished products has the same cost per unit as the ending inventory. The work-in-process inventory is negligible.

Factory Overhead Information

Indirect materials	$ 10,000
Miscellaneous supplies and tools	5,000
Indirect labor	40,000
Supervision—fixed	80,000
Payroll taxes and fringe benefits	75,000
Maintenance costs—fixed	20,000
Maintenance costs—variable	10,000
Depreciation	70,000
Heat, light, and power—fixed	8,710
Heat, light, and power—variable	5,090
Total	$323,800

Selling and Administrative Expense Information

Advertising	$ 60,000
Sales salaries	200,000
Travel and entertainment	60,000
Depreciation—warehouse	5,000
Office salaries	60,000
Executive salaries	250,000
Supplies	4,000
Depreciation—office	6,000
Total	$645,000

Required Prepare the following:

1. Production budget.
2. Raw materials purchase budget.
3. Direct labor budget.
4. Factory overhead budget.
5. Cost of goods sold budget, with schedule of ending inventory.
6. Selling and administrative expense budget.
7. Budget income statement.

(CMA Adapted)

9–39 PURCHASE AND CASH BUDGET D. Tomlinson Retail seeks your assistance in developing cash and other budget information for May, June, and July. At April 30, the company will have cash of $5,500, accounts receivable of $437,000, inventories of $309,400, and accounts payable of $133,055. The budget is to be based on these assumptions:

- **Sales.** Each month's sales are billed on the last day of the month. Customers are allowed a 3 percent discount if payment is made within 10 days after the billing date. Receivables are booked gross; 60 percent of the billings are collected within the discount period; 25 percent are collected by the end of the month; 9 percent are collected by the end of the second month; and 6 percent are likely to be uncollectible.

- **Purchases.** 54 percent of all purchases of material and selling, general, and administrative expenses are paid in the month purchased and the remainder in the following month. Each month's units of ending inventory are equal to 130 percent of the next month's units of sales. The cost of each unit of inventory is $20. Selling, general, and administrative expenses, of which $2,000 is depreciation, are equal to 15 percent of the current month's sales.

Actual and projected sales are:

	Dollars	Units
March	$354,000	11,800
April	363,000	12,100
May	357,000	11,900
June	342,000	11,400
July	360,000	12,000
August	366,000	12,200

Required

1. Determine the budgeted purchases for May and June.
2. Determine the budgeted cash disbursements during June.
3. Determine the budgeted cash collections during May.
4. Determine the budgeted number of units of inventory to be purchased during July.

(CMA Adapted)

9–40 CASH BUDGET The Russon Corporation is a retailer whose sales are all made on credit. Sales are billed twice monthly, on the 10th of the month for the last half of the prior month's sales, and on the 20th of the month for the first half of the current month's sales. The terms of all sales are 2/10, net/30. Based on past experience, accounts receivable are collected as follows:

Within the discount period	80%
On the 30th day	18
Uncollectible	2

Russon's average markup on its products is 20 percent of the sales price. All sales and purchases occur uniformly throughout the month.

The sales value of shipments for May and the forecasts for the next four months follow:

	Revenues
May (actual)	$500,000
June	600,000
July	700,000
August	700,000
September	400,000

Russon purchases merchandise for resale to meet the current month's sales demand and to maintain a desired monthly ending inventory of 25 percent of the next month's sales. All purchases are on credit with terms of net/30. Russon pays for 50 percent of a month's purchases in the month of purchase and 50 percent in the month following the purchase.

Required

1. How much cash can Russon plan to collect in September from sales made in August?

2. What is the budgeted dollar value of inventory on August 31?

3. How much cash can Russon Corporation plan to collect from accounts receivable collections during July?

4. Determine how much merchandise should be purchased during June.

5. Determine the amount that should be budgeted in August for the payment of merchandise.

(CMA Adapted)

9–41 **DIRECT MATERIALS PURCHASES BUDGET** The Press Company manufactures and sells industrial components. The Whitmore Plant is responsible for producing AD–5 and FX–3. Plastic, brass, and aluminum are used in the production of these two products.

Press Company had adopted a 13-period reporting cycle in all of its plants for budgeting purposes. Each period is four weeks long and has 20 working days. The projected inventory levels for AD–5 and FX–3 at the end of the current (seventh) period and the projected sales for these two products for the next three four-week periods follow:

	Projected Inventory Level (in units)	Projected Sales (in units)		
	End of Seventh Period	Eighth Period	Ninth Period	Tenth Period
AD–5	3,000	7,500	8,750	9,500
FX–3	2,800	7,000	4,500	4,000

Past experience has shown that adequate inventory levels for AD–5 and FX–3 can be maintained if 40 percent of the next period's projected sales are on hand at the end of a reporting period. Based on this experience and the projected sales, the Whitmore Plant has budgeted production of 8,000 AD–5 and 6,000 FX–3 in the eighth period. Production is assumed to be uniform for both products within each four-week period.

The raw material specifications for AD–5 and FX–3 are:

	AD–5	FX–3
Plastic	2.0 lb.	1.0 lb
Brass	0.5 lb.	—
Aluminum	—	1.5 lb

Sales of AD–5 and FX–3 do not vary significantly from month-to-month. Consequently, the safety stock incorporated into the reorder point for each of the raw materials is adequate to compensate for variations in the sale of the finished products.

Raw material orders are placed the day the quantity on hand falls below the reorder point. Whitmore Plant's suppliers are very dependable, so the given lead times are reliable. The outstanding orders for plastic and aluminum are due to arrive on the tenth and fourth working days of the eighth period, respectively. Payments for all raw material orders are remitted in the period of delivery. Purchase data and raw material inventory status are:

	Standard Purchase Price per Pound	Purchase Lot (in pounds)	Reorder Point (in pounds)	Projected Inventory Status at the End of the Seventh Period (in pounds)		Lead Time in Working Days
				On Hand	On Order	
Plastic	$0.40	15,000	12,000	16,000	15,000	10
Brass	0.95	5,000	7,500	9,000	—	30
Aluminum	0.55	10,000	10,000	14,000	10,000	20

Required Whitmore Plant is required to submit a report to corporate headquarters of Press Company summarizing the projected raw material activities before each period commences. The data for the eighth period report are being assembled. Determine the following items for plastic, brass, and aluminum for inclusion in the eighth-period report:

1. Projected quantities (in pounds) of each raw material to be issued to production.
2. Projected quantities (in pounds) of each raw material ordered and the date (in working days) the order is to be placed.
3. The projected inventory balance (in pounds) of each raw material at the end of the period.
4. The payments for purchases of each raw material.

(CMA Adapted)

9–42 **BUDGET INCOME STATEMENT** The *Metropolitan News*, a daily newspaper, serves a community of 100,000. The paper has a circulation of 40,000, with 32,000 copies delivered directly to subscribers. The rate schedule for the paper is

Single issue price: $0.15 daily; $0.30 Sunday
Weekly subscription: $1.00 (includes daily and Sunday)

The paper has experienced profitable operations as can be seen from the income statement for the year ended September 30, 20X3 (in thousands):

Revenue:			
Newspaper sales		$2,200	
Advertising sales		1,800	$4,000
Costs and expenses:			
Personnel costs:			
Commissions:			
Carriers	$ 292		
Sales	73		
Advertising	48		
Salaries:			
Administration	250		
Advertising	100		
Equipment operators	500		
Newsroom	400		
Employee benefits	195	$1,858	
Newsprint		834	
Other supplies		417	
Repairs		25	
Depreciation		180	
Property taxes		120	
Building rental		80	
Automobile leases		10	
Other		90	
Total costs and expenses			3,614
Income before income taxes			$386
Income taxes			154
Net income			$ 232

The Sunday edition usually has twice as many pages as the daily editions. Direct edition variable costs for 20X3–X4 are shown here:

	Cost per Issue	
	Daily	**Sunday**
Paper	$0.050	$0.100
Other supplies	0.025	0.050
Carrier and sales commissions	0.025	0.025
	$0.100	$0.175

The company has scheduled the following changes in operations for the next year and anticipates some increased costs:

1. The building lease expired on September 30, 20X4, and has been renewed with a change in the rental fee provisions from a straight fee to a fixed fee of $60,000 plus 1 percent of newspaper sales.

2. The advertising department will eliminate the payment of a 4 percent advertising commission on contracts sold on a contract basis in the past. The salaries of the four employees who solicited advertising will be raised from $7,500 each to $14,000 each.

3. Automobiles will no longer be leased. Employees whose jobs require automobiles will use their own and be reimbursed at $0.15 per mile. The leased cars were driven 80,000 miles in 20X3–X4, and it is estimated that the employees will drive some 84,000 miles next year on company business.

4. Cost increases estimated for next year:
    * Newsprint, $0.01 per daily issue and $0.02 for the Sunday paper
    * Salaries:
    Equipment operators, 8 percent
    Other employees, 6 percent
    * Employee benefits (from 15 percent of personnel costs excluding carrier and sales commissions to 20 percent), 5 percent

5. Circulation increases of 5 percent in newsstands and home delivery are anticipated.

6. Advertising revenue is estimated at $1,890,000 with $1,260,000 from employee-solicited contracts.

Required

1. Prepare a projected income statement for *Metropolitan News* for the 20X3–X4 fiscal year using a format that shows the total variable costs and total fixed costs for the newspaper (round calculations to the nearest thousand dollars).

2. The management of *Metropolitan News* is contemplating one additional proposal for the 20X3–X4 fiscal year—raising the rates for the newspaper to the following amounts:

    Single issue price: $0.20 daily; $0.40 Sunday
    Weekly subscription: $1.25 (includes daily and Sunday)

    The company estimates that the newspaper's circulation would decline to 90 percent of the currently anticipated 20X3–X4 level for both newsstand and home delivery sales if this change is initiated. Calculate the effect on the projected 20X3–X4 income if this proposed rate increase is implemented.

(CMA Adapted)

9–43 **CASH BUDGET** The Barker Corporation manufactures and distributes wooden baseball bats. The bats are manufactured in Georgia at its only plant. This is a seasonal business with a large portion of its sales occurring in late winter and early spring. The production schedule for the last quarter of the year is heavy to build up inventory to meet expected sales volume.

The company experiences a temporary cash strain during this heavy production period. Payroll costs rise during the last quarter because overtime is scheduled to meet the increased production needs. Collections from customers are low because the fall season produces only modest sales. This year the company's concern is intensified because prices are increasing during the current inflationary period. In addition, the sales department forecasts sales of fewer than 1 million bats for the first time in three years. This decease in sales appears to be caused by the popularity of aluminum bats.

The cash account builds up during the first and second quarters as sales exceed production. The excess cash is invested in U.S. Treasury bills and other commercial paper. During the last half of the year, the temporary investments are liquidated to meet the cash needs. In the early years of the company, short-term borrowing was used to supplement the funds released by selling investments, but this has not been necessary in recent years. Because costs are higher this year, the treasurer asks for a forecast for December to judge if the $40,000 in temporary investments will be adequate to carry the company through the month with a minimum balance of $10,000. Should this amount ($40,000) be insufficient, she wants to begin negotiations for a short-term loan.

The unit sales volume for the past two months and the estimate for the next four months are

October (actual)	70,000
November (actual)	50,000
December (estimated)	50,000
January (estimated)	90,000
February (estimated)	90,000
March (estimated)	120,000

The bats are sold for $3 each. All sales are made on account. Half of the accounts are collected in the month of the sale, 40 percent are collected in the month following the sale, and the remaining 10 percent in the second month following the sale. Customers who pay in the month of the sale receive a 2 percent cash discount.

The production schedule for the six-month period beginning with October reflects the company's policy of maintaining a stable year-round workforce by scheduling overtime to meet the following production schedules:

October (actual)	90,000
November (actual)	90,000
December (estimated)	90,000
January (estimated)	90,000
February (estimated)	100,000
March (estimated)	100,000

The bats are made from wooden blocks that cost $6 each. Ten bats can be produced from each block. The blocks are acquired one year in advance so they can be properly aged. Barker pays the supplier one-twelfth of the cost of this material each month until the obligation is retired. The monthly payment is $60,000.

The plant is normally scheduled for a forty-hour, five-day work week. During the busy production season, however, the work week may be increased to six 10-hour days. Each worker can produce 7.5 bats per hour. Normal monthly output is 75,000 bats. Factory employees are paid $4 per hour (up $0.50 from last year) for regular time and time and one-half for overtime.

Other manufacturing costs include variable overhead of $0.30 per unit and annual fixed overhead of $280,000. Depreciation charges totaling $40,000 are included among the fixed overhead. Selling expenses include variable costs of $0.20 per unit and annual fixed costs of $60,000. Fixed administrative costs are $120,000 annually. All fixed costs are incurred uniformly throughout the year. The controller has accumulated the following additional information:

1. The balances of selected accounts as of November 30, 20X0, are

Cash	$ 12,000
Marketable securities (cost and market are the same)	40,000
Accounts receivable	96,000
Prepaid expenses	4,800
Accounts payable (arising from raw material purchases)	300,000
Accrued vacation pay	9,500
Equipment note payable	102,000
Accrued income taxes payable	50,000

2. Interest to be received from the company's temporary investments is estimated at $500 for December.

3. Prepaid expenses of $3,600 will expire during December, and the balance of the prepaid account is estimated at $4,200 for the end of December.

4. Barker purchased new machinery in 20X0 as part of a plant modernization program. The machinery was financed by a 24-month note of $144,000. The terms call for equal principal payments over the next 24 months with interest paid at the rate of 1 percent per month on the unpaid balance at the first of the month. The first payment was made on May 1, 20X0.

5. Old equipment, which has a book value of $8,000, is to be sold during December for $7,500.

6. Each month the company accrues $1,700 for vacation pay by charging Vacation Pay Expense and crediting Accrued Vacation Pay. The plant closes for two weeks in June when all plant employees take a vacation.

7. Quarterly dividends of $0.20 per share will be paid on December 15 to stockholders of record. Barker Corporation has authorized 10,000 shares. The company has issued 7,500 shares, and 500 of these are classified as treasury stock.

8. The quarterly income taxes payment of $50,000 is due on December 15, 20X0.

Required

1. Prepare a schedule that forecasts the cash position at December 31, 20X0. What action, if any, will be required to maintain a $10,000 cash balance?

2. Without regard to your answer in requirement 1, assume Barker regularly needs to arrange short-term loans during the November-to-February period. What changes might Barker consider in its methods of doing business to reduce or eliminate the need for short-term borrowing?

(CMA Adapted)

9–44 CASH BUDGET The Triple-F Health Club (Family, Fitness, and Fun) is a not-for-profit family-oriented health club. The club's board of directors is developing plans to acquire more equipment and expand the club facilities. The board plans to purchase about $25,000 of new equipment each year

 *Service*

331

and wants to establish a fund to purchase the adjoining property in four or five years. The adjoining property has a market value of about $300,000.

The club manager, Jane Crowe, is concerned that the board has unrealistic goals in light of the club's recent financial performance. She has sought the help of a club member with an accounting background to assist her in preparing a report to the board supporting her concerns.

The club member reviewed the club's records, including this cash basis income statement:

TRIPLE-F HEALTH CLUB
Statement of Income (Cash Basis)
For Years Ended October 31 (in thousands)

	20X1	20X0
Cash revenues:		
Annual membership fees	$355.0	$300.0
Lesson and class fees	234.0	180.0
Miscellaneous	2.0	1.5
Total cash received	591.0	481.5
Cash expenses:		
Manager's salary and benefits	36.0	36.0
Regular employees' wages and benefits	190.0	190.0
Lesson and class employees' wages and benefits	195.0	150.0
Towels and supplies	16.0	15.5
Utilities (heat and light)	22.0	15.0
Mortgage interest	35.1	37.8
Miscellaneous	2.0	1.5
Total cash expenses	496.1	445.8
Cash income	$ 94.9	$ 35.7

- Other financial information as of October 31, 20X1:
    Cash in checking account, $7,000
    Petty cash, $300
    Outstanding mortgage balance, $390,000
    Accounts payable arising from invoices for supplies and utilities that are unpaid as of October 31, 20X1, $2,500

- No unpaid bills existed on October 31, 20X1.

- The club purchased $25,000 worth of exercise equipment during the current fiscal year. Cash of $10,000 was paid as of October 31, 20X1.

- The club began operations in 19X9 in rental quarters. In October 19X9, it purchased its current property (land and building) for $600,000, paying $120,000 down and agreeing to pay $30,000 plus 9 percent interest annually on November 1 until the balance was paid off.

- Membership rose 3 percent during 20X1. The club has experienced approximately this same annual growth rate since it opened.

- Membership fee increased by 15 percent in 20X1. The board has tentative plans to increase the fees by 10 percent in 20X2.

- Lesson and class fees have not been increased for three years. The board policy is to encourage classes and lessons by keeping the fees low. The members have taken advantage of this policy, and the number of classes and lessons has increased significantly each year. The club expects the percentage growth experienced in 20X1 to be repeated in 20X2.

- Miscellaneous revenues are expected to grow at the same rate as experienced in 20X1.

- Operating expenses are expected to increase:
    Hourly wage rates and the manager's salary: 15 percent
    Towels and supplies, utilities, and miscellaneous expenses: 25 percent

Required

1. Prepare a cash budget for 20X2 for the Triple-F Health Club.

2. Identify any operating problems that this budget discloses for the Triple-F Health Club. Explain your answer.

3. Is Jane Crowe's concern that the board's goals are unrealistic justified? Explain your answer.

(CMA Adapted)

9–45 ESTIMATE SALES REVENUE Multiplex Electronics Corporation manufactures custom-designed central processing computer chips for specialized applications. The firm expects to sell 9 million units during the coming year. Total foreign sales are approximately 80 percent of the units sold domestically.

International

Since the inception of the firm five years ago, the foreign currency exchange rates have been stable. The firm receives $30 per unit and earns a contribution margin of $15 per unit for all units sold. However, financial crises started in September of this year in several countries in the region where the firm exports most of its foreign sales substantially decreased the firm's sales revenue in U.S. dollars.

For the coming year, the firm expects the exchange rate to be about 60 percent of the level before the devaluation.

Required

1. Estimate the total sales and contribution margin for the coming year if the firm chooses not to alter the selling prices in foreign currencies.

2. Determine the unit selling price for foreign sales for the coming year if the firm desires to receive $30 per unit.

3. Compute the unit selling price for the coming year for all units (for both domestic and foreign markets) if the firm desires to earn the same total amount of contribution margin in U.S. dollars as before the financial crises.

9–46 SMALL BUSINESS BUDGET Small businesses are usually the first organizations to feel the effects of a recessionary economy and are generally the last to recover. Two major reasons for small business financial difficulties are managerial inexperience and inadequate financing or financial management.

Small business managers frequently have problems in planning and controlling profits, including revenue generation and cost reduction activities. These important financial methods are especially critical during a recessionary period. The financial problems of small business are further compounded when there are poor accounting records and inexperience in the management of money.

Required

1. Profit planning is critical for the planning and controlling of profits of a small business. Identify key features that need to be considered when developing a profit plan.

2. The management accountant can help assure that good accounting records exist in an organization. Discuss the key features that form the basis for a good accounting system that will support management decisions.

3. Explain how the management accountant can assist an organization in adopting measures to assure appropriate money management.

(CMA Adapted)

9–47 ETHICS IN BUDGETING Norton Company, a manufacturer of infant furniture and carriages, is in the initial stages of preparing the annual budget for 20X1. Scott Ford has recently joined Norton's accounting staff and is interested in learning as much as possible about the company's budgeting process. During a recent lunch with Marge Atkins, sales

Ethics

333

manager, and Pete Granger, production manager, Ford initiated the following conversation:

Ford: "Since I'm new around here and am going to be involved with the preparation of the annual budget, I'd be interested to learn how the two of you estimate sales and production numbers."

Atkins: "We start out very methodically by looking at recent history, discussing what we know about current accounts, potential customers, and the general state of consumer spending. Then, we add that usual dose of intuition to come up with the best forecast we can."

Granger: "I usually take the sales projections as the basis for my projections. Of course, we have to make an estimate of what this year's closing inventories will be, and that sometimes is difficult."

Ford: "Why does that present a problem? There must have been an estimate of closing inventories in the budget for the current year."

Granger: "Those numbers aren't always reliable since Marge makes some adjustments to the sales numbers before passing them on to me."

Ford: "What kind of adjustments?"

Atkins: "Well, we don't want to fall short of the sales projections so we generally give ourselves a little breathing room by lowering the initial sales projection anywhere from 5 to 10 percent."

Granger: "So, you can see why this year's budget is not a very reliable starting point. We always have to adjust the projected production rates as the year progresses and, of course, this changes the ending inventory estimates. By the way, we make similar adjustments to expenses by adding at least 10 percent to the estimates; I think everyone around here does the same thing."

Required

1. Marge Atkins and Pete Granger have described the use of budgetary slack.
    a. Explain why Atkins and Granger behave in this manner, and describe the benefits they expect to realize from the use of budgetary slack.
    b. Explain how the use of budgetary slack can adversely affect Atkins and Granger.

2. As a management accountant, Scott Ford believes that the behavior described by Marge Atkins and Pete Granger may be unethical and that he may have an obligation not to support this behavior. By citing the specific standards of competence, confidentiality, integrity, and/or objectivity from Standards of Ethical Conduct for Management Accountants, explain why the use of budgetary slack may be unethical.

(CMA Adapted)

9–48 **BUDGET REVISION** Mark Fletcher, president of SoftGro Inc., was looking forward to seeing the performance reports for the month of November because he knew the company's sales for the month had exceeded budget by a considerable margin. SoftGro, a distributor of educational software packages, had been growing steadily for approximately two years; Fletcher's biggest challenge at this point was to ensure that the company did not lose control of expenses during this growth period. When Fletcher received the November reports, he was dismayed to see the large unfavorable variance in the company's Monthly Selling Expense Report that is presented in this problem.

Fletcher called in the company's new controller, Susan Porter, to discuss the implications of the variances reported for November and to plan a strategy for improving performance. Porter suggested that the reporting format that the company had been using might not be giving Fletcher a true picture of the company's operations and proposed that SoftGro revise the budget to correspond with the output level achieved for operation evaluation purposes. Porter offered to redo the Monthly Selling Expense Report for November based on the actual units sold.

Porter discovered the information presented below about the behavior of SoftGro's selling expenses. Using this information and pertinent data from the original Monthly Selling Expense Report, Porter believed she would be able to redo the report and present it to Fletcher for his review.

- The total compensation paid to the sales force consists of both a monthly base salary and commission; the commission varies with the sales dollars.

- Sales office expense is a mixed cost with the variable portion related to the number of orders processed. The fixed portion of office expense is $3,000,000 annually and is incurred uniformly throughout the year.

- Subsequent to the adoption of the annual budget for the current year, SoftGro decided to open a new sales territory. As a consequence, approval was given to hire six additional salespersons effective November 1, 20X3. Porter decided that these additional six people should be recognized in her revised report.

- Per diem reimbursement to the sales force, while a fixed stipend per day, is variable with the number of salespersons and the number of days spent traveling. SoftGro's original budget was based on an average sales force of 90 persons throughout the year with each salesperson traveling fifteen days per month.

- The company's shipping expense is a mixed cost with the variable portion, $3.00 per unit, dependent on the number of units sold. The fixed portion is incurred uniformly throughout the year.

Required

1. Cite the benefits of redoing the budget based on the output level achieved to explain why Susan Porter would propose that SoftGro use the revised budget in this situation.

2. Prepare a revised Monthly Selling Expense Report for November that would permit Mark Fletcher to more clearly evaluate SoftGro's control over selling expenses. The report should have a line for each selling expense item showing the appropriate budgeted amount, the actual selling expense, and the monthly dollar variance.

SOFTGRO INC.
Monthly Selling Expense Report
November 20X3

	Annual Budget	November Budget	November Actual	November Variance
Unit sales	2,000,000	280,000	310,000	30,000
Dollar sales	$80,000,000	$11,200,000	$12,400,000	$1,200,000
Orders processed	54,000	6,500	5,800	(700)
Salespersons per month	90	90	96	(6)
Advertising	$19,800,000	$ 1,650,000	$ 1,660,000	$ 10,000U
Staff salaries	1,500,000	125,000	125,000	—
Sales salaries	1,296,000	108,000	115,400	7,400U
Commissions	3,200,000	448,000	496,000	48,000U
Per diem expense	1,782,000	148,500	162,600	14,100U
Office expense	4,080,000	340,000	358,400	18,400U
Shipping expense	6,750,000	902,500	976,500	74,000U
Total expenses	$38,408,000	$ 3,722,000	$ 3,893,900	$171,900U

(CMA Adapted)

Service

9–49 BUDGET REVISION The Mason Agency, a division of General Service Industries, offers consulting services to clients for a fee. The corporate management of General Service is pleased with the performance of the Mason Agency for the first nine months of the current year and has recommended that the division manager of the Mason Agency, Richard Howell, submit a revised forecast for the remaining quarter, as the division has exceeded the annual plan year-to-date by 20 percent of operating income. An unexpected increase in billed hour volume over the original plan is the main reason for this gain in income. The original operating budget for the first three quarters for the Mason Agency follows:

THE MASON AGENCY
20X0–1 Operating Budget

	First Quarter	Second Quarter	Third Quarter	Total Nine Months
Revenue				
Consulting fees				
Management consulting	$315,000	$315,000	$315,000	$ 945,000
EDP consulting	421,875	421,875	421,875	1,265,625
Total consulting fees	$736,875	$736,875	$736,875	$2,210,625
Other revenue	10,000	10,000	10,000	30,000
Total revenue	$746,875	$746,875	$746,875	$2,240,625
Expenses				
Consultant salary	$386,750	$386,750	$386,750	$1,160,250
Travel and related	45,625	45,625	45,625	136,875
General & admin.	100,000	100,000	100,000	300,000
Depreciation	40,000	40,000	40,000	120,000
Corporate allocation	50,000	50,000	50,000	150,000
Total expenses	$622,375	$622,375	$622,375	$1,867,125
Operating income	$124,500	$124,500	$124,500	$ 373,500

When comparing the actual for the first three quarters to the original plan, Howell analyzed the variances and will reflect the following information in his revised forecast for the fourth quarter:

- The division currently has 25 consultants on staff, 10 for management consulting and 15 for EDP consulting, and has hired three additional management consultants to start work at the beginning of the fourth quarter in order to meet the increased client demand.

- The hourly billing rate for consulting revenues is market acceptable and will remain at $90 per hour for each management consultant and $75 per hour for each EDP consultant. However, due to the favorable increase in billing hour volume when compared to plan, the hours for each consultant will be increased by 50 hours per quarter. There is no learning curve for billable consulting hours for new employees.

- The budgeted annual salaries and actual annual salaries, paid monthly, are the same at $50,000 for a management consultant and 8 percent less for an EDP consultant. Corporate management has approved a merit increase of 10 percent at the beginning of the fourth quarter for all 25 existing consultants, while the new consultants will be compensated at the planned rate.

- The planned salary expense includes a provision for employee fringe benefits amounting to 30 percent of the annual salaries; however, the improvement of some corporatewide employee programs will increase the fringe benefit allocation to 40 percent.

- The original plan assumes a fixed hourly rate for travel and other related expenses for each billing hour of consulting. These are expenses that are not reimbursed by the client, and the previously determined hourly rate has proven to be adequate to cover these costs.

- Other revenues are derived from temporary rental and interest income and remain unchanged for the fourth quarter.

- General and administrative expenses have been favorable at 7 percent below the plan; this 7 percent savings on fourth-quarter expenses will be reflected in the revised plan.

- Depreciation for office equipment and microcomputers will stay consistent at the projected straight-line rate.

- Due to the favorable experience for the first three quarters and the division's increased ability to absorb costs, the corporate management at General Service Industries has increased the corporate expense allocation by 50 percent.

Required

1. Prepare a revised operating budget for the fourth quarter for the Mason Agency that Richard Howell will present to General Service Industries. Be sure to furnish supporting calculations for all revised revenue and expense amounts.

2. Discuss the reasons why an organization would prepare a revised forecast.

(CMA Adapted)

9–50 **STRATEGY, PRODUCT LIFE CYCLE, AND CASH FLOW**   The Burke Company manufactures various electronic assemblies that it sells primarily to computer manufacturers. Burke's reputation has been built on quality, timely delivery, and products that are consistently on the cutting edge of technology. Burke's business is fast-paced. The typical product has a short life; the product is in development for about a year and in the growth stage, with sometimes spectacular growth, for about a year. Each product then experiences a rapid decline in sales as new products become available.

Strategy

Burke has just hired a new vice president of finance, Devin Ward. Shortly after reporting for work at Burke, Ward had a conversation with Andrew Newhouse, Burke's president. A portion of the conversation follows.

Newhouse: "The thing that fascinates me about this business is that change is its central ingredient. We knew when we started out that a reliable stream of new products was one of our key variables—in fact, the only way to cope with the threat of product obsolescence. You see, our products go through only the first half of the traditional product life cycle— the development stage and then the growth stage. Our products never reach the traditional mature product stage or the declining product stage. Toward the end of the growth stage, products die as new ones are introduced."

Ward: "I suppose your other key variables would be cost controls and efficient production scheduling?"

Newhouse: "Getting the product to market on schedule, whether efficiently or not, is important. Some firms in this business announce a new product in March to be delivered in June, and they make the first shipment in October, or a year from March, or sometimes, never. Our reputation for delivering on schedule may account for our success as much as anything."

Ward: "Where I previously worked, we also recognized the importance of on-time deliveries. Our absorption cost system set 93 percent on-time as a standard."

Newhouse: "The key variable that is your responsibility is cash management. It took us a while to recognize that. At first, we thought that profit was the key and that cash would naturally follow. But now we know that cash is the key and that profits naturally follow. Still, we don't do cash management well. Improving our cash management is the main thing we expect from you."

Required

1. Discuss the cash-generating and cash-usage characteristics of products in general in each of the four stages of the product life cycle—development, growth, maturity, and decline.

2. Describe the cash management problems confronting the Burke Company.

3. Suggest techniques that Devin Ward might implement to cope with Burke Company's cash management problems.

(CMA Adapted)

9–51 **CONTINUOUS BUDGET**   WestWood Corporation is a woodstove manufacturer located in southern Oregon. WestWood manufactures three models—small stoves for heating a single room, medium-sized units for use in mobile homes and as a supplement to central heating systems, and large stoves with the capacity to provide central heating.

The manufacturing process consists of shearing and shaping steel, fabricating, welding, painting, and finishing. Molded doors are custom built at an outside foundry in the state, brass plated at a plater, and fitted with custom etched glass during assembly at WestWood's plant. The finished stoves are delivered to dealers either directly or through regional warehouses located throughout the western United States. WestWood owns the three tractor trailers and one large truck used to ship stoves to dealers and warehouses.

The budget for the year ending February 28, 20X2, was finalized in January of 20X1 and was based upon an assumption of the continuation of the 10 percent annual growth rate that WestWood had experienced since 20X0.

Stove sales are seasonal, and the first quarter of WestWood's fiscal year is usually a slack period. As a consequence, inventory levels were down at the start of the current fiscal year on March 1, 20X1.

WestWood's sales orders for the first quarter ended May 31, 20X1, were up 54 percent over the same period last year and 40 percent above the first quarter budget. Unfortunately, not all of the sales orders could be filled due to the reduced inventory levels at the beginning of the quarter. WestWood's plant was able to increase production over budgeted levels, but not in sufficient quantity to compensate for the large increase in orders. Therefore, there is a large backlog of orders. Furthermore, preliminary orders for the busy fall season are 60 percent above the budget and the projections for the winter of 20X1–6 indicate no decrease in demand. WestWood's president attributes the increase to effective advertising, the products' good reputation, the increased number of installations of woodstoves in new houses, and the bankruptcy of WestWood's principal competitor.

Required

1. WestWood Corporation's sales for the remainder of the 20X1–2 fiscal year will be much greater than were predicted five months ago. Explain the effect this increase will have on the operations in the following functional areas of WestWood.
   a. Production.
   b. Finance and accounting.
   c. Marketing.
   d. Personnel.

2. Some companies follow the practice of preparing a continuous budget.
   a. Explain what a continuous budget is.
   b. Explain how WestWood Corporation could benefit by the preparation of a continuous budget.

(CMA Adapted)

SOLUTIONS TO SELF-STUDY PROBLEMS

1. Master Budget

1.

HANSELL COMPANY
Sales Budget
For July 20X0

Budgeted sales in units		6,000
Budgeted selling price per unit	× $	40
Budgeted sales		$240,000

2.

HANSELL COMPANY
Production Budget (in units)
For July 20X0

Desired ending inventory (July 31)		
(The higher of 100 and 7,000 × 0.1)		700
Budgeted sales for July 19X8	+	6,000
Total units needed for July 19X8		6,700
Beginning inventory (July 1)		
(The higher of 100 and 6,000 x 0.1)	−	600
Units to manufacture in July		6,100

3.

HANSELL COMPANY
Production Budget (in units)
For August 20X0

Desired ending inventory (8,000 × 0.1)		800
Budgeted sales	+	7,000
Total units needed		7,800
Beginning Inventory	−	700
Units to manufacture in August		7,100

4.

HANSELL COMPANY
Direct Materials Purchases Budget (in pounds)
For July 20X0

	Direct Materials	
	Dura–1000 **(4 lb. each)**	**Flexplas** **(2 lb. each)**
Materials required for budgeted production (6,100 units of DuraFlex)	24,400	12,200
Add: Target inventories (lower of 1,000 or 5 percent of August production needs)	+ 1,000	+ 710
Total materials requirements	25,400	12,910
Less: Expected beginning inventories (lower of 1,000 or 5 percent)	− 1,000	− 610
Direct materials to be purchased	24,400	12,300

5.

HANSELL COMPANY
Direct Materials Purchases Budget (in dollars)
For July 20X0

	Budgeted Purchases (Pounds)	Expected Purchase Price per Unit	Total
Dura–1000	24,400	$1.25	$30,500
Flexplas	12,300	$5.00	61,500
Budgeted purchases			$92,000

6.

HANSELL COMPANY
Direct Manufacturing Labor Budget
For July 20X0

	Direct Labor-Hours per Batch	Number of Batches	Total Hours	Rate per Hour	Total
K102 Hours	1	61	61	$50	$ 3,050
K175 Hours	10	61	610	$20	12,200
Total			671		$15,250

2. Cash Budget and Budgeted Income Statement

1.

HANSELL COMPANY
Cash Budget
July 20X0

<u>Cash available</u>		
Cash balance, beginning		$ 10,000
Add: Cash receipts		
July cash sales	$240,000 × 20% = $48,000	
Collections of receivables:		
From sales in June		
Collection within the discount period		
	5,500 × $40 × 80% × 60% × 98% = $103,488	
Collection after the discount period		
	5,500 × $40 × 80% × 25% = 44,000	
From sales in May		
	5,400 × $40 × 80% × 10% = 17,280	212,768
Total cash available in July		$222,768
<u>Cash disbursement</u>		
Material purchases		
June purchases	($25,000 + $22,000) × 20% × 98% = $ 9,212	
July purchases	$92,000 × 80% × 98% = 72,128	$ 81,340
Direct manufacturing labor		15,250
Variable factory overhead	($200 × 61 + $30 × 671) × 60% =	19,398
Fixed factory overhead	$50,000 − $20,000 =	30,000
Variable marketing, customer services, and administrative expenses		
	[($600,000 − $270,000) ÷ $2,000,000] × $240,000 =	39,600
Fixed marketing, customer services, and administrative expenses		
	($270,000 − 150,000) ÷ 12 =	10,000
Total disbursements		$195,588
Cash balance before financing		$ 27,180
<u>Financing</u>		
Amount to borrow		13,000
Cash balance, July 31, 20X0		$ 40,180

2.

HANSELL COMPANY
Budget Income Statement
July 20X0

Sales			$240,000
Cost of goods sold*	$22.80 × 6,000 =		136,800
Gross margin			$103,200
Selling and administrative expenses			
Variable		$39,600	
Fixed	$270,000 ÷ 12 =	22,500	62,100
Net income			$ 41,100

*Cost per unit:

Direct materials:			
Dura–1000	4 lb. × $1.25 =	$ 5.00	
Flexplas	2 lb. × $5.00 =	10.00	$15.00
Direct labor:			
K102 labor	.01 hour × $50 =	$0.50	
K175 labor	.1 hour × $20 =	2.00	2.50
Factory overhead:			
Applied based on batch:	$200 ÷ 100 =	$2.00	
Applied based on direct labor-hour:	$30 × .11 hour =	3.30	5.30
Cost per unit			$22.80

Decision Making with a Strategic Emphasis

10

After studying this chapter you should be able to . . .

Define the decision-making process and identify the types of cost information relevant for decision making 1

Use relevant cost information in making special order decisions 2

Use relevant cost information in the make, lease, or buy decision 3

Use relevant cost information in the decision to sell before or after additional processing 4

Use relevant cost information in the decision to keep or drop products or services 5

Use relevant cost information in evaluating programs 6

Analyze relevant cost decisions with multiple products and limited resources 7

Discuss the behavioral and implementation issues in using relevant cost information 8

Jeff Greenberg/Photo Edit

Our policy is to reduce the price, extend the operations, and improve the article. You will notice that the reduction of price comes first. We have never considered costs as fixed. Therefore we first reduce the price to the point where we believe more sales result. Then we go ahead and try to make the prices. We do not bother about the costs. The new price forces the costs down. The more usual way is to take the costs and then determine the price, and although that method may be scientific in the narrow sense, it is not scientific in the broad sense, because what earthly use is it to know the cost if it tells you that you cannot manufacture at a price at which the article can be sold? But more to the point is the fact that although one may calculate what a cost is, and of course all of our costs are carefully calculated, no one knows what a cost ought to be. One of the ways of discovering is to name a price so low as to force everybody in the place to the highest point of efficiency. The low price makes everybody dig for profits. We make more discoveries concerning manufacturing and selling under this forced method than by any method of leisurely investigation.

HENRY FORD, MY LIFE AND WORK
(GARDEN CITY, NY: DOUBLEDAY & COMPANY, 1923), P. 146.

Many years ago, Henry Ford reflected on the relevance of costs in decision making, the focus of this chapter. A firm faces both long-term and short-term decisions, from infrequent decisions about major new investments to daily decisions about scheduling the production and delivery of customer orders. Short-term decisions are those for which most fixed costs are expected to remain the same throughout the period affected by the decision; a period of approximately a year is commonly used. Long-term decisions are covered throughout the text, but especially in capital budgeting (Chapter 11) and strategic management (Chapters 2 and 5).

Short-term decisions are the focus of this chapter. They include whether to accept a one-time customer order; to replace or repair equipment; to make or buy a component of a product; to lease or to buy equipment; and to modify, keep, or delete a product. Managers make short-term decisions by analyzing relevant costs.

BusinessWeek

Can Ford Overtake the Toyota Camry?

In the redesign of the Taurus for the 1996 model year, Ford engineers set their sights high—to move giant steps toward parity with a key competitor, the Toyota Camry. While the Taurus was the best-selling car in the United States, many car buyers gave the Camry much higher marks for quality and engineering excellence. Particularly, car buyers were unhappy with the Taurus's high wind noise, noisy doors, and other examples of lower quality relative to the Camry. So Ford engineers and designers were told, from CEO Trotman and throughout the organization, to improve quality and features. The result was a much better car than the previous Taurus, but also a more expensive car—labor time per car went up to 12 hours from 11 hours, and total costs increased by $750 per car. At the same time, Toyota was using target costing and redesigning the Camry to *decrease* its production cost, so that its price could, in turn, be reduced. The Camry has since gained first place in the United States auto market.

Q: Was Ford's strategy sound? Should it have shifted its focus to short-term profitability versus long-term potential? *Find out on page 358 of this chapter.*

RELEVANT COST INFORMATION FOR DECISION MAKING

Understanding how to identify and use relevant costs is critical to effective decision making. This section explains the concept of relevant cost and its role in the decision-making process.

Relevant Cost Information

Relevant costs are costs to be incurred at some future time; they differ for each option available to the decision maker. A cost that does not differ among the decision maker's options is irrelevant because that choice has no effect on the cost. For example, in choosing which new car to buy, a consumer can ignore the cost of licenses and fees as long as these costs are the same for all cars. Also, a cost that has occurred already or has been committed to is irrelevant; the decision cannot influence these costs. Thus, the cost of the buyer's present car is irrelevant. The only relevant amount for the old car is the future amount—its potential trade-in value. The decision maker's rule is *only future costs that differ among options are relevant for the decision.* (See Exhibit 10–1.)

A relevant cost can be either a variable or a fixed cost. Generally, variable costs are relevant for decision making because they differ between options and have not been committed. In contrast, fixed costs are often irrelevant, since typically they do not differ between options. Note that a fixed cost sometimes is irrelevant because the same fixed cost is incurred in the future under either decision option. At other times, the fixed cost is irrelevant because it has been incurred in the past and cannot differ among the options.

Overall, often variable costs are relevant and fixed costs are not. So the use of the concept of relevant cost follows naturally from the development of the methods we used in cost estimation, cost-volume-profit analysis, and master budgeting.

Occasionally some variable costs are not relevant. For example, assume a manager is considering whether to replace or repair an old machine. If the electrical power requirements of the new and old machines are the same, then the variable cost of power is not relevant. Also, some fixed costs can be relevant. For example, if the new machine requires significant modifications to the plant building, the cost of the modifications (which are fixed costs) are relevant because they are not yet committed.

Assume the old machine was purchased for $4,200 a year ago, that the equipment is depreciated over two years at $2,100 per year, and it has no trade-in or dis-

Relevant costs are costs to be incurred at some future time; they differ for each option available to the decision maker.

LEARNING OBJECTIVE 1 ▶
Define the decision-making process and identify the types of cost information relevant for decision making.

Exhibit 10–1	Relationships among Types of Cost and Relevant Cost

Cost Classification and Cost Relevance
(With examples for the car purchase decision)

	Committed, or "Sunk" (Generally, in the Past)	Not Committed, Discretionary (Generally, in the Future)
Costs That Differ Among Options	Not Relevant Example: Insurance (which is likely to be the same whichever new car is purchased)	Relevant Costs Example: Price of new car
Costs That Are the Same	Not Relevant Example: Price of old car	Not Relevant Example: American Auto Club membership

---

[1]   The development and use of cost information for decision making is often called relevant cost analysis. It is also called incremental analysis, cost analysis, contribution margin analysis, or differential cost analysis. See Chapter 3 for additional clarification of these concepts.

posal value. At the end of the first year the machine has a net book value of $2,100 ($4,200 − $2,100). Also assume that the purchase price of the new machine is $7,000, and it is expected to last for two years with little or no expected trade-in or disposal value. The repair of the old machine would cost $3,500 and would be sufficient for another two years of productive use. The power for either machine is expected to cost $2.50 per hour. Also, the new machine is semiautomated, so that a less-skilled operator is required, resulting in a reduction of average labor costs from $10.00 to $9.50 per hour for the new machine. If the firm is expected to operate at a 1,000-hour level of output for each of the next two years, the two-year total variable costs for power will be 2,000 × $2.50 = $5,000, and labor costs will be $19,000 ($9.5 × 2,000) and $20,000 ($10 × 2,000) for the new and old machines respectively.

Data for Machine Replacement Example

Old Machine	
Current net book value	$2,100
Useful life (if repaired)	2 years
Operating cost (labor)	$10 per hour
New Machine	
Purchase price	$7,000
Useful life	2 years
Operating cost (labor)	$9.50 per hour

The summary of relevant costs for this decision is in Exhibit 10–2, showing a $2,500 advantage for repairing the old machine. The $1,000 decrease in labor costs for the new machine is less than the $3,500 difference of replacement cost over repair cost ($7,000 − $3,500). Note that the power costs and the depreciation on the old machine are omitted because they are irrelevant for the decision.

To show that the analysis based on total costs provides the same answer, Exhibit 10–3 shows the analysis for total costs that includes the power costs and the purchase price of the old machine; neither cost is relevant. The left portion of Exhibit 10–3 is the same as Exhibit 10–2. Note that both analyses lead to the same conclusion. The relevant cost approach in Exhibit 10–2 is always preferred, however, because it is simpler, less prone to error, and provides better focus for the decision maker.

There's more to the decision process than the discovery of relevant costs. The manager must also consider strategic issues, and the nature of the variable costs and the fixed costs in the analysis.

Strategic Relevant Cost Analysis

A management decision usually touches on several strategic issues. For example, focusing on the short-term monthly and annual periods should not lead the manager to ignore the long-term strategic factors about markets and production processes. Failing

Exhibit 10–2	**Relevant Cost Analysis in Equipment Replacement**		
		Relevant Costs	**Difference**
			Replace Minus Repair
	Repair	**Replace**	
Variable costs (for two years at 1,000 hours per year)			
Labor*	$20,000	$19,000	($1,000)
Fixed costs (for two years)			
Old machine repair cost	3,500		(3,500)
New machine		7,000	7,000
Total costs:	$23,500	$26,000	$ 2,500
Repair cost lower by: $2,500			

* $20,000 = 1,000 hours × 2 years × $10 per hour
$19,000 = 1,000 hours × 2 years × $9.50 per hour

Exhibit 10–3	Relevant Cost and Total Cost Analysis in Equipment Replacement

	Relevant Costs		Total Costs		Difference
	Repair	**Replace**	**Repair**	**Replace**	**Replace − Repair**
Variable costs (for two years at 1,000 hours per year)					
Labor	$20,000	$19,000	$20,000	$19,000	($1,000)
Power			5,000	5,000	-0-
Fixed costs (for two years)					
Old machine					
Depreciation			2,100	2,100	-0-
Repair cost	3,500		3,500		(3,500)
New machine					
Depreciation		7,000		7,000	7,000
Total costs	$23,500	$26,000	$30,600	$33,100	$2,500
Repair cost lower by		$2,500		$2,500	

Determining Relevant Costs vs. Strategic Relevant Cost Analysis	
Determine Relevant Costs	**Strategic Relevant Cost Analysis**
Short-term focus	Long-term focus
Not linked to strategy	Linked to the firm's strategy
Product cost focus	Customer focus
Focused on individual product or decision situation	Integrative; considers all customer-related factors

to attend to the long-term, strategic factors could cause the firm to be less competitive in the years ahead. Consider Henry Ford's comments at the start of the chapter. These words are as relevant today as in the early days of the automobile industry. Ford addressed the need for accurate cost information for decision making, while indicating that important strategic factors must be considered in effective decision making. Strategic factors include choices about the nature and amount of manufacturing capacity, product diversity, and product design for cost efficiency. The strategic factors have an effect on the determination of what Ford says a cost "ought to be."

For example, a strategic decision to design the manufacturing process for high efficiency to produce large batches of product reduces overall production costs. At the same time, it might reduce the firm's flexibility to manufacture a variety of products and thus could increase the cost of producing small, specialized orders. The decision regarding cost efficiency cannot be separated from the determination of marketing strategy; that is, deciding what types and sizes of orders can be accepted.

By identifying only relevant costs, the decision maker fails to link the decision to the firm's strategy. The decision maker also must consider strategic issues. For example, the decision to buy rather than to make a part for the firm's product might make sense on the basis of relevant cost, but might be a bad strategic move if the firm's competitive position depends on product reliability that can be maintained only by keeping the manufacture of the part in-house. A good indication of a manager's failing to take a strategic approach is that there will be a product cost focus to the analysis, while a strategic relevant cost analysis also addresses broad and difficult-to-measure strategic issues. The strategic analysis directly focuses on adding value to the customer, going beyond only cost issues.

Variable Costs and Cost Drivers

While for many decisions most of the relevant costs are variable, the concept of variable cost does not mean only a cost tied to changes in the output level. A variable cost is a cost that varies directly with changes in a given cost driver, whether that be the number of products produced, the number of batches of product produced, or the number of design features for each product. For example, certain costs that would be fixed at the output level (e.g., the cost of setting up machinery) would be variable at the batch level because setup costs are incurred with each new batch of product. If we add features to a product, costs increase not only at the output level (additional direct materials and labor) but also at the batch level (increased setup costs) and the product level (increased engineering design costs, inspection and testing costs). In determining the costs that differ between options, managers must consider variable costs in the broadest possible sense as costs that might vary at any level of manufacture—units of output, batches, and products.

Consider the decision in Exhibit 10–2 to repair rather than to replace the old machine. Assume the new machine, because of its simpler design, allowed the firm to reduce setup time for each batch to 25 percent of the time required for the old machine. Assume further that the average of 1,000 hours of operation per year produces 60 batches of product, and that the time required for setup labor is four hours per setup. Of the 1,000 hours, then, 240 hours (60 × 4) are required for setup and 760 hours (1,000 − 240) are direct labor-hours. For the new machine, the setup time is less, 60 hours (60 × 1). The analysis of setup costs is

Setup Costs for New Machine	Setup Costs for Old Machine
$9.50 per hour for labor × 60 setups per year × 1 hour per setup × 2 years = $1,140	$10 per hour for labor × 60 setups per year × 4 hours per setup × 2 years = $4,800

It is apparent that the new machine saves $3,660 ($4,800 − $1,140) in setup costs for the two-year period as well as $760 in direct labor (760 hours × 2 years × $10/hr = $15,200 for the old machine versus 760 × 2 × $9.50 = $14,440 for the new machine; $15,200 − $14,440 = $760). The total labor savings is $4,420 ($3,660 + $760) over the two-year period. This more than offsets the excess of the cost of the new machine over the cost of repair, $3,500 ($7,000 − $3,500), for a net benefit of replacing the machine of $4,420 − $3,500 = $920. See the revised analysis in Exhibit 10-4.

Fixed Costs and Depreciation

There is a common misperception that depreciation of facilities and equipment is a relevant cost. In fact, depreciation is a portion of a committed cost (the allocation

Exhibit 10–4 Relevant Costs in Equipment Replacement (Including Consideration of Setup Costs)

	Relevant Costs		Total Costs		Difference	
	Repair	Replace	Repair	Replace	Replace	Repair
Variable costs (for two years)						
Labor						
Direct	$15,200	$14,440	$15,200	$14,440	($ 760)	
Setup	4,800	1,140	4,800	1,140	(3,660)	
Total labor	$20,000	$15,580	$20,000	$15,580	(4,420)	
Power			5,000	5,000	-0-	
Fixed costs (for two years)						
Old machine						
Depreciation			2,100	2,100	-0-	
Repair cost	3,500		3,500		(3,500)	
New machine						
Depreciation		7,000		7,000	7,000	
Total costs:	$23,500	$22,580	$30,600	$29,680	($ 920)	
Replace cost lower by:		$920		$920		

of a purchase cost over the life of an asset); therefore, it is sunk and irrelevant. There is an exception to this rule—when tax effects are considered in decision making. In this context, depreciation has a positive value in that, as an expense it reduces taxable income and tax expense. If taxes are considered, then depreciation has a role to the extent it reduces tax liability. The decision maker often must consider the impact of local, federal, and sometimes international tax differences on the decision situation.

The Decision-Making Process

In deciding among alternative choices for a given situation, managers employ a five-step process outlined in Exhibit 10–5. The first step, and in many ways the most important, is to consider the broad strategic issues regarding the decision context. This helps focus the decision maker on answering the right question, in part by identifying a comprehensive list of decision options. Strategic thinking is important to avoid decisions that might be best only in the short run. For example, a plant manager might incorrectly view the choice is to either make or buy a part for a manufactured product, when the correct decision might be to determine whether the product should be redesigned so the part is not needed.

The manager's second step is to specify the criteria by which the decision is to be made. Most often the manager's principal objective is an easily quantified, short-term, achievable goal, such as to reduce cost, improve income, or maximize return on investment. Market forces such as strong competition or interested parties (owners or shareholders) have their own criteria for decisions. Therefore, managers most often are forced to think of multiple objectives—both the quantifiable short-term goals and the more strategic, difficult-to-quantify goals.

In the third step, the manager performs an analysis in which the relevant information is developed and analyzed. This step incorporates three sequential activities. The manager (a) develops relevant information about the decision, (b) makes predictions about the future cash flows, and (c) chooses a decision-making model. The decision model we have described in this chapter is *relevant cost analysis*, as illustrated in Exhibits 10–3 and 10–4.

Fourth, based on the relevant cost analysis, the manager selects the best alternative and implements it. In the fifth and final step, the manager evaluates the performance of the implemented decision as a basis for feedback to a possible reconsideration of the decision. The decision process is thus a closed system in which the manager continually evaluates the results of prior analyses and decisions to discover

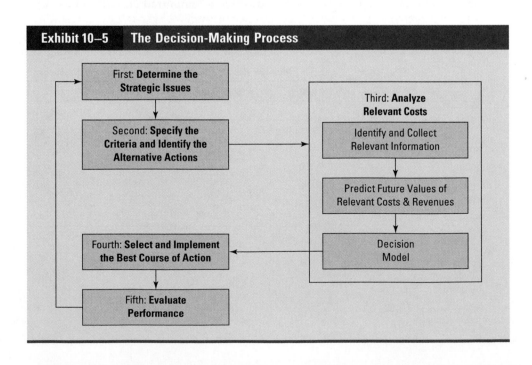

Exhibit 10–5   The Decision-Making Process

any opportunity for continual improvement in the process. Relevant cost analysis is a critical part of the decision process.

Other Relevant Information

Relevant cost information is often an important input for management decisions. Other types of crucial information include strategic information and information about capacity usage and opportunity cost.

Strategic information is important to keep the decision maker focused on the crucial, strategic goals of the firm. It includes information about competitive products and the relevant strengths and weakness of the firm's products and services—basic information about how successfully the firm competes. For example, a manufacturer of high-quality furniture might not want to accept a special order for inexpensive furniture even if the relevant cost analysis were favorable, because the sale of the low-cost line could damage the firm's image as a high-quality furniture producer. Knowledge of the firm's competitive advantage, high-quality furniture, is critical strategic information.

In their decision process managers should include information about the capacity usage of the plant. Capacity usage information is a critical signal of the potential relevance of *opportunity costs*, the benefit lost when one chosen option precludes the benefits from an alternative option. When the plant is operating at full capacity, opportunity costs are an important consideration because the decision to produce a special order or add a new product line can cause the reduction, delay, or loss of sales of products and services currently offered. In contrast, a firm with excess capacity might be able to produce for current demand as well as handle the special order or new product; thus, no opportunity cost is present. When opportunity costs are relevant, the manager must consider the value of lost sales as well as the contribution from the new order or new product.

Other important factors are covered in later chapters. One factor is the *time value of money* that is important when deciding among alternatives with cash flows over two or more years. These decisions are best handled by the methods described in Chapter 11. Another factor is that managers must estimate future costs on an incomplete and subjective basis, so there is *significant uncertainty*. Here the manager can turn to statistical methods such as regression analysis (Chapter 7).

Differences in quality, functionality, timeliness of delivery, reliability in shipping, and service after the sale could strongly influence a manager's final decision, and should be considered in addition to the analysis of relevant costs. Although these factors often are considered in a qualitative manner, when any factor is strategically important, management may choose to quantify it and include it directly in the analysis.

USING RELEVANT COST INFORMATION IN DECISION MAKING

The six decisions in relevant cost analysis are (1) to accept or reject a one-time special order; (2) to make, lease, or buy equipment or components of manufactured products; (3) to sell a product with or without the additional processing costs that would enhance its value; (4) to keep or to delete a product line; (5) to evaluate programs or projects; and (6) to determine service offerings in a not-for-profit organization.

◄ **LEARNING OBJECTIVE 2**
Use relevant cost information in making special order decisions.

Recall that relevant cost analysis refers only to the development and use of relevant cost information. As shown in Exhibit 10–5, the complete decision-making process requires the consideration of strategic issues, decision implementation, and performance evaluation. These aspects of the decision are part of a complete decision-making process.

The Special Order Decision

One of the most common applications of relevant cost analysis occurs when a firm has an occasional option to sell a special order—a specified quantity of goods or services that is not a part of the core business. To make this decision, managers need critical information about relevant costs, revenues, and any opportunity costs. Consider, for example, the special order situation facing Tommy T-Shirt, Inc. (TTS). TTS is a small manufacturer of specialty clothing, primarily T-shirts and sweatshirts with imprinted slogans and brand names. TTS has been offered a contract by a local college fraternity, Alpha Beta Gamma (ABG) for 1,000 T-shirts printed with art work publicizing a fund-raising event. The fraternity offers to pay $6.50 for each shirt. TTS normally charges $9.00 for shirts of this type for this size order.

TTS's master budget of manufacturing costs for the current year is given in Exhibit 10–6. The budget is based on expected production of 225,000 T-shirts from an available capacity of 250,000. The 225,000 units are expected to be produced in 200 different batches. The three groups of cost elements are

1. **Unit-level costs** vary with each shirt printed and include the cost of the shirt ($3.25 each), ink ($.95 each), and labor ($.85).

2. **Batch-level costs** vary, in part, with the number of batches produced. The batch-level costs include machine setup, inspection, and materials handling. These costs are part variable (change with the number of batches) and part fixed. For example, setup costs are $130 per setup ($26,000 for 200 setups) plus $29,000 fixed costs that do not change with the number of setups (e.g., setup tools or software). Total setup costs are $55,000 ($26,000 + $29,000). Similarly, inspection costs are $30 each plus $9,000 fixed costs—$15,000 total ($30 × 200 + $9,000). Materials handling costs are $40 per batch plus $7,000 fixed costs—$15,000 total ($40 × 200 + $7,000).

3. **Plant-level costs** are fixed and do not vary with either the units produced or the batches. These costs include depreciation and insurance on machinery ($315,000) and other fixed costs ($90,000).

TTS analyzes the relevant costs in Exhibit 10–7. The Alpha Beta Gamma order requires the same unprinted T-shirt, ink, and labor time as other shirts, for a total of $5.05 per unit. In addition, TTS uses $200 of batch-level costs for each order.

	Analysis of Contribution from the Alpha Beta Gamma Order	
Sales	1,000 units @ $6.50	$ 6,500
Relevant costs	1,000 units @ $5.25	5,250
Net contribution	1,000 units @ $1.25	$ 1,250

Exhibit 10–6	**Master Budget for TTS's Manufacturing Costs** (Expected Output of 225,000 units in 200 batches)

	Unit-Level Costs		Batch-Level Costs			Plant-Level Costs (all fixed)	
			Variable Costs		Fixed Costs		
Cost Element	Amount	Per Unit	Amount	Per Batch			Total
Shirt	$731,250	$3.25					$731,250
Ink	213,750	.95					213,750
Operating labor	191,250	.85					191,250
Subtotal	$1,136,250	$5.05					$1,136,250
Setup			$26,000	$130	$29,000		55,000
Inspection			6,000	30	9,000		15,000
Materials handling			8,000	40	7,000		15,000
Subtotal			$40,000	$200	$45,000		85,000
Machine-related						$315,000	315,000
Other						90,000	90,000
Total	$1,136,250	$5.05	$40,000	$200	$45,000	$450,000	$1,626,250

Exhibit 10–7	Special Order Decision Analysis for TTS	

Cost Type	Unit Costs	Total Cost for One Batch of 1,000 units
Relevant Costs		
Unit-level costs		
Unprinted shirt	$3.25	$3,250
Ink and other supplies	.95	950
Machine time (operator labor)	.85	850
Total unit-level costs	5.05	$5,050
Batch-level costs (Costs that vary with the number of batches)		
Setup		130
Inspection		30
Materials handling		40
Total ($200/batch; $.20/unit)	.20	$ 200
Total relevant costs	$5.25	$5,250
Nonrelevant Costs		
Fixed batch-level costs ($45,000/225,000)	$ .20	
Plant-level costs		
Machine-related ($315,000/225,000)	1.40	
Other ($90,000/225,000)	.40	
Total nonrelevant costs	$2.00	
Total cost	$7.25	

The correct analysis for the decision is to identify the relevant costs of $5.25, and then to compare the relevant costs to the special order price of $6.50. The nonrelevant costs are not considered because they remain the same whether or not TTS accepts the Alpha Beta Gamma order. There is a $1.25 ($6.50 − 5.25) contribution to income for each shirt sold to Alpha Beta Gamma, or a total contribution of $1,250, so the order is profitable and should be accepted.

A common *incorrect* analysis of this information would focus on the total unit cost of $7.25 per shirt. If TTS's manager had not recognized that $2.00 of nonrelevant cost was not affected by the decision, TTS could have incorrectly rejected the order, thinking that unit costs ($7.25) exceeded the unit sales price ($6.50).

Strategic Issues

The relevant cost analysis developed for TTS gives a useful answer regarding the profitability of the order. However, for a full decision analysis, TTS also should consider strategic factors—capacity utilization, short-term versus long-term pricing, the trend in variable costs, and the use of activity-based costing.

Is TTS Now Operating at Full Capacity? TTS now has 25,000 units of excess capacity—more than enough for the ABG order. But what if TTS is operating at or near full capacity; would accepting the Alpha Beta Gamma order cause the loss of other possibly more profitable sales? If so, TTS should consider the opportunity cost arising from the lost sales. Assume that if TTS is operating at full capacity, accepting the Alpha Beta Gamma order would cause the loss of sales of the other T-shirts that have a higher contribution of $3.75 ($9.00 − $5.25). The opportunity cost is $3.75 per shirt and the proper decision analysis would be

Contribution from Alpha Beta Gamma order	$ 1,250
Less: Opportunity cost of lost sales (1,000 units × $3.75)	(3,750)
Net contribution (loss) for the order	$(2,500)

Exhibit 10–8 shows the effect if TTS had accepted the Alpha Beta Gamma order at full capacity, including the irrelevant fixed costs and the irrelevant variable costs—under full capacity the Alpha Beta Gamma order would reduce total profits by $2,500 due to lost sales.

Exhibit 10–8	**Special Order Decision for TTS under Full Capacity**	
	With ABG Order	**Without ABG Order**
Sales:		
250,000 units at $9.00		$2,250,000
249,000 at $9.00; 1,000 at $6.50	$2,247,500	
Variable cost at $5.25	1,312,500	1,312,500
Contribution margin	935,000	937,500
Fixed cost (per Exhibit 10–6)	450,000	450,000
Operating income	485,000	487,500
Advantage in favor of rejecting the ABG order		$2,500

Excessive Relevant Cost Pricing?   The relevant cost decision rule for special orders is intended only for those infrequent situations when income can be increased by doing a special order. Done on a regular basis, relevant cost pricing can erode normal pricing policies and lead to a loss in profitability for firms like TTS. The failure of large companies in the airline and steel industries has been attributed to excessive relevant cost pricing in these industries because a strategy of continually focusing on the short term can deny a company a successful long term. Special order pricing decisions should not become the centerpiece of a firm's strategy. Doing so can lead to a disaster such as Braniff Airline's—that company used special order pricing so extensively that overall profits fell and bankruptcy followed.[2]

Decline of Variable Costs as a Portion of Total Cost   In looking to the long term, TTS should consider that its costs are likely to shift so that variable costs are a smaller portion of total costs. Variable costs decline due to the automation and streamlining of manufacturing processes in most industries. As a consequence, relevant cost analysis is likely to become more important, because nonrelevant costs have a larger share of total costs. On the other hand, as variable costs fall it becomes more important that special order pricing does not become the centerpiece of the firm's strategy. Excessive short-term pricing can hurt a firm when variable costs are relatively low.

Role of Activity-Based Costing   Activity-based costing has an important role in special order decision making—to provide accurate product cost information. Activity-based costing identifies how costs change at each activity level: units, batches, and products, thereby providing a complete analysis of relevant costs. The TTS example in Exhibits 10–6 and 10–7 illustrates the importance of batch-level costs in relevant cost analysis.

LEARNING OBJECTIVE 3 ▶
Use relevant cost information in the make, lease, or buy decision.

Other Important Factors   In addition to capacity utilization and long-term pricing issues, TTS should consider Alpha Beta Gamma's credit history, any potential complexities in the design that might cause production problems, and other strategic issues such as whether the sale might lead to additional sales of their other products.

Make, Lease, or Buy

Generally, a firm's products are manufactured according to specifications set forth in what is called the **bill of materials.** The bill of materials is a detailed listing of the components of the manufactured product. A bill of materials for the manufacture of furniture is illustrated in Chapter 12. An increasingly common decision for manufacturers is to choose which of these components will be manufactured in the firm's plant, and which will be purchased from outside suppliers.

The **bill of materials** is a detailed listing of the components of the manufactured product.

---

[2] See John K. Shank and Vijay Govindarajan, *Strategic Cost Management* (New York: Free Press, 1993).

All firms occasionally face the additional decision to lease or buy a piece of equipment or a service. For example, electronic equipment such as copiers and computers often are leased from the manufacturer. The terms of the lease may combine fixed and variable costs; for example, a copier lease agreement can include a fixed annual fee plus a per-page charge.

To illustrate the lease or buy decision, we use the example of Quick Copy, Inc., a firm that provides printing and duplicating services and other related business services. Quick Copy uses one large copy machine to complete most large jobs. The machine is leased from the manufacturer on an annual basis that includes general servicing. The annual lease includes both a fixed fee of $40,000 and a per copy charge of $.02 per copy.

The copier manufacturer has suggested that Quick Copy upgrade to the latest model copier that is not available for lease but must be purchased for $160,000. The purchased copier would be useful for one year, after which it could be sold back to the manufacturer for one-fourth the purchase price ($40,000). In addition, the new machine has a required annual service contract of $20,000. Quick Copy's options for the coming year are to renew the lease for the current copier or to purchase the new copier. The relevant information is outlined in Exhibit 10–9. The cost of paper, electrical power, and employee wages will not change if the new machine is purchased, so these costs are irrelevant and are excluded from the analysis. Also, for simplicity we ignore potential tax effects of the decision.

The initial step in the analysis is to determine which machine produces a lower cost. The answer depends on the expected annual number of copies. Using cost-volume-profit analysis (Chapter 8 and Exhibit 10–10), Quick Copy's manager determines the indifference point, the number of copies at which both machines cost the same. The calculations are as follows, where Q is the number of copies:

Exhibit 10–9	**Quick Copy Lease or Buy Information**	
	Lease Option	**Purchase Option**
Annual lease	$40,000	N/A
Charge per copy	.02	N/A
Purchase cost	N/A	$160,000
Annual service contract	N/A	$ 20,000
Value at end of period	N/A	$ 40,000
Expected number of copies a year	6,000,000	6,000,000

Exhibit 10–10   **The Lease-or-Buy Example**

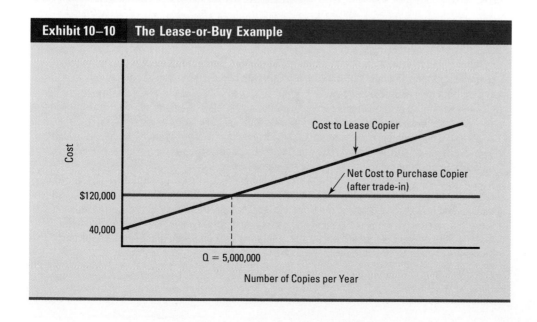

Cost to Lease Copier

Net Cost to Purchase Copier (after trade-in)

Cost

$120,000

40,000

Q = 5,000,000

Number of Copies per Year

$$\text{Lease cost} = \text{Purchase cost}$$

$$\text{Annual fee} = \text{Net purchase cost} + \text{Service contract}$$

$$\$40,000 + \$.02 \times Q = (\$160,000 - \$40,000) + \$20,000$$

$$Q = \$100,000/\$.02$$

$$= 5{,}000{,}000 \text{ copies per year}$$

The indifference point, 5,000,000 copies, is lower than the expected annual machine usage of 6,000,000 copies. This indicates that Quick Copy will have lower costs with the purchase of the new machine. Costs will be lower by $20,000:

$$\textit{Cost of lease minus Cost of purchase}$$

$$(\$40,000 + \$.02 \times 6{,}000{,}000) - (\$160{,}000 - \$40{,}000 + \$20{,}000)$$

$$= \$160{,}000 - \$140{,}000$$

$$= \$20{,}000$$

In addition to the relevant cost analysis, Quick Copy should consider noncost factors such as the quality of the copy, the reliability of the machine, the benefits and features of the service contracts, and any other factors associated with the use of the machine that might properly influence the decision. While this illustration is for the lease-or-buy decision, a very similar analysis is done for the make-or-buy decision.

Strategic Issues

The make-lease-buy decision often raises strategic issues. For example, a firm using value-chain analysis may find that certain of the firm's activities in the value chain can be more profitably performed by other firms. When a firm chooses to have a basic service function provided by an outside firm, it is called outsourcing. Make-or-buy analysis has a key role in the decision to outsource. It provides an analysis of the relevant costs. Many firms in recent years have considered outsourcing manufacturing and data processing, janitorial, or security, services to improve profitability. For example, Eastman-Kodak Corporation has outsourced the data processing

---

A Type of Make-or-Buy Decision—Outsourcing to Reduce Costs: American Airlines, Mitsubishi, and Sears

One of the key developments of recent years is the growth of outsourcing, in which a firm contracts with another firm to provide key services. For example, large firms such as Kodak, Sears, Lucent Technologies, and others have contracted out significant areas of the data processing services previously done in-house. The reason is primarily to reduce costs, as the information systems providers (IBM, EDS, and others) are more effective at controlling costs and utilizing new technologies.

Cost savings also can be achieved in outsourcing because the contract labor is usually local labor paid local wages in contrast to the relatively higher wage scales at the large national firms. For example, American Airlines contracts out ticketing work to Johnson Controls because of wage differentials. APAC, a telemarketing company, has won contracts from Compaq, Sears, and other companies for the same reason.

Changes in currencies around the world also can affect a firm's motivation to outsource. Large Japanese firms such as Toyota and Mitsubishi began to purchase parts outside Japan and built manufacturing plants in the United States and elsewhere during the early 1990s when the yen was rising steadily against the dollar and other currencies. Moving the manufacturing out of Japan reduced overall manufacturing costs for their global manufacturing and sales of cars. In effect, the manufacturing was done in cheaper currencies.

Source: "Outsourced—And Out of Luck," *Business Week,* July 17, 1995; "Let's Order Out for Technology," *Business Week,* May 13, 1996; "What the Strong Yen Is Breeding: Japanese Multinationals," *Business Week,* April 10, 1995.

requirements of its firm, and some of the airlines are outsourcing food preparation, baggage handling, and reservations systems.

IBM, Texas Instruments, Digital Equipment, and other firms have taken the idea of outsourcing a step further, to what is called **contract manufacturing,** in which another manufacturer (sometimes a direct competitor) manufactures a portion of the firm's products. When there is excess capacity or expertise in one firm and lack of capacity or know-how in the other, this can be a cost-effective strategy for both contracting firms. As for the other decisions we have considered, relevant cost analysis and consideration of related strategic factors provide the proper analysis.[3]

> **Contract manufacturing** is when another manufacturer (sometimes a direct competitor) manufactures a portion of the firm's products.
>
> ◄ **LEARNING OBJECTIVE 4**
> Use relevant cost information in the decision to sell before or after additional processing.

Sell before or after Additional Processing

A common decision problem arises when a firm has the option of selling a product or service at an intermediate processing step or adding further processing and then selling the product or service for a higher price. The additional processing might add features or functionality to a product, or add flexibility or quality to a service. For example, a travel agent preparing a group tour faces many decisions related to the features to be offered on the tour—optional side-trips, optional sleeping quarters, and optional entertainment. And a manufacturer of consumer electronics faces a number of decisions regarding the nature and extent of features to offer on its products.

The analysis of features also is important for manufacturers in determining what to do with defective products. Generally, they can either be sold in the defective state to outlet stores and discount chains, or be repaired for sale in the usual manner. The decision problem is, should the product be sold with or without additional processing? Relevant cost analysis is again the appropriate method to analyze these decisions.

To continue with the TTS example, assume a piece of equipment used to print its T-shirts has malfunctioned, and 400 shirts are not of acceptable quality because of missing or faded colors. TTS can sell the defective shirts to outlet stores at a greatly reduced price ($4.50), or run the shirts through the printing machine again. A second run will produce a salable shirt in most cases. The cost of running the T-shirts through the printer a second time is the ink, supplies, and labor cost of $1.70 per shirt, plus the setup, inspection, and materials handling costs for a batch of product. See the relevant cost analysis in Exhibit 10–11.

The analysis shows there is an $880 advantage to reprinting the shirts rather than selling the defective shirts to discount stores.

Exhibit 10–11	**Analysis of Reprinting 400 Defective T-Shirts**	
	Reprint	**Sell to Discount Store**
Revenue (400 @ $9.00, $4.50)	$ 3,600	$1,800
Relevant costs		
Supplies and ink ($.95)	380	
Labor ($.85)	340	
Setup	130	
Inspection	30	
Materials handling	40	
Total relevant costs	920	
Contribution margin	$2,680	$1,800
Net advantage to reprint	$2,680 − $1,800 = $880	
Irrelevant costs		
Cost of unprinted T-shirt	$ 3.25	$ 3.25
Plant fixed costs per shirt	2.00	2.00

---

[3] See "The Airlines to Labor: Buy in—or Get Bashed," *Business Week*, November 1, 1993, p. 40; also "Farming Out Work—To IBM, DEC, NCR . . . ," *Business Week*, May 17, 1993, pp. 92–94.

Strategic Issues

Strategic concerns arise when considering selling to discount stores. Will this affect the sale of T-shirts in retail stores? Will the cost of packing, delivery, and sales commissions differ between these two types of sales? TTS management must carefully consider these broader issues in addition to the key information provided in the relevant cost analysis in Exhibit 10–11.

Profitability Analysis: Keep or Drop Products or Services

An important aspect of management is the regular review of product profitability. This review should address such issues as:

- Which products are most profitable?
- Are the products priced properly?
- Which products should be promoted and advertised most aggressively?
- Which product managers should be rewarded?

These and related issues can be addressed through relevant cost analysis. To illustrate, we use Windbreakers, Inc., a manufacturer of sport clothing. Windbreakers manufactures three jackets—"Calm" (for a light breeze), and "Windy" and "Gale" for sterner weather conditions. Management has requested an analysis of the Gale product due to its low sales and low profitability (see Exhibit 10–12).

The analysis of Gale should begin with the important observation that the $3.61 fixed cost per unit is irrelevant for the analysis of the current profitability of the three products. Because the $171,500 total fixed costs are unchangeable in the short run, they are irrelevant for this analysis. That is, no changes in product mix, including the deletion of Gale, would affect the total fixed costs to be expended in the coming year. The fact that the fixed costs are irrelevant is illustrated by comparing the contribution income statements in Exhibit 10–13, which assumes Gale is deleted, and Exhibit 10–14, which assumes that Gale is retained. The only changes caused by the deletion of Gale are the loss of Gale's revenues and the elimination of variable costs. Thus, the deletion of Gale causes

Exhibit 10–12	Sales and Cost Data for Windbreakers, Inc.			
	Calm	**Windy**	**Gale**	**Total**
Units sold last year	25,000	18,750	3,750	47,500
Price	$30.00	$32.00	$40.00	
Relevant costs				
Unit variable cost	25.00	27.00	36.00	
Unit contribution margin	5.00	5.00	4.00	
Nonrelevant fixed costs	3.61	3.61	3.61	$171,500
Income per unit	1.39	1.39	.39	

Exhibit 10–13	Contribution Income Statement Profitability Analysis: Gale Deleted		
	Calm	**Windy**	**Total**
Sales	$750,000	$600,000	$1,350,000
Relevant costs			
Variable cost	625,000	506,250	1,131,250
Contribution margin	125,000	93,750	218,750
Nonrelevant costs			
Fixed cost			171,500
Net income without Gale			$ 47,250

Exhibit 10–14	**Contribution Income Statement** **Profitability Analysis: Gale Retained**			
	Calm	**Windy**	**Gale**	**Total**
Last year's sales	$750,000	$600,000	$150,000	$1,500,000
Relevant costs				
Variable cost	625,000	506,250	135,000	1,266,250
Contribution margin	125,000	93,750	15,000	233,750
Nonrelevant costs				
Fixed cost				171,500
Net income with Gale				$ 62,250

Exhibit 10–15	**Profitability Analysis: Including Traceable Advertising Costs**			
	Calm	**Windy**	**Gale**	**Total**
Last year's sales	$750,000	$600,000	$150,000	$1,500,000
Relevant costs				
Variable cost	625,000	506,250	135,000	1,266,250
Contribution margin	125,000	93,750	15,000	233,750
Other relevant costs				
Advertising	20,375	15,000	5,000	40,375
Contribution after all				
relevant costs	104,625	78,750	10,000	193,375
Nonrelevant costs:				
Fixed cost				$131,125
Net income with Gale				$ 62,250

a reduction in total contribution margin of $4.00 per unit of Gale times 3,750 units of Gale sold, or $15,000, and a corresponding loss in net income. Alternatively:

Benefit: Saved variable costs of Gale	$135,000	($36 × 3,750)
Cost: Opportunity cost of lost sales of Gale	(150,000)	($40 × 3,750)
Decrease in profit from decision to drop Gale	($ 15,000)	($ 4 × 3,750)

Assume that further analysis shows $40,375 of the $171,500 fixed costs are advertising costs to be spent directly on each of the three products—$ 20,375 for Calm, $15,000 for Windy, and $5,000 for Gale. The remainder of the fixed costs, $171,500 − $40,375 = $131,125, are not traceable to any of the three products and are therefore allocated to each product as before. Because advertising costs are directly traceable to the individual products, and assuming the advertising plans for Gale can be canceled without additional cost, the $5,000 of advertising costs for Gale should be considered a relevant cost in the decision to delete Gale. This cost will differ in the future.

For the proper analysis, see Exhibit 10–15, which shows the total contribution margin after all relevant costs for Gale is $10,000; therefore, the loss associated with deleting Gale would be $10,000. Note that the loss is $5,000 less than that shown in Exhibits 10–13 and 10–14 because a portion of what was considered fixed cost, the $5,000 of advertising cost for Gale, is now correctly identified as a relevant, and therefore avoidable, cost. The contribution after all relevant costs in Exhibit 10–15 is a useful measure of the short-term profitability of each product line. For example, the loss of the entire sales of Windy would have a profit impact of $78,750; for Calm, the impact would be $104,625.

Strategic Issues

In addition to the relevant costs analysis, the decision to keep or drop a product line should include relevant strategic factors, such as the potential that the loss of one product line will affect sales of another. For example, some florists price cards, vases, and other related items at or below cost to better serve and attract customers to the most profitable product, the flower arrangements.

Other important factors include the potential effect on overall employee morale and organizational effectiveness if a product line is deleted. Moreover, managers should consider the sales growth potential of each of the products. Will a product considered for deletion place the firm in a strong competitive position sometime in the future? A particularly important consideration is the extent of available production capacity. If production capacity and production resources (such as labor and machine time) are limited, consider the relative profitability of the products, and the extent to which the products require different quantities of these production resources.

Profitability Analysis: Evaluating Programs

LEARNING OBJECTIVE 6 ▶
Use relevant cost information in evaluating programs.

Managers use the concept of relevant cost analysis to measure the financial effectiveness of programs or projects. A good example of such an analysis is the evaluation of the Health and Weight Loss Program, a primary component of the Health Management Program at Kimberly-Clark Corporation in Neenah, Wisconsin.[4] Kimberly-Clark has traced costs to this program and measured the dollar benefits of the program in three categories: (1) health care savings, (2) sick leave and absenteeism savings, and (3) program fees for the participating employees. Exhibit 10–16 shows the relevant cost analysis of the profitability of this program.

Profitability Analysis: A Not-for-Profit Example

The Triangle Women's Center (TWC) uses relevant cost analysis to determine the desirability of new services. TWC provides several services to the communities in and around a large southeastern city. TWC has not offered child care services but

---

BusinessWeek

 Is Ford Taurus on the Road to Success?

(Continues from page 343)

A: It's too early to tell …

The redesign of the 1996 Taurus significantly improved the car, but at the same time made the car more costly and less competitive with the Camry. Redesigning for lower costs, along with the fall of the yen against the dollar in the late 1990s, helped Toyota set competitive prices on the Camry. Cost-conscious car buyers moved to the Camry, which in 1997 replaced the Taurus as the best-selling car in the United States. Does this mean Ford's strategy failed? That's yet to be seen.

Ford's success in the Taurus was built in part on huge fleet sales to corporations and auto rental agencies. Ford recognized the need to attract younger buyers, those who predominantly bought import cars. The strategy of the redesign was to achieve parity with the imports, especially the Camry, and to get a larger share of the individual buyer's market where higher profits could be obtained.

Ford's strategy sacrificed short-term profitability for the long-term potential to meet the competition in customer acceptance of the import autos, particularly the Camry and Honda Accord. In order to succeed, Ford will have to achieve cost savings that will make it more competitive in price, as customers are now favoring the lower-priced imports over the improved Taurus.

For further reading, see the following sources: "The Shape of a New Machine," *Business Week,* July 24, 1995, and "Autos," *Business Week,* January 12, 1998.

---

[4] The application is described in Kenneth J. Smith, "Differential Cost Analysis Techniques in Occupational Health Promotion Evaluation," *Accounting Horizons,* June 1988, pp. 58–66.

Exhibit 10–16	Health and Weight Loss Program Income Statement for Kimberly-Clark Corporation	

Revenues		
Health care cost savings		$ 9,416
Sick leave absenteeism savings		4,973
Program fees		2,168
Total revenues		$16,557
Relevant costs		
Program materials		112
Consultant's salary		7,804
Total relevant costs		$ 7,916
Contribution after relevant costs		$ 8,641

Exhibit 10–17	Triangle Women's Center Analysis of Child Care Services

Relevant costs	
Salary of director	$29,000
Salary for two part-time assistants	18,000
Variable costs for 20 children at $60 per month	14,400
Total relevant costs	$61,400
Total funding	
United Way	$25,000
City Council	30,000
	$55,000
Expected deficit in the first year	$ 6,400

Sales Commissions at IBM

The use of relevant costs in the analysis of product profitability is important also in motivating and rewarding the sales staff. Since the best measure of short-term profitability is *contribution after relevant costs,* this measure also should be used for sales commissions—to motivate the sales staff to sell the most profitable products, that is, those with the highest contribution margin. The common approach of using sales revenue as a basis for commissions is not consistent with the goal of improving profitability. IBM Corporation recognized the importance of this idea by tying 60 percent of its sales commissions to the *profit* generated by the products sold.

The IBM plan also attends to important strategic factors, such as customer satisfaction. To make sure that salespeople don't simply push for sales of high-margin products, IBM is linking the remaining 40 percent of their commissions to customer satisfaction. Thus the compensation plan makes salespeople think like managers—their focus is on profits and customer satisfaction, as is the focus of top management.

Source: Based on information in *Business Week,* February 7, 1994, p. 110.

has received a large number of requests in recent years. Now TWC is planning to add this service. The relevant cost analysis follows. TWC expects to hire a director ($29,000) and two part-time assistants ($9,000 each) for the child care service. Also, variable costs per child are estimated at $60 per month. No other costs are relevant because none of the other operating costs of TWC are expected to change. TWC expects to receive funding of $25,000 from the United Way plus $30,000 from the city council. The analysis for the first year of operation is shown in Exhibit 10–17 that assumes 20 children, the maximum number, will be enrolled in the service.

The TWC analysis shows that the child care service will have a deficit of approximately $6,400 in the first year. Now TWC can decide whether the deficit can be made up from current funds or by raising additional funds. Relevant cost analysis provides TWC a useful method to determine the resource needs for the new program.

> ### Relevant Cost Analysis Used Incorrectly in Not-for-Profit Organizations
>
> 1. The Massachusetts State Workfare program trains welfare parents to enter the workforce and pays for the child care costs incurred during the training period. An analysis of the program showed that the benefits in removing participants from welfare exceeded the costs of supporting the participants during the training period. However, a closer look showed that many of the participants in the training programs would have left welfare, even without the training. Thus, the calculation of relevant benefits was flawed. It assumed that the training program was the only relevant factor in removing the participants from welfare, which turned out not to be the case.
>
> 2. Relevant cost analysis also was used incorrectly in the cost/benefit analysis of replacing an existing hospital with a new hospital. The revenue currently earned by the present hospital was incorrectly counted as a relevant benefit of the new hospital, when only the incremental revenue of the hospital should have been counted. The current revenue of the present hospital is irrelevant because it would have continued if the old hospital had not been replaced.
>
> **Source:** Based on information from R. J. Herzlinger and Denise Nitterhouse, *Financial Accounting and Managerial Control for Nonprofit Organizations* (Cincinnati: South-Western Publishing, 1994), p. 468.

MULTIPLE PRODUCTS AND LIMITED RESOURCES

LEARNING OBJECTIVE 7 ▶
Analyze relevant cost decisions with multiple products and limited resources.

The preceding profitability analysis was simplified by using a single product and assuming sufficient resources to meet all the demands. The analysis changes significantly when there are two or more products and limited resources. The revised analysis is considered in this section. We continue the example of Windbreakers, Inc., except we assume the Calm product is manufactured in a separate plant under contract with a major customer. Thus, the following analysis focuses *only on the Windy and Gale products,* which are manufactured in a single facility.

A key question for the profitability analysis is, What is the most profitable sales mix for Windy and Gale? If there are no production constraints, the answer is clear; we manufacture what is needed to meet demand for both Windy and Gale. However, when demand exceeds production capacity, management must make some trade-offs about the quantity of each product to manufacture, and therefore, what demand is unmet. The answer comes from considering the production possibilities given by the production constraints. There are two important cases: (1) one production constraint, and (2) two or more production constraints.

One Production Constraint

Assume the production of Windy and Gale requires an automated sewing machine to assemble the jackets, and that this production activity is a limited resource—sales demand for the two products exceeds the capacity on the three automated sewing machines in the plant. Each machine can be run up to 20 hours per day five days per week, or 400 hours per month, which is its maximum capacity allowing for maintenance. This gives 1,200 (3 × 400) available hours for sewing each month. Assume further that the machine requires three minutes to assemble a Windy and two minutes to assemble a Gale. We calculate the contribution for each jacket and for each hour of production in Exhibit 10–18.

Windbreakers will produce the jacket that provides the greatest income, the Gale jacket. While the Windy jacket provides the greatest contribution margin per jacket, the greatest contribution per hour of available machine time is provided by Gale ($100/hour for Windy; $120/hour for Gale). Machine time is a limited resource, so the machine-time-based contribution provides the relevant analysis. Because only 1,200 hours of machine time are available per month, and the Gale jacket requires less machine time, more Gale jackets can be made in a month than Windy jackets. The maximum number of Windy jackets is 24,000 jackets per month (1,200

Exhibit 10–18	Windbreakers Data for the Windy and Gale Plant (One Constraint: The Sewing Machine)		
		Windy	**Gale**
Since:			
Contribution margin/unit		$5	$4
Sewing time per jacket		3 min	2 min
Then, because sewing time is limited to 1,200 hours per month, we determine the contribution margin per machine-hour:			
Number of jackets per hour		20	30
(60 min/3 min = 20; 60/2 = 30)			
Contribution margin per hour		$100	$120
(20 × $5; 30 × $4)			
Also, the maximum production for each product, given the 1,200-hour constraint			
For Windy: 1,200 × 20		24,000	
For Gale: 1,200 × 30			36,000

Exhibit 10–19	Windbreakers Production and Sales Possibilities (One Production Constraint—The Sewing Machine)

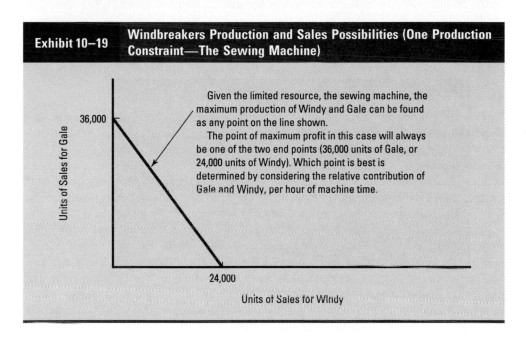

Given the limited resource, the sewing machine, the maximum production of Windy and Gale can be found as any point on the line shown.

The point of maximum profit in this case will always be one of the two end points (36,000 units of Gale, or 24,000 units of Windy). Which point is best is determined by considering the relative contribution of Gale and Windy, per hour of machine time.

hours times 20 jackets per hour, at 3 minutes per jacket). Similarly, if the sewing machine were devoted entirely to Gale jackets, then 36,000 jackets per month could be produced (1,200 times 30 jackets per hour).

There is a continuous trade-off possibility between the extreme situations—zero output of Windy and 36,000 of Gale, and 24,000 of Windy and zero of Gale. These production and sales mix possibilities can be shown graphically—all the sales mix possibilities are represented by all possible points on the line in Exhibit 10–19. The line in Exhibit 10–19 can be determined by the high-low method explained in Chapter 7:

$$\text{Slope} = -36,000/24,000 = -3/2$$

$$\text{Intercept} = 36,000$$

The line in Exhibit 10–19 is thus given by:

$$\text{Units of Gale} = 36,000 - 3/2 \times \text{Units of Windy}$$

To illustrate, assume Windbreakers is producing 12,000 units of Windy. Then:

$$\text{Units of Gale} = 36,000 - 3/2 \times 12,000 = 18,000$$

361

To see that this production mix uses all available capacity of 1,200 hours:

$$\text{Hours for Gale} + \text{Hours for Windy} = \text{Total Hours}$$

$$\frac{\text{Units of Gale}}{\text{Number of Gales/Hour}} + \frac{\text{Units of Windy}}{\text{Number of Windys/Hour}} = \text{Total Hours}$$

$$18{,}000/30 + 12{,}000/20 = 1{,}200 \text{ hours}$$

Now that we know the production possibilities, we can determine the best product mix. Note from Exhibit 10–18 that Gale has the highest overall contribution margin, $120 per hour (30 jackets per hour × $4 per jacket). Because 1,200 machine-hours are available per month, the maximum total contribution from the production possibilities is to produce only Gale and achieve the total contribution of 1,200 × $120 = $144,000 per month. If Windbreakers were to produce and sell only Windy, the maximum total contribution margin would be 1,200 hours × $100 per hour (20 jackets per hour × $5 per jacket), or $120,000 per month, a $24,000 reduction over the contribution from selling only Gale. *Thus, when there is only one production constraint and excess demand, it is generally best to focus production and sales on the product with the highest contribution per unit of scarce resource.* Of course, it is unlikely in a practical situation that a firm would be able to adopt the extreme position of deleting one product and focusing entirely on the other. However, the previous results show the value of considering a strong focus on the more profitable product based on the contribution per unit of a scarce resource.

Two or More Production Constraints

When the production process requires two or more production consraints, the choice of sales mix involves a more complex analysis, and in contrast to one production constraint, the solution can include both products. To continue with the Windbreakers case, assume that in addition to the automated sewing machine, a second production activity is required. The second activity inspects the completed jackets, adds labels, and packages the completed product. This operation is done by 40 workers, who can complete the operation for the Windy jacket in 15 minutes and for the Gale jacket in 5 minutes (because of differences in material quality, less inspection time is required for the Gale jacket). This means that 60/15 = 4 Windy jackets can be completed in an hour, or 60/5 = 12 Gale jackets. Because of the limited size of the facility, no more than 40 workers can be employed effectively in the inspection and packaging process. These employees work a 40-hour week, which means 35 hours actually performing the operation, given time for breaks, training, and other tasks. Thus, 5,600 hours (40 workers × 35 hours × 4 weeks) are available per month for inspecting and packing.

The maximum output per month for the Windy jacket is 5,600 hours times 4 jackets per hour = 22,400 jackets completed per month. Similarly, the maximum output for the Gale jacket is 67,200 jackets. This information is summarized in Exhibit 10–20.

Look at the production possibilities for two constraints in Exhibit 10–21. Here, in addition to the production possibilities for machine time, we show the production possibilities for inspection and packing. The shaded area indicates the range of possible outputs for both Gale and Windy. Note that it is not possible to produce beyond the 22,400 units of Windy, because all 40 workers inspecting and packing full time would not be able to handle more than 22,400 units of Windy, even though the sewing machine is capable of producing 24,000 units. Similarly, though Windbreakers could pack and ship 67,200 units of Gale by having all 40 packers work full time on Gale, it could only manufacture 36,000 of Gale because of limited capacity on the sewing machine.

The production planner can determine the best production mix by examining all the possible production–sales possibilities in the shaded area, from 36,000 on the Gale axis to point A, and then to point 22,400 on the Windy axis. It can be shown that the sales mix with the highest contribution is one of these three points—

Exhibit 10–20	Windbreakers Data for the Windy and Gale Plant (The Second Constraint: Inspecting and Packing)		
		Windy	**Gale**
Since:			
	Contribution margin/unit	$5	$4
	Inspection and packaging time per jacket	15 min	5 min
Then:			
	Number of jackets per hour	4	12
	Contribution margin per hour (4 × $5; 12 × $4)	$20	$48
Also:			
	The maximum production for each product, given the 5,600-hour constraint		
	For Windy: 5,600 × 4	22,400	
	For Gale: 5,600 × 12		67,200

Exhibit 10–21	Windbreakers Production and Sales Possibilities (Two Production Constraints—Sewing Machine and Inspection)

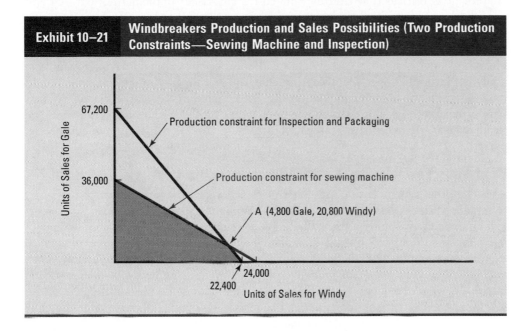

36,000 of Gale, point A, or 22,400 units of Windy. The solution achieved by examining the graph indicates the highest profit mix is for production at point A, 20,800 units of Windy and 4,800 units of Gale.[5]

Strategic Issues

The analysis of sales mix and production constraints is a useful way for managers to understand both how a difference in sales mix affects income and how production limitations and capacities can significantly affect the proper determination of the most profitable sales mix. Similar to the examples in Chapter 5 for the theory of constraints, this method helps managers identify the production constraints and manage them to most effectively utilize scarce resources.

---

[5] The point A, 20,800 for Windy and 4,800 for Gale, is obtained by solving the two equations:

$$15W + 5G = 35 \times 40 \times 4 \times 60 = 336,000 \text{ minutes}$$
$$3W + 2G = 400 \times 3 \times 60 = 72,000 \text{ minutes}$$

Linear programming, a mathematical method, permits the solution of much larger problems involving many products and production activities. A full presentation of the method is beyond the scope of this text. It is covered in most operations research and mathematical programming texts, for example, F. S. Hillier and G. J. Lieberman, *Introduction to Mathematical Programming*, (New York: McGraw-Hill, 1990). The analysis of profitability with multiple products and limited resources is applied in a practical case by Robert J. Campbell, "Pricing Strategy in the Automotive Glass Industry," *Management Accounting*, July 1989, pp. 26–34.

BEHAVIORAL AND IMPLEMENTATION ISSUES

LEARNING OBJECTIVE 8 ▶
Discuss the behavioral
and implementation issues
in using relevant cost
information.

The behavioral and implementation issues of relevant cost analysis include (1) management incentives under relevant cost analysis that distort effective decision making, (2) the incentive to replace variable costs with fixed costs, and (3) the tendency to focus on irrelevant information. Of particular importance are the strategic issues introduced early in the chapter and well summarized in Henry Ford's quote. We are directly concerned with the broader strategic issues involved in each decision context.

Managerial Incentives

A well-known problem in business today is the tendency of managers to focus on short-term goals and neglect the long-term strategic goals, because their compensation is based on short-term accounting measures such as net income. This issue has been raised by many critics of relevant cost analysis. As noted throughout the chapter, it is critical that the relevant cost analysis be supplemented by a careful consideration of the long-term, strategic concerns of the firm. Without strategic considerations, management could improperly use relevant cost analysis to achieve a short-term benefit and potentially suffer a significant long-term loss. For example, a firm might choose to accept a special order because of a positive relevant cost analysis, without properly considering that the nature of the special order could have a significant negative impact on the firm's image in the marketplace, and perhaps a negative effect on sales of the firm's other products. The important message for managers is to keep the strategic objectives in the forefront in any decision situation.

Replacing Variable Costs with Fixed Costs

Another potential incentive associated with relevant cost analysis is for managers to replace variable costs with fixed costs. This might happen if mid-level and lower-level managers realize that since they rely on relevant cost analysis, upper management tends to overlook fixed costs. Lower-level managers might choose to replace their assets and other productive resources in such a way as to reduce variable costs, even though fixed costs are increased significantly. For example, a new machine might replace direct labor. Here the overall costs increase because of the cost of the machine, though variable costs under the manager's control decrease and the contribution margin increases. Management's proper goal is to maximize contribution margin and to minimize fixed operating costs at the same time. Relevant cost analysis should be used as a tool to maximize contribution, and managers also must develop methods to manage fixed costs.[6]

Focus on Irrelevant Factors

Another possible problem area of cost analysis is that managers may fail to properly identify relevant costs. In particular, it is common for untrained managers to include irrelevant, sunk costs in their decision making.[7] Similarly, many managers fail to see that allocated fixed costs are irrelevant. When fixed costs are "unitized" in this manner, many managers tend to improperly find them relevant. It is easier for these managers to see the fixed cost as irrelevant when it is given in a single sum.

These are illustrations of the pervasive biases present in many managers' decision making. To repeat, effective use of relevant cost analysis requires careful iden-

---

[6] D. L. Heerema and R. L. Rogers ("Is Your Cost Accounting System Benching Your Team Players?" *Management Accounting*, September 1991, pp. 35–40) give useful illustrations of the improper use of relevant cost analysis in the automobile industry, the military, and elsewhere.

[7] Prospect theory suggests that people underweight alternatives that are uncertain in comparison to alternatives known to be certain. The theory has been offered as a potential explanation of the tendency people have to include sunk costs in decision making. See D. Kahneman and A. Tversky, "Prospect Theory: An Analysis of Decision under Risk," *Econometrica*, March 1979, pp. 263–92; and Glen Whyte, "Escalating Commitment to a Course of Action: A Reinterpretation," *Academy of Management Review* 11, no. 2 (1986), pp. 311–21.

tification of relevant costs, those future costs that differ among decision alternatives, and to correctly recognize sunk costs and unit fixed costs as irrelevant in the short term.

SUMMARY

Relevant costs are defined as those future costs that differ among the decision maker's options. The principle of relevant cost decision making can be applied in a number of specific decisions involving manufacturing, service, and not-for-profit organizations. The decisions considered in the chapter included (1) the special order decision, for which the relevant costs are the direct manufacturing costs and any incremental fixed costs; (2) the make, lease, or buy decision, for which the relevant costs are the direct manufacturing costs, lease costs, and any avoidable fixed costs; (3) the decision to sell before or after additional processing, for which the relevant costs are the additional processing costs; (4) the decision to keep or drop a product or service, for which the relevant costs are the direct costs and those fixed costs that change if the product or service is deleted; and (5) evaluating programs and projects.

When two or more products or services are involved, another type of decision arises—determining the correct product mix. The solution depends on the number of production activities that are at full capacity. If there is one production constraint, then the answer is to produce and sell as much as possible of the product that has the highest contribution margin per unit of time on the constrained activity. If there are two or more constrained activities, the analysis uses graphical and quantitative methods to determine the correct product mix.

The key limitations of relevant cost analysis have caused it to be used in ways that do not give sufficient attention to the long-term, strategic objectives of the firm. Too strong a focus on relevant costs can cause the manager to overlook important opportunity costs and strategic considerations. Other limitations include the tendency to replace variable costs with fixed costs when relevant cost analysis is used in performance evaluation, and the pervasive tendency of people not to correctly view fixed costs as sunk but to view them as somehow controllable and relevant.

KEY TERMS

Bill of materials   352

Contract manufacturing   355

Relevant costs   344

SELF-STUDY PROBLEMS

(For solutions, please turn to the end of the chapter.)

1. SPECIAL ORDER PRICING

HighValu Inc. manufactures a moderate-price set of lawn furniture (a table and four chairs) that it sells for $225. It currently manufactures and sells 6,000 sets per year. The manufacturing costs include materials of $85 and labor of $45 per set. The overhead charge per set is $35 that consists entirely of fixed costs.

HighValu is considering a special purchase offer from a large retail firm, which has offered to buy 600 sets per year for three years at a price of $150 per set. HighValu has the available plant capacity to produce the order, and no other orders or profitable alternative uses of the plant capacity are expected.

Required   Should HighValu accept the offer?

2. THE MAKE-OR-BUY DECISION

Assume that HighValu Inc., as just described, is currently purchasing the chair cushions for its lawn set from an outside vendor for $15 per set. HighValu's chief operations officer wants an analysis of the comparative costs of manufacturing these cushions, to see whether bringing the manufacturing in-house would save the firm some money. Additional information shows that if HighValu were to manufacture the cushions, the materials cost would be $6 and the labor cost would be $4 per set, and in addition, cutting and sewing equipment would have to be purchased, which would add $10,000 to annual fixed costs.

Required Should HighValu make the cushions or continue to purchase them from the vendor?

3. PROFITABILITY ANALYSIS

Consider again the Windbreakers firm described in the text. Suppose Windbreakers determines that deleting the Gale product line will release production capacity so that additional units of Windy can be manufactured. Assume that, as described in the text, the two production constraints are the automated sewing machine and the inspection and packing operation. The automated sewing machine can make 20 Windys or 30 Gales per hour. As before, the inspection operation requires 15 minutes for a Windy (4 per hour) and 5 minutes for a Gale (12 per hour). Currently, 3,750 Gales and 18,750 Windys are being manufactured and sold. Sales projections show that sales of Windy could be increased to 30,000 units if additional capacity were available.

Required

1. If Windbreakers deletes Gale entirely, how many units of Windy can be manufactured with the released capacity?

2. What is the dollar effect on net income if Windbreakers deletes production and sale of Gale and uses the released capacity for production and sale of Windy?

3. What other factors should be considered in the decision to delete Gale and use the released capacity to produce additional units of Windy?

QUESTIONS

10–1 What are relevant costs? Provide a few examples for the decision to repair or replace a piece of equipment.

10–2 Define outsourcing and explain how relevant cost analysis is used in the outsourcing decision.

10–3 List at least four different decisions wherein relevant cost analysis can be used effectively.

10–4 How does relevant cost analysis differ between manufacturing and service firms?

10–5 Define contract manufacturing and provide a couple of examples.

10–6 List four to six strategic factors that are often important in the make-or-buy decision.

10–7 Explain what is meant by nonrelevant cost and provide two examples.

10–8 Why are variable costs usually more relevant than fixed costs in short-term decision making?

10–9 Give an example of how a firm can decrease variable costs by increasing fixed costs.

10–10 Provide an example of how a firm can decrease fixed costs by increasing variable costs.

10–11 How do short-term evaluations affect a manager's incentives and performance?

10–12 List four or five important limitations of relevant cost analysis.

10–13 How do strategic factors affect the proper use of relevant cost analysis?

10–14 List some of the behavioral and implementation problems to be anticipated in the use of relevant cost analysis.

10–15 How is relevant cost analysis affected by the presence of one production constraint? Two or more production constraints?

10–16 What is the relationship, if any, between relevant cost analysis and cost-volume-profit analysis?

10–17 Explain why depreciation is a nonrelevant cost.

PROBLEMS

10–18 **RELEVANT COSTS** FasTech Inc., a computer consulting firm, is considering the replacement of a computer network (hardware and software) that originally cost $250,000; it has accumulated depreciation of $180,000, and an estimated salvage value of $10,000. FasTech has the opportunity to purchase a new network that would cost $300,000, have a five-year useful life, and have an estimated salvage value of $50,000.

Service

Required What are the relevant costs in the decision to replace the computer network?

10–19 **RELEVANT COSTS** Carla Mays is the owner of HeadBeans Corporation, which processes coffee beans. Mays has engaged a consulting firm to help her decide whether the corporation should upgrade its facilities. The consultants gave her the following information and their bill:

Old machinery	
Original cost	$300,000
Accumulated depreciation	$250,000
Machine salvage value	$ 20,000
Useful life	2 years
New machinery	
Purchase price	$400,000
Salvage value	$ 60,000
Useful life	6 years
Upgraded old machine	
Cost to upgrade	$200,000
Salvage value	$ 10,000
Useful life	4 years
Consulting Fee	$ 5,000

Required What are the relevant costs associated with Mays's decision whether to keep her old machinery, upgrade it, or replace it?

10–20 **RELEVANT COST PROBLEMS**

1. **Make or Buy** Pitch Inc. manufactures machine parts for aircraft engines. CEO Bucky Walters is considering an offer from a subcontractor to provide 2,000 units of product OP89 for a price of $104,000. If Pitch does not purchase these parts from the subcontractor it must produce them in-house with these costs:

Costs per Unit	
Direct materials	$26
Direct labor	16
Variable overhead	6
Fixed overhead	4

In addition to these costs, if Walters produces part OP89, he would also have a retooling and design cost of $8,000.

Required Should Pitch Inc. accept the offer from the subcontractor? Why or why not?

2. **Disposal of Assets** A company has an inventory of 2,000 different parts for a line of cars that has been discontinued. The net book

value of inventory in the accounting records is $50,000. The parts can be either remachined at a total additional cost of $25,000 and then sold for a total of $30,000, or scrapped for $2,500. What should be done?

3. **Replacement of Asset**   A boat, costing $90,000 and uninsured, was wrecked the first day it was used. It can be either disposed of for $9,000 cash and replaced with a similar boat costing $92,000, or rebuilt for $75,000 and be brand-new as far as operating characteristics and looks are concerned. What should be done?

4. **Profit from Pocessing Further**   Almond's Corporation manufactures products A, B, and C from a joint process. Joint costs are allocated on the basis of relative sales value at the end of the joint process. Additional information for Almond's Corporation:

	A	B	C	Total
Units produced	12,000	8,000	4,000	24,000
Joint costs	$144,000	$60,000	$36,000	$240,000
Sales value after joint processing	?	?	60,000	400,000
Additional costs for further processing	28,000	20,000	12,000	60,000
Sales value if processed further	280,000	120,000	80,000	480,000

Required   Should product B be processed further and then sold?

5. **Make Or Buy**   Strawn Company needs 20,000 units of a part to be used in the production of one of its products. If Strawn buys the part from McMillan Company instead of making it, Strawn could not use the released facilities in another manufacturing activity. Fifty percent of the fixed overhead will continue regardless of CEO Donald Mickey's decision. The cost data are

Cost to make the part	
Direct materials	$30
Direct labor	11
Variable overhead	19
Fixed overhead	20
	$80
Cost to buy the part	$75

Required   Determine which alternative is more attractive to Strawn and by what amount.

6. **Selection of the most Profitable Product**   Video Company produces two basic types of video games, Bash and Gash. Pertinent data for Video Company:

	Bash	Gash
Sales price	$200	$140
Costs:		
Direct materials	56	26
Direct labor	30	50
Variable factory overhead*	50	25
Fixed factory overhead*	20	10
Marketing costs (all variable)	28	20
Total costs	$184	$131
Operating income	$ 16	$ 9

*Based on labor hours

The video craze is at its height so that either Bash or Gash alone can be sold to keep the plant operating at full capacity. However, there is insufficient labor capacity in the plant to meet the combined demand for both games. Bash and Gash are processed through the same production departments.

Required Which product should be produced? Briefly explain your answer.

10–21 **SPECIAL ORDER ANALYSIS** VanderMeer Corporation recently was approached by Tihon Company regarding manufacturing a special order of 4,000 units of product CRB2B. Tihon would reimburse VanderMeer for all direct production costs plus 35 percent. The *per-unit* data are

Unit sales price	$28
Variable manufacturing costs	13
Variable marketing costs	5
Fixed manufacturing costs	4
Fixed marketing costs	2

VanderMeer would have a retooling cost of $10,000, but there is otherwise sufficient capacity in the plant to manufacture the order. No marketing costs would be incurred for this special order.

Required Should the special order be accepted, or should the regular units be produced and sold?

10–22 **SPECIAL ORDER ANALYSIS** Marquard Industries produces high-quality automobile seat covers. It has been successful in the industry due to its quality, though all of its customers, the automakers, are very cost conscious and negotiate for price cuts on all large orders. Noting that the auto supply business is becoming increasingly competitive, Marquard is looking for a way to meet the challenge. It is negotiating with JepCo, Inc., a large mail-order auto parts and accessories retailer, for a large order of seat covers. Much of Marquard's business is seasonal and cyclical, fluctuating with the varying demands of the large automakers. Marquard would like to keep its plants busy throughout the year, by reducing these seasonal and cyclical fluctuations. Keeping the flow of product moving through the plants at a steady level is helpful in keeping costs down; extra overtime and machine setup and repair costs are incurred when production levels fluctuate. JepCo has agreed to a large order, but only if the price is reduced to $38. The special order can be produced within available capacity. Marquard prepared these data:

 *Strategy*

Next month's operating information		
Sales	10,000	units
Sales price per unit	$45	
Per unit costs:		
Variable manufacturing costs	25	
Variable marketing costs	8	
Fixed manufacturing costs	6	
Fixed marketing costs	3	
Special order information		
Sales	2,000	units
Sales price per unit	$38	

There are no variable marketing costs associated with the special order, but Ruby Marquard, the president of the firm, has spent $2,000 during the past three months trying to get JepCo to purchase this special order.

Required

1. How much will the special order change Marquard Industries' total operating income?
2. How might the special order fit into Marquard's competitive situation?

10–23 **SPECIAL ORDER** BallCards Inc. manufactures baseball cards sold in packs of 15 in drugstores throughout the country. It is the third leading firm in an industry with four major firms. BallCards has been approached by Pennock Cereal Inc., which would like to order a special edition of cards

 *Strategy*

to use as a promotion with its cereal. BallCards would be solely responsible for the design and production of the cards. Pennock would like to order 25,000 sets and has offered $23,750 for the total order. Each set will consist of 33 cards. BallCards Inc. currently produces cards in sheets of 132.

Production, marketing, and other costs (per sheet)	
Direct materials	$1.20
Direct labor	.20
Variable overhead	.40
Fixed overhead	.15
Variable marketing	.10
Fixed marketing	.35
Insurance, taxes, and administrative salaries	.10
Costs for special order:	
Design	$2,000
Other fixed costs	5,500

No marketing costs would be incurred for the special order. BallCards has the capacity to accept this order without interrupting regular production.

Required

1. Should the special order be accepted? Support your answer with appropriate computations.

2. What are the important competitive issues in the decision?

Ethics

10–24 **SPECIAL ORDER** GrassPlus Inc. manufactures lawn fertilizer and often receives special orders from agricultural research groups because of the quality of its fertilizers. For each type of fertilizer sold, each of the bags is carefully filled to have the precise mix of fertilizer components that are advertised for that type of fertilizer. GrassPlus's operating capacity is 22,000 one-hundred-pound bags per month, and it currently is selling 20,000 bags. The firm just received a request for a special order of 5,000 one-hundred-pound bags of fertilizer for $125,000 from APAC, a research company. The production costs would be the same, though delivery and other packaging and distribution services would cause a one-time $2,000 cost for GrassPlus. The following information has been provided:

Sales and production cost data for 20,000 bags		
Sales price	$28	per unit
Variable manufacturing costs	17	
Variable marketing costs	2	
Fixed manufacturing costs	4	
Fixed marketing costs	2	
Special order		
Sales price	$125,000	
Delivery services	2,000	

There would be no marketing costs associated with the special order.

Required

1. Should GrassPlus accept the special order? Explain why or why not.

2. What would be the change in operating income if the special order is accepted?

3. Suppose that after GrassPlus accepts the special order, it finds that unexpected production delays mean it cannot supply all 5,000 units from its own plants and meet the promised delivery date. It can provide the same materials by purchasing them in bulk from a competing firm. The materials would then be packaged in GrassPlus bags to complete the order. GrassPlus knows the competitor's materials are very good quality, but it cannot be sure

that the quality meets its own exacting standards. There is not enough time for careful testing to determine the quality of the competitor's product. What should GrassPlus do?

10-25 SPECIAL ORDER; OPPORTUNITY COSTS   Bears Inc. is working at full production capacity producing 20,000 units of a unique product. Manufacturing costs per unit for the product are

Direct materials	$ 4
Direct labor	6
Manufacturing overhead	10
Total manufacturing cost	$20

The unit manufacturing overhead cost is based on a variable cost per unit of $4 and fixed costs of $120,000. The nonmanufacturing costs, all variable, are $8 per unit and the sales price is $40 per unit.

A customer, the Sports Headquarters Company (SHC), has asked Bears Inc. to produce 4,000 units of a modification of the new product. This modification would require the same manufacturing processes. Sports Headquarters Co. has offered to share equally the nonmanufacturing costs with Bears Inc. The modified product would sell for $30 per unit.

Required

1. Should Bears produce the special order for SHC? Why or why not?

2. Suppose Bears Inc. had been working at less than full capacity producing 16,000 units of the product at the time the modified product offer was made. What is the minimum price Bears Inc. should accept for the modified product under these conditions?

10-26 MAKE OR BUY   Three Stars Inc. manufactures prefabricated houses. The firm's president, Michelle Brown, is interested in determining whether it would be better to manufacture the doors used in the houses or to buy them from a supplier. The following information, based on production of 500 doors, has been gathered to help determine the best option:

	Costs per Unit
Direct materials	$ 35
Direct labor	50
Variable overhead	10
Fixed overhead	
Administrative salaries	$ 7
Property taxes	2
Insurance	5
Utilities	5
Miscellaneous fixed overhead	6
Total costs	$120

Of the fixed overhead accounts, $5 per unit of miscellaneous fixed overhead would be saved if the doors were purchased from a supplier, and all other fixed costs would be allocated elsewhere. The cost to purchase 500 doors would be $55,000.

Required   Should Three Stars Inc. make or purchase the doors? What is the savings per unit?

10-27 MAKE OR BUY   (Continuation of 10-26)   Three Stars Inc. does not sell as many prefabricated homes in the winter as it does in the spring, summer, and fall. In the winter builders usually are unable to construct them due to inclement and unpredictable weather. Thus, in the winter months Brown is always faced with the option of closing down her facility and laying off her employees or using her facilities for an alternative purpose. The best alternative use involves constructing doors

 *Ethics*

and selling them to retail hardware and home center stores. Last year's financial data for the sale of doors included this information:

Revenues	$250,000
Direct costs	225,000
Fixed overhead costs	75,000
Net loss	($50,000)

Required Should Three Stars continue to manufacture the doors? Include both quantitative and qualitative reasons. What responsibility does Three Stars have to its employees about providing year-around employment, if any?

10–28 **MAKE OR BUY; SPECIAL ORDER** Winona Johnson is the president of Johnson Manufacturing, which manufactures coats. She is trying to decide whether to make 3,000 men's overcoats or purchase them from a subcontractor to fill a rush order she just received. There are no marketing costs on the rush order. Acceptance of the rush order would not necessitate any premium pay for overtime work or additional fixed costs. Johnson Manufacturing has supplied the following:

Cost Data for Men's Overcoats	
Sales price	$42
Direct materials	15
Direct labor	9
Fixed manufacturing overhead	3
Variable manufacturing overhead	6
Variable marketing costs	3
Fixed marketing costs	1
Fixed administrative overhead	2

Required

1. At what purchase price per unit would Johnson be indifferent whether her firm manufactured the coats or purchased them from a subcontractor?

2. What strategic factors should influence Johnson's decision regarding manufacturing the coats or purchasing them?

10–29 **MAKE OR BUY; SPECIAL ORDER** Lester-Smith Company manufactures three wood construction components: wood trusses, wood floor joists, and beams. The plant is operating at full capacity. It can produce 200 trusses, 1,000 joists, and 600 beams per month and sells everything it produces. The monthly revenues and expenses for the three products are

Sales revenues	
Trusses	$ 12,000
Joists	40,000
Beams	90,000
Total revenue	$142,000
Expenses	
Variable cost	
Trusses	$ 10,000
Joists	24,000
Beams	48,000
Total variable cost	$ 82,000
Fixed cost allocated:	
Trusses	$ 4,000
Joists	12,000
Beams	24,000
Total fixed cost	40,000
Total cost	$122,000
Total profit	$ 20,000

Required

1. The firm makes wood trusses mainly to satisfy certain customers by offering a full line of wood components. Lately, it has had a problem making a profit on the trusses and is considering buying them from another manufacturer at $55 a truss. Should the firm buy these trusses or continue to make its own?

2. Lester-Smith has an opportunity to produce an additional 400 beams for a customer at a price of $100 each. If it accepted this special order, the firm would not be able to produce trusses because the plant is operating at full capacity. Should the firm take on this special order?

10–30 **MAKE OR BUY** The Crown Company must decide whether to make or buy part 128PC. Although Crown's idle equipment could be used to produce up to 10,000 units of the part, the company presently needs only 7,000 units. The following shows the estimated cost of making part 128PC.

Allocated general manufacturing overhead	$50,000	
Depreciation on existing equipment	15,000	
Annual additional setup and maintenance costs	20,000	
Total fixed costs	$85,000	
Direct materials	$ 5	
Direct labor	6	
Variable overhead	4	
Total variable manufacturing costs	$15	per unit

Reuten Company offers to sell part 128PC to the Crown Company for $20 per unit.

Required Determine whether Crown should make or buy the part, and explain why.

10–31 **SELL OR PROCESS FURTHER** SNAPA Auto Parts makes a muffler/pipe assembly for a cost of $15.60 each ($10.00 fixed and $5.60 variable). SNAPA has the opportunity to modify this assembly to a more-fuel-efficient model for an additional cost of $5.35 and sell it for $85.00. The muffler/pipe assembly is now selling to customers for $68.00 each. Variable selling and distribution costs would be the same at $25 per unit. Projected sales volume is 60,000 units per year for the new model, an increase of 30,000 units over the current sales level. Labor resources are very tight at present but machine capacity is underutilized.

Required

1. Should SNAPA modify the existing assembly or turn down the extra 60,000 units/year?

2. What would be the increase/decrease in profit if SNAPA modifies the assembly?

3. How will the labor constraint affect the decision?

10–32 **DISCONTINUING A DIVISION** Leonard Financial Services is planning to discontinue one of its divisions that has a contribution margin of $20,000. In addition, $50,000 of Leonard's corporate overhead is allocated to the division. Of the $50,000, $5,000 can be eliminated if the division is discontinued.

Required What would be the increase or decrease in Leonard Industries's pretax income if this division is discontinued?

10–33 **PROFITABILITY ANALYSIS** The Maitax Corporation, located in Buffalo, New York, is a retailer of high-tech products known for their excellent quality and durability. Recently the firm conducted an analysis of one of

Service

its product lines that has only two products, RAM and ROM. The sales for ROM are decreasing and the purchase costs are increasing. The firm might discontinue ROM and sell only RAM.

At Maitax Corporation the fixed costs are allocated to products on the basis of sales revenue. When the president of Maitax saw the income statement, he agreed that ROM should be dropped. If ROM is dropped, sales of RAM are expected to increase by 10 percent next year; the firm's cost structure will remain the same.

	RAM	ROM
Sales	$180,000	$260,000
Variable cost of goods sold	70,000	130,000
Contribution margin	$110,000	$130,000
Expenses:		
Fixed corporate costs	50,000	75,000
Variable selling and administration	18,000	50,000
Fixed selling and administration	12,000	21,000
Total expenses	80,000	146,000
Net income	$ 30,000	$(16,000)

Required

1. Find the expected change in annual net income if ROM is discontinued and only RAM is sold.
2. What strategic factors should be considered?

10–34 **PROFITABILITY ANALYSIS; SCARCE RESOURCES** Graybill Company has met all production requirements for the current month and has an opportunity to produce additional units of product with its excess capacity. Unit selling prices and unit costs for three models of one of its product lines are as follows:

	No Frills	Standard Options	Super Deluxe
Selling price	$30	$35	$50
Direct materials	9	11	10
Direct labor ($5/hour)	5	12	15
Variable overhead	3	7	11
Fixed overhead	6	3	5

Variable overhead is charged to products on the basis of direct labor dollars, while fixed overhead is charged to products on the basis of machine-hours.

Required

1. If Graybill Company has excess machine capacity and can add more labor as needed (neither machine capacity nor labor is a constraint), the excess production capacity should be devoted to producing which product or products?
2. If Graybill Company has excess machine capacity but a limited amount of labor time, the excess production capacity should be devoted to producing which product or products?

10–35 **PROFITABILITY ANALYSIS; JUST-IN-TIME** The controller for Walsh Manufacturing is trying to implement some of the characteristics of a just-in-time (JIT) inventory system. She has accumulated data on Walsh's present inventory system and obtained some projections and estimates of what the results of a JIT system would be.

Estimated annual direct material requirements	360,000
Unit cost for orders of 100,000+ units	$23.00
75,000+ units	23.50
50,000+ units	24.00
25,000+ units	24.50
less than 25,000	25.00
Inventory holding cost (per unit/per month)	.75

Walsh currently purchases 120,000 units every four months. Under a JIT system Walsh would purchase 30,000 units every month. The monthly inventory schedule and the controller's estimate for a JIT system follow:

Average Inventory Balance

Month	Current System	JIT System
January	105,000	15,000
February	75,000	15,000
March	45,000	15,000
April	15,000	15,000
May	105,000	15,000
June	75,000	15,000

(Assume this trend continues throughout the year.)

Required   Which system should Walsh use, and why?

10–36   **MAKE OR BUY; REVIEW OF LEARNING CURVES**   The Henderson Equipment Company has produced a pilot run of 50 units of a recently developed cylinder used in its finished products. The cylinder has a one-year life, and the company expects to produce and sell 1,650 units annually. The pilot run required 14.25 direct labor-hours for the 50 cylinders, averaging .285 direct labor-hours per cylinder. Henderson has experienced an 80 percent learning curve on the direct labor-hours needed to produce new cylinders. Past experience indicates that learning tends to cease by the time 800 parts are produced.

Henderson's manufacturing costs for cylinders are

Direct labor	$12.00	per hour
Variable overhead	10.00	per hour
Fixed overhead	16.60	per hour
Material	4.05	per unit

When pricing products, Henderson factors in selling and administrative expenses at $12.70 per direct labor-hour. All selling and administrative expenses except sales commissions (2 percent of sales) are independent of sales or production volume.

Henderson has received a quote of $7.50 per unit from the Lytel Machine Company for the additional 1,600 cylinders needed. Henderson frequently subcontracts this type of work and has always been satisfied with the quality of the units produced by Lytel.

Required

1. If the cylinders are manufactured by Henderson Equipment Company, determine
   a. The average direct labor-hours per unit for the first 800 cylinders (including the pilot run) produced. Round calculations to three decimal places.
   b. The total direct labor-hours for the first 800 cylinders (including the pilot run) produced.
2. After completing the pilot run, Henderson Equipment Company must manufacture an additional 1,600 units to fulfill the annual requirement of 1,650 units. Without regard to your answer in requirement 1, assume that

- The first 800 cylinders produced (including the pilot run) required 100 direct labor-hours.
- The 800th unit produced (including the pilot run) required .079 hour.

Calculate the total manufacturing costs for Henderson to produce the additional 1,600 cylinders required.

3. Determine whether Henderson Equipment Company should manufacture the additional 1,600 cylinders or purchase the cylinders from Lytel Machine Company. Support your answer with appropriate calculations.

(CMA Adapted)

Strategy

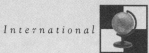

International

10-37 SPECIAL ORDER; STRATEGY; INTERNATIONAL The Sommers Company, located in southern Wisconsin, manufactures a variety of industrial valves and pipe fittings that are sold to customers in nearby states. Currently, the company is operating at about 70 percent capacity and is earning a satisfactory return on investment.

Management has been approached by Glasgow Industries Ltd. of Scotland with an offer to buy 120,000 units of a pressure valve. Glasgow Industries manufactures a valve that is almost identical to Sommers' pressure valve; however, a fire in Glasgow Industries' valve plant has shut down its manufacturing operations. Glasgow needs the 120,000 valves over the next four months to meet commitments to its regular customers; the company is prepared to pay $19 each for the valves.

Sommers' product cost for the pressure valve, based on current attainable standards, is

Direct materials	$ 5.00
Direct labor (.5 hr per valve)	6.00
Manufacturing overhead (1/3 variable)	9.00
Total manufacturing cost	$20.00

Additional costs incurred in connection with sales of the pressure valve are sales commissions of 5 percent and freight expense of $1.00 per unit. However, the company does not pay sales commissions on special orders that come directly to management.

In determining selling prices, Sommers adds a 40 percent markup to product cost. This provides a $28 suggested selling price for the pressure valve. The marketing department, however, has set the current selling price at $27 to maintain market share.

Product management believes that it can handle the Glasgow Industries order without disrupting its scheduled production. The order would, however, require additional fixed factory overhead of $12,000 per month in the form of supervision and clerical costs.

If management accepts the order, 30,000 pressure valves will be manufactured and shipped to Glasgow Industries each month for the next four months. Shipments will be made in weekly consignments, FOB shipping point.

Required

1. Determine how many additional direct labor hours would be required each month to fill the Glasgow Industries order.

2. Prepare an analysis showing the impact of accepting the Glasgow Industries order.

3. Calculate the minimum unit price that Sommers' management could accept for the Glasgow Industries order without reducing net income.

4. Identify the strategic factors that Sommers Company should consider before accepting the Glasgow Industries order.

5. Identify the factors related to international business that Sommers Company should consider before accepting the Glasgow Industries order.

(CMA Adapted)

10–38 PROFITABILITY ANALYSIS; REVIEW OF MASTER BUDGET; STRATEGY

Strategy

RayLok Incorporated has invented a secret process to improve light intensity and manufactures a variety of products related to this process. Each product is independent of the others and is treated as a separate profit/loss division. Product (division) managers have a great deal of freedom to manage their divisions as they think best. Failure to produce target division income is dealt with severely; however, rewards for exceeding one's profit objective are, as one division manager described them, lavish.

The DimLok Division sells an add-on automotive accessory that automatically dims a vehicle's headlights by sensing a certain intensity of light coming from a specific direction. DimLok has had a new manager in each of the three previous years because the predecessor manager failed to reach RayLok's target profit. Donna Barnes has just been promoted to manager and is studying ways to meet the current target profit for DimLok.

The two profit targets for DimLok for the coming year are $800,000 (20 percent return on the investment in the annual fixed costs of the division) plus an additional profit of $20 for each DimLok unit sold. Other constraints on division operations are

- Production cannot exceed sales because RayLok's corporate advertising program stresses completely new product models each year, even though the newness of the models may be only cosmetic.

- The DimLok selling price may not vary above the current selling price of $200 per unit but may vary as much as 10 percent below $200.

- A division manager can elect to expand fixed production or selling facilities; however, the target objective related to fixed costs is increased by 20 percent of the cost of such expansion. Furthermore, a manager may not expand fixed facilities by more than 30 percent of existing fixed cost levels without approval from the board of directors.

Barnes is now examining data gathered by her staff to determine whether DimLok can achieve its target profits of $800,000 **and** $20 per unit. A summary of these reports shows the following:

- Last year's sales were 30,000 units at $200 per unit.

- The present capacity of DimLok's manufacturing facility is 40,000 units per year, but capacity can be increased to 80,000 units per year by an increase in annual fixed costs of $1,000,000.

- Present variable costs amount to $80 per unit, but DimLok's vendors are willing to offer raw material discounts amounting to $20 per unit, beginning with unit number 60,001.

- Sales can be increased up to 100,000 units per year by committing large blocks of product to institutional buyers at a discounted unit price of $180. However, this discount would apply only to sales in excess of 40,000 units per year.

Barnes believes these projections are reliable, and she is now trying to determine what DimLok must do to meet the profit objectives assigned by RayLok's Board of Directors.

Required

1. Determine the dollar amount of DimLok's present annual fixed costs.

2. Determine the number of units that DimLok must sell to achieve both profit objectives. Be sure to consider all constraints in determining your answer.

3. Without regard to your answer in requirement 2, assume Barnes decides to sell 40,000 units at $200 per unit and 24,000 units at $180 per unit. Prepare a master budget income statement for DimLok showing whether Barnes's decision will achieve DimLok's profit objectives.

4. Assess DimLock's competitive strategy.

5. Identify the strategic factors that DimLok should consider.

(CMA Adapted)

SOLUTIONS TO SELF-STUDY PROBLEMS

1. Special Order Pricing

The key to this exercise is to recognize that the variable manufacturing costs of $130 ($85 material and $45 labor) are the relevant costs, and that the fixed overhead costs, since they will not change, are irrelevant.

Thus, the correct decision is to accept the offer, since the price of $150 exceeds the variable manufacturing cost of $130. HighValu also should consider strategic factors. For example, will the three-year contract be desirable? Perhaps there will be a change in the market conditions so that HighValu will have more profitable uses of the capacity in the coming years. Will the special order enhance or diminish the firm's competitive position?

2. The Make-or-Buy Decision

The relevant costs for this analysis are the outside purchase cost of $15 per set versus the make costs of $10 per set ($6 material plus $4 labor), and $10,000 annual fixed costs.

First, determine the amount of annual savings from the reduction in variable costs for the make option:

$$6,000 \text{ annual sales} \times (\$15 - \$10) = \$30,000 \text{ annual savings}$$

Second, compare the savings in variable costs to the additional fixed costs of $10,000 per year. The net savings, and advantage to make rather than buy, is $20,000 ($30,000 − $10,000).

HighValu also should consider relevant strategic factors, such as the quality and reliability of the supply for the cushion. How will the released capacity at the HighValu plant be employed? Are any employees' jobs affected?

3. Probability Analysis

1. To determine the number of Windys that can be manufactured if the 3,750 units of Gale are no longer produced, we consider the capacity released for each of the two constraints.

   For the automated sewing machine: The machine produces 20 Windys per hour or 30 Gales per hour, so that the number of Windys that could be produced from the released capacity of Gale is

$$3,750 \times 20/30 = 2,500 \text{ Windys}$$

   For the inspection and packing operation: The operation requires 15 minutes for Windy (4 per hour) and 5 minutes for Gale (12 per hour), so the number of Windys that could be inspected and packed in the released time is

$$3{,}750 \times 4/12 = 1{,}250 \text{ Windys}$$

In this case, the inspection and packing is the effective limitation, so that if Gale is deleted, we can produce *1,250 Windys* with the released capacity.

2. If 3,750 units of Gale are replaced with 1,250 units of Windy, the proper relevant cost analysis would consider the contribution margins of the two products:

	Windy	Gale
Unit contribution margin	$ 5	$ 4
Units sold (giving up 3,750 units of Gale gives 1,250 of Windy, per part 1)	1,250	3,750
Total contribution margin	$6,250	$15,000

Thus the deletion of Gale and replacement with Windy would reduce the total contribution margin by $8,750 ($15,000 − $6,250).

3. Since the effect on total contribution is significant (as shown in part 2), Windbreakers should continue to make Gale. Other factors to consider are

   a. At existing sales levels of 18,750 of Windy and 3,750 of Gale, Windbreakers is operating at full capacity; if there are additional sales opportunities for Windy, the firm should consider adding to available capacity so that the current sales of Gale can be made plus the additional sales of Windy. The analysis of the cost/benefit of adding additional capacity is best addressed through the techniques of capital budgeting as described in Chapter 11.

   b. The effect of the loss of Gale on the image of the firm and therefore the potential long-term effects on the sales of Windy.

   c. The long-term sales potential for Gale. Will the sales of Gale likely exceed the current 3,750 level in future years?

Capital Budgeting 11

After studying this chapter, you should be able to . . .

Identify major processes in capital investment decisions **1**

Select appropriate data for analyzing capital investments including total **2** initial outlays, net cash flow returns throughout the useful life of the investment, and impact of the final disposition of the investment on cash flow return

Use capital budgeting techniques including the payback period, accounting rate of return, net **3** present value, and internal rate of return methods to assess capital investments and explain the advantages and limitations of these techniques

Identify the underlying assumptions of the discounted cash flow methods and use these methods **4** properly in evaluating capital investments

Discuss the relationships between strategic cost management and capital budgeting **5**

Identify behavioral factors in capital budgeting decisions **6**

Jean Marc Giboux/Gamma Liaison

My interest is in the future because I am going to spend the rest of my life there.

CHARLES FRANKLIN KETTERING

Businesses and organizations often are required to commit large sums to projects with expenditures and benefits expected to stretch well into the future. Such projects are known as **capital investments** and include purchasing new equipment, constructing new facilities, developing and introducing new products, and expanding into new sales territories.

A good capital investment generates cash or decreases cash outlays over its projected lifetime to earn back the capital committed to the project and a desirable profit. A poor capital investment leads to financial hardship, ties up resources for extended periods, curtails opportunities available to the firm, and dooms the organization.

Successful firms often are the result of good capital investment by visionary entrepreneurs. The Ford Motor Company grew by leaps and bounds in the early twentieth century as a result of Henry Ford's visionary investment in new manufacturing techniques at the time. Many venture capitalists have profited handsomely by making capital investments in new ideas. Conversely, the demise of an organization often results from one or a series of poor capital investments. The soundness of capital investment decisions is critical to organizations, whether profit-making or not-for-profit. The process of making capital investment decisions often is referred to as capital budgeting.

A **capital investment** requires committing a large sum of funds to projects with expenditures and benefits expected to stretch well into the future.

CAPITAL BUDGETING PROCESSES

A capital budgeting process consists of three successive steps: project identification, evaluation, and periodic postaudit and review.

◄ LEARNING OBJECTIVE 1
Identify major processes in capital investment decisions.

Project Identification and Definition

The starting point of a capital budgeting process is project identification and definition. A majority of the firms responding to a survey of capital budgeting practices regarded this step as the most critical and the most difficult for a successful capital investment.[1]

BusinessWeek

? ### Can Olympic Hosts and Sponsors Grab the Gold?

When it comes to being a host city or corporate sponsor of the Olympics, the long-term result can be a boon ... or a bust. Not only do host cities face possible destruction to their image (e.g., Munich, 1972; Atlanta, 1996), but they may also suffer economic setbacks (e.g., Montreal, 1976). Of course, that's the negative side. Other host cities have benefited enormously from this large investment, building up their city's image and infrastructure, and increasing recognition of corporate sponsors (e.g., Seoul, 1988; Barcelona, 1992). How large is the investment made by host cities? For the Atlanta 1996 games, an estimated $1.57 billion was raised.

Q: What's the risk of this particular investment? How can hosts and sponsors ensure a gold-medal return? *Find out on page 416 of this chapter.*

---

[1] Of the three stages of capital budgeting process, 51 percent of the firms participating in a survey consider the project identification and definition stage to be the most critical stage for a successful capital investment. Forty-four percent of them also consider this step to be the most difficult. James M. Fremgen, "Capital Budgeting Practices: A Survey," *Management Accounting* 54 (May 1973), pp. 19–25.

Initial proposals for capital investments often come from the local or branch level. This is especially true for equipment replacement or improvement or projects requiring only marginal change from current operations. In contrast, higher management often initiates major changes such as construction of new plants, adoption of just-in-time or flexible manufacturing systems, development of new products, and expansion into new territory.

Management must define a clear boundary of an investment project. It must not only know what a project will do but also have a good understanding of what the project will not do. Lack of a clear definition of a proposed investment project increases the difficulty of estimating revenues, costs, and cash flows. Furthermore, a project without a clear boundary may grow into a huge undertaking that exceeds the resources available to the firm or organization.

Evaluation and Selection

Evaluation of capital investments requires projection of revenues or benefits, costs, and cash flows for the entire life cycle of the project. Knowing the benefits and costs of a project gives management a grasp of its impact on the firm's resources and a way to gauge whether the firm is capable of absorbing the cost. The benefits and costs include both financial and nonfinancial aspects.

Uncertainty about future events often makes estimating revenues or benefits, costs, and cash flows of a capital investment project a difficult task, especially for projects with long lives. Changes in technology; shifts in market demand; actions of other firms in the same or a related industry; and the effects of international, national, regional, and local economies are among the general factors to be considered. In addition, specific factors relating to the project must be identified. Many techniques are available to help us make projections. (See Chapter 7 on cost behavior patterns and cost estimation and Chapter 10 on decision making.)

Financial effects are not the only consideration in evaluating and selecting capital investments. Firms undertake capital investment projects for reasons other than their financial benefits to the organization. Among the nonfinancial reasons for committing major capital expenditures are the safety of employees or the public; employees' convenience or comfort; social concerns; pollution control; legal requirements; contractual commitments; and protection of existing programs, product lines, or market shares.[2]

The critical importance of one or more nonfinancial factors in undertaking a capital investment does not imply that there is no need to conduct a financial evaluation of the project. Even though a firm needs to add pollution abatement equipment to satisfy a legal requirement, it still needs a financial analysis to know the costs and benefits of the project.

Monitoring and Review

A successful capital investment requires continual monitoring and review of the project. Making careful evaluations before selecting a project is only the beginning step. As the project progresses, situations change, new variables surface, and fresh opportunities arise. The firm needs to modify the original plan, incorporate new developments, and alter the course of action, if necessary, to attain the best result for the firm.[3]

---

[2] Nonfinancial reasons often lead to using urgency as a criterion in capital investment projects. Such a concern is especially prevalent in projects undertaken by government. For example, a bridge is rebuilt because the existing bridge was hazardous. A highway is built because the legislator from the district convinces the Department of Transportation that it is urgent to have a new highway through the area. For more examples, see "Report to the Congress of the United States by the Comptroller General," in *Federal Capital Budgeting: A Collection of Haphazard Practices* (Washington, DC: General Accounting Office, 1981).

[3] Twenty-three percent of the firms participating in the capital budgeting survey conducted by James Fremgen consider this stage to be the most critical to the success of an investment.

DATA FOR CAPITAL BUDGETING

Data used for capital investment decisions differ from data generated for accounting records and reports in two respects: their characteristics and the factors relevant to decisions.

Characteristics of Capital Budgeting Data

The characteristics of the data used for capital budgeting differ from those used for financial reporting purposes in three ways: the data period, the measurement object, and the time horizon. Exhibit 11–1 contrasts data characteristics for capital budgeting and those for financial reporting.

Data Period

Two underlying concepts of financial reporting data are periodicity and accrual basis accounting. *Periodicity* requires firms to record and report accounting data at specified regular intervals: monthly, quarterly, or annually. *Accrual basis* accounting requires firms to include in the accounting data and the financial statements for the period all figures pertaining to revenues earned and expenses incurred in a period. Receipt or disbursement of cash is not a factor in determining the period to which the amount is to be included and reported.

Most capital budgeting techniques, however, require evaluating an investment over its complete life cycle, not in one accounting period. A decision to introduce a new product, for example, needs to consider not only the investment required to develop and market the product initially but also the expected revenues and costs during all the years the product is to be on the market. An accrual basis accounting system typically separates the life cycle of the new product into several time periods and focuses on only one period at a time.

Measurement Object

A capital budget focuses on cash flows, not on accrual-based revenues and expenses. Thus, a noncash sale in a period is not included in the capital budget for that period if the firm receives no cash from the sale. Similarly, an expense is not included in capital budgeting if no cash is paid for that expense during that period. In contrast, an accrual-based accounting procedure includes both the noncash sale and the unpaid expense in the period.

Time Horizon

Another difference between capital budgeting data and financial reporting data is in their time horizon. Capital budgeting data focus on future transactions and events, while financial reporting data are based on historical transactions and events. A proper financial report is one that records and reports all transactions and events that have occurred during the period and the consequences of past actions. In contrast, historical data are seldom included in capital budgeting; they are included only to the extent of their effects on current and future cash flows.

Relevant Factors in Capital Budgeting

The ultimate concern of a firm and its investors is its cash position. The relevant factor in capital budgeting, therefore, is the cash flows affected by the capital investment.

◄ **LEARNING OBJECTIVE 2**
Select appropriate data for analyzing capital investments including total initial outlays, net cash flow returns throughout the useful life of the investment, and impact of the final disposition of the investment on cash flow return.

Exhibit 11–1	Capital Budgeting and Financial Reporting Data Characteristics	
Characteristic	**Capital Budgeting**	**Financial Reporting**
Data period	Life of the project	Annual
Measurement object	Cash flows	Accrual revenues and expenses
Time horizon	Future events and transactions	Historical events and transactions

A business firm's managers expect capital investments to improve periodic profits. This interest in profit leads many firms to focus their attention on periodic net income when they consider capital investments. Although net income is a measure of profit, overemphasizing the importance of net income alone can lead to erroneous capital investment decisions because net income is not a good measure of return on a capital investment.

Both the periodicity reporting requirement and the arbitrary process involved in determining net income lessen the usefulness of net income as an objective criterion. Net income is the result of applying selected accounting methods to transactions. The net income of a period can be substantially different when the firm chooses to use different, yet equally acceptable, accounting methods.

Cash flow is the relevant measure of return in capital budgeting. Items affecting cash flows are incorporated in capital budgeting whether they are accounting revenues or expenses of the period. A noncash item, such as depreciation expense, is included in capital budgeting calculations only to the extent that it affects tax obligation cash flows.

Depreciation expenses are not cash payments and are by themselves irrelevant in capital budgeting. This is true even though they are expenses for income determination purposes. A depreciation expense is relevant to a capital budget only because it has an effect on the payment of income taxes. In the same vein, the entire amount of cash paid in a period to purchase an asset is a relevant item for capital budgeting purposes, even though the entire amount may not be an expense for that period in computing net income.

Cash Flows

A capital investment often starts with a cash outflow that is a payment or commitment of funds. Depending on the objectives of the investment, the investment return can decrease cash expenditures, generate cash inflows, or both. Funds also may be needed for more capital investments during the life of the project.

Cash flows occur at three stages of the capital investment project:

1. **Project initiation**   Cash flows at project initiation include:
   - Cash outflows to acquire the investment and to initiate operations.
   - Cash commitments for working capital needed for the operations.
   - Cash inflow from or outflow for the disposal of the replaced or displaced assets.

2. **Project operation**   Cash flows during the operation of a capital investment include:
   - Outflows for operating expenditures and additional capital investment after the initial investment.
   - *Commitments for* additional working capital needed in operations.
   - *Inflows from cash* generated by the investment (revenues and cash savings) and cash released from working capital no longer needed in operations.

3. **Final disposal**   Cash flows at final disposal include:
   - Cash inflows from or outflows for the disposal of the investment.
   - Cash inflows from release of working capital no longer committed to the investment.

Determining Cash Flows in Capital Budgeting

Cash received increases the cash available to the organization, while cash paid or committed decreases the cash available to the organization. The immediate effect a cash receipt or cash payment or commitment has on cash flows often is referred to as the *direct effect*. An event or transaction often changes the tax obligations of a tax-paying organization. The effect an event or transaction has on the amount of an organization's tax payment for the period is the *tax effect*. The total of the direct effect and the tax effect is the *net effect* on cash flow.

Effects of Cash Flow

A. **Direct Effect:** Cash Receipt, Cash Payment, or Cash Commitment

B. **Tax Effect:** Changes in Tax Payments

C. **Net Effect:** Direct Effect + Tax Effect

A $10,000 cash revenue *for a for-profit firm* in the 30 percent tax bracket represents a net cash inflow of $7,000, not $10,000, because the additional $10,000 revenues increase the taxes of the firm by $3,000. A $6,000 cash payment for expenses by the same firm has a net cash outflow of $4,200, because the $6,000 expense decreases the firm's tax expenses by $1,800.

Noncash revenues or expenses also can affect cash flows through tax effects. Because tax liability is figured on accrual-based income, a noncash revenue such as a credit sale does not increase the amount of cash available, but it does increase taxable income for the period, which increases the amount of cash needed for taxes. Thus, noncash revenue *decreases*, not increases, cash available to the firm. The amount of the decrease is the increase in taxes due to the noncash revenue.

Noncash revenue of $10,000 for a firm in the 30 percent tax bracket reduces by $3,000 the cash available to the firm. Although the firm receives no cash from a noncash revenue, it nevertheless increases the tax liability of the firm by $3,000. Therefore, for a taxpaying organization, *a noncash revenue is a cash outflow*, not a cash inflow.

An increase in expenses, on the other hand, decreases taxable income, which reduces the taxes to be paid for the period. A noncash expense, therefore, increases, not decreases, cash flow. Depreciation is a noncash expense that does not require a cash payment in the period the expense is recognized. The expense, however, reduces the tax payment of the firm for the period. This increases cash available for other uses.

Activities at various stages of a capital investment differ and have varying effects on cash flows. Cash flows occur at the initial investment, during project operation, and at the final disposal of capital investments.

Initial Investment

Activities at the inception of a capital investment often involve:

1. Acquisition of the investment.
2. Commitment of working capital needed for operating the investment.
3. Disposal of assets replaced.

Effects of Initial Investment Acquisition on Cash Flow   At the initial investment stage, cash payments for constructing or buying a new facility; purchasing, installing, and testing new equipment; and training personnel are some of the activities that entail cash outflows. The bulk of the direct cash outflow for an investment usually occurs at the beginning of the investment. In capital budgeting the time when initial cash outflows occur for the acquisition is referred to as *time 0 (or year 0)*.

Investment cash outflows also have tax effects. Acquisition costs such as hiring or training of personnel may be treated as expenses in the period they are incurred. An increase in expense reduces income taxes. Decreases in tax payments reduce cash outflows or increase cash inflows.

Another effect on cash flows derived from the investment is depreciation expense. Depreciation expenses themselves have no immediate cash or tax effect. As a noncash expense that decreases operating (and taxable) income in subsequent periods, the depreciation expense of the investment reduces the tax obligation in subsequent years. A reduction in the tax obligation is a cash inflow for a tax-paying organization.

In Exhibit 11–2 we summarize the cash flow effects often entailed during a project's initiation stage.

Smith Company manufactures high-pressure pipe for deep-sea oil drilling. The firm is considering the purchase of a milling machine for $500,000. The cost of installation will be approximately $5,000. Testing and adjusting before placing the machine in production will cost $10,000. After its expected useful life of four years, the equipment is expected to sell for $100,000. Machine removal and site cleaning expenses will cost the firm $20,000. The firm uses straight-line depreciation with an estimated salvage value of $75,000 for the investment. The controller expects the firm to be in the 34 percent federal income tax bracket and the state to levy 6 percent income taxes.

The first segment (year 0) of Exhibit 11–3 shows that the initial cash outflow for the investment will be $515,000. The firm uses straight-line depreciation for the equipment.[4] The depreciation expense for this equipment therefore is $110,000 per year for the next four years, as shown in Exhibit 11–3. The depreciation expense itself has no direct effect on cash flow because the expense requires no cash payment. The depreciation expense, however, does have a tax effect; it acts as a tax shield. It decreases the taxable income of the firm and reduces the tax liability. For a for-profit firm in the 40 percent tax bracket (34 percent federal, 6 percent state income taxes), a $110,000 decrease in net income reduces tax liability by $44,000. The firm enjoys this reduced tax liability, a cash inflow, each year of the life of the capital project.

Effects of Working Capital Commitment on Cash Flow *Working capital* is the excess of cash, receivables, and inventory over current liabilities needed for the operations. An investment in plant and equipment often calls for additional working capital to pay for added payroll and other expenditures, inventories of materials, and supplies required for operations of the investment.

Committing funds to working capital means that funds are not available for other uses. Restricting funds for working capital is a cash outflow in the year the firm com-

---

Exhibit 11–2	Effects of Investment Acquisition on Cash Flow

Direct Effect (Outflow)

- Cost of purchasing, constructing, or manufacturing buildings and equipment.
- Cost of installing and testing equipment.
- Hiring and training personnel.

Tax Effect (Inflow)

- Decrease in income taxes for acquisition costs treated as expenses.
- Decrease in income taxes due to depreciation on the investment.

---

[4] Most spreadsheet programs provide a way to calculate depreciation expense. For example, Lotus and Microsoft EXCEL calculate depreciation expense using the straight-line depreciation method if you enter (preceded with @ for Lotus or = for EXCEL):

SLN (Cost, Salvage Value, Number of Years)

The function for depreciation expense using sum-of-the-years'-digits method is

SYD (Cost, Salvage Value, Number of Years, Period)

where *period* is the year for which depreciation expense is desired. You will enter *1,* for example, if you want to know the depreciation expense for the first year.

The function for depreciation expense using the double-declining balance method is

DDB (Cost, Salvage Value, Number of Years, Period, factor)

where *factor* is the rate at which the balance declines. If factor is omitted, it is assumed to be *2* (the double-declining balance method).

To calculate depreciation expenses using other methods such as the ACRS (Accelerated Cost Recovery System) or MACRS (Modified Accelerated Cost Recovery System), refer to the depreciation schedule described for each method in the Internal Revenue Code (see the appendix to this chapter).

Exhibit 11–3	Effects of Asset Acquisition on Cash Flow

Year 0

Cost of equipment	$500,000
Installation cost	5,000
Testing and adjusting	10,000
Total cash *outflow* in year 0	$(515,000)

Year 1 through Year 4

Total cost for depreciation purposes	$515,000
Expected salvage value at the end of useful life	75,000
Total to be depreciated	$440,000
Years of useful life for depreciation purposes	4
Depreciation expense per year, straight-line basis	$110,000
Income tax rate (34% ⊦ 6%)	40%
Total cash *inflow* (tax deduction) each period due to depreciation expense	$ 44,000

Alternative Schematic Form

			Time Period		
Description	Year 0	Year 1	Year 2	Year 3	Year 4
Cost of equipment	$(500,000)				
Installation cost	(5,000)				
Testing and adjusting	(10,000)				
Tax saving on depreciation expense		$44,000	$44,000	$44,000	$44,000
Total	$(515,000)	$44,000	$44,000	$44,000	$44,000

Exhibit 11–4	Direct Effects on Cash Outflow in Year 0

Cost of equipment, installing, and testing	$(515,000)
Working capital needed for operations	$(200,000)
Tax effect	0
Net investment (total cash outflow in year 0)	$(715,000)

mits the funds. Committing working capital, however, directly affects only cash flow. There are no indirect tax implications because the commitment of working capital has no effect on either revenue or expense and, therefore, no effect on taxes.

Not all investments require additional working capital. The amount of working capital needed for some operations may even decrease as a result of an investment. The amount of such a decrease represents a cash inflow in the period in which the firm reduces its need for working capital. Just-in-time and computer-integrated manufacturing systems are investments that may decrease working capital. Firms investing in these manufacturing systems often reduce their need for inventory—raw materials, work-in-process, or finished goods. These firms enjoy cash inflows from the reduced working capital because investment in new manufacturing technologies increases their operating efficiency through reduced inventory levels and other reductions in operating costs.

The milling machine the Smith Company is considering would require $200,000 in addition to increases in accounts payable and other current liabilities to cover inventories needed for operations and accounts receivable expected to arise from the investment. This $200,000 tied up in inventories and accounts receivable will not be available for other uses during operations. Earmarking the funds has the direct effect of increasing the cash *outflow* for the investment in year 0 from $515,000 to $715,000 (see Exhibit 11–4).

Effect of Disposal of the Assets Replaced on Cash Flow Disposing of assets it no longer needs has both direct and tax effects on a firm's cash flows.

Effect of Asset Disposal on Cash Flow

DIRECT EFFECT

- **Inflow:** Proceeds from disposal
- **Outflow:** Expenditures for equipment removal and site restoration

TAX EFFECT

- **Inflow:** Tax effect on loss of the disposal
- **Outflow:** Tax effect on gain of the disposal

Exhibit 11–5   Net Effect of Asset Disposal on Cash Flow

Terminology

Net Book Value:	Original cost	− Accumulated depreciation
Net Proceeds:	Proceeds from disposal	− Expenditures for removal and restoration
Gain on Disposal:	Net proceeds > Net book value	
Loss on Disposal:	Net proceeds < Net book value	

Net Cash Effect (Inflow)

For Gain: Net proceeds − (Gain on disposal × Tax rate)
For Loss: Net proceeds + (Loss on disposal × Tax rate)

Direct effects are cash proceeds the firm receives from the sale or disposal of an asset net of cash payments made for its disposal. *Tax effects* derive from gains or losses from the disposal. A firm gains if the net proceeds from disposing of an asset exceed the net book value of the asset. The net book value of an asset is the difference between the original cost of the asset and the accumulated depreciation on the asset. A gain on the disposal of an asset is taxable. The net cash inflow from the disposal is decreased by the tax liability on the gain.

A firm suffers a loss if the net proceeds from disposing of an asset are less than the net book value of the asset. A loss reduces the tax obligation of the firm. The effect of the disposal on cash inflow is the sum of (1) the net cash proceeds from the disposal and (2) the savings in taxes due to the loss from the disposal. Exhibit 11–5 summarizes how to determine the net effect of asset disposal on cash flow.

The new machine enables the Smith Company to dispose of another milling machine acquired seven years ago for $320,000. The accumulated depreciation for the old machine is $200,000 as of the replacement date. A used equipment broker has found a buyer willing to pay $80,000 for the old milling machine. Smith Company, however, must pay all the removal expenses. The broker's commission is 10 percent of the selling price. Smith Company estimates that removal of the equipment will cost about $2,000.

Subtracted from the $80,000 selling price for the equipment are the $8,000 commission for the broker and $2,000 equipment removal expenses. The net proceeds to the Smith Company are $70,000. Smith Company, however, can expect even more cash flow returns from the sale of the old milling machine.

The Smith Company suffers a loss on its disposal of the machine. The firm bought it for $320,000 and has taken $200,000 depreciation on the equipment. This leaves a net cost or book value of $120,000 as of the date of disposal. The net proceeds of $70,000 from the sale are $50,000 less than the net book value, a $50,000 loss. This loss decreases taxable income for the period and reduces the firm's income tax liability. At the 40 percent tax rate, the loss from the disposal of the old milling equipment reduces Smith Company's tax bill by $20,000. The cash inflow from the tax saving, however, occurs at the end of the tax year (see Exhibit 11–6).

Exhibit 11–6	Cash Flows from Disposal of Equipment		
Immediate Cash Effect			
Selling price			$ 80,000
Expenses related to the disposal of the equipment:			
Brokers' commission (10 percent of $80,000)		$8,000	
Equipment removal expenses		2,000	10,000
Net proceeds from the disposal of the equipment			$ 70,000
Cash Effect at End of Year (Tax Saving from the Disposal)			
Acquisition cost of the equipment			$320,000
Accumulated depreciation			200,000
Net book value as of disposal date			$120,000
Net proceeds from the disposal			70,000
Loss from the disposal			$ 50,000
Income tax rate			40%
Income tax saving from the loss on disposal			$ 20,000
Total cash inflow from disposal			$ 90,000

Project Operation

A firm invests in a project to increase its revenues, decrease its expenses, or both. The expected changes in revenues or expenses influence cash flows through either direct or tax effects. Unlike other types of cash flows that occur perhaps once or twice during the life of the investment, cash flows from operations occur every year during the life of the investment.

Increases in sales revenue have direct effects on cash inflows. The Smith Company expects its investment to bring in $1,000,000 in cash revenue from increases in production volume in each of the next four years. This investment will have a direct effect of $1,000,000 cash inflow in each of the next four years.

An investment also increases the activity, expenses, and cash expenditures of the firm. Increases in cash expenditures offset the increases in cash from revenues. The $1,000,000 increase in revenues the Smith Company expects from its milling machine investment requires $750,000 cash expenditures for operating expenses. These include direct materials, direct labor, manufacturing overhead, and selling and administrative expenses. The net cash inflow from the investment, therefore, is $250,000 per year. At a 40 percent tax rate, the additional $250,000 can increase the firm's tax obligation by $100,000. This leaves a net after-tax cash inflow of $150,000 per year before considering the depreciation tax shield for each of the four years of the investment and an additional one-time expenditure in the first year of the investment.

Smith Company also expects other additional costs in the first year of operating the new milling machine. These costs include expenditures for employee training, work adjustments, and learning effects. The firm expects these costs to be $50,000. These costs reduce the net after-tax cash inflow in the first year of the investment to $120,000.

In addition, an investment may entail increases in amortized costs and allocated expenses. An investment in plant and equipment also increases the depreciation expenses of the firm, thus raising its amortized costs, which are tax deductible. Although depreciation expenses do not take the form of cash payments, they reduce tax liabilities and therefore cause cash *outflows* to decrease. You can see this tax effect in Exhibit 11–3, where the savings in taxes from the depreciation expenses of Smith's milling machine investment serve to decrease cash outflows by $44,000 each year for 10 years. The decreases in cash outflows due to the depreciation expenses increase the cash flow returns from the investment to $164,000 and $194,000 for year 1 and year 2 through 4, respectively.

An investment can increase the allocation base of the division and, thus, increase the indirect expenses allocated to the division. Suppose the headquarters allocates its expenses to divisions at a rate of $0.025 per dollar of sales. The investment brings in $1,000,000 additional sales per year and results in an additional charge of $25,000 in headquarters expenses to the division each year. The total expenses of the division thus will increase by $25,000 in each of the four years of the investment. The increase in a division's sales, however, does not increase the total costs of the overall company. The $25,000 additional charge to the division is not a cash outflow and, therefore, is not considered in capital budgeting. Also, there is no saving due to the tax effect because the total expenses of the firm remain unchanged.

Panel A of Exhibit 11–7 summarizes the effects of periodic operations on cash flow. Panel B shows an alternative financial approach to determine the same effect. Panel C reports in schematic form the total effects of initial acquisition activities and periodic operations on the cash flows of each period. In Exhibit 11–8 we summarize the determinations of the cash flow effects of various operating items.

Final Disinvestment

Direct Cash Effects   The disposal of the investment at the end of its useful life affects cash flows. A sale brings in cash. The disposal, however, often requires expen-

---

Exhibit 11–7   Effects on Cash Flow

Panel A: Effect of Operations on Cash Flows

Cash Revenue or Expense

Revenues	$1,000,000
Cash operating expenditures	750,000
Increase in cash inflows before taxes	$ 250,000
Income taxes (at 40 percent)	100,000
Increase in cash inflows from operations	$ 150,000

Noncash Expense

Depreciation expenses	$ 110,000
Income tax rate	40%
Decrease in cash outflows due to taxes	$ 44,000
Total cash *inflows* in each period	$ 194,000

*Panel B: Alternative Financial Approach
to Determine Periodic Cash Flow Effects*

Revenues		$1,000,000
Operating expenses:		
Cash expenditures	$ 750,000	
Noncash expenditures: Depreciation	110,000	860,000
Operating income before taxes		$ 140,000
Income taxes (at 40 percent)		56,000
Operating income		$ 84,000
Noncash expenditures: Depreciation		110,000
Increase in cash inflow from operations		$ 194,000

Panel C: Total Effect on Cash Flow in Schematic Form

Description	Time Period				
	Year 0	**Year 1**	**Year 2**	**Year 3**	**Year 4**
Cost of equipment	$(500,000)				
Installation cost	(5,000)				
Testing and adjusting	(10,000)				
Working capital	(200,000)				$200,000
Disposal of the displaced machine	90,000				
Cash flow return from operations (Panel A)		$194,000	$194,000	$194,000	194,000
One-time expenditure (net of taxes)		(30,000)			
Total	$(625,000)	$164,000	$194,000	$194,000	$394,000

---

ditures either to prepare the asset for sale or to do cleanups and restoration of the site after the disposal.

A disinvestment also can decrease the need for personnel. A firm is likely obligated to pay severance or relocation and retraining expenses for employees associated with the operations to be disinvested. These payments or expenses are cash outflows at the time the firm terminates the investment. Anticipating decreasing needs for employees, many firms phase out employees a few years before the final year of an investment by encouraging early retirement, leaving vacated positions unfilled, and transferring to other divisions. Thus, some severance pay, relocation expenses, and retraining costs may occur a few years before the final disposal.

Tax Effects A gain or loss from disposal of an asset has tax implications for a tax-paying firm. The firm pays taxes on any gain and receives tax credit benefits for any loss by way of decreased tax liability because of the loss.

Released Working Capital Working capital committed to an investment is no longer needed once the firm terminates the investment. The funds tied up in working capital for the investment are available for other uses, and the released working capital is a cash inflow without any tax consequence at the time the funds are released. In Exhibit 11–9 we summarize how to determine the effects of the final disposal of the investment on cash flows.

Effect of Final Disposal on Cash Flow—Smith Company The Smith Company expects to sell the milling machine and related peripheral equipment at the end of the fourth year for $100,000. The estimated salvage value for depreciation purposes, however, is $75,000. The cost of removal and cleanup is $20,000.

The disposal thus has a direct cash inflow of $80,000 ($100,000 − $20,000). The estimated salvage value for depreciation purposes is irrelevant in determining the direct cash effect of the disposal, although it does have a tax effect.

After terminating the investment, Smith Company can reassign all but 10 employees to other divisions without incurring significant expenses. The firm expects a cost of $150,000 for relocation, retraining, and work adjustment for these 10 employees. This $150,000 is a cash outflow in the year that the firm discontinues the investment.

Exhibit 11–8   Effects of Periodic Operation

Transaction	Effects on Cash Flow
Cash receipts	Amount received × (1 − tax rate)
Cash expenditures	Amount paid × (1 − tax rate)
Depreciated initial cost	Tax shield: Depreciation expense × tax rate
Allocated cost	No effect

Exhibit 11–9   Determining the Net Effect of Final Disposal on Cash Flow

Cash proceeds from disposal

−

Cash expenditures for preparation, removing, cleaning, and restoration

+

Loss on disposal × tax rate

or, −

Gain on disposal × tax rate

−

Severance pay and relocation and retraining expense × (1 − tax rate)

+

Released working capital

=

Net effect on cash flow from final disposal

Exhibit 11–10	Effects of Final Disinvestment on Cash Flow		

	Disposal of Machine		
Direct Effect	**Cash Flows**	**Gain**	**Net Cash Flow**
Proceeds from sale of machine	$ 100,000		
Machine removal and site cleanup expenses	(20,000)		
Net proceeds from sale of machine		$80,000	$ 80,000
Tax Effect			
Cost of the milling machine	$ 515,000		
Accumulated depreciation	440,000		
Book value of the milling machine		75,000	
Gain on sale of the milling machine		$ 5,000	
Income taxes (at 40 percent)		× 40%	2,000
Net after-tax cash proceeds from disposal of machine			$ 78,000
	Other Expenditures		
Direct Effect			
Relocation cost of displaced employees	$(150,000)		
Tax Effect			
Income taxes (at 40 percent)	60,000		
Net after-tax cash outflow for relocation of employees			$ (90,000)
	Released Working Capital		
Direct Effect			
Working capital no longer needed			200,000
Total effect of the final disposal on cash *inflow*			$188,000

The net proceeds Smith Company receives from the milling machine disposal represent a $5,000 gain ($80,000 net proceeds − $75,000 book value). At the 40 percent tax rate, Smith Company has to pay $2,000 on this gain. After taxes, Smith Company has a $78,000 cash inflow from the disposal.

Other cash expenditures also have tax implications. At the 40 percent tax rate, the $150,000 relocation cost to transfer employees decreases the tax liability of the firm by $60,000. The net after-tax effect the relocation expense has on cash flow, therefore, is a $90,000 cash outflow.

The $200,000 working capital Smith Company committed to the milling machine investment at the commencement of the investment is no longer needed once the investment has been terminated. The release of working capital adds a $200,000 *cash inflow* at the end of the fourth year. There is no tax effect for this item because a decrease in working capital is not a gain. The addition of the $200,000 cash inflow released from the working capital that is no longer needed brings the total cash inflow from termination of the investment to $188,000.

In Exhibit 11–10 you can see the effects of the final disposal of the investment on the cash flows of the Smith Company. In Exhibit 11–11 we summarize the effects on the Smith Company's cash flows the milling machine investment has in each year of its life.

CAPITAL BUDGETING TECHNIQUES

Many techniques are available for evaluating capital investments. The three most widely used are

1. Payback period.
2. Accounting rate of return.
3. Discounted cash flow.

LEARNING OBJECTIVE 3 ▶
Use capital budgeting techniques including the payback period, accounting rate of return, net present value, and internal rate of return methods to assess capital investments and explain the advantages and limitations of these techniques.

Exhibit 11–11	**Effects of Investment in Project B on Cash Flows** (in thousands)				

			Years		
Initial Investment	**0**	**1**	**2**	**3**	**4**
Cost of equipment	$(500)				
Installation cost	(5)				
Testing and adjusting	(10)				
Working capital	(200)				
Disposal of the displaced machine	90				
Operations					
Revenues		$1,000	$1,000	$1,000	$ 1,000
Operating expenses:					
Cash items		$ 800	$ 750	$ 750	$ 750
Noncash item					
Depreciation		110	110	110	110
Total operating expenses		$ 910	$ 860	$ 860	$ 860
Operating income before taxes		$ 90	$ 140	$ 140	$ 140
Income taxes (40 percent)		36	56	56	56
Operating income		$ 54	$ 84	$ 84	$ 84
Noncash expense: Depreciation		110	110	110	110
Cash flow returns from operations		$ 164	$ 194	$ 194	$ 194
Final Disinvestment (Net of taxes)					
Working capital released					$200
Disposal of investment					78
Employee relocation, retraining, or					
severance pay					(90)
Net effect on cash flow	$(625)	$ 164	$ 194	$ 194	$ 382

Each of these methods has its merits and shortcomings. None is definitely superior to the others in all aspects. In a survey of capital budgeting practices, Klammer, Koch, and Wilner found several different capital budgeting techniques in use.[5] Furthermore, a firm may use different methods for different types of projects or use more than one method to evaluate a capital investment. Thirty-nine percent of the responding firms use at least one secondary technique to supplement the primary analytical method for replacement projects.

Data for Capital Budgeting   In discussing capital-budgeting techniques we again use data for the Smith Company. In addition to the previous investment project, called project B, Jennifer O'Clock, the manager, received a similar investment proposal for project A. Project A also has a four-year expected useful life and requires total initial investments of $555,000 in year 0. O'Clock expects project A to generate a revenue of $900,000 each year for four years. The operating expense will be $660,000 each year, in addition to depreciation expenses and other allocated headquarters' expenses.

Project A does not require additional working capital and has a salvage value of $60,000 for depreciation purposes. O'clock expects to sell the investment for $200,000 at the end of the fourth year. The total expenses for relocation, retraining, and severance pay for the displaced employees and for all other expenses relating to the disinvestment are expected to be $240,000.

In Exhibit 11–12 we summarize pertinent data for both projects.

---

5   Thomas Klammer, Bruce Koch, and Neil Wilner, "Capital Budgeting Practices—A Survey of Corporate Use," *Journal of Management Accounting Research*, Fall 1991, pp. 113–30.

Exhibit 11–12	Data for Projects A and B	
Project A		
Required initial investment	$ 555,000	
Estimated salvage value	$ 60,000	
Annual operating data		
Revenues	$ 900,000	per year for four years
Cash operating expense	$ 660,000	per year for four years
Final disinvestment		
Cash proceeds from disposal	$ 200,000	
Employee relocation, retraining, and severance pay	$ 240,000	
Project B		
Required initial investment	$ 625,000	
Estimated salvage value	$ 75,000	
Annual operating data		
Revenues	$1,000,000	per year for four years
Cash operating expense	$ 750,000	per year for four years
Other operating data		
Additional cash expenditure	$ 50,000	year 1 only
Final disinvestment		
Cash proceeds from disposal	$ 100,000	
Machine removal and site cleanup	$ 20,000	
Employee relocation, retraining, and severance pay	$ 150,000	
Company		
Depreciation method:	Straight-line	
Income tax rate:	40 percent for combined federal, state, and local taxes	

The Payback Period Method

How long will it take to get my money back? is a question investors often ask in making investment decisions. The payback period answers this question.

The **payback period** of an investment is the length of time required for the cumulative total net cash inflows from an investment to equal the total initial cash outlays of the investment. At that point in time, the investor has recovered the amount of money invested in the project.

> The **payback period** of an investment is the length of time required for the cumulative total net cash inflows from an investment to equal the total initial cash outlays of the investment.

Determining the Payback Period

The first step in computing a payback period is determining the after-tax cash flows from the investment for each year of the project's life. Look at Exhibits 11–13 and 11–14 to see the cash flows of projects A and B, respectively, over their useful lives. The after-tax net cash flow returns (Column 8) for project A are uniform over the years, while those for project B are uneven. Although the principle for calculating payback periods is the same, the details in determining payback periods differ with various cash flow patterns.

Determining the Payback Period with Uniform Annual Cash Flows   Project A generates a revenue of $900,000 each year for four years (column 2, Exhibit 11–13). The cash operating expenses are $660,000 per year, as reported in column 3, in addition to a $123,750 depreciation expense (column 5) per year. The taxable income therefore is $116,250. At a 40 percent tax rate, the income taxes on the operating income generated by project A are $46,500 per year (column 7). The cash flow return before taxes, however, is $240,000 per year ($900,000 − $660,000). After paying for cash operating expenses and income taxes, project A generates net cash flow returns of $193,500 ($240,000 − $46,500), as reported in column 8. Column 9 of Exhibit 11–13 shows the cumulative net cash proceeds starting from the first period of operation of the project.

The payback period of project A is the total number of periods it takes the cumulative total cash flow (column 9) to equal the initial investment in the project. Project A generates $193,500 net after-tax cash flow returns each year for the first three

Exhibit 11–13	**Payback Period with Uniform Cash Flow Returns** Project A: Total Initial Investment: $555,000							
(1)	(2)	(3)	(4)	(5)	(6)	(7)	(8)	(9)
Period	Revenue	Operating Expenses	Cash Flow Returns Before Taxes	Depreciation Expense*	Operating Income Before Taxes	Income Taxes (40 percent)	Cash Flow Returns (4) – (7)	Cumulative Cash Flow Returns
1	$900,000	$(660,000)	$240,000	$(123,750)	$116,250	$(46,500)	$193,500	$193,500
2	900,000	(660,000)	240,000	(123,750)	116,250	(46,500)	193,500	387,000
3	900,000	(660,000)	240,000	(123,750)	116,250	(46,500)	193,500	580,500
4	1,100,000†	(900,000)‡	200,000	(123,750)	16,250§	(6,500)	193,500	

* Depreciation expense is $123,750 per year [($555,000 − $60,000)/4].

† $900,000 revenue per year plus the $200,000 selling price of the investment.

‡ $660,000 operating expenses per year plus disinvestment expenses of $240,000.

§ Operating income: $1,100,000 − 660,000 − 123,750 − 240,000 (employees' relocation) − 60,000 (estimated salvage value) = $16,250

Exhibit 11–14	**Payback Period with Uneven Cash Flow Returns** Project B: Total Initial Investment—($625,000)	
Years	Net After-Tax Cash Flow Returns	Cumulative Net After-Tax Cash Flow Returns
1	$164,000	$164,000
2	194,000	358,000
3	194,000	552,000
4	382,000	

years and will have cumulative net proceeds of $387,000 by the end of year 2, which is $168,000 short of the initial investment of $555,000 in the project. In the absence of detailed data on cash flow patterns during the year, we assume that revenues and operating expenses flow evenly throughout the year. The firm needs .87 year in the third year to generate $168,000 net cash flow returns. The payback period of project A, therefore, is 2.87 years, or 2 years and 10.4 months.

Alternatively, the payback period for a project with equal cash flow returns every year can be determined by dividing the expected annual cash flow returns into the total initial capital investment:

$$\text{Payback period} = \frac{\text{Total original investment}}{\text{Annual net after-tax cash flow return}}$$

For Project A, the payback period is

$$\text{Payback period} = \frac{\$555,000}{\$193,500} = 2.87 \text{ years}$$

Determining Payback Period with Uneven Annual Cash Flows Column 2 of Exhibit 11–14 reproduces the information in the last row of Exhibit 11–11 and provides the data for finding the payback period of project B. With uneven net cash flow returns, the analysis determines the payback period by calculating the cumulative net cash flow returns starting from the beginning of the investment. The length of time it takes for the cumulative net cash flow returns to equal the initial cash outlay is the payback period of the investment.

Project B has cumulative net proceeds of $552,000 by the end of year 3. This amount is $73,000 short of the initial cash investment of $625,000. The estimated net cash flow returns in year 4 are $382,000. It takes 0.19 of a year in year 4 to earn $73,000. The payback period for project B therefore is 3.19 years, as the following computation shows:

$$3 \text{ years} + \frac{\$73,000}{\$382,000} = 3.19 \text{ years}$$

Evaluation of the Payback Period Method

Advantages   The payback period is easy to compute and understand; it provides a quick estimate of the time needed for an investment to return the amount of cash invested. After the payback period the investment starts to bring in more cash than the amount initially paid for the investment.

Many investors consider the length of payback period a measure of the risk of the investment. The longer the payback period of an investment, the riskier it is. This is true for two reasons: First, the farther into the future a payback period is, the more likely it is that the projected revenues and expenses will not occur as predicted. Second, the longer it takes to recover the investment, the more likely it is that the product or service it provides will become obsolete or attract competition, making it more difficult to earn cash flow returns as projected.

In addition, a payback period can serve as an indicator on the liquidity available to the firm. A project with a four-year payback period is likely not as liquid an investment as one with a payback period of three years or less.

The payback period method emphasizes quick payoffs, an important consideration in some instances. Firms in industries with a high risk of obsolescence often require short payback periods. This was true recently in high-technology industries such as computer chip manufacturing and personal computer production and distribution. Short payback periods often become the determining factor for investments in these industries.

Limitations   Among the limitations of the payback period method are its failures to consider the total profitability of an investment project and the time value of money. The payback period method considers cash flows from the initiation of the project until the point at which the total cash flow returns of the project equal the required initial investment. It ignores all cash flows after the payback period.

The second limitation is that it disregards the time value of money. The payback period method considers only the length of time required to recover the investment, regardless of differences in the timing or pattern of cash flows. As long as the cash flow return amounts are the same, the payback period treats them as equal to the firm, even though the firm may receive some of them many years before it receives others. The payback period method considers a $5,000 cash inflow in year 5, for example, to be exactly the same as a $5,000 cash inflow in year 1.

To illustrate the effects of these two limitations of the payback period method, assume a firm has to select one of two investments. The expected cash flows for these two projects are

Project	Year 0	Year 1	Year 2	Year 3	Year 4	Payback Period
P	$(100,000)	$90,000	$ 5,000	$ 5,000	$80,000	3 years
Q	(100,000)	5,000	95,000	10,000	10,000	2 years

Both projects require the same amount of initial investment. Of the two projects, project Q has a shorter payback period. According to the payback period method, project Q is the preferred investment of the two.

Project Q would be the preferred investment only if we can ignore both the amount of the total net cash flow returns and the patterns of the cash flow returns. The fact that project P brings in $180,000 and project Q brings in only $120,000 over the four-year period is ignored when using the payback period method.

Furthermore, the cash flow patterns show that project P brings in substantially more cash flow returns than project Q in the first year of operations. If the firm invests all the cash inflows from investments and earns a 10 percent return, project P has a shorter payback period than project Q (1.71 years versus 1.99 years).[6] Only by ignoring project P's early cash flow returns can project Q be the preferred investment.

One common error in using the payback period method is to demand too short a payback period. Companies may require short payback periods to maintain a liquid financial position, fulfill the need to finance other investments, and avoid extended projections. Demanding too short a payback period, however, often hampers wise investing by causing firms not to invest in large long-term improvements. After all, an investment in hand tools takes a very short time to pay back its initial outlay, while an investment in a new technology—such as a computer-integrated-manufacturing (CIM) system—usually takes years to earn back the amount invested. A firm that stresses short payback periods in investments and avoids investments in projects that require long payback periods would most likely not fare very well in today's competitive global market.

The Accounting Rate of Return Method
Determining Accounting Rate of Return

The accounting rate of return method is another common way to evaluate capital investments. The **accounting rate of return** is the return (net income) from the investment as a percentage of its book value.

$$\text{Accounting rate of return} = \frac{\text{Net income}}{\text{Investment (Book value)}}$$

The **accounting rate of return** is the net income or the return from an investment as a percentage of its book value.

Both figures are data normally appearing in financial statements, thus the term *accounting rate of return*. It is an unadjusted rate of return because the procedure does not consider the time value of money.

The numerator is the average annual expected net income from the investment over its useful life. The denominator is either the initial total investment or the average investment (book value) over the useful life of the project. Both denominator amounts are used in practice. Some prefer the original investment because it is objectively determined and is not affected by either the depreciation method chosen or the estimation of the salvage value. No matter which approach is used in determining the investment, the same approach should be used for all investments.

Recall the situation that Jennifer O'Clock faces, as described in Exhibit 11–12. She can expect project A to earn a net income of $69,750 per year:

$$\text{Net income} = \text{Revenues} - \frac{\text{Cash operating}}{\text{expenses}} - \frac{\text{Noncash operating}}{\text{expenses}} - \frac{\text{Income}}{\text{taxes}}$$

$$= \$900,000 - \$660,000 - \frac{\$555,000 - \$60,000}{4} - \$46,500$$

$$= \$69,750$$

---

[6] We assume that operating cash flows occur uniformly throughout the year. The estimated payback periods are

	Project P	Project Q
Initial investment	$100,000	$100,000
Cash inflow in year 1	90,000	5,000
Additional cash inflow needed to pay back the initial investment	$ 10,000	$ 95,000
Cash inflow in year 2		
From operations	5,000	95,000
From interest earned (10%) on the cash flow return of year 1	9,000	500
Total cash inflow in year 2	$ 14,000	$ 95,500

Therefore, payback periods are:

$$\text{Project P: } 1 \text{ year} + \frac{\$10,000}{\$14,000} \text{ year} = 1.71 \text{ years}$$

$$\text{Project Q: } 1 \text{ year} + \frac{\$95,000}{\$95,500} \text{ year} = 1.99 \text{ years}$$

The only noncash expense for project A is the depreciation expense of the equipment, determined by using the straight-line depreciation method.

The average investment is the average of the amount the firm carries for the investment in its accounting records each year during the life of the investment. (See Exhibit 11–15 for project A.)

Project A requires an initial investment of $555,000 with $60,000 estimated salvage value after four years. The firm uses straight-line depreciation. The average investment in a year is the average of the investment at the beginning of the year and the balance of the investment at the end of the year. According to the accounting records, the amount of investment is $555,000 at the beginning of year 1 and $431,250 at the end of the same year. The average investment for year 1, therefore, is $493,125. The average investment for the life of the investment is the sum of the average investments for each of the years divided by the number of years. With a total average investment of $1,230,000 over a 4-year period, the average investment over the entire 10-year period is $307,500 ($1,230,000/4).

And the accounting rate of return for project A is 22.68 percent,

$$\frac{\$69,750}{\$307,500} = 22.68 \text{ percent}$$

A firm that uses the straight-line depreciation method can compute the average investment by taking the simple average of the initial investment and the salvage value of the investment at the end of its useful life:

$$\text{Average investment} = \frac{\text{Original cost} + \text{Salvage value}}{2}$$

$$= \frac{\$555,000 + \$60,000}{2} = \$307,500$$

This shortcut computation for average investment is not applicable to situations where the depreciation method is not the straight-line method because the amount of decrease in investment in accounting records is not constant over the years. Exhibit 11–16 shows a determination of the average investment for project A when the firm uses the double-declining-balance depreciation method.

Some firms choose to calculate accounting rates of return on the original cost (investment). The accounting rate of return for project A will be 12.57 percent if the firm chooses to use the original investment as the denominator.

$$\frac{\$69,750}{\$555,000} = 12.57 \text{ percent}$$

Expected annual net income for project A remains stable throughout the project's useful life. The average net income thus is the same as its expected annual income. In contrast, the expected net income for project B varies from year to year. The firm, therefore, needs to calculate the average expected net income of project B before computing the accounting rate of return for project B.

Exhibit 11–15	Average Investment for Project A		
Year	Investment at the Beginning of the Year	Investment at the End of the Year	Average Investment for the Year
1	$555,000	$431,250	$ 493,125
2	431,250	307,500	369,375
3	307,500	183,750	245,625
4	183,750	60,000	121,875
Total			$1,230,000

Average book value = $1,230,000/4 years = $307,500

	Determining Average Investment with the Double-Declining-Balance Depreciation Method			
Exhibit 11–16				
Year	**Investment at the Beginning of the Year**	**Depreciation Expense for the Year**	**Investment at the End of the Year**	**Average Investment for the Year**
1	$555,000	$277,500	$277,500	$416,250
2	277,500	138,750	138,750	208,125
3	138,750	69,375	69,375	104,063
4	69,375	9,375	60,000	64,687
Total				$793,125

Average book value = $793,125/4 years = $198,281

In Exhibit 11–11 we show that the net incomes of project B over its four-year useful life are $54,000, $84,000, $84,000, and $84,000. The average net income per year is $76,500:

$$\frac{\$54,000 + \$84,000 + \$84,000 + \$84,000}{4} = \$76,500$$

The average investment is $295,000:

$$\frac{\$515,000 + \$75,000}{2} = \$295,000$$

And the unadjusted rate of return is 25.93 percent using the average investment, or 14.85 percent using the total initial investment.

$$\frac{\$76,500}{\$295,000} = 25.93 \text{ percent} \qquad \frac{\$76,500}{\$515,000} = 14.85 \text{ percent}$$

Evaluation of the Accounting Rate of Return Method

Advantages The accounting rate of return method uses data generated by the same procedures as those used in preparing financial reports. No special efforts are required to generate data in the analysis when projected financial statements are prepared for the investment. Thus, the cost of generating the data to analyze a capital investment using the accounting rate of return method is lower than any other method. Also, because managers often are evaluated on the basis of the accounting rate of return, using the same procedure in both the decision-making stage and the periodic-evaluation stage ensures consistency. The fact that these data are audited using generally accepted accounting principles can add reliability.

In addition, the accounting rate of return enables decision makers to gauge the effect of the capital investment on the financial performance of the division or the firm. The firm also can easily measure the impact the capital investment may have on debt covenants or other contractual agreements.

The accounting rate of return has an additional advantage over the payback period method in that it includes the entire period of an investment in its analyses of the profitability of the capital investment. Unlike the payback period method, which uses the data only up to the point of recapturing the amount of the original investment, the accounting rate of return method considers all net incomes over the entire life span of the project and provides a measure of the profitability on the investment.

Limitations The accounting rate of return method ignores the time value of money, a limitation it shares with the payback period method. Another limitation of the method is the use of accounting figures in both the denominator and the numerator in determining the accounting rate of return. Accounting figures depend on the choice of accounting procedures. Different accounting procedures can lead to substantially different amounts of net income and book values for the same investment.

Net income based on the straight-line depreciation method is different from (usually greater than) the net income for the same period using, say, a declining-balance depreciation method. As a result, the calculated accounting rates of return are different, even though nothing except the accounting procedures are different. This condition is undesirable because, in a capital investment, the result should differ only if the underlying factors of the capital investment vary; the result should not vary because of a change in the accounting procedures.

Also, whereas accounting income may be a useful measure of the firm's profitability as a whole, cash flows are a better measure of performance over the life of the project for the reasons cited earlier. Furthermore, inclusion of only the book value of the invested asset as the total investment ignores the fact that a project requires the commitment of working capital as well as other outlays.

Neither the payback period method nor the accounting rate of return method considers the time value of money in evaluating capital investment projects. Next, we examine two discounted cash flow methods that explicitly consider the time value of money.

The Discounted Cash Flow Methods

The **discounted cash flow methods (DCF methods)** evaluate a capital investment by considering equivalent present values of all future cash flow returns after the initial investment.

The margin note: **The discounted cash flow methods (DCF methods)** evaluate a capital investment by considering future cash flow returns after the initial investment at their equivalent present values.

An investment has cash flows throughout the useful life of the project. A dollar of cash flow return in the first year of an investment is worth more than a dollar of cash flow return in a later year. A simple addition or subtraction of money received or paid at different points in time to arrive at the total effect of an investment ignores the important consideration of the time value of money in investments. The DCF methods consider explicitly the time value of money in evaluating capital investments.

Two alternative approaches of the DCF methods are in general use—the net present value method and the internal rate of return method. The *net present value (NPV) method* uses a specified discount rate to bring all the subsequent cash flow returns after the initial investment to their present values (the time of the initial investment). The focus of the NPV method is on the dollar amount at the time of the investment.

In contrast, the *internal rate of return (IRR) method* estimates the discount rate that makes the present value of all the subsequent cash flow returns after the initial investment equal to the initial cash outlays for the investment. The focus of the IRR method is on the rate of return.

Although these two approaches differ in their focus, they are variations of the same concept and use the same factors in evaluating capital investments. These factors are

1. The total initial investment.
2. The expected future cash receipts and disbursements.
3. The investor's desired rate of return.

The first two factors have been discussed already. The following section examines issues regarding the third factor, the desired rate of return.

Desired Rate of Return

The margin note: **The desired rate of return** is the minimum rate of return the investing firm requires for the investment.

The **desired rate of return** can be defined as the minimum rate of return the investing firm requires for the investment. The minimum rate can be the rate of return the firm would have earned by investing the same funds in the best available alternative investment that bears the same risk. Such a return also is called the opportunity cost.

Determining the desired rate of return based on the best alternative opportunity available often proves to be difficult in practical terms. Management usually does not know all investment opportunities available to the firm; the task of conducting an exhausting search and examining all opportunities can be very costly, time-consuming, or both.

Rather than using the true opportunity cost, firms often use an alternative measure for the desired rate of return. Among the alternative measures of the desired rate of return are

1. Minimum rate of return.
2. Cost of capital.

Frequently a firm has a minimum return requirement for all its investments and considers only capital project proposals that meet it. Among the factors considered in determining the required minimum rate of return are the strategic plan of the firm, industry average, and other investment opportunities.

Cost of capital often serves as a gatekeeper to ensure that a capital investment project will at least recover the firm's cost in obtaining the necessary funds for the investment. *Statements on Management Accounting No. 4A* by the Institute of Management Accountants defines **cost of capital** as "a composite of the cost of various sources of funds comprising a firm's capital structure."[7] A firm obtains funds by issuing preferred or common stocks; borrowing money using various forms of debt such as notes, loans, or bonds; or retaining earnings. Each of these sources of capital has its own cost and the cost of capital varies as the mix of the capital structure changes.

The minimum cost of the debt is the after-tax interest rate on the debt. The minimum cost of the equity securities is the dividend yield on the stock. The cost of capital for an investment, however, is higher than the minimum costs. Why? Because borrowing affects a firm in other ways in addition to the interest the firm has to pay for the loan. Although a firm may be able to raise the necessary capital for the investment under consideration by issuing bonds bearing 10 percent interest, it may have to issue future bonds at a higher interest rate, offer better terms on preferred stock, or sell common stock at a lower price when it needs funds for other investments in the future. This is because of the reduced liquidity or increased risk due to the financing for the current investment project. In addition to the cost of obtaining the present funds, a firm must take into account such factors as control, risk, flexibility, and the effect the transaction has on the cost of funding future capital needs.

A common approach to incorporate relevant factors in arriving at the cost of capital is to use the weighted average after-tax cost of capital. The **weighted average after-tax cost of capital** is the after-tax cost to the firm of securing funds with a given capital structure. The after-tax cost of each source of capital is weighted by the fraction of the source in the total capital. The sum of the weighted after-tax costs of all the sources of capital is the firm's weighted after-tax cost of capital.

As an example, take a firm in a 40 percent tax bracket for federal and state taxes combined. This firm has raised 25 percent of its total capital from selling bonds that cost 10 percent, 35 percent from issuing preferred stocks that cost 10 percent, and 40 percent from issuing common stocks that cost 15 percent; it has a weighted cost of capital of 11 percent as computed here:

Bond	0.25×10 percent $\times (1 - 0.4) =$	1.5 percent
Preferred stock	0.35×10 percent $=$	3.5 percent
Common stock	0.40×15 percent $=$	6.0 percent
Weighted cost of capital		11.0 percent

The after-tax cost of the 10 percent bond to the firm is 6 percent ($10\% - 10\% \times 40\%$) because bond interest is deductible for tax purposes. Taxes are not subtracted from the cost of common stocks or preferred stock dividends to calculate the cost of these stocks because dividends are not deductible for tax purposes.

The Net Present Value Method

Determining the Net Present Value The **net present value (NPV)** of an investment is the excess of the present value of future cash flow returns over the initial

*The **cost of capital** is a composite of the cost of various sources of funds comprising a firm's capital structure.*

Weighted average after-tax cost of capital is the after-tax cost to the firm of securing funds with a given capital structure.

*The **net present value (NPV)** of an investment is the excess of the present value of future cash flow returns over the initial investment.*

---

[7] Institute of Management Accountants, *Statement Number 4A: Cost of Capital* (Montvale, NJ, 1984), p. 1.

The **present value** of a cash flow return is the current equivalent dollar value of the cash flow, given the desired rate of return.

investment. The **present value** of a future cash flow return is the current equivalent dollar value of the cash flow, given the desired rate of return. The present value for $5,000 received a year from now by an investor with a 10 percent desired rate of return is $4,545:

$$\$5,000 \times 0.909 = \$4,545$$

where 0.909 is the discount factor for 10 percent in one period. The discount factor can be found in the present value table on page 820. With a 10 percent desired rate of return, receiving $4,545 now or $5,000 a year from now is the same to the investor. To verify, let us calculate the total amount the investor has on hand one year after receiving $4,545:

Cash received now	$4,545
Interest for one year: $4,545 × 10 percent =	455
Total cash on hand one year from now	$5,000

Thus, $4,545 is the present value equivalent of the $5,000 to be received one year from now.

The NPV is the excess of the present value of the expected net future cash flow return over the total initial investment.

Present Value of Cash Flow Return

$$
\begin{array}{ccccc}
\text{Net} & \text{Present value} & & \text{Present value} & \text{Total net} \\
\text{present} = & \text{of cash} & - & \text{of cash} & - & \text{initial} \\
\text{value} & \text{receipts} & & \text{expenditure} & \text{investment}
\end{array}
$$

The net present value is the amount in current dollars the investment earns for the investor after yielding the desired return in each period.

The first step in determining the net present value of an investment is to determine the net cash flow return in each year of the investment. The net cash flow returns are converted, based on the desired rate of return, into their present value dollar amounts. The net present value is the remainder after subtracting the total initial cash outlays for the investment from the sum of the present values of all the future net cash flow returns. These steps summarize how to find the NPV of a project:

1. Determine net cash flow return in each year.
2. Select the desired rate of return.
3. Find the discount factor for each of the years based on the desired rate of return selected in step 2.
4. Multiply steps 1 and 3 to determine the present values of the cash flow returns.
5. Sum the amount in step 4 for all the years.
6. Subtract the initial investment from the amount obtained in step 5.

A capital project is desirable, according to the NPV method, if it has a positive NPV and undesirable if it has a negative NPV.

Determining NPV with Uniform Cash Flow Returns   Jennifer O'Clock desires to earn a 10 percent after-tax rate of return on investments. These calculations show the determination of the present value of cash flow returns from project A:

$$\text{Present value of cash flow returns} = \$193,500 \times 3.17$$

$$= \$613,395$$

The amount 3.17 is the discount factor for an annuity of four years at 10 percent. An annuity is a constant sum received or paid each year for a number of years. The discount factor varies according to the number of years and the rate of the desired return. The present value tables on page 821 present discount factors for computing present values of annuities.

Project A generates a yearly after-tax net cash inflow of $193,500 for four years. The preceding calculation shows that at a 10 percent interest rate these yearly net cash flow returns have a present value of $613,395.

Project A requires an initial investment of $555,000. The payment for the initial investment is made at the beginning of the investment and is the present value of the initial investment. Subtracting the initial investment of $555,000 from the present value of net cash flow returns yields $58,395, the NPV of this investment.

$$\text{NPV of project A} = \$613,395 - \$555,000 = \$58,395$$

The NPV indicates that a $555,000 investment in project A will earn $58,395 in current dollars for the investor, in addition to earning a 10 percent return each year for four years on the $555,000 investment.

Using a Spreadsheet Program to Determine NPV   Most spreadsheet programs can quickly determine the present value of cash flow returns.

For both Lotus 1–2–3 and Quattro: @NPV (Rate, Range)

For Microsoft EXCEL: =NPV (Rate, Range)

where *rate* is the interest rate and *range* is the consecutive rows or columns in the spreadsheet that comprise cash flows of the investment. The first amount specified in *range* is the initial cash outflow entered as a negative amount. The second amount is the net cash flow return at the end of the first year of the investment, and so on.

Interpretation of NPV   An investment that earns the same rate of return as the desired rate of return has an NPV of zero. The NPV will be greater than zero (as it is in this case) when an investment earns a rate of return greater than the desired rate of return. The NPV will be a negative amount when an investment earns a return less than the desired rate of return. Project A has an NPV of $58,395. This suggests that project A earns a rate of return greater than the desired return of 10 percent and is a desirable investment. The investment will earn a 10 percent return and $58,395 (in current dollars).

There are, however, alternative investments. The positive NPV of project A does not necessarily mean that project A is the best investment available. The net present value simply shows that the return from investing in project A is greater than the discount rate used in the computation. Other investment opportunities may yield even higher returns. O'Clock must check alternative investments, such as project B in our example, before she makes the final decision.

Determining NPV with Uneven Cash Inflows   Project B has uneven cash flow returns over the years. As a result, the computation of its NPV requires more detailed calculations than those for the NPV of project A. Exhibit 11–17 shows the calculations of the NPV of project B. The procedure starts with the net after-tax cash flow returns generated each year by the investment during its useful life. These cash flows then are discounted using the present value discount factors on page 820, as shown in the last column of Exhibit 11–17.

Exhibit 11–17	NPV of Uneven Cash Flow Returns for Project B		
Years	Net After-Tax Cash Inflow	Discount Factor	Present Value
1	$164,000	0.909	$149,076
2	194,000	0.826	160,244
3	194,000	0.751	145,694
4	382,000	0.683	260,906
Total present value of cash flow returns			$715,920
Less: Initial investment			625,000
Net present value			$ 90,920

The sum of the last column in Exhibit 11–17 tells us that the total present value of the cash flow returns from the investment over the years is $715,920. After subtracting the initial investment from the present value of future cash flow returns, the NPV of project B is $90,920. The positive NPV suggests that project B also is a desirable investment.

Present Value (or Discounted) Payback Period   The payback period methods use cash flows to estimate the payback period of an investment; often they are criticized for ignoring the time value of money. Alternatively, you can use the present values of cash flow returns to determine the payback period of an investment. This payback period is the **present value payback period** that some users refer to as **breakeven time (BET).**

The **present value payback period or breakeven time (BET) method** uses the span of time required for the cumulative present value of cash inflows to equal the initial investment of the project.

The present value payback period method uses the *present values* of cash flow returns, rather than the undiscounted dollar amounts of cash flow returns, to determine the payback period. As in the NPV method, the present value of cash flow returns from the investment is estimated using the firm's cost of capital. The span of time required for the cumulative present value of cash flow returns to equal the initial investment of the project is the present value payback period. The present value payback period of project A is 3.56 years, as calculated in Exhibit 11–18, in contrast to 2.87 years for the simple payback period.

The present value or discounted payback period method has an advantage over the simple payback period method in that it considers one dollar today to be more valuable than one dollar in the future. Nevertheless, it suffers the same weakness as the payback period in other aspects. Both methods emphasize quick payoffs and ignore profitability and cash flow returns after the payback period.

Internal Rate of Return Method

The **internal rate of return (IRR) method** is a discounted cash flow method that estimates the discount rate that makes the present value of subsequent cash flow returns equal the initial investment.

The **internal rate of return (IRR) method** is a DCF method that estimates the discount rate that makes the present value of subsequent cash flow returns equal the initial investment. This rate makes the NPV of the investment zero. The IRR method evaluates capital investments by comparing the internal rate of return to the criterion rate of return. The criterion can be the desired rate of return of the firm, the rate of return from the best alternative investment, or whatever the firm chooses to use.

Determining the Internal Rate of Return

Like the NPV method, the IRR method considers the time value of money, initial cash investment, and all cash flows after the investment. Unlike the NPV method, the computation procedure of the IRR method does not use the desired rate of return (the cost of capital). The IRR method determines the rate of return of an investment and then compares it to the desired rate of return to assess the desirability of the investment. In using this method, the investor asks the question: What is the rate of return of the investment, and how does it compare to the desired return of the firm?[8]

The computation procedures for IRR vary somewhat with cash flow return patterns over the useful life of an investment.

Uniform Cash Flows   The IRR method estimates the discount rate that makes the present value of cash flow returns equal to the initial total cash disbursements and commitments. The first step in using the IRR method, therefore, is to determine the total net initial cash disbursements and commitments for the investment and the net cash flow returns from the investment in each of the years of the investment.

---

[8]   The accounting rate of return method discussed earlier appears to address the same issue; it provides a rate of return on investment. The IRR method, however, considers the time value of money while the accounting rate of return method does not. Also, the IRR method uses cash flows while the accounting rate of return method uses the net income computed by the accounting procedures the firm chooses to use in estimating the rate of return.

Exhibit 11–18   Present Value Payback Period for Project A

Year	Net After-Tax Cash Flow Return	Discount Factor at 10 Percent	Present Value of Cash Flow Return	Cumulative Present Value of Cash Flow Return
1	$193,500	0.909	$175,892	$175,892
2	$193,500	0.826	159,831	335,723
3	$193,500	0.751	145,318	481,041
4	$193,500	0.683	132,161	

Amount needed in year 4 to reach the payback period:

$$\$555,000 - \$481,041 = \$73,959$$

$$\text{Present value payback period} = 3 \text{ years} + \frac{73,959}{132,161} = 3.56 \text{ years}$$

The discount rate that makes the total initial investment and the present value of subsequent cash flow returns from the investment equal is the internal rate of return on the investment. The following equation summarizes this procedure:

$$A_{r,n} = \frac{\text{Total initial cash disbursements and commitments for the investment}}{\text{Annual equal cash flow returns from the investment}}$$

where $A_{r,n}$ is the annuity discount factor that makes the present value of the net cash flow returns over the life of the project equal to the initial investment, n is the number of periods for the project, and r is the discount rate.

The discount rate for the calculated discount factor, $A_{r,n}$, is the interest rate that has the same discount factor as $A_{r,n}$ in the annuity table along the row for n periods, or the closest to it. This discount rate is the internal rate of return of the investment. The IRR for project A is determined as follows:

$$\$555,000 = \$193,500 \times A_{r,4}$$

$$\text{Rearrange, } A_{r,4} = \frac{\$555,000}{\$193,500} = 2.868$$

Using the annuity factor in the present value tables (pp. 820–821) on the four-year row:

$$r \approx 15 \text{ percent}$$

The computed internal rate of return is compared to the firm's desired rate of return or some other chosen criterion to assess the desirability of the investment. An investment is desirable if the computed internal rate of return exceeds the desired rate of return. The computed 15 percent internal rate of return of project A is greater than the 10 percent rate of return that the firm set for this investment. Project A is, therefore, a desirable investment.

When the available annuity table does not have a discount factor that is reasonably close to the computed discount factor for the project, the IRR method requires an interpolation procedure to estimate the IRR.[9]

Uneven Cash Flows The procedure for estimating the internal rate of return of a project with uneven cash flow returns involves trial and error and interpolation.

---

[9] To illustrate the interpolation procedure, let us assume that this is the only annuity table available:

n/r	12%	14%	16%
4	3.037	2.914	2.798

The $A_{r,4}$ for project A is 2.868. The annuity table, however, does not have a discount factor of 2.868 for a four-year project. The discount factor is 2.914 at 14 percent and 2.798 at 16 percent. The IRR, which has a discount of 2.868, is between these two discount rates. The following interpolation procedure estimates the IRR:

(Footnote continues on next page)

Exhibit 11–19	Present Values of Project B with Interest Rates of 14 and 16 Percent				
Year	Net After-Tax Cash Flow	Discount Factor at 16 Percent	Present Value at 16 Percent	Discount Factor at 14 Percent	Present Value at 14 Percent
1	$164,000	0.862	$141,368	0.877	$143,828
2	194,000	0.743	144,142	0.769	149,186
3	194,000	0.641	124,354	0.675	130,950
4	382,000	552	210,864	0.592	226,144
Total			$620,728		$650,108

	Discount Rate	Total Cash Flow Returns	
	14%	$650,108	$650,108
	?		625,000
	16	620,728	
Difference:	2%	$ 29,380	
	?		$ 25,108

Internal rate of return:

$$14\% + 2\% \times \frac{\$25,108}{\$29,380} = 15.71\%$$

The determination of the IRR for project B, as shown in Exhibit 11–19, illustrates this procedure.

The present value of cash flow returns is $650,108 at a discount rate of 14 percent and $620,728 at 16 percent. A 2 percent increase in interest rates from 14 percent to 16 percent decreases the present value of cash flow returns by $29,380. With $625,000 initial investment in the project, the IRR procedure calls for an increase in the discount rate from 14 percent so the present value of cash flow returns will decrease from $650,108 to $625,000, a decrease of $25,108. The needed increase in the discount rate from 14 percent is 0.855 of the 2 percent increase from 14 percent to 16 percent—an increase of approximately 1.71 percent from 14 percent.

Using a Spreadsheet Program to Determine IRR Many spreadsheet programs are easy to use to estimate internal rates of return. For example, Lotus 1–2–3, Quattro, and Microsoft EXCEL offer an IRR function to determine internal rates of return. The required inputs for the programs are

Lotus 1–2–3 and Quattro: @IRR(estimated rate of return in decimal, range)

Microsoft EXCEL: =IRR(range, estimated rate of return in decimal)

	Interest Rate		Discount Factor	
At lower rate	14%	14%	2.914	2.914
Target rate		?		2.868
At higher rate	16		2.798	
Difference	2%		0.116	
		?		0.046

The difference in discount factors between the interest rates on either side of the target discount factor (2.868), discount factors for 14 and 16 percent, is 0.116. This suggests that an increase of 2 percent in interest rates from 14 percent to 16 percent decreases the discount factor by 0.116.

The interest rate we are looking for has a discount factor of 2.868, a decrease of 0.046 from the discount factor for interest rate of 14 percent. The interest rate, therefore, needs to be increased from 14 percent so the discount factor decreases from 2.914 to 2.868. The needed decrease in the discount factor, 0.046, is 40 percent of the difference in the discount factors between 14 percent and 16 percent. With an increase of 2 percent in interest rates from 14 percent to 16 percent, the discount factor decreases by 0.116. The needed increase in interest rate to decrease the discount factor by 0.046, therefore, is 40 percent of the 2 percent, or 80 percent as shown here:

$$14\% + \left(\frac{0.046}{0.116} \times 2\% \right) = 14\% + (0.4 \times 2\%) = 14\% + 0.8\% = 14.80\%$$

The user needs to provide a rough starting point for estimating the rate of return.[10] The *range* is the location of the data in the spreadsheet. The first cell of the range is the initial cash outlay expressed as a negative amount, followed by subsequent cash flow returns.[11]

COMPARISON OF THE NET PRESENT VALUE AND THE INTERNAL RATE OF RETURN METHODS

Among methods for analyzing capital investments the discounted cash flow (DCF) methods are the most theoretically sound. The two DCF methods suggest the same answers in most instances. Sometimes, however, the DCF methods yield significantly different results. To use capital budgeting techniques properly you must recognize situations in which the two DCF methods may reach different conclusions and the reasons for the differences.

Results from analyses using the NPV method and the IRR method may differ when capital investment projects have (1) different initial investment amounts, (2) dissimilar cash flow patterns, or (3) different useful lives. In addition, these two methods may differ in situations with varying costs of capital over the life of a project and in examining multiple investments.

◀ **LEARNING OBJECTIVE 4**
Identify the underlying assumptions of the discounted cash flow methods and use these methods properly in evaluating capital investments.

Amount of Initial Investment

Although both the NPV and the IRR methods use cash flow returns in evaluating capital investments, they do so differently. The NPV method examines the present value of future cash flow returns that an investment will generate over the initial investment in the project. The project that has the highest net present value among the investments under consideration is the choice of the NPV method.

The net present value of a project with a large initial investment is likely to have a higher net present value than another one with a small investment. Consider two investment projects with these initial investments, years of useful life, and annual net cash flow returns:

Project	Initial Investment	Annual Cash Inflow	Years of Useful Life	NPV at 10 percent	IRR
P	$5,000	$1,000	10	$1,145	15.13%
Q	1,000	300	10	843	27.38

NVP vs. IRR Results

Results from NPV and IRR may differ if projects differ in

1. Required initial investment
2. Cash flow pattern
3. Length of useful life
4. Varying cost of capital
5. Multiple investments

---

[10] Microsoft EXCEL assumes the estimated rate of return is 0.1 if none is provided.

[11] Microsoft EXCEL offers two additional programs, MIRR and XIRR, for estimating the internal rate of return. MIRR is for situations where the firm finances the needed cash outflows at a different rate than the expected rate for cash inflows.

$$=MIRR \text{ (range, finance rate, reinvest rate)}$$

XIRR is used when cash flows are not necessarily periodic.

$$=XIRR \text{ (range, dates, estimated rate)}$$

The dates need to correspond with the values specified in the range.

Project P has a higher net present value than that of project Q. A comparison of the NPVs would suggest that project P is the better investment of the two.

In contrast, the IRR method favors project Q. Project Q has an IRR of 27.38 percent while project P only has an IRR of 15.13 percent. One reason project P has a higher NPV than project Q is because it has a much larger investment than project Q, and the NPV method does not take into consideration the difference in the initial investments.

Although the initial investment for project P is five times the amount for project Q, project P is not generating five times the cash flow returns of project Q. The NPV method suggests that project P is the better investment of the two because the criterion is the size of the net present values.

A comparison of net present values of investments requiring substantially different amounts of investment yields no meaningful results. The project that has the largest net present value is not necessarily the project having the highest return among all projects considered, if it requires a substantially larger amount of initial investment than the other projects.

The internal rate of return method uses percentages in evaluating the relative profitability of the investments. The amount of initial investment has no effect on the relative profitability of investments.

Patterns of Cash Flow Returns

Firms invest and earn additional returns on cash flow returns generated from investments. Variations in patterns of cash flow returns such as the timing and the amount of cash flow returns affect the overall returns on projects and can alter capital investment decisions. Also, an investment project with varying directions of cash flow returns over the years can render internal rates of return of the investment uncertain.

Timing and Amounts of Cash Flow Return

Investment projects often differ in cash flow returns at different points in time. Some projects receive the bulk of their cash flow returns at early stages of the project. Others may not provide many cash flow returns until the last years of the project. Some projects have relatively constant cash flow returns throughout the period of the investment. Other projects have rather irregular cash flow returns. Differences in the timing and amount of cash flow returns affect a project's internal rate of return.

Paton Implement Manufacturing Company considers two capital investments in September 20X3, project A and project B. Both projects require $100,000 initial investments and have 10 years of useful life. Project A will generate most of its cash flow returns in the early years of the project, while project B will earn the bulk of its cash flow returns toward the end of the project. Columns 2 and 3 of Exhibit 11–20 contain the expected after-tax cash flow returns for projects A and B respectively. The cost of capital is 10 percent.

Project B's small cash flow returns in the early years increase over the years. The cash flow returns of project A follow the opposite pattern. At a 10 percent cost of capital, project B has a higher net present value than project A. The IRR method suggests the opposite. The internal rates of return are 19.34 percent for project B and 26.18 percent for project A.

Which project is the better investment? The preceding section suggests possible conflicting results from the two DCF methods when projects require different initial investments. However, the two projects, A and B, require the same amount of initial investment.

The two DCF methods have different assumptions on earnings of cash flow returns from an investment. The NPV method assumes that all cash flow returns of an investment earn the cost of capital or the discount rate employed in calculating the net present value of the investment (10 percent in the previous example). The

| Exhibit 11–20 | Effects of Patterns of Cash Flow Returns on the Evaluation of Capital Investment Using DCF Methods | | | | |

(1) Period	(2) Cash Flow Return of A	(3) Cash Flow Return of B	(4) 10 Percent Factor	(5) Present Value of A	(6) Present Value of B
0	$(100,000)	$(100,000)	1.000	$(100,000)	$(100,000)
1	$ 45,000	$ 13,000	.909	$ 40,905	$ 11,817
2	39,000	14,800	.826	32,214	12,225
3	25,000	16,600	.751	18,775	12,467
4	17,000	20,200	.683	11,611	13,797
5	23,000	23,800	.621	14,283	14,780
6	20,000	27,400	.564	11,280	15,454
7	17,000	35,500	.513	8,721	18,212
8	15,000	49,000	.467	7,005	22,883
9	13,000	49,000	.424	5,512	20,776
10	13,000	43,000	.386	5,018	16,598
Total	$ 227,000	$ 292,300		$ 155,324	$ 159,009
NPV				$ 55,324	$ 59,009
IRR				26.18%	19.34%

IRR method assumes that cash flow returns from a project will earn the same rate of return as the internal rate of return of the project.

Project A has an internal rate of return of 26.18 percent. In arriving at this rate the IRR method assumes that all cash flow returns of project A will earn 26.18 percent in each of the subsequent years until the end of its useful life. The $45,000 cash flow returns of project A in year 1 will earn the firm $11,781 ($45,000 × 0.2618) by the end of year 2 and $14,865 [($45,000 + $11,781) × 0.2618] by the end of year 3, and so on until the end of the useful life of project A.

The internal rate of return of project B is 19.34 percent. Thus, the IRR method assumes that all cash flow returns of project B will earn 19.34 percent in each of the subsequent years.

Having earlier cash flow returns and a higher internal rate of return than those of project B, project A raises its IRR in two ways. First, the firm earns returns on the early cash flow returns over a longer period of time than those from the late cash flow returns. Second, all cash flow returns, including the early cash flow returns, earn a higher rate of return.

Which rate of return, the internal rate of return of the project or the discount rate employed in the NPV method, is more realistic for the cash flow returns that an investment generates? Earning a certain rate of return on a project does not imply that the cash flow returns of the project also will earn the same rate of return. Yet the IRR method assumes that *all* cash flow returns of a project earn the *same* rate of return as the internal rate of return of the project.

The most desirable investment may have such a high internal rate of return that other investments are unlikely to earn the same high rate of returns. To expect the cash flow returns of an investment with a high rate of return to also earn the same high return is an overly optimistic and most likely an unrealistic assumption for a firm.

The IRR method assumes that the cash flow returns from project B will earn a lower rate of return in subsequent years than those generated by project A because the internal rate of return of project B is lower, only 19.34 percent. Surely cash available for investment in a given year will not earn a different rate of return because the cash is from a different project.

The NPV method assumes that all cash flow returns will earn the same rate as the discount rate employed in calculating the net present value of the project. The discount rate used by the NPV method usually is the cost of capital for the firm. This is usually a more conservative and more realistic expectation.

The current cost of capital or the discount rate may not be the rate of return that subsequent cash flow returns will earn. To avoid misguided capital investment decisions, management should carefully estimate the rates of return that can be expected of cash generated by an investment.

Changes in Cash Flow Direction

A typical capital investment incurs cash outflows in the early stage of the project and generates cash flow returns thereafter. In practice not every capital investment project follows such a cash flow pattern. After the initial investment some projects require additional investments that exceed the cash flow returns from the project for the same period. The project then would have a net cash outflow, or negative cash flow return, for the period. In a survey on capital budgeting practices, Fremgen found that 32 percent of the respondents frequently experienced one or more mixed directions in cash flows.[12] A mixed cash flow pattern may result in the project's having more than one internal rate of return, as the next example demonstrates.

A firm invests $1,323 in a project that will bring in $3,000 in cash proceeds after one year. The required cost for equipment disposal and site restoration makes the net effect on cash flow at the end of year 2 an outflow of $1,700.

Exhibit 11–21 shows that the project has two internal rates of return. The net present value is zero at a discount rate of 10 percent and again at 16 percent. This project has two internal rates of return because the cash flow direction changes from a cash outflow to a cash inflow and then to a cash outflow again. Theoretically, an investment project can have as many internal rates of return as there are changes in direction of cash flows.

Having multiple internal rates of return usually makes the real rate of return of the investment a puzzle. The Fremgen survey found that 15 percent of the respondents who used the IRR method had experienced multiple internal rates of return. Fortunately, most projects have only one internal rate of return even when there are changes in their cash flow directions.

Users of the IRR method should be cautious in applying it to projects with mixed cash flow directions. The estimated rate of return may not be the only internal rate of return for the project.

Length of Useful Life

The IRR method considers each additional useful year of a project another year that the cash flow returns of the project will earn a return equal to the project's internal rate of return. As a result, IRR favors projects with long useful lives.

Assume that the Paton Implement Manufacturing Company also considers project C. The investment requirement and expected cash flow returns for the first 10 years of project C are the same as those of project A. Project C has a useful life of

Exhibit 11–21	An Investment with Multiple Rates of Return				
(1)	(2)	(3)	(4)	(5)	(6)
Period	Cash Flow	Discount Factor at 10 Percent	Present Value with 10 Percent Discount Rate	Discount Factor at 16 Percent	Present Value with 16 Percent Discount Rate
0	$(1,323)	1.000	$(1,323)	1.000	$(1,323)
1	3,000	.909	2,727	.862	2,586
2	(1,700)	.826	(1,404)	.743	(1,263)
NPV			0		0

---

[12] James M. Fremgen, "Capital Budgeting Practices: A Survey", *Management Accounting* 54 (May 1973), pp. 19–25.

Exhibit 11–22	Effect of the Length of Useful Life on the Evaluation of Capital Investment Using DCF Methods				

Period	Cash Flow of A	Cash Flow of C	10 Percent Discount Factor	Present Value of A	Present Value of C
0	$(100,000)	$(100,000)	1.000	$(100,000)	$(100,000)
1	$ 45,000	$ 45,000	.909	$ 40,905	$ 40,905
2	39,000	39,000	.826	32,214	32,214
3	25,000	25,000	.751	18,775	18,775
4	17,000	17,000	.683	11,611	11,611
5	23,000	23,000	.621	14,283	14,283
6	20,000	20,000	.565	11,300	11,300
7	17,000	17,000	.513	8,721	8,721
8	15,000	15,000	.467	7,005	7,005
9	13,000	13,000	.424	5,512	5,512
10	13,000	13,000	.386	5,018	5,018
11		1,000	.350		350
12		1,000	.319		319
13		1,000	.290		290
14		1,000	.263		263
15		1,000	.239		239
Total	$ 227,000	$ 232,000		$ 155,344	$ 156,805
NPV				$ 55,344	$ 56,805
IRR				26.18%	26.29%

15 years. The cash flow returns of the last five years are $1,000 per year, a 1 percent return for a $100,000 investment. Exhibit 11–22 shows that the internal rate of return of project C is 26.29 percent. Recall that the internal rate of return of project A is 26.18 percent. Project C earns a higher return than project A, even though project C earns a mere 1 percent return in each of its last five years of useful life.

This result is not unique to the IRR method. The NPV method also favors projects with long useful lives as long as the project earns a positive net cash inflow during the additional years. Exhibit 11–22 shows that, even though project C earns only a small net cash flow return in each of the last five years, the NPV increases from $55,344 to $56,805. As long as the cash flow return in a year is positive, no matter how small the cash flow return is, the net present value increases and the desirability of the project improves.

Maintaining an investment ties up resources that the firm can use elsewhere. Even if the project requires no additional out-of-pocket financial outlays in its last years, the firm is paying for the continuation of the project in the form of lost opportunities. The firm can use the space occupied by the project for some other projects. Or the managers can guide other projects better if they do not have to spend time on this project. Or, with the proceeds from the project's termination, the firm can earn a higher return elsewhere.

Varying Cost of Capital

A firm's cost of capital can vary as situations change over the years. A firm may enjoy a low cost of capital when it has excess internal funds available or the capital market has abundant funds. A firm may face a high cost of capital when it experiences adverse operating results or economic conditions are tight. During the course of an investment a firm can have different costs of capital. There are situations where the desired rate of return on investment for different years varies because of variations in competition, the national economy, global situations, or other factors over the years. A proper capital budgeting procedure needs to incorporate changes in the firm's cost of capital or desired rate of return in evaluating capital investments.

The NPV method can accommodate different rates of return in different periods. Jennifer O'Clock realizes that the desired rates of return for project B should be different for different years because of expected changes in the economy, government fiscal policy, international money supply, or other factors. Column 3 of Exhibit 11–23 depicts her desired rate of return at different years. She still can determine the NPV of project B by following the procedure to determine net present values. By using appropriate discount factors for different discount rates, she can determine the net present value of project B as shown in the last column of Exhibit 11–23.

The IRR method yields only one rate of return for the entire life span of an investment project. As a result, the IRR method cannot easily handle situations with varying desired rates of return. The IRR procedure determines a single rate that reflects the return of the project under consideration. The firm then compares the single rate of return to the firm's cost of capital or desired rate of return in assessing the desirability of a project. The procedure does not allow for different rates of return in different years.

Addable Criterion Measures

The NPV method evaluates investment projects in present value dollar amounts while the IRR method evaluates investment projects in percentages or rates. Dollars earned from multiple projects are addable while percentages or rates of return on multiple projects are not. The total net present value of independent projects is the simple sum of the net present values of these projects. If the net present value of a $120,000 investment is $35,000 and the net present value of a $50,000 investment in another independent project is $20,000, the total net present value of investing $170,000 in these two projects is $55,000, the sum of the two net present values. Because the net present values of investment projects are addable, a firm can easily and quickly evaluate investments in multiple projects.

Internal rates of return are not addable. Investments of $120,000 in one project that earns a 10 percent rate of return and $50,000 in another project that earns a 15 percent rate of return do not make the rate of return from the entire $170,000 25 percent. The overall internal rate of return from investing in a number of projects is not the sum of the individual internal rates of return of the projects. A

Exhibit 11–23	Net Present Values of Project B with Different Desired Rates of Return over the Years			
Year	**Net After-Tax Cash Inflow**	**Desired Rate of Return**	**Discount Factor**	**Present Value**
1	$164,000	0.10	0.909	$149,076
2	194,000	0.12	0.797	154,618
3	194,000	0.13	0.694	134,636
4	382,000	0.15	0.572	218,504
Total PV				$656,834
Initial Investment				625,000
NPV				$ 31,834

Exhibit 11–24	A Comparison of NPV and IRR Methods
NPV	**IRR**
Not meaningful for comparing projects with different amounts of initial investments	Easy to compare projects with different amounts of initial investments
NPVs of multiple projects are additive	IRRs of multiple projects are not additive
Assumes cash proceeds can be reinvested to earn the same rate of return as in the computation	Assumes cash proceeds can be reinvested to earn the same rate as the IRR on that particular project
Allows for multiple discount rates	Allows for only one discount rate

Exhibit 11–25	Summary of Factors Affecting Results of Analyses Using the DCF Methods	

Factor	NPV Method	IRR Method
Amount of initial investment	Favors projects with large initial investment	No effect
Rate of return on reinvestment of cash flow returns	The same as the cost of capital or the discount rate used in calculations	The same as the internal rate of return of the investment
Cash flow pattern		
• Timing and amount	Moderate effect	Effects are in proportion to the internal rate of return
• Cash flow direction	No effect	May have multiple rates of return for projects with multiple cash flow directions
Length of useful life	Moderately favors projects with long, useful lives	Favors projects with long, useful lives and in proportion to the internal rate of return
Multiple costs of capital	Incorporates easily	Difficult to incorporate
Addable results	Yes	No

change in the projects under consideration always requires a complete recalculation of the overall internal rate of return.

Exhibit 11–24 contrasts the two DCF methods. Exhibit 11–25 summarizes situations that may lead the NPV method and the IRR method to reach different conclusions in evaluating the same investment project.

STRATEGIC COST MANAGEMENT AND CAPITAL BUDGETING

Capital investment is a critical factor for an organization's continuous success and needs to be tailored to the strategy being followed by the firm or its business units. Moreover, a capital investment can change or reshape an organization's strategy. A capital investment analysis that includes only immediate value-added activities and costs of the firm can be too narrowly focused and fail to capture the full impact of investment to the firm. A proper analysis of a capital investment needs to include the firm's competitive advantage, assessments of the effect of the firm's value chain, and inclusion of strategic cost drivers.

LEARNING OBJECTIVE 5
Discuss the relationships between strategic cost management and capital budgeting.

Competitive Strategy and Capital Budgeting

As discussed in Chapter 2, competitive strategy is the way a firm chooses to compete to achieve its strategic goals or mission. A firm may choose a mission to build, to hold, or to harvest. Exhibit 11–26 shows the effect of differences in strategic missions on capital budgeting.

An organization that chooses a build mission often faces many uncertainties, uses technologies that are still evolving, and traverses on environments that change rapidly. Capital budgeting processes in these firms often are less formal, use more nonfinancial and nonquantifiable data, and adopt subjective criteria in evaluating investment projects. In contrast, a firm with a harvest mission is more likely to be a mature organization or to have products with mature markets. Its capital budgeting processes are more likely to be formalized. Also, most of the data for its capital budgeting are likely to be quantifiable and financial in nature.

In addition, uncertainty faced by an organization with a build mission often requires the firm to look at longer terms. This would involve the expectation of a longer payback and use of relatively low hurdle rates in evaluating capital projects. The high risk involved also requires project approval by a relatively high level of management.

Exhibit 11–26   Strategic Missions and Capital Budgeting

Factors in Capital Budgeting	Strategic Mission		
	Build	Hold	Harvest
Formalization of capital expenditure decisions	Less formal DCF analysis	→	More formalized DCF analysis
Capital expenditure evaluation criteria	More emphasis on nonfinancial data (market share, efficient use of R&D dollars, etc.)	→	More emphasis on financial data (cost efficiency; straight cash on cash incremental return)
	Longer payback	→	Shorter payback
Hurdle rates	Relatively low	→	Relatively high
Capital investment analysis	More subjective and qualitative	→	More quantitative and financial
Project approval limits at business unit level	Relatively high	→	Relatively low
Frequency of postaudit	Frequent	→	Less frequent

Source: Vijay Govindarajan and John K. Shank, "Strategic Cost Management: Tailoring Controls to Strategies," *Journal of Cost Management,* Fall 1992, pp. 14–25.

A mature market is likely ripe for change. By necessity, the payback period for a capital investment in such a market needs to be short, and the hurdle rate has to be at least the firm's average rate of return. A firm that decides to continue its harvest mission will most likely not undertake projects with major innovations. Capital investment projects can be handled at a relatively low management level.

A firm, however, should never consider its strategic mission as a given in its capital investment analysis. Assuming a continuing stable operating environment can be a fatal mistake. Moreover, a capital investment also helps managers in defining strategy, establishing goals, and planning tactics to accomplish those goals. As a tool for analyzing long-term investment opportunities, capital budgeting is guided by strategy and goals; but it is also instrumental in redefining or enhancing the way the firm has chosen to compete. A new manufacturing technology acquired by a harvesting firm with a low-cost competitive position can transform the firm into a different competitive position, such as product differentiation with an increased emphasis of to build. For instance, adoption of a host of new technologies enables Levi-Strauss to make individually tailored designer jeans embroidered with the name of the owner. Cost is no longer the most critical factor in achieving high profitability for the firm. The firm transformed its market from a commodity market to a highly differentiated product.

Value Chain and Capital Budgeting

Critics often charge conventional capital budgeting techniques are inadequate tools that render an incomplete analysis for today's firms that face global competition and rapid changes in both technology and the markets of their products or services. A common criticism is that the conventional capital budgeting techniques are project-oriented; they start from the inception of a project and finish at the delivery of goods and services to market in the short run, and with disposal of the project at the end of the project's useful life. Such an analysis fails to capture the full impact of a capital investment, especially when the investment involves technology change.

Through its activities, a firm adds or creates values and occupies a node in the linked set of value-creating activities all the way from basic raw materials to the ultimate end-use product delivered into the final consumers' hands. (This process has been defined as a value chain by John K. Shank.) Even though it may partake in only a segment of the entire value chain, the firm needs to analyze the impact of its capital investments throughout the entire value chain.

Shank and Govindarajan conducted a field study and demonstrated the importance of value-chain analysis in capital budgeting.[13] A firm undertook a conventional capital budgeting analysis that included only the benefits to the operation where the investment was to be made. The analysis showed no financial gain to the firm and no capital investment was to be made. A value-chain analysis that included impacts to both upstream and downstream operations showed that the firm could save an estimated $33.6 million per year in just one of the firm's locations. The value-chain analysis showed unequivocally the benefit from the investment. The firm changed its decision.

Cost Driver Analysis

Volume frequently is the only identified cost driver in conventional capital budgeting analyses. In many capital investments, however, structural and executional cost drivers are more critical factors than volume. A sound capital budgeting process needs to involve structural and executional cost drivers, in addition to volume as the cost driver.

Structural cost drivers are factors that relate to the firm's strategic choices regarding economic structure. These strategic choices include technology, scale, product-line complexity, scope of vertical integration, or experience. These cost drivers are not volume-based. The strategic cost drivers are more likely to be found at levels in which the firm chooses to compete (Chapter 2).

A capital investment decision to not invest in a new technology mandates the firm to continue to operate with the same set of cost drivers. The cost drivers or their levels can be entirely different should the firm decide to invest in the new technology. The cost of a business unit with a complex product line is not the same as another one with a product line that is easy to make, service, and sell. McDonnell Douglas Corporation's decision in 1996 not to make the estimated $15 billion investment necessary to compete directly with larger rivals reduced the firm to a minor player in the commercial-jet business.[14] A capital budgeting decision can change the structural cost drivers of the firm, and the impacts of structural cost drivers are important considerations in capital budgeting.

Executional cost drivers are major determinants of a firm's cost position that hinge on its ability to work successfully within the economic structure it chooses. Executional cost drivers that are likely to be important include:

- Workforce involvement (participative management).
- Workforce commitment to continuous improvement.
- Adherence to total quality management concepts.
- Utilization of effective capacity.
- Efficiency of production flow layout.
- Effectiveness of product design or formulation.
- Exploitation of linkages with suppliers and customers all along the value chain.[15]

Motorola's cost advantage derives from its ability to reduce defect rates to only three units per million in manufacturing integrated circuits achieved through years of continual capital investments in quality trainings and process improvements. This example shows the impact of an executional cost driver. The cost advantage led Motorola to enter the business of making billets for fluorescent lamps. They believe that their quality skills provide them with a strategic advantage for a successful entry into this new business.

---

[13] John K. Shank and Vijay Govindarajan, "Strategic Cost Analysis of Technological Investments," *Sloan Management Review,* Fall 1992, pp. 39–51.

[14] *The Wall Street Journal,* October 29, 1996, p. A3. The firm eventually was acquired by Boeing, its main rival in the United States.

[15] Shank and Govindarajan, "Strategic Cost Analysis," p. 47.

BEHAVIORAL ISSUES IN CAPITAL BUDGETING

LEARNING OBJECTIVE 6 ▶
Identify behavioral factors
in capital budgeting
decision.

Successful capital budgeting is a result of efforts by individuals and teams. While it is a vital part of corporate decision making, a proper and carefully designed capital investment procedure does not necessarily lead to a successful capital investment. Human behavior often plays an important role in successful capital investments.

A successful manager often is viewed as one who manages a large division or a growing division. Big or growing enterprises require capital investments. Furthermore, a new capital asset is visible and often viewed as "progress" or an "accomplishment." This fact leads many managers to be overly eager to promote capital investments. Firms need to carefully contain aggressive managers who overestimate projections in attempts to earn approval of capital investment for their divisions.

Studies have found escalating commitment a too common phenomenon in capital investments. In an attempt to recoup past losses a decision maker often considers past costs or losses relevant in deciding capital investments. Escalating commitments are even more likely when these managers are also responsible for negative consequences from past actions.[16]

Although sunk costs should have no effect on decisions, research in prospect theory has found that sunk costs play an important role influencing the framing of decisions. Sunk costs do not enter into the computation to determine whether the benefits of a particular course of action exceed the costs. The existence of a negative balance, however, may result in the subsequent decisions being framed as a choice between losses.[17] A positive balance results in the subsequent decisions being framed as a choice between gains. Decision makers are likely to minimize losses while max-

---

BusinessWeek

Can the Olympics Turn Hosts and Sponsors into Champions?

(Continues from page 381)

A: When you go for the gold, you've got to be prepared for a few risks . . .

Like the athletes who invest years of their lives training to reach the Olympics, with risks and returns encountered along the way, host cities and corporate sponsors face a similar scenario. These financial sponsors understand the risks involved, but they also recognize the potential long-term gain—whether it is to their city's image or to its bottom line. Take the most recent Winter Olympics in Nagano, Japan. "It's hard to allocate the costs and returns, but thanks to the Olympics we got a new bullet train to Tokyo, new expressway, and more sewers," says Shigekazu Nakamura, deputy managing editor of *Shinano Mainichi Shimbun,* Nagano's biggest newspaper. Although these improvements add up to approximately $12.1 billion, Nagano and Olympic corporate sponsors believe that the long-term return is definitely worth the initial investment. For example, Eastman Kodak Company, long-time sponsor of the Olympics, believes their investment (a minimum of $40 million) is money well spent. "We've always seen an uptick in revenues, in brand awareness [after the Olympics]," says Carl E. Gustin Jr., a senior vice president at Kodak. So, like the Olympic athletes, financial sponsors have to be ready for a potential stellar performance . . . or a less-than-fulfilling experience.

For further reading, see "Sponsorship: The Risks and Rewards of Going for the Gold," *Business Week,* February 9, 1998; "Atlanta's Big Leap," *Business Week,* July 29, 1996; and "A High Hurdle in Atlanta," *Business Week,* May 3, 1993.

---

[16] Whyte, "Escalating Commitment to a Course of Action: A Reinterpretation," *Academy of Management Review* 11 (1986), pp. 311–21.

[17] D. Kanamen and D. Tversky, "Prospect Theory: An Analysis of Decisions under Risk," *Econometrica* 47 (1979), pp. 263–90.

imizing gains. Many studies in human decision making have found this to be true, even though a rational decision suggests otherwise.

The amount of work and time required to secure approval of a capital investment project often allows much-needed capital investments to be bypassed. In their place smaller projects are built, costing less than the amount that requires approval. Managers may undertake a series of small additions to plant and equipment, rather than undertaking a major capital investment project such as computer-integrated-manufacturing or flexible manufacturing systems. Failure to make necessary major investments can reduce the competitiveness, erode the market share, and jeopardize long-term profitability and even survival of the firm.

Intolerance of uncertainty often leads managers to require short payback periods for capital investments. Once a project pays for itself, the amount of risk is reduced. This makes projects with short payback periods the preferred choice to some decision makers. Not all critical capital investments can have a short payback period, however. Many important projects require a lengthy time for installation, testing, adjusting, personnel training, and market acceptance. Some examples are investments in new manufacturing technologies, new product development, and expanding into new territories, especially a foreign country. Requiring too short a payback period makes the acceptance of such projects very unlikely.

SUMMARY

Capital investment decisions are among the most important decisions for the success of a firm or organization. No business firm can survive for long without good capital investments. No governmental organization can provide good services to its constituents without carefully considered capital investments.

Capital budgeting processes include project identification, project evaluation and selection, and monitoring and review. Initial proposals for capital investment often are made at the local or business subunit level. Investments that involve major technology change are more likely initiated at top management level, however.

Capital investment focuses on events that will unfold in the future. In analyzing capital investments, the primary focus often is on cash flow. An investment is not a good investment if the investor receives less cash from the investment than the amount the investor put in.

Cash flows in investments occur at three stages. These stages are initial acquisition, operations, and final disinvestment. Cash flows at initial acquisition include cash disbursement for the purchase of equipment and facilities, commitment of working capital needed during operation of the investment, and cash proceeds from disposal of the asset the investment replaced or cash disbursement for disposing of the replaced assets and facilities.

An investment generates net cash flow returns during its operation either through increases in revenues or through decreases in expenses. The final disinvestment may generate additional cash proceeds through sales of the investment. On the other side of the ledger, final disinvestment leads to cash expenditures for disposing of the assets, for restoring the facilities the investment occupies, and for terminating, relocating, or retraining of personnel no longer needed when the investment ends. All cash flows for a business firm should be net of tax effects.

Many techniques are available for analyzing capital investments. Among the techniques most often used are undiscounted methods such as payback period and accounting rate of return and discounted cash flow methods such as net present value and internal rate of return. Exhibit 11–27 summarizes the definitions, computation procedures, advantages, and weaknesses of these methods.

A capital investment analysis needs to take into consideration the firm's competitive advantage, effects of the investment on both upstream and downstream activities in the firm's value chain, and impact of strategic structural and executional cost drivers.

417

Exhibit 11–27	**Capital Budgeting Techniques**			
Method	**Definition**	**Computation Procedure**	**Advantages**	**Weaknesses**
Payback period	Number of years to recover the initial investment	Uniform flow: $$\frac{\text{Investment}}{\text{Net cash flow}}$$ Uneven flow: number of years for the cumulative cash flow equal to the investment	1. Simple to use and understand 2. Measures liquidity 3. Allows for risk tolerance	1. Ignores timing and time value of money 2. Ignores cash flows beyond payback period
Accounting rate of return	Ratio of average annual net income to the initial investment or average investment (book value)	$$\frac{\text{Average net income}}{\text{Investment}}$$ Investment is the original total investment or average book value of the investment	1. Data readily available 2. Consistent with other financial measures	1. Ignores timing and time value of money 2. Uses accounting numbers rather than cash flows
Net present value	Difference between the initial investment and the present value of subsequent net cash flow returns discounted at a given interest rate	Present value of cash flow return − Initial investment	1. Considers time value of money 2. Uses realistic discount rate for reinvestment 3. Additive for combined projects	1. Not meaningful for comparing projects requiring different amounts of investments
Internal rate of return	Discount rate that makes the initial investment equal to the present value of subsequent net cash flow returns	Solving the following equation for discount rate i: Present value factor of i × Cash flow returns = Initial investment	1. Considers time value of money 2. Easy for comparing projects requiring different amounts of investment	1. Assumption on reinvestment rate of return may be unrealistic 2. Complex to compute if done manually

APPENDIX

Modified Accelerated Cost Recovery System (MACRS)

Commonly firms use different depreciation methods for various depreciable assets and even for the same type of asset. In an effort to bring more uniformity into computations of depreciation and to encourage businesses to invest in new plant and equipment by allowing them to recover the investment quickly through depreciation, Congress introduced the Accelerated Cost Recovery System (ACRS) in 1981. ACRS was replaced in 1986 by the Modified Accelerated Cost Recovery System (MACRS). As a result, there are currently several systems for determining the depreciation expenses of tangible assets.

The amount of depreciation for a particular asset is determined by two factors: (1) when the asset was placed in service and (2) the nature of the asset. All assets placed in service after 1986 use MACRS. ACRS is used for assets placed in service after 1980 but before 1987. Assets placed in service before 1981 can use either the straight-line or an accelerated depreciation method. This appendix discusses MACRS only. If you need information about other depreciation systems, obtain Publication 534 entitled "Depreciation" from the Internal Revenue Service (IRS).

MACRS assigns all depreciable assets to one of eight classes, referred to as recovery periods in the tax law. Exhibit 11–28 describes these classes and their depreciation methods with examples of assets in each class.

MACRS does not use disposable value; depreciation is calculated based on the entire original cost. With the exception of residential and nonresidential real properties in the last two classes, a half-year convention is used to determine the depreciation for the first year the asset is placed in service, and, if the firm owns the depreciable asset for the entire recovery period, for the year following the end of the recovery period.

A half-year convention allows a half year of depreciation for the first year the firm places the property in service, regardless of when the property is placed in service during the year. To illustrate, the first year depreciation for a five-year property would have been 40 percent (200 percent of the straight-line rate) of the original cost without the half-year convention. Because of the half-year convention, the allowable depreciation for the first year is 20 percent. The depreciation for each of the remaining years of the recovery period is determined by using the 200 percent declining-balance method. The depreciation for the second year of a five-year property, for example, is 40 percent of the remaining 80 percent, which is 32 percent of the original cost. Exhibit 11–29 shows the depreciation rates for properties other than residential or nonresidential real properties.

Under a special rule, a mid-quarter convention, instead of a half-year convention, may have to be used. Residential and nonresidential rental properties use a mid-month convention in all situations. You should consult IRS publications or tax professionals for details.

Tax planning is a complex matter. The discussion in this appendix barely scratches the surface. Many issues such as loss carrybacks and carryforwards, qualification for capital assets, state income taxes, and foreign tax credits are not discussed. Always consult a tax professional to make sure that you include all tax considerations.

Exhibit 11–28	Asset Classes (Recovery Periods) under MACRS	
Class	**Depreciation Method**	**Example**
3-year property	200% declining-balance	Light tools and handling equipment
5-year property	200% declining-balance	Computers and peripheral equipment, office machinery, automobiles, light trucks
7-year property	200% declining-balance	Office furniture, appliances, carpet, and furniture in residential rental property and any asset that does not have an assigned class
10-year property	200% declining-balance	Manufacturing assets for food products, petroleum refining, tobacco
15-year property	150% declining-balance	Road and shrubbery, telephone distribution plant
20-year property	150% declining-balance	Multipurpose farm structures
27.5 year property	Straight-line	Residential rental property
31.5 year property	Straight-line	Nonresidential real property, office building, warehouse

Exhibit 11–29	MACRS Depreciation Rate					
Year	**3-year**	**5-year**	**7-year**	**10-year**	**15-year**	**20-year**
1	33.33	20.00	14.29	10.00	5.00	3.75
2	44.45	32.00	24.49	18.00	9.50	7.22
3	14.81	19.20	17.49	14.40	8.55	6.68
4	7.41	11.52*	12.49	11.52	7.70	6.18
5		11.52	8.93*	9.22	6.93	5.71
6		5.76	8.92	7.37	6.23	5.28
7			8.92	6.55*	5.90*	4.89
8			4.47	6.55	5.90	4.52
9				6.56	5.91	4.46*

*First year of switching to the straight-line method.

SELF-STUDY PROBLEM

(For solution, please turn to the end of the chapter.)

Capital Budgeting for Expanding Productive Capacity

Ray Summers Company operates at a full capacity of 10,000 units per year. The firm, however, is still unable to meet the demand for its product, estimated at 15,000 units annually. This level of demand is expected to continue for the next four years.

To expand productive capacity to meet the demand, the firm can acquire equipment costing $580,000. This equipment has a useful life of four years and can be sold for $50,000 at the end of the fourth year. The engineering division estimates that installation, testing, and adjusting of the machine will cost $12,000 before the machine can be put into production.

An adjacent vacant warehouse can be leased for the duration of the project for $10,000 per year. The warehouse needs renovations at a cost of $58,000 to make it suitable for manufacturing. The lease terms call for restoring the warehouse to its original condition on expiration of the lease. The restoration is estimated to cost $20,000. Analysis of current operating data provides this information:

			Per Unit
Sales price			$200
Variable costs:			
Manufacturing	$ 60		
Marketing	20	$ 80	
Fixed costs:			
Manufacturing	$ 25		
Marketing and administrative	15	40	120
Net income			$ 80

The new equipment has no effect on the variable costs per unit. All current fixed costs are expected to continue with the same total amount. Depreciation expenses are included in the current fixed costs. Fixed costs per unit are $5 for manufacturing and $4 for marketing and administration.

Additional fixed manufacturing costs of $140,000 (excluding depreciation) will be incurred annually if the equipment is purchased. The firm will need to hire an additional marketing manager to serve new customers. The annual cost for the new marketing manager, supporting staff, and office expense is estimated to be approximately $100,000. The accountant expects the firm to be in the 40 percent tax bracket for combined federal and state income taxes in the next four years. No investment credit is currently in effect. The firm requires a minimum rate of return of 12 percent on investments and uses straight-line depreciation.

Required

1. What is the total cash outflow needed for the initial investment in year 0?
2. What effect will the acquisition of the new machine have on net income in each of the four years?

3. What effect will the acquisition of the new machine have on cash flows in each of the four years?
4. Compute the payback period of the investment.
5. Compute the accounting rate of return based on the average investment.
6. Compute the net present value.
7. Compute the internal rate of return.
8. The firm expects the unit variable manufacturing cost to increase with the new machine. What is the most that the unit variable cost can increase and the firm still earn the required rate of return on the investment?

QUESTIONS

11–1 What are the major factors in capital budgeting decisions?

11–2 "If I have to name the one most important concern in capital budgeting, I'll say it is the effect on the bottom line." Do you agree? What factor might have led this company executive with more than 20 years of experience to come to this conclusion?

11–3 What cash flows might a hospital incur after it installs a CAT scanner?

11–4 What are costs for abandoning a chemical factory that the firm has operated for the last 20 years?

11–5 What is a direct cash effect? Can you give some examples of direct cash effects in acquiring a new factory?

11–6 What is tax effect? Can you give some examples of tax effects in acquiring a new factory?

11–7 "Book value is nothing but a bookkeeper's figure and is irrelevant in capital budgeting." Do you agree?

11–8 What are the major deficiencies of the payback period? Does the present value payback period method overcome these deficiencies?

11–9 Does the accounting rate of return method provide a true measure of return on investment? How about the internal rate of return?

11–10 What should be the decision criterion when we use the NPV method to assess capital investments? Does the IRR method use the same criterion?

11–11 "Let's be more practical. DCF is not the only gospel. Many managers have become too absorbed with DCF." Can such a statement be justified? Why?

11–12 "Because business executives don't know how to run the numbers, companies are not acting decisively to put these technologies to work. . . Urgently needed are new cost/benefit formulas and measurements. . . that go beyond the usual return on investment (ROI) evaluations." Do you agree? Why? If you agree, what cost/benefit have we left out in ROI evaluations?

11–13 What criterion should be used in choosing investment projects for a firm with unlimited funds at a cost of 10 percent to the firm? Can the firm use the same criterion if it has only a limited amount of funds available for investments?

11–14 List at least three important behavioral factors in capital budgeting.

11–15 When do differences in results arise between the NPV method and the IRR method?

11–16 How does the size of the initial investment affect the IRR method and NPV method?

11–17 "The net present value method weighs early receipts of cash much more heavily than late receipts of cash." Do you agree?

11–18 How does a depreciation expense affect capital investment decisions?

11–19 A firm may alter its desired rate of return from year to year. What factors could have contributed to the changes?

11–20 Answer yes or no and your reasons in the following two situations:

   a. In evaluating capital projects, if a firm's cost of capital is 10 percent and the internal rate of return of a project is 11 percent, should the firm accept the project? Consider only quantitative factors.

   b. In evaluating a capital project that requires $150,000 initial investment, if the firm's cost of capital is 10 percent and the present value of the expected net increases in cash inflow from the project is $148,000, should the firm accept the project? Consider only quantitative factors.

11–21 How would a firm with a build mission use capital budgeting differently from a firm with a harvest mission? Why might they differ?

11–22 Yale, president of Hotchikiss, Inc., your client, recently attended a seminar at which a speaker discussed planning and control of capital expenditures, which he referred to as capital budgeting. Yale tells you that he is not quite sure he understands that concept.

Required

   a. Explain the nature and identify several uses of capital budgeting.

   b. What are the basic differences between the payback (payout) method and the net present value method of capital budgeting? Explain.

   c. Define cost of capital.

   d. Financial accounting data are not entirely suitable for use in capital budgeting. Explain.

   (CPA Adapted)

PROBLEMS

11–23 **BASIC CAPITAL BUDGETING TECHNIQUES: UNIFORM CASH FLOW RETURNS.**   Irv Nelson, Inc., purchased a $500,000 machine to manufacture a specialty tap for electrical equipment. This tap is in high demand and Nelson can sell all it can manufacture for the next 10 years. The government has exempted taxes on profits from new investments to encourage capital investments. This legislation is not expected to be altered in the foreseeable future. The equipment is expected to have 10 years' useful life with no salvage value. The firm uses straight-line depreciation. The net cash inflow is expected to be $120,000 each year for 10 years. Nelson uses 12 percent in evaluating capital investments.

   Required   Compute for the capital investment

   1. Payback period.
   2. Accounting rate of return based on (a) initial investment and (b) average investment.
   3. Net present value.
   4. Present value payback period.
   5. Internal rate of return.

11–24 **BASIC CAPITAL BUDGETING TECHNIQUES: UNEVEN CASH FLOW RETURNS WITH TAXES**   Use the same information for this problem as you did for Irv Nelson, Inc., except that the investment is subject to taxes and that the net operating cash inflow is

Year	Cash Inflow
1	$ 50,000
2	80,000
3	120,000
4	200,000
5	240,000
6	300,000
7	270,000
8	240,000
9	120,000
10	40,000

Irv Nelson, Inc., has been paying 30 percent for combined federal and state income taxes. This rate is not expected to change during the period of this investment. The firm uses a straight-line depreciation method.

Required Compute for the project

1. Payback period.
2. Accounting rate of return based on (a) initial investment and (b) average investment.
3. Net present value.
4. Internal rate of return.

11-25 **BASIC CAPITAL BUDGETING TECHNIQUES: UNEVEN CASH FLOW RETURNS AND MACRS** Use the data in problem 11-24 for Irv Nelson, Inc., and use MACRS for depreciation for 5-year property.

Required Compute for the investment

1. Payback period.
2. Accounting rate of return based on (a) initial investment and (b) average investment.
3. Net present value.
4. Internal rate of return.

11-26 **EQUIPMENT REPLACEMENT: COST SAVING IN CAPITAL BUDGETING**
The management of Devine Instrument Company is considering the purchase of a new drilling machine, model RoboDril 1010K. According to the specifications and testing results, RoboDril will substantially increase productivity over AccuDril X10, the machine Devine is currently using.

Strategy

AccuDril X10 was acquired 8 years ago for $120,000 and is being depreciated over its 10 years of expected useful life with an estimated salvage value of $20,000. The engineering department expects that AccuDril X10 can be kept going for yet another three years with a major overhaul at the end of its expected useful life at an estimated cost of $100,000. The machine then will be depreciated using straight-line depreciation with no salvage value for the equipment. The overhaul will improve the operating efficiency by 20 percent. No other operating conditions will be affected by the overhaul.

RoboDril 1010K is selling for $250,000. Installation, testing, rearrangement, and training will cost another $30,000. The manufacturer is willing to take the AccuDril as a trade-in for $40,000. The new equipment will be depreciated using straight-line depreciation with no salvage value. New technology most likely would make RoboDril obsolete to the firm in five years.

Variable operating cost for either machine is the same: $10 per hour. Other pertinent data are

	AccuDril X10	RoboDril 1010K
Units of output (per year)	10,000	10,000
Machine-hours	8,000	4,000
Selling price per unit	$ 100	$ 100
Variable manufacturing cost (not including machine-hours)	$ 40	$ 40
Other annual expenses (tooling & supervising)	$95,000	$55,000
Disposable value—today	$25,000	
Disposable value—in five years	-0-	$50,000

Devine Instrument Company's cost of funds is 12 percent and it is in the 40 percent tax bracket.

Required

1. Determine the effect on cash flow for items that differ between the two alternatives.

2. Compute the payback period for purchasing RoboDril 1010K rather than having AccuDril X10 overhauled in two years.

3. What is the present value for each of the alternatives?

4. What other factors, including strategic issues, should the firm consider before making the final decision?

Strategy

11–27 SENSITIVITY ANALYSIS AND PERFORMANCE EVALUATION Use the information in problem 11–26 to answer the following questions:

Required

1. To what extent can the estimated improvement in machine efficiency be in error and the replacement decision still be a correct decision financially?

2. New technologies developed since the purchase of AccuDril X10 make it possible to overhaul this machine now for $80,000. The overhaul will improve productivity by 20 percent and reduce the cost of a major overhaul two years from now to $30,000. All overhaul costs will be depreciated using straight-line depreciation. With either overhaul, the machine will have no salvage value. Either overhaul can be scheduled during regular maintenance and will not affect production. Despite the old saying, "If it isn't broke, don't fix it," should you conduct the overhaul now assuming that no funds currently are available to purchase RoboDril 1010K?

3. Undertaking the overhaul now also improves product quality. Management is of the opinion that the improvement in quality is rather subtle and very difficult to quantify. Should the firm overhaul now?

11–28 COMPARISON OF CAPITAL BUDGETING TECHNIQUES Nil Hill Corporation has been using its present facilities at their annual full capacity of 10,000 units for the last three years. However, the company still is unable to keep pace with continuing demand for the product that is estimated to be 25,000 units annually. This level of demand is expected to continue at least for the next four years. To expand productive capacity to take advantage of the demand, equipment costing $995,000 must be acquired. The machine will double the current production quantity. This equipment has a useful life of 10 years and can be sold for $195,000 at the end of year 4 or $35,000 at the end of year 10. Analysis of current operating data provides the following information:

		Per Unit
Sales price		$195
Variable costs		
Manufacturing	$90	
Marketing	10	$100
Fixed costs		
Manufacturing	$45	
Other	25	70	170
Net income		$ 25

The fixed costs include depreciation expense of the current machine. The new equipment will not change variable costs, but additional fixed manufacturing costs (excluding depreciation) of $250,000 will be incurred annually. An additional $200,000 in fixed marketing costs per year is expected. Nil Hill is in the 30 percent tax bracket. Management has set a minimum rate of return of 14 percent before capital investments are considered any further.

Required

1. What is the effect of the acquisition of the new machine on net income in each of the four years?
2. What is the effect of the acquisition of the new machine on cash flows in each of the four years?
3. Compute the payback period of the investment.
4. Compute the accounting rate of return based on the average investment.
5. Compute the net present value.
6. Compute the internal rate of return.
7. Management is unsure of the reliability of the estimated figures for either the selling price or the unit variable cost. What is the maximum deviation allowed for the original decision to remain unchanged in each of the independent situations described below?
   a. The total variable cost if the change will affect only the variable cost of the additional units to be manufactured by the new machine.
   b. The selling price per unit if the change will affect the unit selling price of all the units sold by the Nil Hill Corporation.

11–29 REPLACING A MACHINE WITH A LARGER-CAPACITY MACHINE: CAPITAL BUDGETING TECHNIQUES AND SENSITIVITY ANALYSIS The Hightec Corporation has a seven-year contract with Magichip Company to supply 10,000 units of XT–12 at $5.00 per unit. Increases in materials and other costs since the signing of the contract two years ago make this product a cash drain to the Hightec Corporation. As the manager of the subsidiary that manufactures and sells XT–12, you discovered that the purchase of a new machine SP1000 would increase productivity and, hopefully, profits. The following is a summary of pertinent information:

	Machine in Use	SP1000
Capacity	10,000 units/year	18,000 units/year
Materials	$ 4 per unit	$ 3 per unit
Labor and other variable costs	$ 1 per unit	$0.2 per unit
Maintenance costs	$ 1 per unit	$0.1 per unit

(For simplicity, assume all revenues and expenses are received and paid at year-ends.)

The current machine can be sold for $3,000 today. The salvage value will be $1,000 if the machine is used for another five years. The new machine costs $100,000, will be depreciated over a five-year life, and will have a net disposal value of $5,000 in five years. The company's cost of capital is 6 percent. If the company decides to keep the old machine, which is fully depreciated, it will be able to continue production with it for at least another five years. All machines are depreciated on a straight-line basis with no salvage value. The firm expects to continue to pay approximately 20 percent for both federal and state income taxes into the foreseeable future. At present the Magichip Company is the only user of XT–12.

Required Compute

1. Effects on cash flow if the new machine is purchased.
2. The net present value of the new machine.
3. The payback period of the new machine, assuming the annual cash flow returns in the original problem were $25,000.
4. The internal rate of return on the new machine, assuming the annual cash flow returns of the new machine in the original problem were $25,000 and there is no salvage value for the new machine SP1000 at the end of its useful life.
5. The internal rate of return assuming that the after-tax cash flow returns for each of the years are

Year 1	$20,000
Year 2	$22,000
Year 3	$25,000
Year 4	$30,000
Year 5	$40,000

6. Refer to the original problem. By how much can the variable costs of the new machine increase (or decrease) and the company be indifferent on the equipment replacement, assuming all the other costs will be as estimated?

11–30 SUM-OF-YEARS'-DIGITS DEPRECIATION Bernie Company purchased a new machine with an estimated useful life of five years and no salvage value for $45,000. The machine is expected to produce cash flow returns from operations, net of income taxes, as follows:

1st year	$ 9,000
2nd year	12,000
3rd year	15,000
4th year	9,000
5th year	8,000

Bernie will use the sum-of-the-years'-digits method to depreciate the new machine in its accounting records. Bernie uses 10 percent for evaluating capital investments and is currently in a 24 percent income tax bracket.

Required Compute

1. Payback period.
2. Net present value.
3. Internal rate of return.

(CPA Adapted)

11–31 WORKING BACKWARD: DETERMINE INITIAL INVESTMENT BASED ON ACCOUNTING RATE OF RETURN The Bread Company is planning to purchase a new machine that it will depreciate on a straight-line basis over a 10-year period. A full year's depreciation will be taken in the year of acquisition. The machine is expected to produce cash flows from operations, net of income taxes, of $3,000 in each of the 10 years. The accounting (book value) rate of return is expected to be 10 percent on the initial increase in required investment. The firm's tax rate is 20 percent.

Required What is the cost of the new machine?
(CPA Adapted)

11–32 WORKING BACKWARD: DETERMINE INITIAL INVESTMENT BASED ON INTERNAL RATE OF RETURN   Gene, Inc., invested in a machine with a useful life of six years and no salvage value. The machine was depreciated using the straight-line method and it was expected to produce an annual cash inflow from operations, net of income taxes, of $2,000. Gene has determined that the time-adjusted rate of return on the investment is 10 percent.

Required   What was the amount of the original investment?
(CPA Adapted)

11–33 WORKING BACKWARD: DETERMINE PERIODIC CASH FLOW BASED ON ACCOUNTING RATE OF RETURN   Dillon, Inc., purchased a new machine for $60,000 on January 1, 20X3. The machine is being depreciated on the straight-line basis over five years with no salvage value. The accounting (book-value) rate of return is expected to be 15 percent on the initial increase in required investment. The machine will generate a uniform cash flow.

Required   What is the expected annual cash flow from operations, net of income taxes, from this investment?
(CPA Adapted)

11–34 MACHINE REPLACEMENT AND SENSITIVITY ANALYSIS WITHOUT CONSIDERING TAXES   Ann & Andy Machine Company bought a cutting machine, Model KC12, on March 5, 20X4, for $5,000 cash. The estimated salvage value was $600 and the estimated life was 11 years. On March 5, 20X5, Ann, the CEO of the company, learned that she could purchase a different cutting machine for $8,000 cash. The new machine, Model AC1, would save the company an estimated $750 per year in operating costs compared to KC12. AC1 has an estimated salvage value of $400 and an estimated life of 10 years. The company could get $3,000 for KC12 on March 5, 20X5. The company uses the straight-line method for depreciations and 12 percent rate of return.

Required

1. Compute, for AC1
   a. Payback period.
   b. Accounting rate of return using the average investment.
   c. Net present value.
   d. Internal rate of return.
2. Should AC1 be purchased? Why?
3. What is the minimum (or maximum) savings AC1 has to have without altering your decision in 2?

11–35 VALUE OF ACCELERATED DEPRECIATION   Freedom Corporation acquired a fixed asset at a cost of $100,000. The estimated life was four years, and there was no estimated salvage value. Assume a relevant interest rate of 8 percent and an income tax rate of 40 percent.

Required

1. What is the present value of the tax benefits resulting from using sum-of-the-years'-digits depreciation as opposed to straight-line depreciation on this asset?
2. What is the present value of the tax benefits resulting from using double-declining-balance depreciation as opposed to straight-line depreciation on this asset?

(CPA Adapted)

11–36 STRAIGHTFORWARD CAPITAL BUDGETING WITH TAXES   Dorothy & George Company is planning to acquire a new machine at a total cost of $30,600. The estimated life of the machine is six years and estimated salvage value is $600. Dorothy & George Company estimates annual cash savings from using this machine will be $8,000. Assume the company's cost of capital is 8 percent and its income tax rate is 40 percent. The company uses straight-line depreciation.

Required

1. What are the annual after-tax net cash benefits of this investment?

2. If the annual after-tax net cash benefits of this investment were $5,000, what would the payback period be?

3. If the annual after-tax net cash benefits of this investment were $5,000, what would the net present value of this investment be?

(CPA Adapted)

11–37 **CAPITAL BUDGETING WITH SENSITIVITY ANALYSIS** Meidi Johnson has owned a medical professional building for the last 20 years. Johnson leased the land from an adjacent medical school 22 years ago for 30 years and had the building constructed. At the end of the lease period, the medical school becomes the sole owner of the land, its improvements, and any structures on the land. The construction took two years. The building is in excellent condition and fully occupied at favorable rental rates. There has been considerable appreciation on the value of the property. Because depreciation is based on the original construction cost, Meidi's taxable income is unusually large.

George Kardell, a commercial real estate broker, has approached Meidi with a proposal from a group of investors. Kardell believes that Johnson can sell the building and the balance of the leasehold at a price that will be profitable to all parties. The sale, if made, would be a cash sale that will provide Johnson with cash she needs for another project. She is currently negotiating with a bank for its financing. The bank is asking for 12 percent interest. Johnson, however, would use 10 percent as her cost of capital if the building can be sold for cash. The potential investor group's cost of capital is 12 percent.

The buyer is in the 30 percent tax bracket. Johnson believes that she has been paying a marginal income tax rate of 40 percent in the last five years and she expects no change in the next eight years. Unfortunately for her, the tax law in effect since last year eliminates any special tax rate for capital gains earned. This condensed income statement is taken from Johnson's latest tax return.

Income Statement for 20X2		
Rental revenue		$2,000,000
Expenses		
Operations	$950,000	
Administration	70,000	
Property taxes	280,000	
Depreciation (straight-line)	100,000	1,400,000
Net income before taxes		$ 600,000
Income taxes at 40 percent		240,000
Net income after taxes		$ 360,000

The buyer will use the straight-line depreciation method. No change in either rental revenue or expenses is expected.

Required

1. What is the most the buyer should pay?

2. What is the minimum selling price Johnson can accept if she has to pay a 5 percent commission to Kardell?

3. What is the most the buyer would be willing to pay if the buyer believes that the purchase is a MACRS five-year property?

11–38 **CASH FLOW ANALYSIS AND NPV** Lou Lewis, the president of the Lewisville Company, has asked you to give him an analysis of the best use of a warehouse owned by the company.

   a. The Lewisville Company is currently leasing the warehouse to another company for $5,000 per month on a year-to-year basis.

   b. The estimated sales value of the warehouse is $200,000. A commercial Realtor believes that the price is likely to remain unchanged in the near future. The building originally cost $60,000 and is being depreciated at $1,500 annually. Its current net book value is $7,500.

   c. The Lewisville Company is seriously considering converting the warehouse into a factory outlet for furniture. The remodeling will cost $100,000. The remodeling would be extremely modest because the major attraction will be rock-bottom prices. The remodeling will be depreciated over the next five years using the double-declining-balance method.

   d. The inventory, cash, and receivables needed to open and sustain the factory outlet would be $600,000. This total is fully recoverable whenever operations terminate.

   e. Lou Lewis is fairly certain the warehouse will be condemned to make room for a new highway in 10 years. The firm most likely would receive $200,000 from the condemnation.

   f. Estimated annual operating data, exclusive of depreciation, are

Sales	$900,000
Operation expenses	$500,000

   g. Nonrecurring sales promotion costs at the beginning of year 1 are expected to be $100,000.

   h. Nonrecurring termination costs at the end of year 5 are $50,000.

   i. The minimum annual rate of return desired is 14 percent. The company is in the 40 percent tax bracket.

Required

   1. Show how you would handle the individual items in determining whether the company should continue to lease the space or convert it to a factory outlet. Use the company's analysis form, which is set up as follows:

			Cash Flows in Year					
Item	Description	Net Present Value	0	1	2	3	4	5
a.								
b.								
.								
.								
.								
i.								

Indicate any item that is irrelevant.

   2. After analyzing all the relevant data, compute the net present value. Indicate which course of action, based on the data alone, should be taken.

11–39 **MACHINE REPLACEMENT WITH TAX CONSIDERATIONS** A computer chip manufacturer spent $2,500,000 to develop a special-purpose molding machine. The machine will be obsolete after four years. The machine has been used for one year. The firm uses straight-line depreciation for this equipment.

At the beginning of the second year, a machine salesman offers a new machine that is vastly more efficient. It will cost $2,000,000, will reduce annual cash manufacturing costs from $1,800,000 to $1,000,000, and will have zero disposal value at the end of three years. The management also decided to use double-declining-balance depreciation method for tax purposes if this machine is purchased.

The scrap value of the old machine is $300,000 now and will be $50,000 three years from now; however, no scrap value is provided in calculating straight-line depreciation for tax purposes.

Required   Assume that income tax rates are 45 percent. The minimum rate of return desired, after taxes, is 8 percent. Using the net-present-value technique, show whether the new machine should be purchased.

11–40 SIMPLE CAPITAL BUDGETING PROBLEM   The Gravina Company is planning to spend $6,000 for a machine that it will depreciate on a straight-line basis over a 10-year period with no salvage value. The machine will generate additional cash revenues of $1,200 a year. Gravina will incur no additional costs except for depreciation. The income tax rate is 35 percent.

Required

1. What is the payback period?
2. What is the accounting (book-value) rate of return on the initial increase in required investment?

(CPA Adapted)

11–41 BASIC CAPITAL BUDGETING   Rockyford Company must replace some machinery. This machinery has zero book value but its current market value is $1,800. One possibility is to invest in new machinery costing $40,000. This new machinery would produce estimated annual pretax operating cash savings of $12,500. Assume the new machinery will have a useful life of four years and have depreciation of $10,000 each year for book and tax purposes. It will have no salvage value at the end of four years. The investment in this new machinery would require an additional investment in working capital of $3,000.

If Rockyford accepts this investment proposal, the disposal of the old machinery and the investment in the new equipment will take place on December 31 of this year. The cash flows from the investment will occur during the next four calendar years.

Rockyford is subject to a 40 percent income tax rate for all ordinary income and capital gains and has a 10 percent after-tax cost of capital. All operating and tax cash flows are assumed to occur at year-end.

Required   Determine

1. The present value of the after-tax cash flow arising from the disposal of the old machinery.
2. The present value of the after-tax cash flows for the next four years attributable to the operating cash savings.
3. The present value of the tax shield effect of depreciation at the end of year 1.
4. Which one of the following is the proper treatment for the $3,000 working capital required in the current year?
   a. It should be ignored in capital budgeting, because it is not a capital investment.
   b. It is a sunk cost that needs no consideration in capital budgeting.
   c. It should be treated as part of the initial investment when determining the net present value.

d. It should be spread over the four-year life of the asset as a cash outflow in each of the years.

e. It should be included as part of the cost of the new machinery and depreciated.

(CMA Adapted)

11–42 **EQUIPMENT REPLACEMENT** The Oilers Company makes a microcomputer desk that it sells for $30 under a contract to a large computer retailer. The company operates one shift in its Ohio plant. The annual normal capacity is 100,000 units.  *Ethics*

Direct labor is paid at the rate of $8.00 per hour. An employee can produce a desk in two hours. Each desk requires eight board feet of hard board costing $0.25 per board foot. Indirect manufacturing costs (manufacturing overhead) at normal capacity of 100,000 units are described by the following budget line:

Total Costs = Fixed costs + Variable cost per unit
Total Costs = $25,000 + $0.30/unit

Some years ago, the Oilers Company installed a saw that presently has a carrying value (book value) of $20,000 and is being depreciated at $2,000 a year. At the time of installation, it was estimated that the saw would have no scrap value at the end of its useful life because the scrap value would equal its dismantling costs.

A sales agent from the Whalers Company is encouraging the Oilers Company to replace the old saw the firm currently uses with a numerically controlled saw. In addition to being able to perform precision cutting, the new machine also will cut the time in half and reduce the direct labor hours required to produce one desk from two hours to one hour. However, because the new saw is more powerful than the present machine, it is expected that utility costs will increase by $0.10 per unit.

The new saw will cost $100,000, including installation charges and transportation. The estimated useful life of the new saw is 10 years; it will be depreciated by the straight-line method. At the end of 10 years, the salvage value is estimated to be $10,000.

The Whalers Company agrees that if Oilers will buy the new saw, Whalers will buy the old saw for $4,000 with no dismantling costs to be charged to Oilers. The income tax rate is 40 percent. The Oilers Company management expects a return on investment of 15 percent. For income tax purposes, the loss on trade-in of the old machine is allowable as a tax deduction.

Required

1. As financial analyst for the Oilers Company you are charged with analysis of the purchase of the new equipment. In the preparation of a report for the president, you will need to determine for consideration by management:

a. The contribution margin per unit under current operating conditions.

b. The standard overhead rate (applied rate) per unit under current operating conditions.

c. The budget line for indirect manufacturing costs (manufactured overhead), assuming the new saw is purchased and installed.

d. The manufacturing overhead standard rate (applied rate) of the new machine if normal capacity of 100,000 units is expected to remain the same.

e. The contribution margin per unit assuming the sales price remains unchanged, if the new saw is purchased and installed.

       f.   The net additional investment of the machine, assuming the Oilers Company decides to install the new saw.

       g.   The expected net additional cash flow per year if the new saw is installed—assume the company sells all that it produces.

2.   The firm will be able to lay off approximately half of the hourly production workers currently on its payroll when the new machine is installed and fully operational. The plant has been in its current location for over 50 years and over 40 percent of the households in this small Southeast town have at least one member who works for the firm. Should the firm purchase the state-of-the-art equipment?

(IMA Adapted)

11–43 EQUIPMENT REPLACEMENT, MACRS   VacuTech is a high-technology company that manufactures sophisticated testing instruments for evaluating microcircuits. These instruments sell for $3,500 each and cost $2,450 each to manufacture. An essential component of the company's manufacturing process is a sealed vacuum chamber where the interior approaches a pure vacuum. The technology of the vacuum pumps that the firm uses to prepare its chamber for sealing has been changing rapidly. On June 1, 19X9, VacuTech bought the latest in electronic high speed vacuum pumps, a machine that allowed the company to evacuate a chamber for sealing in only six hours. The company paid $400,000 for the pump. Recently, the manufacturer of the pump approached VacuTech with a new pump that would reduce the evacuation time to two hours.

VacuTech's management is considering the acquisition of this new pump and has asked Doreen Harris, the company controller, to evaluate the financial impact of replacing the existing pump with the new model. Harris has gathered the following information prior to preparing her analysis.

- The new pump would be installed on May 31, 20X2, and placed in service on June 1, 20X2. The cost of the pump is $608,000, and the costs for installing, testing, and debugging the new pump will be $12,000. The pump would be assigned to the three-year class for depreciation under the Modified Accelerated Cost Recovery System (MACRS) and is expected to have a salvage value of $80,000 when sold at the end of four years. Depreciation on the equipment would be recognized starting in 20X2, and the MACRS depreciation rates would be

Year 1	33%
Year 2	45
Year 3	15
Year 4	7

- The old pump is being depreciated under the Modified Accelerated Cost Recovery System (MACRS) and will be fully depreciated at the time the new pump is placed in service. If the new pump is purchased, arrangements will be made to sell the old pump for $50,000, the estimated salvage value at the time of purchase.

- At the current rate of production, the new pump's greater efficiency will result in annual cash savings of $125,000.

- VacuTech is able to sell all the testing instruments it can produce. Because of the increased speed of the new pump, output is expected to increase by 30 units in 20X2, 50 units in both 20X3 and 20X4, and 70 units in 20X5. For all additional units produced, the manufacturing costs would be reduced by $150 per unit.

- VacuTech is subject to a 40 percent tax rate. For evaluating capital investment proposals, VacuTech's management assumes that annual cash flows occur at the end of the year and uses a 16 percent after-tax discount rate.

Required

1. Determine whether VacuTech should purchase the new pump by calculating the net present value at January 1, 20X2, of the estimated after-tax cash flows that would result from the acquisition.

2. Describe the factors, other than the net present value, that VacuTech should consider before making the pump replacement decision.

(CMA Adapted)

11–44 JOINT VENTURE Perez Group has the opportunity to enter into a joint venture with investors in an emerging country in which it would retain a 49 percent ownership. The firm would be required to invest the entire $3,000,000 initial outlay needed for the venture and receive 80 percent of the expected $900,000 yearly profit for 10 years. At the end of 10 years, the ownership will be turned over to the local investors. Cost of capital is 10 percent. Perez will accept projects only if return on its investment is greater than 20 percent.

International

Required Should Perez invest in the project?

11–45 RISK AND NPV A new investment opportunity was submitted to J. Morgan of SparkPlug Inc. It involves taking over a production facility from B.R. Machine Company, which has been running it for the last 20 years. The acquisition cost will be $1,500,000 and the after-tax cash flow returns will be $275,000 per year for 12 years. However Morgan is unsure about what the cost of capital should be in the computation of the NPV of this project. SparkPlug currently uses 12 percent for its cost of capital. Morgan, however, feels that the cost of capital should be 16 percent because of the declining demand for Sparkplug products.

Required

1. Should the project be accepted if the cost of capital is 12 percent?

2. If Morgan is correct and 16 percent is used, does that change the investment decision?

11–46 SENSITIVITY ANALYSIS Griffey & Son operates a plant in Cincinnati and is considering opening a new facility in Seattle. The initial outlay will be $3,500,000 and should produce after-tax cash flow returns of $600,000 per year for 15 years. However due to the effects of the ocean air in Seattle, the plant's useful life may only be 12 years. The cost of capital is 14 percent.

Required

1. Will the project be accepted if 15 years is assumed? What if 12 years is used?

2. What is the number of years needed for the facility in Seattle to earn at least a 14 percent return?

11–47 UNEVEN CASH FLOWS MaxiCare Corporation, a not-for-profit organization, specializes in health care for older people. Management is considering whether to expand operations by opening a new chain of care centers in the inner cities of large metropolises. Initial cash outlays for lease rental, renovations, working capital, training, and other costs are expected to be about $15 million in year 0. The firm expects the cash inflows of each new facility in its first year of operation to be equal to the total cash outlays for the year. Net cash inflows are expected to increase to $1 million in each of years 2 and 3, $2.5 million in year 4, and $3 million in each of years 5 through 10. The lease agreement for

Service

the facility will expire at the end of year 10 and the firm expects the cost for closing a facility will pretty much exhaust all cash proceeds from the disposal. The cost of capital for the firm is 12 percent.

Required Compute the net present value for this venture.

SOLUTION TO SELF-STUDY PROBLEM

Capital Budgeting for Expanding Production Capacity

1.

Cost of the new equipment	$580,000
Installation, testing, and training	12,000
Renovation cost for the leased warehouse	58,000
Total cash outflow in year 0	$650,000

Thus, the total cash outflow for the initial investment is $650,000.

2.

Sales	$200 × 5,000 =	$1,000,000
Cost of goods sold:		
Variable manufacturing costs per unit	$ 60	
Fixed manufacturing costs:		
Additional fixed manufacturing overhead:		
($140,000 + 10,000)/5,000 units =	30	
Depreciation on new equipment		
(650,000 − $50,000)/4 = $150,000 per year		
$150,000/5,000 units per year =	30	
Manufacturing cost per unit	$ 120	
Number of units	× 5,000	600,000
Gross margin		$ 400,000
Marketing and administrative expenses:		
Variable marketing expenses per unit	$ 20	
Number of units	× 5,000 $100,000	
Additional fixed marketing expenses	100,000	200,000
Net income before taxes		$ 200,000
Income taxes		80,000
Net income		$ 120,000

The firm can expect its net income to increase by $120,000 each year in years 1, 2, and 3. The increase in net income in year 4 will be $108,000 as computed here:

Net income before restoration expenses		$ 120,000
Restoration expenses	$ 20,000	
Decrease in income taxes	8,000	12,000
Increase in net income in year 4		$ 108,000

3.

	Each of Years 1 to 3	Year 4
Net income after taxes	$120,000	$108,000
Add: expenses not requiring cash disbursement:		
Depreciation included in fixed costs		
$30 × 5,000 =	150,000	150,000
Cash inflow from disposal of equipment		50,000
Total cash flow return	$270,000	$ 308,000

Thus, the cash flow return will be $270,000 each year for the first three years, and the cash flow return in year 4 will be $308,000.

4.

$$\text{Payback period} = \frac{\$650,000}{\$270,000} = 2.407 \text{ years}$$

Or 2 years and 5 months.

5. Average investment = ($650,000 + $50,000)/2 = $350,000
    Average net income = ($120,000 × 3 + $108,000)/4 = $117,000
    Accounting rate of return = $117,000/$350,000 = 33.43 percent

6. PV of cash inflows in year 1 to year 3:
    $270,000 × 2.402 = $648,540
    PV of cash inflows in year 4:
    $308,000 × 0.636 =   195,888
    Total PV of cash flow returns $844,428
    Initial investment   650,000
    NPV   194,428

7. PV of cash flow returns at 25 percent $653,320 $653,320
    PV of the projected cash flow returns $650,000
    PV of cash flow returns at 30 percent   598,120
    Difference in PV of cash flow returns $ 55,200 $ 3,320

Therefore, the internal rate of return is

$$24\% + \frac{\$15,154}{\$23,668} \times 2\% = 25.28\%$$

8. The most the after-tax cash flow return per year can be
    decreased is $194,428/3.037 = $64,020
    Add: income taxes   42,680
    The most variable cost per year can increase $106,700

Therefore, the variable cost per unit can increase by $106,700/5,000, or $21.34 per unit, and the firm still will earn 12 percent on the investment.

Part IV
Cost Management
Systems

Job Costing

TI Systems Group... We are listening.
How can we help?

http://www.ti.com

AP/Wide World Photos

438

No business can be successful over the long run without effective procedures for tracking costs and revenues.

MODERN ECONOMIST

Product costing is the process of accumulating, classifying, and assigning direct materials, direct labor, and factory overhead costs to products or services. Product costing provides useful cost information for both manufacturing and nonmanufacturing firms for (1) product and service cost determination and inventory measurement; (2) management planning, cost control, and performance evaluation; and (3) strategic and operational decision making.

> **Product costing** is the process of accumulating, classifying, and assigning direct materials, direct labor, and factory overhead costs to products or services.

Many strategic and operational decisions managers must make are based primarily on information about the cost of products or services. These decisions include:

1. Determining product or service pricing.
   - What is the minimum rate a gas company must charge residential users to cover its costs?
   - How should a restaurant price its menu to cover costs?
2. Assessing the financial effect of adding or deleting a product, division, or subsidiary.
   - Should an automobile manufacturer add an off-road vehicle to its product line?
   - Should a department store close its sporting goods section?
3. Deciding to make or buy.
   - Should a medical clinic do its own blood tests or purchase services from an outside laboratory?
   - Should a toy manufacturing company make or buy some of the plastic components?
4. Evaluating product, service, or division performance.
   - What was last month's printer product line profit for a computer peripheral manufacturing company?
   - What profit was made last year in the deluxe fishing boat product line of a boat manufacturing company?

Before discussing the uses of cost data for these purposes, we explain how to design and select a good cost system, how cost data are gathered, and how costs are determined.

COST SYSTEM DESIGN/SELECTION GUIDELINES

Several different types of product costing systems are available; these include the (1) cost accumulation method—job or process costing systems; (2) cost measurement method—actual, normal, or standard costing systems; (3) overhead assignment method—traditional or activity-based costing systems; and (4) treatment of fixed factory overhead costs—variable or absorption costing systems.

◄ **LEARNING OBJECTIVE 1**
Describe some major choices in designing or selecting product costing systems.

BusinessWeek

How Did TI Overcome Its Twist of Fate?

Ten years ago, Dallas-based Texas Instruments Inc. (TI) was the dinosaur of the semiconductor industry. The inventor of the digital watch and early entrant into personal computers, TI was no longer the leader of the pack, posting a loss of $39 million in 1989. CEO Jerry R. Junkins knew TI had to redefine its basic business if it ever hoped to regain its past glory. And that's exactly what TI did—making a turnaround in recent years with a strategy that increased its revenues and earnings.

Q: How did TI turn it around?   *Find out on page 442 of this chapter.*

The choice of a particular system depends on (1) the nature of the industry and the product or service; (2) the firm's strategy and its management information needs; and (3) the costs and benefits of acquiring, designing, modifying, and operating a particular system.

Cost Accumulation: Job or Process Costing

In a job costing system, the jobs or batches of products or services are the cost objects. This means that for the purposes of determining product cost, all manufacturing costs incurred are assigned to jobs. In a process costing system, on the other hand, production processes or departments are the cost objects. For example, the metal fabrication division might be one cost center and the assembly division another.

The job costing system usually is used by firms having a wide variety of distinct products. A job costing system is appropriate in any environment where costs can be readily identified with specific products, batches, contracts, or projects.

The process costing system, on the other hand, usually is used by firms having homogeneous products. These firms engage in continuous mass production of one or a few products.

Cost Measurement: Actual, Normal, and Standard Costing

Costs in either a job or process costing system can be measured in their actual, normal, or standard amount. An actual costing system uses actual amounts of costs incurred for all product costs including direct materials, direct labor, and factory overhead. Actual costing systems rarely are used because they can produce unit product costs that fluctuate from period to period or even from batch to batch. This fluctuation can cause serious problems in pricing, adding/dropping product line decisions, and performance evaluations. Most of the actual factory overhead costs will be known only at or after the end of the period, rather than at the completion of the batch of products. Thus, actual costing systems cannot provide accurate unit product cost information on a timely basis.

A normal costing system uses actual costs for direct materials and direct labor, and normal costs for factory overhead using predetermined rates. Predetermined factory overhead rates are assigned to cost centers based on the predetermined factory overhead application rate and the activity of the cost center. The predetermined factory overhead rate is derived by dividing budgeted annual factory overhead costs by budgeted volume or activity levels. A normal costing system provides a timely estimate of the cost of producing each batch of product.

A standard costing system uses standard rates (costs) and quantities for all three types of manufacturing costs—direct materials, direct labor, and factory overhead. Standard costs are predetermined target costs the firm should attain. Standard costing systems provide good cost control, performance evaluation, and process improvement in many environments.

Overhead Assignment: Traditional or Activity-Based Costing

Traditional product costing systems often allocate overhead to products or jobs on a volume-based cost driver, such as direct labor dollars or hours. An automated factory environment often requires only a minimal direct labor cost and a significantly higher fixed factory overhead than an older labor intensive factory. Some factory overhead costs are not volume-based. For example, machine setup cost is batch-based and product design cost is product-based. The traditional volume-based overhead allocation based on direct labor-hours or machine-hours may cause serious distortion in product costing by overcosting or undercosting these products.

Under activity-based costing systems, factory overhead costs would be allocated to products using cause-and-effect criteria with multiple cost drivers. Activity-based costing systems use both volume-based and nonvolume-based cost drivers to more accurately allocate factory overhead costs to products based on resource consumption during various activities.

Treatment of Fixed Factory Overhead: Variable and Absorption Costing

Fixed factory overhead is one of the manufacturing cost elements. But it is not always treated the same way as other manufacturing cost elements, such as direct materials and direct labor. Some firms treat fixed overhead costs as other manufacturing costs and include them as part of the unit cost calculation. Such a system is called an absorption costing system. A product cost in such a system includes, or absorbs, both variable and fixed manufacturing costs necessary for the manufacturing of the product. In contrast, a variable costing system includes only variable manufacturing costs in the product cost and treats the fixed factory overhead as the period cost (expense).

Generally accepted accounting principles and tax regulations require an absorption costing method for external reporting purposes. For internal managerial planning and control purposes, many firms prefer to use a variable costing method that includes only direct materials, direct labor, and variable factory overhead as product costs.

Design/Selection Guidelines

Product costing system design or selection is not an easy task. Management accountants follow these guidelines in designing or selecting an appropriate product costing system:

1. **Understand the nature of the business, its products, and the changing manufacturing environment.** Firms with a wide variety of distinct products usually use the job costing system. This system is applied to high-cost/low-volume goods and services. Firms with homogeneous products over a significant time period use the process costing system. This system is applied to high-volume/low-cost goods, where individual units cannot be specifically identified and assigned a cost. In practice, many firms appropriately use job costing for some products or departments and process costing for other products or departments. Automobile manufacturing firms are an example; their product not only has many common features but also has unique features. Automakers cannot use either a pure job costing or a pure process costing system.

A standard cost system is suitable when production processes or activities are repetitive. A normal or actual costing system is more commonly found in a relatively small-size firm, or a new firm, or an industry that manufactures nonstandard or custom-made products.

Many firms' manufacturing environments are changing rapidly. To provide meaningful information, a product costing system must keep up with the constantly changing manufacturing environment. Many firms change their product costing systems from single cost driver systems to multiple cost driver activity-based costing systems due to changes in their manufacturing environments.

2. **Provide useful cost information for management's strategic and operational decision needs.** For management cost control purposes, job costing is more suitable than process costing because it provides more focused and timely information. Job costing is also best for the differentiation strategy.

Standard costing systems provide management with better cost control, performance evaluation, and process improvement information than normal costing or actual costing systems.

Activity-based costing systems provide more accurate product cost information than traditional volume-based costing systems enabling managers to make various strategic decisions.

Variable costing systems separate variable costs from fixed costs. They usually are better suited to cost control, profit planning, and decision making than absorption costing. In the United States, however, variable costing is not an acceptable method of inventory valuation for either external reporting or income taxation.

3. **Consider the cost/benefit of acquiring, designing, modifying, and operating a particular system.** Because the job costing system focuses more on a detailed level

of jobs and cost centers, it requires more time and cost to design and operate than the process costing system.

A standard costing system is more difficult and time-consuming to design and update than a typical normal or actual costing system. However, it requires less clerical cost to operate than an actual costing system.

An activity-based costing system is more costly and time-consuming to design and update than the traditional volume-related costing system.

A variable costing system is more difficult and time-consuming to design than an absorption costing system. It takes less time to operate because it does not require allocating fixed factory overhead to products or services.

A firm may use one product costing system for some purposes, products, or departments and another system for other purposes, products, or departments; then the overall integrated costing system must be flexible enough to permit the use of both.

THE STRATEGIC ROLE OF JOB COSTING

LEARNING OBJECTIVE 2 ▶
Describe the strategic role of job costing.

Job costing systems provide information for managers to make strategic choices regarding products and customers, manufacturing methods, pricing decisions, and other long-term issues. Job costing information is strategically important for a firm for three reasons.

First, a firm competes by using either the cost leadership or the differentiation strategy. If a firm is following the cost leadership strategy, and overheads are complex, then the traditional volume-based job costing (which is simpler than either process costing or activity-based costing) does not provide much help. When a firm is a differentiator, job costing may be more appropriate because management focus should be on critical success factors that create differentiation rather than careful cost tracing to a process or several activities.

Second, an important strategic issue and a potential ethical issue for job costing involves the decisions the firm makes about the basis for allocating overhead, and proration of overapplied or underapplied overhead. For example, if a firm is manu-

---

BusinessWeek

✔ How Did TI Turn the Tables?
(Continues from page 439)

A: By turning to its clients...

Texas Instruments Inc. knew it had to drastically change its strategy and culture to increase revenues and earnings. So TI scrapped its plans to build a billion-dollar consumer business, and shifted its focus to *high-tech corporate clients*—building partnerships and using job costing information to analyze customer profitability and control costs.

With technology advancing and competition intensifying, customers were demanding more complex, customized chip products. One way to overcome this market disadvantage, in CEO Jerry R. Junkins' view, was to start jointly designing chips with key customers. By collaborating with clients, Junkins believed TI would not only start making chips that had guaranteed buyers but also become an indispensable partner. "We're looking for shared dependence," says Junkins. Moreover, joint development would expand TI's technology capabilities, allowing it to make complex chips that could be sold to a wider audience. The company now gets almost 50 percent of its revenues from high-margin products such as microprocessors and customized chips, compared with just 25 percent or so in 1988.

And despite the competition, TI's business relationships are growing. True, the company may not be the market leader it once was—but it seems to have made a turn for the better.

For further reading, see "TI Is Moving Up in the World," Business Week, August 2, 1993.

facturing products for two types of markets—one is price competitive, and the other is not (e.g., cost-plus government contracts)—the manner of overhead allocation is a strategic and an ethical issue. When manufacturing cost-plus products, managers may be tempted to overcost them by choosing an allocation basis or proration method that achieves the desired result.

Third, job costing is suitable in a service firm, especially a professional services firm. The tracing of direct costs is not the major issue, and the allocation of overhead is not complex or difficult. Therefore, the use of job costing would facilitate the effective management of a professional services firm.

Fourth, a job cost sheet could be expanded into a strategic balanced scorecard performance report with four dimensions: financial, customers, internal business processes, and learning and growth.

JOB VERSUS PROCESS COSTING SYSTEMS

Two basic types of product costing systems used in different industries are job costing and process costing. After comparing them, we devote the balance of the chapter to discussing job costing.

Job Costing

Job costing is a product costing system that accumulates and assigns costs to a specific job. Typically it is used by firms having a wide variety of products or services. The production departments of these firms perform tasks that often vary from product to product. Because each product or service may require different operations, the best way to determine the cost of a product or service is to accumulate costs according to jobs or batches. Therefore, in job costing the product or service costs are obtained by gathering and assigning costs to a specific job or individual customer order for one or more products. The unit cost of each product or service is calculated by dividing total job costs by units produced or served. Job costing is used when the products or services are especially tailored to the customers' needs as in the examples that follow for Topnotch Auto Repair and Sally Industries.

Industries that use job costing are printing shops; shipbuilders; custom furniture-manufacturing plants; contractors; film producing companies; accounting firms; law firms; advertising agencies; consulting firms; medical clinics; custom-made machine tools or equipment companies; construction companies; and research, engineering, and development services. Each job in these businesses is likely to be different.

> **Job costing** is a product costing system that accumulates and assigns costs to a specific job.

Process Costing

Process costing accumulates product or service costs by process or department and then assigns them to a large number of nearly identical products. Firms continuously mass producing one or a few homogeneous products or services use process costing. It is not economically feasible to keep track of the detailed cost elements applied to each of the units. In a process costing system, product or service costs are accumulated by process or department rather than by product, as in job costing. Unit product or service cost is calculated by accumulating process costs and dividing the total process costs of the period by units produced or served.

> **Process costing** accumulates product or service costs by process or department and then assigns them to a large number of nearly identical products.

Topnotch Auto Repair Shop

The Topnotch Auto Repair Shop is a business well suited to job costing. The firm typically performs a wide variety of tasks, ranging from changing tires to fixing engines. Although it is likely that the shop personnel are asked to do some of the tasks several times a day, rarely are they asked to do the same task throughout the day. For example, two customers may ask for engine tune-ups, but they have different models of cars that vary in their complexity—and in the cost of repair. One of the customers may ask them to rotate the tires on the car. Therefore, it makes more sense for Topnotch to keep track of the costs of repairing each car, rather than the total monthly costs of the individual tasks.

Sally Industries Uses Job Costing for Entertainment Robots

Sally Industries, Inc., is a small manufacturer of animatronic figures known as entertainment robots such as E.T., the Extraterrestrial. Because entertainment robots are custom orders, Sally Industries uses a job costing system to help managers make project planning, cost control, performance measurement, and pricing decisions. Each job cost sheet is broken down into direct materials, direct labor, and factory overhead. Since Sally Industries is still a small business, it has a relatively simple job costing system that is done largely on spreadsheets.

Source: Based on Thomas Barton and Frederick M. Cole, "Accounting for Magic," *Management Accounting,* January 1991, pp. 27–31.

Exhibit 12–1	Differences between Job and Process Costing

Job Costing	**Process Costing**
1. Costs accumulated by job.	1. Costs accumulated by process or department.
2. Wide variety of different products or services.	2. Mass production of homogeneous products or services.
3. Unit cost computed by dividing total job costs by units produced or served at the end of the job.	3. Unit cost computed by dividing the total process costs of the period by units produced or served at end of the monthly period.

Detergent manufacturing is an example of a business suitable for process costing. Because all the boxes of detergent processed during an accounting period are identical, there is no need to separately record costs for each unit or batch produced during that period. It is much more cost beneficial to find the average cost of performing each process during the period, and then sum these process average costs to arrive at the average cost per box of detergent for the period.

Industries usually employing process costing include chemical plants; food processors; household appliance manufacturers; textile companies; petroleum product manufacturers; paper, lumber, and pulp mills; glass factories; bakeries; wineries; cement factories; and sugar factories.

Comparison of Job and Process Costing Systems

Job costing and process costing are similar in their overall purpose, the basic set of manufacturing accounts, and the flow of costs through manufacturing accounts. The overall purpose of both product costing systems is the proper assignment of direct materials, direct labor, and factory overhead manufacturing costs to products. Both systems use the same basic set of manufacturing accounts, including Materials Control, Work-in-Process Control, Factory Overhead Control, and Finished Goods Control. And the flow of costs through the manufacturing accounts is basically the same in the two systems.

LEARNING OBJECTIVE 3 ▶
Contrast job costing and process costing and identify the types of firms that would use each system.

There are three major differences between job and process costing. First, in a job costing system, costs are accumulated by jobs while in a process costing system, costs are accumulated by production departments. Second, job costing has a wide variety of different products or services; it uses the job cost sheet to accumulate and control costs for a specific job. Process costing has mass production of homogeneous products or services; it uses the production cost report to accumulate and control costs for a particular department. Third, in job costing, the unit cost is calculated by job when each job is completed; in process costing, the unit cost is calculated by department at the end of each accounting period using an equivalent-units-of-production concept. Exhibit 12–1 summarizes these three major differences between job costing and process costing.

JOB COSTING: GENERAL DESCRIPTION

Job Cost Sheet

The basic supporting document in a job costing system is the job cost sheet. A **job cost sheet** records and summarizes the costs of direct materials, direct labor, and factory overhead for a particular job.

The job cost sheet is initiated when production or processing of a job begins. Spaces are provided on a job cost sheet for all cost elements and other detailed data chosen by management. The job cost sheet follows the product as it goes through the production process, with all costs recorded on the sheet. On completion of production, the total of all the costs recorded on the job cost sheet is the total cost of the job. The average cost per unit is determined by dividing the number of units in the job by the total cost of the job. See the job cost sheet in Exhibit 12–2.

All costs recorded in a job cost sheet are included in the Work-in-Process Control account. The subsidiary accounts to the Work-in-Process Control account (such as direct materials, direct labor, and various factory overhead accounts) consist of job cost sheets that include the manufacturing costs incurred during or prior to the current period for processing jobs. The total on all job cost sheets equals the total amount on the debit side of the Work-in-Process Control account. This amount is the total manufacturing cost to account for. This total is reported on the statement of cost of goods manufactured.

Because a separate job cost sheet is prepared for each job, the cost sheets for jobs started but not finished represent a subsidiary ledger that supports the work-in-process inventory control account. When a job is complete, the appropriate cost sheet is placed in a group of cost sheets representing the cost of goods manufactured.

A **job cost sheet** records and summarizes the costs of direct materials, direct labor, and factory overhead for a particular job.

Direct Materials Costs

When materials are purchased at $2,200, the accountant (1) checks the supporting documents of purchase orders, receiving reports, and invoices, and (2) records the purchase amounts in the receipts column of the subsidiary ledger, the Material Ledger. These support the following journal entry:

Exhibit 12–2 Job Cost Sheet

Smith Job Shop
Job Cost Sheet

| Product | Robot | | | | | | | | | | | | | Job No. | 351 |

Date begun: June 6, 19X8 — Quantity: 2
Date completed: July 15, 19X8 — Unit Cost: $3.761

		Direct Materials				Direct Labor					Factory Overhead			
Dept.	Date	Requisition Number	Unit	Cost	Date	Hours	Rate	Ticket	Amount	Machine-Hours	Application Rate	Amount	Total Cost
A	6/6	A–4024	20	$1,500	6/6 to 6/25	100	10	A–1101 through A–1150	$1,000	50	10.00	$ 500	$3,000
B	6/26	B–3105	15	400	6/26 to 6/30	60	15	B–308 through B–320	900	60	6.70	402	1,702
C	7/2	C–5051	10	300	7/1 to 7/15	140	12	C–515 through C–500	1,680	35	24.00	840	2,820
Total				$2,200					$3,580			$1,742	$7,522

(1)	Materials Control	2,200	
	Accounts Payable		2,200

A general ledger control account sums up the similar detailed account balances in the related subsidiary ledger. The Materials Control account amount is the sum of all the direct and indirect materials in the subsidiary ledger.

A product costing system uses material requisition forms to document and control all materials issued. A **material requisition form** is a source document that the production department supervisor uses to request materials for production. The production department prepares material requisition forms to request materials from the warehouse, with copies sent to the cost accounting department. The warehouse releases the materials based on the material requisition. The material requisition indicates the departments, jobs, and projects charged with the materials used. The production department enters this information in computers in an online computer environment.

Based on the information in material requisition forms, costs of direct materials issued to production are recorded on the job cost sheet. This document is the source document for determining materials costs for individual jobs. Notice that the material requisition form in Exhibit 12–3 specifically identifies the job in which the materials will be used.

For example, the Smith Job Shop's department A incurred $1,500 cost of direct materials for Job 351, with the following journal entry:

(2)	Work-in-Process Control	1,500	
	Materials Control		1,500

Indirect materials are treated as part of the total factory overhead cost. Typical indirect materials are factory supplies and lubricants. They are recorded in the Overhead Cost Sheet subsidiary ledger and the Factory Overhead Control general ledger account. The journal entry to record issuing an indirect materials cost of $50 to support departments is

(3)	Factory Overhead Control	50	
	Materials Control		50

Exhibit 12–4 describes direct materials and indirect materials cost flows of transactions (1), (2), and (3) through related general ledger T-accounts, subsidiary ledgers, and various source documents.

Direct Labor Costs

Direct labor costs are recorded on the job cost sheet by means of a time ticket prepared daily for each employee. A **time ticket** shows the time an employee worked

---

A **material requisition form** is a source document that the production department supervisor uses to request materials for production.

LEARNING OBJECTIVE 4 ▶
Delineate the flow of costs by using the manufacturing accounts in a job costing system.

A **time ticket** shows the time an employee worked on each job, the pay rate, and the total cost chargeable to each job.

Exhibit 12–3	Material Requisition Form

MATERIAL REQUISITION FORM   No. A–4024

Job Number	351	Date	June 6, 19X8
Department	A	Received by	Tom Chan
Authorized by	Juanita Peres	Issued by	Ted Mercer

Item Number	Description	Quantity	Unit Cost	Total Cost
MJ 428	Microprocessors	20	$75	$1,500

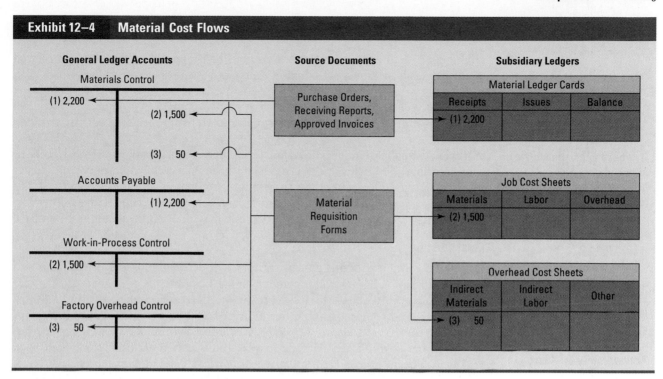

Exhibit 12–4 **Material Cost Flows**

Exhibit 12–5 **Time Ticket**

TIME TICKET

Employee Number _____ 013 _____ Date _____ June 6, 19X8 _____
Employee Name _____ Dale Johnson _____ Job Number _____ # 351 _____
Operation _____ Assembly _____ Approved by _____ Juanita Peres _____

Time Started	Time Completed	Hours Worked	Rate	Cost
8:00 a.m.	11:00 a.m.	3.00	$10.00	$30.00
Total Cost				$30.00

on each job, the pay rate, and the total cost chargeable to each job. Analysis of the time tickets provides information for assigning direct labor costs to individual jobs. Note the typical time ticket form in Exhibit 12–5. The cost of the $1,000 direct labor incurred in the Smith Job Shop's department A for Job 351 is recorded by the following journal entry:

(4)	Work-in-Process Control	1,000	
	Accrued Payroll Control		1,000

In addition to time tickets, clock or time cards are widely used for cost assignment and payroll. The times reported on an employee's time tickets are compared with the related clock cards as an internal check on the accuracy of the payroll computation.

Indirect labor costs are treated as part of the total factory overhead cost. Indirect labor usually includes such items as salaries or wages for supervisors, inspectors, rework labor, and warehouse clerks. They are recorded in the indirect labor column of the Overhead Cost Sheet subsidiary ledger. The following is a journal entry to record the $100 indirect labor cost incurred:

| (5) | Factory Overhead Control | 100 | |
| | Accrued Payroll Control | | 100 |

Exhibit 12–6 describes direct labor and indirect labor cost flows through related general ledger T-accounts, subsidiary ledgers, and various source documents.

Factory Overhead Costs

Cost allocation is a process of assigning costs to the appropriate products, services, or jobs.

Overhead application or allocation is a process of assigning overhead costs to the appropriate jobs. Allocation is necessary because overhead costs are not traceable to individual jobs. There are three approaches in assigning overhead costs to various jobs: actual costing, normal costing, and standard costing. This chapter discusses the first two approaches. Standard costing is discussed in Chapters 14 and 15.

> **Overhead application or allocation** is a process of assigning overhead costs to the appropriate jobs.

Actual Costing

An **actual costing** uses actual costs incurred for direct materials and direct labor and assigns or applies actual factory overhead to various jobs.

Actual factory overhead costs are costs incurred in an accounting period for indirect materials, indirect labor, and other indirect factory costs, including factory rent, insurance, property tax, depreciation, repairs and maintenance, power, light, heat, and employer payroll taxes for factory personnel. Different firms have used such terms as *manufacturing overhead*, *overhead*, or *burden* in referring to factory overhead.

Indirect materials of $50 and indirect labor of $100 have been discussed in transactions (3) and (5), respectively. Other factory overhead costs such as depreciation, utilities, and insurance are accumulated in an Overhead Cost Sheet subsidiary ledger under the Other column. The documents to support these costs include vouchers, invoices, and memos. This journal entry records the actual overhead costs of factory utilities, depreciation, and insurance:

> An **actual costing** uses actual costs incurred for direct materials and direct labor and assigns or applies actual factory overhead to various jobs.
>
> **Actual factory overhead** costs are costs incurred in an accounting period for indirect materials, indirect labor, and other indirect factory costs, including factory rent, insurance, property tax, depreciation, repairs and maintenance, power, light, heat, and employer payroll taxes for factory personnel.

(6)	Factory Overhead Control	350	
	Accounts Payable		80
	Accumulated Depreciation—Plant		150
	Prepaid Insurance		120

The actual factory overhead costs applied to various jobs based on allocation bases such as direct labor-hours, number of employees, and square footage are recorded in the overhead column of the Job Cost Sheets subsidiary ledger. The journal entry to record the overhead application to the Smith Job Shop's department A Job 351 ($50 + $100 + $350 = $500) is

| (7) | Work-in-Process Control | 500 | |
| | Factory Overhead Applied | | 500 |

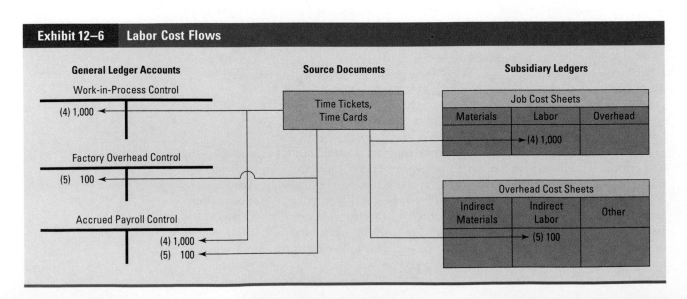

Exhibit 12–6   Labor Cost Flows

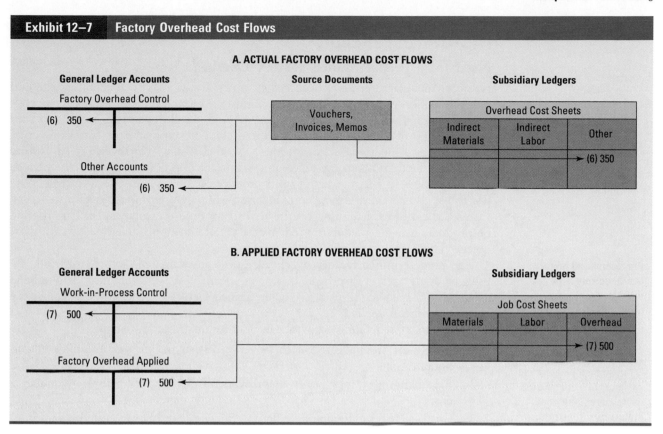

Exhibit 12–7 Factory Overhead Cost Flows

A. ACTUAL FACTORY OVERHEAD COST FLOWS

In Exhibit 12–7, we describe actual factory overhead and applied factory overhead cost flows through related general ledger T-accounts, subsidiary ledgers, and source documents.

Normal Costing

For most manufacturers, actual factory overhead costs are not always readily available at the end of a production process or period, nor can they be traced easily to individual products. In practice, many firms adopt a **normal costing** that uses actual costs for direct materials and direct labor and applies factory overhead to various jobs using a predetermined basis.

The motive for normalizing factory overhead costs is to avoid the fluctuations in cost per unit per period resulting from changes in the volume of units produced in a period. Using a predetermined annual factory overhead rate normalizes overhead cost fluctuations; hence the term *normal costing*.

We discuss the major reasons for using the predetermined overhead rate and the way it applies or allocates factory overhead costs to the specific jobs in a later section.

Normal costing uses actual costs for direct materials and direct labor and applies factory overhead to various jobs using a predetermined basis.

Unit Cost Calculation

When a job is complete, the finished products are transferred from the production department to finished goods. The management accountant finds the total cost incurred on the job cost sheet and transfers the total $3,000 cost (Direct Materials $1,500 + Direct Labor $1,000 + Factory Overhead $500) to the Finished Goods Control account from the Work-in-Process Control account with this journal entry:

(8)	Finished Goods Control	3,000	
	Work-in-Process Control		3,000

As costs of completed jobs are transferred from the Work-in-Process file to the Finished Goods file, the Work-in-Process Control account has a balance at the end of the period, only if there is unfinished work in the factory.

The unit cost for a job ($150) is calculated at the end of the job by dividing the total job cost ($3,000) by the number of units in the job (20).

JOB COSTING: USE OF PREDETERMINED FACTORY OVERHEAD

Need for a Predetermined Factory Overhead Rate

For most manufacturers, overhead costs are not always readily available at the end of a production process or period, nor can they easily be traced to individual products. Thus, for some firms a convenient way to handle overhead costs is to wait until the end of the accounting period and compute product cost based on actual overhead costs incurred. This procedure is *actual costing*. However, actual costing may cause fluctuations in costs per unit for products produced in different periods due to changes in the number of units produced. Consequently, most firms choose not to use the actual overhead costs incurred when computing manufacturing costs. Instead, these firms determine overhead costs for final cost objects, such as the job or product, using a predetermined overhead rate to apply overhead to the cost object. This latter approach is *normal costing*.

The **predetermined factory overhead rate** is an estimated factory overhead rate used to apply factory overhead cost to a specific job. The amount of overhead assigned to a specific job using a predetermined factory overhead rate is called the **factory overhead applied.**

To obtain a predetermined overhead rate, follow these four steps:

1. Determine the budgeted factory overhead costs for an appropriate operating period, usually a year.
2. Select the most appropriate cost drivers for charging the factory overhead costs.
3. Estimate the total amount or activity level of the chosen cost drivers for the operating period.
4. Divide the budgeted factory overhead costs by the estimated activity level of the chosen cost drivers to obtain the predetermined overhead rates.

There are at least two reasons why some firms favor the use of a predetermined factory overhead rate. One reason is to normalize the overhead cost included in each unit of the product. *Normalizing* is using long-term average unit costs such as annualized overhead rates rather than period or monthly overhead rates to determine overhead costs. This avoids the fluctuations in cost per unit per period resulting from changes in the volume of units produced in a period.

A substantial portion of factory overhead costs are period costs that remain constant regardless of the units produced, whereas the output level of firms seldom

> **Predetermined factory overhead rate** is an estimated factory overhead rate used to apply factory overhead cost to a specific job.
>
> **Factory overhead applied** is the amount of overhead assigned to a specific job using a predetermined factory overhead rate.

Monthly Per-Unit Fixed Factory Overhead Cost Fluctuation at Steece Machine Tools, Inc.

Steece Machine Tools, Inc., has a monthly total fixed factory overhead of $60,000 and variable manufacturing costs per unit of $10 for its only product. The firm produced 50,000 units in January but only 10,000 units in February, because it had a large inventory of unsold goods at the end of January. The unit costs would be as follows if actual cost data were used to determine the manufacturing cost per unit.

Month	Production Units	Variable Cost per Unit	Fixed Cost per Unit	Total Unit Cost
January	50,000	$10	$60,000/50,000 = $1.20	$11.20
February	10,000	$10	$60,000/10,000 = $6.00	$16.00

This fluctuation in unit cost is certainly not representative of the actual costs of production of the identical products, and therefore it is not desirable. Predetermined overhead rates are easy to apply and also reduce volatility and fluctuations in job costs caused by changes in the production volume and/or overhead costs throughout the year.

remains the same from period to period. Thus, if the actual overhead cost were used to determine the cost of goods manufactured, the cost assigned to each unit would vary from one period to the next. In periods with low production, the per-unit cost would be high, whereas in periods with high production, the per-unit cost would be low.

The second reason firms favor using a predetermined application overhead rate in the costing process is that this procedure allows management to stay current on production costs. If, for example, the management of a furniture manufacturing firm wants to know the cost of desks manufactured on completion of a job, the controller of the firm can give the actual material and labor costs incurred immediately because this information is readily available. The controller, however, usually could not compute the actual per-unit overhead cost of the desks until the end of the accounting period or until some later time when all bills of factory overhead items arrived from the vendors. The costs for overhead elements such as electricity and repair and maintenance, for example, most likely would not be known until the end of the period or later. Management certainly would not be satisfied with having to wait until the end of the period to learn the manufacturing costs if the firm wants to bill customers promptly. Use of a predetermined factory overhead rate thus enables the controller to determine the cost of the product immediately.

Cost Drivers for Factory Overhead Allocation

The basis for applying a predetermined overhead rate can be either a volume- or activity-based cost driver measure. The important consideration is that it be closely related to the behavior of the total overhead costs. Otherwise, substantial discrepancies may emerge between the overhead applied and the overhead incurred and, worse, the product cost may be misleading or distorted. The base for applying factory overhead also is called the cost driver. The best choice of a cost driver is the activity or output measure that best represents what drives or causes overhead.

Direct labor-hours, direct labor costs, and machine-hours are among the most frequently used volume-based cost drivers for applying factory overhead. Other activity-based cost drivers include the number of setups, orders, manufacturing cycle time, and inspection hours. The overhead cost driver rate is determined by dividing the estimated total overhead cost by the estimated total units of the cost driver for the relevant period. The proper bases or cost drivers for a labor-intensive firm would probably be direct labor-hours, direct labor costs, or some labor-related activity measure. In contrast, if factory overhead costs are predominantly related to the equipment operation, the proper cost driver would probably be machine-hours or a related measure. Alternatively, if most overhead costs consist of purchasing, production scheduling, setup, and expediting, the proper cost driver would be the number of orders instead of direct labor-hours or machine-hours.

Applying Factory Overhead Costs

The predetermined overhead rate usually is calculated at or before the beginning of the year as follows:

◄ **LEARNING OBJECTIVE 5**
Compute a predetermined factory overhead rate and use it in a job costing system.

$$\text{Predetermined overhead rate} = \frac{\text{Budgeted factory overhead amount for the year}}{\text{Expected level of cost driver for the year}}$$

For example, Smith Lighting Company produces lighting fixtures to fill customers' orders. It has a total budgeted factory overhead cost of $200,000 for the coming year. At Smith Lighting Company, total overhead costs vary directly with the total machine-hours worked. Thus, management decided to use the machine-hour as the cost driver for overhead application. The company has the following budgeted and actual data:

Budgeted annual overhead	$200,000
Expected annual machine-hours	100,000
Actual machine-hours for job 11	3,000
Actual units for job 11	300

Thus, the predetermined overhead rate is

$$\frac{\text{Budgeted overhead}}{\text{Expected machine-hours}} = \frac{\$200,000}{100,000} = \$2 \text{ per machine-hour}$$

Based on these estimates, the overhead application rate for Smith Lighting Company for the coming year would be $2 per machine-hour ($200,000/100,000 hours). The overhead cost applied to job 11 would be $6,000, and the overhead cost per lighting fixture would be $20:

$$\text{Overhead applied to job 11 is } \$2 \times 3,000 = \$6,000$$

$$\text{Overhead cost per unit of lighting fixture is } \frac{\$6,000}{300} = \$20$$

The applied factory overhead costs are recorded in the overhead column of the job cost sheets. This journal entry records the application of factory overhead to job 11:

Work-in-Process Control—Job 11	6,000	
Factory Overhead Applied		6,000

Firms lacking a Factory Overhead Applied account credit the Factory Overhead Control account. We use the separate Factory Overhead Applied account to clearly distinguish between actual and applied factory overhead costs.

When using a predetermined overhead rate to apply overhead cost to products, total overhead applied to the units produced exceeds the actual total overhead incurred in periods when production is higher than expected. On the other hand, in a period with lower-than-expected production, the total overhead charged to the units produced during the period is less than the actual total overhead incurred. If the overhead application rate has been properly determined over a long period of time—usually a complete operating cycle—the amount overapplied should be approximately the same as the amount underapplied. Nevertheless, some differences between the actual amount incurred and the amount applied usually remain. A small difference results in no serious distortions in the cost of goods sold and inventory figures.

Underapplied and Overapplied Factory Overhead

The total factory overhead applied for a given period is likely to be different from actual overhead cost incurred for the period. Applied overhead can be greater than actual overhead because the actual level of the cost driver exceeded the estimate, or because actual overhead was less than expected. When the applied overhead cost, which has been recorded as a credit on the Factory Overhead Applied or Factory Overhead Control account, is more than the actual overhead cost recorded on the debit of the Factory Overhead Control account, we call it overapplied overhead. **Overapplied overhead** is the amount of factory overhead applied that exceeds the actual factory overhead cost.

When the applied overhead cost, which has been recorded on the credit side of the Factory Overhead Applied account, is less than the actual overhead cost recorded on the debit side of the Factory Overhead Control account, the firm has underapplied overhead. **Underapplied overhead** is the amount that actual factory overhead exceeds the factory overhead applied.

Disposition of Underapplied and Overapplied Overhead

What do we do with the discrepancy between factory overhead applied and the actual amount of overhead incurred? Since actual production costs should be reported in the period they were incurred, total product costs at the end of the accounting period should be based on actual rather than applied overhead.

Underapplied or overapplied overhead can be disposed of in two ways:

1. Adjust the Cost of Goods Sold account.
2. Adjust the production costs of the period; that is, prorate the discrepancy among the amounts of the current period's applied overhead remaining in

Overapplied overhead is the amount of factory overhead applied that exceeds the actual factory overhead cost.

Underapplied overhead is the amount that actual factory overhead exceeds the factory overhead applied.

the ending balances of the Work-in-Process Control, the Finished Goods Control, and the Cost of Goods Sold accounts.

When the amount of underapplied or overapplied overhead is not a material amount, it generally is treated as a period cost and adjusted to the cost of goods sold. On the other hand, if the amount is significant, proration often is performed.

Adjustment to Cost of Goods Sold

Adjusting to Cost of Goods Sold is the more expedient of the two methods for disposing of overhead discrepancies. The difference between the actual factory overhead incurred and the amount applied to production is disposed of by adding to or subtracting from the Cost of Goods Sold account for the period, whichever is appropriate.

Suppose the Smith Lighting Company applied $200,000 of overhead but found at the end of the year that the actual total amount of overhead incurred was $205,000. The $5,000 discrepancy represents underapplied overhead. The appropriate adjusting entry to the Cost of Goods Sold account would be

◄ **LEARNING OBJECTIVE 6**
Calculate underapplied and overapplied overhead and dispose of them properly at the end of the period.

Cost of Goods Sold	5,000	
Factory Overhead Applied	200,000	
Factory Overhead Control		205,000
To record the disposition of underapplied overhead.		

This entry closes the Factory Overhead Control and Factory Overhead Applied accounts. It also increases the cost of goods sold for the period by $5,000.

To only dispose of a variance in the Cost of Goods Sold account ignores the fact that some portion of current production costs also may be in ending work in process or ending finished goods. Closing the variance to cost of goods sold is acceptable from a practical point of view when the amount is not material and does not significantly distort the financial results.

If underapplied overhead for the Smith Lighting Company is less than 5 percent of the net income, then this is probably an immaterial amount, and closing the underapplied overhead to cost of goods sold is appropriate. After disposal of underapplied factory overhead, the cost of goods sold for the period increases. On the other hand, disposal of overapplied factory overhead decreases the cost of goods sold for the period.

Even if the amount of the variance is significant, the underapplied or overapplied factory overhead may still be disposed of in the Cost of Goods Sold account if the difference is a result of some operating characteristics pertaining only to the current period. When the variance is a result of the current operations of a firm, it should be considered an expense in the current period and therefore be treated in the same manner.

Proration among Inventories and Cost of Goods Sold Accounts

Proration is the process of allocating underapplied or overapplied overhead to Work-in-Process Control, Finished Goods Control, and Cost of Goods Sold accounts.

Because factory overhead is one of the manufacturing cost elements that entered into the Work-in-Process Control account, underapplied or overapplied overhead affects the value of work in process, which, in turn, affects the amount transferred out of the Work-in-Process Control account and charged to the Finished Goods Control account. Eventually, the amount in the Cost of Goods Sold account for the period also is affected because it is determined by the amount in the Finished Goods Control account.

If all the units placed into production are completed and sold at the end of a period, adjusting for any discrepancy between actual overhead and applied overhead can be accomplished with entries in the Cost of Goods Sold account as just explained. If, on the other hand, all units processed are not completed and/or all units completed are not sold at the end of the period, then the adjustment made for underapplied or overapplied overhead affects the Work-in-Process Control account and the Finished

Proration is the process of allocating underapplied or overapplied overhead to Work-in-Process Control, Finished Goods Control, and Cost of Goods Sold accounts.

Goods Control account, in addition to the Cost of Goods Sold account. For these ending inventories to reflect the actual cost incurred, the amount of overapplied or underapplied overhead must be allocated to or prorated among the three accounts.

The proration of the variance is based on the current period's applied overhead in the ending inventories of the Work-in-Process Control and the Finished Goods Control, and Cost of Goods Sold accounts at the end of the period. To determine the ratios for the proration, we compute the sum of the applied overhead in the ending inventories of the Work-in-Process Control and the Finished Goods Control, and the Cost of Goods Sold at the end of the period. The ratio of each of the components to this sum is the amount of the underapplied or overapplied overhead that should be prorated to the cost of the component.

To illustrate the proration of an overhead variance, assume that Smith Lighting Company's accounts had the following applied overhead balances for the end of period:

Smith Lighting Company Operational Data

Work-in-Process ending inventory	$ 20,000
Finished Goods ending inventory	30,000
Cost of Goods Sold	150,000
Total Factory Overhead Applied	$200,000
Factory Overhead Control (Actual)	$205,000

Suppose that Smith Lighting Company uses the Factory Overhead Control account to record the actual overhead incurred, and the Factory Overhead Applied account to record the application of overhead to the job. The proration of the $5,000 underapplied factory overhead among the Work-in-Process Control, Finished Goods Control, and Cost of Goods Sold accounts is computed as follows:

Amount	Applied Overhead	Percentage of Total	Underapplied Overhead Prorated
Work-in-Process	$ 20,000	10	$ 500
Finished Goods	30,000	15	750
Cost of Goods Sold	150,000	75	3,750
Total	$200,000	100	$5,000

The appropriate adjusting entry would be

Factory Overhead Applied	200,000	
Work-in-Process Control	500	
Finished Goods Control	750	
Cost of Goods Sold	3,750	
Factory Overhead Control		205,000

To record the proration of the underapplied overhead.

Some firms prefer to use the balances of work-in-process inventory, finished goods inventory, and cost of goods sold accounts, rather than the applied overhead in the accounts to calculate the percentages.

When there is a substantial variance between the actual factory overhead incurred and the factory overhead applied, the total manufacturing cost as recorded on the debit side of the Work-in-Process Control account is understated (underapplication) or overstated (overapplication). Left unadjusted, the inventory and cost of goods sold accounts would be substantially distorted.

No matter which method is used, underapplied or overapplied overhead usually is adjusted only at the end of a year. Nothing needs to be done about any variances during the year because the predetermined factory overhead rate is based on annual figures. A variance is expected between the actual overhead incurred and the amount applied in a particular month or quarter because of seasonal fluctuations in the operating cycle of the firm, or other incidental events. Furthermore, an underapplied factory overhead in one month is likely to be offset by an overapplied amount in another month (and vice versa).

AN ILLUSTRATION OF A JOB COSTING SYSTEM

Thomasville Furniture Industries, Inc. (TFI), located in Thomasville, North Carolina, has been a large manufacturer of high-quality home and office furniture for over a century. TFI's products are made from the finest materials, including hardwoods such as cherry, poplar, maple, elm, mahogany, and oak, and high-quality upholstery materials. The tables and chairs are produced in plants located in and around Thomasville, North Carolina, while the upholstered products, such as sofas and chairs, are made in the western part of the state.

The production process for a furniture product requires several steps, including cutting, assembling, and finishing. The materials used in the production of each piece of furniture are described in detail in the *bill of materials*. The bill of materials is a list of different materials needed to manufacture a product or part. For example, the bill of materials for TFI's Georgian end table includes 30 different items; a portion of that bill of materials appears in Exhibit 12–8. See the table in Exhibit 12–9.

TFI has hundreds of production jobs in process at any time. For our illustration, we consider simplified, fictitious data from production job X4J–14531 for Georgian end tables. The related transactions, also using fictitious numbers, follow.

Materials Purchased and Used

The eight parts to a Georgian end table include a table top, drawer front panel, side panels, and front apron rail. Each part consists of several materials. The table top, for example, includes one piece of the top, one-half piece of the top core, one piece of top core side bands, and two pieces of top core front and back bands. The drawer front panel includes one piece of drawer front, two pieces of drawer side, one piece of drawer back, one piece of drawer bottom, one piece of female drawer guide, one piece of male drawer guide, and one piece of hardware pull. The Georgian end table top requires a sheet of $27 \times 21 \times \frac{9}{16}$ inch 5-ply elm.

Assume that the Materials Control account has a $10,000 balance on January 1, 19X8. This journal entry records the purchase of $25,000 of materials during January:

(1)	Materials Control	25,000	
	Accounts Payable		25,000
	To record the purchase of materials.		

Assume that the company has a $5,000 beginning balance in the Work-in-Process Control account. During January, the company issued $20,000 in direct materials to its production departments for this job. The use of direct materials is recorded on the credit side of the Materials Control account and on the debit side of the Work-in-Process Control account:

(2)	Work-in-Process Control	20,000	
	Materials Control		20,000
	To record the use of direct materials.		

In addition, the company used $3,000 in indirect materials for this job. The issuance of indirect materials to production is recorded on the debit side of the Factory Overhead Control account and on the credit side of the Materials Control account:

(3)	Factory Overhead Control	3,000	
	Materials Control		3,000
	To record the use of indirect materials.		

Labor Costs Incurred

TFI incurred $70,000 in direct labor cost for job X4J–14531. This cost is recorded by debiting the Work-in-Process Control account and crediting the Accrued Payroll Control account:

(4)	Work-in-Process Control	70,000	
	Accrued Payroll Control		70,000
	To record direct labor cost incurred.		

Exhibit 12–8   Bill of Materials

Thomasville Furniture Industries, Inc.
Bill of Materials

PLANT ___"T"___   ARTICLE ___"END TABLE"___   DATE ___6-19-98___   CHANGES FOR 14521-211

STYLE ___14531-210___   SHEET ___1___ OF ___1___

LINE	NO. PCS.	DESCRIPTION	FINISH SIZE L	FINISH SIZE W	FINISH SIZE T	BS	MULT	ROUGH SIZE L	ROUGH SIZE W	ROUGH SIZE T	FOOTAGE	SKETCH
1	1 14531-210 ONLY	TOP	26	20	13/16		1	27	21	9/16		
2	1/2	TOP CORE					1	17	47 1/2	3/4		
3	1	TOP CORE SIDE BANDS	47 1/2	2	3/4		1	47 1/2	2	4/4		4/4 POP CORE
4	2	TOP CORE FRT. & BK. BANDS	21	2	3/4		1	21	2	4/4		4/4 POP CORE
5												
6	2	SIDE PANELS	22 3/8	4 15/16	3/4	2 13/8	4	23 7/8	2 13/4	5/8		
7	2	SIDE APRON RAIL	22 3/8	1 7/8	17/16	2 13/8	1	23 3/8	2 1/8	8/4		
8	1	BACK PANEL	16 3/8	4 15/16	3/4	15 3/8	4	17 7/8	2 13/4	5/8		
9	1	BACK APRON RAIL	16 3/8	1 7/8	17/16	15 3/8	1	17 3/8	2 1/8	8/4		
10	2	FRONT POST	22 3/4	2 1/2	2 1/2		1	23 3/4	2 3/4	3 pcs 5/4		
11	2	BACK POST	22 3/4	2 1/2	2 1/2		1	23 3/4	2 3/4	3 pcs 5/4		
12												
13	1 14531-210 ONLY	DRAWER FRONT	14 7/8	3 7/8	3/4		3	16 7/16	16 5/16	5/8		4/4 POP CORE
14	2	DWR. SIDES	20	3	7/16		1	21	3 1/4	5/8		
15	1	DWR. BACK	14 11/16	2 7/8	7/16							
16	1	DWR. BOTTOM	14 1/4	19 13/16	3/16	19 13/16	1	15 3/4	20 7/8	R.C.		
17	1	DWR. GUIDE—FEMALE	20 1/2	13 1/32	9/16		1	21 1/2	2 1/4	4/4		
18	1	DWR. GUIDE—MALE	22 1/2	1	1/2		1	23 1/2	1 1/4	4/4		
19	1	DWR. HOWE PULL										
20												

Exhibit 12–8 Continued

21													
22		1	PART. FRT. RAIL BOTT.	16 1/2	1 1/2	3/4	15 3/8	1	17 1/2	1 3/4	4/4		
23		1	DUST FRM. BK. RAIL BOTT.	16 1/2	1 1/2	3/4	15 3/8	1	17 1/2	1 3/4	4/4		
24		2	DUST FRM. END RAIL	20 9/16	1 1/4	3/4	19 9/16	1	21 5/8	1 1/2	4/4		
25													
26		1	FRONT APRON RAIL	16 3/8	1 7/8	17/16	15 3/8	1	17 3/8	2 1/8	8/4		
27		1	TOP FRT. PART. RAIL	16 1/2	1 3/4	3/4	15 3/8	1	17 1/2	2	4/4		
28		1	TOP FRT. PAR. RAIL MLDG.	15 3/8	3/4	3/4		1	16 3/8	1	4/4		
29		1	DWR. BOTT. FILLER MLDG.	15 3/8	3/16	11/16		1	16 3/8	7/16	4/4		
30		2	DWR. END FILLER MLDG.	4 3/8	3/16	11/16		3	16 3/8	7/16	4/4		
31		3	TOP BACK SCREW CLEAT	12	3/4	3/4		1	13	1	4/4		
32													
33													
34													
35		4	PLASTIC FLOOR GUIDES										
36													
37													
38			{ SAME AS 14531-210 EXCEPT OMIT LINE #1-#13										
39			# 14531 - 211 { AND ADD THE FOLLOWING										
40													
41	14531-211 ONLY	1	TOP	26	20	13/16		1	27	21	9/16		
42	14531-211 ONLY	1	DWR. FRONT	14 7/8	3 7/8	3/4		3	16 3/8	13 1/8	5/8		4/4 POP CORE
43													
44													
45													

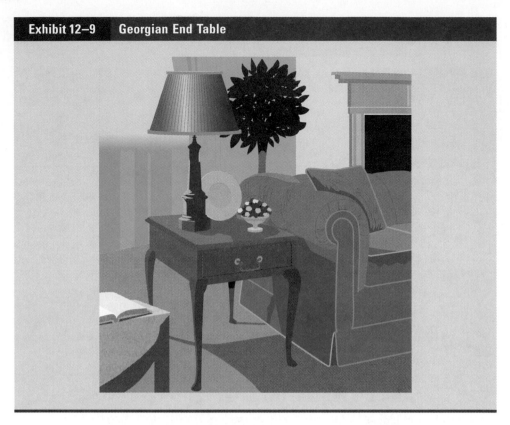

Exhibit 12–9   Georgian End Table

The company also incurred $2,500 in indirect labor costs including the salaries of supervisors, inspectors, and material handlers. The total indirect labor cost is recorded in the books of the company by debiting the Factory Overhead Control account and crediting the Accrued Payroll Control account:

(5)	Factory Overhead Control	2,500	
	Accrued Payroll Control		2,500
	To record indirect labor cost incurred.		

Actual and Applied Factory Overhead Costs

Unlike direct materials and direct labor, the actual factory overhead is not entered directly into the Work-in-Process Control account, as evidenced by the recording of indirect materials and indirect labor costs incurred earlier. The actual factory overhead incurred is recorded on the debit side of the Factory Overhead Control account. Thus, the debit side of the Factory Overhead account includes indirect materials used, indirect labor incurred, and other factory overhead expenses.

TFI incurred other factory overhead expenses for this job including utilities ($1,000), depreciation on factory equipment ($4,000), and insurance on factory equipment ($500). These amounts are recorded on the debit side of the Factory Overhead Control account and on the credit side of other appropriate accounts:

(6)	Factory Overhead Control	5,500	
	Accounts Payable		1,000
	Accumulated Depreciation—Factory		4,000
	Prepaid Insurance		500
	To record actual factory overhead costs.		

TFI applies factory overhead on the basis of direct labor cost. Suppose the firm estimated its total factory overhead for the year as $30,000,000, and the direct labor cost as $200,000,000. The factory overhead thus was applied at the rate of $.15

($30,000,000/$200,000,000) per $1 of direct labor costs. The actual direct labor cost for this job was $70,000; therefore the factory overhead applied was $10,500 (.15 × $70,000).

The $10,500 of factory overhead charged to production is recorded by debiting the Work-in-Process Control account and crediting the Factory Overhead Applied account:

(7)	Work-in-Process Control	10,500	
	Factory Overhead Applied		10,500
	To record the application of factory overhead to the job.		

Completion of a Job

On completion of a production job, the total production costs of the completed units are transferred out of the Work-in-Process Control account and entered into the Finished Goods Control account. Suppose TFI had a $5,000 beginning balance in the Finished Goods Control account. The company completed $80,000 of goods during January 19X8. This amount was transferred out of the Work-in-Process Control account and entered into the Finished Goods Control account by crediting the Work-in-Process Control and debiting the Finished Goods Control account:

(8)	Finished Goods Control	80,000	
	Work-in-Process Control		80,000
	To record the cost of goods completed.		

Exhibit 12–10 contains a cost estimate sheet in use at Thomasville Furniture Industries, Inc.

During the manufacturing process spoilage sometimes occurs. Management accountants have to distinguish between normal spoilage and abnormal spoilage because each is treated differently. Normal spoilage occurs under efficient operating conditions and is charged to a specific job or allocated to all jobs. Abnormal spoilage is not expected under efficient operating conditions and treated as a loss in the period it is detected.

Sale of Goods

Assume that TFI sold most of the furniture from job X4J–14531 with a total cost of $70,000 in January 19X8. The firm records the journal entry by debiting the Cost of Goods Sold account and crediting the Finished Goods Control account:

(9)	Cost of Goods Sold	70,000	
	Finished Goods Control		70,000
	To record the cost of goods sold.		

In addition, an entry must record the revenue received from the sale of the goods. Assume TFI marks up its products at 200 percent of cost. The journal entry to record the sales revenues received from the sale in January 19X8 would be:

(10)	Accounts Receivable	210,000	
	Sales		210,000
	To record the sale of goods.		

Mechanics of Job Costing:

1. Record the costs of direct materials and direct labor used for each job in the work-in-process control.
2. Compute and record the amount of overhead assigned to each job.
3. Determine the total cost and unit cost of the job.

Exhibit 12–10	Sample Cost Estimate

DATE _____

PLANT _____

SUITE NO. _____   ITEM NO. _____   DESCRIPTION _____

Lumber:	Net Mat'ls	Price	Drawer Stock:	Net Mat'ls	Price
4/4					
4/4					
5/4					
6/4			Total Drawer Stock	➡	$
8/4			Carvings:		
Total Lumber	➡	$	Total Carvings w/o waste	xxxxxx	
Face Veneer:			Total Carvings Incl. waste 7	➡	$
			Cabinet Hdwe.		
			Total Cab. Hdwe. w/o waste	xxxxxx	
			Total Cab. Hdwe Incl. waste 4	➡	$
			Hard Board:		
			Total Hard Board	➡	$
			Finishing Materials:	➡	$
			Mirrors & Glass:		
Total Face w/o waste	xxxxxx		Total M & G w/o waste	xxxxxx	
Total Face Incl. waste 7–8	➡	$	Total M & G Incl. waste 2	➡	$
Commercial Veneer:			Stone:		
			Total Stone w/o waste	xxxxxx	
			Total Stone Incl. waste 5	➡	$
			Trim Hdwe.		
Total Commercial Veneer	➡	$			
Glue:		7			
	➡	$			
Chipcore:					
			Tot. Trim w/o waste	xxxxxx	
			Tot. Trim Incl. waste 5	➡	$
			Packing	➡	$
Total Chipcore	➡	$	Crating	➡	$
Plastic F & B					
Total Plastic F & B w/o waste	xxxxxx				
Total Plastic F & B Incl. waste 5	➡	$			
Molded Plastic Parts:					
			Total Material	$	
			Labor Hrs. @$ /hr.	$	
			Direct Overhead	$	
			Period Overhead	$	
			Factory Cost	$	
Total Mold Plastic w/o waste	xxxxxx		S & A %	$	
Total Mold Plastic Incl. waste 4	➡	$	Total Cost	$	
			Chair Seat	$	
			Total Chair Cost	$	

Assume TFI had the following selling and administrative expenses in January in addition to factory overhead costs:

Advertising expenses	$20,000
Sales commissions	21,000
Office salaries	30,000
Depreciation, office equipment	2,000
Other administrative expenses	7,000

Exhibit 12–11	General Ledger Accounts for Thomasville Furniture Industries

Materials Control

Bal. 10,000	(2) 20,000
(1) 25,000	(3) 3,000
Bal. 12,000	

Accounts Payable

	(1) 25,000
	(6) 1,000
	(11) 27,000

Work-in-Process Control

Bal. 5,000	(8) 80,000
(2) 20,000	
(4) 70,000	
(7) 10,500	
Bal. 25,500	

Factory Overhead Control

(3) 3,000	(12) 11,000
(5) 2,500	
(6) 5,500	
Total 11,000	

Factory Overhead Applied

(12) 10,500	(7) 10,500

Accrued Payroll Control

	(4) 70,000
	(5) 2,500
	(11) 51,000

Finished Goods Control

Bal. 5,000	(9) 70,000
(8) 80,000	
Bal. 15,000	

Accumulated Depreciation

	(6) 4,000
	(11) 2,000

Cost of Goods Sold

(9) 70,000	
(12) 500	

Prepaid Insurance

	(6) 500

Sales

	(10) 210,000

Accounts Receivable

(10) 210,000	

Selling Expense Control

(11) 41,000	

Administrative Expense Control

(11) 39,000	

The first two items are selling expenses while the last three are administrative expenses. The following compound journal entry records these expenses:

(11)	Selling Expense Control	41,000	
	Administrative Expense Control	39,000	
	Accounts Payable		27,000
	Accrued Payroll Control		51,000
	Accumulated Depreciation—Factory		2,000

Underapplied Overhead

From journal entries (3), (5), and (6) TFI incurred total actual factory overhead costs of $11,000, but only $10,500 of factory overhead was applied to Work-in-Process Control in journal entry (7). The underapplied overhead amount is

Actual factory overhead:

Indirect materials	$ 3,000
Indirect labor	2,500
Other factory overhead	5,500
Total	11,000
Applied factory overhead	10,500
Underapplied overhead	$ 500

If we assume that TFI closed the underapplied overhead to the Cost of Goods Sold account, then the required journal entry is

(12)	Cost of Goods Sold	500	
	Factory Overhead Applied	10,500	
	Factory Overhead Control		11,000

Posting Journal Entries to the General Ledger

In Exhibit 12–11 we show cost flows through related general ledger T-accounts in the Thomasville Furniture Industries job costing example.

Schedule of Cost of Goods Manufactured and Sold

Schedule of cost of goods manufactured and sold shows the manufacturing costs incurred, the change in the work-in-process inventory, the cost of goods sold, and the change in finished goods inventory during the period.

Many manufacturing firms periodically prepare a **schedule of cost of goods manufactured and sold** for management use; other firms prepare two separate schedules— a schedule of cost of goods manufactured and a schedule of cost of goods sold. The single schedule shows the manufacturing costs incurred, the change in the work-in-process inventory, the cost of goods sold, and the change in finished goods inventory during the period. Cost of goods manufactured is the total cost of direct materials, direct labor, and factory overhead transferred from the Work-in-Process Control account to the Finished Goods Control account during an accounting period.

Exhibit 12–12	Schedule of Cost of Goods Manufactured and Sold

THOMASVILLE FURNITURE INDUSTRIES, INC.
Schedule of Cost of Goods Manufactured and Sold*
For the Month Ended January 31, 19X8

Direct materials:		
Beginning materials inventory	$ 10,000	
Purchase of materials	25,000	
Total materials available	$ 35,000	
Deduct: Ending materials inventory	(12,000)	
Indirect materials used	(3,000)	
Direct materials used		$ 20,000
Direct labor		70,000
Factory overhead applied		10,500
Total manufacturing costs incurred		$100,500
Add: Beginning work in process		5,000
Total manufacturing costs to account for		$105,500
Deduct: Ending work in process		(25,500)
Cost of goods manufactured		$ 80,000
Add: Beginning finished goods		5,000
Cost of goods available for sale		$ 85,000
Deduct: Ending finished goods		(15,000)
Normal cost of goods sold		$ 70,000
Add: Underapplied overhead		500
Cost of goods sold (adjusted for underapplied overhead)		$ 70,500

*The figures are fictitious.

462

Exhibit 12–13	Income Statement

THOMASVILLE FURNITURE INDUSTRIES, INC.
Income Statement*
For the Month Ended January 31, 19X8

Sales		$210,000
Cost of goods sold (from Exhibit 12–12)		(70,500)
Gross margin		$139,500
Selling and administrative expenses		
Selling expenses	$ 41,000	
Administrative expenses	39,000	(80,000)
Net income		$ 59,500

*The figures are fictitious.

Exhibit 12–12 displays the January 19X8 schedule of cost of goods manufactured and sold for Thomasville Furniture Industries. The schedule shows the costs of direct materials, direct labor, applied factory overhead, and cost of goods manufactured carried at normal cost rather than the actual cost. It also shows the normal cost of goods sold before adjustment for the underapplied overhead, and the adjusted cost of goods sold after adjustment for the underapplied overhead. Exhibit 12–13 contains the company's income statement.

THE CONTEMPORARY MANUFACTURING ENVIRONMENT

Plantwide Rate

Many firms have two or more production departments. They can assign factory overhead costs to jobs or products using either a single plantwide overhead rate or a separate departmental overhead rate for each production department.

A **plantwide overhead rate** is a single overhead rate used throughout the entire production facility. It is computed by dividing total plant factory overhead by an activity base or cost driver common to all jobs worked in all departments.

In some production processes, the relationship between factory overhead costs and various cost drivers differs substantially among production departments. For example, some production departments may be labor intensive while other production departments are highly automated. It would be inappropriate therefore for a firm to use a single plantwide overhead application rate for jobs processed by various departments. A labor-intensive department may use a factory overhead application rate based on direct labor, while a highly automated department may use an application rate based on machine usage. The use of departmental overhead rates may be required because it produces more accurate overhead cost assignments for individual jobs.

A **plantwide overhead rate** is a single overhead rate used throughout the entire production facility.

Departmental Overhead Rate

A **departmental overhead rate** is an overhead rate calculated for a single production department. It is computed by dividing total budgeted departmental factory overhead by the budgeted level of a cost driver that is common to all jobs worked or processed by the department. Firms that use a departmental overhead rate keep separate Factory Overhead Control and Applied accounts for each department.

The ideal criterion for choosing an allocation base is a cause-and-effect relationship. A plantwide rate is appropriate when all products pass through the same processes, or all departments are similar. Departmental rates are appropriate when the converse is true.

Western Furniture Company illustrates the misuse of a single plantwide overhead rate. Assume that this manufacturer has two departments: a cutting department and a finishing department. The cutting department is a machine-intensive department

The **departmental overhead rate** is an overhead rate calculated for a single production department.

while the finishing department is labor intensive. The company has budgeted the following for the year:

	Cutting Department	Finishing Department	Total
Budgeted overhead	$600,000	$300,000	$900,000
Budgeted labor-hours	10,000	50,000	60,000
Budgeted machine-hours	30,000	3,000	33,000

Assume that the company uses a single plantwide labor-hour overhead rate as the base for overhead allocation. The single predetermined overhead rate would be computed as:

$$\frac{\text{Budgeted overhead}}{\text{Budgeted labor-hours}} = \frac{\$900,000}{60,000} = \$15 \text{ per labor-hour}$$

During the first week of the year the company works on two jobs 1XA3 and 2YQ4. Job 1XA3 is labor intensive while job 2YQ4 is machine intensive. The company has the following information on the labor- and machine-hours required to complete the work:

	Cutting Department	Finishing Department
Job 1XA3:		
Labor-hours	100	800
Machine-hours	200	20
Job 2YQ4:		
Labor-hours	100	200
Machine-hours	400	40

You can see the factory overhead costs applied to the two jobs using the labor-hour-based plantwide overhead rate in Exhibit 12–14. Notice that the overhead allocation is inaccurate under a single plantwide rate. That is, job 1XA3 uses 220 machine-hours while job 2YQ4 uses 440 machine-hours; yet job 1XA3 has almost three times as much applied overhead. Because more of the overhead (depreciation, maintenance, etc.) relates to the use of machines, job 2YQ4 should be charged with the greater amount of overhead.

To obtain more accurate product costing information, assume that Western Furniture Company decides to use two separate departmental overhead rates for overhead costs, with a machine-hour-based overhead rate for the cutting department and a labor-hour-based overhead rate for the finishing department. The departmental predetermined overhead rates are calculated:

Cutting Department Overhead Rate

$$\frac{\text{Budgeted overhead}}{\text{Budgeted machine-hours}} = \frac{\$600,000}{30,000} = \$20 \text{ per machine-hour}$$

Finishing Department Overhead Rate

$$\frac{\text{Budgeted overhead}}{\text{Budgeted labor-hours}} = \frac{\$300,000}{50,000} = \$6 \text{ per labor-hour}$$

Using departmental overhead rates, the factory overhead cost assigned to the two jobs is shown in Exhibit 12–15.

These calculations show that the applied overhead costs with the single plantwide overhead rate would be $4,700 ($13,500 − $8,800) higher for job 1XA3 and $4,700 ($9,200 − $4,500) lower for job 2YQ4 than if the firm were using the two departmental overhead rates. Job 2YQ4 requires considerably more machine-hours than job 1XA3, but the overhead cost allocation to jobs with the single rate does not consider these differences. Using departmental rates, product cost more accurately reflects the different amounts and types of machine and labor work performed on the two jobs.

Exhibit 12–14	Western Furniture Company's Factory Overhead Allocation Using a Plantwide Overhead Rate	

	Job	
	1XA3	**2YQ4**
Cutting department		
$15 × 100	$ 1,500	
$15 × 100		$1,500
Finishing department		
$15 × 800	12,000	
$15 × 200		3,000
Total overhead applied	$13,500	$4,500

Exhibit 12–15	Western Furniture Company's Factory Overhead Allocation Using Departmental Overhead Rates	

	Job	
	1XA3	**2YQ4**
Cutting department: Machine-hours		
$20 × 200	$4,000	
$20 × 400		$8,000
Finishing department: Labor-hours		
$6 × 800	4,800	
$6 × 200		1,200
Total overhead applied	$8,800	$9,200

The departmental overhead allocation is more accurate than the single plantwide overhead for Western Furniture because it makes two improvements: departmental rates and different bases. Prices based on the plant rate would be inaccurate and lead to pricing errors. In this case, job 1XA3 is significantly overcharged using the plant rate, leading to noncompetitive prices. Similarly, job 2YQ4 is underpriced. On balance, Western Furniture is losing 1XA3 business (which is profitable to the firm) and getting too much 2YQ4 business (which is not profitable, because the firm's prices are too low). In the long run the firm would become less and less profitable.

Cost Drivers and Activity-Based Costing

The recent effort to make U.S. companies more competitive in the world market has created a demand for new cost management systems. Traditional cost accounting systems do a poor job of product costing because they use only volume-based cost drivers. Often they do not reflect changes in major cost categories that follow increasing plant automation.

Traditional product costing systems allocate overhead to products or jobs on a volume-based cost driver, such as direct labor dollars or hours. An automated factory environment requires only a minimal direct labor cost and a significantly higher fixed factory overhead than an older manual factory. Using direct labor dollars or hours as the cost driver to allocate overhead seriously distorts product costs in an automated factory. In addition, some factory overhead costs are not volume based. For example, machine setup cost is batch-based and product design cost is product-based. Thus, traditional volume-based overhead allocation may lead to inaccurate product costing.

Under activity-based costing (ABC), factory overhead costs are assigned to products or services using cause-and-effect criteria with multiple cost pools. The use of both volume-based and nonvolume-based cost drivers is based on the consumption of resources in performing various activities. ABC systems help firms achieve their strategies.

◄ **LEARNING OBJECTIVE 7**
Explain why multiple overhead rates and cost drivers may be preferred to a single, plantwide overhead rate.

Exhibit 12–16	Southern Instruments' Overhead and Cost Driver Information		
Overhead Cost Pool	**Budgeted Overhead Cost**	**Cost Driver for This Cost Pool**	**Expected Activity Level**
Power	$50,000	Machine-hours	5,000
Material handling	40,000	Material weight (lb.)	20,000
Machine setups	60,000	Number of setups	200
Quality control	50,000	Number of inspections	500
Total	$200,000		

Southern Instruments, Inc., uses multiple cost drivers as overhead allocation bases. The company makes specialized instruments for customers to detect water contamination. Its budgeted overhead cost for each cost pool and cost driver information are shown in Exhibit 12–16.

Suppose that while completing job 5ZN1 with 200 units and job 10XY1 with 800 units, the firm consumed the following resources:

	Job 5ZN1	Job 10XY1
Machine-hours	1,000	4,000
Material handling (pounds)	5,000	15,000
Number of setups	100	100
Number of inspections	200	300

The firm uses machine-hours as the single plantwide cost driver to apply overhead costs to job 5ZN1 and job 10XY1:

1. Predetermined overhead rate for the machine-hour cost driver:
   $200,000/5,000 = $40 per machine-hour
2. Overhead costs applied using traditional costing:
   Job 5ZN1 $40 × 1,000 = $ 40,000
   Job 10XY1 $40 × 4,000 = $160,000

The firm's management accountant recently attended an activity-based costing seminar and proposes to use multiple cost drivers of machine-hours, material weight, number of setups, and number of inspections to apply different overhead costs to jobs. Using the activity-based costing approach, the allocation of overhead costs to job 5ZN1 and job 10XY1 would involve the following steps:

1. Compute predetermined cost driver rates:
   Power $50,000/5,000 = $10 per machine-hour
   Material handling $40,000/20,000 = $2 per pound
   Machine setups $60,000/200 = $300 per setup
   Quality control $50,000/500 = $100 per inspection
2. Apply overhead costs to jobs using activity level and cost driver rates:

	Job 5ZN1	Job 10XY1
Power	$10,000	$ 40,000
Material handling	10,000	30,000
Machine setups	30,000	30,000
Quality control	20,000	30,000
Total overhead assigned	$70,000	$130,000

Note that the traditional plantwide volume-based overhead method overcosts the high-volume job 10XY1 by $30,000 ($160,000 − $130,000), and undercosts the low-volume job 5ZN1 by $30,000 ($70,000 − $40,000). This overcosting or undercosting may lead management to incorrect pricing decisions, and false information on the size of gross profits earned.

JOB COSTING FOR SERVICE INDUSTRIES

Job costing is used extensively in service industries such as advertising agencies, banks, construction companies, hospitals, and repair shops, as well as in consulting, architecture, accounting, and law firms. Instead of using the term *job*, accounting and consulting firms use the term *client* or *project*, while hospitals and law firms have the term *case*, and advertising agencies and construction companies use the term *contract* or *project*. Many firms use the term *project costing* to indicate the use of job costing in service industries.

Job costing in service industries uses recording procedures and accounts similar to those illustrated earlier in this chapter, except for direct materials involved (there may be none or an insignificant amount). The primary focus is on direct labor performance. The overhead costs usually are applied to jobs based on direct labor-hours or dollars.

Suppose Freed and Swenson, a Los Angeles law firm, has the following budget for 19X8:

◄ **LEARNING OBJECTIVE 8**
Apply job costing concepts to service industries.

Compensation of professional staff	$ 500,000
Other costs	500,000
Total budgeted costs for 19X8	$1,000,000

Other costs include indirect labor costs for office support people, indirect materials and supplies, photocopying, computer-related expenses, insurance, office rent, utilities, training costs, accounting fees, and other office expenses.

Freed and Swenson has a policy of charging overhead costs to clients or jobs at a predetermined percentage of the professional salaries charged to the client. The law firm's recent data show that chargeable hours average 80 percent of available hours for all categories of professional personnel. The nonchargeable hours are regarded as additional overhead. This nonchargeable time might involve training, idle time, inefficiency in resource allocation, and similar factors.

Using these data, the firm's budgeted direct labor costs and budgeted overhead costs are calculated:

1. Budgeted direct labor costs:
   $ 500,000 × 80% = $ 400,000

2. Budgeted overhead costs:

Other costs	$500,000
Salary costs for nonchargeable hours:	
$500,000 − $400,000 =	100,000
	$600,000

The predetermined overhead rate is:

$$\frac{\text{Budgeted overhead costs}}{\text{Budgeted direct labor costs}} = \frac{\$600,000}{\$400,000} = 150\%$$

In Exhibit 12–17 we present relevant data and job costs for the law firm's recent client, George Christatos.

Job Costing of an Advertising Agency

The job costing system used in a New York City advertising agency provided information that assisted management in identifying highly profitable and extremely unprofitable accounts. The advertising agency used its job costing system to discover that a certain account was being served by personnel at a supervisory level, while less expensive staff-level personnel would have been adequate. The firm then decided to assign staff personnel to the account, resulting in considerable savings. The job costing system also aided in budgeting of costs and revenues for various accounts, so that account managers could more effectively manage them. Overall, the system helped the firm improve its planning, control, and performance evaluation processes.

Source: Based on William B. Mills, "Drawing Up a Budgeting System for an Ad Agency," *Management Accounting*, December 1983, pp. 47–49.

Exhibit 12–17 Job Costing for Freed and Swenson Law Firm

Client: George Christatos

Employee Charges	Hours	Salary Rates	Billing Rates (300 percent)
Partners	10	$80	$240
Managers	20	50	150
Associates	100	20	60
	130		

Total revenues and costs for this client's job:

Service revenues:

$$(\$240 \times 10) + (\$150 \times 20) + (\$60 \times 100) = \$11,400$$

Cost of services:

Direct labor ($80 × 10) + $ (50 × 20)
                        + ($20 × 100)   = $3,800
Overhead $3,800 × 150%   = 5,700

Total costs of services	9,500
Operating income	$1,900

Job Costing at Gallup Organization

Gallup Organization, Inc., a firm that provides nationwide opinion polls, developed a job costing system to manage its cost information for 32 cost categories and more than 300 overlapping jobs per year. The system provided timely reports of job costs by cost category (data entry, mailroom, marketing, travel, computer, ballot cost) and by job phase (planning, design, production, report). The job cost report by job phase is illustrated in Exhibit 12–18. The information provided by the firm's job costing system assisted management in estimating costs and bidding more accurately, in controlling cost better, and in increasing profits.

Source: Based on Michael A. Kole, "Controlling Costs with a Database System," *Management Accounting,* June 1988, pp. 31–35.

Exhibit 12–18 Gallup Organization's Job Cost Report

JOB G085001 **MICROCOMPUTERS*** Group—LAW Study Director—JAM

Cost Group	Job Phase				Total		Estimated Cost	Average Percent
	Planning	Design	Production	Report	Cost	Percent		
Professional salaries	$ 700	$ 800	$1,000	$ 900	$ 3,400	30%	$ 3,500	31
Staff salaries	600	700	900	800	3,000	27	3,000	27
Direct costs	500	600	800	700	2,600	23	2,300	20
Total direct	$1,800	$2,100	$2,700	$2,400	$ 9,000		$ 8,800	
Shared costs	400	500	700	600	2,200	20	2,500	22
Total	$2,200	$2,600	$3,400	$3,000	$11,200		$11,300	
Estimated cost	$2,000	$2,800	$3,300	$3,200	$11,300			
Average percent	80%	25%	29%	28%				

*The figures are fictitious.

Source: Michael A. Kole, "Controlling Costs with a Database System," *Management Accounting,* June 1988, p. 33.

Operation costing is a hybrid costing system that uses job costing to assign direct materials costs and process costing to assign conversion costs to products or services.

OPERATION COSTING

Operation costing is a hybrid costing system that uses job costing to assign direct materials costs as well as process costing to assign conversion costs to products or services.

Operation costing is used in manufacturing operations where the conversion activities are very similar across high-volume production of several product lines, but the direct materials used in the various products differ significantly. After direct labor and factory overhead conversion costs are accumulated by operations or departments, accountants use process costing methods to assign these costs to products or services. On the other hand, direct materials costs are accumulated by jobs or batches, and job costing assigns these costs to products or services.

Industries suitable for applying operation costing include clothing, food processing, textiles, shoes, furniture, metalworking, jewelry, and electronic equipment. For example, chair manufacturing has two standard operations: cutting and assembling. Different jobs, however, require different wood and fabric materials. Therefore, an operation costing system is well suited for this situation.

◄ LEARNING OBJECTIVE 9
Describe an operation costing system.

SUMMARY

Product costing is the process of accumulating, classifying, and assigning direct materials, direct labor, and factory overhead costs to products or services. Product costing provides useful cost information for both manufacturing and non-manufacturing firms for (1) product and service cost determination and inventory valuation; (2) management planning, cost control, and performance evaluation; and (3) managerial decisions.

Several different product costing systems are available and can be classified by the (1) cost accumulation method—job or processing costing systems; (2) cost measurement method—actual, normal, or standard costing systems; (3) overhead assignment method—traditional or activity-based costing systems; and (4) treatment of fixed factory overhead costs—variable or absorption costing systems. The choice of a particular system depends on the nature of the industry and the product or service; the firm's strategy and its management information needs; and the costs and benefits of acquiring, designing, modifying, and operating a particular system.

Job costing systems provide information for managers to make strategic decisions regarding products and customers, manufacturing methods, pricing, overhead allocation methods, and other long-term issues.

Job costing and process costing are two major types of product costing systems. Job costing accumulates costs by jobs; it applies to industries with a wide variety of different orders, products, or services. Process costing accumulates cost by processes or departments; it applies to industries with mass production of homogeneous products or services.

Job costing uses several general ledger accounts to control the product cost flows. Direct materials costs are debited to the Materials Control account at purchase time and debited to the Work-in-Process Control account when materials are requested to production. Direct labor costs are debited to the Work-in-Process Control account when they are incurred. Actual factory overhead costs are debited to the Factory Overhead Control account when they are incurred. Factory overhead applied using the predetermined factory overhead rate in normal costing is debited to the Work-in-Process Control account and credited to the Factory Overhead Applied account. When a job is complete, the cost of goods manufactured is transferred from the Work-in-Process Control account to the Finished Goods Control account.

The predetermined factory overhead rate is an estimated factory overhead rate used to apply factory overhead cost to a specific job. The application of a predetermined overhead rate has four steps: (1) budget the factory overhead costs for an appropriate operating period, usually a year; (2) determine the most appropriate cost drivers for charging the factory overhead costs; (3) budget the total amount or activity level of the chosen cost drivers for the operating period; and (4) divide the budgeted factory overhead costs by the budgeted activity level of the chosen cost drivers to obtain the predetermined factory overhead rates.

The difference between the actual factory overhead cost and the amount of the factory overhead applied is the overhead variance. It is either underapplied or overapplied. It can be disposed of in two ways: (1) adjust the Cost of Goods

Sold account, or (2) prorate the discrepancy among the amounts of the current period's applied overhead remaining in the ending balances of the Work-in-Process Control, the Finished Goods Control, and the Cost of Goods Sold accounts.

The ideal criterion for choosing an allocation base is a cause-and-effect relationship. A plantwide rate is appropriate when all products pass through the same processes, or all departments are similar. In some production processes, the relationship between factory overhead costs and various cost drivers differs substantially among production departments. Then multiple overhead rates with multiple volume-related and nonvolume-related cost drivers based on activity consumption should be used.

Job costing is used extensively in service industries such as advertising agencies, banks, construction companies, hospitals, and repair shops, as well as in consulting, architecture, accounting, and law firms.

KEY TERMS

Actual costing   **448**

Actual factory overhead   **448**

Departmental overhead rate   **463**

Factory overhead applied   **450**

Job cost sheet   **445**

Job costing   **443**

Material requisition form   **446**

Normal costing   **449**

Operation costing   **468**

Overapplied overhead   **452**

Overhead application or allocation   **448**

Plantwide overhead rate   **463**

Predetermined factory overhead rate   **450**

Process costing   **443**

Product costing   **439**

Proration   **453**

Schedule of cost of goods manufactured and sold   **462**

Time ticket   **446**

Underapplied overhead   **452**

SELF-STUDY PROBLEM

(For solution, please turn to the end of the chapter.)

Journal Entries and Accounting for Overhead

Watkins Machinery Company uses a normal job costing system. The company has this partial trial balance information on March 1, 19X8, the last month of the fiscal year:

Materials Control (X, $3,000; Y, $2,000; Indirect Materials, $5,000)	$10,000
Work-in-Process—Job 101	6,000
Finished Goods—Job 100	10,000

These transactions relate to the month of March:

1. Purchased direct materials and indirect materials with the following summary of receiving reports:

Material X	$10,000
Material Y	10,000
Indirect Materials	5,000
Total	$25,000

2. Issued direct materials and indirect materials with this summary of requisition forms:

	Job 101	Job 102	Total
Material X	$5,000	$3,000	$ 8,000
Material Y	4,000	3,000	7,000
Subtotal	$9,000	$6,000	$15,000
Indirect materials			8,000
Total			$23,000

3. Factory labor incurred is summarized by these time tickets:

Job 101	$12,000
Job 102	8,000
Indirect labor	5,000
Total	$25,000

4. Factory utilities, factory depreciation, and factory insurance incurred is summarized by these factory vouchers, invoices, and cost memos:

Utilities	$ 500
Depreciation	15,000
Insurance	2,500
Total	$18,000

5. Factory overhead costs were applied to jobs at the predetermined rate of $15 per machine-hour. Job 101 incurred 1,200 machine-hours while job 102 used 800 machine-hours.

6. Job 101 was completed while job 102 was still in process at the end of March.

7. Job 100 and job 101 were shipped to the customers during March. Both jobs had gross margins of 20 percent based on manufacturing cost.

The company closed the overapplied or underapplied overhead to the Cost of Goods Sold account at the end of March.

Required

1. Prepare journal entries to record the transactions and events. Number your entries from 1 to 7.

2. Compute the ending balance of the Work-in-Process Control account.

3. Compute the overhead variance and indicate whether it is overapplied or underapplied.

4. Close the overhead variance to Cost of Goods Sold account.

QUESTIONS

12–1 What is the purpose of a product costing system?

12–2 Give three ways management uses product costs.

12–3 Distinguish between job costing and process costing.

12–4 Explain when companies are likely to use a job costing system or a process costing system. Provide some examples.

12–5 Which product costing system is extensively used in the service industry for hospitals, law firms, or accounting firms? Explain why.

12–6 What document is prepared to accumulate costs for each separate job in a job costing system? What kind of costs are recorded in the document?

12–7 Explain how predetermined factory overhead rates are computed and why they are used in applying factory overhead to units of products instead of actual overhead costs.

12–8 What is the role of material requisition forms in a job costing system? Time tickets? Bills of materials?

12–9   What is meant by the statement that there is an important cost-benefit issue in accounting for overhead? Why is that issue important?

12–10   Describe the flow of costs through a job costing system.

12–11   Explain what is meant by underapplied overhead and overapplied overhead. How are these amounts disposed of at the end of a period?

12–12   Why are some manufacturing firms switching from direct labor-hours to machine-hours as the cost driver for a factory overhead application?

12–13   What is a plantwide overhead rate? Under what circumstances is using multiple overhead rates preferred to using a single plantwide overhead rate?

12–14   Explain why overhead might be overapplied in a given period.

12–15   Distinguish between an actual costing system and a normal costing system. What are components of the actual manufacturing costs and the components of the normal manufacturing costs?

12–16   Factory overhead includes a variety of costs that vary greatly with respect to the production process. What is the best way to choose an appropriate cost driver in applying factory overhead?

12–17   What is the difference between normal cost of goods sold and adjusted cost of goods sold?

PROBLEMS

12–18   **JOB VS. PROCESS COSTING**   For each of these firms, indicate whether job or process costing is more suitable:

1. Food processing
2. Manufacturing textile products
3. Printing shop
4. Automobile repair shop
5. Accounting firm
6. Oil refining
7. Manufacturer of custom-built houses
8. Consulting firm
9. Manufacturer of electronics
10. Cement manufacturer

12–19   **BASIC JOB COSTING**   Davis Inc. is a job-order manufacturing company. The company uses a predetermined overhead rate based on direct labor-hours to apply overhead to individual jobs. For 19X8, estimated direct labor-hours are 95,000, and estimated factory overhead is $579,500. The following information is for September 19X8. Job A was completed during September, and job B was started but not finished.

September 1, 19X8, inventories:	
Materials Control	$ 7,500
Work-in-Process Control (All job A)	31,200
Finished Goods Control	67,000
Material purchases	$104,000
Direct materials requisitioned:	
Job A	$ 45,000
Job B	33,500
Direct labor-hours:	
Job A	4,200
Job B	3,500
Labor costs incurred:	
Direct labor ($5.50/hour)	$ 42,350
Indirect labor	13,500
Supervisory salaries	6,000

Rental costs:	
Factory	$ 7,000
Administrative offices	1,800
Total equipment depreciation costs:	
Factory	$ 7,500
Administrative offices	1,600
Indirect materials used	$ 12,000

Required

1. What is the total cost of job A?
2. What is the total factory overhead applied during September?
3. What is the overapplied or underapplied overhead for September?

12–20 **JOURNAL ENTRIES** Marita Company uses a job costing system. Normal costing is used and factory overhead is applied on the basis of machine-hours. At the beginning of the year, management estimated that the company would incur $1,007,500 of factory overhead costs and use 77,500 machine-hours.

Marita Company recorded the following events during the month of May:

1. Purchased 180,000 pounds of materials on account; the cost was $2.50 per pound.
2. Issued 120,000 pounds of materials to production. Of this amount, 15,000 pounds were used as indirect materials.
3. Direct labor costs incurred were $240,000 and indirect labor costs incurred were $50,000.
4. Depreciation on equipment for the month amounted to $15,700.
5. Insurance costs were $3,500 for the manufacturing property.
6. Paid $8,500 cash for utilities and other miscellaneous items for the manufacturing plant.
7. Job H11 costing $6,500 and job G28 costing $77,000 were completed during the month and transferred to the Finished Goods account.
8. Job G28 was shipped to the customer during the month. The job was invoiced at 35 percent above cost.
9. During May 7,800 machine-hours were used.

Required

1. Compute Marita Company's predetermined overhead rate for the year.
2. Prepare journal entries to record the events that occurred during May.
3. Compute the amount of overapplied or underapplied overhead and prepare a journal entry to close overapplied or underapplied overhead into cost of goods sold on May 31.

12–21 **ACCOUNTING FOR OVERHEAD** XYZ Company listed the following data for 19X8:

Budgeted factory overhead	$870,000
Budgeted direct labor-hours	60,000
Budgeted machine-hours	20,000
Actual factory overhead	864,500
Actual direct labor-hours	60,500
Actual machine-hours	19,700

Required

1. Assume XYZ applied overhead based on direct labor-hours. Calculate the company's predetermined overhead rate for 19X8.

2. Assume XYZ applies overhead based on machine-hours. Calculate the company's predetermined overhead rate for 19X8.

3. Calculate the overapplied or underapplied overhead if overhead is applied based on direct labor-hours.

4. Calculate the overapplied or underapplied overhead if overhead is applied based on machine-hours.

5. Prepare the journal entry to dispose of overapplied or underapplied overhead if overhead is applied based on direct labor-hours. Assume no proration is done.

6. Prepare the journal entry to dispose of overapplied or underapplied overhead if overhead is applied based on machine-hours. Assume no proration is done.

International

12–22 ACCOUNTING FOR OVERHEAD Yamashita Company is a furniture manufacturing firm in a suburb of Tokyo, Japan. The company uses a job costing system. Factory overhead costs in yen are applied on the basis of direct labor-hours. At the beginning of 19X8, management estimated that the company would incur ¥284,000 of factory overhead costs for the year and work 71,000 direct labor-hours.

During the year the company actually worked 75,000 direct labor-hours and incurred these factory overhead costs:

a. Paid ¥75,400 cash for utilities, power, and other miscellaneous items for the manufacturing plants.

b. Recognized depreciation on manufacturing property, plant, and equipment of ¥58,000 for the year.

c. Paid ¥25,000 cash for the insurance premium on manufacturing property and plant.

d. Incurred advertising costs, ¥10,000.

e. Incurred indirect labor costs, ¥54,600.

f. Incurred indirect material costs, ¥53,000.

g. Paid the ¥55,000 salary of the factory superintendent.

h. Accrued sales and administrative salaries, ¥85,000.

Required

1. Compute the firm's 19X8 predetermined overhead rate.

2. Compute the amount of factory overhead that should be applied to the Work-in-Process account for the year.

3. Compute the amount of overapplied or underapplied overhead to be closed into the Cost of Goods Sold account at the end of the year.

4. Check the most recent issue of *The Wall Street Journal* to find the exchange rate between the U.S. dollar and the Japanese yen.

International

12–23 REVIEW OF JOB COSTING; GENERAL LEDGER RELATIONSHIPS Asiana Company is a Malaysian company that manufactures custom-made products. A job costing system is used to accumulate and record costs in the company's plant. Factory overhead costs in ringgits (M$) are charged to production on the basis of machine-hours. The following budget information is for 19X8:

Budgeted total factory overhead	M$4,200,000
Budgeted total machine-hours	300,000 hours

During January, the firm worked on two jobs:

Job 133:
Direct materials	M$27,000
Direct labor	M$33,000
Machine-hours	9,500 hours

Job 243:
Direct materials	M$45,000
Direct labor	M$51,000
Machine-hours	15,500 hours

The beginning and ending inventories follow. Job 133 was completed and sold during the month.

Inventories, January 1, 19X8
Materials (all direct)	M$33,000
Work-in-process (Job 133)	M$24,000
Finished goods	0

Inventories, January 31, 19X8
Materials (all direct)	M$26,000
Work-in-process (Job 243)	?
Finished goods	0

During January, actual factory overhead costs incurred were M$385,000.

Required

1. Compute the predetermined overhead rate for 19X8.
2. What is the amount of direct materials purchased in January?
3. What is the cost of goods manufactured for 19X8?
4. What is the balance of Work-in-Process at January 31, 19X8?
5. What is the amount of total factory overhead applied in January 19X8?
6. Compute the amount of overapplied overhead or underapplied overhead.
7. Prepare a journal entry to close overapplied or underapplied overhead into the cost of goods sold account.
8. Check the most recent issue of *The Wall Street Journal* to find the exchange rate between the U.S. dollar and the Malaysian ringgit.

12–24 **JOURNAL ENTRIES AND ACCOUNTING FOR OVERHEAD** Humming Company manufactures highly sophisticated musical instruments for professional musicians. The company uses a normal costing system, in which manufacturing overhead is applied on the basis of direct labor-hours. For 19X8, the company estimated that it would incur $120,000 in manufacturing overhead costs and 8,000 direct labor-hours. The April 1, 19X8, balances in inventory accounts are:

Materials	$27,000
Work-in-process (S10)	10,500
Finished goods (J21)	54,000

Job S10 is the only job in process on April 1, 19X8. The following transactions were recorded for the month of April.

a. Materials were purchased on account, $90,000.
b. Materials were issued to production amounting to $91,000; $4,000 of this was for indirect materials. Direct materials issued:

Job S10	$23,000
Job C20	42,000
Job M54	22,000

c. Payroll cost incurred and paid, $20,460:

Direct labor ($13/hour; total 920 hours)

Job S10	$ 6,110
Job C20	4,030
Job M54	1,820
Indirect labor	$ 2,500
Selling and administrative salaries	$ 6,000

d. Depreciation recognized for the month

Manufacturing asset	$ 2,200
Selling and administrative asset	1,700

e. Advertising expenses paid	$ 6,000
f. Factory utilities costs incurred	$ 1,300
g. Other factory overhead costs incurred	$ 1,600

h. Factory overhead was applied to production on the basis of direct labor-hours.

i. Job S10 was completed during the month and transferred to finished goods warehouse.

j. Job J21 was sold on account for $59,000.

k. Collections on account from customers during the month were $25,000.

Required

1. Calculate the company's predetermined overhead rate.
2. Prepare journal entries for the transactions that occurred in April.
3. What is the balance of the materials inventory on April 30, 19X8?
4. What is the balance of the work-in-process inventory on April 30?
5. What is the amount of underapplied or overapplied overhead?

12–25 UNDERAPPLIED OR OVERAPPLIED OVERHEAD Tyson Company uses a job costing system in which factory overhead is applied on the basis of direct labor-hours. There was no job in process on February 1. During the month of February, the company worked on these three jobs:

	Job Number		
	A23	C76	G15
Direct labor ($8/hour)	$24,000	?	$8,800
Direct materials	42,000	61,000	?
Overhead applied	?	24,750	6,050

During the month, the company completed and transferred job A23 to the finished goods inventory at the cost of $82,500. Jobs C76 and G15 were not completed and remain in work in process at the cost of $148,650 at the end of the month. Actual factory overhead costs during the month totaled $48,600.

Required

1. Compute the amount of underapplied or overapplied overhead for February.
2. What is the predetermined factory overhead rate?
3. Compute the cost of direct materials issued to production during the month.
4. Prepare a journal entry showing the transfer of the completed job into the finished goods inventory.

12–26 APPLICATION AND PRORATION OF FACTORY OVERHEAD Getaway Company uses job costing in which factory overhead is applied on the basis of direct labor-hours. The company's factory overhead budget for 19X8 included the following estimates:

Budgeted total factory overhead	$568,000
Budgeted total direct labor-hours	71,000

At the end of the year, the ledger of the company shows the following results:

Actual factory overhead	$582,250
Actual direct labor-hours	69,500

And the following amounts of the year's applied factory overhead remained in the various manufacturing accounts.

	Applied Factory Overhead Remaining
Work-in-Process inventory	$139,000
Finished Goods inventory	216,840
Cost of Goods Sold	200,160

Required

1. Compute the firm's predetermined factory overhead rate for 19X8.
2. Calculate the amount of overapplied or underapplied overhead.
3. Prepare a journal entry to prorate overapplied or underapplied overhead to Work in Process, Finished Goods, and Cost of Goods Sold accounts.

12–27 JOURNAL ENTRIES, APPLICATION AND PRORATION OF OVERHEAD

Hartford Company uses job costing in which factory overhead is applied on the basis of direct labor cost. Any overapplied or underapplied overhead is allocated between the Work-in-Process, Finished Goods, and Cost of Goods Sold accounts. The April 1, 19X8, balances in selected accounts are

Inventories, April 1:	
Materials (all direct)	$124,000
Work in Process (Job 354)	113,400
Finished Goods (Job 243)	178,200

Job 354 was the only job in the manufacturing process at the end of March. Job 243 was completed during March but not yet sold.

These transactions occurred during April 19X8:

a. Materials were purchased on account, $143,000.

b. Materials were requisitioned for use in production:
Direct materials:

Job 354	$ 23,000
Job 475	?
Job 523	72,500
Indirect Materials	18,700

c. An analysis of labor time cards reveals the following labor usage for April:
Direct labor

Job 354	?
Job 475	$102,000
Job 523	36,500
Indirect labor	97,000

d. Depreciation of the factory building and equipment during April amounted to $76,000.

e. Rent for the warehouse was paid in cash, $6,500.

f. Insurance cost covering the factory operation was paid in cash, $11,000.

g. Other factory overhead costs amounted to $63,000.

h. $287,500 of factory overhead cost was applied to production on the basis of direct labor cost.

i. Job 354 and job 475 were completed and transferred to the Finished Goods account. The balance of the Work-in-Process account on April 30, 19X8, was $154,625.

j. Job 243 and job 354 were sold on account during the month. The cost of goods sold for these jobs was $520,475. The balance of the Finished Goods account on April 30 showed $254,875.

Required

1. Prepare journal entries for the transactions that occurred during April.

2. What was the amount of factory overhead applied to job 523?

3. Calculate the firm's predetermined factory overhead rate as a percentage of direct labor cost.

4. What was the cost of goods manufactured in April?

5. What was the direct materials cost incurred in April to initiate and complete job 475?

6. What was the direct labor cost incurred in April to complete job 354?

7. What was the balance of materials account on April 30, 19X8?

8. Calculate the amount of overapplied or underapplied overhead in April.

9. Prepare a journal entry to allocate overapplied or underapplied overhead among Work-in-Process inventory, Finished Goods inventory, and Cost of Goods Sold accounts.

12-28 APPLICATION AND DISPOSITION OF FACTORY OVERHEAD Department 203: Work-in-process, beginning of period

Job	Material	Labor	Overhead	Total
1376	$17,500	$22,000	$33,000	$72,500

Department 203: Costs for 19X8

	Incurred by jobs			
Jobs	Material	Labor	Other	Total
1376	$ 1,000	$ 7,000	—	$ 8,000
1377	26,000	53,000	—	79,000
1378	12,000	9,000	—	21,000
1379	4,000	1,000	—	5,000
	Not incurred by jobs			
Indirect materials and supplies	15,000	—	—	15,000
Indirect labor	—	53,000	—	53,000
Employee benefits	—	—	$23,000	23,000
Depreciation	—	—	12,000	12,000
Supervision	—	20,000	—	20,000
Total	$58,000	$143,000	$35,000	$236,000

Department 203: Overhead rate for 19X8

Budgeted overhead:	
Variable	
Indirect materials	$ 16,000
Indirect labor	56,000
Employee benefits	24,000
Fixed	
Supervision	20,000
Depreciation	12,000
Total	$128,000
Budgeted direct labor dollars	$ 80,000
Rate per direct labor dollar ($128,000/$80,000)	160%

Required

1. What was the actual factory overhead for department 203 for 19X8?
2. What was department 203's underapplied overhead for 19X8?
3. Job 1376 was the only job completed and sold in 19X8. What amount was included in cost of goods sold for this job?
4. What was the amount of work-in-process inventory at the end of 19X8?
5. Assume that factory overhead was underapplied in the amount of $14,000 for department 203. If underapplied overhead were distributed between cost of goods sold and inventory, how much of the underapplied overhead was charged to the year-end work-in-process inventory?

(CMA Adapted)

12–29 **REVIEW OF JOB COSTING** Hogan Company uses a job costing system and applies factory overhead cost to products on the basis of direct labor-hours. Management prepared this overhead budget for 19X8:

Budgeted direct labor-hours	59,000
Budgeted factory overhead	$678,500

During 19X8, an economic recession caused the curtailment of production and a buildup of inventory in Hogan Company's warehouse. The company's ledger shows the following operating data:

Direct labor ($8/hour; 36,000 hours)	$288,000
Inventories, January 1, 19X8:	
Materials (all direct)	$ 35,000
Work-in-process	198,000
Finished goods	450,000
Inventories, December 31, 19X8:	
Materials (all direct)	50,000
Work-in-process	125,000
Finished goods	634,000
Cost of goods sold after adjusting	
for underapplied overhead	987,000

The firm closed underapplied or overapplied overhead directly into the Cost of Goods Sold account. After the adjustment for underapplied overhead, Cost of Goods Sold was increased by $18,000.

Required

1. Compute the company's predetermined factory overhead rate for 19X8.
2. Determine the actual overhead for 19X8.
3. What is the cost of goods manufactured for 19X8?
4. What is the amount of direct materials purchased during the year?

12–30 REVIEW OF JOB COSTING; JOURNAL ENTRIES AND GENERAL LEDGER
Manning Corporation uses a job costing system for its production costs.
Factory overhead cost is applied on the basis of direct labor-hours. The
January 1, 19X8, balances of selected inventory accounts are

Materials (all direct)	$2,500
Work-in-process	1,900
Finished goods	3,900

During January 19X8, these events occurred:

a. Materials were purchased on account, $3,250.

b. Materials issued to production, $4,150.

c. Direct labor cost per hour was $11 and the total direct labor cost
amounted to $3,872.

d. During the month, sales revenue was $8,200, and selling and
administrative expenses were $1,700.

e. The Cost of Goods Sold account during the month amounted to
$7,800.

f. Actual factory overhead costs incurred during the month, $4,826.

The January 31, 19X8, balances of Work-in-Process inventory and
Finished Goods inventory were $3,244 and $7,354, respectively. The firm
closes underapplied or overapplied overhead directly into the Cost of
Goods Sold account.

Required

1. Prepare journal entries to record the events described.

2. What was the balance of the Materials inventory account on
January 31?

3. What was the amount of cost of goods manufactured during
January?

4. What is the firm's predetermined factory overhead rate?

5. Calculate the amount of overapplied or underapplied overhead in
January.

6. What was the operating profit for January?

12–31 REVIEW OF JOB COSTING; GENERAL LEDGER RELATIONSHIP MTT
Company manufactures products to customers' specifications. A job
costing system is used to accumulate production costs. Factory overhead
cost is applied at 115 percent of direct labor cost. Selected data
concerning the past year's operation of the company are

Inventories:	1/1		12/31
Materials (all direct)	$64,000		$42,000
Work-in-process	50,000		35,000
Finished goods	95,000		84,000
Other data:			
Direct materials purchased		$270,000	
Cost of goods available for sale		790,750	

Required

1. What was the cost of direct materials used for production?

2. What was the cost of goods manufactured during the year?

3. What was the cost of goods sold for the year?

4. What was the amount of applied factory overhead cost during the
year?

12–32 SCHEDULE OF COST OF GOODS MANUFACTURED Benaline Company
uses a job costing system for its production costs. A predetermined
factory overhead rate based on direct labor costs is used to apply factory
overhead to jobs. During the month of July, the firm processed three jobs:

A12, C46, and M24. A small fire in the administration office during the wee hours of August 1 left only these fragments of the company's factory ledger:

Inventories, July 1:	
Materials (all direct)	$42,500
Work-in-process (job A12)	54,000
Finished goods	75,000
Inventories, July 31:	
Materials (all direct)	?
Work-in-process (job C46 and job M23)	?
Finished goods	$96,080
Cost of goods sold, July	102,000
Direct materials purchased, July	$25,000
Direct materials issued to production	$63,340
Job A12	$21,340
Job C46	26,000
Job M23	16,000
Factory labor-hours used ($5.50/hour)	
Job A12	2,800
Job C46	3,800
Job M23	1,700
Indirect labor	900
Other factory overhead costs incurred:	
Rent	$29,500
Utilities	8,600
Repairs and maintenance	4,600
Depreciation	27,100
Other	6,600

Job A12 is the only job completed during the month, with $123,080 cost of goods manufactured.

Required

1. Compute the predetermined factory overhead rate.
2. Compute the amount of factory overhead applied during the month of July.
3. Compute the actual factory overhead cost incurred during the month of July.
4. What was the ending balance of the Work-in-Process inventory account?
5. Compute the amount of overapplied overhead or underapplied overhead.
6. Prepare a schedule of cost of goods manufactured.

12–33 **SCHEDULE OF COST OF GOODS MANUFACTURED AND SOLD** Oak Hill Fishery is a canning company in Portland. The company uses a normal costing in which factory overhead is applied on the basis of direct labor costs. Budgeted factory overhead for 19X8 was $621,000, and management budgeted $270,000 of direct labor costs. During the year, the company incurred these actual costs:

Direct materials used	$320,000
Direct labor	255,000
Factory overhead	598,000

The January 1, 19X8, inventory account balances are

Materials (all direct)	$58,000
Work-in-process	34,000
Finished goods	22,000

The December 31, 19X8, balances of these inventory accounts are 15 percent lower.

Required

1. Compute the predetermined factory overhead rate.
2. What is the amount of cost of goods manufactured for the year?
3. What is the amount of direct materials purchased during the year?
4. Calculate underapplied or overapplied overhead for the year. Prepare a journal entry to close the amount directly into the Cost of Goods Sold account.
5. What is the amount of cost of goods sold after the adjustment?
6. Prepare a schedule of cost of goods manufactured and sold.

12-34   JOURNAL ENTRIES, SCHEDULE OF COST OF GOODS MANUFACTURED
Apex Corporation manufactures eighteenth-century, classical style furniture. It uses job costing in which factory overhead is applied on the basis of direct labor-hours. Budgeted factory overhead for 19X8 was $1,235,475 and management budgeted 86,700 direct labor-hours. These transactions were recorded during August:

a. 5,000 square feet of oak were purchased on account at $25 per square foot.
b. Fifty gallons of glue were purchased on account at $36 per gallon (indirect material).
c. 3,500 square feet of oak and 30.5 gallons of glue were requisitioned for production.
d. Payroll costs incurred and paid were $187,900. Of this amount, $46,000 were indirect labor costs and direct labor personnel earned $22 per hour on average.
e. A factory utility bill of $15,230 was paid in cash.
f. August's insurance cost was $3,500 on the manufacturing property and equipment. The premium had been paid in March.
g. Depreciation on manufacturing equipment for August amounted to $8,200.
h. Depreciation on an administrative asset also was recorded at $2,400.
i. Advertising expenses of $5,500 were paid in cash.
j. Other factory overhead costs incurred and paid were $13,500.
k. Miscellaneous selling and administrative expenses incurred were $13,250.
l. Factory overhead was applied to production on the basis of direct labor-hours.
m. Goods costing $146,000 to manufacture were completed during the month.
n. Sales on account for August amounted to $132,000. The cost of goods sold was $112,000.

Required

1. Compute the firm's predetermined factory overhead rate for 19X8.
2. Prepare journal entries to record the events in August.
3. Calculate the amount of overapplied or underapplied overhead to be closed into Cost of Goods Sold on August 31, 19X8.
4. Prepare a schedule of cost of goods manufactured and sold.
5. Prepare the income statement for August.

12–35 PLANTWIDE VS. DEPARTMENTAL OVERHEAD RATE Telefax Corporation manufactures a popular fax. Cost estimates for one unit of the product for the year 19X8 are

Direct materials	$200
Direct labor ($12/hour)	240
Machine-hours	20

The model requires 12 hours of direct labor in department A and 8 hours in department B. However, it requires 5 machine-hours in department A and 15 machine-hours in department B. The factory overhead costs estimated in these two departments are

	A	B
Variable cost	$146,000	$ 77,000
Fixed cost	94,000	163,000

Management expects the firm to produce 1,000 units of products during 19X8.

Required

1. Assume that factory overhead is applied on the basis of direct labor-hours. Compute the predetermined factory overhead rate.
2. If factory overhead were applied on the basis of machine-hours, what would be the plantwide overhead rate?
3. If the company produced exactly 1,000 units during the year, what will be the total amount of applied factory overhead in each department in requirements 1 and 2?
4. If you were asked to evaluate the performance of each department manager, which allocation basis would you use? Why?
5. Compute the departmental overhead rates for each department.

12–36 ACTIVITY-BASED COSTING, COST DRIVERS The controller for Southern Metals Company has established these overhead cost pools and cost drivers for 19X8:

 *Strategy*

Overhead Cost Pool	Budgeted Overhead	Cost Driver	Expected Activity Level
Machine setups	$117,868	Number of setups	40
Power	341,120	Machine-hours	21,320
Material handling	85,000	Material weight	34,000 lb.
Quality control	143,500	Number of units	82,000 units
Other overhead	184,500	Direct labor-hours	14,760 hours
	$871,988		

During March 19X8, an order for 1,500 machine tools was received and produced. The order required:

Machine setups	7
Machine-hours	3,250
Materials	4,250 lb.
Direct labor-hours	2,750 hours

Required

1. Calculate the predetermined factory overhead rates for cost drivers.
2. What is the total factory overhead assigned to fill the order under the activity-based costing approach?
3. Suppose that a single predetermined factory overhead rate based on machine-hours is used to apply factory overhead. What is the

predetermined factory overhead rate? And what is the amount of factory overhead applied to the order?

4. Which product costing system would you prefer? Why?

5. Examine the implications of your answers to requirements 2 and 3 for the Southern Metals' pricing and product-emphasis strategy.

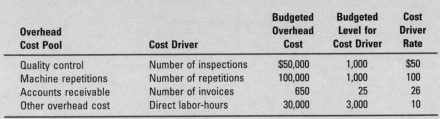

Strategy

12–37 ACTIVITY-BASED COSTING, COST DRIVERS
The Robertson Company manufactures laser printers. It has outlined the following factory overhead cost drivers:

Overhead Cost Pool	Cost Driver	Budgeted Overhead Cost	Budgeted Level for Cost Driver	Cost Driver Rate
Quality control	Number of inspections	$50,000	1,000	$50
Machine repetitions	Number of repetitions	100,000	1,000	100
Accounts receivable	Number of invoices	650	25	26
Other overhead cost	Direct labor-hours	30,000	3,000	10

Robertson has an order for 500 laser printers. Following are the production requirements for the order:

Number of inspections	25
Number of repetitions	200
Number of invoices processed	250
Labor-hours	300

Required

1. What is the total factory overhead assigned to the 500 units under the activity-based costing approach?

2. What is the cost per laser printer?

3. If Robertson expressed its factory overhead rate in direct labor-hours, how much overhead would be applied to the entire order of 500 laser printers?

4. How do you explain the difference?

5. Examine the implications of your answers to requirements 1 and 3 for Robertson's pricing and product-emphasis strategy.

12–38 ACTIVITY-BASED COSTING, COST DRIVERS

			Overhead Cost Pool		
Overhead Cost Pool		Budgeted Overhead Cost	Budgeted Level for Cost Driver	Cost Driver	Rate
Materials handling		$120,000	3,000 pounds	Weight	$ 40
Machine setup		9,750	325 repetitions	Number of repetitions	30
Machine repair		1,045	5 units	Units of time*	209
Inspections		8,100	135 inspections	Number of inspections	60

Requirements for Job 747

Materials handling	100 pounds
Machine setups	25 repetitions
Machine repair time	0.5 hour
Inspections	10 inspections

*One unit equals 15-minute intervals

Required Use the multiple cost drivers to compute the total factory overhead that should be assigned to job 747.

Service

12–39 OVERHEAD RATE, PRICING
Buckey Associates is an advertising agency in Columbus, Ohio. The controller of the company estimated that the company would incur $325,000 in overhead costs for 19X8. Because the overhead costs of each project changes in direct proportion to the

amount of direct professional hours incurred, the controller decided that overhead should be applied on the basis of professional hours. The estimated professional hours for the year were 25,000. During October, the following costs were incurred to make a 20-second TV commercial for Central Ohio Bank:

Direct material	$32,000
Direct professional hours ($23/hour)	1,200

Actual overhead costs to make the commercial were $14,700. It is customary in the industry to bill customers at 150 percent of total cost.

Required

1. Compute the predetermined overhead rate.
2. What is the total amount of the bill to be sent to Central Ohio Bank?

12–40 COST SYSTEM SELECTION, UNDERAPPLIED OR OVERAPPLIED OVERHEAD
The Whittier Clinic is a large, profitable medical complex staffed by doctors who provide a variety of services. When patients go to an appointment, the doctor fills out a computerized form that states what services were provided during the visit. The patient receives the completed form with prices noted in the mail as the bill.

Service

Required

1. Should Whittier Clinic use a job costing system or should it try another system? Why?
2. The applied overhead for Whittier Clinic was $103,475. The clinic found out that actual overhead was $113,775. Is this overhead underapplied or overapplied? What is the amount?
3. What would be your answer if the clinic's applied overhead were $133,850, and actual overhead were $122,950?
4. Should there be a difference between overhead applied and the actual overhead?
5. Using the numerical answer you got in requirement 2, describe with journal entries how you would deal with the underapplied or overapplied overhead amount. Explain why you did it this way and when this procedure should be done.

12–41 BASIC JOB COSTING Daetwyler and Koo public accounting firm has the following budget for 19X8:

Service

Direct labor (for professional hours charged to clients)	$106,000
Overhead:	
Indirect materials	$ 5,000
Indirect labor	75,000
Depreciation—Building	25,000
Depreciation—Furniture	2,500
Utilities	6,000
Insurance	2,400
Property taxes	2,600
Other expenses	1,500
Total	120,000

The firm uses direct labor cost as the cost driver to apply overhead to clients.

During January the firm worked for many clients, two of which are

Davila account:	
Direct materials	$ 200
Direct labor	1,500
Jackson account:	
Direct materials	$2,690
Direct labor	6,300

Required

1. Compute Daetwyler and Koo CPA's budgeted overhead rate. Explain how this is used.
2. Compute the amount of overhead to be charged to the Davila and Jackson accounts using the predetermined overhead rate calculated previously.
3. Compute the separate job cost for the Davila and Jackson accounts.

12–42 JOB COST SHEETS Decker Screw Manufacturing Company produces special screws made to customer specifications. During June, the following data pertained to these costs:

Summary of Direct Material Requisitions

Department Number	Job Number	Requisition Number	Quantity	Cost per Unit
1	2906	B9766	4,550	$ 1.34
2	2907	B9767	110	22.18
1	2908	B9768	1,000	9.00
1	2906	B9769	4,430	1.35
2	2908	B9770	23	48.00

Summary of Direct Labor Time Tickets

Department Number	Job Number	Ticket Number	Hours	Cost per Unit
1	2906	1056–1168	1,102	$6.50
2	2907	2121–2130	136	8.88
1	2908	1169–1189	151	6.50
2	2908	2131–1239	32	8.88
1	2906	1190–1239	810	6.50

Summary of Factory Overhead Application Rates

Department Number	Basis of Application Rates
1	$3 per direct labor-hour
2	150% of direct labor cost

Decker had no beginning Work-in-Process inventory for June. Of the jobs begun in June, job 2906 was completed and sold on account for $30,000, job 2907 was completed but not sold, and job 2908 was still in process.

Required

1. Calculate the direct materials, direct labor, factory overhead, and total costs for each of the three jobs started in June.
2. Perform the same calculations as requirement 1, assuming that both direct materials quantity used and cost per unit have increased by 15 percent. Also, both direct labor-hours and rate per hour have increased by 10 percent.

12–43 JOB COST DETAILS   Hannah Cabinets Inc. is a small business that produces wood cabinets. The company collected the following data:

Job order number:	2809		Quantity ordered:	50
Product:	Tiger Bookcases		Date started:	10/10/X8
Date ordered:	10/03/X8		Date wanted:	10/20/X8
			Date completed:	10/18/X8

	Cutting Department	Assembly Department	Finishing Department
Material used	$800 (Req. 665)	$160 (Req. 681)	$70 (Req. 688)
Direct labor rate	5.40	6.10	8.00
Direct labor-hours	10	35	18.5
Applied factory overhead	$5 per MH*	80% of DLC†	$3 per DLH*‡
Machine-hours	8.25	0	0

*Machine-hour
†Direct labor cost
‡Direct labor-hour

The company uses a 30 percent markup on total factory cost to determine the selling price.

Required

1. Calculate the costs of direct materials, direct labor, applied factory overhead for each department, and the total cost of the job.
2. Calculate the selling price and the gross margin for the job.

12–44 ASSIGNING OVERHEAD TO JOBS   Aero Systems is a manufacturer of airplane parts and engines for a variety of military and commercial aircraft. The company's 40 percent business is based on government contracts. It has two production departments. Department A is a machine-intensive department while department B is a labor-intensive department. Aero Systems has adopted a traditional plantwide rate using the direct labor-hour-based overhead allocation system. Recently, the company has conducted a pilot study using a departmental overhead rate costing system. The new system will use two overhead allocation bases: machine-hours for department A and direct labor-hours for department B. The study shows that the new system, while more accurate and timely, will result in lower costs being assigned to the government jobs, and higher costs being assigned to the company's other private business jobs. Apparently, the current (less accurate) direct labor-based costing system has overcosted government jobs and undercosted private business jobs. On hearing of this, top management has decided to scrap the plans for adopting the new departmental overhead rate costing system, because government jobs constitute 40 percent of Aero Systems' business, and the reduced cost will reduce the price and thus the profit for this part of Aero Systems' business.

 *Ethics*

Required   As the management accountant participating in this pilot study project, how do you see your responsibility when you hear of the decision of top management to cancel the plans for the new departmental overhead rate costing system? Can you ignore your professional ethics code in this case? What would you do?

SOLUTION TO SELF-STUDY PROBLEM

Journal Entries and Accounting for Overhead

1. Journal entries:

(1) Materials Control 25,000
    Accounts Payable 25,000
    To record the purchase of direct materials and indirect materials.

(2) Work-in-Process Control 15,000
    Factory Overhead Control 8,000
      Materials control 23,000
    To record direct and indirect materials issued.

(3) Work-in-Process Control 20,000
    Factory Overhead Control 5,000
      Accrued Payroll Control 25,000
    To record factory labor incurred.

(4) Factory Overhead Control 18,000
    Accounts Payable 500
    Accumulated Depreciation—Factory 15,000
    Prepaid Insurance 2,500
    To record actual overhead costs incurred, including factory utilities, depreciation, and insurance.

(5) Work-in-Process Control 30,000
    Factory Overhead Applied 30,000
    To record the application of factory overhead to jobs.

Summary of factory overhead applied:	
Job 1 ($15 × 1,200)	$18,000
Job 2 ($15 × 800)	12,000
Total	$30,000

(6) Finished Goods Control 45,000
    Work-in-Process Control 45,000
    To record the job finished.

Total manufacturing cost for job 101:	
Beginning inventory	$ 6,000
Direct materials added	9,000
Direct labor incurred	12,000
Factory overhead applied	18,000
Total	$45,000

(7) Accounts Receivable 66,000
    Sales 66,000
    To record the total sales revenue of two jobs.

Cost of Goods Sold 55,000
    Finished Goods Control 55,000
    To record the total cost of goods sold.

Summary of the total cost in shipping orders:	
Job 100	$10,000
Job 101	45,000
Total	$55,000

Sales = $55,000 × 120% = $66,000

2. Ending balance of the Work-in-Process Control for

Job 102	
Direct materials	$ 6,000
Direct labor	8,000
Factory overhead applied	12,000
Total ending balance	$26,000

3. Factory overhead variance:

Actual factory overhead		
Indirect materials	$ 8,000	
Indirect labor	5,000	
Utilities	500	
Depreciation	15,000	
Insurance	2,500	$31,000
Applied factory overhead		30,000
Underapplied factory overhead		$ 1,000

4. To record the disposition of underapplied factory overhead by closing both
Factory Overhead Control and Factory Overhead Applied accounts to the
Cost of Goods Sold account.

Factory Overhead Applied	30,000	
Cost of Goods Sold	1,000	
Factory Overhead Control		31,000

Process Costing

Ron McMillan/Gamma Liaison

When you are drowning in numbers, you need a system to separate the wheat from the chaff.

ANTHONY ADAMS, VICE PRESIDENT,
CAMPBELL SOUP COMPANY, *NEW YORK TIMES*, APRIL 1988

In today's global competition environment, it is vital that managers know product costs for good decision making. Imagine a big corporation's top manager trying to decide whether to discontinue a product without knowing what it cost to produce. Cost information is needed by managers for setting goals; forming strategy; and developing long- and short-term planning; as well as for control, performance measurement, and decision-making purposes.

Process costing is a product costing system that accumulates costs by processes or departments and assigns them to a large number of nearly identical products. The typical firm that uses a process costing system employs a standardized production process to manufacture homogeneous and indistinguishable products.

Firms need to set clear goals and form good strategies to stay competitive. Once strategies are determined, tactics to achieve those must be put into place and monitored continuously. Process costing allows monthly or periodic monitoring of the unit costs of any product a firm manufactures. By monitoring and examining these unit costs, managers can determine whether to improve processes or change tactics. Also, process costing allows accountants to determine unit costs needed for valuing inventory and the cost of goods sold for external financial reports.

THE STRATEGIC ROLE OF PROCESS COSTING

Process costing systems provide information for managers to make strategic decisions regarding products and customers, manufacturing methods, pricing decisions, and other long-term issues. Why is process costing information strategically important for a firm?

First, a firm competes by using either a cost leadership or a differentiation strategy. If it is following the cost leadership strategy and overheads are complex, then a firm should change its traditional volume-based job costing to an activity-based process costing system to provide useful information to management. For example, Boeing Aircraft once had a job costing system using volume-based direct labor cost as the cost driver. Under this system, production managers had no direct responsibility for controlling factory overhead costs. The company decided to control total

◄ LEARNING OBJECTIVE 1
Describe the strategic role of process costing.

BusinessWeek

? How Did Whirlpool Make a Splash Internationally?

Whirlpool's acquisition of Philips Electronics' European appliance business unit was the first step in its plan to transform its largely domestic operation into a global powerhouse. Whirlpool acquired 47 percent of this Dutch consumer-good giant's European appliance business in 1989 and the rest in 1991. So far, Whirlpool's European experience puts it far ahead of Maytag, General Electric, and Electrolux in building an integrated global business. "Whirlpool gets very high marks in its global strategy," says Jerry Herman, an analyst at Kemper Securities Inc. in Cleveland. "They are outpacing the industry dramatically." For instance, operating income for 1994's first three quarters hit 6.5 percent, up from 3.6 percent in 1990, and market share was up from 11.5 percent to 13 percent, just behind No. 2, Bosch-Siemens Hausgerate.

Q: How did Whirlpool improve its operating income, and what is its strategy for continued success internationally? *Find out on page 517 of this chapter.*

costs by changing to an activity-based process costing system.[1] The new process costing system allows factory overhead costs to be assigned to processes regardless of whether managers have direct responsibility for controlling costs. The new system also produces costs more closely related to activities performed.

An ABC/ABM process costing system helps a firm to achieve its low-cost strategy by identifying key activities, drivers, and ways to improve designs and/or processes to reduce cost. For example, potato chip production has three major steps: preparing, processing, and packaging. There are four activities in the preparing step: cleaning, selecting, slicing, and shaping. There are also four activities in the processing step: cooking, frying, salting, and flavoring. For health-conscious customers, the salting activity is a non-value-added activity.

A second important strategic issue is also potentially an ethical issue for process costing because of the decisions the firm makes about (1) the basis for allocating overhead, and (2) the proration of overapplied or underapplied overhead. Say, for example, a firm is manufacturing products for two markets: one is price competitive, and the other is not (e.g., cost-plus government contracts); the manner of overhead allocation is a strategic and an ethical issue. Management may be motivated to overcost the cost-plus products through its choice of an allocation basis or proration method to achieve the desired result.

Third, providing superior customer value is another business strategy to achieve a competitive advantage. One approach is to use value chain analysis in the process costing system. A firm can apply ABC/ABM, target costing, and life-cycle costing methods to reduce the internal value-chain process costs of research and development, design, production, marketing, distribution, and customer service. For example, Milliken & Co. uses ABC/ABM process costing to sharpen its competitive edge by allowing managers to focus on the actual costs for each process and to reduce non-value-added work within a process.[2] A firm can also work with external value-chain stakeholders such as suppliers to reduce its materials-handling costs and customers to improve its production scheduling efficiency.

Fourth, a process costing production cost sheet can also be expanded to be a periodic balanced scorecard performance report with four dimensions: financial, customers, internal business processes, and learning and growth. The balanced scorecard measures tie directly to a firm's strategy and its critical success factors.

CHARACTERISTICS OF PROCESS COSTING SYSTEMS

In this section we identify the types of firms for which a process costing system is most suitable, discuss the concept of equivalent units, and describe five steps in process costing.

When Should a Process Costing System Be Used?

LEARNING OBJECTIVE 2 ▶
Identify the types of firms or operations for which a process costing system is most suitable.

Process costing is used by firms having homogeneous products that pass through a series of similar processes or departments. These firms usually engage in continuous mass production of a few similar products. The work done by the production departments or processes does not vary because all the units are essentially the same. Manufacturing costs are accumulated in each process. The departmental production cost report is a key document to keep track of production quantity and cost information. Unit product cost is calculated by dividing process costs in each department by the equivalent units produced during the period.

Process cost systems are used in many industries such as chemicals, oil refining, textiles, paints, flour, canneries, rubber, steel, glass, food processing, mining, automobile production lines, electronics, plastics, drugs, paper, lumber, leather goods,

---

[1] Robert J. Bowlby, "How Boeing Tracks Costs, A to Z," *Financial Executive*, November–December 1994, pp. 20–23.

[2] James Don Edwards, Cynthia D. Heagy, and Harold W. Rakes, "How Milliken Stays on Top," *Journal of Accountancy*, April 1989, pp. 73–74.

metal products, sporting goods, cement, and watches. Process costing also can be used by service organizations with homogeneous services and repetitive processes such as check processing in a bank or mail sorting by a courier.

Equivalent Units

A manufacturing firm typically has partially completed units at the end of an accounting period. Under the job costing system, these partially completed units are not difficult to handle because job costs are available on job cost sheets.

◀ **LEARNING OBJECTIVE 3**
Explain and calculate equivalent units.

In a process costing system, however, product costs for partially completed units are not readily available. Here, the focus in cost accounting has shifted from jobs to processes or departments. Accordingly, the interest is in the unit cost of performing a certain *process* for a given period. The goal is to find the combined unit cost of all the product units processed in that period, including those that are partially completed at either the beginning or the end of the accounting period. Note that by partially complete we mean partially complete for that department—a unit may be complete for a given department but still be in the work-in-process inventory account if it is not the final department.

The calculation of the product cost begins with determining the production cost per unit in each of the production departments. These unit costs are incorrect if the amount of work done on partially completed units is not considered. Therefore, the cost calculations need to be adjusted for partially completed units so that all units included in the computations reflect work actually done in the period.

With both complete and partially completed units, we need a measure to reflect the proper amount of production work performed during a period. An equivalent unit is one such measure. The problem of equivalent units arises because we take a continuous process and break it into separate, distinct time periods. The process is continuous, but the reporting is periodic, such as monthly or yearly.

Equivalent units are the number of like or similar completed units that could have been produced given the amount of work actually performed on both completed and partially completed units. Equivalent units are not the same as physical units. A firm produced 30 television sets last month with 20 completed sets and 10 partially completed sets (roughly 50% complete). The physical units were 30 sets, but equivalent units were only 25 sets [20 + (10 × 50%)].

Equivalent units are the number of like or similar completed units that could have been produced given the amount of work actually performed on both completed and partially completed units.

The equivalent units should be calculated separately for direct materials, direct labor, and factory overhead because the proportion of the total work performed on the product units in the work-in-process inventories is not always the same for each cost element. Often partially completed units are complete for direct materials but incomplete for direct labor and factory overhead. Examples include chemical making or brewing processes where direct materials are dumped in at the beginning but the cooking process can extend over hours or days. Some firms divide costs into direct materials and conversion cost categories. *Conversion costs* are the sum of direct labor and factory overhead costs.

Milliken's State-of-the-Art Cost Accounting Helps Sharpen Its Competitive Edge

Milliken & Company, a leading textile manufacturer in Spartanburg, South Carolina, uses a process costing system to accumulate its manufacturing costs at each production process or cost center.

In the past few years, the company has improved its costing system by simplifying its standard process costing system and implementing nonfinancial measures. Specifically, the improved cost accounting system allows man-agers to focus on actual costs for each process and to reduce non-value-added work within a process. The new system provides actual cost-per-unit trend charts by product for each plant. It also provides seven nonfinancial measures: (1) reduction in lead or throughput time; (2) reduction in change or setup time; (3) reduction in down-time; (4) reduction in turnaround time for customer samples; (5) increase in on-time deliveries; (6) audits of machinery maintenance; and (7) audits of quality assurance.

The new cost accounting system has helped Milliken managers to improve operations and reduce costs; and it helps the company to stay on top.

Source: Based on James Don Edwards, Cynthia D. Heagy, and Harold W. Rakes, "How Milliken Stays on Top," *Journal of Accountancy,* April 1989, pp. 63–74.

Conversion Costs

For a labor intensive firm, factory overhead and direct labor often are combined under the heading of conversion costs for the purpose of computing equivalent units of production. Linking these two production elements is possible because the formula for applying factory overhead in a labor-intensive industry often uses either direct labor-hours or direct labor-costs as the basis. Thus, these elements often are added in identical proportions to the product units.

Many manufacturing operations incur conversion costs uniformly throughout production. The equivalent units of conversion costs are therefore the result of multiplying the percentage of work completed during the period by the number of units on which work is partially completed. For example, for 1,000 units with an estimated 30 percent complete in the work-in-process ending inventory, the equivalent units of conversion costs in the period are 300 [the work completed (30 percent) × 1,000 units]. However, for 1,000 units with 40 percent complete in the work-in-process beginning inventory, the number of equivalent units of conversion work in the current period is 600. Equivalent units, in this case, are calculated by multiplying 1,000 units by the percentage of work remaining to be completed, 60 percent (100 percent − 40 percent = 60 percent).

In firms using nonlabor-based cost drivers (such as machine-hours or the number of setups) for their factory overhead costs, it is more appropriate to calculate separate equivalent units of production for factory overhead and direct labor costs.

Direct Materials

Direct materials can be added to the product units gradually in various proportions at discrete points of manufacturing, continuously over production. If the materials are added uniformly, then the proportion used for computing equivalent units of direct materials is the same as the proportion for conversion costs. However, if the materials are added all at once, then the proportion used in the computation depends on whether the point in the process where the materials are added has been reached.

Exhibit 13–1 illustrates the determination of equivalent units in direct materials for two different examples. The amounts are for 1,000 and 1,500 product units with 30 percent complete in the beginning and 50 percent complete in the ending work-in-process inventories. If direct materials are added gradually and uniformly throughout the process, 700 equivalent units of direct materials must be added during this period to finish the work-in-process beginning inventory; the work-in-process ending inventory has 750 equivalent units of direct materials. If all materials are added at the beginning of the period, we do not need to add any equivalent units of direct materials to finish the work-in-process beginning inventory; the work-in-process ending inventory has 1,500 equivalent units of direct materials.

Steps in Process Costing

A **production cost report** is a report that summarizes the physical units and equivalent units of a department, the costs incurred during the period, and costs assigned to both units completed and transferred out and ending work-in-process inventories.

The key document in a typical process costing system is the production cost report, prepared at the end of each period for a production process or department. The **production cost report** is a report that summarizes the physical units and equivalent

Exhibit 13–1	Equivalent Units for Direct Materials under Different Assignments					
				Equivalent Units This Period*		
Type of Inventory	Physical Units Partially Complete	Percentage of Completion	Materials Added Gradually	All Materials Added at the Beginning	All Materials Added at 40 Percent Point	All Materials Added at the End
Beginning work-in-process inventory	1,000	30%	1,000 × (1 − 30%) = 700	-0-	1,000 × 100% = 1,000	1,000 × 100% = 1,000
Ending work-in-process inventory	1,500	50%	1,500 × 50% = 750	1,500 × 100% = 1,500	1,500 × 100% = 1,500	-0-

*Equivalent units added to complete the beginning work-in-process inventory during the period, or equivalent units for the ending work-in-process inventory.

Boeing Tracks Aircraft Costs with Process Costing

Boeing Company used to have a job cost accounting system that assigned factory overhead based on direct labor cost. Production managers were almost powerless to control total product cost other than by reducing the direct labor-hours. The company decided to switch to a process costing system in 1994.

Under the new system, unit weighting converts different parts or products to common production units. After the process cost center production unit is calculated, the cost for a particular part is determined by multiplying the cost per production unit times the number of units assigned to that part.

The new process costing system allows factory overhead costs to be assigned to processes where managers have direct responsibility for controlling costs. The new system also produces costs more closely related to the activities performed.

Source: Based on Robert J. Bowlby, "How Boeing Tracks Costs, A to Z," *Financial Executive*, November–December 1994, pp. 20–23.

Five Key Steps in Determining Process Costs

1. Analyzing physical flow of production units.

2. Calculating equivalent units of production for all manufacturing cost elements.

3. Determining total cost for each manufacturing cost element.

4. Computing cost per equivalent unit for each manufacturing cost element.

5. Assigning the total manufacturing costs to units completed and transferred out and units of work in process at the end of the period.

units of a department, the costs incurred during the period, and costs assigned to both units completed and transferred out and ending work-in-process inventories. The preparation of a production cost report includes these five steps:

◄ LEARNING OBJECTIVE 4
Describe five steps in process costing.

Step 1: Analysis of Physical Units

The first step answers the questions: What units were on hand at the beginning of the period? How many were started or received? What units were completed and transferred out? What units are in the ending work-in-process inventory?

The analysis of physical units includes accounting for both input and output units. Input units include the beginning work-in-process inventory and all units that enter a production department during an accounting period. Output units include units that have been completed and transferred out from a production department or are in the work-in-process inventory at the end of a period. (See Exhibit 13–8, Step 1.)

Step 2: Calculation of Equivalent Units

The purpose of calculating equivalent units of production for direct materials, direct labor, and factory overhead is to measure the total work efforts expended on production during an accounting period. The partially completed physical units are converted into the equivalent number of whole units. (See Exhibit 13–8, Step 2.)

Step 3: Determination of Total Costs to Account for

The total manufacturing costs to be accounted for include the current costs incurred and the costs of the units in the work-in-process beginning inventory. (See Exhibit 13–8, Step 3.) The amount of these costs is obtained from material requisitions, labor time cards, and factory overhead allocation sheets.

Step 4: Computation of Unit Costs

The purpose of computing direct materials, direct labor, and factory overhead costs per equivalent unit of production is to have a proper product costing and income determination for an accounting period. (See Exhibit 13–8, Step 4.)

Step 5: Assignment of Total Costs

The objective of the production cost report is to assign total manufacturing costs incurred to the units completed and transferred out during the period and the units that are still in process at the end of the period. The total costs assigned in step 5 should be equal to the total costs to be accounted for in step 3. (See Exhibit 13–8, Step 5.)

Companies generally divide the five-step production cost report into three parts: production quantity information; unit cost determination; and cost assignment. The first part includes step 1, analysis of physical units, and step 2, calculation of equivalent units. The second part includes step 3, determination of total costs to account for, and step 4, computation of equivalent unit cost. The third part includes step 5, assignment of total costs (total costs accounted for).

Process Costing Methods

The two methods of preparing the departmental production cost report in process costing practices are the weighted-average method and the first-in, first-out method (FIFO). The **weighted-average method** includes all costs in calculating the unit cost. This includes both those costs incurred during the current period and those costs incurred in the prior period that are shown as the beginning work-in-process inventory of this period. In this method, prior period costs and current period costs are averaged together; hence, the name weighted-average. The **FIFO method** includes only costs incurred and work effort during the current period in calculating the unit cost. FIFO considers the beginning inventory as a batch of goods separate from the goods started and completed within the same period. FIFO assumes that the first work done is to complete the beginning work-in-process inventory. Thus, all the beginning work-in-process inventories are assumed completed before the end of the current period.

Under the weighted-average method, it makes no difference when a product is started; all units completed in the same period or in the ending inventory of that period are treated the same. When this method is used, all that is considered is the status of the product at the end of the period.

On the other hand, the status of the product at both the end and beginning of a period has to be taken into consideration when the FIFO method is used in determining product costs. That is, the FIFO method looks at the input as well as output of the production process, whereas the weighted-average method looks at only the output of the production process (completed and transferred out and ending work-in-process inventory).

> The **weighted-average method** includes all costs, both those incurred during the current period and those incurred in the prior period that are shown as the beginning work-in-process inventory of this period, in calculating the unit cost.
>
> **FIFO method** includes only costs incurred and work effort during the current period in calculating the unit cost.

ILLUSTRATION OF PROCESS COSTING

Basic Data

To illustrate these two process costing methods, assume Hsu Toy Company has two production departments: the molding department and the finishing department. In the molding department, direct materials (plastic vinyl) are placed into production

---

Kunde Estate Winery Uses a Hybrid Product Costing System

Kunde Estate Winery, located in California's Sonoma Valley, uses a hybrid product costing system to determine the cost of a bottle of wine. Costs are traced through the various wine-making processes or departments for each job (each lot of grapes).

This hybrid job/process costing system has two major steps. First, the cost of initial harvested grape lots is assigned to jobs based on the amount of grapes allocated to the various types of wine to be produced. Second, costs are accumulated by depart-ments and allocated to each wine batch based on the amount of time the wine spends in each department.

The information provided by the product costing system is useful to managers who must decide how to use the grapes harvested each year to produce different wines.

Source: Based on John Y. Lee and Brian Gray Jacobs, "Kunde Estate Winery: A Case Study in Cost Accounting," *CMA Magazine*, April 1993, pp. 15–18.

at the beginning of the process. Direct labor and factory overhead costs are incurred gradually throughout the process with different proportions. The molding department uses machine-hours as the cost driver to apply factory overhead costs.

In Exhibit 13–2 we present a summary of toy units and costs in the molding department during June of 19X8.

Weighted-Average Method

The weighted-average method makes no distinction between the cost incurred prior to the current period and the cost incurred in the current period. As long as a cost is on the current period's cost sheet of the production department, it is treated the same as any other cost, regardless of when the cost was incurred. Consequently the average cost per equivalent unit includes costs incurred during the current period, in addition to costs incurred in the prior period that carry over into this period through beginning work-in-process inventory. We use the familiar five-step procedure to assign direct materials, direct labor, and factory overhead costs to the cost object—the molding department.

Step 1: Analysis of Physical Units

The first step is to analyze the flow of all units through production. Exhibit 13–3 presents the procedures for this step.

The two sections in Exhibit 13–3 show the two aspects of physical units flowing through production—*input units* and *output units*. This procedure ensures that all units in production are accounted for. Input units include all units that enter a production department during an accounting period or entered during the prior period but were incomplete at the beginning of the period. These units come from two sources: (1) beginning work-in-process inventory started in a previous period that was partially completed at the end of the preceding period, which is 10,000 units in our example, and (2) work started or received in the current period, 40,000 units in our example. The sum of these two sources, 50,000 units here, is referred to as the number of units to account for. **Units to account for** are the sum of beginning inventory units and the number of units started during the period.

Output units include units that have been completed and transferred out and units not yet completed at the end of a period. These units can be in one of the two categories: the 44,000 units completed or the 6,000 units in the ending work-in-process inventory. The sum of these two categories, 50,000 units, is referred to

Exhibit 13–2	Basic Data for Hsu Toy Company—Molding Department for Month of June 19X8	
Work-in-process inventory, June 1:		10,000 units
Direct materials: 100 percent complete		$ 10,000
Direct labor: 30 percent complete		1,060
Factory overhead: 40 percent complete		1,620
Beginning work-in-process inventory		$ 12,680
Units started during June		40,000 units
Units completed during June and transferred out of the molding department		44,000 units
Work-in-process inventory, June 30:		6,000 units
Direct materials: 100 percent complete		
Direct labor: 50 percent complete		
Factory overhead: 60 percent complete		
Costs incurred during June:		
Direct materials		$ 44,000
Direct labor		22,440
Factory overhead		43,600
Total costs incurred		$110,040

Exhibit 13–3	Analysis of Physical Units—Molding Department

Input	Physical Units
Work-in-process inventory, June 1	10,000
Units started during June	40,000
Total units to account for	50,000
Output	
Units completed and transferred out during June	44,000
Work in-process-inventory, June 30	6,000
Total units accounted for	50,000

Exhibit 13–4	Calculation of Equivalent Units—Molding Department *(Weighted-Average Method)*

	Physical Units	Completion Percentage	Equivalent Units Direct Materials	Direct Labor	Factory Overhead
Work-in-process, June 1	10,000				
Direct materials		100%			
Direct labor		30			
Overhead		40			
Units started	40,000				
Units to account for	50,000				
Units completed	44,000	100%	44,000	44,000	44,000
Work-in-process, June 30	6,000				
Direct materials		100	6,000		
Direct labor		50		3,000	
Overhead		60			3,600
Units accounted for	50,000				
Total equivalent units			50,000	47,000	47,600

Units accounted for are the sum of the units transferred out and ending inventory units.

as the number of units accounted for. This number should match the number of units to account for. **Units accounted for** includes the sum of units completed and transferred out and the ending inventory units.

The primary purpose of this first step is to make sure that all the units in production are accounted for before we compute the equivalent units of production for each of the production elements.

Step 2: Calculation of Equivalent Units

The second step in the process costing procedure is to calculate the equivalent units of production activity for direct materials, direct labor, and factory overhead. A table of equivalent units, presented in Exhibit 13–4, is based on the table of physical units prepared in step 1 (Exhibit 13–3). Beginning work-in-process inventory units are not included in the calculation of equivalent units because they are completed during the month, and are not treated separately under the weighted-average method.

The weighted-average method computes the total equivalent units produced to date. The units in production in the current period for each of the manufacturing production elements includes both (a) the units from previous periods that are still in production at the beginning of the current period, and (b) the units placed into production in the current period.

In Exhibit 13–4, 44,000 physical units were completed and transferred out of the molding department. These units were 100 percent complete. Thus, they represent 44,000 equivalent units for direct materials, direct labor, and factory overhead. Note that the 44,000 units include 10,000 units placed into production prior to June and completed in June, and 34,000 units (44,000 units − 10,000 units) started and completed in June.

The 6,000 units in the ending work-in-process inventory are complete with respect to direct materials because direct materials are added at the beginning of the process. Thus, they represent 6,000 equivalent units of direct materials. However, they are only 50 and 60 percent complete with respect to direct labor and factory overhead. Therefore, the ending work-in-process inventories represent 3,000 equivalent units of direct labor (6,000 physical units × 50 percent complete), and 3,600 equivalent units of factory overhead (6,000 physical units × 60 percent complete).

As you can see in Exhibit 13–4, the total number of equivalent units is calculated as follows:

Completed and transferred out units

+ Ending work-in-process equivalent units

= Total equivalent units of production

Combining completed units and ending work-in-process equivalent units, the equivalent units of production for the molding department under the weighted-average method are 50,000 units of direct materials, 47,000 units of direct labor, and 47,600 units of factory overhead.

Step 3: Determination of Total Costs to Account for

The third step determines how many dollars were spent both in the beginning work-in-process inventory and current production for direct materials, direct labor, and factory overhead.

Exhibit 13–5 summarizes the total manufacturing costs to account for. As given in our example data, total manufacturing costs ($122,720) consist of the beginning work-in-process inventory balance, $12,680, plus the current costs added during June, $110,040.

Step 4: Computation of Unit Costs

For the fourth step in the process costing procedure, computation of equivalent unit costs of production for direct materials, direct labor, and factory overhead, see Exhibit 13–6. The equivalent per-unit cost for direct materials ($1.08) is computed by dividing the total direct materials cost ($54,000), including the cost of the beginning work-in-process ($10,000) and the cost added during June ($44,000), by the total equivalent units (50,000). Similar procedures are used for direct labor and factory overhead costs. Notice that the total equivalent unit cost of $2.50 can be determined only by adding the unit direct materials cost of $1.08, the unit direct labor cost of $0.50, and the unit factory overhead cost of $0.95.

Exhibit 13–5	**Determination of Total Costs to Account for—Molding Department**	
Beginning work-in-process inventory		
Direct materials	$10,000	
Direct labor	1,060	
Factory overhead	1,620	
Total		$ 12,680
Current costs added during June		
Direct materials	$44,000	
Direct labor	22,440	
Factory overhead	43,600	
Total costs added		110,040
Total costs to account for		$122,720

Exhibit 13–6	Computation of Unit Costs—Molding Department (Weighted-Average Method)			
	Direct Materials	Direct Labor	Factory Overhead	Total
Costs (from Exhibit 13–5):				
Work-in-process, June 1	$10,000	$ 1,060	$ 1,620	$ 12,680
Costs added during June	44,000	22,440	43,600	110,040
Total costs to account for	$54,000	$23,500	$45,220	$122,720
Divide by equivalent units (from Exhibit 13–4):	50,000	47,000	47,600	
Equivalent unit costs	$ 1.08 +	$ 0.50 +	$ 0.95 =	$ 2.53

Exhibit 13–7	Assignment of Total Costs—Molding Department (Weighted-Average Method)		
	Completed and Transferred out	Ending Work-in-Process	Total
Goods completed and transferred out:			
(44,000 × $2.53)	$111,320		$111,320
Ending work-in-process:			
Materials (6,000 × $1.08)		$ 6,480	6,480
Labor (3,000 × $0.50)		1,500	1,500
Overhead (3,600 × $0.95)		3,420	3,420
Total costs accounted for	$111,320	$11,400	$122,720

Step 5: Assignment of Total Costs

The final step of the process costing procedure is assigning total manufacturing costs to units completed and to units in the ending work-in-process inventory. Exhibit 13–7 presents a summary of the cost assignment schedule. Various unit numbers come directly from Exhibit 13–4 while various unit costs come from Exhibit 13–6. Note that the total costs accounted for in this step ($122,720) should equal the total costs to account for in step 3 (Exhibit 13–5).

Production Cost Report

Steps 1 through 5 provide all the information needed to prepare a production cost report for the molding department for June. This report is in Exhibit 13–8.

First-In, First-Out (FIFO) Method

Another way of handling inventory in a process costing application is the first-in, first-out (FIFO) method. This method assumes that the first units to enter a production process are the first units to be completed and transferred out. The same holds true of the units in inventories. The FIFO method accounts separately for the cost of the units started in the previous period; that cost was carried into the current period through the beginning work-in-process inventory.

LEARNING OBJECTIVE 6 ▶
Demonstrate the FIFO method of process costing.

Our illustration of the FIFO method of process costing again uses the Hsu Toy Company's molding department data (see Exhibit 13–2). Unlike the weighted-average method, the FIFO method does not combine beginning inventory costs with current costs when computing equivalent unit costs. The FIFO method considers the beginning inventory as a batch of goods separate from the goods started and completed within the same period. The costs from each period are treated separately. We follow the same five steps as in the weighted-average method, however, in determining product costs.

Exhibit 13–8	**Production Cost Report—Molding Department** *(Weighted-Average Method)*

Production Quantity Information

	(Step 1)		(Step 2)		
			Equivalent Units		
	Physical Units	**Completion Percentage**	**Direct Materials**	**Direct Labor**	**Factory Overhead**
Input					
Work-in-process, June 1	10,000				
Direct materials		100%			
Direct labor		30			
Overhead		40			
Units started	40,000				
Units to account for	50,000				
Output					
Units completed	44,000	100%	44,000	44,000	44,000
Work-in-process, June 30	6,000				
Direct materials		100	6,000		
Direct labor		50		3,000	
Overhead		60			3,600
Units accounted for	50,000				
Total equivalent units			50,000	47,000	47,600

Unit Cost Determination

(Step 3) **Total Costs to Account for**	**Direct Materials**	**Direct Labor**	**Factory Overhead**	**Total**
Work-in-process, June 1	$10,000	$ 1,060	$ 1,620	$ 12,680
Costs added during June	44,000	22,440	43,600	110,040
Total costs to account for	$54,000	$23,500	$45,220	$122,720

(Step 4)				
Divide by equivalent units	50,000	47,000	47,600	
Equivalent unit costs	$ 1.08	$ 0.50	$ 0.95	$ 2.53

Cost Assignment

(Step 5) **Cost Assignment**	**Completed and Transferred out**	**Ending Work-in-Process**	**Total**
Goods completed and transferred out:			
(44,000 × $2.53)	$111,320		$111,320
Ending work-in-process:			
Materials (6,000 × $1.08)		$ 6,480	6,480
Labor (3,000 × $0.50)		1,500	1,500
Overhead (3,600 × $0.95)		3,420	3,420
Total costs accounted for	$111,320	$11,400	$122,720

Step 1: Analysis of Physical Units

The physical flow of product units is unaffected by the process costing method used. Therefore, step 1 is the same as the weighted-average method in Exhibit 13–3.

Step 2: Calculation of Equivalent Units

The FIFO method considers the beginning inventory as a batch of goods separate from the goods started and completed within the same period. The equivalent units in the beginning work-in-process—work done in the prior period—are not counted as part of the FIFO method equivalent units. Only that part of the equivalent units of the beginning work-in-process to be completed this period is counted.

There are two equivalent, alternative procedures to calculate equivalent units of production under the FIFO method.

Procedure One The first procedure is to subtract the equivalent units in the beginning work-in-process from the weighted-average equivalent units to obtain the FIFO method equivalent units, as shown in the last three rows of Exhibit 13–9. The 10,000 physical units in the June 1 work-in-process have 100 percent of direct materials, so they have 10,000 equivalent units of direct materials prior to the current period. However, these units are only 30 percent and 40 percent complete with respect to direct labor and factory overhead, so they contribute only 3,000 equivalent units of direct labor (10,000 × 30%) and 4,000 equivalent units of factory overhead (10,000 × 40%) prior to the current period. Notice that the $10,000 direct materials cost in the beginning work-in-process inventory are excluded from this calculation. Only current costs added in June are used in computing the equivalent unit cost under the FIFO method.

To calculate the total number of FIFO equivalent units, the following equations are given:

$$\text{Completed and transferred out units}$$
$$+ \text{ Ending work-in-process equivalent units}$$
$$= \text{ Weighted-average equivalent units}$$
$$- \text{ Beginning work-in-process equivalent units}$$
$$= \text{ FIFO equivalent units of work done during this period}$$

Exhibit 13–9 shows that the Hsu Toy Company has to account for a total of 50,000 units. Of these, 44,000 units are completed units and 6,000 units are ending work-in-process inventory that is 100 percent complete for direct materials. The

Exhibit 13–9	**Calculation of Equivalent Units—Molding Department** **(FIFO Method—Procedure One)**				
				Equivalent Units	
	Physical Units	**Completion Percentage**	**Direct Materials**	**Direct Labor**	**Factory Overhead**
Input					
Work-in-process, June 1	10,000				
Direct materials		100%	10,000		
Direct labor		30		3,000	
Overhead		40			4,000
Units started	40,000				
Units to account for	50,000				
Output					
Units completed	44,000	100%	44,000	44,000	44,000
Work-in-process, June 30	6,000				
Direct materials		100	6,000		
Direct labor		50		3,000	
Overhead		60			3,600
Units accounted for	50,000				
Total equivalent units (Weighted-average method)			50,000	47,000	47,600
Less: equivalent units in June 1 work-in-process			−10,000	− 3,000	− 4,000
Equivalent units for work done in June only (FIFO method)			40,000	44,000	43,600

total equivalent units for the period for direct materials under the weighted-average method is 50,000. Of the 44,000 units completed during the period, 10,000 units were in the beginning work-in-process inventory. These 10,000 units already have all the direct materials added in the prior period. Subtracting 10,000 units from the 50,000 total equivalent units for the period, the FIFO equivalent units for work done only in June for direct materials is 40,000 units. Following the same procedure, equivalent units of production for the molding department using the FIFO method are 44,000 units of direct labor and 43,600 units of factory overhead.

The difference between the weighted-average method and the FIFO method is that under the weighted-average method the equivalent units of production completed prior to the current period are not subtracted from the total completed units. So equivalent units under the weighted-average method are always as large as or larger than those under the FIFO method.

Procedure Two   An alternative way of determining the equivalent units using the FIFO method is to add equivalent units of work done in the current period for each of the components constituting the output. These three components are (1) equivalent units added to complete the beginning work-in-process inventory, (2) units started and completed during the period, and (3) equivalent units of the ending work-in-process inventory. Exhibit 13–10 presents the FIFO equivalent units computation using the second procedure. Notice that under the FIFO method, the equivalent units in the beginning work-in-process inventory from last month's work effort are not added to equivalent units of work done this month.

For example, the 10,000 units of beginning work-in-process inventory was 30 percent complete for direct labor. The Hsu Toy Company completed the beginning work-in-process inventory by adding the remaining 70 percent of the direct labor work during the current period to complete production. In addition, the firm started another 40,000 units into production during the period. Of these 40,000 units, the firm completed the production of 34,000 units, and the remaining 6,000 units were

Exhibit 13–10	Calculation of Equivalent Units—Molding Department (FIFO Method—Procedure Two)				
			Equivalent Units		
	Physical Units	**Completion Percentage**	**Direct Materials**	**Direct Labor**	**Factory Overhead**
Input					
Work-in-process, June 1	10,000				
Direct materials		100%	10,000		
Direct labor		30		3,000	
Overhead		40			4,000
Units started	40,000				
Units to account for	50,000				
Output					
Completed and transferred out:					
From work-in-process, June 1	10,000				
Direct materials 10,000 × (1 − 100%)			0		
Direct labor 10,000 × (1 − 30%)				7,000	
Overhead 10,000 × (1 − 40%)					6,000
Started and completed					
(44,000 − 10,000) =	34,000	100%	34,000	34,000	34,000
Work-in-process, June 30	6,000				
Direct materials		100	6,000		
Direct labor		50		3,000	
Overhead		60			3,600
Units accounted for	50,000				
Equivalent units for work done in June only			40,000	44,000	43,600

still in the manufacturing process at the end of the period. The firm has completed only 50 percent of the total direct labor to the ending work-in-process inventory, or an equivalent of 3,000 units. To summarize the direct labor spent during the period, the firm spent an equivalent of 7,000 units of direct labor work to complete the beginning work-in-process inventory on hand, started and completed 34,000 units, and spent an equivalent of 3,000 units to complete 50 percent of the 6,000 units of ending work-in-process inventory. The total direct labor work of the period is equivalent to a production of 44,000 FIFO units.

Step 3: Determination of Total Costs to Account for

The total costs incurred to manufacture product units are unaffected by the process costing method used. Therefore, step 3 is the same as the weighted-average method in Exhibit 13–5.

Step 4: Computation of Unit Costs

Under the FIFO method, equivalent unit costs are calculated by dividing the costs incurred during the current period by the equivalent units for work done only during the current period. No cost in the work-in-process beginning inventory is included in determining equivalent unit costs for cost elements. Exhibit 13–11 presents such calculations. The equivalent unit cost for direct materials ($1.10) is computed by dividing the direct materials cost added during June ($44,000) by the equivalent units for work done in June only (40,000). Similar procedures are used for direct labor and factory overhead costs. Notice that the total equivalent unit cost of $2.61 can be determined only by adding the unit direct materials cost of $1.10, the unit direct labor cost of $0.51, and the unit factory overhead cost of $1.10.

Step 5: Assignment of Total Costs

The final step of the process costing procedure is assigning total manufacturing costs to units completed and to units in the ending work-in-process inventory. Like the weighted-average method, the FIFO method assigns its total costs of a period to the units completed and transferred out, and the units still in process at the end of the period. Unlike the weighted-average method, however, the FIFO method accounts for different batches of the completed units separately because work done on different batches may be different.

The manufacturing process for units in the beginning work-in-process overlaps two periods. Thus, units completed from the beginning work-in-process inventory incurred costs prior to the current period as well as during the current period. This fact makes the assignment of costs to units completed during a period a two-part process. In the first part, the total manufacturing cost for units completed from the beginning work-in-process is determined. In the second part, the total manufacturing costs for units started and completed during the manufacturing process in the current period are calculated.

Exhibit 13–11	**Computation of Unit Costs—Molding Department** *(FIFO Method)*			
	Direct Materials	**Direct Labor**	**Factory Overhead**	**Total**
Costs (from Exhibit 13–5):				
Work-in-process, June 1				$ 12,680
Costs added during June	$44,000	$22,440	$43,600	110,040
Total costs to account for				$122,720
Divide by equivalent units (from Exhibit 13–9):	40,000	44,000	43,600	
Equivalent unit costs	$ 1.10 +	$ 0.51 +	$ 1.00 =	$ 2.61

Part 1: Total Cost of Units Completed from Beginning Work-in-Process Inventory
The manufacturing process for units in the beginning work-in-process overlaps two periods. To determine the total manufacturing costs for the units completed from the beginning work-in-process, the firm needs to add the manufacturing costs applied to the units during the current period to the costs from preceding periods already assigned to these units.

The total additional cost incurred in the current period to complete these units is the sum of the equivalent units of each cost element added to complete the element. These are applied to the units in the beginning work-in-process and multiplied by the average unit cost for the cost element.

The costs assigned to the 10,000 units of the beginning work-in-process inventory that were completed and transferred out during the current period are calculated as follows:

Work-in-process inventory, June 1, 10,000 units	$12,680
Costs added during June to complete the beginning inventory:	
Direct labor 7,000 equivalent units × $0.51	3,570
Factory overhead 6,000 equivalent units × $1.00	6,000
Total for beginning inventory	$22,250

Part 2: Total Cost for Units Started and Completed   The production cost of units started and completed in the current period can be computed by multiplying the number of units in this category by the cost per equivalent unit of the period.

The number of units started and completed in the period is the difference between the units completed and the number of units in the beginning work-in-process. In the molding department example, we compute the units started and completed as:

Units completed − Beginning work-in-process = Units started and completed

44,000 units − 10,000 units = 34,000 units

Then the cost assigned to units started and completed is

34,000 units × $2.61 = $88,740

The total costs transferred out are the sum of total cost from the beginning inventory and total cost for units started and completed; that is

$22,250 + $88,740 = $110,990

Ending Work-in-Process Inventory   The cost amount assigned to ending work-in-process units is derived by multiplying the average unit costs for the period of each manufacturing cost element by the equivalent units of the ending work-in-process inventory.

The cost of 6,000 units in ending work-in-process inventory of the molding department is computed as follows:

Direct materials, 6,000 equivalent units × $1.10	$ 6,600
Direct labor, 3,000 equivalent units × $0.51	1,530
Factory overhead, 3,600 equivalent units × $1.00	3,600
Total ending work-in-process inventory	$11,730

Looking at Exhibit 13–12, you can see that the sum of the costs assigned to goods transferred out and in ending work-in-process inventory equals the total costs accounted for of $122,720. This amount should be equal to the total costs to account for in step 3 (see Exhibit 13–5).

Production Cost Report

Steps 1 through 5 provide all the information needed to prepare a production cost report for the molding department for June. (See this report in Exhibit 13–13.)

Exhibit 13–12   Assignment of Total Costs—Molding Department
(FIFO Method)

	Completed and Transferred out	Ending Work-in-Process	Total
Goods completed and transferred out:			
Beginning work-in-process	$ 12,680		$ 12,680
Costs added during June:			
Direct materials	0		0
Direct labor (7,000 × $0.51)	3,570		3,570
Overhead (6,000 × $1.00)	6,000		6,000
Total for beginning inventory	$ 22,250		$ 22,250
Started and completed:			
(34,000 × $2.61)	88,740		88,740
Total costs completed and transferred out	$110,990		$110,990
Ending work-in-process:			
Direct material (6,000 × $1.10)		$ 6,600	$ 6,600
Direct labor (3,000 × $0.51)		1,530	1,530
Overhead (3,600 × $1.00)		3,600	3,600
Total costs accounted for	$110,990	$11,730	$122,720

Exhibit 13–13   Production Cost Report—Molding Department
(FIFO Method)

	Production Quantity Information				
	(Step 1)		**(Step 2)**		
				Equivalent Units	
	Physical Units	Completion Percentage	Direct Materials	Direct Labor	Factory Overhead
Input					
Work-in-process, June 1	10,000				
Direct materials		100%	10,000		
Direct labor		30		3,000	
Overhead		40			4,000
Units started	40,000				
Units to account for	50,000				
Output					
Units completed	44,000	100%	44,000	44,000	44,000
Work-in-process, June 30	6,000				
Direct materials		100	6,000		
Direct labor		50		3,000	
Overhead		60			3,600
Units accounted for	50,000				
Total equivalent units (Weighted-average method)			50,000	47,000	47,600
Less: equivalent units in June 1 work-in-process			−10,000	− 3,000	− 4,000
Equivalent units for work done in June only (FIFO method)			40,000	44,000	43,600

(continued)

Exhibit 13–13	Continued

Unit Cost Determination

(Step 3)	Direct Materials	Direct Labor	Factory Overhead	Total
Work-in-process, June 1				$ 12,680
Costs added during June	44,000	22,440	43,600	110,040
Total costs to account for				$122,720

(Step 4)				
Divide by equivalent units (from Step 2)	40,000	44,000	43,600	
Equivalent unit costs	$ 1.10	$ 0.51	$ 1.00	$ 2.61

Cost Assignment

(Step 5)	Completed and Transferred out	Ending Work-in-Process	Total
Goods completed and transferred out:			
Beginning work-in-process	$ 12,680		$ 12,680
Costs added during June:			
Direct labor (7,000 × $0.51)	3,570		3,570
Overhead (6,000 × $1.00)	6,000		6,000
Total for beginning inventory	$ 22,250		$ 22,250
Started and completed:			
(34,000 × $2.61)	88,740		88,740
Total costs completed and transferred out	$110,990		$110,990
Ending work-in-process:			
Direct materials (6,000 × $1.10)		$ 6,600	$ 6,600
Direct labor (3,000 × $0.51)		1,530	1,530
Overhead (3,600 × $1.00)		3,600	3,600
Total costs accounted for	$110,990	$11,730	$122,720

COMPARISON OF WEIGHTED-AVERAGE AND FIFO METHODS

The key difference between the weighted-average and FIFO methods is the handling of partially completed beginning work-in-process inventory units. The FIFO method separates the units in the beginning inventory from the units started and completed during the period. By contrast, the weighted-average method makes no separate treatment of the units in the beginning work-in-process inventory.

The FIFO method separates costs of the beginning work-in-process inventory from the current period costs, and it uses only the current period costs and work effort to calculate equivalent unit costs. As a result, the FIFO method separately calculates costs for units in the beginning inventory and units that were started during the period. In contrast, the weighted-average method uses the calculated average unit cost for all units completed during the period, including both the beginning work-in-process inventory and units started and completed during the period. By conducting a cost–benefit analysis, firms can decide whether to use the FIFO or the weighted-average method.

The weighted-average method generally is easier to use because the calculations are simpler. This method is most appropriate when direct materials prices, conversion costs, and inventory levels are stable. The FIFO method is most appropriate when direct materials prices, conversion costs, or inventory levels fluctuate.

Firms with a cost leadership strategy prefer the FIFO method to the weighted-average method. Calculating costs per unit for each period independent of other periods (which the weighted-average method does not allow) makes the FIFO

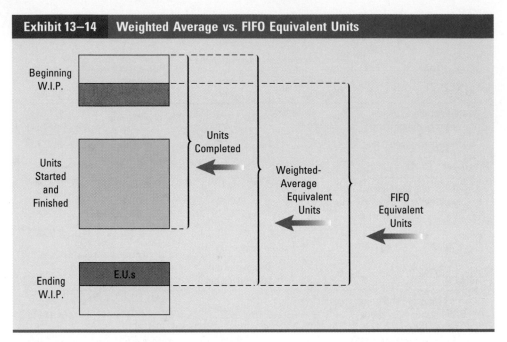

Exhibit 13–14   Weighted Average vs. FIFO Equivalent Units

method preferable for control. The FIFO method also is related more closely to the continuous improvement concept.

In Exhibit 13–14 we present a graphic summary of the difference between the weighted-average and FIFO equivalent units.

Many firms prefer the FIFO method over the weighted-average method for purposes of cost control and performance evaluation because the cost per equivalent unit under FIFO represents the cost for the current period's efforts only. Firms often want to evaluate department managers' performance on just current period costs without mixing in the effects of performance during different periods. Under the weighted-average method, the costs of the prior period and the current period are mixed together, and deviations in performance in the current period may be concealed by interperiod variations in unit costs.

The advantage of the weighted-average method is its simplicity, although computers can reduce this advantage. This method would be inappropriate when a firm's beginning and ending inventories or manufacturing costs per unit change dramatically from period to period.

PROCESS COSTING WITH MULTIPLE DEPARTMENTS

Most manufacturing firms have several departments or use processes that require several steps. As the product passes from one department to another, so does the cost pass from department to department. The costs from the prior department are called transferred-in costs or prior department costs. This section discusses the concept of transferred-in costs and describes both the weighted-average and FIFO methods of cost flow assumptions in firms with multiple departments.

Transferred-In Costs

Transferred-in costs are costs of work done in the prior department that are transferred into the current department.

Transferred-in costs (TI) are costs of work done in the prior department that are transferred into the current department. Including these costs is a necessary part of process costing because we treat each department as a separate entity, and each department's production cost report includes all costs added to the product up to that point. If transferred-in costs were not included, each completed unit transferred out of a department would include only the value of the work done on it by that department. It may help you to think of transferred-in costs as similar to the direct materials introduced at the beginning of the production process. The equivalent units of production of transferred-in costs can be computed in the same manner as direct materials that are added at the beginning of a process. The difference between the direct materials cost and the transferred-in cost is that the former comes from the storeroom while the latter comes from another production department.

The transferred-in cost of the work-in-process ending inventory is almost always 100 percent. In this text the equivalent units of the transferred-in cost for the ending work-in-process inventory always is assumed to be the same as the number of units in the ending work-in-process inventory. Remember, transferred-in costs are treated as if they are added at the beginning of the production process for the department. As units are finished in one department and transferred to a second department for further processing, all transferred-in costs during a period are carried at one unit cost regardless of the cost flow method used by the previous departments. Because all units in process are complete for prior departments' costs, by definition the number of equivalent units is the number of physical units to account for (the weighted-average method in Exhibit 13–16) or the number of physical units transferred in (the FIFO method in Exhibit 13–20).

Basic Data

Suppose Hsu Toy Company's molding department transfers its production units to the finishing department. In the finishing department, direct materials are added at the end of the process. Conversion costs (direct labor and factory overhead) are applied evenly throughout the finishing department's process. The finishing department uses direct labor as the cost driver to apply factory overhead costs.

Data for the finishing department for June 19X8 are shown in Exhibit 13–15.

Weighted-Average Method

Follow the familiar five-step procedure as we illustrate the weighted-average method for process costing with multiple departments.

◄ **LEARNING OBJECTIVE 7**
Analyze process costing with multiple departments.

Steps 1 and 2: Physical Units and Equivalent Units

The first step is to analyze the physical units of production. The second step is to calculate equivalent units. In Exhibit 13–16, we present a summary of the computation of physical units and equivalent units.

In Exhibit 13–16, the 50,000 physical units that were completed were 100 percent complete. Thus, they represent 50,000 equivalent units for transferred-in, direct materials, and conversion costs. Note that the 50,000 units include 14,000 units transferred from the molding department in May and completed in June, and 36,000 units (50,000 units − 14,000 units) transferred from the molding department and also completed in June.

Exhibit 13–15	Basic Data for Hsu Toy Company—Finishing Department
Work-in-process, June 1: 14,000 units	
Direct materials: 0 percent complete	
Transferred-in: 100 percent complete	$ 34,250
Conversion: 50 percent complete	7,000
Beginning work-in-process inventory	$ 41,250
Units transferred-in during June	44,000 units
Units completed	50,000 units
Work-in-process, June 30	8,000 units
Transferred-in: 100 percent complete	
Conversion: 50 percent complete	
Costs added during June	
Direct materials	$ 25,000
Conversion	47,000
Costs transferred-in during June	
Weighted-average method	$111,320
FIFO method	110,990

Exhibit 13–16	**Calculation of Physical Units and Equivalent Units—Finishing Department** *(Weighted-Average Method)*				

	(Step 1)		(Step 2)		
				Equivalent Units	
	Physical Units	**Completion Percentage**	**Transferred-in Costs**	**Direct Materials**	**Conversion Costs**
Input					
Work-in-process, June 1	14,000				
Direct materials		0%			
Transferred-in costs		100			
Conversion costs		50			
Transferred-in	44,000				
Units to account for	58,000				
Output					
Units completed	50,000	100%	50,000	50,000	50,000
Work-in-process, June 30	8,000				
Direct materials		0			
Transferred-in costs		100	8,000		
Conversion costs		50			4,000
Units accounted for	58,000				
Total equivalent units			58,000	50,000	54,000

The 8,000 units in the ending work-in-process inventory are 100 percent complete with respect to transferred-in costs because they are 100 percent complete at the prior department. There is no direct materials component because materials are added at the end of the finishing department. Because the ending work-in-process inventory is only 50 percent complete with respect to conversion costs, the ending work-in-process inventories represent 4,000 equivalent units of conversion costs (8,000 physical units × 50 percent complete).

As Exhibit 13–16 shows, the total number of equivalent units is calculated as follows:

Completed units

+ Ending work-in-process equivalent units

= Total equivalent units of production

That is, by using the weighted-average method, the equivalent units of production for the finishing department are 58,000 units of transferred-in, 50,000 units of direct materials, and 54,000 units of conversion.

Steps 3 and 4: Computation of Total Costs and Unit Costs

The third step is to determine the total manufacturing costs to account for, while the fourth step is the computation of equivalent unit costs for transferred-in, direct materials, and conversion costs.

In Exhibit 13–17, we summarize the total manufacturing costs to account for and unit costs for all cost components. Total manufacturing costs to account for ($224,570) consist of the beginning work-in-process inventory balance, $41,250, plus the current costs added during June, $183,320 ($25,000 + $47,000 + $111,320).

The equivalent unit cost for units transferred in ($2.5099) is computed by dividing the total transferred-in cost ($145,570), including the cost of the beginning work-in-process ($34,250) and the cost added during June ($111,320), by the total equivalent units transferred in (58,000). Similar procedures are used for direct materials and conversion costs.

Exhibit 13–17	Computation of Total Costs and Unit Costs—Finishing Department (Weighted-Average Method)			
(Step 3)	**Transferred-in Costs**	**Direct Materials**	**Conversion Costs**	**Total**
Work-in-process, June 1	$ 34,250	$ 0	$ 7,000	$ 41,250
Costs added during June	111,320	25,000	47,000	183,320
Total costs to account for	$145,570	$25,000	$54,000	$224,570
(Step 4)				
Divide by equivalent units (from Exhibit 13–16):	58,000	50,000	54,000	
Equivalent unit costs	$ 2.5099 +	$ 0.50 +	$ 1.00 =	$ 4.0099

Step 5: Assignment of Total Costs

The final step of the process costing procedure is the assignment of total manufacturing costs to units completed and to units in the ending work-in-process inventory. In Exhibit 13–18, we summarize the cost assignment schedule. Note that the total costs accounted for in this step 5 ($224,574) should equal or be approximately equal to the total costs to account for in step 3 ($224,570) as shown in Exhibit 13–17; where slight differences occur, there may be a rounding error.

Production Cost Report

Steps 1 through 5 provide all the information needed to prepare a production cost report for the finishing department for June. This report appears in Exhibit 13–19.

FIFO Method

Now we illustrate the FIFO method of process costing for multiple departments using data from the Hsu Toy Company's finishing department (see Exhibit 13–15).

Steps 1 and 2: Physical Units and Equivalent Units

In Exhibit 13–20, we summarize the physical flow units and equivalent units of production for the finishing department.

The physical flow of product units is unaffected by the process costing method used. Therefore, step 1 is the same as the weighted-average method.

The 14,000 physical units in the June 1 work-in-process have 100 percent of transferred-in costs, so they represent 14,000 equivalent units of transferred-in work. Because the materials are added at the end of the finishing department, there are zero equivalent units of direct materials for work-in-process inventory on hand on June 1. The beginning work-in-process inventory is only 50 percent complete with respect to conversion activity, so this department has 7,000 equivalent units of conversion costs (14,000 × 50%).

As you can see in Exhibit 13–20, the total number of equivalent units is calculated as follows:

Completed units

+ Ending work-in-process equivalent units

− Beginning work-in-process equivalent units

= Equivalent units of work done during this period

That is, equivalent units of production for the finishing department using the FIFO method are 44,000 units of transferred-in, 50,000 units of direct materials, and 47,000 units of conversion activity.

Exhibit 13-18 Assignment of Total Costs—Finishing Department
(Weighted-Average Method)

(Step 5)	Completed and Transferred out	Ending Work-in-Process	Total
Goods completed and transferred out:			
(50,000 × $4.0099)	$200,495		$200,495
Ending work-in-process:			
Transferred-in (8,000 × $2.5099)		$20,079	20,079
Conversion (4,000 × $1.00)		4,000	4,000
Total costs accounted for	$200,495	$24,079	$224,574

Exhibit 13-19 Production Cost Report—Finishing Department
(Weighted-Average Method)

Production Quantity Information

	(Step 1)		(Step 2)		
			Equivalent Units		
	Physical Units	Completion Percentage	Transferred-in Costs	Direct Materials	Conversion Costs
Input					
Work-in-process, June 1	14,000				
Direct materials		0%			
Transferred-in costs		100			
Conversion costs		50			
Transferred in	44,000				
Units to account for	58,000				
Output					
Units completed	50,000	100%	50,000	50,000	50,000
Work-in-process, June 30	8,000				
Direct materials		0			
Transferred-in costs		100	8,000		
Conversion costs		50			4,000
Units accounted for	58,000				
Total equivalent units			58,000	50,000	54,000

Unit Cost Determination

(Step 3)	Transferred-in Costs	Direct Materials	Conversion Costs	Total
Work-in-process, June 1	$ 34,250	$ 0	$ 7,000	$ 41,250
Costs added during June	111,320	25,000	47,000	183,320
Total costs to account for	$145,570	$25,000	$54,000	$224,570

(Step 4)				
Divide by equivalent units (from Step 2)	58,000	50,000	54,000	
Equivalent unit costs	$ 2.5099	$ 0.50	$ 1.00	$ 4.0099

Cost Assignment

(Step 5)	Completed and Transferred out	Ending Work-in-Process	Total
Goods completed and transferred out:			
(50,000 × $4.0099)	$200,495		$200,495
Ending work-in-process:			
Transferred-in (8,000 × $2.5099)		$20,079	20,079
Conversion (4,000 × $1.00)		4,000	4,000
Total costs accounted for	$200,495	$24,079	$224,574

Exhibit 13–20	Calculation of Physical Units and Equivalent Units—Finishing Department (FIFO Method)

	(Step 1)		(Step 2)		
			Equivalent Units		
	Physical Units	**Completion Percentage**	**Transferred-in Costs**	**Direct Materials**	**Conversion Costs**
Input					
Work-in-process, June 1	14,000				
Transferred-in		100%	14,000		
Direct materials		0		0	
Conversion		50			7,000
Transferred-in	52,000				
Units to account for	66,000				
Output					
Units completed	50,000	100%	50,000	50,000	50,000
Work-in-process, June 30	8,000				
Transferred-in		100	8,000		
Direct materials		0		0	
Conversion		50			4,000
Units accounted for	58,000				
Total equivalent units (Weighted-average method)			58,000	50,000	54,000
Less: equivalent units in June 1 work-in-process			−14,000	− 0	− 7,000
Equivalent units for work done in June only (FIFO method)			44,000	50,000	47,000

Steps 3 and 4: Computation of Total Costs and Unit Costs

Exhibit 13–21 shows the computation of total costs to account for and equivalent unit costs for the finishing department.

The total costs incurred to manufacture product units are unaffected by whether the weighted-average or FIFO method is used. In Step 3, therefore, there is no difference between methods.

The equivalent unit cost for transferred-in ($2.5225) is computed by dividing the transferred-in cost during June ($110,990) by the equivalent units for work done only in June (44,000). Similar procedures are used for direct materials and conversion costs. Notice that the costs of beginning inventory are excluded from this calculation. The calculations use only current costs added in June.

Step 5: Assignment of Total Costs

The final step of the process costing procedure is the assignment of total manufacturing costs to units completed and to units in the ending work-in-process inventory. In Exhibit 13–22, we summarize the cost assignment schedule.

The costs assigned to the first batch of goods completed and from the 14,000 units of the beginning work-in-process are calculated as follows:

Work-in-process, June 1, 14,000 units	$41,250
Costs added during June to complete the beginning inventory:	
Direct material 14,000 equivalent units × $0.50	7,000
Conversion costs 7,000 equivalent units × $1.00	7,000
Total for beginning inventory	$55,250

The costs assigned to the 36,000 units started and completed during June are calculated:

513

Exhibit 13–21	Computation of Total Costs and Unit Costs—Finishing Department *(FIFO Method)*

(Step 3)	Transferred-in Costs	Direct Materials	Conversion Costs	Total
Work-in-process, June 1				$ 41,250
Costs added during June	$110,990	$25,000	$47,000	182,990
Total costs to account for				$224,240
(Step 4)				
Divide by equivalent units (from Exhibit 13–20):	44,000	50,000	47,000	
Equivalent unit costs	$ 2.5225 +	$ 0.50 +	$ 1.00 =	$ 4.0225

Exhibit 13–22	Assignment of Total Costs—Finishing Department *(FIFO Method)*

(Step 5)	Completed and Transferred out	Ending Work-in-Process	Total
Goods completed and transferred out:			
Beginning work-in-process	$ 41,250		$ 41,250
Costs added during June:			
Direct materials (14,000 × $0.50)	7,000		7,000
Conversion (7,000 × $1.00)	7,000		7,000
Total from beginning inventory	$ 55,250		$ 55,250
Started and completed:			
(36,000 × $4.0225)	144,810		144,810
Total costs completed and			
transferred out	$200,060		$200,060
Ending work-in-process:			
Transferred-in (8,000 × $2.5225)		$20,180	$ 20,180
Conversion costs (4,000 × $1.00)		4,000	4,000
Total costs accounted for	$200,060	$24,180	$224,240

$$50,000 \text{ units} - 14,000 \text{ units} = 36,000 \text{ units}$$

$$36,000 \text{ units} \times \$4.0225 = \$144,810$$

And the total costs completed are the sum of total costs from beginning inventory and total costs for units started and completed; that is,

$$\$55,250 + \$144,810 = \$200,060$$

The cost of the finishing department's 8,000 units in ending work-in-process is computed:

Transferred-in: 8,000 equivalent units × $2.5225	$20,180
Conversion: 4,000 equivalent units × $1.00	4,000
Total ending work-in-process inventory	$24,180

In Exhibit 13–22, the sum of the costs assigned to goods completed and ending work-in-process inventory is $224,240. Note that the amount of total costs accounted for in this step 5 should equal the total costs to account for in step 3 (as shown in Exhibit 13–21).

Production Cost Report

Steps 1 through 5 provide all the information needed to prepare a production cost report for the molding department for June. This report appears in Exhibit 13–23.

JOURNAL ENTRIES FOR PROCESS COSTING

Process costing uses the same general ledger manufacturing accounts as job costing discussed in the preceding chapter. However, instead of tracing product costs to specific jobs, we accumulate costs in production departments or other cost centers. Each department has a separate work-in-process inventory account. These journal entries for the Hsu Toy Company use weighted-average method data from Steps 3 and 5 of both Exhibit 13–8 (molding department) and Exhibit 13–19 (finishing department).

◀ **LEARNING OBJECTIVE 8**
Prepare journal entries to record the flow of costs in a process costing system.

Direct materials requisitioned and used:

(1) Work-in-Process Inventory—Molding Department   44,000
      Work-in-Process Inventory—Finishing Department   25,000
        Materials Inventory   69,000
      To record direct materials costs added during June.

Direct labor incurred:

(2) Work-in-Process Inventory—Molding Department   22,440
      Work-in-Process Inventory—Finishing Department   23,500
        Accrued Payroll   45,940
      To record direct labor costs incurred during June. Assume that
      50 percent of the conversion costs in finishing department are direct labor.
      ($47,000 × 50% = $23,500)

Factory overhead applied:

(3) Work-in-Process Inventory—Molding Department   43,600
      Work-in-Process Inventory—Finishing Department   23,500
        Factory Overhead Control   67,100
      To record the application of factory overhead to departments.

Transferred-in costs from the molding department:

(4) Work-in-Process Inventory—Finishing Department   111,320
        Work-in-Process Inventory—Molding Department   111,320
      To record the weighted-average method of the cost of goods completed in the
      molding department and transferred out to the finishing department.

Product units finished:

(5) Finished Goods Inventory   200,495
        Work-in-Process Inventory—Finishing Department   200,495
      To record the weighted-average method of the cost of goods completed in the
      finishing department.

EFFECTS OF THE NEW MANUFACTURING ENVIRONMENT

Just-In-Time Systems

In recent years many firms have adopted just-in-time (JIT) systems to minimize inventories and improve quality control. Under the JIT philosophy, raw materials are received right before going into production. In multiple department situations, production departments assemble goods and subassemblies just in time for the product to be sold. Thus, direct materials inventory, work-in-process inventory, and finished goods inventory are either eliminated or kept to a minimal level.

◀ **LEARNING OBJECTIVE 9**
Characterize the impact of the new manufacturing technologies on process costing.

JIT methodology has three major impacts on process costing procedures: First, the difference in unit cost between the FIFO and weighted-average methods is reduced by the decreased inventory units. Second, under JIT there is much less difference between units completed and work-in-process ending inventory. Three, new cost drivers or activity bases (other than direct labor) are needed to assign

515

Exhibit 13–23	**Production Cost Report—Finishing Department** *(FIFO Method)*

Production Quantity Information

	(Step 1)		(Step 2)		
			Equivalent Units		
	Physical Units	Completion Percentage	Transferred-in Costs	Direct Materials	Conversion Costs
Input					
Work-in-process, June 1	14,000				
Transferred-in		100%	14,000		
Direct materials		0		0	
Conversion		50			7,000
Transferred-in	44,000				
Units to account for	58,000				
Output					
Units completed	50,000	100%	50,000	50,000	50,000
Work-in-process, June 30	8,000				
Transferred-in		100	8,000		
Direct materials		0		0	
Conversion		50			4,000
Units accounted for	58,000				
Total equivalent units			58,000	50,000	54,000
(Weighted-average method)					
Less: equivalent units in					
June 1 work-in-process			−14,000	− 0	− 7,000
Equivalent units for work					
done only in June			44,000	50,000	47,000
(FIFO method)					

Unit Cost Determination

(Step 3)	Transferred-in Costs	Direct Materials	Conversion Costs	Total
Work-in-process, June 1				$ 41,250
Costs added during June	$110,990	$25,000	$47,000	182,990
Total costs to account for				$224,240

(Step 4)				
Divide by equivalent units				
(from Step 2):	44,000	50,000	47,000	
Equivalent unit costs	$ 2.5225	$ 0.50	$ 1.00	$ 4.0225

Cost Assignment

(Step 5)	Completed and Transferred out	Ending Work-in-Process	Total
Goods completed and transferred out:			
Beginning work-in-process	$ 41,250		$ 41,250
Costs added during June:			
Direct materials (14,000 × $0.50)	7,000		7,000
Conversion (7,000 × $1.00)	7,000		7,000
Total from beginning inventory	$ 55,250		$ 55,250
Started and completed:			
(36,000 × $4.0225)	144,810		144,810
Total costs transferred out	$200,060		$200,060
Ending work-in-process:			
Transferred in (8,000 × $2.5225)		$20,180	$ 20,180
Conversion (4,000 × $1.00)		4,000	4,000
Total costs accounted for	$200,060	$24,180	$224,240

BusinessWeek

How Is Whirlpool Improving Its Operating Income?

(Continues from page 491)

A: By pooling its resources . . .

It all comes down to cost management by reducing product and asset costs. Whirlpool's biggest change and challenge are in reducing manufacturing costs. To start, Whirlpool had its national designers and researchers merge into pan-European teams that work closely with Whirlpool's U.S. designers. The result? The creation of common platforms that allow different models to share the same underlying structure and parts, which in turn has led to a significant reduction in product costs across Whirlpool products.

Whirlpool also reduced asset costs by rationalizing Philips' scattered assets. By the end of 1994, it slashed $400 million in annual costs. Whirlpool also shut a surplus plant in Barcelona, trimmed 36 warehouses to 8, and centralized inventory control, cutting Philips's 1,600 suppliers in half. Together, these moves cut inventories by one-third. So far, Whirlpool's product and asset cost reduction strategy has paid off—making a big splash in the international appliance industry.

For further reading, see "Call It Worldpool," Business Week, November 28, 1994.

factory overhead to processes and products. Under JIT process costing becomes very simple because of reduced inventory. To find the unit cost, we simply divide the total cost of the period by the number of units produced to get a close approximation.

Flexible Manufacturing and Cellular Manufacturing Systems

More manufacturing firms are moving toward flexible manufacturing systems (FMS) and cellular manufacturing systems (CMS). A FMS is an automated production system that produces one or more items in a family of parts in a flexible manner. It uses robots and computer-controlled materials-handling systems to link several stand-alone numerical control machines that quickly and efficiently switch from one production run to another.

The effect of FMS on product costing is like that of JIT. Under a FMS environment, process costing is more useful than job costing because more accounting reports are based on time periods rather than the closing of job orders.

A CMS forms a cell containing the machinery and equipment needed to manufacture parts with similar processing requirements. To improve production efficiency, most parts travel in the same direction from one end of a cell to the other. A collection of cells assigned to make a product forms a focused factory. CMS changes the structure of the manufacturing process so that it is by product line rather than process. Under the CMS traditional process costing is less useful than the activity-based costing with cell-level cost pools.

SUMMARY

Process costing is a product cost system that accumulates costs in processing departments and allocates them to all units processed during the period, including both completed and partially completed units. It is used by firms producing homogeneous products on a continuous basis to assign manufacturing costs to units in production during the period. Firms that use process costing include paint, chemical, oil refining, and food processing companies.

Process costing systems provide information so managers can make strategic decisions regarding products and customers, manufacturing methods, pricing options, overhead allocation methods, and other long-term issues.

Equivalent units are the number of like or similar completed units that could have been produced given the amount of work actually performed on both complete and partially completed units.

The key document in a typical process costing system is the production cost report that summarizes the physical units and equivalent units of a department, the costs incurred during the period, and costs assigned to both completed goods and transferred out as well as to ending work-in-process inventories. The preparation of a production cost report includes five steps: (1) analysis of physical units, (2) calculation of equivalent units, (3) determination of total costs to account for, (4) computation of unit costs, and (5) assignment of total costs.

The two methods of preparing the departmental production cost report in process costing are the weighted-average method and first-in, first-out method (FIFO). The weighted-average method includes all costs in calculating the unit cost. It includes those costs incurred in both the current and prior periods that are shown as the beginning work-in-process inventory of this period. The FIFO method includes only costs incurred during the current period in calculating equivalent unit cost. It considers the beginning inventory as a batch of goods separate from the goods started and completed within the same period. FIFO assumes that all the beginning work-in-process inventories were completed before other work is done during the current period.

Under the weighted-average method, it makes no difference when a product is started; all units completed in the same period are treated the same. When this method is used, all you have to know is the status of the product at the end of the period. On the other hand, the status of the product both at the end and at the beginning of a period has to be taken into consideration when the FIFO method is used in determining product costs. That is, the FIFO method looks at input as well as output of the production, whereas the weighted-average method looks at only the output of the production.

Most manufacturing firms have several departments or use processes that require several steps. As the product passes from one department to another, the cost has to follow. The costs that come from the prior department are transferred-in costs or prior department costs. Process costing with multiple departments should include the transferred-in cost as the fourth cost element in addition to direct materials, direct labor, and factory overhead costs.

Process costing uses the same manufacturing accounts as job costing discussed in the preceding chapter. Journal entries are essentially the same as in job costing. However, instead of tracing product costs to specific jobs, we accumulate costs in production departments or cost centers.

For firms that adopt either just-in-time or flexible manufacturing systems, choosing between the weighted-average or the FIFO method of process costing is not so important because the new systems reduce inventory units. Such firms also need new cost drivers other than direct labor cost to assign factory overhead to products.

APPENDIX

Spoilage in Process Costing

In today's contemporary manufacturing environment, firms adopt various quality improvement programs to reduce spoilage, scrap, and rework units. *Spoilage* denotes unacceptable units that are discarded or sold for disposal value. *Scrap* is the part of the product that has little or no value. *Rework* units are product units that are economically reworked so they can be sold through regular channels.

There are two types of spoilage: normal spoilage and abnormal spoilage. *Normal spoilage* occurs under efficient operating conditions. It is uncontrollable in the short term and is considered a part of product cost. That is, lost unit costs are absorbed by the good units produced. *Abnormal spoilage* exceeds expected losses under efficient operating conditions and is charged as a loss to operations in the period detected.

For example, Diamond Company has the following data for the current period:

	Units	Cost
Beginning work-in-process inventory:	2,000	
Direct materials (100 percent complete)		$100,000
Conversion costs (75 percent complete)		80,000
Units started in the period	8,000	
Costs incurred during the period:		
Direct materials		300,000
Conversion costs		405,000
Ending work-in-process inventory:	2,000	
Direct materials (100 percent complete)		
Conversion costs (80 percent complete)		
Completed and transferred out	7,000	
Normal spoilage is 10 percent of good production		

The company uses the FIFO process costing method. With 7,000 good production units, the normal spoilage units total 700. Abnormal spoilage units are 300 units, which is the difference between total input of 10,000 units (beginning work-in-process inventory 2,000 + started 8,000) and the sum of total output units (ending work-in-process inventory 2,000 + completed and transferred out 7,000) and normal spoilage units (700).

In Exhibit 13–24, we show the five-step procedure for FIFO process costing including normal spoilage and abnormal spoilage.

Exhibit 13–24   Diamond Company's FIFO Production Cost Report

Production Quantity Information

	(Step 1)		(Step 2)	
			Equivalent Units	
	Physical Units		**Direct Materials**	**Conversion Costs**
Input				
Work-in-process				
beginning inventory	2,000		(100%)	(75%)
Started this period	8,000			
Total units to account for	10,000			
Output				
Completed	7,000		7,000	7,000
Normal spoilage (10 percent)	700		700	700
Abnormal spoilage	300		300	300
Work-in-process				
ending inventory	2,000	(80%)	2,000	1,600
Total units accounted for	10,000			
Total work done to date			10,000	9,600
Work-in-process				
beginning inventory			(2,000)	(1,500)
Total work done this period			8,000	8,100
(Total equivalent units)				

Cost Determination

(Step 3) Costs Incurred	Total	Direct Materials	Conversion Costs
Work-in-process			
beginning inventory	$180,000	$100,000	$ 80,000
Current cost	705,000	300,000	405,000
Total costs to account for	$885,000	$400,000	$485,000
(Step 4)		($300,000/ 8,000) =	($405,000/ 8,100) =
Cost per equivalent unit	$ 87.50	$ 37.50	$ 50.00

(continued)

Exhibit 13–24   Continued

Cost Assignment

(Step 5)	Total	Direct Materials	Conversion Costs
Units completed (1,000):			
From work-in-process, beginning inventory	$180,000	$100,000	$ 80,000
Current costs incurred completing units	25,000	0	25,000
Total cost from beginning inventory	$205,000	$100,000	$105,000
Normal spoilage	61,250	26,250	35,000
Units started and completed this period	437,500	187,500	250,000
Total cost of units completed	$703,750	$313,750	$390,000
Abnormal spoilage (300)	26,250	11,250	15,000
Work-in-process ending inventory		(2,000 × $37.5)	(1,600 × $50)
	155,000	= $ 75,000	= $ 80,000
Total costs accounted for	$885,000		

The journal entries for the Diamond Company are

Finished Goods Inventory	703,750	
Work-in-Process Inventory		703,750
To record the total cost of units completed.		
Loss from Spoilage	26,250	
Work-in-Process Inventory		26,250
To record the abnormal spoilage cost.		

KEY TERMS

Equivalent units **493**

FIFO method **496**

Production cost report **494**

Transferred-in costs **508**

Units accounted for **498**

Units to account for **497**

Weighted-average method **496**

SELF-STUDY PROBLEMS

(For solutions, please turn to the end of the chapter.)

1. Weighted-Average Method vs. FIFO Method

The chip-mounting production department of the Smith Electronic Company had 300 units of unfinished product, each 40 percent complete on September 30, 19X8. During October of the same year, another 900 units were put into production, and 1,000 units were completed and transferred to the next production department. At the end of October, 200 units of unfinished product, 70 percent completed, were recorded in the ending work-in-process inventory. Smith Company introduces all direct materials when the production process is 50 percent complete. Direct labor and factory overhead (i.e., conversion) costs are added uniformly throughout the process.

Following is a summary of production costs incurred during October:

	Direct Materials	Conversion Costs
Beginning work-in-process		$2,202
Current cost	$9,600	6,120
Total costs	$9,600	$8,322

Required

1. Prepare a production cost report for October 19X8, using the weighted-average method.

2. Prepare a production cost report for October 19X8, using the FIFO method.

2. Weighted-Average Method vs. FIFO Method with Transferred-In Cost

The Reed Company has two departments, a machining department and a finishing department. The following information relates to the finishing department: work-in-process, November 1, 19X8, 10 units, 40 percent completed, consisting of $100 transferred-in costs, $80 direct materials, and $52 in conversion costs. Production completed for November was 82 units; work-in-process, November 30, 19X8, 8 units, 50 percent completed. All finishing department direct materials are introduced at the start of the process, while conversion costs are incurred uniformly throughout the process. Transferred-in costs from the machining department during November were $800; direct materials added were $720 while conversion costs incurred were $861. Following is the summary data of the Reed Company's finishing department.

Work-in-process, November 1, 10 units:	
Transferred-in: 100 percent complete	$ 100
Direct materials: 100 percent added	80
Conversion: 40 percent complete	52
Balance in work-in-process, November 1	$ 232
Units transferred in from machining department during November	80 units
Units completed during November and transferred out to finished goods inventory	82 units
Work-in-process, November 30	8 units
Transferred-in: 100 percent complete	
Direct materials: 100 percent added	
Conversion: 50 percent complete	
Costs incurred during November:	
Transferred-in	$ 800
Direct materials	720
Conversion	861
Total current costs	$2,381

Required

1. Prepare a production cost report for November using the weighted-average method.

2. Prepare a production cost report for November using the FIFO method.

QUESTIONS

13–1 What are the typical characteristics of a company that should adopt a process costing system?

13–2 List three types of industries in which process costing would likely be used.

13–3 Explain the primary differences between job costing and process costing.

13–4 What is meant by the term *equivalent units*?

13–5 How is the equivalent unit calculation affected when direct materials are added at the beginning or end of the process rather than uniformly throughout the process?

13–6 What is a production cost report? What are five key steps in preparing a production cost report?

13–7 What is the distinction between equivalent units under FIFO and equivalent units under the weighted-average method?

13–8 Identify the conditions under which the weighted-average method of process costing would be inappropriate.

13–9 Specify the advantages of the weighted-average method of process costing in contrast to the first-in, first-out method.

13–10 From the standpoint of cost control, why is the FIFO method superior to the weighted-average method? Is it possible to monitor cost trends using the weighted-average method?

13–11 What are transferred-in costs?

13–12 Suppose that manufacturing is done in sequential production departments. Prepare a journal entry to show a transfer of partially completed units from the first department to the second department.

13–13 Under the weighted-average method all units transferred out are treated in the same way. How does this differ from the FIFO method of handling units transferred out?

13–14 Under the FIFO method only current period costs and work are included in unit costs and equivalent units computation. Under the weighted-average method, what assumptions are made when unit costs and equivalent units are computed?

13–15 What is the main difference between journal entries in process costing and in job costing?

13–16 What is the difference between process costing and operation costing?

13–17 Describe the effect of automation on the process costing system.

PROBLEMS

13–18 PHYSICAL UNITS In each case, fill in the missing amount.

1. Work-in-process inventory, February 1   80,000 units
   Work-in-process inventory, February 28   ?
   Units started during February   60,000 units
   Units completed during February   75,000 units

2. Work-in-process inventory, June 1   ?
   Work-in-process inventory, June 30   55,000 gallons
   Units started during June   75,000 gallons
   Units completed during June   83,000 gallons

3. Work-in-process inventory, September 1   5,500 tons
   Work-in-process inventory, September 30   3,400 tons
   Units started during September   ?
   Units completed during September   7,300 tons

4. Work-in-process inventory, November 1   45,000 units
   Work-in-process inventory, November 30   23,000 units
   Units started during November   57,000 units
   Units completed during November   ?

13–19 EQUIVALENT UNITS; WEIGHTED-AVERAGE METHOD The Washington Fisheries, Inc., processes salmon for various distributors. Two departments are involved, processing and packaging. Data relating to tons of salmon sent to the processing department during May 19X8 are

		Percent Completed	
	Tons of Salmon	**Materials**	**Conversion**
Work-in-process inventory, May 1	1,500	80%	70%
Work-in-process inventory, May 31	2,300	50	30
Started processing during May	6,500		

Required

1. Calculate the number of tons completed and transferred out during the month.
2. Calculate equivalent units for units completed and ending work-in-process inventories, assuming the company uses the weighted-average method.

13–20 EQUIVALENT UNITS; WEIGHTED-AVERAGE METHOD Western Oregon Lumber Company grows, harvests, and processes timber for use as building lumber. The following data pertain to the company's sawmill:

Work-in-process inventory, January 1 (materials 60 percent, conversion 40 percent)	25,000 units
Work-in-process inventory, December 31 (materials 70 percent, conversion 60 percent)	15,000 units

During the year the company started 150,000 units in production.

Required Prepare a quantity schedule and compute the equivalent units of both direct materials and conversion for the year, using the weighted-average method.

13–21 EQUIVALENT UNITS; FIFO METHOD Englewood Chemical Company refines a variety of petrochemical products. These data are from the firm's Houston plant:

Work-in-process inventory, September 1	3,000,000 gallons
Direct materials	100 percent completed
Conversion	25 percent completed
Units started in process during September	1,850,000 gallons
Work-In-process inventory, September 30	2,400,000 gallons
Direct materials	100 percent completed
Conversion	80 percent completed

Required Compute the equivalent units of direct material and conversion for the month of September. Use the FIFO method.

13–22 EQUIVALENT UNITS; FIFO METHOD Adams Company has the following information for December 1, 19X8, to December 31, 19X8. All direct materials are 100 percent complete; beginning materials cost $12,000.

Work-in-Process

Beginning balance December 1, 200 units, 9 percent complete	$14,000	Completed 800 units and transferred to finished goods inventory	$140,000
Raw material	54,000		
Direct labor	34,000		
Factory overhead:			
Property taxes	$ 6,000		
Depreciation	32,000		
Utilities	18,000		
Indirect labor	4,000		
Ending balance December 31, 300 units, 11.6 percent complete	$22,000		

Required Calculate equivalent units using the FIFO method.

13–23 EQUIVALENT UNITS; FIFO UNIT COST   Young Company calculated the cost for an equivalent unit of production using the FIFO method.

Data for June 19X8	
Work-in-process inventory, June 1: 30,000 units	
Direct materials: 100 percent complete	$ 80,000
Conversion: 20 percent complete	24,000
Balance in work-in-process, June 1	104,000
Units started during June	50,000
Units completed and transferred	60,000
Work-in-process inventory, June 30	
Direct materials: 100 percent complete	20,000
Conversion: 70 percent complete	
Cost incurred during June:	
Direct materials	$150,000
Conversion costs	
Direct labor	120,000
Applied overhead	145,000
Total conversion costs	$265,000

Required: Compute cost per equivalent unit.

International

13–24 WEIGHTED-AVERAGE METHOD   China Pacific Company manufactures a variety of natural fabrics for the clothing industry in a suburb of Shanghai. The following data in Chinese money called renminbi pertain to the month of October 19X8.

Work-in-process inventory, October 1	25,000 units
Direct materials: 60 percent complete	57,000 renminbi
Conversion: 30 percent complete	45,000 renminbi
Cost incurred during October	
Direct materials	736,000 renminbi
Conversion	1,094,950 renminbi

During October, 175,000 units were completed and transferred out. At the end of the month, 30,000 units (direct materials 80 percent and conversion 40 percent complete) remain in the work-in-process inventory.

Required   Calculate each of the following amounts using weighted-average process costing.

1. Equivalent units of direct materials and conversion.
2. Unit costs of direct materials and conversion.
3. Cost of goods completed and transferred out during October.
4. Cost of the work-in-process inventory at October 31.
5. Check the most recent issue of *The Wall Street Journal* to find out the exchange rate between the U.S. dollar and the Chinese renminbi.

International

13–25 FIFO METHOD   Refer to information in Problem 13–24.

Required   Do problem 13–24 using the FIFO method.

13–26 WEIGHTED-AVERAGE METHOD   Yamamoto Company manufactures a single product that goes through two processes, mixing and cooking. These data pertain to the mixing department for August 19X8:

Work-in-process inventory, August 1 Conversion: 80 percent complete	27,000 units
Work-in-process inventory, August 31 Conversion: 40 percent complete	17,000 units
Units started into production	60,000 units
Units completed and transferred out	?
Costs	
Work-in-process inventory, August 1	
Material X	$ 64,800
Material Y	89,100
Conversion	119,880
Costs added during August	
Material X	152,700
Material Y	138,400
Conversion	302,520

Material X is added at the beginning of work in the mixing department. Material Y also is added in the mixing department, but not until units of product are 60 percent complete with regard to conversion. Conversion costs are incurred uniformly during the process. The company uses the weighted-average cost method.

Required

1. Calculate equivalent units of material X, material Y, and conversion.
2. Calculate costs per equivalent unit for material X, material Y, and conversion.
3. Calculate the cost of units transferred out.
4. Calculate the value of ending Work-in-Process Inventory.

13–27 **FIFO METHOD** Refer to information in problem 13–26.

Required Do problem 13–26 using the FIFO method.

13–28 **WEIGHTED-AVERAGE METHOD** Ito produces a single model of popular digital watches in large quantities. A single watch moves through two departments: assembly and testing. The manufacturing costs in the assembly department during March were

Direct materials added	$137,500
Conversion costs	184,500
	$322,000

There was no beginning inventory of work-in-process. During the month 25,000 watches were started, but only 23,000 were fully completed and transferred to the testing department. All the parts had been made and placed in the remaining 2,000 watches, but only 80 percent of the labor had been completed. The company is using the weighted-average method of processing costing to accumulate product costs.

Required

1. Compute the equivalent units and equivalent unit costs for March.
2. Compute the costs of units completed and transferred to the testing department.
3. Compute the costs of the ending work-in-process.

13–29 **FIFO METHOD** Carolina Pulp Company processes wood pulp for manufacturing various paper products. The company employs a process costing system for its manufacturing operations. All direct materials are added at the beginning of the process, and conversion costs are incurred uniformly throughout the process. This is the company's production quantity schedule for May:

	Tons of Pulp	**Percent Completed**	
		Materials	**Conversion**
Work-in-process inventory, May 1	1,500	100	70
Units started during May	5,000		
Total units to account for	6,500		
Units from beginning work-in-process, which were completed and transferred out during May	1,500		
Units started and completed during May	4,000		
Work-in-process inventory, May 31	1,000	100	60
Total units accounted for	6,500		

And the following cost data are available.

Work-in-process inventory, May 1:	
Direct materials	$20,750
Conversion	23,470
Costs incurred during May	
Direct materials	$80,000
Conversion	58,880

Required

1. Calculate equivalent units of direct materials and conversion during May. Use the FIFO method.

2. Calculate the cost per equivalent unit, for both direct materials and conversion, during May. Use the FIFO method.

13-30 **WEIGHTED-AVERAGE METHOD**   Refer to the information in Problem 13-29.

Required   Do Problem 13-29 using the weighted-average method.

13-31 **FIFO METHOD**   Skyblue Corporation manufactures paint that goes through three processes—cracking, mixing, and cooking. This information was obtained for the mixing department for the month of July:

Work-in-process, July 1	3,000	units	
Transferred-in costs	$35,000	(100 percent complete)	
Costs added by the department			
Direct materials	$17,400	(100 percent complete)	
Conversion	8,100	(60 percent complete)	
	$60,500		

During the month of July, 12,000 units were transferred in from the cracking department at the cost of $240,000, and $103,180 of costs were added by the mixing department.

Direct materials	$58,300
Conversion	44,880

During the month, 8,000 units were completed and transferred to the cooking department. At July 31, the degree of completion of work-in-process was as follows:

Direct materials	80 percent
Conversion	45 percent

Required   Prepare the production cost report of the mixing department for the month of July, using the FIFO method.

13-32 FIFO METHOD Jenice Company uses FIFO process costing to account for the costs of its single product. Production begins in the fabrication department, where units of raw material are molded into various connecting parts. After fabrication is complete, the units are transferred to the assembly department, where no material is added. After assembly is complete, the units are transferred to the packaging department, where units are packaged for shipment. After the units have been packaged, the final products are transferred to the shipping department. A partially completed production cost report for the month of May in the fabrication department follows:

JENICE COMPANY
Fabrication Department—Production Cost Report
For the Month Ended May 31, 19X8

Quantity schedule	Units		
Units to be accounted for:			
Work-in-process inventory, May 1	3,000		
(materials 100 percent, conversion 40 percent)			
Started into production	?		
Total units to be accounted for	?		
Units accounted for as follows:			
Transferred to department Y:			
Units from the beginning inventory	?		
Units started and completed this month	?		
Work-in-process inventory, May 31	4,000		
(materials 100 percent, conversion 60 percent)			
Total units accounted for	?		

Equivalent units and unit costs	Materials	Conversion	Total
Cost added during May	$172,500	?	?
Equivalent units	?	?	
Unit cost	?	?	?

Cost reconciliation			
Cost to be accounted for			
?			
Cost accounted for as follows:			
?			

The cost incurred in the work-in-process inventory of the fabrication department at May 1 is $13,800. The production cost report of the assembly department for the month of May shows that the number of transferred-in units is 68,000, costing $393,400.

Required

1. Fill in the missing amounts in the quantity schedule and complete the equivalent units and costs.

2. Complete the cost reconciliation part of the production cost report.

13-33 JOURNAL ENTRIES NYI Corporation manufactures decorative window glass in two sequential departments. These data pertain to the month of August:

	Department 1	Department 2
Direct materials used for production	$ 55,000	$ 32,000
Direct labor	160,000	320,000
Applied factory overhead	340,000	250,000
Costs of goods completed and transferred	850,000	740,000

Required   Prepare journal entries to record these events:

1. Incurrence of direct materials and direct labor. Application of factory overhead in department 1.
2. Transfer of products from department 1 to department 2.
3. Incurrence of direct materials and direct labor. Application of factory overhead in department 2.
4. Transfer of complete products from department 2 to finished goods inventory.

13–34 **IDENTIFYING COST METHOD; PRODUCTION COST REPORT**   Clearwater Corporation manufactures a single product that goes through two departments, X and Y. A partially completed production cost report for the month of April in department X follows:

CLEARWATER CORPORATION
Department X—Production Cost Report
For the Month Ended April 30, 19X8

Quantity Schedule	Units
Units to be accounted for:	
Work-in-process, April 1	5,000
(materials 100 percent, conversion 60 percent)	
Started into production	?
Total units to be accounted for	71,000
Units accounted for as follows:	
Transferred to department Y:	
Units from the beginning inventory	?
Units started and completed this month	?
Work-in-process, April 30	4,500
(materials 100 percent, conversion 40 percent)	
Total units accounted for	?

Equivalent units and unit costs	Materials	Conversion	Total
Cost added during April	$115,500	$146,925	$262,425
Equivalent units	66,000	?	
Unit cost	?	?	?

Cost reconciliation
Cost to be accounted for
?
Cost accounted for as follows:
?

Required

1. By scrutinizing the partially completed production cost report, identify two ways in which you can tell whether the company is using the weighted-average cost method or the FIFO cost method.
2. Fill in the missing amount in the quantity schedule and equivalent units and unit costs.
3. Assume that the cost in the work-in-process inventory amounted to $9,270 (materials $5,400 and conversion $3,870) at April 1. Complete the cost reconciliation part of the production cost report.

13–35 **IDENTIFYING A PROCESS COSTING METHOD**   Western Auto Products manufactures an expensive car wax compound that goes through three processing departments: grinding, mixing, and cooking. Raw materials are introduced at the start of the grinding process. A partially completed production cost report for the month of May in the grinding department follows:

WESTERN AUTO PRODUCTS
Grinding Department—Production Report
For the Month Ended May 31, 19X8

Quantity schedule	Units
Units to be accounted for:	
Work-in-process inventory, May 1	4,000
(materials 100 percent, conversion 60 percent)	
Started into production	?
Total units to be accounted for	69,000
Units accounted for as follows:	
Transferred to mixing department:	?
Work-in-process inventory, May 30	3,500
(materials 100 percent, conversion 40 percent)	
Total units accounted for	?

Equivalent units and unit costs	Materials	Conversion	Total
Cost of work-in-process inventory, May 1	$21,600	$?	$?
Cost added during May	?	228,970	?
Equivalent units	?	?	
Unit cost	?	?	?

Cost reconciliation

Costs to be accounted for
?
Costs accounted for as follows:
?

The production cost report of the mixing department reveals that the transferred-in cost for the month of May is $589,500 (materials $360,250 and conversion $229,250).

Required

1. By scrutinizing the partially completed production cost report, identify two ways in which you can tell whether the company is using the weighted-average cost method or the FIFO cost method.
2. Fill in the missing amount in the quantity schedule and equivalent units and unit costs.
3. Complete the cost reconciliation part of the production cost report.

13–36 FIFO METHOD The Lester-Smith Company has a department that manufactures wood trusses. The following information is for the production of these trusses for the month of February:

 *Ethics*

Work-in-process inventory, February 1:	10,000 trusses
Direct materials cost: 100 percent complete	$100,000
Conversion: 20 percent complete	$115,000
Units started during February	15,000 trusses
Units completed during February and transferred out	20,000 trusses
Work-in-process inventory, February 29:	5,000 trusses
Direct materials: 100 percent complete	
Conversion cost: 40 percent complete	
Costs incurred during February:	
Direct materials	$50,000
Conversion	$95,000

Required Using the FIFO method, calculate the following:

1. Costs per equivalent unit.
2. Cost of goods completed and transferred out.
3. Cost remaining in the ending work-in-process inventory.

4. Assume that you are the controller of the Lester-Smith Company. The production department's February unit cost is higher than the target or standard cost. If the manager of the first department asks you to do him a favor by increasing the ending inventory completion percentage from 40 to 60 percent to lower the unit costs, what should you do?

Ethics

13–37   WEIGHTED-AVERAGE METHOD   Refer to the information in problem 13–36.

Required   Do Problem 13–36 using the weighted-average method.

13–38   FIFO METHOD; JOURNAL ENTRIES   You are engaged in the audit of the December 31, 19X8, financial statements of Epworth Products Corporation. You are attempting to verify the costing of the work-in-process and finished goods ending inventories that were recorded on Epworth's books as follows:

	Units	Cost
Work-in-process (50 percent complete as to labor and overhead)	300,000	$660,960
Finished goods	100,000	504,900

Materials are added to production at the beginning of the manufacturing process and overhead is applied to each product at the rate of 60 percent of direct labor costs. There was no finished goods inventory on January 1, 19X8. Epworth uses the FIFO costing method. A review of Epworth's 19X8 inventory cost records disclosed the following information:

		Costs	
	Units	Materials	Labor
Work-in-process inventory, January 1, 19X8 (80 percent complete as to labor and overhead)	200,000	$ 200,000	$ 315,000
Units started	1,000,000		
Units completed	900,000		
Current period costs		1,300,000	1,995,000

Required   Prepare a production cost report to verify the inventory balances and prepare necessary journal entries to correctly state the inventory of finished goods and work-in-process, assuming the books have not been closed.

13–39   WEIGHTED-AVERAGE METHOD   Hawes House Inc. uses weighted-average process costing in accounting for its production activities. Materials are added at the beginning of the process and conversion costs are incurred uniformly throughout the process.

October's production records indicate this information:

Quantities	
Beginning work-in-process inventory	1,500 units
Started during October	8,500 units
Completed and transferred out	7,000 units
Ending work-in-process inventory (60 percent complete)	3,000 units

Beginning inventory costs	
Direct materials	$ 800
Direct labor	1,000
Factory overhead	440

October production costs

Direct materials	$4,400
Direct labor	9,000
Factory overhead	3,870

Required   Prepare a production cost report for Hawes House Inc.

13–40   **WEIGHTED-AVERAGE METHOD; TRANSFERRED-IN COSTS**   Choi Corporation manufactures a popular model of business calculators in a suburb of Seoul, South Korea. The production process goes through two departments, assembly and testing. The following information (in South Korean money called won) pertains to the testing department for the month of July.

International

Work-in-process inventory, July 1	4,000 units	
Transferred-in costs	38,800 won	(100 percent complete)
Costs added by the department		
Direct materials	23,400 won	(100 percent complete)
Conversion	23,360 won	(80 percent complete)

During the month of July, 15,000 units were transferred in from the assembly department at the cost of 141,700 won, and costs of 194,265 won were added by the mixing department.

Direct materials	84,125 won
Conversion	110,140 won

During the month, 16,000 units were completed and transferred to the warehouse. At July 31, the completion percentage of work-in-process was:

Direct materials	90 percent
Conversion	60 percent

Required

1. Prepare the production report of the testing department for the month of July, using the weighted-average process costing.

2. Check the most recent issue of *The Wall Street Journal* to find out the exchange rate between the U.S. dollar and the South Korean won.

13–41   **FIFO METHOD; TRANSFERRED-IN COSTS**   Wood Glow Manufacturing Company produces a single product, a wood refinishing kit that sells for $17.95. The final processing of the kits occurs in the packaging department. An internal quilted wrap is applied at the beginning of the packaging process. A compartmented outside box printed with instructions and the company's name and logo is added when units are 60 percent through the process. Conversion costs consisting of direct labor and applied overhead occur evenly throughout the packaging process. Conversion activities after the addition of the box involve package sealing, testing for leakage, and final inspection. Rejections in the packaging department are rare and may be ignored. The following data pertain to the activities of the packaging department during the month of October.

- Beginning work-in-process inventory was 10,000 units, 40 percent complete as to conversion costs.
- 30,000 units were started and completed in the month.
- There were 10,000 units in ending work-in-process, 80 percent complete as to conversion costs.

The packaging department's October costs were

Quilted wrap	$80,000
Outside boxes	50,000
Direct labor	22,000
Applied overhead ($3.00 per direct labor dollar)	66,000

The costs transferred in from prior processing were $3.00 per unit. The cost of goods sold for the month was $240,000, and the ending finished-goods inventory was $84,000. Wood Glow uses the first-in, first-out method of inventory valuation.

Wood Glow's controller, Mark Brandon, has been asked to analyze the activities of the packaging department for the month of October. Brandon knows that to properly determine the department's unit cost of production, he must first calculate the equivalent units of production.

Required

1. Prepare an equivalent units of production schedule for the October activity in the packaging department. Be sure to account for the beginning work-in-process inventory, the units started and completed during the month, and the ending work-in-process inventory.

2. Determine the cost per equivalent unit of the October production.

3. Assuming that the actual overhead incurred during October was $5,000 more than the overhead applied, describe how the value of the ending work-in-process inventory would be determined.

(CMA Adapted)

Ethics

13–42 FIFO METHOD Superior Brands, Inc., manufactures a medium-quality rubber cement product that goes through two departments. Cost and production data for the first department are given for June 19X8:

Work-in-process inventory, June 1	15,000 units
Conversion 40 percent complete	
Work-in-process inventory, June 30	25,000 units
Conversion 65 percent complete	
Units started into production	80,000 units
Units completed and transferred out	?
Costs	
Work-in-process inventory, June 1:	
Direct materials	$ 72,500
Conversion	12,937.50
Costs added during May	
Material A	260,000
Material B	403,750
Conversion	461,437.50

Material A is added at the beginning of work in the first department. Material B also is added in the first department, but it is not added until units of product are 50 percent complete with regard to conversion. Conversion costs are incurred uniformly during the process. The company uses the FIFO cost method.

Required

1. Calculate equivalent units of material A, material B, and conversion.

2. Calculate costs per equivalent unit for material A, material B, and conversion.

3. Calculate the cost of units transferred out.

4. Calculate the value of ending Work-in-Process Inventory.

5. Assume that you are the controller of Superior Brands, Inc., and the first department's June unit cost is higher than the target or standard

cost. If the manager of the first department asks you to do her a favor by increasing the ending inventory completion percentage from 65 to 80 percent to lower the unit costs, what should you do?

13–43 WEIGHTED-AVERAGE METHOD; TWO DEPARTMENTS An automotive exhaust system manufacturer has two departments in muffler processing, the fabrication and assembly departments. All materials for the fabrication department were added at the beginning. Data recorded for January 19X8 are

	Units	Percent Completed	Direct Materials	Conversion
Fabrication Department				
Work-in-process inventory, January 1	5,000	50%	$15,000	$20,000
Units transferred to assembly department in January	50,000			
Work-in-process inventory, January 31	3,000	30		
Assembly Department				
Work-in-process inventory, January 1 (Transferred-in cost: $78,000)	10,000	40		$200,000
Units completed and transferred out in January	55,000			
Work-in-process inventory, January 31	5,000	40		
Costs incurred in January:				
Fabrication department			$117,500	$310,850
Assembly department				$723,400

Required Calculate the following using the weighted-average method:

1. Equivalent units of direct materials and conversion in the fabrication department.
2. Unit costs of direct materials and conversion in the fabrication department.
3. Cost of goods transferred to the assembly department from the fabrication department in the month of January.
4. Cost of the work-in-process ending inventory in the fabrication department.
5. Equivalent units of transferred-in and conversion in the assembly department.
6. Unit costs of transferred-in and conversion in the assembly department.
7. Cost of the goods transferred to finished goods from the assembly department in January.
8. Cost of the work-in-process ending inventory in the assembly department.

13–44 FIFO METHOD; TWO DEPARTMENTS The Graybill Company produces plastic photo frames. There are two departments involved in the manufacturing: the molding department and the finishing department. In the molding department, molds are filled with hot liquid plastic, left to cool, and then opened. The finishing department removes the plastic frame from the mold and strips the edges of the frames of extra plastic. The following information is available for the month of January:

	January 1		January 31	
Work-in-process Inventory	Quantity (pounds)	Cost	Quantity (pounds)	Cost
Molding department	None	—	None	—
Finishing department	5,000	$15,000	2,000	?

The work-in-process inventory in the finishing department is estimated to be 25 percent complete both at the beginning and end of January. Costs of production for January are

Costs of Production	Materials Used	Conversion
Molding department	$300,000	$50,000
Finishing department	—	40,000

The material used in the molding department weighed 50,000 pounds. The firm uses the FIFO method of process costing.

Required Prepare reports for both the molding and finishing departments for the month of January. The answer should include: equivalent units of production (in pounds), total manufacturing costs, cost per equivalent unit (pounds), cost of ending work-in-process inventory, and cost of goods completed and transferred out.

13–45 WEIGHTED-AVERAGE METHOD; FIFO METHOD; TWO DEPARTMENTS

Porter Company's one product is manufactured by a process that requires two departments. The production starts in department A and is completed in department B. Materials are added at the beginning of the process in department A. Additional materials are added when the process is 50 percent complete in department B. Conversion costs are incurred proportionally throughout the production processes in both departments.

On April 1, department A had 500 units in production estimated to be 30 percent complete, while department B had 300 units in production estimated to be 40 percent complete. During April, department A started 1,500 units and completed 1,600 units, while department B completed 1,400 units. The work-in-process ending inventory on April 30 in department A is estimated to be 20 percent complete and the work-in-process ending inventory in department B is estimated to be 70 percent complete.

The cost sheet for department A shows that the units in the work-in-process beginning inventory had $3,000 in direct materials costs and $1,530 for conversion costs. The production element costs incurred in April were $12,000 for direct material and $10,710 for conversion. The work-in-process beginning inventory in department B on April 1 was $6,100. Department B incurred $38,000 in direct materials costs and $24,350 in conversion costs in April.

The cost per unit in March for department A is $14 per unit regardless of which process costing method is used in determining costs. Porter Company uses the FIFO method for department A and the weighted-average method for department B.

Required

1. Prepare a production cost report for department A.
2. Prepare a production cost report for department B.

13–46 (APPENDIX: SPOILAGE) WEIGHTED-AVERAGE METHOD; TRANSFERRED-IN COSTS

JC Company employs a process cost system. A unit of product passes through three departments—molding, assembly, and finishing—before it is completed. The following activity took place in the finishing department during May:

	Units
Work-in-process inventory—May 1	1,400
Units transferred in from the assembly department	14,000
Units spoiled	700
Units transferred out to finished goods inventory	11,200

Direct materials are added at the beginning of the processing in the finishing department without changing the number of units being processed. The work-in-process inventory was 70 percent complete as to conversion on May 1 and 40 percent complete as to conversion on May 31. All spoilage was discovered at final inspection before the units were transferred to finished goods; 560 of the units spoiled were considered acceptable.

JC Company employs the weighted-average costing method. The equivalent units and the current costs per equivalent unit of production for each cost factor are

	Equivalent Units	Current Costs per Equivalent Unit
Cost of prior department	15,400	$5.00
Direct materials	15,400	1.00
Conversion cost	13,300	3.00
		$9.00

Required

1. What is the cost of production transferred to the finished goods inventory?

2. What is the cost assigned to the work-in-process inventory on May 31?

3. If the total costs of prior departments included in the work-in-process inventory of the finishing department on May 1 amounted to $6,300, what is the total cost transferred in from the assembly department to the finishing department during May?

4. What is the cost associated with the abnormal spoilage?

(CMA Adapted)

13–47 **CHOOSING THE PROCESS COST METHOD** Peter Chou is a perfume company that produces a wide line of fragrances for men and women. Each fragrance has to go through certain cycles to acquire the desired scent. This information from February includes the production of perfume for Valentine's Day:

Strategy

	Units
Work-in-process inventory (February 1, 19X8)	3,750
Percent completed with respect to conversion	50%
Units started in February	41,250
Work-in-process inventory (February 28, 19X8) (50%)	4,000

Required

1. Prepare a schedule of equivalent units for Peter Chou for the month of February. Show the results for weighted-average and FIFO methods. Assume that direct materials are added at the beginning.

2. The following costs went into producing the fragrances this month. Calculate the total manufacturing costs and the costs of goods manufactured for February (use FIFO).

	Direct Materials	Conversion Costs	Total
Current cost	$82,500	$452,375	$534,875
Work-in-process inventory (February 1, 19X8)	5,250	6,000	11,250

3. How would the answer to requirement 2 change if the weighted-average method were used?

4. If the company takes a cost leadership strategy, which process costing method (weighted-average or FIFO) should the company adopt? Why?

13-48 CHOOSING THE PRODUCT COSTING SYSTEM The owner of Galletas Americanas, the cookie company, would like to choose a product costing system to assign production costs to the company's products. She has a choice of either a job costing system or a process costing system. The company produces different types of cookies such as chocolate chip, M&M, and peanut butter. All the different types are made of the same basic ingredients: flour, eggs, butter, and baking soda. The two production departments are the dough department and the baking department.

March 1 beginning work-in-process:

Direct materials: $500
Direct labor: 800 hours at $7.50 per hour
Factory overhead: $16,770
Direct materials cost incurred during March: $550
Conversion cost incurred during March: $23,800

The work-in-process balance on March 31 is zero. The units completed and transferred out in March total 3,100.

Required

1. Choose the most appropriate product costing system for Galletas Americanas and indicate why.

2. Compute the unit costs and explain the difference between the two methods.

Strategy

13-49 CHOOSING THE PROCESS COSTING METHOD Kristina Company, which manufactures quality paint sold at premium prices, uses a single production department. Production begins with the blending of various chemicals that are added at the beginning of the process and ends with the canning of the paint. Canning occurs when the mixture reaches the 90 percent stage of completion. The gallon cans are then transferred to the shipping department for crating and shipment. Labor and overhead are added continuously throughout the process. Factory overhead is applied on the basis of direct labor-hours at the rate of $3.00 per hour.

Prior to May, when a change in the process was implemented, work-in-process inventories were insignificant. The change in the process allows greater production but results in considerable amounts of work-in-process for the first time. The company always has used the weighted-average method to determine equivalent production and unit costs. Now, production management is considering changing from the weighted-average method to the FIFO method.

These data relate to actual production during the month of May:

	Costs for May
Work-in-process inventory, May 1	
(4,000 gallons 25 percent complete):	
Direct materials—chemicals	$45,600
Direct labor ($10 per hour)	6,250
Factory overhead	1,875
May costs added:	
Direct materials—chemicals	228,400
Direct materials—cans	7,000
Direct labor ($10 per hour)	35,000
Factory overhead	10,500

	Units for May
Work-in-process inventory, May 1 (25 percent complete)	4,000
Sent to shipping department	20,000
Started in May	21,000
Work-in-process inventory, May 31 (80 percent complete)	5,000

Required

1. Prepare a schedule of equivalent units for each cost element for

the month of May using the weighted-average method and then the first-in, first-out method.

2. Calculate the cost (to the nearest cent) per equivalent unit for each cost element for the month of May using the weighted-average method and the first-in, first-out method.

3. If the company takes a cost leadership strategy, which process costing method (weighted-average or FIFO) should the company adopt? Why?

(CMA Adapted)

13–50 FIFO METHOD Trezevant and Wang, an individual income tax preparation firm, uses the FIFO method of process costing for the monthly reports. The following shows its March 19X8 information:

Service

Returns in process, March 1 (30% complete)	100
Returns started in March	1,100
Returns in process, March 31 (90% complete)	200
Labor and overhead costs for returns in process, March 1	$330
Labor and overhead costs incurred in March	$138,000

Required Calculate the following amounts using the FIFO method:

1. Equivalent units
2. Cost per equivalent unit
3. Cost of completed returns for the month of March
4. Cost of returns in process as of March 31

SOLUTIONS TO SELF-STUDY PROBLEMS

1. Weighted-Average Method vs. FIFO Method

1. Weighted-Average Method

SMITH ELECTRONIC COMPANY
Chip-Mounting Production Department
Weighted-Average Production Cost Report

Production Quantity Information

	(Step 1)	(Step 2)	
		Equivalent Units	
	Physical Units	**Direct Materials**	**Conversion Costs**
Input			
Work-in-process beginning inventory	300		
Completion percentage:			
Direct materials 0 percent			
Conversion 40 percent			
Started this period	900		
Total units to account for	1,200		
Output			
Completed	1,000	1,000	1,000
Work-in-process ending inventory	200		
Completion percentage:			
Direct materials 100 percent		200	
Conversion 70 percent			140
Total units accounted for	1,200		
Total work done to date (Total equivalent units)		1,200	1,140

(continued)

Cost Determination

(Step 3) Costs Incurred	Total	Direct Materials	Conversion Costs
Work-in-process beginning inventory	$ 2,202		$2,202
Current cost	15,720	$9,600	$6,120
Total costs to account for	$17,922	$9,600	$8,322
(Step 4)		($9,600/1,200)	($8,322/1,140)
Cost per equivalent unit	$ 15.30	$ 8.00	$ 7.30

Cost Assignment

(Step 5)	Total	Direct Materials	Conversion Costs
Units completed and transferred out	$15,300 (= $15.30 × 1,000)		
Work-in-process ending inventory	2,622	(200 × $8) $1,600	(140 × $7.30) $1,022
Total manufacturing costs accounted for	$17,922		

2. FIFO METHOD

SMITH ELECTRONIC COMPANY
Chip-Mounting Production Department
FIFO Production Cost Report

Production Quantity Information

	(Step 1)	(Step 2) Equivalent Units	
	Physical Units	Direct Materials	Conversion Costs
Input			
Work-in-process beginning inventory	300		
Completion percentage:			
Direct materials 0 percent		0	
Conversion 40 percent			120
Started this period	900		
Total units to account for	1,200		
Output			
Completed	1,000	1,000	1,000
Work-in-process ending inventory	200		
Completion percentage:			
Direct materials 100 percent		200	
Conversion 70 percent			140
Total units accounted for	1,200		
Total work done to date		1,200	1,140
Work-in-process beginning inventory	300	-0	-120
Total work done this period (Total equivalent units)		1,200	1,020

(continued)

Cost Determination

(Step 3) Costs Incurred	Total	Direct Materials	Conversion Costs
Work-in-process beginning inventory	$ 2,202		$2,202
Current cost	15,720	$9,600	6,120
Total costs to account for	$17,922	$9,600	$8,322
(Step 4)		($9,600/1,200)	($6,120/1,020)
Cost per equivalent unit	$14.00	$8.00	$6.00

Cost Assignment

(Step 5)	Total	Direct Materials	Conversion Costs
Units completed (1,000): From work-in-process beginning inventory	$ 2,202		
Current costs incurred completing units	3,480	(300 × $8) = $2,400	(180 × $6) = $1,080
Total cost from beginning inventory	$ 5,682		
Units started and completed this period	9,800	[$8(1,000 − 300) + $6(1,000 − 300)] = $14(1,000 − 300)	
Total cost of units completed and transferred out	$15,482		
Work-in-process ending inventory	2,440	(200 × $8) = $1,600	(140 × $6) = $840
Total costs accounted for	$17,922		

2. Weighted-Average Method vs. FIFO Method with Transferred-In Cost

1. Weighted-Average Method

REED COMPANY
Finishing Department
Weighted-Average Production Cost Report

Production Quantity Information

	(Step 1)	(Step 2)		
		Equivalent Units		
	Physical Units	Transferred in	Direct Materials	Conversion Costs
Input				
Work-in-process, November 1	10 (40%)			
Started this month	80			
Total units to account for	90			
Output				
Completed	82	82	82	82
Work-in-process, November 30	8 (50%)	8	8	4
Total units accounted for	90			
Total work done to date (Total equivalent units)		90	90	86

(continued)

Unit Cost Determination

(Step 3) Costs Incurred	Total	Transferred- in	Direct Materials	Conversion Costs
Work-in-process, November 1	$ 232	$ 100	$ 80	$ 52
Current costs	2,381	800	720	861
Total costs to account for	$2,613	$ 900	$ 800	$ 913
(Step 4)		($900/90)	($800/90)	($913/86)
Cost per unit	$29.51	$10.00	$ 8.89	$10.62

Cost Assignment

(Step 5)	Total	Transferred- in	Direct Materials	Conversion Costs
Units completed (82):	$2,420 = 82 × $29.51			
Work-in-process, November 30 (8)	193	(8 × $10) = $80	(8 × $8.89) = $71	(4 × $10.62) = $42
Total costs accounted for	$2,613			

2. FIFO Method

REED COMPANY
Finishing Department
FIFO Production Cost Report

Production Quantity Information

	(Step 1)	(Step 2)		
		Equivalent Units		
	Physical Units	Transferred- in	Direct Materials	Conversion Costs
Input				
Work-in-process, November 1	10 (40%)			
Started this month	80			
Total units to account for	90			
Output				
Completed	82	82	82	82
Work-in-process, November 30	8 (50%)	8	8	4
Total units accounted for	90			
Total work done to date		90	90	86
Work-in-process, November 1		−10	−10	− 4
Total work done this month—				
Total equivalent units		80	80	82

Unit Cost Determination

(Step 3) Costs Incurred	Total	Transferred- in	Direct Materials	Conversion Costs
Work-in-process, November 1	$ 232			
Current costs	2,381	$ 800	$ 720	$ 861
Total costs to account for	$2,613			
(Step 4)		($800/80)	($720/80)	($861/82)
Cost per unit	$29.50	$10.00	$ 9.00	$10.50

(continued)

Cost Assignment

(Step 5)	Total	Transferred-in	Direct Materials	Conversion Costs
Units completed (82):				
From work-in-process, November 1 (10)	$ 232			(6 × $10.50)
Current costs added	63			= $63
Total from beginning inventory	$ 295			
Units started and completed (82 − 10 = 72)	2,124	(72 × $10) + (72 × $9) + (72 × $10.5) = 72 × $29.50		
Total cost of units completed and transferred out	$2,419			
Work in process, November 30 (8)	194	(8 × $10) = $80	(8 × $9) = $72	(4 × $10.5) = $42
Total costs accounted for	$2,613			

Cost Allocation: Service Departments and Joint Product Costs

Amy C. Etra/Photo Edit

After studying the chapter, you should be able to . . .

Identify the objectives of cost allocation **1**

Explain the strategic role of cost allocation **2**

Use the three steps of departmental cost allocation **3**

Explain the problems in implementing the different **4** departmental cost allocation methods

Explain the use of cost allocation in service firms **5**

Use the three joint product costing methods **6**

Use the four by-product costing methods **7**

Everything should be made as simple as possible, but not more so.

ALBERT EINSTEIN

One of the most pervasive problems in management accounting is determining how the costs of a shared facility, program, production process, or service should be allocated among its users. Solving this problem is called *cost allocation*. Cost allocation arises in two main contexts, both of which are covered in this chapter: (1) departmental cost allocation and (2) joint product costing. Cost allocation can become quite complex if the number of facilities, processes, products, users, and relationships among them becomes large. In allocating costs, management accountants must focus on a small number of objectives, as Einstein's statement suggests, to keep the allocation simple and interpretable.

OBJECTIVES OF COST ALLOCATION

The objectives of cost allocation are to achieve effective cost management through methods that:

1. *Motivate* managers to exert a high level of effort to achieve the goals of top management.
2. Provide the right *incentive* for managers to make decisions that are consistent with the goals of top management.
3. *Fairly determine the rewards* earned by the managers for their effort and skill, and for the effectiveness of their decision making.

To achieve the first objective, motivating managers, cost allocation can be designed to reward department managers and product managers for reducing costs as desired. A key motivation issue is whether the allocated cost is *controllable* by the manager. For example, when a department's cost allocation for equipment maintenance is based on the number of machine breakdowns in that department, the manager has an incentive to reduce the breakdowns and therefore reduce the maintenance costs. On the other hand, when the cost of maintenance is allocated on the basis of a department's square feet of floor space, the manager—who cannot affect the amount of floor space—is not motivated.

◀ **LEARNING OBJECTIVE 1**
Identify the objectives of cost allocation.

The second objective, providing the incentive for decision making consistent with management's goals, is achieved when cost allocation effectively addresses the incentives of the individual manager, including the manager's relative risk aversion (see the section entitled "The Effect of Risk Preferences on Motivation and Decision Making" in Chapter 3).

BusinessWeek

❓ What's the Skinny on Cost Reduction?

General Electric (GE) is working hard to reduce the costs of its products and services. One technique is to improve work processes that speed the production of appliances and reduce inventories. GE is looking at administrative services as well, including such tasks as payroll, billing customers, and paying vendors. So is Union Carbide Corporation, which was alarmed to find that it spent almost $10 processing a single vendor invoice for payment. These firms were concerned that administrative services were too costly and needed the close look that had been given to production costs in earlier years. Ford, Xerox, and Johnson & Johnson are pursuing the same idea.

Q: How are these firms getting their arms around administrative costs?   *Find out on page 545 of this chapter.*

The third objective, fairness, is met when the cost allocation is clear, objective, and consistently applied. The most objective basis for cost allocation exists when a *cause-and-effect relationship* can be determined. For example, the allocation of maintenance costs on the basis of the number of equipment breakdowns is more objective and more fair than an allocation based on square feet, the number of products produced, or labor costs in the department. The reason is the objective cause-and-effect relationship between maintenance costs and the number of breakdowns; square feet or labor costs do not have a close relationship to maintenance costs.

In some situations, cause-and-effect bases are not available and alternative concepts of fairness are used. One such concept is *ability-to-bear*, which is commonly employed with bases related to size, such as total sales, total assets, or the profitability of the user departments. Other concepts of fairness are based on equity perceived in the circumstance, such as *benefit received*, which often is measured in a nonquantitative way. For example, the cost of a firm's computer services might be allocated largely or entirely to the research and development department because the computer is more critical to this department's functioning and is used by this department more than other departments.

THE STRATEGIC AND ETHICAL ROLES OF COST ALLOCATION

LEARNING OBJECTIVE 2 ▶
Explain the strategic role of cost allocation.

A number of strategic and ethical issues are important in cost allocation. First, ethical issues arise when costs are allocated for products or services that are produced for both a competitive market and a public agency or government department. Although government agencies very often purchase on a cost-plus basis, products sold competitively are subject to price competition. The incentive in these situations is for the manufacturer, using cost allocation methods, to shift manufacturing costs from the competitive products to the cost-plus products. Evidence of this was shown in a 1984 study reported by former Secretary of the Navy John F. Lehman. The study, performed for the Navy by a CPA firm, found that defense contractors' profits on military work were higher than profits on nonmilitary work.

A second and related issue in implementing cost allocation methods is the equity or fair share issue that arises when government reimburses the costs of a private institution, or when government provides a service for a fee to the public. In both cases, cost allocation methods are used to determine the proper price or reimbursement amount. While there is no single measure of equity in these cases, the

---

Cost Basis for Governmental Services: The Federal Aviation Agency

Because of an expected shortfall in the federal government's aviation trust fund, the Federal Aviation Agency (FAA) must look for ways to reduce costs. Some suggestions include:

1. Determine the cost of providing the FAA's services. For example, no one knows the costs of providing the air traffic control (ATC) system, even though the ATC is approximately 70 percent of the FAA's budget. Based on accurate cost information, users of the ATC could be charged fairly for the services provided.

2. The importance of charging for the use of the ATC system is illustrated by the fact that ATC controllers spend as much time directing a small, twin-engine business jet as a large commercial aircraft. Why not have the airlines pay for each minute that the controller speaks to the aircraft pilots? Perhaps a formula also could be devised that would charge the smaller aircraft at a lower rate, using the "ability to bear" principle. But the service would not be free to all.

3. The FAA should charge aircraft manufacturers for its licensing and certification services. FAA's David Hinson says FAA engineers spent 125,000 hours on Boeing's new 777. There should have been a large fee for this service.

Similar arguments could be made about the nation's interstate highways and coastal and intercostal navigation systems.

Source: Based on information in "How to End the Free Ride at the FAA," *Business Week*, May 6, 1997, p. 36.

objectives of cost allocation identified at the beginning of the chapter are a useful guide.

A good example of the equity issue in cost allocation is the reimbursement of large research universities for what is called overhead on research projects sponsored by the government. The payment of overhead is intended to reimburse the university for the cost of facilities and other expenses necessary to maintain the faculty and equipment for the research. Sometimes, what is considered an indirect cost for this purpose is a matter of judgment. For example, in 1990 Stanford University was investigated by federal auditors who found that the overhead charges included expenses for the dining and entertainment areas of the university president's home. These costs were denied, the university repaid some of the overcharges, and the overhead rate was reduced by the Office of the Chief of Naval Research.[1]

A third important strategic issue in cost allocation is the effect of the chosen allocation method on the costs of products sold to or from foreign subsidiaries. The cost allocation method usually affects the cost of products traded internationally and therefore the amount of taxes paid in the domestic and the foreign countries. Firms can reduce their worldwide tax liability by increasing the costs of products purchased in high-tax countries, or countries where the firm does not have favorable tax treatment. For this reason, international tax authorities closely watch the cost allocation methods used by multinational firms. The methods most acceptable to these authorities are based on sales and/or labor costs.[2]

A major advantage of cost allocation systems is that they draw managers' attention to shared facilities. The cost allocation provides a strong incentive for individual and team efforts to manage the cost of these facilities. Also, it can have the benefit of reminding managers of the service and thereby encouraging them to use it. For example, allocation of corporate overhead components such as data processing can have the effect of reminding managers of this corporate service. It thereby can encourage managers to use these services to improve the performance of their units.

BusinessWeek

What's the Secret to GE and Union Carbide's Cost Reduction Diet?

(Continues from page 543.)

A: Eliminate low-value activities!...

General Electric, Union Carbide, and other firms are giving closer scrutiny to their administrative costs, particularly the finance function costs of sending out bills to customers, preparing the payroll, and paying vendors. They are finding that the main way to manage and reduce these costs is to consolidate and centralize operations. The effect is that there are fewer service functions (or departments) than in the past, and these are done only at regional, divisional, or even corporate offices. The idea is that rather than to focus on the proper *allocation* of service department costs, the firm is alternatively looking for ways to *eliminate* these costs. This approach is consistent with the strategic methods described in Chapter 2, for example, the value chain. The firm examines all the activities in the value chain it is involved in to produce a valued product or service, and pinpoints those activities that give the firm a competitive advantage. The noncritical activities are outsourced, reduced, or eliminated altogether. This is how GE, Union Carbide, and other firms are looking at their administrative service department.

For further reading, see "A Day of Reckoning for Bean Counters," *Business Week*, March 14, 1994, pp. 75–76.

---

[1]   "Navy Cuts Interim Overhead Rate," *The Stanford Observer*, March–April 1991.

[2]   Eric G. Tomsett, "Allocation of Central Costs in an International Group," *World Tax* (a publication of Deloitte & Touche International), January 1992.

SERVICE AND PRODUCTION DEPARTMENT COST ALLOCATION

LEARNING OBJECTIVE 3 ▶
Use the three steps of departmental cost allocation.

The preceding chapters on job costing (Chapter 12) and process costing (Chapter 13) provide a useful context for introducing cost allocation. In those chapters we saw that overhead costs are allocated either directly to products (job costing), or indirectly in an allocation first to production departments and then to the products (process costing), as illustrated in Exhibit 14–1. The direct allocation approach pools all overhead into a single amount and allocates overhead using a single rate. In contrast, the departmental approach pools overhead costs in departmental cost pools and allocates overhead from each department to the products using a separate rate, one for each department. We explain in Chapter 12 that the departmental allocation is preferred because it more accurately traces overhead costs to the products that use these costs. This is particularly important when different products require different amounts of resources in the various production departments.

In this further refinement of the departmental approach, we recognize that overhead costs are incurred in service departments as well as production departments. Service departments provide human resources, maintenance, engineering and other services to the production departments, while production departments directly assemble and complete the product. There are three phases to this extended departmental approach: (1) trace all direct costs and allocate overhead costs to both the service departments and the production departments, (2) allocate the service department costs to the production departments, and finally (3) allocate the production

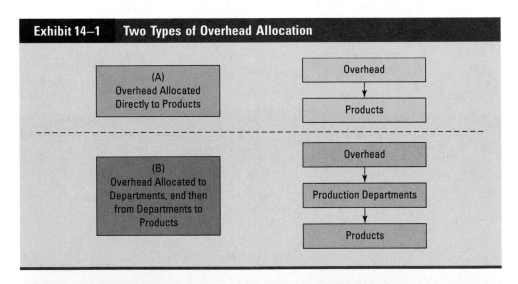

Exhibit 14–1   Two Types of Overhead Allocation

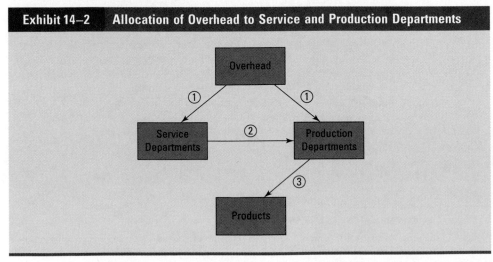

Exhibit 14–2   Allocation of Overhead to Service and Production Departments

department costs to the products. These steps are illustrated in Exhibit 14–2. This allocation is more accurate than the departmental method illustrated in Chapter 12 because service department costs are included.[3]

This section explains the common methods for allocating service and production department costs to a firm's products and services. We assume here that costs directly traceable to a department are charged directly to that department. A cost can be traced when there is a clear cause-and-effect relationship between the cost and the cost object. For example, the cost of paint used in the painting department is directly traceable to the painting department. When the cost cannot be directly traced to a department or product, then cost allocation comes into play.

The three phases of cost allocation are illustrated in Exhibit 14–3.

First Phase: Initial Allocation to Departments

The first phase in departmental cost allocation has two parts: (1) to trace the direct manufacturing costs in the plant to each service and production department that used them, and (2) to identify the indirect manufacturing costs in the plant and allocate them to each of the service and production departments.

For the first-phase allocation, see the information for the Beary Manufacturing Company in Exhibit 14–4. Beary manufactures two products and has two manufacturing departments and two service departments. Two types of indirect costs are common to all four departments—indirect labor and indirect materials. Beary uses both labor-hours and machine-hours for allocating the indirect costs.

Look at the first-phase allocation for the Beary Company in the first-phase panel of Exhibit 14–5. Total direct costs of $36,000 are traced directly to the four departments, while the indirect costs are allocated using labor-hours (for indirect labor) and machine-hours (for indirect materials). At the top of the exhibit, the allocation bases contain information about labor-hour and machine-hour usage.

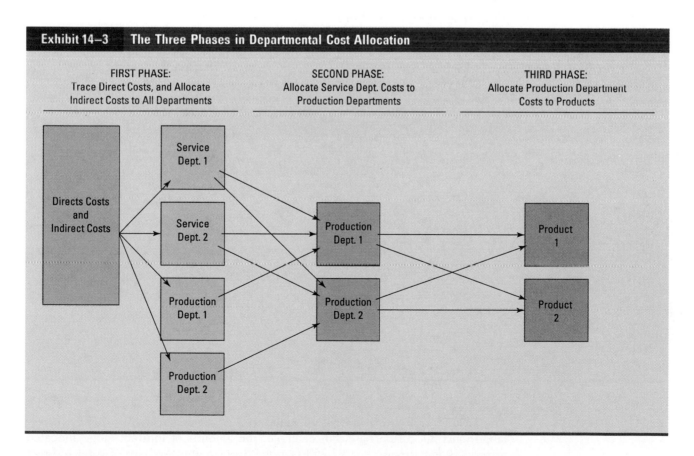

Exhibit 14–3   The Three Phases in Departmental Cost Allocation

FIRST PHASE:
Trace Direct Costs, and Allocate Indirect Costs to All Departments

SECOND PHASE:
Allocate Service Dept. Costs to Production Departments

THIRD PHASE:
Allocate Production Department Costs to Products

---

[3]   Activity-based costing (Chapter 4) can be viewed as an additional refinement of these methods because it takes the allocation one step further, from the department to the individual production activity.

| Exhibit 14–4 | Data for Beary Manufacturing Company |

	Service Department 1	Service Department 2	Production Department 1	Production Department 2	Total
Labor-hours	1,800	1,200	3,600	5,400	12,000
Machine-hours	320	160	1,120	1,600	3,200
Direct costs	$1,600	$5,500	$15,500	$13,400	$36,000
Indirect labor					$25,000
Indirect materials	←		Not Traceable	→	$ 5,000

| Exhibit 14–5 | Departmental Allocation Using the Direct Method (Beary Company) |

		Departments				Product	Product	
Departmental Allocation Bases	Base	Service 1	Service 2	Production 1	Production 2	1	2	Total
Direct labor-hour (DLH)		1,800	1,200	3,600	5,400			12,000
percent		15%	10%	30%	45%			100%
Machine-hour (MH)		320	160	1,120	1,600			3,200
percent		10%	5%	35%	50%			100%
FIRST PHASE: Trace Direct Costs and Perform Initial Allocation of Indirect Costs								
Direct costs		$ 1,600	$ 5,500	$ 15,500	$ 13,400			$36,000
Indirect costs:								
Indirect Labor	DLH	3,750	2,500	7,500	11,250			$25,000
		= .15 × $25,000	= .1 × $25,000	= .3 × $25,000	= .45 × $25,000			
Indirect Materials	MH	500	250	1,750	2,500			$ 5,000
		= .1 × $5,000	= .05 × $5,000	= .35 × $5,000	= .5 × $5,000			
Totals for all departments		**$ 5,850**	**$ 8,250**	**$ 24,750**	**$ 27,150**			**$66,000**
SECOND PHASE: Reallocate Service Department Costs to Production Departments: The Direct Method								
Service 1 Service percent to producing departments				30%	30%			
Allocation percent per the direct method				50.0% = 30%/60%	50.0% = 30%/60%			
Allocation amount		$(5,850)		$ 2,925 = .3 × $5,850	$ 2,925 = .3 × $5,850			
Service 2 Service percent to producing departments				30%	60%			
Allocation percent per the direct method				33.33% = 30%/90%	66.67% = 60%/90%			
Allocation amount			$(8,250)	$ 2,750 = ⅓ × $8,250	$ 5,500 = ⅔ × $8,250			
Totals for production departments				**$ 30,425**	**$ 35,575**			**$66,000**
THIRD PHASE: Allocate Production Department Costs to Products								
Base: Direct labor-hours for each product						1,800	1,800	3,600
percent						50%	50%	
Machine-hours						400	1,200	1,600
percent						25%	75%	
Production 1	DLH			$(30,425)		$15,213 = .5 × $30,425	$15,213 = .5 × $30,425	
Production 2	MH				$(35,575)	8,894 = .25 × $35,575	26,681 = .75 × $35,575	
Totals for each product*						**$24,106**	**$41,894**	**$66,000**

*Small differences due to rounding.

The $25,000 of indirect labor is allocated to the four departments using the direct labor-hours allocation base. For example, the amount of indirect labor allocated to service department 1 is $3,750 (service department 1's share of total indirect labor, or 15% × $25,000). The allocations of indirect labor costs to the other departments are done in the same way. Similarly, the $5,000 of indirect materials cost is allocated to the four departments using machine-hours. The amount of indirect materials allocated to service department 1 is $500 (.1 × $5,000). The totals for direct costs and allocated indirect costs are

Service department 1	$ 5,850
Service department 2	8,250
Production department 1	24,750
Production department 2	27,150
Total	$66,000

Second Phase: Allocation of Service Department Costs to Production Departments

The second phase allocates the costs from the service departments to the producing departments. This is the most complex of the allocation phases because services flow back and forth between the service departments. Often these are called **reciprocal flows.** For example, assume that 40 percent (720 hours) of service department 1's 1,800 labor hours are spent serving service department 2. Also, assume that 10 percent of service department 2's time is spent serving service department 1. You can see these two reciprocal flows for the Beary Company in Exhibit 14–6.

The percentage of service relationships is commonly determined by reference to labor-hours, units processed, or some other allocation base that best reflects the service provided in the departments. In the Beary Company, the service flow percentages for each service department are determined by the labor-hours used for services provided to the other service department and the production departments. Beary Company's first service department spends 40 percent of its labor time serving the second service department and 30 percent serving each of the two production departments. The second service department serves the first service department 10 percent of the time, the first production department 30 percent of the time, and the second production department 60 percent of the time.

Accountants use three common methods to allocate costs from one department to another when there are reciprocal flows. There are three methods for allocating the costs of the service departments. Each of these methods provides a means for dealing with reciprocal service department flows: (1) the direct method, (2) the step method, and (3) the reciprocal method.

The Direct Method

The **direct method** is the simplest of the three methods because it ignores the reciprocal flows. The cost allocation is done by using the service flows *only to production departments* and determining each production department's share of that service. For example, for the first service department, the share of time for each production department is 50 percent of the total production department service.

> **Reciprocal flows** represent the movement of services back and forth between service departments.

> The **direct method** of cost allocation is done by using the service flows *only to production departments* and determining each production department's share of that service.

Exhibit 14–6 Reciprocal Relationships in Beary Company

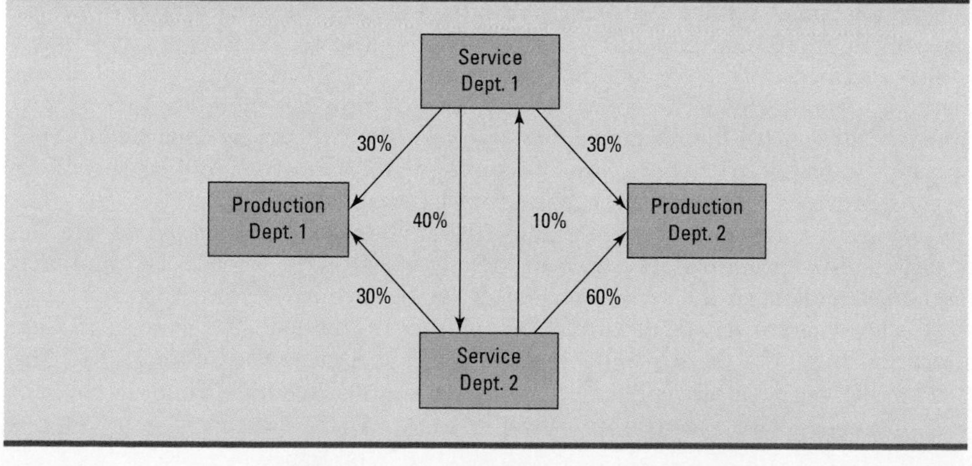

For the first service department:

Net service to both production departments for service department 1:
= 100% − time of service to second service department
= 100% − 40% = 60%

Production department 1's share: 30 percent/60 percent = 50 percent

Production department 2's share: 30 percent/60 percent = 50 percent

For the second service department:

Net service to both production departments for service department 2:
100 percent − 10 percent = 90 percent

Production department 1's share: 30 percent/90 percent = 33.33%

Production department 2's share: 60 percent/90 percent = 66.67%

These percentage shares are used to allocate the costs from service departments to production departments, as shown in the second-phase panel of Exhibit 14–5. In that panel, for example, $5,850 of service department 1's costs are allocated equally to the production departments; 50 percent each is $2,925. The $8,250 of service department 2's costs are allocated one-third or $2,750 to the first production department and two-thirds or $5,500 to the second production department. Total costs in the first and second production departments at the end of the phase-two allocations are $30,425 and $35,575, respectively.

The third and final phase is much like the first phase. The allocation from production departments to products typically is based on the labor-hours or machine-hours in the production departments where the products are produced. For the Beary Company, production department 1 is allocated on the basis of labor-hours, and production department 2 is allocated on the basis of machine-hours; see the third-phase panel of Exhibit 14–5. The production of product 1 required 1,800 of production department 1's total labor time of 3,600, and thus is allocated 50 percent (1,800/3,600) of the total cost in production department 1. Similarly, because product 1 required 400 of the 1,600 machine-hours used in production department 2, it is allocated 25 percent (400/1,600) of the costs of production department 2. Product 2's costs are determined in a similar manner, as shown in Exhibit 14–5. The total cost of $66,000 is allocated as $24,106 to product 1 and $41,894 to product 2.

The Step Method

The **step method** uses a sequence of steps in the allocation of service department costs to production departments.

The second method for allocating service department costs is the **step method,** so-called because it uses a sequence of steps in the allocation of service department costs to production departments. In the first step, one of the service departments is selected to be allocated fully, that is, to the other service department as well as to each of the production departments. The department to be allocated fully usually is chosen based on the amount of service to other service departments. Because Beary Company's service department 1 provides more service (40%) to service department 2 (10%) it goes first in the allocation. The second service department is allocated only to the production departments in the same manner as the direct method. Overall, this means that the step method provides more accurate allocations because one of the reciprocal flows between the two service departments (the one in the first step) is taken into account in the allocation, unlike the direct method in which all the reciprocal flows are ignored.

Looking at the step method in Exhibit 14–7, notice that the first phase (tracing of direct costs and initial allocation of indirect costs) is the same as for the direct method. However, in the second phase, service department 1, which is in the first step, is allocated to service department 2 and the two production departments. The allocation to service department 2 is $2,340 (.4 × $5,850). The allocations for the two production departments are determined in a similar manner. Then, in the sec-

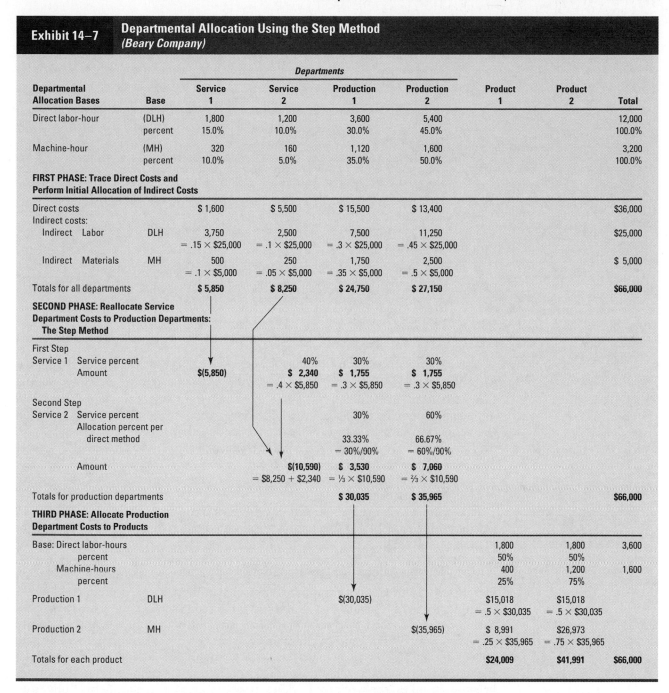

Exhibit 14–7 **Departmental Allocation Using the Step Method**
(Beary Company)

Departmental Allocation Bases	Base	Service 1	Service 2	Production 1	Production 2	Product 1	Product 2	Total
Direct labor-hour	(DLH)	1,800	1,200	3,600	5,400			12,000
	percent	15.0%	10.0%	30.0%	45.0%			100.0%
Machine-hour	(MH)	320	160	1,120	1,600			3,200
	percent	10.0%	5.0%	35.0%	50.0%			100.0%

FIRST PHASE: Trace Direct Costs and Perform Initial Allocation of Indirect Costs

	Base	Service 1	Service 2	Production 1	Production 2	Product 1	Product 2	Total
Direct costs		$ 1,600	$ 5,500	$ 15,500	$ 13,400			$36,000
Indirect costs:								
Indirect Labor	DLH	3,750	2,500	7,500	11,250			$25,000
		= .15 × $25,000	= .1 × $25,000	= .3 × $25,000	= .45 × $25,000			
Indirect Materials	MH	500	250	1,750	2,500			$ 5,000
		= .1 × $5,000	= .05 × $5,000	= .35 × $5,000	= .5 × $5,000			
Totals for all departments		**$ 5,850**	**$ 8,250**	**$ 24,750**	**$ 27,150**			**$66,000**

SECOND PHASE: Reallocate Service Department Costs to Production Departments: The Step Method

	Base	Service 1	Service 2	Production 1	Production 2	Product 1	Product 2	Total
First Step								
Service 1 Service percent			40%	30%	30%			
Amount		$(5,850)	$ 2,340	$ 1,755	$ 1,755			
			= .4 × $5,850	= .3 × $5,850	= .3 × $5,850			
Second Step								
Service 2 Service percent				30%	60%			
Allocation percent per direct method				33.33%	66.67%			
				= 30%/90%	= 60%/90%			
Amount			$(10,590)	$ 3,530	$ 7,060			
			= $8,250 + $2,340	= ⅓ × $10,590	= ⅔ × $10,590			
Totals for production departments				**$ 30,035**	**$ 35,965**			**$66,000**

THIRD PHASE: Allocate Production Department Costs to Products

	Base	Service 1	Service 2	Production 1	Production 2	Product 1	Product 2	Total
Base: Direct labor-hours						1,800	1,800	3,600
percent						50%	50%	
Machine-hours						400	1,200	1,600
percent						25%	75%	
Production 1	DLH			$(30,035)		$15,018	$15,018	
						= .5 × $30,035	= .5 × $30,035	
Production 2	MH				$(35,965)	$ 8,991	$26,973	
						= .25 × $35,965	= .75 × $35,965	
Totals for each product						**$24,009**	**$41,991**	**$66,000**

ond step, service department 2 is allocated to the two production departments using the direct method in the same manner as in Exhibit 14–5. The only difference is that the total cost in service department 2 ($10,590) is now the combination of the original cost in service department 2 ($8,250) plus the cost allocated from service department 1 in the first step ($2,340).

The third phase of the step method is completed in the same manner as for Exhibit 14–5. The only difference is that the total costs in the two production departments are different. Using the step method, the total cost allocated to product 1 is $24,009 and the total cost allocated to product 2 is $41,991, for a total of $66,000.

The Reciprocal Method

The **reciprocal method** is the most preferred of the three methods because, unlike the others, it takes into account *all* the reciprocal flows between the service departments. This is accomplished by using simultaneous equations; the reciprocal flows are simultaneously determined in a system of equations.

The **reciprocal method** takes into account all the reciprocal flows between service departments through simultaneous equations.

Each service department has an equation to represent the cost to be allocated, consisting of the first-phase allocation costs plus the cost allocated from the other department. For Beary Company, the equation for the first service department is as follows, using the symbol S1 to represent service department 1 and the symbol S2 to represent service department 2.

Allocated S1 Costs = Initial allocation + Cost allocated from S2

$$S1 = \$5,850 + .1 \times S2$$

Similarly, the equation for the second service department is as follows:

Allocated S2 Costs = Initial allocation + Cost allocated from S1

$$S2 = \$8,250 + .4 \times S1$$

These two equations can be solved for S1 and S2 by substituting the second equation into the first as follows:

$$S1 = \$5,850 + .1 \times (\$8,250 + .4 \times S1)$$

$$S1 = \$6,953.13$$

And substituting S1 back into the second equation:[4]

$$S2 = \$11,031.25$$

These values for S1 and S2 are allocated to the producing departments using the percentage service figures for each department. We illustrate the process for the Beary Company in Exhibit 14–8. Note that since the reciprocal method has taken all reciprocal service department activities into account, the allocation is based on the actual service percentages for each production department. For example, production department 1, which receives 30 percent of service department 1's work, is allocated 30 percent of service department 1's cost, $2,086 (.3 × $6,953.13). The allocations are done in a similar manner for service department 2's costs and for production department 2.

The third phase analysis in Exhibit 14–8 is done in the same manner as in Exhibits 14–5 and 14–7. The total cost allocated to product 1 is $24,036 and for product 2, $41,964.

Third Phase: Allocation to Products

For the third phase, allocating production department costs to products, look at Exhibits 14–5, 14–7, and 14–8. Note that while total costs are the same ($66,000), the amounts allocated to the two products vary. Although these amounts do not vary greatly at Beary Company, in practice, wide variations can occur. When there are significant differences, a management accountant should consider the value of the reciprocal method, which is more complete and accurate than the others because it takes the reciprocal flows between service departments fully into account.

---

[4] The solution of equations explained here can become very tedious for three or more service departments. In this case, spreadsheet and other software programs such as LOTUS 1–2–3 or EXCEL can be used. In EXCEL, the solution requires the use of the functions MINVERSE and MMULT, which perform the matrix operations to determine the inverse of a matrix and the product of two matrices, respectively. In LOTUS 1–2–3, the functions for matrix inversion and multiplication are under the Range/Analyze menu. To solve the equations in matrix format, first obtain the equations in the following form (for the Beary Company data):

$$S1 - .1S2 = 5,850$$

$$-.4S1 + S2 = 8,250$$

There are three matrices: the A matrix is taken from the above coefficients (1, −.1; −.4, 1); the B matrix is (5850, 8250); the C matrix is the solution that equals the inverse of A multiplied by B.

Exhibit 14–8	**Departmental Allocation Using the Reciprocal Method** *(Beary Company)*

| | | **Departments** | | | | | | |
Departmental Allocation Bases	Base	Service 1	Service 2	Production 1	Production 2	Product 1	Product 2	Total
Direct labor-hour	(DLH)	1,800	1,200	3,600	5,400			12,000
	percent	15.0%	10.0%	30.0%	45.0%			100.0%
Machine-hour	(MH)	320	160	1,120	1,600			3,200
	percent	10.0%	5.0%	35.0%	50.0%			100.0%

FIRST PHASE: Trace Direct Costs and
Perform Initial Allocation of Indirect Costs

Direct costs		$1,600	$5,500	$ 15,500	$ 13,400			$36,000
Indirect costs:								
Indirect Labor	DLH	3,750	2,500	7,500	11,250			$25,000
		= .15 × $25,000	= .1 × $25,000	= .3 × $25,000	= .45 × $25,000			
Indirect Materials	MH	500	250	1,750	2,500			$ 5,000
		− .1 × $5,000	= .05 × $5,000	= .35 × $5,000	= .5 × $5,000			
Totals for all departments		**$5,850**	**$8,250**	**$ 24,750**	**$ 27,150**			**$66,000**

SECOND PHASE: Reallocate Service
Department Costs to Production Departments:
  The Reciprocal Method

First: Solve the simultaneous equations for Service 1 and Service 2:
  Amount allocated from Service 1 $ 6,953.13
  Amount allocated from Service 2 $11,031.25
Second: Allocate to Producing Departments:

Service 1 Service percent				30%	30%			
Amount				$ 2,086	$ 2,086			
				= .3 × $6,953	= .3 × $6,953			
Service 2 Service percent				30%	60%			
Amount				$ 3,309	$ 6,619			
				= .3 × $11,031	= .6 × $11,031			
Totals for production departments				$ 30,145	$ 35,855			**$66,000**

THIRD PHASE: Allocate Production
Department Costs to Products

Base: Direct labor-hours						1,800	1,800	3,600
percent						50%	50%	
Machine-hours						400	1,200	1,600
percent						25%	75%	
Production 1	DLH			$(30,145)		$15,073	$15,073	
						= .5 × $30,145	= .5 × $30,145	
Production 2	MH				$(35,855)	$ 8,963	$26,891	
						= .25 × $35,855	= .75 × $35,855	
Totals for each product						**$24,036**	**$41,964**	**$66,000**

Implementation Issues

The four issues to consider when using departmental cost allocation methods are (1) difficulty in determining an appropriate allocation base, (2) separating variable and fixed costs (called dual allocation), (3) use of budgeted rather than actual amounts, and (4) cases when allocated costs exceed the outside purchase price.

◀ **LEARNING OBJECTIVE 4**
Explain the problems in implementing the different departmental cost allocation methods.

Difficulty in Determining the Allocation Base

Determining an appropriate allocation base and a percentage figure for service provided by the service departments is often difficult. For example, it may be inappropriate to use labor-hours in an automated plant where labor is a small part of total cost. Similarly, square feet of floor space may be inappropriate to allocate certain costs where there is a great deal of idle space. Furthermore, the use of square feet of floor space can have undesirable motivational consequences. For example, if we are allocating plantwide maintenance costs to production departments using floor space as a base, there is inadequate incentive for a department to limit its use of maintenance expense. Since the actual use of maintenance is unrelated to floor space, by increasing its usage of maintenance, a given department increases total maintenance cost without proportionally increasing its allocated share of the cost. Other departments pay for the increased maintenance cost as well, as illustrated in Exhibit 14–9. Here, department A increases its use of maintenance (from part 2 to part 3 in Exhibit 14–9), while department B's usage stays the same. The effect of department A's increased usage is that department B pays one-half the increased cost, when allocation is based on square feet. A preferred approach in this example would be to allocate on the basis of maintenance requests, to achieve the desired objectives of motivation and fairness. Exhibit 14–10 provides some suggested allocation bases that can address some of these difficulties.

Separate Fixed and Variable Costs: Dual Allocation

A preferred allocation approach separates variable and fixed costs, and traces the variable costs directly to the departments that caused the cost. The tracing of variable costs in this way satisfies the allocation objectives of motivation and fairness. However, a firm sometimes finds it difficult or uneconomical to separate the variable and fixed costs of the departments. The firm then allocates the total costs (both variable and fixed) in the same manner. Because variable costs are not

---

Exhibit 14–9   Disincentive Effects of Certain Allocation Methods

	Department A	Department B	Total Maintenance Cost
Part 1: Basic information			
Square feet of floor space	5,000	5,000	
Average number of maintenance requests	50	50	
Total maintenance costs			$200,000
Part 2: Maintenance cost allocation in an average month using square feet of floor space			
Allocated maintenance cost	$100,000	$100,000	$200,000

Part 3: Maintenance cost allocation based on square feet for a month when department A increases usage of maintenance from 50 to 80 maintenance requests, while department B's usage remains the same at 50 requests. Total maintenance costs increase to $260,000. Here we assume that maintenance costs are variable with the number of maintenance requests, or $2,000 per request ($200,000/(50 + 50) or $260,000/(50 + 80)).

	Department A	Department B	Total Maintenance Cost
Allocated maintenance cost:	$130,000	$130,000	$260,000

Exhibit 14–10   Allocation Bases for Certain Types of Costs

Personnel-related costs—number of employees

Payroll-related costs (pensions, fringe benefits, payroll taxes)—labor cost

Material-related costs—materials cost or quantity used

Space-related costs—square feet or cubic feet

Energy-related costs—motor capacity

Research and development—estimated time, sales, or assets employed

Public relations—sales

Executives' salaries—sales, assets employed

Property taxes—square feet, real estate or insurance valuation, market value of assets

Source: Based on The Institute of Management Accountants' Statement Number 4B, "Allocation of Service and Administrative Costs," Montvale, New Jersey.

traced, the latter approach does not meet the allocation objectives as well as dual allocation.

Budgeted vs. Actual Amounts

When the allocation base is determined from actual amounts (for example, labor-hours incurred in the current period), then each department's allocation of cost is affected by the other department's actual usage of the allocation base. The reason is that each department's actual usage affects total actual usage. Unfavorable incentives arise, because one department's usage now affects the amount allocated to the other departments. Exhibit 14–11 continues the example of allocating maintenance costs used in Exhibit 14–9, except maintenance is allocated on the basis of direct labor-hours. Also, we assume that maintenance costs are both variable and fixed relative to direct labor-hours; there are $100,000 in total fixed costs and a $5 per direct labor-hour variable cost. In Exhibit 14–11 department B's allocated costs increased from $100,000 (part 2) to $112,500 (part 3) even though department B did not increase its usage of direct labor-hours or of maintenance requests. The reason is that department A reduced its usage of direct labor from 10,000 hours to 6,000 hours. As a result, the $100,000 *total fixed costs in maintenance are allocated over a smaller number of total labor hours*, thus increasing department B's total cost allocation. The direct labor-hours-based allocation is unfair and unmotivating for department B.

For this reason it is preferable to use budgeted or predetermined amounts rather than actual amounts for allocating fixed costs. When budgeted direct labor-hours are used, each department's fixed cost allocation is predictable, and not influenced by the usage in other departments. In contrast, it is preferable to allocate variable costs on the basis of actual usage, since variable costs can be directly traced to the different users. This is another reason why it is important to separate variable and fixed costs, as noted above. An important limitation of the use of budgeted rates is that sometimes the budget may be difficult to obtain. For example, the method would be difficult to implement when the allocation base varies significantly from period to period or is difficult to predict accurately.

Allocated Costs Exceed External Purchase Cost

Another limitation of the three departmental allocation methods is they can allocate a cost to a department that exceeds the cost of that department's service if it were provided by an outside supplier. Should the department pay more for a service internally than an outside vendor would charge? To motivate managers to be efficient and to make the right decisions, the allocation should be based on the cost

Exhibit 14–11	Disincentive Effects of Actual-Usage-Based Allocation Methods		
	Department A	**Department B**	**Total Maintenance Cost**
Part 1: Basic Information			
Actual number of direct labor-hours	10,000	10,000	
Budgeted number of direct labor-hours	10,000	10,000	
Average number of maintenance requests	50	50	
Total maintenance costs			$200,000
Part 2: Maintenance cost allocation in an average month using the number of direct labor-hours.			
Allocated maintenance cost	$100,000	$100,000	$200,000
Part 3: Maintenance cost allocation based on direct labor-hours for a month when department A decreases usage of direct labor-hours from 10,000 to 6,000 hours, while department B's usage remains the same at 10,000 hours. Total maintenance costs decrease to $180,000. Here we assume that maintenance costs have both a variable ($5 per direct labor-hour) and fixed ($100,000) component.			
Allocated maintenance cost	$ 67,500 (6,000/16,000) × $180,000	$112,500 (10,000/16,000) × $180,000	$180,000

Exhibit 14–12	**Cost Allocation Using External Prices**						

(A) User Department	(B) Direct Labor-Hours	(C) Direct Labor-Hours Allocation Base	(D) Cost Allocation Based on Labor-Hours	(E) Outside Price	(F) Allocation Base for Outside Price	(G) Allocation Based on Outside Price
A	3,000	30% (3,000/10,000)	$ 300	$ 360	30% (360/1,200)	$ 300
B	4,000	40% (4,000/10,000)	400	600	50% (600/1,200)	500
C	1,000	10% (1,000/10,000)	100	120	10% (120/1,200)	100
D	2,000	20% (2,000/10,000)	200	120	10% (120/1,200)	100
Total	10,000	100%	$1,000	$1,200	100%	$1,000

if each department had to obtain the service outside the firm. Consider the data in Exhibit 14–12 for a firm with four departments that share a common data processing service costing $1,000. Data processing costs are allocated using direct labor-hours in each of the departments as shown in columns (B), (C), and (D) of Exhibit 14–12. The data processing service also can be obtained from an outside firm at the cost shown in column (E).

The direct labor-hours allocation base in this example penalizes department D, which can obtain the service outside the firm at $80 less than the inside cost ($200 − $120), perhaps because of the simplified nature of the requirements in department D. In contrast, department B can obtain the service outside only at a much higher price ($600 versus $400 inside), perhaps because of the specialized nature of the service. In this case, the allocation based on the *outside price* (the right-hand column in Exhibit 14–12) is fair to both departments B and D. It is a better reflection of the competitive cost of the service. The question of whether, and under what conditions, the department should be allowed to purchase outside the firm is a different issue, which is addressed in the coverage of management control in chapters 18 and 19.

COST ALLOCATION IN SERVICE INDUSTRIES

LEARNING OBJECTIVE 5 ▶
Explain the use of cost allocation in service firms.

The concepts presented in this chapter apply equally well whenever joint costs are incurred in manufacturing, service, and not-for-profit organizations, as we show with two examples.

Blue Cross–Blue Shield of North Carolina (BCBS), a health insurance provider, uses departmental allocation methods to allocate the costs of the many support departments within the company. These include claims management, customer billing, premium accounting, financial accounting, actuarial, operations, marketing and sales, and facilities management. BCBS allocates these costs to key service businesses—commercial health programs, small firm health plans, state employee health plans, health maintenance plans, and many more. Cost allocation is strategically important, helping BCBS to determine not only which programs are most profitable but also how to price these programs effectively.

Financial institutions such as commercial banks also use cost allocation. To illustrate how the allocation would be done, we use the Community General Bank (CGB), which provides a variety of banking services, including deposit accounts, mortgage loans, installment loans, investment services, and other services. Currently, CGB is analyzing the profitability of its mortgage loan department, which has two main businesses—commercial construction loans and residential construction loans. An important part of the analysis of these loan businesses is determining how costs should be traced or allocated between the two businesses.

The cost allocation begins by identifying which departments directly support the two mortgage loan businesses—the loan operations department and the marketing department. The *operations department* handles the processing of loan applications, the safekeeping of appropriate documents, billing, and maintenance of accounts for both commercial and residential loans. The *marketing department* provides direct advertising, promotions, and customer service for both types of loans.

Other departments support the two loan businesses indirectly, by supporting the operations and marketing departments. Two important support departments are the administrative services department and the accounting department. The *administrative services department* provides legal and technical support. The *accounting department* provides financial services, including regular financial reports and the maintenance of customer records. The administrative services and accounting departments provide services to each other as well as to the operations and marketing departments, as illustrated in Exhibit 14–13. Each of the four departments has labor and certain supplies costs that can be traced directly to the department. In addition, CGB's human resources department and computer services department provide services to all four departments.

CGB uses the step method to allocate costs from support departments to the loan businesses. See the step method in Exhibit 14–14, which follows the same approach as for the Beary Company in Exhibit 14–7. The top panel of Exhibit 14–14 shows the allocation bases CGB uses to allocate human resources costs and computer services costs to each of the departments. The allocation base for human resources costs is the number of employees, or the headcount, in each department, while the allocation of computer services costs is based on the number of computers in each department.

The first phase of the allocation in Exhibit 14–14 shows tracing the totals of $1,560,000 of direct labor and $33,000 for supplies costs to each department as well as the allocation of the human resources costs ($80,000) and computer services costs ($66,000), using the allocation bases identified earlier. The result is that the total cost of $1,739,00 is allocated as follows

Accounting department	$ 253,700
Administrative services department	381,500
Operations department	623,700
Marketing department	480,100
Total cost	$1,739,000

In the second phase, the accounting and administrative service department costs are allocated to the operations and marketing departments, using the step method and the service percentages in Exhibit 14–13. The result is that the $1,739,000 of total cost is now allocated to the operations department ($934,958) and the marketing department ($804,043).

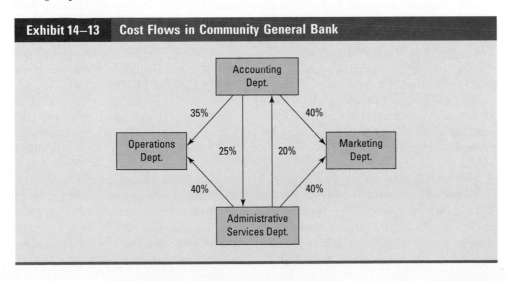

Exhibit 14–13   Cost Flows in Community General Bank

Exhibit 14–14   Cost Allocation at Community General Bank

Departmental Allocation Bases	Base	Accounting	Administrative Services	Operations	Marketing	Commercial Loans	Residential Loans	Total
Headcount	(HC)	80	100	160	60			400
	percent	20.0%	25.0%	40.0%	15.0%			100.0%
Number of computers	(NC)	60	60	150	30			300
	percent	20.0%	20.0%	50.0%	10.0%			100.0%

FIRST PHASE: Trace Direct Costs and Perform Initial Allocation of Indirect Costs

Direct Costs								
Labor		$ 221,000	$ 339,500	$ 554,500	$ 445,000			$1,560,000
Supplies		3,500	8,800	4,200	16,500			33,000
Indirect Costs:								
Human Resources	HC	16,000	20,000	32,000	12,000			80,000
Computer Services	NC	13,200	13,200	33,000	6,600			66,000
Totals for All Departments		$ 253,700	$ 381,500	$ 623,700	$ 480,100			$1,739,000

SECOND PHASE: Reallocate Accounting and Administrative Costs to Operations & Marketing
** The Step Method**

First Step								
Accounting Dept.	Service percent		25%	35%	40%			
	Amount	$(253,700)	$ 63,425	$ 88,795	$ 101,480			
Second Step								
Administrative Services	Service percent			40%	40%			
	Allocation percent per direct method			50%	50%			
	Amount		$(444,925)	$ 222,463	$ 222,463			
Totals for Production Departments*			–	$ 934,958	$ 804,043			$1,739,000

THIRD PHASE: Allocate Operations and Marketing Costs to Commercial and Residential Loans

Base: Number of banking transactions						15,000	10,000	25,000
	percent					60%	40%	
Number of loans						900	3,600	4,500
	percent					20%	80%	
Operations	Number of Transactions			$(934,958)		$560,975	$373,983	
Marketing	Number of Loans				$(804,043)	$160,809	$643,234	
Totals for commercial and residential loans						$721,783	$1,017,217	$1,739,000

*Small differences due to rounding.

In the third and final phase, the costs from the operations and marketing departments are allocated to the two businesses—commercial and residential loans. The allocation base CGB uses to allocate operations department costs is the number of banking transactions handled within operations (15,000 for commercial loans and 10,000 for residential loans), and the allocation base for marketing costs is the number of loans of either type (900 commercial loans and 3,600 residential loans). The result of the final allocation is that the total cost of $1,739,000 is allocated to the commercial loans department ($721,783) and the residential loans department ($1,017,217), as illustrated in the bottom panel of Exhibit 14–14.

Cost allocation provides CGB a basis for evaluating the cost and profitability of its services. By taking the allocated operating costs just determined, the cost of funds provided, and the revenue produced by both commercial and residential loans, a profitability analysis of mortgage loans can be completed, as illustrated in Exhibit 14–15.

The profitability analysis in Exhibit 14–15 shows that the relatively high allocated operating costs of the residential loan department are an important factor in its overall poor performance (only 19.8 percent contribution per dollar of revenue in contrast to more than 30 percent for the commercial loan area). In contrast, it appears the cost of funds is comparable for both types of loans (43.58 percent of revenues for commercial loans and 46.27 percent of revenues for residential loans).

Exhibit 14–15	Profitability Analysis of Mortgage Loans Community General Bank	
	Commercial Loans	**Residential Loans**
Revenues	$2,755,455	$2,998,465
Less expenses:		
Cost of funds	1,200,736	1,387,432
Allocated operating costs	721,783	1,017,217
Contribution	$ 832,936	$ 593,816
Key ratios:		
Contribution/revenue	30.23%	19.80%
Cost of funds/revenues	43.58%	46.27%

The analysis points the way to further study of the profitability of residential loans, and in particular, to the cost of operations and marketing for these loans.

JOINT PRODUCT COSTING

Cost allocation is also needed when a firm has joint products. Joint products are produced simultaneously in the same production departments before being moved to subsequent production departments as separate products. Many manufacturing plants yield more than one product from a joint manufacturing process. For example, the petroleum industry processes crude oil into multiple products: gasoline, naphtha, kerosene, fuel oils, and residual heavy oils. Similarly, the semiconductor industry processes silicon wafers into a variety of computer memory chips with different speeds, temperature tolerances, and life expectancies. Beef and hides are products linked together in the meatpacking process; neither one of these items can be produced without producing the other. Other industries that yield joint products include lumber production, food processing, soap making, grain milling, dairy farming, and fishing.

Joint products and by-products are derived from processing a single input or a common set of inputs. **Joint products** are products from the same production process that have relatively substantial sales values. Products whose total sales values are minor in comparison to the sales value of the joint products are classified as **by-products.**

A change in market demand or production technology can change the status of a by-product or a joint product. Chips of wood bark are a log-processing by-product because all the manufacturer can do is sell them at only a token price to a landscaping company to use for mulch. Bark chips would become a joint product, however, if a pharmaceutical company could extract from them a valuable ingredient that raised their value.

Joint products and by-products both start their manufacturing life as part of the same raw material. Up until a certain point in the production process, no distinction can be made between the products. The point in the production process at which individual joint products can be identified for the first time is called the **split-off point.** Thereafter, separate production processes may be applied to the individual products. At the split-off point, joint products or by-products may be salable or may require further processing in order to be salable, depending on their nature.

Joint costs include all the manufacturing costs incurred prior to the split-off (including direct materials, direct labor, and factory overhead). For financial reporting purposes, these costs are allocated among the joint products. Additional costs incurred after the split-off point that can be identified directly with individual products are called **additional processing costs** or **separable costs.**

Other outputs of joint production include scrap, waste, spoilage, and defective units. Scrap is the residue from a production process that has little no recovery value. Waste, such as chemical waste, is a residual material that has no recovery

◄ **LEARNING OBJECTIVE 6**
Use the three joint product costing methods.

Joint products are products from the same production process that have relatively substantial sales value.

By-products are products whose total sales values are minor in comparison with the sales value of the joint products.

The **split-off point** is the first point in a joint production process in which individual products can be identified.

Additional processing costs or **separable costs** are those that occur after the split-off point and can be identified directly with individual products.

value, and firms are required to properly dispose of it. In addition to waste and scrap, some products do not meet quality standards and may be reworked for resale. Spoiled units are not reworked for economic reasons. Defective units are reworked to become salable units.

Methods for Allocating Joint Costs to Joint Products

The most frequently used methods to allocate joint costs to joint products are (1) physical measures, (2) sales values, and (3) net realizable values.

The Physical Measure Method

The **physical measure** method uses a physical measure such as pounds, gallons, yards, or units or volume produced at the split-off point to allocate the joint costs to joint products.

The **average cost method** uses units of output to allocate joint costs to joint products.

The **physical measure method,** naturally enough, uses a physical measure such as pounds, gallons, yards, or units or volume produced at the split-off point to allocate the joint costs to joint products. The first step is to select the proper physical measure as the basis for allocation. We can use units of input or units of output. For example, if we are costing pork products, the production of 100 hams each having an average weight of 4 lbs would have an input measure of 400 lbs and an output measure of 100 hams. When units of output are used, this also is called the **average cost method.**

Assume that Johnson's Foods produces pork chops and fresh ham for distribution to restaurants and supermarkets in the southeastern United States. The cost of 14,000 pounds of raw, unprocessed pork plus the direct labor and overhead for cutting and processing whole pigs into pork chops and ham is the joint cost of the process. The flow of production is illustrated in Exhibit 14-16.

The production process starts at point 1. A total $16,000 joint cost ($7,000 direct materials, $5,000 direct labor, and $4,000 factory overhead) is incurred. Point 2 is the split-off point where two joint products are separated: 2,000 pounds of pork chops and 8,000 pounds of ham. The remaining 4,000 pounds of by-products, scrap, and waste are not accounted for. (In the appendix to the chapter we explain how to account for by-products.) If we use a physical measure method, the joint cost of $16,000 is allocated as shown in Exhibit 14–17.

Based on the physical quantities (pounds in this example) of the joint products at the split-off point, we can compute the relationship of each of the joint products

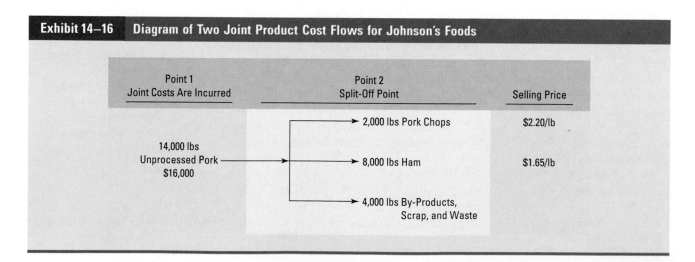

Exhibit 14–16   Diagram of Two Joint Product Cost Flows for Johnson's Foods

Point 1 Joint Costs Are Incurred	Point 2 Split-Off Point	Selling Price
	→ 2,000 lbs Pork Chops	$2.20/lb
14,000 lbs Unprocessed Pork $16,000	→ 8,000 lbs Ham	$1.65/lb
	→ 4,000 lbs By-Products, Scrap, and Waste	

Exhibit 14–17   Physical Measure Method

Product	Physical Measure	Proportion	Allocation of Joint Cost	Cost per Pound
Pork chops	2,000 lbs	0.20	$16,000 × .2 = $ 3,200	$1.60
Fresh ham	8,000 lbs	0.80	16,000 × .8 = 12,800	1.60
Total	10,000 lbs	1.00	$16,000	

to the sum of the total units. The joint cost allocated to the products is the average cost per pound of the joint cost, which is $1.60 per pound.

The physical measure used in determining the relative weights for allocating the joint cost should be the quantities of the products at the *split-off point*, not the quantities when the production of the products is completed. Thus, the relevant quantities in the example are 2,000 pounds of pork chops and 8,000 pounds of ham.

The production costs per pound for both products are

$$\text{Pork chops } \$1.60 \text{ per pound} = \$3,200/2,000 \text{ pounds}$$

$$\text{Ham} \qquad \$1.60 \text{ per pound} = \$12,800/8,000 \text{ pounds}$$

In this example, the physical measure method produced the same cost per pound for pork chops and ham because the units of *input* (pounds) are used. The cost per pound would be different if we used *output* of 2,000 pork chops and 2,000 hams as the physical measure. The per-unit cost of each chop and each ham would be $4 ($16,000/4,000 units), while the cost per pound would be (each chop is one lb, and a ham is 4 lbs):

$$\text{Pork chops } \$4/1 = \$4/lb$$

$$\text{Ham} \qquad \$4/4 = \$1/lb$$

Advantages and Limitations   Among the advantages of the physical measure method are that (1) it is easy to use, and (2) the criterion for the allocation of the joint costs is objective. This method, however, ignores the revenue-producing capability of individual products that can vary widely among the joint products and have no relationship at all to any physical measure. Also, each product may have a unique physical measure (gallons for one, pounds for another) and hence the method may not be applicable. The following method addresses these limitations.

The Sales Value at Split-Off Method

An alternative and widely used method is the sales value at split-off method. The **sales value at split-off method** (or more simply, sales value method) allocates joint costs to joint products on the basis of their relative sales values at the split-off point. This method can be used only when joint products can be sold at the split-off point. If we assume that a pound of pork chops can be sold for $2.20 and a pound of ham for $1.65, and Johnson's Foods has produced 2,000 pounds of pork chops and 8,000 pounds of ham, then the $16,000 joint cost should be allocated between the products as shown in Exhibit 14–18.

The first step in the sales value method (Exhibit 14–18) is to compute the total sales value of the joint products at the split-off point. Note that the sales value is the sales price multiplied by the production units, *not the actual sales units*. Determination of the proportion of the sales value of each joint product to the total sales value is the second step. Finally, we allocate the total joint cost among the joint products based on those proportions.

In the Johnson's Foods example, the sales value of pork chops is $4,400 and the sales value of ham is $13,200, a total of $17,600. The weights of the individual sales values of the products to the total sales value are 0.25 ($4,400/$17,600) for pork chops and 0.75 ($13,200/$17,600) for ham. The allocated costs are $4,000 to pork chops and $12,000 to ham.

> The **sales value at split-off method** allocates joint costs to joint products on the basis of their relative sales values at the split-off point.

Exhibit 14–18	Sales Value at Split-off Method					
Product	**Units**	**Price per unit**	**Sales Value**	**Weight**	**Joint Cost Allocated**	**Cost per Pound**
Pork chops	2,000 lbs	$2.20	$ 4,400	0.25	$16,000 × .25 = $ 4,000	$2.00
Ham	8,000 lbs	1.65	13,200	0.75	16,000 × .75 = 12,000	1.50
Total			$17,600	1.00	$16,000	

The production costs per pound for both products are calculated

Pork chops	$2.00 per pound = $4,000/2,000
Ham	$1.50 per pound = $12,000/8,000

Note that pork chops have a higher unit cost for the sales value method than for the physical unit method. The reason is that pork chops have a higher sales value. If the sales prices are estimated accurately and if there are no additional processing costs, the sales value at the split-off point method generates the same gross margin percentage for both pork chops and ham as shown in Exhibit 14–19.

Advantages and Limitations The advantages of the sales value method are that (1) it is easy to calculate, and (2) it is allocated according to the individual product's revenues. This method is superior to the physical measure method because it allocates the joint costs in proportion to the products' ability to absorb these costs. This is an application of the ability-to-bear concept of fairness included in the objectives of cost allocation at the beginning of the chapter.

One limitation of the sales value method is that in some industries market prices change constantly. Also, the sales price at split-off may not be available because additional processing is necessary before the product can be sold.

The Net Realizable Value Method

> The **net realizable value (NRV)** of a product is the estimated sales value of the product at the split-off point, made by subtracting the additional processing and selling costs beyond the split-off point from the ultimate sales value of the product.

Not all joint products can be sold at the split-off point. Thus, there is no market price to attach to some products at the split-off point. In these cases, the concept of net realizable value is used. The **net realizable value (NRV)** of a product is the estimated sales value of the product at the split-off point, made by subtracting the additional processing and selling costs beyond the split-off point from the ultimate sales value of the product.

$$NRV = \text{Sales value} - \text{Additional processing cost}$$

In the Johnson's Foods example, assume that in addition to pork chops and ham products, the firm also processes bacon from raw, unprocessed pork. Assume further that 14,000 pounds of pork yield at the split-off point 2,000 pounds of pork chops and 8,000 pounds of ham as before, but in addition 2,000 pounds of raw bacon. The remaining 2,000 pounds are scrap, waste, and by-products. There is no market for raw bacon; it must be processed further for sale to restaurants and supermarkets for $2.50 per pound. The additional total processing cost is $600. In Exhibit 14–20 we present an overview of this situation.

Exhibit 14–21 shows the joint cost allocation calculation using the net realizable value method.

If Johnson's Foods sold all the products it produced during the period, its gross margin amounts for the products would be as shown in Exhibit 14–22. Note that the gross margin percentage is lower for bacon than for pork chops because of the additional processing cost of $600.

Advantages and Limitations The net realizable value method is superior to the physical measure method because, like the sales value at split-off method, it produces

Exhibit 14–19	Product-Line Profitability Analysis	
	Pork Chops	**Ham**
Sales	$2.20 × 2,000 = $4,400	$1.65 × 8,000 = $13,200
Cost of goods sold	$2.00 × 2,000 = 4,000	$1.50 × 8,000 = 12,000
Gross margin	$ 400	$ 1,200
Gross margin percent	9.09%	9.09%

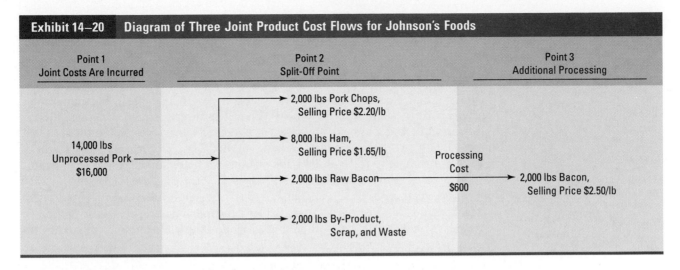

Exhibit 14–20   Diagram of Three Joint Product Cost Flows for Johnson's Foods

Point 1 Joint Costs Are Incurred	Point 2 Split-Off Point	Point 3 Additional Processing
14,000 lbs Unprocessed Pork $16,000	2,000 lbs Pork Chops, Selling Price $2.20/lb 8,000 lbs Ham, Selling Price $1.65/lb 2,000 lbs Raw Bacon 2,000 lbs By-Product, Scrap, and Waste	Processing Cost $600 → 2,000 lbs Bacon, Selling Price $2.50/lb

Exhibit 14–21   Net Realizable Value Method

Product	Units	Unit Price	Sales Value	Additional Processing	Net Realizable Value	Weight	Allocated Cost	Total Cost	Cost per Pound
Pork chops	2,000	$2.20	$ 4,400	–	$ 4,400	.2	$ 3,200	$ 3,200	$1.60
Ham	8,000	1.65	13,200	–	13,200	.6	9,600	9,600	1.20
Bacon	2,000	2.50	5,000	$600	4,400	.2	3,200	3,800	1.90
Total	12,000		$22,600	$600	$22,000	1.0	$16,000	$16,600	

Exhibit 14–22   Product-Line Profitability Analysis

	Pork Chops	Ham	Bacon
Sales	$2.20 × 2,000 = $4,400	$1.65 × 8,000 = $13,200	$2.50 × 2,000 = $5,000
Cost of goods sold	$1.60 × 2,000 = 3,200	$1.20 × 8,000 = 9,600	$1.90 × 2,000 = 3,800
Gross margin	$1,200	$ 3,600	$1,200
Gross margin percent	27.27%	27.27%	24%

an allocation that yields a predictable, comparable level of profitability among the products. The physical measure method might provide misleading guidance to top management regarding product profitability, and it can be very frustrating to product-line managers.

However, the net realizable value method is less objective than the sales value method. Because the sales value method uses an objective, market price at the split-off, it is preferred over both the physical measure method and the net realizable value method, and it is used whenever a market value for the product at the split-off point is available.

SUMMARY

This chapter introduces the objectives, concepts, and methods of cost allocation. There are two main cost allocation applications—departmental cost allocation and joint product costing. The three phases of departmental cost allocation are (1) the tracing of direct costs and initial allocation of indirect costs, (2) the allocation of service department costs to production departments, and (3) the allocation of production department costs to products. The second phase is the most complex. There are three methods for allocating service department costs to production departments: the direct method, the step method, and the reciprocal method. The three methods differ in how they deal with service flows among service departments. The direct method ignores these flows, while the step method includes some of them, and the reciprocal method includes all. For this reason, the reciprocal method is preferred.

Joint product costing arises when two or more products are made simultaneously in a given manufacturing process. There are three methods for costing joint products: (1) the physical measures method, (2) the sales value at split-off method, and (3) the net realizable value method. The physical measure method is the most simple to use but also has a significant disadvantage. Because the allocation ignores sales value, the gross margins of joint products can differ in significant and unreasonable ways. In contrast, the sales value and net realizable value methods tend to result in similar gross margins among the joint products. The sales value at split-off method is used when sales value at split-off is known, and otherwise the net realizable value is used.

APPENDIX

By-Product Costing

LEARNING OBJECTIVE 7 ►
Use the four by-product costing methods.

A by-product is a product of relatively small sales value that is produced simultaneously with one or more joint products. Two approaches are used for by-product costing: (1) the asset recognition method and (2) the revenue method. The main difference between these approaches lies in whether they assign an inventoriable cost to by-products in the period in which they are produced. The asset recognition method records by-products as inventory at net realizable values; the value of the by-product is therefore recognized when the by-product is produced. In contrast, the revenue method does not assign costs to the by-products in the period of production but recognizes by-product value in the period sold.

Both approaches contain two alternative methods, depending upon the way in which by-products are reported in the income statement. The two asset recognition approaches are:

Method 1: *Net Realizable Value Method*   Method 1 shows the net realizable value of by-products on the balance sheet as inventory and on the income statement as a deduction from the total manufacturing cost of the joint products. This is done in the *period in which the by-product is produced.*

Method 2: *Other Income at Production Point Method*   Method 2 shows the net realizable value of by-products on the income statement as an other income or other sales revenue item. This is done in the *period in which the by-product is produced.*

The two revenue methods are:

Method 3: *Other Income at Selling Point Method*   Method 3 shows the net sales revenue from a by-product sold *at time of sale* on the income statement as an other income or other sales revenue item.

Method 4: *Manufacturing Cost Reduction at Selling Point Method*   Method 4 shows the net sales revenue from a by-product sold *at time of sale* on the income statement as a reduction of the total manufacturing cost.

In Exhibit 14–23 we summarize the four major by-product costing methods.

Asset Recognition Methods

To illustrate the asset recognition methods, assume Johnson's Foods believes additional profit can be made by selling pork feet as well as pork chops, ham, and bacon. However, the selling price of the pork feet is expected to be relatively low, 50 cents per pound. Moreover, additional processing and selling costs of 30 cents per pound would be necessary for cleaning, packaging, and distributing the product. Since the sales value of pork feet is relatively low, the firm decides to treat pork chops, ham,

Exhibit 14–23	A Summary of By-Product Costing Methods	
	Place in Income Statement	
Time to Recognize	**As Other Income**	**As a Deduction of Manufacturing Cost**
At time of production (Asset recognition methods)	Other income at time of production	Net realizable value method; Reduction in joint product cost at time of production
At time of sale (Revenue methods)	Other income at time of sale	Reduction in cost of joint products at time of sale

Exhibit 14–24	Diagram of Three Joint Products and One By-Product Cost Flows for Johnson's Foods

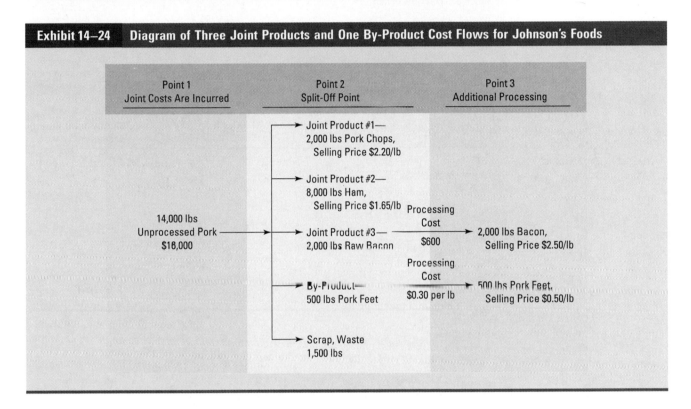

and bacon as joint products and pork feet as a by-product. Suppose the firm sold all production of pork chops, ham, and bacon, but sold only 400 of the 500 pounds of pork feet produced. In Exhibit 14–24 we show the cost flows of the three joint products and one by-product.

From Exhibit 14–21, the total sales value of pork chops, ham, and bacon is $22,600 ($4,400 + $13,200 + $5,000) and the total cost of goods sold is $16,600 ($3,200 + $9,600 + $3,800). The net realizable value (NRV) of the 500 pounds of pork feet produced is

$$\text{NRV} = \text{Sales value} - \text{Additional processing cost}$$

$$= \$0.50 \times 500 - \$0.30 \times 500$$

$$= \$100$$

Johnson's accounting for the by-product using the net realizable value method and the other income at production point method appears in Exhibit 14–25.

Asset recognition methods are based on the financial accounting concepts of asset recognition, matching, and materiality. By-products are *recognized* as assets with probable future economic benefits because a market exists for them. Asset recognition methods also have the preferred effect of *matching* the value of the by-product with its manufacturing cost; when the by-product is sold, its inventory cost is shown as the cost of sales. If the net realizable value of a by-product is *material* (that is, it

Exhibit 14–25	By-Product Costing—Asset Recognition Methods	
	Method 1 **Net Realizable** **Value Method**	**Method 2** **Other Income at** **Production Method**
Sale of joint products	$22,600	$22,600
Cost of goods sold:		
Cost of joint products sold	$16,600	$16,600
Less net realizable value of by-product	(100)	—
Cost of goods sold	$16,500	$16,600
Gross margin	$ 6,100	$ 6,000
Other income at production	—	100
Income before tax	$ 6,100	$ 6,100

Exhibit 14–26	By-Product Costing—Revenue Methods	
	Method 3 **Other Income at** **Selling Point Method**	**Method 4** **Manufacturing Cost** **Reduction Method**
Sales of joint products	$22,600	$22,600
Cost of goods sold:		
Cost of joint products sold	$16,600	$16,600
Less net sales revenue of by-product sold ($.50 − $.30) × 400	—	(80)
Cost of goods sold	$16,600	$16,520
Gross margin	$ 6,000	$ 6,080
By-product revenue	80	—
Income before tax	$ 6,080	$ 6,080

will have a significant effect on inventory or profit), then the asset recognition methods should be used, because of the matching concept.

Revenue Methods

Revenue methods recognize by-products at the time of sale. In Exhibit 14–26 we illustrate the two methods.

Revenue methods are justified on the financial accounting concepts of revenue realization, materiality, and cost-benefit. These methods are consistent with the argument that by-product net revenue should be recorded at the time of sale because this is the *point revenue is realized*. Also, revenue methods are appropriate when the value of the by-product is *not material*, that is, very small in relation to net income. For *cost–benefit* considerations, many firms use a revenue method because of its simplicity.

KEY TERMS

Additional processing (separable) costs 559

Average cost method 560

By-products 559

Direct method 549

Joint products 559

Net realizable value (NAV) 562

Physical measure method 560

Reciprocal flows 549

Reciprocal method 551

Sales value at split-off method 561

Split-off point 559

Step method 550

SELF-STUDY PROBLEM

(For solution, please turn to the end of the chapter.)

Joint Product Costing

The Northern Company processes 100 gallons of raw materials into 75 gallons of product GS–50 and 25 gallons of GS–80. GS–50 is further processed into 50 gallons of product GS-505 at a cost of $5,000, and GS–80 is processed into 50 gallons of product GS–805 at a cost of $2,000. In Exhibit 14–27 we depict this manufacturing flow.

Exhibit 14–27	Joint Cost Flows for Northern Comapny

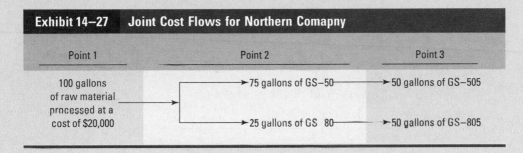

Point 1	Point 2	Point 3

100 gallons of raw material processed at a cost of $20,000
→ 75 gallons of GS–50 → 50 gallons of GS–505
→ 25 gallons of GS 80 → 50 gallons of GS–805

The production process starts at point 1. A total of $20,000 in joint manufacturing costs are incurred in reaching point 2. Point 2 is the split-off point of the process that manufactures GS–50 and GS–80. At this point GS–50 can be sold for $300 a gallon and GS–80 can be sold for $60 a gallon. The process is completed at point 3—products GS–505 and GS–805 have a sales price of $500 a gallon and $140 a gallon, respectively.

Required   Allocate the joint product costs using each of the three methods.

QUESTIONS

14–1   What are the objectives of cost allocation? Which are most important in a retail firm? In a manufacturing firm? In a service firm?

14–2   Explain the difference between joint products and by-products.

14–3   Explain the difference between spoilage, waste, rework, and scrap.

14–4   What are the three methods for departmental cost allocation? Explain how they differ, and which is the most preferred and why.

14–5   What are the three phases in departmental cost allocation? What happens at each phase?

14–6   Give two or three examples of how cost allocation can be used in service industries and not-for-profit organizations.

14–7   What are the four methods used in by-product costing, and how do they differ? Which is the preferred method and why?

14–8   What are the limitations of joint product cost allocation?

14–9   What are the limitations of departmental cost allocation?

14–10 What is the role of cost allocation from a strategic point of view?

PROBLEMS

14–11 **COST ALLOCATION, GENERAL**   An organization's service and administrative costs can be substantial, and some or all of these costs usually are allocated to cost objects. Thus, the allocations of service and administrative costs can have a significant impact on product cost and pricing, asset valuation, and segment profitability.

Required

1. What are service and administrative costs?

2. When service and administrative costs are allocated, the costs are grouped into homogeneous pools and then allocated to cost objects according to some allocation base.

    a. Compare and contrast the benefit and cost criteria for selecting an allocation base.

    b. Explain what is meant by the ability-to-bear costs criterion for selecting an allocation base and discuss why this criterion has limited use.

(CMA Adapted)

Service

14–12 DEPARTMENTAL COST ALLOCATION The HomeLife Life Insurance Company has two service departments (actuarial and premium rating) and two production departments (marketing and sales). The distribution of each service department's efforts to the other departments is

From	To			
	Actuarial	**Premium**	**Marketing**	**Sales**
Actuarial	—	80%	10%	10%
Premium	20%	—	20%	60%

The direct operating costs of the departments (including both variable and fixed costs) are

Actuarial	$80,000
Premium rating	15,000
Marketing	60,000
Sales	40,000

Required

1. Determine the total cost allocated to the marketing and sales departments using the direct method.

2. Determine the total cost allocated to marketing and sales using the step method.

3. Determine the total cost allocated to marketing and sales using the reciprocal method.

14–13 DEPARTMENTAL COST ALLOCATION The Johnson Products Company has two service departments (S1 and S2) and two production departments (P1 and P2). The distribution of each service department's efforts to the other departments is

From	To			
	S1	**S2**	**P1**	**P2**
S1	—	10%	30%	?%
S2	10%	—	?%	40%

The direct operating costs of the departments (including both variable and fixed costs) are

S1	$160,000
S2	60,000
P1	50,000
P2	120,000

Required

1. Determine the total cost allocated to P1 and P2 using the direct method.

2. Determine the total cost allocated to P1 and P2 using the step method.

3. Determine the total cost allocated to P1 and P2 using the reciprocal method.

14–14 DEPARTMENTAL COST ALLOCATION; OUTSOURCING The Thompson Company produces two software products (NetA and NetB) in two separate departments (A and B). These products are very highly regarded network maintenance programs. NetA is used for small networks and NetB is used for large networks. Thompson is known for the quality of its products and its ability to meet dates promised for software upgrades.

Strategy

Net A is produced in department A, and Net B is produced in department B. The production departments are supported by two support departments, systems design and programming services. The source and use of the support department time are summarized as:

From	To				Total Labor-Hours
	Design	Programming	Department A	Department B	
Design	—	2,000	3,000	5,000	10,000
Programming	600	—	600	800	2,000

The costs in the two service departments are as follows:

	Design	Programming
Labor and materials (all variable)	$16,000	$25,000
Depreciation and other fixed costs	28,000	45,000
Total	$44,000	$70,000

Required

1. What are the costs allocated to the two production departments from the two service departments, using the direct method, the step method (both possible sequences), and the reciprocal method?

2. The company is considering outsourcing programming services to JBF Services, Inc., for $25 per hour. Should Thompson do this?

14–15 DEPARTMENTAL COST ALLOCATION McKeoun Enterprises is a large machine tool company now experiencing alarming increases in maintenance expense in each of its four production departments. Currently, maintenance costs are allocated to the production departments on the basis of labor-hours incurred in the production department. To provide pressure for the production departments to use less maintenance work, and to provide an incentive for the maintenance department to become more efficient, McKeoun has decided to look into new methods of allocating maintenance costs. One suggestion now being evaluated is a form of outsourcing: the producing departments could purchase maintenance service from an outside supplier. That is, they would have the choice of either using an outside supplier of maintenance or being charged an amount based on their use of labor-hours. This table shows the labor-hours in each department, the allocation of maintenance cost based on labor-hours, and the cost of providing the equivalent level of maintenance service by an outside maintenance provider.

Production Department	Direct Labor-Hours Allocation Base (Percent)	Allocated Cost	Outside Price
A	20%	$ 90,000	$115,000
B	30	135,000	92,000
C	10	45,000	69,000
D	40	180,000	184,000
Total	100%	$450,000	$460,000

Required

1. As a first step in moving to the outsourcing approach, McKeoun is considering an allocation based on the price of the outside maintenance supplier for each of the four departments. Calculate the cost allocation on this basis and compare it to the current labor-hour basis.

2. If McKeoun follows the proposed plan, what is likely to happen to the overall use of maintenance, and how will each department manager be motivated to increase or decrease the use of maintenance? What are the overall effects of going to the new plan?

14–16 DEPARTMENTAL COST ALLOCATION Boa Corporation distributes its service department overhead costs to product departments. This information is for the month of June:

	Service Departments	
	Maintenance	Utilities
Overhead costs incurred	$20,000	$10,000
Service provided to departments:		
Maintenance	—	10%
Utilities	20%	—
Producing—A	40	30
Producing—B	40	60
Totals	100%	100%

Required What is the amount of maintenance department costs distributed to producing department A for June using (1) the direct method, (2) the step method, and (3) the reciprocal method?

14–17 DEPARTMENTAL COST ALLOCATION Hermo Company has just completed a hydroelectric plant at a cost of $21,000,000. The plant will provide the company's power needs for the next 20 years. Hermo will use only 60 percent of the power output annually. At this level of capacity, Hermo's annual operating costs will amount to $1,800,000, of which 80 percent are fixed.

Service

Quigley Company currently purchases its power from Norton Electric at an annual cost of $1,200,000. Hermo could supply this power, thus increasing the output of its plant to 90 percent of capacity. This would however reduce the estimated life of the plant to 14 years.

Required

1. If Hermo were to supply power to Quigley, it would need to be compensated for the decrease in the life of the plant and the appropriate variable costs. Hermo has decided that the charge for the decreased life should be based on the original cost of the plant calculated on a straight-line basis. What is the minimum annual amount that Hermo would charge Quigley?

2. What is the maximum amount Quigley would be willing to pay Hermo annually for the power?

(CMA Adapted)

14–18 JOINT PRODUCTS Lowe Company manufactures products A and B from a joint process. Sales value at split-off was $700,000 for 10,000 units of A and $300,000 for 15,000 units of B. Using the sales value at the split-off approach, joint costs properly allocated to A were $140,000.

Required What were the total joint costs?

14–19 JOINT PRODUCTS Axe Company produces joint products J, K, and B from a process. This information concerns a batch produced in April at a joint cost of $60,000:

| | | After Split-off | |
Product	Units Produced	Total Additional Costs	Total Market Values
J	1,000	$20,000	$70,000
K	2,000	10,000	30,000
B	4,000	2,000	7,000

Required How much of the joint cost should be allocated to each of the joint products using the net realizable value method?

14–20 JOINT PRODUCTS Ohio Corporation manufactures liquid chemicals A and B from a joint process. Joint costs are allocated on the basis of sales value at split-off. It costs $4,560 to process 500 gallons of product A and 1,000 gallons of product B to the split-off point. The sales value at split-off is $10 per gallon for product A and $14 for product B. Product B requires an additional process beyond split-off at a cost of $1 per gallon before it can be sold.

Required What is Ohio's cost to produce 1,000 gallons of product B?

14–21 JOINT PRODUCT COSTING; BY-PRODUCTS (APPENDIX) Malcom Company produces 10,000 units of A, 20,000 units of B, and 10,000 units of C from the same manufacturing process at a cost of $300,000. A and B are joint products, whereas C is regarded as a by-product. The unit selling prices of the products are $25 for A, $10 for B, and $5 for C. None of the products require any further processing. Of the units produced, 5,000 units of A, 12,000 units of B, and 8,000 units of C are sold. Malcom Company uses the net realizable value method to allocate joint costs.

Required

1. What is the value of the ending inventory of Product A?
2. What is the value of the ending inventory of Product C?

14–22 JOINT PRODUCT COSTING The Killian Company manufactures two skin care lotions, Liquid Skin and Silken Skin, out of a joint process. The joint costs incurred are $420,000 for a standard production run that generates 180,000 gallons of Liquid Skin and 120,000 gallons of Silken Skin. Liquid Skin sells for $2.40 per gallon while Silken Skin sells for $3.90 per gallon.

Required

1. Assuming both products are sold at the split-off point, what is the amount of joint cost of each production run allocated to Liquid Skin on a net realizable value basis?
2. If no additional costs are incurred after the split-off point, what is the amount of joint cost of each production run allocated to Silken Skin on a physical-quantity basis?

3. If additional processing costs beyond the split-off point are $1.40 per gallon for Liquid Skin and 90 cents per gallon for Silken Skin, what is the amount of joint cost of each production run allocated to Silken Skin on a net realizable value basis?

4. If additional processing costs beyond the split-off point are $1.40 per gallon for Liquid Skin and 90 cents per gallon for Silken Skin, what is the amount of joint cost of each production run allocated to Liquid Skin on a physical quantity basis?

(CMA Adapted)

14–23 **JOINT PRODUCT COSTING** Sonimad Sawmill manufactures two lumber products from a joint milling process. The two products developed are mine support braces (MSB) and unseasoned commercial building lumber (CBL). A standard production run incurs joint costs of $300,000 and results in 60,000 units of MSB and 90,000 units of CBL. Each MSB sells for $2 per unit, and each CBL sells for $4 per unit.

Required

1. Assuming no further processing work is done after the split-off point, what is the amount of joint costs allocated to commercial building lumber (CBL) on a physical quantity allocation basis?

2. If there are no further processing costs incurred after the split-off point, what is the amount of joint cost allocated to the mine support braces (MSB) on a sales value basis?

3. Assume the commercial building lumber is not marketable at split-off but must be further planed and sized at a cost of $200,000 per production run. During this process, 10,000 units are unavoidably lost; these spoiled units have no value. The remaining units of commercial building lumber are salable at $10.00 per unit. The mine support braces, although salable immediately at the split-off point, are coated with a tarlike preservative that costs $100,000 per production run. The braces are sold then for $5 each. Using the net realizable value (NRV) basis, what is the completed cost assigned to each unit of commercial building lumber?

4. Should Sonimad Sawmill choose to process the mine support braces beyond the split-off? What would be the contribution?

(CMA Adapted)

14–24 **JOINT PRODUCTS; BY-PRODUCTS (APPENDIX)** Grafton Company produces joint products A and B in department 1 from a process that also yields by-product W. Product A and by-product W are sold after separation, but product B must be further processed in department 2 before it can be sold. The cost assigned to the by-product is its market value less 40 cents per pound for delivery expense (NRV method). The following information relates to a batch produced in July:

Product	Production (in pounds)	Sales Price per Pound	
A	2,000	$4.50	
B	4,000	9.00	
W	500	1.50	
Joint cost in department 1			$18,000
Product B additional process cost in department 2			$10,000

Required

1. For joint cost allocation purposes, what is the NRV at the split-off point of product B?

2. How much of the joint cost incurred in department 1 should be allocated to the joint products?

(CMA Adapted)

14–25 **JOINT PRODUCTS** Watkins Company produces three products, X, Y, and Z, from a joint process. Each product may be sold at the point of split-off or processed further. Additional processing requires no special facilities, and the production costs of further processing are entirely variable and traceable to the products involved. Last year all three products were processed beyond split-off. Joint production costs for the year were $60,000. Sales values and costs needed to evaluate Watkins' production policy follow:

 *Strategy*

Product	Units Produced	Sales Value at Split-off	If Processed Further	
			Sales Value	Additional Costs
X	6,000	$25,000	$42,000	$9,000
Y	4,000	41,000	45,000	7,000
Z	2,000	24,000	32,000	8,000

Required

1. Determine the unit cost and gross profit for each product if Watkins allocates joint production costs in proportion to the relative physical volume of output.

2. Determine unit costs and gross profit for each product if Watkins allocates joint costs using the relative sales value method.

3. Should the firm sell all of its products after further processing?

4. The firm has been selling all of its products at the split-off point. Selling any of the products after further processing will entail direct competition with some of Watkins' major customers. What strategic factors does Watkins need to consider in deciding whether to process any of the products further?

14–26 **JOINT PRODUCTS; BY-PRODUCTS (APPENDIX)** Multiproduct Corporation is a chemical manufacturer that produces two main products (Pepco–1 and Repke–3) and a by-product (SE–5) from a joint process. If Multiproduct had the proper facilities, it could process SE–5 further into a main product. The ratio of output quantities to input quantity of direct material used in the joint process remains consistent with the processing conditions and activity level.

Multiproduct currently uses the physical method of allocating joint costs to the main products. The FIFO (first-in, first-out) inventory method is used to value the main products. The by-product is inventoried at its net realizable value, and the net realizable value of the by-product is used to reduce the joint production costs before the joint costs are allocated to the main products.

Jim Simpson, Multiproduct's controller, wants to implement the relative sales value method of joint cost allocation. He believes that inventory costs should be based on each product's ability to contribute to the recovery of joint production costs. The net realizable value of the by-product would be treated in the same manner as with the physical method.

Data regarding Multiproduct's operations for November 19X9 are presented in the following report. The joint cost of production amounted to $2,640,000 for November 19X9.

| | Main Products | | By-Product |
	Pepco–1	Repke–3	S–5
Finished goods inventory in gallons on November 1, 19X9	20,000	40,000	10,000
November sales in gallons	800,000	700,000	200,000
November production in gallons	900,000	720,000	240,000
Sales value per gallon at split-off point	$2.00	$1.50	$.55*
Additional process costs after split-off	$1,800,000	$720,000	—
Final sales value per gallon	$5.00	$4.00	—

*Disposal and selling costs of 5 cents per gallon are incurred to sell the by-product.

Required

1. Describe the sales value method and explain how it accomplishes Jim Simpson's objective.

2. Assuming Multiproduct Corporation adopts the sales value method for internal reporting purposes,
   a. Calculate how the joint production cost for November 19X9 would be allocated.
   b. Determine the dollar values of the finished goods inventories for Pepco–1, Repke–3, and SE–5 as of November 30, 19X9.

3. Multiproduct Corporation plans to expand its production facilities to enable the further processing of SE–5 into a main product. Discuss how the allocation of the joint production costs under the relative sales value method would change when SE–5 becomes a main product.

(CMA Adapted)

Ethics

14–27   JOINT PRODUCTS   Alderon Industries is a manufacturer of chemicals for various purposes. One of the processes used by Alderon produces SPL–3, a chemical used in swimming pools; PST-4, a chemical used in pesticides; and RJ–5, a by-product sold to fertilizer manufacturers. Alderon uses the net realizable value of its main products to allocate joint production costs, and the first-in, first-out (FIFO) inventory method to value the main products. The by-product is inventoried at its net realizable value, and this value is used to reduce the joint production costs before the joint costs are allocated to the main products. The ratio of output quantities to input quantities of direct material used in the joint process remains consistent from month to month.

Data regarding Alderon's operations for the month of November 19X9 follow. During this month, Alderon incurred joint production costs of $1,702,000 in the manufacture of SPL–3, PST–4, and RJ–5.

	SPL–3	PST–4	RJ–5
Finished goods inventory in gallons (November 1, 19X9)	18,000	52,000	3,000
November sales in gallons	650,000	325,000	150,000
November production in gallons	700,000	350,000	170,000
Sales value per gallon at split-off	—	$3.80	$.70*
Additional processing costs	$874,000	$816,000	—
Final sales value per gallon	$4.00	$6.00	—

*Disposal costs of 10 cents per gallon are incurred to sell the by-product.

Required

1. Determine Alderon Industries' allocation of joint production costs for the month of November 19X9. Be sure to present appropriate supporting calculations.

2. Determine the dollar values of the finished goods inventories for SPL–3, PST–4, and RJ–5 as of November 30, 19X9.

3. Alderon Industries has an opportunity to sell PST–4 at the split-off point for $3.80 per gallon. Prepare an analysis showing whether Alderon should sell PST–4 at the split-off point or continue to process this product further.

4. As a production supervisor for Alderon, it has come to your attention that the critical chemical compound in PST–4 may be present in small quantities in SPL–3. What should you do?

(CMA Adapted)

14–28 **JOINT PRODUCTS; BY-PRODUCTS; REVIEW OF CHAPTERS 8 AND 10**
Lond Company produces joint products Jana and Reta, together with by-product Bynd. Jana is sold at split-off, whereas Reta and Bynd undergo additional processing. Production data pertaining to these products for the year ended December 31, 19X9, were

	Jana	Reta	Bynd	Total
Joint costs				
Variable				$ 88,000
Fixed				148,000
Separate costs				
Variable		$120,000	$ 3,000	$123,000
Fixed		90,000	2,000	92,000
Production in pounds	50,000	40,000	10,000	100,000
Sales price per pound	$4.00	$7.50	$1.10	

There were no beginning or ending inventories. No materials were spoiled in production. Bynd's net realizable value is deducted from joint costs. Joint costs are allocated to joint products to achieve the same gross margin percentage for each joint product.

Although 19X9 performance could be repeated for 19X0, Lond is considering possible operation of the plant at its full capacity of 120,000 pounds. The relative proportions of each product's output with respect to cost behavior and production increases would be unchanged. Market surveys indicate that prices of Jana and Bynd would have to be reduced to $3.40 and $0.90, respectively. Reta's expected price decline cannot be determined.

Required

1. Prepare the following schedules for Lond Company for the year ended December 31, 19X9:
    a. Total gross margin.
    b. Allocation of joint costs to Jana and Reta.
    c. Separate gross margins for Jana and Reta.

2. Compute Lond's breakeven point in pounds for the year ended December 31, 19X9.

3. Prepare the following schedules for Lond Company for the year ending December 31, 19X0:
    a. Projected production in pounds for each product at full capacity.
    b. Differential revenues (excluding Reta).
    c. Differential costs.
    d. Sales price required per pound of Reta in order for Lond to achieve the same gross margin as that for 19X9.

(CPA Adapted)

14–29 **DEPARTMENTAL COST ALLOCATION** Marfrank Corporation is a manufacturing company with six functional departments—finance, marketing, personnel, production, research and development (R&D), and information systems—each administered by a vice president. The

 *Strategy*

information systems department (ISD) was established in 19X8 when Marfrank decided to acquire a mainframe computer and develop a new information system.

While systems development and implementation is an ongoing process at Marfrank, many of the basic systems needed by each of the functional departments were operational at the end of 19X9. Thus, calendar year 19X0 is considered the first year for which the ISD costs can be estimated with a high degree of accuracy. Marfrank's president wants the other five functional departments to be aware of the magnitude of the ISD costs by reflecting the allocation of ISD costs in their reports and statements prepared at the end of the first quarter of 19X0. The allocation to each of the departments was based on their actual use of ISD services.

Jon Werner, vice president of ISD, suggested that the actual costs of ISD be allocated on the basis of pages of actual computer output. This basis was suggested because reports are what all the departments use in evaluating their operations and making decisions. The use of this basis resulted in the following allocation:

Department	Percentage	Allocated Cost
Finance	50%	$112,500
Marketing	30	67,500
Personnel	9	20,250
Production	6	13,500
R & D	5	11,250
Total	100%	$225,000

After the quarterly reports were distributed, the finance and marketing departments objected to this allocation method. Both departments recognized that they were responsible for most of the report output, but they believed that these output costs might be the smallest of ISD costs and requested that a more equitable allocation basis be developed.

After meeting with Werner, Elaine Jergens, Marfrank's controller, concluded that ISD provided three distinct services—systems development, computer processing represented by central processing unit (CPU) time, and report generation. She recommended that a predetermined rate be developed for each of these services based on budgeted annual activity and costs. The ISD costs would then be assigned to the other functional departments, using the predetermined rate times the actual activity used. Any difference between actual costs incurred and costs allocated to the other departments would be absorbed by ISD.

Jergens and Werner concluded that systems development could be charged on the basis of hours devoted to systems development and programming, computer processing based on CPU time used for operations (exclusive of database development and maintenance), and report generation based on pages of output. The only cost they thought should not be included in any of the predetermined rates was purchased software; these packages usually were acquired for a specific department's use. Thus, Jergens concluded that purchased software would be charged at cost to the department for which it was purchased. To revise the first-quarter allocation, she gathered this information on ISD costs and services:

Information Systems Department Services

	Estimated Annual Costs	Actual First-Quarter Costs	Percentage Devoted to		
			Systems Development	Computer Report	
				Processing	Generation
Wages/benefits					
Administration	$100,000	$25,000	60%	20%	20%
Computer operators	55,000	13,000		20	80
Analysts/programmers	165,000	43,500	100		
Maintenance					
Hardware	24,000	6,000	75	25	
Software	20,000	5,000	100		
Output supplies	50,000	11,500		100	
Purchased software	45,000	16,000*	—	—	—
Utilities	28,000	6,250	100		
Depreciation					
Mainframe computer	325,000	81,250	100		
Printing equipment	60,000	15,000		100	
Building improvements	10,000	2,500	100		
Total department costs	$882,000	$225,000			

*All software purchased during the first quarter of 19X0 was for the benefit of the production department.

Information Systems Department Services

	Systems Development	Computer Operations (CPU)	Report Generation
Annual capacity	4,500 hours	360 CPU hours	5,000,000 pages
Actual usage during first quarter, 19X0			
Finance	100 hours	8 CPU hours	600,000 pages
Marketing	250	12	360,000
Personnnel	200	12	108,000
Production	400	32	72,000
R&D	50	16	60,000
Total usage	1,000 hours	80 CPU hours	1,200,000 pages

Required

1. a. Develop predetermined rates for each of the service categories of ISD—systems development computer processing and report generation.

   b. Using the predetermined rates developed in requirement 1a, determine the amount each of the other five functional departments would be charged for services provided by ISD during the first quarter of 19X0.

2. With the method proposed by Elaine Jergens for charging the ISD costs to the other five functional departments, there may be a difference between ISD's actual costs incurred and the costs assigned to the five user departments.

   a. Explain the nature of this difference.

   b. Discuss whether this proposal will improve cost control in ISD.

3. Explain whether Jergen's proposed method of charging user departments for ISD costs will improve planning and control in the user departments.

4. Assume a finance manager has suggested that ISD should be outsourced. What are the factors Marfrank should consider in deciding whether or not to outsource ISD?

(CMA Adapted)

Strategy

International

14–30 JOINT AND BY-PRODUCT COSTING   Doe Corporation is a worldwide grower, processor, canner, and wholesaler of three main pineapple products—sliced pineapple, crushed pineapple, and pineapple juice. Doe's growers are located in Hawaii, with processing and canning plants in Hawaii, California, and Mexico. The markets are worldwide; Doe's two main competitors also compete worldwide.

Doe's production process begins when pineapples are processed in the cutting department. The pineapples are washed and the outside skin is cut away. Then the pineapples are cored and trimmed for slicing. The three main products (sliced, crushed, juice) and the by-product (animal feed) are recognizable after processing in the cutting department. Each product then is transferred to a separate department for final processing.

The trimmed pineapples are forwarded to the slicing department where the pineapples are sliced and canned. Any juice generated during the slicing operation is packed in the cans with the slices.

The pieces of pineapple trimmed from the fruit are diced and canned in the crushing department. Again, the juice generated during this operation is packed in the can with the crushed pineapple.

The core and surplus pineapple generated from the cutting department are pulverized into a liquid in the juicing department. There is an evaporation loss equal to 8 percent of the weight of the good output produced in this department, which occurs as the juices are heated.

The outside skin is chopped into animal feed in the feed department.

The Doe Corporation uses the sales value method to assign costs of the joint process to its main products. The by-product is inventoried at its market value.

A total of 270,000 pounds were entered into the cutting department during May. This schedule shows the costs incurred in each department, the proportion by weight transferred to the four final processing departments, and the selling price of each end product.

Department	Costs Incurred	Proportion of Product by Weight Transferred to Departments	Selling Price per Pound of Final Products
Cutting	$60,000	—	—
Slicing	4,700	35%	$.60
Crushing	10,580	28	.55
Juicing	3,250	27	.30
Animal feed	700	10	.10
Total	$79,230	100%	

Required

1. The Doe Corporation uses the net realizable value method to determine inventory values for its main products and by-products. Calculate:

   a. The pounds of pineapple that result as output for pineapple slices, crushed pineapple, pineapple juice, and animal feed.

   b. The net realizable value at the split-off point of the three main products.

   c. The amount of cutting department cost assigned to each of the three main products and to the by-product in accordance with corporate policy.

   d. The gross margins for each of the three main products.

2. Comment on the significance to management of the gross margin information by main products.

3. What are some of the important issues Doe faces as a global company? What are its critical success factors? Which key issues arise because Doe operates in several countries? Should any of these issues affect the way Doe allocates cost, as done in requirement 1 above?

(CMA Adapted)

SOLUTION TO SELF-STUDY PROBLEM

Joint Product Costing

Physical Measure Method

If we use a physical measure method, the joint cost of $20,000 is allocated as shown in Exhibit 14–28.

The production costs per gallon for both products are the same:

Product GS–50: $15,000/75 = $200

Product GS–80: $ 5,000/25 = $200

The Sales Value at Split-Off Method

Assume that a gallon of GS 50 can be sold for $300 and a gallon of GS–80 for $60, and the Northern Company has sold 60 gallons of GS–50 and 20 gallons of GS–80. Then the $20,000 joint cost should be allocated among the products as shown in Exhibit 14–29.

Note that the quantities sold do not figure in the analysis, which is based on *units produced* only. The production costs per gallon for both products are calculated:

Product GS–50 $18,750/75 = $250

Product GS–80 $ 1,250/25 = $ 50

The Net Realizable Value Method

Assume that the processing of GS–50 into GS–505 and GS–80 into GS–805 requires the additional separable costs of $5,000 and $2,000 respectively. Then the net realizable values of GS–50 and GS–80 are $20,000 and $5,000 as shown in Exhibit 14–30. The allocated costs are $16,000 to GS–50 and $4,000 to GS–80.

The costs per gallon for products GS–505 and GS–805 are calculated:

Product GS–505   ($16,000 + $5,000)/50 = $420

Product GS–805   ($ 4,000 + $2,000)/50 = $120

Exhibit 14–28   Physical Measure Method

Product	Physical Measure	Weight	Allocation of Joint Cost
GS–50	75 gallons	.75	$20,000 × .75 = $15,000
GS–80	25 gallons	.25	20,000 × .25 = 5,000

Exhibit 14–29   Sales Value at Split-off Method

Product	Units	Price	Sales Value	Weight	Joint Cost Allocated
GS–50	75	$300	$22,500	.9375	$20,000 × .9375 = $18,750
GS–80	25	60	1,500	.0625	20,000 × .0625 = 1,250
Total			$24,000	1.00	$20,000

Exhibit 14–30		Net Realizable Value Method					
Product	Production Units	Price	Sales Value	Separable Cost	Net Realized Value	Weight	Joint Cost Allocated
GS–50	50	$500	$25,000	$5,000	$20,000	.8	$20,000 × .8 = $16,000
GS–80	50	140	7,000	2,000	5,000	.2	20,000 × .2 = 4,000
Total	100		$32,000	$7,000	$25,000	1.0	$20,000

Part V

Cost Accounting and Operational Control

581

The Flexible Budget and Standard Costing:

Direct Materials and Direct Labor

After studying this chapter, you should be able to . . .

1 Evaluate the effectiveness and efficiency of an operation, and calculate and interpret the operating income variance

2 Develop and use flexible budgets to conduct further analyses of the operating income variance for control of operations and performance evaluation, as well as calculate and interpret the sales volume and flexible budget variances

3 Set proper standard costs for planning, control, and performance evaluation

4 Identify factors that contribute to an operating income flexible budget variance; and analyze and explain sales price variance, direct materials price and usage variances, and direct labor rate and efficiency variances

5 Assess the influence of the contemporary manufacturing environment on operational control and standard costing

6 Recognize behavioral implications in implementing standard cost systems

7 Describe cost flows through general ledger accounts and prepare journal entries for acquisition and uses of direct materials and direct labor in a standard cost system

Michael Newman/Photo Edit

He who controls the past controls the future.

GEORGE ORWELL

A successful firm carries out its operations as planned. Operating conditions, however, often do not occur exactly as forecast at the time the plan is prepared. Periodic review and evaluations enable the firm to learn from the past and, as George Orwell says, control the future.

EVALUATING OPERATING RESULTS

Two aspects of operations are generally of interest to management in assessing operations: effectiveness in attaining goals and efficiency in carrying out operations.

Effectiveness

An operation is **effective** if the firm has attained or exceeded the goal or goals set for the operation. A firm that sets out to earn $50 million net operating income for the year and earns $50 million is effective. A student who sets out to earn a 3.0 grade point average for the semester and receives a 3.25 is effective. A social service organization that has a goal of serving 50,000 hot meals to homeless people and serves 55,000 hot meals has an effective operation.

A firm is ineffective that has a goal of gaining 10 percent of total market share and gains only 6 percent at the end of the year. A student with a grade point average of 2.75 was not effective, though two part-time jobs may not have been part of the plan when the 3.0 goal was chosen.

Effective operations are essential for a successful strategy. Ineffective operations, on the other hand, can lead to a disaster. Firms with ineffective operations often suffer disappointing bottom lines and drain cash and other resources of the firm. Repeated ineffective operations often force the firm to either abandon or modify the strategy. Intel's effective operations enable the firm to be successful in carrying out its strategy of bringing new computer chips to the market before the competition. Intel has enjoyed high profitability and dominated the market since the mid 1980s. A series of setbacks in its operations, on the other hand, forced IBM to retreat and redirect its strategies several times since the early 1980s. IBM is no longer the computer giant that it once was.

Most organizations have multiple strategic goals. Effectiveness in attaining each of these goals should be assessed so that management has a clear grasp of the overall effectiveness of operations and the feasibility of attaining the strategic goals.

Some firms measure their effectiveness by analyzing one or a few of their critical success factors. A business firm may assess whether it earns the desired amount of

◀ **LEARNING OBJECTIVE 1**
Evaluate the effectiveness and efficiency of an operation and calculate and interpret the operating income variance.

An **effective operation** attains the goal set for the operation.

BusinessWeek

? How Has Benchmarking Made Its Mark on U.S. Business?

Benchmarking—it's certainly no stranger to today's business world. An uncommon business term and practice 20 years ago, ever since the Japanese began offering world-class products (and in turn, competition) in the '70s, benchmarking has become a key player in today's business environment. Take Xerox Corporation, for example. In 1979, Canon introduced a midsize copier for under $10,000. Xerox couldn't believe that Canon could produce a better product, assuming that Canon had priced it below fair value to buy market share. Instead, Xerox soon learned that Canon had in fact produced a quality product that cost less.

Q: How did Canon do it, and what was Xerox's response? *Find out on page 592 of this chapter.*

operating income, gains the target market share, introduces new products by the deadlines, or attains the rate of return on net assets as specified in the master budget. School districts may use the average SAT score of their high school graduates as a measure of their effectiveness. Students may assess their effectiveness by the number of credit hours completed or the grade point average earned.

A master budget often is based on the desired operating results for the period. As a result, many firms use the master budget of a period as the starting point in assessing the effectiveness of their operations.

Efficiency

An **efficient operation** wastes no resources in operations.

A firm with an **efficient operation** wastes no resources. An operation is inefficient if the firm spent more than the amount of resources necessary or specified for the task completed. A firm that incurred $40,000 to manufacture and sell 10,000 units is efficient if the standard calls for a cost of $4 per unit. The same firm would be inefficient if it incurred costs of $50,000 for the same 10,000 units.

Assessments of efficiency are independent of assessments of effectiveness. A firm can be effective through attaining the goal or goals set for its operation, yet still be inefficient. Conversely, a firm can be efficient yet not be effective if it fails to attain the goal for its operations. Consider the previous manufacturing firm. If it made and sold 9,000 units in a period when its master budget specified manufacturing and selling 10,000 units for the period, the firm was ineffective. It did not meet its sales goal of 10,000 units. If the firm spent $35,000 to manufacture and sell the 9,000 units, it was efficient. The firm was effective if it manufactured and sold 12,000 units and attained the goal for the period. The firm was not efficient, however, if it spent $60,000 to manufacture 12,000 units, or $5 per unit instead of the $4 standard cost.

Assessing Effectiveness

An important short-term goal for a company is to earn the operating income projected for the period. The effectiveness of a company often is measured by comparing the actual amount of operating income to the master budget amount. The difference between the actual operating income and the master budget operating income is the **operating income variance.**

The **operating income variance** of a period is the difference between the actual operating income of the period and the master budget operating income projected for the period.

Consider the analysis of operations for Schmidt Machinery Company in Exhibit 15–1. The budgeted operating income for the period is $200,000 in column (2), while the actual operating income for the period is $128,000 in column (1). The operating income variance for the period, therefore, is $72,000 unfavorable in column (3). Schmidt Machinery Company was not effective in attaining its goal for the period; its operation is 36 percent short of the budgeted operating income.

Exhibit 15–1	Comparing Operating Results with Master Budget					
SCHMIDT MACHINERY COMPANY **Analysis of Operations** **For the period ended October 31, 20X6**						
	(1) Actual		(2) Master Budget		(3) Variance		(4) Actual as Percent of Master Budget
Units sold	780		1,000		220	U*	78.00%
Sales	$639,600	100%	$800,000	100%	$160,400	U	79.95
Variable expenses	350,950	55	450,000	56	99,050	F†	77.99
Contribution margin	$288,650	45%	$350,000	44%	$ 61,350	U	82.47
Fixed expenses	160,650	25	150,000	19	10,650	U	107.10
Operating income	$128,000	20%	$200,000	25%	$ 72,000	U	64.00

*U denotes an *unfavorable* effect on the budgeted operating income.

†F denotes a *favorable* effect.

Besides the operating income variance, we can determine a variance for each item by finding the difference between the master budget and the actual result. Notice that the variance between the actual sales and the expected sales stands out. Actual sales are 220 units and $160,400 less than the budgeted amounts. On the other hand, the variable expenses variance is favorable—$99,050 less than the budgeted amount. This comparison probably would lead us to conclude that the primary reason for the failure of the Schmidt Machinery Company to attain its budgeted net income is the shortfall in sales. The shortfall is so large that even with good control of expenses, evidenced by the substantial favorable variance in variable expenses, the firm still suffers a substantial decrease in operating income.

That conclusion, however, is only half-correct at best and may be misleading. Direct comparisons between the actual amounts incurred and the master or static budget amounts for variable expenses are often meaningless. The variable expenses in the master or static budget are for operations at a higher level than that actually achieved. Variable expenses at the 780-unit level of the budgeted operation should be less than the variable expenses at the 1,000-unit level. Thus, Schmidt Machinery Company should not give credit to its management for having good control of its expenses based only on this comparison. Differences between the actual amount and the master budgeted amount for variable expenses are not measures of effectiveness. Nor are they measures of efficiency, as we discuss later.

The operating income variance reveals only whether the firm has achieved the budgeted operating income for the period; it does not point out causes for the deviation or help the firm identify courses of action to reduce or eliminate similar deviations in the future. The firm needs to conduct further analyses to learn not only whether the firm is on target but also the reason for missing the target. One approach to finding this knowledge is to conduct an analysis on the efficiency of the operation. The flexible budget for the period at the attained level of operation is a useful tool for such an analysis.

The Flexible Budget

As operating conditions change, an organization needs a budget that incorporates the changes. The master or static budget is useful for initial planning and coordinating efforts for the budget period. The planning and evaluating done near and at the end of the period should incorporate the actual events as much as possible. One tool to use is a flexible budget.

The **flexible budget** is a budget that adjusts revenues and expenses for changes in output achieved. With changes in output (units manufactured or sold for a manufacturing firm, number of patient-days for a hospital, or number of students for a school district) revenues and expenses of the firm also deviate from the budgeted amount.

Flexible budgets can help management answer many important questions about an operation. The data for the Schmidt Machinery Company in Exhibit 15–1 show that the operating income of the period is $72,000 below the budgeted amount. On receiving the report, management likely would want to know:

1. Why has net income gone down?
2. Why has the cost of sales gone from 69 to 71 percent? Can management do something to prevent the same thing from happening next year?
3. Why have selling and general expenses increased $10,650?
4. What are the reasons for the deterioration in operating results? Is it because of changes in
   a. units sold?
   b. sales price?
   c. sales mix?
   d. manufacturing or merchandising cost?
   e. selling and general expenses?

Flexible budgeting allows management to analyze the operating results and changes in operating conditions in detail, helping to find answers to these questions.

◀ **LEARNING OBJECTIVE 2**
Develop and use flexible budgets to conduct further analyses of the operating income variance for control of operations and performance evaluation, as well as calculate and interpret the sales volume and flexible budget variances.

The **flexible budget** is a budget that adjusts revenues and costs for changes in output achieved.

Flexible budgets differ from the master budget in the number of budgeted output units. Other factors, such as *unit* sales prices, *unit* variable costs, and *total* fixed expenses, in flexible budgets are the same as the master budget. Exhibit 15–2 illustrates flexible budgets for Schmidt Machinery Company. As sales units change, the total sales and total variable expenses change. As a result, the total contribution margin and operating income also change. The unit selling price, unit variable cost, and total fixed expense, however, remain the same.

For a sales level that is 80 percent of the master budget sales level, sales, variable expenses, and contribution margin for the flexible budget are 80 percent of the corresponding amounts of the master budget. The fixed expenses remain at the $150,000 level for flexible budgets at the 80 percent and 110 percent levels. Also, the operating income for the flexible budget at 80 percent is not 80 percent of the amount in the flexible budget at 100 percent (master budget). In this example, the operating income of the flexible budget at 80 percent ($130,000) is only 65 percent of the operating income of the master budget ($200,000). The fixed expenses account for the lower percentage because the $150,000 fixed expenses are a much greater proportion of the smaller sales level.

Total sales and total expenses for a flexible budget are calculated using this formula:

Total sales = Number of units sold × Budgeted sales price per unit

Total expenses = Total variable expenses + Total fixed expenses

= (Number of units sold × Budgeted variable cost per unit)

+ Budgeted total fixed expenses

A firm can prepare flexible budgets for different levels of operation or activity. In addition, flexible budgets can differ from the master or static budget in the timing of their preparation and in their levels of detail. A firm can prepare flexible budgets anytime—before, during, or after an operation—while a firm prepares a master budget only before the operation starts.

Flexible budgets also typically contain fewer details than master budgets, facilitating analysis of selected aspects of an operation. Exhibit 15–3 highlights some of these differences.

Assessing Efficiency

Two aspects of efficiency are usually of interest to firms that manufacture and sell products. These are the flexible budget variance and the sales volume or activity

Exhibit 15–2	**Flexible Budgets of Schmidt Machinery Company**					
	(1) Flexible Budget at 80 Percent		**(2)** Flexible Budget at 100 percent		**(3)** Flexible Budget at 110 percent	
Units sold	800		1,000		1,100	
Sales ($800)	$640,000	100.00%	$800,000	100.00%	$880,000	100.00%
Variable expenses ($450)	360,000	56.25	450,000	56.25	495,000	56.25
Contribution margin ($350)	$280,000	43.75%	$350,000	43.75%	$385,000	43.75%
Fixed expenses	150,000	23.44	150,000	18.75	150,000	17.05
Operating income	$130,000	20.31%	$200,000	25.00%	$235,000	26.70%

Exhibit 15–3	**The Master Budget and the Flexible Budget Compared**	
	Master Budget	**Flexible Budget**
Time prepared	Before the period	Before, during, or after the period
Activity levels	Single level	One or more levels
Levels of detail	All aspects of operations	Selected aspects

variance. The **flexible budget variance** is the difference between the actual operating result and the flexible budget amount at the actual operating level of the period. A flexible budget variance measures efficiency in using input resources to attain the operating results of the period. The difference between the flexible budget and the master or static budget is the sales volume or activity variance.

Sales Volume (Activity) Variance

The **sales volume or activity variance** measures the effect on sales, expenses, contribution margins, or operating income of changes in units of sales. In column (4) of Exhibit 15–4 you can see the sales volume variances for Schmidt Machinery Company's operations in October 20X6.

Schmidt Machinery Company sold 780 units during the month, while the master budget in column (5) planned a sale of 1,000 units for the period. Column (3) shows the flexible budget at the level of the actual units sold during the period. Comparing these budgets, we find the sales volume (activity) variance to be 220 units unfavorable in units and $77,000 unfavorable in operating income, as reported in column (4). Note that the operating income sales volume (activity) variance is the same as the contribution margin sales volume (activity) variance. These variances always are identical because fixed expenses do not change when considering the effect of changes in sales volumes on operating income. Alternatively, the operating income sales volume (activity) variance is the product of the budgeted contribution margin per unit in the master budget and the difference in units of sales between the actual units sold and the units in the master (static) budget.

$$\begin{array}{ccc} \text{Operating} & & \left[\begin{array}{cc}\text{Actual} & \text{Budgeted}\\ \text{units} - & \text{sales in}\\ \text{sold} & \text{units}\end{array}\right] & \begin{array}{c}\text{Master budget}\\ \times \quad \text{contribution}\\ \text{margin per unit}\end{array} \end{array}$$

$$= (780 - 1{,}000) \times \$350$$

$$= \$77{,}000 \text{ U}$$

The operating income sales volume variance shows that when the sales volume decreases by 220 units, the operating income of the firm decreases by $77,000.

> The **flexible budget variance** is the difference between the actual operating result and the flexible budget at the actual operating level of the period.
>
> The **sales volume or activity variance** measures the effect on sales, expenses, contribution margins, or operating income of changes in units of sales.

Exhibit 15–4   **Assessing Operating Results with a Flexible Budget**

SCHMIDT MACHINERY COMPANY
Analysis of Operations
For the period ended October 31, 20X6

Data Item for Analysis	(1) Actual	(2) Flexible Budget Variance		(3) Flexible Budget	(4) Sales Volume (Activity) Variance		(5) Master (Static) Budget
Units sold	780	0		780	220	U	1,000
Sales	$639,600	$15,600	F	$624,000	$176,000	U	$800,000
Variable expenses	350,950	50	F	351,000	99,000	F	450,000
Contribution margin	$288,650	$15,650	F	$273,000	$ 77,000	U	$350,000
Fixed expenses	160,650	10,650	U	150,000	0		150,000
Operating income	$128,000	$ 5,000	F	$123,000	$ 77,000	U	$200,000

Analysis of Operating Income Variances

Total operating income variance
= $128,000 − $200,000 = $72,000 U

Flexible budget variance	Sales volume variance
= $128,000 − $123,000	= $123,000 − $200,000
= $5,000 F	= $77,000 U

587

Sales volume (activity) variances can have significant implications on strategic management. A significant unfavorable sales volume variance can be an indication that the market may be smaller than the level planned at the time the firm set the strategy. The firm may need to modify or abandon its strategy. An insignificant sales volume variance confirms the firm's strategy. A significant favorable sales volume variance can be an indication that the firm needs to pursue the strategy more aggressively.

Operating Income Flexible Budget Variance

> The **operating income flexible budget variance** is the difference between the flexible budget operating income for the units sold and the actual operating income.

The **operating income flexible budget variance** is the difference between the flexible budget operating income for the actual units sold and the actual operating income earned during the period. In Exhibit 15–4, the operating income flexible budget variance is the difference in operating income between columns (1) and (3). Column (1) reports the actual operating income earned from selling 780 units. Column (3) shows the budgeted operating income the firm would have earned if the firm operates at the budgeted efficiency in the manufacturing and selling of 780 units. The $5,000 difference in operating income is due to the differences in sales price, variable expenses, and/or fixed expenses.

Flexible budget operating income variances measure efficiencies in operations that are primarily internal to the firm. Unfavorable flexible budget operating income variances can diminish the feasibility of the strategy and jeopardize continuation of the strategy.

The remainder of this chapter and the next chapter examine the flexible budget operating income variance in more detail. This detailed analysis isolates the portion of the variance due to differences in sales price, variable expenses, and/or fixed expenses. This further examination of the factors that contribute to a flexible budget operating income variance requires a good understanding of standard costs, so we turn to that topic next.

STANDARD COST

LEARNING OBJECTIVE 3 ▶
Set proper standard costs for planning, control, and performance evaluation.

How many strokes should a golfer take to play a course? How much should it cost the Ford Motor Company to manufacture an Explorer? How much should it cost Wal-Mart to sell a hair dryer? How much should it cost a New York City mission to serve a hot meal to a homeless person?

A golfer uses the par for the course as a gauge for performance. *Par* is the number of strokes golfers expect to take to cover a course competently; it is the *standard* golfers strive to attain. The costs that the Ford Motor Company, Wal-Mart, and the mission in New York City set for their operations are standard costs. A

> A **standard cost** is the cost a firm ought to incur for an operation.

standard cost is the ideal predetermined expenditure a firm ought to incur for an operation or a specific objective.

Standard costs are among the foundations for a firm's planning and control activities. These activities include budget preparation, monitoring and control operations, and performance evaluation. A furniture manufacturer budgets the dollar amount of direct materials required to produce 5,000 entertainment centers based on the standard usage of direct materials per entertainment center and standard prices of the materials. If the standard calls for 3 square feet of plexiglass for each entertainment center at $15 per square foot, the firm has a materials budget of 15,000 square feet of plexiglass and $225,000 ($15 × 15,000). The firm also uses the $15 price per foot and the 3-foot standard per unit in monitoring its manufacturing operations and assessing performance.

Components of a Standard Cost System

A standard cost prescribes what expected performances should or ought to be. A complete standard cost for an operation is composed of carefully established standards for each of the operating cost elements, including manufacturing costs, selling expenses, and administrative expenses. Although the discussions in this and the next chapter focus on standard cost systems for manufacturing operations, these concepts and procedures also can be applied to standard cost systems for other operations.

A manufacturing operation has three manufacturing cost elements: direct materials, direct labor, and factory overhead. This chapter focuses on standard costs for direct materials and direct labor. Chapter 16 discusses the standard cost for factory overhead costs.

Standard costs can differ with different types of standards. Next we discuss the different types of standards that firms use.

Types of Standards

Not all firms have similar expectations for their standards. Differences in expectation levels lead to two types of standards—ideal and currently attainable.

Ideal Standard

An **ideal standard** is a standard that demands perfect implementation and maximum efficiency in every aspect of the operation. A firm can meet the ideal standard set for its operations only if all factors turn out exactly as expected and the firm carries out its operations exactly as prescribed. An ideal standard is a forward-looking standard; rarely is it a historical standard.

Suppose the ideal standard for manufacturing a tabletop calls for cutting two 4-by-4-foot tabletops from one 8-by-4-foot sheet of plywood so that each tabletop measures exactly 4-by-4-foot. According to the ideal standard, producing 1,000 tabletops requires 500 sheets of plywood. A firm can meet such a standard if all equipment and instruments are in proper working condition, there is no defective plywood, and workers cut all pieces perfectly.

An ideal standard is not easily attained. During an operation, accidents happen, unexpected events arise, and undesirable circumstances manifest themselves. Perfect performance, however, is not impossible. Today's highly competitive environment and demands for total quality management in all aspects of an operation have made many firms realize the importance of attaining ever higher ideal standards in all their operations. This is often called a continuous improvement strategy.

At times an ideal standard can be met only if everybody involved, including people performing the task and those in supporting functions, exert extraordinary efforts throughout the operation. Extraordinary efforts to achieve an ideal standard, while possible, may lead to undue stress over a long period, which, in turn, decreases morale, increases apathetic attitudes among employees, and decreases the long-term productivity of the organization. Such concerns have led firms to adopt ideal standards for their operations only infrequently. Some firms set ideal standards for their operations because they are facing a crisis and need extraordinary efforts.

Firms that use ideal standards often modify performance evaluations and reward structures so that employees are not frustrated by failure to attain the ideal standard immediately. A firm, for example, may use progress toward the ideal standard, rather than deviations from the standard, as the primary factor in its performance evaluation and reward system.

Currently Attainable Standard

A **currently attainable standard** sets the performance criterion at a level that workers with proper training and experience can attain most of the time without extraordinary effort. A currently attainable standard emphasizes normality and allows for some deviations.

Suppose a firm sets the standard for the plywood to produce 1,000 tabletops at 525 sheets of plywood, although two tabletops can be cut from one sheet of plywood. The additional 25 sheets allow for such things as less than ideal input quality, occasional maladjustment of the equipment used in production, and varying experience and skill levels of the personnel involved in the production. With a standard that allows for some deviations, the firm usually can reach a currently attainable standard with reasonable effort.

An **ideal standard** is a standard that demands perfect implementation and maximum efficiency in every aspect of the operation.

A **currently attainable standard** sets the performance criterion at a level that workers with proper training and experience can attain most of the time without extraordinary effort.

Selection of a Standard

Which standards—ideal or currently attainable—should a firm use in its standard cost system? There is no single answer for all situations. The most suitable standard for a firm is the one that helps it to attain its strategic goals.

For many firms struggling for survival in intensely competitive industries, an ideal standard appropriately motivates workers to put forth extraordinary effort. An ideal standard is not effective, however, if frequent failures to meet the standard discourage employees or lead them to ignore the standards.

Conversely, a currently attainable standard allows for inefficiencies. This allowance is strategically unwise in the intensely competitive environment in which most firms operate. A standard that allows 25 additional sheets of plywood conveys to production workers that they have attained an excellent performance as long as they do not make more than 25 mistakes for every 500 sheets of plywood they cut.

Inefficiencies cost the firm and decrease its operating income. Inefficiencies also can cause the competitive position of the firm to decline. An ideal standard prescribes a high-yet-achievable performance. Any deviation from the ideal standard is an imperfection and undesirable to the firm. A world-class firm can ill afford any inefficiency and, most likely, would use ideal standards for its operations.

Today's dynamic and intensely competitive environment requires all organizations to reexamine standards periodically and maintain continuous improvement. New technologies, equipment, and production processes often make existing standards obsolete. Without continuous updating of standards, a firm finds survival in a fiercely competitive global economy that demands total quality and high efficiency difficult.

Nonfinancial Measures

Although most measures in standard cost systems eventually are expressed in dollar amounts as costs to the firm, nonfinancial measures often play important roles in standard cost systems. Managers do not manage costs; they manage activities. Managers must control all activities that are strategically important for meeting the firm's goals. Some of these activities, such as friendly service, on-time delivery, and quality, do not have financial measures. For example, management at McDonald's considers QSCV (quality, service, cleanliness, and value) to be the foremost factors for its success, yet none of them can be reflected directly by a financial measure.

Sources of the Standards

Firms often use several sources in determining appropriate standards for their operations. These sources include activity analysis, historical data, standards for similar operations in other firms (a technique known as benchmarking), market expectations (target costing), and strategic decisions.

Activity Analysis

Activity analysis is the process of identifying, delineating, and evaluating the activities required to complete a job, project, or operation. A thorough activity analysis includes all the input factors and activities required to complete the task efficiently. The analysis involves personnel from several functional areas including product engineers, industrial engineers, management accountants, and production workers.

Because each product is different, product engineers need to specify the components of the products in detail. Based on the facilities and equipment of the firm and the design of the product, the industrial engineers then analyze the steps or procedures necessary to complete the task or product. Management accountants work with engineers to complete the analyses.

For example, an activity analysis for preparing a hamburger at a fast-food restaurant starts with an assessment of the ingredients of the hamburger and the tasks involved in preparing, cooking, and wrapping it. It specifies the quantities and qualities of onion, lettuce, tomato, pickle, ground beef, buns, and other ingredients. The analysis then determines the tools, the steps or procedures, and the time needed to chop onions, cut lettuce, slice tomatoes and pickles, cook the hamburger, and wrap the product. The analysis specifies the required skill level of the workers, experience of workers, equipment to be used, and other relevant factors affecting performance. The management accountant adds the cost of the ingredients, wage rates of workers with the required skill levels, and overheads to arrive at the total standard cost.

Activity analysis, if properly executed, offers the most precise specification for determining standards. Activity analysis, however, is time consuming and expensive.

Historical Data

Historical data for making a similar product often can be a good source for determining the standard cost of an operation when reliable and accurate data are available. When data for determining the standard are lacking or insufficient and the cost of developing standards through activity analysis or other alternative methods is prohibitively high, the firm may use historical data to establish the standard. The high cost of developing standards through an alternative method leaves small businesses with little choice but to rely on historical data if they want to take advantage of standard costing and flexible budget systems.[1]

By carefully analyzing historical data for manufacturing a product or executing a task, management can determine appropriate standards for operations. A common practice is to use the average or the median of historical amounts for an operation as the standard of the operation. A firm determined to excel, however, would use as the standard the best performance in the past.

Analysis of historical data is usually much less expensive than an activity analysis for determining standards. Analysis of historical data also has the advantage of including all manufacturing factors concerning the way a firm operates in determining the standard for the firm. A standard based on the past may, however, be biased and perpetuate past inefficiencies. Furthermore, historical standards are more attainable than ideal standards and are not necessarily consistent with continuous improvements required of many firms in today's worldwide competitive environment.

Benchmarking

Associations of manufacturers often collect industry information and have data available that managers can use in determining operation standards. Current practices of similar operations in other firms, not necessarily firms in the same industry, also can be good guidelines for setting the standard.

In recent years many world-class firms were not satisfied with using the best operations of firms in the same industry; they have adopted as standards the best operations of any firm. Bath Iron Works, the fourth-largest shipyard in the United States, uses as benchmarks the German firm Thyssen for pipe bending, Walt Disney World for preventive maintenance, and L.L. Bean for receipt inspection and paper reduction. IBM's plant in Austin, Texas, uses for benchmarks such plants as Tatung, Sampo, and DTK in Taiwan. For its circuit board manufacturing, Allen-Bradley benchmarks a Hewlett-Packard Company plant in Colorado and Digital Equipment Company.

The advantage of using benchmarking is that a firm is using the best performance anywhere as the standard. Using such a standard can help the firm maintain a competitive edge in today's global competition. A firm that reviews its benchmark periodically and compares its standards with the best operations worldwide can regularly maintain its edge over competitors. Data from trade associations or other firms, however, may not be completely applicable to the unique situation in which a firm operates.

---

[1]   William C. Lawler and John Leslie Livingstone, "Profit and Productivity Analysis for Small Businesses," *Journal of Accountancy*, December 1986, pp. 190–96.

BusinessWeek

How Did Xerox Make Its Comeback—and Raise the Bar?

(Continues from page 583)

A: Through ten key steps . . .

It took Xerox more than a year to decide that "we had to get back on track or roll over and die," recalls Robert C. Camp, manager of benchmarking competency at Xerox Corporation. Recognizing that Canon and other Japanese companies were becoming more competitive by taking a close look at its competition, Xerox decided to take similar action—adopting benchmarking as its comeback technique. Specifically, Xerox adapted various Japanese techniques, cutting its unit-production costs in half, reducing inventory costs by two-thirds, and in turn increasing its share of the U.S. copier market by 50 percent, to approximately 15 percent.

But Xerox didn't stop there. Camp took what Xerox learned in manufacturing and created a "10-step recipe for achieving quantum leaps in the performance of any department or process." The recipe included determining the best practices in the industry, developing a strategy to match what the best would probably be in the future, and employing this strategy over and over again. For example, when Xerox started out on its comeback in the early '80s, it went to L.L. Bean Inc., a known leader in order fulfillment. By looking to the standards of a leader, Xerox learned what was necessary to be the best in order-fulfillment processes and cut its warehousing costs by 10 percent. In addition to obtaining a stronger bottom line, Xerox also learned that looking beyond its competition and benchmarking with leaders in other industries is a step in the right direction.

For further reading, see "Beg, Borrow—and Benchmark," *Business Week,* November 30, 1992; "Quality," *Business Week,* November 30, 1992.

Market Expectations and Strategic Decisions

Market expectations and strategic decisions often play important roles in standard setting, especially for firms using target costing (Chapter 5). With a set sales price for which the firm can or desires to sell the product, the *target cost* is the cost that yields the desired profit margin for the product. It is computed as the difference between the sales price and the desired profit margin of the product. Detailed standards then are determined for manufacturing the product at the target cost.

A firm that has a target sales price of $200 and desires to earn a gross profit margin of 25 percent of the sales price has a target cost of $150. The total standard cost for manufacturing the product then would be set not to exceed $150.

Strategic decisions also have effects on the standard cost of a product. A strategic decision to strive for continuous improvement (known by the Japanese term *kaizen*) and zero defects would require the firm to set the standard for the product at the most challenging level continuously. As another example, the strategic decision to replace a manual drilling machine with a high-precision automatic drilling machine would require the firm to alter the standard for its manufacturing process.

Standard Setting Procedures

Using one or more of these sources of standards as the starting point, a firm may use either an authoritative procedure or participation in setting the standard of the firm.

An **authoritative standard**
is determined solely or
primarily by management.

A **participative standard**
calls for active
participation throughout
the standard-setting
process by workers
affected by the standard.

An **authoritative standard** is determined solely or primarily by management. In contrast, a **participative standard** calls for active participation throughout the standard-setting process by workers affected by the standard. A firm uses an authoritative process to ensure proper consideration for all operating factors, incorporate the desires or expectations of management, or expedite the standard-setting process. Firms using an authoritative process in standard setting, however, should keep in mind that a perfect standard is useless if it is not accepted and implemented by the employees affected by the standard.

Employee participation in setting a standard makes it more likely that they will accept the standard. It also reduces the chance that employees will view the stan-

An Exemplary Participative Standard Setting

Merrill-Continental Company, Inc. attributes the successful implementation of its standard cost system to the fact that the standards essentially were designed on the shop floor by the operating supervisors, and not by an outside industrial engineering department. The performance standards, as a result, were accepted and used enthusiastically by employees.

Source: Based on Thomas A. Faulhaber, Fred A. Coad, and Thomas J. Little, "Building a Process Cost Management System from the Bottom Up," *Management Accounting,* May 1988, pp. 58–62.

dard as unreasonable and makes it more likely they will buy into or adopt the standard as their own.

Establishing Standard Cost

Establishing a standard cost is a joint effort of management, product design engineers, industrial engineers, management accountants, production supervisors, the purchasing department, the personnel department, and the employees affected by the standard. Although not all of them are always involved, they participate at various points in establishing the standard cost.

Costs are the results of activities to create products or render services, and as we have said, activities, not costs, are what managers manage. All standards, therefore, should be established for cost drivers underlying the costs associated with the product or service cost object.

Establishing Standard Cost for Direct Materials

A standard cost for direct materials for a given product has three facets: quality, quantity, and price.

The first step in establishing a standard cost is to specify clearly the quality of the direct materials for the manufacturing process or product. The quality of direct materials often affects the quantity of the direct materials needed in the process, their price, the time required to process them, and the extent and frequency of supervision needed to complete the process.

Often trade-offs are needed between using more expensive, higher-quality direct materials and less expensive, lower-quality direct materials in operations. The marketing department, engineering department, production department, and management accountants need to assess these trade-offs and determine the quality of the direct materials for the product.

Once the quality of the direct materials has been specified, several departments including the industrial engineering department, the production department, and management accountants need to work together to set standards for the quantity of direct materials to be consumed by the manufacturing process or product. Among factors considered in setting quantity standards are product design, cost drivers of manufacturing activities, quality of the direct materials, and the conditions of the production facility and equipment to be used in manufacturing the product.

A firm determines its price standards for direct materials with considerations for quality, quantity, and, at times, the timing of purchases. In a competitive environment, many companies emphasize long-term relationships with selected suppliers that are reliable in delivering quality materials on time. Then, the price standard needs to be revised only when the underlying long-term factors in the determination of price change.

Establishing Standard Cost for Direct Labor

Direct labor costs vary with the type of work involved, complexity of the product, skill level of workers, nature of the manufacturing process, and type and condition of the equipment to be used. Based on these factors, the industrial engineering department, production department, labor union, personnel department, and management accountants determine jointly the quantity standard for direct labor.

593

Exhibit 15-5   **Standard Cost Sheet**

SCHMIDT MACHINERY COMPANY
Standard Cost Sheet

Product: XV-1

Description	Quantity	Unit Cost	Subtotal	Total
Direct materials:				
Aluminum	4 pounds	$25	$100	
PVC	1 pound	40	40	$140
Direct labor	5 hours	40		200
Factory overhead (based on direct labor-hours):				
Variable	5 hours	12	60	
Fixed	5 hours	24	120	180
Standard Cost per Unit				$520

The personnel department determines the standard wage rate for the type and skill level of workers needed for the manufacturing process. The standard labor rate, for either direct or indirect labor, includes not only compensation paid but also fringe benefits granted to employees and required payroll taxes associated with wages and salaries. Fringe benefits include health and life insurance, pension plan contributions, and paid vacations. Payroll taxes include unemployment taxes and the employer's share of an employee's Social Security.

Standard Cost Sheet

A **standard cost sheet**
specifies the standard
price and quantity of each
manufacturing cost
element for the production
of one product.

A **standard cost sheet** specifies the standard price and quantity of each manufacturing cost element for the production of one product.

In Exhibit 15-5 is a simplified standard cost sheet for the Schmidt Machinery Company. Not included in the standard cost sheet is the budgeted variable selling and administrative expense of $50 per unit.

Schmidt's standard cost sheet specifies that the standard cost for one unit of XV-1 is 4 pounds of aluminum at $25 per pound, 1 pound of PVC at $40 per pound, 5 hours of direct labor at $40 per hour, and factory overhead of $36 ($12 + $24) per direct labor-hour.

OPERATING INCOME FLEXIBLE BUDGET VARIANCE

LEARNING OBJECTIVE 4 ▶
Identify factors that
contribute to an operating
income flexible budget
variance; and analyze and
explain sales price
variance, direct materials
price and usage
variances, and direct
labor rate and efficiency
variances.

The **sales price variance**
is the difference between
the total actual sales
revenue and the total
flexible budget sales
revenue for the units sold
during a period.

Factors that contribute to an operating income flexible budget variance include deviations of sales price, variable expense, and fixed expense from their standard amounts. Deviations of fixed expenses are discussed in Chapter 16.

Sales Price Variance

A **sales price variance** is the difference between the total actual sales revenue and the total flexible budget sales revenue for the units sold during the period. The same sales units are used in calculating the total actual sales revenues of the period and the total flexible budget. The difference between total sales revenue in the actual operating result of the period and in the flexible budget can be attributed to the difference in sales price.

Exhibit 15-4 shows that Schmidt Machinery Company sold 780 units of XV-1 for $639,600, or $820 per unit. The budgeted sales price, however, is $800 per unit. At the budgeted selling price of $800 per unit, the total sales revenue in the flexible budget for 780 units is $624,000. The difference, $15,600, is due to the actual selling price being $20 per unit higher than the budgeted selling price for the 780 units sold. This is the calculation of the sales price variance:

A Standard Cost Sheet of Merrill-Continental Company, Inc.

Product letter		A	B	C
Color		Black	Black	White
Felt		Y	N	Y
Width	Inches	48	48	48
Thickness of rubber	Inches	0.060	0.080	0.060
Roll length	Feet	100	80	100
Package type		1	2	1
Production rate	Feet/Min	6	4	6
Trim loss	Percent	5.0%	5.0%	10.0%
Trim recovery	Percent	2.0%	3.0%	5.0%
Glue usage	Pounds/sf	0.05	0.05	0.10
Materials				
Compound 1 $/lb	0.41	1	1	0
Compound 1 S.G.	1.60			
Compound 2 $/lb	0.41	0	0	1
Compound 2 S.G.	1.58			
Felt 1 $/S.F.	0.06	1	0	0
Felt 2 $/S.F.	0.08	0	0	1
Glue 1 $/lb	0.60	1	0	0
Glue 2 $/lb	0.80	0	0	1
Package 1 $/Each	2.00	1	0	1
Package 2 $/Each	4.00	0	1	0
Labor	**$/Hour**			
Direct —Extruder	$10.00	1.00	1.00	1.00
—Operator	$6.00	3.00	2.00	3.00
Indirect —Maintenance	$12.00	0.50	0.50	0.50
—Forklift	$8.00	0.30	0.30	0.30
Changeover—Setup				
Line hours	Each	0.50	0.50	0.50
Scrap	S.F. Each	500	500	50

Source: Thomas A. Faulhaber, Fred A. Coad, and Thomas J. Little, "Building a Process Cost Management System from the Bottom Up," *Management Accounting*, May 1988, p. 60.

$$\begin{array}{l} \text{Sales} \\ \text{price} \\ \text{variance} \end{array} = \left[\begin{array}{c} \text{Actual selling} \\ \text{price per} \\ \text{unit} \end{array} - \begin{array}{c} \text{Flexible budget} \\ \text{sales price} \\ \text{per unit} \end{array} \right] \times \begin{array}{c} \text{Actual} \\ \text{units} \\ \text{sold} \end{array}$$

$$= (\$820 - \$800) \times 780 \text{ units}$$

$$= \$15,600 \text{ Favorable}$$

Flexible Budget Variable Expense Variance

The **flexible budget variable expense variance** is the difference between the actual variable expenses incurred and the total standard variable expenses in the flexible budget for the units sold during the period. This variance reflects the deviation of actual variable expenses from the standard variable expenses for the number of units sold during the period.

In Exhibit 15–4 we see that Schmidt Machinery Company incurred a total variable expense of $350,950 for the period to produce and sell 780 units of XV–l. On the standard cost sheet in Exhibit 15–5, the standard variable manufacturing expense is $400 per unit, including $140 for direct materials, $200 for direct labor, and $60 for variable manufacturing overhead. For 780 units, the total standard

> The **flexible budget variable expense variance** is the difference between the actual variable expenses incurred and the total standard variable expenses in the flexible budget for the units sold during the period.

variable manufacturing expense is $312,000. In addition, the standard variable selling and administrative expense is $50 per unit, or $39,000 in total. This brings the total variable expense for manufacturing and selling 780 units to $351,000.

The total actual variable expense incurred in October, $350,950, is $50 less than the standard expense for manufacturing 780 units of XV–1, $351,000. This suggests that the operation met the standards set in the standard cost sheet.

Need for Further Analysis of the Flexible Budget Variable Expense Variance

The flexible budget variable expense variance is the sum of variances of cost elements that constitute the total variable expense. They include direct materials variances, direct labor variances, variable overhead variances, and variable selling and administrative expense variances. Different factors may drive each of these variances. Aggregations of variances can mask poor performance in one or more of the cost components or operating divisions, especially when there are offsetting material, labor, manufacturing overhead, or selling and administrative variances, as is true in the operating results of the Schmidt Machinery Company.

The operating results of Schmidt Machinery Company for the period show a $50 favorable flexible budget variable expense variance. Further analyses of the expenses shown in Exhibit 15–6 reveal that Schmidt Machinery Company spent $94,380 for 3,630 pounds of aluminum to manufacture 780 units of XV–1. The standard cost for aluminum for 780 units of XV–1 is 3,900 pounds for a total cost of $78,000. The aluminum cost incurred exceeds the standard cost allowed by $16,380, or 21 percent. In contrast, the labor and variable overhead variances are favorable. Conducting separate analyses of variances for different costs can prevent offsetting of an inefficient use of one resource by efficient uses in one or more other resources. Looking only at the total costs can mislead the manager.

Exhibit 15–6	Comparison of Actual Variable Expenses and Flexible Budget Variable Expenses

SCHMIDT MACHINERY COMPANY
October 20X6

Product: XV–1
Units Manufactured: 780
Operating Results

Direct materials:			
Aluminum	3,630 pounds at $26	$94,380	
PVC	720 pounds at $41	29,520	$123,900
Direct labor	3,510 hours at $42		147,420
Variable factory overhead			40,630
Total variable cost of goods manufactured			$311,950
Variable selling and administrative expenses			39,000
Total variable expense incurred			$350,950

Flexible Budget

Total standard variable cost of goods manufactured:		
Standard variable manufacturing cost per unit (from Exhibit 15–5)	$400	
Number of units manufactured	× 780	$312,000
Standard variable selling and administrative expenses	780 × $50	39,000
Total standard variable expense		$351,000
Flexible budget variable expense variance		$ 50 F*

*F denotes a *favorable* result.

Direct Materials Variances

The flexible budget direct materials variance is the difference between the actual total direct materials cost incurred and the total standard direct materials cost for the units of the product manufactured during the period.[2] This variance reflects the overall efficiency in buying and using the direct materials in operations. Attaining efficiency in buying and using materials requires good control over both the price paid for the materials and the quantity of the materials used in the operation. We must analyze the total direct materials variance further into a direct material price variance (PV) and a direct material quantity variance or usage variance (UV), so that the firm can gain a better understanding of the causes of cost variations.

In the next two exhibits, we use the Schmidt Machinery Company's data to illustrate these analyses. Exhibit 15–7 shows that the Schmidt Machinery Company used 3,630 pounds of aluminum at a total cost of $94,380 to manufacture 780 units of product XV–1. The standard cost sheet reported in Exhibit 15–5 indicates that

Exhibit 15–7	Detailed Comparison of Actual and Standard Costs

SCHMIDT MACHINERY COMPANY
October 20X6

Product: XV–1
Units Manufactured: 780
Operating Result

Direct materials:			
Aluminum	3,630 pounds at $26	$94,380	
PVC	720 pounds at $41	29,520	$123,900
Direct labor	3,510 hours at $42		147,420
Variable factory overhead			40,630
Total variable cost of goods manufactured			$311,950
Variable selling and administrative expenses			39,000
Total variable expense incurred			$350,950

Flexible Budget

Direct materials:			
Aluminum	780 units × 4 pounds × $25 =	$78,000	
PVC	780 units × 1 pound × $40 =	31,200	$109,200
Direct labor	780 units × 5 hours × $40 =		156,000
Variable factory overhead	780 units × 5 hours × $12 =		46,800
Total standard variable cost of goods manufactured			$312,000
Variable selling and administrative expenses			39,000
Total flexible budget variable expense			$351,000
	($350,950 − $351,000)		$ 50 F*

Variances

Direct materials:			
Aluminum	$ 94,380 − $ 78,000 = $16,380 U[†]		
PVC	29,520 − 31,200 = 1,680 F		$14,700 U
Direct labor	147,420 − 156,000 =		8,580 F
Variable factory overhead	40,630 − 46,800 =		6,170 F
Flexible Budget Variable Manufacturing Cost Variance			$ 50 F
Variable selling and administrative expense variance			0
Flexible Budget Variable Expense Variance			$ 50 F

*F denotes a *favorable* result.

†U denotes an *unfavorable* result.

---

[2] Variable and fixed overhead variances are covered in Chapter 16.

the standard cost for one unit of XV–1 is 4 pounds of aluminum at $25 per pound. Exhibit 15–8 shows computations for variances relating to the usage of aluminum to manufacture 780 units of XV–1 for the period.

Total Direct Materials Standard Cost for the Period

The total standard cost for direct materials is based on the unit output of the period. The total standard cost of direct materials is determined using these three steps:

Step 1: Find that 780 units of product XV–1 were manufactured from accounting records.

Step 2: Determine the standard units of the cost element, aluminum, per unit of XV–1 from the standard cost sheet—4 pounds of aluminum per unit of XV–1. We then multiply 4 pounds by 780 units from step 1 to determine the total standard units of aluminum allowed for the actual units of the product XV–1 manufactured. The result shows that the total standard allowed quantity of aluminum for 780 units of XV–1 is 3,120 pounds.

Step 3: Find the unit standard cost of the cost element, aluminum ($25 per pound), from the standard cost sheet. Multiply that cost by the amounts in step 2 to arrive at the total standard cost of aluminum for the actual units of XV–1 manufactured during the period. The total standard cost for 780 units of XV–1 is $78,000.

Direct Materials Flexible Budget Variance

Direct materials flexible budget variance is the difference in direct material costs between the actual cost incurred and the total standard cost in the flexible budget for the units manufactured during the period. The flexible budget variance for aluminum for the Schmidt Machinery Company is the difference between the actual cost incurred, $94,380, and the total standard direct material cost in the flexible budget for the 780 units manufactured during the period, $78,000, or $16,380 unfavorable.

> **Direct materials flexible budget variance** is the difference in direct material costs between the actual amount incurred and the total standard cost in the flexible budget for the units manufactured during the period.

Exhibit 15–8	Direct Materials—Aluminum Variances		

Actual Input at Actual Cost	Actual Input at Standard Cost	Standard Cost for Actual Output
3,630 pounds × $26 = $94,380	3,630 pounds × $25 = $90,750	3,120 pounds × $25 = $78,000

PV = ($26 − $25) × 3,630
= $3,630 U

UV = (3,630 − 3,120) × $25
= $12,750 U

Or,

PV = $94,380 − $90,750
= $3,630 U

UV = $90,750 − $78,000
= $12,750 U

Flexible budget variance
= $94,380 − $78,000 = $16,380 U

Or,
Or,
= $ 3,630 U + $12,750 U = $16,380 U

Price Variance:		**Usage Variance**	
Actual price	$26	Standard quantity allowed (780 units × 4 pounds)	3,120
Standard price	− 25	Actual quantity used	− 3,630
Difference	$ 1 U	Difference	510 U
Actual usage (and purchase)	× 3,630	Standard price	× 25
	$3,630 U		$12,750 U

Further Analyses of the Direct Materials Flexible Budget Variance

Price Variance A **direct materials price variance** is the difference between the actual and standard unit price of the direct materials multiplied by the actual quantity of the direct materials purchased. Schmidt Machinery Company paid $26 to purchase aluminum while the standard cost sheet specifies a price of $25 per pound for aluminum. The firm paid $1 per pound more than the standard unit price. With a total of 3,630 pounds purchased, the price variance for aluminum for the period therefore is $3,630 unfavorable (Exhibit 15–8).

$$PV_{DM} = (AP_{DM} - SP_{DM}) \times AQ_{DM}$$

$$PV_{Aluminum} = (AP_{Aluminum} - SP_{Aluminum}) \times AQ_{Aluminum}$$

$$= (\$26 - \$25) \times 3,630$$

$$= \$1 \times 3,630 = \$3,630 \text{ Unfavorable}$$

A **direct materials price variance** is the difference between the actual and standard unit price of the direct materials multiplied by the actual quantity of the direct materials purchased.

Usage Variance A *direct materials usage variance* is the difference between the actual units of direct materials used and the total standard units of direct materials that should have been used for the units of the product manufactured multiplied by the standard unit price of direct materials. The total standard units of the direct materials that should have been used for the units of the product manufactured are also the flexible budget units for direct materials. Some users call usage variances efficiency or quantity variances.

Schmidt Machinery Company used 3,630 pounds to manufacture 780 units of the final product XV–1. According to the standard cost sheet, each unit of XV–1 requires 4 pounds of aluminum. The total standard quantity of aluminum allowed for the production of 780 units is 3,120 pounds (780 units × 4 pounds per unit). The 3,630 pounds of aluminum used in production is 510 pounds more than the total standard quantity allowed for the 780 units of XV–1 manufactured during the period. At the standard price of $25 per pound, the usage variance is $12,750 unfavorable (Exhibit 15–8).

$$UV_{DM} = (AQ_{DM} - SQ_{DM}) \times SP_{DM}$$

$$UV_{Aluminum} = (AQ_{Aluminum} - SQ_{Aluminum}) \times SP_{Aluminum}$$

$$= (3,630 - 3,120) \times \$25$$

$$= 510 \times \$25 = \$12,750 \text{ Unfavorable}$$

Interpreting the Direct Materials Price Variance

A direct materials price variance may be a result of failure to take purchase discounts, an unexpected price change for the materials, change in freight costs, variation in grades of the purchased items, or other causes. The purchasing department is often the office most likely to provide an explanation for materials price variances.

Care must be taken in interpreting a price variance. A favorable direct materials price variance may lead to high manufacturing costs if the low-cost materials are of poor quality. Downstream costs such as scrap, rework, schedule disruptions, or field services could exceed the price savings from lower materials prices. A firm with a differentiation strategy is most likely to fail when it pursues favorable price variances through purchases of low-quality materials. A firm that competes on low cost also is likely be doomed if the quality of its products is below the minimum criterion its customers expect.

Similarly, a firm with a cost-effective purchasing department that has several warehouses full of materials and supplies, all purchased in bulk at low prices, may have a higher total overall cost than a firm that buys in small quantities, as needed, and pays higher purchase prices to maintain only a minimum amount of direct materials on hand. Carrying costs and additional material handling costs may cost the firm more than its savings in purchase prices.

A useful measure for evaluating the performance of purchasing departments, besides the traditional price variance, is the **materials usage ratio,** a ratio of quantity used

The **materials usage ratio** is the ratio of quantity used over quantity purchased.

over quantity purchased. A low materials usage ratio suggests that the purchasing department may have made purchases for stocks, not for operational needs for the period. Such a move can be costly if the firm considers all costs. The benefit of any favorable price variance should be evaluated together with the cost of inventory storage of the surplus purchases.

A genuine favorable material price variance can be an indication that the firm needs to pursue the market more aggressively. An unfavorable price variance that cannot be eliminated suggests to the firm that it may need to reevaluate its strategy.

Interpreting the Direct Materials Usage Variance

A direct materials usage variance says that the units of direct materials used in manufacturing processes is different from the units that should have been used for the operation. This discrepancy may measure efficiency in using the direct materials. A direct materials usage variance can result from the efforts of production workers, substitutions of the material for other materials or production factors, variation from standard in the quality of direct materials, inadequate training or inexperienced workers, poor supervision, excess spoilage, or other factors.

Direct Labor Variances

A direct labor flexible budget variance also can be divided into rate (price) and efficiency (quantity) variances. The procedure for further analysis of the total direct labor variance is similar to the procedure followed for further analyses of total direct materials variances. Exhibit 15–9 shows the direct labor rate variance (RV) and direct labor efficiency variance (EV) incurred when Schmidt Machinery Company manufactured 780 units of XV–1.

Direct Labor Rate Variance

A **direct labor rate variance** is the difference between the actual and standard hourly wage rate multiplied by the actual direct hours used in production.

The **direct labor rate variance** is the difference between the actual and standard hourly wage rate multiplied by the actual direct labor-hours used in the production.

Schmidt Machinery Company paid an average wage rate of $42 per hour during the period and used 3,510 direct labor-hours in production. The standard cost sheet calls for a wage rate of $40 per hour. The firm paid $2 per hour more than the standard hourly rate. With a total of 3,510 hours, the total direct labor rate variance is $7,020 unfavorable.

Exhibit 15–9	Direct Labor Variances	
Actual Input at Actual Cost	**Actual Input at Standard Cost**	**Standard Cost for Actual Output**
3,510 hours × $42 = $147,420	3,510 hours × $40 = $140,400	3,900 hours × $40 = $156,000

	Rate Variance (RV)	**Efficiency Variance (EV)**
Or,	= ($42 − $40) × 3,510 = $7,020 U	= (3,510 − 3,900) × $40 = $15,600 F
	= $147,420 − $140,400 = $7,020 U	= $140,400 − $156,000 = $15,600 F

Flexible budget variance
= $7,020 U + $15,600 F = $8,580 F

Or,

Flexible budget variance
= $147,420 − $156,000
= −$8,580 or $8,580 F

The direct labor rate variance reflects the effect on the operating income of the difference in hourly wage rates between the actual hourly wage rate paid and the standard hourly wage rate specified in the standard-cost sheet. A direct labor rate variance may be a result of the firm's not paying the same hourly wage as specified in the standard cost sheet or not using the same skill-level workers as specified in the standard cost sheet.

The personnel department usually is responsible for direct labor rate variances. Production, however, may be responsible for the variance if it chooses to use workers with a higher skill level than specified in the standard cost sheet.

Direct Labor Efficiency Variance

The **direct labor efficiency variance** is the difference between the actual and standard direct labor hours allowed for the units manufactured multiplied by the standard hourly wage rate. Schmidt Machinery Company used 3,510 direct labor-hours to manufacture 780 units of XV–1 during the period. The standard cost sheet allows 5 direct labor-hours for 1 unit of XV–1. The total standard hours allowed for 780 units of XV–1, therefore, is 3,900 hours (780 × 5). Thus, Schmidt Machinery Company used 390 fewer direct labor-hours than the total labor-hours called for to manufacture 780 units of XV–1. At a standard wage rate of $40 per hour, the total direct labor efficiency (quantity) variance is $15,600 favorable.

The direct labor efficiency variance reflects the effect on operating income of the difference between the hours used manufacturing the output and the total standard hours allowed for the units manufactured. Because this difference is a result of the difference in labor-hours, the resulting variance is called a direct labor *efficiency* variance and is the responsibility of the production department.

Besides the efficiency of the workers in carrying out their tasks, several other factors can lead to a direct labor efficiency variance. Among them are

1. Workers or supervisors who are new on the job or inadequately trained.
2. Workers' skill levels are different from those specified in the standard cost sheet.
3. Batch sizes are different from the standard size.
4. Materials are different from those specified.
5. Machines or equipment are not in proper working condition.
6. Supervision is inadequate.
7. Scheduling is poor.

Identification of variances helps managers to become aware of deviations from the expected performance. To realize the full benefit of determining and reporting variances, managers need to recognize variances in a timely manner.

Timing of Variance Recognition

A direct materials price variance can be identified either at the *time of purchase* or at the *time materials are issued* to production. The primary difference lies in the timing of variance identification and the way in which direct materials are recorded in the materials control account. Early recognition of variances such as when a price variance is recorded at the time of purchase allows the firm to know early any discrepancy between the actual purchase price paid and the standard price for the purchase. The materials inventory also can be carried at the standard cost. Thus, the same materials purchased at different times with different purchase prices carry the same unit cost in the books.

When a direct materials price variance is recorded at the time materials are issued to production, the direct materials inventory is carried at actual purchase prices. Deviations of actual prices from the standard may not be known until the direct materials are issued to production. In either case, the costs of direct materials involved in the work in process are recorded at the standard cost.

When a direct materials price variance is recognized at the time of purchase, the purchase price variance is computed based on the actual quantity purchased, not

The **direct labor efficiency variance** is the difference between the actual and standard direct labor hours for the units manufactured multiplied by the standard hourly wage rate.

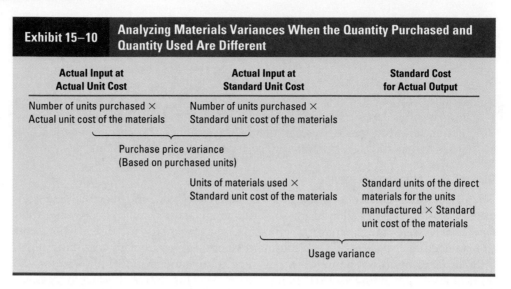

Exhibit 15–10	Analyzing Materials Variances When the Quantity Purchased and Quantity Used Are Different

Actual Input at Actual Unit Cost	Actual Input at Standard Unit Cost	Standard Cost for Actual Output
Number of units purchased × Actual unit cost of the materials	Number of units purchased × Standard unit cost of the materials	

Purchase price variance
(Based on purchased units)

	Units of materials used × Standard unit cost of the materials	Standard units of the direct materials for the units manufactured × Standard unit cost of the materials

Usage variance

the actual quantity used in the production.[3] Consequently, the actual quantity purchased is used in the price variance computation, while the actual units consumed in production are used in the computation of the usage variance, as shown in Exhibit 15–10.

The analysis of variances for direct labor costs does not need to be split into two steps because direct labor has no inventory. The actual hours for which workers receive wages are always the same as the actual hours worked in production during the period.

EFFECT OF THE NEW MANUFACTURING TECHNOLOGY

LEARNING OBJECTIVE 5 ►
Assess the influence of the contemporary manufacturing environment on operational control and standard costing.

Recent advances in manufacturing technology have had a great impact on manufacturing and standard costs. No distinction between units purchased and units used is necessary in computing variances for direct materials for firms that maintain a minimal inventory or firms that use a just-in-time (JIT) system. In these firms the quantity purchased in a period is almost the same as, if not exactly equal to, the amount used during the period.

Furthermore, firms using JIT systems have less interest in materials purchase price variances. The reason is that they purchase materials from suppliers under long-term contracts and the prices they negotiate are not subject to short-term fluctuation. Also, JIT firms emphasize the total cost of operations, not just materials purchase costs. Factors such as quality, reliability, and availability often outweigh the purchase cost.

The arrival of new manufacturing technologies such as automation, flexible manufacturing systems, and cluster or cell manufacturing also decreases the importance of direct labor variances. Firms that use automated manufacturing systems such as that employed by Hewlett-Packard Company at its factory in Fort Collins, Colorado, use little or no direct labor. These firms attach little importance to labor rate and efficiency variances.

Contemporary firms emphasize zero-defect and continuous improvement in quality. The utmost concerns of these firms are satisfying customers and providing better products than the competition. A well-managed firm is not the one with the lowest unfavorable variances or the highest favorable variances. It is the one with happy customers and consistently better products.

The theory of constraint in Chapter 5 emphasizes that the focus on improving the overall efficiency of a firm lies in improving throughput time from the beginning of the process till completion and delivery. While decreasing unfavorable labor

---

[3]   Some writers refer to a price variance computed on the quantity used in production as a usage price variance.

efficiency variances of nonbottleneck operations might give managers satisfaction, such efforts would not affect the overall efficiency of the firm.

BEHAVIORAL AND IMPLEMENTATION ISSUES

A standard cost system provides guidance and criteria for operations and performance evaluations. Variances from the standard should be used strictly as inputs to gain a better understanding of the operations and to improve the operations; they should never be used to find a scapegoat. Research in organizational behavior has shown that successful operations are often the result of proper rewards. The focus in using a standard cost system should be on influencing behavior through positive reinforcements and appropriate motivation. Seldom does long-term success result from penalties and punishments.

◄ **LEARNING OBJECTIVE 6**
Recognize behavioral implications in implementing standard cost systems.

The way that managers and employees perceive a standard cost system affects its success or failure. A negative perception or motivation often is the result of unreasonable standards, secrecy in setting standards, authoritarian control procedures, poor communication, excessive pressure, inflexibility, uneven reward systems, or excessive emphasis on profits. These situations can make a good standard cost system a failure. Managers or employees with highly negative perceptions may feel discouraged and adopt protective or defensive behavior, or even sabotage the system. These tactics include padding budgets, subtle attempts to beat the system, decreases in product and service quality, absenteeism, lackadaisical attitudes, decreased initiative, and sharing trade secrets. On the other hand, managers and other employees who like a standard cost system show enthusiasm, creativity, and productivity.

The controller and supporting staff are responsible for reporting to all levels of management the actual results of operations compared with the budgeted goals including variances. They are staff personnel and principally concerned with service. The controller and supporting staff should not usurp line authority, nor give the impression that they can. Staff personnel should not be directed to exercise authority over operating line personnel.

Nor should the controller reprimand operating personnel for unfavorable results reflected on performance reports. Any corrective action resulting from either favorable or unfavorable results is strictly a line function. The controller is responsible for designing an effective system of cost control. The line executives and supervisors, however, have direct responsibility for implementing cost control.

How Monsanto, DuPont, American Express, and Other Firms Improve Performance

After examining practices in several companies including Monsanto, Xel, DuPont, American Express, Xaloy, GTE, and Black Box, *Business Week* concludes the factors that make performance pay work are

- **Set attainable goals**

- **Set meaningful goals** You can neither motivate nor reward by setting targets employees can't comprehend. Complex financial measures and jargon-heavy reports mean nothing to most employees.

- **Bring workers in** Give workers a say in developing performance

measures and listen to their advice on ways to change work systems.

- **Keep targets moving** Performance pay plans must be constantly adjusted to meet the changing needs of workers and customers. The life expectancy of a plan may be no more than three or four years.

- **Aim carefully** Know what message you want to send. Make sure the new scheme doesn't reward the wrong behavior.

Source: Based on "Bonus Pay: Buzzword or Bonanza?" *Business Week,* November 14, 1994.

Not all variances should be treated equally. The favorable efficiency variance of a *nonbottleneck* operation has little benefit to the firm. Nor does an unfavorable direct labor efficiency variance of the same operation affect the firm other than in the increased level of manufacturing costs. An unfavorable direct labor efficiency variance in a *bottleneck* operation, on the other hand, can lead to sizable negative ripple effects on the firm's total manufacturing costs and operations. When the unfavorable efficiency variance occurs in an upstream operation that is a bottleneck, the output in all downstream operations may have to be curtailed. A series of unfavorable efficiency variances in bottleneck operations can severely cripple the operation of the firm.

COST FLOWS IN GENERAL LEDGERS USING A STANDARD COST SYSTEM

LEARNING OBJECTIVE 7 ▶
Describe cost flows through general ledger accounts and prepare journal entries for acquisition and use of direct materials and direct labor in a standard cost system.

Manufacturing costs in a standard cost system flow through the Materials Inventory Control account, Accrued Payroll account, Factory Overhead Control account, Work-in-Process Inventory Control account, and Finished Goods Inventory Control account, as in other manufacturing cost systems. In addition, each variance has its own separate ledger account that allows the accumulation and monitoring of that variance.

When direct materials are purchased, the standard cost for the purchased materials is recorded in the Materials Inventory Control account. The discrepancy between the standard cost and the actual price paid for the materials is recorded in the Materials Purchase Price Variance account. Direct labor costs incurred are recorded in the Accrued Payroll account. Then, as direct materials and labor are placed into the manufacturing processes, standard costs flow from Materials Inventory Control and Accrued Payroll accounts to the Work-in-Process Inventory Control account.

The difference between the standard cost for the direct materials issued to production and the standard cost for direct materials recorded in the Work-in-Process Inventory Control account is recorded in the Direct Materials Usage Variance account. The total labor variance between the direct labor incurred and the standard direct labor cost recorded in the Work-in-Process Inventory Control account is recorded in either or both the Direct Labor Rate Variance or the Direct Labor Efficiency Variance accounts. On completion of production, the standard cost of the units completed is transferred from the Work-in-Process Inventory Control account to the Finished Goods Inventory Control account at the standard total product cost. Exhibit 15–11 shows the flow of costs through relevant accounts in a standard cost system.

To illustrate, on October 7, Schmidt Machinery Company purchased 3,630 pounds of aluminum at $26 per pound and 720 pounds of PVC at $41 per pound. According to the standard cost sheet (Exhibit 15–5), the standard costs are $25 and $40 per pound for aluminum and PVC, respectively. The firm makes the following journal entries for the purchases:

Oct. 7	Materials Inventory Control (3,630 × $25)	$90,750	
	Materials Purchase Price		
	Variance—Aluminum (3,630 × $1)	3,630	
	Accounts Payable (3,630 × $26)		$94,380
	Purchase of 3,630 pounds aluminum from Dura-Igor		
	Corporation at $26 per pound. Terms 1/EOM, n/180.		
	Standard price $25 per pound.		
7	Materials Inventory Control (720 × $40)	$28,800	
	Materials Purchase Price		
	Variance—PVC (720 × $1)	720	
	Accounts Payable (720 × $41)		$29,520
	Purchase of 720 pounds PVC from TVC Chemical Inc.		
	at $41 per pound. Terms 2/10, n/30. Standard price		
	$40 per pound.		

Exhibit 15–11	Cost Flows and Ledger Entries in a Standard Cost System

Materials Inventory Control

Beginning inventory at standard cost		Units issued to production × Standard price per unit	$78,000 28,800
Number of units purchased × Standard price per unit	$90,750 28,800		

Materials Purchase Price Variance

Unfavorable Variances	$3,630 720	Favorable Variances	

Materials Usage Variance

Unfavorable Variances	$12,750 2,400	Favorable Variances	

Accrued Payroll

	Actual direct labor hours spent × Actual hourly wage rate	$147,420

Labor Rate Variance

Unfavorable Variances	$7,020	Favorable Variances	

Labor Efficiency Variance

Unfavorable Variances		Favorable Variances	$15,600

Accounts Payable

	Number of units purchased × Actual unit price	$94,380 29,520

Work-in-Process Inventory Control

Beginning inventory at standard cost		Number of units completed × Standard cost per unit	$405,600
Standard units of direct materials for the units of product manufactured × Standard direct materials unit price	$90,750 31,200		
Standard direct labor hours for the units of the product manufactured × Standard hourly wage rate	156,000		

Finished Goods Inventory Control

Beginning inventory at standard cost		Actual unit sold × Standard cost per unit
Actual units completed × Standard cost per unit	$405,600	

Cost of Goods Sold

Actual units sold × Standard cost per unit	

The production department requests 3,630 pounds of aluminum and 720 pounds of PVC on October 9 for the production of 780 units of XV–1.

9	Work-in-Process Inventory Control		
	(780 × 4 = 3,120; 3,120 × $25)	$78,000	
	Materials Usage Variance—Aluminum (510 × $25)	12,750	
	Materials Inventory Control (3,630 × $25)		$90,750
	Issued 3,630 pounds of aluminum to production for the production of 780 units of XV–1. Standard usage is 4 pounds per unit of XV–1.		

9	Work-in-Process Inventory Control		
	(780 × 1 = 780; 780 × $40)	$31,200	
	Materials Usage Variance—PVC (60 × $40)		$ 2,400
	Materials Inventory Control (720 × $40)		28,800
	Issued 720 pounds of PVC to production for the production of 780 units of XV–1. Standard usage is 1 pound per unit of XV–1.		

The production department incurs a total of 3,510 hours of direct labor at a total cost of $147,420 to complete the production of 780 units of XV–1 on October 15. The standard calls for 5 hours per unit of XV–1 and a standard hourly wage of $40.

15   Work-in-Process Inventory Control
       (780 × 5 = 3,900; 3,900 × $40) $156,000
     Labor Rate Variance (3,510 × $2)   7,020
          Labor Efficiency Variance (390 × $40) $ 15,600
          Accrued Payroll (3,510 × $42)   147,420
     Incurred 3,510 hours to manufacture 780 units of XV–1.
     Standard cost allows 5 hours per unit of XV–1 at
     $40 per hour.

The standard cost sheet (Exhibit 15–5) specifies that the total standard cost per unit of XV–1 is $520. These journal entries record the completion of production and transferring of 780 units of XV–1:

15   Finished Goods Inventory Control (780 × $520) $405,600
          Work-in-Process Inventory Control $405,600
     Completion of 780 units of XV–1. Standard
     cost is $520 per unit.

SUMMARY

Measures of effectiveness and efficiency help managers assess their operations. Managers are interested in effectiveness in attaining the goals set for the operation and efficiency in carrying out operations during a period. A commonly used measure of effectiveness is the operating income variance, which is the difference between the actual and master budget operating income.

An operation is efficient if the firm wastes no resources in operations. A flexible budget can play an important role in assessing operating efficiency. Using the flexible budget for the operation attained in the period, the operating income variance can be separated into the sales volume and flexible budget variances. The sales volume variance is the difference between the master budget and the flexible budget. It measures the effects of changes in sales units on sales, expenses, contribution margins, and operating income. The flexible budget variance is the difference between the actual operating result and the flexible budget. It measures efficiency in using resources.

Establishing a standard requires careful analysis of operations. A standard can be an ideal standard or a currently attainable standard. A manufacturing operation usually has a standard cost sheet that details the standard quantity and standard cost for all the significant manufacturing elements of the operation. A firm uses activity analysis, historical data, benchmarking, market expectation, and strategic considerations to set standards. Typical standards include standards for direct materials and direct labor. Comparing actual direct materials and direct labor costs to standard costs for direct materials and direct labor, respectively, a firm can identify the materials purchase price variance, materials usage variance, labor rate variance, and labor efficiency variance. Exhibit 15–12 summarizes the relationships of these variances. Used properly, these variances can be a powerful tool for controlling operations, identifying factors that may have contributed to favorable or unfavorable operating results, and evaluating performance.

Recent advances in manufacturing technology such as JIT, flexible manufacturing, total quality management, and the theory of constraints have had great impacts on manufacturing and standard costs. Among the impacts are the decreased significance of materials purchase price variance, labor variances, and variances of nonbottleneck operations.

The focus in using a standard cost should be on influencing behavior with positive reinforcements and motivation rather than imposing penalties and punishments. Unreasonable standards, secrecy in standard settings, authoritarian control, poor communication, inflexibility, unfair performance evaluation, uneven rewards, and excessive emphasis on profits, among other factors, often make a good standard cost system a failure.

Exhibit 15–12	Hierarchy of Variances

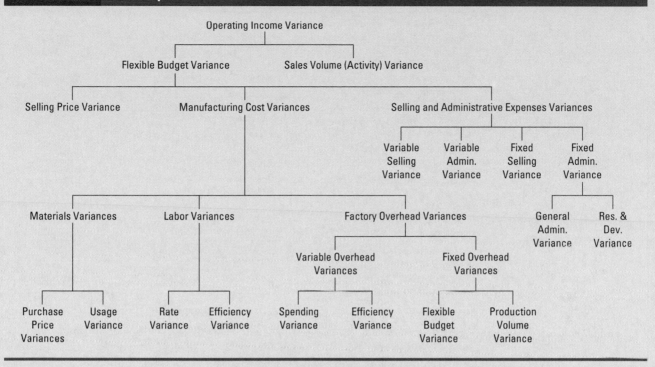

KEY TERMS

SELF-STUDY PROBLEMS

(For solutions, please turn to the end of the chapter.)

1. Sales Volume and Flexible Budget Variances

Solid Box Fabrications manufactures boxes for workstations. The firm's standard cost sheet and the operating result of October 20X2 are

	Standard Cost per Unit		Operating Result October 20X2
Units			9,500
Sales	$50.00		$551,000
Variable costs:			
Direct materials			
5 pounds at $2.4 per pound =	$12.00	48,000 pounds × $3 =	$144,000
Direct labor			
.5 hour at $14 per hour =	7.00	4,800 hours × $16 =	76,800
Variable manufacturing overhead	2.00		19,000
Variable selling and			
administrative expenses	5.00		55,100
Total variable cost	$26.00		$294,900
Contribution margin	$24.00		$256,100
Fixed costs:			
Manufacturing costs	$50,000		$ 55,000
Selling and administrative	20,000		24,000
Total fixed costs	$70,000		$ 79,000
Operating income			$177,100

In preparing the master budget for October 20X2, the firm had several expected changes from the standard cost sheet. The sales price would increase by 8 percent. Its suppliers notified the firm that materials prices would increase by 5 percent starting October 1. The labor contract that started on October 1 increased wages and benefits by 10 percent. Fixed manufacturing costs would increase $5,000 for insurance, property taxes, and salaries. For fixed selling and administrative expenses, there would be a $2,000 increase in managers' salaries. Furthermore, the firm plans to spend an additional $2,000 for advertising during October 20X2. The unit sales for October 19X2 was expected to be 10,000 units. Solid Box Fabrications uses JIT systems in all of its operations including materials acquisitions and product manufacturing.

Required

1. Prepare the master budget and flexible budgets at 9,500 units and at 11,000 units for October 20X2.

2. Compute the sales volume operating income variance, flexible budget operating income variance, sales price variance, and flexible budget variable cost variance for October 20X2.

3. Determine the direct materials price variance, direct materials usage variance, direct labor rate variance, and direct labor efficiency variance.

2.   Direct Materials Price and Usage Variances, Direct Labor Rate and Efficiency Variances, and Journal Entries

Chemical, Inc., has set up the following standards for direct materials and direct labor for each 20-pound bag of Weed-Be-Doom.

	Per Bag
Direct materials: 25 pounds XF–2000 @ $0.08	$2.00
Direct labor: 0.05 hour @ $32	1.60

The firm manufactured 2,000,000 pounds of Weed-Be-Doom during December using 2,700,000 pounds of materials and 5,200 direct labor-hours. The firm purchased 3,000,000 lbs. of XF–2000 at $0.075 per pound and incurred a total payroll of $182,000 for direct labor during the month. The firm identifies all variances at the time it incurs the costs.

Required

1. Compute the price and usage variances for direct materials and the rate and efficiency variances for direct labor.

2. Prepare journal entries to record the company's data.

QUESTIONS

15–1   Tobias Company earned $5 million last year from selling 25,000 units of a special dental drill that deadens sounds that could annoy dental patients. The master budget calls for sales of 30,000 units and $7.5 million in operating income. The operating income in the flexible budget for 25,000 units, however, is $4.5 million. A member of the operation review committee comments that the firm was neither efficient in its operations nor effective in attaining the operating goal. What is a possible rationale for reaching such a conclusion? Do you agree with this assessment?

15–2   Can a standard cost system be used in job order costing? In process costing?

15–3   Which of the following is the best basis on which cost standards should be set for measuring controllable production efficiencies: engineering standards based on ideal performance, engineering standards based on attainable performance, or recent average historical performance?

15–4   Why should management want to separate direct labor variances into rate variances and efficiency variances?

15–5   The manager of a firm is happy to receive a report that shows a favorable total materials variance of $75. Given that, the manager decides no further action is needed. Do you agree?

15–6   What is the normal year-end treatment of immaterial variances recognized in a cost accounting system utilizing standards?

15–7   What is the difference between a standard and a budget?

15–8   Verbatim Company's budget for last year included $80,000 for prime costs. The total actual prime costs for the period were $72,000. Can we say that the plant manager has done a better-than-expected job in controlling the cost if actual production were 80 percent of the budgeted production?

15–9   Which variances would be directly affected by the relative position of a production process on a learning curve?

15–10 Will excess direct labor wages resulting from overtime premiums affect direct labor variances? Which variances?

15–11 Should management feel distressed if all the variances of a period are unfavorable?

15–12 Portfolio management is a powerful concept in finance and marketing. The marketing application of the concept is to develop and manage a balanced portfolio of products. Market share and market growth can be used to classify products for portfolio purposes, and the product classifications often are extended to the organizational units that make the product. The market share/growth classifications can be depicted like this:

Market Growth Rate	Market Share	
	High	Low
High	Rising Star	?
Low	Cash Cow	Dog

Question marks are products that show high-growth rates but have small market shares, such as new products that are similar to their competitors. Rising stars are high-growth, high-market-share products that tend to mature into cash cows. Cash cows are slow-growing established products that can be milked for cash to help the question marks and introduce new products. The dogs are low-growth, low-market-share items that are candidates for elimination or segmentation. Understanding where a product falls within this market share/growth structure is important when applying a standard cost system.

Required

1. Discuss the major advantages of using a standard cost accounting system.
2. Describe the kinds of information that are useful in setting standards and the conditions that must be present to support the use of standard costing.
3. Discuss the applicability or nonapplicability of using standard costing for a product classified as a
   a. Cash cow.
   b. Question mark.

(CMA Adapted)

15–13 At the end of its fiscal year, Graham Company had several substantial variances from standard variable manufacturing costs. Which one of the following scenarios is the most justifiable for the firm to allocate the resulting variances between inventories and cost of sales?
   a. Additional cost of raw materials acquired under a speculative purchase contract.
   b. A breakdown of equipment.
   c. Overestimates of production volume for the period resulting from failure to predict an unusual decline in the market for the company's product.
   d. Increased labor rates won by the union as a result of a strike.

(CMA Adapted)

15–14 What is the difference between a master budget and a flexible budget?

15–15 Do flexible budgets adapt to changes in both inflation rate and activity?

15–16 Todco planned to produce 3,000 units of its single product, Teragram, during November. The standard specifications for one unit of Teragram include 6 pounds of material at $.30 per pound. The firm uses JIT in all of its operations. Actual production in November was 3,100 units of Teragram. The accountant computed a favorable materials purchase price variance of $380 and an unfavorable materials usage variance of $120. Which one of the following conclusions is best supported by these variances?
   a. More materials were purchased than were used.
   b. More materials were used than were purchased.
   c. The actual cost of materials was less than the standard cost.
   d. The actual usage of materials was less than the standard allowed.
   e. The actual cost and usage of materials were both less than standard.

(CMA Adapted)

15–17 Firms using JIT systems often have a minimal interest in materials price variances. Why?

15–18 Identify effects that new technologies such as JIT, flexible manufacturing systems, and TQM have on standard cost systems.

15–19 Discuss behavioral concerns in establishing and implementing a standard cost system.

15–20 When should journal entries recording variances be posted?

15–21 Can an organization be effective but not efficient in its operation? Efficient but not effective?

PROBLEMS

15–22 **MATERIALS PURCHASE PRICE** Kennedy Company's direct materials costs are

Standard unit price	$3.60
Actual quantity purchased	1,600
Total standard quantity for units manufactured	1,200
Actual quantity used in production	1,500
Materials purchase price variance—favorable	$240

Required

1. What was the actual purchase price per unit, rounded to the nearest penny?
2. What was the direct materials usage variance?

15–23 **MATERIALS PRICE VARIANCE** Wagner Company's direct materials costs are

Direct materials purchased	20,000
Direct materials used	16,000
Total direct materials purchased costs	$40,000
Standard price per unit of direct materials	$2.10
Direct materials usage variance—favorable	$4,200

Required Compute for Wagner Company

1. Actual price per unit of direct materials.
2. Direct materials price variance.
3. Total standard quantity of direct materials for the operation.

15–24 **MATERIALS PRICE VARIANCE** Rex Company's direct materials costs for May are

Increase in direct materials inventories	2,000 pounds
Actual quantity of direct materials used	30,000 pounds
Actual cost of direct materials	$90,000
Unfavorable direct materials usage variance	$3,000
Standard quantity of direct materials allowed for May production	29,000 pounds

Required Compute for the month of May

1. Standard cost per pound of the direct material.
2. Total purchases (in pounds) of direct materials during the period.
3. Direct materials price variance.

15–25 **MATERIALS VARIANCES** Perkins Company, which has a standard cost system, had 500 gallons of raw materials X in its inventory on June 1, which were purchased in May for $1.20 per gallon and carried at a standard cost of $1. The following information pertains to raw materials X for the month of June:

Number of gallons purchased	1,400
Standard number of gallons allowed for production in June	1,300
Standard cost per gallon	$1.00
Actual cost per gallons in June	$1.10
Direct materials inventory, June 30	400 gallons

Required Compute the materials purchase price and usage variances for raw materials X for June.

15-26 MATERIALS PRICE AND USAGE VARIANCES During March, Younger Company's direct materials costs for the manufacturer of product T were

Actual unit purchase price	$6.50
Standard quantity allowed for the units of T produced	2,100
Decrease in direct materials inventories	100
Quantity of direct materials used in production	2,300
Standard unit price	$6.25

Required What were Younger's direct materials price and usage variances for March?

15-27 MATERIALS PRICE AND USAGE VARIANCES A company uses a standard cost system to account for its only product. The materials standard per unit was 4 pounds at $5.10 per pound. Operating data for April were

Total flexible budget variance for materials	$580 unfavorable
Materials purchased	8,000 pounds
Number of finished units produced	2,000
Increase in direct materials inventory	200 pounds

Required Calculate

1. The materials price and usage variances for April.
2. Actual cost of direct materials per pound.

15-28 STANDARD DIRECT MATERIALS COST Each finished unit of product DX-25 contains 60 pounds of raw materials. Twenty-five percent of the material in the final product evaporates during the manufacturing process. The budget allows the raw materials to be purchased for $2.50 a pound under terms of 2/10, n/30. The company takes all cash discounts. Determine the standard direct materials cost for each unit of DX-25.

15-29 MATERIALS PRICE AND USAGE VARIANCES Durable Company installs shingle roofs on houses. The standard materials cost for a Type R house is $1,250, based on 1,000 shingles at a cost of $1.25 per shingle. During April, Durable installed roofs on 20 Type R houses, using 22,000 shingles at a total actual cost of $26,400. The firm maintains no inventory. What are Durable's materials price and usage variances for April?

15-30 MATERIALS USAGE VARIANCE Buckler Company manufactures desks with vinyl tops. The standard materials cost for the vinyl used per Model S desk is $27.00, based on 12 square feet of vinyl at a cost of $2.25 per square foot. A production run of 1,000 desks in March resulted in usage of 12,600 square feet of vinyl at a cost of $2 per square foot. What was the usage variance resulting from that production run?

15-31 LABOR RATE VARIANCE Barber Company's direct labor costs for the month of January were

Actual direct labor-hours	34,500
Total standard direct labor-hours	35,000
Total payroll for direct labor	$241,500
Direct labor efficiency variance	$3,200 favorable

Required What is Barber's

1. Standard hourly rate?
2. Direct labor rate variance?

15-32 STANDARD LABOR RATE AND EFFICIENCY VARIANCE Hanley's direct labor costs for the month of January were

Direct labor hourly rate paid	$7.50
Total standard direct labor-hours allowed	11,000
Actual direct labor-hours	10,000
Direct labor rate variance	$5,500.00 favorable

Required Compute

1. The standard direct labor rate in January.
2. Direct labor efficiency variance.

15–33 **STANDARD LABOR RATE AND TOTAL HOURS** Thorp Company's records for April disclosed these data relating to direct labor:

Actual cost	$10,000
Rate variance	1,000 favorable
Efficiency variance	1,650 unfavorable

Actual direct labor-hours for April amounted to 2,000.

Required Compute for Thorp

1. Standard direct labor rate per hour.
2. Total standard direct labor hours allowed.

15–34 **LABOR EFFICIENCY VARIANCE** Lion Company's direct labor costs for the month of January were

Actual direct labor-hours	20,000
Total standard direct labor-hours	21,000
Direct labor rate variance—unfavorable	$3,000
Total payroll for direct labor	$126,000

Required What was Lion's direct labor efficiency variance?

15–35 **LABOR RATE AND EFFICIENCY VARIANCES** The direct labor standards for producing a unit of Targo are two hours at $10 per hour. Budgeted production for the period was 1,000 units of Targo. The firm manufactured 900 units of Targo and spent $19,000 for 2,000 direct labor-hours.

Required What are the direct labor rate and efficiency variances?

15–36 **LABOR RATE AND EFFICIENCY VARIANCES** A company's direct labor costs for manufacturing its only product in October were

Standard direct labor-hour per unit of product	1
Number of finished units produced	10,000
Standard rate per direct labor-hour	$10
Total payroll for direct labor	103,500
Actual rate per direct labor-hour	$9

Required Determine for October the

1. Direct labor rate variance.
2. Direct labor efficiency variance.

15–37 **LABOR RATE AND EFFICIENCY VARIANCES** Using this information, determine the labor rate and efficiency variances:

Standard labor cost per hour	$20
Standard labor cost per gallon of output at 20 gallon/hour	$1
Standard labor cost for 8,440 gallons of the actual output	$8,440
Total payroll for direct labor: (410 hours at $21.00/hr)	$8,610

15–38 **ACTUAL LABOR HOURS** Westcott Company's direct labor costs are

Standard direct labor-hours	10,000
Standard direct labor rate	$22.50
Actual direct labor rate	$21.00
Direct labor efficiency variance—unfavorable	$27,000

Required What were the actual hours worked, rounded to the nearest hour?

15–39 **ACTUAL LABOR HOURS**   Tub Company uses a standard cost system. The following information pertains to direct labor for product B for the month of October:

Standard hours allowed for actual output	2,000
Actual labor rate paid per hour	$8.40
Standard labor rate per hour	$8.00
Labor efficiency variance	$1,600 U

Required   What were the actual hours worked?

15–40 **TOTAL PAYROLL**   Townsend Company's direct labor costs for May are

Standard direct labor rate	$20.00
Standard direct labor-hours	20,000
Actual direct labor-hours	21,000
Direct labor rate variance—favorable	$63,000

Required   What is Townsend's total direct labor payroll for May?

15–41 **TOTAL PAYROLL**   Sullivan Corporation's direct labor costs for the month of March are

Standard direct labor-hours	42,000
Actual direct labor-hours	40,000
Direct labor rate variance—favorable	$8,400
Standard direct labor rate per hour	$6.30

Required   What was Sullivan's total direct labor payroll for the month of March?

15–42 **STANDARD DIRECT LABOR COST PER UNIT**   Each unit of product XK–46 requires three direct labor-hours. Employee benefit costs are treated as direct labor costs. Data on direct labor are

Number of employees	25
Weekly productive hours per employee	35
Estimated weekly wages per employee	$504
Employee benefits (related to weekly wages)	25%

Required   Determine the standard direct labor cost per unit of product XK–46.

15–43 **ACTUAL AND STANDARD LABOR RATES**   Data relating to Goodman Company's direct labor costs are

Standard direct labor-hours	30,000
Actual direct labor-hours	29,000
Direct labor rate variance—favorable	$17,400
Total payroll	$330,600

Required

1. What was Goodman's actual direct labor rate?
2. What was Goodman's standard direct labor rate?

15–44 **TOTAL DIRECT MATERIALS COST IN FLEXIBLE BUDGET**   RedRock Company uses flexible budgeting for cost control. RedRock produced 10,800 units of product during March, incurring a direct materials cost of $13,000. Its master budget for the year has a direct materials cost of $180,000 for 144,000 units.

Required

1. Compute the direct materials cost in the flexible budget for March production.

2. Determine the direct materials flexible budget variance.

(CMA Adapted)

15–45 STANDARD COST IN PROCESS COSTING; ALL VARIANCES, AND JOURNAL ENTRIES Dash Company adopted a standard cost system several years ago. The standard costs for the prime costs of its single product are

| Material | (8 kilograms × $5.00/kg) | $40.00 |
| Labor | (6 hours × $8.20/hr.) | $49.20 |

All materials are issued at the beginning of processing. These operating data were taken from the records for November:

In-process beginning inventory	none	
In-process ending inventory	800	units, 75 percent complete as to labor
Units completed	5,600	units
Budgeted output	6,000	units
Purchases of materials	50,000	kilograms
Total actual labor costs	$300,760	
Actual hours of labor	36,500	hours
Material usage variance	$1,500	unfavorable
Total material variance	$750	unfavorable

Required

1. Compute for November:
   a. The labor efficiency variance.
   b. The labor rate variance.
   c. The actual kilograms of material used in the production process during the month.
   d. The actual price paid per kilogram of material during the month.
   e. The total amounts of material and labor cost transferred to the finished goods account.
   f. The total amount of material and labor cost in the ending balance of work-in-process inventory at the end of November.

2. Prepare journal entries to record all transactions including the variances in requirement 1.

(CMA Adapted)

15–46 JOINT DIRECT MATERIALS VARIANCES Benderboard produces corrugated board containers used by the nearby wine industry to package wine in bulk. Benderboard buys kraft paper by the ton, converts it to heavy-duty paperboard on its corrugator, then cuts and glues it into folding boxes that are opened and filled with a plastic liner and then with the bottles of wine.

Many other corrugated board converters are in the area and competition is strong. Therefore, Benderboard is eager to keep its costs under close control. Management has a standard cost system that has been in use for several years. Responsibility for variances has been established. For example, the purchasing agent has been charged with the raw materials price variance, while the general foreman has been answerable for the raw materials usage variance.

Recently, the industrial engineer and the accountant participated in a workshop sponsored by the Institute of Management Accountants at which there was some discussion of variance analysis. It was noted during the workshop that responsibility for some variances was properly dual. The accountant and engineer reviewed their system and were not sure how to adapt the new analysis to it.

The firm has the following standards for its raw materials:

Standard direct raw materials per gross of finished boxes
is 4½ tons of kraft paper at $10 per ton = $45.00.

During May, the accountant assembled the following data about raw materials:

Finished product: 5,000 gross of boxes
Actual cost of raw materials during month: $300,000 (25,000 tons at $12 per ton)
Actual direct raw materials put into production (used): 25,000 tons
Benderboard began and finished the month of May with no inventory.

Required Determine for Benderboard:

1. Direct materials price variance.
2. Direct materials efficiency (usage) variance.
3. Direct materials joint variance.

(CMA Adapted)

15–47 BASIC ANALYSIS OF DIRECT LABOR VARIANCES Day-Mold was founded several years ago by two designers who developed several popular lines of living room, dining room, and bedroom furniture for other companies. The designers believed that their design for dinette sets could be standardized and would sell well. They formed their own company and soon had all the orders they could complete in their small plant in Dayton, Ohio.

From the beginning the firm was successful. The owners bought a microcomputer and software to produce financial statements. The owners thought all the information they needed was contained in these statements.

Recently, however, the employees have been requesting raises. The owners wonder how to evaluate the employees' requests. At the suggestion of Day-Mold's CPA, who prepares the tax return, the owners have hired a consultant who is a CMA to implement a standard cost system. The consultant believes that the calculation of variances will aid management in setting responsibility for labor's performance.

The foremen believe that under normal conditions the dinette set can be assembled with five hours of direct labor at a cost of $20 per hour. The consultant has assembled labor cost information for the most recent month and would like your advice in calculating direct labor variances.

During the month, the actual direct labor wages paid were $127,600 to employees who worked 5,800 hours. The factory produced 1,200 dinette sets during the month.

Required

1. Compute for management's consideration direct labor variances.
2. Provide management with reasons for the variances.

(CMA Adapted)

Strategy

15–48 STANDARD COST SHEET ColdKing Company is a small producer of fruit-flavored frozen desserts. For many years, ColdKing's products have had strong regional sales because of brand recognition; however, other companies have begun marketing similar products in the area, and price competition has become increasingly important. Janice Wakefield, the company's controller, is planning to implement a standard cost system for ColdKing and has gathered considerable information from her co-workers about production and materials requirements for ColdKing's products. Wakefield believes the use of standard costing will allow ColdKing to improve cost control, make better pricing decisions, and enhance strategic cost management.

ColdKing's most popular product is raspberry sherbet. The sherbet is produced in 10-gallon batches, and each batch requires six quarts of good raspberries and 10 gallons of other ingredients. The fresh raspberries are sorted by hand before entering the production process. Because of imperfections in the raspberries and normal spoilage, one quart of berries is discarded for every four quarts of acceptable raspberries. Three minutes is the required standard direct labor time for sorting required to obtain one quart of acceptable raspberries. The acceptable raspberries are then blended with the other ingredients; blending requires 12 minutes of direct labor time per batch. After blending, the sherbet is packaged in quart containers. Wakefield has gathered the following price information:

- ColdKing purchases raspberries at a cost of 80 cents per quart. All other ingredients cost a total of 45 cents per gallon.
- Direct labor is paid at the rate of $9 per hour.
- The total cost of materials and labor required to package the sherbet is 38 cents per quart.

Required

1. Develop the standard cost for the direct cost components of a 10-gallon batch of raspberry sherbet. For each direct cost component of a batch of raspberry sherbet, the standard cost should identify the:
   a. Standard quantity.
   b. Standard rate.
   c. Standard cost per batch.

2. As part of the implementation of a standard cost system at ColdKing, Wakefield plans to train those responsible for maintaining the standards in the use of variance analysis. She is particularly concerned with the causes of unfavorable variances.
   a. Discuss the possible causes of unfavorable materials price variances, identify the individuals who should be held responsible for these variances, and comment on the implications of these variances on strategic cost management.
   b. Discuss the possible causes of unfavorable labor efficiency variances, identify the individuals who should be held responsible for these variances, and comment on the implications of these variances on strategic cost management.

(CMA Adapted)

Strategy

15–49 **SALES VOLUME VARIANCE** The following information is available for the Mitchelville Products Company for the month of July:

	Master Budget	Actual
Units	4,000	3,800
Sales revenue	$60,000	$53,200
Variable manufacturing costs	16,000	19,000
Fixed manufacturing costs	15,000	16,000
Variable selling and administrative expense	8,000	7,700
Fixed selling and administrative expense	9,000	10,000

Required

1. Compute for the month of July sales volume variance and flexible budget variance in contribution margin and operating income.

2. Discuss implications of the variances on strategic cost management.

(CMA Adapted)

15–50 **STANDARD COST SHEET** Singh Company is a small manufacturer of wooden household items. Al Rivkin, corporate controller, plans to implement a standard cost system. Rivkin has information from several co-workers that will help him in developing standards for Singh's products.

One product is a wooden cutting board. Each cutting board requires 1.25 board feet of lumber and 12 minutes of direct labor time to prepare and cut the lumber. The cutting boards are inspected after they are cut. Because they are made of a natural material that has imperfections, one board is normally rejected for each five boards accepted. Four rubber foot pads are attached to each good cutting board. A total of 15 minutes of direct labor time is required to attach all four foot pads and finish each cutting board. The lumber for the cutting boards costs $3 per board foot, and each foot pad costs 5 cents. Direct labor is paid at the rate of $8 per hour.

Required

1. Develop the standard cost for the direct cost components of the cutting board. For each direct cost component of the cutting board, the standard cost should identify the
   a. Standard quantity
   b. Standard rate
   c. Standard cost per unit

2. Identify the advantages of implementing a standard cost system.

3. Explain the role of each of the following persons in developing standards:
   a. Purchasing manager.
   b. Industrial engineer.
   c. Cost accountant.

(CMA Adapted)

15–51 **FILL IN MISSING DATA** Ohio Valley Precision Machinery Company maintains no inventory and has these data for its fiscal year just ended:

	Actual Operating Result	Flexible Budget Variance	Flexible Budget	Sales Volume Variance	Master Budget
Units	600		a	b	800
Sales revenue	$7,200	d	c	e	$8,800
Variable cost:					
Manufacturing	h	$600 F	g	$1,200 F	f
Selling and administrative	i	k	j	l	$1,600
Contribution margin	$2,400	m	n	q	p
Fixed cost	r	v	t	u	s
Operating income	$1,200	x	w	y	$1,400

Required Find the amounts of the missing items a through y.

15–52 **FILL IN MISSING DATA** V-Grip Company uses the JIT system in all its operations and has these data for its fiscal year just ended:

	Actual Operating Result	Flexible Budget Variance	Flexible Budget	Sales Volume Variance	Master Budget
Units	b		a	100 F	1,500
Sales revenue	e	$1,600 U	d	c	$37,500
Variable cost:					
Manufacturing	h	$1,600 U	f	g	$24,000
Selling and administrative	$4,000	i	3,200	k	j
Contribution margin	l	m	n	p	q
Fixed cost	r	u	s	v	t
Operating income	$1,000	w	$3,600	y	x

Required

1. Find the amounts of the missing items *a* through *y*.
2. Compute the actual selling price per unit.

15–53 FLEXIBLE BUDGET AND VARIANCE Phoenix Management helps rental property owners find renters and charges property owners one-half of the first month's rent tenants pay. For August 20X2, Phoenix expects to find renters for 100 apartments with an average first month's rent of $700. Budgeted cost data per tenant application for 20X2 are

Service

- Professional labor: 1.5 hours at a rate of $20 per hour.
- Checks on credit worthiness: $50.

Phoenix expects other costs, including a lease payment for the building, secretarial help, and utilities, to be $3,000 per month. On average, Phoenix is successful in placing one tenant for every three applicants.

Actual rental applications in August 20X2 were 270. Phoenix paid $9,500 for 400 hours of professional labor. Credit-worthiness checks went up to $55 per application. Other support costs for August 20X2 were $3,600. The average first month rentals for August 20X2 were $750 per apartment unit for 90 units.

Required

1. Compute for August 20X2 the amount of operating income attributable to flexible budget and sales volume variances.
2. Determine the professional labor rate and efficiency variances for August 20X2.
3. What factors should be considered in evaluating the effectiveness of professional labor?

15–54 ACQUISITION COSTS Amy Booker is the newly appointed manager of the consumer electronics division of Price Mart. Price Mart is among the largest retailers of consumer goods in several states in the United States, Canada, and Mexico. Booker has just come back from a tour of the division's suppliers in several countries including several potential suppliers in emerging countries.

Ethics

Booker is pondering using companies in emerging countries as suppliers for some of its most popular electronic products. Switching to these suppliers will greatly enhance the firm's competitive position. With the switch the firm can reduce the purchase cost of a personal cassette player, for example, from $12 to $8. The standard acquisition cost for the cassette player is $11 per unit. Booker's predecessor tried for more than two years and could never meet the standard.

International

Price Mart relies heavily on data from its standard cost system in performance evaluations. Booker knows that she may become CEO of the company in two years if she performs.

Two companies, Free Enterprise and Continental Electronic, have agreed to sell up to 1 million personal cassette players at $8, F.O.B. shipping point. Booker, however, is somewhat uncomfortable in doing business with both companies. In its recent annual report, Amnesty International stated that most workers of Free Enterprise are prisoners. Continental Electronic is a state-owned company. The president of Continental Electronic demands as a term of sale that an additional 1 percent be deposited in a "scholarship" fund account he has set up at a small bank in New York City.

Required

1. What variances might be reported if Booker purchases personal cassette players from either one of these two companies?

2. What ethical issues do Amy Booker and Price Mart face in preparing variance reports?

International

15–55 PRICE VARIANCE Applied Materials Science (AMS) purchases its materials from several countries. As part of its cost control program, AMS uses a standard cost system for all aspects of its operations including materials purchases. The standard cost for each material is established at the beginning of the fiscal year, and the standards are not revised until the beginning of the next fiscal year.

Pat Butch, the purchasing manager, is happy with the result of the year just ended. He believes that the purchase price variance for the year will be favorable. He is very confident that his department meets, at least, the standard prices. The preliminary report from the controller's office confirms his jubilation. This is a portion of the preliminary report:

Total quantity purchased	36,000 kilograms
Average price per kilogram	$50
Standard price per kilogram	$60
Budgeted quantity per quarter	4,000 kilograms

In the fourth quarter the purchase department had to increase purchases from the budgeted normal volume of 4,000 to 24,000 kilograms as a result of the firm's success in a fiercely competitive bidding. The substantial increase in the volume to be purchased forced the purchasing department to search for alternative suppliers. After frantic searches, the purchasing department found suppliers in several foreign countries that would be able to meet the firm's needs. The quality of the materials from these suppliers is higher than that of the firm's regular suppliers. The purchasing department, however, was very reluctant to make the purchase because the negotiated price was $76 per kilogram including shipping and import duty.

The actual cost of the purchases, however, was much lower because of the currency devaluations right before deliveries started. The currency devaluation was a result of the financial turmoil of several countries in the region.

Patricia Rice, the controller, does not share the euphoria of the purchasing department. She is fully aware of the following quarterly purchases:

	First Quarter	Second Quarter	Third Quarter	Fourth Quarter
Quantity	4,000	4,000	4,000	24,000
Purchase price (per kilogram)	$68	$69	$73	

Required

1. Calculate price variances for the fourth quarter and for the year.
2. Evaluate the performance of the purchasing department.

SOLUTIONS TO SELF-STUDY PROBLEMS

1. Sales Volumes and Flexible Budget Variances

1.

	Master Budget October 20X7	Flexible Budget	
Units	10,000	9,500	11,000
Sales	$540,000	$513,000	$594,000
Variable costs:			
Direct materials	$126,000	$119,700	$138,600
Direct labor	77,000	73,150	84,700
Variable manufacturing overheads	20,000	19,000	22,000
Variable selling and administrative expenses	50,000	47,500	55,000
Total variable cost	$273,000	$259,350	$300,300
Contribution margin	$267,000	$253,650	$293,700
Fixed costs:			
Manufacturing costs	$ 55,000	$ 55,000	$ 55,000
Selling and administrative	24,000	24,000	24,000
Total fixed costs	$ 79,000	$ 79,000	$ 79,000
Operating income	$188,000	$174,650	$214,700

2. Sales volume operating income variance:
$174,650 − 188,000 = $13,350 Unfavorable

Flexible budget operating income variance:
$177,100 − $174,650 = $2,450 Favorable

Sales price variance = $551,000 − 513,000 = $38,000 Favorable

Flexible budget variable cost variance:
$294,900 − $259,350 = $35,550 Unfavorable

3.

Direct Materials

$3 × 48,000 lb = $144,000 $2.52 × 48,000 lb = $120,960 $2.52 × 47,500 lb = $119,700

Price variance
= $144,000 − $120,960
= $23,040 Unfavorable
or
= ($3 − $2.52) × 48,000
= $0.48 × 48,000

Usage variance
= $120,960 − $119,700
= $1,260 Unfavorable
or
= (48,000 lb − 47,500 lb) × $2.52
= 500 × $2.52
= $1,260 Unfavorable

Direct Labor

$16 × 4,800 hrs = $76,800 $15.4 × 4,800 hrs = $73,920 $15.4 × 4,750 hrs = $73,150

Rate variance
= $76,800 − $73,920
= $2,880 Unfavorable
or
= ($16 − $15.4) × 4,800
= $0.6 × 4,800

Efficiency variance
= $73,920 − $73,150
= $770 Unfavorable
or
= (4,800 hrs − 4,750 hrs) × $15.4
= 50 × $15.4
= $770 Unfavorable

2. Direct Materials Price and Usage Variances, Direct Labor Rate and Efficiency Variances, and Journal Entries

1.

Direct Materials—XF–2000

$0.075 × 3,000,000 pounds
= $225,000

$0.08 × 3,000,000 pounds
= $240,000

$0.08 × 2,700,000 pounds
= $216,000

$0.08 × 2,500,000 pounds
= $200,000

Price variance
= $225,000 − $240,000
= $15,000 Favorable
or
= ($.075 − $0.08) × 3,000,000
= $0.005 × 3,000,000
= $15,000 Favorable

Usage variance
= $216,000 − $200,000
= $16,000 Unfavorable
or
= (2,700,000 pounds − 2,500,000 pounds) × $0.08
= 2,000,000 × $0.08
= $16,000 Unfavorable

Direct Labor

$35 × 5,200 hours
= $182,000

$32 × 5,200 hours
= $166,400

$32 × 5,000 hours
= $160,000

Rate variance
= $182,000 − $166,400
= $15,600 Unfavorable
or
= ($35 − $32) × 5,200
= $3 × 5,200
= $15,600 Unfavorable

Efficiency variance
= $166,400 − $160,000
= $6,400 Unfavorable
or
= (5,200 hours − 5,000 hours) × $32
= 200 × $32
= $6,400 Unfavorable

2.
Materials Inventory Control (3,000,000 × $.08)	$240,000	
Materials Purchase Price Variance (3,000,000 × $.005)		$ 15,000
Accounts Payable (3,000,000 × $.075)		225,000

Purchase 3,000,000 pounds of XF–2000 at $.075/per pound from Johnson Chemical Suppliers.

Work-in-Process Inventory Control ($0.08 × 2,500,000)	$200,000	
Materials Usage Variance (200,000 × $.08)	16,000	
Materials Inventory Control (2,700,000 × $.08)		$216,000

    Issued 2,700,000 pounds of XF–2000 for the production
    of 100,000 bags of Weed-Be-Doom.

Work-in-Process Inventory Control (5,000 × $32)	$160,000	
Labor Rate Variance (5,200 × $3)	15,600	
Labor Efficiency Variance (200 × $32)	6,400	
Accrued Payroll (5,200 × $32)		$182,000

    Direct labor wages for the manufacturing of 100,000 bags
    of Weed-Be-Doom for 5,200 hours at $35 per hour.

Standard Costing: Factory Overhead

16

After studying this chapter, you should be able to ...

Establish proper standard costs for variable overhead **1**

Calculate and interpret a variable overhead flexible budget variance, spending variance, and efficiency variance **2**

Determine the total standard fixed overhead and the standard fixed overhead application rate **3**

Compute and interpret the fixed factory overhead total variance, spending (budget) variance, production volume variance, and overapplied or underapplied fixed factory overhead **4**

Use alternative two-way or three-way procedures to analyze and interpret factory overhead variances **5**

Dispose of variances through the financial accounting system **6**

Apply a standard cost system to service organizations **7**

Describe the effects of recent advances in new manufacturing technologies and rapid changes in operating environments on standard cost systems, and adapt a standard cost system to these changing environments **8**

Determine whether to conduct further investigations of variances **9**

A. Carey/The Image Works

A man should never be ashamed to own that he has been in the wrong, which is but saying in other words, that he is wiser today than yesterday.

JONATHAN SWIFT

Although reporting a variance in a standard costing system is not analogous to saying there is something wrong in the operation, it is true that the most important function of a standard costing system is to help the firm attain a better operating result. In Chapter 15 we discussed the basic concepts of a standard cost system, its applications to direct materials and direct labor, and the recording of standard costs. Building on that material, we examine the application of the standard costing system to variable and fixed overhead. In addition, we examine further the effects recent advances in manufacturing technologies and rapid changes in operating environments have had on the use of the standard cost system. Using a hospital setting, we also illustrate the applications and benefits of using standard cost systems in service organizations.

STANDARD COSTS FOR FACTORY OVERHEAD

Typically a firm has both variable and fixed factory overhead costs. Like direct materials or direct labor costs, the amount of variable factory overhead varies with the activity of the firm. The procedure for analyzing variable factory overhead variances is similar to the procedures for analyzing direct materials or direct labor variances. Because fixed factory overheads have a different cost behavior pattern than variable factory overheads, the procedure for analyzing them is different as well.

◄ **LEARNING OBJECTIVE 1**
Establish proper standard costs for variable factory overhead.

Standard Variable Factory Overhead

Uses of a standard cost system for variable factory overhead include establishing standard variable factory overhead rates, using the standard to monitor and control variable factory overhead costs during operations, and evaluating operations based on the standard.

Establishing the Standard Cost for Variable Factory Overhead

Establishing the standard variable factory overhead cost for an operation involves four steps:

1. Determining the behavioral patterns of variable factory overhead costs.
2. Selecting one or more appropriate cost drivers for applying variable factory overhead to cost objects such as products, services, or divisions.

BusinessWeek

? Does TQM Have a Dark Side?

When TQM (total quality management) hit U.S. businesses in the early '80s, Varian Associates, Inc., was one of the many companies that got caught up in the quality whirlwind. Varian, a scientific equipment maker, jumped in full force—essentially reinventing the way it did business and achieving stellar results. For instance, the unit that made vacuum systems for computer clean rooms boosted on-time delivery by 50 percent, and the radiation-equipment-service department was ranked number one for prompt customer visits. Despite such efforts and seemingly strong results, Varian's sales only grew by 3 percent in 1990, and it posted a $4.1 million loss after a $32 million profit in 1989.

Q: Where did Varian's quality efforts go astray? *Find out on page 654 of this chapter.*

3. Ascertaining the intended level of operation and estimating the total variable factory overhead and the corresponding total of the cost driver.

4. Computing the standard variable factory overhead rate.

Determining the Behavioral Pattern of Variable Factory Overhead. A manufacturing process often has hundreds of variable factory overhead items. Although the total variable factory overhead changes as the activity level changes, not all variable factory overhead items vary at the same rate. For example, the amount of sandpaper used by a furniture manufacturer varies mostly with the total pieces of furniture manufactured during a period, while the amount of oil used for equipment in the factory can be a step function of the units manufactured during the interval. For example, if a piece of equipment needs one gallon of fresh oil for every 5,000 units, the change in oil cost occurs in discrete steps, rather than in direct proportion to the units produced, as for direct materials. In Exhibit 16–1 we illustrate one such overhead pattern. Other variable factory overhead items can have widely divergent variation rates. An operation typically has several rates of change for its variable factory overhead; each varies with changes in a different manufacturing activity.

Changes in some factory variable overhead costs, however, are not due entirely to changes in manufacturing activity. Some overhead cost changes are the result of management decisions. Setup costs are examples of such costs. The manufacture of 10,000 units, for example, might have a total setup cost of $5,000 if the 10,000 units are manufactured in one batch. The setup cost increases to, say, $9,800 if the firm manufactures the 10,000 units in two batches, and to $14,000 for three batches.

In general, the standard variable factory overhead for a manufacturing operation is a function of the number of units manufactured and possibly other activities of the manufacturing processes. The beginning step in determining standard costs for variable factory overhead is to understand their cost behavioral patterns. Because a number of cost drivers influence variable overhead costs, standard costs for variable overhead should be based on a careful selection of the appropriate cost drivers. These cost drivers can be volume-based or activity-based.

Selecting the Cost Drivers to Apply Variable Factory Overhead An operation usually has a vast number of variable factory overheads involving many usage patterns. Finding a single cost driver that changes in the same proportion as all the variable factory overheads is an impossible task. One solution is to use a different cost driver for each factory overhead item that has a different use pattern. Such a solution, however, often cannot be justified in view of its implementation cost.

Many firms use a single cost driver, such as direct labor-hours or direct labor cost, as the cost driver for applying variable factory overhead. This practice is satisfactory as long as the total variable factory overhead is small or the total variable fac-

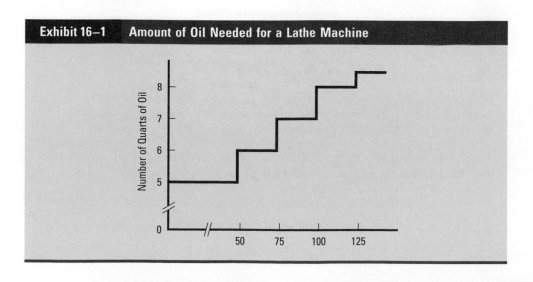

Exhibit 16–1   Amount of Oil Needed for a Lathe Machine

tory overhead relates to the selected cost driver. The increasing importance of factory overhead and the decreasing amount of direct labor-hours in many operations in recent years, however, have led many firms to reexamine this conventional practice. Their efforts to find more appropriate cost drivers have led to greater uses of activity-related factory overhead cost drivers.

An activity-based cost driver applies factory overhead to products or services according to the activity level of manufacturing operations. Using activity-based factory overhead cost drivers requires identifying activities that cause factory overhead costs to change. Items that change as a result of similar activities are grouped together.

Cooper identifies activities that change the amount of factory overhead as unit-based, batch-based, product-based, and facility-based factory overhead.[1] Unit-based cost drivers include machine-hours, direct labor-hours, and units of materials. Batch-based cost drivers include the number of times materials and parts are moved during manufacturing, the number of setups, and the number of times materials and parts are received and inspected. Product-based cost drivers include the number of products, number of processes, and number of schedule changes. Facility-based cost drivers mostly relate to the size of operations, not production activities.[2]

For simplicity of illustration the early part of this chapter uses a single cost driver—direct labor-hours. A later example uses multiple cost drivers for variable factory overhead. Exhibit 16–2 contains the standard cost sheet of Schmidt Machinery Company originally presented as Exhibit 15–5. This standard cost sheet shows that the firm applies variable factory overhead at the rate of $12 per direct labor-hour.

Determining the Level of Operation and Estimating the Total Variable Factory Overhead and the Total Cost Drivers Cost drivers for different variable factory overhead items can be different. Furthermore, these cost drivers may not vary proportionately with changes of operating levels. A firm thus needs to decide the level of its operation and estimate the total variable factory overhead and the total selected cost driver at that level of operation before determining the standard variable factory overhead rate.

Schmidt plans to manufacture 1,000 units. At this level of operation, the accountant estimates its total variable factory overhead to be $60,000 and the total amount of the selected cost driver, direct labor-hours, to be 5,000 hours.

Exhibit 16–2	Standard Cost Sheet

SCHMIDT MACHINERY COMPANY
Standard Cost Sheet

Product Number XV–1

Description	Quantity	Unit Cost	Subtotal	Total
Direct materials:				
Aluminum	4 pounds	$25	$100	
PVC	1 pound	40	40	$140
Direct labor	5 hours	40		200
Factory overhead (based on 5,000 direct labor-hours):				
Variable	5 hours	12	60	
Fixed	5 hours	24	120	180
Standard Cost per Unit				$520

[1] Robin Cooper, "Cost Classification in Unit-Based and Activity-Based Manufacturing Cost Systems," *Journal of Cost Management for the Manufacturing Industry*, Fall 1990, pp. 4–14.

[2] Robert D. McIlhattan, "How Cost Management Systems Can Support the JIT Philosophy," *Management Accounting*, September 1987, pp. 20–26.

Determining the Standard Variable Factory Overhead Rate   The standard variable factory overhead rate is determined by dividing the amount of the selected cost driver into the estimated total variable factory overhead.[3] Schmidt's accountant determines its standard variable factory overhead rate by dividing the 5,000 direct labor-hours of the cost driver into the total variable factory overhead to arrive at the standard variable factory overhead rate of $12 per direct labor-hour.

Analyzing Variable Factory Overhead

LEARNING OBJECTIVE 2 ▶
Calculate and interpret a variable factory overhead flexible budget variance, spending variance, and efficiency variance.

The total variable factory overhead variance is the difference between total actual variable factory overhead incurred and total standard variable factory overhead for the output of the period.

The first step in analyzing variable factory overhead is to determine the total variable factory overhead variance. This total variance can be further analyzed into detailed variances.

Determining the Total Variable Factory Overhead Variance   The **total variable factory overhead variance** of a period is the difference between the total actual variable factory overhead incurred and the total standard variable factory overhead allowed for the output (manufactured) of the period. Some companies refer to the total variable factory overhead variance as the *variable factory overhead flexible budget variance*.

Schmidt Machinery Company used 3,510 direct labor-hours and incurred a total factory variable overhead cost of $40,630 to manufacture 780 units of XV–1 during October 20X6. The amount of the total actual variable factory overhead for the period is the sum of the amounts in the subsidiary ledgers of variable factory overhead items.

Exhibit 16–3 shows that the total standard variable factory overhead for the period is $46,800. The procedure to determine the total standard variable factory overhead

---

Steps in Determining a Standard Variable Factory Overhead Rate

1. Decide the level of operation.
2. Determine total variable factory overhead for the operation.
3. Select an activity basis for variable factory overhead and determine the amount for the operation.
4. Divide the amount in step 2 by the amount in step 3 to arrive at the standard variable overhead rate.

Exhibit 16–3   Variable Factory Overhead Flexible Budget Variance

SCHMIDT MACHINERY COMPANY
Variable Factory Overhead Flexible Budget Variance
For the Month of October 20X6

Total actual variable factory overhead		$40,630
Total standard variable factory overhead:		
1. Find the number of units manufactured.	780 units	
2. Determine for the units manufactured the standard quantity of the substitute cost driver for applying variable factory overhead.		
a. Find the cost driver the firm uses.	Direct labor-hours	
b. Find the standard quantity of the substitute cost driver for one unit of the product.	× 5 Direct labor-hours	
c. Compute the total standard quantity of the substitute cost driver for the units manufactured.	3,900 Direct labor-hours	
3. Find the standard variable overhead rate.	× $12 per Direct labor-hour	
4. Compute the total standard variable overhead.		= 46,800
Variable factory overhead flexible budget variance		$ 6,170 F

---

[3]   An alternative procedure is to use the multiple regression analysis procedure discussed in Chapter 4 to determine the standard variable factory overhead rates. This permits the use of multiple cost drivers such as one that includes machine-hours, labor-hours, number of setups, and so forth.

allowed for a period is similar to the procedures for determining the total standard costs allowed for direct materials and direct labor costs. The only exception is that a substitute cost driver or cost drivers for variable factory overhead costs are used in the procedure, instead of quantities of the variable factory overhead items themselves.

Schmidt's accountant determines the total standard variable factory overhead allowed for its operations during October 20X6 by first calculating the total standard direct labor-hours allowed for the output of the period, 780 units of XV–1. Direct labor-hours is the substitute cost driver that Schmidt Machinery Company uses to apply its variable factory overhead to the units manufactured during the period.

Schmidt manufactured 780 units of XV–1 in its October 20X6 operations. At 5 direct labor-hours for each unit of XV–1 manufactured, the total standard direct labor-hours for October are 3,900. Schmidt's accountant determined its standard variable factory overhead rate to be $12 per direct labor-hour. The total standard variable factory overhead for its operations in October, therefore, is $46,800 (3,900 hours × $12 per hour).

The difference between the total variable factory overhead incurred and the total standard variable factory overhead is the variable factory overhead flexible budget variance. Schmidt Machinery Company incurred a total actual variable factory overhead of $40,630 in its operations during October 20X6. The total standard variable factory overhead allowed for the output of the period as calculated based on the substitute cost driver, direct labor-hours, is $46,800, as determined by the procedure described earlier. The variable factory overhead flexible budget variance, therefore, is $6,170, favorable ($46,800 − $40,630).

Commonly managers refer to variable factory overhead flexible budget variances as overapplied if they are favorable or underapplied if unfavorable. In October 20X6, Schmidt Machinery Company has an overapplied, favorable, variable factory overhead of $6,170.

Further Analysis of the Variable Factory Overhead Flexible Budget Variance

Many firms analyze the variable factory overhead flexible budget variance further into two detailed variances based on the substitute cost driver for applying variable factory overhead. The **variable factory overhead spending variance** is the difference between the actual variable factory overhead incurred and the total standard variable factory overhead for the actual quantity of the substitute cost driver for applying variable factory overhead. The remainder is the **variable factory overhead efficiency variance.** This variance shows the difference between the total standard variable factory overhead for the actual quantity of the substitute cost driver for applying the overhead and the standard variable factory overhead allowed for the output of the period.

In Exhibit 16–4 we illustrate this procedure using the October 20X6 operating data of Schmidt Machinery Company. Schmidt uses direct labor-hours to apply variable factory overhead to its products. Further analysis of its variable factory overhead flexible budget variances thus is based on direct labor-hours.

The procedures for further analysis of variable factory overhead flexible budget variances are similar to those for direct materials or direct labor flexible budget variances. The procedures differ, however, in the activity measure of the cost item being analyzed. Further analysis of the direct materials or direct labor flexible budget variance uses a direct measure of the cost item. In contrast, there is no direct measure of variable factory overhead because variable factory overhead is the total of various overhead activities—inspection, setup, materials handling, and so forth, each of which may vary with a different cost driver.

Schmidt Machinery Company used 3,510 direct labor-hours in October 20X6. At the standard rate of $12 per hour the standard variable factory overhead for the actual direct labor-hours during the period is $42,120, shown in point B in Exhibit 16–4. Using this amount, we can separate the variable factory overhead flexible budget variance into two components. The difference between the actual variable factory overhead incurred, point A, and the total standard variable factory overhead for the actual quantity of the cost driver to apply the variable factory overhead, point B, is the variable factory overhead spending variance. This is $1,490, favorable.

The **variable factory overhead spending variance** is the difference between variable factory overhead incurred and total standard variable factory overhead based on the actual quantity of the cost driver to apply the overhead.

The **variable factory overhead efficiency variance** is the difference between the total standard variable factory overhead for the actual quantity of the substitute cost driver for applying variable factory overhead and the total standard variable factory overhead cost for the units manufactured during the period.

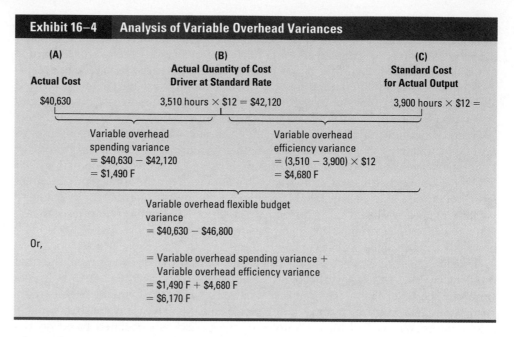

Exhibit 16–4 **Analysis of Variable Overhead Variances**

(A) Actual Cost	(B) Actual Quantity of Cost Driver at Standard Rate	(C) Standard Cost for Actual Output
$40,630	3,510 hours × $12 = $42,120	3,900 hours × $12 =

Variable overhead
spending variance
= $40,630 − $42,120
= $1,490 F

Variable overhead
efficiency variance
= (3,510 − 3,900) × $12
= $4,680 F

Variable overhead flexible budget
variance
= $40,630 − $46,800

Or,

= Variable overhead spending variance +
Variable overhead efficiency variance
= $1,490 F + $4,680 F
= $6,170 F

The difference between point B and the total standard variable factory overhead allowed for the output of the period, point C, is the variable factory overhead efficiency variance, $4,680, favorable.

Differences between Variable Factory Overhead Variances and Direct Materials and Direct Labor Variances

Although analyzing variable factory overhead costs is similar to analyzing direct materials and direct labor variances as described in Chapter 15, the procedures differ in at least two respects. First, prime costs and overhead costs often differ in the way that total costs change. In addition to varying with volume, the total variable factory overhead cost also varies with activities that change categorically or at intervals such as the number of production runs, number of batches, and the type of products. In contrast, total direct materials or total direct labor costs vary in proportion only to changes in production volume.[4]

Second, firms use a single cost driver such as pounds of materials or hours of direct labor to assign direct materials or direct labor costs to cost objects. In contrast, a firm may use two or more cost drivers to assign factory overhead costs because of the many different overhead activities involved.

Some managers perceive the amount of work needed to maintain a multiple-cost-drivers costing system for detailed identification and measurement of all overhead activities exceeds the benefit derived. As a result, these firms assign factory overhead to cost objects through a single cost driver such as direct labor-hours, machine-hours, or direct material cost.

When a single cost driver is used for a number of overhead activities, the relationship between factory overhead and the cost driver is not perfect. The amount of factory overhead incurred per machine-hour, for example, may vary from 1 cent to $5 depending on what transpires during the hour measured, even though the firm applies, say, $2 of factory overhead per machine-hour to cost objects. The imperfect relationships can have significant effects on the results of variance analysis for factory overhead.

Interpretation and Implications of Variable Factory Overhead Variances

The imperfect relationships between variable factory overhead items and their cost drivers require us to interpret and draw conclusions about variable factory overhead vari-

---

[4] Exceptions are firms with guaranteed wages or employment. The guaranteed portions of labor costs are fixed costs.

ances with care. The meaning and implications of variable factory overhead variances are not the same as their counterparts for direct materials or direct labor variances.

Variable Factory Overhead Spending Variance The counterparts of the variable factory overhead spending variance are the direct materials price and direct labor rate variances. These variances measure the effect of differences between actual unit prices and the standard unit prices on manufacturing cost. In addition to the effects of price deviations, a variable factory overhead spending variance may contain some or all the effects of quantity deviations.

Assume, for example, a firm uses machine-hours as the cost driver to apply variable factory overhead. The standard calls for one machine-hour with 2 ounces of oil per machine-hour at $2.50 per ounce or $5 per machine-hour, for the production of 10 units.[5] The firm used 6,000 machine-hours and 12,500 ounces of oil at a cost of $31,250 (2,500 × $2.50) to manufacture 55,000 units during the period just completed.

According to the standard, the manufacture of 55,000 units should have taken 5,500 machine-hours and 11,000 (2 × 5,500) ounces of oil. The accountant calculates variable factory overhead efficiency variances based on the difference in machine-hours because the firm applies variable factory overhead using machine-hours. The operation used 500 machine-hours more than the standard allowed for the manufacture of 55,000 units. At the standard application rate of $5 per machine-hour, the firm has an unfavorable efficiency variance of $2,500 (500 × $5), as shown in part 1 of Exhibit 16–5. The efficiency variance represents the

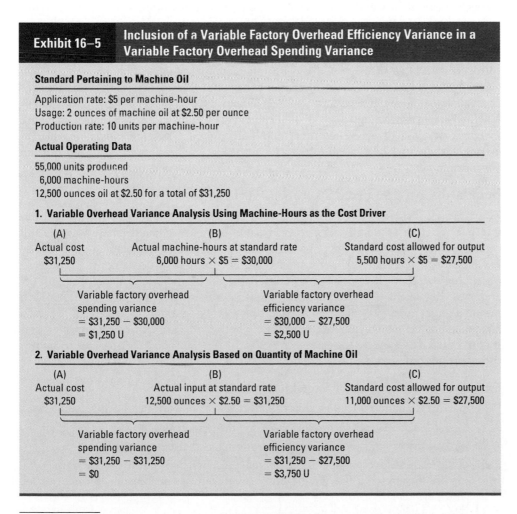

Exhibit 16–5	**Inclusion of a Variable Factory Overhead Efficiency Variance in a Variable Factory Overhead Spending Variance**

Standard Pertaining to Machine Oil

Application rate: $5 per machine-hour
Usage: 2 ounces of machine oil at $2.50 per ounce
Production rate: 10 units per machine-hour

Actual Operating Data

55,000 units produced
 6,000 machine-hours
12,500 ounces oil at $2.50 for a total of $31,250

1. Variable Overhead Variance Analysis Using Machine-Hours as the Cost Driver

(A)	(B)	(C)
Actual cost	Actual machine-hours at standard rate	Standard cost allowed for output
$31,250	6,000 hours × $5 = $30,000	5,500 hours × $5 = $27,500

Variable factory overhead spending variance
= $31,250 − $30,000
= $1,250 U

Variable factory overhead efficiency variance
= $30,000 − $27,500
= $2,500 U

2. Variable Overhead Variance Analysis Based on Quantity of Machine Oil

(A)	(B)	(C)
Actual cost	Actual input at standard rate	Standard cost allowed for output
$31,250	12,500 ounces × $2.50 = $31,250	11,000 ounces × $2.50 = $27,500

Variable factory overhead spending variance
= $31,250 − $31,250
= $0

Variable factory overhead efficiency variance
= $31,250 − $27,500
= $3,750 U

---

[5] The cost of oil is a direct cost if we know that the firm manufactures 10 units per machine-hour and uses 2 ounces of oil per machine-hour. The firm may treat the cost of oil as a direct cost if the cost is a significant amount. However, the cost of oil needed to operate machinery is most likely an insignificant amount and is, therefore, an overhead item.

excess variable overhead cost that the firm would have incurred because of the excess machine-hours.

The firm used 12,500 ounces of oil during the operation, an excess of 1,500 ounces over the standard. At the standard price of $2.50 per ounce, the efficiency variance would have been $3,750 unfavorable using the same procedure as we used for analyzing direct materials usage variances in Chapter 15, as shown in part 2 of Exhibit 16–5.

Here we see that a part of the variable factory overhead efficiency variance is included in the variable factory overhead spending variance. The difference between the actual quantity of oil used during the operation, 12,500 ounces, and the standard quantity of oil for the actual machine-hours operated, 12,000 ounces, is 500 ounces. At $2.50 standard price per ounce, the 500-ounce excess usage costs $1,250. Both the $1,250 and the $2,500 are results of excess usage of oil. The $1,250, however, is included in the variable factory overhead spending variance when the variable factory overhead is analyzed using machine-hours as the cost driver. The inclusion of both the price variance and a portion of the efficiency variance in a variable factory overhead spending variance must be taken into consideration in interpreting and determining the implications of the variance.

Variable Factory Overhead Efficiency Variance

The use of a single cost driver for applying variable factory overhead renders any interpretation of variable factory overhead variances difficult because of the imperfect relationship between the chosen cost driver and variable factory overhead.

Each element of variable factory overhead (lubricant, indirect labor, setup materials, and labor) often has a unique cost driver. Therefore, the use of a single cost driver for all the elements of variable factory overhead imperfectly measure the usage (efficiency variance) for many of them. In response, the management accountant breaks the variable factory overhead into its elements, chooses the appropriate cost driver for each element, and calculates the spending and efficiency variances for each element. Thus, if lubricant, indirect labor, and setup cost are significant variable factory overhead items, we would have a spending and an efficiency variance for each of these three elements, rather than a single spending and a single efficiency variance for all variable factory overhead. The importance of choosing an appropriate cost driver, therefore, cannot be overemphasized.

Standard Cost for Fixed Factory Overhead

Many firms consider establishing a standard cost for fixed factory overhead an integral part of their standard cost system because of GAAP requirements to use full costing for financial reporting. An additional incentive is the mandate to include fixed factory overhead in pricing for federal government procurement. Many genuinely believe that all costs of an operation should be included in the product cost and that they can assign fixed factory overhead costs to products or operations with reasonable accuracy. Other firms believe that using a standard cost system for fixed factory overhead allows them to determine whether their operations incur fixed factory overheads as expected, to assess the effectiveness of their facilities and to review the appropriateness of the size of these facilities.

Establishing Standard Cost for Fixed Factory Overhead

LEARNING OBJECTIVE 3 ▶
Determine the total standard fixed factory overhead for an operation and a standard fixed factory overhead application rate.

Determining the standard fixed factory overhead involves four essential elements:

1. Total *budgeted fixed factory overhead* for the operation.
2. A *cost driver* or drivers for applying the fixed factory overhead.
3. The normal level of operations as reflected by the quantity of the cost driver for applying the fixed factory overhead, or the *denominator activity* for the period.
4. The standard fixed factory overhead *application rate*.

Total Budgeted Fixed Factory Overhead   Fixed factory overhead items are period expenditures that do not vary with the activity level of the period. Once the activity level has been determined, the total fixed factory overhead for the period remains relatively constant regardless of the level of operations.

Cost Driver for Applying Fixed Factory Overhead   Fixed factory overhead usually is assigned to cost objects via one or more alternative activity measures. Because the total fixed factory overhead does not vary with changes in the activity level, while the quantity of the activity measure for applying fixed factory overhead does change, there is in effect no activity measure for fixed factory overhead during the period.[6] To include fixed factory overheads in product costs, firms commonly use the same cost driver they use for the variable factory overhead to apply fixed factory overhead to products or operations.

Denominator Activity and Fixed Factory Overhead Application Rate   The denominator activity is the desired operating level at the expected operating efficiency for a period, expressed in the quantity of the cost driver for applying fixed factory overhead. A **fixed factory overhead application rate** is the rate at which the firm applies fixed overhead costs to cost objects. A firm determines its fixed factory overhead application rate by dividing the denominator activity into the total budget fixed factory overhead for the period.

Schmidt Machinery Company uses direct labor-hours as the cost driver to apply its factory overhead; its normal manufacturing activity level is 1,000 units of product XV–1 per period. With a desired labor standard of 5 direct labor-hours per unit of XV–1, the denominator activity per period is 5,000 direct labor-hours. Schmidt has a total budget fixed factory overhead of $120,000 per period and a denominator activity of 5,000 direct labor-hours. The fixed factory overhead application rate, therefore, is $24 per direct labor-hour.

Analyzing Fixed Factory Overhead Variances

Although the total fixed factory overhead of a firm may change over a long period, it typically remains relatively stable in the short run. A firm expects the total actual fixed factory overhead for a period to be the same as the budgeted amount, regardless of the level of production attained. Schmidt Machinery Company has a budgeted monthly total fixed factory overhead of $120,000. The total fixed factory overhead for the period, therefore, is expected to be $120,000.

The total flexible variance for a variable cost is the difference between the amount incurred for the variable cost and the flexible budget amount allowed for the actual output of the period. The actual output of a period may not be the master budget amount. In contrast, the total flexible variance of a fixed factory overhead is the difference between the actual amount incurred and the budget allowance amount for the period. This budget allowance amount is the same in both the master and the flexible budget. The amount of the fixed factory overhead in a flexible budget of the period is identical to the amount in the master budget because the fixed cost does not differ at different levels of output.

The **denominator activity** is the desired operating level at the expected operating efficiency for the period, expressed in the quantity of the cost driver for applying fixed factory overhead.

A **fixed factory overhead application rate** is the rate at which the firm applies fixed overhead costs to cost objects.

◄ **LEARNING OBJECTIVE 4**
Compute and interpret the fixed factory overhead total variance, spending (budget) variance, production volume variance, and overapplied or underapplied fixed factory overhead.

Steps in Determining a Fixed Factory Overhead Rate

1. Determine the total budgeted fixed factory overhead for the period.
2. Select a cost driver for applying fixed factory overhead.
3. Calculate the denominator quantity for the selected cost driver.
4. Compute the fixed factory overhead application rate by dividing step 3 into step 1.

---

[6]   Recent studies on activity-based costing reveal that many so-called fixed factory overheads in the past do vary with some activities. For these cost items, firms need to find appropriate activity levels and bases for proper product cost determinations.

The **fixed factory overhead spending (budget) variance** is the difference between the actual amount incurred and the budgeted allowance for the fixed factory overhead.

Fixed Factory Overhead Spending Variance The fixed factory overhead spending variance is the difference between the actual amount incurred and the amount budgeted for the fixed factory overhead. This variance also is called the *fixed factory overhead (flexible) budget variance.* Schmidt Machinery Company incurred a total of $130,650 actual fixed factory overhead during October 20X6 (see Exhibit 16–6, point A). The budgeted fixed factory overhead allowance was $120,000 for the month (see Exhibit 16–6, point B). The difference between the total actual fixed factory overhead incurred (point A) and the budgeted allowance for fixed factory overhead for the period (point B) is $10,650, unfavorable. The firm, therefore, has an unfavorable fixed factory overhead spending (flexible budget) variance of $10,650 for the month (see the calculation on the left side of Exhibit 16–6).

The **fixed factory overhead production volume variance** is the difference between the budget allowance for fixed factory overhead for the period and the applied fixed factory overhead.

Fixed Factory Overhead Production Volume Variance The fixed factory overhead production volume variance is the difference between the budgeted allowance for fixed factory overhead for the period and the applied fixed factory overhead. Fixed factory overheads are applied based on the standard fixed factory overhead application rate to the operation of the period. The operation of the period is measured by its units of outputs.

A fixed factory overhead production volume variance arises whenever the firm's actual operating level is not the same as the budgeted level for its operations. Schmidt manufactures 780 units of XV–1 in October 20X6, which, according to the standard cost sheet, requires 3,900 standard direct labor-hours (780 units × 5 hours). At a standard fixed factory overhead application rate of $24 per direct labor-hour, the total standard fixed factory overhead applied to October 20X6 is $93,600 (3,900 hours × $24 per hour), see point C in Exhibit 16–6. With a budget fixed factory overhead allowance of $120,000, Schmidt has an unfavorable fixed factory overhead production volume variance of $26,400 for October (see the right side of Exhibit 16–6).

The difference between the budget fixed factory overhead allowance and the fixed factory overhead applied is a production volume variance, because the difference is a result of the difference between the number of units manufactured and the budget (denominator) volume. The denominator is the number of units the firm bud-

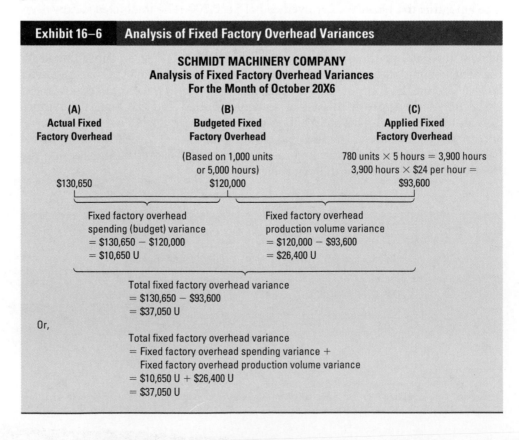

Exhibit 16–6   Analysis of Fixed Factory Overhead Variances

SCHMIDT MACHINERY COMPANY
Analysis of Fixed Factory Overhead Variances
For the Month of October 20X6

(A) Actual Fixed Factory Overhead	(B) Budgeted Fixed Factory Overhead	(C) Applied Fixed Factory Overhead
	(Based on 1,000 units or 5,000 hours)	780 units × 5 hours = 3,900 hours 3,900 hours × $24 per hour =
$130,650	$120,000	$93,600

Fixed factory overhead spending (budget) variance
= $130,650 − $120,000
= $10,650 U

Fixed factory overhead production volume variance
= $120,000 − $93,600
= $26,400 U

Total fixed factory overhead variance
= $130,650 − $93,600
= $37,050 U

Or,

Total fixed factory overhead variance
= Fixed factory overhead spending variance +
  Fixed factory overhead production volume variance
= $10,650 U + $26,400 U
= $37,050 U

geted to manufacture during the period. Note in Exhibit 16–7 the alternative computations for the amounts in points B and C in Exhibit 16–6. This exhibit shows clearly that the production volume variance arises from a difference between the budgeted (denominator) and the actual units of output. The production volume variance is favorable when the firm manufactured more units during the period than the budgeted (denominator) units and unfavorable when the actual production is below the budgeted units. There is no production volume variance when the number of units manufactured during the period is the same as the denominator number of units the firm budgeted (1,000 units).

Some firms also view production volume variances as a measure of facility or capacity utilization. A production volume variance reflects capacity utilization because it is the difference between the planned and the actual uses of the firm's facility or capacity. Schmidt planned to operate 5,000 direct labor-hours. The production of 780 units in October 20X6 indicates that the firm operates only at the level of 3,900 direct labor-hours (780 units × 5 standard direct labor-hours per unit). The firm underused its facility by 1,100 hours (5,000 − 3,900). At the standard fixed factory overhead application rate of $24 per hour, the production volume is $26,400, unfavorable (see the bottom panel of Exhibit 16–7). This unfavorable variance indicates an operation below the planned level that may cost the firm $26,400.

Total Fixed Factory Overhead Variance The sum of the fixed factory overhead spending and production volume variances is the total fixed factory overhead variance of the period. This is the difference between the fixed factory overhead incurred and the standard fixed factory applied to the output of the period. It also is referred to as the amount of the underapplied or overapplied fixed factory overhead.

Schmidt Machinery Company incurred $130,650 fixed factory overhead during October 20X6 in manufacturing 780 units of XV–1. The total applied fixed factory overhead for 780 units is $93,600. Schmidt Machinery Company, therefore, has a total fixed factory overhead variance or underapplied fixed factory overhead of $37,050 for the period.

Interpretation of Fixed Factory Overhead Variances

The various ways that fixed factory overhead spending and production volume variances can be distinguished from variable factory overhead variances mandate that the

Exhibit 16–7	Determinants of a Production Volume Variance	
(A) **Actual Fixed** **Factory Overhead**	**(B)** **Budgeted Fixed** **Factory Overhead**	**(C)** **Applied Fixed** **Factory Overhead**

	Budgeted units	1,000	Actual units	780
	× Hours per unit	5	× Hours per unit	5
		5,000 hours		3,900 hours
	× Fixed overhead rate	$24	× Fixed overhead rate	$24
$130,650		$120,000		$93,600

Fixed factory overhead production volume variance
= (Budgeted units − Actual units) × Standard hours per unit ×
   Standard fixed factory overhead application rate per hour
= (1,000 − 780) × 5 hours × $24 per hour
= $26,400 U

Or,

= Underused (overused) capacity in hours × Standard fixed
   factory overhead application rate per hour
= (Planned level of operation in standard hours − Actual
   operating level attained in standard hours) × Standard
   fixed factory overhead application rate per hour
= (5,000 hours − 3,900 hours) × $24
= $26,400 U

fixed factory overhead variances be interpreted differently. These variances have different implications than variable factory overhead spending and efficiency variances.

Fixed Factory Overhead Spending Variance   A fixed factory overhead spending variance may arise from one or more of these causes. One cause is that the budget procedure fails to anticipate or incorporate changes in fixed factory overhead. A budget may have inadvertently neglected scheduled raises for factory managers, changes in property taxes on factory buildings and equipment, or purchases of new equipment. A significant fixed factory overhead spending variance that results from an ineffective budget procedure suggests that the firm may need to revise its budgeting process.

A second cause is excessive spending due to improper or inadequate control of operations. Events such as emergency repairs, impromptu replacement of equipment, or the addition of managers for an unscheduled second shift increase fixed factory overhead for the period. Management needs to investigate the causes of such unfavorable fixed factory overhead spending variances to prevent similar events from occurring in future periods.

A third cause is that the firm's cost classifications may not reflect the actual cost behavior patterns. Classifying a cost item that is not entirely fixed as fixed overhead would lead to an unfavorable fixed factory overhead spending variance when the actual production exceeds the budgeted amount. It would lead to a favorable fixed factory overhead spending variance when the actual production is below the budgeted level.

In many operations, no factory overhead item's cost is strictly variable or fixed. A small amount of the fixed factory overhead spending variance that resulted from imprecise classifications of factory overhead items need not alarm management. A large variance, however, should prompt management to investigate the cause of the variance, including reexamining cost behavior patterns of factory overhead.

Fixed Factory Overhead Production Volume Variance   A fixed factory overhead production volume variance reflects the *effectiveness* of the firm in attaining a goal set for the period, rather than its *efficiency* in controlling costs. Schmidt Machinery Company had a budget to manufacture 1,000 units in October 20X6, but it actually manufactured 780 units. As a result, the firm has an unfavorable fixed factory overhead production volume variance of $26,400. Schmidt was ineffective in attaining the goal set for October. In contrast, all the other variances discussed so far reflect efficiencies of operation.

A fixed factory overhead production volume variance may result from management decisions, an unexpected change in demand for the product, or problems in manufacturing operations. Management may alter a production plan in view of a new market outlook or strategic considerations. It may decide to phase out or increase the production of a product because of knowledge gained about a new technology since the preparation of the budget. Or the sales volume since the beginning of the year may suggest a larger or smaller market than expected in the budget. Management, therefore, may decide to step up or reduce production of the product. A fixed factory overhead production volume variance that results from one or more of these causes most likely is beyond the control of factory management.

Unexpected production problems also can be a source of fixed factory overhead production volume variance. Among the production problems a factory may encounter are equipment not functioning properly due to inadequate maintenance or unexpected breakdowns, a product not designed for easy production, or unexpected high labor turnovers. A production volume variance that results from manufacturing problems very likely is the responsibility, either partially or fully, of the factory management.

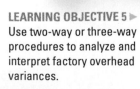

LEARNING OBJECTIVE 5 ▶
Use two-way or three-way procedures to analyze and interpret factory overhead variances.

Alternative Analyses of Factory Overhead Variances

Not all firms want or need as detailed an analysis of factory overhead as the four-way analysis just discussed. Alternative ways of analyzing factory overheads that are less detailed are the three-way and two-way analyses of variances.

Three-Way Analysis of Factory Overhead Variances

A three-way analysis of factory overhead variances separates the difference between the total factory overhead incurred and the standard factory overhead costs applied to the operations of the period for both variable and fixed factory overheads into three variances. A three-way analysis often is necessary because the company's chart of accounts does not separate variable and fixed factory overhead costs or management does not consider a more detailed analysis cost effective.

The three-way analysis of factory overhead combines the variable factory overhead spending variance and the fixed factory overhead spending (budget) variance into the (total) factory overhead spending variance. The three factory overhead variances from this analysis thus are factory overhead spending, variable factory overhead efficiency, and production volume variances. The *factory overhead spending variance* is the difference between the actual total factory overhead incurred and the expected total factory overhead for the actual quantity of the cost driver for overhead applications.

Schmidt Machinery Company has an unfavorable (total) factory overhead spending variance of $9,160, the sum of a $1,490 favorable variable factory overhead spending variance and a $10,650 unfavorable fixed factory overhead budget variance in the four-way analysis of factory overhead. Exhibit 16–8 illustrates the process of performing a three-way analysis for factory overhead variances.

Computing three variances requires four distinct points, as we show in Exhibit 16–8. Point A is the actual total factory overhead incurred during the period. Point B is the standard factory overhead applied to the actual quantity of the selected cost driver for applying factory overhead incurred during the period. Point C is the total standard factory overhead cost allowed for the output of the period. Point D is the total standard factory overhead cost applied based on the standard quantity of the selected cost driver for the units manufactured during the period.

The total fixed factory overheads in points B and C are always identical. Both points use the budgeted total fixed factory overhead, $120,000 in the example. The only difference between these two points is in their amounts of the standard variable factory overhead. The standard variable factory overhead in point B is based on the *actual quantity of the cost driver* for applying factory overhead. Schmidt Machinery Company, which uses direct labor-hours as the cost driver for applying factory overhead, spent 3,510 direct labor-hours in operations during October 20X6. At a standard variable factory overhead rate of $12 per direct labor-hour, the total variable factory overhead at point B is $42,120 (3,510 × $12). Adding the budgeted fixed factory overhead of $120,000, the total factory overhead at point B is $162,120.

The difference between points A and B is a factory overhead spending variance. Schmidt has a total factory overhead incurred, identified as point A, of $171,280 and $162,120 for point B. Its factory overhead spending variance therefore is $9,160, unfavorable.

Exhibit 16–8	**Three-Way Analysis of Factory Overhead Variances**			
	(A) Actual Cost Incurred	**(B)** Actual Input at Standard Rate	**(C)** Flexible Budget for the Output	**(D)** Total Applied to the Output
Variable	$ 40,630	$ 42,120	$ 46,800	$ 46,800
Fixed	+ 130,650	+ 120,000	+ 120,000	+ 93,600
Total	$171,280	$162,120	$166,800	$140,400

Spending variance = $9,160 U   Efficiency variance = $4,680 F   Production volume variance = $26,400 U

Underapplied factory overhead $30,880

The amount of factory overhead at point C is the total standard factory overhead for the operation of the period. The total standard variable factory overhead is the product of the total standard quantity of the cost driver for applying variable factory overhead for the units manufactured during the period and the standard variable factory overhead application rate. Schmidt manufactures 780 units of XV–1 during October 20X6. With 5 standard direct labor-hours per unit of XV–1 and the application rate of $12 standard variable factory overhead per direct labor-hour, the total standard variable factory overhead for the period is $46,800 (780 units × 5 hours per unit × $12 variable overhead rate per hour). This amount also is the variable factory overhead flexible budget amount. In fact, both the variable and the fixed factory overhead at point C are the flexible budget amounts for the units manufactured during the period. The fixed factory overhead in the flexible budget is $120,000. Thus, the total factory overhead at point C is $166,800.

The difference between points B and C is a factory overhead efficiency variance. Schmidt Machinery Company has $162,120 for point B and $166,800 for point C. Schmidt thus has a favorable factory overhead efficiency variance of $4,680 for its operations during October 20X6.

Point D is the total standard factory overhead applied to the units manufactured during the period. The total standard variable factory overhead applied to units manufactured during the period is the same as the flexible budget amount. Schmidt applies $12 variable factory overhead for each direct labor-hour. For the 780 units manufactured in October 20X6, which has total standard direct labor-hours of 3,900, the total variable factory overhead applied is $46,800.

Schmidt Machinery Company budgets a total of $120,000 fixed factory overhead for the month and applies fixed factory overhead at the rate of $24 per direct labor-hour. The total fixed factory overhead applied to the 780 units of XV–1 manufactured during the period therefore is $93,600 (780 units × 5 hours × $24). The sum of the applied variable factory overhead of $46,800 and the applied fixed factory overhead of $93,600 is the total factory overhead applied to operations of October 20X6, which is $140,400, shown as point D in Exhibit 16–8. The difference between points C and D is a factory overhead production volume variance. For Schmidt's operations during October 20X6, this amount is $26,400, unfavorable.

A four-way analysis of variances requires separate tracking of variable and fixed factory overheads and provides a more detailed analysis of an operation. Yet if this additional analysis of variances provides little useful information to management, a three-way analysis of variances is sufficient. A three-way analysis of variances also is used in situations where a firm's cost accounting system makes no distinction between variable and fixed factory overhead.

Two-Way Analysis of Factory Overhead Variances

A two-way analysis of factory overhead variances analyzes the difference between the total factory overhead incurred and the total factory overhead applied into two variances. These two variances are factory overhead flexible budget variance and factory overhead production volume variance. The factory overhead flexible budget variance also is called a factory overhead controllable variance. In Exhibit 16–9 we show a two-way analysis of factory overhead variances for the October 20X6 factory overhead costs of Schmidt Machinery Company.

Note in Exhibit 16–9 that a two-way analysis of variances uses three of the four points employed in the three-way analysis. Point A is the total actual factory overhead incurred during the period. Point C is the factory overhead in the flexible budget for the units manufactured during the period. Point D is the total standard factory overhead applied to the units manufactured during the period. Point B in Exhibit 16–8, the three-way analysis of variances, is not used.

The difference between points A and C is a factory overhead flexible budget variance. This variance also can be determined by merging the spending and efficiency variances from the three-way analysis.

Schmidt Machinery Company incurred a total factory overhead of $171,280 to manufacture 780 units of XV–1 during October 20X6. The total standard variable

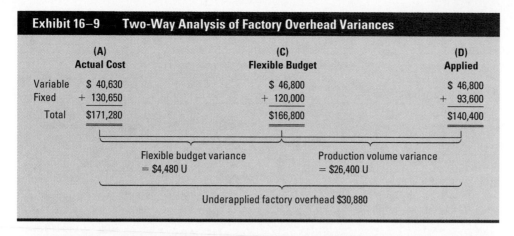

Exhibit 16-9   Two-Way Analysis of Factory Overhead Variances

	(A) **Actual Cost**	**(C)** **Flexible Budget**	**(D)** **Applied**
Variable	$ 40,630	$ 46,800	$ 46,800
Fixed	+ 130,650	+ 120,000	+ 93,600
Total	$171,280	$166,800	$140,400

Flexible budget variance = $4,480 U

Production volume variance = $26,400 U

Underapplied factory overhead $30,880

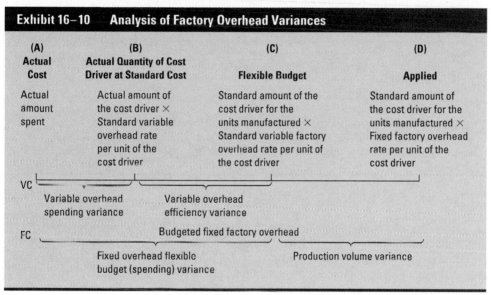

Exhibit 16-10   Analysis of Factory Overhead Variances

(A) **Actual** **Cost**	**(B)** **Actual Quantity of Cost** **Driver at Standard Cost**	**(C)** **Flexible Budget**	**(D)** **Applied**
Actual amount spent	Actual amount of the cost driver × Standard variable overhead rate per unit of the cost driver	Standard amount of the cost driver for the units manufactured × Standard variable factory overhead rate per unit of the cost driver	Standard amount of the cost driver for the units manufactured × Fixed factory overhead rate per unit of the cost driver

VC

Variable overhead spending variance

Variable overhead efficiency variance

FC

Budgeted fixed factory overhead

Fixed overhead flexible budget (spending) variance

Production volume variance

factory overhead for 780 units of XV-1 is $46,800. The total budgeted fixed factory overhead for the period is $120,000. The total amount at point C, therefore, is $166,800. Schmidt has an unfavorable factory overhead flexible budget variance of $4,480 for its operations during October 20X6. Alternatively, we can determine the factory overhead flexible budget variance by combining, from the three-way analysis of factory overhead variances, the unfavorable spending variance of $9,160 and the favorable efficiency variance of $4,680.

Summary of Factory Overhead Variances

A firm may analyze factory overhead variances separately for its variable and fixed factory overhead costs, or it may perform the variance analyses without distinguishing the variances from either variable or fixed factory overhead. When variable and fixed factory variances are both divided into two detailed variances, the analysis is a four-way analysis of factory overhead variances. In Exhibit 16-10 you can see the determination of factory overhead variances using a four-way analysis. In Exhibit 16-11 we summarize the analyses presented earlier for the operations of the Schmidt Machinery Company in October 20X6.

Firms often can achieve a more effective control when the analysis is done at a more detailed level. Effective controls also require separate analyses for factory overhead items that have different cost drivers. Analyses at an aggregated level, say, a single cost driver for all the factory overhead items, may mask significant variations in one or more of the individual overhead items. Separate analyses for factory overhead items with different cost drivers follow the procedure discussed earlier.

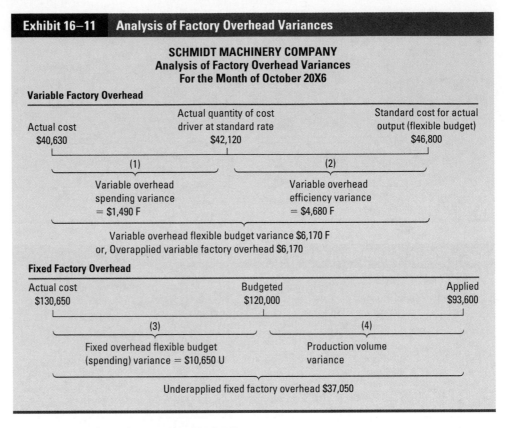

Exhibit 16–11   Analysis of Factory Overhead Variances

SCHMIDT MACHINERY COMPANY
Analysis of Factory Overhead Variances
For the Month of October 20X6

Variable Factory Overhead

| Actual cost $40,630 | Actual quantity of cost driver at standard rate $42,120 | Standard cost for actual output (flexible budget) $46,800 |

(1)
Variable overhead spending variance = $1,490 F

(2)
Variable overhead efficiency variance = $4,680 F

Variable overhead flexible budget variance $6,170 F
or, Overapplied variable factory overhead $6,170

Fixed Factory Overhead

| Actual cost $130,650 | Budgeted $120,000 | Applied $93,600 |

(3)
Fixed overhead flexible budget (spending) variance = $10,650 U

(4)
Production volume variance

Underapplied fixed factory overhead $37,050

DISPOSITION OF VARIANCES

LEARNING OBJECTIVE 6 ▶
Dispose of variances through the financial accounting system.

A standard cost system provides standard costs for cost of goods sold and inventories. The firm, however, might have incurred an actual cost that differed from the standard cost in carrying out operations of the period. How should a firm dispose of the variance, if any?

A financial accounting system may treat a variance as an item pertaining to the current period and dispose of the variance in the income statement of the period. Alternatively, it may consider the variance's effect on the entire operations of the period and allocate it to the inventory and expense accounts.

Variance as a Current Period Savings or Expense

Firms that consider unfavorable manufacturing cost variances as expenses or losses include the variances in the income statement of the period. An unfavorable (favorable) manufacturing variance is added to (subtracted from) the cost of goods sold of the period. A favorable (unfavorable) sales price variance is added to (subtracted from) the amount of the total sales in standard selling prices to arrive at the total actual sales of the period. Other variances are included in appropriate places in the income statement of the period. Schmidt Machinery Company disposes of its manufacturing cost variances in the period they occur. Schmidt's condensed income statement appears in Exhibit 16–12.

This procedure is easy and inexpensive. Firms often elect to dispose of variances in this manner at year-ends when manufacturing variances are relatively small.

Even when the variance is a significant amount, a firm may include the entire cost variance in the cost of goods sold whether the variances are the result of efficient or inefficient operations of the period. A variance resulting from operating efficiency should be included in the report for the operating results of that period; no part of such a variance should be included in the ending inventories of the period. This can be achieved by including the entire cost variance in the period's cost of goods sold.

Furthermore, separate reports of cost variances draw management's attention to significant manufacturing variances. A well-managed firm pays attention to vari-

Exhibit 16–12	Income Statement

SCHMIDT MACHINERY COMPANY
Income Statement
For the Period Ended October 31, 20X6

Sales	$624,000	
Add: Sales price variance	15,600 F	
Net sales		$639,600
Cost of goods sold (at standard):	$405,600*	
Add: Manufacturing cost variances	+ 37,000† U	
Total cost of goods sold		442,600
Gross margin		$197,000
Selling and administrative expenses		69,000
Operating income		$128,000

*Standard manufacturing cost per unit (Exhibit 15–5)	$ 520	
Number of units manufactured and sold	× 780	
Total standard cost of goods manufactured and sold	$405,600	

†Total variable manufacturing cost variance (Exhibit 15–6)	$ 50	F
Total fixed manufacturing cost variance (Exhibit 16–6)	37,050	U
Total manufacturing cost variance	$37,000	U

Exhibit 16–13	Proration of Manufacturing Cost Variance

Accounts	Cost at Standard	Percent of Total	Proration of Variance	Adjusted Total Cost
Work in Progress, Ending	$ 36,400	7%	$37,000 × 0.07 = $ 2,590	$ 38,990
Finished Goods, Ending	78,000	15	$37,000 × 0.15 = 5,550	83,550
Cost of Goods Sold	405,600	78	$37,000 × 0.78 = 28,860	434,460
Total	$520,000	100%	$37,000	$557,000

ances, and management accountants can assist such attention-directing by providing management with separate reports of cost variances instead of burying variances in myriad accounts.

Proration of Variance

An alternative to disposing of variances as a current period cost is to prorate manufacturing cost variances among the cost of goods sold and the ending inventories. Assume that in addition to the 780 units sold with $405,600 in standard costs, Schmidt Machinery Company has $36,400 of work-in-process inventory and $78,000 of finished goods inventory as of the end of October 20X6. The firm prorates manufacturing cost variances among ending inventories and the cost of goods sold of the period.[7] The total manufacturing cost variance in October 20X6 is $37,000, unfavorable. In Exhibit 16–13 we show the proration of the manufacturing cost variances.[8]

Prorations of manufacturing cost variances among ending inventories and the cost of goods sold have the effect of carrying the saving or cost of the efficient or inefficient operations of a period to future periods. When Schmidt Machinery Company sold the finished goods ending inventory in 20X7, the unfavorable variance

---

[7] This example assumes Schmidt carries no materials ending inventories. When materials purchased differ from materials used, however, the proration of the materials price variance should include direct materials ending inventory as well as the direct materials usage variance.

[8] When different cost drivers are used for different cost elements, the proration should be done separately for each of the cost elements based on the cost driver for the cost element.

added to the finished goods ending inventory of October 20X6 increased the cost of goods sold of 20X7 by $5,550. As a result the operating income of 20X7 decreases by $5,550 because of the unfavorable variance in 20X6. If the increase in manufacturing cost is due to an inefficient operation in 20X6, it is inappropriate to have the effect of the inefficient operation reflected in the operating income of a different period. Such a mixture of performance from one period to another renders analyses and performance evaluations for a period ambiguous.

Prorations of manufacturing cost variances among ending inventories of work-in-process and finished goods and cost of goods sold are appropriate, however, if the cost variance is a result of inappropriate standards or bookkeeping errors. In these circumstances management needs to revise the standard or take action so that the same bookkeeping error does not recur.[9]

STANDARD COST IN SERVICE INDUSTRIES

LEARNING OBJECTIVE 7 ▶
Apply a standard cost system to service organizations.

A standard cost system facilitates budget preparation, assists monitoring and controlling operations and performance evaluation, and aids management in making decisions about product pricing and resource management. These benefits are not limited to manufacturing firms. Firms or organizations of all types and in all businesses, including those in service industries, can benefit from using standard cost systems.

In today's highly competitive environment, many managers in service industries have found that methods such as product line planning, productivity monitoring, quality control, and advance cost measurement are necessary to run an efficient, competitive, and profitable service organization. To use these methods, managers need cost standards to thoroughly grasp the behavior of cost items in operations, to determine the efficiency and profitability of their organizations, to identify deviations from the expected course of action, and to target areas that need attention.

A standard cost system can best serve its function if the organization adapts the system to its own operating characteristics and objectives. We discuss the application of a standard cost system to health care organizations to illustrate its use by service organizations. Before considering the applications, however, we examine how the general characteristics of service organizations differ from those of manufacturing firms.

General Characteristics of Service Organizations

Among characteristics that distinguish service organizations from manufacturing firms are the absence of output inventory and labor-intensive products, the predominance of fixed costs, and the lack of a uniform measure for outputs.

Service outputs cannot be stored for use in a future period. Vacant service bays in an automobile repair shop today do not increase the service bays available tomorrow. Empty airline seats on a flight do not increase the seats available for the next flight. Vacant hospital beds today do not increase the beds available tomorrow. Thus, service outputs cannot be generated before they are needed; a service output exists only when there is a customer. In contrast, a manufacturer can make products to sell before a customer has expressed interest in buying these products. Consequently, instead of a production volume variance, a service firm has the sales volume variance that has a direct effect on the operating income of the firm.

Services are provided by people. As a result, most service organizations are labor intensive and incur the bulk of their expenses in salary and wage-related expenditures. With material costs mostly incidental expenses, the major cost items of many service organizations are labor costs and overhead. As a result, labor-related measures such as the labor rate and efficiency variances are much more important than

---

[9]   Neither GAAP nor the Internal Revenue Code specifically addresses the issue of proration. Given that the total amount of variance is most likely an immaterial amount, firms can use either of the methods to dispose of variances. Many firms, however, prorate variances in financial reports and for tax purposes.

materials and variable overhead variances to managers of service firms. Labor-intensiveness leads service firms to monitor activities and gauge operating results using labor-based measures.

Equipment in service organizations helps staff members provide better services. Service organizations acquire equipment to (1) replace labor, (2) reduce production costs, (3) improve process efficiency, and (4) improve the quality of services. Cost reduction may not be the primary goal.

New equipment added to a service organization often increases, rather than decreases, the total operating cost and cost of its services. A hospital that adds a piece of equipment, for example, improves the quality of treatment it provides; the equipment, however, adds to the cost of treatment. A multimedia classroom improves quality of instruction while increasing the cost of that instruction. A simple cost/output ratio often is not a good efficiency measure; if used improperly, it may be detrimental to the ultimate objective of the service organization—to provide better services to customers.

Most costs in service organizations are fixed costs. The bulk of labor costs are for professional personnel who usually are paid monthly salaries. Variations in salaries from one period to the next are few, if any. Overhead costs often consist of expenses related to facilities and equipment and are fixed in amounts for each time period. The predominance of fixed costs in service organizations increases the importance of monitoring fixed cost variances for profit improvements.

Unlike a manufacturing firm that produces many identical products, a service organization produces unique outputs. As two patients check out of a hospital, their conditions and the care they received while there most likely are not the same. The likelihood of two students receiving degrees from the same institution at the same time having received the same education is almost nil.

Furthermore, service organizations often use measures other than units of output to gauge their output. Hospitals use patient-days to measure their product. Colleges and universities use credit-hour production to show their output. Such surrogate output measures often are not perfect indicators of the products a service organization produces. Patients or their families are likely to place different values on the same number of patient-days depending on the results of treatment. A patient who is cured of a disease is more likely to be pleased with the care received than is the family of a patient who died of the same disease, even though the patient-days were identical for both. In addition, the amount and type of work performed to complete an output unit of a service organization often varies from one client to the next, or from one patient-day to another. The amounts and types of work performed during 30 patient-days of care for two heart-disease patients may be vastly different, even though the number of patient-days is identical.

Educational institutions are other service organizations that often do not use their outputs—students graduated—as the measure of their output. Credit-hour production is frequently cited by these institutions as the measure of their output. One hundred credit hours of mediocre instruction do not have the same value as one hundred hours of excellent instruction. Intangible attributes, in addition to units of output, play dominant roles in determining the value of outputs from a service organization. These characteristics often lead service firms to rely on input-related measures such as patient-days and the number of credit hours produced to measure and monitor operations.

The differences in operating characteristics between service organizations and typical manufacturing firms make it necessary to modify standard cost systems before applying them to service organizations. In Exhibit 16–14 we list some measures of output often used by service organizations.

A Standard Cost System in a Hospital

The differences in operating characteristics between service organizations and typical manufacturing firms make it necessary to modify standard cost systems before

Exhibit 16–14	**Surrogate Output Measures of Service Organizations**
Type of Organization	**Surrogate Output Measure**
Airline	Revenue passenger-miles
Hospital	Patient-days
Hotel	Occupancy rate or number of guests
Accounting, legal, and consulting firms	Professional staff hours
Colleges and universities	Credit hours
Primary and secondary schools	Number of students

applying them to service organizations.[10] Even so, not all service organizations are identical. We have chosen a hospital to illustrate the use of the standard cost system in service organizations.

Hospitals generally have three types of costs: direct, transferred, and allocated. Different types of costs require different methods of measurement, must be interpreted individually, and have different implications for the organizations when they vary from standard measures.

Direct Costs

Direct costs are costs conveniently and economically traceable to a patient care unit. Nursing cost, supplies, physicians' fees, laboratory fees, radiology fees, and pharmaceutical costs are examples. Direct cost variances can be attributed to either price or quantity factors and are analyzed using a procedure analogous to that of analyzing direct cost variances for manufacturing firms. As is true for many service organizations, most direct costs in a hospital are labor costs.[11]

To best use standard cost systems, the cost drivers should be clearly identified for all direct costs. Among cost drivers used in hospitals are patient-days, operating procedures, laboratory tests, and radiology procedures.

Data generated routinely by a hospital's accounting information system usually can provide the figures needed for analyzing direct costs. Labor rate and efficiency variances usually can be determined using data available from payroll or personnel accounting systems. Price and usage variances for medical fees of hospital-based physicians can be analyzed using data from the hospital patient system. Inventory control or accounts payable systems can provide data for analyzing price and usage variances for items maintained in inventory and other nonlabor cost items.

In Exhibit 16–15 you can see the standard cost for the pediatrics floor of Lancaster County Hospital. The standard cost sheet separately depicts standards for direct expenses, transferred expenses, and allocated expenses. Variable expenses are specified with two elements: standard rate/price per unit of the cost driver and standard quantity of the cost driver. For example, the standard rate for registered nurses is $15 per hour and the standard quantity per patient-day is 1.3 hours.[12] The "Fixed" column specifies the standard fixed cost per period. Thus, the salaries for supervisors are $4,500 per month. The "Quantity" column delineates the standard charge per patient-day and mixed expenses. Housekeeping expense is an example of mixed expenses. In addition to 0.40 hour per patient-day and 1.50 hours per discharge, there is a fixed housekeeping expense of 48 hours per month.

---

[10]   This section is based on the American Hospital Association's *Managerial Cost Accounting for Hospitals* (Chicago: American Hospital Association, 1980), Chapters 8–10. Numbers used in this section have been adjusted and may not reflect reality.

[11]   Direct materials, if identified, tend to be a small fraction of the total cost. Exceptions are some very expensive prescription drugs. Hospitals, therefore, usually spend little time analyzing direct materials variance.

[12]   All labor costs in this section include wages or salaries, fringe benefits, and other employer's payroll costs.

Exhibit 16–15	Standard Cost Sheet

LANCASTER COUNTY HOSPITAL
Standard Cost Sheet for Pediatrics Floor

Direct Expenses	Rate/Price	Quantity	Fixed
Salaries and wages:			
Supervisors			$4,500
RNs	$15.00 per hour	1.3 hours per patient-day	
LPNs	10.00 per hour	1.7 hours per patient-day	
Nursing assistants	6.50 per hour	0.9 hour per patient-day	
Supplies—inventory	0.20 per unit	10 units per patient-day	
Supplies—noninventory			300
Pediatrician fees	100 per hour	0.5 hour per patient-day	
Other direct expenses			250
Transferred Expenses			
Housekeeping	5.00 per hour	48 hours + 0.4 hour per patient-day + 1.50 hours per patient discharge	
Laundry	0.25 per pound	500 pounds + 15 pounds per patient-day + 30 pounds per discharge + 50 pounds per surgery	
Allocated Expenses			
Personnel	0.08 per hour	242 hours + 3.9 hours per patient-day	
Other administrative and general	3.00 per hour	118 hours + 0.05 hour per patient-day + 1.5 hours per patient discharge	

Exhibit 16–16 contains relevant operating data for October 20X6. In Exhibit 16–17 we show a performance report on direct costs of the pediatrics floor.[13]

On receiving the performance report, the pediatric unit manager prepares the following report relating to direct expenses.[14]

Date: November 5, 20X6
To: Cynthia DeCamp, Hospital Director
From: Stan DeVine, Pediatric Unit Manager
Subject: Direct expenses, October 20X6

Direct Labor. During the previous month, my unit recruited three new RNs at the entry-level pay scale, replacing two retired RNs who had been with us for more than 20 years and were at the top of the pay scale. The average hourly salary for all RNs on the unit was reduced to $14 per hour, resulting in a favorable labor rate variance. The replacements, however, increased my RN nursing hours per patient-day to 1.5 hours, resulting in an unfavorable labor efficiency variance in last month's average daily staffing. To compensate for the increased RN staffing, one LPN was transferred to the Emergency Room, which needs his help. This resulted in both a favorable rate and efficiency variance for LPNs. We expect, however, the favorable rate variance will be lost in approximately six months when the RNs reach the next pay level. Therefore, I recommend that plans be made to replace one RN with one LPN.

---

[13] Based on Table 14 in *Managerial Cost Accounting for Hospitals* (Chicago: American Hospital Association, 1980), p. 97.

[14] Ibid., pp. 98–99.

Exhibit 16–16   Operating Data

LANCASTER COUNTY HOSPITAL
Operating Data for Pediatrics Floor
October 20X6

Direct Expenses	Rate/Price	Quantity	Fixed
Salaries and wages:			
Supervisors			$4,500
RNs	$ 14.00 per hour	720 hours	
LPNs	9.50 per hour	770 hours	
Nursing assistants	7.00 per hour	480 hours	
Supplies—inventory	0.172 per unit	4,800 units	
Supplies—noninventory			520
Pediatrician fees	120.00 per hour	288 hours	
Other direct expenses			275
Transferred Expenses			
Housekeeping	5.50 per hour	160 hours	
Laundry	0.30 per pound	10,000 pounds	
Allocated Expenses			
Personnel		2,200 hours	
Other administrative and general		300 hours	

Exhibit 16–17   Performance Report

LANCASTER COUNTY HOSPITAL
Pediatrics Floor Performance Report
For the Month of October 20X6

	Actual	Standard	Variance	Price/Rate	Efficiency
Service units:					
Patient-days	480				
Average daily census	16				
Patient discharges	96				
Surgeries	20				
Direct Expenses					
Salaries and wages:					
Supervisors	$ 4,500	$ 4,500	—	—	—
RNs	10,080	9,360	$ 720 U	$ 720 F	$1,440 U
LPNs	7,315	8,160	845 F	385 F	460 F
Nursing assistants	3,360	2,808	552 U	240 U	312 U
Supplies—inventory	825	960	135 F	135 F	—
Supplies—noninventory	520	300	220 U	—	220 U
Pediatrician fees	34,560	24,000	10,560 U	5,760 U	4,800 U
Other direct expenses	275	250	25 U		25 U
Total direct expenses	$61,435	$50,338	$11,097 U	$4,760 U	$6,337 U
Transferred Expenses					
Housekeeping	$ 880	$ 960	$ 80 F	—	$ 80 F
Laundry	3,000	2,895	105 U	—	105 U
Total transferred	$ 3,880	$ 3,855	$ 25 U		$ 25 U
Allocated Expenses					
Personnel	$ 176	$ 169	$ 7 U		$ 7 F
Other administrative and general	900	858	42 U		42 U
	$ 1,076	$ 1,027	$ 49 U		$ 49 U
Total department expense	$66,391	$55,220	$11,171 U	$4,760 U	$6,411 U

For a period of five consecutive days in the middle of the month, the unit had over 20 patients and required the use of 48 overtime hours for the nurse assistants, causing an unfavorable rate and efficiency variance for this group.

Supplies—Inventory   Uses of inventory supplies followed the standard level of 10 items per patient-day. However, two brands were changed. The purchasing department informs me the brands are less expensive and resulted in a $135 savings last month. Furthermore, the new items appear to be better than the previous brands. We will continue to use them.

Supplies—Noninventory   The unfavorable quantity variance resulted primarily from purchasing items that had been deferred the last several months. Year-to-date spending on these items, however, still remains favorable.

Pediatrician fees   The resident pediatrician, Dr. Kiddear, and other staff were required to provide some overtime night-shift service during the period that the patient census was more than 20 patients. Overtime night-shift work is paid at a higher rate than standard, thus causing an unfavorable price variance. The 48 additional hours for overtime night-shift work were responsible for the unfavorable usage variance.

Transferred Costs

Transferred costs are costs accumulated in patient care support cost centers including laboratory, laundry, food services, and housekeeping. Other units could not operate without the services these cost centers provide, so these expenses are transferred to the patient care units.

Costs accumulated in these cost centers consist of variable and fixed costs. For example, the cost of laundering uniforms, gowns, sheets, and other garments every day the unit is open is constant, regardless of the level of activity of the unit. On the other hand, the laundry cost does vary with the number of patient-days, number of surgical procedures performed, and number of discharges or transfers of patients. Total laundry for the pediatric floor is determined as follows:

Pounds of laundry = 500 pounds + (15 pounds × number of patient-days) +
(30 pounds × number of discharges or transfers) +
(50 pounds × number of surgeries)

There may be both price and usage variances for a transferred cost. The user department, however, usually has no control over unit prices of transferred costs and thus no price variance for transferred costs is calculated for the user department. The performance report includes only usage variances for the transferred costs.

Allocated Costs

Allocated costs are costs incurred in general and administrative cost centers. They usually are fixed in amount for each time period. The amounts of allocated costs are a result of management decisions to provide a given level of service for the anticipated range of activity.

The total cost for the admission office of a hospital is $300,000 per year when admissions range between 150 and 250 patients per day. The total cost increases to $400,000 if management anticipates admissions in the range of 400 to 600 patients per day. The difference results from hiring added staff, buying new equipment, and performing similar factors of operation.

Organizations usually analyze only the spending (flexible budget) variances of allocated costs for user departments. A variance relating to activity volumes, computed by multiplying the standard cost for the activity and the difference between the budgeted and the actual activity volume, is calculated for long-term evaluation and planning purposes. Because user departments often have no control over activities relating to allocated costs, an analysis of activity variances for allocated costs for short-run performance evaluation may be misleading and may even cause undesirable behavior.

STANDARD COSTS IN THE NEW MANUFACTURING ENVIRONMENT

LEARNING OBJECTIVE 8 ▶
Describe the effects of recent advances in new manufacturing technologies and rapid changes in operating environments on standard cost systems, and adapt a standard cost system to these changing environments.

The new manufacturing environment and new management techniques emphasize continual improvement, total quality control, and managing activity rather than cost. These emphases have changed product costing, strategic and operational decisions, and cost allocation methods, as discussed in the preceding chapters. They also influence how a standard cost system and variance analyses are used as management tools, including applications to the preparation of flexible budgets, selection of evaluation criteria, and judging the implications of variances of manufacturing cost elements.

Effect of the New Manufacturing Environment on Flexible Budgeting

Under the conventional approach, flexible budgets are prepared using a single-cost driver for all factory overhead. Exhibit 16–18 contains a typical conventional flexible budget for an output of 2,000 units (5,000 direct labor-hours) when the firm has a master budget for an output of 3,000 units (7,500 direct labor-hours) and the firm uses direct labor-hours as the cost driver to assign factory overhead to cost objects. The firm spent 5,200 direct labor-hours to manufacture 2,000 units. In Exhibit 16–19 we show the actual cost during the period and a typical conventional performance report for the operations.

Many firms in new manufacturing environments no longer use a single cost driver, such as direct labor-hours or machine-hours, to measure overhead costs and

---

Exhibit 16–18   **Master Budget and a Conventional Flexible Budget**

Cost Function			Flexible Budget 2,000 Units (5,000 direct labor-hours)	Master (Static) Budget 3,000 Units (7,500 direct labor-hours)
Variable	**Fixed**			
$20/unit		Direct materials	$ 40,000	$ 60,000
6/Direct labor-hours		Direct labor	30,000	45,000
2/Direct labor-hours		Indirect material	10,000	15,000
1/Direct labor-hours		Repair and maintenance	5,000	7,500
	$ 5,000	Receiving	5,000	5,000
	30,000	Engineering support	30,000	30,000
	80,000	Setup	75,000	75,000
		Total	$195,000	$237,500

Exhibit 16–19   **A Conventional Performance Report**

	Actual Cost	Flexible Budget	Variance
Direct material	$ 50,000	$ 40,000	$10,000 U
Direct labor	36,000	30,000	6,000 U
Indirect material	11,000	10,000	1,000 U
Repair and maintenance	6,500	5,000	1,500 U
Receiving	3,000	5,000	2,000 F
Engineering support	30,000	30,000	—
Setup	50,000	75,000	25,000 F
Total	$186,500	$195,000	$ 8,500 F

assign them to cost objects. Recent advances in activity-based costing lead many firms to measure and monitor overheads based on activities that drive overhead cost. These firms also can prepare flexible budgets using direct cost drivers for factory overhead. The budgeted total factory overhead no longer varies with changes in a surrogate cost driver; instead, it varies with changes in several direct cost drivers for overhead costs. In Exhibit 16–20 you can see the preparation of flexible budgets using an activity-based approach. Exhibit 16–21 contains a performance report that uses the activity-based cost functions in determining the flexible budget for the product manufactured during the period.

The total manufacturing cost variance for the period changed from $8,500, favorable, as reported in the conventional performance report that uses a single-cost-driver cost function (Exhibit 16–19), to $15,000, unfavorable, derived when using an activity-based flexible budget in preparing a performance report for the period (Exhibit 16–21). In Exhibit 16–22 we compare these performance reports.

Note in Exhibit 16–22 that variances identified using a conventional approach (single cost driver) may be misleading. Substantial differences are found in variances for the cost items repair and maintenance, receiving, and setups. The conventional approach considers repair and maintenance as a variable cost that varies with direct labor-hours. In contrast, the activity-based approach identifies repair and maintenance as a mixed cost with the variable portion of the cost varying with machine-hours. As a result, the cost variance incurred for repair and maintenance decreases from $1,500 unfavorable to $500 unfavorable. The conventional approach considers both receiving and setups as fixed costs, while the activity-based costing

Exhibit 16–20   Cost Functions of Manufacturing Costs

Cost Item	Cost Driver	Cost Function Variable	Fixed	Flexible Budget	Master (Static) Budget
	Number of units			2,000 units	3,000 units
Direct materials	Number of units	$20/unit	—	$ 40,000	$ 60,000
Direct labor	Number of units	15/unit	—	30,000	45,000
	Direct labor-hours			5,000 hours	7,500 hours
Indirect material	Direct labor-hours	$2/direct labor-hours	—	10,000	15,000
	Machine-hours			300,000 hours	450,000 hours
Repair and maintenance	Machine-hours	$0.01/machine-hours	$3,000	6,000	7,500
	Number of setups			2 setups	3 setups
Receiving	Number of setups	$1,500/setup	$500	3,500	5,000
Setup	Number of setups	25,000/setup	—	50,000	75,000
Engineering support	Per period		$30,000	30,000	30,000
Total				$169,500	$237,500

Exhibit 16–21   A Performance Report Using Activity-Based Costing

	Cost Incurred	Flexible Budget	Variance
Direct materials	$ 50,000	$ 40,000	$10,000 U
Direct labor	36,000	30,000	6,000 U
Indirect material	11,000	10,000	1,000 U
Repair and maintenance	6,500	6,000	500 U
Receiving	3,000	3,500	500 F
Engineering support	30,000	30,000	—
Setup	48,000	50,000	2,000 F
Total	$184,500	$169,500	$15,000 U

Exhibit 16–22	A Comparison of Conventional and Activity-Based Costing Performance Reports		
	Variances		
	Conventional	**Activity-Based**	**Difference**
Direct material	$10,000 U	$10,000 U	$ —
Direct labor	6,000 U	6,000 U	—
Indirect material	1,000 U	1,000 U	—
Repair and maintenance	1,500 U	500 U	1,000
Receiving	2,000 F	500 F	1,500
Engineering support	—	—	—
Setup	25,000 F	2,000 F	23,000
Total	$ 8,500 F	$15,000 U	$25,500

approach classifies these two costs as setup-related costs. The net result of these changes in cost variances is a $25,500 total difference in cost variances.

Should All Variances Be Calculated?

In today's new manufacturing environment, not all firms choose to calculate and report all the variances reported under a conventional standard cost system. Among variances that are no longer computed and reported by some firms are materials price, materials usage, labor efficiency, variable overhead budget, and overhead production volume variances. (Chapter 15 discussed materials and labor variances.) Next we examine overhead variances in a new manufacturing environment.

Overhead Flexible Budget Variance

Using an activity-based costing system enables a firm to calculate overhead variances in more detail for each overhead cost driver. This system provides an opportunity for more detailed variance analyses that can reveal more of the operations leading to the variances. Firms should not, however, overemphasize individual overhead variances. The focus should be on the total factory overhead variance, not variances of individual overhead items. An unfavorable setup variance may encourage excessively large production runs. Overconcern with unfavorable factory overhead variances may cause minimal inspections or preventive maintenance.

Production Volume Variance

The production volume variance is calculated by multiplying the deviation in units manufactured from the units budgeted to be manufactured by the standard fixed factory overhead rate. The standard fixed factory overhead rate is determined by dividing the denominator activity into the total budgeted allowance for fixed factory overhead.

Firms need to use the capacity of the equipment or division that is the bottleneck of the manufacturing process as the denominator. Where there is more than one bottleneck, the denominator should be the smallest capacity among the bottleneck production processes. Using a nonbottleneck activity as the denominator leaves all the divisions that use the standard fixed factory overhead rate to manufacture the denominator quantity to minimize their production volume variances. The excess units that nonbottleneck divisions or equipment manufacture over the production capacity of the bottleneck divisions or equipment increase work-in-process inventories; they do not increase productivity or the operating efficiency of the manufacturing process, or the operating income of the firm. In fact, a favorable production volume variance of nonbottleneck equipment or divisions is not favorable to the firm; rather, it increases work and costs for the firm.[15]

---

[15]   Eliyahu M. Goldratt, *The Goal* (Croton-on-Hudson, NY: North River Press, 1986).

A division can achieve a favorable production volume variance by stepping up production activities to increase the units manufactured. This favorable production volume variance may be achieved, however, by manufacturing for inventory—a practice in which a JIT firm should never engage. The production volume variance should never be calculated and reported for performance evaluation purposes because it encourages this unwanted behavior. If calculated, the fixed factory overhead production volume variance should be reported only to top managers. Never should it be used to evaluate the performances of lower operating units.

Furthermore, the production volume variance should never be reported alone; it should be accompanied by the ratio of units used or shipped to the total units manufactured. As long as the ratio is 1 or very close to 1, any production volume variance can have only long-term implications; it has no significance in short-term evaluation of operations.

INVESTIGATION OF VARIANCES

Identification and report of variances are the first steps toward controlling variances and improving operations. An effective standard cost system requires that management respond properly to variances because a variance left uncorrected can affect the firm for many periods. An unnecessary corrective action, on the other hand, wastes resources and can cause performance to regress.

◄ **LEARNING OBJECTIVE 9**
Determine whether to conduct further investigations of variances.

Not all variances call for investigation and corrective action. The proper response to a variance depends on the type of standard the firm uses, the expectation of the firm, the magnitude and impact of variances, and the causes and controllability of variances.

Type of Standard

A firm may use either a currently attainable standard or an ideal standard in its standard cost system. Proper actions for variances from these two standards differ. A material variance from a currently attainable standard, either favorable or unfavorable, often requires management's immediate attention. The same variance from an ideal standard, in contrast, may require no action on the part of management, except noting improvement or deterioration in operations as indicated by the magnitude and direction of the variance. As long as the organization is making good progress toward the ideal standard over time, management may not need to take any corrective action, even if the variance for the period is rather substantial in amount.

Expectations of the Firm

Firms have different expectations for their operations. A firm experiencing a crisis needs and demands peak performance from all of its employees. A struggling firm may need to attain the established standards in all cases and tolerate no exceptions, even an ambitious ideal standard. In contrast, a highly profitable firm may be satisfied with making steady progress toward its established standard, especially when using an ideal standard to communicate to staff members the firm's desired ultimate goal. The firm may not be overly alarmed by minor deviations from the standard. Companies with good management and caring workers, however, care about the standards regardless of whether the firm is struggling or profitable.

Experience also may affect an organization's reaction to a variance. A firm in the early stages of using an ideal standard may not be alarmed by small deviations, while a firm further along the path toward an ideal standard may see the same amount of deviation as a setback that requires corrective action.

Magnitude, Pattern, and Impact of a Variance

The magnitude of a variance and its impact on future operations affect the firm's reaction to the variance. Rarely do operating results meet the standards exactly. Small variances are expected and most of them need no special attention from the management, unless a pattern develops. A persistent small unfavorable variance may require management's attention because the cumulative effect of the small variances on operating results can be quite substantial and may reflect deteriorating operations.

A large variance usually catches the attention of management, and management responds with immediate corrective action. Such a response, however, may not be warranted. A large variance does not require action if it is not representative of the underlying operations or if it is a one-time occurrence. A large unfavorable factory overhead efficiency variance identified with direct labor-hours as the base for applying factory overhead may not be an indication of runaway factory overhead costs if the bulk of factory overhead is driven by activities other than direct labor-hours. Similarly, a large unfavorable direct materials usage variance requires no further action if the variance is a result of, for example, a poorly adjusted machine that has since been repaired.

Causes and Controllability

The degree to which an organization can control a variance determines whether corrective actions are needed. No action is needed if management has no control over the variance even though it has a significant impact on the firm's operations.

Causes of variances can be classified into two categories: random and systematic. Among underlying factors leading to systematic variances are: prediction, modeling, measurement, and implementation. Each of these factors has its own implications for further investigation or for the optimal managerial action to correct the variance. Exhibit 16–23 shows controllability, actions to be taken, and classifications of variances.

Random variances arise beyond the control of management, either technically or financially, and are often considered as *uncontrollable variances*. Standards often are point estimates of the long-run average performance of operations. Small variances in either direction occur in operations and the firm usually cannot benefit from investigating or responding to these variances. For example, prices of goods or services acquired in open markets fluctuate with, among other factors, supply and demand at the time of acquisition and the amount of time allowed to acquire the goods or services. Such a variance is a random variance and requires no action by the management.

Systematic (controllable) variances are persistent and most likely recur unless corrected. Systematic variances that are material in amount require management to take proper action. Among causes for these variances are: prediction, modeling, measurement, and implementation. Variances resulting from different sources call for different actions. In Exhibit 16–23 you can see a classification of variances.

Prediction errors result from inaccurate estimates of the amounts for variables used in the standard-setting process. A prediction error would include allowing a

Random variances are variances beyond the control of management, either technically or financially, that often are considered as uncontrollable variances.

A **prediction error** is a deviation from the standard because of an inaccurate estimation of the amounts for variables used in the standard-setting process.

Exhibit 16–23	Classification of Variances		
Controllability	**Types of Variances**	**Actions to Be Taken**	**Examples**
Uncontrollable (Random)	Random error	None	Overtime wages paid to make up lost time due to employees ill with the flu. Materials lost in a fire.
Controllable (systematic)	Prediction error	Modify standard-setting processes	Materials prices increased faster than expected.
	Modeling error	Revise model or modeling process	Learning curve effect not considered. Not allowing normal materials lost.
	Measurement error	Adjust accounting procedures	Attributed bonus to the period paid, not the period earned. Assigned costs to wrong jobs.
	Implementation error	Take proper corrective actions	Failed to provide proper training for the tasks.

5 percent increase for the price of a direct material when the actual price increased 10 percent or expecting to have adequate $10-per-hour workers available when a shortage forced a firm to hire workers at $15 per hour.

Modeling errors result from failing to include all the relevant variables or including wrong or irrelevant variables in the standard-setting process. A modeling error occurs when a firm uses as standards the production rates of experienced workers even though most of its workers are newly hired with little or no experience. The unfavorable direct labor efficiency variance the firm experienced is a result of the modeling error, not of inefficient operations. The standard of making 100 gallons of output from every 100 gallons of input material is a modeling error when the manufacturing process has a 5 percent normal evaporation rate.

Corrective actions for both prediction and modeling errors usually occur when the firm establishes the standard for operations.

Measurement errors are incorrect numbers caused by improper or inaccurate accounting systems or procedures. Including bonuses earned by employees for their extraordinary productivity as a cost of the period the bonuses were paid rather than the period in which the workers earned the bonuses is a measurement error. Charging overhead incurred for setups based on direct production labor-hours rather than setup times would also be a measurement error. Corrective actions for measurement errors include redesigning the accounting systems or procedures used by the firm and proper training of cost accountants.

Failure to correct prediction, modeling, or measurement errors would, in the long run, frustrate employees and lead them to focus on showing the best reported results, even at the expense of bettering the overall performance of the firm. Employees of firms using standard cost systems that have uncorrected prediction, modeling, or measurement errors often lose confidence in all accounting reports.

An **implementation error** is a deviation from the standard that occurs during operations as a result of operators' errors. Materials of lesser quality than specified in the standard might have been used in productions. Workers with a different skill level than the one called for in the standard may be assigned. The cutting machine may be set to cut tubes in lengths of 2 feet 9.7 inches instead of 2 feet 10 inches as required.

Implementation errors either can be temporary or persist until corrected. An incorrectly set cutting machine continues to manufacture products with wrong lengths until corrected. Use of wrong or excessive materials in production, on the other hand, may occur only for one production run.

Among the tools that can help managers keep track of variances and determine the need to investigate variances are statistical control charts.

Statistical Control Chart

A widely used tool that helps managers identify out-of-control variances is a control chart that plots variances over time. In Exhibit 16–24 we show such a chart.

A control chart enables managers to grasp the size and the trend, if any, of variances over time. In Exhibit 16–24 you can see an upward trend of unfavorable variances beginning in March and repeating in September. An alert manager would very likely monitor the operations closely starting from, say, April or May. Were corrective actions taken in April or May, the upward pattern of unfavorable variances starting in September might not have occurred. The chart also suggests that in December the firm is likely to have a larger unfavorable variance than in any of the previous months unless the firm takes corrective actions.

Firms often include control limits in control charts. Typically, there are two limits: upper and lower. Although the limits in Exhibit 16–24 are equal in distance from the standard cost, they are not necessarily so, especially where it is more costly to the firm to incur unfavorable variances than favorable variances. In such cases, firms may allow a narrower band for the upper limit than for the lower limit.

Variances within the limits are deemed random variances and no further action is needed unless a pattern emerges.

When the control limits are established using a statistical procedure, the chart is called a **statistical control chart.** A common practice is to set the control limits

A modeling error is a deviation from the standard because of failure to include all the relevant variables or inclusion of wrong or irrelevant variables in the standard-setting process.

Measurement errors are incorrect numbers caused by improper or inaccurate accounting systems or procedures.

An **implementation error** is a deviation from the standard that occurs during operations as a result of operators' errors.

Statistical control charts set control limits using a statistical procedure.

at plus and minus three standard deviations from the standard cost. The control limits, however, vary with the type of standard the firm uses and the expectation of the management.

The chapter appendix examines a cost-benefit approach in evaluating the decision to investigate variances under uncertainty.

Company Practices

Experienced managers usually have a good intuitive feel for whether a variance requires further investigation. Others follow a magnitude rule of thumb, either in dollar amounts or in percentage of variation, to determine whether to further investigate variances. Often, signals that a process is out of control occur and the cause for the variance is corrected before a variance report is available. Through visual inspections the operator of a cutting machine may notice that cuttings are not square as required. The operator may adjust the alignment that caused the improper cutting and correct the problem even before the manager receives the variance report.

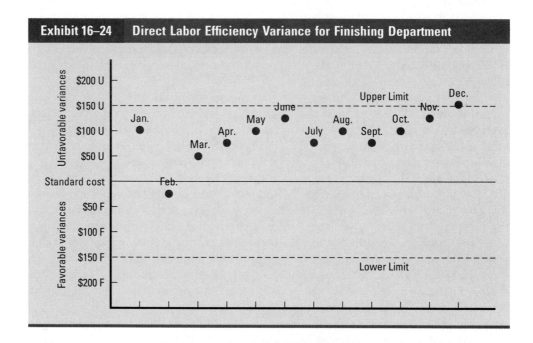

Exhibit 16–24   Direct Labor Efficiency Variance for Finishing Department

---

BusinessWeek

✔ **Varian Uses TQM to Reduce Operating Costs**
(Continues from page 625)

A: By refocusing its efforts . . .

Varian's slow sales growth and losses are due in part to its single-minded focus on quality. Varian isn't the only company that has faced disappointment with its quality efforts; in fact, this realization led Varian to refocus its energies—keeping the quality effort in mind, but also working to reduce operating costs, while meeting important customer expectations. For example, when faced with customer dissatisfaction on the amount of time it took to set up radiology equipment at hospitals, Varian took a hard look at hundreds of possible solutions. It ended up changing the way it shipped cables, using plastic bags rather than "popcorn" filler (which saved 30 minutes of cleanup time), and redesigning key parts to fit together more easily. In the end, it saved 95 hours in setup time, which equated to $50,000 per order to hospitals, and saved Varian $1.8 million a year—a change that went a long way toward pleasing customers *and* reducing company operating costs. It also helped Varian see the bright side once again.

For further reading, see the following sources: "How to Make It Pay," *Business Week,* August 8, 1994; "Quality," *Business Week,* November 30, 1992.

The following survey of U.S. managers showed vastly different approaches to investigating direct materials and direct labor variances.

Company Practice on Investigating Direct Material and Direct Labor Variances*

	Percent	
	Direct Materials	Direct Labor
All variances investigated	6.9%	5.3%
Variances over prescribed dollar limits investigated	34.8	31.0
Variances over prescribed percentage limits investigated	12.2	14.1
Statistical procedures used to select cases for investigation	0.9	0.9
Judgment used to decide if investigation is needed	45.2	47.8
Variances never investigated	0.0	0.9
Total	100.0%	100.0%

*B. Gaumnitz and F. Kollaritsch, "Manufacturing Variances: Current Practice and Trends," *Journal of Cost Management*, Spring 1991, pp. 58–64.

SUMMARY

Establishing standard variable factory overhead for an operation requires determination of cost behavioral patterns of overhead cost items, selection of proper activity cost drivers, and calculation of the overhead application rate. In Exhibit 16–25 we summarize an analysis of factory overhead variances.

The variable factory overhead flexible budget variance or the total variable factory overhead variance, shown as (A) in Exhibit 16–25, is the difference between the total actual variable factory overhead cost and the total standard variable factory overhead for the number of units manufactured. Variable factory overhead spending and efficiency variances are detailed analyses of the total variance. The variable factory overhead spending variance, (B), is the difference between the variable factory overhead incurred and the standard variable factory overhead for the actual quantity of the cost drivers for applying variable factory overhead. The variable factory overhead efficiency variance, (C), is the difference between the standard variable factory overhead for the actual quantity of the cost drivers for applying variable factory overhead and the standard variable factory overhead for the output of the period. Because of the imperfect association between the cost driver or drivers for applying overhead and the variable factory overhead costs, a variable factory overhead spending variance may include both price and usage variances, while a variable factory overhead efficiency variance may not measure efficiency in the usage of variable factory overhead items, but merely efficiency in use of the cost driver.

Uses of standard costs for fixed factory overhead include determining the total budgeted fixed factory overhead for the operation, selecting a cost driver or drivers for applying the fixed factory overhead, and choosing the denominator activity level for the period as measured by the chosen cost driver. The fixed factory overhead application rate is determined by dividing the quantity of the cost driver at the denominator activity level into the budgeted total fixed factory overhead. Fixed factory overhead variances include the fixed factory overhead spending (budget) variance and the production volume variance. The fixed factory overhead spending variance, (E), is the difference between the actual and the budgeted fixed factory overhead for the period. Neither the actual units manufactured nor the actual level of the cost driver incurred during the period has any effect on the amount of the fixed factory overhead spending variance. The production volume variance, (F), is the difference between the budgeted total fixed

Exhibit 16–25   Analysis of Factory Overhead

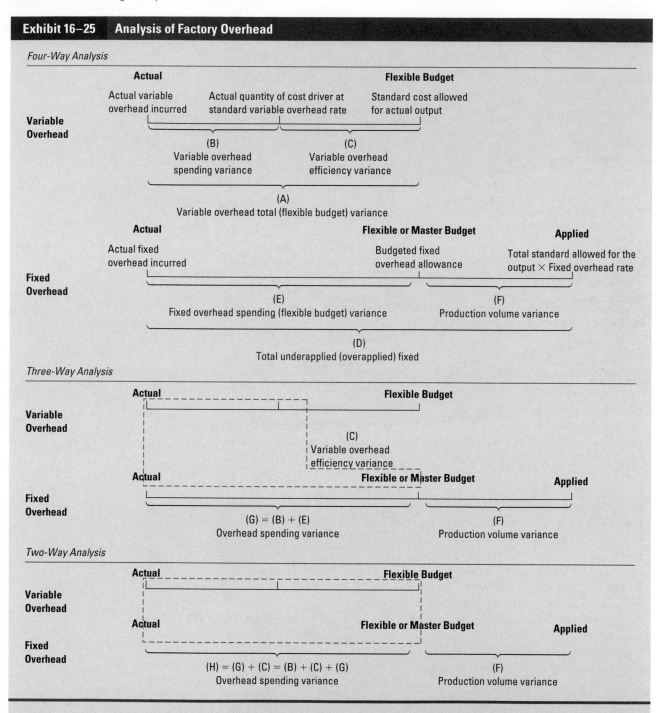

Four-Way Analysis

Variable Overhead

| **Actual** | | **Flexible Budget** |
| Actual variable overhead incurred | Actual quantity of cost driver at standard variable overhead rate | Standard cost allowed for actual output |

(B)
Variable overhead spending variance

(C)
Variable overhead efficiency variance

(A)
Variable overhead total (flexible budget) variance

Fixed Overhead

| **Actual** | **Flexible or Master Budget** | **Applied** |
| Actual fixed overhead incurred | Budgeted fixed overhead allowance | Total standard allowed for the output × Fixed overhead rate |

(E)
Fixed overhead spending (flexible budget) variance

(F)
Production volume variance

(D)
Total underapplied (overapplied) fixed

Three-Way Analysis

Variable Overhead

Actual ---------- **Flexible Budget**

(C)
Variable overhead efficiency variance

Fixed Overhead

Actual ---------- **Flexible or Master Budget** ---------- **Applied**

(G) = (B) + (E)
Overhead spending variance

(F)
Production volume variance

Two-Way Analysis

Variable Overhead

Actual ---------- **Flexible Budget**

Fixed Overhead

Actual ---------- **Flexible or Master Budget** ---------- **Applied**

(H) = (G) + (C) = (B) + (C) + (G)
Overhead spending variance

(F)
Production volume variance

factory overhead allowance and the total fixed factory overhead applied to the units manufactured during the period. The difference between the actual and the applied fixed factory overhead (or the sum of spending and production volume variances), (D), also is referred to as underapplied or overapplied fixed factory overhead.

The variances identified for variable factory overhead and fixed factory overhead can be combined into a total of either three or two variances. The three-way analysis creates a factory overhead spending variance, (G), by combining variable factory overhead spending and fixed factory overhead spending variances into one variance. The other two factory overhead variances remain intact. The three variances, therefore, are the factory overhead spending variance (G), the factory overhead efficiency variance (C), and the production volume variance (F). The two-way analysis further combines the factory overhead spending variance, (G), with the factory overhead efficiency variance, (C). The combined variance is the factory overhead flexible budget variance, (H).

A firm can dispose of variances in the income statement of the period in which the variance incurs by charging them to the cost of goods sold. Alternatively, the firm can prorate the variances among the cost of goods sold and ending inventories.

Benefits from using a standard cost system are not limited to manufacturing operations; service firms and other types of operations also can benefit from using standard cost systems. Because operating characteristics of service firms often differ from those of manufacturing firms, modifications may be needed and emphases may be different when using standard costs in a service organization. Among operating characteristics that may differ are absences of output inventory, labor-intensive operations, the predominance of fixed costs, and ambiguity of output measures in service organizations.

Changes in manufacturing environments in recent years affect the application of standard cost systems. Firms in new manufacturing environments no longer use a single cost driver to measure and apply overhead. An increasing number of firms are using ideal, rather than currently attainable, standards. To be globally competitive, many firms mandate continual improvement and striving for perfection. Also, not all variances are calculated. The theory of constraint points out that the denominator activity level should be set at the level of the bottleneck activity of the operation.

Whether to conduct further investigations of variances depends on the type of standard the firm uses, the expectations of the firm, the magnitude and impact of variances, and the causes and controllability of variances.

APPENDIX

Variance Investigation Decisions under Uncertainty

Investigations of variances cost time and money. Firms need to weigh the costs of investigation against the benefits in determining whether to conduct further investigations for a variance. The purpose of investigation is to determine the states of nature or the underlying cause of the variance. Management can then take proper action.

The states of nature underlying a variance can be either random or systematic. The alternative courses of action available to management when facing a variance are either to conduct an investigation or to take no action. With two possible states of nature and two courses of action, there are four combinations, each of which implies a different cost to the firm. These four combinations are

IR Investigate and find the reported variance to be a random fluctuation. No further action is needed.

IN Investigate, find the reported variance is a result of systematic or nonrandom causes, and take corrective action.

NR Do not investigate and the reported variance is a result of random variations.

NN Do not investigate and the reported variance is a result of systematic or nonrandom causes.

Payoff Table

The cost to the firm of each course of action is different as are the effects and implications of each possible state of nature underlying the variance. In Exhibit 16–26 we show the consequences of alternative management action under different states of nature. When the variance is a result of a nonrandom factor, the cost to the firm to correct the variance is C. The cost of correction includes the cost to correct the nonrandom factor that led to the variance and the cost of the variance the firm continues to experience until the variance is corrected. If management decides not to investigate the reported variance and the variance is systematic and persistent, the firm then suffers a total cost, L. L is the present value of all the losses the firm will suffer before the next decision time.

The decision not to conduct an investigation is a correct one when the variance is a random occurrence. The firm wastes no resources at all. The firm will, however, suffer a loss of L if the reported variance is a result of a nonrandom cause.

Management also needs to estimate the likelihood of the operation being in control or out of control, based on its understanding of the operation. The operation being in control implies that the reported variance is a random phenomenon. The operation being out of control suggests that the reported variance is a result of one or more systematic causes. The estimated probabilities of the states of nature enable management to compute the expected costs for each of the alternative courses of action. The expected costs then serve as the input to the variance investigation decision.

Upon receiving the variance report, management estimates that the probability the reported variance is due to a random fluctuation at 90 percent. The cost of investigation is approximately $1,000. Corrective actions, if needed, will likely cost the firm approximately $5,000, including the loss from the variance that the firm will continue to incur before its cause is corrected. The firm will suffer losses with a present value of $30,000 if no investigation is conducted and the variance stemmed from a nonrandom cause. In Exhibit 16–27 we summarize this information.

Management has a 90 percent chance of finding the variance is merely a random fluctuation and the investigation is, therefore, a waste of time and resources. However, there is a 10 percent chance the variance is a result of nonrandom factors that need to be corrected to avoid further losses. With the cost of investigation, $1,000, and the cost of corrective action, $5,000, the total cost to the firm will be $6,000 if the investigation finds the cause of the variance is nonrandom. The expected value of investigation is, therefore, $1,500, as shown in this computation:

$$E(\text{Investigate}) = (\$1,000 \times .9) + (\$6,000 \times .1) = \$1,500$$

If management decides not to investigate, there is still a 90 percent chance that the variance is random and the firm incurs no cost. There is, however, a 10 percent chance that the variance is a result of nonrandom factors. In this latter case, the firm is likely to suffer a total loss of $30,000. Thus, the expected cost of not investigating the cause of the variance is $3,000, as shown here:

$$E(\text{Do not investigate}) = (\$0 \times .9) + (\$30,000 \times .1) = \$3,000$$

With the expected cost of investigation of $1,500 being lower than the $3,000 cost of not investigating, the recommended course of action according to the payoff table is to conduct an investigation to find the cause of the reported variance.

Exhibit 16–26   Payoff Table for Investigation of a Variance

	States of Nature	
Management Action	**Random**	**Nonrandom**
Investigate	I	$I + C$
Do not investigate	none	L

Exhibit 16–27   A Decision Using a Payoff Table

	States of Nature		
Management Action	**Random** .9	**Nonrandom** .1	**Expected Value**
Investigate	$1,000	$6,000	$1,500
Do not investigate	$0	$30,000	$3,000

Exhibit 16–28	Using a Payoff Table to Determine Indifference Probability	

	States of Nature	
Management Action	**Random** $1 - p$	**Nonrandom** p
Investigate	I	$I + C$
Do not investigate	0	L

Indifference Probability

A payoff table also can determine the maximum level of probability for a nonrandom variance to occur and management to favor not investigating the cause of the reported variance. Let p be the probability of a nonrandom variance. Then the probability of a random variance is $1 - p$. In Exhibit 16–28 we show the payoff table.

The expected costs of management actions can be represented by

$$E(\text{Investigate}) = I \times (1 - p) + (I + C) \times p, \text{ and}$$

$$E(\text{Do not investigate}) = L \times p$$

If the cost of both actions is the same, then it makes no difference to the firm which course of action is taken. That is, for management to be indifferent between the courses of action (to investigate or not to investigate), the expected costs of the courses of action have to be equal. At the indifference point,

$$I \times (1 - p) + (I + C) \times p = L \times p$$

Simplifying the equation, we get

$$I - C \times p = L \times p$$

which can be rewritten as

$$p = \frac{I}{L - C}$$

Using these data, the indifference probability is 4 percent:

$$p = \frac{\$1,000}{\$30,000 - \$5,000} = .04$$

The result suggests that the optimal action for management is to conduct an investigation when the probability of nonrandom variance exceeds 4 percent. Our calculation earlier confirms this conclusion. The probability of nonrandom variance was estimated to be 10 percent and the payoff table suggests that the recommended course of action is for the firm to conduct an investigation on the cause of the variance.

KEY TERMS

Denominator activity   633

Fixed factory overhead application rate   633

Fixed factory overhead production volume variance   634

Fixed factory overhead spending variance (fixed factory overhead flexible budget variance)   634

Implementation error   653

Measurement error   653

Modeling error   653

Prediction error   652

Random variances   652

Statistical control charts   653

Total variable factory overhead variance   628

Variable factory overhead efficiency variance   629

Variable factory overhead spending variance   629

SELF-STUDY PROBLEMS

(For solutions, please turn to the end of the chapter.)

1. Analysis of Overhead Variance

Simpson Manufacturing has the following standard cost sheet for one of its products:

Direct materials	5 pounds at $ 2	$10
Direct labor	2 hours at $25	50
Variable factory overhead	2 hours at $ 5	10
Fixed factory overhead	2 hours at $20	40

Factory overhead is to be applied based on direct labor-hours and the factory overhead rate is determined based on manufacturing of 400 units of the product.

The firm has the following actual operating results for the year just completed:

Units manufactured	360	
Direct materials purchased and used	1,800 pounds	$19,800
Direct labor incurred	750 hours	20,250
Variable factory overhead incurred		4,800
Fixed factory overhead incurred		15,800

Before the closing of periodic accounts, the balances in selected accounts are

Account	Debit (total)	Credit (total)
Work-in-Process Inventory Control	$153,000	$134,640
Finished Goods Inventory Control	134,640	111,690
Cost of Goods Sold	111,690	

Required

1. Determine the
   a. Total standard variable factory overhead for the period.
   b. Total variable factory overhead applied during the period.
   c. Total budgeted fixed factory overhead.
   d. Total fixed factory overhead applied.

2. Compute the following variances using four-way analysis of variances:
   a. Total variable factory overhead variance.
   b. Variable factory overhead spending variance.
   c. Variable factory overhead efficiency variance.
   d. Total underapplied or overapplied variable factory overhead variance.
   e. Fixed factory overhead spending variance.
   f. Production volume variance.
   g. Total fixed factory overhead variance.
   h. Total underapplied or overapplied fixed factory overhead variance.

3. Compute the following variances using three-way analysis of variances:
   a. Factory overhead spending variance.
   b. Factory overhead efficiency variance.
   c. Production volume variance.

4. Compute the factory overhead flexible budget and production volume variances using two-way analysis of variances.

5. Make proper journal entries for
   a. Incurrence of factory overhead costs.
   b. Application of factory overhead costs to production.
   c. Identification of factory overhead variances assuming that the firm uses the four-way analysis of variances identified in requirement 2.
   d. Close all factory overhead cost items and their variances of the period if
      (1) The firm closes all variances to the cost of goods sold of the period.

(2) The firm prorates variances to the inventory accounts and cost of goods sold of the period.

2. Variance Investigation (Appendix)

David Smiley is the manager of Photobonics Manufacturing. He notices that the operation has an unfavorable materials efficiency variance of $25,000 in the last few weeks. He is trying to decide whether to investigate this variance. If he conducts an investigation and discovers that the process is indeed out of control, corrective actions will cost the firm $5,000. The cost of an investigation is $2,500. The firm could suffer a total loss of $55,000 if it continues with the operation that is out of control. Smiley estimates the probability that the operation is out of control to be 0.60.

Required

1. What are the expected costs of investigating and of not investigating? Should the operation be investigated?

2. At what level of probability that the operation is out of control would Smiley be indifferent on the course of action to be taken?

QUESTIONS

16–1   Verbatim Company's budget for factory overheads for last year was $80,000. The actual cost for the period is identical with the budgeted amount even though the actual production was 90 percent of the budgeted production. Can we say that the plant manager has done a good job in controlling the factory overhead if (a) the firm has only fixed factory overhead? (b) the firm has both variable and fixed factory overheads?

16–2   What is the relationship between the variable factory overhead efficiency variance and the direct labor efficiency variance for firms that use direct labor-hours for applying factory overheads?

16–3   What is the relationship among factory overhead spending variance, variable factory overhead spending variance, fixed factory overhead budget variance, and variable factory overhead efficiency variance?

16–4   What is a factory overhead flexible budget variance?

16–5   "Whether the variance is favorable or unfavorable need not be considered when deciding whether to investigate a variance." Do you agree?

16–6   "As long as the actual factory overhead does not vary significantly from the standard cost of the factory overhead required for a given operation there is no need for further analyses of the factory overhead variance." Do you agree?

16–7   Why do some firms choose to use two-way, instead of three-way or four-way, analysis of their manufacturing overhead cost variances?

16–8   What is the difference between the applied variable factory overhead and the total variable factory overhead in the flexible budget? Between the applied fixed factory overhead and the total fixed factory overhead in the master budget?

16–9   Would the choices of denominator level affect the amount of fixed factory overhead (flexible) budget variance? Production volume variance?

16–10 Sipple Furniture's annual master budget includes $360,000 for fixed production supervisory salaries at a monthly volume of 500 units. Supervisory salaries are expected to be incurred uniformly through the year. During August, 450 units were produced and production supervisory salaries incurred were $29,000. What is Sipple Furniture's supervisory salary's flexible budget variance for August?

16–11 Baxter Corporation's master budget calls for the production of 5,000 units of product monthly. The master budget includes indirect labor of $144,000 annually; Baxter considers indirect labor to be a variable overhead. During the month of April, 4,500 units of product were produced and indirect labor costs of $10,100 were incurred. What amount would be reported as flexible budget variance for indirect labor if Baxter Corporation prepares a performance report using flexible budget based on the units manufactured during the period?
(CMA Adapted)

16–12 Can the differences between the actual and the standard factory overhead be separated into price and efficiency variances as when analyzing direct material or direct labor variances?

16–13 List causes that may lead to a variable factory overhead spending variance.

16–14 List causes that may lead to a variable factory overhead efficiency variance.

16–15 List causes that may lead to a fixed factory overhead spending variance.

16–16 List causes that may lead to a production volume variance.

16–17 What are differences in characteristics between service and manufacturing firms? Discuss effects, if any, these differences in characteristics may have on using standard costing system in service firms.

16–18 Why do many firms in today's new manufacturing environment no longer compute and report a direct materials price variance?

16–19 What factors need to be considered in determining whether to investigate a variance?

PROBLEMS

16–20 **FACTORY OVERHEAD RATES** The machining department of the Walkenhorst Company expects to finish the current year with 42,000 units and is preparing the budget for the coming year using the following estimates:

Maximum capacity	50,000 units
Machine-hours per unit	2
Variable factory overhead	$3.00 per hour
Fixed factory overhead	$360,000

The firm has decided to prepare the budget at 80 percent of the maximum capacity. The department uses machine-hours as the basis to apply factory overhead.

Required Determine for the budget year
1. The factory overhead application rate.
2. The budgeted total factory overhead.

16–21 **FACTORY OVERHEAD FLEXIBLE BUDGET** Redline Company uses flexible budgeting for cost control. Redline produced 10,800 units of products during March, incurring a total factory overhead of $13,000, of which $2,500 is for fixed factory overhead. Its master budget for the year reflected a total factory overhead cost of $175,200 at a production volume of 144,000 units, with $60,000 budgeted for fixed factory overhead.

Required What is the factory overhead cost in the flexible budget for March production?

Service

16–22 **FLEXIBLE BUDGET** Somson SuperKlean Service's master budget shows straight-line depreciation on equipment of $258,000. The master budget was prepared at an annual volume of 103,200 chargeable hours. This volume is expected to occur uniformly throughout the year. During September, Somson engaged 8,170 chargeable hours, and the accounts reflected actual depreciation on equipment of $20,500.

Required Determine the flexible budget amount for depreciation on equipment for September.

16–23 **THREE-WAY VARIANCE ANALYSIS** The following information is available from the Swinney Company for its operations in March:

Actual factory overhead	$20,000
Fixed overhead expenses, actual	$ 8,000
Fixed overhead expenses, budgeted	$ 9,000
Actual hours	4,200
Standard hours for the units manufactured	4,000
Total budgeted hours	4,500
Standard variable overhead rate per DLH	$ 2.50

Swinney uses a three-way analysis of factory overhead variances.

Required Compute for Swinney Company

1. Factory overhead spending variance.
2. Variable factory overhead efficiency variance.
3. Factory overhead production volume variance.

16–24 **OVERHEAD APPLIED** Overhead cost information for Danielson Company for the month of October is

Total actual overhead incurred	$28,800
Fixed overhead budgeted	$ 7,200
Total standard overhead rate per DLH	$ 4.00
Standard variable overhead rate per DLH	$ 3.00
Standard production hours allowed	3,500

Required

1. What is the total factory overhead flexible budget variance?
2. What is the total underapplied or overapplied factory overhead?
3. What is the factory overhead production volume variance?

16–25 **TWO-WAY ANALYSIS OF VARIANCES** Information on Conehead Company's overhead costs for May is

Standard applied overhead	$60,000
Flexible budget overhead for the units produced	54,000
Budgeted overhead based on master budget	72,000
Actual overhead incurred	63,000

Required

1. What is the total flexible budget overhead variance?
2. What is the factory overhead production volume variance?
3. What is the total underapplied or overapplied factory overhead?

16–26 **OVERHEAD AT TWO ACTIVITY LEVELS AND FOUR-WAY ANALYSIS**
Greenhat Company used a flexible budget system and prepared this information for the year:

	Level of Operation	
	80 percent	100 percent
Standard direct machine-hours (MH)	20,000	25,000
Variable factory overhead	$72,000	?
Total factory overhead rate per MH	$12.60	

Greenhat applied factory overhead based on the 90 percent capacity level. The standard calls for 2 machine-hours per unit manufactured. During 20X6, Greenhat operated 23,000 machine-hours to manufacture 11,300 units. The actual factory overhead was $12,000 more than the flexible budget amount for the actual units manufactured, of which $5,000 was due to fixed factory overhead.

Required

1. What is the budget allowance for total fixed factory overhead at 80 percent level of operation? At 100 percent level of operation?

2. What is the standard variable factory overhead rate? Standard fixed factory overhead rate?

3. What is the total factory overhead flexible budget amount for the operation of the period?

4. Using four-way analysis compute for Greenhat Company,
    a. Variable factory overhead spending variance.
    b. Variable factory overhead efficiency variance.
    c. Fixed factory overhead spending variance.
    d. Factory overhead production volume variance.

16–27 **THREE-WAY ANALYSIS**   Use the data for Greenhat Company in problem 16–26.

Required   Compute the following variances using three-way analysis.

1. Factory overhead spending variance.

2. Variable factory overhead efficiency variance.

3. Factory overhead production volume variance.

16–28 **TWO-WAY ANALYSIS**   Use the data for Greenhat Company in problem 16–26.

Required   Compute the following variances using two-way analysis.

1. Factory overhead flexible budget variance.

2. Factory overhead production volume variance.

16–29 **TWO-WAY ANALYSIS AND DIRECT LABOR VARIANCE**   The following information relates to the month of April for Marilyn, Inc., which uses a standard cost system and a two-way analysis of overhead variances:

Actual total cost for direct labor	$43,400
Actual hours worked	14,000
Standard hours allowed for good output	15,000
Direct labor rate variance—unfavorable	$ 1,400
Actual total overhead	$32,000
Budgeted fixed costs	$ 9,000
Normal activity in hours	12,000
Total overhead application rate per standard direct labor-hour	$ 2.25

Required

1. What was Marilyn's direct labor efficiency variance for April?

2. What was Marilyn's factory overhead flexible budget (controllable) variance for April?

3. What was Marilyn's production volume variance for April?

(CPA Adapted)

16–30 **WORKING BACKWARD**   Shonburger Company applies factory overhead based on machine-hours (MH) and had a total favorable factory overhead variance of $120,000 for 20X1. Additional data pertaining to 20X1 are:

Variable overhead:	
Applied based on standard machine-hours allowed	$600,000
Total standard amount for actual machine-hours	500,000
Fixed overhead:	
Applied based on standard machine-hours allowed	$360,000
Budgeted	300,000

Required

1. What is the total overhead incurred in 20X1 if the total favorable overhead variance includes production volume variance?

2. What is the total overhead incurred in 20X1 if the total favorable overhead variance is defined as the flexible budget overhead variance?

16-31 **BASIC FACTORY OVERHEAD VARIANCES** Shateau Job Shop has the following operating data for its operations in 20X2:

Budgeted fixed overhead	$20,000
Standard variable overhead (2 machine-hours at $3 each)	$6 per unit
Actual fixed overhead	$21,400
Actual variable overhead	$32,500
Budgeted volume (5,000 units × 2 machine-hours)	10,000 MH
Actual machine-hours	9,500
Units produced	4,500

Required Compute for Shateau Company

1. Variable factory overhead spending variance.
2. Variable factory overhead efficiency variance.
3. Fixed factory overhead spending variance.
4. Factory overhead production volume variance.
5. Factory overhead spending variance using three-way analysis.
6. Factory overhead flexible budget variance using two-way analysis.

16-32 **TWO COST DRIVERS** Alden Company uses a two-way analysis of overhead variances. Selected data for the 20X0 production activity are

Budgeted fixed factory overhead costs:	$ 64,000	
Setup (for 32 setups)	200,000	$264,000
Other		$480,000
Actual factory overheads incurred		
Variable factory overhead rate		$600
per setup		$5
per machine-hour	32,000 hours	
Standard machine-hour	35,000 hours	
Actual machine-hour	28	

Required Compute the budget (controllable) variance for 20X0.

16-33 **ALL MANUFACTURING VARIANCES** Eastern Company manufactures special electrical equipment and parts and employs a standard cost accounting system with separate standards established for each product.

A special transformer is manufactured in the transformer department. Production volume is measured by direct labor-hours in this department and a flexible budget system is used to plan and control department overhead.

Standard costs for the special transformer are determined annually in September for the coming year. The standard cost of a transformer for the year was computed at $67 per unit, as shown here:

Direct materials:		
Iron	5 sheets × $2	$10
Copper	3 spools × $3	9
Direct labor	4 hours × $7	28
Variable overhead	4 hours × $3	12
Fixed overhead	4 hours × $2	8
Total		$67

Overhead rates were based on normal and expected monthly capacity for the year, both of which were 4,000 direct labor-hours. Practical capacity for this department is 5,000 direct labor-hours per month. Variable overhead costs are expected to vary with the number of direct labor-hours actually used.

During October, 800 transformers were produced. This was below expectations because a work stoppage occurred during contract negotiations with the labor force. Once the contract was settled, the department scheduled overtime in an attempt to catch up to expected production levels.

The following costs were incurred in October:

Direct Material	Purchased	Used
Iron	5,000 sheets at $2.00/sheet	3,900 sheets
Copper	2,200 spools at $3.10/spool	2,600 spools

Direct Labor
Regular time: 2,000 hours at $7.00 and 1,400 hours at $7.20.
Overtime: 600 of the 1,400 hours were subject to overtime premium. The total overtime premium of $2,160 is included in variable overhead in accordance with company accounting practices.

Factory overhead:
Variable:	$10,000
Fixed:	$ 8,800

Required

1. What is the most appropriate time to record any variance of actual materials prices from standard?
2. What is the labor rate (price) variance?
3. What is the labor efficiency variance?
4. What is the materials price variance?
5. What is the materials quantity variance?
6. What is the variable overhead spending variance?
7. What is the variable overhead efficiency variance?
8. What is the budget (spending) variance for fixed overhead?
9. What is the factory overhead production volume variance?

(CMA Adapted)

16–34 **FOUR-WAY ANALYSIS**   Derf Company applies overhead on the basis of direct labor-hours. Two direct labor-hours are required for each product unit. Planned production for the period was set at 9,000 units. Manufacturing overhead is budgeted at $135,000 for the period, of which 20 percent is fixed. The 17,200 hours worked during the period resulted in production of 8,500 units. Variable manufacturing overhead cost incurred was $108,500 and fixed manufacturing overhead cost was $28,000. Derf Company uses a four-variance method for analyzing manufacturing overhead.

Required   Compute for Derf Company

1. The variable overhead spending variance for the period.
2. The variable overhead efficiency (quantity) variance for the period.
3. The fixed overhead budget (spending) variance for the period.
4. The factory overhead production volume variance for the period.

(CMA Adapted)

16–35 **FOUR-WAY ANALYSIS**   Able Control Company, which manufactures electrical switches, uses a standard cost system and carries all inventory at standard. The standard factory overhead costs per switch are based on direct labor-hours:

Variable overhead	(5 hours at $8.00/hour)	$ 40
Fixed overhead	(5 hours at $12.00*/hour)	60
Total overhead		$100

*Based on budget of 300,000 direct labor-hours per month.

The following information is for the month of October:

- 56,000 switches were produced although 60,000 switches were scheduled to be produced.
- 275,000 direct labor-hours were worked at a total cost of $2,550,000.
- Variable overhead costs were $2,340,000.
- Fixed overhead costs were $3,750,000.

The production manager argued during the last review of the operation that the operation needs to have a more up-to-date base for charging factory overhead costs to operations. She commented that her factory has been highly automated in the last two years and has hardly any direct labor. The factory hires only highly skilled workers to set up productions and to do periodic adjustments of machinery whenever the need arises.

Required Compute for Able Control Company:

1. The fixed overhead spending variance for October.
2. The factory overhead production volume variance for October.
3. The variable overhead spending variance for October.
4. The variable overhead efficiency variance for October.
5. Comment on the implications of the variances and suggest any action that the firm should take to improve its operations.

(CMA Adapted)

16–36 **COMPREHENSIVE** Organet Stamping Company manufactures a variety of products made of plastic and aluminum components. During the winter months, substantially all of the production capacity is devoted to lawn sprinklers for the following spring and summer season. Other products are manufactured during the remainder of the year. Because a variety of products are manufactured throughout the year, factory volume is measured by production labor-hours rather than units of production.

Production and sales volume have grown steadily for the past several years, as can be seen from the following schedule of standard production labor:

This year	32,000 hours
1 year ago	30,000 hours
2 years ago	27,000 hours
3 years ago	28,000 hours
4 years ago	26,000 hours

The company has developed standard costs for its several products. Standard costs for each year are set in the preceding October. The standard cost of a sprinkler this year was $4.00, computed as follows:

Direct materials		
Aluminum	0.2 pound × $0.40 per pound	$0.08
Plastic	1.0 pound × $0.38 per pound	0.38
Production labor	0.3 hour × $9.00 per hour	2.70
Overhead*		
Variable	0.3 hour × $1.60 per hour	0.48
Fixed	0.3 hour × $1.20 per hour	0.36
Total		$4.00

*Calculated using 30,000 production labor-hours as normal capacity.

During February of this year, 8,500 good sprinklers were manufactured. The following costs were incurred and charged to production:

Materials requisitioned for production:		
Aluminum	(1,900 pounds × $0.40 per pound)	$ 760
Plastic: Regular	(6,000 pounds × $0.38 per pound)	2,280
Low grade†	(3,500 pounds × $0.38 per pound)	1,330
Production labor		
Straight time	(2,300 hours × $10.00 per hour)	23,000
Overtime	(400 hours × $15.00 per hour)	6,000
Overhead		
Variable		5,200
Fixed		3,100 8,300
Costs charged to production		$41,670

Materials price variations are not charged to production but to a materials price variation account at the time the invoice is entered. All materials are carried in inventory at standard prices. Materials purchases for February were

Aluminum	(1,800 pounds × $0.48 per pound)	$ 864
Plastic		
Regular grade	(3,000 pounds × $0.50)	1,500
Low grade†	(6,000 pounds × $0.29)	1,740

†Due to plastic shortages, the company was forced to purchase lower-grade plastic than called for in the standards, which increased the number of sprinklers rejected on inspection.

Required Compute:

1. The total variance from standard cost of the costs charged to production for February.

2. The spending or budget variance for the fixed portion of the overhead costs for February.

3. The labor efficiency variance.

4. The labor rate variance (assume overtime premium is not charged to overhead).

5. The total variable cost variance.

6. The variable overhead spending, efficiency, and flexible budget variances.

7. The factory overhead production volume variance.

8. Materials variances, and comment on the effects of using materials of different grades.

(CMA Adapted)

16–37 **COMPREHENSIVE** Cain Company has an automated production process, and consequently machine-hours are used to describe production activity. A full absorption costing system is employed by the company. The annual profit plan for the coming fiscal year is finalized in April of each year. The profit plan for the fiscal year ending May 31 called for 6,000 units to be produced, requiring 30,000 machine-hours. The full absorption costing rate for the fiscal year was determined using 6,000 units of planned production. Cain develops flexible budgets for different levels of activity for use in evaluating performance. A total of 6,200 units was actually produced during the fiscal year requiring 32,000 machine-hours. This schedule compares Cain Company's actual costs for the fiscal year with the profit plan and the budgeted costs for two different activity levels:

CAIN COMPANY
Manufacturing Cost Report
For the Fiscal Year Ended May 31
(in thousands of dollars)

Item	Profit Plan (6,000 units)	Flexible Budgets for 31,000 Machine-Hours	Flexible Budgets for 32,000 Machine-Hours	Actual Costs
Direct material				
G27 aluminum	$ 252.0	$ 260.4	$ 268.8	$ 270.0
M14 steel alloy	78.0	80.6	83.2	83.0
Direct labor				
Assembler	273.0	282.1	291.2	287.0
Grinder	234.0	241.8	249.6	250.0
Manufacturing overhead				
Maintenance	24.0	24.8	25.6	25.0
Supplies	129.0	133.3	137.6	130.0
Supervision	80.0	82.0	84.0	81.0
Inspector	144.0	147.0	150.0	147.0
Insurance	50.0	50.0	50.0	50.0
Depreciation	200.0	200.0	200.0	200.0
Total cost	$1,464.0	$1,502.0	$1,540.0	$1,523.0

Required Compute:

1. The actual cost of material used in one unit of product.
2. The cost of material that should be processed per machine-hour.
3. The budgeted direct labor cost for each unit produced.
4. The variable manufacturing overhead rate per machine-hour in a flexible budget formula.
5. The manufacturing overhead production volume variance for the current year.
6. The manufacturing overhead spending variance using the three-way to analyze manufacturing overhead variance for the year.
7. The total budgeted manufacturing cost for an output of 6,050 units.

(CMA Adapted)

16–38 **REVISING BASE CAPACITY** Yuba Machine Company manufactures nut shellers at its Sutter City plant. The machines are purchased by nut processors throughout the world. Since its inception, the family-owned business has used actual factory overhead costs in costing factory output. However, on December 1, 20X8, Yuba began using a predetermined factory overhead application rate in order to determine manufacturing costs on a more timely basis. This information is from the 20X8–9 budget for the Sutter City plant:

Strategy

Plant practical capacity	100,000 direct labor-hours
Variable factory overhead costs	$3.00 per direct labor-hour
Fixed factory overhead costs	
Salaries	$ 80,000
Depreciation and amortization	50,000
Other expenses	30,000
Total fixed factory overhead	$160,000

Based on these data, the predetermined factory overhead application rate was established at $4.60 per direct labor-hour.

A variance report for the Sutter City plant for the six months ended May 31, 20X9, follows. The plant incurred 40,000 direct labor-hours that represent one-half of the company's expected activity in the master budget.

Variance Report

	Actual Costs	Budgeted Costs*	Variance[†]
Total variable factory overhead	$120,220	$120,000	$ (220)
Fixed factory overhead			
Salaries	$ 39,000	$ 32,000	$ (7,000)
Depreciation and amortization	25,000	20,000	(5,000)
Other expenses	15,300	12,000	(3,300)
Total fixed factory overhead	$ 79,300	$ 64,000	$(15,300)

*Based on 40,000 direct labor-hours.

[†]Favorable (Unfavorable)

Yuba's controller, Sid Thorpe, knows from the inventory records that one-quarter of the applied fixed factory overhead costs remain in the work-in-process and finished goods inventories. Based on this information Thorpe has included $48,000 of fixed factory overhead as part of the cost of goods sold in the following interim income statement:

YUBA MACHINE COMPANY
Interim Income Statement
For Six Months Ended May 31, 20X9

Sales	$625,000
Cost of goods sold	380,000
Gross profit	$245,000
Selling expense	44,000
Depreciation expense	58,000
Administrative expense	53,000
Operating income	$ 90,000
Provision for income taxes (40%)	36,000
Net income	$ 54,000

Required

1. Define practical capacity and explain why it may not be a satisfactory basis for determining a fixed factory overhead application rate.

2. Prepare a revised variance report for Yuba Machine Company using the expected activity in its master budget as the basis for applying fixed factory overhead.

3. Determine the effect on Yuba Machine Company's reported operating income of $90,000 at May 31, 20X9, if the fixed factory overhead rate was based on the expected activity in Yuba's master budget rather than practical capacity.

4. What capacity should the firm use in determining its factory overhead application rate if the firm 1) deems the product a cash cow, or 2) is striving to capture market share and to expand the total market size?

(CMA Adapted)

16–39 **VARIABLE OVERHEAD VARIANCES** Use the data in problem 16–29 for Marilyn, Inc.

Required Compute, using three-way analysis:

1. Variable overhead spending variance.
2. Variable overhead efficiency variance.

(CMA Adapted)

16–40 **FOUR-WAY ANALYSIS** Nolton Products developed its overhead application rate from the current annual budget. The budget is based on an expected actual output of 720,000 units requiring 3,600,000 direct labor-hours. The company is able to schedule production uniformly throughout the year.

A total of 66,000 units requiring 315,000 direct labor-hours was produced during May. Actual overhead costs for May amounted to $375,000. The actual costs as compared with the annual budget and one-twelfth of the annual budget follow.

Nolton uses a standard-costing system and applies factory overhead on the basis of direct labor-hours.

	Annual Budget				
	Total Amount	Per Unit	Per Direct Labor-Hour	Monthly Budget	Actual Costs for May 20X3
Variable					
Indirect	$ 900,000	$1.25	$ .25	$ 75,000	$ 75,000
labor	1,224,000	1.70	.34	102,000	111,000
Supplies					
Fixed	648,000	.90	.18	54,000	51,000
Supervision	540,000	.75	.15	45,000	54,000
Utilities	1,008,000	1.40	.28	84,000	84,000
Depreciation	$4,320,000	$6.00	$1.20	$360,000	$375,000

Required Calculate the following amounts for Nolton Products for May 20X3.

1. Applied overhead costs
2. Variable overhead spending variance
3. Variable overhead efficiency variance
4. Fixed overhead spending variance
5. Production volume variance

Be sure to identify each variance as favorable (F) or unfavorable (U).
(CMA Adapted)

16–41 **PRORATION OF VARIANCES** Butrico Manufacturing Corporation uses a standard cost system that records raw materials at actual cost, records materials price variance at the time that raw materials are issued to work-in-process, and prorates all variances at year-end. Variances associated with direct materials are prorated based on the direct materials balances in the appropriate accounts, and variances associated with direct labor and manufacturing overhead are prorated based on the direct labor balances in the appropriate accounts.

The following Butrico information is for the year ended December 31:

Finished goods inventory at 12/31:	
Direct materials	$ 87,000
Direct labor	130,500
Applied manufacturing overhead	104,400
Raw materials inventory at 12/31	$ 65,000
Cost of goods sold for the year ended 12/31:	
Direct materials	$348,000
Direct labor	739,500
Applied manufacturing overhead	591,600
Direct materials price variance (unfavorable)	10,000
Direct materials usage variance (favorable)	15,000
Direct labor rate variance (unfavorable)	20,000
Direct labor efficiency variance (favorable)	5,000
Manufacturing overhead incurred	690,000

There were no beginning inventories and no ending work-in-process inventory. Manufacturing overhead is applied at 80 percent of standard direct labor.

Required Compute

1. The amount of direct materials price variance to be prorated to finished goods inventory at December 31.

2. The total amount of direct materials in finished goods inventory at December 31, after all materials variances have been prorated.

3. The total amount of direct labor in finished goods inventory at December 31, after all variances have been prorated.

4. The total cost of goods sold for the year ended December 31, after all variances have been prorated.

(CMA Adapted)

16–42 **WORKING BACKWARD—TWO-WAY ANALYSIS** Beth Company had budgeted fixed factory overhead costs of $50,000 per month and a variable factory overhead rate of $4 per direct labor-hour. The standard direct labor-hours allowed for October production were 18,000. An analysis of the factory overhead indicates that in October Beth had an unfavorable budget (controllable) variance of $1,000 and a favorable production volume variance of $500. Beth uses a two-way analysis of overhead variances.

Required Compute

1. The actual factory overhead incurred in October.

2. Beth's applied factory overhead in October.

(CMA Adapted)

16–43 **FOUR-WAY ANALYSIS** Edney Company employs a standard system for product costing. The standard cost of its product is

Raw materials	$14.50
Direct labor (2 direct labor-hours × $8)	16.00
Manufacturing overhead (2 direct labor-hours × $11)	22.00
Total standard cost	$52.50

The manufacturing overhead rate is based on a normal annual activity level of 600,000 direct labor-hours. Edney planned to produce 25,000 units each month during the year. The budgeted annual manufacturing overhead is

Variable	$3,600,000
Fixed	3,000,000
	$6,600,000

During November, Edney produced 26,000 units. Edney used 53,500 direct labor-hours in November at a cost of $433,350. Actual manufacturing overhead for the month was $260,000 fixed and $315,000 variable. The total manufacturing overhead applied during November was $572,000.

Required Determine for November

1. The variable manufacturing overhead spending variance.

2. The variable manufacturing overhead efficiency variance.

3. The fixed manufacturing overhead spending (budget) variance.

4. The manufacturing overhead production volume variance.

(CMA Adapted)

16–44 **COMPUTE ALL VARIABLE VARIANCES** Aunt Molly's Old Fashioned Cookies bakes cookies for retail stores. The company's best-selling cookie is chocolate nut supreme, which is marketed as a gourmet cookie and regularly sells for $8 per pound. This is the standard cost per pound of chocolate nut supreme, based on Aunt Molly's normal monthly production of 400,000 pounds:

Cost Item	Quantity	Standard Unit Cost	Total Cost
Direct materials			
Cookie mix	10 ounces	$ .02/ounce	$ .20
Milk chocolate	5 ounces	.15/ounce	.75
Almonds	1 ounce	.50/ounce	.50
			$1.45
Direct labor*			
Mixing	1 minute	14.40/hour	.24
Baking	2 minutes	18.00/hour	.60
			.84
Variable overhead†	3 minutes	32.40/hour	1.62
Total standard cost per pound			$3.91

*Direct labor rates include employee benefits.

†Applied on the basis of direct labor-hours.

Aunt Molly's management accountant, Karen Blair, prepares monthly budget reports based on these standard costs. April's contribution report compares budgeted and actual performance:

Contribution Report
April 20X5

	Budget	Actual	Variance
Units (in pounds)	400,000	450,000	50,000 F
Revenue	$3,200,000	$3,555,000	$355,000 F
Direct material	580,000	865,000	$285,000 U
Direct labor	336,000	348,000	12,000 U
Variable overhead	648,000	750,000	102,000 U
Total variable costs	1,564,000	1,963,000	$399,000 U
Contribution margin	$1,636,000	$1,592,000	$ 44,000 U

Justine Molly, president of the company, is disappointed with the results. Despite a sizable increase in cookies sold, the product's expected contribution to the overall profitability of the firm decreased. Molly has asked Blair to identify the reasons why the contribution margin decreased. Blair has gathered this information to help in her analysis of the decrease:

Usage Report
April 20X5

Cost Item	Quantity	Actual Cost
Direct materials		
Cookie mix	4,650,000 ounces	$ 93,000
Milk chocolate	2,660,000 ounces	532,000
Almonds	480,000 ounces	240,000
Direct labor		
Mixing	450,000 minutes	108,000
Baking	800,000 minutes	240,000
Variable overhead		750,000
Total variable costs		$1,963,000

Required

1. Explain the $44,000 unfavorable variance between the budgeted and actual contribution margin for the chocolate nut supreme cookie product line during April 20X5 by calculating these variances. Assume that all materials are used in the month of purchase.

a. Sales price variance.
b. Materials price variance.
c. Materials quantity variance.
d. Labor efficiency variance.
e. Variable overhead efficiency variance.
f. Variable overhead spending variance.
g. Contribution margin volume variance.

2. a. Explain the problems that might arise in using direct labor-hours as the basis for allocating overhead.
   b. How might activity-based costing (ABC) solve the problems described in requirement 2a?

(CMA Adapted)

Ethics

16–45 COMPARE ACTUAL WITH BUDGETED COSTS   Talbot Company manufactures shirts sold to customers for embossing with various slogans and emblems. Bob Ricker, manufacturing supervisor, recently received the following November production report; the November budget is based on the manufacture of 80,000 shirts.

November 20X2 Production Report

Cost Item	Standard	Actual	Variance
Direct materials	$160,000	$162,000	$ (2,000)
Direct labor	240,000	246,000	(6,000)
Factory overhead	200,000	241,900	(41,900)

Ricker was extremely upset by the negative variances in the November report as he has worked very closely with his people for the past two months to improve productivity and to ensure all workers are paid their standard wage rates. He immediately asked to meet with his boss, Chris Langdon. Also disturbed by the November results, Langdon suggested that Ricker meet with Sheryl Johnson, Talbot's manager of cost accounting, to see if he can gain further insight into the production problems. Johnson was extremely helpful and provided Ricker with the additional information on the annual budget and these actual amounts for November:

Variable Overhead Expenditures

	Annual	Per Unit	November
Indirect material	$ 450,000	$ .45	$36,000
Indirect labor	300,000	.30	33,700
Equipment repair	200,000	.20	16,400
Equipment power	50,000	.05	12,300
Total	$1,000,000	$1.00	$98,400

Fixed Overhead Expenditures

	Annual	November
Supervisory salaries	$ 260,000	$ 22,000
Insurance	350,000	29,500
Property taxes	80,000	6,500
Depreciation	320,000	34,000
Heat, light, telephone	210,000	21,600
Quality inspection	280,000	29,900
Total	$1,500,000	$143,500

- Factory overhead at Talbot includes both variable and fixed components and is applied on the basis of direct labor-hours. The company's 20X2 budget includes the manufacture of 1 million shirts and the expenditure of 250,000 direct labor-hours.

- The standard labor rate at Talbot is $12 per hour, and the standard materials cost per shirt is $2.
- Actual production for November was 82,000 shirts.

With these data, Johnson and Ricker prepared to analyze the November variances, paying particular attention to the factory overhead variance because of its significance. Johnson knows that part of the problem is caused by Talbot's not using flexible budgeting, and she will be able to explain this to Ricker as they analyze the data.

Required

1. By calculating the following four variances, prepare an explanation of the $41,900 unfavorable variance between budgeted and actual factory overhead during the month of November 20X2:
   a. Budget volume variance for total factory overhead.
   b. Variable overhead efficiency variance.
   c. Variable overhead spending variance.
   d. Fixed overhead spending variance.
2. Describe the likely behavioral impact on Bob Ricker of the information provided by the calculations in requirement 1. Be sure to make specific reference to the variances calculated, indicating Ricker's responsibility in each case.

(CMA Adapted)

16–46 INVESTIGATION OF VARIANCE UNDER UNCERTAINTY, APPENDIX The internal auditor of the Transnational Company estimates that the probability of its internal control procedure being in control is .8. She estimates the costs of conducting an investigation at about $20,000 and the cost of revising and improving the internal control procedure to be approximately $50,000. The present value of savings from having the new procedure is expected to be $250,000.

Required

1. Construct a payoff table for the firm to determine the best course of action to the firm.
2. What is the expected cost to the firm if it conducts an investigation? Does not conduct an investigation?
3. Should the firm conduct an investigation?

16–47 INVESTIGATION OF VARIANCE UNDER UNCERTAINTY, APPENDIX The manager of MMX Digital is deciding whether to embark on a advertising campaign for the firm's newest multimedia computer chip. There has been some discussion among division managers about the market condition for the product. To simplify the discussion and decision, probabilities were assessed by the marketing department regarding a strong market (.6) and a weak market (.4).

The manager, with the help of the marketing staff, has estimated the profits she believes the firm could earn:

Profits with advertising:	Strong market	$10 million
	Weak market	4 million
Profits without advertising:	Strong market	8 million
	Weak market	5 million

Required

1. Should the firm inaugurate the advertising campaign?
2. What is the probability level regarding the state of the market that will render the manager indifferent between the courses of action?
3. What is the maximum amount the firm should pay to obtain the perfect information regarding the state of the market, if such information is available?

16–48 **INVESTIGATION OF VARIANCE UNDER UNCERTAINTY, APPENDIX** A student organization is planning to raise funds by selling flower bouquets on Saint Valentine's Day. The bouquet will be a special arrangement for the members of the student organization. The sales booth costs $100, which can be sold to another student organization for $30 after the sales project. The bouquets can be purchased at $7 each and will be sold for $12 each. The cost of having bouquets delivered to the booth is $20 per delivery. Once delivered, no bouquet can be returned.

Required

1. The organization predicts sales to be 60 units. If actual sales are 48 units, what is the cost of the prediction error?

2. The organization has to place its order in 12-bouquet bundles. With good weather the organization can sell 100 bouquets. The number of bouquets will most likely be 36, however, if the weather turns out to be nasty. A member of the organization majoring in meteorology predicts, after consulting with meteorologists at the National Weather Bureau and local TV stations, that there is a 60 percent chance of having good weather on Saint Valentine's Day.

   a. Construct a payoff table for the situation faced by the organization.

   b. What is the best course of action to the organization?

   c. What is the expected value of perfect information?

16–49 **INVESTIGATION OF VARIANCE UNDER UNCERTAINTY, APPENDIX** Ron Bagley is contemplating whether or not to investigate a labor efficiency variance in the assembly department. It will cost $6,000 to undertake the investigation and another $18,000 to correct operations if the department is found to be operating improperly. If the department is operating improperly and Bagley failed to make the investigation, operating costs from the various inefficiencies are expected to amount to $33,000. At which probability of improper operation would Bagley be indifferent between investigating and not investigating the variance?

Service

International

16–50 **TWO-WAY ANALYSIS OF VARIANCE** International Finance Incorporated issues letters of credit to importers for overseas purchases. The company charges a nonrefundable application fee of $3,000 and, on approval, an additional service fee of 2 percent of the amount of credit requested.

The budget for the firm for the year just completed includes fixed expenses for office salaries and wages of $500,000, for leasing of office space and equipment of $50,000, and for utilities and other operating expenses of $10,000. In addition, the budget also includes variable expenses for supplies, and other variable overhead costs of $1,000,000. The firm estimated its variable overhead cost to be $2,000 for each letter of credit approved and issued. The firm approves, on average, 80 percent of the applications received.

During the year the firm received 600 requests and approved 75 percent of the requests. The total variable overheads were 10 percent higher than the standard amount applied while the total fixed expenses were 5 percent below the amount allowed.

In addition to these expenses, the firm also paid a $270,000 insurance premium for the letters of credit issued. The insurance premium is 1 percent of the amount of credits issued in U.S. dollars. The actual amount of credit issued often differs from the amount requested due to fluctuations in exchange rates and variations in the amount shipped from the amount ordered by the importer. The strength of the dollar during the year decreased the insurance premium by 10 percent.

Required

1. Calculate the variable and fixed overhead application rates for the year.
2. Prepare an analysis of the overhead variances for the year just completed.

SOLUTIONS TO SELF-STUDY PROBLEMS

1. Analysis of Overhead Variance

1. a.

Units manufactured during the period	360
Standard direct labor-hours per unit	× 2
Total standard direct labor-hours for the units manufactured during the period	720
Standard variable factory overhead rate per direct labor-hour	× $5.00
Total standard variable factory overhead for the period	$3,600

b. The total variable factory overhead applied $3,600

c.

Budgeted units of production	400
Standard direct labor-hours per unit	× 2
Total standard direct labor-hours for the units budgeted for the period	800
Standard fixed factory overhead rate per direct labor-hour	× $20.00
Total budgeted fixed factory overhead for the period	$16,000

d.

Total standard direct labor-hours for the units manufactured during the period (from 1a)	720
Standard fixed factory overhead rate per direct labor-hour	× $20.00
Total fixed factory overhead applied	$14,400

2. a, b, and c.

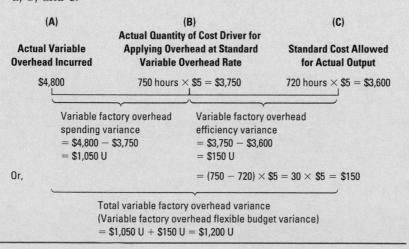

(A)	(B)	(C)
Actual Variable Overhead Incurred	Actual Quantity of Cost Driver for Applying Overhead at Standard Variable Overhead Rate	Standard Cost Allowed for Actual Output
$4,800	750 hours × $5 = $3,750	720 hours × $5 = $3,600

Variable factory overhead spending variance
= $4,800 − $3,750
= $1,050 U

Variable factory overhead efficiency variance
= $3,750 − $3,600
= $150 U

Or, = (750 − 720) × $5 = 30 × $5 = $150

Total variable factory overhead variance
(Variable factory overhead flexible budget variance)
= $1,050 U + $150 U = $1,200 U

d. Total underapplied variable factory overhead variance is $1,200.

e, f, and g.

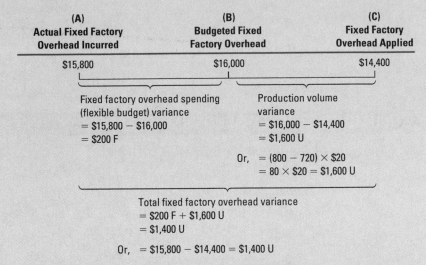

(A) **Actual Fixed Factory Overhead Incurred**	(B) **Budgeted Fixed Factory Overhead**	(C) **Fixed Factory Overhead Applied**
$15,800	$16,000	$14,400

Fixed factory overhead spending
(flexible budget) variance
= $15,800 − $16,000
= $200 F

Production volume
variance
= $16,000 − $14,400
= $1,600 U

Or, = (800 − 720) × $20
= 80 × $20 = $1,600 U

Total fixed factory overhead variance
= $200 F + $1,600 U
= $1,400 U

Or, = $15,800 − $14,400 = $1,400 U

   h. Total under-applied fixed factory overhead variance = $1,400

3. a. Factory overhead spending variance
= Variable factory overhead spending variance + Fixed factory
overhead spending variance
= $1,050 U + $200 F = $850 U

   b. Factory overhead efficiency variance = Variable factory
overhead efficiency variance = $150 U

   c. Production volume variance = $1,600 U

4. Factory overhead flexible budget variance = Factory overhead
spending variance + Factory overhead efficiency variance =
$850 U + $150 U = $1,000 U

Production volume variance is $1,600 U, the same as those in
either the four-way or three-way analysis of variances.

5. a. Factory Overhead Control   20,600
      Cash, Sundry Payable accounts, Prepaid
      accounts, or Accumulated Depreciations   20,600

   b. Work-in-process Inventory Control   18,000
      Factory Overhead Applied   18,000

   c. Factory Overhead Applied   18,000
      Variable Factory Overhead Spending Variance   1,050
      Variable Factory Overhead Efficiency Variance   150
      Production Volume Variance   1,600
        Factory Overhead Control   20,600
        Fixed Factory Overhead Spending Variance   200

   d. (1) Cost of Goods Sold   2,600
        Fixed Factory Overhead Spending Variance   200
          Variable Factory Overhead Spending Variance   1,050
          Variable Factory Overhead Efficiency Variance   150
          Production Volume Variance   1,600
      (2) Ending balances at standard are:
        Work-in-Process Inventory Control
         ($153,000 − $134,640) $ 18,360
        Finished Goods Inventory Control
         ($134,640 − $111,690)   22,950
      Cost of Goods Sold $111,690
        Total $153,000

Account	Cost at Standard	Percent of Total	Proration of Variance	Adjusted Total Cost
Work-in-Process, Ending	$ 18,360	12%	$2,600 × 0.12 = $ 312	$ 18,672
Finished Goods, Ending	22,950	15	2,600 × 0.15 = $ 390	23,340
Cost of Goods Sold	111,690	73	2,600 × 0.73 = $1,898	113,588
Total	$153,000	100%	$2,600	$155,600

Cost of Goods Sold	1,898	
Work-in-Process Control	312	
Finished Goods Control	390	
Fixed Factory Overhead Spending Variance	200	
Variable Factory Overhead Spending Variance		1,050
Variable Factory Overhead Efficiency Variance		150
Production Volume Variance		1,600

2. Variance Investigation (Appendix)

Courses of Action

A_1: Investigate the operation to determine the causes of the efficiency variance.
A_2: Do not investigate the operation.

States of Operation

S_1: The operation is in control.
S_2: The operation is out of control.

Cost and Probability

I = Cost of investigation = $2,500
C = Cost of corrective action, if an out of control is found = $5,000
L = Losses from the operation being out of control and no correction is made = $55,000
P = Probability of the operation being in control = .40

Payoff Table

	States of Operation	
	In Control (Random)	Out of Control (Systematic)
Management Action	.4	.6
Investigate	$2,500	$2,500 + $5,000
Do not investigate	0	$55,000

1. $E(\text{Investigate}) = .4 \times \$2,500 + .6 \times \$7,500 = \$5,500$
   $E(\text{Not to Investigate}) = .6 \times \$55,000 = \$33,000$

   The expected total cost to the firm will be lower if Smiley investigates the variance and takes proper action to correct the cause of the variance if the operation is found to be out of control.

2. Smiley would be indifferent if the probability of in control (P) renders the expected costs of investigation to be equal to the expected cost of not investigating.

$$\$2,500P + \$7,500(1 - P) = \$55,000(1 - P)$$

$$50,000P = 47,500$$

$$P = .95$$

As long as the probability of the operation being in control is .95 or lower, Smiley should investigate the cause of variances.

Daniel Nichols/Gamma Liaison

17

Managing Productivity and Marketing Effectiveness

After studying this chapter, you should be able to . . .

1 Describe productivity and implications of changes in productivity

2 Compute and interpret operational and financial partial productivity

3 Distinguish among productivity change, input price change, and output change

4 Identify the advantages and limitations of applying productivity measures to firms in service and not-for-profit organizations

5 Separate a sales volume variance into sales mix and sales quantity variances

6 Explain how market size and market share variances lead to sales quantity variances

> Productivity is not everything, but in the long run it is almost
> everything.
>
> PAUL KRUGMAN

PART ONE: MANAGING PRODUCTIVITY

Most organizations want to improve productivity so they can do more with less. The desire to produce more with less is, in the final analysis, a leading driver for humanity's progress. Productivity in making and moving things has increased by more than 45-fold in the last 125 years in industrialized countries. As a result, the average working hours per year per worker have decreased from more than 3,000 hours to around 1,800 hours in the United States. The productivity explosion also paid for the 10-fold expansion of education and for the even greater expansion of health care. Productivity has become the wealth of nations.[1]

Firms that use fewer materials, workers, machines, or other production resources than their competitors to manufacture the same product with equal or higher quality enjoy competitive advantages. These firms usually earn higher-than-average returns and command long-term success. For this reason, producing more with less is often a strategic critical success factor for business firms.

Firms that compete as cost leaders have to be able to perform all tasks with fewer resources than their competitors to be successful. Firms competing on differentiation or focus strategies also can increase their profit margins by not using any more resources than their competitors. Governments and not-for-profit organizations often require their employees to do more with the limited resources at their disposal. Economists and

◀ **LEARNING OBJECTIVE 1**
Describe productivity and implications of changes in productivity.

Productivity in USAA

Many firms have improved their productivity continuously over the years. For example, USAA, a financial services firm located in San Antonio, has pursued increases in employee productivity for more than 30 years. The company's financial assets have increased 100-fold while the total number of employees has increased by a factor of only five.

Source: Based on "Solving the Productivity Puzzle," *The Wall Street Journal,* March 4, 1994.

BusinessWeek

? What's the Big Deal with Deere?

John Deere & Company knows what it's like to have bumper years and not-so-abundant years. For instance, in 1991, Deere had a loss of $20 million versus 1990 profits of $411 million. What happened? With the demand for farm equipment on the downturn and competition on the upswing, Deere faced a tough environment and some tough decisions. The lean years not only caused thin sales but it also led to the company downsizing its workforce to meet the shrinking farm market. By 1994, however, Deere made a turnaround, with profits sharply increasing and its net income up 35 percent from 1993.

Q: How did Deere increase profits with a smaller workforce in a shrinking market? *Find out on page 690 of this chapter.*

---

[1] Peter F. Drucker, *Managing for the Future* (New York: Truman Tolley Books, 1993), pp. 93–94.

financial analysts often use the amount of output produced per unit of input resource as an indicator of the competitiveness and economic well-being of a country. Almost everywhere we look, the ability to do more with less is critically important.

WHAT IS PRODUCTIVITY?

Productivity is the ratio of output to input.

Productivity is the relationship between what is produced and what is required to produce it.

$$\text{Productivity} = \frac{\text{Output}}{\text{Input}}$$

A firm that spent five days to manufacture 100 units has a productivity of 20 units per day. A social service worker who processed 75 cases over a four-week period has a productivity of 3.75 cases per day. A firm that uses 24.5 pounds of material to manufacture one unit is more productive than another firm that uses 25 pounds of the same materials to manufacture one unit of the same product.

A primary objective in measuring productivity is to improve operations either by using fewer inputs to produce the same output or to produce more output with the same inputs. Improvements in productivity require benchmarks or criteria to assess changes in productivity and to determine needed improvements to attain the goal. Among criteria often used are past productivity measures of the firm, productivity measures of another division of the same firm or other firms in the same industry, the industry standard, or a benchmark established by top management as the goal for the firm to attain.

MEASURING PRODUCTIVITY

Operational productivity is the ratio of output to the number of units of an input factor.

Financial productivity is the ratio of output to the dollar amount of one or more input factors.

Partial productivity is a productivity measure that focuses only on the relationship between one of the inputs and the output attained.

A measure of productivity can be either an operational or a financial productivity. An **operational productivity** measure is essentially a physical measure with both the input and the output in physical units. A **financial productivity** measure uses dollar amounts for the input. For example, the number of tables made per sheet of plywood is an operational productivity while the number of tables per dollar cost of plywood is a financial productivity.

A productivity measure that focuses on only the relationship between one of the inputs and the output attained is a **partial productivity** measure. Common partial productivity measures include

- Direct materials yield productivity such as output/units of materials.
- Workforce productivity such as output per labor-hour or output per person employed.
- Process (or activity) productivity such as output/machine-hours or output per kilowatt hour.

A productivity measure that includes all the input resources used in production is *total productivity*. The number of tables manufactured per dollar of manufacturing costs is a total productivity measure because the denominator, manufacturing costs, includes all manufacturing costs incurred to make the tables. In Exhibit 17–1 we show different productivity measures.

Exhibit 17–2 contains an example of data used to measure productivity—production data for Er-Cat Precision Tool Company in 20X2 and 20X3 for manufacturing DB2 drill bits. The manufacturing costs include a total fixed factory overhead of $300,000 per year and variable manufacturing costs consisting of metal alloy (direct materials) and direct labor-hours.

The firm earned $1,100,000 operating income in 20X3, a 17 percent increase from the $940,000 earned in 20X2. Without examining the operating data in detail, management probably would be very happy with the operating result. The increase in operating income, however, compares unfavorably to the 20 percent increase in total sales. Because fixed costs are the same in both years, the less than proportional increase in the operating income is a result of a higher than proportional increase in the firm's variable costs—direct materials and direct labor costs.

Exhibit 17–1	Productivity Measures

Productivity {
Partial productivity
   Operational partial productivity, or
   Financial partial productivity

Total productivity (financial productivity)

Exhibit 17–2	Operating Data

ER-CAT PRECISION TOOL COMPANY
20X2 and 20X3 Operating Data for DB2
(dollars in 000s)

	20X2	20X3
Units of DB2 manufactured and sold	4,000	4,800
Total sales ($500 per unit)	$2,000	$2,400
Direct materials (25,000 pounds at $24/pound and 32,000 pounds at $25/pound)	600	800
Direct labor (4,000 hours at $40 per hour and 4,000 hours at $50/hour)	160	200
Other operating costs	300	300
Operating income	$940	$1,100

A multitude of factors, however, may have contributed to the increase in these two costs. Among them are increases in the number of units manufactured and sold; changes in the amounts of the inputs, such as direct materials or direct labor-hours, used in production; and increases in unit costs of resources. The firm needs to identify the factors that caused the change in total costs so that management can improve operating income by decreasing manufacturing costs. (Chapters 15 and 16 discuss analyses based on the standard costs of the firm for the period to determine the effect that changes in cost elements, such as wage rates, labor-hours, materials prices, and materials usage, have on the production cost of the period.)

Productivity measurements discussed in this chapter examine the effect of a firm's productivity on the operating income of the firm. An increase in productivity decreases costs and increases operating income. Changes in the productivity of different resources, however, are not always in the same direction or at an equal pace. A firm can improve its productivity in using direct materials while its productivity for direct labor deteriorates or improves at a slower pace. Worse, productivity of different resources may be in conflict. For instance, management of a furniture manufacturer can increase materials productivity by reducing waste due to improper cutting. To reduce improper cuttings, however, employees need to spend more labor-hours in cutting boards carefully—a decrease in labor-hour productivity. Management needs to know the effects of productivity changes on operating income to best use its resources.

Partial Productivity

A *partial productivity measure* describes the relationship between the output of a period and a required input for the production of the output.

$$\text{Partial productivity} = \frac{\text{Units of output manufactured}}{\text{Units or cost of a single input resource used}}$$

The denominator is the quantity or cost of a manufacturing factor such as direct materials or direct labor-hours, while the numerator is the unit or value of the goods or services produced.

◀ **LEARNING OBJECTIVE 2**
Compute and interpret operational and financial partial productivity.

A partial productivity of the direct materials for DB2 for the Er-Cat Precision Tool Company in 20X2 is 0.16:

$$\text{Partial productivity of DM in 20X2} = \frac{4,000}{25,000} = 0.16$$

Operational Partial Productivity

An operational partial productivity shows the conversion ratio of an input resource into the output. The numerator, the output, is the number of units produced while the denominator is the units of the input resources used in attaining the output. Looking at Exhibit 17–3 you can see the operational partial productivity of Er-Cat Precision Company in 20X2 and 20X3. The partial productivity of 0.16 for the direct materials in 20X2 says that the firm manufactured 0.16 unit of output for every pound of direct materials used in production.

A comparison of partial productivity over time shows changes in productivity of the input resource. The operating results of Er-Cat Company show that the partial productivity of the direct materials decreased over time. The firm manufactured 0.16 unit of DB2 for each pound of direct materials in 20X2 and only 0.15 unit of DB2 for each pound in 20X3, a 6.25 percent decrease in productivity [(0.16 − 0.15) ÷ 0.16 = 0.0625]. The partial productivity of direct labor, however, improved during the same period. The firm manufactured one unit of DB2 per direct labor-hour in 20X2 and 1.2 units per direct labor-hour in 20X3, a 20 percent increase in productivity [(1.2 − 1) ÷ 1 = 0.20].

The changes in productivity also can be examined by computing the amount of input resources that the firm would have used in 20X3 had the firm maintained the same partial productivity as in 20X2, as shown in Exhibit 17–4. Had the firm maintained the same partial productivity, the 4,800 units of DB2 manufactured and sold in 20X3 would have required only 30,000 pounds of direct materials (4,800 ÷ 0.16). The decrease in partial productivity of direct materials necessitated the use of an additional 2,000 pounds in 20X3 (32,000 − 30,000). Similarly, the firm would have spent 4,800 direct labor-hours in 20X3 had the firm had the same direct labor partial productivity in 20X3 as in 20X2. The firm saved the cost of 800 hours of direct labor (4,800 − 4,000) when it increased its partial productivity in 20X3 for direct labor from 1.0 to 1.2.

Financial Partial Productivity

LEARNING OBJECTIVE 3 ▶
Distinguish among productivity change, input price change, and output change.

The bottom half of Exhibit 17–3 reports the financial partial productivity of direct materials and direct labor. A financial partial productivity shows the number of units of output manufactured for each dollar of the input resource the firm spent. The 20X3 financial partial productivity for direct materials is determined by dividing the actual cost incurred in 20X3, $800,000, into the actual output of 20X3, 4,800 units.

Exhibit 17–3	Partial Productivity

ER-CAT PRECISION TOOL COMPANY
Partial Productivity—Direct Materials and Direct Labor

Product: DB2

Operational Partial Productivity

	20X2	20X3
Direct materials	4,000 ÷ 25,000 = 0.16	4,800 ÷ 32,000 = 0.15
Direct labor	4,000 ÷ 4,000 = 1.00	4,800 ÷ 4,000 = 1.20

Financial Partial Productivity

	20X2	20X3
Direct materials	4,000 ÷ $600,000 = 0.0067	4,800 ÷ $800,000 = 0.006
Direct labor	4,000 ÷ $160,000 = 0.025	4,800 ÷ $200,000 = 0.024

This productivity, 0.006, indicates that for every dollar Er-Cat spent on direct materials, the firm manufactured 0.006 unit of DB2. The data also show that the partial productivity decreased from 20X2 to 20X3 by 10 percent [(0.006667 − 0.006) ÷ 0.006667].

The financial partial productivity of direct labor is 0.025 for 20X2 and 0.024 for 20X3, a decrease in productivity of 4 percent [(0.025 − 0.024) ÷ 0.025]. This result contradicts the operational partial productivity for direct labor reported earlier, which showed a 20 percent improvement in the partial productivity of direct labor. These results suggest that, even though the workers increased their productivity per hour, the increase in cost due to increases in hourly wages is more than the gain in productivity per hour. We can see this more clearly by dividing the changes in financial partial productivity as shown in Exhibit 17–5.

Differences in operating results can be a result of differences in output level, input cost, or productivity. The top portion of Exhibit 17–5 shows the framework for analyses to determine effects from each of these factors. Point A is the actual operating result of 20X3. All three factors at point A are 20X3 figures: units of output, input cost, and productivity. The only difference between A and B is the productivity. Point B is the cost to manufacture the 20X3 output at the *20X2 productivity* level and 20X3 input cost. Thus, the difference between points A and B is a result of changes in productivity between 20X3 and 20X2.

The difference between points B and C is in the unit price for the input resource. Point B uses a *20X3 unit price* while point C uses a *20X2 unit price* of the input resource. The other two factors, units of output and productivity, remain the same at both points. The difference between points B and C, therefore, is due to changes in the input prices.

Point D is the cost to manufacture the *20X2 output* at the 20X2 productivity with the input resource at the 20X2 unit cost. Recall that point C is the cost to manufacture the 20X3 output at the 20X2 productivity and the 20X2 unit cost of the input resource. Any difference in the costs is due to the difference in the output levels. Because both points C and D use the same productivity and unit cost of the input resource, the ratios of output to input at these two points are always identical.

The analysis shows that, of the 10 percent decrease in financial partial productivity of direct materials (from .0067 to .006, Exhibit 17–3), only 6 percent (.0004/.0067, Exhibit 17–5) can be attributed to productivity change. The remaining 4 percent (.000267/.0067, Exhibit 17–5) is due to the price change per pound of direct materials from $24 in 20X2 to $25 in 20X3. The total change in financial partial productivity of direct labor is a 4 percent decrease from 20X2 (from .025 to .024, Exhibit 17–3). The partial productivity of direct labor did increase by 16 percent (.004/.025, Exhibit 17–5). The 25 percent increase in wages, however, more than offset any gain in productivity of labor. As a result, the total direct labor cost increased.

Operational vs. Financial Partial Productivity

An operational partial productivity measure uses physical units in both the numerator and the denominator. Therefore, it is easily understood by operational

			Exhibit 17–4		Changes in Partial Productivity

ER-CAT PRECISION TOOL COMPANY
Effects of Changes in Partial Productivity of Direct Materials
and Direct Labor in the Production of DB2

Input Resource	20X3 Output	20X2 Operational Partial Productivity	Input That Would Be Used in 20X3 at 20X2 Productivity	Input Used in 20X3	Saving or (Loss) in Units of Input
Direct materials	4,800	0.16	30,000	32,000	(2,000)
Direct labor	4,800	1.00	4,800	4,000	800

| Exhibit 17–5 | Decomposition of Financial Partial Productivity |

ER-CAT PRECISION TOOL COMPANY
Decomposition of Financial Partial Productivity

Framework

	A	B	C	D
Output	20 × 3	20 × 3	*20 × 3*	*20 × 2*
Productivity	*20 × 3*	*20 × 2*	20 × 2	20 × 2
Input cost	20 × 3	20 × 3	*20 × 2*	20 × 2

| | Productivity Change | Input Price Change | Output Change |

Operating Data for Decomposing Financial Partial Productivity

	Actual 20X3 Operating Results	20X3 Output at 20X2 Productivity and 20X3 Input Cost	20X3 Output at 20X2 Productivity and 20X2 Input Cost	Actual 20X2 Operating Results
Output units:	4,800	4,800	4,800	4,000
Input units and costs:				
Direct materials	32,000 × $25 = $ 800,000	30,000 × $25 = $750,000	30,000 × $24 = $720,000	25,000 × $24 = $600,000
Direct labor	4,000 × $50 = 200,000	4,800 × $50 = 240,000	4,800 × $40 = 192,000	4,000 × $40 = 160,000
Total	$1,000,000	$990,000	$912,000	$760,000

Decomposition

20X3 Operation			20X2 Operation

	20X3 output ÷ (20X3 input × 20X3 input costs)	20X3 output ÷ (20X2 input for the 20X3 output × 20X3 input costs)	20X3 output ÷ (20X2 input for the 20X3 output × 20X2 input costs)	20X2 output ÷ (20X2 input × 20X2 input costs)
Direct materials	4,800/$800,000 = 0.006	4,800/$750,000 = 0.0064	4,800/$720,000 = 0.006667	4,000/$600,000 = 0.006667
Direct labor	4,800/$200,000 = 0.024	4,800/$240,000 = 0.02	4,800/$192,000 = 0.025	4,000/$160,000 = 0.025

	Productivity change	Input price change	Output change
Direct materials	0.006 − 0.0064 = 0.0004 U	0.0064 − 0.006667 = 0.000267 U	0.006667 − 0.006667 = 0
Direct labor	0.024 − 0.02 = 0.004 F	0.02 − 0.025 = 0.005 U	0.025 − 0.025 = 0

Summary of Results

Productivity Change from 20X2

	Productivity Change		Input Price Change		Output Change		Total Change
Direct materials	0.0004 U	+	0.000267 U	+	0	=	0.000667 U
Direct labor	0.004 F	+	0.005 U	+	0	=	0.001 U

Change as Percent of 20X2 Productivity

	Productivity Change		Input Price Change		Output Change		Total Change
Direct materials	6% U	+	4% U	+	0%	=	10% U
Direct labor	16 F	+	20 U	+	0	=	4 U

personnel. In addition, an operational productivity measure is simpler because it is unaffected by price changes or other factors, which makes it easier to benchmark.

By focusing on the physical measure of one input resource at a time, an operational partial productivity measure enables management to know the effect on operations of changes in the productivity of the input resource. Executives in the auto industry often use partial productivity measures to compare labor productivity in the United States to that in Japan as a gauge of their competitive positions in the market.

A financial partial productivity has the advantage of considering the effects of both cost and quantity of an input resource on productivity. At a management level, the effect of cost, not merely the physical quantity, is of concern. In addition, financial partial productivity can be used in operations that use more than one production factor. An operational partial productivity, on the other hand, can measure only one direct material or type of direct labor at a time.

Limitations of Partial Productivity Analysis

A partial productivity measure has several limitations. First, it measures only the relationship between an input resource and the output; it ignores any effect that changes in quantities of other manufacturing factors have on the productivity. An improved partial productivity measure may have been gained at the expense of the decreased productivity of one or more other input resources. For example, Er-Cat Company could have decided to use less direct labor and more direct materials.

A second limitation is that partial productivity ignores any effect that changes in the production factor have on productivity. An example is a change in the quality of the production factor. The labor-hours the Er-Cat Company uses in 20X3 might have a higher skill level than those of 20X2. As a result, the partial productivity of labor increases. The average hourly wage rate, however, also increased. Is it worthwhile, then, for the firm to make the trade-off? Unfortunately, an analysis of operational partial productivity cannot provide us with an answer.

Third, partial productivity also ignores any effect that changes in the operating characteristics of the firm may have on the productivity of the input resource. The labor operational partial productivity improves when the firm installs high-efficiency equipment. The improvement in labor operational partial productivity can hardly be attributed to increased labor productivity.

Fourth, no efficiency standard is involved in partial productivity measures, and there may be no relationship between a partial productivity measure and the efficiency variance as determined in Chapter 15.

Total Productivity

Total productivity measures the relationship between the output attained and the total input costs of all required input resources for the production of the output. Total productivity provides a measure of the productivity of all required input resources combined.

$$\text{Total productivity} = \frac{\text{Units or sales value of output manufactured}}{\text{Total costs of all input resources}}$$

Total productivity is a financial productivity measure. The sum of all input resources in their physical measures usually is not meaningful. Dollars represent a common factor that allows measures of different resources such as materials, labor, and other production factors to be added together.

The first panel of Exhibit 17–6 shows the computation of the total productivity of the firm's total variable manufacturing costs for 20X2 and 20X3. The computation of total productivity involves three steps: First, determine the outputs of each of the periods—4,000 units in 20X2 and 4,800 units in 20X3. Second, calculate the total variable costs incurred to produce the output. The total variable manufacturing costs for DB2 are $760,000 in 20X2 and $1,000,000 in 20X3. Third, compute total productivity by dividing the output quantity by the total cost of variable input resources. The results are 0.005263 in 20X2 and 0.0048 in 20X3. For every dollar of variable cost incurred in 20X2 the firm manufactured 0.005263 unit of the output, while manufacturing only 0.0048 unit in 20X3, a decrease of 0.000463 unit or 8.8 percent in productivity [(0.005263 − 0.0048) ÷ 0.005263].

Alternatively, we can substitute total sales revenue for the units manufactured in the numerator to compute the total productivity, as shown in the second panel of

Total productivity
measures the relationship between the output attained and the total input costs of all the required input resources.

Exhibit 17–6	Total Productivity

ER-CAT PRECISION TOOL COMPANY
Total Productivity for DB2

Total productivity in unit

	20X2	20X3
(a) Total units manufactured	4,000	4,800
(b) Total variable manufacturing costs incurred	$760,000	$1,000,000
(c) Total productivity: (a) ÷ (b)	0.005263	0.0048
(d) Decrease in productivity: 0.005263 − 0.0048 = 0.000463 (8.8%)		

Total productivity in sales dollar

	20X2	20X3
(a) Total sales	$2,000,000	$2,400,000
(b) Total variable manufacturing costs incurred	$760,000	$1,000,000
(c) Total productivity: (a) ÷ (b)	$2.6316	$2.4
(d) Decrease in productivity: $2.6316 − $2.4 = $0.2316 (8.8%)		

Exhibit 17–6. In 20X2, the firm generated $2.6316 in sales for each dollar of variable costs the firm spent. The productivity decreases to $2.40 in 20X3, a drop of $0.2316 in sales, or 8.8 percent [(2.6316 − 2.4) ÷ 2.6316].

Of the two alternative measures of total productivity, the productivity of all the required resources to manufacture the output units often is used in assessing production operations. Achieving higher productivity by making more units is an important beginning step for a successful firm. A firm needs to generate higher revenue for each dollar spent on input resources to be successful.

Advantages and Limitations of Total Productivity

Total productivity measures the combined effects of changes in all the operating factors. As such, using a total productivity measure decreases the possibility of manipulating one or two manufacturing factors to improve the measure. The same cannot be said for partial productivity measures. To the extent that partial productivity of direct labor can be improved at the expense of the partial productivity of materials, a manager whose firm uses the partial productivity of direct labor as the primary basis of performance evaluation may not pay due care to minimizing scraps.

By necessity, total productivity is a financial productivity measure. Personnel at the operational level often find it difficult to link financial productivity measures to their day-to-day operations. A deterioration in total productivity can result from increased costs of resources, which may be beyond the control of manufacturing people. Such ambiguity in the relationship between the performance measure and the reward system may defeat the very purpose of having a measurement of productivity.

Another consideration in using a total productivity is that the basis for assessing changes in productivity may change over time. For instance, Er-Cat Precision Tool Company assesses the change in productivity in 20X3 from 20X2 using 20X2 as the criterion. The evaluation of the change in productivity in 20X2 from 20X1 would have used the productivity in 20X1 as the criterion. Such a procedure makes it impossible to compare changes in productivity from 20X2 to 20X3 to those of changes from 20X1 to 20X2 because the two measures use different years as the base. This problem can be mitigated by using a constant base year.

In addition, productivity measures may ignore the effects on productivity of changes in demand, changes in selling prices of the goods or services, and special purchasing or selling arrangements.

Changes in demand alter the size of operations. The size of operations may affect total productivity as well as partial productivity for materials, workforce, or process.

Economies of scale often mean that productivity per unit of input differs at various levels of operation.

Increases or decreases in selling prices of the output goods or services change productivity in dollars of output for each unit of input either in part or in total. An increase in the selling price of a product to $12 from $10 would have increased productivity per dollar of materials cost by 20 percent if no other changes occurred for the operations. Thus, if the same firm increased its productivity per dollar of materials cost from $4.00 to $4.50 of sales, the firm actually had a decrease, not an increase, in its productivity.

Special arrangements either in sales of the output or in purchases of input resources also may disrupt the underlying relation between input and output in computing productivity. A special arrangement to sell products at a discount decreases the productivity in dollars of output for input units. Alternatively, a special purchase of materials increases financial productivity. Neither can be attributed to a loss or gain in productivity.

PRODUCTIVITY IN THE NEW MANUFACTURING ENVIRONMENT

Productivity and Total Quality Management

Too often managers believe improvements in quality can be attained only at the expense of productivity because of the need for additional resources or decreases in units of good output. The experience of many firms is the opposite—improvements in quality *increase* productivity.

First, quality improvements often decrease waste and spoiled units, and thus decrease the amount of input resources needed. Improvements in quality at Kangall Manufacturing decreased the rejected units from 10 percent of the total units manufactured to 2 percent. The improvement in quality improved the firm's productivity from 1.6 to 1.74.[2]

Second, improvements in quality decrease the resources needed in production. Improvements in quality decrease or eliminate reworks and spoiled units. Decrease or elimination of reworks or spoiled units makes the materials, production hours, and processes (machine-hours, energy, space) they consume unnecessary. Productivity improves because less input is required to produce output.

Productivity and Business Process Reengineering

Productivity and business process reengineering go hand in hand; these two important approaches can help a firm attain a higher level of profitability and improve competitiveness.

Improving productivity requires answering the question: How can we manufacture a product or complete a task with fewer inputs, including materials, time, and facility? Productivity improvement need not be restricted to efforts on reducing the inputs needed for the same output or increasing the level of output from the same inputs.

A thorough improvement in productivity goes deeper. The first questions in efforts to increase productivity, especially in service organizations, should be: What is the task? What are we trying to accomplish? Why do it at all?[3] These are the very same questions that business process reengineering asks. The easiest and perhaps the largest increases in productivity come from redefining the task to be done, especially by eliminating activities to be done and from redesigning the processes to perform the task.

---

[2]   If the firm spent $3,937.50 to manufacture 7,000 units, of which 700 units were rejected, the productivity of the firm is 6,300/$3,937.50 = 1.6. A decrease in the rejection rate to 2 percent of the total units produced would enable the firm to turn out 6,860 good units. The productivity improves to 6,860/$3,937.50 = 1.74. In fact, the firm can spend an additional 8.9 percent in costs ($350) for quality improvements and still maintain the same productivity.

[3]   Drucker, *Managing for the Future.*

Productivity and Employee Turnover

Individual employees are important conduits of learning and productivity. When employees leave the company, they take learning with them and productivity suffers. That is especially true in service firms. Manufacturing firms may mitigate the consequence of employee turnover by automating machinery and improving factory design.

The best companies inspire loyalty and reduce employee turnover by sharing productivity gains with employees. An Atlanta-based fast-food chain, Chick-fil-A, shares store profits with their employees on a fifty-fifty basis. As a result, the firm's employees earn 50 percent more than the competition and employee turnover is 5 percent a year versus 35 percent for competitors. The firm has grown to 600 stores without ever tapping the stock market.

Source: Based on Frederick F. Reichheld, "Solving the Productivity Puzzle," *The Wall Street Journal,* March 4, 1996.

BusinessWeek

✔ How Did Deere Do More with Less?
(Continues from page 681)

A: It starts with the little people ...

John Deere & Company's Chief Executive Hans W. Becherer recognized that the fastest way to adapt to its tough environment was to reach out to its workforce. He believed that employees held the key to improved quality and costs—"It's often the people at the root of the company, on the shop floor, who will provide the best answers," says Becherer. With that thought in mind, Deere initiated a number of labor innovations throughout the company. It enlisted workers in new jobs, expanded employee training programs, and created cost-reduction teams and self-directed work teams—soliciting advice on "everything from cutting production costs to improving product quality." As an example of the extent of Deere's innovations, managers asked John Soliz, a United Auto Workers member and assembly-line worker, to travel across North America to talk with dealers and farmers about Deere products. By taking Soliz out of his traditional job and providing him with training and new skills, the end result was "win-win-win": a satisfied worker with new skills, farmers and dealers with improved customer service, and a company with increased profits.

For further reading, see "The New Soul of John Deere," *Business Week,* January 31, 1994.

Productivity often is computed for all inputs and processes, including both value-added and non-value-added activities. An improvement in productivity for a non-value-added activity is not the best use of resources. Non-value-added activities should be eliminated through reengineering, not improved. Efforts to improve productivity should be focused only on value-added activities. Productivity should be assessed only on value-added activities.

To be productive is to do better what we already do well. To be competitively productive requires continuous improvements. Continuous improvements entail continuous learning and process reengineering. Only with continuous productivity improvements can a firm remain competitive in the long run.

Finally, productivity improvement is not a synonym for employee layoffs or capacity shrinkage. Although laying off workers and closing plants raises the level of productivity, these methods are one-time shots and they do not improve growth rates. When demands pick up, the firm may not be able to fulfill the potential. The cost of lost profit, yielding of opportunities to competitors, and deteriorated competitive position can far exceed the benefits of slimming down and restructuring. Boeing benefited from trimming its fat in the early 1990s. As the demand for aircraft rose, the firm struggled and failed to keep pace with the demand. Production bottlenecks forced Boeing to delay scheduled deliveries in October 1997 and opened up opportunities for Airbus, its chief rival.

PRODUCTIVITY IN SERVICE AND NOT-FOR-PROFIT ORGANIZATIONS

Service and not-for-profit organizations employ more than half the total workforce in the United States and continue to account for an increasing portion of both the national and global economy. Improving productivity in the service industry and not-for-profit organizations is critical for continued economic progress.

The basic concepts for measuring productivity in service and not-for-profit organizations are similar to those for measuring productivity in manufacturing firms. To the extent that the output and the required tasks for attaining the output of a service firm or not-for-profit organization can be defined clearly and identified as comparable from period to period, organizations can use the procedure discussed earlier for manufacturing operations to examine productivity changes. The productivity change of a shelter for the homeless can be measured by the ratio of the number of persons the shelter housed to the total expenses the shelter incurred. An airline can gauge productivity by computing the ratio of paid-passenger-miles to total operating expenses.

Unfortunately, many of the outputs and required tasks of service firms and not-for-profit organizations cannot be measured precisely. Hospitals often use patient-days to measure their outputs and productivity. Although the number of patient-days can be measured unequivocally, not all patient-days require the same amount of work or generate the same revenue. The care needed during a patient-day for an open-heart surgery patient most likely is much greater than that for a normal childbirth.

Indefinite relationships between the output and input resources required in a service firm often lead its management to measure only financial productivity. Here both the numerator and denominator of the ratio are measured in dollar amounts. An open-heart patient demands more input resources than does a mother during a routine delivery. On the other hand, the patient-day of the open-heart patient also generates higher revenue than does the patient-day of the maternity patient. Financial productivity can serve as a good measure for service firms if there is a relatively constant relationship between the revenue generated and the cost of the input resources required to generate the revenue, and the dollar amount is a major critical factor for the organization. Unfortunately for measurement purposes, dollar amounts can hardly represent a major objective of not-for-profit organizations, and revenues of service firms are more likely determined by the quality of the services rendered, not the cost of input resources.

One additional difficulty in measuring productivity in a not-for-profit organization is the absence of revenue as the common measure for output. The output of a higher education institution includes the number of students graduated, total credit hours taught, contributions to the advancement of knowledge, and services to the community. Not only is it difficult to obtain a clear measure for some of these outputs but also there is no revenue attached to most, if not all, of these outputs. Consequently, it is impossible to have a revenue-based financial measure of the output of a higher education institution.

◀ **LEARNING OBJECTIVE 4**
Identify the advantages and limitations of applying productivity measures to firms in service and not-for-profit organizations.

PART TWO: MANAGING MARKETING EFFECTIVENESS

A market is where a firm earns profits, fulfills its strategic goals, and attains long-term successes. No firm can gain long-term success without marketing effectiveness. Marketing effectiveness includes:

- Achieving budgeted operating income.
- Attaining budgeted market share.
- Adapting to changes in the market.

Factors affecting marketing effectiveness include selling price, sales quantity, product mix, market size, and market shares of the firm. Variances in any of these

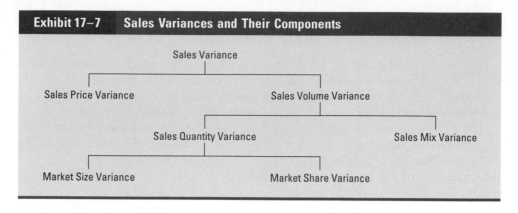

Exhibit 17–7   Sales Variances and Their Components

factors can lead the firm astray in short-run performance objectives, strategic goals, and long-term success. Exhibit 17–7 depicts the relationships of sales variances.

When the actual sales revenues differ from the master budgeted levels, the causes of the difference can be in either sales prices or sales volumes. A sales volume variance can result from sales quantity and sales mix variances. From a marketing effectiveness perspective, deviations in sales quantity can be explained by market size or market share variances.

SALES PRICE AND SALES VOLUME VARIANCES

A *sales price variance* is the difference between the actual dollar amount received from all the units sold and the dollar amount the firm would have received had the firm sold these units at the budgeted selling price per unit.

Sales price variance measures the impact of deviations of the actual selling prices from the master budgeted selling prices on contribution margin and operating income. A firm computes its sales price variance by multiplying the difference between the actual and the budgeted selling prices per unit of the product by the actual units of the product sold. This variance also is the sales revenue flexible budget variance.

$$\begin{array}{l} \text{Sales} \\ \text{price} \\ \text{variance} \end{array} = \left[\begin{array}{l} \text{Actual} \\ \text{selling price} \\ \text{per unit} \end{array} - \begin{array}{l} \text{Budgeted} \\ \text{selling price} \\ \text{per unit} \end{array} \right] \begin{array}{l} \text{Actual} \\ \times \text{ number of} \\ \text{units sold} \end{array}$$

A *sales volume (activity) variance* is the difference between the budgeted contribution margin for the actual total units sold (flexible budget contribution margin) and the budgeted contribution margin for the budgeted units (master budget contribution margin). This variance measures the effect on contribution margin and operating income when the quantity sold for one or more products differs from the quantity in the master budget for the period. The sales volume variance was introduced in Chapter 15 as part of the analysis of flexible budget variances. Exhibit 15–4 is reproduced here as Exhibit 17–8 to provide a starting point for further analyses of the sales volume variance into the separate factors that lead to the sales volume variance.

Schmidt Machinery Company's budget included an operating income of $200,000 through sales of 1,000 units of XV–1 at a selling price of $800 per unit ($800,000 ÷ 1,000 units), while incurring a variable expense of $450 per unit ($450,000 ÷ 1,000 units), and a total fixed expense of $150,000 for the month. The actual operating results showed that the firm sold 780 units for $639,600, or an average selling price of $820 per unit. The average actual selling price per unit exceeds the budgeted unit selling price by $20. Thus, the firm has a favorable sales price variance of $15,600 ($20 per unit × 780 units sold).

The master budget calls for total sales of 1,000 units; however, the firm sold 780 units, or 220 units less than the budgeted units for the period. At a standard contribution margin of $350 per unit ($800 − $450 or $350,000 ÷ 1,000 units), the

Exhibit 17–8	Actual and Budget Operating Data

SCHMIDT MACHINERY COMPANY
Analysis of Operations
For the Month Ended October 31, 20X2

	Actual	Flexible Budget Variances*	Flexible Budget	Sales Volume Variances	Master Budget
Units sold (XV–1)	780	0	780	220	1,000
Sales	$639,600	$15,600 F	$624,000	$176,000 U	$800,000
Variable expenses	350,950	50 F	351,000	99,000 F	450,000
Contribution margin	$288,650	$15,650 F	$273,000	$ 77,000 U	$350,000
Fixed expenses	160,650	10,650 U	150,000	—	150,000
Operating income	$128,000	$ 5,000 F	$123,000	$ 77,000 U	$200,000

*Including both price and efficiency variances.

shortfall in units sold reduces both the total contribution margin and the operating income by $77,000 ($350 × 220 units). This is the sales volume or activity variance. It is the difference between the contribution margin (and the operating income) of the flexible budget amount and the corresponding master (static) budget contribution margin (operating income), or the difference between the actual units sold and the sales units budgeted in the master budget times the budgeted contribution margin per unit.

$$\begin{array}{l} \text{Sales} \\ \text{volume} \\ \text{variance} \end{array} = \begin{bmatrix} \text{Number} & \text{Number of} \\ \text{of units} & - & \text{units in the} \\ \text{sold} & & \text{master budget} \end{bmatrix} \times \begin{array}{l} \text{Budgeted} \\ \times \text{ contribution} \\ \text{margin per unit} \end{array}$$

$$= (780 - 1,000) \times \$350 = \$77,000 \text{ U}$$

Several factors may contribute to a sales volume variance. Among them are sales quantity and sales mix variances, which we examine next.

SALES MIX VARIANCE

Two major contributing factors to a sales volume variance are deviations in sales mix and changes in sales quantities. To begin, we consider changes in sales mix.

Sales mixes fluctuate for multiproduct firms. Assume that Schmidt Machinery Company carries another product, FB–33, in addition to XV–1 as shown in Exhibit 17–8. Exhibit 17–9 shows a condensed master budget for the month and Exhibit 17–10 shows the operating results for November 20X2.

During November 20X2, Schmidt sold 780 units of XV–1 at an average price of $800 per unit ($624,000 ÷ 780 units = $800). The actual average selling price per unit is the same as the budgeted selling price per unit for the product. The firm also sold 3,220 units of FB–33 at $600 per unit ($1,932,000 ÷ 3,220 units = $600), the same price as the budgeted selling price per unit. Thus, the firm had no sales price variance.

Notice that the actual variable expenses *per unit* for both XV–1 and FB–33 (Exhibit 17–10) are identical to those of budgeted variable expenses *per unit* for the products (Exhibit 17–9); also, the actual fixed expense is the same as the budgeted fixed expense. There is no variance due to deviations of the actual operating expenses from the standard or budgeted amounts. Also, the total units sold, 4,000 units, is the same as the budgeted units for the month. Thus, there is no sales volume variance. Given that the actual selling prices, variable expenses, fixed expenses, and total sales volume are all identical to the budgeted amounts, the actual operating income should be identical to the budgeted operating income.

A comparison of the budgeted operating income in Exhibit 17–9 and the actual operating income reported in Exhibit 17–10 shows, however, that the actual

◄ **LEARNING OBJECTIVE 5**
Separate a sales volume variance into sales mix and sales quantity variances.

Exhibit 17–9   Master Budget

SCHMIDT MACHINERY COMPANY
Master Budget
For the Month Ended November 30, 20X2

| | XV–1 | | FB–33 | | Both Products | |
	Total	Per Unit	Total	Per Unit	Total	Per Unit
Units	1,000		3,000		4,000	
Sales	$800,000	$800	$1,800,000	$600	$2,600,000	$650.00
Variable expenses	450,000	450	960,000	320	1,410,000	352.50
Contribution margin	$350,000	$350	$840,000	$280	$1,190,000	$297.50
Fixed expenses	150,000		450,000		600,000	
Operating income	$200,000		$390,000		$590,000	

Exhibit 17–10   Income Statement

SCHMIDT MACHINERY COMPANY
Income Statement
For the Month Ended November 30, 20X2

| | XV–1 | | FB–33 | | Both Products |
	Total	Per Unit	Total	Per Unit	Total
Units	780		3,220		4,000
Sales	$624,000	$800	$1,932,000	$600	$2,556,000
Variable expenses	351,000	450	1,030,400	320	1,381,400
Contribution margin	$273,000	$350	$ 901,600	$280	$1,174,600
Fixed expenses	150,000		450,000		600,000
Operating income	$123,000		$ 451,600		$ 574,600

operating income is $15,400 below the budgeted amount. With all the operating factors—selling prices, variable expenses, total fixed expenses, and total units sold—seemingly identical to those in the master budget, why does the firm have an unfavorable operating income variance of $15,400?

The answer is that the operating income variance arises from a change in sales mix. Schmidt Machinery Company carries two products. You may have noticed that the actual sales units for products XV–1 and FB–33 are not the same as the budgeted quantities, even though the combined sales volume for the products is the same as the amount in the master budget for the period. The sales of XV–1 during the period are 220 units less than the budgeted quantity, while the sales of FB–33 are 220 units higher than the budgeted quantity. In this example, the deviations of individual sales quantities from the respective budgeted amounts for different products contribute to the operating income variance of the period. For a multiproduct firm, selling the *total* number of units specified in the master budget does not imply that the flexible budget operating income of the period will be the same as the master budget operating income.

Most firms carry multiple products or provide more than one service. Budgets for these firms specify the quantities, prices, and costs for each of their products or services just as Schmidt's budgets do. **Sales mix** is the proportion of units of each product or service to the total unit of all products or services. When not all the quantities of products sold or services rendered during a period are the same as their amounts in the budget, the firm has two sales mixes: budgeted sales mix and actual sales mix.

With separate budgeted selling prices, budgeted costs, and contribution margins per unit for different products or services, a firm that carries multiple products has

The **sales mix** of a firm is the proportion of units of each product or service to the total unit of all products or services.

separate amounts for each of its products or services in the flexible or master budgets. Typically, not all products have the same contribution margins per unit. Thus, even if the total units sold is exactly the same as the total unit sales in the master budget, the total contribution margin in the firm's flexible budget will differ with the total contribution margin in the master budget when the actual sales mix deviates from the budgeted sales mix. Deviations of the actual sales mix from the budgeted sales mix can affect the total contribution and operating income of the firm.

The **sales mix variance** of a product is the product of the difference between these two ratios, the actual total units of *all* products sold, and the budgeted contribution margin per unit of the product:

$$
\begin{matrix}
\text{Sales mix} \\
\text{variance for} = \\
\text{a product}
\end{matrix}
\begin{bmatrix}
\text{Actual sales} & & \text{Budget sales} \\
\text{mix percentage} & - & \text{mix percentage} \\
\text{for the product} & & \text{for the product}
\end{bmatrix}
\times
\begin{matrix}
\text{Actual total} \\
\text{units of} \\
\text{all products} \\
\text{sold}
\end{matrix}
\times
\begin{matrix}
\text{Budgeted unit} \\
\text{contribution} \\
\text{margin of} \\
\text{the product}
\end{matrix}
$$

> The **sales mix variance** of a product is the product of the difference between the actual and budgeted sales mix, the actual total units of all products sold, and the budgeted contribution margin per unit of the product.

A product's sales mix variance measures the effect on contribution margin and operating income due to the deviation of the actual sales mix from the budgeted sales mix. The computation of a sales mix variance starts with determining the actual sales mix ratio and the budgeted sales mix ratio for each of the products of the firm. The budget and actual sales mixes for XV–1 and FB–33 for November 20X2 are

Product	Budget Units	Budget Sales Mix	Actual Units Sold	Actual Sales Mix
XV–1	1,000	1,000 ÷ 4,000 = 0.25	780	780 ÷ 4,000 = 0.195
FB–33	3,000	3,000 ÷ 4,000 = 0.75	3,220	3,220 ÷ 4,000 = 0.805
Total	4,000	1.00	4,000	1.00

Using the data in Exhibit 17–9, the sales mix variances are

Sales mix
variance $= (0.195 - 0.25) \times 4{,}000 \text{ units} \times \$350 = \$77{,}000 \text{ U}$
of XV–1

Sales mix
variance $= (0.805 - 0.75) \times 4{,}000 \text{ units} \times \$280 = \$61{,}600 \text{ F}$
of FB–33

Total sales mix variance $= \$77{,}000 \text{ U} + \$61{,}600 \text{ F} = \$15{,}400 \text{ U}$

The actual units of XV–1 sold, 780 units, are 19.5 percent of the total products sold during the month. The budget, on the other hand, calls for XV–1 to account for 25 percent of the total units sold. Given the actual total sales of 4,000 units and the budgeted contribution margin of $350 per unit of XV–1, the sales mix for XV–1 is $77,000 unfavorable.

Similarly, we can determine that the sales mix variance for FB–33 is $61,600 favorable. This variance is favorable because the actual sales mix, 80.5 percent, is greater than the budgeted sales mix of 75 percent. The total sales mix variance of the firm is the sum of the sales mix variances of all the products, which is $15,400 unfavorable for the Schmidt Machinery Company.

SALES QUANTITY VARIANCE

The second major contributing factor to the sales volume variance of a multiple product firm is the difference between the budgeted and actual sales quantities. The **sales quantity variance** of a product is the product of the difference between the budgeted and the actual total sales quantity, the budgeted sales mix of the product, and the budgeted contribution margin per unit of the product. The computation of a sales quantity variance involves three factors: the difference between the budgeted and the actual total sales quantity of all products of the operation, the budgeted sales mix of the product, and the budgeted contribution margin per unit of the product. For each product the sales quantity variance is the product of these three factors.

> The **sales quantity variance** of a product is the product of the difference between the budgeted and actual total sales quantity, the budgeted sales mix of the product, and the budgeted contribution margin per unit of the product.

A sales quantity variance measures the effect on the contribution margin and operating income due to the deviation of the actual total sales units from the budgeted total units. With the focal point of a sales quantity variance being the difference between actual and budgeted total sales units, to determine a sales quantity variance we use the budgeted amounts for the other two elements in the computation of the variance. To calculate the sales quantity variance for each product:

$$\begin{array}{l}\text{Sales} \\ \text{quantity} \\ \text{variance for} \\ \text{a product}\end{array} = \left[\begin{array}{l}\text{Actual total} \\ \text{units of all} \\ \text{products sold}\end{array} - \begin{array}{l}\text{Budgeted total} \\ \text{sales units of} \\ \text{all products}\end{array}\right] \times \begin{array}{l}\text{Budgeted} \\ \text{sales mix} \\ \text{percentage} \\ \text{of the product}\end{array} \times \begin{array}{l}\text{Budgeted} \\ \text{contribution} \\ \text{margin per unit} \\ \text{of the product}\end{array}$$

Notice the calculation of the sales quantity variance for each of the products uses the budgeted sales mix and the budgeted contribution margin per unit of the product. Also, the quantity difference is the difference between the actual *total* units and the budgeted *total* units of all the products of the operation.

The previous example for the November 20X2 operation of Schmidt Machinery Company has no sales quantity variances because the actual total units sold are the same as the budgeted total sales units. To illustrate determination of a sales quantity variance, let us examine operating data from another month.

In December 20X2, Schmidt sold 1,600 units of XV–1 and 3,400 units of FB–33, all at the budgeted unit selling prices, budgeted unit variable expenses, and budgeted total fixed expenses. Exhibit 17–11 shows the actual operating result of December 20X2. The budget for December is exactly the same as the budget for November of 20X2. With total budgeted sales of 4,000 units, the total quantity sold in December 20X2 of 5,000 units is 1,000 units more than the budgeted units.

With no difference between the actual and the budgeted selling prices for both products, there is no selling price variance. The selling price variance shown in Exhibit 17–12 confirms this conclusion. The difference between the actual operating income ($912,000 from Exhibit 17–11) and the budgeted operating income ($590,000 from Exhibit 17–9), $322,000 favorable, thus can be attributed to a sales volume variance. The bottom panel of Exhibit 17–12 confirms this result. This sales volume variance can be separated further into a sales mix variance and a sales quantity variance.

Following the procedure for calculating the sales quantity variance, we see that Schmidt has a total $297,500 favorable sales quantity variance in December 20X2, as shown in Exhibit 17–13.

The total sales quantity variance can help managers examine the effect of increases or decreases in total units sold on operating income. The previous example shows that had the firm maintained the budgeted sales mix, the budgeted contribution margins per unit, and budgeted fixed costs, it could have earned $297,500 more in operating income from the higher actual sales quantity (1,000 units over budget) than the budgeted amount. Exhibit 17–14 verifies this analysis.

Had the firm sold the 5,000 units at the budgeted sales mix, Schmidt would have sold 1,250 units of XV–1 and 3,750 units of FB–33. With the budgeted contribu-

---

Exhibit 17–11   **Income Statements for Two Products**

SCHMIDT MACHINERY COMPANY
Income Statement
For the Month Ended December 31, 20X2

	XV–1	FB–33	Total
Units	1,600	3,400	5,000
Sales	$1,280,000	$2,040,000	$3,320,000
Variable expenses	720,000	1,088,000	1,808,000
Contribution margin	$ 560,000	$ 952,000	$1,512,000
Fixed expenses	150,000	450,000	600,000
Operating income	$ 410,000	$ 502,000	$ 912,000

Exhibit 17–12	Selling Price and Sales Volume Variance

SCHMIDT MACHINERY COMPANY
Selling Price and Sales Volume Variances
For December 20X2

Selling price variance

XV–1	($800 − $800) × 1,600 = 0
FB–33	($600 − $600) × 3,400 = 0
Total	0

Sales volume variance

XV–1	(1,600 − 1,000) × $350 = $210,000 F
FB–33	(3,400 − 3,000) × $280 = $112,000 F
Total	$322,000 F

Exhibit 17–13	Sales Quantity Variance

SCHMIDT MACHINERY COMPANY
Sales Quantity Variance
For December 20X2

$$\begin{matrix} \text{Sales quantity} \\ \text{variance for} \\ \text{a product} \end{matrix} = \begin{bmatrix} \text{Actual total} \\ \text{units of all} \\ \text{products sold} \end{bmatrix} - \begin{bmatrix} \text{Budgeted total} \\ \text{units of sales} \\ \text{for all products} \end{bmatrix} \times \begin{matrix} \text{Budgeted sales} \\ \text{mix percentage} \\ \text{of the product} \end{matrix} \times \begin{matrix} \text{Budgeted contribution} \\ \text{margin per unit for} \\ \text{the product} \end{matrix}$$

XV–1	(5,000 − 4,000) × 0.25 × $350 = $ 87,500 favorable
FB–33	(5,000 − 4,000) × 0.75 × $280 = $210,000 favorable
Total	$297,500 favorable

Exhibit 17–14	Further Analysis of Sales Quantity Variance

SCHMIDT MACHINERY COMPANY
Further Analysis of Sales Quantity Variance
For December 20X2

Product	Budgeted Sales Mix	Total Units at the Budgeted Mix	Contribution Margin per Unit	Total Contribution Margin
XV–1	0.25	5,000 × 0.25 = 1,250	$350	$350 × 1,250 = $ 437,500
FB–33	0.75	5,000 × 0.75 = 3,750	$280	$280 × 3,750 = 1,050,000
Total contribution margin of the total units sold at the budgeted mix				$1,487,500
Budgeted fixed expenses				600,000
Operating income from the sale of the total actual units at the budgeted mix				$ 887,500
Operating income of the master budget				590,000
Sales quantity variance				$ 297,500

tion margin of $350 and $280 per unit of XV–1 and FB–33, respectively, the firm would have earned a total contribution margin of $1,487,500. After subtracting the budgeted fixed cost of $600,000, the firm would have an operating income of $887,500, $297,500 higher than the budgeted operating income.

The company, however, did not sell its products at the budgeted sales mix in December 20X2, as shown here:

Product	Units Sold	Actual Sales Mix	Budgeted Sales Mix
XV–1	1,600	0.32	0.25
FB–33	3,400	0.68	0.75
Total	5,000	1.00	1.00

The firm had sales mix variances for the period. Exhibit 17–15 computes the sales mix and sales quantity variances using a columnar form similar to those used in Chapters 15 and 16.

The left column in Exhibit 17–15 is the flexible budget for the actual total units sold with the *actual sales mixes* the firm experienced. The middle column is the flexible budget for the actual total units sold with the *budgeted sales mixes*. The right column is the master budget for the period.

Schmidt Machinery Company sold 1,600 units of XV–1 and 3,400 units of FB–33 in December. The actual sales mixes in the left column are 32 percent and 68 percent for XV–1 and FB–33, respectively.

The middle point in Exhibit 17–15 uses the number of units the firm would have sold had the total actual units sold matched the budgeted sales mix. Schmidt sold a total of 5,000 units. According to the budgeted sales mix, 25 percent of the total units sold would be XV–1. Had the firm sold the 5,000 units at the budgeted sales mix, the number of units of XV–1 sold would have been

$$5{,}000 \text{ units} \times 25 \text{ percent} = 1{,}250 \text{ units}$$

All three points use the same budgeted contribution margin per unit. Thus, the only difference between the left point and the middle point is in the sales mix. The left point uses the actual sales mix while the middle point uses the budgeted sales mix. The difference in total contribution margins between these two points results from the difference in their sales mixes, or the sales mix variance.

Exhibit 17–15	Sales Mix and Quantity Variances

SCHMIDT MACHINERY COMPANY
Sales Mix and Quantity Variances
For December 20X2

Scheme

Total units	Actual	Actual	Budget
Sales mix	*Actual*	*Budget*	Budget
Contribution margin	Budget	Budget	Budget

              Sales mix variance   Sales quantity variance

Flexible Budget with Actual Sales Mix	**Flexible Budget with Budgeted Sales Mix**	**Master Budget**
Total actual units of all products sold × *Actual* sales mix × Budgeted contribution margin per unit	Total **actual units** of all products sold × *Budgeted* sales mix × Budgeted contribution margin per unit	Total **budgeted units** of sales for all products × Budgeted sales mix × Budgeted contribution margin per unit

Product XV–1

$5{,}000 \times 0.32 \times \$350$	$5{,}000 \times 0.25 \times \$350$	$4{,}000 \times 0.25 \times \$350$
$= 1{,}600 \times \$350$	$= 1{,}250 \times \$350$	$= 1{,}000 \times \$350$
$= \$560{,}000$	$= \$437{,}500$	$= \$350{,}000$

          Sales mix variance   Sales quantity variance
        = $560,000 − $437,500   = $437,500 − $350,000
        = $122,500 F   = $87,500 F

               Sales volume variance
               = $560,000 − $350,000
               = $210,000 F

To verify: Sales volume variance
      = Sales mix variance + Sales quantity variance
      = $122,500 F   + $87,500 F
      = $210,000 F

(continued)

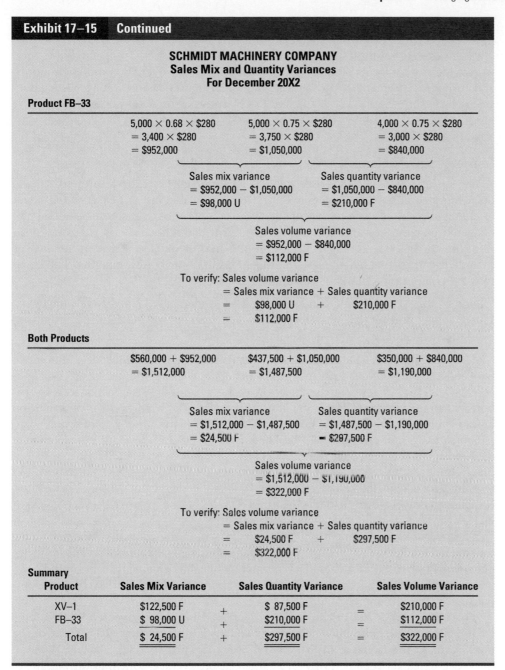

Exhibit 17–15   Continued

SCHMIDT MACHINERY COMPANY
Sales Mix and Quantity Variances
For December 20X2

Product FB–33

5,000 × 0.68 × $280	5,000 × 0.75 × $280	4,000 × 0.75 × $280
= 3,400 × $280	= 3,750 × $280	= 3,000 × $280
= $952,000	= $1,050,000	= $840,000

Sales mix variance
= $952,000 − $1,050,000
= $98,000 U

Sales quantity variance
= $1,050,000 − $840,000
= $210,000 F

Sales volume variance
= $952,000 − $840,000
= $112,000 F

To verify: Sales volume variance
= Sales mix variance + Sales quantity variance
= $98,000 U   + $210,000 F
= $112,000 F

Both Products

$560,000 + $952,000	$437,500 + $1,050,000	$350,000 + $840,000
= $1,512,000	= $1,487,500	= $1,190,000

Sales mix variance
= $1,512,000 − $1,487,500
= $24,500 F

Sales quantity variance
= $1,487,500 − $1,190,000
= $297,500 F

Sales volume variance
= $1,512,000 − $1,190,000
= $322,000 F

To verify: Sales volume variance
= Sales mix variance + Sales quantity variance
= $24,500 F   + $297,500 F
= $322,000 F

Summary

Product	Sales Mix Variance		Sales Quantity Variance		Sales Volume Variance
XV–1	$122,500 F	+	$ 87,500 F	=	$210,000 F
FB–33	$ 98,000 U	+	$210,000 F	=	$112,000 F
Total	$ 24,500 F	+	$297,500 F	=	$322,000 F

The difference between the middle point and the right point is in the total units of all products sold. The middle point uses the total actual units of all products sold, while the right point uses the total budgeted sale units of all products. Both points use the budgeted sales mix and the budgeted contribution margin per unit. The difference between these two points stems from the difference in the total units—a sales quantity variance.

The sum of the sales quantity variance and the sales mix variance, for each of the individual products and for the firm, should be the same as the sales volume variance. The summary of Exhibit 17–15 confirms this result.

MARKET SIZE AND MARKET SHARE VARIANCES

Two of the contributing factors to a sales quantity variance are changes in the total market size and the firm's share of the market. A *market size variance* measures the effect on the total contribution margin and the operating income of changes in the size of the total market for the firm's product. A *market share variance* assesses the

◀ LEARNING OBJECTIVE 6
Explain how market size and market share variances lead to sales quantity variance.

effect on the total contribution margin and the operating income of changes in a firm's proportion of the total market.

At the time Schmidt's accountant prepared its budget, it expected the total worldwide market for its products, XV–1 and FB–33, to be 40,000 units each month and to have 10 percent of the total market. The master budget data for December was reported in Exhibit 17–9. Exhibit 17–11 showed the actual operations for the month. Exhibit 17–13 reports that the firm has a favorable total sales quantity variance of $297,500.

Market Size Variance

Market size variance measures the effect of changes in the total market size on the firm's total contribution margin and operating income.

A **market size variance** measures the effect that changes in the total market have on a firm's total contribution margin and operating income. To capture the effect of changes in the size of the total market, the computation compares the actual and budgeted market sizes and assumes that the firm maintains exactly the same positions in all other factors as specified in the master budget. These other factors include the firm's market share, sales mix, and unit contribution margins. The equation for computing a market size variance is

$$\begin{matrix} \text{Market} \\ \text{size} \\ \text{variance} \end{matrix} = \begin{bmatrix} \text{Actual total} & \text{Budgeted total} \\ \text{units of the} & - \text{units of the} \\ \text{market} & \text{market} \end{bmatrix} \times \begin{matrix} \text{Budgeted} \\ \times \text{market} \\ \text{share} \end{matrix} \times \begin{matrix} \text{Weighted-average} \\ \text{budgeted contribution} \\ \text{margin per unit} \end{matrix}$$

The first term on the right side is the focus of the variance: the difference between the total actual size (in units) of the market and the anticipated or budgeted size. The last term in the equation is the weighted-average budgeted contribution margin per unit. The computation uses the weighted-average contribution margin of all the products the firm has in the same market, not the budgeted contribution margin of an individual product. This is because the market size variance deals with the market of all the products the firm has in the market. In our example, Schmidt budgeted to sell a combined total of 4,000 units of XV–1 and FB–33 to earn a total contribution margin of $1,190,000, as shown in Exhibit 17–9. Thus, the budgeted average contribution per unit is $297.50 for the period ($1,190,000 ÷ 4,000).

The budgeted total market is 40,000 units, of which the company expects to have a budgeted market share of 10 percent, or 4,000 units. The total market for December turned out to be 31,250 units. The market size has changed. In Exhibit 17–16 we show the calculation of the market size variance for Schmidt Machinery Company, $260,312.50 unfavorable.

The total market size of the industry decreased from the expected 40,000 units to 31,250. Because Schmidt Machinery Company expects to have 10 percent of the market share, the decrease in market size of 8,750 units (40,000 − 31,250) would have decreased its total sales by 875 units. At an average contribution margin of

Exhibit 17–16	Market Size and Market Share Variances

SCHMIDT MACHINERY COMPANY
Market Size and Share Variances
For December 20X2

Market Size Variance Calculation

(31,250 − 40,000) × 0.1 × $297.50 = $260,312.50 unfavorable

Market Share Variance Calculation

31,250 × (0.16 − 0.10) × $297.50 = $557,812.50 favorable

Reconciliation of the Market Size Variance, Market Share Variance, and Sales Quantity Variance

Market size variance	$260,312.50 unfavorable
Market share variance	$557,812.50 favorable
Sales quantity variance	$297,500.00 favorable

$297.50 per unit, the total decrease in unit sales would have decreased Schmidt's operating income by $260,312.50.

As the size of the total market for a firm's products changes, the total sales of the firm are likely to change with it. When the total market size for a firm's products expands, the total sales of the firm likely would increase. A firm that failed to increase its total sales in proportion to the increase in the total market is not keeping up with the market and is losing its marketing position.

Market Share Variance

A **market share variance** compares the firm's actual market share to its budgeted market share and measures the effect of changes in the firm's market share on its total contribution margin and operating income. To determine a market share variance, we need three items: the difference between the actual and the budgeted market shares of the firm, the total *actual market size*, and the weighted-average budgeted contribution margin per unit. Notice that the computation uses the *actual*, not budgeted, total market size and the *budgeted*, not actual, weighted-average contribution margin per unit. The product of these three factors—the difference in market shares, total actual market size, and weighted-average budget contribution margin per unit—is the market share variance. The equation is

$$\begin{array}{c}\text{Market}\\\text{share}\\\text{variance}\end{array} = \begin{bmatrix}\text{Actual}&\text{Budgeted}\\\text{market}-\text{market}\\\text{share}&\text{share}\end{bmatrix} \times \begin{array}{c}\text{Actual total}\\\text{units of the}\\\text{industry}\end{array} \times \begin{array}{c}\text{Weighted-average}\\\text{budgeted contribution}\\\text{margin per unit}\end{array}$$

In Exhibit 17–16 we show the calculation of the market share variance for Schmidt Machinery Company's December 20X2 operations.

Even though the total market for the industry has decreased to 31,250, Schmidt Machinery Company's total sales are higher than the budgeted sales for the period. As a result, its market share increases from the budgeted 10 percent to 16 percent (5,000 units ÷ 31,250 units = 16%). Given the actual total market size of 31,250, the increase in the market share of 6 percent would have increased Schmidt's total sales units by 1,875 units above the level expected in the budget. At a budgeted weighted-average contribution of $297.50 per unit, this increase in units would have increased its operating income by $557,812.50.

Together, the market size variance and market share variance account for the sales quantity variance of the period. Look at the bottom of Exhibit 17–16 to confirm this result. For December 20X2, Schmidt has an unfavorable market size variance of $260,312.50 and a favorable market share variance of $557,812.50. The total of these two variances is $297,500 favorable, the same as the sales quantity variance reported earlier.

In Exhibit 17–17 we calculate market size and market share variances using a columnar form. The left point, A, is the total budgeted contribution margin the firm would have earned from the units it actually sold. Seen from the perspective of the total market size of the industry, the total actual units sold by the firm is the product of the total actual market size of the industry and the actual market share of the firm:

$$31{,}250 \text{ units} \times 16 \text{ percent} = 5{,}000 \text{ units}$$

At the left point, the average budgeted contribution margin per unit is $297.50 and the total contribution margin from 5,000 units is $1,487,500.

The middle point, B, is the total budgeted contribution margin the firm would have earned had it maintained the budgeted market share. With total market size of 31,250 the firm would have sold 3,125 total units were the firm to maintain its budgeted market share of 10 percent. At the average budgeted contribution margin of $297.50 per unit, total contribution would have been $929,687.50. The difference between this point and point A is due entirely to the difference in market shares. The difference, $557,812.50, is a market share variance. The variance is favorable because the firm has an actual market share of 16 percent as opposed to only a 10 percent market share anticipated at the time of budgeting.

Market share variance compares the firm's actual market share to its budgeted market share and measures the effect of changes in the firm's market share on its total contribution margin and operating income.

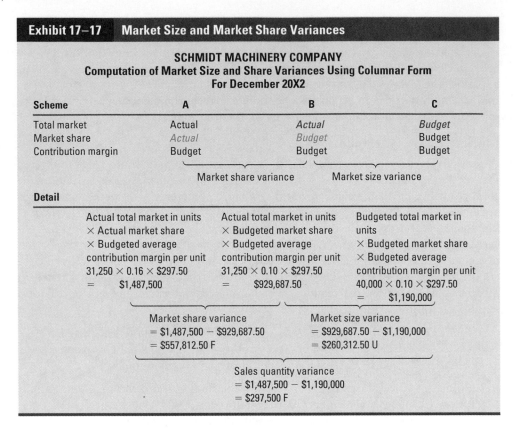

Exhibit 17–17   Market Size and Market Share Variances

SCHMIDT MACHINERY COMPANY
Computation of Market Size and Share Variances Using Columnar Form
For December 20X2

Scheme	A	B	C
Total market	Actual	*Actual*	*Budget*
Market share	*Actual*	*Budget*	Budget
Contribution margin	Budget	Budget	Budget

        Market share variance   Market size variance

Detail

Actual total market in units × Actual market share × Budgeted average contribution margin per unit	Actual total market in units × Budgeted market share × Budgeted average contribution margin per unit	Budgeted total market in units × Budgeted market share × Budgeted average contribution margin per unit
31,250 × 0.16 × $297.50	31,250 × 0.10 × $297.50	40,000 × 0.10 × $297.50
= $1,487,500	= $929,687.50	= $1,190,000

Market share variance
= $1,487,500 − $929,687.50
= $557,812.50 F

Market size variance
= $929,687.50 − $1,190,000
= $260,312.50 U

Sales quantity variance
= $1,487,500 − $1,190,000
= $297,500 F

The right point, C, is the master budget. The budgeted total unit sales here is the product of the budgeted market size and the budgeted market share:

$$40,000 \times 10 \text{ percent} = 4,000 \text{ units}$$

The only difference between the middle point, B, and the master budget, C, is in the total market size. The middle point uses the actual market size, while the right point uses the budgeted market size. The difference, therefore, is a market size variance, which is $260,312.50 in our example. The variance is unfavorable because the actual market size is smaller than the firm anticipated at the time it prepared the master budget for December 20X2.

MARKETING VARIANCES AND STRATEGIC MANAGEMENT

Businesses have as goals earning higher operating income and increasing their market shares through increasing either total sales or sales of higher-margin items. Firms fulfill these and other operating and strategic goals through sales activities. Sales variances, including sales price, sales volume, sales mix, sales quantity, market share, and market size variances, help managers in planning, monitoring, and assessing the effectiveness of sales activities in attaining budgeted goals. These variances can have tremendous impacts on the firm's strategic planning and implementation, in addition to being important inputs to the performance evaluations of managers and divisions.

Strategic Implications of a Sales Price Variance

A price change is a tactical action. A *tactical action* involves few organizational resources, is relatively easy to implement, and can be reversed in a relatively short time. McDonald's decrease of the price of its Big Mac to 99 cents and an airline's temporary reduction of round-trip airfare between Chicago and Paris to, say, $250 are tactical actions. Price decreases are tools that firms often use as competitive weapons to expand market shares, or to implement the strategy of converting the firm into a low-cost provider. Other firms may raise prices to implement a differentiation strategy.

Decreasing sales prices to secure higher sales volumes or market shares, however, can jeopardize the firm's profitability if the unfavorable sales price variance exceeds the favorable sales volume variance. Similarly, an increase in total quantity sold may not benefit a firm that sold low-margin items at the expense of high-margin products because the unfavorable sales mix variance is greater than the favorable sales quantity variance.

Firms need to take into consideration their current positions and the likely reactions of competitors before taking actions to change sales prices. An action such as a price change taken by a market leader is likely to bring immediate responses from competitors and a high probability of imitation of the action. For example, competitors usually follow immediately any reduction in airfares by other airlines. The result can be a decrease in total sales for all airlines with either no significant increase in the total number of passengers or no change in each airline's market share. An unfavorable market price variance experienced by a market leader is likely to be repeated as competitors cut prices. Unless accompanied by other actions, any gain in market shares by the market leader through price reductions is likely short-lived.

A favorable market price variance experienced by a market leader without meaningful deterioration in the firm's market share suggests a successful implementation of the tactical action.

An unfavorable market price variance experienced by a nonmarket leader without a significant gain in market shares suggests that the price-cutting action may be questionable.

A nonmarket leader with a meaningful gain in market share and an unfavorable market price variance needs to assess its ability to sustain the gained market share and the difference between the unfavorable sales price variance and the favorable market share variance. To the extent that the gained market share is sustainable and the unfavorable sales price variance is less than the favorable market share variance, the tactical action is a successful strategic implementation.

A favorable market price variance experienced by a nonmarket leader without a significant loss of market share may indicate that the market perceives the firm having a differentiated product and the firm could follow a differentiation strategy.

A firm needs to assess the difference between the favorable price variance and the unfavorable market share variance if it has a favorable market price variance with a significant loss of the firm's market share.

Strategic Implications of a Market Share Variance

A firm that has an unfavorable sales price variance may be following an appropriate strategy if it intends to build its market share because of the great potential of its products. A favorable market share variance is evidence of the success of such a strategy. In this instance, the firm may place less significance on the overall unfavorable contribution margin or operating income variance as long as it achieves a favorable market share variance.

Management should always be on the lookout for declines in the firm's market shares. A decrease in market shares should alert management to the erosion of the firm's competitive position and the encroachment of competitors. Ignoring declining market shares can lead to the eventual demise of the firm.

The wisdom of attaining a favorable market share variance at the expense of unfavorable sales price variances may be questionable if the products are in a mature market. The strategy is likely furtive or even devastating if these products are the firm's cash cows.

A firm implementing a differentiation strategy typically does not hold large shares of the markets it serves. The high profitability of its products, however, makes it very important for the firm to monitor its sales quantity and market share. A small change in sales quantity and market share can have a very significant impact on the firm's current and future operating income.

The primary product of Unifi, a North Carolina textile manufacturer, is textured polyester. Polyester's popularity peaked in the early 1970s. The total market decreased by more than 50 percent in 10 years, from a demand of over 1.4 billion pounds in 1975 to 650 million pounds in 1985.

Unifi's chairman, Allen Mebane, saw the shrinking demand for polyester as an opportunity to become a dominant player and spent heavily to purchase state-of-the-art equipment to improve Unifi productivity and product quality. Through its investments, Unifi became the low-cost high-quality producer in the industry and forced out many of its competitors. By 1994 the firm became the world's largest producer of textured polyester and had more than 70 percent of the U.S. market.

What about profit? Over a recent five-year period the firm earned an average annual return of 37 percent for its shareholders.

Source: Michael Hitt, R. D. Ireland, and R. E. Hoskisson, *Strategic Management* (St. Paul, MN: West Publishing, 1995), p. 100.

Strategic Implications of a Market Size Variance

Misdirected expansions undertaken during periods of declining market size could lead to overcapacities, decline in revenues, or financial distresses. Shrinking market sizes, however, do not necessarily mean downsizing as the experience of textile manufacturer Unifi demonstrates. Unifi has earned an average return of 37 percent for its shareholders despite a declining market for its product—textured polyester.

Unifi also shows that the market size for a product may not be rigidly defined or correctly perceived by the majority of the industry. Facing a declining market, Unifi explored and developed new uses for textured polyester in automobiles and home furnishings. As a result, Unifi's market size is larger than its competitors'. Indeed, we have abundant evidence of firms that took action to redefine and expand the market size of their products. Often, the results of such actions include high profitability enjoyed by these firms. McDonald's expansion in the early 1980s into Japan and Taiwan—countries where people seldom consumed beef products and hated cheese—redefined that firm's total market size. For many years, McDonald's franchises in Japan and Taiwan have been among the most profitable.

SUMMARY

Increasing global competition and rapid changes in technologies make it mandatory for management to be constantly alert to changes in the productivity of input resources as well as opportunities and changes in marketing. Management needs to be aware of levels and changes in the productive factors such as materials, workforces, energy, and processes. To manage marketing effectively, management needs to be fully informed on the effects of changes in selling prices, sales volumes, sale mixes, market sizes, and market shares on operations and the strategy of the firm. The effects of these changes on operating results need to be monitored so management can take appropriate actions at the earliest time.

Productivity is the ratio of output to input. Improvements in productivity enable a firm to do more with fewer resources. A productivity measure often is compared to the performance of prior periods, other firms, or a benchmark.

A partial productivity is the ratio of the output level attained to the amount of an input resource. The higher the ratio is, the better. An operational partial productivity is the required physical quantity of an input resource for the production of one unit of the output. A financial partial productivity is the number of units of output manufactured for each dollar of the input resource the firm spent. A financial partial productivity measure can be separated into changes due to productivity change, input price change, and output change. Productivity change is the difference between the actual and the expected quantity of input resources for the manufacturing of the output. The input price change accounts for the effects of differences in prices for the input resource between the actual price paid and the budgeted (or a benchmark) price, while the output change variance accounts for the change in cost due to changes in units of output.

A total productivity measures the relationship between the output attained and the total input costs. This measure usually is a financial productivity.

The same concepts for measuring productivity as in manufacturing firms are also applicable to service industries and not-for-profit organizations. Some of the limitations of measuring productivity in service industries and not-for-profit organizations are imprecise output measures, lack of definite relationships between output and input resources, and the absence of revenue for not-for-profit organizations.

The sales volume variance accounts for the difference in contribution margins or operating incomes between the flexible budget amount and the master (static) budget. For a single product firm, the sales volume variance is the product of the standard contribution margin per unit of product and the difference between the actual units sold and the budgeted sales units. Sale volume variances of firms with multiple products need to be analyzed further into sales mix and sales quantity variances. The product's sales mix variance is the product of three elements: (1) the difference between the actual sales mix and the budget sales mix, with sales mix defined as the ratio of the unit of the product to the total units of all products, (2) the total units of all products sold during the period, and (3) the standard contribution margin of the product. The sales quantity variance of a product is the product of three elements: (1) the difference between the actual and the budgeted total units of the firm, (2) the budget sales mix of the product, and (3) the standard contribution margin of the product.

A sales mix variance measures the effect of deviation of the actual from the budgeted mixtures. The sales mix variance of a product is favorable if the firm sells more than the budgeted proportion of the product. A sales quantity variance assesses the effect on total contribution margin and operating income when the total actual units sold deviates from the budgeted total units.

A sales quantity variance can be separated further into the market size and the market share variances. The market size variance assesses the effect on the firm's total contribution margin and operating income of changes in the total market size of the industry. It is determined by the product of three factors: (1) the difference between the actual and the budgeted total units of the market, (2) the budgeted market share of the firm, and (3) the weighted-average budgeted contribution margin per unit. The market size variance is favorable if the actual total market size is greater than the expected market size at the time the master budget was prepared. The market share variance measures the effect of changes in the firm's market share on operating income. The market share is the product of three elements: (1) the actual total units of the market, (2) the difference between the actual and the budgeted market share of the firm, and (3) the average budgeted standard contribution margin per unit.

KEY TERMS

Financial productivity   682

Market share variance   701

Market size variance   700

Operational productivity   682

Partial productivity   682

Productivity   682

Sales mix   694

Sales mix variance   695

Sales quantity variance   695

Total productivity   687

SELF-STUDY PROBLEMS

(For solutions, please turn to the end of the chapter.)

1.   Productivity Variances

Carlson Automotive Company manufactures fuel-injection systems. It manufactured and sold 60,000 units in 20X3 and 64,000 units in 20X4 at $25 per unit. In 20X3 the firm used 75,000 pounds of alloy TPX–45 at $7.20 per pound and spent 10,000 direct labor-hours at an hourly wage rate of $30. In 20X4 the firm used 89,600 pounds of alloy TPX–45 at $6.80 per pound and spent 10,847 direct labor-hours at an hourly wage rate of $32. The total amount for all other expenses remains the same at $450,000 each year. Jerry Olson, CEO, was disappointed that while the total sales increased, the $195,616 operating income earned in 20X4 is only 93 percent of the amount earned in 20X3, which was $210,000.

Required   Analyze the

1.   Operational partial productivity of the direct material and direct labor for both 20X3 and 20X4.
2.   Financial partial productivity of the direct material and direct labor for both 20X3 and 20X4.
3.   Detailed compositions of financial partial productivity.
4.   Total productivity for 20X3 and 20X4 as measured in both units and sales dollars.

2.   Sales Variance

Springwater Brewery has two main products—premium and regular ale. Its operating results and master budget for 20X2 (000 omitted) are

	Operating Results of 20X2			Master Budget for 20X2		
	Premium	**Regular**	**Total**	**Premium**	**Regular**	**Total**
Barrels	180	540	720	240	360	600
Sales	$28,800	$62,100	$90,900	$36,000	$43,200	$79,200
Variable expenses	16,200	40,500	56,700	21,600	27,000	48,600
Contribution margin	$12,600	$21,600	$34,200	$14,400	$16,200	$30,600
Fixed expenses	10,000	5,000	15,000	10,000	5,000	15,000
Operating income	$ 2,600	$16,600	$19,200	$ 4,400	$11,200	$15,600

Pam Kuder, CEO, estimated at the time she prepared the master budget that total industry sales would be 1,500,000 barrels during the period. After the year was over Mark Goldfeder, the controller, reported that total industry sales were 1,600,000 barrels.

Required   Calculate the

1.   Selling price variances for the period for each of the products and for the firm.
2.   Sales volume variances for the period for each of the products and for the firm.
3.   Sales quantity variances for the firm and for each of the products.
4.   Sales mix variances for the period for each of the products and for the firm.
5.   The sum of the sales quantity variance and sales mix variance and verify that this total equals the sales volume variance.
6.   Market size variances.
7.   Market share variances.
8.   The sum of market size variance and market share variance and verify that this total equals the sales quantity variance.

QUESTIONS

17–1 What is productivity?

17–2 Discuss why improving productivity is important for a firm that follows a strategy of being the cost leader.

17–3 List benchmarks or criteria that often are used in assessing productivity and discuss their advantages and disadvantages.

17–4 What is an operational productivity? A financial productivity?

17–5 What is a partial productivity? A total productivity?

17–6 "A financial productivity measure contains more information than an operational productivity measure does." Do you agree?

17–7 "A total productivity measure encompasses all partial productivity measures." Do you agree?

17–8 "Partial productivity measures need to be calculated only for value-added activities." Do you agree?

17–9 Why do manufacturing personnel prefer operational productivity measures over financial productivity measures?

17–10 "An activity productivity measure such as machine-hour productivity is more important in a JIT environment than in a non-JIT environment." Do you agree?

17–11 List important measurements for assessing marketing effectiveness.

17–12 What are components of sales variances?

17–13 Distinguish between a *sales price variance* and a *sales volume variance*.

17–14 What is the difference between a *sales quantity variance* and a *sales volume variance*?

17–15 "As long as a firm sells more units than the number of units specified in the master budget, the firm will not have an unfavorable sales volume variance." Do you agree? Why?

17–16 What are the relationships among a selling price variance, a sales mix variance, a sales quantity variance, and a sales volume variance?

17–17 Distinguish between a *market size variance* and a *market share variance*.

17–18 "A favorable sales quantity variance indicates that the marketing manager has done a good job." Do you agree? Can you give an example where a market size variance or market share variance rendered an opposite indication than the sales quantity variance suggested?

17–19 What are the relationships between a market size variance, a market share variance, a sales quantity variance, and a sales volume variance?

17–20 An improvement in earnings growth can be achieved at the expense of market shares (an unfavorable market share variance). Do you agree?

PROBLEMS

17–21 TRUE OR FALSE? Which of the following statements is true?

a. The lower the partial productivity ratio, the greater the productivity.

b. Productivity has improved when the partial productivity increased.

c. Prices of inputs are incorporated in the partial productivity ratio.

d. The partial productivity ratio measures the number of outputs produced per multiple input.

17–22 OPERATIONAL PARTIAL PRODUCTIVITY Darwin, Inc., provided the following information for a production factor:

Budgeted production	10,000 units
Actual production	9,500 units
Budgeted input	9,750 gallons
Actual input	8,950 gallons

What is the operational partial productivity ratio of the production factor?

  a. 0.97 unit per gallon.

  b. 1.02 units per gallon.

  c. 1.06 units per gallon.

  d. 1.12 units per gallon.

  e. none of the above.

17–23 FINANCIAL PARTIAL PRODUCTIVITY HFD Corporation makes small parts from steel alloy sheets. HFD's management has some ability to substitute direct materials for direct manufacturing labor. If workers cut the steel carefully, HFD can manufacture more parts out of a metal sheet, but this requires more direct manufacturing labor-hours. Alternatively, HFD can use fewer direct manufacturing labor-hours if it is willing to tolerate more waste of direct materials. HFD provides this information for the years 20X1 and 20X2:

	20X1	20X2
Output units	400,000	486,000
Direct manufacturing labor-hours used	10,000	13,500
Wages per hour	$26	$25
Direct materials used	160 tons	180 tons
Direct materials cost per ton	$3,375	$3,125

Required Carry four digits after the decimal point in all your computations.

  1. Compute for 20X1 and 20X2 the financial partial productivity for both input manufacturing factors.

  2. Calculate HFD's total productivity in units for 20X1 and 20X2.

  3. Evaluate management's decision in 20X2 to substitute one production factor for another.

17–24 OPERATIONAL PARTIAL PRODUCTIVITY Frisen Communication Inc. manufactures a scrambling device for cellular telephones. The main component of the scrambling device is a very delicate part, CSU10. Unless handled very carefully during manufacturing, CSU10 is easily damaged. Once damaged, the part has to be discarded. Only skilled laborers are hired to manufacture and install CSU10; however, damages still occur. Robotic instruments process all other parts. The operating data of Frisen Communication Inc. for the years 20X1 and 20X0:

	20X1	20X0
Units manufactured	500,000	600,000
Number of CSU10 used	800,000	825,000
Direct labor-hours spent	150,000	200,000
Cost of CSU10 per unit	$156	$135
Direct labor wage rate per hour	$56	$63

Required

  1. Compute the operational partial productivity ratios for 20X0 and 20X1.

2. On the basis of the operational partial productivity you computed, what conclusions can you draw on the productivity of the firm in 20X1 relative to 20X0?

17–25 FINANCIAL PARTIAL PRODUCTIVITY Use the data for Frisen Communication Inc. in problem 17–24 to do the required items.

Required

1. Compute the financial partial productivity ratios for 20X0 and 20X1.

2. On the basis of the financial partial productivity you computed, what conclusions can you draw on the productivity of the firm in 20X1 relative to 20X0?

3. Separate the changes in the financial partial productivity ratios from 20X0 to 20X1 into productivity changes, input price changes, and output changes.

4. Is there any additional insight on the relative productivity between 20X0 and 20X1 from the detailed information provided by the separations of the change of the financial partial productivity ratios?

17–26 TOTAL PRODUCTIVITY Use the data for Frisen Communication Inc. in problem 17–24 to do the required items.

Required

1. Compute the total productivity ratios for 20X0 and 20X1.

2. On the basis of the total productivity you computed, what conclusions can you draw on the productivity of the firm in 20X1 relative to 20X0?

17–27 OPERATIONAL AND FINANCIAL PARTIAL PRODUCTIVITY In the fourth quarter of 20X1 Simpson Company embarked on a major drive to improve productivity. The drive included redesigned products, reengineered manufacturing processes, and productivity improvement courses. The drive was completed in the last quarter of 20X2. The controller's office has gathered the following year-end data for the assessment of the drive.

	20X1	20X2
Units manufactured and sold	15,000	18,000
Selling price of the product	$40	$40
Materials used (pounds)	12,000	12,600
Cost per pound of materials	$8	$10
Labor-hours	6,000	5,000
Hourly wage rate	$20	$25
Power (kwh)	1,000	2,000
Cost of power per kwh	$2	$2

Required

1. Prepare a summary contribution-approach income statement for each year and calculate the total change in profits.

2. Compute the operational partial productivity ratios for each of the production factors for 20X1 and 20X2.

3. Compute the financial partial productivity ratios for each of the production factors for 20X1 and 20X2.

4. On the basis of the operational and financial partial productivity you computed, what conclusions can you draw on the productivity of the firm in 20X2 relative to 20X1?

5. Separate the changes in the financial partial productivity ratios from 20X1 to 20X2 into productivity changes, input price changes, and output changes.

6. Discuss additional insights on the relative productivity between 20X1 and 20X2 from the detailed information provided by the separations of the change in the financial partial productivity ratios.

17–28 OPERATIONAL AND FINANCIAL PARTIAL PRODUCTIVITY Varceles Design has two alternative approaches, identified as MF and LI, to produce next year's fashion for men. The firm expects the total demand to be 20,000 suits. Varceles can produce the same output with either approach using these combinations of input resources:

	Materials (yds.)	Labor (hrs.)
MF	300,000	100,000
LI	200,000	120,000

The cost of materials is $8 per yard; the cost of labor is $25 per hour.

Required

1. Compute the partial operational productivity ratios for each alternative production approach. Which approach would you select based on the partial operational productivity ratios?

2. Calculate the partial financial productivity ratios for each alternative production approach. Which approach would you select based on the partial financial productivity ratios?

3. Compute the total productivity ratios for each alternative production approach. Which approach would you select based on the total productivity ratios?

Service

17–29 OPERATIONAL PARTIAL PRODUCTIVITY Software Solution (SOS) helps subscribers to solve software problems. All transactions are done over the telephone. Most of the firm's software engineers are recent graduates. For the year 20X2, 10 engineers handled 100,000 calls. The average yearly salary for software engineers was $45,000.

Starting in 20X3 the firm retained and hired only software engineers with at least two years' experience. SOS raised the engineers' salary to $60,000 per year. In 20X3, eight engineers handled 108,000 calls.

Required

1. Calculate the operational partial productivity for both years.

2. Calculate the financial partial productivity for both years.

3. Did the firm make the right decision in hiring only software engineers with at least two years' experience?

4. List some other factors that need to be considered in assessing the decision.

Strategy

17–30 DIRECT LABOR RATE AND EFFICIENCY VARIANCES, PRODUCTIVITY MEASURES, AND STANDARD COSTS Textron Manufacturing Inc. assembles industrial testing instruments. The firm has two departments: assembly and testing. Operating data for 20X0 and 20X1 are

	20X0	20X1
Assembly department:		
Actual direct labor-hours per instrument	25	20
Actual wage rate per hour	$30	$36
Standard direct labor-hours per instrument	24	21
Standard wage rate per hour	$28	$35
Testing department:		
Actual direct labor-hours per instrument	12	10
Actual wage rate per hour	$20	$24
Standard direct labor-hours per instrument	14	11
Standard wage rate per hour	$21	$25

The firm assembled and tested 20,000 instruments in both 20X0 and 20X1.

Required

1. Calculate the direct labor rate and efficiency variances for both years at both departments.

2. Compute the direct labor operational partial productivities in both years for both departments.

3. Determine the financial partial productivity for both departments for both years.

4. Compare your answers for requirements 2 and 3. Comment on your results.

5. How do the productivity measures differ from the variance analysis? Do they offer different perspectives for strategic decisions of the firm?

17–31 **PRODUCTIVITY AND ETHICS**   Janice Interiors installs custom interiors for luxury mobile homes. In its most recent negotiation with the union, the firm proposed to share equally productivity gains in direct labor. In return the union agreed not to demand wage increases. Most union members, however, are very skeptical about the honesty of the management in calculating the productivity measures. Nevertheless, union members voted to give the program a try. Kim Tomas, the management accountant responsible for determining productivity measures, collected these data at the end of 20X2:

Ethics

	20X2	20X1
Number of installations	560	500
Direct labor-hours	112,000	99,000

Steve Janice, the CEO, is very anxious to demonstrate the firm's good intentions by showing the labor union a positive result. He suggests to Tomas that some of the direct labor-hours are actually indirect. He believes that the hours spent on details are indirect because these hours cannot be allocated to specific types of work. Following his suggestion, Tomas reclassifies 12,000 hours as indirect labor.

Required

1. Evaluate whether Janice's suggestion to reclassify some of the direct labor-hours as indirect labor is ethical.

2. Would it be ethical for Tomas to modify his calculations?

17–32 **MARKET SIZE, MARKET SHARE, WORKING BACKWARD**   Triple Delight's sales forecast for 20X1 estimated that the firm would sell three cheeseburgers and one fishwich for every four hamburgers sold. The following data were culled from its operation analyses for 20X1:

Total operating income variance:	Hamburger	$18,000	Unfavorable
	Cheeseburger	50,000	Favorable
	Fishwich	10,000	Unfavorable
Sales quantity variance:	Hamburger	14,000	Favorable
	Cheeseburger	15,000	Favorable
	Fishwich	?	
Sales mix variance:	Hamburger	2,240	Unfavorable
	Cheeseburger	4,800	Unfavorable
	Fishwich	1,600	Favorable
Fixed costs variances:		—0—	
Market share variance:		$ 96,000	Unfavorable
Market size variance:		126,000	Favorable
Change in market share:		4%	
Fixed cost flexible budget variance:		—0—	

The estimated total volume for the fast-food industry in the region was 2,500,000 units. Industry statistics compiled at the end of 20X1 showed the total units sold to be 4,000,000 units.

Required Determine the

1. Budget weighted-average contribution margin.
2. Budget and actual market shares.
3. Budget and actual total units of sales.
4. Sales quantity variances for fishwich.
5. Budget contribution margin of each of the products.
6. Actual sales mix of each of the products.
7. Budget and actual sales for each of the products.

17–33 FLEXIBLE BUDGET, SALES VOLUME, SALES MIX, AND SALES QUANTITY VARIANCES Melinda Company has two products code named A and B. Melinda's budget for August 20X2 is

	Product A	Product B	Total
Master Budget			
Sale	$200,000	$300,000	$500,000
Variable costs	120,000	150,000	270,000
Contribution margin	$ 80,000	$150,000	$230,000
Fixed costs	100,000	90,000	190,000
Operating income	$ (20,000)	$ 60,000	$ 40,000
Selling price per unit	$100	$50	

On September 1, these operating results for August were reported:

	Product A	Product B	Total
Operating Results			
Sale	$180,000	$320,000	$500,000
Variable costs	120,000	140,000	260,000
Contribution margin	$ 60,000	$180,000	$240,000
Fixed costs	100,000	90,000	190,000
Operating income	$ (40,000)	$ 90,000	$ 50,000
Units sold	1,900	5,000	

Required Determine the following variances in contribution margins:

	Product A	Product B
Flexible budget variance	_____	_____
Sales volume variance	_____	_____
Sales quantity variance	_____	_____
Sales mix variance	_____	_____

17–34 FLEXIBLE BUDGET, SALES VOLUME, SALES MIX, AND SALES QUANTITY VARIANCES Jerry Tidwell, CEO and a major stockholder of the Tidwell Company, was not very happy with its operating results in 20X0. Tidwell Company manufactures two environmentally friendly industrial cleaning machines used primarily in automobile repair shops, gas stations, and auto dealerships. The master budget and operating results of the year (000s omitted except for the selling price per unit) are

	Master Budget			Actual Result		
	SK–100	SK–50	Total	SK–100	SK–50	Total
Sales	$100,000	$50,000	$150,000	$90,000	$60,000	$150,000
Variable costs	50,000	20,000	70,000	50,000	22,000	72,000
Contribution margin	$ 50,000	$30,000	$ 80,000	$40,000	$38,000	$ 78,000
Fixed costs	20,000	20,000	40,000	30,000	20,000	50,000
Operating income	$ 30,000	$10,000	$ 40,000	$10,000	$18,000	$ 28,000
Unit selling price	$ 100	$ 50				
Units sold				900	1,200	

Required

1. Compute the flexible budget variance, sales volume variance, sales quantity variance, and sales mix variance for each of the products and for the firm.

2. Explain to Jerry Tidwell the implications of the variances you just computed on planning and control of operations.

17-35 MARKET SIZE, MARKET SHARE, AND SALES QUANTITY VARIANCES, SINGLE PRODUCT Prolite Company manufactures one product. Its budget and operating results for 20X0 are

	Budgeted	Actual
Units sold	90,000	100,000
Unit contribution margin	$ 8.00	$10.00
Unit selling price	$20.00	$21.00

Industry volume was estimated to be 1,500,000 units at the time the budget was prepared. Actual industry volume for the period was 2,000,000 units.

Required

1. What is the market size variance?
2. What is the market share variance?
3. What is the sales quantity variance?

17-36 MARKET SIZE, MARKET SHARE VARIANCES Lau & Lau, Ltd., of Hong Kong manufactures two products that sell to the same market. Its budget and operating results for 20X0 are

	Budgeted	Actual
Unit sales		
Product A	30,000	35,000
Product B	60,000	65,000
Unit contribution margin		
Product A	$ 4.00	$ 3.00
Product B	$10.00	$12.00
Unit selling price		
Product A	$10.00	$12.00
Product B	$25.00	$24.00

Industry volume was estimated to be 1,500,000 units at the time the budget was prepared. Actual industry volume for the period was 2,000,000 units.

Required

1. What is the budgeted average unit contribution margin?
2. What is the sales volume contribution margin variance for each product?
3. What is the sales mix contribution margin variance for each product?
4. What is the sales quantity contribution margin variance for each product?
5. What is the market size contribution margin variance?
6. What is the market share contribution margin variance?
7. What is the total flexible budget contribution margin variance?
8. What is the total variable cost price variance if the total contribution margin price variance is $50,000 favorable?
9. What is the total variable cost efficiency variance if the total contribution margin price variance is $50,000 favorable?

17-37 **SALES MIX AND VOLUME VARIANCES**   CompuWorld sells two RISC chips to small machine tool manufacturers: R66 and R100. Pertinent data for 20X0:

	Budgeted		Actual	
	R66	**R100**	**R66**	**R100**
Selling price per chip	$50	$160	$55	$155
Variable cost per chip	40	90	43	95
Contribution margin	$10	$ 70	$12	$ 60
Fixed cost per chip	6	30	5	25
Operating income	$ 4	40	$ 7	$ 35
Sales in units	1,200	400	1,000	1,000

Required

1. What is the R66 sales quantity variance?
    a. $ 400 F
    b. $1,000 F
    c. $1,200 F
    d. $3,000 F
    e. $3,600 F

2. What is the R100 sales mix variance?
    a. $20,000 F
    b. $30,000 F
    c. $35,000 F
    d. $40,000 F
    e. $70,000 F

3. What is the total sales volume variance?
    a. $10,000 F
    b. $12,400 F
    c. $13,000 F
    d. $22,000 F
    e. $40,000 F

17-38 **MARKET SHARE, MARKET SIZE, AND SALES VOLUME VARIANCES**
C. W. McCall sells a gold-plated souvenir mug; it expects to sell 1,600 units in 20X0 for $45 each to earn a $25 contribution margin per unit. Janice McCall, president, expects the total market to be 32,000 units for the year. In 20X0, the local college won the national hockey championship and the total market was 100,000 units and C. W. McCall sold 3,000 at $75 each. The variable cost to the firm is $40 per unit.

Required

1. What is the market share variance?
    a. $ 8,000 U
    b. $11,200 U
    c. $40,000 U
    d. $50,000 U
    e. $70,000 U

2. What is the market size variance?
    a. $ 51,000 F
    b. $ 68,000 F
    c. $ 71,400 F
    d. $ 85,000 F
    e. $119,000 F

3. What is the sales volume variance for C. W. McCall?
    a. $ 35,000 F
    b. $ 49,000 F

c. $ 51,000 F
d. $ 85,000 F
e. $135,000 F

17–39 SALES VOLUME, SALES QUANTITY, AND SALES MIX VARIANCES The
Varner Performing Arts Center has a capacity of 7,500 seats: 2,000 center
seats, 2,500 side seats, and 3,000 balcony seats. The budgeted and actual
tickets sold for a Broadway musical show are

Service

	Ticket Price	Budgeted Seats Sold	Actual Seats Sold
Center	$60	80%	95%
Side	50	90	85
Balcony	40	85	75

The actual ticket prices are the same as budgeted. Once a show is
booked, there is no variable cost relating to the total number in
attendance.

Required Compute for the show

1. The budgeted and actual sales mix percentages for different types
   of seats.
2. The budgeted average contribution margin per seat.
3. The total sales quantity variance and the total sales mix variance.
4. The total sales volume variance.

17–40 SALES VOLUME, SALES QUANTITY, AND SALES MIX VARIANCES I Can't
Believe It's Gelatin operates several stores in a major metropolitan city
and its suburbs. Its budget and operating data for 20X0 follow:

	Budgeted Data for 20X0			Actual Operating Results in 20X0		
Flavor	Gallons	Selling Price per Gallon	Variable Costs per Gallon	Gallons	Selling Price per Gallon	Variable Costs per Gallon
Vanilla	250,000	$1.20	$0.50	180,000	$1.00	$0.45
Chocolate	300,000	1.50	0.60	270,000	1.35	0.50
Strawberry	200,000	1.80	0.70	330,000	2.00	0.75
Anchovy	50,000	2.50	1.00	180,000	3.00	1.20

Required

1. Compute for the individual flavors and total sold:
   a. Sales volume variances.
   b. Sales mix variances.
   c. Sales quantity variances.
2. Assess the operation of 20X0 based on your analyses.

17–41 MARKET SIZE AND MARKET SHARE VARIANCES Use the data in
problem 17–40 for I Can't Believe It's Gelatin. The total market for ice
creams, yogurt, and gelatin was expected to be 10 million gallons. The
industry group for the area reported that the gallons sold for the year
totaled 9,600,000.

Required Compute the market size and market share variances for I
Can't Believe It's Gelatin.

**17–42 SALES VOLUME, SALES QUANTITY, AND SALES MIX VARIANCES;
WORKING BACKWARD** DOA Alive is a group of aspiring musicians,
actors, and actresses that perform in theaters and dinner clubs. It has two

Service

Strategy

shows: matinee and evening. These operating data pertain to the month of July:

Master Budget Data
Total operating income	$10,000
Total monthly fixed cost	$39,200
Total number of shows	100
Contribution margin per show: matinee	$240
evening	$600

Actual Operating Results
Total sales quantity variance	$4,920 U

The actual matinees were 150 percent of the evening shows.

Required

1. Calculate for each type of show and the total:
   a. Sales mix variances.
   b. Sales quantity variances.
   c. Sales volume variances.
2. What strategic conclusions can you draw from the variances?

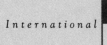

International

Service

17–43 MARKET SIZE AND SHARE VARIANCES   TransPacific Airlines (TPA) budgeted 80 million passenger-miles, or 5 percent of the total market for the route, for the year just completed at a contribution margin of 40 cents per mile. The budgeted variable cost is 12 cents per mile.

The operating data for the year show that TPA flew 69.12 million passenger-miles with an average price of 48 cents per passenger-mile. The unexpected financial crises of several countries in the region decreased the total miles flown by all airlines by 10 percent. There is no flexible budget variance for all costs.

Required   Assess for the firm the effects of the price, sales volume, market size, and market share on its operating results for the year.

17–44 SMALL BUSINESS MARKET SIZE AND SHARE VARIANCES   Diane's Designs is a small business run out of the house of its owner. For the past six months, the company has been selling two products, welcome signs and birdhouse signs. The owner has become concerned about the market effectiveness of the company. The master budget and actual results for the month of March 19X9 are:

Master Budget

	Welcome Signs	Birdhouses	Total
Units	50	25	75
Sales	$1,000	$250	$1,250
Variable costs	900	120	1,020
Contribution margin	$ 100	$130	$ 230
Fixed costs	75	75	150
Operating income	$ 25	$ 55	$ 80

Actual Results

	Welcome Signs	Birdhouses	Total
Units	45	35	80
Sales	$ 675	$420	$1,095
Variable costs	580	270	850
Contribution margin	$ 95	$150	$ 245
Fixed costs	75	75	150
Operating income	$ 20	$ 75	$ 95

The industry totals for welcome signs for the last six months are 3,000 budgeted and 2,550 actual.

Required

1. Show a comparison of Diane's Designs' market shares.
2. What is the market share variance?
3. What is the market size variance?
4. Explain possible reasons for these variances.
5. How might Diane's Designs improve in the future?

(Contributed by Stacy Armstrong)

SOLUTIONS TO SELF-STUDY PROBLEMS

1. Productivity Variances

1. Operational partial productivity

	20X3			20X4		
	Output	Input Resource Used	Partial Productivity	Output	Input Resource Used	Partial Productivity
TPX–45	60,000 ÷	75,000 =	0.8	64,000 ÷	89,600 =	0.7143
Direct labor	60,000 ÷	10,000 =	6.0	64,000 ÷	10,847 =	5.9002

2. Financial partial productivity

	20X3			20X4		
	Units of Output	Cost of Input Resource Used	Partial Productivity	Units of Output	Cost of Input Resource Used	Partial Productivity
TPX–45	60,000 ÷	$540,000 =	0.1111	64,000 ÷	$609,280 =	0.105
Direct labor	60,000 ÷	300,000 =	0.2	64,000 ÷	$347,104 =	0.1844

3. Separation of financial partial productivity

	(A) 20X4 Output with 20X4 Productivity at 20X4 Input Costs	(B) 20X4 Output with 20X3 Productivity at 20X4 Input Costs	(C) 20X4 Output with 20X3 Productivity at 20X3 Input Costs	(D) 20X3 Output with 20X3 Productivity at 20X3 Input Costs
Direct materials	64,000/$609,280 = 0.105	64,000/$544,000 = 0.1176	64,000/$576,000 = 0.1111	60,000/$540,000 = 0.1111
Direct labor	64,000/$347,104 = 0.1844	64,000/$341,333 = 0.1875	64,000/$320,000 = 0.2	60,000/$300,000 = 0.2
Direct materials	Productivity change 0.105 − 0.1176 = 0.0126 U	Input price change 0.1176 − 0.1111 = 0.0065 F	Output change 0.1111 − 0.1111 − 0	
Direct labor	0.1844 − 0.1875 = 0.0031 U	0.1875 − 0.2 = 0.0125 U	0.2 − 0.2 = 0	

Summary of result

	Productivity Change	Input Price Change	Total Change	Change as Percent of 20X3 Productivity		
				Productivity Change	Input Price Change	Total Change
Direct materials:						
TPX–45	0.0126 U	0.0065 F	0.0061 U	11.34% U	5.85% F	5.49% U
Direct labor	0.0031 U	0.0125 U	0.0156 U	1.55% U	6.25% U	7.8% U

4. Total productivity
   Total productivity in units

	20X3	20X4
(a) Total units manufactured	60,000	64,000
(b) Total variable manufacturing costs incurred	$840,000	$956,384
(c) Total productivity (a) ÷ (b)	0.071429	0.066919
(d) Decrease in productivity	0.071429 − 0.066919 =	0.00451

Total productivity in sales dollars

	20X3	20X4
(a) Total sales	$1,500,000	$1,600,000
(b) Total variable manufacturing costs incurred	$840,000	$956,384
(c) Total productivity (a) ÷ (b)	$1.7857	$1.6730
(d) Decrease in productivity	$1.7857 − $1.6730 =	$0.1127

2. Sales Variance

1. Selling price variances (in 000)

Flexible budget sales:

	Master Budget for 20X2		Budgeted Selling Price Per Unit		Total Units Sold in 20X2		Flexible Budget Sales
	Total Sales	Units					
Premium	$36,000 ÷	240 =	$150	×	180	=	$27,000
Regular	$43,200 ÷	360 =	$120	×	540	=	$64,800

	Premium			Regular		
	Actual	Flexible Budget	Selling Price Variance	Actual	Flexible Budget	Selling Price Variance
Barrels	180	180		540	540	
Sales	$28,800	$27,000	$1,800 F	$62,100	$64,800	$ 2,700 U

Total selling price variance of the firm = $1,800 F + $2,700 U = $900 U

2. Sales volume variances for the period for each of the products and for the firm.

Flexible budget variable expenses:

	Master Budget for 20X2		Budgeted Variable Expenses per Unit		Total Units Sold in 20X2		Flexible Budget Variable Expenses
	Total Variable Expenses	Number of Units					
Premium	$21,600 ÷	240 =	$90	×	180	=	$16,200
Regular	$27,000 ÷	360 =	$75	×	540	=	$40,500

	Premium			Regular		
	Flexible Budget	Master Budget	Sales Volume Variance	Flexible Budget	Master Budget	Sales Volume Variance
Barrels	180	240		540	360	
Sales	$27,000	$36,000		$64,800	$43,200	
Variable expenses	16,200	21,600		40,500	27,000	
Contribution margin	$10,800	$14,400	$3,600 U	$24,300	$16,200	$8,100 F
Fixed expenses	10,000	10,000	—	5,000	5,000	—
Operating income	$ 800	$ 4,400	$3,600 U	$19,300	$11,200	$8,100 F

Total sales volume variance of the firm = $3,600 U + $8,100 F = $4,500 F

3. Sales quantity variances for the firm and for each of the products. (See below.)

4. Sales mix variances for the period for each of the products and for the firm (000 omitted).

   Calculation for sales mixes:

	Budgeted		Actual	
	Total Sales in Units	**Sales Mix**	**Total Sales in Units**	**Sales Mix**
Premium	240	0.40	180	0.25
Regular	360	0.60	540	0.75
Total	600	1.00	720	1.00

Flexible Budget		**Master Budget**
Total actual units of all products sold × Actual sales mix × Standard contribution margin per unit	Total actual units of all products sold × Budgeted sales mix × Standard contribution margin per unit	Total budgeted units of sales for all products × Budgeted sales mix × Standard contribution margin per unit

Premium

$720 \times 0.25 \times \$60 = \$10,800$ $\quad 720 \times 0.40 \times \$60 = \$17,280$ $\quad 600 \times 0.40 \times \$60 - \$14,400$

Sales mix variance = $6,480 U

Sales quantity variance = $2,880 F

Sales volume variance
= $10,800 − $14,400
= $3,600 U

To verify: Sales volume variance
= Sales mix variance + Sales quantity variance
= $6,480 U   + $2,880 F
= $3,600 U

Regular

$720 \times 0.75 \times \$45 = \$24,300$ $\quad 720 \times 0.60 \times \$45 = \$19,440$ $\quad 600 \times 0.60 \times \$45 = \$16,200$

Sales mix variance = $4,860 F

Sales quantity variance = $3,240 F

Sales volume variance
= $24,300 − $16,200
= $8,100 F

To verify: Sales volume variance
= Sales mix variance + Sales quantity variance
= $4,860 F   + $3,240 F
= $8,100 F

Total

Sales mix variance   = $6,480 U + $4,860 F = $1,620 U
Sales quantity variance = $2,880 U + $3,240 F = $6,120 F

5. Verification

	Sales mix variance	+ Sales quantity variance	=	Sales volume variance
Premium	$6,480 U	$2,880 F		$3,600 U
Regular	$4,860 F	$3,240 F		$8,100 F
Total	$1,620 U	$6,120 F		$4,500 F

6. Market size variances. (See below.)

7. Market share variances (000 omitted. See below.)

Weighted average budgeted contribution margin per unit:

Master budget total contibution margin	$30,600
Master budget total sales units	÷ 600
Weighted-average budgeted contribution margin per unit	$ 51

Calculation for market shares:

Budgeted: Total sales in units 600 ÷ Total sales of the industry 1,500 = 0.40
Actual: Total sales in units 720 ÷ Total sales of the industry 1,600 = 0.45

Calculation for variances:

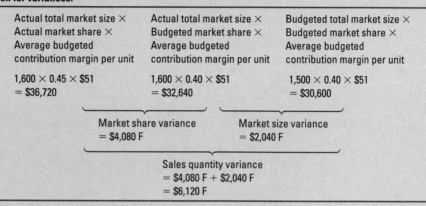

Actual total market size ×	Actual total market size ×	Budgeted total market size ×
Actual market share ×	Budgeted market share ×	Budgeted market share ×
Average budgeted	Average budgeted	Average budgeted
contribution margin per unit	contribution margin per unit	contribution margin per unit
$1,600 \times 0.45 \times \$51$	$1,600 \times 0.40 \times \$51$	$1,500 \times 0.40 \times \$51$
= $36,720	= $32,640	= $30,600

Market share variance
= $4,080 F

Market size variance
= $2,040 F

Sales quantity variance
= $4,080 F + $2,040 F
= $6,120 F

---

8. The sum of market size variance and market share variance and verification that this total equals the sales quantity variance.

Total market size variance	+	Total market share variance	=	Total quantity variance
$2,040 F		$4,080 F		$6,120 F

Part VI

Management Control

A. Ramey/Photo Edit

18

Management Control and Strategic Performance Measurement

After studying this chapter, you should be able to . . .

1   Identify the objectives of management control

2   Identify the types of management control systems and show where they are used

3   Define strategic performance measurement and show how it can be applied in centralized, decentralized, and team-oriented organizations

4   Explain the objectives and applications of strategic performance measurement in three common strategic business units: cost SBUs, revenue SBUs, and profit SBUs

5   Explain the role of the balanced scorecard in strategic performance measurement

6   Explain the role of strategic performance measurement in service and not-for-profit organizations

We must ask where we are and whither we are tending.

ABRAHAM LINCOLN

President Lincoln was aware of the need to regularly assess how one is doing, whether it be the individual, the firm, or the government. In this chapter we look at the role of performance evaluation within firms and other organizations.

PERFORMANCE EVALUATION AND CONTROL

Performance evaluation is the process by which managers at all levels gain information about the performance of tasks within the firm and judge that performance against preestablished criteria as set out in budgets, plans, and goals. Performance evaluation is applied for each of the three management functions—operations, marketing, and finance. In *operations*, the focus of performance evaluation is on the activities of production managers and production supervisors who report to them. In *marketing*, the evaluation is applied to the activities of sales executives, sales managers, and individual salespersons. In *finance*, performance evaluation monitors the financing activities of the firm, including the maintenance of adequate liquidity, cash flow management, the cost of capital, and other financing activities.

Also, performance evaluation is applied at many different levels in the firm—top management, mid-management, and the operating level of individual production and sales employees. In operations, the performances of individual production supervisors at the *operating level* are evaluated by plant managers, who in turn are evaluated by executives at the *management level*. Similarly, individual salespersons are evaluated by sales managers who are evaluated in turn by upper-level sales management, and so on. There are often no operating-level employees involved in financial management, so the performance of financial managers is typically evaluated at the upper-management level only.

Management control refers to the evaluation by upper-level managers of the performance of mid-level managers. **Operational control** means the evaluation of operating-level employees by mid-level managers. Operational control is covered in Part V. Management control is covered in Part VI, which begins with this chapter.

Operational Control versus Management Control

In contrast to operational control, which focuses on detailed short-term performance measures, management control focuses on higher-level managers and long-term,

Performance evaluation is the process by which managers at all levels gain information about the performance of tasks within the firm and judge that performance against preestablished criteria as set out in budgets, plans, and goals.

◄ **LEARNING OBJECTIVE 1**
Identify the objectives of management control.

Management control refers to the evaluation by upper-level managers of the performance of mid-level managers.

Operational control means the evaluation of operating level employees by mid-level managers.

BusinessWeek

? **Can R&D Give Companies a Jump on the Competition?**

Effective use of research and development (R&D) is an important part of any firm's competitive strategy. For firms that face global competition, as most firms do, R&D can be critical. Some firms take an incrementalist approach to R&D, striving to add value to their products and services through continuous improvements. Other firms take the opposite approach, looking specifically for breakthrough results from R&D. The breakthrough results are those that fundamentally change the nature of products and services, and the nature of competition in the industry. An example of breakthrough results is General Electric's digital X-ray technology, first sold in 1996, that uses digital imaging to replace the conventional film-based technology. Many firms employ both approaches.

Q: How do companies determine which R&D approach to implement? And how do they accurately evaluate the results?

Find out on page 743 of this chapter.

strategic issues. Operational control has a management-by-exception approach; that is, it identifies units or individuals whose performance is not in compliance with expectations, so that the problem can be promptly corrected. In contrast, management control is more consistent with the management-by-objectives approach, wherein long-term objectives such as growth and profitability are determined, and performance is periodically measured against these goals.

Also, management control has a broader and more strategic objective—to evaluate the overall profitability of the unit as well as the performance of the manager of the unit, to decide whether the unit should be retained or deleted, and to motivate the manager to achieve top management's goals. Because of this broader focus, there are multiple objectives for management control, and generally there are multiple measures of performance rather than a single financial or operating measure, as is sometimes true in operational control. Exhibit 18–1 shows an organizational chart that illustrates the different roles of management control and operational control.

Objectives of Management Control

In a management-by-objectives approach, top management assigns a set of responsibilities to each mid-level manager. The nature of these responsibilities, and therefore the precise nature of the objectives of top management, depends on the functional area involved (operations, marketing, or finance) and on the scope of authority of the mid-level manager (the extent of the resources under the manager's command). Often, these areas of responsibility are called *strategic business units* (SBUs), and the term *SBU manager* is used in place of mid-level manager. A **strategic business unit** consists of a well-defined set of controllable operating activities over which the SBU manager is responsible. Generally, managers have autonomy for making decisions and for managing the human and physical resources of the SBU. The objectives of management control are to:

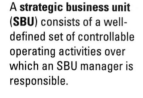

A **strategic business unit (SBU)** consists of a well-defined set of controllable operating activities over which an SBU manager is responsible.

1. *Motivate* managers to exert a high level of effort to achieve the goals of top management.
2. Provide the right *incentive* for managers to make decisions consistent with the goals of top management.
3. *Fairly determine the rewards* managers earn for their effort and skill, and for the effectiveness of their decision making.

A concise summary of top management's objectives is to provide fair compensation to the manager for working hard and making the right decisions, all within the

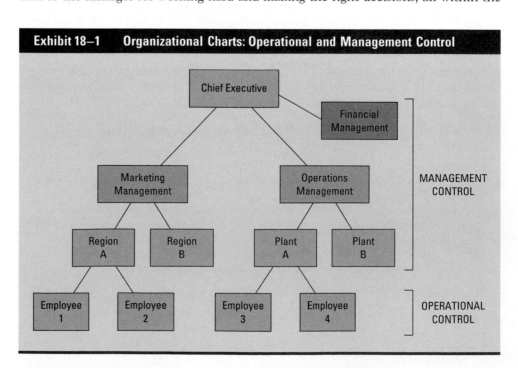

Exhibit 18–1   Organizational Charts: Operational and Management Control

context of autonomous action by the SBU manager. A common mechanism for achieving these multiple objectives is to develop an **employment contract** between the manager and top management that covers each of the previous points. Assuming that managers act in autonomous self-interest, the contract is designed to provide incentives for managers to act independently while simultaneously achieving top management's objectives and also earning the desired compensation. (This is called **goal congruence.**) The contract specifies the desired behaviors of the manager and the compensation to be awarded for specific outcomes. The contract can be written or unwritten, explicit or implied; some contracts may be legal and enforceable by the courts.[1] For clarity and effectiveness, organizations often choose explicit, written contracts.

Employment Contracts

An economic model called the **principal-agent model** is a prototype that contains the key elements contracts must have to achieve the desired objectives. The model sets out two important aspects of management performance that affect the contracting relationship, uncertainty and lack of observability.

> Uncertainty. Each manager operates in an environment that is influenced by factors beyond the manager's control—operating factors such as unexpected and unpreventable machine breakdowns and external factors such as fluctuations in market prices and demands. The manager's lack of control means there is some degree of *uncertainty* about the effectiveness of the manager's actions, independent of the efforts and abilities the manager brings to the job.

> Lack of observability. The efforts and often decisions made by the manager are *not observable to top management*. Also, the manager generally possesses information not accessible to top management. Because of the independent and unobservable action of the manager, top management is able to observe only the concrete outcomes of the manager's actions, and not the efforts that led to these outcomes.

The presence of uncertainty in the job environment and the lack of observability and existence of private information for the manager complicate the contracting relationship. Ideally, with no uncertainty and perfect observability, the manager and top management would base their contract on the amount of effort the manager was to supply. If effort is observable, both parties would be assured of the desired outcome. However, the presence of uncertainty and the lack of observability mean that the contract between the manager and top management must specifically incorporate both uncertainty and the lack of observability. This can be accomplished by understanding and applying the three principles of employment contracts:

1. Because of uncertainty in the manager's environment, the contract should recognize that other factors inside and outside the firm also influence the outcomes of the manager's efforts and abilities. Therefore, the contract should separate the outcome of the manager's actions from the effort and

An **employment contract** is an agreement between the manager and top management, designed so that the manager acts independently to achieve top management's objectives.

Goal congruence is achieved when the manager acts independently in such a way as to simultaneously achieve top management's objectives.

The **principal-agent model** is a conceptual model that contains the key elements contracts must have to achieve the desired objectives.

The Three Principles of Effective Contracting

1. Separate the outcome of the manager's actions from the effort and decision-making skill of the manager.
2. Exclude known uncontrollable factors.
3. Make adjustment for the expected relative risk aversion of the manager.

---

[1] For a good overview of the use of contracts in management control, see Kenneth A. Merchant, *Rewarding Results* (Boston: Harvard Business School Press, 1989), especially Chapters 1 and 2.

Exhibit 18–2   The Principal-Agent Model

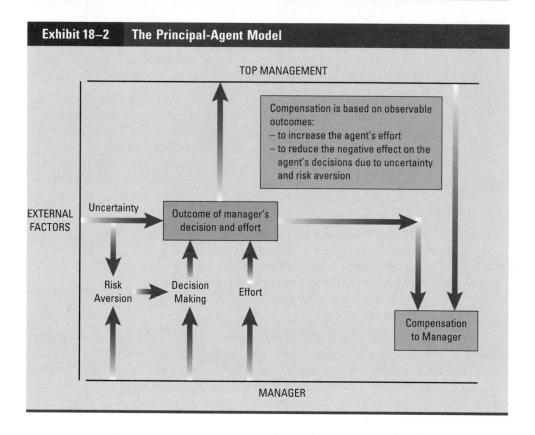

decision-making skills employed by the manager; that is, separate the performance of the manager from the performance of the SBU.

2. The contract must include only factors controllable by the manager. This concept is similar to the first principle, which separates the manager from the SBU, while the second principle excludes *known* uncontrollable factors from the contract.

3. Because of uncertainty and lack of observability, a *risk-averse manager is improperly biased* to avoid decisions with uncertain outcomes. In contrast, top management would prefer to see these relatively risky decisions implemented because of top management's greater tolerance for risk.

In effect, the contract between top management and the manager should recognize the risk aversion of the manager and the role of uncertainty—the need to understand and to apply the three principles of contracting.

In the principal-agent model in Exhibit 18–2, top management supplies compensation to the manager who operates in an environment of uncertainty. The manager supplies effort and decision-making skills, as well as a degree of risk aversion. The effect of the effort and decision-making skills on the factors in the environment produces the outcomes (i.e., amount of sales achieved and reduction in manufacturing costs). Based on the reported outcomes, top management determines the compensation for the manager. In this way, the principal-agent model shows the relationships among the key factors that affect the manager's performance and the manager's compensation.

DESIGN OF MANAGEMENT CONTROL SYSTEMS

The first choice in developing a management control system is to clearly identify the who, what, and when for the evaluation of something or someone. We start with the *who*, that is, who is interested in evaluating the performance of the organization? There are four recipients of performance reports: (1) the owners, directors, or shareholders; (2) the creditors; (3) the community or governmental units affected by the operations of the firm; and (4) the employees of the firm. Each has a different view about what performance is desired.

◀ **LEARNING OBJECTIVE 2**
Identify the types of management control systems and show where they are used.

Another aspect of management control is *what* is being evaluated. Commonly the evaluation is of the individual manager, to assess the effectiveness and efficiency of the manager's performance. Alternatively, the focus of the evaluation might be the SBU under the manager's control for the purpose of determining whether or not to expand or to divest the SBU. Rather than focusing on the individual manager, the evaluation might be directed to a team of managers. Also, a manager's performance can be compared either with that of other managers or with the manager's previous performance. Comparison to other managers is common, but comparison to the manager's own prior performance is preferable when comparison to others is inappropriate or unfair in some way.

A final aspect of management control is *when* the performance evaluation is done. There are two considerations here: First, the evaluation can be done on the basis of either resources input to the manager or outputs of the manager's efforts. The first approach uses the master budget (Chapter 9), while the second uses the flexible budget (Chapter 15). The focus is on inputs when it is difficult to measure the outputs of the manager's efforts, or the nature and extent of the manager's control over the outputs is not clear. Then, the evaluation of the manager is done *ex ante*, before the manager's efforts and decisions have been made. In effect, the manager negotiates with top management for the amount of resources needed. This approach is common in service and not-for-profit organizations, for which the outputs are often difficult to measure. In contrast, in manufacturing, where the inputs and outputs are often relatively easy to measure, it is more common to see the *ex post* approach based on actual outputs.

Another timing option is to tie the evaluation to the product life cycle. The life cycle of a product or service is the time from its introduction to its removal from the market. In the early stages of a product's sales life cycle, management's focus is primarily on nonfinancial factors such as market penetration and success in developing certain customers. The appropriate performance measures at this time include revenues by customer class and area, the number of back orders, the number of new customers, and customer satisfaction. As the product achieves market acceptance, profitability and asset management become more important, and the performance

Culture and Management Control

The determination of who is doing the evaluation is especially important for companies with multinational ownership. As Hofstede points out, "accounting and management control systems are manifestations of culture and reflect basic cultural assumptions." For example, Hofstede goes on to explain that Japanese firms and Japanese investors are more likely to reward collectivist rather than individual behavior—that is, behavior that helps the organization rather than an individual unit. Also, Japanese managers are more accustomed to thinking in long-term goals and are more likely to reward behavior that has a long-term focus than are managers in other countries, including the United States.

Source: Based on information in G. W. Hofstede, *Cultures and Organizations* (New York: McGraw-Hill, 1991).

measures change. Finally, when the product is in its mature phase—when the nature of the competition is established and the future of the market is clear—the focus on profitability continues, but in addition there is a new interest in strategic issues such as customer satisfaction, information regarding product modifications, and potential new markets. Top management must choose the types of performance measures that are appropriate for the sales life cycle stage of the product or service, as illustrated in Exhibit 18–3.

The management accountant first determines the who, what, and when of management control and then designs a system to accomplish it. The systems for management control are of two types—formal and informal. Formal systems are developed from explicit management guidance, while informal systems arise from the unmanaged, and sometimes unintended, behavior of managers and employees. Informal systems reflect the managers' and employees' reactions and feelings that arise from the positive and negative aspects of the work environment. An example is the positive feelings of security and acceptance of an employee in a company that has a successful product and generous employee benefits.

Informal Systems

Informal Systems at the Individual Level

Informal systems arise in firms at both the individual and the group levels. At the individual level, employees' performance is influenced by the individual drives and aspirations they bring to the workplace; these are apart from any incentives and guidance provided by management. Such individual motivators explain performance differences between employees.

Informal Systems at the Team Level

When informal systems exist at the work group or team level, shared team norms, such as a positive attitude to help the firm achieve quality goals or to improve sales, influence the performance of those on the team. At a broader level, organization-level norms can influence the behavior of teams and of individual employees. For example, firms such as IBM and Wal-Mart have a culture of commitment to customer service, while others have a culture devoted to quality (Ford, Milliken) or

Exhibit 18–3	Sales Life Cycle of Management Control
Stage of Product's Sales Life Cycle	**Appropriate Performance Evaluation Measures**
Early	Revenue, Market penetration
Growth	Profitability, Asset management
Mature	Profitability, Strategy

Exhibit 18–4   Systems for Management Control

		INFORMAL SYSTEMS	FORMAL SYSTEMS
	INDIVIDUAL	Aspiration Level Personal Drives	Hiring Practices Promotion Procedures STRATEGIC PERFORMANCE MEASUREMENT
	TEAMS	Peer Norms Organization Culture	Keiretsu Shared Responsibility

innovation (Rubbermaid, Hewlett-Packard). Management accountants must consider these informal systems to properly develop formal systems that have the desired impact on employees' performance.

Formal Systems

Formal Systems at the Individual Level

The three important formal management control systems at the level of the individual employee are (1) hiring practices, (2) promotion policies, and (3) strategic performance measurement systems. In each of these systems, management sets expectations for desired employee performance. Hiring and promotion policies are critical in all companies and are a supplement to strategic performance measurement systems. Strategic performance measurement systems are the most common method for evaluating managers.

Formal Systems at the Team Level

There are no known formal systems for management control at the team or group level, though the increased emphasis on teamwork in recent years is likely to produce demand for such systems. The *keiretsu* system of shared responsibility prevalent in Japanese companies is being adopted by some U.S. companies, and is a likely starting place for such a development. The four management control systems are summarized in Exhibit 18–4.

STRATEGIC PERFORMANCE MEASUREMENT

> "The difference in companies is people. I would rather have a first-class manager running a second-rate business than a second-class manager running a first-class business."
>
> JACK E. REICHERT, CEO OF BRUNSWICK CORPORATION

◄ **LEARNING OBJECTIVE 3**
Define strategic performance measurement and show how it can be applied in centralized, decentralized, and team-oriented organizations.

Strategic performance measurement is an accounting system used by top management for the evaluation of SBU managers.

Strategic performance measurement is a system used by top management for the evaluation of SBU managers. It is used when responsibility can be effectively delegated to SBU managers, and there are adequate measures for evaluating the performance of the managers. Before designing strategic performance measurement systems top managers determine when delegation of responsibility (called *decentralization*) is desirable and choose the appropriate measures used in the system.

Decentralization

A firm is decentralized if it has chosen to delegate a significant amount of responsibility to SBU managers. In contrast, a centralized firm reserves much of the decision making at the top management level. For example, in a centralized multistore

---

The Value of Decentralization at Kids 'R' Us

For certain firms, local knowledge can be critical, as the example of Kids 'R' Us illustrates. Kids 'R' Us, a retailer of children's clothing, recently attempted to break into the retail clothing market in Puerto Rico. The objective was to take advantage of the Puerto Rican love for retail shopping—Puerto Ricans spend 55 percent of their disposable income in retail stores. Kids 'R' Us made a big push on back-to-school clothing sales, but failed to take into account that most Puerto Rican kids wear uniforms to school. In addition, much of the clothing was too heavy and not suitable to the warm Puerto Rican climate. Jeff Handler, the company's marketing director, explained that the firm's central purchasing and planning policies and procedures had caused the errors. Local knowledge was critical for the effective management of the stores in Puerto Rico.

Source: Based on information in *Business Week*, February 28, 1994, p. 8.

retail firm, all pricing decisions, product purchasing, and advertising decisions are made at the top management level, typically by top-level marketing and operations executives. In contrast, a decentralized retail firm allows local store managers to decide which products to purchase and the type and amount of advertising to use, as well as to make other marketing and operating decisions.

The benefit of the centralized approach is that top management retains control over key business functions, so that a desired level of performance is assured. Additionally, with top management involvement in most decisions, the expertise of top management can be effectively utilized, and the activities of the different units within the firm can be effectively coordinated. For many firms, however, a decentralized approach is preferable. The main reason is that top management cannot effectively manage the operations at a very detailed level; they lack the necessary local knowledge. Decisions at lower levels in the firm must be made on a timely basis using the information at hand, to make the firm more responsive to the customer. For example, often the retail store manager must make quick changes in the store inventory, pricing, and advertising to respond to local competition and to changing customer buying habits and tastes.

While the main reason for decentralization is the use of local or specialized knowledge by SBU managers, there are other important incentives. First, many managers would say that decentralized strategic performance measurement is more motivating because it provides managers an opportunity to demonstrate their skill and their desire to achieve, and to receive recognition and compensation for doing so. Second, because of the direct responsibility assumed by SBU managers, the decentralized approach provides a means for training new top-level managers. Finally, most managers would agree that the decentralized approach is a better basis for performance evaluation. It is perceived to be more objective and to provide more opportunity for the advancement of hard-working, energetic managers.

There is a downside as well. Decentralization may hinder coordination within the firm because of the greater autonomy at lower management levels. Also, because of the increased focus on competition, there may be greater conflict among lower-level managers, which can lead to counterproductive actions and reduced overall profits.

Different Types of Strategic Business Units

The four types of strategic business units (SBUs) are cost SBUs, revenue SBUs, profit SBUs, and investment SBUs. **Cost SBUs** are a firm's production or support SBUs that provide the best quality product or service at the lowest cost. Examples of cost SBUs include the assembly department in a plant, the data processing department, and the shipping and receiving department. When the focus is on the selling function, SBUs are called **revenue SBUs** and are defined either by product line or by geographical area. When an SBU both generates revenues and incurs the major portion of the cost for producing these revenues, the SBU is a **profit SBU.** Profit SBU managers are responsible for both revenues and costs and therefore want to achieve a desired operating profit. The use of profit SBUs is an improvement over

Cost SBUs are production or support SBUs within the firm that have the goal of providing the best quality product or service at the lowest cost.

A **revenue SBU** is defined either by product line or by geographical area.

A **profit SBU** both generates revenues and incurs the major portion of the cost for producing these revenues.

Benefits and Drawbacks of Decentralization	
BENEFITS OF DECENTRALIZATION	**DRAWBACKS OF DECENTRALIZATION**
• Uses local knowledge	• May hinder coordination among SBUs
• Allows timely and effective response to customers	• Can cause potential conflict among SBUs
• Trains managers	
• Motivates managers	
• Offers objective method of performance evaluation	

cost and revenue SBUs in many firms, because they align the manager's goals more directly with top management's goal to make the firm profitable.

The choice of a profit, cost, or revenue SBU also depends on the nature of the production and selling environment in the firm. Products that have little need for coordination between the manufacturing and selling functions are good candidates for cost centers. These include many commodity products such as food and paper products. For such products there are relatively few times when the production manager has to adjust the functionality of the product or the production schedule to suit a particular customer. For this reason, production managers should focus on reducing cost while sales managers focus on sales; this is what cost and revenue SBUs accomplish.

In contrast, sometimes close coordination is needed between the production and selling functions. For example, high-fashion and consumer products require close coordination so that consumer information coming into the selling function reaches the design and manufacturing function. Cost and revenue SBUs could fail to provide the incentive for coordination—production managers would be focusing on cost and not listening to the ever-changing demands coming from the selling function. A preferred option is to use the profit center for both the revenue and production managers, so that both coordinate to achieve the highest overall profit.

When a firm has many different profit SBUs because it has many different product lines, it may be difficult to compare their performance because they vary greatly in size and in the nature of their products and services. A preferred approach is to use **investment SBUs,** a concept that includes assets employed by the SBU as well as profits in the performance evaluation. Investment SBUs are covered in Chapter 19.

> An **investment SBU** is a concept that includes assets employed by the SBU as well as profits.

COST-BASED STRATEGIC BUSINESS UNITS

Cost SBUs include direct manufacturing departments such as assembly and finishing and manufacturing support departments such as materials handling, maintenance, and engineering. The direct manufacturing and manufacturing support departments are often evaluated as cost SBUs since these managers have significant direct control over costs but little control over revenues or decision making for investment in facilities.

> ◀ **LEARNING OBJECTIVE 4**
> Explain the objectives and applications of strategic performance measurement in three common strategic business units: cost SBUs, revenue SBUs, and profit SBUs.

The Strategic Role of Cost SBUs

Several strategic issues arise when implementing cost SBUs. One is cost shifting, a second is excessively focusing on short-term objectives, and the third is the tendency of managers and top management to miscommunicate because of the pervasive problem of budget slack.

Cost Shifting

Cost shifting occurs when a department replaces its controllable costs with noncontrollable costs. For example, the manager of a production cost SBU that is evaluated on controllable costs has the incentive to replace variable costs with fixed costs. The reason is the manager generally is not held responsible for increases in noncontrollable fixed costs. The net effect might be higher overall costs for the firm, though controllable costs in the manager's department might decrease. Fixed costs go up while variable costs go down. The effective use of cost SBUs requires top management to anticipate and to prevent cost shifting by requiring analysis and justification of equipment upgrades and any changes in work patterns that affect other departments. Top management's attention to cost shifting is particularly important because the foundation of strategic performance measurement systems is an SBU manager who is responsible for only controllable costs. The focus on controllable costs is necessary to achieve the objectives of motivation and fairness. However, as explained earlier, excessive focus on controllable costs can result in dysfunctional cost shifting.

Cost-shifting issues arise in not-for-profit as well as other firms. For example, many governmental units do not distinguish between direct and indirect costs in their performance reporting. This can lead to poor decision making, as illustrated by the U.S. Forest Service:

> Inappropriate accounting measures allegedly caused the United States Forest Service to cut down trees that an ordinary business would have left standing ... the Forest Service is not charged for the cost of constructing roads into remote areas to reach the lumber. The Forest Service's response to these measures of its performance is to cut down a great deal of lumber and to construct costly, intricate roads to reach it. The Service already has 342,000 miles of logging roads and plans to build yet another 262,000 by 2040. Critics contend that these roads are constructed to reach increasingly poor quality timber and that they inflict considerable environmental damage. They recommend new measures of its performance that account for the full cost of logging, including the cost of raising the timber, building the roads to reach it, and replacing it.[2]

The Forest Service's failure to identify the full cost of the logging, including the costs of the roads as well as the logging of the trees, caused poor decision making. The costs of the roads were improperly shifted away from the Forest Service.

Also, not-for-profit entities have an incentive for cost shifting because certain services are reimbursed on a cost-plus basis while other services are charged fixed fees. Cost shifting in this context means the allocation of joint costs from the fixed-charge to the cost-plus services. The cost shifting can be done in a variety of ways. A number of hospitals, for example, have found it necessary to shift the costs of Medicare and Medicaid (fixed-fee) patients to private (cost-plus) patients.[3] Cost shifting undermines the motivation and fairness of the performance evaluation systems within these hospitals.

In a related example, cost shifting can occur *within* the hospital:

> Kevin Schulman, a medical economist at Georgetown Medical School, tells of a hospital where the radiology department decided to save money by sending out only one copy of a report, instead of separate copies to each care provider. It won a hospital efficiency award, while the medical clinic in the same hospital had to hire someone to reproduce that lone report for all the doctors who needed a copy.[4]

---

[2] Regina E. Herzlinger and Denise Nitterhouse, *Financial Accounting and Managerial Control for Nonprofit Organizations* (Cincinnati: South Western Publishing, 1994), p. 419. Also, Cox et al., "Responsibility Accounting and Operational Control for Governmental Units," *Accounting Horizons*, June 1989, pp. 38–48, show the results of a survey of 830 governmental units in the United States and Canada with a principal finding that the strategic performance measurement systems in three-fourths of these units did not distinguish between controllable and uncontrollable costs.

[3] See "Cost-Shifting: How One Hospital Does It," *The Wall Street Journal*, December 9, 1991.

[4] "Hospitals Attack a Crippler: Paper," *Business Week*, February 21, 1994, pp. 104–106.

The cost shifting was from one department in the hospital to another, rather than from one type of patient to another.

Excessive Short-Term Focus

Another strategic issue is the broad concern that many performance measurement systems focus excessively on annual cost figures; this motivates managers to attend to only short-term costs and neglect long-term strategic issues. This concern is an important reason why cost SBUs should use nonfinancial strategic considerations as well as financial information on costs.

Budget Slack

A third strategic issue is to recognize both the negative and the positive roles of budget slack. **Budget slack** is the difference between budgeted and expected performance. The majority of firms have some amount of slack, evidenced by a budgeted cost target that is somewhat easier to attain than would be reasonably expected. Managers often plan for a certain amount of slack in their performance budgets to allow for unexpected unfavorable events. However, a significant amount of slack might result from SBU managers' attempts to make their performance goals easier, and therefore indicate an overall lower level of performance than should have been achieved.

> **Budget slack** is the difference between budgeted performance and expected performance.

The positive view of slack is that it addresses effectively the decision-making and fairness objectives of performance evaluation. By limiting managers' exposure to environmental uncertainty, it reduces the relative risk aversion of the managers. The resulting evaluation therefore satisfies fairness, and the reduced risk helps the managers make decisions that are more nearly congruent with the goals of top management.

Producing and Support Departments

There are two methods for implementing cost SBUs for producing and support departments, the discretionary-cost method and the engineered-cost method. These two methods differ in their underlying cost behavior, and their focus on inputs or outputs. When costs are predominantly fixed, an input-oriented planning focus is appropriate because fixed costs are not controllable in the short term. The planning approach is taken so that top management can effectively budget for expected costs in each cost SBU; the focus is on beginning-of-period planning for expected costs rather than end-of-period evaluation of the amount of costs expended. In contrast, if costs are primarily variable and therefore controllable, then an output-oriented approach, based on end-of-period evaluation of controllable costs, would be appropriate. The input-oriented approach is called the **discretionary-cost method** because costs are considered largely uncontrollable and discretion is applied at the planning stage. The output-oriented approach is called the **engineered-cost method,** since costs are variable and therefore "engineered," that is, controllable.

> The **discretionary-cost method** is input-oriented, since costs are considered largely uncontrollable and discretion is applied at the planning stage.

Another factor in choosing between discretionary-cost and engineered-cost SBUs is the complexity of the work environment. SBUs that have relatively ill-defined outputs (for instance, research and development) will have less well-defined goals and are therefore more likely to be evaluated as discretionary-cost SBUs, while SBUs for which the operations are well defined and the output goals are more clearly determined will be engineered-cost SBUs.

> The **engineered-cost approach** is the output-oriented approach since costs are variable and therefore engineered, that is, controllable.

SBUs for Production and Support Departments	
Discretionary-Cost Approach	**Engineered-Cost Approach**
Costs are mainly fixed, uncontrollable	Costs are mainly variable, controllable
Firms use an input-oriented planning focus	Firms use an output-oriented evaluation focus
Operations are ill-defined	Operations are well-defined

Cost behavior in a production SBU is therefore important in choosing the cost SBU method. As explained in Chapter 3, the behavior of a cost driver depends upon the level of analysis: the facility, the product, the batch of production, or the unit of production. Similarly, when studying a cost SBU, we must know on which level of analysis it operates. For example, costs in the engineering department are driven primarily by product-level cost drivers—the number of new products or product changes. Also, costs in the inspection department are driven primarily by batch-level cost drivers—the number of production runs or setups.

There are relatively few cost drivers at the facility level because most of the facility-related costs are fixed and do not fluctuate with changes in production level, production mix, or product. Costs at the facility level have few cost drivers; therefore, most departments at this level are evaluated as discretionary-cost SBUs.

For cost SBUs at the unit, batch, and product levels, managers commonly implement the engineered-cost method based on the appropriate cost driver for that production activity. For example, for the engineering department where the cost driver is at the product level, the engineered-cost method uses the number of engineering changes to new and existing products as the cost driver and evaluates the performance of the engineering department on its costs for each engineering change completed. Similarly, for the inspection department where the cost driver is at the batch level (inspection is done for each batch), the appropriate cost-SBU method would again be the engineered-cost method, in which management reviews the cost incurred versus the number of batches inspected.

Some production departments are more difficult to classify as batch, product, or facility level. For example, the maintenance department can be viewed as a facility-level activity because much of the demand for maintenance is for plant and equipment that is not influenced by production level (units or batches). However, because the wear on equipment is greater at a higher level of production or for a larger number of batches, batch and unit cost drivers also may be appropriate. The choice of a method depends in part on management's objectives. If management wants to motivate a reduction in the use of maintenance (because costs have been rising or because of overall budget constraints), then the engineered-cost method is appropriate since it rewards cost reduction.[5] In contrast, if management is concerned about the low overall serviceability of plant and equipment (due perhaps to a prior lack of maintenance), then the discretionary-cost method provides the right incentive, by reducing the maintenance manager's risk aversion and thereby motivating proper additional expenditures on maintenance.

Another option for management control of the engineering department or maintenance department is to treat each of these as profit SBUs and to charge users a price for their services. The effect of using a profit SBU method would be added emphasis on cost control and an incentive for the SBU to provide quality service and perhaps seek markets outside the firm.

General and Administrative Departments

Administrative support departments such as personnel management, research and development, data processing, and printing and duplicating also are commonly evaluated as cost SBUs. There is often no source of revenue, but most of the costs are controllable by the department managers, so the cost SBU method is appropriate.[6]

---

[5] Note, however, that Robin Cooper and Robert S. Kaplan, in "Activity-Based Systems: Measuring the Costs of Resource Usage," *Accounting Horizons*, September 1992, explain that methods like the engineered-cost method do not necessarily achieve a reduction in costs unless the supply of resources is reduced following a reduction in the usage of resources.

[6] Occasionally, top management chooses to regard one of the support SBUs as a profit SBU to encourage the department to become competitive with outside providers of equivalent services, and also to encourage the department to offer these services to customers outside the firm. This method is becoming more common in particular for data processing departments, printing and duplicating, and customer service departments.

The choice of a discretionary-cost or engineered-cost method for these departments depends on cost behavior in the department and on management's philosophy and objectives, as explained earlier. Also, the proper choice of method might change over time. For example, when cost reduction is a key objective, the data processing department might be treated as an engineered-cost SBU for a time. Later it might be changed to a discretionary-cost SBU to motivate data processing managers to focus on long-term goals such as the design of new computer information systems.

Cost behavior in administrative support SBUs is often a step-fixed cost, as illustrated in Exhibit 18–5. As clerical and/or service support personnel are added, labor costs increase in a step-fixed pattern. Suppose that one clerk is required to process 100 new employee applications per month and that each clerk is paid $1,200 per month. If there are 250 applications per month, then three clerks are required at a total cost of $3,600 per month. If the discretionary-cost method is used, the supervisor of personnel management is likely to have negotiated for three clerks *at the beginning of the year,* and therefore the budget is $3,600 and there is no meaningful *ex post* evaluation. The discretionary-cost method is represented by the horizontal line in Exhibit 18–5.

Recognizing that each application in effect costs $12 ($1,200/100), management might choose to use an engineered-cost method in which the personnel department manager is evaluated by comparing the budget of $3,000 (250 applications times $12 per application) to the actual expenditure of $3,600. Because there can be slack or overcapacity due to the nature of the step-fixed cost, an unfavorable cost variance is likely; only when the operation is exactly at one of the full-capacity points (100, 200, 300 . . .) will there be no variance. Therefore, the interpretation of the cost variances must include both the productivity of labor and the underutilization of labor due to excess capacity.

Outsourcing the Cost SBU

Outsourcing is the term used to describe a firm's decision to have a service or product currently provided by a support department supplied by an outside firm in the future. For example, H. J. Heinz, Eastman-Kodak, and the Vatican in Rome are among the organizations that have chosen to outsource their data processing.[7] These

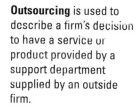

Outsourcing is used to describe a firm's decision to have a service or product provided by a support department supplied by an outside firm.

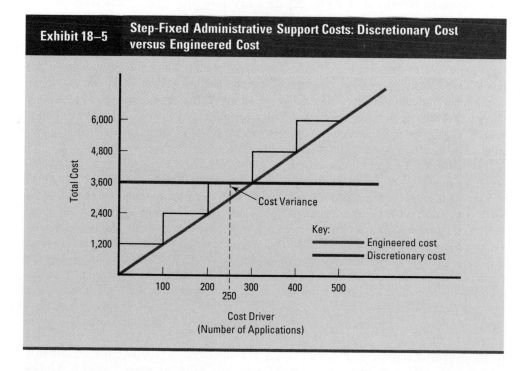

| Exhibit 18–5 | **Step-Fixed Administrative Support Costs: Discretionary Cost versus Engineered Cost** |

7 *CIO Magazine,* special issue on outsourcing, October 1991; and John J. Keller, "More Firms 'Outsource' Data Networks," *The Wall Street Journal,* March 11, 1991.

The Growth in Outsourcing

DATA PROCESSING

A number of large firms, including AT&T, Kodak, Ameritech, Rubbermaid, Aetna, DuPont, and J. P. Morgan, are outsourcing significant parts of their data-processing operations. Approximately 20 percent of the largest U.S. companies are doing it, says Howard Anderson of Yankee Group Research Inc. The motivations for outsourcing data processing are twofold: One is to reduce the overall cost of data processing. The other, perhaps stronger reason is that the firms want to keep up with advancing technology. Firms are more likely to do so if they have an accomplished technology partner.

HUMAN RESOURCES MANAGEMENT

"The human resources function of the not-too-distant future will be a small, highly leveraged, cost-effective internal management consultancy . . . Most of the functions associated with human resources today will be outsourced or administered by line business units."

CUSTOMER SERVICE

Matrixx Marketing is one of the growing number of firms that provide customer service activities for large retail and manufacturing clients. For example, Matrixx handles the customer service needs of ConAgra, Microsoft, and the American Red Cross. As many firms strategically reorient themselves and return to a focus on their core businesses, they outsource many of the operations for which they are not experts to leading providers such as Matrixx.

Source: Based on information in *Business Week,* May 13, 1996, p. 47; David White, Lotus Development Corp., quoted in *Fortune,* May 13, 1996, p. 176; and "New Industry Flourishes on Downsizing," *USA Today,* April 26, 1995.

firms have found that the outside source is an effective way to obtain reliable service at a reasonable cost without the risk of obsolescence and other potential management problems. It can also be an effective way to gain access to new technologies. The cost of outsourcing is that the firm loses control over a potentially strategic resource and must rely on the outside firm's competence and continued performance. For this reason firms analyze this decision thoroughly, select the vendors carefully, and develop precisely worded contracts. Outsourcing is an increasingly favorable option used by many firms for their data processing, printing and duplicating, engineering, and other services.

Cost Allocation

A pervasive issue when using cost SBUs is how the jointly incurred costs of service departments—such as data processing, engineering, human resources, or maintenance—are to be allocated to the departments using the service. The various cost allocation methods are explained in Chapter 14. The choice of method affects the amount of cost allocated to each cost SBU, and therefore it is critical in effective cost SBU evaluation. For example, if the cost of maintenance is allocated based on the square feet of space in each production department, the departments with more space have higher costs. The incentives of such an allocation method are not clear because the production departments likely cannot control the amount of space they occupy. Alternatively, if maintenance costs are allocated on the basis of the number of maintenance jobs requested, then the production departments can control their allocated maintenance costs by controlling usage.

The criteria for choosing the cost allocation method, as explained in Chapter 14, are the same as the objectives for management control, to (1) motivate managers to exert a high level of effort, (2) provide an incentive for managers to make decisions consistent with top management's goals, and (3) provide a basis for a fair evaluation of managers' performance. For example, when management wants to encourage production departments to reduce the amount of maintenance, allocation based on usage provides the desired incentive. In contrast, if management wants the departments to increase the use of maintenance to improve the serviceability of the equipment, the most effective incentive might be to not allocate the maintenance cost, or perhaps to subsidize it in some way.

A useful guide in choosing the cost allocation method, in addition to the three criteria just explained, is to use dual allocation. **Dual allocation** is a cost allocation method in which fixed and variable costs are separated. Variable costs are directly traced to user departments, and fixed costs are allocated on some logical basis. For example, the variable costs of maintenance such as supplies, labor, and parts can be traced to each maintenance job and charged directly to the user department. This

Dual allocation is a cost allocation method in which fixed and variable costs are separated. Variable costs are directly traced to user departments, and fixed costs are allocated on some logical basis.

approach is both fair and motivating. In contrast, the fixed costs of the maintenance department (training, manuals, equipment, etc.) that cannot be traced to each maintenance job should be allocated to the user departments using a basis that fairly reflects each department's use of the service. For example, those departments whose maintenance jobs require more expensive equipment might be allocated a higher proportion of the maintenance department's fixed costs.

REVENUE-BASED STRATEGIC BUSINESS UNITS

The marketing department can be viewed as both a revenue SBU and a cost SBU. The revenue SBU responsibility stems from the fact that the marketing department manages the revenue-generating process. The marketing manager must therefore report revenues, typically by product line, and sometimes also by sales area and salesperson. The revenue reports are used by top management to assess the performance of the marketing manager in achieving desired sales goals. Often this analysis is performed at a detailed level to determine the separate effects of price changes, quantity changes, and sales mix changes on the overall sales dollars.[8]

It is common for management to use revenue drivers in the evaluation of the performance of revenue SBUs. **Revenue drivers** in manufacturing firms are the factors that affect sales volume, such as price changes, promotions, discounts, customer service, changes in product features, delivery dates, and other value-added factors. In service firms the revenue drivers focus on many of the same factors, with a special emphasis on the quality of the service—is it courteous, helpful, and timely?

> **Revenue drivers** are the factors that affect sales volume, such as price changes, promotions, discounts, customer service, changes in product features, delivery dates, and other value-added factors.

The marketing department also can be a cost SBU. In the pharmaceuticals, cosmetics, software, games and toys, and specialized electrical equipment industries, the cost of advertising and promotion is a significant portion of the total cost of producing and selling the product. The marketing department incurs two types of costs—order-getting and order-filling costs. **Order-getting costs** are expenditures to advertise and promote the product. Included are samples, demonstrations, advertising and promotion, travel and entertainment expenses, commissions, and marketing research. Since showing how these costs have directly affected sales is often difficult, managers view order-getting costs as a discretionary-cost SBU and focus on planning these expenditures rather than evaluating their effectiveness. In contrast, other firms have developed extensive analyses of order-getting costs to determine which are the most effective activities for improving sales. Such additional analyses might consist of statistical analyses of general economic data and the firm's sales and operating data, together with operational analyses consisting of ratios of sales per salesperson, sales per number of follow-ups on inquiries, and returns and allowances per product and salesperson.

> **Order-getting costs** are expenditures to advertise and promote the product.

A second category of marketing costs is order-filling costs. **Order-filling costs** include freight, warehousing, packing and shipping, and the cost of collections. These costs have a relatively clear relationship to sales volume, and as a result they often can be effectively managed as an engineered-cost SBU. The engineered-cost method could be implemented by developing appropriate operating ratios—average shipping cost per item, average freight cost per sales dollar, and so on.

> **Order-filling costs** include freight, warehousing, packing and shipping, and the cost of collections.

PROFIT-BASED STRATEGIC BUSINESS UNITS

The profit SBU manager's goal is profits. A key advantage of the profit SBU is that it places the incentives of the manager in congruence with those of top management, to improve the profitability of the firm. Moreover, the profit SBU also should motivate individual managers because by earning profits they are contributing

---

[8] This is explained in Chapter 17. Also, some marketing managers have a relatively broad view of the responsibility of the marketing function, which includes responsibility for sales and cost of sales. This is suggested, for example, by the Institute of Marketing's definition: "Marketing is the management process for identifying, anticipating, and satisfying customer requirements profitably."

directly to the success of the firm. For these reasons, the profit SBU meets the management control objectives of motivation and decision making explained earlier.

The Strategic Role of Profit SBUs

Three strategic issues cause firms to choose profit SBUs rather than cost or revenue SBUs. First, profit SBUs provide the incentive for the desired coordination among the marketing, production, and support functions. The handling of rush orders is a good example. A rush order would be viewed unfavorably by a cost SBU because of the potential added cost associated with the disruption of the production process, while the order would be viewed favorably by a revenue SBU. If they are in separate cost and revenue SBUs, there is little incentive for the production manager to coordinate with the marketing manager to meet the rush order. In contrast, if the production SBU is a profit SBU, the production manager accepts the order if it improves the SBU's profit, a decision consistent with both the production SBU's and top management's goals.

A second reason firms use profit SBUs rather than cost SBUs is to motivate managers to think of their product as marketable to outside customers. Production departments that provide products and services primarily for other internal departments may find that they can market their product or service profitably outside the firm, or that the firm might be able to purchase the product or service more cheaply outside the firm. For example, American Airlines earns several million dollars per year providing contract maintenance and other services for other airlines. Skill Dynamics, a unit of IBM that previously provided training service only for IBM staff, provides training services for others as well.

Some profit SBUs motivate internal departments to compete with outside suppliers. For example, First Union Bank of Charlotte, North Carolina, has viewed its printing and duplicating department this way. And within IBM, as former IBM Chief Executive John Akers noted:

> Each plant is responsible for putting a firm price on what it makes or does including subassembly work headed for another IBM plant. The plant has to deliver at that price and make a profit. If the price is too high, the receiver of that work is free to look elsewhere—either inside or outside the company—to obtain an alternate source. In other words, every step of our manufacturing process is compared to what is going on outside the business. Each step has to compete as a source of supply.[9]

The third reason for choosing profit SBUs is to motivate managers to develop new ways of profit making from their products and services. For example, a growing number of companies are finding that service contracts (for home entertainment equipment, business equipment, appliances, and so on) are a significant source of profit, in addition to sales of the product. In the software industry, revenues from service and upgrades may be as important as the original sales price of the software. Coordination between marketing, production, and design is critical for the success of these efforts, and since many of these contracts are for three years or more, careful analysis must be done of the expected future costs of the service. In a profit SBU, managers have the incentive to develop creative new products and services, because the profit SBU evaluation rewards the incremental profits.[10]

The Contribution Income Statement

The **contribution margin income statement** is based on the contribution margin developed for each profit SBU and for each relevant group of profit SBUs.

A common form of profit SBU evaluation is the contribution margin income statement. The **contribution margin income statement** is based on the contribution margin developed for each profit SBU and for each relevant group of profit SBUs. The contribution income statement is illustrated in Exhibit 18–6 for Machine Tools,

9 John Naisbitt and Patricia Aburdene, *Re-inventing the Corporation* (New York: Warner Books, 1985), p. 64.

10 See "Slugfest in the Service Biz," *Business Week*, February 28, 1994, p. 106.

| | | | | Exhibit 18–6 | Machine Tools, Inc. Contribution Income Statement (000s omitted) | | |

	Company as a Whole	Company Breakdown into Two Divisions		Breakdown of Division B by Product			
		Division A	Division B	Not Allocated	Product 1	Product 2	Product 3
Net revenues	$2,000	$600	$1,400		$400	$700	$300
Variable costs	900	200	700		100	350	250
Total contribution margin	$1,100	$400	$ 700		$300	$350	$ 50
Short-term controllable fixed costs	250	100	150	$ 25	25	100	-0-
Short-term controllable margin	$ 850	$300	$ 550	(25)	$275	$250	$ 50
Long-term controllable fixed costs	400	120	280	20	10	130	120
Contribution by SBU (CSBU)	$ 450	$180	$ 270	$(45)	$265	$120	$ (70)
Untraceable costs	200						
Operating income	$ 250						

Inc. (MTI). MTI has two operating divisions—division A and division B. The level of detail at which the contribution income statement is developed varies depending on management's needs. For a firm with a limited number of products, the level of detail in Exhibit 18–6 is common. For a firm with several products, a more extensive contribution income statement would be required to provide sufficient detail for management analysis.

This contribution margin income statement is an extension of the income statement illustrated in Chapter 10: Exhibits 10–14 and 10–15. Exhibit 10–14 introduces the idea of traceable fixed costs; that is, fixed costs that can be traced directly to a product line or production unit. Exhibit 10–15 shows both contribution margin and contribution margin less traceable fixed costs, which we call **contribution by SBU (CSBU)**. The concept of CSBU is important, because it measures *all* the costs that are traceable to, and therefore controllable by, the individual profit SBUs. CSBU is a more complete and fair measure of performance than either the contribution margin or profit.

This chapter expands the contribution margin income statement by distinguishing short-term and long-term controllable (i.e., traceable) fixed costs. **Short-term controllable fixed costs** are those fixed costs that the profit SBU manager can influence in approximately a year or less. That is, the manager typically budgets these costs in the annual budget; some costs involve contractual relationships for a year or less. Examples include advertising; sales promotion; certain engineering, data processing, and research projects; and management consulting. In contrast, **long-term controllable fixed costs** are those that are not controllable within a year's time; usually these include facilities-related costs such as depreciation, taxes, and insurance.

As illustrated in Exhibit 18–6, the firm develops a useful measure of the profit SBU manager's short-term performance by subtracting short-term controllable fixed cost from the contribution margin, to get the **short-term controllable margin.** In contrast, to measure the manager's performance in managing both short- and long-term costs, the CSBU measure is most appropriate since it includes both short-term and long-term fixed costs.

One complication in completing the contribution income statement is that some costs that are not traceable at a detailed level are traceable at a higher level of aggregation. The not-traceable column in the income statement represents costs traceable to division B but not traceable to any of the product lines. For example, the $25,000 short-term controllable fixed costs might consist of the cost of advertising that was done at the division level to benefit all three products.

In addition to providing useful measures of the manager's performance in managing both short-term and long-term controllable costs, the contribution margin income statement can be used to determine whether a profit SBU should be deleted or retained, much like our contribution margin analysis in Exhibit 10–15.

The **contribution by SBU (CSBU)** measures all the costs that are traceable to, and therefore controllable by, the individual profit SBUs.

Short-term controllable fixed costs are those fixed costs that the profit SBU manager can influence in approximately a year or less.

Long-term controllable fixed costs are those that are not controllable within a year's time, and these usually include facilities-related costs such as depreciation, taxes, and insurance.

Short-term controllable margin is determined by subtracting short-term controllable fixed costs from the contribution margin.

The analysis is now enhanced because of our ability to distinguish short-term and long-term controllable fixed costs. For example, using the analysis in Exhibit 18–6, MTI can figure that if product 3 is deleted, the short-term effect will be to reduce profit by $50,000, the amount of the short-term controllable margin. All the costs involved in the determination of the short-term controllable margin are avoidable within a period of one year. Taking the longer-term view, MTI could ultimately save an additional $120,000 of long-term controllable fixed costs by deleting product 3. Thus, in the long term, MTI can save $70,000 by deleting product 3, the amount of the contribution by profit SBU (CSBU) for product 3.

Variable Costing versus Absorption Costing

The use of the contribution margin income statement often is called variable costing because it separates variable and fixed costs. Only variable costs are included in determining the cost of sales and the contribution margin. In contrast, absorption costing is a cost system in which fixed cost is included in product cost and cost of sales. Absorption costing is the conventional costing system, as it is required by financial reporting standards and by the Internal Revenue Service for determining taxable income.

The advantage of variable costing is that it meets the three objectives of management control systems by showing separately those costs that can be traced to, and controlled by, each SBU. In this section we see an additional reason for using variable costing—while net income determined using absorption costing is affected by changes in inventory levels, net income using variable costing is not affected. In Exhibit 18–7 we show how net income is affected using absorption costing.

The first of the three panels in Exhibit 18–7 shows the data used in the illustration, including units produced and sold and costs for two periods. The second panel shows both the absorption and variable cost income statements for two periods. Two periods are used to show the differences for both possible cases: inventory is increasing or decreasing. The third panel shows a brief explanation of why the income figures differ for the two methods.

In period one, inventory increases by 40 units because production of 100 units exceeds sales of 60 units. Inventory decreases by the same amount in period two. Using absorption costing, the unit product cost is $30 variable plus $40 fixed, or $70 per unit in both periods. The $70 unit cost is used to calculate the cost of goods sold on the income statements in periods one and two for absorption costing. The selling and administrative costs ($5 variable and $1,200 fixed) are deducted after gross margin to get the net income of $300 in period one and $2,300 in period two.

The variable cost income statement uses variable cost only to determine product cost. The cost of sales and inventory figures are determined using a variable manufacturing cost of $30 per unit. To get the total contribution margin, the variable selling and administrative costs of $5 per unit sold are deducted along with variable cost of sales of $30 per unit. The result is a total contribution margin of

Exhibit 18–7	Comparison of Absorption and Variable Costing		
Data Summary	**Period 1**	**Period 2**	
Units			
Beginning inventory	0	40	
Price	$ 100	$ 100	
Sold	60	140	
Produced	100	100	
Unit variable costs			
Manufacturing	$ 30	$ 30	
Selling and administrative costs	$ 5	$ 5	
Fixed costs			Per unit
Manufacturing	$4,000	$4,000	$40
Selling and administrative costs	$1,200	$1,200	

Exhibit 18–7   Continued

Comparison of Absorption and Variable Costing

Period One Income Statement

	Absorption Costing		Variable Costing	
Sales (60 × $100)	$6,000		$6,000	
Cost of goods sold				
Beginning inventory	$ 0		$ 0	
+ Cost of goods produced	7,000		3,000	
	(= 100 × $70)		(= 100 × $30)	
= Cost of goods available for sale	7,000		3,000	
− Ending inventory	2,800		1,200	
	(= 40 × $70)		(= 40 × $30)	
= Cost of goods sold		4,200		1,800
Less: Variable selling and				
administrative costs		N/A		300
Gross margin		**$1,800**		
Contribution margin				**$ 3,900**
Less other costs				
Less: Fixed manufacturing costs	N/A		$4,000	
Less: Selling and administrative costs				
Variable	300		N/A	
Fixed	1,200		1,200	
Total other costs		1,500		5,200
Net income		$ 300		$(1,300)

Period Two Income Statement

	Absorption Costing		Variable Costing	
Sales (140 × $100)	$14,000		$14,000	
Cost of goods sold				
Beginning inventory (from period one)	2,800		1,200	
+ Cost of goods produced (for 100				
units, same as period one)	7,000		3,000	
= Cost of goods available for sale	9,800		4,200	
Ending inventory	0		0	
= Cost of goods sold		9,800		4,200
Less: Variable selling and administrative		N/A		700
Gross margin		**$ 4,200**		
Contribution margin				**$ 9,100**
Less: Other costs				
Less: Fixed manufacturing costs	N/A		4,000	
Less: Selling and administrative costs				
Variable	700		N/A	
Fixed	1,200		1,200	
Total other costs		1,900		6,200
Net income		$ 2,300		$ 3,900

Reconciling the Difference in Net Income between Absorption and Variable Costing

	First Period	Second Period
Change in inventory in units	40	(40)
Multiply times fixed overhead rate	$40	$40
= Difference in net income	$1,600	$(1,600)
(Negative number means variable		
costing net income is higher.)		

Key to exhibit: N/A = not applicable

$3,900 in period one and $9,100 in period two. In variable costing, all fixed costs (both manufacturing fixed cost of $4,000 and selling and administration fixed costs of $1,200) are deducted from the contribution margin, to get a $1,300 loss in period one and $3,900 profit in period two.

The difference in net income in period one between absorption and variable costing is $1,600 ($300 profit compared to a $1,300 loss), which is exactly the amount of fixed cost put into the increase in inventory under absorption costing ($1,600 = 40 units multiplied by $40 per unit fixed cost). Note that the amount of ending inventory in period one differs by $1,600 ($2,800 for absorption cost versus $1,200 for variable costing). This amount is also the difference in net income between variable and absorption costing for both period one and period two, when inventory decreases by 40 units. The useful guide then is that *absorption cost net income exceeds variable cost net income (by the amount of fixed cost in the inventory change) when inventory increases and variable costing net income is greater than absorption cost net income when inventory decreases*.

The important point is that variable costing is not affected by the change in inventory because all fixed costs are deducted from income in the period in which they occur; fixed costs are not included in inventory, so that inventory changes do not affect net income. For this reason, variable cost net income can be considered a more reliable measure and is preferable for use in strategic performance measurement. When absorption costing is used (as is required for financial reporting), the management accountant must use special caution in interpreting the amount of net income and attempt to determine what portion of profit, if any, might be due to inventory changes. This is especially important if net income is used as a basis for performance evaluation, as it is in profit SBUs.

STRATEGIC PERFORMANCE MEASUREMENT AND THE BALANCED SCORECARD

LEARNING OBJECTIVE 5 ▶
Explain the role of the balanced scorecard in strategic performance measurement.

Cost, revenue, and profit SBUs are widely used methods to achieve strategic performance measurement. A common characteristic of these SBUs in practice is they use little or no nonfinancial information. However, a complete strategic performance evaluation necessarily attends to all the critical success factors of the business, including many nonfinancial factors. A useful approach for a complete strategic performance evaluation is to include both financial and nonfinancial factors for the SBU, using the balanced scorecard. The balanced scorecard measures the SBU's performance in four key areas: (1) customer satisfaction, (2) financial performance, (3) internal business processes, and (4) learning and growth. Cost, revenue, and profit SBUs focus on the financial dimension. The main concept of the balanced scorecard is that no one measure can properly evaluate the SBU's progress to strategic success. Rather, multiple measures typically grouped in the four key areas provide the desired comprehensive evaluation of the SBU's performance. Moreover, by attending directly to the firm's critical success factors (CSFs), the balanced scorecard effectively links the performance measurement/evaluation process to the firm's strategy.

Caterpillar Corporation provides an example of the application of the balanced scorecard concept to SBUs.[11] Caterpillar developed a new approach for evaluating its SBUs in the early 1990s. The focus of the new approach was to improve achievement of the critical success factors: to improve responsiveness to customers and to improve the flexibility of internal business processes. Prior to that time, Caterpillar used cost SBUs to control divisional operations. Each division's goal was to reduce the cost of designing and manufacturing products. Because there was no direct link to the customer or to profitability, decision making was not strategic.

Caterpillar's new approach included a move from cost SBUs to profit SBUs with the objective of drawing managers' attention to profitability and customer service, and to create a climate of constructive conflict among the SBUs. Moreover, the profit SBUs were evaluated with many nonfinancial measures including customer and employee satisfaction, delivery performance, and process improvement. Thus at Caterpillar, the SBU evaluation is much like a balanced scorecard. Caterpillar plans

---

[11] James A. Hendricks, David G. Defreitas, and Delores K. Walker, "Changing Performance Measures at Caterpillar," *Management Accounting*, December 1996, pp. 18–24.

to increase the development and use of nonfinancial measures. The firm believes that achievement of CSFs leads to even better financial results in the future.

As at Caterpillar, increasingly management accountants are called on to measure and report selected nonfinancial and operating data, the type of information that is relevant for the critical success factors. This information is often presented in the format of a balanced scorecard. Additional examples of potential critical success factors and how they might be measured in a balanced scorecard SBU are in Exhibit 18–8.

Exhibit 18–8	Critical Success Factors and How to Measure Them
Critical Success Factor	**How It Is Measured**
Quality	Number of defects or returns, customer satisfaction
Efficiency	Throughput time
Flexibility	Setup time, cycle time
Effectiveness	Value added versus non–value added
Skill development	Training hours, skill performance
Customer satisfaction	Number of complaints, survey results
Timeliness of delivery	Time from order to customer receipt
Timeliness of new product release	Number of days over/under targeted introduction date
Safety	Number of accidents, related occurrences
Collections	Aging of receivables, number of delinquencies
Manufacturability	Cycle time, setup time, number of design changes
	Complaints, turnover

BusinessWeek

How Did GE, IBM, and Otis Make Great Strides Against Their Competitors?

(Continues from page 723)

A: R&D was a stepping stone . . . Like GE, Otis Elevator and IBM employ the breakthrough approach to investment in R&D, seeking to obtain big results that create a foundation for new markets and dramatic growth. For example, Otis Elevator is completing development of the first elevator capable of providing service to buildings taller than 130 stories—a product that will open a whole new market for Otis, while IBM's current development of silicon-germanium semiconductors promises to fundamentally change the computer industry. Some would argue that a firm needs to have both an incrementalist R&D strategy that focuses on improvements in existing products as well as breakthrough projects. The incrementalist R&D projects help to keep the current product lines competitive, while the breakthrough projects hold out the promise of a successful future.

The decision of which approach to invest in is a difficult one that asks companies to evaluate short-term and long-term goals and strategies. Added into this complex decision is the difficulty surrounding the management and evaluation of R&D projects—with breakthrough projects being especially difficult because of the extensive uncertainty surrounding them. What is clear is that breakthrough projects must be evaluated differently than incrementalist projects, and they cannot be effectively managed as a cost or profit SBU. More patience is required, and the pressure of short-term cost reports is inappropriate. In addition, emphasis must be placed on the skills of the researchers who are responsible for these projects. For example, academic research at Rensselaer Polytechnic Institute shows that the most successful R&D researchers are those who have wide-ranging networks in the research community. In the end, companies recognize that R&D is a necessary part in the effort to set themselves apart from the competition— whether it is in small steps or leaps and bounds.

For further reading, see "Getting to 'Eureka!'" *Business Week,* November 10, 1997.

Exhibit 18–9	**Performance Report for the Consumer Loan Department August 31, 19X4**

Variable Costs:	
Direct labor	$23,446
Supplies	3,836
Short-Term Controllable Costs	
Supervision salaries	15,339
Advertising	6,500
Fees and services	4,226
Other	766
Long-Term Controllable Costs	
Facilities	650
Data processing	2,200
Other	899
Total Costs	$57,862
Operating Performance:	
Number of accounts at end of month	1,334
Number of new accounts	54
Number of closed accounts	22
Number of transactions processed	1,994
Number of inquiries processed	334

MANAGEMENT CONTROL IN SERVICE AND NOT-FOR-PROFIT FIRMS

Management control in service and not-for-profit firms is commonly implemented in the form of either a cost SBU or a profit SBU. As manufacturing and retail firms do, these organizations choose a cost SBU when the critical mission of the manager is to control costs, whereas a profit SBU is preferred when the department manager must manage both costs and revenues or, alternatively (in a not-for-profit firm), manage costs without exceeding budgeted revenues.

LEARNING OBJECTIVE 6 ▶
Explain the role of strategic performance measurement in service and not-for-profit organizations.

The most common type of SBU in service and not-for-profit firms is the cost SBU. For example, the performance of the manager of a bank's consumer loan department often is monitored as a cost SBU, as illustrated in Exhibit 18–9. Note that the structure of the performance report is much like that of the profit SBU analysis in Exhibit 18–6. The difference here is that the focus is on costs, which are separated into variable costs such as labor and supplies, short-term controllable fixed costs such as supervision salaries, and long-term controllable fixed costs such as data processing and facilities management. In addition, the report includes information regarding certain operating measures that are critical to the success of the department—the number of new accounts, number of closed accounts, number of transactions processed, and number of inquiries handled. This information is used to evaluate the manager's performance over time, and perhaps also to compare performance to that of managers in related departments such as the mortgage loan department.

Note that the report does not include the cost of funds provided for the loans, since it is assumed that the department manager cannot control either the supply or the cost of those funds.

SUMMARY

For management control systems the principal focus is on the most commonly used method, the strategic performance measurement. The goal of top management in using strategic performance measurement is to *motivate the managers* to provide a high level of effort, to *guide them to make decisions that are congruent with the goals of top management,* and to provide a basis for *fair compensation* for the managers.

Strategic performance measurement systems are implemented in four different forms, depending on the nature of the manager's responsibilities—the revenue SBU, cost SBU, profit SBU, and investment SBU. The four types of SBUs are employed in manufacturing as well as service and not-for-profit firms. Common manufacturing examples of cost SBUs are production and production-support departments. Cost SBUs often are evaluated as either engineered-cost SBUs or discretionary-cost SBUs. Discretionary-cost SBUs focus on planning desired cost levels, while the engineered-cost method focuses on evaluation of achieved cost levels.

The marketing department can be either a cost SBU or a revenue SBU or both. As a revenue SBU, the marketing department has goals for sales growth, while as a cost SBU, there are goals for managing order-getting and order-filling costs.

The profit SBU is used when there is a need for coordination between the marketing and production areas, as, for example, in handling special orders or rush orders. Evaluation on profit provides the incentive for the departments to work together. Also, profit SBUs are used to set a desirable competitive tone. All departments have the profit incentive to compete with other providers of the product or service, inside or outside the firm. The contribution margin income statement is an effective means to evaluate profit SBUs because it identifies the direct costs for each profit SBU.

The contribution margin income statement is sometimes called variable costing. It has the benefit of not being affected by changes in finished goods inventory. In contrast, the conventional income statement based on absorption costing is affected by inventory changes.

A key issue in the effective use of strategic performance measurement systems is the integration of strategic considerations into the evaluation. This requires an identification of the critical success factors of the firm, and appropriate measurement and reporting of these factors, commonly in the form of a balanced scorecard. In many cases, a substantial portion of these factors are nonfinancial, including operating and economic data from sources external to the firm.

KEY TERMS

SELF-STUDY PROBLEM

(For solution, please turn to the end of the chapter.)

Discretionary-Cost and Engineered-Cost Methods

C. B. (Chuck) Davis is the manager of the claims processing department for Liberty Life Insurance Co. Davis has 12 clerks working for him to process approximately 900 claims per month. Each clerk earns a $2,400 monthly salary, including benefits. The number of claims varies somewhat, and in recent years it has been as low as 810 and as high as 1,020 per month. Davis has argued with Liberty officials that his 12 clerks are not enough to handle 1,000 or more claims; Davis knows from a recent study of his department that it takes a well-trained clerk on the average 121 minutes to process a claim (processing time also varies widely, from as little as a few minutes to several hours, depending on the complexity of the claim). While Liberty management agrees that 12 clerks are not sufficient for a month with 1,020 claims, there are far too many clerks when there are only 810 claims to process. Management figures that 12 clerks is about right. Assume that each clerk works an eight-hour day except for 40 minutes of break time and there are an average 22 working days in each month. In the most recent month, January, the department processed 915 claims.

Required

1. What type of SBU does it appear that Liberty management is using for the claims processing department?

2. Assuming that Liberty uses the discretionary-cost method, what is the budgeted cost in the claims department for January?

3. Assuming that Liberty uses the engineered-cost method, what is the budgeted cost in the claims department for January?

4. If you were Davis, how would you develop a more effective argument for top management to provide you with additional clerks?

QUESTIONS

18–1 What is the difference between management control, performance evaluation, and operational control?

18–2 What is strategic performance measurement, and why is it important for effective management?

18–3 Does an effective performance evaluation focus on individual or team performance?

18–4 Explain the difference between informal and formal control systems. What type of control system is strategic performance measurement?

18–5 Name three types of organizational designs and explain the differences between them.

18–6 What are four types of strategic performance measurement SBUs, and what are the goals of each?

18–7 Since absorption costing is accepted for financial reporting purposes, and variable costing is not, why are we concerned about the difference between them? What is the difference, and why is it important?

18–8 What are some of the important behavioral and implementation issues in strategic performance measurement? How does the management accountant deal with these issues?

18–9 What is the role of cost allocation in strategic performance measurement?

18–10 Can strategic performance measurement be used for service and not-for-profit firms? How?

18–11 In what situations would a cost SBU be most appropriate? A profit SBU? A revenue SBU?

18–12 How do centralized and decentralized firms differ? What are the advantages of each?

18–13 Can the marketing department be both a revenue SBU and a cost SBU? Explain.

PROBLEMS

18–14 DEPARTMENTAL COST ALLOCATION IN PROFIT SBUs Elvis Wilbur owns two adjoining restaurants, the Beef Barn and the Fish Bowl. Each restaurant is treated as a profit SBU for performance evaluation. Although the restaurants have separate kitchens, they share a central baking facility. The principal costs of the baking area include depreciation and maintenance on the equipment, materials, supplies, and labor.

Required

1. Wilbur allocates the monthly costs of the baking facility to the two restaurants based on the number of tables served in each restaurant during the month. In April the costs were $24,000, of which $12,000 is fixed cost. The Beef Barn and the Fish Bowl each served 3,000 tables. How much of the joint cost should be allocated to each of the restaurants?

2. In May fixed and unit variable costs remained the same, but the Beef Barn served 2,000 tables and the Fish Bowl served 3,000. Now, how much should be allocated to each restaurant? Explain your reasoning.

18–15 ALLOCATION OF MARKETING AND ADMINISTRATIVE COSTS; PROFIT SBUs Snodgrass Academy allocates marketing and administrative costs to its three schools based on total annual tuition revenue for the schools. In 19X3 the allocations (000s omitted) were

Service

	Lower School	Middle School	Upper School	Total
Tuition revenue	$700	$600	$900	$2,200
Marketing and administration	255	218	327	$ 800

In 19X4, the Middle and Upper schools experienced no change in revenues, while the Lower School's tuition revenue increased to $1.5 million. Marketing and administrative costs rose to $960,000.

Required

1. Using revenue as an allocation base, how should the costs be allocated for 19X4?

2. What are the shortcomings of this allocation formula?

18–16 ALLOCATION OF CENTRAL COSTS; PROFIT SBUs The Whispering Glen Resorts, Inc., operates four resort hotels in the heavily wooded areas of eastern Texas. The resorts are named after the predominant trees at the resort: Oak Glen, Pine Glen, Magnolia, and Pecan Arbor. Whispering Glen allocates its central office costs to its four guest buildings according to annual revenue generated by each building. For the current year these costs (000s omitted) include:

Service

$ 6,000	Front office personnel
4,000	Administrative and executive salaries
2,000	Interest on resort purchase
300	Advertising
100	Housekeeping
80	Depreciation on reservations computer
80	Room maintenance
50	Carpet-cleaning contract
40	Contract to repaint rooms
$12,650	

Pertinent data relating to the four resorts:

	Pine	Pecan	Oak	Magnolia	Total
Revenue (000s)	$ 3,000	$ 7,000	$ 9,000	$ 5,000	$ 24,000
Square footage	52,500	75,000	32,500	75,000	235,000
Rooms	150	200	100	250	700
Assets (000s)	$65,000	$110,000	$88,000	$45,000	$308,000

Required

1. Based on annual revenue, how many of the central office costs are allocated to each resort? What are the shortcomings of this allocation method?

2. Suppose the current method were replaced with a system of four separate cost pools, with costs collected in the four pools allocated on the basis of revenues, assets invested in each resort, square footage, and number of rooms, respectively. Which costs should be collected in each of the four pools?

3. Using the cost pool system, how much of the central office costs would be allocated to each of the four resorts? Is this system preferable to the single-allocation base system used in requirement 1? Why or why not?

Service

18–17 ALLOCATION OF COMMON COSTS Betty Jones and Penny White are associates at the same law firm in Atlanta. They traveled to New York City together recently to visit their respective clients. From the airport, they shared a cab ride to their hotel. The cab ride for Jones alone would have cost $18, but for two passengers the cost was $22. Had Jones not offered to share the cab ride, White (in deference to her client's frugality) would have taken the bus to Grand Central Station, which is six blocks from the hotel, at a cost of $10.

Required How should the $22 cost of the cab ride be allocated to the two clients?

Service

18–18 ALLOCATION OF ADMINISTRATIVE COSTS Kuldigs Rental Management Services manages four local apartment complexes of varying sizes and degrees of luxury. Kuldigs' president has observed that the luxurious apartments tend to require more of her staff's time than the simpler units. Kuldigs incurs monthly operating expenses of $15,000, and its president desires a profit of 7 percent, for a total monthly billing of $16,050.

	Units	Average Rent per Unit
Pinnacle Point	100	$720
Whispering Woods	355	540
Hollow Rock	300	425
College Villa	550	340

Required How should the $16,050 be allocated to the four apartment complexes? Explain your answer.

18–19 ALLOCATION OF COMMON COSTS Seven businesses rent offices and suites of various sizes in a 3,500-square-foot office building owned by Bill Luckus. He allocates the utility costs among the tenants according to the square footage rented. Tenants now are balking at this arrangement, because last week Dottie's Drapes, a tenant who leases 400 square feet, installed a massive new lighting system and two window-unit air conditioners. The other tenants claim they should not bear the cost of Dottie's extravagant use of electricity.

Required How should Luckus respond to the tenants' complaints?

18–20 RESPONSIBILITY FOR INEFFICIENCY; ETHICS General Hospital leases its diagnostic equipment from Normed Leasing, which also is responsible for maintaining the leased equipment. Recently the hospital's MRI machine fell into disrepair and physicians were required to order expensive nonemergency laboratory tests for their patients to diagnose conditions that could have been diagnosed more easily (and less expensively) using MRI. Rather than bill its patients for the entire costs of these tests, the hospital billed the patients for the cost of MRI and billed the difference to Normed. Normed disputes the charge, claiming that the physicians should have postponed diagnosis of the patients' conditions until the MRI machine could be repaired.  *Ethics*

Required What issues need to be addressed to determine how the charge should be handled properly? How can this type of situation be prevented? If appropriate, include ethical issues in your response.

18–21 ASSIGNING RESPONSIBILITY Kristen Langdon, the sales manager at a large manufacturer of bicycles, has secured an order from a major department store that is due for shipment on November 1. She is eager to please the department store in hopes of getting more of its business in the future. She asks Bryan Collins, the company's purchasing agent, to procure all the necessary parts in time for production to begin on October 10. Collins orders the parts from reputable suppliers, and most of them arrive by October 7. George Watkins, the production manager, begins production as scheduled on October 10, even though the gears Collins ordered were delayed because of some quality control problems at the manufacturer. Collins assures Watkins that the gear shipment will arrive before October 16, when those parts are scheduled to be attached to the bicycles. The shipment finally arrives on October 18, after production has been delayed for two days.

Required Which department should bear the responsibility for the two days' downtime? How can problems like this be avoided in the future?

18–22 RESOLVING DISPUTES AMONG PRODUCTION COST SBUs Red Apple Industries manufactures institutional-use furniture. Department A is responsible for welding the base of the desk to the chair assembly. The desks then are placed on an automatic conveyer to department B, where the desktop is riveted to the chair. The desks continue on the conveyer to department C for further assembly. Wanda Werk, the manager of department A, is responsible for moving 800 welded desks per hour to department B. A faulty circuit in department B causes a delay in processing in the department and prompts Rosie Dan, the department B manager, to ask Werk to stop the conveyer. Werk refuses, necessitating the removal of the welded desks from the conveyer until the riveting can resume. Dan bills Werk's department for the costs of this extra work. Werk disputes the charge, citing her responsibility to convey 800 desks per hour to department B.

Required How should the managers' dispute be resolved? How could it have been avoided?

18–23 RESPONSIBILITY FOR WAGE DIFFERENTIAL Bloomfield University keeps a staff of five computer repair workers during the academic year. During the summer months the school's computers are used infrequently and thus require very little of the repair workers' time. To make full use of these workers, the university reassigns them to the maintenance department, where they assist in the annual cleaning of the classroom buildings. Because of their relatively high skill level, the workers are paid at a rate of $18 per hour year-round, while the maintenance workers with whom they work in the summer are paid $11 an hour.  *Service*

Required What department should bear the costs of the $7 an hour wage differential for the computer repair workers?

18–24 **COMPARISON OF VARIABLE AND ABSORPTION COSTING** The Mane Company manufactures hair brushes that sell at wholesale for $2 per unit. Budgeted production in both 19X5 and 19X6 was 2,000 units. There is no beginning inventory in 19X5. These data summarize the 19X5 and 19X6 operations:

	19X5	**19X6**
Sales	2,000 units	2,200 units
Production costs:	2,400 units	2,000 units
Factory—variable (per unit)	$.60	$.50
—fixed	$1,000	$1,000
Marketing—variable	$.50	$.60
Administrative—fixed	$500	$500

Required

1. Income statements for each year based on absorption costing.

2. Income statements for each of the years based on variable costing.

3. A reconciliation and explanation of the differences in the operating income resulting from using the absorption costing method and variable costing method.

18–25 **ABSORPTION AND VARIABLE COSTING** Seymore Inc. planned and manufactured 300,000 units of its single product in 19X5, its first year of operations. Variable manufacturing costs were $40 per unit of production. Planned and fixed manufacturing costs were $700,000. Marketing and administrative costs (all fixed) were $500,000 in 19X5. Seymore Inc. sold 150,000 units of products in 19X5 at $50 per unit.

Required

1. Determine Seymore Inc.'s operating income using absorption costing.

2. Determine Seymore Inc.'s operating income using variable costing.

3. Explain the difference between the operating incomes in requirements 1 and 2.

18–26 **VARIABLE AND ABSORPTION COSTING** Jason Reynolds, Inc., is the manufacturer of a specialized surgical instrument called the TDR–11. The firm has grown rapidly in recent years because of the product's low price and high quality. However, sales have declined this year due primarily to increased competition and to a decrease in the surgical procedures for which the TDR–11 is used. Reynolds is concerned about the decline in sales, but he is especially concerned about the decline in operating income over the past year. He has hired a consultant to further analyze the firm's profitability. The consultant provided the following information:

	19X4	**19X5**
Sales (units)	2,300	1,900
Production	2,200	1,700
Budgeted production and sales	2,000	2,000
Beginning inventory	850	750
Data per unit (all variable)		
Price	$1,995	$1,885
Direct materials	440	440
Direct labor	255	255
Selling costs	125	125
Period cost (all fixed):		
Manufacturing overhead	$480,000	$480,000
Selling and administrative	160,000	160,000

Required

1. Using the absorption cost method used by Reynold's accountant to prepare the annual financial statements, prepare the income statements for 19X4 and 19X5.

2. Using variable costing, prepare an income statement for each period, and explain the difference in net income from that obtained in requirement 1.

3. Write a brief memo to Reynolds that explains the difference in income between variable costing and absorption costing.

18–27 **CONTRIBUTION MARGIN INCOME STATEMENT FOR PROFIT SBUs; STRATEGY** Music Teachers, Inc., is an educational association for music teachers that had 20,000 members during 19X5. The association operates from a central headquarters but has local membership chapters throughout the United States. Monthly meetings are held by the local chapters to discuss recent developments on topics of interest to music teachers. The association's journal, *Teachers' Forum,* is issued monthly with features about recent developments in the field. The association publishes books and reports and sponsors professional courses that qualify for continuing professional education credits. Their statement of revenue and expense (000s omitted) for the current year is

Strategy

Revenue	$3,275
Expense	
Salaries	$ 920
Personnel costs	230
Occupancy costs	280
Reimbursement to local chapters	600
Other membership services	500
Printing and paper	320
Postage and shipping	176
Instructors' fees	80
General and administrative	38
Total expenses	$3,144
Excess of revenues over expenses	$ 131

The Board of Directors of Music Teachers Inc. requested that a segmented statement of operations be prepared showing the contribution of each profit SBU (i.e., membership, magazine subscriptions, books and reports, continuing education). Mike Doyle was assigned this responsibility and had gathered these data prior to statement preparation:

- Membership dues are $100 per year of which $20 covers a one-year subscription to the association's journal. Other benefits include membership in the association and chapter affiliation. The portion of the dues covering the magazine subscription ($20) should be assigned to the magazine subscriptions profit SBU.

- One-year subscriptions to *Teachers' Forum* were sold to nonmembers and libraries at $30 each. A total of 2,500 of these subscriptions were sold. In addition to subscriptions, the magazine generated $100,000 in advertising revenue. The costs per magazine subscription were $7 for printing and paper and $4 for postage and shipping.

- A total of 28,000 technical reports and professional texts were sold by the books and reports department at an average unit selling price of $25. Average costs per publication were as follows.

Printing and paper	$4
Postage and shipping	$2

- The association offers a variety of continuing education courses to both members and nonmembers. The one-day courses cost $75 each and were attended by 2,400 students in 19X5. A total of 1,760 students took two-day courses at a cost of $125 for each course. Outside instructors were paid to teach some courses.

- Salary and occupancy data are

	Salaries	Square Footage
Membership	$210,000	2,000
Magazine subscriptions	150,000	2,000
Books and reports	300,000	3,000
Continuing education	180,000	2,000
Corporate staff	80,000	1,000
	$920,000	10,000

The books and reports department also rents warehouse space at an annual cost of $50,000. Personnel costs are 25 percent of salaries.

- Printing and paper costs other than for magazine subscriptions and books and reports relate to the continuing education department.

- General and administrative expenses include all other costs incurred by the corporate staff to operate the association.

Doyle has decided to assign all revenue and expense to the profit SBUs that can be:

1. Traced directly to a profit SBU.
2. Allocated on a reasonable and logical basis to a profit SBU.

The expenses that can be traced or assigned to corporate staff as well as any other expenses that cannot be assigned to profit SBUs will be grouped with the general and administrative expenses and not allocated to the profit SBUs. Doyle believes that allocations often tend to be arbitrary and are not useful for management reporting and analysis. He believes that any further allocation of the general and administrative expenses associated with the operation and administration of the association would be arbitrary.

Required

1. Prepare a contribution margin income statement for Music Teachers, Inc.
2. What is the strategic role of the contribution margin income statement for Music Teachers, Inc.?
3. Mike Doyle is considering the possibility of not allocating indirect or nontraceable expenses to profit SBUs.
   a. What reasons often are presented for not allocating indirect or nontraceable expenses to profit SBUs?
   b. Under what circumstances might the allocation of indirect or nontraceable expenses to profit SBUs be acceptable?

(CMA Adapted)

International

Strategy

18–28 **CONTRIBUTION MARGIN INCOME STATEMENT FOR PROFIT SBUs; STRATEGY, INTERNATIONAL** Stratford Corporation is a diversified company whose products are marketed both domestically and internationally. The company's major product lines are pharmaceutical products, sports equipment, and household appliances. At a recent meeting of Stratford's board of directors, there was a lengthy discussion on ways to improve overall corporate profitability without new acquisitions. New acquisitions are problematic, as the company already is heavily leveraged. The members of the board decided that they required additional financial information about individual corporate operations to target areas for improvement. Dave Murphy, Stratford's controller, has been asked to provide additional data that would assist the board in its investigation. Stratford is not a public company and, therefore, has not prepared complete income statements by product line. Murphy regularly has prepared an income statement by product line through contribution margin. However, Murphy now believes that income statements prepared through operating income along both product lines and geographic areas would provide the directors with the required insight into corporate operations. Murphy has the following data available:

| | Product Lines | | | |
	Pharmaceutical	Sports	Appliances	Total
Production/Sales in units	160,000	180,000	160,000	500,000
Average selling price per unit	$8.00	$20.00	$15.00	
Average variable manufacturing cost per unit	4.00	9.50	8.25	
Average variable selling expense per unit	2.00	2.50	2.25	
Fixed factory overhead excluding depreciation				$500,000
Depreciation of plant and equipment				400,000
Administrative and selling expense				1,160,000

Murphy had several discussions with the division managers from each product line and compiled this information:

- The division managers concluded that Murphy should allocate fixed factory overhead on the basis of the ratio of the variable costs expended per product line or per geographic area to total variable costs.

- Each of the division managers agreed that a reasonable basis for the allocation of depreciation on plant and equipment would be the ratio of units produced per product line or per geographical area to the total number of units produced.

- There was little agreement on the allocation of administrative and selling expenses so Murphy decided to allocate only those expenses that were directly traceable to the SBU being delineated; that is, manufacturing staff salaries to product lines and sales staff salaries to geographic areas. Murphy used these data for this allocation:

Manufacturing Staff		Sales Staff	
Pharmaceutical	$120,000	United States	$ 60,000
Sports	140,000	Canada	100,000
Appliances	80,000	Europe	250,000

- The division managers provided reliable sales percentages for their product lines by geographical area:

| | Percentage of Unit Sales | | |
	United States	Canada	Europe
Pharmaceutical	40%	10%	50%
Sports	40	40	20
Appliances	20	20	60

Murphy prepared this product-line income statement:

STRATFORD CORPORATION
Statement of Income by Product Lines
For the Fiscal Year Ended April 30, 19X7

| | Product Lines | | | | |
	Pharmaceutical	Sports	Appliances	Unallocated	Total
Sales in units	160,000	180,000	160,000		
Sales	$1,280,000	$3,600,000	$2,400,000	—	$7,280,000
Variable manufacturing and selling costs	960,000	2,160,000	1,680,000	—	4,800,000
Contribution margin	$ 320,000	$1,440,000	$ 720,000	—	$2,480,000
Fixed costs					
Fixed factory overhead	$ 100,000	$ 225,000	$ 175,000	—	$ 500,000
Depreciation	128,000	144,000	128,000	—	400,000
Administrative and selling expense	120,000	140,000	80,000	$ 820,000	1,160,000
Total fixed costs	$ 348,000	$ 509,000	$ 383,000	$ 820,000	$2,060,000
Operating income (loss)	$ (28,000)	$ 931,000	$ 337,000	$(820,000)	$ 420,000

Required

1. Prepare a contribution margin income statement for Stratford Corporation based on the company's geographic areas of sales.

2. As a result of the information disclosed by both income statements (by product line and by geographic area), recommend areas where Stratford Corporation should focus its attention to improve corporate profitability.

3. What changes would you make to Stratford's strategic performance measurement system? Include the role, if any, of the firm's international business operations in your response.

(CMA Adapted)

18–29 DESIGN OF STRATEGIC BUSINESS UNIT   Hamilton-Jones, a large consulting firm in Los Angeles, has experienced rapid growth over the last five years. To better service its clients and to better manage its practice, the firm decided two years ago to organize into five strategic business units, each of which serves a significant base of clients—accounting systems, executive recruitment and compensation, client-server office information systems, manufacturing information systems, and real-estate consulting. Each of the client SBUs is served by a variety of administrative services within the firm, including payroll and accounting, printing and duplicating, report preparation, and secretarial support. Management of Hamilton-Jones watches closely the trend in the total costs of each of administrative support areas on a month-to-month basis. Management has noted that the costs in the printing and duplicating area have risen by 40 percent over the last two years, a rate that is twice that of any of the other support areas.

Required   Should Hamilton-Jones evaluate the five strategic business units as cost or profit SBUs? Why? How should the administrative support areas be evaluated?

18–30 DESIGN OF STRATEGIC BUSINESS UNIT   Martinsville Manufacturing Company develops parts for the automobile industry. The main product line is interior systems, especially seats and carpets. Martinsville operates out of a single large plant that has 30 manufacturing processes—dyeing of carpet, fabrication of seat frame, cutting of fabric, and so on. In addition to the 30 manufacturing units, there are six manufacturing support departments, including maintenance, engineering, janitorial support, scheduling, materials receiving and handling, and information systems. The costs of the support departments are allocated to the 30 manufacturing units on the basis of direct labor cost, materials costs, or the square feet of floor space in the plant occupied by the unit. In the case of the maintenance department, the cost is allocated on the basis of square feet. Maintenance costs have been relatively stable in recent years, but the firm's accountant advises that the amount of maintenance cost is a little high relative to the industry average.

Required What are the incentive effects on the manufacturing units of the current basis for allocating maintenance costs? What would be a more desirable way, if any, for allocating these costs? Explain your answer.

18–31 **DESIGN OF STRATEGIC BUSINESS UNIT** MetroBank is a fast-growing bank that serves the region around Jacksonville, Florida. The bank provides commercial and individual banking services, including investment and mortgage banking services. The firm's strategy is to continue to grow by acquiring smaller banks in the area to broaden the base and variety of services it can offer. There are now 87 strategic business units in the bank, which represent different areas of service in different locations. To support the growth of the firm, MetroBank has invested several million dollars in upgrading its information services function. The number of networked computers and the number of support personnel have more than doubled in the last four years, and now account for 13 percent of total operating expenses. Two years ago, MetroBank decided to charge information services to the SBUs based on the headcount (number of employees) in each of the SBUs. Recently, some of the larger SBUs have complained that this method has overcharged them, and that some of the smaller SBUs are actually using a larger share of the total information services resources. MetroBank's controller has decided to follow up on these complaints. His inquiry of the director of the information services department revealed that, while generally the larger departments used more services, there were in fact some small departments that "kept (him) pretty busy." Based on this response, the controller is considering changing the charges for information services to the basis of actual service calls in each of the SBUs rather than headcount.

Service

Required Is the information services department at MetroBank a profit SBU or a cost SBU? Which type of unit should it be, and why? Evaluate the controller's decision regarding the basis for charging information services costs to the SBUs.

18–32 **DESIGN OF STRATEGIC BUSINESS UNIT** Advanced Electronic Devices (AED) is a large manufacturer of electronic parts used in the manufacture of computers, automobiles, and a variety of consumer products. There are approximately 3,500 different products that AED manufactures each year. Approximately 10 percent of these are new products, while another 10 percent are dropped each year. AED is organized into 16 profit SBUs that cover the main areas of AED's business. In addition, there are 14 manufacturing support departments, each of which is charged to the profit SBUs on the basis of product cost. The head of engineering, one of the largest support departments, has argued that the current system is dysfunctional. It does not encourage the longer-term type of engineering projects that she thinks are critical to the success of the firm. She argues that it is the longer-term engineering projects that will develop the key improvements in the products and production processes that will maintain the firm's "competitive edge."

Required Assess the arguments of the head of the engineering department. Is the engineering department currently evaluated as a cost SBU or profit SBU? How do you think the support departments, including engineering, should be evaluated, and how should their costs be charged to the manufacturing departments?

SOLUTION TO SELF-STUDY PROBLEM

Discretionary-Cost and Engineered-Cost Methods

1. Liberty management is apparently using a cost SBU for the claims department because no revenues are generated there. Since management has chosen not to adjust the number of clerks for the changing number of claims each month, it appears to be using a discretionary-cost method to budget these costs. That is, management has determined it is more effective to provide a reasonable resource (12 clerks) for the claims processing area, and not to be directly concerned with the efficiency with which the clerks are working, the slack that is created during slow times, or the hectic pace that is necessary at peak load times. Their view is that the work averages out over time.

2. If Liberty uses the discretionary-cost method, the budget would be the same each month and would not depend on the level of claims to be processed. The budget would be the costs of providing the number of clerks that management judges to be adequate for the job (12 clerks × $2,400 per month) or $28,800 per month.

3. If Liberty uses the engineered-cost method, there is a budgeted cost for each claim that is processed based on the average time as determined from a study of the work flow. Assume that each clerk works an eight-hour day except for 40 minutes of break time, then (assuming 22 working days) the number of claims a clerk can process each month is

$$\frac{[(8 \text{ hours} \times 60 \text{ minutes}) - 40] \times 22 \text{ days}}{121 \text{ minutes}} = 80 \text{ claims per month}$$

And thus the cost per claim is

$$\$2,400/80 = \$30 \text{ per claim}$$

The engineered-cost budget for January is

$$915 \text{ claims} \times \$30 \text{ per claim} = \$27,450$$

The unfavorable variance for January using the engineered-cost method would be $1,350 ($28,800 actual expenditure less $27,450 budgeted expenditure). This unfavorable variance is best interpreted as the cost of unused capacity for processing claims. Since the capacity for processing claims is $80 \times 12 = 960$ claims, there is unused capacity of 45 claims ($960 - 915 = 45$ claims), or approximately one-half of one clerk.

4. Davis could make the strategic argument that the claims processing department should be staffed for peak capacity rather than for average capacity, to ensure promptness and accuracy during the busy months and to provide a better basis for employee morale, which is an important factor in performance during the low-volume months as well.

19

Strategic Investment Units and Transfer Pricing

After studying this chapter, you should be able to ...

Gamma Liaison

I know the price of success—dedication, hard work and an unremitting devotion to the things you want to see happen.

FRANK LLOYD WRIGHT

This chapter continues the development of strategic performance measurement introduced in Chapter 18, in which the four types of SBUs (revenue, cost, profit, and investment units) were explained and revenue, cost, and profit SBUs were developed in some detail. We consider investment SBUs in Part One of this chapter. Part Two explains transfer pricing, a method to handle the pricing problem that arises when a firm exchanges products or services between SBUs.

PART ONE: STRATEGIC INVESTMENT UNITS

Most firms use profit SBUs and investment SBUs to evaluate managers.[1] Profit SBUs are commonly used because of their strong effect on the motivation and goal congruence objectives of SBUs; managers are rewarded for their units' contribution to the firm's total profit. However, firms cannot use profit alone to compare one business unit to other business units or to alternative investments. The reason is the other business units and alternative investments are likely to be of different sizes or have different operating characteristics. The desired level of profit for a unit depends on its size and operating characteristics. Thus, while profit alone can be used effectively to evaluate a unit's performance over time, it should not be used to evaluate performance relative to other units or to alternative investments. What is needed is a means to compare a unit to other units and to alternative investments. The profit per dollar invested for each unit, usually called **return on investment (ROI)**, can be used to compare a unit to others or to the profitability of alternative investments. Investment SBUs are based on the concept of return on investment.

> **Return on investment (ROI)** is profit divided by investment in the business unit.

BusinessWeek

What's Kodak's Vision for the Future?

Critics have charged that George Fisher, Kodak CEO, has been too much of the nice guy, and hasn't made the cost cuts necessary to keep the firm a major player in the global photo-imaging business. They charge that competitors, such as Fuji of Japan and new entries Sony, Canon, and Hewlett-Packard, seem to be more nimble and aggressive than the 118-year-old film and camera manufacturer. George Fisher came to Kodak to trim things, and succeeded in divesting the chemical business and in reorienting much of top management. However, new investments in digital imaging have required huge investments ($500 million per year) and are slow in paying off. Fisher says the company's future lies in successful new products in digital photography technology. Critics say that the firm needs to tighten its belt to become the global competitor that is its birthright.

Will Fisher's long-term focus keep Kodak competitive? *Find out on page 770 of this chapter.*

---

[1] The majority of U.S. firms that responded to three recent surveys used either profit SBU or investment unit strategic performance measurement to evaluate their business units. J. S. Reece and W. A. Cool, "Measuring Investment Center Performance," *Harvard Business Review*, May–June 1978; V. Govindarajan, "Profit Center Measurement: An Empirical Study," working paper, The Amos Tuck School of Business Administration, Dartmouth College, 1994; and A. S. Keating, "Metrics for Division Manager Performance Evaluation," working paper, Simon Graduate School of Business, University of Rochester, March 1996.

THE STRATEGIC ROLE OF INVESTMENT UNITS

The strategic role of investment SBUs is the same as those for the other SBUs. The objectives are to:

1. Motivate managers to exert a high level of effort to achieve the goals of the firm.

2. Provide the right incentive for managers to make decisions that are consistent with the goals of top management.

3. Determine fairly the rewards earned by the managers for their effort and skill.

LEARNING OBJECTIVE 1 ▶
Identify the objectives of strategic investment units.

How do investment SBUs achieve these three objectives? The first objective, motivation, is achieved because the goal of increasing return on investment is clear and intuitive, and generally within the manager's control. The second objective, goal congruence, is achieved since return on investment is a critical financial performance measure for the firm as a whole. Each successful investment SBU contributes directly to the success of the firm. The third objective, fairness of rewards, is achieved because the use of investment SBUs provides a sound basis for comparing the performance of units of different size—profits are measured relative to the amount of investment. Moreover, return on investment contributes to achieving fairness because it is a clear, quantitative measure that is well understood by managers, and over which they typically have a great deal of control.

The principal measure of investment SBU performance is return on investment. In addition, there are two related measures: residual income (RI) and economic value added (EVA). We consider each in the following sections.

RETURN ON INVESTMENT

LEARNING OBJECTIVE 2 ▶
Explain the use of return on investment (ROI) and identify its advantages and limitations.

The most commonly used investment SBU measure is return on investment (ROI). ROI is a percentage, and the larger the percentage, the better the ROI. ROIs for successful firms range from 10 to more than 50 percent, though each firm's ROI must be evaluated in light of the industry average ROI and the economic factors facing that particular firm. Profit is typically determined from generally accepted accounting principles. However, for internal purposes, the firm can choose to use alternative definitions of profit, as for example the variable costing approach explained in Chapter 18.[2]

The amount of investment often is determined from the assets of the business unit, based also on generally accepted accounting principles. Alternatively, investment can be measured by the value of the ownership interest. The value of the ownership interest is determined from the shareholders' equity of the financial statements of a publicly owned firm. For a nonpublic firm, it is determined from the amount of total assets less liabilities. When the value of the ownership interest is used for investment, return on investment often is called **return on equity (ROE).** ROE is of special interest to shareholders and business owners because it is a direct measure of the firm's returns to them. Because our focus in this chapter is on the performance of managers in meeting top management's goals, we hereafter focus only on return on assets. The evaluation of the firm from the viewpoint of the shareholder is considered again in Chapter 20.

Return on equity (ROE) is the return determined when investment is measured as shareholders' equity.

ROI Equals Return on Sales × Asset Turnover

We can enhance the ROI measure's usefulness by showing it as the product of two components:

$$ROI = \text{Return on sales} \times \text{Asset turnover}$$

$$ROI = \frac{\text{Profit}}{\text{Sales}} \times \frac{\text{Sales}}{\text{Assets}}$$

---

[2]   Generally accepted accounting principles are the body of accounting rules, methods, and procedures that are set forth as acceptable by the accounting profession for use in preparing financial statements.

Return on sales (ROS), a firm's profit per sales dollar, measures the manager's ability to control expenses and increase revenues to improve profitability.[3] **Asset turnover,** the amount of dollar sales achieved per dollar of investment, measures the manager's ability to increase sales from a given level of investment. Together, the two components of ROI tell a more complete story of the manager's performance and enhance top management's ability to evaluate and compare the different units.

> **Return on sales (ROS),** a firm's profit per sales dollar, measures the manager's ability to control expenses and increase revenues to improve profitability.
>
> **Asset turnover,** the amount of sales achieved per dollar of investment, measures the manager's ability to produce increased sales from a given level of investment.

Illustration of Evaluation Using Return on Investment

Assume CompuCity is a retailer with three product lines—computers, software, and computer help books. CompuCity has stores in three regions—the Carolinas, the Boston area, and South Florida. CompuCity's profits for the Carolinas have declined in the recent year, due in part to increased price competition in the computer unit.

Because of the recent decline in profits, top management uses ROI to study the performance of the Carolinas region. Each of the three product lines is considered an investment SBU. CompuCity knows that the markups are higher in software, and lowest for computers because of growing price competition. Investment in each of the units consists of inventory for sale and the value of the real estate and improvements of the retail stores. Inventory is relatively low in the computer unit since merchandise is restocked quickly from the manufacturers. Also, inventory is low in the book unit because about 40 percent of CompuCity's books are on consignment from publishers.

The value of the real estate and improvements is allocated to each of the three units on the basis of square feet of floor space used. The software unit occupies the greatest amount of floor space, followed by computers and books. The top of Exhibit 19-1 shows the income, sales, and investment information for CompuCity in 19X6 and 19X7. The bottom section of Exhibit 19-1 shows the calculation of ROI, including return on sales and asset turnover, for the Carolinas region for both 19X6 and 19X7.

Exhibit 19-1	**ROI, Return on Sales, and Asset Turnover for CompuCity (Carolinas Region)**

Income, Investment, and Sales for CompuCity

	Income		Investment		Sales	
	19X6	**19X7**	**19X6**	**19X7**	**19X6**	**19X7**
Computers	$ 8,000	$ 5,000	$ 50,000	$ 62,500	$200,000	$250,000
Software	15,000	16,000	100,000	80,000	150,000	160,000
Books	3,200	5,000	32,000	50,000	80,000	100,000
Total	$26,200	$26,000	$182,000	$192,500	$430,000	$510,000

Return on Sales, Asset Turnover, and ROI for CompuCity

	Return on Sales		Asset Turnover		ROI	
	19X6	**19X7**	**19X6**	**19X7**	**19X6**	**19X7**
Computers	4% = 8,000/200,000	2% = 5,000/250,000	4.00 = 200,000/50,000	4.00 = 250,000/62,500	16% = 8,000/50,000	8% = 5,000/62,500
Software	10% = 15,000/150,000	10% = 16,000/160,000	1.50 = 150,000/100,000	2.00 = 160,000/80,000	15% = 15,000/100,000	20% = 16,000/80,000
Books	4% = 3,200/80,000	5% = 5,000/100,000	2.50 = 80,000/32,000	2.00 = 100,000/50,000	10% = 3,200/32,000	10% = 5,000/50,000
Total	6.10% = 26,200/430,000	5.10% = 26,000/510,000	2.36 = 430,000/182,000	2.65 = 510,000/192,500	14.40% = 26,200/182,000	13.50% = 26,000/192,500

---

[3] ROI based on asset turnover and return on sales is often referred to as the *DuPont approach*, since it was originated by Donaldson Brown, chief financial officer of DuPont Corporation early in the 1900s.

Exhibit 19–1 shows that CompuCity's ROI has fallen (from 14.4 percent in 19X6 to 13.5 percent in 19X7) due mainly to a decline in overall return on sales (from 6.1 percent in 19X6 to 5.1 percent in 19X7). Further analysis shows that the drop in return on sales is due to the sharp decline in ROS for the computer unit (from 4 percent in 19X6 to 2 percent in 19X7). The decline in ROS in the computer unit is likely the result of the increased price competition in that unit.

The analysis also shows that software is the most profitable business unit (the highest ROI of 20 percent), and this is so primarily because of the relatively high return on sales (ROS is highest at 10 percent since the markup on software products is relatively high). In contrast, the computer and book units have higher asset turnovers due to the lower required levels of inventory and floor space for the computer unit, and the large percentage of consignment inventory for the book unit. Also, ROI has improved significantly for the software unit because of the decline in investment, due either to a reduction in inventory or a decrease in floor space for software (recall that investment is allocated to the units on the basis of floor space).

Strategic Analysis Using ROI

Using ROI enables CompuCity to evaluate the managers of the three units and also to complete a strategic analysis of the entire firm. CompuCity can set performance goals for managers in terms of both return on sales and asset turnover. The unit managers then have very clear goals to increase sales and reduce costs, reduce inventory, and use floor space effectively. To be effective, the goals should recognize differences in the competitive factors among the units. For example, lower ROS should be expected of the computer unit because of competitive pricing in that unit.

Exhibit 19–1 also shows how competitive factors in the computer unit and how business relationships affecting inventory in the computer and book units affect the firm's profitability. This provides a useful basis for an improved strategic analysis—for determining how the firm should position itself strategically. How should CompuCity's competitive approach be changed in view of recent and expected changes in the competitive environment? Perhaps the computer unit should be reduced and the software unit expanded. Which stores in the Carolinas are successful, and why? A value chain analysis might provide insight into strategic competitive advantage and opportunity. For example, CompuCity may find it more profitable to reduce its computer unit, and replace it with products that are potentially more profitable—printers, pagers, cell phones, fax machines, supplies, and computer accessories.

Overall, ROI provides a useful basis not only for evaluating the performance of the unit manager but also for strategically evaluating the performance of the entire firm.

Using Return on Investment

For ROI to be useful, income and investment must be determined consistently and fairly. This means:

1. Income and investment must be measured in the same way for each unit. For example, all units must use the same inventory cost flow assumption (FIFO or LIFO) and the same depreciation method.

2. The measurement method must be reasonable and fair for all units. For example, if some of the units have much older assets than other units, then the use of historical cost-based net book value for assets can significantly bias the ROI measures in favor of the older units.

In the following sections, we consider the measurement issues affecting both the determination of income and investment.

Measuring Income and Investment: Effect of Accounting Policies

Accounting policies regarding the measurement of investments and the determination of income have a direct affect on ROI. The two main types of accounting policies that affect ROI are: (1) revenue and expense recognition policies, and (2) asset measurement methods. Revenue and expense recognition policies affect ROI by determining when a sale is recognized as revenue and when an expenditure is recognized as an expense. These policies affect the timing of sales and expenses. For example, cash-based accounting systems recognize sales and expenses when the cash is received or disbursed, while accrual systems recognize sales (and related expenses) when the product or service is delivered or provided. Moreover, for accrual systems, revenue may be recognized either when the order is received, when goods are shipped, or when the customer is billed. The firm's policy for revenue and expense recognition should be considered carefully, since any differences between units might significantly influence the proper interpretation of ROI.

Similarly, the firm has accounting policies for measurement of inventory and long-lived assets that affect income and investment:

For Long-Lived Assets

1. **Depreciation policy.** The determination of the useful life of the asset and the depreciation method affect both income and investment. Larger depreciation charges reduce ROI.

2. **Capitalization policy.** The firm's capitalization policy states when an item is expensed or capitalized as an asset. If an item is expensed, the effect will be to reduce ROI. (This is illustrated in Exhibit 19–2.)

For Inventory

3. **Inventory measurement methods.** The choice of inventory cost flow assumption (FIFO, LIFO) affects income and the measurement of inventory. Methods that increase cost of goods sold and decrease inventory, as is often the effect with LIFO in times of rising prices, reduce ROI.

4. **Absorption costing** (explained in Chapter 18). The effect of absorption costing is to create an upward bias on net income and therefore on ROI when inventory levels are rising, and the reverse when inventory levels are falling.

5. **Disposition of variances** (explained in Chapter 16). Standard cost variances may be closed to the cost of goods sold or prorated to the inventory accounts; the choice will have a direct effect on income and the inventory balances.

These five measurement issues affect the proper interpretation of net income and investment, and therefore of ROI.[4] To ensure comparability, all business units must

Exhibit 19–2	Effect of Capitalizing Certain Costs on ROI for CompuCity (Carolinas Region)

ROI Prior to Capitalizing Display Materials (same as Exhibit 19–1)

	Computer Unit	Book Unit
Assets	$62,500	$50,000
Income	$ 5,000	$ 5,000
ROI	8%	10%

Book Unit Expenses Display Costs, while the Computer Unit Capitalizes These Costs

	Computer Unit	Book Unit
Assets	$64,000 = $62,500 + $1,500	$50,000
Income	$6,500 = $5,000 + $1,500	$ 5,000
ROI	10.2% = $6,500/$64,000	10%

---

[4] Another important point is that each of the policies has the effect of either simultaneously increasing income and increasing investment, or simultaneously decreasing income and decreasing investment. Since ROI is a ratio that normally is between zero and one, an increase in income increases ROI even though investment also has increased by the same amount, and vice versa.

use the same policies. Moreover, when interpreting ROI, top management should consider that the existing accounting policies may have a bias to overstate (or understate) income and investment.[5]

To illustrate the effect of an accounting policy, assume that all units of CompuCity have the policy of expensing all the furniture and other items used to display products; these items cost $1,500 per year. Suppose the computer unit decides to capitalize these expenses. What is the effect on ROI? Exhibit 19–2 compares the computer unit to the books unit, before the change (in the top panel) and after (in the bottom panel).

The illustration shows how the decision to capitalize the display costs has increased the computer unit's assets, income, and ROI. While the book unit has the higher ROI when both units expense display costs, the decision of the computer unit to capitalize these costs, while the book unit does not, has caused the computer unit to have the higher ROI.

Other Measurement Issues for Income

In addition to the firm's accounting policies, other effects on income should be considered when using ROI:

1. **Nonrecurring items.** Income can be affected by nonrecurring charges or revenues, and then it would not be comparable to income of prior periods or of other business units. For example, the high promotion costs for introducing a new product might significantly distort net income in the period involved.

2. **Income taxes.** Income taxes may differentially affect the various units, with the result that after-tax net income may not be comparable. This may be true, for example, if the business units operate in different countries with different tax rates and tax treaties.

3. **Foreign exchange.** Business units that operate in foreign countries are subject to foreign exchange rate fluctuations that can affect the income and the value of investments of these units.

4. **Joint cost sharing.** When the business units share a common facility or cost, such as the cost of a personnel department or data processing, the cost often is allocated to the units on some fair-share basis. For example,

---

The Effect of Accounting Policies on Return on Investment: The Case of International Accounting Standards

Because of an expected change in international accounting standards in January 1995, European firms, especially Swiss pharmaceuticals Roche Holding Ltd and Sandoz Ltd., were paying high prices to purchase U.S. firms in 1994. Why? The reason is a different accounting rule for goodwill. Goodwill is the difference between the value of the assets purchased and the purchase price. Beginning January 1, 1995, European companies had to write off goodwill over 20 or more years instead of the pre-1995 regulations that allowed them to write off goodwill against taxes in the

year of the purchase, for large savings in taxes.

As a result of the new rule in Europe, many European companies were looking in 1994 to buy other firms to avoid the tax losses associated with the 1995 rule. For example, the Swiss company Sandoz decided to bid for Gerber Products Company because Sandoz had a potential $3.2 billion tax write-off from the goodwill on the purchase. This is why, for example, Sandoz bid so high for Gerber—its offer was 53 percent higher than the other bids.

And perhaps most important, the

goodwill write-off makes the acquiring company look much more profitable. Because its assets are reduced by the amount of the write-off, a company's *return on investment looks a lot higher.* For example, if the European firm Nestlé had followed the capitalization rule in its acquisition of Perrier and Carnation Company, its return on investment would have fallen from approximately 16 percent to a less admirable 9 percent in 1993.

Source: Based on information in "The Swiss Are Coming," *Business Week,* June 6, 1994, p. 31.

---

[5] Frances L. Ayres summarizes the accounting policies that can affect income in "Perceptions of Earnings Quality: What Managers Need to Know," *Management Accounting,* March 1994, pp. 27–29.

square feet of floor space is used to allocate plant-level costs. (See Chapter 14 for a discussion of allocation objectives and methods.) Different allocation methods result in different costs for each unit, and therefore they have an effect on the units' income.

Each of these effects on income can influence the proper interpretation of ROI and should be considered when using ROI to evaluate investment SBUs.

Measuring Investment: Which Assets to Include?

A common method for calculating ROI is to define investment as the cost of long-lived assets plus working capital.[6] A key criterion for including an asset in ROI is the degree to which it is controllable by the unit. For example, if the unit's cash balance is controlled at the firmwide level, then only a portion or perhaps none of the cash balance should be included in the amount of investment for the purpose of calculating ROI. Similarly, receivables and inventory should only include those controllable at the unit level.

Long-lived assets commonly are included in investment if traceable to the unit (for shared assets, see the next section). Management problems arise, however, if the long-lived assets are leased, or if some significant portion of these assets is idle. Leasing requires a clear firmwide policy regarding how the lease will be treated in determining ROI, so unit managers are properly motivated to lease or not to lease, as is the firm's policy. In general, the leased assets should be included as investments since they represent assets used to generate income, and the failure to include them can cause a significant overstatement of ROI.

For idle assets, the main issue is again controllability. If the idle assets have an alternative use or are readily saleable, then they should be included in the investment amount for ROI. Also, if top management wants to encourage the divestment

---

Factors Affecting the Proper Interpretation of Return on Investment

Accounting Policies That Affect Return on Investment

1. Revenue and expense recognition policy
2. Inventory and long-lived asset measurement
   Inventory:
      Cost flow assumption (FIFO, LIFO)
      Absorption costing
      Disposition of standard cost variances
   Long-lived assets:
      Depreciation policy
      Capitalization policy

Other Effects on Income

1. Nonrecurring items
2. Income taxes
3. Foreign exchanges gains and losses
4. Joint cost sharing

Other Effects on Investment

1. Determining which assets are included
2. Joint asset sharing
3. Current cost

---

[6] Working capital is defined as current assets less current liabilities. For a discussion of the determination of assets for ROI, see R. N. Anthony and V. Govindarajan, *Management Control Systems*, 8th ed. (Burr Ridge, IL: Richard D. Irwin, 1995), pp. 221–39.

of idle assets, including idle assets in ROI would motivate the desired action, since divestment would reduce investment and increase ROI. Alternatively, if top management sees a potential strategic advantage to holding the idle assets, then excluding idle assets from ROI would provide the most effective motivation, since holding idle assets would not reduce ROI.

Measuring Investment: Allocating Shared Assets

When shared facilities are involved, such as a common maintenance facility for the auto and truck fleets of different units, management must determine a fair sharing arrangement. As in joint cost allocation (Chapter 14), top management should trace the assets to the business units that used them and allocate the assets that cannot be traced on a basis that is as close to actual usage as possible. For example, the investment in the maintenance facility might be allocated on the basis of the number of vehicles in each unit, or on the total value of the vehicles in each unit.

Alternatively, sometimes the required capacity and therefore the investment in the joint facility are large because the user units require high levels of service at periods of high demand. The assets should be allocated by the *peak demand* of each individual unit; units with higher peak-load requirements that cause the need for capacity then receive a relatively higher portion of the investment. For example, a computer services department might require a high level of computer capacity because certain users require a large amount of service at certain times of the month.

Measuring Investment: Current Values

Historical cost is the value of current assets plus the net book value of the long-lived assets.

Net book value is the historical cost of the asset less accumulated depreciation.

The amount of investment is typically the historical cost of the assets.[7] The **historical cost** amount is the book value of current assets plus the net book value of the long-lived assets. **Net book value** is the historical cost of the asset less accumulated depreciation. A problem arises when the long-lived assets are a significant portion of total investment because most long-lived assets are stated at historical cost, and price changes since the purchase of these assets can make the historical cost figures irrelevant and misleading.

If the relatively small historical cost value is used for investment in ROI, the result is that ROI *can be significantly overstated* relative to ROI determined with the current value of the assets. The consequence is that the use of historical cost ROI can mislead strategic decision making, since the inflated ROI figures can create an illusion of profitability. The illusion is removed when the assets are replaced later at their current value, and the amount of income may not have been sufficient to support the replacement of the asset at the current higher value.

For example, a firm that enjoys a relatively high ROI of 20 percent based on net book value (e.g., income of $200,000 and net book value of $1,000,000) would find that *if* replacement cost of the assets were four times book value ($4 \times \$1,000,000 = \$4,000,000$), the ROI after replacement would become a relatively low 5 percent ($200,000 over $4,000,000). Strategically, the firm should have identified the low profitability in a timely manner. Historical cost ROI can delay this recognition. A proper strategic approach is to use an investment value in ROI that takes into consideration replacing the assets at their current market value, so decisions are made on the basis of the current and future profitability of the firm's products and services, and not on the basis of their past profitability alone.

In addition to its strategic value, the use of current value helps to reduce the unfairness of historical cost net book value when comparing among business units with *different aged assets*. Units with older assets under the net book value method have significantly higher ROIs than units with newer assets, because of the effect of price changes and of accumulating depreciation over the life of the assets. If the old and new assets are contributing equivalent service, then the bias in favor of the

---

[7] Ninety-nine out of a hundred firms use historical cost measurement of investment, as reported by Reece and Cool, "Measuring Investment Center Performance," and Govindarajan, "Profit Center Measurement." Of these, 9 out of 10 use net book value and the rest use gross book value.

unit with older assets is unfair to the manager of a unit with newer assets. The difference also is misleading for strategic decision making. The use of current values helps to reduce this bias since current values are not as strongly affected by age of assets as are historical cost-based net book values.

Measures of Current Values   The three methods for developing or estimating the current market values of assets are (1) gross book value, (2) replacement cost, and (3) liquidation value. **Gross book value (GBV)** is the historical cost without the reduction for depreciation. It is an estimate of the current value of the assets. Gross book value improves on net book value because it removes the bias due to differences in the age of assets among business units. However, it does not deal with potential price changes in the assets.

> **Gross book value (GBV)** is the historical cost without the reduction for depreciation.

The other two approaches, replacement cost and liquidation value, effectively handle both the issues of age of assets and current cost. **Replacement cost** represents the current purchase price to replace the assets at the current level of service and functionality. In contrast, **liquidation value** is the price that could be received for the sale of the assets. In effect, replacement cost is a purchase price and liquidation value is a sales price. Generally, replacement cost is higher than liquidation value.

> **Replacement cost** represents the current cost to replace the assets at the current level of service and functionality.
> **Liquidation value** is the price that could be received for the sale of the assets.

Gross book value is preferred by those who value the objectivity of a historical cost number; purchase cost is a reliable, verifiable number. In contrast, replacement cost is preferred when ROI is used to evaluate the manager or the unit as a continuing enterprise, because the use of replacement cost is consistent with the idea that the assets will be replaced at the current cost, and the business will continue. On the other hand, the liquidation value is most useful when top management is using ROI to evaluate the business unit for potential disposal, and the relevant current cost is the sales value of the assets, or liquidation value.

To illustrate, consider CompuCity's three marketing regions: (1) the Carolinas (shown in Exhibit 19–1), (2) the Boston area, and (3) South Florida. CompuCity has 15 stores in the Carolinas, 18 in the Boston area, and 13 in Florida. Each store is owned and managed by CompuCity. Exhibit 19–3 shows the net book value, gross book value, replacement cost, and liquidation value for the stores in each region.[8]

The stores in the Boston area, where CompuCity began, are among the oldest and are located in areas where real estate values have risen considerably. The newer stores in the Carolinas and Florida are also experiencing significant appreciation in

Exhibit 19–3	**Investment Data and ROI for CompuCity in Its Three Marketing Regions** (000s omitted)				
Region	**Income**	**Net Book Value**	**Gross Book Value**	**Replacement Cost**	**Liquidation Value**
Financial Data					
Carolinas	$26,000	$195,500	$250,500	$388,000	$ 332,000
Boston area	38,500	212,000	445,000	650,000	1,254,600
South Florida	16,850	133,000	155,450	225,500	195,000
Return on Investment					
Carolinas		13.30%	10.38%	6.70%	7.83%
Boston area		18.16	8.65	5.92	3.07
South Florida		12.67	10.84	7.47	8.64

---

[8]   The values in Exhibit 19–3 represent the simple average of beginning of year and end of year values for gross and net book values (beginning and ending values are not shown). Replacement cost and liquidation value are determined as of the point in time when ROI is calculated. The use of the simple average is a common approach when determining the value of investment using gross book value or net book value in the calculation of ROI. Because income is measured for the entire period, investment is also measured as the average cost of the assets over the entire period.

real estate values. ROI based on net book value shows the Boston area to be the most profitable. But a further analysis based on gross book value shows that when we take into account that the Boston area stores are somewhat older, the ROI figures for all three regions are comparable. This illustrates the potentially misleading information from ROI based on net book value.

Replacement cost is useful in evaluating the performance of the region managers because it best measures the investment in the continuing business. The ROI figures show that all three regions are somewhat comparable, with South Florida slightly in the lead.

Liquidation value provides a somewhat different answer. The ROI based on liquidation value for the Boston area is very low relative to the other two areas. Because of the significant appreciation in real estate values at the Boston area stores, the liquidation value for the Boston region is quite high. The replacement cost figure is lower than liquidation cost because the assumption is made that if CompuCity replaced its stores in the Boston area, they would be located where the real estate values are somewhat lower. The analysis of liquidation-based ROIs is useful for showing CompuCity management that the real estate value of these stores may now exceed their value as CompuCity retail locations. Perhaps CompuCity should sell these stores and locate elsewhere in the Boston area, where the values are near that of the suggested replacement cost figure.

Strategic Issues in Using Return on Investment

In addition to the measurement issues described earlier, two key issues must be considered in using ROI for evaluating investment SBUs: First, use the balanced scorecard to avoid an excessive focus on short-term results. Second, ROI has a disincentive for new investment by the most profitable units.

The Balanced Scorecard: Avoiding Excessive Short-Term Focus

ROI evaluation, much like profit SBUs and cost SBUs, focuses the manager's attention on the costs and revenues of the current period, discouraging new investment that would increase profits, unless there is a quick and significant improvement in income. The result is what is often called investment myopia, in which managers tend to avoid new investment because the returns may be uncertain and may not be realized for some time. If the manager is evaluated on current ROI performance, the urgency of meeting the current period's ROI target tends to drive out efforts to improve long-term profits.[9] The ROI-based incentive is for the manager to reduce research and development spending, advertising, and productivity improvements in the interest of improving the current ROI; strategically these decisions might have disastrous long-term effects.

The effects of an excessive focus on short-term results can be addressed by using ROI as *only one part* of an overall evaluation of a strategic investment unit. A good approach would be to use a balanced scorecard, in which ROI plays an important role in the financial dimension of critical success factors. In addition, the balanced scorecard evaluation considers critical success factors in the other three dimensions: (1) customer satisfaction, (2) internal business processes, and (3) learning and growth. The main concept of the balanced scorecard is that no one measure properly evaluates the SBU's progress to strategic success. Moreover, by attending directly to the firm's CSFs, the balanced scorecard effectively links the performance measurement/evaluation process to the firm's strategy. Chapter 18 shows an example of how Caterpillar Corporation uses the balanced scorecard in strategic performance measurement.

---

[9] Investment myopia is discussed widely. See, for example, Judith H. Dobrzynski, "A Sweeping Prescription for Corporate Myopia," *Business Week*, July 6, 1992; Kenneth A. Merchant, *Rewarding Results: Motivating Profit Center Managers* (Boston: Harvard Business School Press, 1989), Chap. 4; and John Dearden, "The Case Against ROI Control," *Harvard Business Review*, May–June 1969.

ROI and Investment in Information Technology at Otis Elevator

The chief information officers of several large firms explained that their firms' investments in information technology sometimes could not be justified on the basis of ROI, but that long-term issues were the basis of the decision to invest.

Don Lucas, CIO at Otis Elevator Company, noted that while Otis's information technology investments are in line with those of other manufacturing firms, the company gets more benefit from its investment by focusing less on traditional systems that tend to emphasize cost savings and more on strategic systems. The strategic systems can benefit the revenues side, which is more important to Otis.

Lucas says, "Otis's profits have been increasing, and we in information systems like to think a certain part of that is due to our contribution. I know a lot of people won't build systems unless they can quantify their return on investment, but in this environment that's a dangerous thing. I absolutely believe that some of the key strategic systems at many companies never get off the drawing board because it's too difficult to get the return on investment. Just because all your projects have a high rate of return doesn't mean you're a winner."

Source: Based on information in "The ROI Polloi," by David Freedman, *CIO Magazine,* April 1990, pp. 30–40.

Exhibit 19–4   ROI for Purchase of Switch by CompuCity

	First Year	Second Year	Third Year
Depreciation expense	$7,500 = $22,500/3	$7,500	$7,500
Net book value at year-end	$15,000 = $22,500 − $7,500	$7,500 = $15,000 − $7,500	$0 = $7,500 − $7,500
Average net book value for the year	$18,750 = ($22,500 + $15,000)/2	$11,250 = ($15,000 + $7,500)/2	$3,750 = ($7,500 + $0)/2
ROI	$13.33\% = \dfrac{\$10,000 - \$7,500}{\$18,750}$	$22.22\% = \dfrac{\$10,000 - \$7,500}{\$11,250}$	$66.67\% = \dfrac{\$10,000 - \$7,500}{\$3,750}$

Disincentive for New Investment by the Most Profitable Units

Business units evaluated on ROI bear an important disincentive that conflicts with their achieving the objectives of investment SBUs. ROI encourages units to invest only in projects that earn *higher than the unit's current ROI*, so that the addition of the investment improves the unit's overall ROI right away. Thus, there is a corresponding disincentive for the most profitable units to invest in any project that does not exceed the unit's current ROI, even though the project would have a good return. A good return can be defined as an ROI in excess of some minimum threshold; for example, a firm might strive for a firmwide ROI of 12 percent, so that only a project earning an ROI of 12 percent or greater should be accepted.

The disincentive for new investment hurts the firm strategically in two ways. First, investment projects that would be beneficial for the firm are declined. Second, although the firm wants the units with highest ROI to grow, to take advantage of the unit's apparent management skill, ROI evaluation provides a disincentive for the best units to grow. In contrast, the units with the lowest ROI have an incentive to take on new projects to improve their ROI. But management skills may be lacking in the low-ROI units.

The disincentive can be illustrated if we assume the Boston region of CompuCity has an option to purchase a telephone switch for $22,500. The switch would increase the capacity of its 800 service number and reduce operating costs by $10,000 per year. The switch is expected to last for three years and have no salvage value. Exhibit 19–4 shows the determination of ROI for the purchase of the switch using the straight-line method of depreciation. The ROI for the purchase of the

BusinessWeek

Can Kodak Keep Its Objectives in Focus?

(Continues from page 759)

A: Well, it won't be a snap . . .

Especially with the critics watching. While many say Kodak needs to focus on short-term cost cutting, CEO Fisher remains focused primarily on his long-term goals for new products—advanced film–camera systems and digital photography. Taking on the same role he had at his previous firm, Motorola, Fisher has concentrated on turning out technologically advanced products in these photography segments in the hope of big profits in the next millennium. The company is turning out a wide array of digital products—cameras, scanners, and other devices—and sales of these items are up 25 percent over the prior year. Kodak is said to be far ahead of other firms in digital imaging sales. However, competitors such as Hewlett-Packard make Kodak's future prospects uncertain. Strong competitors in the film business, such as Fuji, are also squeezing Kodak's profits, leading to disappointing profits in the second quarter of 1997. Fisher maintains that these are short-term problems, and not a problem with his strategy. "When you're trying to do as many things as we're doing, there's bound to be some things that don't improve as fast as you planned," says Fisher.

A key issue in the debate is the focus of many investors on short-term profit results, in apparent conflict with Fisher's focus on costly investments that promise long-term competitiveness. Kodak must both satisfy the demands of current shareholders for profits and share price appreciation, and build a strategy for the long-term success of the firm. Accounting results as measured by profit alone cannot capture the complexity of the competitive situation he faces. Only time will tell if Fisher can create picture-perfect results for Kodak.

For further reading, see "Can George Fisher Fix Kodak?" *Business Week,* October 20, 1997; "Commentary: Kodak's Focus May Be Too Narrow," *Business Week,* November 24, 1997; and "A Dark Kodak Moment," *Business Week,* August 4, 1997.

switch is 13.33 percent in the first year, and 22.22 percent and 66.67 percent in the second and third years.[10]

Using average net book value, the ROI of the Boston region is currently 18.16 percent (Exhibit 19–3). This means that the Boston unit might not purchase the switch because the first year's return for the switch of 13.33 percent is less than the current ROI. Buying the switch would reduce Boston's ROI from 18.16 percent to 17.77 percent [($38,500 + $10,000 − $7,500)/($212,000 + $18,750)] in the first year. In later years, the ROI from the switch would substantially exceed Boston's current ROI, but the manager may not be able to wait for that improvement, when there is strong pressure for current profits.

Moreover, from a firmwide perspective, since the return on the switch in each of the years exceeds the firm's threshold return of 12 percent, the Boston region should purchase the switch. Thus, a significant limitation of ROI is it can cause SBU managers to decline some investments in conflict with firmwide interests. A useful way to address this limitation is to use an alternative measure of investment SBU profitability, called residual income.

RESIDUAL INCOME

In contrast to ROI, which is a percentage, **residual income** is a dollar amount equal to the income of the business unit less a charge for the investment in the unit. The

LEARNING OBJECTIVE 3 ▶
Explain the use of residual income and identify its advantages and limitations.

Residual income is a dollar amount equal to the income of the business unit less a charge for the investment in the unit.

---

10   Using the discounted cash flow methods explained in Chapter 11, the purchase of the switch has an internal rate of return of approximately 16 percent ($22,500/$10,000 = 2.250; the PV factor for 16 percent and three years is 2.246). As noted in Chapter 11, the discounted internal rate of return provides a summary return for the entire life of a multiyear project, in contrast to ROI for which the return increases each year over the life of the project under most depreciation methods.

charge is determined by taking the firm's desired minimum rate of return and multiplying it by the amount of the investment. Residual income can be interpreted as the income earned after the unit has paid a charge for the funds necessary to provide the investment in the unit.

The calculation of residual income for CompuCity is illustrated in Exhibit 19–5, using a minimum rate of return of 12 percent. Note that since all three units have ROI greater than 12 percent, all also have a positive residual income. Note too that the ranking of units on ROI is the same as the ranking of units on the basis of residual income—the Boston area unit has the highest ROI and residual income.

The issues regarding the measurement of investment and income for residual income are the same as discussed for ROI. Because of the effect of different accounting policies and the tendency of net book value to understate investment, the residual income measure must be interpreted carefully. The advantage of residual income is that a unit pursues an investment opportunity as long as the return from the investment exceeds the minimum rate of return set by the firm. For example, using residual income the Boston region would accept the opportunity to purchase the telephone switch described in Exhibit 19–4 because the telephone switch would contribute to residual income. The residual income in the first year after the investment in the switch would be $13,310 [($38,500 + $10,000 − $7,500) − .12($212,000 + $18,750)], a $250 improvement over the unit's residual income without the switch, $13,060 (Exhibit 19–5).

An additional advantage of residual income is that a firm can adjust the required rates of return for differences in risk and types of assets. For example, a firm can include a risk adjustment in the evaluation of SBUs. Units with higher business risk can be evaluated at a higher minimum rate of return. The increased risk might be due to obsolete products, increased competition in the industry, or other economic factors affecting the business unit.

Another advantage is that it is possible to calculate a different investment charge for different types of assets. For example, one might use a higher minimum rate of return for long-lived assets that are more likely to be specialized in use and thus not as readily salable. Because of the advantages of residual income, more than one-third of investment SBUs use it.[11]

Limitations of Residual Income

While the residual income measure deals effectively with the disincentive problem of ROI, it has limitations. A key limitation is that since residual income is not a

Exhibit 19–5	Illustration of Residual Income for CompuCity	
	Income	**Average Net Book Value**
Financial data		
Carolinas	$26,000	$192,500
Boston area	38,500	212,000
South Florida	16,850	133,000
Return on investment		
Carolinas	13.51%	
Boston area	18.16	
South Florida	12.67	
Residual income	(minimum rate of return = 12 percent)	
Carolinas	$ 2,900 = $26,000 − .12 × $192,500	
Boston area	$13,060 = $38,500 − .12 × $212,000	
South Florida	$ 890 = $16,850 − .12 × $133,000	

---

[11] See Reece and Cool, "Measuring Investment Center Performance," and Govindarajan, "Profit Center Measurement."

Exhibit 19–6	The Effect of the Size of the Unit and the Minimum Desired Rate of Return on Residual Income	
	Business Unit A	**Business Unit B**
Investment	$10,000,000	$750,000
Income	$1,500,000	$112,500
ROI	15% = $1,500,000/$10,000,000	15% = $112,500/$750,000
Residual income, at a minimum desired return of 12 percent	$300,000 = $1,500,000 − .12 × $10,000,000	$22,500 = $112,500 − .12 × $750,000

Exhibit 19–7	Advantages and Limitations of ROI and Residual Income	
	Advantages	**Limitations**
ROI	– Easily understood – Comparable to interest rates and to rates of returns on alternative investments – Widely used	Disincentive for high ROI units to invest in projects with ROI greater than the minimum rate of return but less than the unit's current ROI
Residual income	– Supports incentive to accept all projects with ROI greater than the minimum rate of return – Can use the minimum rate of return to adjust for differences in risk – Can use a different minimum rate of return for different types of assets	– Favors large units when the minimum rate of return is low – Not as intuitive as ROI – May be difficult to obtain a minimum rate of return
Both ROI and residual income	– *Congruent* with top management goals for return on assets – *Comprehensive financial measure;* includes all the elements important to top management: revenues, costs, and investment – *Comparability;* expands top management's span of control by allowing comparison across business units	– *May mislead strategic decision making;* not as comprehensive as the balanced scorecard, which includes customer satisfaction, internal processes, and learning as well as financial measures; the balanced scorecard is linked directly to strategy – *Measurement issues;* variations in the measurement of inventory and long-lived assets; also, variations in the treatment of nonrecurring items, income taxes, foreign exchange effects, and the use/cost of shared assets – *Short-term focus;* investments with long-term benefits may be neglected

percentage, it suffers the same problem of profit SBUs in that it is not useful for comparing units of significantly different sizes. It favors larger units that would be expected to have larger residual incomes, even with relatively poor performance. Moreover, relatively small changes in the minimum rate of return can dramatically affect the residual income for different size units, as illustrated in Exhibit 19–6. While both unit A and unit B have the same ROI of 15 percent, the amount of residual income differs significantly—$300,000 for unit A and only $22,500 for unit B. The difference would be greater for a smaller minimum return.

ROI and residual income can complement each other in the evaluation of investment SBUs. The advantages and limitations of each measure are summarized in Exhibit 19–7.

Economic value added (EVA) is a business unit's income after taxes and after deducting the cost of capital.

LEARNING OBJECTIVE 4 ▶
Explain the use of economic value added (EVA) in evaluating strategic investment units.

ECONOMIC VALUE ADDED

Economic value added (EVA) is a business unit's income after taxes and after deducting the cost of capital.[12] The idea is very similar to what we have explained

---

[12] G. Bennett Stewart III, "EVA Works—But Not If You Make These Common Mistakes," *Fortune*, May 1, 1995, pp. 117–18.

as residual income. The objectives of the measures are the same—to effectively motivate investment SBU managers and to properly measure their performance. In contrast to residual income, EVA uses the firm's cost of capital instead of a minimum rate of return. The *cost of capital* is usually obtained by calculating a weighted average of the cost of the firm's two sources of funds—borrowing and selling stock. For many firms the minimum desired rate of return and the cost of capital are very nearly the same, with small differences due to adjustments for risk and for strategic goals such as the desired growth rate for the firm. Also, while residual income is intended to deal with the undesirable effects of ROI, EVA is used to focus managers' attention on creating value for shareholders, by earning profits greater than the firm's cost of capital.

Another difference is that users of EVA do not follow conventional, conservative accounting policies. Expenses that contribute to the long-term value of the company are capitalized. These expenses usually are expensed under generally accepted accounting principles. Such expenses include research and development, certain types of advertising, and training and employee development. A number of firms, such as CSX, Coca-Cola, Briggs & Stratton, and AT&T, have adopted EVA in recent years and attribute improvements in profitability to the change. These developments indicate a renewed interest in residual income, with modifications, and some evidence of its usefulness for evaluating investment SBUs.

PART TWO: TRANSFER PRICING

Transfer pricing is the determination of an exchange price when different business units within a firm exchange products or services. The products may be final products that are sold to outside customers or intermediate products that are components of the final product.

Transfer pricing is one of the most strategic activities in SBU management. It not only directly affects the strategic objectives of the firm (such as the decision of which parts of the value chain the firm should occupy) but also requires coordination among the marketing, production, and financial functions. It affects materials and parts sourcing decisions, tax planning, and potentially the marketing of the final and intermediate products. Because significant decision-making autonomy is desirable to enhance the motivation of the business units, it is also desirable that the transfer price be set in an arm's-length manner between the units; that is, the units should behave as if they were independent businesses. Determining the transfer price in this manner is desirable not only from a management perspective but also for tax purposes, as explained in the next section. However, the arm's-length approach is not always possible, for example, when there are no alternative suppliers. The transfer pricing methods explained here include techniques for handling a variety of circumstances.

> **Transfer pricing** is the determination of an exchange price when different business units within a firm exchange products or services.

When Is Transfer Pricing Important?   Transfers of products and services between business units is most common in firms with a high degree of vertical integration. Vertically integrated firms occupy a number of different value-creating activities in the value chain. Wood product, food product, and consumer product firms are of this type. For example, a manufacturer of computers must determine transfer prices if it prepares the chips and boards and other components of the computer, as well as assembles the computer itself. (See Exhibit 2–13 in Chapter 2: Value Chain for the Computer Manufacturing Industry.) A useful way to visualize the transfer pricing context is to create a graphic such as Exhibit 19–8 that shows the business units involved in the transfer of products and services and identifies whether they are inside or outside the firm, international or domestic. Exhibit 19–8 shows the transfers for a hypothetical computer manufacturer, High Value Computer (HVC) that purchases a key component, the x-chip, from both an internal and an external supplier. The internal unit that manufactures x-chips sells them both internally and externally, and other components are purchased from international sources. The

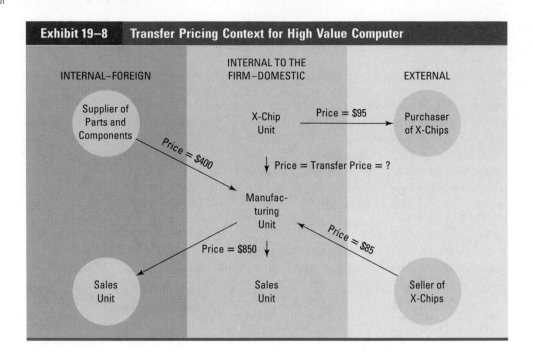

Exhibit 19–8 **Transfer Pricing Context for High Value Computer**

INTERNAL–FOREIGN | INTERNAL TO THE FIRM–DOMESTIC | EXTERNAL

Supplier of Parts and Components

X-Chip Unit

Price = $95

Purchaser of X-Chips

Price = $400

Price = Transfer Price = ?

Manufacturing Unit

Price = $850

Price = $85

Sales Unit

Sales Unit

Seller of X-Chips

manufactured units are transferred to both domestic and foreign sales units. Where known, the price of the transfer is shown in Exhibit 19–8.

The management accountant's role is to determine the proper transfer price for the internal sales of the x-chip. We begin by considering the objectives of transfer pricing.

OBJECTIVES OF TRANSFER PRICING

LEARNING OBJECTIVE 5 ▶
Explain the objectives of transfer pricing, the different transfer pricing methods, and when each method should be used.

The objectives for transfer pricing are the same as for SBUs. These objectives are (1) to motivate managers, (2) to provide an incentive for managers to make decisions consistent with the firm's goals, and (3) to provide a basis for fairly rewarding the managers.

In satisfying these objectives, the determination of the transfer price also must recognize firmwide strategic goals. For example, an important strategic objective for transfer pricing is to minimize taxes locally and internationally. By setting a high transfer price for goods shipped into a relatively high tax country, the firm can reduce overall firm-level tax liability. This would increase the cost and thus reduce the income of the purchasing unit in the high tax country, thereby minimizing taxes there. At the same time, the higher profits shown by the selling unit (as a result of the high transfer price) would be taxed at lower rates in the seller's home country.

Other strategic objectives of transfer pricing include developing strategic partnerships. A relatively high transfer price might be used to encourage internal units to purchase from an external supplier, to encourage an external business relationship the firm wants to develop because of the quality of the supplier, or to gain entrance to a market in a new country. It also might assist a newer or weaker unit to grow, or build up a unit for spin-off or sale to outside investors.

International Transfer Pricing Objectives

With the globalization of business, the international aspect of transfer pricing is becoming a critical concern. This is particularly true of tax issues. Other international objectives include minimizing customs charges, dealing with currency restrictions of foreign governments, and dealing with the risk of expropriation by foreign governments. **Expropriation** occurs when a foreign government takes ownership and control of assets the domestic investor has invested in that country. In managing the relationship with any one country, the management accountant attempts to find a strategic balance among these sometimes conflicting objectives.

Expropriation occurs when a foreign government takes ownership and control of assets the domestic investor has invested in that country.

Minimization of Customs Charges The amount of the transfer price can affect the overall cost, including the customs charges, of goods imported from a foreign unit. For example, for High Value Computer, if customs charges are significant on the parts and components imported by the domestic manufacturing unit, a relatively low transfer price on these imports would be beneficial to the overall firm to reduce the amount of customs charges.

Currency Restrictions As a foreign unit accumulates profits, a problem arises in some countries that place limits on the amount and/or timing of repatriation of these profits to the parent firm. One way of dealing with these restrictions is to set the transfer price so that profits accumulate at a relatively low rate. This objective must be considered together with other transfer pricing objectives.

Risk of Expropriation When there is a significant risk of expropriation, the domestic firm can take appropriate actions such as limiting new investment, developing improved relationships with the foreign government, and setting the transfer price such that funds are removed from the foreign country as quickly as possible.

TRANSFER PRICING METHODS

The four methods for determining the transfer price are variable cost, full cost, market price, and negotiated price. Each has advantages and limitations, and the choice of method depends on a careful consideration of the circumstances.

The variable cost method sets the transfer price equal to the variable cost of the selling unit. This method is desirable when the selling unit has excess capacity, and the chief objective of the transfer price is to satisfy the internal demand for the goods. The relatively low transfer price encourages buying internally. However, this method is not suitable when the selling unit is a profit or investment SBU because it would adversely affect the seller's profit.

The full cost method is the most commonly used.[13] An advantage of this approach is that it is well understood and the information is readily available in the accounting records. A key disadvantage is that it includes fixed costs, which can cause improper short-term decision making.

The market price method is the most preferred and the next most common.[14] The key advantage is that it is objective; it best satisfies the arm's-length criteria desired for both management and tax purposes. A key disadvantage is that the market price often is not available, especially for intermediate products.

The negotiated price method involves a negotiation process and sometimes arbitration between units to determine the transfer price. This method is desirable when the units have a history of significant conflict, and negotiation can result in an agreed-on price. The limitation is that the method can reduce the desired autonomy of the units.

Commonly firms use two or more methods; this is called dual pricing. For example, when there are numerous conflicts between two units, standard full cost might be used as the transfer price for the buyer, while market price might be used for the seller.[15] The difference between the two prices is accumulated at the firm level.

The advantages and limitations of the four methods are outlined in Exhibit 19–9.

Choosing the Right Transfer Pricing Method

The three key factors to consider in deciding whether to make internal transfers, and if so, the transfer price:

---

[13] Full cost or cost-plus markup is used by the largest percentage (42 percent) of the firms responding to surveys by Vancil and Govindarajan; Richard Vancil, *Decentralization: Management Ambiguity by Design* (Homewood, IL: Richard D. Irwin, 1979); and Govindarajan, "Profit Center Measurement."

[14] The surveys of Vancil and Govindarajan show that 31 percent of those using transfer pricing use the market price method.

[15] See a discussion of this issue in *The Wall Street Journal*, April 18, 1997, p. B1, regarding Koch Industries.

1. Is there an outside supplier?
2. Is the variable cost of the seller less than the market price?
3. Is the selling unit operating at full capacity?

Exhibit 19–10 shows the influence of these three factors on the choice of a transfer price and on the decision to purchase inside or out.

First: Is there an outside supplier?   If not, there is no market price, and the best transfer price is based on cost or negotiated price. If there is an outside supplier, we need to consider the relationship of the inside seller's variable cost to the market price of the outside supplier, by answering the second question.

Second: Is the variable cost of the seller less than the market price?   If not, it is likely that the seller's costs are far too high, and the buyer should buy outside. On the other hand, if the seller's variable costs are less than the market price, we need to consider the utilization of capacity in the selling unit, by answering the third question.

Third: Is the selling unit operating at full capacity?   That is, will the order from the internal buyer cause the selling unit to deny other sales opportunities? If not, the sell-

Exhibit 19–9	Advantages and Limitations of the Four Transfer Pricing Methods	
Method	**Advantages**	**Limitations**
Variable cost	– Causes buyer to act as desired, to buy inside	– Unfair to seller if seller is profit or investment SBU
Full cost	– Easy to implement – Intuitive and easily understood – Preferred by tax authorities over variable cost	– Irrelevance of fixed cost in decision making; fixed costs should be ignored in the buyer's choice of whether to buy inside or outside the firm – If used, should be standard rather than actual cost (allows buyer to know cost in advance and disallows seller from passing along inefficiencies)
Market price	– Helps to preserve unit autonomy – Provides incentive for the selling unit to be competitive with outside suppliers – Has arm's-length standard desired by taxing authorities	– Often intermediate products have no market price – Should be adjusted for cost savings such as reduced selling costs, no commissions, and so on
Negotiated price	– May be the most practical approach when there is significant conflict	– Need negotiation rule and/or arbitration procedure, and this may reduce autonomy – Potential tax problems; may not be considered arm's length

Exhibit 19–10	Choosing the Right Transfer Price		
		Decision to Transfer	**Transfer Price**
First: If there is *no* outside supply: ──────────────▶		Buy inside	Cost or negotiated price
If there is an outside supply, answer the second question below:			
Second: If the *seller's variable costs are greater than the outside price,* then the seller must look for ways to reduce costs ──────────▶		Buy outside	No transfer price
If seller's variable costs are less than the outside price, answer the third question:			
Third: If *seller has excess capacity,* then ──────────▶		Buy inside	**Low:** variable cost **High:** market price
If the seller is at full capacity ─────▶	And if the contribution of the outside purchase to the whole firm is *greater than* the contribution of the inside purchase ──▶	Buy outside	No transfer price
	And if the contribution of the outside purchase to the whole firm is *less than* the contribution of the inside purchase ──▶	Buy inside	Market price

ing division should provide for the internal buyer, and the transfer price should fall somewhere between variable cost and market price. In contrast, if the selling unit is at full capacity, we need to determine and compare the cost savings of internal sales versus the opportunity cost of lost sales in the selling division. If the cost savings to the inside buyer are greater than the cost of lost sales to the seller, then the buying unit should buy inside, and the proper transfer price should be the market price.

This three-question analysis is from top management's point of view and is thus the desired outcome of the units making these decisions autonomously. A good approach that preserves much of the units' autonomy is to have clear guidelines regarding top management's objectives in transfer pricing. Unit managers should know that autonomous actions favoring one unit over the interests of the firm as a whole are viewed negatively in the unit manager's year-end performance evaluation.

Determining the right transfer price and the right transfer decision can be illustrated using the High Value Computer case (Exhibit 19–8). High Value has the option to purchase the x-chip outside the firm for $85 or to manufacture the chip. The relevant information is presented in the top portion of Exhibit 19–11. The lower portion of Exhibit 19–11 shows the calculation of the relevant costs for each of the options.

A comparison of options one and two in Exhibit 19–11 shows that the firm as a whole benefits under option one when the manufacturing unit purchases the

Exhibit 19–11	Transfer Pricing Example The High Value Computer Company

Key assumptions:
  The manufacturing unit can buy the x-chip inside or outside the firm.
  The x-chip unit can sell inside or outside the firm.
  The x-chip unit is at full capacity (150,000 units).
  One x-chip is needed for each computer manufactured by High Value.

Other information:

Sales price of computer for HVC's computer unit	$850
Variable manufacturing cost of the computer unit (excluding x-chip)	
($400 parts and $250 labor)	650
Variable x-chip manufacturing cost for HVC's x-chip unit	60
Price of x-chip from outside supplier, to HVC computer unit	85
Price of x-chip from HVC's x-chip unit to outside buyer	95

Option One:

High Value manufactures 150,000 computers, using x-chips purchased for $85 from outside supplier; High Value's x-chip unit sells 150,000 units for $95 each to outside buyer.

Contribution Income Statement (000s omitted); it is assumed that fixed costs will not differ between the two options and are excluded from the analysis:

	Computer Manufacturing Unit	X-Chip Unit	Total
Sales (price = $850, $95)	$127,500	$14,250	$141,750
Less: Variable costs			
X-chip ($85)	12,750		12,750
Other costs ($650, $60)	97,500	9,000	106,500
Contribution margin	$ 17,250	$ 5,250	$ 22,500

Option Two:

High Value manufactures 150,000 computers, using x-chips purchased for $60 (variable cost) from the inside supplier.

	Computer Manufacturing Unit	X-Chip Unit	Total
Sales (price = $850, $60)	$127,500	$9,000	$136,500
Less: Variable costs			
X-chip ($60)	9,000		9,000
Other costs ($650, $60)	97,500	9,000	106,500
Contribution margin	$ 21,000	$ —	$ 21,000

x-chip outside, and the x-chip unit also sells outside. The reason is the $25 savings to the manufacturing unit for internal sales of the x-chip ($85 outside price less $60 variable cost) is less than the opportunity cost to the x-chip unit of $35 per unit ($95 outside price less $60 variable cost).

INTERNATIONAL TAX ISSUES IN TRANSFER PRICING

LEARNING OBJECTIVE 6 ▶
Discuss the important international tax issues in transfer pricing.

The **arm's-length standard** says that transfer prices should be set so they reflect the price that would have been set by unrelated parties acting independently.

The **comparable price method** establishes an arm's-length price by using the sales prices of similar products made by unrelated firms.

The **resale price method** is based on determining an appropriate markup, where the markup is based on gross profits of unrelated firms selling similar products.

Two recent surveys have found that more than 80 percent of multinational firms (MNCs) see transfer pricing as a major international tax issue, and more than half these firms said it was the most important issue.[16] Most countries now accept the Organization of Economic Cooperation and Development (OECD) model treaty, which provides that transfer prices should be adjusted using the arm's-length standard, that is, to a price that would have been arrived at by unrelated parties. While the model treaty is widely accepted, there are differences in the way countries apply it. However, there is strong worldwide support for an approach to limit attempts by MNCs to reduce tax liability by setting transfer prices that differ from the arm's-length standard.[17]

The Arm's-Length Standard

The **arm's-length standard** says that transfer prices should be set so they reflect the price that would have been set by unrelated parties acting independently. The arm's-length standard is applied in many ways, but the three most widely used methods are (1) the comparable price method, (2) the resale price method, and (3) the cost-plus method. The **comparable price method** is the most commonly used and the most preferred by tax authorities. It establishes an arm's-length price by using the prices in sales of similar products made by unrelated firms.[18] A limitation is that it depends on the availability of comparable and unrelated prices.

The **resale price method** is used for distributors and marketing units where there is little value added and no significant manufacturing operations. In this method, the transfer price is based on determining an appropriate markup, where the markup is based on gross profits of unrelated firms selling similar products.

Transfer Pricing and Tax Avoidance

The United States versus Japan
By setting a high transfer price from their factories in Japan to their marketing subsidiaries in the United States, Japanese automakers are able to reduce the profit shown by the U.S. subsidiaries and thereby reduce U.S. taxes. President Clinton's staff estimates that the loss from transfer pricing abuses such as this may be as high as $15 billion per year. The magnitude of the problem is shown by a recent Internal Revenue Service study of 3,357 foreign-controlled corporations that found that

the majority understated income on their tax returns. According to the study, Japanese companies were the most likely of any of America's top 10 trading partners to use unfair transfer pricing practices.

Japan versus the United States
Japan also sees itself as the victim of unfair transfer pricing practices. The Japanese National Tax Administration Agency (NTAA) has charged Coca-Cola Co. with $145 million in additional taxes for 1990–1992 because of alleged trans-

fer pricing abuses. They also charged American International Group, Inc., with $87 million in additional taxes for a transfer pricing disagreement.

The Internal Revenue Service response in the United States is that each foreign subsidiary must prove that its transfer price is arm's length; that is, the same as would have been reached by unrelated parties.

Source: Based on information in *Business Week,* July 12, 1993, p. 143; and *Business Week,* May 30, 1994, p. 55.

---

[16]   Based on information from two surveys: (1) the Ernst & Young Transfer Pricing Global Survey of 400 MNCs, as reported in the *Ernst & Young Business UpShot,* October 1997; and (2) a survey of 210 companies in the United States, United Kingdom, Japan, Australia, Netherlands, France, and Germany, as reported in *Accounting Today,* August 21–September 10, 1995.

[17]   For further information on international taxation and transfer pricing, see B. J. Arnold and M. J. McIntyre, *International Tax Primer* (Boston: Kluwer Law International, 1995); also, S. Crow and E. Sauls, "Setting the Right Transfer Price," *Management Accounting,* December 1994, pp. 41–47.

[18]   In this context *unrelated* means the firm has no common ownership interest.

Audit of Transfer Prices

Because of transfer pricing's key role in international taxation, taxing authorities worldwide have begun to focus on transfer prices in tax audits of multinational corporations (MNCs). A recent survey of 400 MNCs reported that the areas most likely to trigger an audit were exchanges of managerial services (52 percent), sales of finished goods (39 percent), technical services (35 percent), and intangibles (36 percent).

Source: Based on information from the *Ernst & Young LLP Business UpShot,* December 1997.

The **cost-plus method** determines the transfer price based on the seller's costs, plus a gross profit percentage determined from comparison of sales of the seller to unrelated parties, or sales of unrelated parties to other unrelated parties.

> The **cost-plus method** determines the transfer price based on the seller's costs, plus a gross profit percentage determined from comparison of sales of the seller to unrelated parties.
>
> **Advance pricing agreements (APAs)** are agreements between the Internal Revenue Service (IRS) and the firm using transfer prices, which sets out the agreed-on transfer price.

Advance Pricing Agreements

Advance pricing agreements (APAs) are agreements between the Internal Revenue Service (IRS) and the firm using transfer prices, which sets out the agreed-on transfer price. The APA usually is obtained before the firm engages in the transfer. The aim of the APA program is to resolve transfer pricing disputes in a timely manner, and to avoid costly litigation. The program supplements the dispute resolution methods already in place: administrative (IRS), judicial, and treaty mechanisms. Two-thirds of the MNCs in a recent survey indicated they expected to use APAs in determining their transfer prices.[19]

[19] *Accounting Today,* August–September 1995, p. 10.

SUMMARY

ROI and residual income are two of the most common and most well-understood financial measures in business today. Because of the advantage of investment SBUs in motivating managers and providing a useful basis for top management to compare business units, the measures are now commonly used in most firms.

As firms move to a focus on strategy and the use of cost management to facilitate strategy, managers must consider carefully the role of ROI and residual income in performance evaluation. Both measures have a short-term focus that can be inconsistent with a strategy-based approach. For this reason, some view ROI and residual income as the dinosaurs of cost management, in need of replacement. However, the wide use of ROI and residual income in practice and the growth in interest in the balanced scorecard and in economic value added (EVA) suggest that firms are continuing to use ROI and residual income, but are also adapting investment SBUs to include the strategic focus.

Transfer pricing is an area where the management accountant can serve an important strategic role by overseeing the many objectives of transfer pricing—performance evaluation, evaluation of business units, tax minimization, management of foreign currencies and risks, and other strategic objectives. Especially for multinational firms, the determination of transfer prices is likely to have important effects on profits and the achievement of strategic goals. Management considers the availability and quality of outside supply, the capacity utilization of the internal selling unit, and the strategic objectives of the firm in determining the proper transfer price—cost-based, market price, or a negotiated price. Value chain analysis can help by identifying strategically important activities in the value chain and by indicating how competitive the firm is in providing these activities within the industry.

Advance pricing agreement (APA) 779

Arm's-length standard 778

Asset turnover 761

Comparable price method 778

Cost-plus method 779

Economic value added (EVA) 772

Expropriation 774

Gross book value (GBV) 767

Historical cost 766

Liquidation value 767

Net book value 766

Replacement cost 767

Resale price method 778

Residual income 770

Return on equity (ROE) 760

Return on investment (ROI) 759

Return on sales (ROS) 761

Transfer pricing 773

SELF-STUDY PROBLEMS

(For solutions, please turn to the end of the chapter.)

1. Return on Investment and Residual Income

Selected data from Irol Inc.'s accounting ledger include:

Sales	$8,000,000
Net book value, beginning	2,500,000
Net book value, end	2,600,000
Net income	640,000
Minimum rate of return	12%

Required

1. Calculate return on investment, return on sales, and asset turnover.

2. Calculate residual income.

2. Determining the Proper Transfer Price

Johnston Chemical Company is a specialty manufacturer of a wide variety of industrial chemicals and adhesives. Much of the raw material is purchased in bulk from other chemical companies. One of the chemicals, T-Bar, is prepared in one of Johnston's own plants. T-Bar is shipped to other Johnston plants at a given internal price.

The Johnston adhesive plant requires 10,000 barrels of T-Bar per month and can purchase T-Bar outside the firm for $150 per barrel. Johnston's T-bar unit has a capacity of 20,000 barrels per month and is presently selling that quantity to outside buyers at $165 per barrel. The difference between the T-Bar unit's price of $165 and the outside firm's T-bar price of $150 is due to short-term pricing strategy only; the materials are equivalent in quality and functionality. The T-Bar unit's selling cost is $5 per barrel, and the T-Bar unit's variable cost of manufacturing is $90 per barrel.

Required

1. Should the adhesive unit purchase T-Bar inside or outside the firm?

2. Based on your answer in requirement 1, what should be the proper transfer price for T-Bar?

3. How would your answer to requirements 1 and 2 change if the T-Bar unit had a capacity of 30,000 barrels per month?

QUESTIONS

19-1 Explain the advantages of investment SBUs. Why would a firm choose investment SBU evaluation rather than profit SBU or cost SBU evaluation?

19-2 What are the three investment SBU evaluation measures?

19–3 What is return on investment, and how is it calculated?

19–4 What are the measurement issues to be concerned about when using return on investment?

19–5 What are the advantages and limitations of return on investment?

19–6 What is meant by the arm's-length standard, and what is it used for?

19–7 What are the components of return on investment, and how is each of them interpreted and used?

19–8 What are the advantages and limitations of residual income?

19–9 What are the objectives of investment SBU evaluation?

19–10 What is return on equity, how is it calculated, and how is it interpreted?

19–11 What are the three methods most commonly used in international taxation to determine the transfer price that is acceptable to tax authorities? Explain each method briefly.

19–12 What is meant by expropriation, and what is the role of transfer pricing in this regard?

19–13 How does the concept of economic value added compare to return on investment and residual income?

PROBLEMS

19–14 **INVESTMENT SBUs; THE SALES LIFE CYCLE** (Review of Chapter 18)
The sales life cycle is used to describe the phases a product goes through from introduction to withdrawal from the market. The four phases are

1. Introduction
2. Growth
3. Maturity
4. Decline and withdrawal

In the introduction phase, the product relies on product differentiation to attract new customers. Then, in the growth phase, the product attracts competition, though differentiation is still an advantage for the firm. In the maturity phase competition is keen, and cost control and quality considerations become important. In the final, decline phase, differentiation again becomes important as well as cost control and quality (see Chapter 5 and Chapter 18 for more detail).

Required At which phases, if any, of the sales life cycle should investment SBU evaluation methods be used, and why?

19–15 **INVESTMENT SBUs; THE COST LIFE CYCLE** As explained in Chapter 5, the cost life cycle consists of the phases the product goes through within a firm to prepare it for distribution and service. The five phases of the cost life cycle are

1. Research and development
2. Design
3. Production
4. Marketing and distribution
5. Customer service

The early phases of the cost life cycle are particularly important in that a relatively high percentage (some say as high as 80 percent or more) of the product's life cycle costs are determined at these phases. That is, the downstream costs of manufacturing, service, and repair are a direct consequence of the quality of the design.

Required At which phases, if any, of the cost life cycle should investment SBU evaluation methods be used, and why?

Service

19–16 ROI AND RESIDUAL INCOME Consider the following data from Coastal States Financial, Inc. Coastal uses investment SBU evaluation to analyze its two main divisions—mortgage loans and consumer loans (in millions):

	Mortgage Loans	Consumer Loans
Total assets	$2,000	$10,000
Operating income	$400	$1,500
Return on investment	25%	15%

Required

1. Which division is more successful? Why?

2. Coastal uses residual income as a measure of management success. What is the residual income for each division if the minimum desired rate of return is (a) 11 percent, (b) 15 percent, (c) 17 percent? Which division is more successful under each of these rates?

19–17 RETURN ON INVESTMENT; COMPARISONS OF THREE COMPANIES
Required Fill in the blanks for this information:

	Companies in the Same Industry		
	A	B	C
Sales	$1,500,000	$750,000	$_____
Income	200,000	75,000	_____
Investment (assets)	500,000	_____	2,500,000
Return on sales	_____	_____	0.5%
Asset turnover	_____	_____	1.5
Return on investment	_____	1%	_____

19–18 CALCULATING ROI AND RI Selected data from Behring Company's accounting records reveal the following:

Sales	$700,000
Average investment	$350,000
Net income	$50,000
Minimum rate of return	12%

Required

1. Calculate the return on investment.

2. Calculate the residual income.

19–19 TARGET SALES PRICE; RETURN ON INVESTMENT Preferred Products, a manufacturer of bicycles, uses normal volume as the basis for the cost figures used in setting prices. That is, prices are set on the basis of long-run volume predictions. The prices are then adjusted only for large changes in pay rates or material prices. You are given the following information:

Materials, wages, and other variable costs	$300 per unit
Fixed costs	$200,000 per year
Target return on investment	20%
Normal volume	1,500 units
Investment (total assets)	$800,000

Required

1. What sales price is needed to attain the target return on investment of 20 percent?

2. What rate of return on investment will be earned at sales volumes of 2,000 and 1,000 units, respectively, given the sales price determined in requirement 1?

19–20 VARIOUS MEASURES OF PROFITABILITY When the Bronx Company formed three divisions a year ago, the president told the division managers an annual bonus would be given to the most profitable division. The bonus would be based on either the return on investment or residual income of the division. Investment is to be measured using gross book value or net book value. The following data are available:

Division	Gross Book Value	Operating Inc.
A	$500,000	$53,500
B	480,000	52,000
C	300,000	33,300

All the assets are long-lived assets that were purchased 15 years ago and have 15 years of useful life remaining. A zero terminal disposal price is predicted. Bronx's minimum return on investment used for computing residual income is 10 percent.

Required Which method for computing profitability would each manager choose? Show supporting calculations. Where applicable, assume straight-line depreciation.

19–21 CALCULATING ROI & RI AND COMPARING RESULTS Morgan Industries manufactures die machinery. To meet its expansion needs, the company recently acquired (19X3) one of its suppliers, Vienna Steel. To maintain Vienna's separate identity, Morgan reports Vienna's operations as an investment SBU. All of Morgan's investment SBUs are monitored on the basis of return on investment. Management bonuses are based on ROI and all investment SBUs are expected to earn a minimum of 12 percent before income taxes.

Strategy

Vienna's ROI has ranged from 14 percent to 18 percent since 19X3. It recently had the opportunity for a new investment that would have yielded 13 percent ROI. However, division management decided against the investment because it believed the investment would decrease the division's overall ROI.

The 19X5 operating statement for Vienna follows. The division's operating assets were $13,000,000 at the end of 19X5, a 6 percent increase over the 19X4 year-end balance.

VIENNA DIVISION
Operating Statement
For Year Ended December 31, 19X5
(000s omitted)

Sales		$25,000
Cost of goods sold		16,600
Gross profit		8,400
Operating expense		
Administration	$2,340	
Selling	3,810	6,150
Income before income taxes		$ 2,250

Required

1. Calculate the following performance measures for 19X5 for the Vienna Division of Morgan Industries:
   a. Return on average investment in operating assets employed.
   b. Residual income calculated on the basis of average operating assets employed.
2. Which performance measure (ROI or residual income) should Morgan Industries use to provide the right incentive for each division to autonomously act in the firm's best interests? Would Vienna's management have been more likely to accept the capital investment opportunity if residual income had been used as a performance measure instead of ROI? Explain.

3. What type of strategic performance measurement do you recommend for Vienna Division? Explain.

Strategy

19–22 **ROI PERFORMANCE MEASURES** T-shirts R Us Inc. operates two divisions that manufactures T-shirts for universities. Each division has its own manufacturing facility. The historical-cost accounting system reports these data for 19X6:

ATLANTIC COAST DIVISION
Income Statement
(000s omitted)

Revenue	$600
Operating costs	470
Operating income	$130

BIG 10 DIVISION
Income Statement
(000s omitted)

Revenue	$600
Operating costs	400
Operating income	$200

T-shirts R Us Inc. estimates the useful life of each manufacturing facility to be 15 years. The company uses straight-line depreciation, with a depreciation charge of $70,000 per year for each division and no salvage value at the end of 15 years. The manufacturing facility is the only long-lived asset of either division. Current assets are $300,000 in each division. At the end of 19X6 the Atlantic Coast Division is four years old and the Big 10 Division is six years old.

An index of construction costs, replacement cost, and liquidation values for manufacturing facilities for production of T-shirts for the six-year period that T-shirts R Us Inc. has been operating is as follows:

			Liquidation Value:	
Year	Cost Index	Replacement Cost	Big 10	Atlantic Coast
19X0	80	$1,000,000	$800,000	$ 800,000
19X1	82	1,000,000	800,000	800,000
19X2	84	1,100,000	700,000	700,000
19X3	89	1,150,000	600,000	700,000
19X4	94	1,200,000	600,000	800,000
19X5	96	1,250,000	600,000	900,000
19X6	100	1,300,000	500,000	1,000,000

Required

1. Compute return on investment for each division using historical cost. Interpret the results.
2. Compute return on investment for each division, incorporating current-cost estimates as follows, using:
   a. Gross book values under historical costs.
   b. Gross book value at historical cost restated to current cost using the index of construction costs.
   c. Net book value of long-lived assets restated at current cost using the index of construction costs.
   d. Current replacement cost.
   e. Current liquidation value.
3. Which of the measures calculated in requirement 2 would you choose for (a) performance evaluation of each division manager, (b) deciding which division is most profitable for the overall firm? What are the strategic advantages and disadvantages to the firm of each measure for both (a) and (b)?

19–23 **TRANSFER PRICING; DECISION MAKING** Daniels Inc. manufactures sports equipment. The company is comprised of several divisions, each operating as its own profit SBU. Division A has decided to go outside the company to buy materials, since it was informed that division B was increasing its selling price of the same materials to $200. Information for division A and division B is as follows:

Outside price for materials	$150
Division A's annual purchases	10,000 units
Division B's variable costs per unit	$140
Division B's fixed costs	$1,250,000
Division B's capacity utilization	100%

Required

1. Will the company benefit if division A purchases outside the company? Assume division B cannot sell its materials to outside buyers.

2. Assume division B can save $200,000 in fixed costs if it does not manufacture the material for division A. Should division A purchase from the outside market?

3. Assume the situation in requirement 1. If the outside market value for the materials drops $20, should A buy from the outside?

19–24 **TRANSFER PRICING; DECISION MAKING** Using the information from problem 19–23, assume division B could sell 10,000 units outside for $210 per unit with variable marketing costs of $8. Should division B sell outside or to division A?

19–25 **TRANSFER PRICING; DECISION MAKING** Phoenix Inc., a cellular communication company, has multiple divisions. Each division's management is compensated based on the operating income of the division. Division A currently purchases cellular equipment from outside markets, and uses it to produce communication systems. Division B produces similar cellular equipment and sells to outside customers, but not currently to division A. Division A's manager approaches division B's manager with a proposal for division A to buy division B's equipment. Division B would incur variable manufacturing costs of $60 per unit if it produces the cellular equipment that division A desires.

Relevant Information about Division B

Sells 50,000 units of equipment to outside customers at $130 per unit.
Operating capacity is currently 80 percent; the division can perform at 100 percent.
Variable manufacturing costs $70 per unit.
Variable marketing costs $8 per unit.
Fixed manufacturing costs are $580,000.

Income per Unit for Division A (assuming parts purchased outside, not from division B):

Sales revenue		$320
Manufacturing costs		
Cellular equipment	80	
Other materials	10	
Fixed costs	40	
Total manufacturing costs		130
Gross margin		190
Marketing costs		
Variable	35	
Fixed	15	
Total marketing costs		50
Operating income		$140

Required

1. Division A wants to buy 25,000 units from division B at $75 per unit. Should division B accept or reject the proposal?

2. How should division A proportion the units purchased internally and externally that would be in the best interest of Phoenix Company?

3. What range will the managers of divisions A and B agree is the best price for their respective divisions?

19–26 **TRANSFER PRICING ISSUES** It often happens that when transfer prices are based on cost, a supplying division has no incentive to reduce cost. For example, a design change that would reduce manufacturing cost in the supplying division would be of benefit only to downstream divisions if the transfer price is based on a markup of cost.

Required What can or should be done to provide the supplying division an incentive to reduce manufacturing costs when the transfer price is cost-based?

International

19–27 **TRANSFER PRICING; INTERNATIONAL TAXATION** The Hirsch Company has a manufacturing subsidiary in Singapore that produces high-end exercise equipment for consumers in the United States. The manufacturing subsidiary has total manufacturing costs of $1,500,000 plus general and administrative expenses of $350,000. The manufacturing unit sells the equipment for $2,500,000 to the marketing subsidiary in the United States, which sells the equipment to the final consumers for an aggregate of $3,500,000. The sales subsidiary has total marketing, general, and administrative costs of $300,000. Assume that Singapore has a corporate tax rate of 33 percent, while in the United States, the tax rate is 46 percent. Assume that no tax treaties or other special tax treatments apply.

Required What would be the effect on total corporate level taxes of the Hirsch Company if the manufacturing subsidiary raises its price to the sales subsidiary 10 percent?

Strategy

19–28 **TRANSFER PRICING; DECISION MAKING** Advanced Manufacturing Inc. (AMI) produces electronic components in three divisions—industrial, commercial, and consumer products. The commercial products division annually purchases 10,000 units of part 23–6711, produced by the industrial division for use in the manufacture of one of its own products. The commercial division is growing rapidly due to rapid growth in its markets. The commercial division is expanding its production and now wants to expand its purchases of part 23–6711 to 15,000 units per year. The problem is that the industrial division is at full capacity. There has been no new investment in the industrial division for some years because top management sees little future growth in its products, so it is unlikely that industrial's capacity will increase soon.

The commercial division also can buy part 23–6711 from HighTech Inc. or from Britton Electric. Britton is a customer of the industrial division, now purchasing 650 units of part 88–461. The sales to Britton would not be affected by the commercial division's decision about part 23–6711.

Industrial division	
Data on part 23–6711	
Price to commercial division	$185
Variable manufacturing costs	155
Price to outside buyers	205
Data on part 88–461	
Variable manufacturing costs	65
Sales price	95
Other suppliers of part 23–6711	
HighTech Inc., price	$200
Britton Electric, price	$210

Required

1. What is the proper decision regarding where to purchase the part for the commercial division, and what is the correct transfer price?

2. What are the strategic implications of your answer to requirement 1? How can AMI become more competitive in one or more of its divisions?

19–29 TRANSFER PRICING; INTERNATIONAL TAXES; ETHICS Target, Inc., is a multinational firm with sales and manufacturing units in 15 countries. One of its manufacturing units, in country X, sells its product to a retail unit in country Y for $200,000. The country X unit has manufacturing costs for these products of $100,000. The retail unit in country Y sells the product to final customers for $300,000. Target is considering adjustments in its transfer prices to reduce overall corporate tax liability.

International

Ethics

Required

1. Assume both country X and country Y have corporate income tax rates of 40 percent and there are no special tax treaties or benefits applicable to Target. What would be the effect on Target's total tax burden if the manufacturing unit raises its price from $200,000 to $240,000?

2. What would be the effect on Target's total taxes if the manufacturing unit raised its price from $200,000 to $240,000 and the tax rate in country X is 20 percent and the tax rate in country Y is 40 percent?

3. Comment on the ethical issues, if any, you observe in this case.

19–30 STRATEGIC PERFORMANCE MEASUREMENT: INTERNATIONAL; STRATEGY; SERVICE INDUSTRY With the growth of the multinational company as a significant business structure throughout the world, a growing problem is developing in the area of analysis of the financial results for these business entities. At the time the incidents in this problem took place, the U.S. dollar was strengthening considerably relative to other currencies. Besides causing economic problems in many of the developing countries, it also creates a problem in the proper evaluation of a multinational's subsidiaries and their contribution to the total results of the company.

International

Strategy

Service

The Security System Corporation provides financial services for dealers and consumers in a variety of construction and consumer products areas. The firm is searching for the proper method of evaluating its subsidiaries. Of concern is their contribution to the overall earnings of the company and how to evaluate whether the specific goals developed by the subsidiaries' management have been met.

In search for answers, the company is concerned with the following concepts:

- Analysis of results—should it be in local currency or U.S. dollars?

- Management's explanation of variances—in local currency or U.S. dollars?

- What should the time frames be for comparative data—plan or forecast?

The firm has six distinctive business segments in the new-residential-housing market: consumer appliance market, commercial nonresidential construction, consumer aftermarket, apparel market, automotive market, and capital goods markets. Last year the company achieved 30 percent of its revenues and 35 percent of its earnings from its international subsidiaries. However, years ago when the British pound sterling was at one pound = $2.33 U.S. (whereas now it's one pound = $1.68 U.S.), the firm achieved 35 percent of its revenue—but more significantly 47 percent of its earnings—from its international subsidiaries. During the past five years, although the U.S. dollar equivalent of earnings from the international subsidiaries has gone down from 47 percent of the total to 35 percent, most of the operations have reported significant, steady gains from year to year in their local currency.

All operations report their monthly financial data to the firm's world headquarters in U.S. dollars. They use the existing exchange rate at the close of business on the last day of the month. The firm reports the exchange based on FASB 52 accounting (except for one or two special situations). The comparisons of the monthly financial data are made against a financial plan that uses a predetermined exchange rate for the various months of the year.

Over the past five years, even as the U.S. dollar has steadily strengthened against foreign currencies, the firm has been analyzing the financial results of its operations totally in U.S. dollars. Its results are compared to a fixed-plan exchange rate.

The firm establishes exchange rates to be used each year, many times optimistically, and then sets an earnings per share target on that basis. Then, if the dollar strengthens even greater, the firm finds itself missing its targets. It then makes statements that a particular group missed its planned targets when, in fact, the group's operations may all have exceeded their local currency plans but are losing on the comparison due to unfavorable exchange rate effects.

Required   How should the firm measure its results to enhance its competitiveness? How can it safeguard its overall EPS target if it uses local currencies in the reporting system? Where does the responsibility for the U.S. dollar attainment of goals lie?

(CMA Adapted)

SOLUTIONS TO SELF-STUDY PROBLEMS

1. Return on Investment and Residual Income

1. Return on sales = Net income/Sales
    = $640,000/$8,000,000
    = .08

    Asset turnover = Sales/Average investment
    = $8,000,000/($2,500,000 + $2,600,000)/2
    = 3.137 times

    ROI = Profit margin × Asset turnover
    = .08 × 3.137
    = 25.1%

2. Residual income = Net income − (Average investment ×
    Minimum rate of return)
    = $640,000 − [($2,500,000 + $2,600,00)/2] × .12
    = $334,000

2. Determining the Proper Transfer Price

1. Since the T-Bar unit is at full capacity, and since the contribution on outside sales of $70 ($165 − $5 − $90) is greater than the cost saving of inside production of $60 ($150 − $90), the T-Bar unit should sell outside, and the adhesive unit should purchase T-Bar for $150 outside the firm.

2. Since the T-bar unit is at full capacity and there is an outside market, the best transfer price is market price for T-bar. The relevant market price is the price that the T-Bar unit can get (assuming it is a reliable, long-term price), $165. This transfer price will cause the adhesive unit to do the correct thing; that is, to buy outside since the outside price is lower.

3. If the T-bar unit has excess capacity, then it can sell T-Bar both internally and externally. The correct transfer price is then the price that will cause the adhesive unit to purchase internally; that is, any price between variable cost of the seller ($90) and the outside market price to the adhesive unit ($150). The units might agree on a price by considering what is a fair return to each unit, and in effect split the profit on the sale between the units. The actual outcome of the negotiations for the transfer price depends on a number of factors, including the negotiation skills of the two managers.

Management Compensation and the Evaluation of the Firm

AP/Wide World Photos

After studying this chapter, you should be able to . . .

1 Identify and explain the types of management compensation

2 Identify the strategic role of management compensation and the different types of compensation used in practice

3 Explain the three characteristics of a bonus plan: the base for determining performance, the compensation pool from which the bonus is funded, and the bonus payment options

4 Describe the role of tax planning and financial reporting in management compensation planning

5 Explain how management compensation plans are used in service firms and not-for-profit organizations

6 Apply the two approaches for evaluating the firm: financial analysis and valuation

There's no praise to beat the sort you can put in your pocket.

MOLIÈRE

The first of this chapter's two parts addresses management compensation, a topic that follows directly from management control (Chapters 18 and 19). The second part goes a step further, to look at the evaluation of the entire firm. Both topics have drawn significant attention in recent years, as shareholders and investors look closely at the performance of the firms and their managers.

PART ONE: MANAGEMENT COMPENSATION

Recruiting, motivating, rewarding, and retaining effective managers are critical in the success of all firms. Effective management compensation plans are an important and integral part of the determination of a strategic competitive advantage, and an important concern of the management accountant.

◀ **LEARNING OBJECTIVE 1**
Identify and explain the types of management compensation.

TYPES OF MANAGEMENT COMPENSATION

Management compensation plans are policies and procedures for compensating managers.[1] Compensation includes one or more of the following: salary, bonus, and benefits or perquisites (perks). **Salary** is a fixed payment, while a **bonus** is based on the achievement of performance goals for the period. **Perks** include special benefits for the employee, such as travel, membership in a fitness club, life insurance, medical benefits, tickets to entertainment events, and other extras paid for by the firm.

Compensation can be paid currently (usually an annual amount paid monthly) or deferred to future years. Salary and benefits are typically awarded currently, while bonuses are either paid currently or deferred, though a wide variety of plans are found in practice.

The compensation plans for high-level managers are generally explained in the firm's proxy statements and must be approved by the shareholders. Base salary usually is an annual cash payment, though it also may include predetermined future cash payments and/or stock awards. Perks are commonly awarded on an annual basis, though there may be future payments or benefits. Base salary and perks are negotiated when the manager is hired, and when the compensation contracts are reviewed and renewed. They are not commonly influenced by the manager's current performance, as is bonus pay. A recent study of the top five executives at 1,070 firms in

Management compensation plans are policies and procedures for compensating managers.

A **salary** is a fixed payment.

A **bonus** is based on the achievement of performance goals for the period.

Perks include special services and benefits for the employee, such as travel, membership in a fitness club, life insurance, medical benefits, tickets to entertainment events, and other extras paid for by the firm.

BusinessWeek

Is It Worth It?

Valuing a firm is a complex task. Consider Intel, the manufacturer of processors for personal computers, which currently has a share price of $73 (January 1998). Some would say that since the firm's earnings have grown at twice the rate of the Standard & Poor's 500 stock index in the last five years, Intel's stock is undervalued at a price/earnings ratio of 18. Others note that Intel's stock price has risen steeply in recent years, and it properly reflects the value of the firm.

Q: Is Intel overpriced or underpriced? *Find out on page 809 of this chapter.*

---

[1] These plans also are referred to as executive compensation plans, executive incentive compensation, employee contracts, compensation contracts, or bonus and incentive contracts.

Wider Use of Bonus Instead of Base Salary: Duracell

In an effort to reduce fixed operating costs, companies are reducing pension and medical benefits for active and retired employees. They also are seeking ways to reduce the basic salary structure, which is primarily fixed cost. If an employee is given a raise, that increase becomes an entitlement and must be paid each year. It also is used to calculate the worker's pension and other company-paid benefits, thus effectively increasing the amount of fixed cost.

Firms can effectively reduce fixed costs by keeping base salary increases to a minimum. In addition, companies are striving to increase the efficiency and productivity of employees at every level, using incentive plans and similar productivity enhancement programs.

For example, Duracell Corp. motivates employees by giving stock options to all full- and part-time employees. "Employees really do have a vested interest in how the company performs, and as we make those hurdles (increase in stock price) there's a real sense of accomplishment," according to Gary Fox, a Duracell manager.

On the other hand, it is a complex and difficult task to establish appropriate salary levels and incentive plans. Incentives tend to lose their effect over time as employees begin to consider the incentive as part of the compensation base.

Source: Based on information in *Coopers & Lybrand Executive Briefing,* November 1991; and "At Duracell, an Early Christmas," *Business Week,* September 30, 1996.

New AT&T CEO Focuses on Pay for Performance

C. Michael Armstrong, CEO of AT&T since October 1997, wants to make the firm more profitable and quicker to respond to customer needs. A key aspect of his plan is pay for performance. Almost 75 percent of all AT&T executives have their bonuses tied to quantitative goals, including sales, costs, and profits. Also, as for other firms such as Kodak, top executives will be required to purchase shares of the company, to further align their incentives and goals with those of the firm's shareholders.

Source: Based on information in "New Boss, New Plan," *Business Week,* February 2, 1998, pp. 122–32.

13 major industries showed that bonus pay is the fastest growing part of total compensation—firms are moving toward linking executive pay to performance. The median bonus was 80 percent of salary for the sampled firms, and in some industries the median bonus was larger than salary. For example, in the financial services industry the median bonus was 255 percent of the average salary.[2]

THE STRATEGIC ROLE AND OBJECTIVES OF MANAGEMENT COMPENSATION

The strategic role of management compensation has three aspects: (1) the strategic conditions facing the firm, (2) the effect of risk aversion on managers' decision making, and (3) certain ethical issues.

Design the Compensation Plan for Existing Strategic Conditions

LEARNING OBJECTIVE 2
Identify the strategic role of management compensation and the different types of compensation used in practice.

The compensation plan should be grounded in the strategic analysis of the firm—its competitive strengths and weaknesses and critical success factors. As the strategic conditions facing the firm change over time, the compensation plan also should change. For example, the firm's strategy changes as its products move through the different phases of the sales life cycle—product introduction, growth, maturity, and decline (Chapter 5). As a firm's product moves from the growth phase to the mature phase, the firm's strategy also moves from product differentiation to cost leadership. When

---

[2] *Deloitte & Touche Review,* April 29, 1996, citing a survey done by the Conference Board for 1994 compensation.

this happens, the compensation plan should change in response to the new strategy. In Exhibit 20–1 we illustrate how the mix of salary, bonus, and perks might change as the firm and its products move through different phases of the sales life cycle.

Note in Exhibit 20–1 that the mix of the three parts of total compensation changes as strategic conditions change. For example, in the mature phase of the products' life cycle, when competition is likely to be the greatest and the firm is interested in maintaining an established market and controlling costs, a balanced compensation plan of competitive salary, bonus, and benefits is needed to attract, motivate, and retain the best managers. In contrast, during the growth phase when the need for innovation and leadership is the greatest, there is an emphasis on relatively large bonuses to effectively motivate managers. In effect, top management considers the specific strategic conditions facing the firm as a basic consideration in developing the compensation plan and making changes as strategic conditions change.

Risk Aversion and Management Compensation

The manager's relative risk aversion can have an important effect on decision making (see Chapter 18, "Employment Contracts"). Risk aversion is the tendency to prefer decisions with assured outcomes over those with uncertain outcomes. It is a relatively common decision-making characteristic of managers. A risk-averse manager is biased against decisions that have an uncertain outcome, even if the expected outcome is favorable.

For example, a risk-averse manager might cancel a planned investment in new equipment that would reduce operating costs if there is a chance that nonoperating costs might increase, due to installation problems or employee training needs or other reasons. In contrast, top management and shareholders of the firm may see the risk of additional nonoperating costs as not significant relative to the potential for reduced operating costs. The difference in perspective comes about because the manager's bonus is likely to be directly and significantly affected by the outcome of the decision, while the outcome is likely to have a relatively small impact on the firm and therefore on top management and shareholders.

Compensation plans can manage risk aversion effectively by carefully choosing the mix of salary and bonus in total compensation. The larger the proportion of bonus in total compensation, the more the incentive to the manager to avoid risky outcomes. To reduce the effect of risk aversion, there should be a relatively large proportion of salary in total compensation, with a smaller portion in bonus. Determining the proper balance between salary and bonus must take all three compensation objectives into account.

Ethical Issues

Two ethical issues arise when designing and implementing compensation plans: (1) the overall level of compensation and (2) unethical actions, such as managers' misreporting their performance.

Exhibit 20–1	Compensation Plans Tailored for Different Strategic Conditions*		
Product Sales Life Cycle Phase:	**Salary**	**Bonus**	**Benefits**
Product introduction	High	Low	Low
Growth	Low	High	Competitive
Maturity	Competitive	Competitive	Competitive
Decline	High	Low	Competitive

*Key to exhibit: "Competitive" lies between low and high.

Source: Adapted from George T. Milkovich and Jerry M. Newman, *Compensation* (Burr Ridge, IL: Richard D. Irwin, 1984), p. 12. Also, V. Govindarajan and J. K. Shank present a similar approach based on the Boston Consulting Group's concepts of the three phases: build, hold, and harvest, in "Strategic Cost Management: Tailoring Controls to Strategies," *Journal of Cost Management*, Fall 1992, pp. 14–24.

When Is Executive Pay Too High?

There is a common concern that executive pay is too high, and that workers are not properly compensated relative to the very high salaries and bonuses of top executives, particularly during periods of corporate downsizing.[3] High executive compensation is unjust, some argue, and compensation plans are unethical. Others point out that most executives are worth their high compensation because they bring far greater value to the firm. Shareholders and bondholders who see their investments appreciate, and attribute this to the executive, are likely to see the compensation plans as just and ethical. For example, when a key manager left Wal-Mart, the firm stock price fell 4 percent the day of the announcement, indicating the very high importance investors placed on this executive.[4] The Internal Revenue Service may deny the firm's right to deduct compensation it determines to be unreasonable. The U.S. Tax Court analyzes 14 compensation factors to determine whether the compensation is reasonable. These factors include the manager's qualifications, the nature of the work, the size and complexity of the firm, and the prevailing economic conditions.[5]

Unethical Actions

Sometimes the management compensation plan provides an incentive for unethical action. A well-known example is the H. J. Heinz Company, which in 1979 discovered management fraud in many of its divisions.[6] The division managers had been using improper billing, accounting, and reporting practices to transfer income from one fiscal period to another. Their purpose was to achieve a target profit level needed to win bonuses. An investigation by the audit committee found that perceived and actual pressures to achieve the goals of Heinz's bonus program were a major reason for the fraud. A lack of top management emphasis on ethics and accounting controls also contributed to the fraud.

Similarly, at one time Sears, Roebuck & Co. paid auto shop employees commissions based on the amount of repair work done. The result was charges for unnec-

---

Executive Pay Too High?

Nearly three-quarters of ordinary Americans feel that corporate bosses are overpaid.

Source: Based on information in Business Week Survey, *Business Week,* May 12, 1997, p. 41.

High CEO Pay Alienates Lower-Level Managers

A study by researchers at Stanford University and the University of Illinois at Urbana found that overpayment of CEOs, relative to industry norms and to the pay levels of lower-level managers, tends to be associated with higher turnover rates of lower-level managers. The implication is that the high CEO pay hurts the loyalty and motivation of lower-level managers.

Source: Based on information from "Where CEO Pay Really Grates," *Business Week,* October 13, 1997.

---

[3]   "Gross Compensation?" *Business Week,* March 18, 1996, pp. 32–34; "Executive Pay," *The Wall Street Journal,* April 11, 1996; "Even Executives Are Wincing at Executive Pay," *Business Week,* May 12, 1997, pp. 40–41; "When Bosses Get Rich from Selling the Company," *Business Week,* March 30, 1998, pp. 33–34.

[4]   *The Wall Street Journal,* March 29, 1996. Bill Fields, a 25-year veteran of Wal-Mart, left his position as chief of the main discount store business department to accept a similar position at Viacom, Inc.

[5]   The 14 factors are set out in the Tax Court ruling in *Pulsar Components International, Inc., v. Commissioner,* T.C. Memo 1996–129 (3/14/96).

[6]   "H. J. Heinz Company, A Case on Ethics in Management," Harvard Business School Case No. 382–034, Harvard Business School, Boston, MA. See, also, H. M. Schilit, *Financial Shenanigans: How to Detect Accounting Gimmicks and Fraud in Financial Reports* (New York: McGraw-Hill, 1993); and John A. Byrne, "Smoke, Mirrors, and the Boss's Paycheck," *Business Week,* October 13, 1997, p. 63.

essary work and work that was never done, as well as overcharges for completed work. The discovery of these fraudulent practices in 1992 damaged Sears' auto shop business, requiring Sears to change policies quickly to win back customers. Again, the presence of a very strong motivation due to a compensation plan, without compensating accounting controls designed to detect and prevent fraud, can lead to unethical behavior.

Objectives of Management Compensation

The key objective of the firm is to develop management compensation plans that support the firm's strategic objectives, as set forth by the firm's management and owners. The objectives of management compensation are therefore consistent with the three objectives of management control as defined in Chapter 18:

1. To motivate managers to exert a high level of effort to achieve the firm's goals.
2. To provide the right incentive for managers, acting autonomously, to make decisions consistent with the firm's goals.
3. To fairly determine the rewards earned by managers for their effort and skill, and for the effectiveness of their decision making.

In Chapter 18 and Chapter 19, these objectives were used to develop performance measurement systems (e.g., cost, profit, and investment SBUs). In this chapter the objectives are used to develop effective management compensation plans.

The first objective is to motivate managers to a high level of effort to achieve the firm's goals. A performance-based compensation plan is best for this purpose. For example, a bonus plan that would reward the manager for achieving particular goals would be appropriate. The goals could be financial or nonfinancial, current or long term.

The second objective is to provide the right incentive for managers to make decisions consistent with the firm's objectives. The firm's objectives are identified in the strategic competitive analysis, from which is derived the firm's critical success factors. Critical success factors include customer satisfaction, quality, service, product development, and innovation in production and distribution. Firms attend to critical success factors by making them part of the manager's compensation.

For example, McDonald's rewards managers who develop its critical success factors—quality, service, cleanliness, and value—as well as the conventional financial performance measures (earnings, growth in sales). Firms such as International Paper Company include nonfinancial factors such as quality, safety, and minority employee development as factors in management compensation plans. Research has shown that firms like these with clear strategic goals specified in critical success factors include these factors in their compensation plans.[7]

In developing compensation plans, the management accountant works to achieve fairness by making the plan simple, clear, and consistent. Fairness also means that a plan focuses only on the controllable aspects of the manager's performance. For example, compensation should not be affected by expenses that cannot be tied directly to the manager's unit. Similarly, the performance of the manager should be separated from that of the manager's unit because economic factors beyond the manager's control are likely to affect the performance of the unit. Fairness in this sense often is achieved by basing the manager's compensation on performance relative to prior years or to agreed-on goals, rather than on comparison to other managers.

---

[7]   C. Ittner and D. Larcker, "Total Quality Management and the Choice of Information and Reward Systems," *Journal of Accounting Research* (1995 Supplement), pp. 1–34; R.R. Bushman, Indejejikian and A. Smith, "CEO Compensation: The Role of Individual Performance Evaluation," *Journal of Accounting and Economics*, April 1996.

BONUS PLANS

Bonus compensation is the fastest growing part of total compensation and often the largest part. There are a wide variety of possible bonus pay plans that can be categorized according to three key aspects:

- The **base of the compensation,** that is, how the bonus pay is determined. The three most common bases are (1) stock price; (2) cost, revenue, profit, or investment SBU–based performance; and (3) the balanced scorecard.

- **Compensation pools,** that is, the source from which the bonus pay is funded. The two most common compensation pools are earnings in the manager's own SBU and a firmwide pool based on total earnings for the firm.

- **Payment options,** that is, how the bonus is to be awarded. The two common options are cash and stock (typically common shares). The cash or stock can either be awarded currently or deferred to future years. Also, the stock can either be awarded directly or granted in the form of stock options.

Bases for Bonus Compensation

LEARNING OBJECTIVE 3 ▶
Explain the three characteristics of a bonus plan: the base for determining performance, the compensation pool from which the bonus is funded, and the bonus payment options.

Bonus compensation can be determined on the basis of stock price, strategic performance measures (cost, revenue, profit, or investment SBU), or the balanced scorecard (critical success factors). For example, when the manager's unit is publicly held, the unit's stock price is a relevant base. When stock price is used, the amount of the bonus depends on the amount of the increase in stock price, or on whether the stock price reaches a certain predetermined goal. Similarly, when strategic performance measures or critical success factors are used, the bonus depends either on the amount of improvement in the measure or on achieving a predetermined goal. The bonus can be determined by comparing the stock price, accounting measures, or critical success factors for a given manager to that of other managers. There are three ways to determine the bonus. It can be based on a comparison to (a) prior years, (b) a budget or predetermined target, or (c) other managers. By using a budget or comparison to prior years firms avoid the influence of uncontrollable factors.

The choice of a base comes from a consideration of the compensation objectives, as outlined in Exhibit 20–2. A common choice is to use cost, revenue, profit, or investment SBUs because they are often a good measure of economic performance; therefore, they are motivating and perceived to be fair. As many firms move to a more strategic approach to cost management, however, the use of critical success factors and stock-price-based measures in compensation is likely to increase. Chrysler Corporation, International Paper Company, and other firms are using critical success factors in this way. Also, SBU-based accounting measures can cause

---

Linking Rewards to Performance Measures at Pioneer Petroleum

Companies understand that strategic goals are more likely achieved if the firm includes them in management compensation. An oil company uses the balanced scorecard as the sole basis for computing incentive compensation. The balanced scorecard–based incentive plan is as follows: 60 percent of executives' bonuses are tied to their achievement of four financial indicators: return on capital, profitability, cash flow, and operating cost. The remaining 40 percent of the bonus is tied to indicators of customer satisfaction, dealer satisfaction, employee satisfaction, and environmental responsibility. The firm's CEO says that linking compensation to the scorecard has helped to align the company with its strategy. "I know of no competitor," he says, "who has this degree of alignment. It is providing results for us."

Source: Based on information in R. S. Kaplan and D. P. Norton, "Using the Balanced Scorecard as a Strategic Management System," *Harvard Business Review,* January–February 1996, pp. 75–85. (Name of actual company disguised by the authors.)

flawed decision making. For example, when a bonus is tied to conventional net income, there is an incentive for managers to build up inventory because an increase in inventory causes an increase in the current period's net income (see Chapter 18).

Bonus Compensation Pools

A manager's bonus can be determined in the so-called **unit-based pool** that is based on the performance of the manager's unit. For example, the bonus pool might be determined as the excess of the unit's earnings over 5 percent of investment in the unit. This would then be the amount available for the manager's bonus. The appeal of the unit-based pool is the strong motivation for effective managers to perform and to receive rewards for their effort—the upside potential to the individual manager is very motivating.

Alternatively, the amount of bonus available to all managers is often a **firmwide pool** set aside for this purpose. For example, a firmwide pool might be the excess of firmwide earnings over 5 percent of firmwide investment. Each unit manager's bonus is then drawn from this common pool. General Electric Corporation's bonus compensation plan includes the following statement regarding the firm's pool:

> "the maximum amount in any year is 10% of the amount by which consolidated net earnings exceed 5% of average consolidated capital investment."
>
> (General Electric Corp., Proxy Statement, 1995)

When the bonus pool is unit-based, the amount of the bonus for any one manager is independent of the performance of the other managers. In contrast, when a firmwide pool is used, the bonus to each manager depends in some predetermined way on the performance of the firm as a whole. The sharing arrangements vary widely, though a common arrangement is for all managers to share equally in the firmwide bonus pool. Generally, the firmwide pool provides an important incentive for coordination and cooperation among units within the firm, since all managers share in the greater overall firm profits that result from cross-unit efforts. Moreover, those who think executive pay is too high also often argue that pay linked to overall firm performance is preferable, since all managers share in the success of the firm. We summarize the advantages and disadvantages of each approach in Exhibit 20–3.

A **unit-based pool** is a method for determining a bonus based on the performance of the manager's unit.

A **firmwide pool** is a method of determining the bonus available to all managers through an amount set aside for this purpose.

Exhibit 20–2	Advantages and Disadvantages of Different Bonus Compensation Bases		
	Motivation	**Right Decision**	**Fairness**
Stock Price	(+/−) Depends on whether stock and stock options are included in base pay and bonus (−) lack of controllability can be unmotivating	(+) consistent with shareholder's interests	(−) lack of controllability
Strategic Performance Measures (cost, revenue, profit and investment SBUs)	(+) strongly motivating if noncontrollable factors are excluded	(+) generally a good measure of economic performance (−) typically has only a short-term focus (−) if bonus is very high, creates an incentive for inaccurate reporting	(+) intuitive, clear, and easily understood (−) measurement issues: differences in accounting conventions, cost allocation methods, financing methods
Balanced Scorecard: Critical Success Factors	(+) strongly motivating if noncontrollable factors are excluded	(+) consistent with management's strategy (−) may be subject to inaccurate reporting	(+) if carefully defined and measured, CSFs are likely to be perceived as fair (−) potential measurement issues, as above

Key: (+) means the base has a positive effect on the objective.
   (−) means the base has a negative effect on the objective.

Exhibit 20–3	Advantages and Disadvantages of Different Bonus Pools		
	Motivation	**Right Decision**	**Fairness**
Unit-Based	(+) strong motivation for an effective manager—the upside potential (−) unmotivating for manager of economically weaker units	(−) provides the incentive for individual managers **not** to cooperate with and support other units, when needed for the good of the firm	(−) does not separate the performance of the unit from the manager's performance
Firmwide	(+) helps to attract and retain good managers throughout the firm, even in economically weaker units (−) not as strongly motivating as the unit-based pool	(+) effort for the good of the overall firm is rewarded—motivates teamwork and sharing of assets among units	(+) separates the performance of the manager from that of the unit (+) can appear to be more fair to shareholders and others who are concerned that executive pay is too high

Key: (+) means the pool has a positive effect on the objective.
 (−) means the pool has a negative effect on the objective.

Incentive Compensation at Owens Corning

Owens Corning began the process of reducing entitlement-style employee benefits on January 1, 1996. All salaried U.S. employees became eligible for rewards, including nonqualified stock options, if the company achieved specific business results. Owens also planned to extend the plan to nonsalary employees.

Owens Corning considered three key measures as a basis for management compensation—earnings per share, cash flow, and sales growth. Managers received a profit-sharing contribution of up to 4 percent of pay and an annual stock bonus worth up to 8 percent, each linked to the three measures of corporate performance.

Source: Based on information in *Business Week,* July 22, 1996, pp. 82–83.

Bonus Payment Options

In recent years there has been a great increase in different payment options for bonus compensation plans. In the competition for top executives, firms are developing innovative ways to attract and retain the best.[8]

We look at the four most common:

Current Bonus (cash and/or stock) based on current (usually annual) performance. This is the most common form of the bonus.

Deferred Bonus (cash and/or stock) earned currently but not paid for two or more years. Deferred plans are used to avoid or delay taxes, or to affect the future total income stream of the manager in some desired way. Also, this type of plan can be used to retain key managers, when the deferred compensation is only paid if the manager stays with the firm.

Stock Options confer the right to purchase stock at some future date at a predetermined price. Stock options are used to motivate managers to increase stock price for the benefit of the shareholders.

Performance Shares are stock granted for achieving certain performance goals over two years or more.

Generally, the current and deferred bonus plans focus the manager's attention on short-term performance measures, most commonly, accounting earnings. In contrast, stock options and performance shares focus the manager's attention directly on shareholder value. See the advantages and disadvantages of the four plans in Exhibit 20–4.

---

[8] "Executive Pay," *Business Week,* March 30, 1992, pp. 52–58.

Exhibit 20-4	Advantages and Disadvantages of Bonus Payment Options		
	Motivation	**Right Decision**	**Fairness**
Current bonus	(+) strong motivation for current performance; stronger motivation than for deferred plans	(−) short-term focus (−) risk-averse manager avoids risky but potentially beneficial projects	(+/−) depends on the clarity of the bonus arrangement and the consistency with which it is applied
Deferred bonus	(+) strong motivation for current performance, but not as strong as for the current bonus plan, since the reward is delayed	as above	as above
Stock options	(+) unlimited upside potential is highly motivating (−) delay in reward reduces motivation somewhat	(+) incentive to consider longer-term issues (+) provides better risk incentives than for current or deferred bonus plans (+) consistent with shareholder interests	as above, plus (−) uncontrollable factors affect stock price
Performance shares	as above	(+) incentive to consider long-term factors that affect stock price (+) consistent with the firm's strategy, when critical success factors are used (+) consistent with shareholder interests, when earnings per share is used	(+/−) depends on the clarity of the bonus arrangement and the consistency with which it is applied

Key: (+) means the payment option has a positive effect.
  (−) means the payment option has a negative effect.

The Hidden Cost of Stock Options

Stock options are used by many firms to provide an effective means of manager compensation. The stock options align managers' interests with shareholders. The stock options also have another important benefit. The cost of this type of compensation *does not affect net income.* Under current accounting rules, the effect of stock options on net income, determined by the Black-Scholes fair value option pricing model, *need only be disclosed in footnotes* to the financial statements. Companies such as Bristol-Myers, PepsiCo, MCI, and many others have granted options that would have affected 1996 earnings significantly. For example:

MCI	$97 million
Bristol-Myers Squibb	55 million
Compaq	21 million

Source: Based on information from "Share the Wealth," *The Wall Street Journal,* January 14, 1997, p. 1; "Executive Pay," *Business Week,* April 21, 1997, pp. 58–66.

TAX PLANNING AND FINANCIAL REPORTING

In addition to achieving the three main objectives of compensation plans, firms attempt to choose plans that reduce or avoid taxes for both the firm and the manager. By combining salary, bonus, and perks accountants can maximize potential tax savings for the firm, while delaying or avoiding taxes for the manager. For example, many types of perks (club memberships, company car, entertainment) are deductible to reduce the firm's tax liability but are not considered income to the manager (and therefore are not taxed).

In contrast, while salary is also a deductible business expense for the firm, it is taxable income to the manager. Bonus plans have a variety of tax effects, as outlined in Exhibit 20–5. Tax planning is complex and dynamic, an integral part of compensation planning. Exhibit 20–5 is intended to suggest general relationships; a thorough coverage of tax planning is beyond the scope of this text.

Firms also attempt to design compensation plans that have a favorable effect on the firm's financial report. For example, present accounting rules do not require current recognition of the expense for grants of stock or stock options in many

◀ **LEARNING OBJECTIVE 4**
Describe the role of tax planning and financial reporting in management compensation planning.

Exhibit 20–5	Tax and Financial Report Effects of Compensation Plans			
			Tax Effect	
		Financial Statement Effect	**On the Firm**	**On the Manager**
Salary		Current expense	Current deduction	Currently taxed
Bonus	Current	Current expense	Current deduction	Currently taxed
	Deferred	Deferred expense	Deferred deduction	Deferred tax
	Stock Options—Nonqualified Plans	Accounting rules encourage but do not require recognition as expense for most stock grants; only footnote disclosure is required	Deduction when exercised	Taxed as ordinary income when exercised
	Stock Options—Qualified Plans	As above	No deduction	Taxed as capital gains when stock is sold, if held 18 months from exercise date
	Performance Shares	As above	Deferred deduction	Deferred tax
Perks	Certain Retirement Plans	Current expense	Current deduction	Deferred tax
	Other Perks	Current expense	Current deduction	Never taxed

compensation cases.[9] This means the financial report effects of stock-based compensation can be delayed, and earnings can be shown as currently higher than under other types of compensation. A thorough coverage of financial reporting rules regarding management compensation is not attempted here. In Exhibit 20–5 we provide an overview of the issues.

MANAGEMENT COMPENSATION IN SERVICE FIRMS

LEARNING OBJECTIVE 5 ▶
Explain how management compensation plans are used in service firms and not-for-profit organizations.

While most compensation arrangements are found at manufacturing or merchandising firms, an increasing number of service firms are using these plans—especially financial and professional service firms. A good example is the compensation plan for the architectural and engineering design firm, Short-Elliott-Hendrickson, Inc. (SEH).[10] The professional services of SEH are provided in a variety of markets, each of which is organized as a profit SBU—airport planning, water resources, waste management, municipal services, structural engineering, architecture, and others. SEH has developed a compensation plan for managers of each profit SBU. The plan uses a balanced scorecard approach that focuses on three areas: (1) financial results, (2) client satisfaction, and (3) improvement in the process of developing and providing the services. Management considers the financial results area to be the most important and has developed the following critical success factors and procedures to assess each manager's financial performance. The financial results of each profit SBU are evaluated on three criteria: profitability, efficiency, and collections of accounts receivable.

1. Profitability is measured by the *profit multiplier*, the ratio of net revenues to direct labor dollars.
2. Efficiency is measured by *staff utilization*, which is determined from the ratio of chargeable (to clients) direct labor-hours to total hours less vacation and holiday time.
3. *Collection of accounts* is measured by two ratios:
   — The percentage of accounts receivable over 90 days, a measure of the ability to collect customer accounts.

---

9 FASB, *Statement No. 123*, "Accounting for Stock-Based Compensation" (Stanford, CT: FASB, 1995).

10 Mark Pederson and Gary A. Lidgerding, "Pay-for-Performance in a Service Firm," *Management Accounting*, November 1995, pp. 40–43.

Exhibit 20–6	Management Compensation Plan for the Water Resources Group of SEH Inc.

1. Profit Multiplier (Ratio: net revenues to direct labor dollars)		2. Staff Utilization (Ratio: chargeable time to total time)		3. Collection of Accounts			
				Percentage of Accounts Receivable > 90 days		Days Revenue Unbilled	
Actual	88%	Actual	79%	Actual	14%	Actual	50 days
Goal	95%	Goal	83%	Goal	10%	Goal	45 days
Variance	7%	Variance	4%	Variance	4%	Variance	5 days
Multiply by weight of	3	Multiply by weight of	3	Multiply by weight of	2	Divide by goal	45 days
Weighted variance	21%	Weighted variance	12%	Weighted variance	8%	Percent variance	11%
Less	100%	Less	100%	Less	100%	Less	100%
Score	79%		88%		92%		89%

Source: Adapted from Mark Pederson and Gary A. Lidgerding, "Pay-for-Performance in a Service Firm," *Management Accounting,* November 1995, p. 42.

> — Average days unbilled work outstanding, a measure of the ability to complete assignments and to bill promptly for them.

In Exhibit 20–6, SEH's compensation plan is based on these four measures. Note that the Water Resources Group fell short of its target in each of the three areas with scores of 79 percent for the profit multiplier, 88 percent for staff utilizaton, and 92 percent and 89 percent respectively for each of the two measures of collections of accounts. The advantage of this compensation plan is it clearly places responsibility for financial results on the three criteria that are important to SEH's strategy. It is therefore consistent with the objectives of management compensation. The objectives of motivation and correct decision making are achieved since profit SBU managers have clear, attainable goals consistent with the firm's strategy. The objective of fairness is achieved by focusing on ratios rather than total profits, which means greater comparability among managers.

MANAGEMENT COMPENSATION IN NOT-FOR-PROFIT ORGANIZATIONS

A good example of compensation-based responsibility accounting in not-for-profit organizations is the bonus arrangement for the manager of the Greensboro, North Carolina, Coliseum. The Greensboro Coliseum is a large indoor arena used for sporting events such as basketball (the Atlantic Coast Conference Basketball Tournament), ice hockey (the National Hockey League team, the Hurricanes), and a variety of musical and other performances. The Coliseum is owned and managed by the city; it has been running deficits of over a million dollars per year in recent years.

To address the need to increase revenues, the Greensboro City Council decided to contract out management of the Coliseum to a management company that would be paid a fee plus a bonus incentive for reducing the deficit. The current director of the Coliseum proposed forming a management company with himself as director. The proposal included a $175,000 fee to the management company, a $125,000 salary for himself as director, and a bonus that would be available if he were able to generate revenues greater than 80 percent of expenses (i.e., reduce the deficit to under 20 percent). The current ratio of revenues to expenses is 75 percent.

The city council was warm to the idea, though the city manager wanted the bonus threshold higher (88 percent), and one council member wanted the bonus arrangement to include both a percent and an amount, "If the amount of the deficit is $3 million, I don't want to pay any incentive. If it is $1 million I will."[11]

---

[11] *Greensboro News & Record,* May 29, 1996.

The management contract is a useful means for Greensboro to achieve its goals for the Coliseum. There is a strong motivation for the director and management company to increase revenues and thereby reduce the city's deficit. However, as in any type of performance measurement system, there must be attention to the measurement issues—how are revenue and expense to be determined?

PART TWO: EVALUATION OF THE FIRM

LEARNING OBJECTIVE 6 ▶
Apply the two approaches for evaluating the firm: financial analysis and valuation.

In this second part of the chapter we examine how to evaluate the performance of the firm as a whole. The goal of strategic cost management is the success of the firm in maintaining competitive advantage, so we must evaluate the overall performance of the firm as well as the performance of individual managers.

The two principal approaches for evaluating a firm's performance are financial analysis and valuation. The *financial analysis* approach uses the balanced scorecard, financial ratio analysis, and economic value added as benchmarks in the evaluation. While this approach evaluates the firm's overall performance, it does not develop a dollar value for the firm. In contrast, the *valuation* of the firm evaluates the firm by estimating its total market value, which can then be compared to the market value for prior periods or for comparable firms.

The Financial Analysis Approach

To illustrate the financial analysis approach—using the balanced scorecard, financial ratio analysis, and economic value added—we use EasyKleen Company, a manufacturer of paper products. For relevant information about EasyKleen, see Exhibit 20–7.

The Balanced Scorecard

The use of the balanced scorecard to evaluate the firm is very much like the use of critical success factors in evaluating and compensating the individual manager. When evaluating the firm on CSFs, the management accountant uses benchmarks from industry information, and considers how the CSFs have changed from prior years. A favorable evaluation results when the CSFs are superior to the benchmarks and to prior years' performance. For example, assume EasyKleen has three CSFs, one each from the three key performance categories:

1. Return on total assets (financial performance).
2. Number of quality defects (business processes).
3. Number of training hours for plant workers (human resources).

A target level of performance is set for each CSF based on a study of the performance of the best firms in the industry. The benchmark is set at 90 percent of the best performance in the industry, and EasyKleen is evaluated on the overall performance, as illustrated in Exhibit 20–8.

EasyKleen management sees from the balanced scorecard that the firm met its goal in the financial area but fell short in both the operations and human resources areas. The scorecard is a guide for rewarding managers and for directing attention to achieving desired goals.

Financial Ratio Analysis

Financial ratio analysis uses financial statement ratios to evaluate the performance of the firm. Two common measures of performance are the liquidity and the profitability of the firm. Liquidity refers to the firm's ability to pay its current operating expenses (usually a year or less) and maturing debt. The five key measures of liquidity are accounts receivable turnover, inventory turnover, the current ratio, the quick ratio, and the cash flow ratio. The greater these ratios, the better, and the higher the evaluation of the firm's liquidity. There are four key profitability ratios: the gross margin percent, return on assets, return on equity, and earnings per share. The five liquidity ratios and four profitability ratios are explained in other finance

Exhibit 20–7	Selected Financial Information

EASYKLEEN COMPANY
Summary of Selected Financial Information
For the Year Ended December 31, 19X8

Financial Statements

Current assets	
Cash	$ 50,000
Accounts receivable	100,000
Inventory	50,000
Investments	–0–
Total current assets	200,000
Long-lived assets	200,000
Total assets	$400,000
Current liabilities	$ 50,000
Long-term debt	200,000
Total liabilities	$250,000
Shareholders' equity	150,000
Total liabilities and equity	$400,000
Sales	$1,000,000 (50% credit sales)
Cost of sales	500,000
Gross margin	500,000
Operating expense	300,000
Operating profit	200,000
Income taxes	100,000
Net income	$100,000

Asset Valuation, Total Assets

Net book value	$400,000
Gross book value	550,000
Replacement cost	700,000
Liquidation value	450,000

Other Information

Depreciation expense	$30,000/year
Current share price	$16.25
Number of outstanding shares	50,000
Training expenses	$30,000 (26 hours per worker)
Capital expenditures	$10,000
Quality defects	350 ppm (parts per million)
Cost of capital	12%
Return on total assets	
Net income/Total assets	
$100,000/$400,000	25%

Net Cash Flow

Net income	$100,000
+ Depreciation expense	30,000
– Increase in working capital	20,000
– Capital expenditures	10,000
Total	$100,000

and accounting texts, and are not covered here. Instead we show how each of the ratios is calculated for EasyKleen Company in Exhibit 20–9. The information is taken from Exhibit 20–7 and assumes that the benchmark level of performance is 90 percent of the best in the industry.

As you can see in Exhibit 20–9, EasyKleen had a very good year financially. Six of its nine goals were met. Profitability is the strongest area, where three of four ratios were exceeded substantially; only the earnings per share target was unmet, by

Exhibit 20–8	Balanced Scorecard

EASYKLEEN COMPANY
Balanced Scorecard

Category	CSF	Target Performance	Actual Performance	Variance
Financial	Return on total assets	22%	25%	3% (exceeded)
Operations	Quality defects	300 ppm	350 ppm	50 ppm (unmet)
Human Resources	Training hours	32 hours per employee	26 hours per employee	6 hours (unmet)

Exhibit 20–9	Financial Analysis

EASYKLEEN COMPANY
Financial Analysis

Ratio (how calculated)	Benchmark	Actual	Percent Achievement
Liquidity Ratios			
Accounts receivable turnover (credit sales/average receivables)	7	5 = $500,000/$100,000	71% (unmet)
Inventory turnover (cost of sales/average inventory)	9	10 = $500,000/$50,000	111% (met)
Current ratio (current assets/current liabilities)	2	4 = $200,000/$50,000	200% (met)
Quick ratio (cash and receivables/current liabilities)	1	3 = ($50,000 + $100,000)/$50,000	300% (met)
Cash flow ratio (net cash flow/current liabilities)	2.5	2 = $100,000/$50,000	80% (unmet)
Profitability Ratios			
Gross margin percent (gross profit/net sales)	35%	50% = $500,000/$1,000,000	143% (met)
Return on assets (net income/average total assets)	22%	25% = $100,000/$400,000	114% (met)
Return on equity (net income less preferred dividends/shareholders' equity)	44%	66.67% = $100,000/$150,000	152% (met)
Earnings per share (net income less preferred dividends/weighted average number of shares outstanding)	$2.15	$2.00 = $100,000/50,000	93% (unmet)

a small margin. The liquidity goals were largely met, though receivables turnover and cash flow fell short. This points to the need for a plan to improve the collection of receivables, which would improve both these ratios. Overall, the financial ratio analysis shows that EasyKleen performed quite well.

Economic Value Added

Economic value added (EVA) is a business unit's income after taxes and after deducting the cost of capital. The cost of capital usually is obtained by calculating a weighted-average of the cost of the firm's two sources of funds—borrowing and selling stock. EVA is used to focus managers' attention on creating value for shareholders. By earning profits greater than the firm's cost of capital, the firm increases the resources within the firm that are available for dividends and/or to finance the continued growth of the firm. Dividends and growth boost stock price and add shareholder value.

EVA for EasyKleen is determined as follows, where invested capital is defined for EVA as total assets less current liabilities. Training expenses of $30,000 are added to total assets and back to net income for EVA calculations, since training expenses are considered an investment for EVA purposes:

$$
\begin{aligned}
\text{EVA} &= \text{EVA net income} - (\text{Cost of capital} \times \text{Invested capital}) \\
&= \text{Net income} + \text{Training expenses} \\
&\quad - .12\text{x}(\text{Total assets} + \text{Training expenses} - \text{Current liabilities}) \\
&= \$100,000 + \$30,000 - .12 \times (\$400,000 + \$30,000 - \$50,000) \\
&= \$84,400
\end{aligned}
$$

The EVA of \$84,400 for EasyKleen is a very positive value, relative to net income and invested capital. It is an indication of the firm's strong profitability, and in particular, of its significant contribution to shareholder value.

Major corporations such as Coca-Cola, Quaker Oats, CSX, and AT&T use EVA in manager compensation to provide a stronger motivation for managers to take actions that add shareholder value. James Meenan of AT&T argues that EVA is far more highly correlated with stock price than any other accounting measure AT&T uses.[12]

The Valuation Approach

An intuitively appealing performance measure for the firm is its market value. Market value is an objective measure that clearly shows what investors think the firm is worth. It also has the advantage of being consistent with the objective of top management to add shareholder value:

> The essence of corporate strategy is to figure out how the corporation, as intermediary, can add value to the business it oversees.... The point here is not that businesses should not be trying to compete effectively in product and service markets; of course they should. But that effort has

---

Dell Computer and CSX Corporation Benefit from Using Economic Value Added (EVA)

Dell Uses Economic Value Added to Improve Competitiveness

Economic value added (EVA) has enabled a number of firms to significantly improve their competitiveness. Dell Computer was suffering from intense price competition with Compaq Corporation and other competitors in early 1993. EVA was introduced to focus managers and operating employees on their role in improving profitability. For example, the marketing department began to calculate the return on investment for each mailing. And the purchasing department computed the cost of unsold inventory. "We spent 15 months educating people about return on invested capital, convincing them they could impact our future," according to Chief Financial Officer Thomas J. Meredith.

EVA Helps CSX Unit Become More Profitable

The Internodal unit at CSX Corporation uses trains to carry freight to trucks or cargo ships. In 1988, the unit was unprofitable, as shown by a negative EVA of \$70 million. The unit managers were told to bring the EVA up to breakeven before 1993 or the unit would be sold. By 1992, the unit had achieved a positive EVA of \$10 million. This was accomplished by careful attention to the use of assets. A focus on idle assets led unit managers to reschedule certain routes. For example, on the route from New Orleans to Jacksonville, Florida, four locomotives pulled a freight train at 28 mph, arriving four to five hours prior to the time needed to load the trucks or freighters in Jacksonville. By removing one of the four locomotives and using a speed of 25 mph, the train arrived in time for the unloading, with an hour to spare. The slow-down and removal of the one locomotive was a significant saving to the unit in both capital costs (the locomotive) and operating costs (less fuel required). Looking at all the routes in a similar manner the Intermodal group was able to achieve significant savings in capital usage and operating costs.

Sources: Based on information from Gary McWilliams, "Whirlwind on the WEB," *Business Week,* April 7, 1997, pp. 132–36; and Shawn Tully, "The Real Key to Creating Wealth," *Fortune,* September 20, 1993, pp. 38–50.

---

[12]   Shawn Tully, "The Real Key to Creating Wealth," *Fortune,* September 20, 1993, pp. 38–50.

Spinoffs of Business Units: Effect on Market Value and Compensation

Why the Spinoff?

Many firms find that spinoffs of business units result in an increase in the market value of these units. The spinoff makes it easier for the market to assess the value of the spunoff business, since it is difficult for analysts and investors to assess the aggregate value of firms with multiple businesses. Research shows that spunoff subsidiaries show better than average growth in sales, income, and capital expenditures. Randall Woolridge of Penn State University finds that business units that are not given a lot of attention by top management tend to suffer and are therefore better off spun off.

Spinoffs and CEO Compensation at ITT

Also, we see that management compensation follows the benefits from spinoffs. The total compensation of Rand V. Araskog, CEO of ITT Corporation, more than doubled in the year that ITT spun off two business units—ITT Industries and ITT Hartford Group. ITT's stock price almost tripled from three years prior. Charles Peck, a senior associate of the Conference Board, a nonprofit business research center in New York, said, "You can make an argument that if a business, through splitting or downsizing, is increasing the earning performance of the company, then the compensation is legitimate. These days, we're going more toward measures of financial performance, rather than the sheer size of the company."

Sources: Based on information in "Confessions of a Corporate-Spinoff Junkie," by Roger Lowenstein, *The Wall Street Journal*, March 28, 1996; and "Araskog's Piece of ITT Empire Shrinks but Compensation More Than Doubles," *The Wall Street Journal*, April 1, 1996.

Shareholder Value and Compensation at Kodak

Chairman Kay Whitmore of Eastman Kodak Company has announced a new focus for the firm. He decided to manage the company to maximize earnings and stock price. "Shareholders have been the most under-served of our constituents," he confessed.

Also, Whitmore placed a special emphasis on earnings growth by changing Kodak's compensation system to link executive compensation to earnings and stock price. The system requires the top 40 executives to hold large amounts of Kodak stock, ranging from one to four times their annual salary. When the plan was introduced, most Kodak executives held only a few shares. The plan allows five years to meet the requirement.

There is some evidence the plan can work. Research by Gerald Sanders at Brigham Young University shows that "high levels of stock ownership appear to produce a long-term orientation among executives."

Source: Based on information from *Business Week,* February 1, 1993, pp. 24–26; see, also, "How Companies Make the Boss Buy Stock, but Soften the Pinch," *New York Times,* February 1, 1998, p. B1.

to be measured not only in terms of its impact on competition in a product or service market, but also in terms of its effect in the market for corporate control (*i.e., in the equity market; stock price*). A company that emphasizes the former at the expense of the latter can find itself in trouble very quickly . . . Many companies in America are moving quickly and confidently in the wrong direction. They believe that they are becoming leaders in their industries; instead, they are becoming leading targets for raids and proxy fights . . . To sum up, companies need strategies for competing in two kinds of markets: the familiar product and service markets, and the market for corporate control. Winning in the latter market depends on creating for shareholders superior value that derives from cash flow returns. (emphasis added)[13]

As this statement predicts, a public firm that advances its competitive position but fails to achieve acceptance in the market through improved stock price will find itself vulnerable in the market for corporate control. That is, the company might be purchased by investors who see that the firm is undervalued in the market. Success in the market is achieved by taking a value-oriented approach within the firm—orienting the firm's strategy to shareholder value. This can mean the spin-off of certain business units, financial restructuring, and outsourcing of certain activities.

---

[13] T. Copeland, T. Koller, and J. Murrin, *Valuation: Measuring and Managing the Value of Companies* (New York: John Wiley, 1992), pp. 3–26.

> ### Fleet Financial Group: Achieving Strategic Goals versus Improving Shareholder Value
>
> Firms must distinguish between two types of performance: (1) achieving strategic goals and (2) improving shareholder value. While closely related, these two goals are separable; achievement on one does not guarantee achievement on the other. For example, Fleet Financial Group, Inc., began a cost reduction effort in 1993 to improve the firm's competitive advantage, with the expectation that stock price would increase; managers would be awarded bonuses on the basis of improved stock price. Unfortunately, while the cost reduction plan was a success, the improvement in stock price did not follow, nor did the bonuses.
>
> **Source:** Based on information from *Business Week,* March 18, 1996, p. 34.

The concept of adding shareholder value requires a new interpretation of management strategy and the value chain. The role of strategy goes beyond the policies and procedures to achieve competitive advantage. It must also include the overarching objective, adding shareholder value. Similarly, the value chain of the firm goes beyond adding value for the customer of the firm, to adding value also to the shareholders.

The Market Value Method

The four methods for directly measuring the value of a firm are (1) market value, (2) asset valuation, (3) the discounted cash flow method, and (4) earnings-based valuation. The first method is the most simple and direct. The value of the firm is determined from the number of outstanding shares multiplied by the current market price of the shares. For the EasyKleen Company, the value determined in this way would be:

$$\text{Number of shares} \times \text{Share price}$$
$$= 50,000 \times \$16.25 = \$812,500$$

The performance of the firm and of top management can be evaluated by changes either in share price or the market value of the firm. The market value method is the most direct and objective measure of the shareholders' assessment of the firm's performance, and of the firm's success in creating value for the shareholders.

For nonpublic firms, and those public firms without frequently traded stock, a relevant stock price is not available, and one of the three other methods is needed to evaluate the firm.

The Asset Valuation Method

Accountants have four options when using the asset valuation method—net book value, gross book value, replacement cost, and liquidation value (see Chapter 19). An important limitation of the net book value and gross book value methods is that they are affected by the accounting policies of the firm, and they can be greatly distorted by the age of the assets. The most desirable valuation is either the replacement cost or liquidation value because they more nearly reflect the actual current value of the assets.

The replacement cost and liquidation value methods have weaknesses, however. Most important, there is rarely an objective measure for replacement cost or liquidation value, since the firm is not likely to be involved in either liquidation or replacement at the time the valuation is made. The asset values in Exhibit 20–10 show quite a range. EasyKleen is not considering liquidation, so the replacement cost of $700,000 is likely to be the more useful of the two measures.

The Discounted Cash Flow Method

The discounted cash flow (DCF) method measures the value of the firm as the discounted present value of the firm's net cash flows. It is based on the same concepts used in Chapter 11 for capital budgeting decisions. Cash flows a year or more into the future are discounted to take into account the time value of money; cash flows in recent periods are more valuable than cash flows in distant periods. Since it is based on cash flows, the DCF method has the additional advantage of not being subject to the bias of different accounting policies for determining total assets and net income, as are the asset valuation and the financial analysis methods. The DCF method is commonly used when the share price is not available or is unreliable.

The DCF method distinguishes two types of value in determining a valuation of the firm. The first is the value of the cash flows for the planning period (usually a three- to five-year period), and the second is the value of the cash flows beyond three to five years. Exhibit 20–11 shows how the method is used for the EasyKleen Company, assuming that the discount rate (the cost of capital) is 12 percent, the planning period is five years, and the net cash flows increase by $10,000 each year and then remain at $150,000 per year for the sixth year and thereafter. In Exhibit 20–11 we show that the total discounted value of net cash flows for the first five years is $424,470.

The present values of the cash flows from the sixth year on are determined using the discount factor for an annuity with a continuing life, which is the inverse of the discount rate ($1/.12 = 8.3333$).[14] This gives a discounted value for these six-year-plus cash flows of $1,249,995. To discount this amount back from the beginning of the sixth year to the present, we discount $1,249,995 by the fifth year discount factor (.567) to arrive at the discounted value of the continuing (six-year-plus) cash flows, $708,747.

Exhibit 20–10

EASYKLEEN COMPANY
Asset Valuation Methods and Values

Method	Value
Net book value	$400,000 (from the financial statements)
Gross book value	550,000 (from the financial statements)
Replacement cost	700,000 (estimated, usually by appraisals of experts in commercial real estate)
Liquidation value	450,000 (estimated, usually by appraisals of experts in commerical real estate)

Exhibit 20–11   DCF Valuation of the EasyKleen Company

Years	Cash Flow	Present Value Factor	Present Value of Cash Flows	
1	$100,000	.893	$ 89,300	
2	110,000	.797	87,670	
3	120,000	.712	85,440	
4	130,000	.636	82,680	
5	140,000	.567	79,380	
Total present value of cash flows in the planning period →			$424,470	(A)
6+	$150,000	8.3333	$1,249,995	(B)
Total present value of 6+ years' cash flows → .567			708,747	(C) = (B) × .567
Marketable securities and investments			–0–	(D)
Market value of debt			200,000	(E)
Value of the firm, shareholder value			$ 933,217	= (A) + (C) + (D) − (E)

---

[14] Typically, the assumption is made that cash flows from the firm continue indefinitely, and thus the use of the discount factor for an annuity in perpetuity (continuing life). This assumption is consistent with the idea that the firm is an ongoing entity with little or no likelihood of bankruptcy. If a shorter period is desired, one can use the appropriate discount factor from the annuity table for the desired number of years. For example, if the desired period, after the planning period, is from the 6th year to the 20th year, the discount factor is found in the annuity table for 15 years (6 through 20), or 6.811. The factor 6.811 would then be used in place of the factor, 8.3333, in the analysis in Exhibit 20–11.

To get the *net* valuation of the firm, we now add the discounted value of the planning period cash flows and the discounted value of six-year-plus cash flows to the value of current nonoperating investments such as marketable securities, and we subtract the market value of long-term debt. The net valuation for the firm is then $933,217. This value is somewhat higher than for the market value method ($812,500) or the replacement cost asset value of $700,000. If the cash flow estimates are reliable, the DCF method provides a useful measure in determining the value of the firm.

Earnings-Based Valuation

The earnings-based method computes value as the product of expected annual accounting earnings times a multiplier. The multiplier often is estimated from the price-to-earnings ratios of the stocks of comparable publicly held firms. The earnings multiplier has important limitations. The accounting treatment of inventory, depreciation, and other important components of earnings might not be comparable to that of other firms in the industry. When earnings are not comparable for these reasons, it is difficult to determine a relevant and useful multiplier.

The price-to-earnings ratio measures the amount the investor is willing to pay for a dollar of the firm's earnings per share. If the price-to-earnings ratio is not available for a given firm, then an average or representative value is taken from the price-to-earnings ratios of other firms in the industry. This ratio may then be adjusted upward to recognize a firm with future profit potential not recognized in current earnings, or vice versa. Assume the relevant price-to-earnings multiple for Easy-Kleen is 8.5. Then, the value of EasyKleen using this method would be determined from:

$$\text{Earnings multiplier} \times \text{Earnings}$$

$$= 8.5 \times \$100,000 = \$850,000$$

The earnings multiplier is easy to apply and can provide a useful evaluation of the firm, subject to the limitations noted.

In practice, it is common for the management accountant to use two or more of the valuation techniques and to evaluate the assumptions in each to arrive at an overall valuation assessment. If the management accountant is confident of the forecasts of net cash flow, a valuation close to $900,000 is appropriate and reasonable.

BusinessWeek

 Is Intel Worth More than You Might Think?

(Continues from page 791)

A: Now that's an understatement!

Michael Murphy, editor of the *California Technology Stock Letter,* reviews all technology firms such as Intel. He argues that reported earnings of these firms understate their potential because the calculation of earnings treats research and development expenditures as a current expense. For example, Intel's price/earnings ratio of 18 is somewhat lower than the S&P average of 22. Firms that spend heavily on research, such as Intel, have deflated earnings, but enhanced prospects. Intel has been able to make its research pay off in profitable products. Thus, when determining the value of technology firms such as Intel, Murphy adds back research and development expenditures to earnings. Using this approach, the value of Intel's stock should be about $100 per share versus its current $73 per share.

The use of research and development in valuation is consistent with the economic value added (EVA) approach to performance measurement described in Chapter 18. EVA adds research and development, as well as training and other investments, back to earnings. This approach provides an earnings number that places a high value on research and training, and rewards firms that make these investments.

For further reading, see "Inside Wall Street," *Business Week,* January 19, 1998; and "Intel," *Business Week,* December 22, 1997.

SUMMARY

In this last chapter we discuss how much managers and their companies are worth. The first part introduces the objectives and methods for compensating managers. There are three principal objectives for management compensation, which follow directly from the objectives for management control—the *motivation* of the manager, the *incentive* for proper decision making, and *fairness* to the manager. There are three main types of compensation—*salary, bonus* and *benefits*. The bonus is the fastest growing part of total compensation and often the largest part. The three important factors in the development of a bonus plan are the base for computing the bonus (strategic performance measures, stock price, and critical success factors), the source of funding for the bonus (the business unit or the entire firm), and the payment options (current and deferred bonus, stock options, and performance shares). The development of an executive compensation plan is a complex process involving these three factors and the three types of compensation, together with the objectives of management control.

Tax planning and financial reporting concerns are important in compensation planning because of management's desire to reduce taxes and to report financial results favorably. Thus, accountants must consider taxes and financial reporting issues in the development of a compensation plan for managers.

The second part of the chapter considers the evaluation of the performance of the entire firm, in contrast to the previous two chapters and the first part of this chapter that focused on the individual manager. The evaluation of the firm is important for investors, and as one part of an overall assessment of the performance of top management. There are two approaches—a financial analysis approach focusing on critical success factors and accounting measures, and a valuation approach focusing on market valuation. There are four methods for assessing the market value of the firm—market value of shares, asset valuation, the discounted cash flow method, and the earnings multiplier.

KEY TERMS

Bonus **791**

Firmwide pool **797**

Management compensation plans **791**

Perks **791**

Salary **791**

Unit-based pool **797**

SELF-STUDY PROBLEM

(For solution, please turn to the end of the chapter.)

Management Compensation Plan

Davis-Thompson-Howard & Associates (DTH) is a large consulting firm that specializes in the evaluation of governmental programs. The lawyers, accountants, engineers, and other specialists in DTH evaluate both the success of potential new government programs and the performance of existing programs. DTH obtains most of its consulting engagements by completing proposals in open bidding for the services desired by governmental agencies. The competition for these proposals has increased in recent years, and as a result DTH's yield (the number of new engagements divided by proposals) has fallen from 49 percent a few years ago to only 26 percent in the most recent year. The firm's profitability has fallen as well. DTH has decided to study its management compensation plan as one step among the many it will take in an attempt to return the firm to its previous level of profitability.

DTH has six regional offices, two located near Washington, D.C., and the others near large metropolitan areas where most of their clients are located. Each office is headed by an office manager who is one of the firm's professional associates. The firm's services in these offices are classified into financial and operational audit services, educational evaluation, engineering consulting, and financial systems. The Washington offices tend to provide most of the financial and audit services, and the other offices all offer their own mix of professional services. No two offices are alike, since each has adapted to the needs of its regional client base. The objective of DTH is to be among the three most competitive firms in its areas of service, and to grow its revenues by at least 10 percent per year.

The compensation plan at DTH awards each office a bonus based on (1) the increase in billings over the prior year and (2) the number of net new clients acquired in the current year. The office manager has the authority to divide the office bonus as he sees fit, though generally these same two criteria are used to allocate the office bonus to the office professionals. Top management is not aware of any problems with the compensation plan. There have been no significant complaints.

One observation by the CEO may suggest a reason for the firm's decline in yield of proposals. The firm has been losing out particularly on new large contract proposals that require large staffs and a significant professional travel commitment. These are jobs for which it would be necessary to coordinate two or more DTH offices. The CEO notes that DTH has as many regional offices as most of its competitors, who now seem to be winning a larger share of these contracts.

Required Discuss the pros and cons of the DTH compensation plan. Is the plan consistent with DTH's objectives and competitive environment?

QUESTIONS

20–1 Identify and explain the three objectives of management compensation.

20–2 Explain the three types of management compensation.

20–3 Explain how a manager's risk aversion can affect decision making, and how compensation plans should be designed to deal with risk aversion.

20–4 Explain how management compensation can provide an incentive to unethical behavior. What methods must be used to reduce the chance of unethical activities resulting from compensation plans?

20–5 From a financial reporting standpoint, what form of compensation is most desirable to the firm?

20–6 From a tax planning standpoint, what form of compensation is least desirable to the manager? To the firm?

20–7 List the three bases for bonus incentive plans; explain how they differ and how each achieves or does not achieve the three objectives of management compensation.

20–8 Identify and explain the five financial ratios used in the evaluation of liquidity as part of the evaluation of the firm.

20–9 What are the two types of bonus pools for bonus incentive plans? How do they differ and how does each achieve or not achieve the three objectives of management compensation?

20–10 List the four types of bonus payment options and explain how they differ. How does each achieve or not achieve the three objectives of management compensation?

20–11 Develop arguments to support your view as to whether executive pay in the United States is too high.

20–12 What are the four valuation methods? Which do you think is superior and why?

20–13 What type of management compensation is the fastest growing part of total compensation? Why do you think this is the case?

20–14 Why do you think it is important for a management accountant to be able to complete an evaluation of the firm, apart from an evaluation of individual managers?

20–15 How does the firm's management compensation plan change over the life cycle of the firm's products?

PROBLEMS

20–16 **EFFECT OF COST ALLOCATION IN COMPENSATION PLANS**   Performance of divisional managers at Leakproof Faucet Corporation is judged by an evaluation of the operating incomes of the divisions. These abbreviated income statements for the year ending 19X6 are for the three divisions of Leakproof Faucet Corporation:

	Newton	Granite	Longview	Totals
Revenues (in 000)	$2,500	$1,250	$1,500	$5,250
Cost of goods sold	1,300	575	600	2,475
Gross margin	1,200	675	900	2,775
Division overhead	250	125	150	525
Corporate overhead*	524	262	314	1,100
Operating income	426	288	436	1,150

*Total corporate overhead is allocated to each division based on the division's proportion of total revenue.

The manager of the Newton division, through increases in manufacturing efficiency, created some additional capacity in 19X6. The only way he could have utilized this capacity would have been to manufacture a model J–5 faucet, which would have had the following impact on the Newton division:

Increase in annual revenues (in thousands) of $750.

Increase in cost of goods sold of $600.

Increase in divisional overhead of $100.

Ross Garrett, the Newton division manager, chose not to manufacture the J–5 faucets; therefore, the additional capacity went unused.

Required

1. Prepare revised income statements for the three divisions for 19X6 assuming that Garrett had chosen instead to utilize the additional capacity to manufacture the model J–5.
2. Calculate the contribution margin of the Newton division for each scenario.
3. Why did Garrett choose not to manufacture the J–5?
4. Would Leakproof Faucets have benefited from the manufacture of the J–5?
5. Identify an advantage and a disadvantage of not allocating any corporate overhead to the divisions.

Service

20–17 **PERFORMANCE EVALUATION AND RISK AVERSION**   Jill Lewis is the office manager of PureBreds, Inc. Her office has 30 employees whose collective job is to process applications by dog owners who want to register their pets with PureBreds. There is never a shortage of applications waiting to be processed, but random events beyond Lewis's control cause fluctuations in the amount of applications that her office can process.

Alex Zale, the district manager that Lewis reports to, has no way to observe her effort other than to monitor the number of applications that are processed.

Required

1. If Lewis is risk adverse, how should Zale compensate her? Why?

For requirements 2 and 3 assume that the correctness of the information that is entered into the computers at Lewis's office is as important as the volume of processed applications.

2. What are the disadvantages of a compensation package that is influenced by the number of processed applications, but not by the correctness of the data input?

3. List at least two ways Zale could measure how accurately Lewis's office is processing the applications.

20–18 PERFORMANCE EVALUATION AND RISK AVERSION Heartwood Furniture Corporation has a line of sofas marketed under the name NightTime Sleepers. The management at Heartwood is considering several compensation packages for Amy Johnson, the general manager at NightTime. As general manager, Johnson makes all investing and operating decisions for NightTime.

Required

1. Johnson is risk neutral, and she prefers to get the maximum reward for her hard work. Do you recommend compensation based on flat salary, an ROI-based bonus, or a combination of both? Why?

2. If Johnson does not make investing decisions for NightTime, is ROI still a good performance measure? If so, then explain why. If ROI is not a good measure, then suggest an alternative.

20–19 PERFORMANCE EVALUATION; DIFFERENT PERFORMANCE MEASURES Heartwood Furniture wants to evaluate Amy Johnson, the NightTime Sleepers division manager, on the basis of a comparison of NightTime's ROI to Stiles Furniture's ROI. Stiles Furniture operates in a business environment similar to NightTime, and both companies have the same capabilities. However, Stiles uses a significantly different manufacturing strategy than NightTime.

Required

1. Would evaluating Johnson with this benchmark be fair?

2. Would using residual income instead of ROI offer any advantages?

3. What are the drawbacks to evaluating Johnson on total sales instead of ROI?

20–20 ALTERNATIVE COMPENSATION PLANS ADM, Inc., an electronics manufacturer, uses growth in earnings per share (EPS) as a guideline for evaluating executive performance. ADM executives receive a bonus of $5,000 for every penny increase in EPS for the year. This bonus is paid in addition to fixed salaries ranging from $500,000 to $900,000 annually.

 *Strategy*

Cygnus Corporation, a computer components manufacturer, also uses EPS as an evaluation tool. The executives at Cygnus receive a bonus equal to 40 percent of their salary for the year if the EPS for Cygnus fall in the top third on a list ranking Cygnus and its 12 competitors' EPS ratios.

Required

1. Why are companies like ADM, Inc., and Cygnus Corporation switching from stock option incentives to programs more like the ones listed above? What does the use of these plans by the two firms say about each firm's competitive strategy?

2. What are the weaknesses of incentive plans based on EPS?

20–21 COMPENSATION; MACHINE REPLACEMENT Choco-Lots Candy Co. makes chewy chocolate candies at a plant in Winston-Salem, North Carolina. Brian Main, the production manager at this facility, installed a packaging machine last year at a cost of $400,000. This machine is expected to last for 10 more years with no residual value. Operating costs for the projected levels of production are $80,000 annually.

Main has just learned of a new packaging machine that would work much more efficiently in Choco-Lots' production line. This machine would cost $420,000 installed, but the annual operating costs would only be $30,000. This machine would be depreciated over 10 years with no residual value. Main could sell the current packaging machine this year for $150,000.

Main has worked for Choco-Lots for seven years. He plans to remain with Choco-Lots for about two more years, which is when he expects to move into a vice president of operations position at his father-in-law's company. Choco-Lots pays Main a fixed salary with an annual bonus of 1 percent of net income for the year.

Assume Choco-Lots uses straight-line depreciation and has a 10 percent required rate of return. Ignore income tax effects.

Required

1. As the owner of Choco-Lots, would you want Main to keep the current machine or purchase the new machine?

2. Why might Main not prefer to make the decision desired by the owner of Choco-Lots?

Ethics

20–22 COMPENSATION; PERKS; ETHICS DuMelon Publishing Inc. is a nationwide company headquartered in Boston, Massachusetts. The perquisites provided for the employees at DuMelon are a significant element of their compensation. All professional employees at DuMelon receive company-paid benefits including medical insurance, term life insurance, vacations, and holidays. All DuMelon professionals also receive reimbursement for travel expenses when conducting business for DuMelon and a 25 percent match from DuMelon for money deposited by the professionals in the company-sponsored 401(k) plan.

There are variations in these perquisites depending on the employee's salary and level in the company. For example, the amount of vacation days increases as a professional works up the corporate ladder. Also, the maximum amount that can be contributed to the 401(k) plan increases as a person's salary increases.

When an employee at DuMelon attains a position of vice president of a function, such as operations or sales, then that person qualifies for a special class of additional perquisites. Vice presidents receive their own company cars, larger offices with decoration allowances, and access to the executive suite at the Boston office. (The executive suite features a dining room and lounge for the executives' use.) Also, these executives are reimbursed for all business travel expenses, whereas other employees have a $100/day maximum reimbursement.

Required

1. Explain the implications for employee behavior and performance of DuMelon having two levels of perquisites for professional employees.

2. Suppose that the policy for perquisites is not applied strictly at DuMelon. As a result, the following instances have occurred:
   a. The travel expenses of VPs' spouses have been occasionally paid by the company. The company policy is unclear as to whether or not this is allowed.
   b. Some VPs have special-ordered their company-provided vehicles, which costs the company an average of an additional $3,300 for each occurrence.
   c. Passes to the executive suite have been lent to other professionals at DuMelon.

d. Some of the VPs' offices are much larger than other VPs' offices. There appear to be no factors determining who gets the nicest offices.

How might this situation affect the behavior of VPs and other professionals at DuMelon, and what are the underlying implications for perquisite cost control? Use specific examples when applicable.

20–23 **INCENTIVE PAY IN THE HOTEL INDUSTRY** Jorge Martinez is the general manager of Classic Inn, a local mid-priced hotel with 100 rooms. His job objectives include providing resourceful and friendly service to the hotel's guests, maintaining an 80 percent occupancy rate, improving the average rate received per room to $58 from the current $55, and achieving a savings of 5 percent on all the hotel's costs. The hotel's owner, a partnership of seven people who own several hotels in the region, want to structure Martinez's future compensation in such a way that he would be objectively rewarded for achieving these goals. In the past he has been paid an annual salary of $42,000, with no incentive pay. The incentive plan the partners developed has each of the goals weighted as follows:

Service

Measure	Percent of Total Responsibility
Occupancy rate (also reflects guest service quality)	40%
Operating within 95 percent of expense budget	25
Average room rate	35
	100%

If Martinez achieved all his goals, the partners thought his performance should merit total pay of $46,000. It was agreed that for the incentive plan to be effective, it should comprise 50 percent of Martinez's total pay, $23,000.

The goal measures used to compensate Jorge are as follows:

Occupancy goal: 29,200 room-nights = 80 percent occupancy rate × 100 rooms × 365 days

Compensation: 40 percent weight × $23,000 target reward = $9,200
$9,200/29,200 = 31.5 cents per room-night

Expense goal: 5 percent savings

Compensation: 25 percent weight × $23,000 target reward = $5,750
$5,750/5 = $1,150 for each percentage point saved

Room rate goal: $3.00 rate increase

Compensation: 35 percent weight × $23,000 target reward = $8,050
$8,050/300 = $26.83 per each cent increase

Martinez's new compensation plan will thus pay him a $23,000 salary plus 31.5 cents per room-night sold plus $1,150 for each percentage point saved in the expense budget plus $26.83 per each cent increase in average room rate.

Required

1. Based on this plan, what will Martinez's total compensation be if his performance results are:
   a. 29,200 room-nights, 5 percent saved, $3.00 rate increase?
   b. 25,000 room-nights, 3 percent saved, $1.15 rate increase?
   c. 28,000 room-nights, 0 saved, $1.03 rate increase?
2. Comment on the expected effectiveness of this plan.

20–24 **INCENTIVE PAY FORMULA DEVELOPMENT** Use the concepts in problem 20–23 to complete the following requirements.

Service

Required

1. Design an incentive pay plan for a restaurant manager whose goals

are to serve 300 customers per day at an average price per customer of $6.88. The restaurant is open 365 days per year. These two goals are equally important. The incentive pay should comprise 40 percent of the manager's $32,000 target total compensation.

2. Calculate the manager's total compensation if 280 customers per day are served at an average price of $6.75.

Strategy

20-25 EVALUATING AN INCENTIVE PAY PLAN; STRATEGY Anne-Marie Fox is the manager at a new and used boat dealership. She has decided to reevaluate the compensation plan offered to her sales representatives to ascertain if it encourages the success of the dealership. The representatives are paid no salary, but they receive 20 percent of the sales price of every boat sold, and they are granted the authority to negotiate the boats' prices as far down as their wholesale cost if necessary.

Required Is this plan in the strategic best interest of the dealership?

20-26 CHOOSING BETWEEN INCENTIVE PLANS Flash Brogdon is a ski instructor looking for employment in the Oregon mountains. He has received full-time job offers from two ski lodges and must choose between them. The two jobs seem equally attractive, so Brogdon wants to choose the lodge that pays the higher compensation. Running Elk Lodge offers a wage of $8 per hour for a 40-hour week, plus 30 percent of the fees paid by walk-in pupils desiring private lessons, plus 40 percent of fees from pupils who specifically request a private lesson from Brogdon. Blustery Ridge Lodge offers a wage of only $6 per hour, plus 25 percent of walk-in private lesson fees, 45 percent of requested private lesson fees, and 15 percent of the fees paid by walk-in groups. Both lodges charge skiers $50 for private lessons and $100 per 5-person group for group lessons. Brogdon's previous experience leads him to expect weekly volume of 15 walk-in private lessons, 6 private lesson requests, and 20 walk-in group lessons.

Required Which job should Brogdon accept? What factors should Brogdon consider in making his choice?

20-27 COMPENSATION POOLS; RESIDUAL INCOME; REVIEW OF CHAPTER 19 Household Products Inc. (HPI) manufactures household goods in the United States. The company made two acquisitions in previous years to diversify their product lines. In 19X4, Household Products Inc. acquired glass and plastic producing companies. HPI now (19X6) has three divisions: glass, plastic, and paper. The following information (000s omitted) presents operating revenue, operating income, and invested assets of the company over the last three years.

Operating Revenue	19X4	19X5	19X6
Paper	$12,000	$13,000	$14,000
Plastic	5,000	4,500	4,200
Glass	7,000	7,200	7,400
Operating Income			
Paper	$ 3,000	$ 3,200	$ 3,500
Plastic	500	300	120
Glass	1,100	900	700
Invested assets			
Paper	$ 7,000	$ 7,400	$ 7,900
Plastic	2,000	1,500	1,200
Glass	4,000	4,200	4,800

The following table shows the number of executives covered by HPI's current compensation package:

	19X4	19X5	19X6
Paper	300	350	375
Plastic	40	40	37
Glass	120	140	175

The current compensation package is an annual bonus award. The senior executives share in the bonus pool. The pool is calculated as 12 percent of the annual residual income of the company. The residual income is defined as operating income minus an interest charge of 15 percent of invested assets.

Required

1. Use asset turnover, return on sales, and ROI to explain the differences in profitability of the three divisions.

2. Compute the bonus amount to be paid during each year; also, compute individual executive bonus amounts.

3. If the bonuses were calculated by divisional residual income, what would be the bonus amounts?

4. Discuss the benefits and problems of basing the bonus on HPI's residual income compared to divisional residual income.

20–28 **COMPENSATION; STRATEGIC ISSUES** Mobile Business Incorporated (MBI) is a worldwide manufacturing company that specializes in high technology products for the aerospace, automotive, and plastics industries. State of the art technology and business innovation have been key to MBI's success over the last several years. MBI has 10 manufacturing plants in six foreign countries. The products are sold worldwide through sales representatives and sales offices in 23 countries. Performance information from these plants and offices is received weekly and summarized monthly in the Toronto headquarters.

Strategy

International

After a meeting of the board of directors, some employees thought the company was moving away from its goal of striving to maintain and expand their global position through innovative products.

One area of concern was with the company's bonus compensation package. The company's current bonus plan focuses on giving rewards based on the utilization of capital within the company, i.e., management of inventory, collection of receivables, and use of physical assets. The board of directors is concerned with the short-term focus of the compensation package.

Required Develop a bonus package that takes into consideration the strategic goals of MBI and the global environment in which it operates.

SOLUTION TO SELF-STUDY PROBLEM

Management Compensation Plan

DTH's goal is to grow its business by at least 10 percent a year in a very competitive environment. The compensation plan is consistent with this goal because it rewards increases in revenues and number of new clients. However, it is likely that under the current plan each office is focusing only on the client base in its own region.

A problem arises when DTH is faced with proposals that require joint cooperation and participation among two or more offices. The compensation plan does not have an incentive for cooperation. In fact, it could be a distraction and reduce the potential for a substantial bonus for any given office to develop a proposal for a large contract in which other offices might benefit. The cost of the proposal would be borne by the office, while the benefits would accrue to other offices as well as the original office. The cost of the proposal for large contracts must therefore be shared among the offices in some way, or any one office will not have the incentive to spend the time and money necessary to develop a large proposal.

In addition to sharing the cost of the proposal, DTH should consider having a firmwide proposal development group for these large projects. The individual offices would then be charged for the cost of this group, perhaps in proportion to the fees received from large contracts in that office. Clearly, the firm is losing out on the larger contracts, and the compensation and proposal development plans have to provide the needed incentive for each office to aggressively go after them.

Another alternative is to go to a firmwide compensation pool that would provide a direct and strong incentive for each of the offices to cooperate in developing new business. However, a disadvantage of this approach is that it would reduce the motivation for each office to go after business in their own region because the revenues from these individual efforts would be shared firmwide.

Another issue concerning the current compensation plan is the office manager's discretion in dividing the office bonus among the professionals in the office. While no complaints have been heard, it is unlikely that a lower-level professional would complain about the office manager's bonus decisions. The equity of this system should be reviewed to assure that each office manager is using this discretion in a fair and appropriate way.

Table 1 Present Value of $1

Periods	4%	5%	6%	7%	8%	9%	10%	11%	12%	13%	14%	15%	20%	25%	30%
1	0.962	0.952	0.943	0.935	0.926	0.917	0.909	0.901	0.893	0.885	0.877	0.870	0.833	0.800	0.769
2	0.925	0.907	0.890	0.873	0.857	0.842	0.826	0.812	0.797	0.783	0.769	0.756	0.694	0.640	0.592
3	0.889	0.864	0.840	0.816	0.794	0.772	0.751	0.731	0.712	0.693	0.675	0.658	0.579	0.512	0.455
4	0.855	0.823	0.792	0.763	0.735	0.708	0.683	0.659	0.636	0.613	0.592	0.572	0.482	0.410	0.350
5	0.822	0.784	0.747	0.713	0.681	0.650	0.621	0.593	0.567	0.543	0.519	0.497	0.402	0.328	0.269
6	0.790	0.746	0.705	0.666	0.630	0.596	0.564	0.535	0.507	0.480	0.456	0.432	0.335	0.262	0.207
7	0.760	0.711	0.665	0.623	0.583	0.547	0.513	0.482	0.452	0.425	0.400	0.376	0.279	0.210	0.159
8	0.731	0.677	0.627	0.582	0.540	0.502	0.467	0.434	0.404	0.376	0.351	0.327	0.233	0.168	0.123
9	0.703	0.645	0.592	0.544	0.500	0.460	0.424	0.391	0.361	0.333	0.308	0.284	0.194	0.134	0.094
10	0.676	0.614	0.558	0.508	0.463	0.422	0.386	0.352	0.322	0.295	0.270	0.247	0.162	0.107	0.073
11	0.650	0.585	0.527	0.475	0.429	0.388	0.350	0.317	0.287	0.261	0.237	0.215	0.135	0.086	0.056
12	0.625	0.557	0.497	0.444	0.397	0.356	0.319	0.286	0.257	0.231	0.208	0.187	0.112	0.069	0.043
13	0.601	0.530	0.469	0.415	0.368	0.326	0.290	0.258	0.229	0.204	0.182	0.163	0.093	0.055	0.033
14	0.577	0.505	0.442	0.388	0.340	0.299	0.263	0.232	0.205	0.181	0.160	0.141	0.078	0.044	0.025
15	0.555	0.481	0.417	0.362	0.315	0.275	0.239	0.209	0.183	0.160	0.140	0.123	0.065	0.035	0.020
16	0.534	0.458	0.394	0.339	0.292	0.252	0.218	0.188	0.163	0.141	0.123	0.107	0.054	0.028	0.015
17	0.513	0.436	0.371	0.317	0.270	0.231	0.198	0.170	0.146	0.125	0.108	0.093	0.045	0.023	0.012
18	0.494	0.416	0.350	0.296	0.250	0.212	0.180	0.153	0.130	0.111	0.095	0.081	0.038	0.018	0.009
19	0.475	0.396	0.331	0.277	0.232	0.194	0.164	0.138	0.116	0.098	0.083	0.070	0.031	0.014	0.007
20	0.456	0.377	0.312	0.258	0.215	0.178	0.149	0.124	0.104	0.087	0.073	0.061	0.026	0.012	0.005
22	0.422	0.342	0.278	0.226	0.184	0.150	0.123	0.101	0.083	0.068	0.056	0.046	0.018	0.007	0.003
24	0.390	0.310	0.247	0.197	0.158	0.126	0.102	0.082	0.066	0.053	0.043	0.035	0.013	0.005	0.002
25	0.375	0.295	0.233	0.184	0.146	0.116	0.092	0.074	0.059	0.047	0.038	0.030	0.010	0.004	0.001
30	0.308	0.231	0.174	0.131	0.099	0.075	0.057	0.044	0.033	0.026	0.020	0.015	0.004	0.001	0.000
35	0.253	0.181	0.130	0.094	0.068	0.049	0.036	0.026	0.019	0.014	0.010	0.008	0.002	0.000	0.000
40	0.208	0.142	0.097	0.067	0.046	0.032	0.022	0.015	0.011	0.008	0.005	0.004	0.001	0.000	0.000

Table 2 Present Value of Annuity of $1

Payments	4%	5%	6%	7%	8%	9%	10%	11%	12%	13%	14%	15%	20%	25%	30%
1	0.962	0.952	0.943	0.935	0.926	0.917	0.909	0.901	0.893	0.885	0.877	0.870	0.833	0.800	0.769
2	1.886	1.859	1.833	1.808	1.783	1.759	1.736	1.713	1.690	1.668	1.647	1.626	1.528	1.440	1.361
3	2.775	2.723	2.673	2.624	2.577	2.531	2.487	2.444	2.402	2.361	2.322	2.283	2.106	1.952	1.816
4	3.630	3.546	3.465	3.387	3.312	3.240	3.170	3.102	3.037	2.974	2.914	2.855	2.589	2.362	2.166
5	4.452	4.329	4.212	4.100	3.993	3.890	3.791	3.696	3.605	3.517	3.433	3.352	2.991	2.689	2.436
6	5.242	5.076	4.917	4.767	4.623	4.486	4.355	4.231	4.111	3.998	3.889	3.784	3.326	2.951	2.643
7	6.002	5.786	5.582	5.389	5.206	5.033	4.868	4.712	4.564	4.423	4.288	4.160	3.605	3.161	2.802
8	6.733	6.463	6.210	5.971	5.747	5.535	5.335	5.146	4.968	4.799	4.639	4.487	3.837	3.329	2.925
9	7.435	7.108	6.802	6.515	6.247	5.995	5.759	5.537	5.328	5.132	4.946	4.772	4.031	3.463	3.019
10	8.111	7.722	7.360	7.024	6.710	6.418	6.145	5.889	5.650	5.426	5.216	5.019	4.192	3.571	3.092
11	8.760	8.306	7.887	7.499	7.139	6.805	6.495	6.207	5.938	5.687	5.453	5.234	4.327	3.656	3.147
12	9.385	8.863	8.384	7.943	7.536	7.161	6.814	6.492	6.194	5.918	5.660	5.421	4.439	3.725	3.190
13	9.986	9.394	8.853	8.358	7.904	7.487	7.103	6.750	6.424	6.122	5.842	5.583	4.533	3.780	3.223
14	10.563	9.899	9.295	8.745	8.244	7.786	7.367	6.982	6.628	6.302	6.002	5.724	4.611	3.824	3.249
15	11.118	10.380	9.712	9.108	8.559	8.061	7.606	7.191	6.811	6.462	6.142	5.847	4.675	3.859	3.268
16	11.652	10.838	10.106	9.447	8.851	8.313	7.824	7.379	6.974	6.604	6.265	5.954	4.730	3.887	3.283
17	12.166	11.274	10.477	9.763	9.122	8.544	8.022	7.549	7.120	6.729	6.373	6.047	4.775	3.910	3.295
18	12.659	11.690	10.828	10.059	9.372	8.756	8.201	7.702	7.250	6.840	6.467	6.128	4.812	3.928	3.304
19	13.134	12.085	11.158	10.336	9.604	8.950	8.365	7.839	7.366	6.938	6.550	6.198	4.843	3.942	3.311
20	13.590	12.462	11.470	10.594	9.818	9.129	8.514	7.963	7.469	7.025	6.623	6.259	4.870	3.954	3.316
22	14.451	13.163	12.042	11.061	10.201	9.442	8.772	8.176	7.645	7.170	6.743	6.359	4.909	3.970	3.323
24	15.247	13.799	12.550	11.469	10.529	9.707	8.985	8.348	7.784	7.283	6.835	6.434	4.937	3.981	3.327
25	15.622	14.094	12.783	11.654	10.675	9.823	9.077	8.422	7.843	7.330	6.873	6.464	4.948	3.985	3.329
30	17.292	15.372	13.765	12.409	11.253	10.274	9.427	8.694	8.055	7.496	7.003	6.566	4.979	3.995	3.332
35	18.665	16.374	14.498	12.948	11.655	10.567	9.644	8.855	8.176	7.586	7.070	6.617	4.992	3.998	3.333
40	19.793	17.159	15.046	13.332	11.925	10.757	9.779	8.951	8.244	7.634	7.105	6.642	4.997	3.999	3.333

absolute quality conformance (robust quality approach) Conformance that requires all products or services to exactly meet the target value with no variation

account classification method A method that requires the classification of each cost account in the financial records as either a fixed or variable cost

accounting rate of return The net income or the return from an investment as a percentage of its book value

activity analysis The development of a detailed description of the specific activities performed in the operations of a firm

activity-based budgeting A budgeting process that focuses on costs of activities or cost drivers necessary for production and sales

activity-based costing (ABC) An analysis used to improve the accuracy of cost analysis by improving the tracing of costs to cost objects

activity-based management (ABM) An activity analysis used to improve operational control and management control

activity driver A measure of frequency and intensity of demands placed on activities by cost objects

actual costing A costing process that uses actual costs incurred for direct materials and direct labor and assigns or applies actual factory overhead to various jobs

actual factory overhead Costs incurred in an accounting period for indirect materials, indirect labor, and other indirect factory costs, including factory rent, insurance, property tax, depreciation, repairs and maintenance, power, light, heat, and employer payroll taxes for factory personnel

additional processing costs or separable costs Costs that occur after the split-off point and can be identified directly with individual products

advance pricing agreement (APA) An agreement between the Internal Revenue Service (IRS) and the firm using transfer prices, which sets out the agreed-on transfer price

allocation bases The cost drivers used to allocate costs

analysis of variance table A table that separates the total variance of the dependent variable into both error and explained variance components

appraisal costs Costs incurred in the measurement and analysis of data to ascertain if products and services conform to specifications

arm's-length method A standard that says transfer prices should be set so they reflect the price that would have been set by unrelated parties acting independently

asset turnover The amount of sales achieved per dollar of investment; measures the manager's ability to produce increased sales from a given level of investment

authoritative standard A standard determined solely or primarily by management

average cost The total of manufacturing costs (materials, labor, and overhead) divided by units of output

average cost method A method that uses units of output to allocate joint costs to joint products

balanced scorecard An accounting report that includes the firm's critical success factors in four areas: (1) financial performance, (2) customer satisfaction, (3) internal business processes, and (4) innovation and learning

basic engineering The method in which product designers work independently from marketing and manufacturing to develop a design from specific plans and specifications

batch-level activity An activity performed for each batch of products rather than for each unit of production

benchmarking A process by which a firm identifies its critical success factors, studies the best practices of other firms (or other units within a firm) for these critical success factors, and then implements improvements in the firm's processes to match or beat the performance of those competitors

bill of materials A detailed listing of the components of the manufactured product

bonus compensation Based on the achievement of performance goals for the period

breakeven point   The point at which revenues equal total cost and profit is zero

budget   A quantitative plan of operations for an organization; it identifies the resources and commitments required to fulfill the organization's goals for the budgeted period

budgeting   The process of preparing a budget

budget slack   The difference between budgeted performance and expected performance

by-products   Products whose total sales values are minor in comparison with the sales value of the joint products

capital budgeting   A process for evaluating an organization's proposed long-range major projects

capital investment   An investment that requires committing a large sum of funds to projects with expenditures and benefits expected to stretch well into the future

cash budget   A budget that brings together the anticipated effects of all budgeted activities on cash

cause-and-effect diagram   A diagram that maps out a list of causes that affect an activity, process, stated problem, or a desired outcome

comparable price method   Establishes an arm's-length price by using the sales prices of similar products made by unrelated firms

computer-aided design (CAD)   The use of computers in product development, analysis, and design modification to improve the quality and performance of the product

computer-aided manufacturing (CAM)   The use of computers to plan, implement, and control production

computer-integrated manufacturing (CIM)   A totally integrated manufacturing system that integrates all functions of the offices and factories within a company via a computer-based information network, to allow hour-by-hour manufacturing management

concurrent engineering   A new simultaneous engineering approach in which product design is integrated with manufacturing and marketing throughout the product's life cycle

confidence interval   A range around the regression line within which the management accountant can be confident the actual value of the predicted cost will fall

continuous budget   A budgeting system that has in effect a budget for a set number of months, quarters, or years at all times

continuous improvement (The Japanese word is *kaizen*.)   A management technique in which managers and workers commit to a program of continuous improvement in quality and other critical success factors

continuously updated budget   A budget that incorporates new information as the year unfolds

contract manufacturing   When another manufacturer (sometimes a direct competitor) manufactures a portion of the firm's products

contribution by SBU (CSBU)   A measurement of all the costs that are traceable to, and therefore controllable by, the individual profit SBUs

contribution income statement   Focuses on variable costs and fixed costs, in contrast to the conventional income statement which focuses on product costs and non-product costs

contribution margin income statement   An income statement based on contribution margin that is developed for each profit SBU and for each relevant group of profit SBUs

contribution margin ratio   The ratio of the unit contribution margin to unit sales price $(p - v)/p$

control chart   A graph that depicts successive observations of an operation taken at constant intervals

controllable cost   A cost that a manager or employee has discretion in choosing to incur or can significantly influence the amount of within a given, usually short, period of time

conversion cost   Direct labor and overhead combined into a single amount

core competencies   Skills or competencies that the firm employs especially well

correlation A given variable tends to change predictably in the same or opposite direction for a given change in the other, correlated variable

cost When a resource is used for some purpose

cost allocation The process of assigning indirect costs to cost pools and cost objects

cost assignment The process of assigning costs to cost pools, or from cost pools to cost objects

cost driver Any factor that has the effect of changing the level of total cost for a cost object

cost driver analysis The examination, quantification, and explanation of the effects of cost drivers

cost element An amount paid for a resource consumed by an activity and included in a cost pool

cost estimation The development of a well-defined relationship between a cost object and its cost drivers for the purpose of predicting the cost

cost leadership A competitive strategy in which a firm succeeds by producing products or services at the lowest cost in the industry

cost life cycle The sequence of activities within the firm that begins with research and development, followed by design, manufacturing, marketing/distribution, and customer service

cost management information The information the manager needs to effectively manage the firm or not-for-profit organization

cost object Any item or activity for which costs are accumulated for management purposes

cost of capital A composite of the cost of various sources of funds comprising a firm's capital structure

cost of goods manufactured The cost of goods that were finished and transferred out of work-in-process this period

cost of goods sold The cost of the product transferred to the income statement when inventory is sold

cost of quality report A report that shows the costs of prevention, appraisal, internal, and external failures. An important type of cost of quality report is the quality matrix, which shows the different quality costs for each operating and suport function

cost-plus method A method that determines the transfer price based on the seller's costs, plus a gross profit percentage determined from comparison of sales of the seller to unrelated parties

cost pools Costs that are collected into meaningful groups

cost SBU Production or support SBUs within the firm that have the goal of providing the best quality product or service at the lowest cost

costs of conformance Costs of prevention and appraisal

costs of nonconformance Costs of internal failure and external failure

costs of quality Costs associated with the prevention, identification, repair, and rectification of poor quality, and with opportunity costs from lost production time and sales as a result of poor quality

cost tables Computer-based databases that include comprehensive information about the firm's cost drivers

cost-volume-profit (CVP) analysis A method for analyzing how various operating decisions and marketing decisions will affect net income

critical success factors (CSFs) Measures of those aspects of the firm's performance that are essential to its competitive advantage, and therefore to its success

currently attainable standard A level of performance that workers with proper training and experience can attain most of the time without extraordinary effort

CVP graph Illustrates how the levels of revenues and total costs change over different levels of output

degrees of freedom Represents the number of independent choices that can be made for each component of variance

denominator activity The desired operating level at the expected operating efficiency for the period, expressed in the quantity of the cost driver for applying fixed factory overhead

departmental overhead rate An overhead rate calculated for a single production department

dependent variable The cost to be estimated

design analysis A common form of value engineering in which the design team prepares several possible designs of the product, each having similar features that have different levels of performance and different costs

desired rate of return The minimum rate of return the investing firm requires for the investment

differential cost A cost that differs for each decision option and is therefore relevant

differentiation A competitive strategy in which a firm succeeds by developing and maintaining a unique value for the product, as perceived by consumers

direct cost A cost conveniently and economically traced directly to a cost pool or a cost object

direct labor The labor used to manufacture the product or to provide the service

direct labor efficiency variance The difference between the actual and standard direct labor hours for the units manufactured multiplied by the standard hourly wage rate

direct labor rate variance The difference between the actual and standard hourly wage rate multiplied by the actual direct hours used in production

direct materials The cost of the materials in the product and a reasonable allowance for scrap and defective units

direct materials flexible budget variance The difference in direct material costs between the actual amount incurred and the total standard cost in the flexible budget for the units manufactured during the period

direct materials price variance The difference between the actual and standard unit price of the direct materials multiplied by the actual quantity of the direct materials purchased

direct materials usage budget A plan that shows the direct materials required for production and their budgeted cost

direct method Cost allocation using the service flows *only to production departments* and determining each production department's share of that service

discounted-cash flow methods (DCF methods) A method that evaluates a capital investment by considering future cash flow returns after the initial investment at their equivalent present values

discretionary-cost method An input-oriented approach in which costs are considered largely uncontrollable and discretion is applied at the planning stage

drum-buffer-rope system A system for balancing the flow of production through a binding constraint, thereby reducing the amount of inventory at the constraint and improving overall productivity

dual allocation A cost allocation method in which fixed and variable costs are separated. Variable costs are directly traced to user departments, and fixed costs are allocated on some logical basis

dummy variable A variable that represents the presence or absence of a condition

Durbin-Watson statistic A measure of the extent of nonlinearity in the regression

economic value added (EVA) A business unit's income after taxes and after deducting the cost of capital

effective operation The attainment of the goal set for the operation

efficient operation An operation that wastes no resources

employment contract An agreement between the manager and top management, designed so that the manager acts independently to achieve top management's objectives

engineered-cost method An output-oriented method since costs are variable and therefore engineered, that is, controllable

equivalent units The number of like or similar completed units that could have been produced given the amount of work actually performed on both completed and partially completed units

executional cost drivers   Factors such as workforce involvement, design of the production process, and supplier relationships that the firm can manage in the short term to reduce costs

expropriation   A foreign government takes ownership and control of assets the domestic investor has invested in that country

external failure costs   Costs incurred to rectify quality defects after unacceptable products or services reach the customer and lost profit opportunities caused by the unacceptable products or services delivered

facility-sustaining activity   An activity performed to support the production of products in general

factory overhead   All the indirect costs commonly combined into a single cost pool in a manufacturing firm

factory overhead applied   The amount of overhead assigned to a specific job using a predetermined factory overhead rate

FIFO method   A process costing method that includes only costs incurred and work effort during the current period in calculating the unit cost

financial budget   A plan that identifies sources and uses of funds for budgeted operations to achieve the expected operating results for the period

financial productivity   The ratio of output to the dollar amount of one or more input factors

finished goods inventory   The cost of goods that are ready for sale

firmwide pool   A method of determining the bonus available to all managers through an amount set aside for this purpose

first differences   For each variable, the difference between each value and the succeeding value in the time series

fixed cost   The portion of the total cost that does not change with a change in the quantity of the cost driver, within the relevant range

fixed factory overhead application rate   The rate at which the firm applies fixed overhead costs to cost objects

fixed factory overhead production volume variance   The difference between the budgeted allowance for fixed factory overhead for the period and the applied fixed factory overhead

fixed factory overhead spending (budget) variance   The difference between the actual amount incurred and the budgeted allowance for the fixed factory overhead

flexible budget   A budget that adjusts revenues and costs for changes in output achieved

flexible budget variable expense variance   The difference between the actual variable expenses incurred and the total standard variable expenses in the flexible budget for the units sold during the period

flexible budget variance   The difference between the actual operating result and the flexible budget at the actual operating level of the period

flexible manufacturing system (FMS)   A computerized network of automated equipment that produces one or more groups of parts or variations of a product in a flexible manner

focus   A competitive strategy in which a firm succeeds by targeting its attention to a specific segment of a market

F-statistic   A useful measure of the statistical reliability of the regression

functional analysis   A common type of value engineering in which the performance and cost of each major function or feature of the product is examined

goal congruence   The consistency between the goals of the firm and the goals of its employees. It is achieved when the manager acts independently in such a way as to simultaneously achieve top management's objectives

goalpost conformance (zero-defects conformance)   Conformance to a quality specification expressed as a specified range around a target

gross book value   The historical cost without the reduction for depreciation

group technology   A method of identifying similarities in the parts of products a firm manufactures, so the same part can be used in two or more products, thereby reducing costs

high-low method   A method that improves on the accuracy of the account classification and visual fit methods by using algebra to determine a unique estimation line between representative low and high points in the data

histogram   A graphical representation of the frequency of events in a given set of data

historical cost   The value of current assets plus the net book value of the long-lived assets

ideal standard   A standard that demands perfect implementation and maximum efficiency in every aspect of the operation

implementation error   A deviation from the standard that occurs during operations as a result of operators' errors

independent variable   The cost driver used to estimate the value of the dependent variable

indirect cost   A cost that is not conveniently or economically traceable from the cost or cost pool to the cost pool or cost object

indirect labor   Supervision, quality control, inspection, purchasing and receiving, and other manufacturing support costs

indirect materials   The cost of materials used in manufacturing that are not physically part of the finished product

internal accounting controls   A set of policies and procedures that restrict and guide activities in the processing of financial data, with the objective of preventing or detecting errors and fraudulent acts

internal failure costs   Costs incurred as a result of poor quality found through appraisal prior to delivery to customers

internal rate of return (IRR) method   A discounted cash flow method that estimates the discount rate that makes the present value of subsequent cash flow returns equal the initial investment

investment SBU   A concept that includes assets employed by the SBU as well as profits

ISO 9000   A set of guidelines for quality management and quality standards developed by the International Organization for Standardization in Geneva, Switzerland

job costing   A product costing system that accumulates and assigns costs to a specific job

job cost sheet   A cost sheet that records and summarizes the costs of direct materials, direct labor, and factory overhead for a particular job

joint products   Products from the same production process that have relatively substantial sales values

just-in-time (JIT) system   A comprehesive production and inventory system in which materials and parts are purchased or produced as needed and just in time to be used at each stage of the production process

kaizen budgeting   A budgeting approach that explicitly demands continuous improvement and incorporates all the expected improvements in the resultant budget

kanban   A set of control cards that are used to signal the need for materials and products to move from one operation to the next in an assembly line

learning curve analysis   A systematic method for estimating costs when learning is present

learning rate   The percentage by which average time (or total time) falls from previous levels, as output doubles

least squares regression   One of the most effective methods for estimating costs, found by minimizing the sum of the squares of the estimation errors; a statistical method that finds the best-fitting prediction model

life-cycle costing   A management technique used to identify and monitor the costs of a product throughout its life cycle

liquidation value   The price that could be received for the sale of the assets

long-range plan   A plan that identifies which actions are required during the 5- to 10-year period covered by the plan to attain the firm's strategic goal

long-term controllable fixed costs Costs that are not controllable within a year's time; usually these include facilities-related costs such as depreciation, taxes, and insurance

management compensation plans Policies and procedures for compensating managers

management control The evaluation of mid-level managers by upper-level managers

marginal cost The additional cost incurred as the cost driver increases by one unit

margin of safety A measure of the potential effect of the risk that sales will fall short of planned levels

margin of safety ratio A useful measure for comparing the risk of two alternative products, or for assessing the riskiness in any given product

market share variance A comparison of the firm's actual market share to its budgeted market share and measurement of the effect of changes in the firm's market share on its total contribution margin and operating income

market size variance A measure of the effect of changes in the total market size on the firm's total contribution margin and operating income

mass customization A management technique in which marketing and production processes are designed to handle the increased variety that results from delivering customized products and services to customers

master budget A plan of operations for a business unit during a budgeted period

material requisition form A source document that the production department supervisor uses to request materials for production

materials inventory The store of materials used in the manufacturing process or in providing the service

materials usage ratio The ratio of quantity used over quantity purchased

mean squared variance The ratio of the amount of variance of a component to the number of degrees of freedom for that component

measurement errors Incorrect numbers caused by improper or inaccurate accounting systems or procedures

merchandise purchase budget A plan that shows the amount of merchandise the firm needs to purchase during the period

mixed cost The total cost when it includes both variable and fixed cost components

modeling error A deviation from the standard because of failure to include all the relevant variables or inclusion of wrong or irrelevant variables in the standard-setting process

multicollinearity Two or more independent variables that are highly correlated with each other

net book value The historical cost of the asset less accumulated depreciation

net present value (NPV) The excess of the present value of future cash flow returns over the initial investment

net realizable value (NRV) The estimated sales value of the product at the split-off point, made by subtracting the additional processing and selling costs beyond the split-off point from the ultimate sales value of the product

network diagram A flowchart of the work done that shows the sequence of processes and the amount of time required for each

nonconstant variance The condition when the variance of the errors is not constant over the range of the independent variable

non-value-added activity An activity that does not contribute to customer value or to the organization's needs

normal costing A costing process that uses actual costs for direct materials and direct labor and applies factory overhead to various jobs using a predetermined basis

operating budget A plan that identifies resources needed in operating activities and the acquisition of these resources

operating income flexible budget variance The difference between the flexible budget operating income for the units sold and the actual operating income

operating income variance The difference between the actual operating income of the period and the master budget operating income projected for the period

operating leverage   The ratio of the contribution margin to profit

operational control   Mid-level managers monitor the activities of the operating-level managers and employees

operational productivity   The ratio of output to the number of units of an input factor

operation costing   A hybrid costing system that uses job costing to assign direct materials costs and process costing to assign conversion costs to products or services

opportunity cost   The benefit lost when choosing one option precludes receiving the benefits from an alternative option

order-filling costs   Expenditures for freight, warehousing, packing and shipping, and the cost of collections

order-getting costs   Expenditures to advertise and promote the product

outliers   Unusual data points that strongly influence a regression analysis

outsourcing   A firm's decision to have a service or product provided by a support department supplied by an outside firm

overapplied overhead   The amount of factory overhead applied that exceeds the actual factory overhead cost

overhead   All the indirect costs commonly combined into a single cost pool

overhead application or allocation   A process of assigning overhead costs to the appropriate jobs

Pareto analysis   A management tool that shows 20 percent of a set of important cost drivers are responsible for 80 percent of the total cost incurred

Pareto diagram   A histogram of the frequency of factors contributing to the quality problem, ordered from the most to the least frequent

partial productivity   A measure that focuses only on the relationship between one of the inputs and the output attained

participative standard   Active participation throughout the standard-setting process by workers affected by the standard

payback period   The length of time required for the cumulative total net cash inflows from an investment to equal the total initial cash outlays of the investment

performance evaluation   The process by which managers at all levels gain information about the performance of tasks within the firm and judge that performance against preestablished criteria as set out in budgets, plans, and goals

performance measurement   A measurement that identifies indicators of the work performed and the results achieved in an activity, process, or organizational unit

period costs   All nonproduct expenditures for managing the firm and selling the product

perks   Special services and benefits for the employee, such as travel, membership in a fitness club, life insurance, medical benefits, tickets to entertainment events, and other extras paid for by the firm

physical measure method   A method that uses a physical measure such as pounds, gallons, yards, or units or volume produced at the split-off point to allocate the joint costs to joint products

planning and decision making   Budgeting and profit planning, cash flow management, and other decisions related to operations

plantwide overhead rate   A single overhead rate used throughout the entire production facility

predetermined factory overhead rate   An estimated factory overhead rate used to apply factory overhead cost to a specific job

prediction error   A deviation from the standard because of an inaccurate estimation of the amounts of variables used in the standard-setting process

present value   The current equivalent dollar value of a cash flow return, given the desired rate of return

present value payback method or breakeven time (BET)   A method using the span of time required for the cumulative present value of cash inflows to equal the initial investment of the project

prevention costs   Costs incurred to keep quality defects from occurring

prime costs   Direct materials and direct labor combined

principal-agent model A conceptual model that contains the key elements contracts must have to achieve the desired objectives

process costing A costing system that accumulates product or service costs by process or department and then assigns them to a large number of nearly identical products

product and service costing In preparing financial statements, management complies with the financial reporting requirements of the industry and of regulatory agencies

product costing The process of accumulating, classifying, and assigning direct materials, direct labor, and factory overhead costs to products or services

product costs Only the costs necessary to complete the product (direct materials, direct labor, and factory overhead)

production budget A plan for acquiring and combining the resources needed to carry out the manufacturing operations that allow the firm to satisfy its sales goals and have the desired amount of inventory at the end of the budget period

production cost report A report that summarizes the physical units and equivalent units of a department, the costs incurred during the period, and costs assigned to both units completed and transferred out and ending work-in-process inventories

productivity The ratio of output to input

product-sustaining activity An activity performed to support the production of a different product

profit SBU An SBU that generates revenues and incurs the major portion of the cost for producing these revenues

profit-volume graph Illustrates how the level of profits changes over different levels of output

proration The process of allocating underapplied or overapplied overhead to Work-in-Process Control, Finished Goods Control, and Cost of Goods Sold accounts

prototyping A method in which functional models of the product are developed and tested by engineers and trial customers

quality A product or service that meets or exceeds customers' expectations at the price they are willing to pay

random variances The variances beyond the control of management, either technically or financially, that often are considered as uncontrollable variances

rank-order correlation A statistic that measures the degree to which two sets of numbers tend to have the same order or rank

reciprocal flows The movement of services back and forth between service departments

reciprocal method A cost allocation method that takes into account all the reciprocal flows between service departments through simultaneous equations

reengineering A process for creating competitive advantage in which a firm reorganizes its operating and management functions, often with the result that jobs are modified, combined, or eliminated

regression analysis A statistical method for obtaining the unique cost estimating equation that best fits a set of data points

relevant cost A cost with two properties: it differs for each decision option and it will be incurred in the future

relevant range The range of the cost driver in which the actual value of the cost driver is expected to fall, and for which the relationship is assumed to be approximately linear

replacement cost The current cost to replace the assets at the current level of service and functionality

resale price method A transfer pricing method based on determining an appropriate markup, where the markup is based on gross profits of unrelated firms selling similar products

residual income A dollar amount equal to the income of the business unit less a charge for the investment in the unit

resource An economic element that is applied or used in the performance of activities

resource driver A measure of the quantity of resources consumed by an activity

return on equity (ROE) The return determined when investment is measured as shareholders' equity

return on investment (ROI) Profit divided by investment in the business unit

return on sales (ROS) A firm's profit per sales dollar; a measure of the manager's ability to control expenses and increase revenues to improve profitability

revenue drivers The factors that affect sales volume, such as price changes, promotions, discounts, customer service, changes in product features, delivery dates, and other value-added factors

revenue SBU An SBU with responsibility for sales, defined either by product line or by geographical area

risk preferences The way individuals differentially view decision options, because they place a weight on *certain* outcomes that differs from the weight they place on *uncertain* outcomes

robot A computer-programmed and controlled machine that performs repetitive activities

R-squared A number between zero and one. Often it is described as a measure of the explanatory power of the regression; that is, the degree to which changes in the dependent variable can be predicted by changes in the independent variable

salary A fixed payment

sales budget A schedule showing expected sales in units at their expected selling prices

sales life cycle The sequence of phases in the product's or service's life in the market—from the introduction of the product or service to growth in sales and finally maturity, decline, and withdrawal from the market

sales mix The proportion of units of each product or service to the total of all products or services

sales mix variance The product of the difference between the actual and budgeted sales mix, the actual total units of all products sold, and the budgeted contribution margin per unit of the product

sales price variance The difference between the total actual sales revenue and the total flexible budget sales revenue for the units sold during a period

sales quantity variance The product of the difference between the budgeted and actual total sales quantity, the budgeted sales mix of the product, and the budgeted contribution margin per unit of the product

sales value at split-off method A method that allocates joint costs to joint products on the basis of their relative sales values at the split-off point

sales volume or activity variance A measurement of the effect on sales, expenses, contribution margin, or operating income of changes in units of sales

schedule of cost of goods manufactured and sold A schedule that shows the manufacturing costs incurred, the change in the work-in-process inventory, the cost of goods sold, and the change in finished goods inventory during the period

short-term controllable fixed costs Fixed costs that the profit SBU manager can influence in approximately a year or less

short-term controllable margin A margin determined by subtracting short-term controllable fixed costs from the contribution margin

split-off point The first point in a joint production process in which individual products can be identified

standard cost The cost a firm ought to incur for an operation

standard cost sheet A listing of the standard price and quantity of each manufacturing cost element for the production of one product

standard error of the estimate (SE) A measure of the accuracy of the regression's estimates

statistical control charts Charts that set control limits using a statistical procedure

step-fixed cost A cost that varies with the cost driver, but in discrete steps

step method A cost allocation method that uses a sequence of steps in the allocation of service department costs to production departments

strategic business unit (SBU) A well-defined set of controllable operating activities over which an SBU manager is responsible

831

strategic cost management   The development of cost management information to facilitate the principal management function, strategic management

strategic management   The development of a sustainable competitive position

strategic performance measurement   An accounting system used by top management for the evaluation of SBU managers

strategy   A set of goals and specific action plans that, if achieved, will provide the desired competitive advantage

structural cost drivers   Strategic plans and decisions that have a long-term effect with regard to issues such as scale, experience, technology, and complexity

sunk costs   Costs that have been incurred or committed in the past, and are therefore irrelevant

SWOT analysis   A systematic procedure for identifying a firm's critical success factors—its internal strengths and weaknesses, and its external opportunities and threats

Taguchi quality loss function   Depicts the relationship between the total loss to a firm due to quality defects and the extent of quality defects

target costing   The desired cost for a product is determined on the basis of a given competitive price, such that the product will earn a desired profit

task analysis   The activity of each process is described in detail to help identify binding constraints

templating   A design method in which an existing product is scaled up or down to fit the specifications of the desired new product

theory of constraints (TOC)   A strategic technique to help firms effectively improve the rate at which raw materials are converted to finished product

throughput   Sales less direct materials costs, including purchased components and materials handling costs

time ticket   A sheet showing the time an employee worked on each job, the pay rate, and the total cost chargeable to each job

total contribution margin   The unit contribution margin multiplied by the number of units sold

total productivity   The relationship between the output attained and the total input costs of all the required input resources

total quality management (TQM)   A technique in which management develops policies and practices to ensure that the firm's products and services exceed customers' expectations

total variable factory overhead variance   The difference between total actual variable factory overhead incurred and total standard variable factory overhead for the output of the period

transfer pricing   The determination of an exchange price when different business units within a firm exchange products or services

transferred-in costs   The costs of work done in the prior department that are transferred into the current department

trend variable   A variable that takes on values of 1, 2, 3, . . . for each period in sequence

t-value   A measure of the reliability of each of the independent variables; that is, the degree to which an independent variable has a valid, stable, long-term relationship with the dependent variable

two-stage allocation   A procedure that assigns a firm's resource costs, namely factory overhead costs, to cost pools and then to cost objects

underapplied overhead   The amount that actual factory overhead exceeds the factory overhead applied

unit-based pool   A method for determining a bonus based on the performance of the manager's unit

unit contribution margin   The difference between unit sales price and unit variable cost; it is a measure of the increase in profit for a unit increase in sales

unit cost   The total of manufacturing costs (materials, labor, and overhead) divided by units of output

unit-level activity   An activity performed for each unit of production

units accounted for   The sum of the units transferred out and ending inventory units

units to account for   The sum of the beginning inventory units and the number of units started during the period

value-added activity   An activity that contributes to customer value and satisfaction or satisfies an organizational need

value-chain analysis   A strategic analysis tool used to identify where value to customers can be increased or costs reduced, and to better understand the firm's linkages with suppliers, customers, and other firms in the industry

value engineering   Used in target costing to reduce product cost by analyzing the trade-offs between (1) different types and levels of product functionality and (2) total product cost

variable cost   The change in total cost associated with each change in the quantity of the cost driver

variable factory overhead efficiency variance   The difference between the total standard variable factory overhead for the actual quantity of the substitute cost driver for applying variable factory overhead and the total standard variable factory overhead cost for the units manufactured during the period

variable factory overhead spending variance   The difference between variable factory overhead incurred and total standard variable factory overhead based on the actual quantity of the cost driver to apply the overhead

visual fit method   A method that calls for the management accountant to view the cost data from prior periods, in either tabular or graphical form, and estimate the cost on the basis of visual judgment

weighted average after-tax cost of capital   The after-tax cost to the firm of securing funds with a given capital structure

weighted-average method   A method that includes all costs, both those incurred during the current period and those incurred in the prior period that are shown as the beginning work-in-process inventory of this period, in calculating the unit cost

work cells   Small groups of related manufacturing processes organized in clusters to assemble parts of finished products

work-in-process inventory   Accounts for all costs put into manufacture of products that are started but not complete at the financial statement date

work measurement   A cost estimation method that makes a detailed study of some production or service activity to measure the time or input required per unit of output

work sampling   A statistical method that makes a series of measurements about the activity under study

zero-base budgeting   A budgeting process that requires managers to prepare budgets from ground zero